FRIESEN

Developmental Psychology Today

RANDOM HOUSE 🏠 NEW YORK

Developmental Psychology Today

FIFTH EDITION

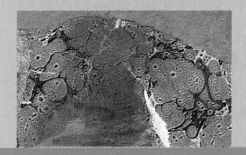

Lois Hoffman
University of Michigan

Scott Paris
University of Michigan

Elizabeth Hall

Robert Schell

Fifth Edition

987654321

Library of Congress Cataloging-in-Publication Data

Developmental psychology today.

   Bibliography: p.
   Includes index.
   1. Developmental psychology.   I. Hoffman, Lois.
BF713.D48   1988   155   87-23317
ISBN 0-394-36169-5

Book and Cover Design: Lorraine Hohman
Cover Collage: Joan Hall
Front cover photos: Spanning seventy years, courtesy of Molly Freund
Back cover photos: Spanning sixty-seven years, courtesy of K. Bendo

Acknowledgments and Copyrights begin on page 589.

To our parents, Gus and Etta, George and Muriel,
Ed and Mae, Joseph and Anna Lee;
and to our children,
Amy and Jill; Jeff, Kristin,
and Julie; Susan and David; and Robby

Preface

DEVELOPMENTAL PSYCHOLOGY TODAY first appeared in 1971. For the past three editions, Robert Schell, a developmental psychologist, and Elizabeth Hall, a professional writer, have collaborated to produce a comprehensive, research-based textbook. Our aim has always been to give students an up-to-date and balanced overview of information, topics, viewpoints, and issues in developmental psychology. As the field of developmental psychology has exploded in every direction, this has become an ever larger task. Researchers are exploring new topics and studying old topics in new ways. The swelling tide of new and important ideas and findings has brought new journals into being — on infancy, on early adolescence, on gender, on almost every aspect of development, even journals to review the findings reported in other journals. For the first time, no single psychologist can possibly organize and synthesize the wealth of research, the complicated issues, and the theoretical debates that now characterize the field.

As we began to plan the fifth edition, we realized that we needed to enlarge our team in order to master the multitude of new findings in every area of development. Our job was not merely to report on this research, but to examine it with an expert eye, sorting it out, and making sense of it for students. When we looked for a developmentalist who understood the critical problems and questions affecting social and emotional development, from the nursery to the nursing home, we turned naturally to Lois Hoffman, professor of developmental psychology at the University of Michigan. Hoffman, who is the coauthor of *Working Mothers,* is the nation's leading expert on the effects of maternal employment on the family. Her recent interest in the adult years enlarged her area of research to include older adults and made her an ideal member of our team. When we looked for a developmentalist who not only understood the way research and theories were challenging old assumptions but also applying theories and findings to real problems, we immediately went to Scott Paris, who is professor of psychology and education at the University of Michigan and director of its Center for Research on Learning and Schooling. His years of research on memory development in young children has questioned old views, and his research with school children is aimed at helping teachers turn reluctant pupils into self-regulated learners. In addition, his experience as coauthor of an introductory psychology text has made him aware of students' needs. At the same time, Robert Schell's interests were moving away from research and toward his private practice, which is devoted to helping children solve their personal and academic problems. It seemed only natural to ask Hoffman and Paris to take charge of the new edition. Although Schell was not able to take a major role in this revision, his imprint remains on our final product.

THE NEW FIFTH EDITION

Sweeping changes in the field of developmental psychology have led to a major reorganization and rewriting of DEVELOPMENTAL PSYCHOLOGY TODAY. Yet we have retained the research-based orientation of past editions and our determination to keep the text interesting and readable remains firm. The accent of this fifth edition is on change. Our guiding theme is that development occurs in the context of a changing society. Instead of assuming that development is always the same, we take the position that broad changes in the way we live alter the experience of every life stage. While presenting development within today's society, we note trends that could affect development in the future. Although we have enlarged our presentation of specific theories, we have continued to integrate theory and research, so that coverage is not tied to a single theory or theorist. This approach gives instructors the freedom to emphasize particular theoretical positions as they see fit—either through supplementary lectures, assigned readings, or other means.

New Organization

The fifth edition of DEVELOPMENTAL PSYCHOLOGY TODAY places more emphasis on adulthood than did earlier editions. We have expanded our coverage of adulthood to six chapters. This shift reflects the growing emphasis that developmentalists have placed on adulthood, which has grown out of the realization that people develop and change throughout the life span. Another innovation is our approach to the story of childhood. We have presented development through childhood in three parts: the beginnings of life (from conception to the end of the neonatal period); infancy and early childhood (from one month through the age of three); and childhood (ages four to twelve). This division allows us to explore the beginnings of development at some length and to see the continuity as well as the changes across childhood. It enables us, for example, to present the story of language development in a single chapter. Finally, we have completed our survey of human development in only twenty chapters, in the belief that this rearrangement allows us to present information in a more coherent manner without breaking the flow of our story.

Instructors familiar with previous editions will notice other major and minor changes. In the introductory Part I (Chapters 1 and 2), we have dropped a chapter in order to get the student into the story of development sooner. We have also reorganized our approach to theories, discussing information-processing in a cognitive instead of a behavioral context, and we have emphasized the influence of maturational theories on the study of development. In Part II on the beginnings of life (Chapters 3 and 4), we have placed the discussion of genetics in the prenatal chapter, which is where most instructors like to cover the topic. In the neonatal chapter, we have greatly expanded the discussion of early personality and social relationships, reflecting our theme of development within a social context.

Part III on infancy and early childhood shows similar change. Our exploration of physical development (Chapter 5) shows that the development of motor skills is actually a dynamic process that involves perception, cognition, emotions, and social relations. The chapter on cognition (Chapter 6) blends Piaget and information processing, presenting both approaches separately, but also interweaving them as a way of showing that instead of warring with each other, they present a complementary picture of early development. Our discussion on language (Chapter 7) emphasizes the maturational, cognitive, and social advances out of which language emerges. Our discussion of early social development (Chapter 8) assumes that the norm in today's society is the working mother and the more involved father.

Part IV on childhood pays equal attention to social and cognitive development. In our discussion of the child within the family (Chapter 9), we explore the way parental styles and disciplinary techniques interact with the child's personality to affect personality and social development. As we look at children with peers, at school, and before the television set (Chapter 10), we continue the story of social skills, managing aggression, and sex roles that began in Chapter 9. The advantage of our new coverage of childhood becomes especially apparent in the cognitive chapters, where the new organization allows us to present an integrated view of cognition and to discuss the shift from preoperational to concrete operational thought smoothly, talking about what children *can* do instead of what they cannot (Chapter 11). An entirely new chapter (Chapter 12) examines intelligence, looking at the differences within and between families that affect intellectual development and then turning to the application of that development in school situations. It looks at the cognitive processes involved in reading, writing, and arithmetic, what is required for mastery, how it develops, and the links between motivation and academic success.

Chapters in Part V on the adolescent have been completely reorganized. The first chapter (Chapter 13) looks at the changes that take place during the years from twelve to eighteen: biological changes, cognitive changes, social changes, and changes within the self. After learning about the basic changes of adolescence, students are prepared to understand some of the adolescent problems that receive extensive coverage in the media. They soon discover that adolescent problems have been blown out of proportion, and that adolescents are no more likely than the rest of the population to be in trouble. After exploding such myths, the second chapter (Chapter 14) looks at adolescent drug use, crime, suicide, pregnancy, and eating disorders.

Coverage of adulthood has been expanded to fill Parts VI and VII. The chapters on personality and social development (Chapters 15, 17, 19) have two interwoven themes: adulthood in a changing society and the effect of gender. Two new chapters on cognitive development in adulthood echo the approach taken to intellectual development in the childhood section. The first chapter (Chapter 16) examines changes in intelligence during early (ages eighteen to forty) and middle (ages forty to sixty-five) adulthood. The second chapter (Chapter 18) looks at learning, thinking, and memory in later adulthood, placing them in the context of biological and environmental changes. Our discussion of death (Chapter 20) has been recast to see dying as life's last developmental task that involves a preparation for death.

More Selective Coverage

The goal of previous editions of DEVELOPMENTAL PSYCHOLOGY TODAY was to survey *all* research in *all* areas of development and to look at *all* the issues and topics that concerned developmentalists. Such a goal has become unrealistic. To cover the entire field in such a manner would require a book at least twice the size of this text. For the fifth edition, we have chosen a new goal: to select the most important studies in the most important areas, while devoting more attention to helping students understand what they have read. In this edition, we spend more time analyzing the presented material, explaining the implications of research, synthesizing viewpoints and theories, and discussing their applications. We believe that this approach helps students gain an appreciation for developmental issues that will last long beyond the final exam.

Up-to-Date Research

In order to retain the text's emphasis on development *today,* we have included much of the newest research on issues, methods, and ground-breaking research. In this book, students will encounter early research showing

the effects of PCB consumption during pregnancy on later child development;

the ability of newborns to "count" to two;

longterm predictions of IQ from habituation studies in infancy;

the use of formal rehearsal by three-year-olds in the memorization of word lists;

that Japanese children do better in math than American children because of the way social and parental attitudes affect the school experience; and

the effectiveness of the "birth-cohort" theory in predicting rises and falls in adolescent crime, suicide, and pregnancy rates.

Authentic Examples from Daily Life

In this edition, we have used individuals in the news, specific subjects in studies, and experiences reported by various researchers in a way that brings developmental issues to life for the reader. Such examples are scattered through every chapter. Social effects on development seem clear when, for example, students sit in as parents tell their small son about an impending divorce, or as they watch the morning routine in a two-career family. Adolescent suicide is no longer an abstract problem when students learn about the deaths of four real adolescents in a single town. The effect of aging on memory processes takes on new meaning when psychologists B. F. Skinner and Donald Hebb describe their own memory problems. The case of Karen Quinlan dramatically conveys the importance of various medical definitions of death.

Highlights on Current Issues

Students will find more boxed inserts in this edition of DEVELOPMENTAL PSYCHOLOGY TODAY. The boxes are varied, drawing from in-depth coverage of a particular study or reports from the world outside the research laboratory. They may discuss a particular research technique, illuminate a controversial or newsworthy topic from the standpoint of developmental issues, or present experiences from other cultures. As they read these boxes, students will find out about new technology that allows researchers to watch the spread of neural activity across the living infant brain. They will learn about the boom in gym classes for babies, the mystery of SIDS, how latchkey children actually manage in their parents' absence, the psychological effects of parental battles on watching toddlers, the social effects of China's one-child policy, the negative effects that employment may have on teenagers, or the absence of any connection between IQ and the ability to handicap horses.

Study Aids

In order to assist the learning process, we have expanded our aids to the student. An outline precedes each chapter to serve as an advance organizer. Each chapter is followed by a numbered summary so students can review its content. At its first use, each new term is printed in boldface type. Following each chapter is a list of these key terms, which are also defined in the glossary at the end of the book. Study terms, those important terms that the student is likely to encounter again and again in the text and on tests, are also listed separately and defined again at the end of each chapter.

ACKNOWLEDGMENTS

We would like to acknowledge several people whose contributions to this edition have given us an enormous boost toward our goals. Joseph Adelson, professor of psychology at the University of Michigan, supplied materials and guidance for the revision of the adolescent Part V, Chapters 13 and 14. Adelson is editor of the *Handbook of Adolescent Psychology* and author of *Chronicles of American Culture*. His research on adolescents' understanding of society and his experience as codirector of the University of Michigan's psychological clinic are reflected in these chapters. Marc Bornstein, chief of the section on child and family research at the National Institute of Child Health and Human Development in Bethesda, Maryland, supplied materials and guidance for Part II on the beginnings of life, Chapters 3 and 4. Bornstein is coauthor of *Development in Infancy* (2nd ed., Random House) and coeditor of *Developmental Psychology: An Advanced Textbook*. His research on vision and learning in early infancy informed these chapters. Esther Thelen, professor of psychology at Indiana University supplied materials for the revision of Chapter 5, "Fundamentals of Physical Growth." Thelen's research on the development of motor skills and her dynamic motor theory, which have changed the way we look at physical development in infancy and early childhood, underlie this revision.

The book would not have been possible without the strength and support of the team at Random House. Our special thanks go to our editor, Mary Falcon, who brought our team together and guided the revision; Holly Gordon, our patient and meticulous project editor; and Susan Friedman, whose copyediting was immensely helpful. The book's handsome appearance is the work of Stacey Alexander, our production supervisor, and Elyse Rieder, photo editor.

We are also grateful to the following individuals. Their ideas, comments, and suggestions were of great help to us as we revised this edition.

Ruth Carpenter, *Walters State Community College*
Janet Fritz, *Colorado State University*
Steven Hamilton, *Cornell University*
Michael Kalinowski, *University of New Hampshire*
N. Laura Kamptner, *California State University at San Bernardino*
Joseph LaVoie, *University of Nebraska at Omaha*
Lois Layne, *Western Kentucky University*
Elizabeth Lorch, *University of Kentucky*
Ned W. Schultz, *California Polytechnic State University at San Luis Obispo*
A. Lynn Scoresby, *Brigham Young University*
Stephan Werba, *Catonsville Community College*

Contents

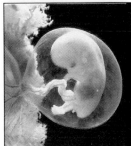

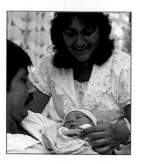

PART III   THE FIRST FOUR YEARS   105

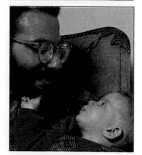

PART V ADOLESCENCE: BUILDING AN IDENTITY 337

PART VI EARLY AND MIDDLE ADULTHOOD 397

PART VII   LATER ADULTHOOD   477

PART I

The Meaning of Development

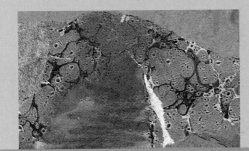

As parents contemplate their newborn infant, they are full of pride and plans. The baby's grandparents recall how, thirty years ago, they reacted in the same way—as did their own parents a quarter of a century before. Thirty years from now, the infant in turn will be a parent gazing down at his or her own child. Around the world, in every culture, the cycle of human development goes ever on. The progression from infant to child to young adult to aging elder is a familiar one, but what does it mean? What is the major force behind development? What sort of processes are responsible for the changes we see? Why do people brought up in the same culture, even living on the same block, turn out so differently? Explaining how babies develop into adults and why their developmental path takes one turning and not another is the province of developmental psychology. Yet it is understanding the general rules of development and not the precise prediction of any one person's life course that is the developmental psychologist's goal. As you will soon discover, explanations of human development vary. Although each has increased our understanding of the mysterious process of development, none can, by itself, adequately describe the progression from cradle to grave.

1

CHAPTER 1

Concepts and Methods in Developmental Psychology

THE NATURE OF HUMAN DEVELOPMENT
Domains of Development / Stages / The Stages of Life

DETERMINANTS OF DEVELOPMENT
Biological Determinants / Environmental Determinants

RESEARCH METHODS IN DEVELOPMENTAL PSYCHOLOGY
Observational Studies / Interview Studies / Experimental Studies / Developmental Designs

THE FIELD OF DEVELOPMENTAL PSYCHOLOGY
Careers in Developmental Psychology / Using Developmental Psychology

In your grandparents' day, many psychologists believed that babies came into the world as alike as peas in a pod. Psychologist John Watson (1924) was so convinced of our initial similarity that he said,

> Give me a dozen healthy infants, well-formed, and my own specified world to bring them up in and I'll guarantee to take any one at random and train him to become any type of specialist I might select — doctor, lawyer, artist, merchant-chief and, yes, even beggar-man and thief, regardless of his talents, penchants, tendencies, abilities, vocations, and race of his ancestors. (P. 104)

Watson believed that a baby's mind was like a blank tablet and that learning inscribed on it the traits, talents, and peculiarities that would appear in the adult. He had no patience with people who suggested that an architect's ability to visualize a structure in space or a chief executive officer's drive to enlarge a corporation might at all be influenced by inborn capacities and limits.

Watson's extreme view of the causes of the differences among us has fallen out of favor. Today, most psychologists agree that we become the

3

kind of people we are through the **interaction** of heredity and environment. Our inherited predispositions influence our environment, which influences our inherited predispositions, in a never-ending spiral that produces a unique individual with specific interests, capabilities, limits, and ways of responding to events. This process of age-related change over the life span, which describes the transition from fertilized egg to aged adult, is known as **development.** Understanding that change is the aim of developmental psychologists.

This chapter explores the nature of human development and the field of developmental psychology. We begin by looking at the characteristics of development and the way it is usually broken up for study. Next we consider the way that development progresses through a series of stages. We then investigate the determinants of development, seeing how they affect each of us. That brings us naturally to a discussion of major research methods and how psychologists study development. The chapter closes with a brief overview of developmental psychology itself, noting the goals, the uses, and the scope of the discipline.

THE NATURE OF HUMAN DEVELOPMENT

A good way to think about development is as a process of change within the individual across the life span. This developmental change has several characteristics:

- Development is *continuous;* changes occur over hours, days, weeks, months, and years (Appelbaum and McCall, 1983), and developmental changes continue throughout life. Instead of seeing childhood experience as rigidly determining the rest of a person's life, developmentalists believe that change and development can occur at every period of life.
- Development is *cumulative;* it builds upon what has gone before. How children and adults respond and what they can learn today depends in part on their earlier experiences in related situations.
- Development is *directional;* infants grow first into children and then into adults.

- Development is *differentiated;* babies who may find it difficult to distinguish among their perceptions, thoughts, feelings, and actions become children who first separate these elements of experience, then make finer distinctions in what they perceive, what they feel, what they think, and what they do (Flavell, 1985).
- Development is *organized;* infants slowly become able to organize and control their actions. Just as babies learn to coordinate their muscle and perceptual functions, adults learn to organize and control the various tasks related to their work and family lives.
- Development is *holistic;* each aspect of development, whether physical, cognitive, or social, depends on every other aspect, and all development is the result of interaction.

Our lives are thus interwoven fabrics of individual change, and each life is a fabric produced in a specific social, cultural, and historical setting, which directs the weaving in special ways.

Domains of Development

Although development is holistic, it is virtually impossible for developmental psychologists to study it that way. So many strands of influence are involved that most developmentalists focus on either the cognitive, social, or physical domain of development. Researchers who focus on cognitive development study perception, learning, language, or thought. Those who focus on social development study emotions, motivation, personality, and relations with other people. Those who focus on physical development study changes within the body, motor skills, health, and nutrition.

Isolating development in this way is artificial, and developmental psychologists are acutely aware of the problem. They know that changes in one domain influence changes in the others. Consider the dilemma facing the psychologist who wants to study the development of intelligence. What aspect of intelligence does she or he examine? A researcher could look at memory, at the way people solve problems, at the effects of accumulated knowledge, at the effects of physical maturation, at the effects of aging, or at the effects of family relationships. All these and other factors interact to shape intellectual development.

Stages

We often resort to the concept of stages when trying to explain someone's behavior. We might say of a difficult toddler, a pouting adolescent, or a middle-aged adult involved in an extramarital affair, "He (or she) is just going through a stage." But this colloquial usage of the term is too loose for developmental psychologists. They would reserve **stage** to describe a particular pattern of abilities, motives, or behavior that is predicted by a specific theory of development. Some developmentalists see development as stagelike, with each stage sharply different from stages that precede or follow it, as a butterfly goes from caterpillar, to pupa, to winged insect. Other developmentalists see development as continuous; they believe that we develop in a smooth, continuous manner, as a daisy grows from a seedling into a mature, blooming plant. In their view, behavior in one stage is not different in quality from behavior in other stages, and the concept of stage is more convenient than meaningful.

This question has been more difficult to resolve than you might think, because the concept of stage involves much more than the fact that some kinds of behavior invariably precede others. According to Flavell (1985), a developmental stage is characterized by structures, qualitative changes, abruptness, and concurrence.

- A stage is characterized by *structures*. Within each stage, various abilities, motives, or skills must be linked in some cohesive pattern.
- A stage is characterized by *qualitative changes*. The abilities, motives, or skills of one stage must be as different from those of the preceding or subsequent stages as apples are from oranges. A child who moves from one stage to the other does not simply know more about the world; he or she thinks in radically different ways.
- A stage is characterized by *abruptness*. The abilities, motives, skills, or behavior that are typical of the stage must change simultaneously. The change may not be as abrupt as that between fetus and newborn infant, but the transition

During the seventeenth century, when Velásquez painted this scene, childhood was just beginning to emerge as a separate period of life. Children still dressed and were treated like miniature adults. *(Scala/Art Resource)*

should be fairly brief. After the transitional period, the person's behavior should remain relatively stable during the rest of the stage.

- A stage is characterized by *concurrence*. The various abilities and behavior that are typical of the stage should develop at about the same pace. For example, a child who develops one concept typical of a particular intellectual stage should also have developed the other concepts that characterize the stage. An adolescent who can reason about hypothetical situations should also be able to solve problems by reasoning in a logical, systematic manner.

Despite their dissatisfaction with the concept of stages, developmental psychologists find stages convenient ways of providing general descriptions of the major phases of life in a particular domain, be it cognition, sexuality, moral judgment, friendship, or careers. Although stages generally follow chronological age, level of function, *not* age, is the developmental marker of stage theories. When they use stages, however, psychologists find it difficult to specify the boundaries between the stages and the transitions from one stage to the next.

The Stages of Life

When we divide the life span into the stages of prenatal development, infancy, childhood, adolescence, and adulthood, we are using stages in a convenient, but not theoretically coherent, way. Such a division makes sense to us, but our view of the life span is not shared by all contemporary societies or even by our own society in earlier times. Today, some societies divide life into three periods (such as infancy, childhood, and adulthood) or only two (infancy and adulthood) (Mead, 1968).

The way in which people in a society view the life span depends largely on their social and economic system. During the Middle Ages, for example, infancy lasted for about seven years; then a young person began working alongside adults (Ariès, 1962). And Western cultures did not view adolescence as a separate stage of life until industrialization and economic productivity freed most young people past the age of puberty from farm and factory labor. More recently, increases in life

expectancy have led to a substantial number of people living well into their eighties. So many of these older adults have remained active and vigorous that the period of later adulthood has been divided into the "young-old" and the "old-old," in order to separate healthy older adults from those who are sickly and frail (Neugarten and Hall, 1987).

The use of physical and mental condition as the dividing line between the young-old and the old-old points up the problem of finding appropriate markers to divide the life span. We are not consistent in choosing our markers and seem unable to decide whether biological, social, or cognitive events give us the best way of sectioning off a person's life. Some biological markers seem to make sense: the moment of birth divides the prenatal period from infancy; puberty divides childhood from adolescence. Social events also make convenient markers of the life span. The assumption of adult roles in work or marriage marks the end of adolescence and the start of adulthood, while the loss of roles — such as retirement from work — is similarly significant. Cognitive events also can be used. Meaningful speech marks the end of infancy and the start of childhood, and mature reasoning divides childhood from adolescence.

Our inconsistency in the selection of life markers highlights one fact about development that evokes general agreement from psychologists. Chronological age is a poor way to divide the life span, and the older people get, the less helpful it is (Salthouse, 1982). During infancy and early childhood, when so many developmental advances depend on biological maturation, chronological age is less misleading than it is during adulthood. When given the age of an adult, about all you can safely conclude is that she or he has lived a certain number of years (Neugarten and Hall, 1987).

The biological, chronological, and social markers roughly coincide with major phases in the life span but rarely fall at exactly the same place (see Figure 1.1). In talking about development, however, it seems convenient to use five chronological periods that more or less correspond to our culture's usage.

The **prenatal period** begins at conception and ends at birth. It is the least arbitrary and easiest to define because its beginning and end are clearly marked by biological events. **Infancy** begins at

Phase	Biological Marker	Age	Psychosocial Marker
PRENATAL	Conception	–9 months	
	Birth	0 1 Month	
INFANCY			Forming attachments
	Walking, Talking	2 years	
CHILDHOOD **Early**			
		6 Years	Mastering basic skills
Later			
	Puberty	11 Years	
ADOLESCENCE			Building personal and sexual identity
	Physical Maturity	20 Years	
ADULTHOOD **Early**			Establishing personal and economic independence
		40 Years	
Middle	Menopause (in Women)		Expanding personal and social involvement and responsibility
		60 Years	
Later			Reformulating social roles and personal goals
	Death		

FIGURE 1.1 Because the phases of human development are based on cultural views of the life span, they vary from one society to another. Each phase of development used in this book is marked by particular biological or psychosocial events.

birth and continues until approximately age two. By the end of the second year, most children have begun to acquire language and symbolic thought. In addition, most adults think of two-year-olds as children rather than as infants, which corresponds to the developmental shift from nonlinguistic to linguistic communication.

The third phase, **childhood,** begins around age two and continues through late childhood, at around age twelve. So much development takes place during this phase that we often find it necessary to use additional terms, such as *toddler* (a transitional stage from about eighteen months until a child's third birthday) and *preschooler* (from about three to six years). Puberty is usually accepted as the end of childhood and the beginning of adolescence. **Adolescence,** the fourth phase, is a less definite period than childhood because its end is not defined as well as the end of other phases of development. Most agree that adolescence ends when a person acquires adult economic and social roles. **Adulthood,** the fifth phase, generally begins in the

More and more Americans are living into late adulthood, a period of life when people generally are more capable than younger members of society realize. *(Ken Heyman)*

late teens or early twenties and continues until death. This is clearly the longest phase, spanning early adulthood, the middle years, and late adulthood (encompassing both the young-old and the old-old).

This convenient division of development makes it easier to discuss behavioral changes that accompany one another. Yet we need to remember that development is always continuous. Each person's life shows a continuity from conception to death, even though development may be relatively rapid at one time and slow at another.

DETERMINANTS OF DEVELOPMENT

Development is the product of many interacting causes. When we examine hereditary influences on development, we need to keep reminding ourselves that heredity (genetic or biological) never operates in isolation from the environment. Environmental determinants may be physical or social. The physical environment may be, in the prenatal period, the mother's uterus or, in childhood, the neighborhood of the inner city, or an Iowa farm. Social environments encompass the effects of other people and social institutions on development. Yet when we look at these environmental influences, we also need to remind ourselves that the same influence may work differently, depending on a person's heredity.

Because developmental psychologists study change across time, they are especially aware that behavior depends on both the genetic makeup of the person and the environment—on *nature* as well as on *nurture*. However, they may disagree about how genes and environments interact and may emphasize either nature or nurture in specific areas of development. Some, for example, believe that personality is heavily influenced by a baby's inborn temperament (nature). Others believe that experiences while growing up are the primary influence (nurture).

Biological Determinants

Biological determinants begin working on us at

These identical twins, separated from birth, were not even aware of each other's identity until they were thirty-nine years old. Is their identical genetic make-up responsible for the uncanny similarity of their lives? *(Enrico Ferorelli/DOT)*

the moment of conception and continue their work until we die. Clearly, biological determinants are powerful in some areas of development. Sitting, standing, and walking depend heavily on the biological maturation of muscles, nerves, and brain. Babies also come into the world biologically prepared to form social bonds, to investigate their surroundings, and to acquire language. Our heredity as a species so strongly disposes human infants to develop these abilities that they will appear in any natural human environment (Scarr, 1983). Only extreme deprivation will prevent their development.

Similarly, our perceptual systems have evolved so that we will be able to extract the sort of information from the environment that we need to survive (Gibson and Spelke, 1983). The abilities to perceive depth, to pick out the sounds of speech from a stream of noise, and to coordinate our eyes, ears, and hands require little learning. If these abilities depended on learning, our species would have disappeared from the earth long ago.

Ethnic differences in temperament may begin with a biological push. Psychologist Daniel Freedman (1979), who tested babies during the first forty-eight hours after birth, found that Caucasian and Chinese babies already resembled cultural stereotypes. Caucasian babies seemed easily excited but Chinese babies remained steady and calm. When researchers pressed a piece of gauze to the babies' noses, Caucasian babies twisted their heads away or batted at the cloth with their hands.

Chinese babies simply lay still and began breathing through their mouths. When the babies were undressed and began to cry, researchers picked them up. The Caucasian babies quieted slowly; the Chinese babies immediately stopped crying. As the babies develop, these tendencies may be strengthened as the mothers' culturally influenced attitudes and behavior interact with the babies' basic excitability or calm.

Our heredity also influences those characteristics that make us different from one another: our individual appearance, our personality, our intelligence. One way to find out how biological determinants might influence these characteristics is to compare identical twins who have been reared apart. Identical twins develop when a single egg cell (fertilized by a single sperm) separates early in development; both twins have exactly the same heredity. At the University of Minnesota, Thomas Bouchard (see Holden, 1980) has been studying pairs of identical twins who were separated at birth. Bouchard has found that such twins score so closely on many personality and ability tests that an uninformed observer would assume that the same person had taken the test twice. Most are similar in other ways as well.

One set of twins—Jim Springer and Jim Lewis—did not meet until the age of 39, yet their lives had followed amazingly similar courses. In school, both had hated spelling but liked math; both had worked part-time as deputy sheriffs, both drove a Chevrolet, and both chewed their fingernails, chain-smoked the same brand of cigarette, drank the same brand of beer, disliked baseball, enjoyed stock-car racing, and had a hobby of carpentry. Their pulse, blood pressure, and sleep patterns were identical. Since they had been eighteen, each twin had suffered from headaches that came on in the afternoon, and at the same age, each had gained ten pounds. Even more startling, each had married twice (each first to a woman named Linda, then to a woman named Betty); both had a son named James Alan; and both owned a dog named Toy. But environmental influences were also apparent. The two Jims had different tastes in music, they combed their hair differently, and they had different ways of expressing themselves—one was good at talking, but the other preferred the written word. Their mannerisms were so different that one reminded a journalist of Clint Eastwood, and

the other seemed more like Dick Van Dyke (Johnson, 1980).

Even some of the similarities between the twins can be explained by environmental influences. Adoption agencies often place separated twins in highly similar environments, and both Jims grew up in working-class homes in Ohio just eighty miles apart, where they were exposed to similar socioeconomic influences and social class values.

Environmental Determinants

Heredity can express itself only in the context of the environment, which continually influences every aspect of development. Influences from the social environment are especially clear in the development of sex roles, where family, friends, and society all shape our ideas of masculinity and femininity. Parents tend to encourage active, exuberant physical play in their young sons and sedentary social play in their young daughters, with fathers being the stronger champions of traditional sex roles (Tauber, 1979). Siblings also take an active role in teaching us what it means to be male or female. (The accompanying box, "Sibling Influences," explores other ways in which siblings can influence development.) Compared to children with siblings of only their own sex, boys have feminine sisters and girls have masculine brothers (Sutton-Smith, 1982). The outside world helps the process along, as children see stereotypical sex roles portrayed in programs and commercials. Two-year-olds get further instruction from peers, as they learn that boys play with boys and girls play with girls—and boys are taught that playing with girls' toys is forbidden (Fagot, 1985). By the time they are three years old, American children (even those who stay at home) know which toys, clothing, tools, household objects, games, and occupations are suitable for boys or girls (Huston, 1983).

The interaction of physical and social determinants was highlighted by a North Carolina study, in which psychologists Philip Zeskind and Craig Ramey (1978, 1981) followed a group of infants who were born suffering from fetal malnutrition. Such babies are generally apathetic, unresponsive to sights and sounds in the environment, and they are cross when aroused. If they grow up in a nonsupportive environment, their early handicap may be maintained—or even made worse. All the

SIBLING INFLUENCES: HOW BROTHERS AND SISTERS FEEL ABOUT ONE ANOTHER

Brothers and sisters have an important influence on one another's development. But the nature of that influence varies from one child to the next, because the nature of the sibling relationship also varies. One pair of siblings may have a close, warm relationship; another pair may be distant; a third pair may spend most of their time squabbling. What determines the kind of sibling relationship that develops? Psychologists Wyndol Furman and Duane Buhrmester (1985) of the University of Denver decided that the best way to find out was to ask some children.

They began by interviewing fifth and sixth graders, asking them such questions as, "What is it like having a brother (or sister)?" and probing the good and bad aspects of the relationship. From the children's replies, Furman and Buhrmester developed a questionnaire, which they gave to other fifth and sixth graders. Their answers provided a glimpse of the factors that affect sibling relationships most strongly.

A sibling's influence depends in part on the quality of the relationship. What determines whether siblings feel close to each other? The closest relationships develop between siblings of the same sex who are near the same age. Such children report greater intimacy and companionship; in addition, a child is more likely to behave altruistically toward a sibling of the same sex. The most distant relationship is between a closely spaced brother and sister.

Power and status, which appear to be determined by age differences, can also increase a sibling's influence. Children who are four or more years older than their brother or sister tend to dominate the relationship and to be nurturant toward the younger sibling. The effect is magnified in large families where there are at least four children. Younger children view their much older siblings of the same sex as especially dominant, and these much older siblings are generally admired by their younger brothers and sisters.

Conflict and sibling rivalry are favorite themes of psychologists, and they can affect the family atmosphere. However, few children voluntarily mentioned these problems. Only 10 percent spoke about

Relationships generally are closest when siblings are the same sex and close in age. Most young boys admire their older brothers and see them as very dominant. (Barbars Rios/Photo Researchers)

competition with a brother or sister, and only 20 percent talked about parents favoring one child over another. Answers to the questionnaire indicated that antagonism and conflict are most intense when siblings are near the same age, with children most likely to quarrel frequently with a slightly older sibling. Children are more likely to engage in rivalry with a younger brother or sister than with an older sibling and are likely to feel that their parents are partial to the younger sibling. The warmth or distance of a relationship apparently had no bearing on whether it was marked by conflict. At first this result seemed puzzling, but the researchers suggest that some siblings in detached relationships may fight frequently; others may simply avoid each other and thus eliminate conflict.

These factors of age, sex, birth order, and family spacing are not the only influences on sibling relationships. Undoubtedly, each child's temperament also affects the way a relationship develops. But in the interaction of determinants, sibling relationships are also likely to affect the characteristics of individual children as well as the relationship between parent and child (Furman and Buhrmester, 1985).

babies were given nutritional supplements and medical care, but one group was also placed in an educational day-care program. At three months, all the babies scored below average on measures of mental development. At eighteen months, the babies in the day-care program were developing normally, but the other babies had lost ground. This disparity grew larger over the next few years, with the babies in the day-care program doing as well as well-nourished babies in the program (see Figure 1.2).

Why did the educational program have such powerful effects? Zeskind and Ramey believe that the sluggish, irritable nature of malnourished babies affects their mothers' behavior, so that the mother tends to withdraw, interacting less with

her baby. That withdrawal initiates a developmental spiral that intensifies the baby's early handicap. Such a detrimental cycle apparently did not get started among the babies in the day-care program, who received extra care and attention. When they were three years old, the babies in day care were more responsive and outgoing than the babies with no day-care experience, and they had much higher intelligence test scores (an average of 96 compared with 70).

Experience can even influence the developmental rate and level of abilities that babies are biologically prepared to develop. In rural Guatemala, babies sometimes spend their first year inside a small, dark, windowless hut. Family members rarely speak to them or play with them, and they are passive, quiet, fearful, and rarely smile. Deprived of the sort of stimulation that most U.S. babies get, these Guatemalan babies are slow to develop. Studies indicate that they are several months behind U.S. babies in reaching such intellectual milestones of infancy as imaginative play, and they begin talking about a year after U.S. babies do (Kagan and Klein, 1973). If the effects of experience can be demonstrated in areas of development that are so heavily influenced by biological determinants, environment clearly plays an important role.

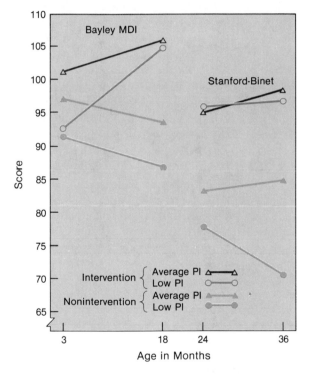

FIGURE 1.2   Intellectual development of infants from three months to three years, as measured by infant (Bayley MDI) and toddler (Stanford-Binet) intelligence tests. Some infants suffered from fetal malnutrition (low PI); the rest were normal (average PI). All the malnourished babies were given nutritional supplements and medical care, but infants in the educational day-care program (intervention group) developed more rapidly than infants who stayed at home (nonintervention group). PI refers to ponderal index, a ratio of weight to length. *(From Zeskind and Ramey, 1981)*

RESEARCH METHODS IN DEVELOPMENTAL PSYCHOLOGY

It seems clear that both biological and environmental determinants influence development. But how can we discover which particular factors are heavily implicated in the development of specific skills and abilities? For example, suppose we want to know whether the experience of being abused by a parent affects a child's emotional development. The first step in identifying various determinants and their effects on human development is to formulate a **hypothesis** about the way a determinant might act. A hypothesis is nothing more than a prediction that we can test by gathering appropriate information. So we might begin our investigation with the hypothesis that being abused affects the way young children respond to another child in distress. The next step is to devise a study in which we can gather the sort of information that would test our hypothesis, and as we will see, a pair of researchers carried out just such a study. From the results of their test, we can draw conclusions about our hypothesis.

This process can be followed in any of several different methods, and the distinctions among them depend on how much *control* we have over various aspects of our study. A researcher may or may not have control over

1. the selection of subjects for study,
2. the experience the subjects have in the study, and
3. the possible responses they can give to that experience.

Each of the methods we might use has advantages and disadvantages, and our choice will depend on our purpose and the circumstances.

A single study, no matter how well executed, cannot answer all our questions. At best, it will support our conclusions or show that they are wrong. The final test comes when other researchers **replicate,** or repeat, our results. A scientific finding is established when several different researchers, in different places, using the same basic method, replicate the results.

The major methods used by developmental psychologists are observational studies, interview studies, and experimental studies, and each allows the researcher a different degree of control (see Table 1.1). When a study is well controlled, all extraneous factors affect all subjects similarly, allowing researchers to assume that the behavior under study is actually affected by the factor they are studying.

Observational Studies

In **observational studies,** a researcher observes people as they go about their daily activities and carefully records their behavior. Observational studies can take place in homes, schools, or offices, on playgrounds and city streets, at parties, parades, or nursing homes. Because people are behaving spontaneously in natural settings, researchers feel fairly confident in generalizing from the results of their observations to other situations. Such studies can produce valuable information about the effects of environmental **variables,** or factors, on behavior. In order for observational studies to be successful, however, researchers must establish explicit rules for categorizing and recording what they see, so that two observers watching the situation will produce comparable records. Researchers use various techniques to record behavior. Some use a checklist, marking off listed actions each time they occur. Some use time sampling, observing each subject for a specified number of minutes and recording behavior of interest. Others, who are interested in recording as much natural behavior as possible, videotape activities, then analyze them frame by frame for behavior that might otherwise go unnoticed. There are two kinds of observational studies: naturalistic and field studies.

Table 1.1
Methods of Studying Development

Method	Advantages	Disadvantages
Observational studies	Situation close to everyday life	No control over selection of participants
		Observations may be unreliable
		Unknown and uncontrolled factors may influence results
Interview	Situation close to everyday life	Unknown and uncontrollable factors may influence results
	Some control over selection of participants	
	Experience and responses of participants may be standardized	Observations may be unreliable
Experiment	Unwanted factors may be controlled or eliminated	Situation may be far removed from daily life
	Generally most efficient and least expensive	

Naturalistic Studies In **naturalistic studies,** researchers simply observe and record what they see, without changing the situation in any way. For example, Mary Main and Carol George (1985) wondered whether young children who had been battered by their parents would be less likely than other youngsters to show concern for a distressed child. Observers went to two nursery schools for battered children and two nursery schools that served "families under stress," recording the social behavior of selected children. All the children were from disadvantaged homes. When the records were analyzed, Main and George discovered that the abused toddlers not only failed to respond sympathetically to the distress of other children, but also became fearful or angry, sometimes threatening a child in distress or even attacking the crying toddler. Toddlers who had never been abused often showed concern or sadness at the other child's distress and almost never became angry (see Figure 1.3). The researchers' hypothesis was confirmed, and the results suggested that the experience of being abused may change very young children's emotional responses to others in a way that should concern us.

Field Studies In the study of abused children just described, researchers had to wait for distress to develop naturally. But sometimes researchers can set up a situation in a natural setting and then observe people's responses. When the investigator introduces some factor into the natural situation that changes it, the research is known as a **field study.** For example, when Laura Adamson and Roger Bakeman (1985) wondered how infants' expression of pleasure during play changed as they grew older, they observed infants playing in their homes. But they set up the situation beforehand, arranging with the babies' mothers so that the babies could be observed playing alone with specific toys provided by the researchers, playing with their mother, and playing with another baby. When Adamson and Bakeman examined videotapes of the babies' play, they found that six-month-old babies showed their pleasure by squealing, smiling broadly, or waving their arms, but that eighteen-month-old babies usually expressed their pleasure vocally. They also found that babies of any age were more likely to show pleasure in social play than when playing by themselves and that babies find it easier to communicate their pleasure

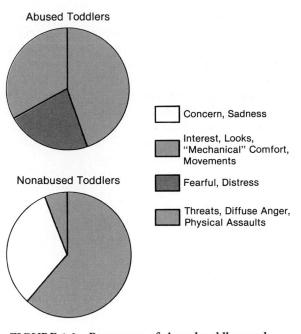

FIGURE 1.3 **Responses of abused toddlers and disadvantaged toddlers to the distress of other children. The figures indicate the average proportion of responses falling into each category.** *(From Main and George, 1985)*

to their mother than to another baby. Adamson and Bakeman concluded that babies use expressions of pleasure as greetings, as social communication, and to communicate about some other object.

Interview Studies

In interview studies, investigators ask questions of their subjects, then analyze the replies. The same method can be applied in a standardized way to each subject, or the psychologist can vary the approach. Depending upon the purpose of the study, the interviews may be in-depth, with the researcher talking separately and at length with each subject; or the interview can take the form of a questionnaire, with each subject replying on a paper-and-pencil form or giving brief answers *(always, never, sometimes)* to standardized questions put by the researcher. The interviews may be used to establish some aspect of development or to evaluate individuals.

Clinical Studies In **clinical studies,** investigators usually conduct in-depth interviews, often supplemented by observation and questionnaire. By using clinical techniques, for example, David Heller (1985) investigated children's ideas about God. One at a time, he interviewed forty children between the ages of four and twelve, hoping to discover how children conceive of God and how their conceptions change with intellectual development. Besides answering a number of direct questions, the children drew pictures of God, acted out with dolls their ideas of God, wrote letters to God, and made up a story about God. As we might expect, the children's home background, religious training, age, sex, and personality all affected their ideas of the deity. Preschoolers associated God with play and merriment, and they invented an additional "all bad" God to handle the dark aspects of life. Among older children, three types of God appeared: a congenial deity who was like an imaginary playmate with extraordinary powers; a highly romanticized figure that served as a focus for mingled religious and sexual feelings; and a healing, nurturant figure who cured all ills. Heller found that, no matter what their age, children tended to weave their most pressing emotional concerns into their views of God. The most nearly universal view was of a God who works through human intimacy and the interconnectedness of lives, with His divine power depending on the actions of men, women, girls, and boys.

Researchers also use clinical studies to explore adult development. For example, Daniel Levinson (1978) conducted extensive interviews with forty men to explore his theory that men's lives tend to fall into similar patterns. In addition to free-ranging biographical interviews (up to twenty hours with each man), Levinson gave each man a standard psychological test, in which the man looked at five pictures and told a story about each one. Then Levinson interviewed the man's wife, and, after a lapse of two years, reinterviewed the man himself. From his clinical study, Levinson concluded that he had uncovered a universal pattern of development that characterizes American men today. (The accompanying box, "A Clinical Study of Parents," provides an example of a clinical study that explores family relationships.)

Case Studies Another way of investigating development is through **case studies**, in which re-

searchers study individuals rather than groups. The researcher uses in-depth interviews and observation but follows the individuals over a period of months or years. Swiss psychologist Jean Piaget used this method successfully to study intellectual development with his own children. He meticulously recorded their development, noting what they did and said, as well as the emotions they conveyed. His "interviews" often took the form of games. For example, when his daughter Jacqueline was one year, one month, and twenty-three days old, Piaget (1951) wrote:

> J. was sitting opposite me. I puffed out my cheeks and then pressed each of them with a forefinger, letting the air escape through my mouth. J. then put the palm of her right hand over her mouth and made a sound like a kiss. She then touched her cheeks but did not succeed in reproducing the complete action. (P. 58)

Case studies were also the main resource on which Sigmund Freud relied when developing his psychodynamic theory of human development. From the detailed records of his patients' treatments, along with all the other information he had about them, Freud constructed a new view of human emotional development, one that has had enormous influence on Western society.

Experimental Studies

An **experiment** is the most objective way to test a hypothesis. It gives the investigator the greatest amount of control over the situation, which can be constructed to eliminate extraneous influences that might be present in a natural setting. In an experiment, researchers examine the effects of selected variables on behavior, controlling and manipulating whatever variable is being studied. Suppose we want to study the effect of aging on memory. We might give young adults and retirees an opportunity to learn word lists, then test them to see how many words each group remembers. The variable that is selected or changed in some way by the investigator is called the **independent variable**: it is independent of whatever subjects do. In our experiment, the independent variable is the word list, which we might vary by changing the number of words in the list, or the categories from which the words are drawn, or the amount of study

A CLINICAL STUDY OF PARENTS: MY FAVORITE CHILD

In the best of all possible worlds, parents would love all their children equally. But as we know, most parents eventually feel closer to one or another of their children. These feelings may not be present when the children are small but develop slowly over the years as parent and child personalities mesh or clash, as children gratify or demolish their parents' hopes and expectations. A trio of researchers from the University of Notre Dame used a clinical study to find out what makes a "favorite child" and why parents regard some of their children as "disappointments." The subjects in this study were 117 middle-class Catholic couples, mostly in their early sixties, with an average of 4.4 grown children. Through computer analysis, the researchers were able to trace the effect of seventeen different independent variables on the parent-child relationship.

Aware that parents are unlikely to say "Catherine is my favorite," Joan Aldous, Elisabeth Klaus, and David Kline (1985) constructed interviews and questionnaires that probed the comfort and sympathy provided by each child and asked which child a parent turned to for help in times of trouble. The answers tended to confirm the old rhyme, "A son is a son till he takes a wife, but a daughter's a daughter the rest of her life." Both fathers and mothers overwhelmingly said that they got the most comfort and sympathy from a daughter. It also helped if the daughter lived nearby (within 50 miles) and had few disagreements with her parents.

No parents were asked whether sons or daughters made the best confidants, but the researchers' analysis of the parents' responses showed a clear split between genders on which child was chosen as confidant. Mothers overwhelmingly confided in their daughters, especially elder daughters who lived nearby and who had shared interests. Fathers chose a child who was himself or herself a parent but preferred to confide in sons over daughters.

The disappointing child was opposite from the comforters and confidants in most respects. In most cases a son, he tended to disagree with his parents and shared no interests with them. Parents did not like the way the disappointing child treated them,

Older mothers often make confidantes out of their grown daughters and feel closer to them than to their other children. (The Picture Cube)

and fathers were disappointed in children who were not parents themselves, who did not go to church regularly, and who had failed to complete college. As one father put it, "John frustrates me by his life style, his lack of ambition, and his goals" (p. 315).

Among these parents, distance seemed unimportant compared with other factors. Their confidants and comfort-givers sometimes lived far away, and their disappointing children sometimes lived nearby. Common interests and goals were more important than proximity, just as they are in friendships between adults. Similarly, when parents had failed to transmit their interests and values to a child, they often expressed disappointment in that son or daughter. The children's experiences, both while growing up and as adults, undoubtedly were involved in the development of favorite children, as were the temperaments of parent and child.

time we allow. The variable that changes in some way because of the introduction of the independent variable is called the **dependent variable**; it usually is some measure of the subjects' behavior. In our experiment, the dependent variable is the number of words recalled. If we compare the performance of younger and older adults in each condition, we would know something about the effects of aging on memory.

As we follow an actual experiment, we can see how researchers can manipulate the independent variable merely by changing the instructions they give to their subjects. Older children have better memories than younger children because they have discovered techniques that help them store information. For example, if we give twelve-year-olds a list of words to learn, they repeat the words, several at a time, varying the words on each repetition. This practice is called *active rehearsal*. Seven-year-olds simply repeat the same word over and over. But what if we taught the younger children how to rehearse words the way older children do? Would they remember as many?

Peter Ornstein and his colleagues (1985) tested this hypothesis in an experiment with second and sixth graders. Some of the second graders were given eighteen easy words to learn; the words were printed on index cards, and as the investigator read a word, the children saw it for five seconds. The only instructions they received were to repeat the words aloud. These children represented the **control group** in the experiment. They would be tested on the words, but they would not have the same experience (instruction in active rehearsal) as the other children. The rest of the children made up the **experimental groups**. All of them—both second and sixth graders—were given instruction in active rehearsal before they started learning the list. But for half of them, the independent variable was manipulated again: they were allowed to see all eighteen words displayed on a board while the words were read aloud. As expected, second graders in the control group did poorly. Second graders who got instructions in active rehearsal did somewhat better. But second graders whose active rehearsal was supported by viewing all the words throughout the learning period did as well as the sixth graders. Second graders apparently need more than instruction in a sophisticated rehearsal technique to equal the performance of older children. Because both groups

of sixth graders remembered about the same number of words, the researchers learned something else from this study. As children develop, the researchers learned, they also gain another skill: the ability to remember the word they are supposed to be rehearsing when the word is not in sight.

Developmental Designs

Because development is age-related change, researchers studying developmental issues have to grapple with a problem that is rarely encountered when they investigate other areas of behavior. The problem is to discover whether age-related changes are due to influences that affect most people at the same point in the life span (such as walking, learning to talk, starting school, reaching puberty, or retiring) or whether some factor in society (such as economic depression, war, television, computers) is responsible. These historical events similarly affect everyone born at about the same time (a group known as a **cohort**), but no two cohorts will be affected in exactly the same way. For example, people born early in the twentieth century may see computers as little more than an annoyance that makes a nightmare out of attempts to correct mistakes in a credit card statement. But people born within the past few years will grow up using computers daily and will find it impossible to think of studying, writing, handling their personal finances, or transacting business without them.

In their studies of development, researchers have used several different designs: cross-sectional, longitudinal, and sequential. Some are less susceptible than others to cohort effects, but each has an important place in the study of development (see Table 1.2).

Cross-Sectional Designs Most of the information we have on development comes from studies that have used a **cross-sectional design**. In this design, researchers study different age groups at the same time and compare the results. The comparisons may be between different age groups within the same stage of life (six-year-olds, eight-year-olds, and twelve-year-olds), or between people at different stages of life (eighteen-year-olds and sixty-year-olds). Just over a decade ago, a researcher estimated that 90 percent of all developmental studies were designed this way (Wohlwill,

Table 1.2
Developmental Designs

Type	Method	Tells Us	Advantages	Disadvantages
Cross-sectional design	Observe several cohorts on one occasion	Age differences in behavior	Quick, inexpensive	Differences may not be developmental, but reflect cohort effects Cannot show differences within individuals
Longitudinal design	Observe one cohort on several occasions	Changes in behavior with time	Shows developmental trends Shows changes within individuals	Differences may reflect changes in society Lengthy, expensive Practice effect, attrition of subjects
Sequential design	Observe several cohorts on several occasions	Age-related changes in behavior	Reveals effects of age, cohort, and societal change	Lengthy, expensive

1973)—and with good reason. Cross-sectional studies are relatively inexpensive, and they can be done quickly. Researchers can gather in a few days the sort of information that would require years, even decades, to obtain through other methods. Earlier in the chapter, we encountered several cross-sectional studies: the naturalistic observation of abused toddlers, the interview study on children's conceptions of God, and the experimental study on rehearsal techniques. The cross-sectional design can be used with any type of study.

Sometimes cohort effects can have a strong influence on the outcome of a study. When this happens, we may make erroneous assumptions about developmental changes. For example, a cross-sectional study of IQ scores in later life might show a curve like that in Figure 1.4. The scores appear to decline with increasing age. But an inspection of the graph reminds us that people studied at age eighty in 1975 were born in 1895, and those studied at age twenty were born in 1955. In the time between those cohorts, the cultural and social environment changed in many ways. Those changes may have affected the development and maintenance of intellectual skills. Longer education and mass communication exposed more people in each cohort tested to the information and skills in abstract thinking required to score well on such tests. In fact, each new generation of Ameri-

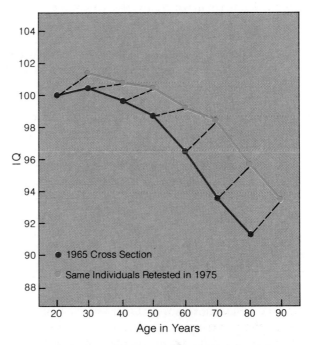

FIGURE 1.4   In this hypothetical example, eight groups of people were tested in 1965; the results of this cross-sectional study, shown by the red line, indicate that IQ declines with age. However, when the same samples were retested a decade later, the results (shown by the blue line) show a rise in IQ for each age group (indicated by dashed lines). Apparently, cohort differences, not aging, are responsible for the downward trend. *(Adapted from Nesselroade, Schaie, and Baltes, 1972)*

cans scores higher on IQ tests (Flynn, 1984), so that younger cohorts score higher on the tests than older cohorts did at the same age. What appears to be a dramatic decline in IQ scores over age is in part an effect of the lower test scores for older groups throughout their lives. Age does affect test scores, but many people are well into their seventies before the first measureable age-related decline appears (Schaie, 1984).

Cross-sectional studies also have another limitation: they may not show the pattern of changes within the individual. Each person is tested only once, so we have only information about differences between individuals. Studies show that most children begin putting two words together just before their second birthday, but each child develops at his or her own pace, and no one can predict when a specific child will begin producing two-word sentences. Similarly, most people's performance on IQ tests begins to decline toward the end of life, yet it is impossible to predict when, why, or how much an individual's scores will decline. In fact, one eighty-two-year-old woman in New York State made higher scores on some parts of an IQ test than she had twenty years earlier (Jarvik, 1973).

Longitudinal Designs Cases like that of the eighty-two-year-old woman are detected in **longitudinal designs,** in which the same people are followed over weeks, months, years, or decades. The same people can be compared with themselves at ages twenty and eight. Cohort differences do not affect the results of longitudinal studies, and changes within the individual become clear. Studying development in this way is an expensive and lengthy way to proceed: a research project may take many years to complete.

Several longitudinal studies have been providing valuable information about development. For example, in the Intergenerational Studies, researchers have been following three groups of Californians for nearly sixty years (Eichorn, Clausen, Haan, Honzik, and Mussen, 1981). Two of the three groups in the study have been studied since their births, in 1928 and 1929; the third group has been studied since 1931, when they were fifth and sixth graders. From information collected on these individuals, we have learned a great deal about intellectual and social development, including factors that affect changes in IQ, political attitudes,

personality, emotional stability, sex roles, careers, and marriage. This study also has given us a detailed picture of the effects of one historical event — the Great Depression of the 1930s — on development (Elder, 1974).

Not all longitudinal studies go on for decades. Earlier we discussed Adamson and Bakeman's (1985) study of infant pleasure in play. This was a longitudinal study, in which babies were observed every three months over a twelve-month period.

Longitudinal studies may escape the errors that cohort differences can cause, but they have their own problems. They may confuse development with historical changes in society, which means that their results cannot be generalized to other cohorts. When people are tested again and again over decades, changes in society may be affecting their behavior. For example, television may be increasing the sophistication of young children, perhaps even influencing the way they process information. And the availability of cheap, reliable contraceptives may be affecting sexual attitudes and behavior. Such environmental changes may have profound — and unsuspected — effects on some aspect of development.

Another problem that limits the conclusions we can draw from longitudinal studies has to do with the subjects themselves. When people are tested repeatedly over many years, they may become familiar with the type of tests that are administered. If this happens, their scores show a "practice effect," so that comparisons with earlier scores may not be completely valid. And in lengthy longitudinal studies, the people in poorest health begin to die, leaving only the healthy, presumably more competent, survivors to be tested (Schaie, 1977). This diminishing pool of participants is accentuated as other subjects move away or refuse to take part in further testing. Taken together, these factors make the sample less representative than it was at the start of the study.

Mixed Designs Because cross-sectional and longitudinal designs have weaknesses, what can researchers do? Some researchers have suggested combining both designs in a single study, which they call a **sequential design** (Baltes, Reese, and Nesselroade, 1977).

Our realization that IQ scores do not decline drastically with age grew out of a sequential study directed by Warner Schaie (1979). This project,

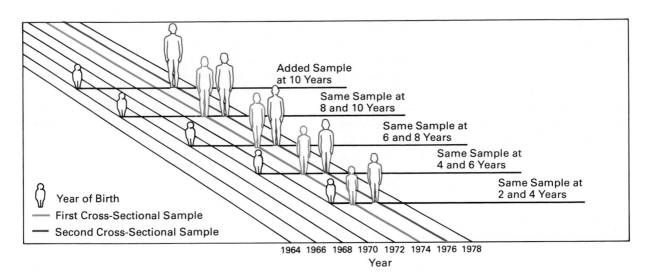

Figure 1.5   A sequential research design that combines cross-sectional and longitudinal research. First, samples of children at each of four ages (two, four, six, and eight) are selected and studied. Two years later the same samples of children are studied again, and another sample of ten-year-olds is included. Using both methods on the same group of children offsets the weaknesses inherent in each type of study.

known as the Seattle Longitudinal Study, began in 1956 with a cross-sectional group of 500 men and women between the ages of 21 and 70. The group was tested again in 1963, 1970, and 1977. On each occasion, another cross-sectional group was added to the study, also to be tested at subsequent points. In addition, researchers tested two different cross-sectional groups toward the close of the study: one in 1974 and the other in 1975 (see Migdal, Abeles, and Sherrod, 1981). Testing these last two groups allowed the researchers to discover whether the performance of the longitudinal groups had been affected by repeated testing. (A somewhat simpler sequential design is shown in Figure 1.5.)

Using a variety of designs and methods increases the confidence that researchers have in their findings. When the results of one study are verified by researchers using a different method or design, psychologists' confidence in their results also is bolstered. In fact, the more ways in which a finding can be verified, the more confident they are. When naturalistic observation, field studies, case studies, clinical studies, and experimental studies, cross-sectional and longitudinal designs yield the same general findings, we can put some confidence in the developmental change that has

been described and the conclusions of the researchers.

THE FIELD OF DEVELOPMENTAL PSYCHOLOGY

Although developmental psychologists focus on age-related changes in behavior, their field has broadened beyond the subject matter usually considered in psychology courses. Because development is affected at several levels of influence, developmental psychologists draw on information from biology, sociology, anthropology, and history to help them understand its course.

From their study of human development, developmentalists hope to achieve a number of goals:

- To *describe* changes with age and experience in physical growth, thinking, and personality. Such descriptions provide a picture of the general course of development.

- To *compare* people from diverse backgrounds, people with different rearing histories, and people with different biological histories. This comparison provides a picture of individual differences.

- To *explain* developmental changes and sequences according to principles, rules, theories, and mechanisms.
- To *predict* patterns of development. Once development can be predicted, we can devise ways to *control* it, and intervention becomes possible. This means that we can *improve* the situation of infants, children, or adults for whom the course of development has gone astray and perhaps *prevent* other developmental problems from arising. Individuals then might develop their capabilities to the utmost and lead more fulfilling lives.
- To *relate* the findings of developmental psychology to the work of other disciplines, so that basic knowledge is useful to educators, health-care providers, parents, therapists, social workers, and scientists.

Careers in Developmental Psychology

Developmental psychologists work in a wide variety of situations. They may conduct research; teach in colleges; or work in schools, clinics, businesses, or foundations. Some specialize in disseminating information about development to the public.

Researchers in developmental psychology usually are on university faculties, although they may carry out their research in schools, hospitals, or the community. They generally specialize in studying a particular age group and focus on a particular area of research. For example, one researcher may specialize in perception in young babies, another may focus on the influence of heredity on development, another on the effects of the family on the competence of preschool children, another on the development of memory in school-age children, and yet another on the effects of various environments on the competence of older adults. Some developmental psychologists do not work with people at all, but do their research with animals, hoping to find parallels to human development in the development of monkeys, kittens, or other species. Because development is influenced at various levels, developmental psychologists often conduct their research in col-

laboration with physicians, nutritionists, endocrinologists, physiologists, sociologists, psychiatrists, or anthropologists.

Some researchers also teach courses in developmental psychology. Many developmental psychologists specialize in teaching at the college level. Others work at schools, clinics, or hospitals, where they serve people who need special counseling. Some work with gifted children or with children who have learning problems; others work with socially isolated children. Some work with emotionally disturbed children or with children whose handicaps either require special counseling or keep them out of the regular school program. Some developmental psychologists work with older adults, who may be newly widowed, confined to nursing homes, or terminally ill.

Developmental psychologists also serve as consultants to business and industry. They might develop children's television programs, for example, or advise companies on the design of toys for children. They might work for foundations, where they would be concerned with research, training, and services related to the foundation's various programs connected with a developmental area such as birth defects. Finally, some developmental psychologists specialize in getting information to the public. They may write columns or articles for newspapers or magazines, they may write scripts for radio and television programs, or they may write books that help people to deal with various developmental tasks or problems.

Using Developmental Psychology

Information about human development in general is used in many ways. Such general information is the result of basic research, in which the potential value of the knowledge is not the primary consideration of the investigator. For example, he or she might be concerned with whether babies can perceive color. Whether a young baby sees the world in shades of gray or in color is a fascinating question. Sometimes, however, developmentalists use research to advance practical goals. For example, in the field of infancy, researchers have developed ways of coaching parents of premature infants, in the hope of preventing destructive interaction patterns between parent and child (Field, 1983). Combined day-care and parent-training programs for highly disadvantaged babies and preschoolers have reduced later school failure and delinquency during adolescence (Clement, Schweinhart, Barnett, Epstein, and Weikart, 1984). Premarital training programs have been devised to train couples in communicating and problem solving, in the hope of making marriages less vulnerable to divorce (Ridley, Avery, Harrell, Haynes-Clements, and McCunny, 1981). A program that teaches coping skills to residents of nursing homes has resulted in healthier, happier older adults whose success in managing daily events has given them a sense of control over their lives (Rodin and Hall, 1987).

The practical application of information about development is not restricted to professionals. Each of us can use information about development to improve our own lives. What we learn about the typical course of development can help us to cope with situations that might otherwise seem overwhelming. We find that our problems of career choice, mate selection, parenting, or coming to terms with aging are not unique, and we begin to see what a wide range of options we can choose among. As we understand the variables that influence human development, we gain insight into our own situation. This insight further widens our choices and opens the way to personal growth.

Studying developmental psychology often provides a new way of looking at development. It is easy to view nonhuman organisms with detachment, for their behavior is removed from anything we have experienced. It is more difficult, at first, to look at the behavior of a human being in a similarly objective fashion. But a major message of psychology is that human behavior has its antecedents and its consequences, that there is a regularity and a degree of lawfulness in development. After reading this book, you should be able to discover why certain types of behavior occur and how conditions may influence later behavior. You will no longer ascribe aggressive behavior to meanness, for example, but will begin to understand how temperament, family background, and experiences with peers can interact to produce a person who frequently fights with others. Our investigation of developmental theories, which occupies the next chapter, will provide you with the various frameworks that have been used to explain development.

SUMMARY

1. **Development,** which is the process of age-related change over the life span, occurs through the **interaction** of heredity and environment. Developmental change within the individual is continuous, cumulative, directional, differentiated, organized, and holistic. A developmental **stage** is characterized by four features. It is structured (its parts link in a cohesive pattern). It displays qualitative change (behavior is radically different from the preceding stage). It appears abruptly (abilities, motives, and skills show only a brief transition). And it displays concurrence (abilities and behavior develop at about the same pace). Developmentalists disagree about whether development is stagelike (and therefore discontinuous) or continuous (and therefore quantitative instead of qualitative). Because chronological age is not always the most helpful way to divide the life span, societies often rely on biological, social, or cognitive markers. The divisions may differ from one society to another; in American society, people divide the life span into a **prenatal period, infancy, childhood, adolescence,** and **adulthood.**

2. Hereditary influences on development (whether genetic or biological) never operate in isolation from the environment. Although developmentalists agree that both nature and nurture are involved in all aspects of development, they disagree about how they interact in specific areas of development.

3. Research in development begins with a **hypothesis** — a prediction that can be tested by gathering appropriate information. Researchers use various methods to test hypotheses; each method produces information about the effects of **variables** (factors) on behavior, and the methods vary in the amount of control

possible in each. **Observational studies,** in which people go about their daily activities, give the researcher the least control. They may be **naturalistic studies** (in which researchers simply observe and record what they see) or **field studies** (in which the researcher introduces some variable that changes the situation). **Interview studies,** in which investigators question their subjects, then analyze their replies, allow a moderate amount of control. Interview studies may be **clinical studies** (in-depth interviews, supplemented by observation and questionnaires) or **case studies** (in which the same individuals are observed and interviewed over a period of months or years). **Experiments,** in which the researcher can control the presence, absence, or intensity of various variables, offer the most control. In an experiment, an **independent variable** is manipulated by the researcher, and this manipulation affects the **dependent variable,** which is usually a measure of the subjects' behavior. The behavior of individuals in the **experimental group** is compared with that of individuals in the **control group,** who are not exposed to the experimental condition.

4. To those who study development, the nature of the experimental design is important. Some age-related changes may simply reflect the influence of historical events on a **cohort** (a group of people born at about the same time). Cohort effects may affect **cross-sectional designs,** in which researchers study different age groups at the same time. **Longitudinal designs,** in which the same people are followed for months or years, are not affected by differences among cohorts, but they may be influenced by changes in society. **Sequential designs** combine cross-sectional and longitudinal designs in a single study.

5. Researchers may either conduct basic developmental research, in which the potential value of their findings is not a primary consideration, or applied research, in which the purpose is to advance practical goals. Developmental psychologists work in a variety of settings, conducting research, teaching, counseling individuals who need special assistance, and serving as consultants to schools, business, and industry. Most researchers specialize in a particular age group and a particular area of development. Underlying the study of development are the convictions that behavior has antecedents and consequences and that development is regular and lawful.

KEY TERMS

adolescence
adulthood
case study
childhood
clinical study
cohort
control group
cross-sectional design

dependent variable
development
experiment
experimental group
field study
hypothesis
independent variable
infancy

interaction
longitudinal design
naturalistic study
observational study
prenatal period
sequential design
stage
variable

STUDY TERMS

cohort The members of a particular age group; a group of people of the same age.

control group A group with the same characteristics as the experimental group but that does not undergo the experimental treatment.

cross-sectional design An experimental design that

compares the performance of different age groups on a single occasion.

experiment   A study in which researchers can control the arrangement and manipulation of conditions, in order to systematically observe particular phenomena.

hypothesis   A prediction based on theory that can be tested by gathering appropriate information in some sort of study—either observational, interview, or a true experiment.

interaction   A spiraling developmental process in which hereditary characteristics influence the environment, which in turn affects further development, and vice versa.

longitudinal design   An experimental design that follows the same subjects over time, comparing their behavior at different ages.

observational study   Any study in which researchers observe people as they go about daily activities and carefully record their behavior. It may be a *naturalistic study*, in which researchers simply observe behavior without interfering in any way, or a *field study*, in which they introduce some factor into the natural situation that changes it.

sequential design   An experimental design that combines elements from cross-sectional and longitudinal designs in a single study.

stage   A particular pattern of abilities, motives, or behavior that is predicted by a specific theory of development; each stage is structured, reflects qualitative changes in behavior, appears abruptly, and has characteristic abilities that develop at about the same pace.

variable   A factor that can vary in size or strength and that may affect the results of a study. The *independent variable* is selected or changed in some way by the investigator (to test a hypothesis); its introduction changes the *dependent variable*.

CHAPTER 2

Theories
of Development

BIOLOGICAL THEORIES
Maturational Theories / Ethological Theories

PSYCHODYNAMIC THEORIES
Freud's Psychosexual Theory / Erikson's Psychosocial Theory

BEHAVIOR-LEARNING THEORIES
Conditioning Theories / Social-Learning Theories

COGNITIVE THEORIES
Piaget's Cognitive-Developmental Theory / Information-Processing Theories

DIALECTICAL THEORIES

UNDERSTANDING HUMAN DEVELOPMENT

The advice given American parents who seek help in rearing their children has varied dramatically over the past sixty years. During the 1920s, pamphlets published by the U.S. Children's Bureau urged parents to curb their babies' sensuous impulses. Parents were to stamp out thumbsucking with mittens sewn over the ends of nightgown sleeves or by pinning the tiny sleeves to the cribsheet. And they were to eliminate masturbation by tying the little feet to bars on opposite sides of the crib, so babies could not get pleasurable sensations by rubbing their thighs together. Ten years later, concern had shifted to another area of child rearing. Parents were told that they must not permit their babies to run the household. If infants were dry, full, and not being stuck by a pin, said the experts, let them cry it out; otherwise parents would be ruled by their babies' whims. Government experts who advised parents during the 1940s were not horrified by thumbsucking and masturbation, but they were still uncomfortable with these activities. Now the advice was to distract the baby with a toy whenever a thumb wandered into the mouth or a little hand strayed to the genitals. At last, however, parents were permitted to pick up a crying child (Wolfenstein, 1955).

25

During the 1950s, experts no longer talked about stifling babies' impulses and attempts at tyranny. Instead the basic message was, "enjoy your baby." Parents were told that development follows a biological plan, one that is deflected only by severe deprivation. Babies would regulate themselves, and parents need only be warm, and loving, and alert to their babies' needs.

Today the message is only slightly different. Parents are still urged to be warm, and loving, and sensitive to their babies' needs, but they are advised to provide stimulation as well. Now that research has established the baby's great ability to learn, experts talk about infant capabilities and how parents can develop social and intellectual skills by talking to their babies and playing games with them. Over the past few decades, most of the restrictions and fears that alarmed our grandparents have been banished from the nursery. How did they get there in the first place? And why do experts say one thing to one generation of parents and something quite different to the next?

The answer to both questions is the same: over the years, theories of development change, and the advice of experts generally reflects whichever theory of development happens to be most influential at the time. A **theory** is a set of logically related statements that generates testable hypotheses and explains some aspect of experience.

How important are theories? Without theories, we would have only a collection of facts without any kind of interpretation. The logical statements of theories indicate which facts are most important for interpreting development and show how our facts about development fit together. Because every theory is built on certain assumptions, theories act like a lens, filtering out certain facts and arranging the others in a particular pattern (Thomas, 1979). The lens both helps to organize the facts and influences their interpretation.

Theories are important for another reason: they guide research. A good theory leads to hypotheses about development. As we saw in Chapter 1, before we can design a study that will tell us something about development, we must have a hypothesis to test — a prediction concerning the relations among the facts we observe. Thus, theories are also important because they enable us to predict the outcome of situations — both in studies and in life. As we consider the major developmental

theories, try to see how each theory filters out some facts and focuses on others.

In this chapter, we explore the major types of developmental theories, noting the perspective of each. In biological theories of development, the evolutionary history of the species and the maturation of the individual are the dominant factors in development. Psychodynamic theories spring from Sigmund Freud's insights into human motivation and sexual development. Behavior-learning theorists focus on the role of environmental experiences. Cognitive theorists, by contrast, focus on activities of the learner and processes of thought. Dialectical theorists look at the interaction between the organism and the environment, stressing the way that development is profoundly altered by historical and cultural influences. Finally, we discover why the different perspectives are so difficult to compare and how each addresses important developmental issues.

BIOLOGICAL THEORIES

Biological theories lean to the nature side of the nature-nurture question, although they recognize the necessary interactions that must occur between the developing person and the environment. All biological theories have been heavily influenced by the ideas of Charles Darwin, which led many developmentalists to look at behavior from an evolutionary perspective. Some biological theories emphasize the maturation of the individual and others focus on the way biologically based behavior increases the child's chances of survival.

Maturational Theories

Developmentalists who propose **maturational theories** believe that development is directed from within, unfolding according to a biological timetable. The major advocate of the biological approach to development was Arnold Gesell. Gesell believed that capabilities appeared when children reached the appropriate stage of maturity. No matter how many opportunities a child had to learn some skill, until muscles, nerves, brain, and bones were ready, all attempts to teach them would be

ARNOLD GESELL

(1880–1961)

(Historical Pictures Service)

Arnold Gesell grew up in a small Wisconsin town located on the banks of the upper Mississippi River. His career spanned several professions: educator, psychologist, physician, and writer. After starting his professional life as an educator, he entered Clark University, where his views of development were influenced by his teacher, G. Stanley Hall. After he became a psychologist and began studying children, he decided that unless he knew more about physiology, he would never understand development. So at the age of 30, he entered medical school.

For fifty years, Gesell worked at the Yale Clinic of Child Development, becoming its director in 1911 and retiring in 1948. He is noted for the detailed studies of children's growth and development that were carried out under his supervision. Gesell was an innovator: he was the first to film his observations of infants and young children, preserving their activities for later frame-by-frame study, and he was a pioneer in the development of infant intelligence tests. Because he applied his theories to child rearing, he has had a major impact on the way American children were reared. His books for the general public (*The First Five Years of Life* [1940]; *The Child from Five to Ten* [1946]; *Youth* [1956]) contained reassuring advice and detailed information about physical and behavioral changes during each year of life, from birth to age sixteen.

futile. Some children walked, talked, and developed self-control early, and some were much slower, but each capability appeared when the child was ready to acquire it.

This belief was accompanied by a faith in self-regulation. Gesell believed that children indicate when they are ready for some developmental step. A newborn baby knows when she is hungry, an older infant knows when he is ready to walk, a toddler knows when she is ready to talk, and so on. If parents follow the baby's signals, instead of trying to impose their own expectations, family life runs more smoothly. As you can see, this advice is similar to the message from government experts during the 1950s — to stop worrying and enjoy your baby.

Gesell believed that development went through a series of stages, with periods of smooth, coordinated behavior sandwiched between transitional periods of unstable behavior, when a child first acquired new ways of doing things and then consolidated them. This process was common to all aspects of development — physical coordination, temperament, personality, and intellectual skills.

Although most psychologists agree that maturation plays an important role in early development, they believe that Gesell's position does not give enough importance to teaching and learning (Crain, 1985). Some contemporary psychologists (such as Scarr, 1985) are influenced by Gesell's views; others believe that optimal development requires an environment that is more than simply adequate.

Ethological Theories

A group of dedicated naturalists who sought to observe development in its natural settings has brought the ideas of Charles Darwin (1809–1882) and the methods of behavioral biology into the field of developmental psychology. These **ethologists** translate biological evolutionary concepts into behavioral terms in order to study human development. Konrad Lorenz and Niko Tinbergen, who worked primarily with animals, pioneered this way of studying behavior. Together with Karl von Frisch, they received the Nobel Prize for their research in 1973.

When seen from the ethological viewpoint, human behavior is best understood by examining the way it enables babies, children, or adults to survive and flourish in an environment similar to the one in which our species evolved. When psychiatrist John Bowlby (1969) examined the bond between infant and mother, for example, he concluded that it was part of a behavioral system that had evolved to protect the developing organism. Because human infants are helpless for so long, their survival depends on protection by mature members of the species. The attachment of babies to their caregivers promotes survival by generally keeping the pair in close proximity. Although attachment is expressed in varying ways in different cultures, some variety of bond between infant and caregiver has been present in every society studied.

If babies develop attachments to keep them near adults, what sort of evolved response guarantees that the adult caregiver will care for a baby's needs? Ethologists believe that the baby's smile, the baby's cuteness, and the baby's cry act as **releasing stimuli,** which are events that regularly evoke certain behavior in members of a species. Darwin (1872/1955) first pointed out that the baby's smile evoked feelings of joy in the caregiver, a "released" response that tends to keep the caregiver nearby. Lorenz (1942–1943) has noted that in most species, adult animals respond to very young animals with caregiving—yet they rarely respond in this way to other adults. In fact, most people respond to cuteness in babies and baby animals by wanting to pick them up and cuddle them. What makes the babies of any species seem cute? Young animals are cute because they have relatively large heads, particularly foreheads, and foreshortened facial features. This combination of features apparently acts as a releasing stimulus, improving the chances of adequate infant care and survival. Finally, the baby's cry also serves as a releaser (Hinde, 1983). Cries may not release joy or an urge to cuddle, but they are extremely effective in bringing an adult to the infant's side.

Ethologists also have noted remarkable similarity in the social behavior of human beings and their nearest primate relatives. This resemblance has led them to see the structure of children's play groups as formed by evolved behavior. These groups invariably have dominance hierarchies, which are so similar to those that characterize monkey and ape troops that they may have the same evolutionary source (Rajecki and Flanery, 1981). Children climb the dominance ladder by means of physical attack, threats, or struggles over objects.

Courtship and greeting rituals also seem to show some sort of evolutionary basis. Irenäus Eibl-Eibesfeldt (1970), who studied groups around the world, found amazing similarities in the facial expressions that accompany these rituals. For example, when a woman greets a man in a flirtatious manner, the eyebrows go up, the head tilts, the gaze lowers, and the eyelids drop. No matter which cultural tradition a woman comes from, she uses the same mannerisms.

Ethological theories suggest that human development is best understood by looking at behavior as partially the product of our evolutionary history. This approach has been most useful when it is applied to infancy, although developmentalists also have begun to look at older age groups. The research method developed by ethologists, which involves careful observation in natural settings, has been adopted by investigators in many areas of developmental psychology.

PSYCHODYNAMIC THEORIES

Most psychodynamic theorists discuss human development in terms of various confrontations between the growing individual and the demands of the social world. They emphasize how the individual must accommodate to society while gratifying basic human drives. Most also emphasize that the child gradually develops a sense of self, an identity against which to judge his or her own behavior.

As a group, psychodynamic theorists have centered their attention on personality development. Their concern has been to understand and explain the development of both rational and irrational feelings and behavior. To some extent, all psychodynamic theorists have tried to account for human

SIGMUND FREUD

(1856–1939)

Sigmund Freud's theories reflect his training in the biological sciences and his clinical experience. He specialized in physiology, received his M.D. degree in Vienna in 1881, and began lecturing and doing research in neuropathology. A grant enabled him to go to Paris and study under the famous neurologist Jean Martin Charcot, who was using hypnosis to treat hysteria.

Freud became interested in personality when he realized that many of his patients' physical symptoms were caused by mental or emotional factors. This led to his development of free association and dream interpretation as therapeutic methods. He found that his adult neurotic patients had repressed their memories of early childhood emotional experiences, which generally involved sex, aggression, or jealousy. Because these experiences were unpleasant, Freud proposed that they became lost to awareness; that is, they were pushed into an unreachable area of the mind, the unconscious.

In his theory of psychosexual development, he interpreted what he learned from treating his patients in the light of embryology and physics. He proposed that the emergence of psychosexual stages was primarily determined by maturation and that mental life followed the law of conservation of energy, which states that energy cannot be created or destroyed, only transformed. People's mental and emotional lives, he believed, show a comparable transformation of psychic energy (libido) from one stage to the next. This energy motivates people's thinking, their perceptions, and their memories, and it remains constant even though it becomes associated with different regions of the body during development.

development by looking at early sexual and emotional experiences that may influence later behavior.

Freud's Psychosexual Theory

As Sigmund Freud (1905/1955) saw it, from earliest infancy human beings are motivated by irrational urges toward pleasure. These urges are an expression of the **libido,** which is the "life force" or "psychic energy" that motivates human behavior. The young child's instincts inevitably conflict with social demands, forcing the youngster to alter his or her behavior in socially acceptable ways. Out of this continual conflict, rational behavior gradually develops. In Freud's psychosexual theory of development, intelligence or adaptation is much less important than a sensuality that has become socialized.

Freud proposed the existence of three conflicting aspects of human personality: the id, the ego, and the superego. In the **id** reside all of the **unconscious** impulses; the person is unaware of these forces. The newborn baby is pure id. The **ego,** which begins to develop when a baby is about six months old, guides a person's realistic coping behavior. It uses memory, reason, and judgment in its task, which is to mediate the eternal conflicts between what one wants to do (the province of the id) and what one must or must not do (the province of the superego). The **superego** is the conscience, which develops in early childhood as a child internalizes parental values and standards of conduct.

Freud's view of human development is in part an evolutionary one. Our biological urges are part of our evolved animal nature, and development proceeds through interaction with external reality. Thus, development is an unfolding of genetic

Table 2.1
Freud's Psychosexual Developmental Stages

Age*	Psychosexual Stage	Focus of Pleasurable Feelings	Characteristic Behavior	Unfavorable Outcome (Fixation)
Birth to 18 months	Oral	Mouth, lips	Seeks oral stimulation Sucks although not hungry	Alcoholism, smoking, nail-biting Immature, demanding personality
18 months to 3 years	Anal	Rectum	Enjoys expelling and retaining feces	Highly rigid conformism Compulsive neatness, miserliness Hostile, defiant personality
3 to 6 years	Phallic	Genitals	Fondles genitals Falls in love with parent of other sex	Sexual problems (impotence, frigidity) Homosexuality Inability to handle competition
6 to 11 years	Latency	—	Mastery of developmental skills	
From puberty	Genital	Other people	Mature sexual relationships	

* Ages approximate.

stages in which instinctual libidinal impulses become attached to various pleasure centers of the body. Freud described the human life cycle in terms of a **psychosexual theory,** tying psychological development to the resolution of the conflicts that characterize each stage of life (see Table 2.1). Unless the growing child successfully navigates a stage, Freud believed, he or she will become **fixated** at that stage and as an adult will have an immature personality in which the characteristic traits of the stage predominate.

Freud saw the third, or phallic, stage of development as particularly critical. At this time, he believed, boys fall in love with their mothers and girls with their fathers. Yet it is clear to the boy that he cannot have his mother to himself, that his father is his rival in the battle for his mother's affections. And it is equally clear to the girl that her wish to possess her father cannot succeed because of her mother. This realization produces psychological turmoil within the child, known as the *Oedipus complex.* Powerless to push the rival parent out of the way and fearing punishment, both boys and girls resolve their Oedipal conflict by identifying with the parent of their own sex. Boys assume their fathers' values, standards, sexual orien-

tation, mannerisms, and other characteristics and girls, their mothers' characteristics. This internalization of parental values produces the superego; now children can feel shame or guilt when they violate the internalized standards.

Once Freud's theories found their way into academic and popular thinking, the field of human development was changed. Today's psychodynamic theories are elaborations and modifications of Freud's thought or reactions to it. Yet it has proved difficult to test Freud's basic concepts, because some are metaphorical and do not lend themselves to testable hypotheses. After analyzing their research into children's views of the family, Kurt Fischer and Malcolm Watson (1981) suggested that most children who live in a nuclear family probably do go through some form of Oedipal conflict but that the four-year-old's jealousy of the same-sex parent develops because the youngster cannot understand family roles. Although they know that girls become mommies and boys become daddies, they can think about only one dimension of a role at a time. And so a four-year-old boy believes that when he grows older, his mother will be the same age as she is today. At about six, children understand that a person can be

ERIK ERIKSON

(b. 1902)

(Olive R. Pierce/Black Star)

Erik Erikson was born in Germany of Danish parents. He graduated from art school and went to Florence, Italy, intending to become an art teacher. In Vienna, where he had gone to teach children of American families, he met Freud and other analysts, and soon entered psychoanalytic training.

When Hitler came to power in Germany, Erikson emigrated to America. He held a series of positions in child-guidance clinics and major universities while maintaining a private practice. During an appointment at Harvard University, Erikson developed an interest in anthropology and studied the Sioux and Yurok Indians. During a subsequent ap-

pointment at the University of California, Berkeley, he studied adolescents, using a technique in which the way young people played with dolls revealed their unconscious thoughts and feelings.

Erikson is one of the few theorists to describe emotional development across the life span. In his theory, personality develops through eight stages, from infancy to the final stage of life. As a person interacts with a widening social world, he or she moves from a universe of self and mother to an image of humankind. Each stage has its own conflict to be resolved, and the failure to resolve any of these conflicts can lead to psychological disorders. Erikson's psychodynamic theory is important for several reasons. Unlike Freud, he believes that neuroses are not necessarily the result of problems in infancy or early childhood. He emphasizes the healthy personality instead of the disturbed individual. He includes society and history as well as the family among forces affecting emotional development.

both a mommy and a wife or a daddy and a husband. They resolve the conflict—not out of fear, as Freud proposed, but because cognitive development has ended the child's confusion about roles.

Erikson's Psychosocial Theory

Erik Erikson (1982) has heavily modified Freud's psychoanalytic theory, turning it into an elaborate stage theory that describes emotional development across the life span. In Erikson's **psychosocial theory,** personality develops according to steps predetermined by the individual's readiness to react with a widening social world, a world that begins with a dim image of mother and ends with an image of humanity. Erikson saw development as consisting of the progressive resolution of conflicts between needs and social demands. At each of eight stages, conflicts must be resolved, at least partially, before progress can be made on the next

set of problems (see Table 2.2). Yet the successful resolution of a conflict does not eliminate the defeated quality (such as mistrust or despair) from the personality. In healthy individuals, the balance merely shifts so that the victorious quality (such as trust or integrity) becomes dominant (Erikson and Hall, 1987). At any stage, a failure to resolve the conflict can result in psychological disorders that affect the rest of the life span.

From Trust to Industry Babies need to develop a relationship in which they can get what they require from a person who is ready and able to provide it—almost always a mother. They need to develop feelings of comfort with their mothers and need to know that a consistent caregiver will be there when they need one. Constant, reliable care promotes the baby's sense of *trust*. This consistency in care enables babies to learn to tolerate frustrations and to delay immediate gratifications,

Table 2.2
Erikson's Psychosocial Developmental Stages

Age*	Psychosocial Stage	Psychosocial Conflict	Favorable Outcome	Unfavorable Outcome
Birth to 18 months	Infancy	Basic trust vs. mistrust	Hope Tolerates frustration; can delay gratification	Suspicion; withdrawal
18 months to 3 years	Early childhood	Autonomy vs. shame, doubt	Will Self-control; self-esteem	Compulsion; impulsivity
3 to 6 years	Play age	Initiative vs. guilt	Purpose Enjoys accomplishments	Inhibition
6 to 11 years	School age	Industry vs. inferiority	Competence	Inadequacy; inferiority
Puberty to early twenties	Adolescence	Identity vs. role confusion	Fidelity	Diffidence, defiance, socially unacceptable identity
Early twenties to 40	Young adulthood	Intimacy vs. isolation	Love	Exclusivity; avoidance of commitment
40 to 60 years	Middle adulthood	Generativity vs. stagnation	Care Concern for future generations, for society	Rejection of others; self-indulgence
From 60 years	Old age	Integrity vs. despair	Wisdom	Disdain; disgust

* Ages approximate. Erikson (Erikson and Hall, 1987) recently has suggested that the period of generativity may last much longer today, now that adults remain healthy and active until an advanced age.

Note: Erikson's first four stages correspond to Freud's psychosexual stages, but Erikson has subdivided Freud's fifth stage into four stages.

because they know that adults around them care and can be trusted to meet their needs. If the baby's needs are not consistently met, he or she may develop a sense of mistrust and react to frustration with anxiety and upset.

After infants begin to walk and to exercise some self-direction, they run into social restraints. During this second stage, they increasingly demand to determine their own behavior ("Me do it!"), but because they have little judgment about their actual capabilities, they need to be gently protected from excesses while granted *autonomy* in those matters that they can handle. It is particularly important at this stage, Erikson suggests, that parents not shame a child into feeling that he or she is incompetent. Shame can be a devastating experience for anyone, and it is particularly difficult for young

children who are struggling for autonomy and who are not yet sure that they can develop any degree of competent self-regulation.

After children have gained a relatively secure sense of autonomy, they enter the third stage of development and are ready to take the initiative in planning their own activities. As Erikson sees it, *initiative* adds to autonomy the quality of undertaking, planning, and attacking a task for the sake of being active and on the move. In the preceding stage, self-will often inspired acts of defiance. In the third stage, children are ready for positive, constructive activities under their own initiative. The potential problem at this period is guilt; children may come to feel that their intrusiveness and activity have evil consequences. This is the period of sexual attraction to the parent of the other sex, of seductive behavior by little girls toward their fathers, and of assertive, manly behavior of little boys toward their mothers. As children resolve these hopeless attractions, they identify with the same-sex parent and develop a conscience. Harsh parental responses to a child's sexual overtures and other initiatives, however, can lead to an overdeveloped, harsh conscience that may always plague the person with guilt.

Erikson theorizes that, once children have come to terms with their families by identifying with the same-sex parent, they enter the fourth stage and are ready to move into the larger world. About this time, in our culture, they go to school. Before children can become adults in any society, they must become workers; they learn that they will gain recognition by producing things *(industry)*. The child, therefore, wants to learn the technical skills that characterize adults. The potential problem in this period lies in a sense of inadequacy and inferiority, which can develop if children are not praised for their accomplishments. In Erikson's theory, this is a decisive stage, for the child must prepare for effective adult roles.

From Identity to Ego Integrity   In the fifth stage, adolescents question all of their previous resolutions to problems of trust, autonomy, initiative, and industry. Rapid body growth and genital maturity create a "physiological revolution" within them at the time that they face adult life. According to Erikson, adolescents search for continuity and sameness within themselves—a sense of *identity* —and in their search they have to refight the battles of earlier years, usually casting their parents in the role of adversaries. They try to discard roles and ways of behaving, then reformulate them and try them again. The potential problem at this period is that an adolescent's identity may become confused. When this happens, adolescents do not learn who they are as people, as sexual beings, as adult workers, as potential parents. They are unable to commit themselves to any goal.

Young adults emerging from the search for identity are eager and willing to fuse their identities with those of others. In terms of Erikson's sixth stage, they are ready for *intimacy*, for relationships with others in which they are strong enough to make sacrifices for another's welfare without losing themselves in another's identity. It

is at this point that true sexual love can emerge. The potential problem at this stage is isolation from others, a failure to commit oneself to loving relationships because of competition or fear.

Generativity characterizes the seventh stage and refers to the adult's concern with establishing and guiding the next generation. Merely producing children does not give a person a sense of generativity; adults must see the role of rearing children as a contribution to humankind and the larger society. Those who are childless can express generativity through productivity in their work and creativity in their lives. Having a sense of accomplishment in adult life depends on giving loving care to others and regarding your own contributions to society as valuable. The possible dangers of this period are self-absorption and a sense of stagnation, a feeling that you are going nowhere, doing nothing important.

In Erikson's theory, the final stage of the life cycle should result in a sense of wholeness, of purposes accomplished and a life well lived. People who develop *ego integrity* see meaning in their lives and believe that they did the best they could under the circumstances. In such a final consolidation of life's stages, death loses its sting. The potential problem in the final stage is regret and despair over wasted chances and unfortunate choices. A despairing person fears death and wishes desperately for another chance. The person with integrity accepts death as the end of a meaningful lifetime.

Although Erikson's theory is complex and vague, researchers have been able to derive hypotheses from it. Most of their studies have focused on college students, who do seem to be considering alternative identities and forming commitments (Waterman, 1982). Adolescents who have been unable to establish their identities often seem maladjusted in ways that Erikson might have predicted. In a longitudinal study of Harvard men (Valliant, 1977), those who seemed most mature and adapted to the world at midlife had mastered the tasks of the first seven stages. By contrast, those whose lives seemed unsuccessful tended to be filled with mistrust, to have problems with autonomy and initiative, to have insecure identities, to have failed in their attempts at intimacy, and were reluctant to assume the responsibility for other adults.

In Erikson's theory, the major developmental task facing young adults is the development of intimacy. Those who cannot commit themselves to a loving relationship risk becoming isolated from others. *(Chris Brown)*

BEHAVIOR-LEARNING THEORIES

The theorists we have just considered, whether maturational or psychodynamic, see development as originating within the person. Developmentalists who take a behavior-learning approach see the major influence as coming from the environment. Although they agree that biological factors set limits on the sort of behavior that develops, behavior-learning theorists lean toward the nurture side of the nature-nurture question. They believe that experience or learning is responsible for most of what babies become and that learning begins before the child leaves the uterus. Because learning theorists reject the notion that development comes primarily from within, they see it as a continuous process—one without stages.

Conditioning Theories

When psychologists explain development in terms of **conditioning theories,** they interpret developmental changes in terms of learning to associate one event with another, either through classical or operant conditioning. These psychologists, whose work is heavily influenced by the theories of behaviorists John B. Watson and B. F. Skinner, believe that conditioning can explain all learning, from how children acquire language to what makes people attend a ballet, cherish free speech, or go to war.

Watson explained all learning in terms of classical conditioning. In **classical,** or respondent, **conditioning,** we learn to associate two events that happen at about the same time. In this form of conditioning, we have no control over either event. Studies of classical conditioning grew out of the work of Ivan Pavlov (1927) in Russia. Pavlov demonstrated that some kinds of behavior, which he called reflexes, were responses to external stimuli. There are two kinds of reflexes: unconditioned reflexes and conditioned reflexes. **Unconditioned reflexes** are responses that a person naturally gives to a specific stimulus. For example, we blink an eye when a puff of air strikes the eyeball, and we salivate when food is placed in the mouth. **Conditioned reflexes** are responses that we *learn* by associating a neutral stimulus, such as a bell or light, with an unconditioned stimulus, such as a puff of air or the taste of food.

We learn these conditioned reflexes through the process of classical conditioning, which works in a predictable way. If the conditioned stimulus occurs repeatedly just before the unconditioned stimulus, we come to respond to the conditioned stimulus much as we originally responded only to the unconditioned stimulus. If a bright light suddenly shines in your eyes, you will squeeze your eyelids shut. This is a reflexive movement; even a newborn baby behaves this way. Suppose that someone sounds a buzzer, then shines a spotlight into your eyes. After this happens several times, you will squeeze your lids shut each time you hear the buzzer, although the light never comes on.

Emotions are particularly subject to classical conditioning. Parents have noticed this process at work in their children and commonly observe that, by the time their baby is one year old, he or she begins to cry at the sight of a nurse who has always been present when the baby got a painful injection. Many of our emotional reactions are conditioned — such as disgust at thought of eating worms or the shudder of fear when a door creaks in a horror film.

Classical conditioning ignores the consequences of a person's responses. In **operant conditioning,** we are still learning to connect two events, but one of the events is our behavior. (We "operate" on the environment.) Operant conditioning is also known as *instrumental conditioning,* because our actions are "instrumental" in producing whatever pleasant or painful consequences follow. In this basic kind of learning, which was described and studied by Skinner (1938), any action that is followed by some pleasant consequence or any action that ends some unpleasant situation is strengthened, or "reinforced."

Reinforcement can take many forms. Positive reinforcement brings us a pleasant consequence; it includes concrete rewards (such as money, toys, or candy), and intangible rewards (such as affection, praise, attention, or the satisfaction that comes with the completion of a difficult task). For example, suppose that a boy sees an adult leave a package behind on a counter. If he receives a reward (a quarter or warm praise) when he runs after the adult and returns the package, the boy will be likely to respond that way again. *Negative reinforcement* removes something unpleasant from our immediate situation. It includes relief from pain, the ending of arguments or cries, or the removal of some barrier that stands between us and something we want. For example, if a baby stops crying when the father picks it up, then the father is likely to pick up the baby the next time he hears his child crying. Responses that are not reinforced decrease in frequency or may even be eliminated (**extinguished**). If the boy gets no reward, he will be less likely to be so helpful in the future; if the baby keeps wailing, the father is unlikely to rush to the crib the next time the baby cries.

When our actions are punished, our tendency to repeat them is weakened. **Punishment** includes any unpleasant consequence, from a spanking or a scolding to the removal of something pleasant, such as the loss of privileges when a teenager is grounded or the loss of money when a speeding motorist is fined.

If we had to experience every situation for conditioning to operate, we would learn very slowly. Yet we learn rapidly, in part because both classical and operant conditioning generalize to other situations — even when the generalization may be inappropriate. For example, the baby who fears the nurse who gives injections may come to fear all people in white uniforms or all rooms that look like an examining room. The child who learns to call mother "Mommy" may also call the caregiver at the day-care center "Mommy."

Operant principles also can be used to develop new behavior. When they are applied in this way, the new behavior is shaped by the technique of **successive approximation.** When using this technique, you initially reward behavior that represents a first step toward the action you want. Then the behavior must resemble the desired response more and more closely. For example, if you are teaching a little girl to draw a circle, you would first reward her (with praise and encouragement) for picking up the pencil, then for holding it correctly, then for drawing a curved line, then for drawings that are more and more circular, until at last she must draw an acceptable circle to get a reward (Bijou, 1976). This method has been used successfully in a wide variety of situations, from toilet training young children and coaching athletic teams, to teaching social and cognitive skills (Semb, 1972). It has also been used to persuade a shy six-year-old who could not utter a word in the classroom to talk normally (Richards and Siegel, 1978).

Social-Learning Theories

Some psychologists considered the conditioning approach too narrow and inflexible. They believed that not all learning could be explained as a result of classical and operant conditioning. In its place, they developed **social-learning theory,** which grew out of earlier behavior-learning views but which stressed that people often learn, not only through shaping and reinforcement, but also by watching others.

With observational learning given such prominence, the process of **imitation** came to play a key role in most social-learning accounts of human development. Many studies have demonstrated the increasing resemblance of the child's social behav-

When youngsters imitate
their parents' actions, they
demonstrate the basis of
social-learning theorists' belief that imitation plays an
essential role in development.
(Owen Franken/Stock, Boston)

ior to that of adult models, and explanations for this resemblance have broadened over the years. The earliest social-learning theorists focused on the child's imitation of his or her parents. Neal Miller and John Dollard (1941) proposed that nurturance from parents becomes the motivating force for a child's imitations. As parents satisfy the child's needs for food, warmth, and affection, they become associated with the satisfaction of those needs and take on reinforcing properties them-selves. Because the parents' behavior is reinforc-ing, the child begins imitating whatever the parent does to reward himself or herself. Subsequently, Jerome Kagan (1958) and John Whiting (1960) pointed out that parents also have more power and control more possessions than the child does. The child envies the parents' status and copies them in the hope that such imitations will bring the child some of the parents' influence and status.

Then Albert Bandura and Richard Walters (1963) stressed that children can learn new re-sponses merely from watching a model. If they see the model rewarded for some behavior, they are as likely to imitate it as if they have been rewarded themselves. Further, when a child is rewarded for imitating a model, the child will tend to imitate the model on later occasions even when not rewarded (Bandura, 1969).

Since that time, social-learning theorists have shifted their emphasis in a radical direction. Ban-dura (1977), who has been one of the theorists responsible for these changes, has restated many aspects of human learning and motivation in terms of **cognition,** which encompasses all the processes we use to gain knowledge about the world. Ac-cording to Bandura, cognitive processes (percep-tion, learning, memory, and thinking) play a cen-tral role in regulating what children and adults attend to, how they describe or think about what they see and hear, and whether they repeat it to themselves and lodge it in memory. Short-lived everyday experiences can leave lasting effects be-cause they are retained in memory in symbolic form. In contemporary social-learning theory, learning from a model is not simply a matter of imitation. As children and adults watch others, they form concepts about possible behavior that will later guide their own actions. As they then observe their actions and the consequences, they can change their concepts and act in different ways.

Children tend to copy a model's complete pat-tern of behavior, instead of slowly learning bits of a pattern in response to reinforcement. When watching a model, children can learn entirely new behavior, although they might not immediately

ALBERT BANDURA

(b. 1925)

(Courtesy Dr. Albert Bandura)

Albert Bandura received his doctorate in clinical psychology from Iowa State University in 1952; after completing a post-doctoral internship, he accepted a position at Stanford University, where he is professor of psychology. His research and writing on personality and social development reflect his background in clinical psychology and his strong interest in child development. Over the past few years, his theories have had a major influence on the thinking of developmental psychologists.

Early in his career, Bandura became dissatisfied with the gaps that existed between the concepts of clinical psychology and those of general psychology. He also believed that behavior-learning views, including social learning, were too narrow to account for socialization and the development of behavior.

To overcome the deficiencies, Bandura developed a broad, integrated sociobehavioral approach to human behavior. According to his view, direct experience is not the only teacher; human beings learn from infancy by simply observing what other people do and noticing what happens to them. Other symbolic models are provided by way of television, books, or magazines, and such models may teach unacceptable as well as acceptable behavior. Bandura emphasizes the importance of distinguishing between learning and performance. He stresses that although people learn to do many things, they are most likely to do the things that they or others consider acceptable or rewarding.

Bandura's work stresses the links among cognitive processes, learning, and performance. Thus, cognitive skills, information, and rules strongly affect what an individual does. And because people can think about what happened to them or what may happen to them, their behavior cannot be manipulated simply by reinforcement. Bandura sees people as freer to choose and to make changes in their lives than did the original behavior-learning theorists.

---

show it. A ten-year-old girl might, for example, watch a television program in which one child helps another who is in trouble. Although there is no observable change in the watching girl, she may go out of her way a week or two later to offer assistance when she sees a child in need of aid.

In this new view, the idea of stimuli as purely external physical events that control behavior has been replaced with the view that stimuli serve as information that help people decide what to do. The person's conception of a stimulus, not the stimulus itself, regulates behavior. Recently, Bandura (1982) has proposed that this sort of cognitive activity affects our behavior through its effect on what he calls "self-efficacy." **Self-efficacy** refers to our judgment of our own competence in a particular situation. Because we tend to avoid activities that we believe are beyond us and to seek out

those that we are good at, these judgments influence whether we will take part in some activity, how hard we will work at it, and how long we will keep trying when we meet obstacles. What determines self-efficacy in a particular situation? Bandura believes that at any time, our judgments about ourselves are based on four kinds of information: our past successes or failures; having watched others in similar situations; the assurances of others that we can be successful; and our physiological state at the moment (whether we feel tired, under stress, or alert).

The power of self-efficacy was demonstrated by manipulating people's judgments of their physical strength. When researchers convinced women that they were strong and physically competent and men that they were weak and less competent, sex differences in physical strength virtually disappeared in a subsequent test of strength (Weinberg, Gould, and Jackson, 1979). By raising children's perceptions of their competence in mathematics, Bandura (Bandura and Schunk, 1981) has helped children who were failing in their arithmetic classes to become more competent at mathematical tasks.

Unlike conditioning theorists, social-learning theorists give human thought and knowledge central importance in explaining development. Other cognitive theorists are less interested in learning than in the processes of thought.

COGNITIVE THEORIES

Cognitive theorists are primarily interested in the development and functioning of the mind. When they turn their attention to some other aspect of development, such as aggression, they explain it in cognitive terms. As we shall see, the approaches and assumptions of various cognitive theorists differ dramatically. During the 1960s and 1970s, the cognitive-developmental theory of Jean Piaget dominated the field. Nearly all research was aimed at extending or refuting his theory. Today, however, the majority of researchers in cognitive development use the concepts and methods of information-processing theorists (Siegler, 1983).

Piaget's Cognitive-Developmental Theory

Piaget produced a strict stage theory of development, in which the child actively constructs his or her knowledge of the world. As the child develops, the mind undergoes a series of reorganizations. With each reorganization, the child moves into a higher level of psychological functioning. These stages are determined by human evolutionary history; children are born with a set of specifically human systems (called *sensoriomotor systems*) that allow them to interact with the environment and to incorporate experience and stimulation.

Piaget's theory gives meaningful continuity to the development of human understanding. In it, cognition is a spontaneous biological process, and the function and characteristics of thought are like those of digestion or respiration—taking in, modifying, and using whatever elements were needed. Piaget called his approach **genetic epistemology**. Epistemology is the study of knowledge—how we know what we know. The term *genetic* here means developmental. Piaget's theory covers the development of intelligence (ways of knowing) over the life span.

For Piaget, all knowledge comes from action. From birth, babies actively engage and use the environment, and they construct their own understanding of it. For example, babies act on objects around them—feel, turn, bang, mouth them—and grow in their knowledge of those objects through structuring their experiences. The baby's knowledge grows neither from the objects themselves nor from the baby but from the interaction of the two and the consequent links between actions and objects.

Schemes   In Piaget's view, a child's understanding of the world (as opposed to the mere recording of it) arises from the coordination of actions and the interrelationships of objects. The infant is a **constructivist**. The baby constructs reality from the relationships of actions and objects, not simply from actions alone nor from the perceptual qualities of objects. For example, infants can shake a rattle or throw it; they can apply those same actions to a small stuffed bear. When the rattle is shaken, it makes a noise; when it is thrown, it lands with a sharp clatter. But the tiny bear is noiseless when shaken and makes only a soft thud when thrown. Yet the bear can be squeezed, whereas the rattle resists the pressure of the baby's fingers. From such ordinary and simple actions on objects, infants come to know the effects of their actions and the properties of objects. They also learn to coordinate their actions—they cannot simultaneously throw and roll an orange, but they can finger it first and then throw or roll it. Grasping, throwing, and rolling are all action patterns, which Piaget called **schemes**. These action schemes are the infant's form of thought. They are the primary units of mental organization; and in babies, action patterns are like concepts without words.

Older children and adults still think in action schemes when they drive a car, type a term paper, or play a piano, but they also have internalized action schemes derived from earlier concrete ex-

JEAN PIAGET

(1896 – 1980)

(Yves de Braine/Black Star)

Jean Piaget was born and reared in Switzerland. As a boy he was a keen observer of animal behavior and, when he was only fifteen, published a paper on shells in a scientific journal. He came by his interest in knowledge and knowing (epistemology) as a result of studying philosophy and logic. Whereas most American psychologists have been influenced by the evolutionary theories of Charles Darwin, Piaget was influenced by the creative evolution of Henri Bergson, who saw a divine agency instead of chance as the force behind evolution.

After receiving his doctorate in biological science at the University of Lausanne in 1918, he became interested in psychology. In order to pursue his interest in abnormal psychology, he went to Paris and, while studying at the Sorbonne, secured a position in Alfred Binet's laboratory. During his work there, he began to pay more attention to children's wrong answers than to their right ones, realizing that the wrong answers provided invaluable clues to the nature of their thinking.

Piaget's interests in children's mental processes shifted and deepened when, in 1929, he began observing his own children. As he kept detailed records of their behavior, he worked at tracing the origins of children's thought to their behavior as babies. Later, he became interested in the thought of adolescents. Piaget's primary method was to present problems in a standardized way to children of different ages. He then asked each child to explain his answers and probed these explanations with a series of carefully phrased questions.

Soon after completing his work in Paris, Piaget accepted an appointment as director of research at the Jean Jacques Rousseau Institute in Geneva. He lived in Geneva until his death, conducting research and writing on cognitive development as professor of experimental psychology and genetic epistemology at the University of Geneva.

perience. These later schemes can be mental actions, which allow them to manipulate objects mentally, classifying them, and understanding their relationships. Mental arithmetic replaces the physical act of counting; logical sequences of thought, such as "If . . . then" statements, replace the younger child's concrete manipulations of cause-effect relations. Older children and adults no longer need physically try out the solution to every problem.

For example, most adults have come to understand the principle of gravity: when released from an elevated position, objects fall. But a ten-month-old baby explores gravity by dropping toys over the side of the crib and watching as they hit the floor. Blocks, stuffed animals, cups, teething rings, every object the baby can reach is dropped, and all fall satisfactorily to the floor. Before long, the baby's scheme of dropping objects in space incorporates information derived from dropping many objects. The baby understands that all objects fall, and the experiments end. And because a toy that is dropped cannot be played with, the baby eventually realizes that manipulating objects and dropping them are not compatible schemes. The carpet around the crib is no longer littered with toys.

Assimilation and Accommodation According to Piaget, children's thinking develops through two processes: assimilation and accommodation. **Assimilation** refers to the incorporation of new knowledge into existing schemes. For example, a child can bang a large variety of objects and assimilate to an existing scheme whether or not "banging" is a primary attribute of each object. Some objects make loud noises, others, soft; some break,

In Piaget's view, to obtain the toy this baby first tries a familiar grasping scheme (assimilation) and then alters it with new knowledge (accommodation) to get the toy through the bars. *(George S. Zimbel/Monkmeyer Press)*

others squeak; and so forth. **Accommodation** refers to the modification of the child's existing schemes to incorporate new knowledge that does not fit them. The processes of assimilation and accomodation always work together in complementary fashion. To assimilate is to use what one already knows how to do; to accommodate is to acquire a new way of doing something. Both processes continue to function throughout the life span.

At any given time, the developing person can change his or her cognitive structures only to a limited extent. There always must be some continuity. The balance, or equilibrium, between assimilation and accommodation is a process of continual readjustment over the life span. **Equilibration** is the most general developmental principle in Piaget's theory; it states that the organism always tends toward biological and psychological balance and that development is a progressive approximation to an ideal state of equilibrium that it never fully achieves. A child's equilibrium at any one stage may be upset by external events, such as new information he or she cannot readily assimilate, or by internal processes that bring the child to a new "readiness" to accommodate. In both cases, the child's previous temporary equilibrium is upset,

and development advances to a new, higher level of organization.

Stages The organization of behavior is qualitatively different at each stage of Piaget's theory. The two essential points are that:

1. stages emerge in a constant order of succession, and
2. neither heredity nor environment can by itself explain the progressive development of mental structures.

Piaget proposed four major stages of intellectual development: a sensorimotor stage, a preoperational stage, a concrete-operational stage, and a formal-operational stage (see Table 2.3). The *sensorimotor stage*, which begins at birth and extends through the first two years of life, is divided into six subperiods. This stage roughly corresponds to infancy. The *preoperational stage* corresponds to the preschool years. It begins at around the age of two, when children start to record experiences symbolically. This advance indicates the dawn of representational thought, when children can think about objects and people that are not present. The preoperational stage ends at about the age of

Table 2.3
Stages in Piaget's Cognitive-Developmental Theory

Stage	Age*	Major Characteristic
Sensorimotor	Infancy (birth to age 2)	Thought confined to action schemes
Preoperational	Preschool (Age 2 to 7)	Representational thought Thought intuitive, not logical
Concrete operational	Childhood (age 7 to 11)	Systematic, logical thought but only in regard to concrete objects
Formal operational	Adolescence and adulthood (from age 11)	Abstract, logical thought

* Ages approximate.

seven — after children in Western cultures have begun formal education. Then children move into the *concrete-operational stage,* when they attain logical thought but only in respect to concrete objects. They then understand new kinds of logical operations in which they can mentally reverse actions. By eleven or twelve, young adolescents begin to develop a formal logic and are able to think in terms of propositions ("If . . . then" statements). At this time, they enter the *formal-operational stage,* which Piaget regarded as the culmination of cognitive development. The ages given for each stage are, of course, approximate. For example, although the concrete-operational stage begins at about age seven, many five- and six-year-olds have already entered it.

Piaget's theory is still influential, but recent research has modified it considerably. Many developmentalists believe that he underestimated the baby's ability to extract information about the world (Harris, 1983). Others have pointed out that the four major stages do not accurately reflect the course of cognitive development and that development in particular areas does not progress exactly as Piaget proposed (Gelman and Baillargeon, 1983). Yet Piaget's insistence on the active role played by the child in learning about the world continues to dominate cognitive theories. In addition, many developmentalists accept his basic idea that cognitive structures influence perception, memory, and the ability to solve problems — although they may disagree about how those structures should be characterized (Flavell, 1982; Gelman and Baillargeon, 1983).

Information-Processing Theories

Cognitive theorists who take an information-processing approach see human beings as manipulators of symbols. People are believed to process information about the world much as another symbol manipulator, the computer, does: both take information from the outside world, register the information in symbolic form (called *encoding*), combine it with other information, store it, retrieve it, and send it back into the world in a decoded form (see Figure 2.1). Using the precise language developed for computer science, researchers try to analyze the way people represent and manipulate information (Siegler, 1983).

The first **information-processing theory** was not developmental, but was a theory of attention in adults. Donald Broadbent (1954), an English psychologist, tried to account for the way different situations affected adults' attention to sounds and the way they remembered them. The system he proposed for processing sounds was so general that it could be applied to all cognitive processes, and its influence is still visible in current information-processing theories.

Unlike Piaget, most information-processing theorists see no major change in the structure of the mind as children grow. They believe that thought and behavior are built upon a small set of primitive processes that are present early in life. These primitive processes include recognition, visual scanning of the environment, the analysis of perceptual events into features, learning, and the integration of the senses (Siegler, 1983). With

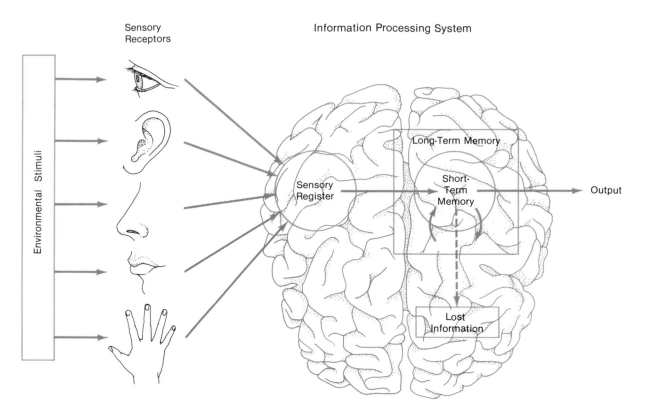

Sensory Receptors

Information Processing System

Environmental Stimuli

Sensory Register

Long-Term Memory

Short-Term Memory

Output

Lost Information

FIGURE 2.1   Information from the environment (sights, sounds, touches, tastes, odors) strikes the sensory receptors, which transmit it to the sensory register in the brain. After brief processing, the information enters short-term (or working) memory, where it can be encoded, elaborated, and rehearsed. These operations facilitate storage in long-term memory. Unless it receives active processing, information in short-term memory is often lost. When we think, plan, talk, or act, information is retrieved from long-term memory and is processed in short-term memory. (This schematic diagram does not indicate physiological locations.)

experience, basic capacities increase, and these processes become faster and more efficient. For example, infants can recognize objects they have seen before; apparently they can store information and get it back again. But they require fairly long exposure to an object, and the range of objects they can recognize is small. Their problem is magnified because they are also easily distracted. With development, their recognition processes will become swift, efficient, and flexible. At a glance, a child who once referred to all trucks, vans, and automobiles as "car" will be able to distinguish a Dodge from a Datsun.

Each of the processes develops in much the same way. Children become able to hold more information in their working memory at one time, which leads to an apparent increase in the basic capacity of the system. They develop more efficient methods of storing information and of getting it back out again. The very young child appears to have few strategies that can make information available, whereas the adolescent and adult have a whole array of them, which they can use to encode information or to recall information that has been stored (Kail and Hagen, 1982). They begin to understand how to use their control processes to manipulate information within the system. They learn to assess their own cognitive skills, direct their attention, plan ahead, and monitor their own progress on cognitive tasks (Paris and Lindauer, 1982).

As this development takes place, children build up a rich network of concepts and a broad knowledge about how things are done (Flavell, 1985).

Their knowledge base keeps increasing. Indeed, some developmentalists believe that children's increased knowledge base may underlie many of the apparent changes in the system's basic capacities and control processes. For instance, Michelene Chi and Randi Koeske (1983) studied a four-year-old boy whose knowledge of dinosaurs surpassed that of most adults. The child not only knew the names of forty-six different kinds of dinosaur, but had an organized store of information about his twenty favorites. He could describe each of them, tell you its nickname, what sort of habitat it lived in, what it ate, how it moved about, and how it defended itself.

How do all these improvements in efficiency and speed come about? Developmentalists are not certain, but Robert Siegler (1983) has proposed three different mechanisms that might be responsible. The first of these mechanisms is *self-modification*. This is the way Piaget explained cognitive development; assimilation and accommodation are examples of a system modifying itself. The second developmental mechanism is *automatization*. As the child grows, mental operations that were conscious become automatic, just as do the operations involved in driving a car. Once this happens, the child's working memory is cleared and he or she has more space to hold information while manipulating it. For example, when young children read, they must decode the words on the paper and understand what they have decoded. But they may have to devote so much attention and effort to decoding the words (translating the letters *d-o-g* into the sound "dawg") that there is little space left in their working memory for comprehending what they have decoded. And even if they understand the word, they may forget it before they can go on to the next word (Wilkinson, 1980). Once the decoding process becomes automatic, the child begins to read more fluently. Finally, children become more *proficient at encoding* information, choosing important features to encode, and establishing relationships among these features.

Today, many studies of cognitive development use an information-processing approach. According to Siegler (1983), it has changed the way we think about development. Yet information processing has been largely limited to the development of cognition and has provided no insight into emotion or personality development. But then,

except for HAL in the movie *2001*, no computer yet has shown joy, love, hate, fear, grief, or anger.

DIALECTICAL THEORIES

According to **dialectical theories,** human development cannot be understood without considering how historical-social changes affect behavior and its development. Knowledge is seen as social, created by society and transmitted to the individual. Neither child nor adult, therefore, processes stimuli as simple reflections of the real world. Instead, both apply internalized historical and cultural factors to their sensations. When development is approached in this way, major cultural changes (such as cars, computers, and television) are seen as perhaps altering how we perceive the world, categorize it, think, and organize our inner consciousness.

Dialectical psychology first became prominent when Soviet psychologists were searching for an approach that would fit comfortably within the Marxist framework. Its major advocate was Lev S. Vygotsky. Shortly after the Russian Revolution, Vygotsky proposed a way of looking at human development that viewed mental activities as taking shape in a matrix of social history. Society, he believed, was essential to human development. Concepts, language, voluntary attention, logical memory — everything that distinguishes the human mind from that of the chimpanzee — comes from the culture and begins between the child and another person. Each of these functions appears twice in a child's development — first shared between the child and a more competent person (an interpersonal process) and then inside the child (an intrapersonal process) (Vygotsky, 1978).

As children reconstruct a process, according to Vygotsky, they move through a series of spiral stages, passing through the same point at each new reconstruction, but on a higher level. With each new level, they gain more and more control of their behavior. Development is neither an accumulation of small changes in behavior nor a single upward line. In each succeeding stage, new responses are carried out in new ways under the

LEV SEMANOVICH VYGOTSKY

(1896–1934)

The Russian, Lev S. Vygotsky, was a contemporary of Piaget and Werner. In 1917 he graduated from Moscow University, and until 1923 he taught both literature and psychology in Gomel. In 1924, just after Soviet psychology had officially adopted "reactology" —an approach to psychology that depended upon behavioral reactions in a Marxist framework (Cole and Scribner, 1978)—Vygotsky returned to Moscow to work at the Institute of Psychology. His views did not coincide with the major European approaches to psychology, which were either introspective or behavioristic (as was reactology). Nor did Vygotsky find the Gestalt psychologists' attempts to study behavior and experience as wholes a very satisfactory solution.

Vygotsky believed that the study of psychology was the study of changing processes, for as people respond to a situation, they alter it. One of his complaints about Piaget's theory was that the Swiss psychologist did not give enough weight to the influence of the environment on the developing child.

Vygotsky believed that the internalization of social and cultural activities was the key to human development and that internalization distinguished human beings from animals.

In some respects, today we might regard Vygotsky as a psychologist who was interested in human cognition, for his primary areas of interest were thought, language, memory, and play. At the end of his life, he worked on the problems of education. But Vygotsky was also trained as a physician and advocated the combination of neurology and physiology with experimental studies of thought processes. Just before his death from tuberculosis in 1934, he had been asked to head the department of psychology in the All-Union Institute of Experimental Medicine.

Vygotsky died at thirty-eight, but his influence on Soviet psychology continued through his students, who hold major positions throughout the Soviet Union. For years after his death, Vygotsky had no influence in North America; but in 1962, *Thought and Language* was translated, and his ideas entered the American psychological community. With each passing year, his notions about the relation of thought and language and the nature and uses of play, have received more attention. In 1978, his essays, *Mind in Society,* were translated and published.

influence of different psychological processes.

Vygotsky also stressed the importance of what he called the **zone of proximal development.** By this term he meant that when children have the guidance of an adult or more capable peer, they are often able to carry out tasks they could never complete by themselves. For example, with an adult standing by to give advice and help out in the difficult places, a child can bake cookies, measuring the ingredients, mixing the dough, forming the cookies and baking them. The skill appears first in interaction with the adult; later the child may learn to bake cookies without any assistance. The width

of this zone varies from child to child. With the help of an adult, one six-year-old may be able to complete a task meant for eight-year-olds; another may be able to handle only tasks meant for children who are six and one-half years old. Vygotsky (1978) believed that instead of waiting until children can learn a task without working at it with an adult, teachers should concentrate on cooperative instruction in the zone of proximal development. He maintained that the only "good learning" is learning that proceeds ahead of development.

In recent years, American psychologists have come to regard dialectics as a helpful tool. When

Important learning takes place in the zone of proximal development where children cannot handle tasks on their own but can complete them with the aid of an adult. *(Elizabeth Crews)*

adopting the dialectical approach, researchers look at development in a new way, one that stresses social interaction and the influence of the wider society. When they study cognitive activity, for example, this approach has led them to look at its goal (remembering an appointment) and to study thought and action together. Formerly, they may have focused narrowly on cognitive processes (memory) and separated thought from action (Rogoff, 1982).

Some American psychologists have adapted Vygotsky's idea of the zone of proximal development to classroom problems. With lessons that require student and teacher to engage in social interaction, researchers have been able to help failing students understand and remember the material in their science and social studies textbooks (Palinscar and Brown, 1984). Other researchers have devised ways of assessing a child's zone of proximal development, on the grounds that traditional achievement and aptitude tests — which require children to work by themselves — fail to pick out those youngsters who could profit from instruction (Campione, Brown, Ferrara, and Bryant, 1984). By uncovering hidden learning potential, these assessment procedures could open the door to instruction that a child might be denied on the basis of an achievement test.

UNDERSTANDING HUMAN DEVELOPMENT

Faced with such an array of developmental theories, we may simply become bewildered. A few common themes are clear. Human growth and development, all theorists agree, is regular; behavior is at least potentially predictable. When we look more closely, however, we find that theorists seem to be living in such different worlds that any comparison of their views is difficult, if not impossible. In the world of most behavior-learning theorists, the individual is passive and development occurs as he or she reacts to changes in the environment. In the world of the cognitive-developmental theorist, the individual is active and takes the lead in the interactions that lead to development. When behavior-learning theorists look at a child, they see an individual who is easily marked by experience, as an aluminum soft-drink can is easily squeezed into a new shape. When maturational theorists look at a child, they see a soft plastic tumbler that rebounds when pressure is removed.

Another obstacle to comparisons is the differing focus of various theories. Psychodynamic theorists are interested in explaining personality

Table 2.4
Developmental Theories

	Nature of Development	Guiding Process	Individual	Shape of Development	Focus
Biological theories	Nature	Maturation	Active	Stage	Observable changes in structure and behavior
Psychodynamic theories	Both	Maturation	Active	Stage	Internal changes in personality structure
Behavioral-learning theories	Nurture	Learning	Passive	Continuous	Observable changes in behavior
Cognitive-developmental theories	Nature	Maturation	Active	Stage	Internal changes in mental structure
Information-processing theories	Nurture	Learning	Active	Continuous	Observable changes in behavior
Dialectical theories	Both	Both	Interactive	Spiral	Relationship between individual and society

Note: Each theory addresses development in its own way. The lens through which the theory interprets development is ground by the way the theory regards the nature of development (what development occurs), the process of development (how it occurs), the role of the individual, the shape of development, and by which aspect of development the theory takes as its major concern.

development; they pay little attention to the development of thought. With cognitive theorists, the pattern is reversed. And this difference in focus can lead to confusion because of differences in language. When using the same words, different theorists may not be talking about the same thing. "Learning," for example, means one thing to a behavior-learning theorist and something different to a cognitive-developmental theorist.

When describing the same process, theorists use different terms — terms that reflect the world view of their own particular theory. Take the relationship between baby and caregiver, called *attachment*. Psychodynamic theorists regard attachment as an outgrowth of the caregiver's satisfying the infant's need to suck — the dominant feature of the oral period. Learning theorists see attachment as the result of conditioning: the primary caregiver both satisfies the infant's basic needs and provides interesting and satisfying stimulation. Ethological theorists view attachment as an evolved response that increases the likelihood of the infant's — and therefore the species' — survival. These descriptions suggest different explanations but they simply focus on different aspects of the process.

So how do we evaluate the theories that we have explored in this chapter? Because each theory is based on different assumptions, we cannot say that one is superior to another. We can say, however, that one theory may do a better job than another in explaining a particular aspect of development. As Neil Salkind (1985) suggests, we can also look at the way each one addresses the important issues in development (see Table 2.4).

One issue has to do with the *nature of development:* what does the theory regard as the major force that influences development? The way a theory answers this question locates it on the nature-nurture issue. All theories regard both as important but stress one side or the other. As we have seen, biologically based theories of development focus on heredity, whereas behavior-learning theorists see environment as primary. The other theories tend to be more strongly interactional, although cognitive-developmental theorists lean slightly toward nature, and dialectical theorists lean toward nurture.

Another issue is the *process that guides development:* what is the underlying process primarily responsible for changes in development? This question asks how development occurs, while the first question asked what is responsible. On this issue, theories align themselves as they did on the first question. Biological theorists see maturation as the underlying process that guides development, while behavior-learning theorists point to learning. Again, the other theorists are less extreme, viewing both processes as important. However, both psychodynamic and cognitive-developmental theorists believe that maturation is essential for the emergence of various stages, and other theorists stress learning. Information-processing theorists regard experience and the development of a knowledge base as essential, whereas dialectical theorists believe that development is impossible without society.

Theories also differ on the *shape of development:* is development smooth and continuous, or do changes occur in abrupt stages? As we saw in Chapter 1, distinguishing clear stages in development is extremely difficult. Among the theories we have explored, maturational, psychodynamic, and cognitive-developmental theories see development as stagelike.

Finally, theories must be able to explain *individual differences;* how does the theory explain differences that appear among individuals? All theorists agree that individual differences develop as hered-

ity interacts with experience. Biological theorists would remind us that we are all born with individual predispositions, and behavior-learning theorists would look at our histories of reinforcement (learning). Psychodynamic theorists would stress the importance of experiences within the family during the first five or six years of life.

Each of the theories we have explored contributes something to our understanding of development, and as you read this book, you will notice that different sections stress different theories. Work that implements cognitive theories is discussed most extensively in chapters on language and intellectual development; psychodynamic theories appear most often in the discussions of personality. Because behavior-learning theorists regard all behavior as learned and because their techniques of study are used by psychologists of many persuasions, behavior-learning work or methods appear throughout the book. Maturational and ethological theories are drawn on wherever they seem to contribute to an explanation of human development.

As we go into the next chapter, our theme changes from general principles to the individual. The rest of the book traces the way a person develops, from the union of two cells at conception to the ending of a long life.

SUMMARY

1. No matter what approach developmentalists take, they work from **theories,** or sets of logically related statements, that allow them to interpret development. Biological theories emphasize the role of nature in development. Arnold Gesell was the major advocate of **maturational theory.** He believed that development is self-regulating and that it unfolds according to a biological timetable. **Ethologists** see behavior as partially the product of evolutionary history; ethological theorists interpret behavior by the way it might have enabled the species to survive.

2. Psychodynamic theorists see development as arising out of confrontations between the individual and the demands of society; they are primarily concerned with personality development. In Freud's **psychosexual theory,** development passes through five stages, each typified by a particular conflict. If a stage is not handled successfully, the individual becomes **fixated** at that stage. The **libido,** or "life force," is the basis of human motivation. Within each person, the **unconscious** forces of the **id** are tempered by the **ego** (which uses memory, reason, and judgment to guide realistic behavior) and the **superego** (conscience). In Erikson's **psychosocial theory,** development passes through eight stages that are predetermined by the organism's readiness to interact with the external world. Each stage is typified by a conflict between inner needs and social demands.

3. Behavioral-learning theorists see development as primarily the result of experience. **Conditioning theories** explain development in terms of two forms of learning: **classical conditioning** and **operant conditioning**. In classical conditioning, **unconditioned reflexes** (or natural responses) become associated with neutral stimuli; in the process, they are transformed into **conditioned reflexes**. In operant conditioning, the association is between some event and our behavior. Our actions are **reinforced** by their consequences; actions that are not reinforced are **extinguished. Social-learning theory,** which emphasizes the role of observation and **imitation,** has expanded conditioning theories to include the role of human thought and knowledge. Albert Bandura has restated learning and motivation in terms of **cognition,** in which stimuli serve as information that affects our behavior through **self-efficacy** (a judgment of personal competence in a particular situation).

4. Jean Piaget's cognitive-developmental theory is a strict stage theory in which the mind is described as undergoing a series of evolutionarily determined reorganizations. This development takes the child through a series of four cognitive stages: sensorimotor, preoperational, concrete operational, and formal operational. Piaget described his approach as **genetic epistemology,** and he believed that the infant was a **constructivist** whose knowledge came from action. Understanding depended on **schemes** (at first, action patterns) with which the child **assimilates** and **accommodates** new knowledge.

The individual always adheres to the principle of **equilibration,** continually striving for a balance between internal schemes and the outside world. According to **information-processing theory,** people process information much as a computer does, with thought and behavior built on a small set of primitive processes that are present early in life. Experience leads to an increase in basic capacities and a faster, more efficient processing of information. These changes may be the result of self-modification, of automatization, or of greater encoding proficiency.

5. In **dialectical theories,** human development is heavily influenced by historical-social changes. Knowledge is social, created by society and transmitted to the individual. At each stage of development a person interacts with society to reach a new level of functioning. Lev Vygotsky, the major dialectical theorist, maintained that the most important learning took place in the **zone of proximal development,** where children learn only with the assistance of a more mature individual.

6. Each group of theories tends to focus on a different aspect of the developmental process. All theorists agree that human growth and development are regular and that behavior is potentially predictable. In evaluating any theory, it is important to consider how it views the nature of development, the process that guides development, the shape of development, and individual differences.

KEY TERMS

accommodation	extinguish	punishment
assimilation	fixated	reinforcement
classical conditioning	genetic epistemology	scheme
cognition	id	self-efficacy
conditioned reflex	imitation	social-learning theory
conditioning theory	information-processing theory	successive approximation
constructivist	libido	superego
dialectical theory	maturational theory	theory
ego	operant conditioning	unconditioned reflex
equilibration	psychosexual theory	unconscious
ethologist	psychosocial theory	zone of proximal development

STUDY TERMS

accommodation　Piaget's term for the modification of schemes to incorporate new knowledge that does not fit them.

assimilation　Piaget's term for the incorporation of new knowledge into existing schemes.

classical conditioning　A simple form of learning, in which one stimulus is associated with another, so that the first evokes the response that normally follows the second stimulus. Also called respondent conditioning.

dialectical theory　Developmental theory that sees development as proceeding in a dialectic between the individual and society, with each interaction leading to a higher level of functioning.

equilibration　Piaget's term for the developmental principle by which the organism always tends toward biological and psychological balance.

information-processing theory　A theory of cognition that see individuals as processing information much as a computer does; thought and behavior are believed to be built on a small set of primitive processes.

maturational theory　Theory of development that sees development as self-regulating and unfolding according to a maturational timetable.

operant conditioning　A form of learning in which a response is strengthened or changed as a result of reinforcement. Sometimes called instrumental conditioning.

scheme　Piaget's term for patterns of action (throwing, chewing) or mental structures (classification of objects) that are involved in the acquisition and structuring of knowledge.

self-efficacy　An individual's judgment of his or her competence in a particular situation, which influences whether a person will take part in some activity, how hard he or she will work at it, and how long the individual will persevere in the face of obstacles.

social-learning theory　A behavior-learning theory that sees development as the result of conditioning, observation, and imitation and that sees stimuli as information.

theory　A set of logically related statements that generates testable hypotheses and explains some aspect of experience.

zone of proximal development　Vygotsky's term for the area in which children, with the help of adults or more capable peers, can solve problems they are unable to solve by themselves.

PART II

The Beginning of Life

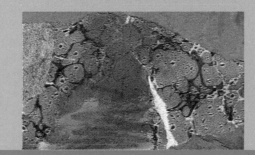

No matter how sophisticated we are, the miracle of birth can reduce us to an awestruck silence. In only thirty-eight weeks, an undifferentiated cluster of cells becomes an individual capable of unassisted life. During those weeks within the uterus, the developing organism is utterly dependent on the mother's body. The moment of birth ruptures this close relationship, forcing infants to rely on their own mouths for sustenance, their own lungs for air, and their own eyes and ears for information about the world. Despite their obvious helplessness, newborns come into the world prepared to gather the information they need to make sense of their new environment. Their heredity, determined at the moment of conception, has provided them with the evolved capabilities of their species as well as with the unique constellation of genes that makes them individuals. In this unit, we see how development within the uterus prepares the newborn for an independent life, and we follow the progress of the first four weeks.

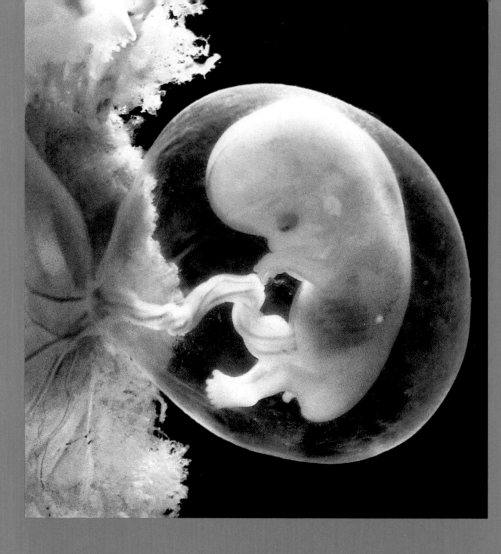

CHAPTER 3

Prenatal Development

Development begins when a cell from the father and a cell from the mother unite deep within the mother's body. At that instant, the inheritance of a new individual is established. The newly fertilized cell, or **zygote,** which is no larger than the period on this page, contains all the instructions for a unique physical appearance and a disposition toward certain personality characteristics and mental abilities. But this genetic composition can only express itself in an environmental context; the two together determine how a person looks and behaves. Their interaction is at the heart of one of the oldest debates in psychology: how much influence inheritance or environment has in producing any given trait. The debate continues in part because even when a characteristic is inherited, life experiences affect the way the trait develops.

Although expectant parents may come to feel that the **prenatal period** lasts forever, only thirty-eight weeks after the two tiny cells come together an independent human being emerges. In no other comparable segment of life will such swift and intricate growth and development occur. The structures and functions that emerge during this brief period form the basis of the individual's body and behavior for the rest of life.

In this chapter, we follow the development of the fertilized egg into a healthy, normal baby who is ready for independent life outside the mother's womb. Before we watch the unfolding of individual development, we examine the workings of heredity and the transmission of specific traits from parent to child. Some of the growing fetus's behavior and capabilities will become apparent, and some problems that can arise in the course of development will be spelled out. As we look at the link between the mother and her unborn child, we will discover the importance of the mother's health, habits, and emotions during the prenatal period.

HOW LIFE BEGINS

The development of each person begins at the moment of conception, when the sperm cell, or **spermatozoon**, from the father unites with the egg, or **ovum**, of the mother. The ovum is the largest cell in the human body; it sometimes can be seen without a microscope. Ova mature in the female's ovaries, which release one egg during each **menstrual cycle** of around twenty-eight days. The freed egg, which probably can be fertilized for less than twenty-four hours, travels down the **Fallopian tube** toward the uterus (Figure 3.1).

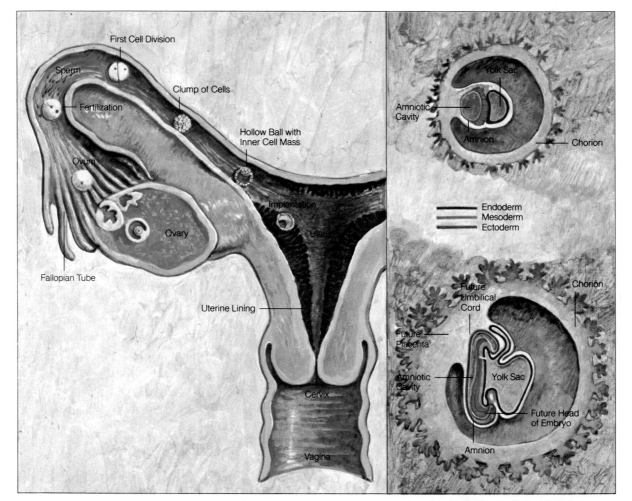

FIGURE 3.1   The early development of the human embryo. Fertilization occurs at the upper end of the Fallopian tube. By the time the fertilized ovum reaches the uterus, it has already divided many times. Within seven or eight days, it is securely implanted in the uterine wall, where the process of prenatal development continues.

When we look at the obstacles that stand in the way of conception, it is a wonder that sperm and egg ever get together. First, the vaginal tract is so acid that millions of sperm die before they can begin their journey. Second, except around the time of ovulation, the small opening in the **cervix,** or lower part of the uterus, is so densely covered with mucus that sperm cannot penetrate it. Third, of the sperm that enter the uterus, only a few will find the correct Fallopian tube, for only one contains an egg. Fourth, the egg must be able to enter the Fallopian tube, which is sometimes blocked by adhesions or scars from pelvic infection. Fifth, the egg must travel down the Fallopian tube fast enough to meet the sperm while both short-lived cells are still capable of fertilization. Sixth, once the sperm finds the egg, it must penetrate several layers of protective material. Such a variety of circumstances must be met before conception takes place that about one couple in ten is unable to conceive. Yet some couples conceive after a single act of sexual intercourse.

Chromosomes and Genes

Parents transmit traits and dispositions to their children through **genes,** which are microscopic bits of a complex chemical called **deoxyribonucleic acid, or DNA.** Each of the approximately 100,000 pairs of genes in a human cell provides a unit of information for the blueprint of heredity — the genetic code. This code specifies the structure of every body cell; it guides the development of bones and eyes, brain and fingernails, and disposes the offspring toward certain behavioral patterns. Within each cell, genes coalesce into beadlike strings called **chromosomes;** a given gene always occurs at the same place on the same chromosome.

The Production of Sex Cells

Most cells of the human body contain twenty-three pairs of chromosomes, direct copies of the

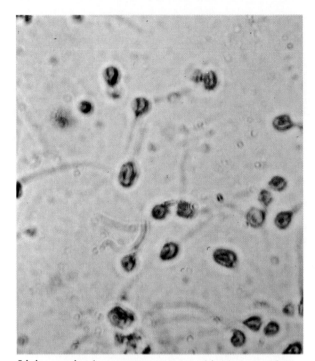

Living, active human spermatazoa, highly magnified. The waving tail propels the sperm to ovum, and the head contains the nucleus, which carries the chromosomes. *(Petit Format/Nestle/Science Source/Photo Researchers)*

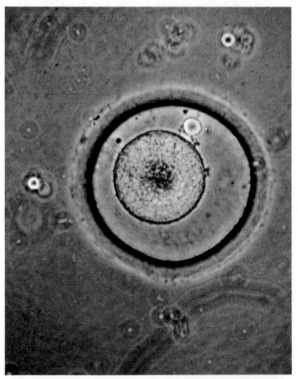

A living human ovum magnified. Unlike the ova of many other vertebrates, the human ovum has little yolk; the fetus must get its nourishment through the placenta. *(From Rugh and Shettles, 1971)*

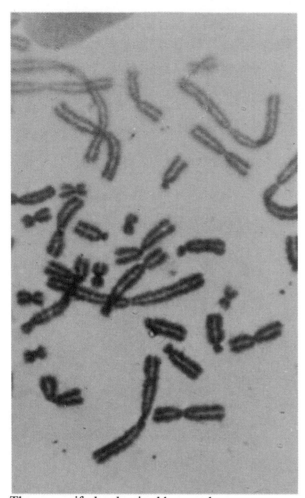

These magnified and stained human chromosomes are getting ready to divide. The form that they have assumed is characteristic of cell division. *(Courtesy Leonard Hayflick. Copyright © the President and Fellows of Harvard College)*

original twenty-three pairs with which each person begins life. There is one major exception to this rule: the **gametes,** or ova and spermatazoa, which are also known as *sex cells.* Gametes can break the rule because they form by a special kind of cell division, called **meiosis.** During meiosis, a normal cell containing twenty-three pairs of chromosomes divides and divides again to produce four cells, each containing twenty-three unpaired chromosomes. We can think of the process as a stately dance, which the chromosomes begin by lining up in pairs within the cell's nucleus. The members of each chromosome pair divide and gravitate to opposite sides of the cell, which then splits into two cells, each containing twenty-three *single* chromosomes rather then twenty-three *pairs.* These cells then duplicate themselves, producing four gametes, each having a set of twenty-three *single* chromosomes. At conception, when a sperm unites with an egg, the result is a single sex cell having twenty-three pairs of chromosomes. Figure 3.2A illustrates meiosis but shows only two of the twenty-three chromosome pairs involved.

With the exception of identical twins, each conception produces a unique individual with a genetic combination unlike that of anyone else in the world. Just over half of the 200,000 genes come from the mother and the rest from the father. The uniqueness of each combination is ensured by a process known as *crossing over.* During a crossover, after the chromosomes have lined up, each pair exchanges corresponding sections before it splits, mingling maternal and paternal genes in a single chromosome (Scarr and Kidd, 1983).

FIGURE 3.2   (A) The production of sex cells. Sex cells divide in a pattern of cell division called *meiosis* to produce gametes—ova and sperm—that have only half the number of chromosomes of the parent cells. For simplicity, only two of the twenty-three pairs of chromosomes are shown here. In meiosis, first the members of each pair split up (first division), and then the chromosomes themselves split in half (second division). In a subsequent step, they regenerate their missing halves (next line). At conception, the union of the gametes results in a zygote that has the full number of chromosomes, half from the mother and half from the father.

(B) Transmission of alleles in the inheritance of PKU. The chromosomes in this pair carry the alleles *N* and *p.* Both parents have both forms of the gene, and therefore they produce gametes with chromosomes bearing either the *N* or the *p* gene in equal numbers. Depending on which gametes happen to unite in conception, the new cell may have the alleles *NN, Np, pN,* or *pp.* Because *p* is a recessive gene, only babies with *pp* will have PKU.

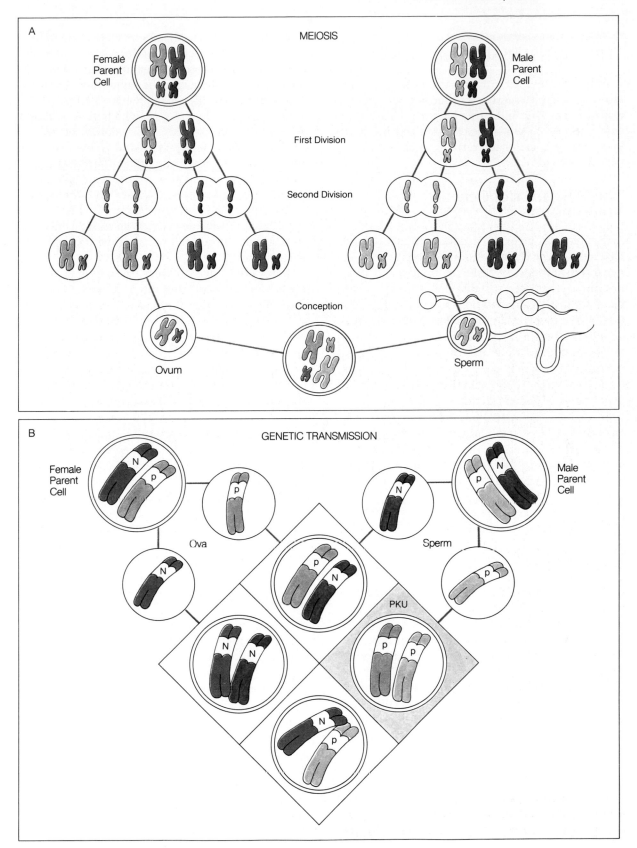

A MEIOSIS

Female Parent Cell

Male Parent Cell

First Division

Second Division

Conception

Ovum

Sperm

B GENETIC TRANSMISSION

Female Parent Cell

Male Parent Cell

Ova

Sperm

PKU

THE TRANSMISSION OF GENES

Children sometimes resemble their parents in certain physical characteristics, but not always. For example, a mother and father both may have brown hair, but one of their three children may be blond. How are physical characteristics passed on from parent to child?

The Mechanics of Genetic Transmission

Although hair color is a common and obvious characteristic, its transmission is complicated. Genetic transmission is easier to understand if we examine a characteristic that depends on a single pair of genes. A dramatic example of single-gene transmission occurs in **phenylketonuria,** or **PKU,** an inherited inability to metabolize phenylalanine (a component of milk and other foods). During normal metabolism, phenylalanine is converted into tyrosine, an amino acid that is essential in the production of chemicals that regulate brain function. In the baby with PKU, phenylpyruvic acid and other metabolic compounds in the blood climb to dangerous levels, and the developing nervous system is damaged. If this metabolic abnormality is left untreated, the child will be mentally retarded within two or three years.

Each person has two genes related to the metabolism of phenylalanine, one on each chromosome of the same pair. Let N symbolize the gene corresponding to normal metabolic ability and p represent the gene for PKU. When a gene can have several forms, the related genes (in this case, N and p) are called **alleles.** Now look at Figure 3.2B, which illustrates these alleles in a single pair of chromosomes. In this example, the mother's and father's cells each carry an Np combination of alleles. When the parent cells divide to form gametes, half of the father's sperm cells and half of the mother's ova will carry the gene for PKU $(p),$ and half will carry a gene for normal metabolic ability $(N).$ When sperm and egg meet, one of four possible combinations will result: NN, Np, pN (which is the same as Np), or pp.

Which of the children will have PKU and which will have normal metabolism? Any baby born with NN will be normal, and any baby born with pp will have PKU. These offspring are homo-

zygous, which means that their cells have matching genes for this characteristic. But what about babies who are **heterozygous,** meaning that their cells have different alleles for the same trait? Are these Np babies normal, or do they have PKU?

The answer depends on which gene is **dominant** and which is **recessive.** A dominant gene is one whose trait appears in the individual even when that gene is paired with a different gene for the trait. The paired gene whose trait fails to appear is recessive. In the case of PKU, the normal gene is dominant over the recessive PKU gene. Therefore, Np babies will have normal metabolism, although they can transmit the PKU gene to their offspring.

This difference between the genes a person carries and the traits that appear illustrates the difference between **genotype** and **phenotype.** The genotype is the specific combination of alleles in a person's genetic make-up (in this case, NN, Np. and pp), and the phenotype is the nature of the trait as it appears in the individual (in this case, normal or PKU). The genotypes NN and Np both produce the normal phenotype because N is dominant over p.

Yet genetic combinations are not the only factors responsible for differences between a person's genetic make-up (genotype) and what that person actually looks like and how he or she behaves (phenotype). Experiences always affect the development of a person's phenotype. For example, when a baby with pp genes is placed at birth on a phenylalanine-free diet, he or she develops more or less normally.

For a variety of reasons, genetic transmission is rarely as simple as it is in the case of PKU. First, dominance is not always all-or-none. Some single-gene traits may be **codominant,** so that either allele may express itself, depending on environmental conditions. Second, the vast majority of human traits are **polygenic,** which means that several genes are required to produce the trait. Sometimes all the genes have an equal and cumulative effect; in other cases, some genes in the combination have more influences than others on the phenotype. In addition, many polygenic traits, such as height, skin color, and resistance to disease, show continuous variation. That is, the trait appears in varying degrees; in the case of height, people range from extremely short to extremely tall (Ehrman and Probber, 1983).

The more scientists study the process of human genetic transmission, the more complex it seems. We cannot point to a single gene that is responsible for a given behavioral trait. Indeed, researchers have been unable to identify the individual genes involved in many polygenic traits (Scarr and Kidd, 1983).

The Importance of X and Y

One pair of chromosomes is different from all the rest. This pair, called the sex chromosomes, is unique because its members do not have matching alleles. All normal ova carry the female chromosome (X), but normal sperm may carry either the female chromosome (X) or the male chromosome (Y). When ovum and sperm join, the zygote will be either female (XX) or male (XY), depending on which type of sperm fertilizes the egg.

The influence of the sex chromosomes goes beyond determining whether the zygote will develop into a boy or a girl. The large X chromosome carries many genes, but the small Y chromosome carries only a few. This means that a boy gets more genes from his mother than from his father, a situation that sometimes has serious consequences. Because there is no corresponding allele for many genes on the X chromosome, the male zygote has no protection against potentially harmful recessive genes carried by the mother (Ehrman and Probber, 1983). One of these sex-linked conditions is hemophilia (a disease in which the blood does not clot); another is colorblindness; a third is a form of muscular dystrophy. These conditions are rare in girls, appearing only if both X chromosomes carry the related gene.

How Do Genes Affect Behavior?

Genes exert their influence throughout the life span. At various points in development, genes "turn on," becoming active in producing substances within the body that create new structures, regulate their functions, or maintain their states. For example, genes may alter the way the nervous system functions, change the sensitivity of sensory systems, alter the threshold level at which cells can be activated by hormones, or modify the timing of developmental events.

Genes always interact with the environment, even during the prenatal period. The genetic make-up of each person has a **reaction range**—a unique range of possible responses to the environments that he or she may encounter. In other words, there are some limits on how any person can respond to good or bad environmental conditions. Take the case of height. Good nutrition from birth will make all of us taller than poor nutrition will, but in both kinds of environments some will be taller than others, as Figure 3.3 indicates. Genes do not specify a particular pattern of height. They specify a pattern of growth that varies with nutrition and other environmental factors. The final height any of us achieves depends on both genetic and environmental factors.

The interaction between good nutrition and

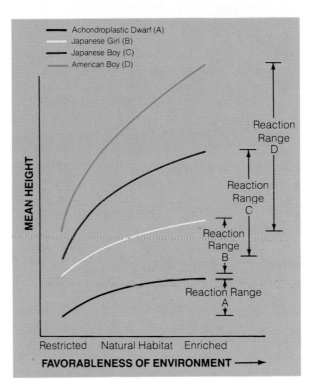

FIGURE 3.3 When the heights of adolescents with four different genetic make-ups are compared, it becomes clear that environment and genes combine to produce development. The Japanese boy (genetic make-up C) who had grown up in an optimum environment would be taller than the American boy (genetic make-up D) who had grown up in a severely restricted environment. But if both environments were natural, severely restricted, or optimum, the American boy would be taller. Under no circumstances could the dwarf (genetic make-up A) be as tall as any of the other three. *(From Gottesman, 1974)*

genes in determining height is easy to grasp, but the way genes and environment might interact to affect behavior is more difficult to discern. Sandra Scarr (1982; Scarr and McCartney, 1983) recently has suggested three ways in which this interaction might occur. First, the home may provide a passive genetic influence. Children not only share their parents' genes, they also live in an environment selected by their parents, where the available experiences are partly determined by the parents' own genes. A child whose parents are both artists will grow up surrounded by art, will experiment with paints and clay at an early age, and will have artists as role models at home. This kind of influence is strongest in childhood, when the home is the dominant environmental influence. Second, a child's genetically influenced appearance and behavior evoke particular responses from others. These responses to the child's attractiveness (or lack of it), physical skills and strength (or lack of them), and temperament will in turn affect the way the child behaves. This kind of influence is probably about the same throughout life. Finally, a child actively seeks out some kinds of experiences and ignores others. Because the child cannot pay attention to everything that goes on, he or she selects experiences that are pleasant, interesting, or challenging. And things that are boring, too easy, or too hard will be avoided. This influence probably gets increasingly stronger as a person get older.

Studying Genetic Influences on Behavior

Researchers have developed several techniques for discovering how genes contribute to the development of individual differences. Some investigators breed other animals and apply principles derived from that research to human genetics. Others study families, on the assumption that the more closely people are related and the more similar a trait, the more likely it is that genetic factors have influenced its development. Only in the case of some abnormal physical traits that are caused by a single gene, such as PKU, have researchers been able to discover just how genes affect development.

Most physical and behavioral traits are polygenic. Appearance is obviously influenced by genetic differences, because genetically related peo-

ple resemble each other more than unrelated people do, whether they grow up together or not. Family resemblances, such as ears that stick out or lie close to the head, are common. Among European royal families, where there was a good deal of inbreeding, genetic traits often became pronounced. The Hapsburg royal family, for example, was noted for the "Hapsburg jaw," a long, protruding chin that was so exaggerated in Charles II of Spain that he could not chew (Durant and Durant, 1963).

Some physiological measures, such as heart rate and blood pressure, show a genetic influence (Claridge and Mangan, 1983), and so do some complicated behavioral disorders. For example, researchers have found that genes are involved in schizophrenia, although the disorder does not appear unless the person's environment fosters its development (Diederen, 1983). Genes also appear to be involved in some forms of reading disorders found in people with normal intelligence. How might genes affect the ability to read? Perhaps certain genetic combinations affect the development of the nervous system, so that children process sounds or letter shapes so slowly that they find it difficult to put the two together (Farnham-Diggory, 1978). Reading disorders tend to run in families and probably take several forms, each influenced by a different genetic combination. Among a group of nine families, 50 of the 84 family members had a similar reading disorder. By analyzing the chromosomes of the family members, researchers discovered that the disorder was apparently linked to a single dominant allele located on chromosome 15 (Smith, Kimberling, Pennington, and Lubs, 1983).

Assessing Genetic Similarity Chromosomal analysis is unlikely to be of much use in the study of normal behavioral traits, because these traits all seem to be polygenic. So instead of analyzing chromosomes, researchers use mathematical techniques to assess the degree of similarity they find through various types of family studies.

Both major types of family studies, twin studies and studies of adopted children, rely on **correlation**. A correlation is a numerical expression of how closely two factors are related; that is, it describes how changes in one factor are associated with changes in the other. The larger the correlation, the more closely two measures correspond, and the better one score can predict the other. Although correlation demonstrates a relationship between the two factors, it does not establish that either factor *causes* the other.

The correlation between the IQ scores of unrelated children reared apart is generally close to .00. As the relatedness between two people increases, the correlation between their IQ scores also increases. Notice that in Table 3.1, the correlations for unrelated children reared together is +.38. Because these children have no common genes, the figure primarily reflects the effect of the environment on IQ. The correlations for siblings (brothers and sisters) are about the same as the correlations for fraternal twins (twins developed from two separate egg cells). This is to be expected, because on the average both siblings and fraternal twins share half their genes. But identical twins (twins developed from a split single egg cell) have identical genetic make-ups, and their IQs show much higher correlations.

Based on such evidence, can we say that genetic make-up is the primary determinant of a person's IQ? Not at all. As relatedness between individuals increases, so does the similarity of their environment. Brothers and sisters share some of their environment, but because they are born at different times and because each has a variety of unique experiences, their environments are not identical. Twins are born at the same time, but this does not eliminate the environmental influence on their IQ scores. In the case of fraternal twins, especially those of the same sex, parents often characterize them ("the smart one," "the dumb one," "the good one," "the naughty one") and then respond to them in those terms. As a result, each twin is treated differently by the parents. Twins also may develop separate interests and may exaggerate the differences between themselves in order to establish their own identities. For these reasons, some psychologists have suggested that the environment of ordinary siblings may be more similar than that of fraternal twins (Hoffman, 1985).

Adoption Studies   Most researchers believe that adoption studies are probably the best way to search for genetic influences on IQ. In Texas, researchers studied 300 adoptive families, comparing the IQs of biological mothers, adoptive parents, and the biological children in the adoptive families (Willerman, 1979). They compared the children whose biological mothers had IQs of 95 or less with those children whose biological mothers had IQs of 120 or more (see Table 3.2). No children of low IQ mothers had IQs of 120 or more, and no children of high IQ mothers had IQs of 95 or less. Children in both groups responded to their good environment, but children of the mothers with high IQs responded the most, indicating that their reaction range for these skills was probably higher.

As this study seems to demonstrate, intellectual skills have a reaction range. No matter how stimulating the environment, few people become Albert Einsteins or Leonardo da Vincis. And unless the environment is extremely deprived, most people do not become mentally retarded. Each of us has a range of at least 25 IQ points in which our IQ score tends to fall, depending on rearing conditions (Scarr, 1981). A good environment allows these skills to develop toward the upper end of that range. Sandra Scarr and Richard Weinberg (1983) tested this idea by studying more than 100 poor black children who were adopted as babies by middle-class white families, in which most of the parents were college graduates. The average IQ score of these children was above the national average of both black and white children, indicating the profound effect of environment on IQ.

Environment affects development by providing

Table 3.1
Correlations of Intelligence Test Scores

Unrelated children reared apart	+.00
Unrelated children reared together	+.38
Siblings reared together	+.54
Fraternal twins reared together	+.53
Identical twins reared apart	+.74
Identical twins reared together	+.86

Note: All data except these in unrelated children reared apart from Rowe and Plomin, 1978. Note that these data are from American studies and do not include data from studies by Sir Cyril Burt.

Source: D. C. Rowe and R. Plomin, "The Burt Controversy: A Comparison of Burt's Data on IQ with Data from Other Studies," *Behavior Genetics,* 8 (1978), 81–84.

Table 3.2
IQ of Adoptees as a Function of Biological Mother's IQ

IQ of Biological Mother	Adoptive Parent's IQ	Adopted Child's IQ	Adoptees ≥ 120 IQ	Adoptees ≤ 95 IQ
Low IQ (89.4) (n = 27)	110.8	102.6	0%	15%
High IQ (121.6) (n = 34)	114.8	118.3	44%	0%

Source: L. Willerman, "Effects of Families on Intellectual Development," *American Psychologist,* 34 (1979), 923–929.

certain stimuli and certain opportunities for people to develop particular characteristics. Genes affect development by responding to given environments in unique ways. Individual differences among people apparently are caused by genetic differences in their reaction ranges *and* by specific differences in their environments. Later in the chapter we will explore some of the issues and complexities involved in genetic transmission.

PRENATAL GROWTH

As soon as sperm and egg unite, development begins and progresses at a rapid rate. The course of prenatal development falls into roughly three periods. During the first two weeks after conception, called the **germinal period,** the zygote is primarily engaged in cell division. During the **embryonic period,** which covers the next six weeks, the organism (now called an **embryo**) begins to take shape, and its various organ systems begin to form. Thereafter, from approximately eight weeks after conception to birth, the developing organism is called a **fetus.** The total **gestation period** usually lasts about 266 days (thirty-eight weeks) from conception or 280 days (forty weeks or nine calendar months) from the beginning of the mother's last normal menstruation. Because most women do not know exactly when they conceived, physicians usually go by **menstrual age;** however, **gestational age** is a more accurate measure of fetal development.

The Germinal Period

Almost immediately after fertilization, the zygote begins the process of cell division that will eventually produce a human body made up of billions of cells. Although an adult's body cells are highly differentiated according to their location and function (for example, nerve cells are quite different in form and function from muscle cells), the cells at this point in development are all identical.

The zygote takes about three days to move through the Fallopian tube into the uterus, where it floats freely for another four or five days before implanting itself in the nutrient-rich uterine wall. By the end of the first two weeks, the cells have multiplied greatly in number and have begun to differentiate themselves according to genetic instructions. An outer membrane (**chorion**) and an inner membrane (**amnion**) form a sac that surrounds and protects the developing organism. By now, the microscope can distinguish the **placenta,** a flexible structure of tissue and blood formed jointly by fetus and mother. From it develops the bluish-red **umbilical cord,** through which oxygen and nourishment pass from maternal to fetal blood vessels and through which fetal wastes are removed. A membrane separates the two circulatory systems and provides the fetus with some protection. Large particles in the mother's blood, such as bacteria, cannot pass through the barrier, but minute particles, such as many viruses and chemical molecules, can slip through the barrier. As we will see, the permeability of this barrier has significant implications for the developing fetus.

If all the embryo's cells are identical, how does a cell know whether it is destined to be part of the nervous system, the skeleton, the heart, the lungs, or the liver? Some scientists believe that substances scattered through the unfertilized egg are activated by fertilization. These gene-regulating substances then reprogram the various embryonic cells, sending them to a particular location and assigning them a function (Kolata, 1979). Other scientists believe that all embryonic cells are essentially neutral and that genetic action is indirect. Somehow, chemicals at various sites in the embryo alter cells to serve the purpose required at that location. For example, researchers have found "instructive molecules" that seem able to direct the nature and growth of nerve cells (Thoenen and Edgar, 1985).

As the germinal period ends, the two-week-old organism is firmly anchored to the lining of the uterus, which maternal hormones have prepared for the developing egg. Life is on its way, although the mother does not yet know she is pregnant.

The Embryonic Period

Within four weeks after conception, the organism is already about one-fifth of an inch long, 10,000 times larger than the original fertilized egg. Its heart is beating to pump blood through microscopic veins and arteries. The beginnings of a brain, kidneys, liver, and a digestive tract have appeared. Indentations at the top will eventually become jaws, eyes, and ears.

The two principles that guide development during the embryonic period, when organs, limbs, and physiological systems form, are the same principles that will guide later growth and development in the fetus, infant, and child. The first principle, called **proximodistal development,** refers to the fact that development generally progresses from the center of the body toward the periphery. During the embryonic period, organs along the central axis of the body develop first; the extremities develop later. Thus, in the early weeks the organism is literally all head and heart. The embryo also follows the principle of **cephalocaudal development:** growth generally progresses from head to foot. So the embryonic head develops first, and only later does the lower part of the body begin to enlarge and to assume its newborn proportion and size. This development follows a pattern of

staggered starts, so that different organs begin to form at different points in the embryonic period.

By the end of the embryonic period, the organism is almost an inch long and has begun to look human. What appear to be the gill slits of a fish are really rudimentary forms of structures in the neck and lower face. What seems to be a primitive tail eventually becomes the tip of the spine; the tail reaches its maximum length at about six weeks and then slowly recedes. The head is clearly distinct from the rounded, skin-covered body and accounts for about half of the embryo's total size. The eyes have come forward from the sides of the head, and eyelids have begun to form. Eyes, nose, lips, tongue, and even the buds of teeth can be distinguished. The knobs that will be arms and legs grow; in a matter of weeks, they will differentiate into hands and feet and then into fingers and toes.

In this early period, the brain sends out impulses that coordinate the functioning of other organ systems. The heart beats sturdily, the stomach produces minute quantities of digestive juices, the liver manufactures blood cells, and the kidneys purify the blood. Testes and ovaries have formed,

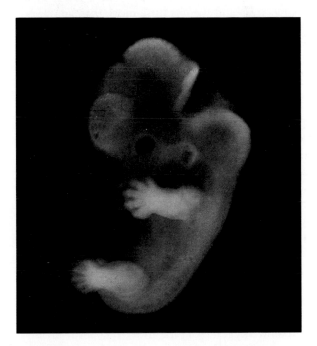

Normal fetus at forty days. Note the rudimentary brain, eye, ear, fingers, and toes. *(From Rugh and Shettles, 1971)*

and the endocrine system has begun to produce hormones. But the embryo has a long way to go. All its organ systems are in a primitive form, and it will be several months before they can be considered fully functional.

The Fetal Period

About eight weeks after conception, when the major organs have taken shape, the fetal period begins. Development shifts from the formation of rudimentary organs to organizing their structure and establishing their function. Now bone cells first appear. By twelve weeks, the fetus has begun to stretch out a little from its C-shaped posture, and the head is more erect. The limbs are nicely molded, and folds for fingernails and toenails are present. A close look could readily determine the sex of the fetus. The lips become separate from the jaws, the nasal passages have formed, the lungs have taken their definitive shape, the brain has attained its general structure, the eye is organized, and the retina is becoming layered. The pancreas secretes bile, and the bone marrow has begun to produce blood. Yet the fetus is only about three inches long and weighs little more than an ounce.

By sixteen weeks the fetus is between six and seven inches long and weighs about four ounces. Until now, its head has been enormous in relation to the rest of its body, but the lower part of the body has grown. Now the head takes up only about one-fourth of the body. The sixteen-week-old fetus looks like a miniature baby. Its face looks human, hair may appear on the head, bones can be distinguished throughout the body, and the sense organs approximate their final appearance.

Although most of the basic systems are present, the fetus could not survive if it were born at this point. Certain functions necessary for life outside the uterus have not yet developed. The fetus floats in a watery world and receives its oxygen through the placenta, so it cannot yet handle the problem of breathing air. Before it can breathe successfully, it must be able to produce the liquid **surfactin**, which coats the air sacs of the lungs and permits them to transmit oxygen from the air to the blood. Around the age of twenty-three weeks, the fetus can begin to produce and maintain surfactin, but if it is born at this time, it often cannot keep surfactin levels high enough. If levels drop too low, the newborn

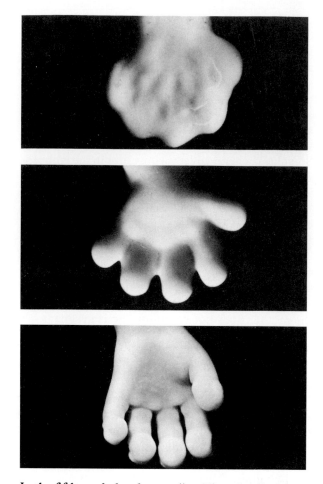

In the fifth week, hands are a "molding plate" with finger ridges. In the sixth week, finger buds form. In the seventh and eighth weeks, fingers, thumbs, and fingerprints form; at this time the touch pads are prominent. *(Courtesy Carnegie Institution of Washington)*

may develop **respiratory distress syndrome** and die. By about thirty-five weeks (sometimes earlier), the fetus develops a new system for maintaining surfactin. This new method allows it to live outside the uterus.

Generally speaking, 161 days (twenty-three weeks or about five and one-half months) is regarded as the minimum possible age at which a fetus may survive. Only in the past few years have babies born this young survived, and not many have done so. A twenty-three-week-old fetus has a highly immature brain and cannot maintain its vital functions without intensive medical assistance. The longer birth is postponed past the twenty-three-week point, the more likely it is that the

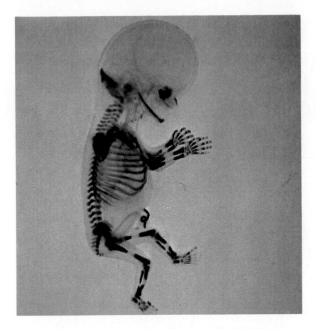

An X-ray of an eight-week-old fetus. The skeleton has developed; the darkened regions indicate advanced bone formation. *(From Rugh and Shettles, 1971)*

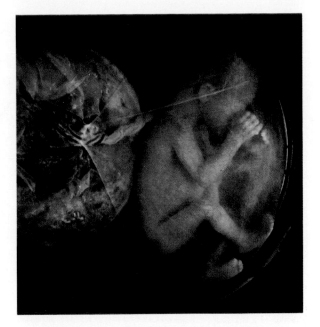

Human fetus at twelve weeks, with the umbilical cord and placenta attached. Through the cord, the developing fetus and mother exchange gases, nutrients, and metabolic wastes. The cord also serves as an entryway for teratogens. *(From Rugh and Shettles, 1971)*

fetus will survive. Fetuses born after 252 days of gestation (thirty-six weeks) are considered to be of normal term, although unusual circumstances may still make special care necessary for the first few days or weeks of life.

A fetus that remains in the uterus much after term also may need special care. About three fetuses in 100 remain in the uterus forty-two weeks or more. As the placenta ages, less and less oxygen and nourishment reach the fetus, so that it begins to lose weight and waste away. At birth, an older fetus may need immediate oxygen and nourishment.

During the final weeks of prenatal development, when the fetus could survive on its own, its organs step up their activity. Its heart rate becomes quite rapid. Fat forms over the entire body, smoothing out the wrinkled skin and rounding out contours. The fetus usually gains about one-half pound a week during the last eight or nine weeks in the uterus. At birth, the average full-term baby is about twenty inches long and weighs a little more than seven pounds, although weights vary from less than three to more than twelve pounds, and length may be less than seventeen or more than twenty-two inches.

PRENATAL BEHAVIORAL DEVELOPMENT

How early in life can the fetus move spontaneously? How soon does it respond to a stimulus? And what kinds of responses does it make? Such questions were not answered until about thirty-five years ago, when Davenport Hooker (1952) had the opportunity to observe the spontaneous behavior and reactions of embryos and fetuses that had been delivered by Caesarean section. They were too immature to survive, but their movements were recorded on film for later study.

Although most mothers say that they feel fetal movement at about sixteen weeks (an event known as *quickening*), by that time the fetus has already been able to move its muscles for approximately eight weeks. Hooker also discovered that by twelve weeks, the fetus can kick its legs, turn its feet, close its fingers, bend its wrists, turn its head, squint, frown, open and close its mouth, and respond to touch.

By twenty-three weeks, the fetus often moves

DOES THE FETUS HAVE A WAY OF DEFENDING ITSELF?

Why doesn't the mother's body invariably reject the fetus growing within her? Once the fetus is born, her body would not tolerate a transplant of skin or an organ from her baby unless she also received a drug to keep her from rejecting it. Yet she harbors the fetus for thirty-eight weeks, nourishing and protecting it until it can survive on its own. Only when things go dreadfully wrong does she miscarry her fetus because of incompatibility. This once happened regularly when there was a crucial difference between mother and baby in an aspect of their blood called the Rh factor. If this happened, a woman with Rh negative blood often became sensitized against the Rh positive blood of her fetus. Physicians now can keep this incompatibility from developing, but their treatment is limited to the Rh factor.

Given the nature of the immune system, all fetuses logically should be rejected. The fetus itself does not touch the mother's body. But the outer layer of the amniotic sac and part of the placenta consist of fetal cells that are in direct contact with the mother's body and her bloodstream. Theoretically, this contact should trigger a massive response from the mother's immune system, with antibodies rushing to repel the alien tissue. Yet the fetus is unharmed. Why is it immune?

Some researchers believe that the fetus hides. It coats the cells that touch the mother's tissue with a substance that fools the mother's immune system. Her body simply does not realize that foreign tissue inhabits it. Other researchers who have been working to solve this puzzle believe that the fetus actively defends itself against expulsion. In this view, the mother's body does recognize the fetal cells as foreign. Her immune system is activated, and it begins producing antibodies to destroy the invading tissue. But before the first antibodies can attack, the fetal cells manufacture a substance that shuts down the mother's immune cells (Wingerson, 1979).

Pediatrician Wade Faulk and cell biologist John McIntyre believe that they have demonstrated this action by mixing a protein from these fetal cells with cells from another animal's immune system. An infinitestimal amount of this protein (25 one-millionths of a gram) reduced the production of antibodies by 97 percent. The researchers speculate that some miscarriages can be traced to fetal cells that are not very efficient at producing this protein. Their hope is to develop an injection that would come to the aid of fetuses whose defense is ineffective. If they are successful, some women who consistently miscarry may one day be able to have healthy babies (see Wingerson, 1979).

---

spontaneously. It sleeps and wakes as a newborn does and even has a favorite position for its naps. At twenty-four weeks, it can cry, open and close its eyes, and look up, down, and sideways. It has developed a grasp reflex and soon will be strong enough to support its weight with one hand. As mothers are uncomfortably aware, during the final eight or nine weeks, the fetus is quite active, often delivering unexpectedly sharp kicks or elbow jabs. These spontaneous actions, which are limited by the increasingly snug fit of the uterus, seem to be embedded in a regular pattern of movement, for the older fetus moves its arms and legs about once each minute, in a cycle similar to that found in newborns (Robertson, Dierker, Sorokin, and Rosen, 1982). Researchers are not sure just how early this pattern develops but have shown that it is not related to other fetal rhythms, such as breathing. As we will see in Chapter 4, most newborn behavior is rhythmic, and some of the rhythms have social meaning.

Behavioral development before birth corresponds to the development of the nervous system and muscles. As early as seven and one-half weeks, the embryo responds when its mouth is stroked with a fine hair; it moves its upper trunk and neck. By nine weeks, the fetus bends its fingers when the palm of its hand is touched and either curls or

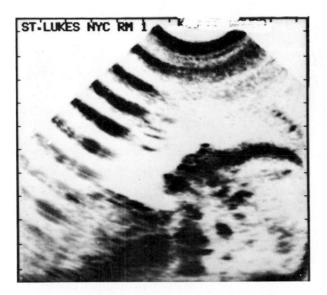

In this sonogram, the fetal head and chest show clearly. Such ultrasound images can be used to detect the presence of twins, gross abnormalities in the fetus, and to observe fetal responses to sound.
(Courtesy of the Ultrasound Department, St. Luke's Medical Center, NYC)

straightens its toes in response to a touch on the sole of the foot. By eleven weeks, the fetus can swallow. As development progresses, the fetus becomes increasingly sensitive to stimulation, and its response changes from a diffuse, general movement of the whole body to a movement limited to the muscles in the stimulated area. Now, for example, a touch on the mouth evokes only movements of the mouth muscles. Within the last few months before birth, the fetus behaves essentially as it does at birth, grasping, sucking, and kicking.

At about this time, the fetus also hears sounds and responds to them. Researchers have established the existence of the capacity by using **ultrasound** to watch fetal movements. In this technique, sound is passed through the mother's abdominal wall, bounced off the fetus, and the echoes are transformed into thousands of dots that appear on a screen. These pictures are called **sonograms.** When researchers made a loud sound next to the mother's abdomen, just over a fetal ear, the fetus started. It squeezed its eyelids shut, averted its head, waved its arms, and extended its leg (Birnholz and Benacerraf, 1983) (see Table 3.3). After observing more than 900 infants this way, the researchers discovered that a fetus who does *not* respond to sounds probably has major developmental problems. Either the fetus is profoundly deaf or there is some significant defect in its nervous system. Every fetus that did not react to the sound was later found to be deaf, structurally deformed, or dangerously ill.

A fetus even may remember sound patterns if they are repeated frequently. The possibility that a fetus may be capable of this sort of rudimentary learning emerged when researchers asked pregnant women to read the same children's story

**Table 3.3
Fetal Hearing**

Gestational Age (Weeks)	*Auditory Response*			
	No Response	*Inconsistent*	*Blink*	*Total*
12–15.9	17	0	0	17
16–19.9	26	0	0	26
20–23.9	32	0	0	32
24–24.9	14	7	0	21
25–25.9	9	14	1	24
26–26.9	5	20	3	28
27–27.9	2	12	9	23
28–28.9	0	3	17	20
29–32	0	0	36	36

Note: Among one group of fetuses studied by Birnholz and Benacerraf, the characteristic startled blink first appeared at 25 weeks, and by 29 weeks all fetuses reacted to the sound.

Source: J. C. Birnholz and B. R. Benacerraf, "The Development of Human Fetal Hearing," *Science,* 22 (1983), 516–518.

aloud twice each day during the last few months of pregnancy. Three days after the babies were born, Anthony DeCasper and Melanie Spence (1986) played a recording of a woman reading both the familiar story and a new one. The babies could regulate the sound by sucking on a pacifier; their sucks kept the sound on. Babies seemed to remember the familiar story and prefer it, sucking more consistently to hear the familiar tale, whether both stories were read by their mother or another woman.

THE BIRTH PROCESS

As the time for birth approaches, the fetus generally lies head down in the uterus. The uterus at this time resembles a large sack that opens into the vagina through the cervix. Exactly what event triggers the birth process? Researchers are not certain, but many believe that the fetus plays a major role in determining its onset.

Labor and Delivery

When the birth process begins, the upper portion of the uterus contracts at regular and progressively shorter intervals while the lower part of the uterus thins out, and the cervix dilates to permit the fetus to pass through the birth canal. Later, the mother's abdominal muscles also contract in a bearing-down motion. Unless drugs deaden her sensations, she usually pushes hard to get the baby out. The entire process is called **labor,** and it may be completed in less than three hours or drag on for more than a day. For first-born infants, the average labor lasts from thirteen to fifteen hours. It is markedly shorter for later-born children.

The first stage of labor lasts until the cervix is completely dilated. It usually begins with faint contractions that grow stronger and more frequent. In the second stage of labor, the fetus passes head first through the birth canal and is born, a process that lasts approximately eighty minutes for first-born children (see Figure 3.4). After birth, the attendant cleans the baby's nose and mouth with a suction apparatus to prevent sub-

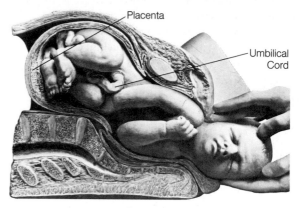

FIGURE 3.4   Models indicating the position of the fetus during passage through the birth canal. *(Reproduced with permission, from the* Birth Atlas, *published by Maternity Center Association, New York)*

stances from entering the lungs and to make breathing easier. Then the umbilical cord is tied and cut. In the final stage of labor, uterine contractions expel the **afterbirth** — the placenta, its membranes, and the rest of the umbilical cord. This process lasts approximately five to twenty minutes, and the afterbirth is immediately examined by the attendant to determine whether it is complete and normal.

Not all deliveries proceed in this normal fashion. In fact, among the mothers in various studies, only 45 percent had no complications of any kind. Most complications are mild or moderate, but in some instances, complications are severe (Grossman, Eichler, and Winickoff, 1980). For example, in a breech delivery, the baby's buttocks appear first in the birth canal, then the legs, and finally the head. In a transverse presentation, the baby lies crosswise in the uterus, and a shoulder, arm, or hand first enters the vagina. Both kinds of delivery can be dangerous because the baby may experience anoxia, or even suffocate, before the head emerges. In **anoxia,** the air supply is cut off temporarily. Its effects may be fleeting, long lasting, or permanent, depending on how long the baby cannot get air, whether the baby is also affected by anesthetics, and the baby's general health.

Because of this danger, physicians have become increasingly likely to deliver babies lying in a breech or transverse position by Caesarean section, in which the baby is removed through an incision in the mother's abdomen. This surgical procedure is also used when the mother's pelvis is too small to permit her baby to pass through; when the mother suffers from diabetes, high blood pressure, or some other ailment; when the mother has active herpes; or when the fetus seems in danger, perhaps from a prolonged delivery.

Immediately after birth, the newborn baby is examined so attendants can determine whether further medical help is needed. Most physicians rely on the baby's **Apgar score** on a test devised by physician Virginia Apgar to assess the newborn's appearance (color), heart rate, reflex irritability, muscle tone, and respiratory effort (Apgar and James, 1962). Each of these five characteristics is rated 0, 1, or 2 (2 being best), and these scores are added to constitute the baby's total Apgar score, which may vary from 0 to 10. At one minute after delivery, most normal newborns achieve a score of 8 to 10.

Another widely used method is the Dubowitz scoring system, which gives a fairly accurate estimate of the newborn's gestational age (Dubowitz, Dubowitz, and Goldberg, 1970). A baby's score on ten neurological signs (such as limb reflexes and hand flexion) and eleven characteristics of appearance (such as skin texture, genitals, and ears) can be determined in less than five minutes (Self and Horowitz, 1979). The highest possible score (70) indicates a baby that is past term. The Dubowitz system has become increasingly popular because it separates the premature baby from the very small, full-term baby.

Methods of Childbirth

Over the past few decades, American methods of childbirth have undergone dramatic change. At one time, all labors were considered difficult and painful. In most American hospitals, drugs were routinely given, and episiotomies (surgical incisions to enlarge the vaginal opening) and forceps were used to speed the birth process. Such practices were considered the best ways to care for mothers and babies. But a growing number of parents and medical personnel began to question these procedures (Hahn and Paige, 1980), and their dissatisfaction seemed to be supported by evidence from other cultures.

Anthropologists reported that childbirth practices varied dramatically around the world. In cultures that regarded birth as something to be hidden, women often had prolonged and difficult labors. But in cultures that regarded birth as an open, easy process, women generally had short, uncomplicated labors (Mead and Newton, 1967).

Grantly Dick-Read (1944), a British physician who had noticed that some of his patients found childbirth a relatively peaceful, painless experience, believed fear generated a tension that produced pain in most women. His urging of what he called "natural childbirth" met with some success, and his techniques, combined with the more recently introduced Lamaze method, have brought about changes in the way many obstetricians handle childbirth. In the Lamaze method, women learn to substitute new responses for learned responses of pain and, by concentrating on breathing, try to inhibit painful sensations (Chabon, 1966). Another feature of this method is a "coach," who stays with the mother during labor to provide psychological encouragement. Since the Lamaze method was introduced, additional methods of natural childbirth have been devised. In all of them, parents learn about the birth process, a coach stays with the mother, and the mother is encouraged to take as little medication as possible and to participate actively in the birth.

The rising popularity of natural childbirth gradually has led many hospitals to change their procedures. In most hospitals, the husband may accompany his wife into the delivery room, where he can offer her emotional support and participate in the birth process. In addition, in many hospitals,

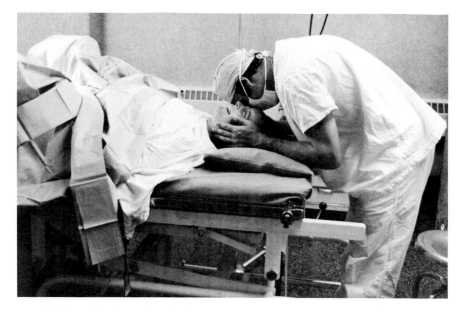

Many fathers are taking an active role in the births of their children. This woman is receiving encouragement and emotional support from her husband in the delivery room. *(Abigail Heyman/Archive)*

some of the routine customs, from automatic medication to episiotomy, that tend to make birth an abnormal and unpleasant procedure, have been eliminated for normal deliveries. The medical profession has come to realize that all family members benefit from sharing the experience of childbirth. Today, professionals urge a more homelike hospital atmosphere, the presence of the father, a bed that allows the mother to give birth in a near sitting position, an opportunity for mother, father, and infant to be together after delivery, and the encouragement of breast-feeding (Interprofessional Task Force, 1978).

FETAL ABNORMALITIES AND BIRTH COMPLICATIONS

Most pregnancies follow a normal course of development, and most babies are normal. On occasion, however, a genetic abnormality affects the developing fetus. Sometimes the process of meiosis goes wrong. At other times, a change takes place in the chemical structure of a single gene, producing a new allele that carries different genetic information—information that can be transmitted to a person's children. Such **mutations** may be spontaneous, or they may be caused by radiation or exposure to environmental chemicals. Most zygotes with chromosomal or genetic abnormalities do not survive; when they die, the mother usually assumes that her menstrual period was late. When an abnormal zygote lives, the defect usually is minor, although some defects require medical or surgical intervention, and a few are so serious that they threaten the life of the baby. By using the techniques described in the box, "Detecting Complications," physicians can discover many serious abnormalities before birth.

Chromosomal Abnormalities

When a cell divides to form a gamete, a pair of chromosomes may fail to separate, so that one of the gametes has one chromosome too many and the other has one too few. When the sex chromosome is involved, the fertilized egg may carry either a single female chromosome (XO), an extra female chromosome (XXY), or an extra male chromosome (XYY). The X chromosome is necessary for development, so a zygote with only a male chromosome (OY) never survives.

Zygotes with the XO pattern develop into girls with **Turner's syndrome,** a condition that affects about one birth in every 2,500 (World Health Organization, 1964). These girls are especially short, have a webbed or shortened neck, a broad-bridged nose, low-set ears, and short, chubby fingers. Un-

DETECTING COMPLICATIONS

Many factors, from drugs taken by the mother during pregnancy to chromosomal abnormalities, can affect the development of the fetus. Some years ago, it was not until a child was born that abnormalities or potentially fatal diseases could be detected. By that time, it was too late to take preventive action. Today, several prenatal diagnostic procedures can answer questions about fetal development. Prospective parents whose relatives have been born with abnormalities or life-threatening conditions can be reassured about their child's normality or prepare themselves to deal with abnormal conditions.

Gross abnormalities in fetal development now can be discovered early in pregnancy by the use of ultrasound (discussed earlier). Sonograms can show visible abnormalities, resolve confusion over the age of the fetus, and uncover such conditions as a placenta that is blocking the birth canal or the presence of more than one fetus.

Ultrasound often is used as a guide for performing other procedures to detect chromosomal abnormalities. In one procedure, known as **amniocentesis,** the physician inserts a hollow needle through the mother's abdomen and draws out a sample of amniotic fluid. The fetus sheds cells into the amniotic fluid, and if the fetal cells in this fluid are grown in a culture, technicians can perform chromosomal analyses that will detect such abnormalities as Down's syndrome and Turner's syndrome. The chemical composition of the amniotic fluid frequently provides clues to other diseases, such as Tay-Sachs (a genetically transmitted disease in which the absence of a fat-metabolizing enzyme leads to death before the age of seven). The fluid also reveals whether the fetus can produce enough surfactin to avoid respiratory distress when it is born. In addition, tests can detect the blood group and sex of the fetus. Amniocentesis carries a slight risk: the chances are one in 200 that it will cause bleeding or spontaneous abortion (Mittenthal, 1984). Because the procedure cannot be done until between the fourteenth and the sixteenth week after conception, and then because results are not known for several weeks, amniocentesis leaves little time for parents to make critical decisions concerning abortion.

In a newer procedure, known as **chorionic villi sampling,** the physician inserts a hollow tube through the vagina and removes cells from the fingerlike projections of the chorion. This technique can be used as early as the eighth week of pregnancy, and results are quicker because no cells need be grown. Instead, the cells are examined directly. Chorionic villi sampling detects the same range of conditions as amniocentesis, and the information is available early enough for an abortion by uterine aspiration. The risk to the embryo is somewhat higher with this sampling technique than with amniocentesis: 1.8 spontaneous abortions per 100 tests (Brozan, 1985).

A simple test, together with amniocentesis, can uncover neural tube defects, another serious condition. If the tube that forms the brain and spinal column fails to close, the fetus is likely to be seriously damaged. The defect occurs in 1.2 births in every thousand; it is found in all population groups. No one knows why it happens in one pregnancy and not another (Leonard, 1981). When the tube fails to close at the top, babies are born without a brain or with an incomplete one. If they are alive at birth, they die within a few days. When the tube fails to close along the spinal column, the babies have a condition known as **spina bifida:** a bundle of nerves protrudes through an opening in the spinal column. These babies generally live, although many are retarded or paralyzed below the waist. In some, fluid does not drain properly from the skull, so that they also have **hydrocephaly,** an accumulation of fluid within the skull that presses on the brain.

Prenatal screening for neural tube defects is a routine part of medical care in the United Kingdom and is becoming more common in the United States. The procedure for detecting neural tube defects is a lengthy one. When the fetus has such a defect, its liver produces excessive amounts of alfa-fetoprotein (AFP). The AFP passes into the amniotic fluid and from there to the maternal bloodstream. An inexpensive test can detect high levels of AFP, but positive results do not mean a defective fetus. The chances are still 48 out of 50 that it is normal. Ultrasound and amniocentesis can pick out cases of neural tube defects from those in which other conditions of pregnancy, such as the presence of twins or an incorrect estimate of fetal age, have led to high AFP levels.

Most often, prenatal diagnostic techniques remove parents' anxiety over possible defects. Even if both parents carry the recessive Tay-Sachs gene, for example, the chances are still three in four that their baby will be normal. If the test indicates an abnormal fetus, parents can discuss the situation with a genetic counselor, who can tell them how extensive the defect may be and what sort of care their child will require.

Based on that information, the parents make their own decision. Among couples interviewed by Michael Gold (1981), for example, the results of prenatal screening for neural tube defects varied widely. All mothers had shown high AFP levels at the initial screening. Anne and Joe discovered their fetus had spina bifida and chose abortion. Within a year, Anne was pregnant again. This time the fetus showed no abnormality. Five months later, they were parents of a normal, healthy baby girl. Like most couples, Steve and Julie found that their fetus was normal; they became parents of a healthy boy. Pat and Tony found that their fetus was seriously deformed but could not bring themselves to consider abortion. Their baby was born with only part of a brain and died almost immediately. Many parents who discover their child is defective follow Pat and Tony's example and decide not to terminate the pregnancy. When their defective baby is born, there is no shock, and they find it easier to form emotional bonds with their baby and to adapt to his or her condition than if they had not been initially prepared.

less they are given female hormones, they do not develop secondary sex characteristics. Although most seem to have normal verbal skills, their spatial skills are significantly below normal (Rovet and Netley, 1982).

About one in 400 babies is born with an XXY pattern, a condition known as **Klinefelter's syndrome.** Some of these boys develop normally, but unless they are given male sex hormones, the majority never develop secondary sex characteristics. These boys are generally passive, dependent, and mentally slow (Rubin, Reinisch, and Haskett, 1981). Zygotes who have inherited an XYY pattern develop into apparently normal boys and men. Only a microscopic examination of their cells reveals the unusual chromosome pattern. However, as men they are often impulsive and antisocial, although they do not seem to be especially violent toward other people (Rubin, Reinisch, and Haskett, 1981).

If the zygote has an extra chromosome 21 (three instead of two), the egg develops into a baby who suffers from **Down's syndrome** (formerly called *mongolism*). Boys and girls with this condition frequently have congenital heart disease and other problems; often they do not live past their teens. Such children usually are mentally retarded, although the extent of retardation varies.

Although Down's syndrome generally is caused by an extra chromosome, sometimes it develops when extra material from chromosome 21 be-

This youngster was born with Down's syndrome, a chromosomal disorder that is caused by an error in cell division. Most Down's syndrome children are mentally retarded, and many attend special schools like this one. *(Alan Cary/The Image Works)*

comes attached to another chromosome. This tendency is extremely rare, and it is inherited. Most cases of Down's syndrome arise when an error in cell division produces an offspring with an entire extra chromosome 21, a genetic make-up unlike that of either parent. This tendency is not inherited. Up to 30 percent of the cases of Down's syndrome are caused by faulty cell division in the sperm; the rest are caused by faulty cell division in the ovum (Gunderson and Sackett, 1982).

The likelihood of producing a Down's syndrome child because of an error in cell division increases as parents age. The risk of producing a child with Down's syndrome is only about 1 in 2,000 for mothers at the age of twenty, 1 in 1,000 at age thirty, and 1 in 500 at age thirty-five. By the age of forty, the ratio rises to about 1 in 100, and by age forty-five, it is 1 in 45 (Omenn, 1983). But older mothers generally are married to older men, and older men may produce faulty sperm. Other abnormalities also occur more frequently in children born to older parents, which is the reason most genetic counselors encourage parents to have their children before the mother reaches forty.

Environmental Hazards

Although the environment within the uterus protects the fetus from many harmful influences, some agents that can alter or kill the developing organism are able to cross the placental barrier (see Table 3.4). It seems ironic that most of these agents, which are called **teratogens,** reach the fetus through the same connections with the mother that bring life-sustaining nutrients and oxygen. Teratogens include diseases, smoking, and environmental pollutants.

Even when the extent of exposure to a destructive agent is known, however, there is no way to predict the extent of its influence on the developing fetus. Timing is apparently the crucial factor in determining whether an environmental influence will produce an abnormality. As noted earlier, different organ systems generate and develop on a staggered schedule. Because organs are most vulnerable during their period of most rapid growth, different teratogens can have the same effect at a given point in fetal development and the same teratogen can have different effects, depending on

the age of the fetus at the time of exposure. Thus, if a destructive agent is introduced at the time an organ is forming, that organ may never develop properly. Yet the same agent may have less serious effects — or no effect at all — on organs already formed or on those that are not yet ready to make their appearance. A general rule is that younger fetuses run much higher risks than older fetuses. Exposure is especially dangerous during the embryonic period, when the mother does not know she is pregnant and is unaware that teratogens are at their insidious work.

Timing is not the only factor that determines the extent of damage. The amount of exposure, the genetic susceptibility of the fetus, and the mother's physical condition can reduce or exaggerate the likelihood of malformation (Johnson and Kochlar, 1983).

Gross physical damage usually is apparent at birth or during early infancy. But some teratogens produce "sleeper effects"; their influence is not apparent until later in the course of development. Either the damage is masked by some compensatory mechanism, or else behavior that is affected by the damage emerges only later (Jacobson, Fein, Jacobson, Schwartz, and Dowler, 1985). Damage to the central nervous system that affects the ability to talk, for example, goes unnoticed until a child is at least two years old; damage that affects the ability to concentrate or to master school skills goes unnoticed until even later.

Disease   If a woman contracts **rubella** (German measles) early in pregnancy, her child may be born blind, deaf, brain damaged, or with heart disease. Fortunately, serious damage seems restricted to the first three months of the prenatal period, and the later the mother catches rubella, the less likely it is that her baby will be infected. In one study, 47 percent of the babies born to mothers who had rubella during the first month of pregnancy and 22 percent of babies whose mothers had the disease in the second month were abnormal, but only 7 percent of those whose mothers contracted it in the third month were seriously affected (Michaels and Mellin, 1960).

Sexually transmitted diseases in the mother also can have unfortunate consequences for the fetus. The organisms that cause **syphilis** pass through the placental barrier, transmitting the disease to the

Table 3.4
Some Substances that May Harm the Fetus*

Danger Established	Danger Suspected	Possible Danger
Definite Evidence of Harm	Appear to Increase the Chances of Death or Disability	Animal Data Are Suggestive, but Human Data Are Limited
Alcohol	Anesthetic gases	Caffeine
Antibiotics (some)	Narcotics	Carbon disulfide
Antitumor drugs	Appetite depressants that work on the nervous system	Chlordane
Cadmium		Insulin
DES	Anticonvulsive drugs (Dilantin)	Lithium
Lead	Quinine	Aspirin
Mercury	Drugs for heart disease or high blood pressure (thiazides, reserpine)	Tranquilizers (Valium, Librium, Meprobamate, phenothiazines)
Oral contraceptives	Cocaine	Barbiturates
Cigarettes		
Thalidomide		
PCBS		
Accutane (acne drug)		

* This sampling from the growing list of harmful substances reinforces the wisdom of the obstetrician's advice to take as little medication during pregnancy as possible.

fetus. If a pregnant woman is in the early stages of syphilis, and if she receives treatment, her baby is likely to be born without ill effects. But if she remains untreated or if she is in a more severe stage of the disease, her baby may be born with congenital syphilis. When the mother is seriously infected, her baby may suffer a wide variety of debilitating and severe abnormalities.

As the fetus moves down the birth canal, it can come into contact with gonococcus, the bacterium that produces **gonorrhea.** A number of years ago, many babies became blind when their eyes were infected by gonococci during the birth process. Because many women have gonorrhea without showing any symptoms, it has become common practice to place drops of silver nitrate or antibiotics in the eyes of all newborn babies. The practice has almost wiped out this kind of blindness. **Chlamydia,** another bacterium, today is more common than gonorrhea. And like gonorrhea, it may be a silent, symptomless infection that lurks in the vagina and enters the baby during labor. About 100,000 babies each year develop eye infections or pneumonia from Chlamydia infections. Although antibiotic ointments can prevent the eye infec-

tions, they seem unable to keep pneumonia from developing (Brody, 1984).

The prospects are less hopeful for a **genital herpes** infection, which represents a real danger for a fetus that picks up the virus while moving down the birth canal. Because the incubation period for this virus is from four to twenty-one days, infected babies may not show any symptoms until after they go home from the hospital. Up to half the babies born to mothers with a genital herpes infection contract the disease, and only about half of them survive it (Babson, Pernoll, Benda, and Simpson, 1980).

Another sometimes sexually transmitted disease that can pass through the placental barrier is **acquired immune deficiency syndrome,** or AIDS. In most cases, the mother contracts the disease when injecting street drugs with a contaminated needle, but whatever the source of the mother's infection, the danger to the baby is the same. The baby's immune system collapses, so that the infant has no protection against any infection he or she may encounter. An exposed baby may not develop an active form of AIDS until later in childhood, but those who live long enough eventually develop degenerative brain disease (Seligmann, 1986).

Drugs A golden rule of obstetric practice has been to advise women to take as little medication during pregnancy as possible. Even aspirin has become suspect; some authorities believe that it can lengthen pregnancy and lead to bleeding in the newborn infant (Babson, Pernoll, Benda, and Simpson, 1980). Heavy consumption of coffee, tea, and cola may shorten pregnancy and lead to poor reflexes and neuromuscular development in newborns (Jacobson, Fein, Jacobson, Schwartz, and Dowler, 1984).

One of the more spectacular examples of drug effects was seen in the 1960s, when women who took the drug thalidomide early in pregnancy (while fetal limbs were forming) gave birth to babies without arms or legs. These infants' hands and feet grew from their bodies like flippers. Accutane, a drug often prescribed today for severe acne, also causes fetal death or serious malformations of the face, skull, brain, heart, and thymus gland (Schmeck, 1985).

Sometimes drugs given to keep a mother from miscarrying can affect the developing fetus. Diethylstilbestrol (DES), for example, a synthetic hormone that was widely prescribed from the 1940s until 1975, has been associated with a rare form of vaginal and cervical cancer in women whose mothers received the drug, with highest damage among those exposed to large doses during the first month of prenatal development. When these exposed women later became pregnant themselves, they were much more likely than other women to miscarry, to have abnormal pregnancies that required surgical termination, and to give birth before term (Sandberg, Riffle, Higdon, and Getman, 1981). Adolescent boys whose mothers received the drug tend to have low sperm counts.

Heroin use creates an added problem. The newborn infant of a heroin or methadone user often must go through withdrawal, because both drugs pass through the placental barrier. These babies have tremors, diarrhea, high temperatures, and convulsions. They are irritable, sleep poorly, and cry a great deal. Many of them are also extremely light; they eat voraciously but do not gain weight. When they are older, they often are restless, find it difficult to sit still, and have short attention spans (Kolata, 1978).

The damage done by cocaine is only now becoming apparent. The widespread availability of "crack" (free-based cocaine that can be smoked) has turned cocaine addiction among newborns and cocaine-related developmental complications into major problems in some large urban hospital nurseries. Addicted babies respond much as heroin- or methadone-addicted babies do. But these babies face additional hazards. They may have strokes or serious respiratory problems. Although some "coke babies" show few symptoms, physicians believe that neurological impairment may lead to sleeper effects in such areas as language skills (Barol, 1986).

One in 750 babies born in the United States shows the effects of **fetal alcohol syndrome.** These babies, who are born to alcoholic mothers, are extremely light, have an odd, conical-shaped head and characteristic facial features, and are mentally retarded. Occasionally, these babies have cleft palates, heart murmurs, hernias, damaged kidneys, and eye, neural tube, or skeletal defects. Studies indicate that heavy alcohol consumption is especially risky before a woman realizes that she is pregnant: human embryos run the greatest danger of gross brain malformation during the third week of development (Sulik, Johnston, and Webb, 1981).

Social drinking also may harm the fetus. Heavy social drinkers have about three times as many stillbirths as light drinkers, and their babies are light, have abnormal heart rates, low Apgar scores, suck weakly, and perform poorly on tests of newborn behavior. Mothers who averaged fourteen drinks a week during pregnancy had children who as four-year-olds had difficulty paying attention and had slowed reaction times (Streissguth et al., 1984), and mothers who averaged five drinks a week during pregnancy had sluggish babies who had trouble adjusting to stimuli (Streissguth, Barr, and Martin, 1983). The danger probably increases among mothers who save their drinking for weekend parties. When blood alcohol levels rise sharply, the umbilical cord appears to collapse, perhaps cutting off the supply of oxygen to the fetal brain (Mukherjee and Hodgen, 1982). Apparently, one drink a day is not as harmful as six days' abstention followed by five drinks on Saturday night.

Smoking   Cigarette smoking has been associated with a wide variety of effects on the fetus, in part because nicotine and increased carbon monoxide in the mother's blood both deprive the fetus of oxygen. Nicotine also crosses the placental barrier, speeding the fetus's heart and depressing its respiratory rate. Smokers are more likely to miscarry and have babies who die early in infancy, and they are twice as likely as nonsmokers to have low birthweight babies. Babies of smokers also have a significantly higher rate of cleft palates and hare lips. As newborns, the babies of women who smoked just under one package of cigarettes a day tend to be slow to cry or to respond to sounds (Jacobson, Fein, Jacobson, Schwartz, and Dowler, 1984). As four-year-olds, the babies of such women tend to have trouble paying attention (Streissguth et al., 1984).

Environmental Pollutants   Chemicals in the air that expectant mothers breathe and in the food they eat may pass through the placental barrier. Lead, mercury, and PCBs (synthetic hydrocarbons) are among the best known environmental pollutants. They accumulate in the body, and from time to time, areas of high contamination provide dramatic proof of their insidious effects on the growing fetus. During the 1970s, for example, Japanese mothers who regularly ate mercury-contaminated fish gave birth to infants with severely damaged nervous systems (Takeuchi, 1972). Those who survived had abnormal motor development, found it difficult to chew or swallow, and were profoundly retarded.

More recently, Sandra Jacobson and her colleagues (Jacobson et al., 1985) have studied the effects of PCB poisoning on the fetus. They discovered that infants born to women who ate PCB-contaminated fish from Lake Michigan (at least twenty-six pounds over the six-year period preceding the birth) were lower in birth weight and had smaller head circumferences and shorter gestation periods than babies born to women who lived in the same area but did not eat fish. By the time the affected infants were seven months old, a sleeper effect had appeared. Although their behavior as newborns seemed normal, these infants now showed memory problems: they found it difficult to recognize objects they had just seen. As with other teratogens, the amount of the pollutant that reached the fetus and the time of exposure were

important. In addition, any genetic predisposition or temporary condition that might sensitize the fetus to the pollutant's harmful effects can either heighten or diminish the damage.

Emotional Stress   Because stress alters a pregnant woman's hormone production, it also alters the environment of her fetus. There is little doubt that these real physiological changes have momentary effects on the fetus, because they divert blood flow away from the fetus and cut back on its oxygen supply (Stechler and Halton, 1982). In one group of women, sudden grief, fear, or anxiety was followed by intense fetal activity, with the fetus moving at ten times its normal level (Sontag, 1966). Can the oxygen deprivation and chemical changes that accompany stress have lasting effects? Mothers who show high levels of anxiety during pregnancy tend to have difficult deliveries, and their infants score poorly on newborn assessment scales (Gunderson and Sackett, 1982). Some studies suggest that severe stress during pregnancy may affect an infant's birth weight, heart rate, motor development, and emotionality (Joffe, 1965; Thompson, 1957).

Intense distress during pregnancy seems to have had lasting effects on one group of children (Blomberg, 1980). Their mothers had been unsuccessful in their search for an abortion. Therefore the mothers' stress was closely associated with the pregnancies. These youngsters performed worse at school, showed more psychosomatic symptoms, and were more often in need of psychiatric treatment than youngsters in a control group of similar age, sex, birth order, and social class. It is possible, however, that the postnatal behavior of these mothers also contributed to the effect.

Anesthetics   In recent years, American women have been asking for fewer pain-relieving drugs during the birth process. Their reluctance to take unnecessary drugs is probably wise, because many of the drugs given for pain cross the placental barrier and have a depressant effect on the fetus. The effects of these drugs may linger for days or even months, depending on the drug, the dosage, and the time of administration. In most studies, babies whose mothers were given drugs performed poorly on standard tests of infant behavior compared with babies whose mothers received no drugs. Among the baby's basic functions that are affected by drugs given their mothers to relieve pain are visual attention, sucking, weight gain, smiling, movement, and responses to various stimuli (Stechler and Halton, 1982).

Prematurity

Any condition that interferes with fetal development can result in a baby's being born before **term,** which refers to a gestational age of thirty-six to forty weeks from conception. All such babies once were called premature and given special medical care. This definition was inadequate, because an early baby sometimes is of normal weight and health, whereas a baby born at term sometimes is seriously underweight and needs intensive medical care. Therefore, physicians began treating all newborns who weighed less than five and one-half pounds (2,500 grams) as premature, regardless of

their gestational age. Then, as tests like the Dubowitz system were developed, it became possible to distinguish between the early baby and the baby who is **small for gestational age,** or SGA. The latter are at higher risk than most early babies, because some aspect of their development usually has gone awry and has inhibited their growth. They also are likely to have physical problems.

Babies who need the most medical attention are those with a gestational age of less than thirty-three weeks (no matter what their weight) or those who weigh less than 2,000 grams (no matter what their age). They need special care, including continual monitoring of their blood pressure, temperature, respiration, and heart rate; feedings of water and milk through a tube directly into the stomach; and careful control of their oxygen supply (too little and they develop cerebral palsy; too much and they become blind). Even with the best of care, about 10 percent of these high-risk babies die (Babson et al., 1980). Among babies with a gesta-

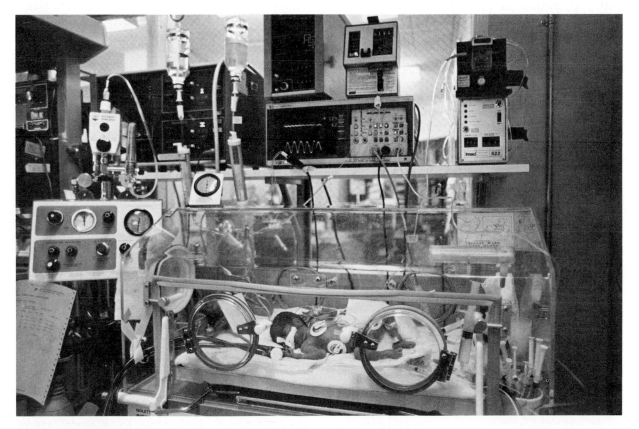

The life-support system of a premature infant. *(David Hurn/Magnum)*

tional age of thirty-seven weeks or less and a birth weight of less than 2,500 grams, about 10 percent show some kind of intellectual impairment (Kopp, 1983).

The prospect of normal development in these early infants has markedly increased from the 1960s, when 15 percent were severely handicapped (Kopp, 1983). Tests of year-old infants indicate that the rate of severe disability is continuing to drop, especially among those who weighed less than 1,500 grams (3 pounds 5 ounces) at birth, although mild effects still might appear when these youngsters enter school (Teltsch, 1985). What is the best predictor of a tiny, sick baby's future? The home environment. Although some medical or physiological problems may produce a degree of disability in any environment, preterm or SGA babies who grow up in advantaged homes generally do well. Often they show no lasting effects from their birth problems. But many babies with similar problems who grow up in disadvantaged homes have learning disabilities or some neurological defect. The worst outcomes generally appear among the poorest babies (Kopp, 1983).

In spite of all the possible complications of the prenatal period, most babies come into the world as normal individuals. As a baby emerges from the dark of the womb, the most intimate human relationship ends. Within the uterus, the child is completely dependent on the mother for the automatic satisfaction of every need. At birth, the baby starts life as a separate individual. In the next chapter, we look at the beginnings of independent life — the world of the newborn child.

SUMMARY

1. Development begins when the father's **spermatozoon** unites with the mother's **ovum,** to form a **zygote.** Each **gamete,** or sex cell, was formed by **meiosis,** which produces cells containing twenty-three single **chromosomes.** Chromosomes are composed of **genes,** tiny bits of **deoxyribonucleic acid (DNA),** which transmit traits and predispositions to the offspring.

2. The complex processes of genetic combination determine the offspring's **genotype,** the unique set of genes carried by the child. The **phenotype,** or physical expression of those genes, often is different from the genotype. This difference is in part due to the fact that, for some single-gene traits, the **dominant** gene masks the **recessive** gene. For example, the inherited metabolic difficulty **PKU** appears when two recessive **alleles** (genes) for the trait are paired; in this case, the offspring are **homozygous** for PKU. When only one PKU allele is present, the offspring is **heterozygous** and the phenotype is normal. Some single-gene traits are **codominant,** and the majority of traits are **polygenic** (produced by many genes).

3. Genes always interact with the environment, and any genotype has a **reaction range** in which it may be expressed. This interaction can affect behavior through passive genetic influence (experience provided by parents), through the responses a child's appearance and behavior evoke from others, and through the child's actively seeking out some experiences and ignoring others. Researchers use animal breeding experiments and family studies (including twin studies and adoption studies) to study genetic influences on development. Results of family studies are expressed as **correlations,** numerical expressions of how closely two factors are related.

4. During a 266-day **gestation period,** the organism rapidly progresses from a **zygote** primarily engaged in cell division (the **germinal period**), to an **embryo** in which organ systems are forming **(embryonic period),** to a **fetus** that increasingly resembles a human being **(fetal period).** During the germinal period, the **placenta** and **umbilical cord** develop; they nourish the organism and carry away its wastes. During the

prenatal period, growth is **proximodistal** (from the center of the body to the periphery) and **cephalocaudal** (from head to toe). After all systems have formed, the fetus still cannot survive on its own, in part because it cannot produce enough **surfactin** to protect it from **respiratory distress syndrome.** Twenty-three weeks is the minimum age at which a fetus might survive outside the uterus.

5. During the birth process **(labor),** uterine contractions push the infant, then the **afterbirth,** through the birth canal. Babies sometimes are delivered by Caesarean section, especially if they are in danger of **anoxia.** Immediately after birth, the baby's appearance and functioning are rated; the most common rating system produces an **Apgar score.**

6. When genetic **mutations** occur during meiosis, the zygote generally dies. Sometimes meiosis produces chromosomal abnormalities, so that the fetus has **Turner's syndrome** (a single female chromosome), **Klinefelter's syndrome** (two female and one male chromosomes), or **Down's syndrome** (an extra chromosome 21). Many abnormalities, including **spina bifida,** can be detected before birth by **amniocentesis** or **chorionic villi sampling,** guided by **ultrasound.**

7. **Teratogens,** agents that can reach the fetus by crossing the placental barrier, include diseases, drugs, smoking, emotional stress, and environmental pollutants. Their effect depends on the timing of the exposure, the dosage, and the genetic susceptibility of the fetus. Babies who need extra attention after birth are generally those who are born more than five weeks before **term** and those who are **small for gestational age (SGA).**

KEY TERMS

acquired immune deficiency syndrome (AIDS)
afterbirth
allele
amniocentesis
amnion
anoxia
Apgar score
cephalocaudal development
cervix
Chlamydia
chorion
chorionic villi sampling
chromosomes
codominant
correlation
deoxyribonucleic acid (DNA)
dominant gene
Down's syndrome
embryo
embryonic period
Fallopian tube

fetal alcohol syndrome
fetus
gametes
genes
genital herpes
genotype
germinal period
gestational age
gestation period
gonorrhea
heterozygous
homozygous
hydrocephaly
Klinefelter's syndrome
labor
meiosis
menstrual age
menstrual cycle
mutation
ovum
phenotype
phenylketonuria

placenta
polygenic
prenatal period
proximodistal development
reaction range
recessive gene
respiratory distress syndrome
rubella
small for gestational age (SGA)
sonogram
spermatozoon
spina bifida
surfactin
syphilis
teratogen
term
Turner's syndrome
ultrasound
umbilical cord
zygote

STUDY TERMS

allele The alternate form of a gene found at a given site on a chromosome. If the allele's corresponding trait appears in an individual even when the allele is paired with a different allele for the same trait, the allele is *dominant;* if its corresponding trait fails to appear in those circumstances; the allele is *recessive.*

cephalocaudal development The progression of growth from head to foot; the head develops and grows before the torso, arms, and legs.

correlation A numerical expression of how closely two factors are related. Correlations range from +1.00 (perfect positive correlation) to −1.00 (perfect negative correlation).

Down's syndrome A condition that results when an extra chromosome 21 is present in the zygote, or when extra material from chromosome 21 becomes attached to another chromosome. It produces various physical abnormalities and mental retardation in the afflicted child.

genotype The specific combination of alleles that makes up each individual's genetic inheritance.

phenotype Physical or behavioral traits as they appear in the individual, reflecting genetic and environmental influences.

proximodistal development The progression of physical and motor growth from the center of the body to the periphery, which first appears during the embryonic period.

reaction range The range of possible responses within which a genetic trait can express itself.

small for gestational age (SGA) The condition in which a baby is underweight for his or her gestational age.

teratogen Any influence that can disrupt fetal growth or cause malformation in the developing organism.

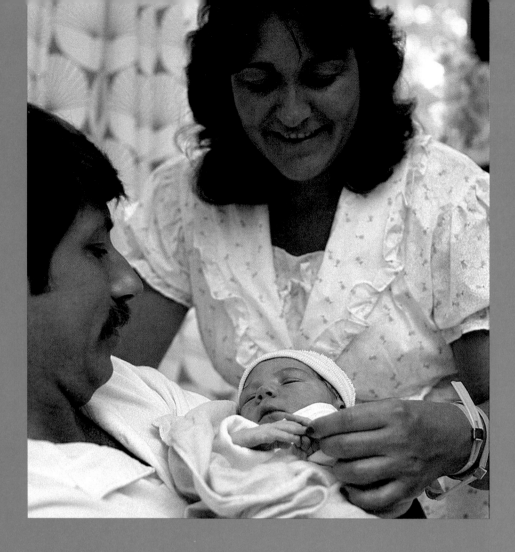

CHAPTER 4

The Newborn's World

THE NEONATE

BASIC FUNCTIONS AND RHYTHMS
Temperature Regulation / Sleep Patterns / Sucking Patterns

REFLEXES
The Rooting Reflex / Grasping and Moro Reflex /
Walking Movements

EARLY PERCEPTUAL DEVELOPMENT
Tasting / Smelling / Hearing / Seeing

ADAPTING TO THE WORLD
Memory and Perceptual Analysis / Learning to Do Things

PERSONALITY AND SOCIAL RELATIONS
Temperament / Social Relations

The newborn infant is suddenly thrust from a warm, dark, watery world into a cold, gaseous universe filled with light. The transition must be a shock. Nearly a century ago, American psychologist William James (1890/1950) supposed the new world must appear terribly chaotic to the naive baby, "assailed by eyes, ears, nose, skin, and entrails at once, [who] feels it all as one great blooming, buzzing confusion. . . ." This new sensory world may not be as confusing as James assumed, for babies enter the world possessing a variety of capacities and skills that help them reduce the confusion and begin to sort out their surroundings.

The baby's vital organs are formed and functional. Unlike the newborn kitten or puppy, a human baby's eyes are open. Babies can see and hear and smell and taste and feel; they can cry and eat and move their limbs. They possess a set of reflexes that help them to cope with their strange new world and sample its character. They are prepared to learn and very quickly begin searching their surroundings for information. Yet babies are helpless. Unlike the newborn calf, who stands within the hour and staggers over to its mother to nurse, the human baby must be carried to the mother and the nipple placed near the tiny mouth before the baby's ability to nurse is of any use. The newborn baby is a curious mixture of competence and incapacity.

In this chapter, we explore the capabilities and limitations of newborn babies, beginning with the natural biological rhythms that keep many of their basic body functions in balance. After a look at the baby's reflexes and their possible significance, we consider early perceptual capabilities and try to establish just what a newborn can taste, smell, hear, and see. Next, we watch babies adapting to their new world and find out how researchers tell whether or how much a baby can learn and remember. Our examination of the newborn's temperament will show that psychologists have been finding the rudiments of personality in the first weeks of life. Finally, we look at the baby's social world, discovering that the way newborn infants look and listen or the way they quiet when upset may provide the roots for their individual social development.

The technical term for a newborn baby is **neonate**, a word derived from Greek and Latin roots meaning newborn. Although some researchers would limit the neonatal period to the first week of life, and others would limit it to the first two weeks, most agree that we can refer to a baby as a neonate until the end of his or her first month of life outside the womb.

THE NEONATE

To most of us, the thought of a little baby brings to mind images of a cuddly, cooing bundle of softness and joy. Although this characterization soon will be apt for most infants, the sight of their new baby sometimes disappoints, if not shocks, parents.

At the moment of birth, neonates emerge blotched with their mother's blood and covered with a white, greasy substance called **vernix**, which has lubricated them for passage through the birth canal. Their puffy, wrinkled appearance derives in part from the presence of fluid and small pads of fat under the skin.

The neonate's head may be oddly shaped or even peaked, from being compressed as it emerged through the mother's pelvis. This compression is possible because the fetal skull is made up of soft, overlapping pieces of cartilage. At the crown of the head, a soft spot, called the **fontanel** (which means "little fountain") lacks cartilage entirely,

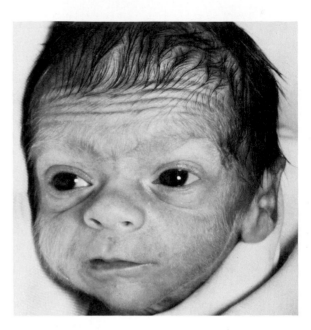

A normal premature baby. The lanugo (hair) on the face is characteristic of premature infants; the shape and proportion of facial features are characteristic of most newborns. *(A. K. Tunstill)*

and it pulsates up and down as the blood supply is pumped about the brain.

Despite this somewhat battered appearance, most parents regard their new baby as attractive. Their reaction to the baby may affect their expectations about their child. Researchers have found that young women and men expect highly attractive neonates to be "good" babies, babies who are cheerful, healthy, responsive to other people, and easy to care for (Stephan and Langlois, 1984). Later we shall see how these expectations might influence the way parents treat their babies.

Most babies are highly alert just after they are born. They generally are responsive in the delivery room, when the parents hold and get acquainted with their new daughter or son. During this first visit, the mother may nurse the baby.

Later, when newborns finally fall asleep for the first time in the world of air, their sleep is usually deep. Even a loud sound may fail to elicit any obvious response. During this sleep, the body is beginning to function on its own. Within the womb, the placenta linked the fetus's circulatory, digestive, temperature-regulation, and excretory system with those of the mother. Now the baby's own physiological equipment must take over these necessary functions.

BASIC FUNCTIONS AND RHYTHMS

Neonates come into the world prepared to keep their bodily systems in balance. Their behavior already seems organized, and many of their basic functions have detectable rhythms that repeat in cycles ranging from seconds to hours. Breathing and sucking, which have cycles measured in seconds, are essential to the maintenance of life. Some rhythms, such as the spontaneous limb movements that occur every minute or so, already are in place before birth, as we saw in Chapter 3. When Steven Robertson (1982) used time-lapse photography to study these movements in neonates, he concluded that they may be linked to the same timing mechanism that in the sleeping newborn produces regular sighs to help maintain efficient breathing. Some rhythms that vary on a daily basis, such as temperature, appear shortly after birth; others, such as rhythmical swaying, rocking, and kicking, appear as neuromuscular pathways develop during the first year (Thelen, 1979). However, the biological clock that responds to the alternation of night and day may already have begun to run, its timing set by signals from the mother's brain (Kolata, 1985).

Temperature Regulation

The efficiency of the neonate's temperature control is quickly put to the test in the first encounter with the hospital environment. Within the watery uterus, the temperature hovers around 98.6 degrees Fahrenheit, but the gaseous environment that greets the baby is usually colder by 20 to 30 degrees. Although many hospitals try to minimize this shock by wrapping the baby in warmed towels, the baby's temperature control system has to begin its work under considerable stress.

Why is the regulation of body temperature so important? It is vital because the functions performed by most of the baby's cells and organs are governed by enzymes that can act only within a narrow range of temperature. If the baby's temper-

ature goes above or below this range, enzyme production is disrupted and body functions are impaired. When the surrounding temperature is too hot, the baby may go into shock; too cold, and the baby's tissues cannot get enough oxygen, and the acid level of his or her blood rises to dangerous levels (Babson, Pernoll, Benda, and Simpson, 1980). For this reason, preterm babies may require a stay in the incubator, just at a time when parents are forming an emotional bond to their child. Whether this separation impedes the bonding process is not known, but it certainly does not enhance the relationship.

Most babies prove equal to the task of temperature regulation. Within fifteen minutes of birth, they are responding to cold by constricting their surface blood vessels and shunting blood from the surface of the body, where it would cool. Although the system works fairly well within a couple of hours, it will not be at peak efficiency until the baby is between four and nine weeks old (Rovee-Collier and Gekoski, 1979). In the meantime, neonates rely on other techniques to meet the stress of cold (Woodson, 1983). They reduce their body surface by drawing up their arms and legs and curling their bodies, thus shrinking heat loss. They become restless and cry, a response that helps them in two ways: the muscular activity required generates heat, and the close contact that results when a caregiver picks them up provides additional warmth from the caregiver's body. If the temperature rises, the neonate can stretch out quietly, increasing body surface and decreasing heat production.

Sleep Patterns

Newborn infants sleep a lot—about sixteen or seventeen out of each twenty-four hours. Unfortunately for most parents, they rarely sleep much more than four hours without waking. The typical newborn begins life by staying awake and alert for a couple of hours, then immediately goes into the regular four-hour sleep/wake cycle (Emde, Swedberg, and Suzuki, 1975). During each cycle, the baby is awake for only about half an hour. Gradually, sleep patterns begin to fall into the day-night cycle. By the time babies are six weeks old, they begin to sleep a little more at night and stay awake

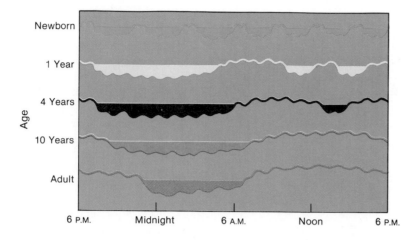

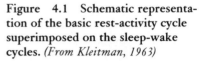

Figure 4.1 Schematic representation of the basic rest-activity cycle superimposed on the sleep-wake cycles. *(From Kleitman, 1963)*

longer during the day. By sixteen weeks, the baby may be sleeping up to six hours at a stretch, and daytime sleep has become naps. And by the last half of the first year, the typical infant sleeps through the night without waking (see Figure 4.1). Each baby's sleep schedule is highly personal, however, as parents of ten-month-olds who still wake up at 2 A.M. ruefully report. Why do neonates sleep so much? Sleep conserves energy, and the sleeping infant has more calories left over to fuel growth. In addition, time spent in sleep is time protected against possible overload from the multitude of stimuli that bombard infants during their waking hours. Sleep might be one way babies cope with what James called a "blooming, buzzing confusion."

From the beginning, newborns' sleep is coordinated with a shorter, hourly rest-activity cycle in which the quality of sleep varies in a rhythmic fashion (Emde, Swedberg, and Suzuki, 1975). There are two general kinds of sleep, distinguished principally by whether rapid eye movement (REM) occurs. During **REM sleep,** or **active sleep,** eye movements are accompanied by faster and more variable respiration, less muscular activity, and more even patterns of brain waves than are seen in non-REM, or **quiet,** sleep (see Figure 4.2). During sleep, babies go from active to quiet sleep in rhythmic cycles, similar to the longer cycles seen in adults. However, newborns go directly into active sleep; not until they are three months old will they begin each cycle with a period of quiet sleep as adults do (Berg and Berg, 1979). At birth, about half of each hour-long sleep cycle is

spent in active sleep, but the proportion soon begins to drop, so that within three months the baby spends twice as much time in quiet sleep. The trend continues, and older preschoolers spend four-fifths of the sleep time in quiet sleep, which is the adult average. Much of the newborn's extra sleep is composed of active sleep.

What do the rapid eye movements of active sleep signify? Adults awakened during active sleep usually report that they have been dreaming. Yet it is unlikely that newborn babies in active sleep experience anything resembling an adult dream. For one thing, their experiences are limited, and whatever "dreams" they might have are probably no more than random patterns of light and sound (McCall, 1979). For another thing, the active sleep of neonates is physiologically different from that of dreaming adults, and the distinctive brain wave patterns that characterize active sleep do not appear until babies are three or four months old (Parmelee and Sigman, 1983).

Scientists have explained the function of young infants' active sleep in several ways. Some suggest that this active sleep reflects a high metabolic rate. Some suggest that it simply indicates immaturity in the neural mechanisms that regulate wakefulness, because active sleep is controlled by lower parts of the brain, but higher brain levels are also involved in quiet sleep. Others believe that periodic neural activity, either from external or internal sources, is necessary for brain development. Because neonates sleep so much and have little opportunity to respond to events in the world around them, they provide their own neurological self-stimulation

—stimulation at a level that they can handle. Indeed, several studies indicate that wakefulness without stress or pain may reduce the need for active sleep (Berg and Berg, 1979). Premature babies show even higher percentages of active sleep than full-term infants do. Babies born as early as twenty-five weeks spend all their time in some sort of active sleep. Perhaps such activity is necessary before birth if neurological development is to proceed normally.

Sucking Patterns

The neonate's sucking is another basic rhythmical behavior that has been studied in great detail. Being able to suck effectively is the foundation of feeding and, therefore, of survival. It is not surprising, then, that most newborns suck competently and precisely.

The young baby sucks rhythmically, in bursts separated by pauses. On the average, the baby puts together approximately five to twenty-four sucks in a single burst, sucking at a rate of approximately one to two and one-half times each second, and then takes a brief rest. Hunger, age, health, and level of arousal all influence the baby's pattern of sucking, but each baby also sucks in his or her own characteristic pattern. No one knows whether these sucking patterns are innate, because sucking at birth is usually affected by drugs that pass through the placenta during pregnancy and labor. Several days later, when these drugs have worn off, a baby's sucking patterns already may have

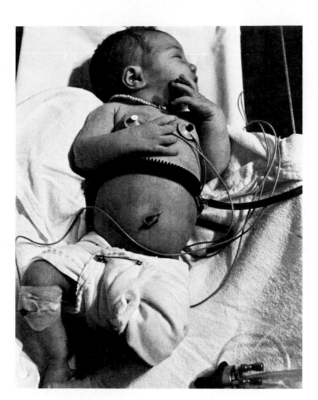

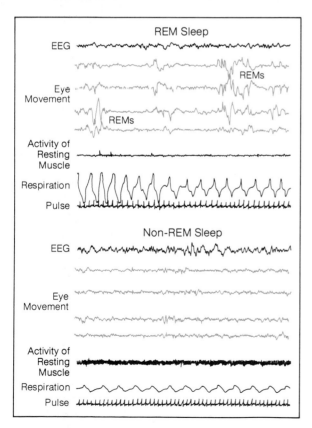

FIGURE 4.2 *(top)* This baby is in a stabilimeter crib, which measures his muscular activity. The belt around his abdomen measures respiration, and the electrodes on his chest produce electrocardiographic records. When electroencephalographic recordings are made, electrodes are placed on the head and at the outer corners of the eyes. Although cumbersome, the apparatus is not uncomfortable for the baby.

(bottom) Recordings showing the differences between thirty seconds of REM sleep and non-REM sleep in a newborn. Besides the heightened eye activity during REM sleep, note the absence of muscle activity, the rapid respiratory rate, and the changing respiratory amplitude. *(Photograph by Jason Lauré; chart after Roffwarg, Dement, and Fisher, 1964)*

been affected by interaction with the mother during feeding (Crook, 1979).

Even if the neonate's feeding performance is a little ragged, within a few days he or she sucks, swallows, and breathes in smooth coordination. The fact that a newborn can swallow almost three times faster than an adult and can suck at the same time he or she takes in air aids in the accomplishment of this feat. Adults who sucked in a liquid and breathed at the same time probably would choke. Babies can manage simultaneous sucking and breathing because they extract milk from the nipple by pressing it against the roof of the mouth instead of by drawing in milk as you would when using a straw.

When sucking, the average baby becomes calm and alert. Head movements cease, so that objects on either side no longer distract the sucking infant. The baby seems to focus intently on objects that are straight ahead and to process these sights more efficiently than when not sucking (Crook, 1979). It appears that the neonate is learning most during the feeding period, when he or she is most likely to be interacting with a parent.

REFLEXES

The possible chaos of the newborn's world is further reduced by some responses that he or she does not have to learn. A neonate comes equipped with more than a dozen **reflexes,** which are unlearned responses to specific stimuli — responses that are not affected by motivation and that are common to all members of the species. Some of these reflexes are adaptive. They may help the baby to avoid danger: babies close their eyes to bright light and twist their bodies or move their limbs away from sources of pain. Some reflexes may help the baby to feed: babies reflexively root, suck, and swallow. Other reflexes appear to be vestiges of the past, left over from our prehuman ancestors whose infants had to be good grabbers to survive. Still others are simple manifestations of neurological circuitry in the baby that later will be suppressed or integrated into more mature patterns of behavior. Some of these reflexes, such as the eyeblink or the cough, are permanent. But most disappear within a few

weeks or months, as the brain matures. When these immature reflexes fail to drop out, it may be a sign of abnormal neurological development.

The Rooting Reflex

All babies have a **rooting reflex** — a tendency to turn the head and mouth in the direction of any object that gently stimulates the corner of the mouth. This reflex has obvious adaptive significance because it helps the baby place the nipple in the mouth, where the sucking and swallowing reflexes will come into play. If you stroke the corner of a newborn's mouth with your index finger, moving sideways from the mouth toward the cheek, the baby may move tongue, mouth, or even the whole head toward the stimulated side. At first, this reflex appears even when you stroke the cheek a long way from the mouth. As the baby gets older, the reflex appears only when the stimulation is at the mouth, and only the baby's mouth responds. Both the rooting and sucking reflexes are present before the baby is born, and the rooting reflex disappears when the baby is three or four months old. Babies learn to suck their thumbs while rooting: if one of their hands happens to brush a cheek, the reflex is triggered and the thumb winds up inside the mouth, where the sucking reflex takes over.

Grasping and Moro Reflex

Babies are born with a strong **grasping reflex.** If you place a week-old baby on his or her back and insert your finger into the baby's hand, the infant will grasp it firmly. Sometimes a grasping newborn can literally hang by one hand. The grasping reflex gets stronger during the first month, then begins to decline in strength, disappearing at about three or four months.

The **Moro reflex** appears when a baby suddenly loses support for both neck and head. It consists of a thrusting out of the arms in an embracelike gesture and a curling of the hands as if to grasp something. The Moro reflex is easy to see. Simply hold a baby with one hand under the head and the other in the small of the back, and then rapidly lower your hands, especially the hand holding the head, and then bring them to an abrupt halt. A second

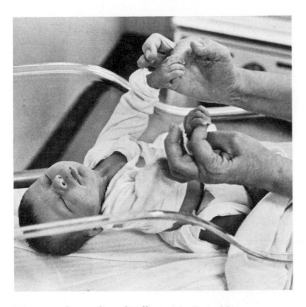

The grasping reflex. *(William MacDonald)*

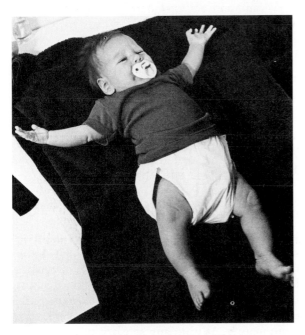

The Moro reflex. *(Lawrence Frank, 1981)*

provides the stimulus for the Moro, you can feel the baby suddenly tighten his or her grip. The Moro reflex appears the strongest after the first week, when the baby is alert, with open or barely closed eyes. It, too, decreases as the baby gets older. The Moro is difficult to elicit after the baby is three months old, and it is almost always gone by five or six months.

Many scientists believe that the grasping and Moro reflexes are once-adaptive responses left over from our prehuman history (Prechtl, 1982). Although they are no longer useful to human babies, the reflexes still are vital among monkeys, whose infants ride on their backs or cling to their stomachs. An infant monkey who loses support and automatically reaches out will grasp its mother's fur or skin and remain safe; one who does not will fall to the ground.

Walking Movements

A baby only a week or two old may look as if he or she is trying to walk. If you hold the baby under the arms while gently lowering him or her to a surface until both feet touch it and the knees bend, the baby will respond with a reflexive **stepping** motion. If you slowly bounce the baby lightly up and down, the baby may straighten out both legs at the knee and hip as if to stand. Then if moved forward, the baby may try stepping motions, as if walking.

Newborns also show a second walking motion, called a **placing reflex**. This reflex is simply the baby's propensity to lift his or her feet onto a surface. If held up and moved toward a table until the top part of the foot touches the edge, the baby is likely to lift up a foot and place it on the table. Both the stepping and the placing responses disappear between the third and fourth month after birth.

Neither behavior has much practical utility, because one- or two-week-old babies have neither the strength nor the balance to walk or step. However, the two reflexes appear to indicate a certain inborn neurological organization that forms the basis for later standing and walking. Early walking movements seem to be under the control of primitive areas of the brain, but researchers cannot agree on just why they disappear. The traditional view has been that as the baby's higher brain

way to obtain the Moro reflex is to lay the baby on his or her back with the head facing straight up and then slap the mattress behind the head with enough force to jerk the head and neck slightly. If your finger is in a baby's hand when somebody else

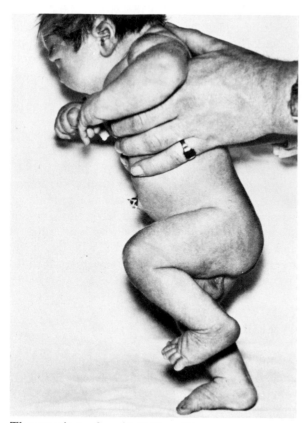

The stepping reflex. *(A. K. Tunstill)*

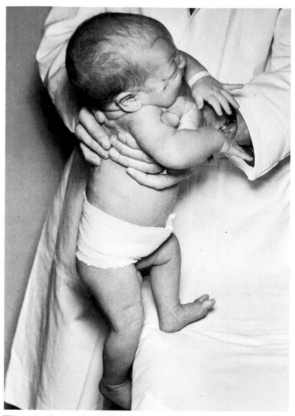

The placing reflex. *(A. K. Tunstill)*

centers mature, they take over control from the lower brain centers and suppress these reflexes (Menkes, 1980). But Philip Zelazo (1983) has argued that the disappearance of walking movements is due primarily to the baby's failure to use them. He notes that when young babies were given practice in stepping for several weeks, they lost the response more slowly and walked about a month sooner than other babies. However, Esther Thelen and her associates (Thelen, Fisher, and Ridley-Johnson, 1984) maintain that babies stop stepping because their legs are gaining fat and other tissue so rapidly that their muscles simply aren't strong enough to lift their heavy legs against gravity. When these researchers weighted the legs of four-week-old babies, the stepping movements dropped by nearly one-third; and when they placed the babies in water—where gravity is less of a burden—the stepping movements nearly doubled. All three explanations may be involved. Once the movements are gone, they reappear as voluntary acts from a baby who is ready to walk.

EARLY PERCEPTUAL DEVELOPMENT

Some years ago, many people believed that the newborn baby's senses were not functional. They assumed that the baby could not see, smell, or taste and could feel only pain, cold, and hunger. However, research has established that neonates' senses, although not as precise as those of adults, do inform them about their surroundings. Some elements of the newborn's sensory systems are not quite mature. Within any sensory system, development occurs from the periphery inward. For example, the eye reaches maturity before the visual cortex, where the signals are interpreted (Bornstein, 1984).

Some of the newborn's sensory systems are further developed than others. The newborn's senses of touch, taste, and smell, for example, are more acute than the sense of hearing; and the baby's sight—although functional—is probably the least highly developed (Gottlieb, 1983). This staggered development of sensory systems probably minimizes the chaotic jumble of sensation a newborn might otherwise have to deal with. If the baby "concentrates" on one sense at a time, he or she does not have to solve the problems involved in adjusting to all the varieties of sensory stimuli at once (Turkewitz and Kenny, 1982).

Researchers believe that knowing about the newborn's sensory capabilities is valuable. If we know what newborn babies can see, hear, smell, taste, and feel, we can discover which events in the environment might influence them. And if we can establish normal sensory levels, we may be able to detect—and help—babies whose sensory systems are not developing normally. For example, deafness often is not discovered until a child is three years old (Meadow, 1978). Detection of deafness early in infancy would keep babies with severe hearing loss from being treated as if they were mentally retarded.

Tasting

Babies' sensitivity to taste is much more highly developed than was believed only a few years ago. When drops of various concentrated solutions are placed on their tongues, newborn babies respond with facial expressions much like those of adults. Jacob Steiner (1979) tested 175 full-term babies before they had their first feeding and found that an extremely sweet liquid brought forth smiles, followed by eager licking and sucking. When they tasted a sour solution, most babies pursed their lips, wrinkled their noses, and blinked their eyes. When a bitter fluid was dripped into their mouths, they stuck out their tongues and spat. Some even tried to vomit. Yet when Steiner placed distilled water on their tongues, the babies simply swallowed, showing no expression at all. A group of twenty premature newborns, given plain water and a sour solution, responded just as the full-term infants had done.

Within a few days, a baby's sensitivity to tastes becomes still more acute (Johnson and Salisbury, 1975). For example, when fed solutions of salt water, sterile water, artificial milk, or breast milk, a baby is likely to show distinctly different patterns of sucking, swallowing, and breathing for each solution. Babies' sensitivity to solutions of

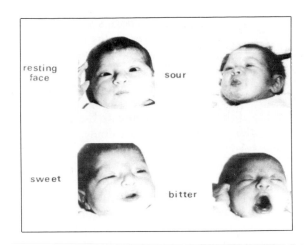

Newborns respond to strong tastes much as adults do. When tested within a few hours of birth, they stick out their tongues, spit, or even vomit when a bitter liquid is dripped onto their tongues. *(From Steiner, 1979)*

different intensities also varies. If they are given stronger solutions, their expressions intensify, a sign that newborns can tell the difference between sweet and very sweet and between bitter and very bitter (Ganchrow, Steiner, and Daher, 1983). Their sucking also changes when a solution becomes sweeter: they suck more slowly and their heart rates increase. These results appear contradictory, because we might expect a baby to suck more vigorously when given something that tastes good. In an attempt to resolve this paradox, Charles Crook and Lewis Lipsitt (1976), who conducted the experiment, suggest that babies are simply enjoying the treat. They slow down to savor the sweet taste, and pleasurable excitement causes their hearts to speed up.

Smelling

Newborns definitely react to strong odors. Babies less than twelve hours old reacted in a recognizable manner to synthetic odors of various foods (Steiner, 1979). When a cotton swab saturated with the odor of rotten eggs or concentrated shrimp was waved beneath their noses, the infants responded as babies in Steiner's previous experiment had responded to bitter tastes. To the aromas of butter, bananas, vanilla, chocolate, strawberry, and honey, the babies responded with expressions of enjoyment and satisfaction.

The keenness of the newborn's sense of smell has been demonstrated by the ability of breast-fed babies to identify their mother's odor. Mothers taped gauze pads to their armpits and kept them there overnight. Then Jennifer Cernoch and Richard Porter (1985) placed the mother's pad on one side of the baby's head, next to the cheek, and on the other side, they placed a similar pad from a woman who had not given birth recently. (Neither woman had used a deodorant.) Because many babies prefer one side or the other, care was taken to alternate the pads' placement. These two-week-old babies spent more time with their heads turned toward their mothers' pads than toward the pads from the other women. Further experiments showed that the babies also recognized and preferred their mothers' pads to pads from another lactating woman but that they did not distinguish between a pad from their father's armpit and one from the armpit of an unfamiliar man. The ability seemed limited to breast-fed babies. Bottle-fed babies showed no preference for a pad from their mother's armpit in any situation. Why do breast-fed babies seem to have keener noses than bottle-fed babies? The researchers believe that the simplest explanation is the breast-fed baby's greater physical intimacy with his or her mother. When babies nurse at the breast, their noses are next to their mothers' bare skin at each feeding. A bottle-fed baby generally is held by a clothed person (and not always the mother), so the baby does not get the same exposure to the mother's scent as does the breast-fed baby.

Hearing

Discovering just what newborns can hear and what they seem to listen to can add to our understanding of the baby's perceptual world. As we saw in Chapter 3, the fetus apparently can hear and respond to sounds by the age of twenty-eight weeks (Birnholz and Benaceraff, 1983). Discovering just what babies hear and listen to is complicated by the fact that there is no unique physiological response to hearing. Researchers can determine what a baby is looking at by observing eye movements and fixations, but the responses to sounds—head-turning, startling, heart rate, and respiration—also can be evoked by other kinds of stimuli (Aslin, Pisoni, and Jusczyk, 1983). Despite this problem, we have learned a good deal from such responses. Two other techniques also have been fairly successful in the discovery of what sounds babies can hear and whether they can distinguish among them: brain waves and sucking patterns in response to sounds. When researchers chart brain waves, they record many of the baby's brain-wave responses to the same stimulus, then use a computer to average the activity. This average is called an **evoked potential**. When researchers use sucking patterns, they give babies a nipple that is attached to electronic recording equipment, which monitors the rate and intensity of sucking. If babies who have been listening to one sound respond to a new sound by sucking faster, researchers assume that the babies have noticed the difference between the two sounds.

What Do Newborns Hear?   For the first few days of life, the middle-ear passages are filled with amniotic fluid, and so the sounds reaching a neonate may be somewhat dampened. Yet all normal newborns can hear, and some can hear very well. Most newborns turn their heads in the direction of a shaking rattle, but instead of turning immediately, they take about two and one-half seconds to respond (Muir and Field, 1979). Preterm babies are even more sluggish in their response; they wait about twelve seconds before turning their heads toward the sound (Aslin, Pisoni, and Jusczyk, 1983).

Human beings distinguish most sounds on the basis of their pitch and their intensity. Generally, the higher a sound's pitch, the louder it must be before we can detect it. Newborns' ears are not as sensitive as the average adult's; at any frequency, a sound must be 10 to 20 decibels louder before a newborn can detect it (Aslin, Pisoni, and Jusczyk, 1983). (The difference between a whisper and normal conversation is about 30 decibels.) The ability to detect sounds improves throughout infancy. Once babies are more than six months old, the difference between the adult's and the baby's ability to detect very shrill sounds, such as high-pitched whistles, is quite narrow (Schneider, Trehub, and Bull, 1980). Whether this similarity in response to shrill sounds is due to higher relative sensitivity on the part of infants or hearing loss on the part of adults is not known.

What Do Newborns Listen To?   Babies seem to prefer some sounds to others, but their preferences probably change, depending on their state. Adults seem to realize this, for the way they talk to an alert baby or one they are trying to rouse differs sharply from the way they talk to a crying baby. When talking to a newborn, parents change their intonation, tempo, and rhythm from their normal speech. The pitch of their voices becomes higher; their intonation rises and falls in an exaggerated fashion; they say only a few words at a time and make lengthy pauses; they often repeat words or phrases (Fernald and Simon, 1984). But when mothers are trying to comfort a crying baby, their voices fall to a pitch lower than their normal speaking voice, and the intonation remains fairly steady.

Newborns seem to prefer the sounds of their mother's voices. When three-day-old babies were given the chance to turn on a recording of their own mothers reading a Dr. Seuss story (by beginning to suck when a tone sounded) or the voice of another woman reading the same story (by beginning to suck after the tone stopped), most quickly adapted their sucking pattern to keep hearing their mother's voice (DeCasper and Fifer, 1980). Because these babies had had no more than twelve hours of contact with their mothers since birth, their preference may have been affected by hearing their mother's voice from within the uterus. As we saw in Chapter 3, other newborns apparently preferred a story their mother had read aloud daily before they were born (DeCasper and Spence, 1986).

Seeing

Just what can neonates see, and which aspects of the world do they notice? Apparently, they can see a lot, but what they see is blurry — almost as if you were to smear Vaseline on a pair of glasses and then inspect your surroundings. As the visual cortex and the pathways between it and the eye mature, vision rapidly improves. By the end of the neonatal period, the infant's sight is clearer and better organized — although it will be several months before he or she can see as well as an adult.

What Do Newborns See?   The clarity of your

The baby's ability to focus and to see details more clearly improves rapidly. *(Linda Ferrer/Woodfin Camp & Associates)*

vision is based on the eye's ability to change focus and how sharply it can resolve objects once they are in focus. Your ability to focus is known as **visual accommodation,** and you can demonstrate it by holding one finger a few inches from your nose and another at arm's length, then quickly alternating your focus from one to the other. The newborn can accommodate, but not very well, tending to overaccommodate for distant objects and to underaccommodate for objects nearby (Banks and Salapatek, 1983). This tendency probably does not bother the baby, because objects seem somewhat blurry even when they are in focus. When the newborn's **acuity,** which is the ability to resolve detail, is translated into terms of the standard eye chart, a week-old baby sees objects at 20 feet about as clearly as the average adult does at 600 feet. Taken together, these factors sharply reduce the amount of *distinctive* visual stimulation that gets through and probably minimize the baby's "blooming, buzzing confusion."

Both accommodation and acuity improve rapidly with experience and with the maturation of the visual system. Accommodation is already better at ten days than at birth; by three months, the baby's accommodation errors are small; and by five months, he or she can accommodate to objects that are only a few inches from the eye. Acuity also improves rapidly; by six months, a baby can detect (and investigate) specks of lint on the carpet that may escape a parent's notice (Banks and Salapatek, 1983).

When you look at an object, you focus both eyes on it. Each eye sees a slightly different image, and by a visual mechanism called **convergence,** the two images come together until only a single object appears. If you hold your finger at arm's length, focus on it, and then move it toward the tip of your nose, you can feel the muscles of your eyes perform this function. The newborn probably sees a lot of misaligned images, much like those you can produce by pressing gently at the side of one eye. Within a month, the neonate's eyes are converging — although not always with much accuracy. By two or three months, the baby's convergence seems fairly competent (Aslin, 1977).

What Do Newborns Notice?   Babies seem organized to acquire information through their eyes. When they are awake, they keep moving their eyes, looking about them even when they are in the dark. Marshall Haith (1980) proposes that a baby is born prepared to seek visual stimulation and that the search has an overriding purpose: to keep cells in the visual cortex firing at a high level. This activity is necessary for maintaining established neural pathways and for developing new ones. The search has an additional benefit: it brings the baby in contact with whatever useful information might be available in the visual field.

Once newborns locate a potentially interesting sight in the world, they generally do not scan the entire shape but concentrate on a side or a corner, where black-white contrast is highest and thus where sensory information is the richest (Bornstein, 1984). As a result, a young baby probably does not perceive entire forms, just their specific features — an angle, an edge. The neonate's concentrated scanning probably means that the very young baby may miss the most interesting and informative part of a stimulus. When a three-week-old looks at your face, he or she is likely to look at the edge, where your hair stands out against the background, or at the edge of your cheek or chin, instead of at your eyes or mouth.

Our exploration of the newborn's perceptual world indicates that it is somewhat less confusing than James supposed. Although the neonate's sensory systems are functioning, a considerable amount of the environment simply is not accessible. In addition, newborn babies are selective about the stimuli they pay attention to: they tune some things in and tune other things out. Although the perceptual world of the newborn would seem fairly simple to us, it may not seem that way to the child.

ADAPTING TO THE WORLD

Babies are born with many ways of sensing events in the world and with various reflex actions that help them in situations they are likely to encounter. If they are to adapt to their environment, however, they must be able to learn. How does the newborn learn about the world?

Memory and Perceptual Analysis

Newborns spend most of their time sleeping, fussing, or crying. The average newborn is alert for only about five or ten minutes at a time. Many parents are fond of putting mobiles and other objects in the crib with their new baby. Is it possible that an infant who is alert for such short periods can become familiar with such objects? That is, can a neonate form a memory of a mobile, retain that memory, and later recognize that mobile as familiar or detect a new one as different?

Alan Slater, Victoria Morison, and David Rose (1984) explored this possibility with babies who were about three days old. While the babies were alert, the researchers showed them a complex stimulus made of colored paper. The stimulus was displayed to the baby until he or she looked away for at least two seconds. Then it was presented again and again (at least six times), until the time the baby spent gazing at the stimulus on three consecutive trials dropped to half or less of the total time spent during the first three trials. When this happened, the infant had habituated. The process of **habituation** is roughly analogous to becoming bored with a stimulus, and it implies that the baby has learned and remembered something about the stimulus. The decline in looking after repeated exposures may mean that the baby has formed a memory of that stimulus. How does the researcher know that the baby is not simply tired or becoming drowsy? To find out whether the baby actually remembered the stimulus, Slater and his associates then showed the baby two stimuli: the original stimulus and a new one, just as colorful and complex as the old one. If the baby looked longer at the new stimulus than at the old one, he or she must have had a memory for the familiar one. When shown the pair of stimuli, the baby must have compared them with the stored information and detected which was a new and interesting sight.

In this experiment, newborns clearly showed that they could form a memory that lasted for at least several seconds, because on two successive trials eight babies spent more time looking at the new stimulus than at the familiar one.

Newborns also can learn to recognize specific sounds. When researchers repeated the word *tinder* again and again, babies soon habituated and stopped turning their heads toward the sound. But when the researchers began saying *beagle*, the three-day-old babies once more turned their heads toward the sound (Brody, Zelazo, and Chaika, 1984). Apparently, they had stored the old sound and compared their memory of it with the new sound.

On the basis of such research, we can conclude that newborns can form a memory of a stimulus, retain that memory for at least ten seconds, and make some kind of comparison between the memory and the new stimulus. That tells us that if the mobile over the crib is suddenly changed, the newborn probably will be aware of the switch, but it does not tell us whether the baby will realize that the mobile placed over the crib today is different from the mobile that hung there yesterday.

Learning to Do Things

Habituation is a kind of learning; babies learn that they have seen an object before. It is a primitive kind of "exposure learning," but it indicates that the baby can perceive, store information, and remember it (Bornstein, 1985). However, learning is much more than simple recognition. Can a newborn learn to connect one event with another?

Until recently, many psychologists believed

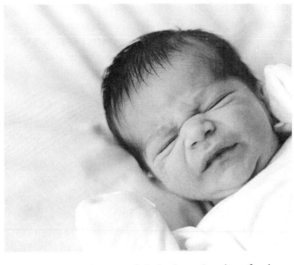

Newborns spend most of their time sleeping, fussing, or crying. *(Elizabeth Crews)*

that babies were incapable of this sort of learning during the first few weeks of life. Yet in one study, three-day-old infants learned to suck a nipple in order to turn on the light in a slide projector so that they could see a brightly colored checkerboard (Werner and Siqueland, 1978). In another study, two-day-old babies learned to associate strokes on their forehead with the taste of a sugar solution (Blass, Ganchrow, and Steiner, 1984). Researchers stroked a baby's forehead, then dropped a sweet solution into the baby's mouth. Soon, the babies began sucking vigorously each time their foreheads were stroked. Some even cried when they were stroked but got nothing sweet afterward, a sign that they expected the sweet fluid.

Yet researchers have found it difficult to show this sort of learning in neonates. Why have they had so much trouble? One reason is that in early studies, babies often were asked to learn responses that had little to do with the way their lives were unfolding. Responses that help the infant to survive — such as head turning and sucking, which are connected with feeding — are fairly easy for the neonate to learn to produce (Sameroff and Cavanagh, 1979). Babies are born "prepared" to make such responses, and they often encounter situations that demand them. Asking babies to kick vigorously in order to see an interesting sight or get a sweet drink is less likely to be successful, because these situations do not resemble anything a baby is likely to encounter naturally. Another important factor that early researchers usually did not consider was the baby's state. A baby's state changes rapidly and with it, the baby's ability to detect sights and sounds. A sound may have to be louder, a design brighter, clearer, or larger, for a baby to detect them as he or she moves from active alertness, to quiet alertness, to drowsiness (Field, 1981). A baby who is hungry responds differently from one who has just eaten or another who is midway in the feeding cycle. Finally, babies who are quietly alert for only five or ten minutes are unlikely to learn in a situation that requires them to be responsive for fifteen minutes.

When alert, healthy neonates are asked to learn by making a response that they are prepared to make, they seem capable of making rudimentary connections between events. This ability is extremely important because these simple connections provide the basis for all later behavior. But even among very young babies, there are individual differences in the ability to learn (Bornstein, 1985). In the habituation experiment, for example, eight babies preferred to look at the new design, one preferred the familiar design, and one showed no preference of any kind (Slater, Morison, and Rose, 1984). And among the eight babies who looked more at the new design, the length of time they looked before habituating ranged from just over one minute to nearly five minutes.

PERSONALITY AND SOCIAL RELATIONS

Only a few years ago, most developmentalists were excited about **bonding,** which is the process by which a mother forms an emotional bond with her baby. Encouraged by their research with a group of mothers, Marshall Klaus and John Kennell (1976) had proposed that there was a brief period, just after birth, while the mother was primed with hormones, when intimate contact with her baby forged this bond. They urged all obstetricians to promote immediate physical contact after birth. However, research in Guatemala, Sweden, Brazil, Jamaica, and the United States has indicated that there is no easy way to promote

maternal motivation. There seems to be no evidence of a special bonding period and, although early contact is certainly an emotionally satisfying experience, it has no clear impact on the mother-infant relationship (Lamb and Hwang, 1982).

Yet the parent-child relationship does begin in the delivery room. Once they have assured themselves that their baby is complete and normal, parents start looking for the first signs of personality in their child. It is difficult to talk about the personality of a newborn. When we think of personality, we have in mind the way verbal, cognitive, and emotional behavior is displayed in a social context. A neonate cannot express personality in this way, but the seeds of the developing personality may be apparent in the baby's **temperament,** which consists of early, observable individual differences in babies' emotional, attentional, and motor behavior (Bornstein, Gaughran, and Homel, 1986).

Temperament

Any parent who has had more than one child is aware that babies are different from the first day of life. Some babies are irritable and fussy; others are easy-going and easy to soothe. Some babies seem interested in the world around them; others seem to pay little attention. Although teratogens and medication during delivery may affect these responses, wide differences are also apparent among babies whose birth was unmedicated and uneventful (Bornstein, Gaughran, and Homel, 1986).

Many researchers believe that a newborn's temperament is determined primarily by his or her genotype (Scarr and McCartney, 1983; Buss and Plomin, 1984). There are, of course, no "sociability" or "irritability" genes. Instead, the baby's level of activity and the way he or she responds to the environment are influenced by genes. Together, they determine the way the baby interacts with others, the way others interact with the baby, and what sorts of experiences the baby seeks out or avoids. As we saw in Chapter 3, behavior geneticists have proposed that genes and the environment interact in this way. As the baby interacts with the environment, aspects of temperament may remain stable, be modulated, or even disappear.

A BOOST FOR
PRETERM BABIES

Babies who are born very early (thirty-three weeks or less after conception) or very small (2,000 grams or less) come into the world at a disadvantage. Their physiological systems are not yet coordinated for survival outside the womb, and their bodies must work desperately hard to adjust. The attempt apparently is stressful, because preterm babies have much higher heart rates than full-term babies. Their hearts beat about thirty times more each minute. They seem to require more active sleep; their sleep is restless; and they are less responsive to stimuli (Rose, 1983).

Because these babies run the risk of intellectual impairment (see Chapter 3), psychologists have been trying to develop programs that would alleviate early stress and increase the infants' chances of normal development. One group of researchers has found that pacifiers, which soothe most babies, also help preterm infants to develop better. Each time the preterm infants were fed by tube, the researchers placed a pacifier in their mouths and left it there until five minutes after the meal had been delivered. The babies who got the pacifier were ready for bottle-feeding several days earlier than a control group of preterm infants, went home from the hospital four days sooner, and had fewer complications (Anderson, Buroughs, and Measel, 1983). How could a simple pacifier have such an effect? Crying, especially hard crying, allows blood to bypass the lungs and circulate without being properly oxygenated. When the babies sucked on a soothing pacifier, they maintained a better supply of oxygen throughout their bodies.

Other researchers have found mild stimulation helpful in settling down preterm babies. With one group of preterm babies, Susan Rose (1983) played a tape-recorded human heartbeat while the infants slept. Babies who heard the sound of the beating heart spent less time in active sleep, were not as restless, and breathed more regularly than other preterm babies — although their heart rates remained elevated. With another group of babies, Frank Sca-

fidi and his associates (Scafidi et al., 1986) found that gentle massage was effective. For ten days, the researchers spent fifteen minutes, three times each day, stroking each tiny baby's head, shoulders, back, arms, hands, legs, and feet. They also gently flexed and then extended the infants' arms and legs. These babies spent more time awake than similar babies in a control group, and they gained weight more rapidly — although they ate the same amount of formula as the other babies. Apparently, the stimulation improved the efficiency of their metabolism. The stimulated babies were able to leave the hospital about six days earlier than the other babies, which reduced the hospital bill of each infant by $3,000.

Although gentle stimulation seems to be helpful, too much stimulation may have the opposite effect. Preterm babies seem able to tolerate stimulation only within a narrow range (Field, 1981). They require more stimulation before they respond. They also are overwhelmed by a level of stimulation that full-term babies find fascinating. This combination can disrupt the relationship between parent and child. For example, a mother who finds that loud cries and pokes are necessary to get her baby's attention is amazed and perhaps hurt when the game soon ends in her baby's apparent aversion or tears.

Because many psychologists believe that normal development depends in good part on the quality of the preterm baby's social interactions, researchers have looked for ways to teach a mother to adapt to her baby's social levels. Tiffany Field (1981) asks mothers to imitate everything their baby does, repeat their words slowly, and fall silent whenever their baby looks away from them. When mothers do this, babies spend much more time looking at their mothers, and the game time is extended. This program slows down and simplifies the mother's actions so that they mesh with her baby's behavior.

None of these programs is complicated, but small interventions early in a preterm baby's life may be as effective as much more complicated interventions at a later age.

Differences in Temperament   One striking difference among newborns is their *activity level.* Some babies are restless and active, waving their arms or legs about; others seem placid and move more slowly. During the first few days, this difference shows more strongly in the energy with which the baby moves, not necessarily the frequency of his or her movements (Korner, Hutchinson, Koperski, Kraemer, and Schneider, 1981). Later this quality may affect how often or how vigorously an infant reaches for, mouths, and bangs objects or attempts to stand and crawl (Bornstein, Gaughran, and Homel, 1986).

Irritability is another aspect of temperament that appears to differ among newborns. Some babies cry a lot during the first few days (up to one-third of the time), and may even cry or fret after a feeding (Korner et al., 1981). Their mood changes often, they have fits of irritability, and they are upset by events that do not bother other babies. They are hard to soothe, and their parents often consider them "difficult" babies. Extremely difficult babies may become difficult toddlers who frequently have clashes with their mothers (Lee and Bates, 1985). Difficult babies sometimes profit by their irritability. Among young Masai babies in Kenya, where food is scarce, difficult babies were more likely than "easy" babies to survive (deVries, 1984). Their continual demands apparently ensured that they got enough food, whereas babies who did not complain sometimes died of malnutrition or disease.

Newborns also differ in their *stimulus sensitivity.* Some respond to a very slight stimulus — a sound, a touch — but others respond only if the stimulus is fairly intense. Babies who are highly responsive seem to enjoy being cuddled, kissed, and rolled about by their parents. In contrast, other babies show little reaction or else resist such affectionate play by stiffening their bodies when they are handled (Schaffer, 1971).

Many studies have documented early personality differences among babies. In a major study, Alexander Thomas and Stella Chess (1977) arrived at nine different aspects of temperament that led them to describe babies as "easy" (40 percent), "difficult" (10 percent), "slow to warm up" (15 percent), and "average" (35 percent, who did not fit into any distinctive category) (see Table 4.1). As they followed these youngsters through childhood, they noted that the characteristics sometimes persisted over the years. For example, a wiggling, active baby became the two-year-old who was "constantly in motion, jumping and climbing," and the seven-year-old who was unable to sit still in the classroom.

Temperament and Interaction   Of course, personality is much more complex than these simple categories of temperament would imply. A child's personality is a developing and evolving set of tendencies to behave in various ways. The ways those tendencies evolve is affected by parent-child interaction. Parents often interpret the smallest behavior as revealing their newborn's personality, and by the time their infant is two weeks old, mothers may develop both a style of relating to their baby and an opinion of his or her personality (Osofsky and Connors, 1979). A baby's characteristics affect the parents' attitudes toward the baby, and they may also affect the parents' feelings about themselves. Parents who had been looking forward to cuddling and kissing their newborn and who find themselves with a noncuddler may falsely infer that their baby dislikes them or that they are somehow inadequate. The negative attitudes they form could color the way they customarily interact with their child. Finally, the parents' own life circumstances and psychological functioning probably color their perceptions of

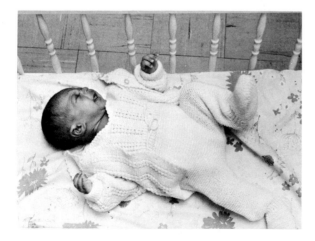

From the moment of birth, newborns display their own individual temperaments. Some are restless, some lie quietly; some are fussy and irritable, some rarely cry; some are highly sensitive to sights and sounds, some pay little attention to them. *(Tyrone Hall/Stock, Boston)*

Table 4.1
Styles of Newborn Temperament

Difficult Child	*Easy Child*	*Slow-to-Warm-Up Child*
Irregular body functions (sleeping, eating, etc.)	Regular body functions (sleeping, eating, etc.)	Low-to-moderate activity level
Intense reactions	Low to mild intensity of reactions	Mild intensity of reactions
Withdraws from unfamiliar situations	Approaches new situations positively	Withdraws at first from new situations
Adapts slowly to new routines	Adapts easily to new routines	Adapts slowly to new situations
Mood generally negative	Mood generally positive	Mood somewhat negative
Cries frequently	Cries infrequently	

Source: Information from Thomas and Chess, 1977.

their baby's temperament (Lamb and Bornstein, 1986).

According to Thomas and Chess (1977), the "goodness of fit" between the child's temperament and the parents' style is the key to personality development. When a baby's temperament and the parents' style mesh comfortably, development generally is healthy. But when they clash, as when an impatient parent has a difficult baby, problems may lie ahead. Parents who are upset by a difficult child's impulsiveness and who react to a twelve-month-old's forays with repeated prohibitions and handslaps may wind up with a two-year-old who is always in trouble, whereas parents who simply keep tempting objects out of a difficult baby's reach may have no more than average trouble with their two-year-old (Lee and Bates, 1985). Rearranging the environment so that an unpleasant characteristic does not manifest itself is probably a common parental response (Campos, Barrett, Lamb, Goldsmith, and Stenberg, 1983). Parents of one highly active toddler who climbed on every available surface simply installed a set of pegs on the wall and hung the kitchen chairs out of reach between meals. Parents of a highly irritable baby learned to arrange their shopping excursions so that they got home before the baby's patience wore out or the next feeding was due. Such adjustments to temperamental characteristics indicate why parents often treat one child differently from another.

An infant's temperament has other practical implications besides provoking different treatment from his or her parents (Lamb and Bornstein, 1986). As babies get older, their temperament be-

comes more consistent, which makes their behavior more predictable. We might say that temperament serves as a form of social communication. Finally, the baby's temperament may lead parents to rearrange the environment in ways that directly form personality and encourage the development of specific characteristics. If parents believe that their baby is inquisitive, they may go out of their way to make experiences available to the child. If they believe that their baby is shy, they may protect the child from interactions with outsiders. Such parental perceptions are potent, whether they are accurate or not, and they are another example of the way genes and environment interact as the child's temperament evokes certain responses from parents.

Social Relations

Social relations in the newborn are primitive by adult standards, yet babies and their parents carry on intricate sorts of nonverbal communication from the first days. Much of it takes place while the baby is feeding, where the neonate gets his or her first lessons in taking turns.

Taking Turns   The design of the human body ensures that the nursing neonate and mother are placed in a situation that facilitates communication. When a mother breast-feeds her newborn baby, the infant is cradled in her arms, with the small face about nine inches from hers — the distance at which the baby's eyes are naturally in focus. The feeding situation may contain the seeds of turn-taking, a skill that is essential to language

Most parents carry on "conversations" with their newborn; after catching the baby's gaze, they speak to their newborn, then interpret the baby's smiles, frowns, hiccups, burps, and cries as replies. *(Elizabeth Crews)*

and social development. Mothers, whether breast- or bottle-feeding, tend either to jiggle the nipple in the baby's mouth or to stroke the baby about the mouth whenever sucking stops. But the baby does not resume sucking until the mother stops jiggling. It appears that the infant's normal sucking routine of bursts and pauses fits naturally into the turn-taking of human dialogue and that mothers use their child's natural feeding rhythm as a basis for developing early social communication (Kaye and Wells, 1980).

Social relations outside the feeding situation also evolve into a turn-taking arrangement. Parents attempt to catch their baby's gaze, smile, blow on the skin or touch it lightly, and jiggle the baby. The baby responds by returning the gaze or by smiling reflexively—at first to touch and later to vocalizations. By the third week, the smile is accompanied by brightened eyes and a near grin, especially if the parent nods the head as he or she talks to the baby. Toward the end of the neonatal period, the baby begins smiling to vigorous physical stimulation—games of pat-a-cake, in which the parent bounces the baby's hands (Field, 1981).

From the very beginning, parents imitate their newborns' sounds and facial expressions. As noted earlier, they speak to their babies in a high-pitched voice; they also interpret their newborns' smiles, noises, and changes in expression as if they were thoughtful answers to their own questions. Parents then act as interpreters, expressing their babies' replies in words, taking both parts of the dialogue. Smiles are considered an indication that the baby understands them. Cries, fretting, or frowns may be seen as signs that the baby either doesn't understand or is trying to figure out what the parent has said (Papoušek and Papoušek, 1984).

Social interaction is possible only when a baby is alert, and as we have seen, the newborn's alertness is confined to brief periods. By analyzing films and videotapes, Hanuš Papoušek and Mechthild Papoušek (1984) have discovered that parents tend to adjust their behavior to the baby's signals. If the baby stops responding or seems drowsy, they stop the play and often ask the baby what is wrong. At the same time, they test the baby's muscle tone, either gently pushing the chin down to open the baby's mouth or trying to open the baby's fist and stretching the fingers. These tests allow parents to tailor their behavior to the baby's state, and afterward they either increase the level of stimulation or end the interaction.

Individual differences among babies affect early social relations in several ways. Babies who return a parent's gaze steadily or who smile early encourage parent's attempts to establish a social relationship. Babies who rarely have periods of quiet alertness but seem to spend all their time either sleeping or crying can frustrate the parent's attempts to communicate (Osofsky and Connors, 1979).

Social Aspects of Crying Perhaps the most obvious method by which the newborn communicates with others is crying. Generally speaking, a neonate cries as a signal of distress, as if to say, "Help me!" Even quite young babies cry in different ways, depending on whether the crying is stimulated by hunger, pain, or pleasure. (A pleasure cry is a wail from a full, dry, comfortable baby.) Each

BABY BLUES AND SOCIAL INTERACTIONS

Could lingering effects from emotional problems during pregnancy alter the interaction between mother and baby? That seemed to be the case among mothers studied by Tiffany Field and her colleagues (Field et al., 1985). Toward the end of their pregnancies, a group of women who were having ultrasound examinations to determine the age of the fetus filled out a questionnaire used to predict **postpartum depression,** an emotional letdown (generally called "baby blues") that often follows the birth of a baby. Typical questions were "Do you often feel that your husband (boyfriend) does not love you?"; "Was your pregnancy unplanned (accidental)?"; and "Do you more or less regret that you are pregnant?" From these women, Field and her colleagues chose a dozen whose answers indicated a risk of postpartum depression and another dozen whose answers indicated no problems. When the woman's babies were a few months old, the researchers videotaped these mothers while they were playing with the baby "as you would at home." Afterward, the women answered various questionnaires meant to tap their emotional outlook, their view of their babies, and their knowledge of child development.

Sure enough, women whose answers during pregnancy signaled the likelihood of postpartum depression scored significantly higher than the others on scales meant to detect depression and anxiety in adults. The depressed women also felt that they had less control over their own lives. Not only did the women in the two groups differ in mood; they also interacted differently with their babies. The videotapes showed that women in the depressed group played fewer games with their babies, imitated them less often, were less active, and were more likely to appear tense and anxious. Their babies seemed less alert and less contented than the other babies, fussing often and squirming restlessly.

Women in both groups were equally informed about child development, but they differed sharply in their views of child rearing. The depressed women tended to favor strictness with children and punitive disciplinary methods. They also saw themselves and their babies as more emotional than the nondepressed mothers did.

This study shows a connection between emotional stress during pregnancy and the later mother-child relationship, but it raises more questions than it answers. Did these women's postpartum depression affect the way they interacted with their babies? Or was it their sense that they had no control over their lives? What caused the babies' lack of alertness and frequent fussing? Was it a lack of stimulation by their mothers? Their exposure to their mothers' depressed behavior? Or did the mothers' stress during pregnancy so alter the prenatal environment that it left lingering effects on the babies?

cry can be distinguished by the pattern of pauses between bursts of crying, by the duration of the cry, and by its tonal characteristics. Mothers are especially effective at distinguishing among these cries (Sagi, 1981), and most mothers can recognize the cry of their own babies before the babies are a week old (Morsbach and Bunting, 1979).

The quality of the baby's cry may affect the nature of the parent-infant relationship. "Difficult" babies have their own special cry; they tend to pause longer between wails than either "average" or "easy" babies do, and their pauses seem to communicate the urgency of the baby's demands.

Researchers have found that other mothers interpret these difficult cries as "spoiled," and the more experience a mother has, the more likely she is to say that the baby is spoiled (Lounsbury and Bates, 1982).

Fathers respond to an infant's wail just as mothers do. As Ann Frodi and her colleagues (Frodi, Lamb, Leavitt, and Donovan, 1978) discovered, there is no detectable difference in the physiological reaction of mothers and fathers to the crying of an unfamiliar baby: in each, blood pressure rises and skin conductance increases. This physiological arousal is accompanied by feelings of annoyance, irritation, and distress. While a parent may be answering a baby's cry for help, he or she is also trying to stop the unpleasant sound.

Yet the response of a mother to her own baby's cry differs from her response to the cry of an unfamiliar baby. When mothers hear their own baby wailing with anger or pain, their hearts slow down, then speed up, as if they were getting ready to take care of the baby's needs. But when they hear the cry of an unfamiliar baby, their hearts slow down—and stay that way (Wiesenfeld and Malatesta, 1982). The researchers who conducted the study that produced these findings suggest that mothers respond to their own baby empathically, but their response to other babies indicates that

they probably have no intention of aiding the baby and feel no obligation to do so.

From the first moment of independent life, babies are different. They differ in their need for sleep, food, and stimulation. Some want to be cuddled; others do not like to be held. Some are placid; some are active. With such a wide span of individual differences at birth, it is no wonder that—given the additional influence of widely different environments—no two children or adults are alike. From the time babies draw their first breath, the differences among them become more and more pronounced. As these differences blossom, each child meets the common tasks and challenges of development in his or her own way.

SUMMARY

1. **Neonates** arrive in the cold, gaseous world covered with **vernix.** In order that their heads may compress to pass through the birth canal, the **fontanel** at the crown of their head entirely lacks protective cartilage.

2. The neonate's basic functions have detectable rhythms, ranging from seconds to hours. Body temperature becomes regulated soon after birth, and within a couple of hours infants are in the regular four-hour sleep/wake cycle. Neonates sleep about sixteen hours each day, and most of their extra sleeptime is spent in **REM,** or **active, sleep.** The sleep/wake cycle seems related to a basic rest/activity cycle, with REM sleep periods equivalent to periods of waking alertness. Neonates suck rhythmically, in bursts separated by pauses, and each baby has a unique sucking pattern.

3. From birth, the newborn is equipped with a set of **reflexes** that are elicited by specific stimuli. These include the **rooting reflex,** the **Moro reflex, stepping,** and **placing** reflexes; most disappear within a few months. Some reflexes, such as the cough and the eyeblink, are permanent.

4. The newborn's sensory systems appear to develop in sequence, with sight being the least highly developed. Neonates react to tastes and smells much as adults do, and breast-fed babies can identify their own mother's odor. Researchers study hearing by monitoring head

turns, startle responses, heart rate, respiration, **evoked potentials,** and sucking patterns. Newborns' hearing is less sensitive than the average adult's; sounds must be somewhat louder before a neonate can detect them. Neonates prefer some sounds to others, depending on their state.

5. Newborns' **acuity** and **visual accommodation** are poor, so that only a limited amount of distinct visual stimulation gets through; however, both improve rapidly. Until a baby is two or three months old, **convergence** is also poor. Newborns actively select visual stimulation, gathering information from the environment. Their patterns of attention and search appear aimed at keeping visual cortex cells firing.

6. Newborns can form memories that last for at least ten seconds, then compare their memory with new sights or sounds. Neonates have shown this capacity in studies that depend on **habituation,** a primitive kind of learning similar to becoming bored with a stimulus. Newborns also can learn to connect one event with another, but their learning ability appears to depend on the type of response they are asked to make and on their physiological state. Even newborns show individual differences in the ability to learn, but they learn most readily when they are alert and the response is one they are "prepared" to make.

7. Researchers have been unable to demonstrate the existence of a special period just after birth when mothers are primed with hormones that facilitates **bonding.** Newborns differ in **temperament.** They show wide differences in activity level, irritability, and stimulus sensitivity. These temperamental predispositions influence the tone of the baby's social relationships, which may in turn affect later personality development. Early social relations often evolve into turn-taking, a skill necessary for language and social development. Parents imitate their newborn's sounds and facial expressions, interpreting the infant's sounds, smiles, and body movements as intelligent replies to the parents' words. The quality of a baby's cry may affect the nature of the parent-infant relationship.

KEY TERMS

active sleep
acuity
bonding
convergence
evoked potential
fontanel
grasping reflex

habituation
Moro reflex
neonate
placing reflex
postpartum depression
quiet sleep
reflex

REM sleep
rooting reflex
stepping reflex
temperament
vernix
visual accommodation

STUDY TERMS

bonding The process through which parents form an emotional attachment to their baby.

habituation Reduced response to a stimulus after repeated or continuous encounters with it; a primitive kind of learning analogous to becoming bored with a stimulus.

neonate The technical term for an infant during the first month of independent life.

quiet sleep Sleep during which there is no movement of the eyes, respiration is slowed, and brain waves show an uneven pattern; also called non-REM sleep.

reflex An unlearned response to a specific stimulus that is not affected by motivation and that is common to all members of a species.

REM sleep Sleep that is characterized by rapid eye movements (REM), rapid respiration, and a relatively even pattern of brain waves; also called active sleep.

temperament Early, observable differences in a baby's emotional responses, motor actions, and attention.

PART III

The First Four Years

I n the course of their first four years, dependent babies become independent, inquisitive children. As their bodies grow, their nervous systems mature, and their experiences deepen, an enormous change takes place. From sensory beings who are sorting out the world, they become youngsters who not only perceive it in detail and act effectively on it but who also remember the past and plot future actions. By the time children approach their fourth birthday, the chubby hands that clumsily shook rattles have become coordinated instruments that throw balls, build sand castles and block towers, and paint glowing pictures. Three-year-olds are competent talkers, whose early cooing and babbling has become an impressive command of language that they use to get things done. They are highly social beings, who make friends with other children and enjoy playing with them. The early attachment to mother has become a comfortable partnership that is preparing children to leave the tight world of the family circle and venture into the ever-expanding world of childhood.

CHAPTER 5

Fundamentals of Physical Growth

A fter thirty-four weeks in the uterus, the chimpanzee baby is born relatively helpless. For several months, it clings to the fur of its mother's chest, where her cradling arm can provide further support. From about five months, this infant takes partial responsibility for its own safety, riding on its mother's back as she scrambles through the brush and swings into the trees. At six months, the chimpanzee baby begins to walk. Chimpanzees reach sexual maturity when they are ten years old, and growth continues for a few more years (Lovejoy, 1981).

The human baby spends thirty-eight weeks in the uterus and is helpless much longer than the chimpanzee. The five-month-old human baby will not sit without support for at least another month and will not walk until about twelve months. Sexual maturity comes when the child is twelve or thirteen years old, and growth continues for approximately another five years. Why does the human baby develop so slowly?

Some researchers believe that the human baby is born "too soon," so that the newborn continues to resemble a fetus both physically and behaviorally. If human babies were born at the same stage of development as other primates, they would spend twenty-one months in the uterus (see Figure

5.1). Instead, they continue to grow at the rapid fetal rate for several months. This rapid postnatal growth makes the large human brain possible. The newborn macaque's brain has reached 65 percent of its adult size; the newborn chimp's brain, 40.5 percent; but the newborn human brain, only 23 percent (Gould, 1977). If the human brain were any larger at birth, the fetus could not pass through the birth canal. And if the birth canal were wide enough for a brain as relatively developed as the chimpanzee's, a woman would not be able to walk upright (Leakey and Lewin, 1977).

Because the brain has so much growing to do, the newborn's skull, as well as the rest of the skeleton, is also exceedingly immature — even though the newborn baby is proportionately heavier compared to maternal weight than any other primate. The baby's nervous system, as immature as it is, is relatively further advanced than the skeleton. The baby's bones are soft and the muscles are weak. Newborns lack the strength and the leverage ei-

ther to support themselves or to direct their limbs and fingers with any precision (Eichorn, 1979). It is no wonder that it will be many months before the human child is strong enough to stand up and walk.

In this chapter, we follow the physical development of infants and toddlers. After exploring the genetically guided physical growth of infancy, we follow the course of brain development. We consider the gradual emergence of the infant's perception of a three-dimensional world, which prepares us to examine the development of motor skills. Our outline of motor development shows that the mastery of these skills is much more than a matter of cortical maturation. In this section, we trace the development of two major skills: skilled control of the hands and walking. The environment, we discover, exerts a powerful influence on the rate and quality of a child's physical development. Finally, we look at the relative roles of maturation and experience in the development of motor skills.

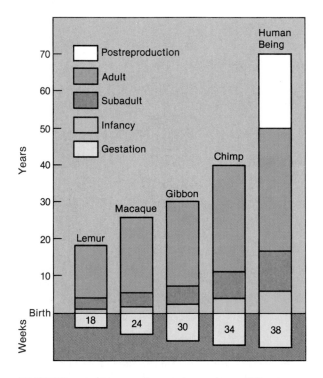

FIGURE 5.1   Progressive prolongation of life phases and gestation in primates. Note the proportionality of the four indicated phases. The postreproductive period is restricted to human beings and is probably a recent development. *(From Lovejoy, 1981)*

THE PROCESS OF PHYSICAL DEVELOPMENT

Physical development results from interaction between the child and the environment. During the process, children grow (they become larger), they develop (their body structure and functions become increasingly complex), and they mature (their size, organic structure, and body build progress toward physiological maturity).

Physical development during infancy and childhood is as orderly and lawful as the development of the fertilized egg into the newborn infant. This regular progress results from the canalization of growth. **Canalization** describes a genetically programmed path of growth that is extremely difficult to deflect from its ordained course (Scarr, 1983b). Although some environmental interaction is necessary for its full expression, the required environmental input is found in any normal human habitat. Canalized growth is also self-stabilizing; if some extreme circumstance momentarily deflects it from its canalized course, internal guidance is so strong that growth returns to its normal path as

Keeping her balance is still a major task for this little girl; until her postural stability improves, she can take only a step or two before she falls. *(Elizabeth Crews)*

soon as the momentary obstruction is removed.

As infants develop, their growth continues to follow the cephalocaudal and proximodistal patterns begun in the fetal period (see Chapter 4). Although the brain still has a lot of growing to do, the newborn's head is closer to its adult size than any other part of the body. Throughout childhood the largest increase in height takes place in the growth of the legs. As the child grows, the head contributes proportionally less to body length, shrinking from one-quarter of the total length at birth to one-twelfth at maturity (Bayley, 1956). The head-to-toe, center-to-periphery patterns also characterize the development of motor control. As body structures and functions become increasingly complex, the baby achieves progressively greater control over movements. Babies gain control over the muscles of the head and neck, then the arms and abdomen, and finally the legs.

They learn to control the movements of their shoulders before they can direct their arms or fingers. They use their hands as a unit before they can control the finer movements of their fingers.

In the process of acquiring such control, babies master a series of tasks (Gentile et al., 1975). First comes the establishment of body stability, which is essential to the mastery of all other motor skills. Babies cannot sit, stand, walk, manipulate objects, or investigate the world effectively unless they can keep their balance. Locomotion, or the ability to move their bodies through the environment, provides a second set of tasks. Crawling, walking, and running depend on the successful coordination of joints and muscles into patterns of action. Limb manipulation, the ability to reach, grasp, and investigate with the fingers, presents a third set of tasks. All of these tasks must be mastered within a constantly changing environment, which keeps altering the nature of each task. Walking up stairs, for example, requires muscles and joints to respond in different ways from walking on a sandy beach.

Norms

Because development is canalized, children master these tasks in a similar and predictable manner. By observing many children, psychologists interested in the normal course of development have produced detailed descriptions of events in the growth process. A number of investigators (Bayley, 1956; Cattell, 1940; Gesell, 1925; Griffiths, 1954; Lenneberg, 1967) have analyzed the sequence in which physical characteristics and motor, language, and social skills emerge. They have discovered that the sequence, as well as the appearance, of various skills is highly canalized and predictable. Such studies have produced **norms,** or typical patterns, that describe the approximate ages at which important attributes and skills appear. Norms are based on simple mathematical calculations that reflect average growth tendencies. They do not explain growth or development; they merely describe it, indicating what is most likely to appear in the development of children at various ages.

Norms can be useful in describing how most children develop. They can help us assess the ef-

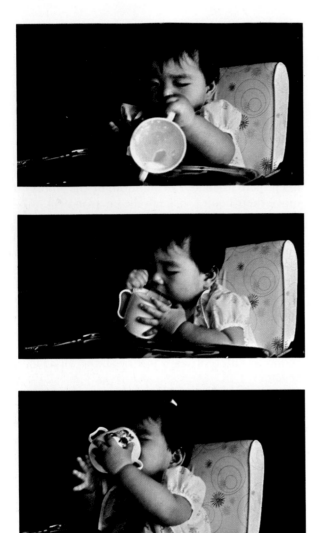

Drinking from a cup requires the integration of specific skills and actions. This year-old infant uses and adjusts her grasping and sucking skills as she learns to drink from a cup. *(Tom Suzuki)*

fects of environmental changes on behavior (such as the effects of separating infants from their mothers), or they can be useful in studying cross-cultural and subcultural variations. Norms also have been used to examine the effects of institutionalization, of gender, and of birth order on a child's development. And they have been helpful in studies of prematurity and of early disorders. The baby whose size or motor development lags

far behind the norm alerts the pediatrician to look for further signs of trouble.

Yet the value of norms as a diagnostic tool for an individual child is limited. In every aspect of growth, normal children vary widely on each side of a norm. Parents who are unaware of the width of the "normal zone" of accomplishment may become unnecessarily alarmed when they see young infants who have been walking for several months while their own, older baby still cannot stand. The wide range of differences in growth showed clearly in a study that Howard Meredith (1963) conducted among Iowa males. At the age of eighteen, the lightest boy in his study weighed no more than the heaviest boy had weighed when he was eight. The boy who was lightest at eight weighed about the same as the heaviest boy when he was two.

Norms for some of the major milestones that occur during the first two years of life are shown in Figure 5.2. The age at which normal children master these skills shows great variability. Some children never creep or crawl but go directly from sitting to taking their first steps. The normal range for the onset of walking is itself large, from as early as eight months to as late as twenty.

In many aspects of growth, norms differ for boys and girls. Girls and boys grow at different rates, and the difference begins before birth. By the time they are halfway through the fetal period, girls' skeletal development is three weeks ahead of boys', and by the time they are born, girls have outstripped boys by four to six weeks in skeletal maturity, although not in size (Tanner, 1978). Some organ systems are more developed at birth in girls, and this may help explain why more girls than boys survive.

During the first few months, boys grow faster than girls, but girls surpass boys from seven months until they are about four years old. From that time until puberty, both sexes grow at the

FIGURE 5.2 Some of the major milestones in motor development that occur over the first two years of life. Each dot indicates the approximate average age of occurrence. Individual infants may demonstrate these skills somewhat earlier or later than the average indicated. *(After Lenneberg, 1967, and Bayley, 1969)*

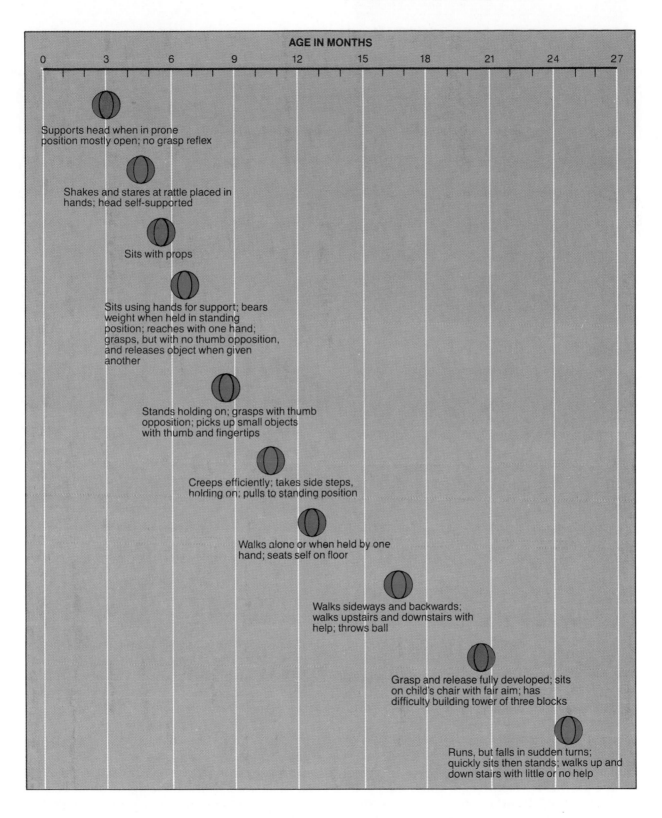

AGE IN MONTHS

0   3   6   9   12   15   18   21   24   27

Supports head when in prone
position mostly open; no grasp reflex

Shakes and stares at rattle placed in
hands; head self-supported

Sits with props

Sits using hands for support; bears
weight when held in standing
position; reaches with one hand;
grasps, but with no thumb opposition,
and releases object when given
another

Stands holding on; grasps with thumb
opposition; picks up small objects
with thumb and fingertips

Creeps efficiently; takes side steps,
holding on; pulls to standing position

Walks alone or when held by one
hand; seats self on floor

Walks sideways and backwards;
walks upstairs and downstairs with
help; throws ball

Grasp and release fully developed; sits
on child's chair with fair aim; has
difficulty building tower of three blocks

Runs, but falls in sudden turns;
quickly sits then stands; walks up and
down stairs with little or no help

same rate. According to an old rule, children reach half their adult height by the end of the second year. This rule is helpful only when parents want to predict the height of boys. Because girls mature earlier than boys, they reach the halfway mark sooner: at about eighteen months.

Individual Growth Patterns

The first thing an observer notices about a group of infants is how different each appears. Marked structural differences have existed among them since soon after conception. Newborn infants differ in such physical variables as height (length), weight, muscularity, hairiness, dental development, and a host of other measureable characteristics. As children grow, these physical differences persist. Some, such as height and weight, become more pronounced; others, such as hairiness, become less noticeable.

The rate of growth differs nearly as much as structure does. Healthy children may grow much more slowly or more quickly than the mythical average child described by norms. Maturation rates seem to be related to body build, which is largely dictated by heredity. A child who is broadly built, large, and strong is likely to grow rapidly, while a slender, long-legged, but small, lightly muscled child is likely to grow more slowly (Bayley, 1956).

Because norms do not provide an adequate yardstick for measuring individual growth, researchers have discovered ways to assess the individual child's growth progress. The rate at which teeth erupt is one fairly accurate measure. Another is skeletal age; the degree of calcification, the shape, and the position of bones reveal how far a child has progressed toward physiological maturity. Because skeletal age is assessed by X-raying the wrist and hand, this measurement is taken only when some medical problem is suspected.

Some children grow much more rapidly than others. Although individual growth patterns are generally stable, severe dietary deficiencies or stress can disrupt them and temporarily slow growth. When the condition responsible for retarded growth is eliminated, a child often goes through a period of **catch-up growth,** when growth accelerates to compensate for the slowdown. For example, newborn babies whose growth has been delayed in the uterus show catch-up growth in both weight and height. This may happen when twins' growth has been slowed because of crowded conditions within the uterus or when a small mother has carried a genetically large child (Tanner, 1978). On the average, from birth to six months or so, smaller babies gain more weight than do larger ones. Newborn catch-up growth is usually completed by the end of the third year.

BRAIN DEVELOPMENT

Within two years, the baby's brain will triple in size, reaching about 75 to 80 percent of its adult weight and dimensions. Perhaps because of its extensive, rapid growth, the baby's central nervous system is more adaptable than it will be later in life. If an infant is born with a malformed major brain tract, the nervous system may be capable of correcting for it, perhaps by developing the same function in a different area. When an infant's brain is damaged, the recovery may be so complete that the baby shows no apparent aftereffects. If, for example, the part of the brain that controls language function should be injured, the baby may develop normal language function anyway. Sometimes the recovery seems complete, but extensive testing can detect damage that is not apparent in most situations (Goldman-Rakic et al., 1983).

Electrical Activity

When newborn babies are awake or asleep, the electrical activity of their brain shows characteristic wave patterns, as we saw in Chapter 4. At this age, a baby's EEG tracings show no alpha waves (a wave pattern that appears in adults when their eyes are closed and they are not actively processing information). A slowed form of alpha rhythm seems to appear at about four months; over the years, it gradually increases in frequency, assuming adult form when the child is about sixteen years old. Because of this regular development,

WINDOW ON THE INFANT BRAIN

In the past few years, researchers have developed a new way of studying brain function. **Positron emission tomography (PET)** is based on the biochemistry of the nervous system. When neurons function, they use glucose for energy, and the more active they are, the more glucose they require. If radioactive glucose is injected into the body, the presence of glucose in the brain can be translated into maps of the brain made by recording the decay of radioactive ions. These maps, called PET scans, provide a window through which researchers can watch the living brain at work.

For the first time, PET scans have been used to trace the development of brain function in babies. Harry Chugani and Michael Phelps (1986) made PET scans of nine nearly normal infants and four severely retarded infants and toddlers. The "normal" infants were developing normally, although they had suffered from some sort of neurological seizure as newborns.

PET scans made on infants between the ages of five days and eighteen months clearly show the gradual spread of function through the developing brain (see PET scans). In the newborn, the most active areas of the brain were the primary motor and sensory areas, the basal ganglia (which integrate information from various parts of the brain), the brainstem (which controls such automatic activities as breathing and circulation), and the cerebellum (which is involved in movement). Little energy was used by the cortex or by the area that initiates and integrates movement. This pattern is consistent with a mostly subcortical control of behavior. At eleven weeks, activity was spreading through the cortex, while energy use had increased in the pri-

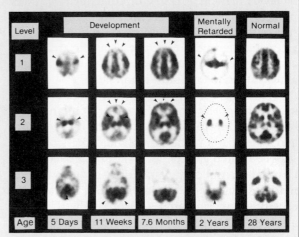

These PET scans show developmental changes in brain function while the babies tested were awake and had their eyes open. The PET scans show brain activity at three levels, with level 1 corresponding to the top of the brain (cortex). The PET scans of the adult brain are reduced in size. (From Chugani and Phelps, 1986)

mary motor and sensory areas. By seven and one-half months, the pattern of activity in the baby's brain resembled that seen in adults.

This pattern did not appear in the PET scans of severely retarded two-year-olds; instead, their brain function resembled that of "normal" newborns. These retarded toddlers, who had suffered severe anoxia at birth, showed little cortical activity. They also had retained many of the neonatal reflexes that disappear in normal infants.

alpha frequency sometimes is used as a measure of brain maturation (Parmelee and Sigman, 1983). Other brain wave patterns, such as the evoked potential (see Chapter 4), show regular maturational changes in speed as well as form. At birth,

babies' responses to new sights and sounds come slowly. At about three months, the response is faster, and by the age of four, the child's brain responds as quickly as the adult's (Parmelee and Sigman, 1983).

Cortical Control

At birth the baby's **cortex** (the mantle of cells covering the two cerebral hemispheres) is exceedingly immature, an indication that much neonatal behavior may be reflexive or controlled by lower parts of the brain. The areas of the brain that control particular sensory and motor functions develop at different rates. Once a specific area in the cortex develops, the corresponding function can appear in the baby's development.

The relationship between cortical maturity and behavior is not so straightforward as it might seem, however. Development in the sensory receptors and other parts of the brain and spinal cord also may be related to the appearance of new behavior (Parmelee and Sigman, 1983). In addition, **neurons** (the basic cells in the brain) that seem to be structurally mature may not be able either to generate nerve impulses or to manufacture the chemicals that transmit nerve impulses across synapses (Goldman-Rakic et al., 1983). Finally, the development of many motor skills may depend as much on the growth of joints and muscles as on neural development (Thelen, in press).

Some researchers have argued that instead of viewing brain growth as leading to increased physical and mental control, we should see the baby's use of the body and nervous system as causing growth in corresponding brain areas. For example, Stephen Rose (1973) suggests that the barrage of sensory information that assails newborns when they emerge from the uterus leads the cortex to grow and neural connections to develop. Research with animals supports this position. Studies with kittens have shown that without stimulation, neuronal connections fail to develop, and connections that are present atrophy (Hubel and Weisel, 1963). Studies with rats have shown that when animals are given environmental stimulation (toys, rat companions, and a view), they have heavier and thicker cortexes than rats raised in standard lab cages with no toys, no view, and no company (Rosenzweig, Bennett, and Diamond, 1972). Research has not been able to establish just how early stimulation can modify the human brain. Arthur Parmelee and Marian Sigman (1983) propose that during the last month before birth, environmental stimulation can affect the brain's organization and

so influence the development of behavior and cognition. They believe that the shift from a purely genetically guided development to a development dominated by the environment is a slow, staggered process, with different systems coming under environmental influence at different times.

PERCEIVING A SOLID WORLD

Motor development depends on the coordination of many developing skills and in turn contributes to the perfection of other skills. For example, if children are to move surely through a three-dimensional world, they must be able to perceive its solidity and depth. Yet the ability to perceive depth may depend in part on the child's experience in locomotion. Depth perception seems to emerge gradually, at some time between three and six months (Banks and Salpatek, 1983).

How soon can babies use visual depth cues as warnings about such dangers as falling off tables or chairs? Eleanor Gibson and Richard Walk (1960) studied this sort of depth perception by placing eight-to twelve-month-old infants on the edge of a "visual cliff." The cliff consisted of a patterned platform covered with Plexiglas and lighted so that it seemed to have a shallow and a deep side. Most babies refused to crawl over the deep side of the cliff, even to reach their mothers (see accompanying photograph). Because the youngest infant in this study was eight months old, Gibson and Walk could not determine whether the refusal to venture over the edge of the cliff was due to the maturation of vision or whether learning played a central role. In a later study using the visual cliff, Sandra Scarr and Philip Salapatek (1970) found that babies younger than seven months old showed no fear when placed on the edge of the cliff. Only babies who were already crawling avoided the edge.

Apparently, some crawling experience is necessary for the baby to discover that depth cues may signal danger. Yet much younger babies can distinguish between the deep and shallow sides of the cliff. When two-month-old babies are placed on the deep side, their hearts slow down, a sign that

Most infants who can crawl will not venture out on the glass surface over the "deep" side of the visual cliff. Not even the sight of mother holding an attractive toy can persuade a baby to cross what appears to be a sudden drop. *(Steve McCarroll)*

suggests they sense some difference between the two sides (Campos, 1976). They probably note a difference in contour density but do not interpret it as indicating depth (Banks and Salapatek, 1983). When nine-month-old babies are placed on the deep side, their response is very different. Their hearts speed up, a sign that suggests they are afraid (Campos, 1976).

THE DEVELOPMENT OF MOTOR SKILLS

Some psychologists view motor development as primarily reflecting the maturation of motor areas of the brain. Others believe that perception, cognition, emotions, and social relationships also help to organize and motivate movement and that motor skills, in turn, are important to further perceptual, cognitive, emotional, and social development (Thelen, in press). Cortical control is only one of many processes that are essential for the emergence of various motor milestones. As a skill develops, the coalition of various muscles and joints on which it is based may change. When this happens, the skill may show an uneven spiral development. That is, instead of steadily increasing in smoothness and accuracy, the skill goes through a period in which it again becomes clumsy or even disappears (Trevarthen, 1982).

Eventually, the emerging motor skill becomes coordinated and controlled. Coordination requires the baby to recruit the correct muscle groups involved in the execution of a particular skill, whether reaching, walking, throwing, or jumping. Control requires the baby to apply those muscle groups in a directed way toward a task. We can trace this gradual, often spiral, development in the control of hand use and walking.

Using the Hand

Skilled hand use—making and using tools—is one of the hallmarks of humanity. We can consider it a sort of manual intelligence, and some researchers (Bruner, 1970) believe that hand use reveals a good deal about the nature of thought and problem solving. Unlike the hands of most primates, the human hand is a despecialized organ—it can do almost anything. This lack of specialization means that the joints and tendons in our fingers, wrists, elbows, shoulders, and trunk can operate independently. It takes years before the child can combine and coordinate them to express full manual intelligence.

Reaching and Grasping Almost from birth,

babies follow moving objects with their eyes. Their ability to reach out and grasp the objects they see develops in a characteristic pattern, seeming to disappear and reappear, as the various components of the grasp rearrange themselves in different ways. In a series of studies, Claes von Hofsten (1982; 1983; 1984) dangled a brightly colored yarn ball in front of a baby. The ball was connected by a rod to an electric motor, which slowly moved the ball in a horizontal path from one side of the infant to the other. As newborns reached rapidly toward the object, their hand opened, and as the hand neared the object, the motion slowed down. But the baby rarely managed to touch the ball of yarn with these swipes. Hofsten emphasizes that motion is not yet functional or goal-oriented. The baby is not attempting to grab and manipulate the object. The reach simply indicates that the baby is paying attention to the object. In these early weeks, the arm and hand act as information-gathering feelers, which infants point toward an object that has attracted their gaze. Although eye-hand coordination is present, the eye does not guide the hand; it simply aims it. The baby probably relies on kinesthetic receptors in the arm and hand muscles, tendons, and joints to direct the swooping arm (Trevarthen, 1982).

When the baby is about two months old, a change appears. The baby reaches out much less often toward the dangling ball. Yet interest is still high; babies spend more time gazing intently at the object whether or not they reach for it. When they do stretch their arm toward the object, they reach with a fist instead of an open hand. Hofsten suggests that the baby's arm and shoulder are controlled by the brainstem, but the coordination of the hand and fingers is guided by the cortex. The cortical system has begun to function but is not yet coordinated with the earlier system that controls gross motor movements. The apparent backsliding in ability indicates that the prestructured motor pattern has broken down so that its constituents can be reassembled in a more mature manner.

By the end of the fourth month, most of the baby's reaches are again open-handed. Now the reach is slower, and the baby often succeeds in grasping—or at least touching—the object. The hand moves toward and with the object at the same time, with the eyes guiding the hand. The baby must be able to see both the hand and the object in order to reach the fascinating toy. The precision of aim and its timing indicate a delicately tuned system of sensorimotor functioning. The baby seems to monitor and correct the reach, because the hand zigs and zags, stops and starts on its way to the target. Once babies grasp an object, they seem to hang on only as long as they pay attention to it. If you now present a second toy, the first one falls from the infant's hand as soon as attention shifts to the new object (Bruner, 1970).

The final stage in reaching appears at about nine months. Once again, the reach is rapid, but now it is highly accurate and direct. Catching hold of some interesting object no longer requires a baby's complete attention. Babies may or may not watch the reaching hand, because the motion has become so skilled and practiced that visual control is not necessary when the path between hand and object is obvious (Bushnell, 1985). By now babies are also skilled graspers. If they have a toy in one hand, they hang onto it, perhaps shifting it to the other hand, in order to free a hand for a new reach. When both hands are full, they deposit an old toy in their lap or place it within easy reach before taking a third toy (Bruner, 1970).

Handedness Handedness develops slowly. Most toddlers tend to use one hand more often than the other, but many children do not settle on the consistent use of one hand until they are about five years old (Goodall, 1980). When lying on their backs, most newborns (65 percent) turn their heads to the right; a few (15 percent) prefer lying with their heads turned to the left; and the rest show no preference for either side. This preference, which is still apparent at two months, predicts which hand the baby is likely to use in reaching for objects at four months (Michel, 1981). However, the preference for the right-handed reach declines during this period. In Hofsten's (1984) study, the percentage of right-handed reaches declined from 72 percent at one week to 55 percent at four months.

By this time, most infants hold a toy longer when it is placed in their right hand than when it is placed in their left. Between six and nine months, many babies tend to rely on their right hands when they reach for an object directly in front of them. But the use of the right hand is not yet stable in all

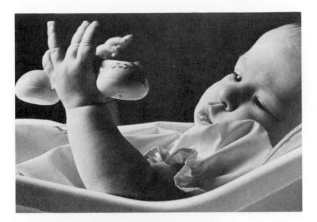

At twenty weeks, infants hold objects without firmly grasping them. By twenty-eight weeks, they can use their palms to close around and pick up an object. By forty weeks, they use the thumb and forefinger in opposition, grasping much as an adult does. *(Steve McCarroll)*

conditions. In one study (Michel, Harkins, and Ovrut, 1986), seven- to nine-month-olds were consistent in using their right hands to reach for a toy, but often used either hand when manipulating an object.

In nearly all adult right-handers and some left-handers, the left side of the brain is primarily responsible for the production and comprehension of language. Therefore several investigators have suggested that both the onset of handedness and the beginnings of speech may be due to the establishment of the left hemisphere's control over motor functions. When Douglas Ramsay (1984; Ramsay and Weber, 1986) followed the development of hand preference, he found that infants start favoring one hand (usually the right) during the same week that they began babbling ("baba-baba"). These events may occur any time between four and one-half and nine months. But the preference is not stable. During the next several months infants go through periods in which their prefer-

ence disappears, and most use either hand indiscriminately. This connection between language and hand preference, together with the subsequent fluctuations in use, may explain why other researchers (Goldfield and Michel, 1986) have found no increase with age in hand preference during the latter half of the first year.

Some children begin relying exclusively on one hand much earlier than others. The timing of this preference interacts with gender in an unusual way. In a longitudinal study of children between the ages of eighteen and forty-two months (Gottfried and Bathurst, 1983), girls whose hand preference (whether right or left) was consistent tested significantly higher on tests of intellectual development than girls with inconsistent hand preference. No relationship appeared for boys. At least half the children showed a steady hand preference throughout the study. In another study (Tan, 1985), four-year-old boys (but not girls) who had failed to develop a consistent hand preference were poorly coordinated. Despite the widespread belief that left-handers tend to be more awkward than right-handers, both groups with consistent hand preferences were equally well coordinated.

Walking

During the first two months, a baby's legs gain a good deal of fat but not much muscle. As we saw in Chapter 4, the chubby legs become too heavy for babies to move unless they have some relief from gravity (Thelen, Fisher, and Ridley-Johnson, 1984). From the time they are about two months old, babies will not step when held upright. Instead, they either draw up both legs as soon as they are lowered toward the ground or extend their legs but keep their feet fixed as if they were glued to the floor (Forssberg, 1985).

Even after newborns' stepping movements disappear, babies continue the same pattern of motor activity while lying on their backs (Thelen, 1985). The infant's rhythmic kicking movements are at first identical with the newborn stepping response. All the joints (hip, knee, ankle) work in unison, and the movement is always the same, no matter how many times a minute the baby kicks. Although the movements are different from those used in mature walking, there are enough parallels between them to suggest that this pattern, which is probably generated in the spinal cord, forms the basis for later walking. Between two and five months, the stereotypical kick breaks down. The action of each joint becomes individualized, only to be reorganized in more mature motor patterns. This temporary disorganization paves the way for the development of voluntary control, so that the baby will be able to turn over, crawl, stand up, walk, and climb.

Before babies can walk, various components of the ability must mature and become coordinated (Thelen, 1984). Babies' body proportions change, shifting the center of gravity downward. Their muscles become strong enough to support their bodies. They develop control over their posture, and their cortex develops, allowing them to integrate and coordinate the components of walking (Zelazo, 1984).

Near their first birthday, most infants take their first steps. But this walking lacks the characteristics that distinguish human walking from walking

This seven-month-old boy is not ready to walk. When his father holds him upright, the baby does not step but keeps his feet fixed as if they were glued to the floor. *(Rae Russel)*

in other primates (Forssberg, 1985). The motion probably is still generated at the spinal cord, as was the early stepping, only now the baby has developed voluntary control over it. Youngsters land on their toes or flat on their feet, instead of striking the ground with their heel, as adults do. They fail to flex their knees to cushion the impact of each step, and their hip motion is also different. The adult walking pattern develops gradually toward the end of the second year, probably in response to (1) changes in its organization and control in the spinal cord and brain or (2) improvements in posture and strength — or both.

The consequences of walking for both child and parent are incalculable. The infant's world widens, and new possibilities open. When young-

Walking brings babies a new feeling of competence, because they now need no assistance to approach others—or to leave them if interaction becomes unpleasant. *(Linda Ferrer/Woodfin Camp & Associates)*

sters master the skill of moving around at will and with comparative ease, systematic changes occur in the way they explore their surroundings. They are likely to feel more competent. Now they can approach other people (fostering social interaction) or leave them (fostering autonomy) (Kopp, 1979). As we saw in Chapter 2, Erik Erikson (1963) views the establishment of autonomy as the toddler's major developmental task. Walking changes children's lives in other ways. Suddenly, they find their actions interrupted as never before. Their explorations of interesting objects that once lasted until they grew weary or bored are abruptly terminated by parents who move them bodily away, distract them from their fascinating forays, begin to shout "No!" and perhaps even slap an infant hand. Parents treat children who can walk differently from infants, seeing them less as "babies" and more as individuals. This shift in perspective leads parents to expect the child to adapt himself or herself to family routines and rules. Walking also exposes the child to accident, and so leads to even more parental intervention.

Play Skills

As the months pass, youngsters become confident walkers. Soon they are testing and refining new motor skills—running, jumping, climbing, and manipulating objects. Around the age of three, boys become more proficient than girls at play that requires strength, such as throwing a ball for distance. But three-year-old girls are more skillful at most activities that do not require power. From the age of four until puberty, strength is the only difference between the sexes in large motor skills.

Coordination, which includes the child's accuracy of movement, poise, smoothness, rhythm, and ease, is the basis of almost all play skills. It provides a fairly good index for determining a child's ability and agility at physical play. A child acquires coordination more slowly than strength or speed, because coordination requires the interplay of sensory and motor skills that often depend on the maturation of small muscles and on practice.

There are, of course, large individual differences in the ages at which children are able to do various things, as well as differences in the degree of their skill and coordination in each activity. Although maturation of muscles and bones plays a large part in the emergence of running, jumping, and skipping, the opportunity to practice and the encouragement of others helps in the mastery and refinement of such abilities.

Among preschoolers, boys are much more likely than girls to engage in rough-and-tumble play. Such play appears in children as young as eighteen months, and Nicholas Blurton-Jones (1976) believes that those who do not begin it early may never engage in it. In a typical bout of rough-and-tumble play, one child chases another, and the chase is followed by scuffling, wrestling, and laughter.

Episodes of rough-and-tumble play combine characteristic patterns of motor activity (Blurton-Jones, 1976). Children run, chase and flee, wrestle, jump up and down with feet together, beat at each other with open hands (but do not actually land blows), laugh, and fall down. When engaged in such play, children also exhibit a typical facial expression—an open-mouthed smile with the lips covering the teeth. During real hostilities, children beat with closed fists, frown, and fix their gaze on each other. Such actions are never part of

Rough-and-tumble play may seem aggressive, but it's all in fun and no blows actually are exchanged. *(Spencer Carter/ Woodfin Camp & Associates)*

rough-and-tumble play. When children begin rough-and-tumble play, it either continues until they are exhausted or turns abruptly into a game that requires rules, such as tag or Superman.

Part of the significant gender difference in rough-and-tumble play may derive from the fact that young girls seem to perceive as a threatening advance the same action that young boys interpret as an invitation to roughhouse. In a group of preschoolers studied by Janet DiPietro (1981), girls showed just as much vigorous activity on the trampoline as boys. Rough-and-tumble play often developed among boys when one tried to take a toy from another. Girls interpreted such actions not as an invitation to play but as a bid for dominance.

The effects of rough-and-tumble play appear to be positive. Children who engage in it generally stay together after the game ends and tend to play together on subsequent occasions. Although no one knows all the functions of rough-and-tumble play, researchers have suggested that it encourages youngsters to form and consolidate friendships (Smith, 1977) and provides a safe way to practice aggression (Suomi, 1977). Blurton-Jones (1976) concludes that because children in several cultures give the same signals (facial expression, laughter, and the like) to indicate its lack of hostility, rough-and-tumble play may have had an important role in the evolution of human beings.

GROWTH AND ENVIRONMENT

No one is sure how environmental factors influence growth during infancy and childhood. The internal mechanism that regulates growth appears to be affected by hormonal and chemical factors. Some researchers believe that nutrition, illness, and stress may affect the composition of these chemicals (Tanner, 1978).

Socioeconomic background, illness, or stress may influence growth in part through an indirect effect on nutrition. For example, in developing nations, family poverty sometimes leads mothers to dilute infant formula, so that babies waste away. And unsanitary conditions may produce contaminated milk, resulting in infant deaths from diarrhea. For these reasons, the World Health Organization encourages breast-feeding and has urged a global ban on the promotion of infant formulas in developing countries (Campbell, 1982).

Nutrition and Health

Because nutrition is a central environmental determinant of normal physical growth, dietary deficiencies often are responsible for abnormal growth patterns. Malnutrition, obesity, and the choice of early feeding methods may have important effects on development.

Malnutrition General malnutrition, in which children simply do not get enough to eat, is marked by a lack of calories as well as a lack of protein, vitamins, and minerals. This near starvation sometimes occurs in developing countries, even when there is no drought (Waterlow and Payne, 1975). As the number of calories available to a young child drops dangerously near the level required for maintenance and growth, the child becomes listless and ceases to play or to explore the environment. When calorie intake drops below the minimum level, growth ceases.

The experience of infants and children who have gone through wartime famine demonstrates the effects of temporary malnutrition. The growth records of these youngsters show periods of delayed growth. Studies of children who were subjected to severe wartime malnutrition in Europe and Asia indicate that when the episode of malnutrition is neither too severe nor too long, the effects of acute malnourishment are usually overcome through catch-up growth. Once these children returned to a normal diet, they caught up with their peers by adolescence (Wolff, 1935; Acheson, 1960). Catch-up growth can be dramatic, as Figure 5.3 indicates. In this case, a little girl who suffered from two periods of malnutrition in infancy and early childhood returned to her normal growth curve before she started school (Tanner, 1978).

Short periods of malnutrition can be overcome, but children who are chronically undernourished may suffer permanent effects. Despite the catch-up growth that follows the return to an adequate diet, they will be smaller as adults than they would have been under normal circumstances. Their height will fall at the low end of their genetic reaction range (see Chapter 3). Severe malnutrition in infancy also can disrupt brain development, affecting connections between neurons and the development of chemicals that transmit signals through the brain (Parmelee and Sigman, 1983). Among a group of malnourished Guatemalan infants, height and weight were good predictors of performance on mental and motor tests (Lasky et al., 1981). Children with a history of severe,

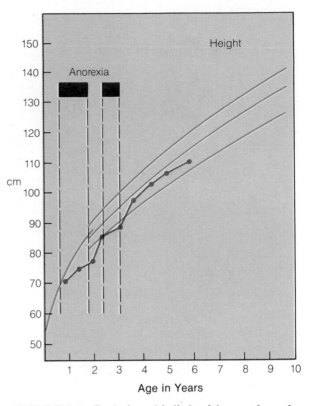

FIGURE 5.3 Each time this little girl went through a period of near starvation (anorexia), her growth slowed and her recorded height fell below her individual growth curve. But the catch-up growth that accompanied adequate nutrition eventually returned her to her own growth curve. *(From Tanner, 1978; redrawn from Prader, Tanner, and von Harnack, 1963, p. 155)*

chronic malnutrition tend to make lower scores on IQ tests and tests of specific cognitive abilities than other children in the same community, and their school achievement also lags behind. The disparity continues even after the children receive an adequate diet. But as Ernesto Pollitt and his associates (Pollitt, Garza, and Leibel, 1984) point out, when testing malnourished youngsters, it is difficult to separate social factors from the physiological effects of malnutrition. In addition, the sluggishness of the malnourished child may lead to lowered motivation when the youngster takes tests.

Deficiencies of specific nutrients also can

When children in low-income families are listless and have trouble paying attention in school, the problem may be anemia—the result of a diet that lacks essential nutrients. *(Nick Sapieha/Stock, Boston)*

Helu, and Howanitz, 1983). Iron is believed to affect brain chemistry, but perhaps the supplements simply improve general health and well-being, so that the child is no longer listless and becomes motivated (Pollitt, Garza, and Leibel, 1984). Anemic youngsters are deficient in folic acid and vitamin B_{12} as well as iron. When children develop anemia, they are listless, unable to pay attention, and have trouble sleeping (Kopp, 1983).

Obesity Another major nutritional problem is **obesity,** or excessive fatness. Genes play some part in its development. Study after study has shown that adopted children's relative weight is more like the weight of their biological parents than of their adoptive parents (Kolata, 1986; Biron, Mongeau, and Bertrand, 1977). In a longitudinal study, William Kessen and Judith Rodin have been comparing children of normal-weight parents with children of overweight parents (Rodin and Hall, 1987). When these children were newborns, three factors predicted whether they would be obese as preschoolers:

1. Obesity in the parents
2. A heightened responsiveness to sweet tastes at birth
3. A heightened responsiveness to environmental stimuli at birth.

Many obese children and adults show a similar heightened responsiveness to environmental cues. Food not only appeals more to them, but when they see it or smell it, their insulin levels rise dramatically (Rodin, 1983). High insulin levels make people eat more and speed the conversion of food to fat.

Fat babies are not necessarily fat children. After reviewing various studies, Alex Roche (1981) found almost no connection between obesity in infancy and obesity at age sixteen. But parents inadvertently can push their preschoolers into obesity. Some become alarmed when their three-year-olds seem to stop eating; so they press food on children who use fewer calories now that their growth has slowed. Other parents are so afraid that their child will become fat that they put rigid restraints on the youngster's food consumption. Dependent on parental guidance, the child never de-

disrupt development. For example, a serious, often fatal disease called **kwashiorkor,** may follow severe, prolonged protein deficiency. This ailment is prevalent among infants in developing countries whose diet consists primarily of breast milk after they are a year old or who are fed a low-protein substitute for breast milk (such as cassava or arrowroot) (Jelliffe and Jelliffe, 1979; Waterlow, 1973). Such infants are profoundly apathetic; they have scaly skin, diarrhea, swollen limbs and abdomen, and liver degeneration. If the disease goes untreated for more than four months, they may be severely retarded (Cravioto and Delicardie, 1970). With adequate protein, infants with kwashiorkor grow rapidly but never catch up with infants of their own age.

Malnutrition this severe is virtually unknown in the United States. But chronic undernutrition is still a problem in some places, as is the deficiency of specific nutrients, especially iron. When infants do not get enough iron, they lag behind other babies on tests of motor and mental development. The link seems fairly well established, because when these infants are given iron supplements, they catch up with other babies (Oski, Honig,

Some researchers have connected the recent increase in weight gain among American children with a heavy diet of television. *(Annette Pelaez/Woodfin Camp & Associates)*

velops any internal psychological controls over eating (Rodin and Hall, 1987). Another factor that seems to affect weight is the speed with which children eat. Overweight preschoolers chew each bite of food less than preschoolers of normal weight, which allows them to take more bites of food (and thus more calories) during a meal (Drabman, Cordua, Hammer, Jarvie, and Horton, 1979). This difference appears as early as eighteen months — the youngest age studied. When obesity lingers until school age, it has a good chance of being permanent. Forty percent of obese seven-year-olds will become obese adults.

More and more American children are becoming obese; in the past twenty years, obesity among six- to eleven-year-olds has increased 54 percent. According to William Dietz, television bears a good part of the responsibility for this increase (Kolata, 1986). He has found that — next to already being fat — the strongest predictor of future obesity is watching lots of television. Dietz explains that children eat more while they watch TV; that TV ads encourage them to eat more; and that their inactivity while watching TV so reduces their energy needs that they gain weight. No matter what factors are linked with obesity, the basic problem remains the same: obesity is the result of consuming more calories that the body can use.

Socioeconomic Factors

Many children in lower socioeconomic classes show normal growth patterns. Yet setbacks to growth are concentrated among low-income groups. Sometimes chronic undernourishment is responsible; sluggish children whose interest is hard to arouse may reflect the low energy levels that accompany poor diets. Diseases of the eyes, skin, and respiratory and gastrointestinal tracts may be prevalent because undernourished children are more vulnerable to infection. Nagging ailments, including badly decayed teeth, may persist because of a lack of medical care.

When all English children born during a single week in 1958 were followed through the preschool years, growth differences between those with fathers in highly skilled occupations and those with fathers in less skilled occupations became steadily larger (Tanner, 1978). Studies conducted in Europe, Asia, Africa, and North and South America (including the United States) support these findings (Meredith, 1984). In each country, children in upper socioeconomic groups were taller, heavier, had larger head circumferences, wider pelvises, and thicker upper arms than their peers in lower socioeconomic groups.

General health status also seems linked to so-

SUDDEN INFANT DEATH SYNDROME

On a cold winter night, parents put their three-month-old son in his crib for the night. The baby has a runny nose but otherwise seems healthy. Early the next morning, they discover that their child has died quietly in his sleep. The baby is the victim of **sudden infant death syndrome (SIDS),** more commonly called "crib death." Each year 7,000 apparently healthy American babies fall victim to this sudden killer, and investigators have been searching diligently for the cause (*New York Times*, 1985).

Most babies who succumb to SIDS are between two and four months old. Babies less than a month old seem immune, and 90 percent of the deaths occur before babies are six months old. Victims of SIDS come from every country, every race, and every socioeconomic level, although deaths are more frequent among babies whose medical histories and family backgrounds include certain risk factors (see "Babies at Risk for SIDS").

Infant victims of SIDS seem normal, but Marie Valdes-Dapena recently testified before a congressional committee that autopsies have shown lesions in the brainstems of these babies (*New York Times*, 1985). The brainstem controls breathing and heart action, so the link with SIDS seems reasonable. However, researchers are uncertain whether the lesions are the cause or the result of SIDS.

Other researchers have focused on **sleep apnea,** or a temporary halt in breathing during sleep. Alfred Steinschneider (1975) has discovered widespread evidence of such episodes among babies and believes that they are common among infants who die of SIDS. The lower a baby's birth weight, the more likely the infant is to stop breathing periodically during sleep. The incidence of apnea also increases when babies have slight respiratory infections. By studying sleeping babies attached to instruments that record body functions, Steinschneider has found that periods of prolonged apnea tend to occur during REM sleep (which was discussed in Chapter 4) and that they often are accompanied by slowed heart rates. Recently, French researchers (Navelet, Payan, Guilhaume, and Benoit, 1984) have discovered that babies who are at risk for SIDS spend more time in REM sleep during the night and are awake less often than other babies. This finding agrees with Steinschneider's observations that heart rates be-

Babies at Risk for SIDS

Male
Black
Younger than six months
Birth weight of $5\frac{1}{2}$ pounds or less
Low Apgar score (7 or less)
Signs of jaundice at birth
Severe respiratory problems at birth
Periods of prolonged apnea
Increased REM sleep, decreased wakefulness at night
Mild upper respiratory infection
Not vaccinated for polio, diphtheria, whooping cough, or tetanus
Bottle-fed
Family of low socioeconomic status
Adolescent mother
Mother failed to complete high school
Mother smokes
Mother anemic at time of birth

Note: Each of these factors increases an infant's risk of developing SIDS. For example, 70 percent of SIDS victims' mothers smoke, as compared with 40 percent of other mothers. None of the factors has been shown to *cause* the syndrome, but all are correlated with it.

Source: Information from Lipsitt, Sturner, and Burke, 1979; McKenna, 1983; Navelet et al., 1984; *New York Times*, 1985.

come slower during long periods of sleep. The longer the sleep period, the greater the possibility of apnea when the heart is beating slowly.

Lewis Lipsitt (1979) believes that the slight head colds found in about half the SIDS victims may implicate a learning problem. Babies are born with unconditioned, defensive reflexes that help them clear their air passages. Unless these reflexes work properly during the neonatal period, babies do not learn to clear obstructions by the time the reflexes drop away. Because babies at risk for SIDS are weaker, not as visually alert, and engage their environment less than other infants, they may have fewer opportunities to learn the voluntary responses that would later save their lives. This tendency would be especially true among bottle-fed infants, because they do not get any practice in learning to breathe when their nose is partially obstructed, as breast-fed babies do.

A final strand in the web of factors leading to

SIDS may be modern child-care practices. Anthropologist James McKenna (1983) notes that our hunting and gathering ancestors carried their infants with them wherever they went by day and slept with them at night. Being continually carried about provides the jiggling, rocking, bouncing stimulation that some researchers believe may be essential for motor, cognitive, and social development (Thoman, Korner, and Beason-Williams, 1977).

Babies also are deprived of rhythmic stimulation by modern sleeping practices. McKenna believes that the practice of putting babies to sleep in cribs by themselves may increase the risk of SIDS. He proposes that the smell, touch, and movement of parents' bodies provide stimulation that helps regulate infant breathing. The regular rise and fall of the parent's chest and the sound of the parent's breathing may "remind" the infant to breathe. The child who suffers from sleep apnea may desperately need that reminder.

Most babies are in no danger from SIDS: the disorder strikes only one in 500 infants. Babies who have had bouts of apnea can be monitored during sleep. Researchers have developed an apnea monitor, a device that sounds an alarm if the baby should go for more than twenty seconds without taking a breath. The alarm alerts the parents, who then can rouse the baby; the rousing restarts the baby's breathing. Steinschneider (1975) has noted that when babies who have had recurrent episodes of sleep apnea are admitted to the hospital, the episodes decrease markedly. He conjectures that the noisy hospital surroundings keep babies from prolonged deep sleep, with its slowed heart rate. Most attacks of SIDS occur after midnight, when the house is likely to be quite. This has led Steinschneider to suggest that a radio playing in a sleeping baby's room might add enough noise to the environment to prevent some episodes of apnea.

---

cioeconomic level. Families living in poverty areas have an infant mortality rate that is 30 percent higher than that of families in other areas (Bronfenbrenner, Moen, and Garbarino, 1984). As we saw in Chapter 3, SGA (small-for-gestational age) babies who grow up in disadvantaged homes frequently have learning disabilities or neurological defects that SGA babies in middle-class homes escape. Children in low-income families are less likely to have a regular source of medical care than other children and so are less likely to have preventive medical attention (Butler, Starfield, and Stenmark, 1984).

Differences in nutrition and medical care may provide only a part of the explanation. Class differences in sleep and exercise habits and in home life generally may contribute to the effect. Meager resources and large families may combine to diminish the quality of maternal care, leading to slowed growth. In England (Acheson, 1960), social workers rated the "efficiency" of mothers (a measure that included how organized the mother seemed to be at meeting her child's basic needs). At all socioeconomic levels, the more efficient the mother, the taller the children. When inefficiency

was combined with poor socioeconomic conditions, the effect on growth was striking. In other studies (Butler, Starfield, and Stenmark, 1984), the mother's education accounted for some of the differences in children's health and the family's use of health services, even after income was accounted for.

Stress

Severe emotional stress can retard growth, apparently by affecting the body's secretion of hormones. Several hormones have important roles in the regulation of growth, but the growth hormone (GH) itself is one of the most important. At one time, children who lacked GH became midgets, perfectly proportioned adults about 4 feet tall. Until 1985, such children received injections of GH taken from human pituitary glands. After physicians discovered that the human extract could transmit lethal viruses, it was removed from the market. Today children who lack GH take Protropin, a synthetic form of GH produced through genetic engineering. Like human GH,

Protropin stimulates rapid catch-up growth. One youngster who took the new drug grew five inches the first year, and by the age of eleven was 52 inches tall. His height was expected to be within the normal range soon (Abramson, 1985).

So far as is known, the level of GH rises in the blood only a few times each day — about an hour or so after children go to sleep, after they exercise, and when they are anxious. GH stimulates the liver to produce the hormone somatomedin, which apparently stimulates growth through its action on cartilage cells at the ends of bones and probably on muscle cells as well. A single dose of GH keeps somatomedin blood levels high for at least twenty-four hours (Tanner, 1978).

In some children, severe psychological stress stops the production of GH. Like children whose bodies do not produce the hormone, they fail to grow. The onset of this condition, called **psychosocial dwarfism,** is associated with severe emotional distress in young children (Powell, Brasel, and Blizzard, 1967). Indeed, if affected children are removed from their disturbed environment, they show rapid catch-up growth.

MATURATION AND EXPERIENCE

How necessary are environmental supports in the mastery of motor skills? When children grow up in an environment that is both socially and physically impoverished, their development may lag severely. In a series of studies conducted in institutions with such environments, Wayne Dennis and his associates (Dennis, 1960; Dennis and Najarian, 1957; Dennis and Sayegh, 1965) found that children who were ignored by adults and surrounded by an unstimulating environment showed retarded motor development from the time they were two months old.

Because motor skills are canalized, however, normal development tends to reassert itself if the unsupportive environment is changed. In the Crèche, a Lebanese foundling home, infants spent most of their first year lying on their backs in cribs. Some of the infants studied by Wayne Dennis and Yvonne Sayegh (1965) were more than a year old but could not sit up. The infants in the experimental group were propped into a sitting position and allowed to spend an hour each day playing with such simple, attractive objects as fresh flowers, pieces of colored sponge, and colored plastic disks strung on a chain. This seemingly small amount of stimulation caused the babies' developmental age to jump dramatically.

Researchers have attempted to assess the relative contribution of maturation and experience to motor skills by using **co-twin control.** In this type of study, the investigator gives one of a pair of twins some experiences believed to be important in learning a skill and withholds or delays those same experiences for the other twin. In Myrtle McGraw's (1935; 1939) classic co-twin control study, one twin received practice in crawling and standing, and the other was kept from all opportunities. Despite the difference in their experience, both twins crawled and walked at the same age.

Yet we know that individual differences do appear in the rate of motor-skill mastery. Some children walk at ten months, others at fifteen. When a culture regularly supplies (or denies) certain experiences, the mastery of a particular skill may be accelerated (or delayed) in most of its members. Among the Kipsigis in Western Kenya, babies sit, stand, and walk earlier than most American babies do. However, they take longer to lift the head, crawl, and turn over. According to Charles Super (1976), Kipsigi mothers deliberately teach their babies to sit, stand, and walk, and the teaching methods are relatively standardized. For example, mothers play with their young babies by holding them under the arms and bouncing them on their laps. The baby responds with the stepping response, which does not disappear among Kipsigi infants. (In Chapter 3, we saw that American newborns who get active practice in the stepping response lose the response more slowly and begin walking early [Zelazo, 1983]). When Kipsigi babies are about seven months old, their mothers begin training them to walk. Mothers hold the infant under the arms or by the hands and, with the baby's feet on the ground, move the infant forward slowly.

This accelerated development of motor skills is significant — but it is not large. On the average,

CREATING SUPERBABIES

The boom in fitness has reached the nursery. Parents are enrolling three-month-old babies in exercise classes at Gymboree or Playorena franchise outlets; others are buying kiddie exercise-kits that include instructional video cassettes, plastic barbells, a baby balance beam, and a clutch ball to encourage eye-hand coordination (Kantrowitz and Joseph, 1986).

Do regular, intensive workouts accelerate motor development? Babies who would otherwise spend their days lying alone in a barren crib probably profit a great deal from such exercise. But these babies are unlikely to be enrolled in classes. No one yet has shown that the extra stimulation provided by exercise classes greatly accelerates the development of children's motor skills. As noted in the text, practice in motor skills appears to speed up the acquisition of skills such as sitting, crawling, or walking by as much as a month. Yet early development is so canalized that the early gains are likely to be washed out before many months pass. When a new motor skill emerges, there are wide differences among babies in their control of the skill. But once the skill becomes part of babies' general behavior pattern, differences between babies shrink markedly (Kopp, 1979). By the age of two, all toddlers act pretty much alike. We can say with some confidence that a history of regular workouts in an infant exercise class is unlikely to put a baby on the road to the Olympics.

Why do parents enroll their infants and toddlers in these classes? The mother of ten-month-old Emily Peterson told journalists that she wanted her daughter to be in good shape (Kantrowitz and Jo-

(Jacques Chenet/Woodfin Camp & Associates)

seph, 1986). Emily, who had been in exercise class since she was three months old, was bouncing on a trampoline and zooming down a miniature slide. Emily's mother was "into fitness." She worked out five times a week in an aerobics class.

Is there any reason to enroll an infant in an exercise class? The classes provide a structured setting that guarantees regular, intensive parent-infant interaction in families where parents are so busy that they let daily play periods slip by. Yet babies have a natural propensity for exercise. They hold their own exercise class in the crib. Their traditional games and nursery play with parents provide additional stimulation. So most babies, given a little space, interesting objects to play with, and plenty of interaction with parents, get all the exercise they need for healthy development.

Kipsigi babies walk about a month sooner than American babies. Similarly, Native American infants who spend their first year bound to cradle-boards and are denied practice in muscular coordination walk about a month later than other American babies. These variations both fall within the normal range of development for human infants. Canalization apparently both limits the amount of delay in the mastery of motor skills and places a ceiling on the degree of acceleration.

SUMMARY

1. Newborns continue to grow at the rapid fetal rate for several months after birth, primarily because they are born at an earlier stage of development than other primates. Infants develop in predictable ways because of the **canalization** of growth; genetic programming is so strong that human development is self-stabilizing and will appear in any normal human environment. Both physical growth and motor development follow the cephalocaudal, proximodistal patterns of development found in the fetus. Motor control involves the mastery of three tasks: bodily stability, locomotion, and limb manipulation. All must be mastered within a constantly changing environment.

2. **Norms** are typical patterns that describe the approximate ages at which important attributes and skills appear. Normal children vary widely on each side of a norm, and maturation rates seem related to body build. An individual's progress toward maturity can be measured by tooth eruption or skeletal age. When growth is disrupted by severe malnutrition or illness, later **catch-up growth** generally returns the child to his or her normal pattern.

3. The development of motor control is correlated with development in specific areas of the **cortex**, although new behavior also depends on development in sensory receptors and the spinal cord and on the growth of joints and muscles. The immature brain is more plastic than the adult brain. Stimulation is necessary for the development of the nervous system, and environmental stimulation may begin modifying the brain during the last month before birth.

4. Depth perception seems to emerge gradually at some time between three and six months. Some crawling experience seems necessary before the baby can use depth cues to keep from falling over edges.

5. As a skill develops, the coalitions of muscles and joints may change, so that the skill either becomes clumsy or temporarily disappears. Babies' skill at reaching out and grasping an object develops through, first, an open-handed swoop among newborns that signifies attention; second, a closed-fisted reach at two months that indicates a breakdown in the reflexive motor pattern; third, an open-handed, visually directed grasp at five months; and fourth, a highly accurate, skilled grasp at nine months that no longer requires the baby's full attention. Handedness is established slowly, with periods when hand preference seems to disappear. By the time they are eighteen months old, about half of children consistently use the same hand; yet some children do not settle on one hand until they are five years old. The newborn's stepping response, which is probably generated in the spinal cord, seems to form the basis for later walking.

6. Children's skill at physical games depends on strength, speed, and coordination. Until children are three years old, there is no difference in strength between the sexes. At three, boys become stronger than girls, and from eighteen months, boys are much more likely than girls to enjoy rough-and-tumble play. Rough-and-tumble play may lead to formation and consolidation of friendships, although it also provides a safe way to practice aggression.

7. Environmental factors, such as nutrition, illness, stress, and the quality of maternal care, can either promote or impede a child's growth. Severe malnutrition in infancy can disrupt brain development, and long-term, severe, chronic malnutrition generally leads to low scores on cognitive tests. **Kwashiorkor,** which is caused by prolonged protein deficiency, leads to slowed growth, severe mental retardation, or even death. **Obesity,** or excessive fatness, is becoming more common among American children. Genes, a heightened responsiveness to environmental stimuli, eating habits, and lack of exercise all seem involved in its development. In all countries, children in upper socioeconomic classes grow more rapidly and are healthier than children in lower socioeconomic classes, perhaps because of differences in nutrition, preventive medical care,

sleep and exercise habits, and general home life. Stress can affect the production of growth hormone, either slowing or stopping normal growth.

8. Psychologists have studied the relative roles of maturation and experience by comparing the age at which infants in different cultures acquire certain skills, by **co-twin control** studies, and by assessing the results of restrictions in a child's experience. Canalization apparently both limits the amount of delay in the mastery of motor skills and places a ceiling on the degree of acceleration.

KEY TERMS

canalization
catch-up growth
cortex
co-twin control

kwashiorkor
neuron
norms
obesity

positron emission tomography (PET)
sleep apnea
sudden infant death syndrome (SIDS)

STUDY TERMS

canalization Genetic programming that is extremely difficult to deflect from its course and that is self-stabilizing when temporarily deflected.

catch-up growth A period of rapid growth that returns a child to his or her normal growth curve after a condition that has been retarding growth is eliminated.

cortex The mantle of neural cells that covers the two cerebral hemispheres; it is heavily involved in sensation, speech, learning, memory and voluntary movements.

norms Typical patterns of growth or performance, describing the approximate ages at which important attributes and skills appear.

CHAPTER 6

Cognition: From Sensing to Knowing

David, who is fifteen months old, has discovered his mother's pen, which was lying open on the coffee table. When his mother comes to check on her quiet son, she finds ink on his mouth, on his hands, and on his clothes. She takes away the pen, puts it on a high shelf and, when David protests, picks him up for a moment. As soon as she puts him down, he toddles over to the shelf, stretches out his arm, opens and closes his fingers, and says "Day-boo"—his word for himself—to indicate that he wants the pen. Although he cannot see the pen, he knows that it is lying on the shelf. David has not always been so persistent. When he was eight months old, he forgot about forbidden playthings when his mother distracted him. But now that he is older, his memory has developed, and he has a mental image of the forbidden toy.

Since the day of his entry into this exciting, often puzzling world, David has taken some important steps on the journey called cognitive development, and he still has many challenging adventures ahead of him.

In this chapter, we follow the development of the child's mind during infancy and toddlerhood. After distinguishing between learning and cognition, we pick up some of the same topics we examined in the neonate. We discover that babies find some things more interesting than others and try to determine what factors attract their attention. Next we look at the basic learning processes, discovering what they tell us about the minds of infants and toddlers. As we watch the development of memory, we find that the process is selective and that the context may determine how much a baby or toddler remembers. We examine the stages of cognitive growth in infancy, tracing the baby's separation of self from the world. Finally, we explore the implications of mental representation, as revealed in the child's understanding of the object concept, egocentrism, search strategies, and pretend play.

LEARNING AND COGNITION

The lengthy story of cognitive development is the story of how children progress from the limited and poorly organized store of knowledge and intellectual skills they possess at birth to the concept-rich, well-ordered store of knowledge that most adults use so well. By the time we complete our tale of the first four years, we will have seen babies and toddlers as remarkably active organisms, curious about the world and themselves and eager to make sense of them both. We will watch them use their varied experiences to construct new hypotheses—about how the parts fit and mesh, and about which of their actions are permissible and which forbidden. We will see them as architects of time, space, and objects and as designers and users of symbols.

During the first half of this century, the description of this process focused on **learning,** which is the process of acquiring new information. At that time, developmental psychologists were heavily influenced by behavior-learning theories, and they were trying to discover the general laws of learning—laws that described the process equally well in rats, in babies, or in college students. Most researchers used studies of classical or operant conditioning to trace the child's growth of understanding. But instead of talking about acquiring "information," psychologists talked about the acquisition of "responses to stimuli" and restricted their definition of learning to

changes in behavior. The child's mind (as well as that of the adult) was a "black box" that few psychologists tried to explore.

Many psychologists became dissatisfied with this approach. Instead of seeing children as learners, they saw them as thinkers. Instead of interpreting their research in terms of responses to stimuli, researchers began talking about children's expectations. They were now interested in what took place between the stimulus and the response. Instead of seeing changed behavior and learning as synonymous, cognitive psychologists regarded behavior as the *result* of learning (Stevenson, 1983). Today, developmentalists study **cognition,** which includes all the processes of representing information and using it: perceiving, using symbols, learning, remembering, thinking, planning, reasoning, and fantasizing. Learning is still regarded as a central aspect of cognition, but it is no longer the entire story. From birth, infants attend to objects and people in their world and learn about the properties and actions of both. Attention is one of the cognitive processes that researchers have studied extensively.

ATTENTION

Attention is important because it plays a key role in the baby's gathering of information. What the baby thinks and learns about depends on what the baby perceives, and this perception is directed by attention. Babies prefer some patterns and colors to others, but they prefer any pattern to a plain stimulus—no matter how colorful it is. Robert Fantz (1961) showed infants ranging in age from two to six months a set of six flat disks. Three of the disks were patterned; the other three had no patterns but were brightly colored. At all ages, babies looked longer at the patterned than at the brightly colored but unpatterned disks (see Figure 6.1). Babies may pay more attention to pattern than to color because pattern is more informative.

As babies grow older, the qualities of a stimulus that *attract* their attention do not change. Bold patterns, large objects, motion, sudden changes of illumination, and loud sounds will attract a baby's attention at any age (Olson and Sherman, 1983).

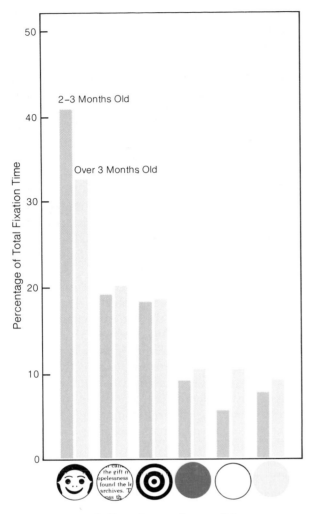

FIGURE 6.1   In Fantz's experiment, disks were shown to infants in a looking chamber. Fixation-time percentages indicate that, whether the infants were younger or older than three months, they looked at pattern longer than at color or brightness. *(Adapted from Fantz, 1961)*

Young babies find human faces the most fascinating objects in their world, and by the age of two months the baby's attention focuses on the eyes. *(Alice Kandell/Photo Researchers)*

But attracting attention and holding it are two different processes (Daehler and Bukatko, 1985). A baby's attention may be momentarily grabbed by a blinking light or the crash of a dropped plate, but when nothing else happens, attention wanders to some other object in the environment. As babies learn more about the world, the characteristics that *hold* their attention change. They prefer increasingly complex sights, such as objects with more angles or more elements. For example, a design with 128 small squares scattered over it holds a four-month-old's attention much longer than a design of the same size with two large squares. Yet both designs are equally fascinating to newborns (Fantz, Fagan, and Miranda, 1975).

After babies are about three months old, their previous experience seems to play an increasing role in determining what holds their attention. Babies seem to watch an object as long as they can glean new information from it. In one study (Hunter, Ames, and Koopman, 1983), researchers placed several toys in front of eight- and twelve-month-olds. Most babies played with toys that were new to them. But if their play session was stopped before they had finished exploring a new toy, the babies went back to it at the next play session instead of picking up a toy they had never seen before.

To investigate the cognitive aspects of attention, some researchers have studied the baby's response to a human face. By two weeks, babies can tell the difference between facelike and nonfacial patterns, and they prefer to look at faces (Fagan, 1979). One-month-olds tend to inspect details along the edge of the face, such as the chin or the ear — where contour is obvious and contrast is

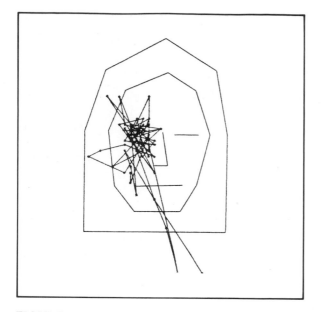

FIGURE 6.2   **This computer-generated pattern reflects the eye movements of an eight-week-old infant when shown a color photograph of a human face; notice the concentration of gaze in the region of the eye, indicating increased attention to internal features of the face.** *(Adapted from Hainline, 1978)*

highest. Two-month-olds gaze instead at features within the face, such as the nose, the mouth, or an eye (Maurer and Salapatek, 1976). The eyes seem to hold a special interest for the two-month-old baby (see Figure 6.2). In one study (Hainline, 1978), eyes drew the attention of two-month-olds under all conditions — whether the face remained still, moved slightly from side to side, or talked. Not even the mouth movements involved in speech draw a baby's attention away from the eyes (Haith, Bergman, and Moore, 1977).

Perhaps babies are attracted from the periphery of the face to the eyes because, as they mature, they come to see the face as a meaningful entity instead of simply as a collection of features. By this time, the eyes may have taken on social meaning. Babies may have learned that when a face is accompanied by speech, fixing their attention on the eyes keeps the sound of the human voice going. Gradually, the infant discovers the invariant features of the face, which remain unchanged from pose to pose, and integrates its parts into a meaningful configuration (Fagan, 1979).

By five months, babies can tell one photographed face from another; they can distinguish between photos of a woman and a baby or a woman and a man; by seven months they can distinguish between two dissimilar men (Fagan, 1979). They also can distinguish between expressions of sorrow and anger, and they do not like an angry face. Five-month-olds keep gazing at the photograph of a sorrowful face but look away when shown an angry face (Schwartz, Izard, and Ansul, 1985). All of these tasks with photographs are much more difficult than recognizing actual familiar people, because photos have so few cues. In their homes, where voices, odors, and the movements of animated faces provide additional cues, babies have been recognizing their mothers and fathers since they were about two months old.

Like the rest of us, babies and toddlers pay close attention to the people and objects that interest them. Toddlers deploy their attention more effectively than babies do, but their selectivity affects what they are likely to notice and remember. In a recent study (Renninger and Wozniak, 1985), researchers used videotapes of two- and three-year-olds at play to identify the youngsters' special interests. Later the children completed a series of tasks that required them to remember objects that were pictured on cards. In each task, pictures of the child's special interest, such as cars, horses, dolls, or bears, were included. No matter what their age, children remembered the pictures of objects they were interested in far better than they remembered other objects.

BASIC LEARNING PROCESSES

When we talk about learning, we are referring to processes that lead to developmental change when the child interacts with the environment. Babies are born into an unfamiliar world and immediately begin gathering information about this strange environment. They learn to recognize specific objects — mother, the juice bottle, a rattle. They learn where objects are located — the cookie jar in the kitchen, the television in the family room, their crib in the bedroom. They learn which events fol-

The same learning processes that psychologists study in the laboratory are demonstrated by babies who indicate that they know their favorite food comes from the big white box in the kitchen. *(Bruce Plotkin/ The Image Works)*

low one another—bedtime follows story hour, playtime comes after Mommy and Daddy arrive home from work, the cat scratches when you pull its tail, and a toy dropped from the highchair falls onto the floor. Infants and toddlers also learn many skills—how to roll a ball, how to climb up on a chair, and how to ride a tricycle.

This wide variety of behavior is based on learning processes, including habituation, conditioning, and imitation. The process of learning itself depends on other cognitive processes—on the way babies perceive a stimulus, how they represent that information, and whether they register it so that it can be retrieved. Unless babies can re-

member what they have seen, heard, and touched, they must rediscover the world anew each day.

Habituation

Most studies of young infants' cognitive abilities rely on habituation, in which babies watch a stimulus until they stop paying attention. As we saw in Chapter 4, their boredom reflects their increasing knowledge about the stimulus and indicates that they have learned something about it. Habituation has given us a window through which we can infer the cognitive processes of infancy. Using this simple form of learning, researchers have tested babies' ability to detect various stimuli, to tell the differences among them, to remember them, to classify them into groups, and to develop concepts (Bornstein and Benasich, 1986).

Babies habituate to some stimuli faster and more efficiently than they do to others. They habituate faster to conspicuous stimuli than to less conspicuous, complex stimuli; faster to happy faces than to other expressions; faster to three-dimensional objects than to photographs or drawings; and faster to stimuli they prefer than to stimuli that they do not find particularly interesting (Bornstein, 1985). Babies also habituate more quickly as they get older: newborns habituate only under special conditions, three-month-olds habituate relatively slowly, and seven-month olds habituate rapidly. This increase in efficiency is due in part to the maturation of the cortex, which gradually takes over control from lower parts of the brain, and in part to the baby's increasing knowledge of the world.

There are wide individual differences in the speed and efficiency with which babies habituate. As we saw in Chapter 4, such differences are apparent in the first week of life. Babies who habituate quickly (often with only a single trial) and show a rapid recovery of interest when they see a novel sight or hear novel sounds are acquiring information about the stimulus rapidly. After reviewing the research, Marc Bornstein and Marian Sigman (1986) found that this pattern of habituation and recovery is associated with intellectual functioning in early childhood. Babies younger than six months who are highly efficient at representing and recalling visual and auditory stimuli tend to have higher than average scores on standard tests of verbal ability as preschoolers. Other longitudinal studies have shown a similar connection between a preference for novel stimuli at six months and the IQ scores of six-year-olds (Rose and Wallace, 1985).

Conditioning

Praise and attention are typical reinforcers that condition youngsters; they strengthen whatever response they customarily follow. Babies who are picked up *only* when they cry learn to cry for attention. They do this because their wails are reinforced, but their other social overtures (smiling, cooing) are not. Older infants whose attempts to communicate are consistently reinforced by parental attention and praise are likely to speak more frequently than infants whose parents seem oblivious to their early words. Toddlers whose forays into the street are quickly punished by angry scolding are less likely to step off the curb again soon. In Chapter 8, we will see that the stereotypical ways in which parents treat their infants and toddlers reinforce independence in boys and dependence in girls.

By arranging for babies to get a reward only for specific actions, researchers have successfully conditioned babies to suck, smile, cry, turn their heads, look, or kick (Lancioni, 1980). The rewards that have proved effective are quite varied. One of them is the privilege to see a sharply focused picture. Ilze Kalnins and Jerome Bruner (1973) placed five- to twelve-week-old babies where they could see a blurred color movie of Eskimo life. When the babies began sucking on a pacifier, an opaque plastic screen rotated away from the camera lens and the picture became sharp. As long as the babies sucked at the rate of 0.75 sucks per second, the picture remained clear. But when sucking lagged, the screen moved back over the lens and the picture blurred. The babies soon learned to increase their rate of sucking. Yet when the control was reversed, so that sucking blurred the picture, the babies were not able to inhibit their sucking even though they averted their gaze from a blurred screen (see Figure 6.3). This difference in response is consistent with the results of conditioning studies reported in Chapter 4: sucking is a response that enhances survival, so the baby is prepared to suck. Asking babies to stop sucking a nipple is asking them to respond in a way that goes against their biological preparation.

How rapidly a baby learns seems to be connected with the baby's temperament. In a study of two- and three-month-olds, infants were given a chance to work a mobile that was suspended above the crib (Dunst and Lingerfelt, 1985). A ribbon tied around one ankle was attached to the mobile, and when the babies kicked that foot, the mobile bounced and swayed. All the babies learned to kick the correct foot in order to make the mobile bounce, but some babies learned more quickly than others. Many of the fast learners were babies whose mothers described them as highly consistent in their sleep-wake cycles, mealtimes, and periods of fussiness. The regularity of their biological functions may have given them an early opportunity to learn about the predictability of events. Babies whose mothers described them as highly attentive to events in their world also learned quickly. It seems reasonable that babies who pay attention to what is going on have an increased opportunity to learn which events follow one another.

From the results of such conditioning experiments, we might suppose that rewarding babies and toddlers is a royal road to easy child rearing. Handing out cookies and praise when children act appropriately would seem to guarantee clever, well-behaved children. Unfortunately, rewards do not always strengthen children's responses. In a lengthy series of experiments, Mark Lepper (1983) has shown that when children are rewarded for some activity they normally enjoy, they become *less* likely to engage in that activity in the future. For example, three-year-olds who enjoyed playing with colored markers were offered "Good Player Awards" (a colored card with a large gold star and a red ribbon) if they used the markers to draw pictures for the researcher. The children eagerly agreed, drew their pictures, and accepted their awards. Other youngsters either were praised (no tangible reward) for drawing pictures or else were given Good Player Awards although they had not expected them. A week later, the children were observed at play. Children who had been praised and those who had received an unexpected award were using the magic markers as frequently as they had before (see Figure 6.4). But children who had received an expected award

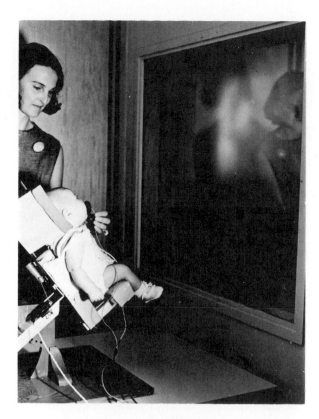

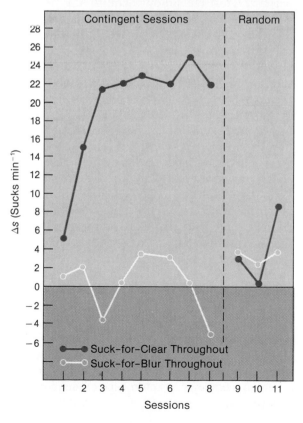

FIGURE 6.3   **When young infants could clear a blurred movie by sucking on a nipple, they quickly learned to keep the picture sharp (contingent). But when their sucking no longer had an effect on the picture (random), it quickly dropped back to normal levels ("0"). Babies whose sucking blurred the picture could not learn to keep it clear; instead, they averted their gaze.** *(Halftones courtesy Dr. Ilze Kalnins; graph from Kalnins and Bruner, 1973)*

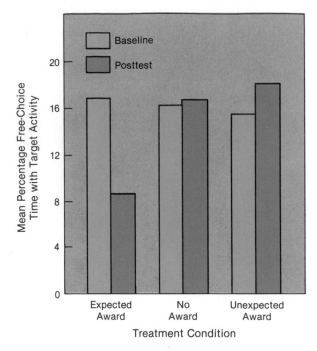

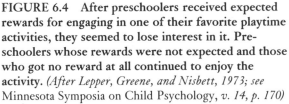

FIGURE 6.4 **After preschoolers received expected rewards for engaging in one of their favorite playtime activities, they seemed to lose interest in it. Preschoolers whose rewards were not expected and those who got no reward at all continued to enjoy the activity.** *(After Lepper, Greene, and Nisbett, 1973; see* Minnesota Symposia on Child Psychology, *v. 14, p. 170)*

were paying little attention to the markers—they spent about half as much time with the pens as they had before they got the awards (Lepper, Greene, and Nisbett, 1973).

Why did the rewards backfire? Mark Twain (1876) explained the process in *Tom Sawyer*: "Work consists of whatever a body is *obliged* to do. . . . Play consists of whatever a body is not obliged to do." When children engage in some activity spontaneously, they see the activity as fun: they are intrinsically motivated. But when children undertake the same activity to get a reward, their spontaneous enjoyment fades. It is Lepper's (1983) contention that in such cases, children perceive that they are being controlled by others, and their intrinsic interest in the activity is undermined. Along with the promised rewards go surveillance by adults (to make certain that the task is completed), the expectation of being evaluated, and the pressure to complete the task by a certain time. Play suddenly becomes work. However, once children are old enough to compare their performance with that of others, rewards that depend on successful performance (an award for the best picture or a place on the Honor Roll) are unlikely to destroy intrinsic interest. They give the child no reason to consider why he or she undertook the activity; instead, they serve as information about the child's competence.

Learning to Control the Environment

The feeling of control over the environment is important even to young babies. Three-month-olds who kicked to make the mobile bounce were not working for a sweet drink or to please an adult. By experimenting, they had learned that kicking was an effective way to get the mobile to do their bidding. Their activity was intrinsically motivated, and they were controlling it. Some years ago, John Watson and Craig Ramey (1972) explored the importance of control and the unpleasant consequences of helplessness. They placed a pressure-sensitive pillow beneath the heads of eight-week-old babies. When the infants turned their heads to the side, a switch inside the pillow tripped, and a colorful mobile above their heads began to move. Before long, the infants began turning their heads to operate the display. From their coos and delighted smiles, it was clear that the infants were pleased. A second group of infants lay beneath the same display, but they had no control over its movements. Instead, the mobile's motions were started and stopped by a timer. These babies soon lost interest in the mobile and rarely smiled. Later, when the pressure-sensitive pillow was placed beneath their heads, the babies made no attempt to control the display. Apparently, they had learned that they were helpless to control the environment.

Infants seem to have an urge to understand the environment and to manage it. They seek out tasks that promote learning and increase their competence. When they succeed in mastering some task, most infants show joy—or at least satisfaction (Dweck and Elliott, 1983). But when infants discover that they are powerless to control the environment, they may develop **learned helplessness.**

If they do, they may become apathetic, unresponsive youngsters who make no effort to master new tasks or to initiate social interactions.

Most infants are in little danger of developing learned helplessness. Their experiences with their parents and other caregivers generally foster their sense of control. Their cries are likely to bring comfort; their smiles and coos to evoke enjoyable social stimulation. As we saw in Chapter 4, newborns already are controlling the rate and pace of social interactions.

Imitation

Babies and toddlers learn a great deal from the successes and failures of their own efforts. But they also learn from watching others. If they were forced to discover everything for themselves, the process of learning how to do things and when—or when not—to do them would make many normal cognitive advances difficult, if not impossible. Because observational learning is so important, developmentalists have tried to discover just how early babies can imitate people around them. Attempts to fix that date have led to a great deal of controversy.

For decades, psychologists have agreed that babies of eight weeks or so will imitate an adult who has first imitated a habitual response of the baby's, but this has been regarded as "pseudoimitation." Not until the latter part of the first year were infants supposed to be able to imitate actions they could neither see nor hear themselves perform, such as opening and closing their eyes or mimicking facial expressions.

Then, in 1977, Andrew Meltzoff and Keith Moore reported that babies of two, three, or six weeks old would stick out their tongues, protrude their lips, open their mouths, and open and close their fists in mimicry of an adult's actions. More recently, Meltzoff and Moore (1983) tested forty newborns who were less than three days old. These babies seemed to be born imitators: they often opened their mouths or stuck out their tongues when the experimenters modeled the action for them. Despite Meltzoff and Moore's consistent success, many researchers have been unable to replicate their findings (e.g., Koepke, Hamm, Legerstee, and Russell, 1983). These researchers suggest that when psychologists find imitation, they inadvertently have influenced the outcome of their experiment. For example, the investigator may stick out his or her tongue until the infant just happens to respond in a similar fashion.

However, if Meltzoff and Moore's findings are generally replicated, there may be a serious rethinking of infant cognitive development. This sort of imitation would require babies to form some mental representation of what they have seen and match it to sensory information from their own mouths, lips, tongues, and fingers. Most theories of cognitive development deny that very young infants can form representations. Yet it seems unlikely that these babies have been conditioned to respond to adult facial contortions. As we saw in Chapter 4, newborns are alert for very short periods and would have had little opportunity for learning.

One possible explanation is that researchers have been studying a releasing mechanism—an unconditioned response that babies automatically tend to make whenever anything moves toward mouth or hands. Sandra Jacobson (1979) has discovered that six-week-old babies also stick out their tongues if a small white ball or a black felt-tipped pen is moved toward their mouths, held there for a few seconds, and then moved away. Other researchers (Abravanel and Sigafoos, 1984) have found that four- to six-week-olds seem to stick out their tongues reflexively but that the response disappears by about the tenth week.

Such an explanation gets some support from research by Annie Vintner (1986), who believes that movement may provide the key to the puzzle. In a study with newborns, she found that babies responded to the moving face, not to the expression. She proposes that movements may not be detected and processed by the cortex, which processes detailed visual information. Instead, the babies may be relying on subcortical visual processes, because at this time most of the babies' actions are under subcortical control. If so, whatever "representations" the babies are using are very different from the symbolic representations that develop during the second year of life.

Toward the end of the first year, the possibility of observational learning develops. For the first time, babies can imitate behavior that is entirely new to them. Now they no longer have to stumble

When this toddler picked up the newspaper and imitated his parents' customary action, his deferred imitation demonstrated his ability to represent information symbolically. *(Jean-Claude Lejeune/Stock, Boston)*

imitated the researcher's actions. But at first, the ability to imitate is limited. In another study, twelve-month-olds also imitated simple actions, such as placing a crown on a doll's head, after a ten-minute delay (Abravanel and Gingold, 1985). But almost none could imitate a simple, repetitive action (such as stacking three blocks in the correct order) or a task that required two different actions in a given order (such as using a drumstick to push a doll out of a clear plastic cylinder). A majority of eighteen-month-olds were successful on such tasks.

Such imitations are primitive symbols and provide evidence for the existence of other symbols within the child's mind. These mental symbols cannot be observed, but adults can infer their presence from the child's actions. When two-year-old Susan watches her father read and the next day picks up a book and pretends to read herself, we can infer that Susan has created a mental image of her father in the act of reading. This memory is a condensed, internal imitation, in thought rather than in action, and it allows the child to imitate some action long after the event. The symbolic nature of imitation makes it a milestone in intellectual development, because symbolic representation forms the basis for human civilization: for language, mathematics, science, and the arts (Piaget, 1951).

MEMORY IN INFANTS AND TODDLERS

Memory is basic to any kind of learning, so infants clearly can remember. Among the questions researchers are trying to answer are "How long can the baby remember?" and "Under what conditions?" As we saw in Chapter 4, newborns can remember a stimulus for five to ten seconds and can detect a difference between that memory and another stimulus. As babies grow, it takes them less time to register sights in memory, and so when they are allowed to look at a pattern or some other stimulus for a specified length of time, they show gradual improvements with age in their ability to retain a memory. But when they are allowed to look at an object until they lose interest, even two-month-old babies seem to remember sights as well

accidentally onto some new action but can learn it by watching others. However, they can only imitate some action immediately after they have seen it performed. Then, during the second year, their ability to imitate what they see and hear advances markedly. They become able to defer their imitations. They can imitate on Wednesday the actions they saw their parents perform on Monday or Tuesday.

The glimmerings of deferred imitation appear soon after a child's first birthday. In an experimental situation, some fourteen-month-olds watched a researcher demonstrate a very simple action that involved pulling apart a small toy held together by a piece of rigid plastic tubing (Meltzoff, 1985). After a twenty-four-hour delay, these youngsters as older babies do. This finding suggests that although there are age differences among babies in the speed of encoding visual information, once it is processed, retention probably does not differ (Werner and Perlmutter, 1979).

Babies begin forgetting almost immediately. Within the first month, babies may forget a design they have been gazing at in less than a minute yet remember a learned response from one day to the next (Olson and Sherman, 1983). By the time they are five or six months old, babies will recognize a black-and-white photograph of a human face after a lapse of two weeks—although within three hours they forget a facelike mask they have seen (Fagan, 1979).

Selective Memory

Forgetting seems to be both selective and a gradual process, with first one, then another aspect of a stimulus fading from memory (Kail, 1985). Such a pattern of forgetting appeared among five-month-olds who looked at various designs (Strauss and Cohen, 1980). A few seconds after the babies looked at a large black arrow, they remembered its size, color, shape, and the direction in which it was pointed. Fifteen minutes later, they remembered only its shape and color. The next day, they remembered only that they had seen an arrow.

Carolyn Rovee-Collier (1984) believes that babies selectively process events and are likely to remember some response that has had an effect on their world. For that reason, she has focused on babies' recognition of a mobile that they have controlled with foot kicks. In a study with Eleanor Vander Linde and Barbara Morrongiello (1985), Rovee-Collier discovered that after a week's delay, two-month-old babies can recognize a mobile that they have operated for eighteen minutes with foot kicks. If two weeks pass before they see the mobile again, they fail to recognize it. But when the sessions are rearranged so that instead of spending one eighteen-minute session with the mobile, the babies get to operate it six minutes at a time in three sessions spread over a week, they can recognize the mobile after a lapse of two weeks (see Figure 6.5).

Why should breaking the training into three short sessions improve a young baby's memory?

The researchers believe that when babies have three opportunities with a mobile, they probably notice different features at each session. Two weeks later, in the test session, there are more cues to remind them of the original situation. Indeed, when babies recognize events after delays of several weeks, the world has probably supplied them with cues to help them locate the events in memory. In an earlier study with Janet Davis, Rovee-Collier (Davis and Rovee-Collier, 1983) showed that when two-month-olds forget how to operate the mobile after two weeks, the memory still may be stored although it is inaccessible. Seventeen days after two-month-olds learned to work a mobile, they watched a researcher operate it—but were not allowed to operate it themselves. The next day, as soon as the ribbon was tied to an ankle, the babies began operating the mobile. Such reencounters with objects and events in the baby's daily life may explain the persistence of memories in young babies. As babies develop, their memory keeps improving; ten- or twelve-month-olds can hold events longer in memory, need fewer cues to remember past events, and find it easier to compare present events with stored knowledge of the past than younger babies.

Recalling the Past

Most research with infants indicates that they can recognize objects they have seen before, but little experimental evidence exists to indicate that they can remember an object that is not present. **Recall** is more complex than recognition, because it takes place in the absence of the object or information to be remembered. By the time they are about seven months old, babies begin to show some evidence of recall in their daily lives. When parents of seven- to eleven-month-old babies were asked to record any incidents of recall, they reported many such instances (Ashmead and Perlmutter, 1980). Most babies remembered where household items, such as baby lotion, belonged and showed surprise when an item was not in its correct place. They searched for people or objects and remembered the routines of such games as peekaboo. The natural surroundings of home helped these babies to remember common routines and objects. The assistance of parents was also an important factor,

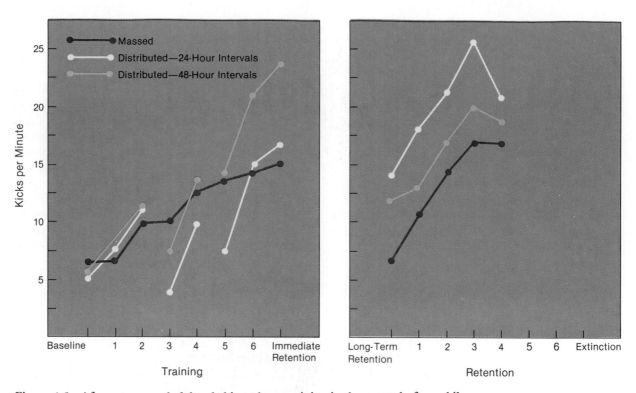

Figure 6.5   **After a two-week delay, babies whose training in the control of a mobile had been distributed over several sessions showed clear evidence that they remembered their formal training. Babies with the same amount of training massed in a single session had to relearn that their kicks controlled the mobile.** *(From Linde, Morrongiello, and Rovee-Collier, 1985)*

for parents generally structure infants' attempts to remember and often provide memory cues during social interactions (Paris, Newman, and Jacobs, 1985).

This parental assistance is especially helpful with toddlers, whose memory skills are improving rapidly. Most families have familiar routines: pets must be fed, baths taken, teeth brushed, prayers said at night. When researchers (Wellman and Somerville, 1980) asked parents of toddlers to see if the youngsters could remember these routines by themselves, many were successful. Even one-year-olds remembered old, established routines, although they sometimes needed slight prompting. Two- and three-year-olds remembered the old routines and learned new ones as well. Parents reported that shortly after they began expecting the toddlers to remember the routines without help, the youngsters showed a marked improvement in their ability to remember them.

The important role played by parents in the toddler's expanding memory skills became clear when researchers observed mothers looking at picture books with their seventeen- to twenty-two-month-old children (Ninio, 1983). The mothers were sensitive to their children's level of knowledge, simply providing labels when children showed that they did not know the word for a pictured object, but asking questions ("Where is the puppy?" "What's that?") when children showed that they understood the word. By requiring youngsters to generate stored information, parents apparently promote children's ability to regulate their own memory (Price, 1984).

By the time they are three years old, most toddlers sing advertising jingles and chant nursery rhymes, and their recall of parental promises is almost perfect. Researchers (Somerville, Wellman, and Cultice, 1983) have studied this sort of intentional memory in two- to four-year-olds.

During repeated picture-book reading, mothers help strengthen their toddlers' memory skills by giving them a chance to generate stored information. *(Robert McElroy/Woodfin Camp & Associates)*

Parents asked children to remind them to do something in the future, such as take the laundry out of the dryer or buy candy for the child at the supermarket. Four-year-olds were much better than two-year-olds when they were supposed to remind parents about dull tasks. But when the task interested the child, two-year-olds' memory was equally good: they remembered to remind their parents about promised treats 80 percent of the time.

Two- and three-year-olds often do poorly on formal tests of memory, especially tests that ask them to recall several objects. When shown nine toys, for example, most three-year-olds remember only two of them. What accounts for the difference between their poor showing in the psychological lab and their extensive recall at home? When toddlers take part in a memory experiment, they are in an unfamiliar setting, and they face tasks that require sophisticated language skills, speedy response, focused attention, cooperation with strangers, and the application of their memory skills to strange tasks that bear little similarity to their daily experiences (Wellman and Somerville, 1982). Many young children also seem unaware of the techniques used by their elders to register information in memory. They use inappropriate search techniques to retrieve the information, and—even when they have the information—their limited verbal ability makes it difficult for them to produce it (Perlmutter, 1980).

By the time children are three years old, however, some have learned to use rehearsal as an aid to recall (Weissberg and Paris, 1986). When three-year-olds were asked to memorize a list of six words, nearly half of them audibly repeated the words to themselves. After a delay of sixty to ninety seconds, the children recalled from 2.5 to 3 words from the list. These children recalled more words when memorizing a list than they did when the memorization was part of a game. The researchers speculated that nursery school experience, wide exposure to televison, and parents' behavior increase young children's familiarity with remembering as a goal itself. In the past few years, American children may have become more likely to use memory-aiding techniques (such as rehearsal) than children in other cultures (Istomina, 1975).

SENSORIMOTOR THOUGHT

A growing memory indicates that a baby's store of knowledge about the world is mounting. But knowing that a baby recognizes a mobile or recalls a game tells us almost nothing about what that toy or game means to the baby. As infants move from reflexive, self-centered creatures to symbol-using individuals who act purposefully on their surroundings, they gradually come to understand the world. The story of this change details the appearance and gradual development of thought. Because Piaget's (1951; 1952; 1954) picture of this transformation is so comprehensive, it provides us with a useful way to look at cognition in infancy.

The baby's own activity spurs cognitive development, and the baby's principal tools are assimilation and accommodation, which were discussed in Chapter 2. When three-month-old babies are offered their first chance to drink from a cup, for example, they first try to assimilate the cup to their current mouth-using skills, sucking at the cup's edge as they suck at a nipple. When this does not work, babies modify, or accommodate, those mouth-using skills so that they are as effective with the hard rim of the cup as they were with the soft nipple. As babies grow, they continue to use old responses on new objects and then modify

While mouthing a hard metal pan, babies first try old responses (assimilation) on the object, then modify those responses (accommodation) as they explore the object's form, texture, solidity, and taste. *(Linda Rogers/Woodfin Camp & Associates)*

those old responses, thus learning to adapt to a widening world.

Piaget developed his account of the **sensorimotor stage** by carefully observing his three children —Jacqueline, Lucienne, and Laurent—and frequently intervening in their activities to study their reactions. He concluded that thought during this period progresses through six substages, in which babies' behavior reflects the contents of their minds (see Table 6.1). Babies move through the substages at different rates, with each substage representing a clear advance in cognitive development.

Substage 1 — Reflex Acts

The first substage covers the neonatal period. During the first month of independent life, babies' responses to sights and sounds, smells and tastes, pressure and touch are not purposeful investigations of the world. Instead they are reflexive responses babies possessed when they entered the

world. Much of their behavior is a response to internal stimulation, and many of their actions seem rigidly programmed. For example, if you brush a baby's mouth or cheek with your finger, the baby will suck reflexively. Yet these seemingly inflexible actions can be affected by experience. As Piaget (1954) observed:

> Laurent, as early as the second day, seems to seek with his lips the breast which has escaped him. . . . From the third day he gropes more systematically to find it. . . . He searches in the same way for his thumb, which brushed his mouth or came out of it. . . . Thus it seems that the contact of the lips with the nipple and the thumb gives rise to a pursuit of those objects, once they have disappeared, a pursuit connected with reflex activity in the first case and with a nascent or acquired habit in the second case. (P. 8)

Habits are acquired through experience; they are learned. Using operant conditioning, Arnold Sameroff (1968) showed how newborns learn to modify their reflexive sucking. One group of infants could get milk only by squeezing the nipple

Table 6.1
Stages of Sensorimotor Thought

Substage 1 (0–1 month)*	Reflex acts	Rigid, stereotyped reflexive actions Reflexive imitation
Substage 2 (1–4 months)	Primary circular reactions	Sensorimotor schemes based on reflexes Pseudoimitation; babies imitate immediate imitations of their own actions
Substage 3 (4–8 months)	Secondary circular reactions	Sensorimotor schemes based on learning True imitation of actions babies already perform, but only if they can see themselves performing the act
Substage 4 (8–12 months)	Coordination of secondary schemes	Intentional acts toward goals Observational learning through immediate imitation of simple actions
Substage 5 (12–18 months)	Tertiary circular reactions	Solution of problems through overt trial and error Immediate imitation of acts, perhaps some deferred imitation of very simple, single actions
Substage 6 (18–24 months)	Symbolic thought	Solution of problems through mental trial and error Representation of objects by mental symbols Deferred imitation of more complicated actions

* Ages approximate

between the tongue and palate; the other group could get milk only by lowering the bottom jaw to create a partial vacuum in the mouth. Both groups of infants quickly adjusted their style of sucking, with the first group steadily squeezing the nipple and the second group just as steadily obtaining milk through suction.

Substage 2 — Primary Circular Reactions

During the second substage, when babies are from one to four months old, they incorporate experi-ence in their reflexive schemes. Through accom-modation, the schemes become acquired adapta-tions, which are the first true sensorimotor schemes. Infants begin to coordinate their senses; they use their eyes to direct their grasp and turn their heads toward the source of a sound. In Chap-ter 3, we saw that newborns show similar coordi-nation but that it seems to be reflexive and disap-pears after the first month. Babies in Substage 2 cannot distinguish their actions from the world and the objects in it.

The hallmark of this stage is what Piaget called the **primary circular reaction.** This term refers to

CAN BABIES COUNT?

Babies may be born to count, for they seem to come into the world possessing basic number skills. That statement may sound farfetched, but some developmental psychologists are convinced that it is so (Gelman, 1982; Keil, 1981). Toddlers spontaneously count the objects in their world, although two-year-olds may count only as far as two and may use invented number words. But long before their second birthday, babies are aware of number.

Studies with newborns in a Baltimore hospital indicate that babies only a day or two old seem to know the difference between two objects and three objects (Antell and Keating, 1983). These babies looked at patterns of dots until they habituated. Each card had the same number of dots on it, but the dots were arranged differently. When they had habituated to a card containing three dots, the babies showed new interest in a two-dot card; and when they had habituated to two dots, they found three dots interesting. But when the numbers increased, the task was beyond them. None of the babies could tell the difference between four dots and six dots.

The babies' responses were apparently no fluke. Similar tests with four- to seven-month-old babies produced the same results: the babies detected the difference between two- and three-dot displays but could not handle four- and six-dot patterns (Starkey and Cooper, 1980). Six- to nine-month-olds also re-sponded differently to slides in which the number of common household objects changed from two to three or back again (Starkey, Spelke, and Gelman, 1980). In this study, babies who habituated to a slide with three objects (such as a scraper, a memo pad, and a comb) showed no interest in another three-object slide, even though it portrayed different objects arranged differently. But a two-object slide immediately attracted their attention.

What does this mean? Young babies apparently detect equivalences, yet they surely cannot reason meaningfully about quantities, and there is no indication that they consciously represent number. Flavell (1985) speculates that babies are born with some sort of inborn neurological process that handles nonverbal counting—a counting scheme of some sort that is similar to a sucking or grasping scheme. Other researchers (Antell and Keating, 1983) suggest that the babies are detecting unchanging environmental features (number). Eleanor Gibson (1969) has proposed that all human perception is based on the ability to select unchanging features in the environment (a dog's ears, legs, tail, and head) from the continually shifting features (the dog's posture, position, and the wagging of its tail). In this view, babies can perceive number because all perception is guided by similar rules.

---

any action that the baby repeats because of the pleasurable stimulation it provides. For example, when babies lie on their backs, unconfined by clothing, they often flail their arms and kick their legs rhythmically. Some developmentalists interpret these rhythmic movements as responses by an infant who is too immature to produce a goal-directed response (Thelen, 1981). Thumbsucking is another typical primary circular reaction, and like most of these reactions, it centers on the baby's own body. Such sucking, grasping, looking, or vocalizing is different from the reflexive actions of the first substage because it is initiated by the baby instead of being a response to internal stimulation.

Sometimes babies imitate the actions of adults, but these primary circular reactions are what Piaget called "pseudoimitation." For example, Piaget (1951) describes how, at ten weeks, Lucienne imitated him. Piaget had observed Lucienne moving her head spontaneously from side to side.

She was upright in her mother's arms opposite me. I began to nod my head up and down. While she was watching, Lucienne kept quite still except for slight movements in order to watch what I was doing. As soon as I stopped, she distinctly reproduced the up and down movement. I then moved my head from left to right and vice versa. Lucienne moved her head slightly as she watched, and as soon as I stopped, reproduced the sideways movement. Her mother, who was holding her, clearly felt the difference in the movements of the spine and muscles. (P. 12)

At this stage, Lucienne, like all babies, could imitate only one of her own customary responses—and only if someone else mimicked that response immediately after she made it.

Substage 3 — Secondary Circular Reactions

Babies in this substage, who are about four to eight months old, are busy with actions they have learned. Their sensorimotor coordination has improved and their new skill at grabbing attractive objects gives them many opportunities for such activity. Now babies' action schemes prolong events that interest the baby. They have become what Piaget called **secondary circular reactions.** In this advance, babies repeat learned responses as opposed to the unlearned behavior that appears in primary circular reactions. Laurent's behavior at four months, while passing a stick from hand to hand, is typical:

> The stick then happens to strike a toy hanging from the bassinet hood. Laurent, immediately interested by this unexpected result, keeps the stick raised in the same position, then brings it noticeably nearer to the toy. He strikes it a second time. Then he draws the stick back but moving it as little as possible as though trying to conserve the favorable position, then he brings it nearer to the toy, and so on, more and more rapidly. (Piaget 1952, p. 176)

Infants in the third substage are capable of "true imitation." They can imitate actions that they see others make—but only if the action is one they already perform and only if they can see themselves perform it. They are also tireless explorers of objects. They look at objects, handle them, mouth them, rotate them, transfer them from one hand to another, and bang them against any available surface. These early explorations seem to be a quest for information; after babies have completed their initial investigation, they seem to lose interest and begin throwing, pushing, or dropping the object (Ruff, 1984).

Perceptions and actions are still so intertwined at this age that babies find it hard to separate them. The infant apparently has no mental image of objects as separate things; instead, he or she represents an object through motor responses. The meaning of the object is intertwined with the actions the baby has connected with it. When babies catch sight of a familiar object, they indicate their recognition by going through a mild version of whatever secondary circular reaction they use with it. Piaget (1952, p. 187) describes Lucienne as "opening or closing her hands or shaking her legs, but very briefly and without effort" when she glimpses a doll she had often manipulated by kicking or striking it as it hung from the bassinet hood.

Substage 4 — Coordination of Secondary Schemes

In the latter part of the first year (eight to twelve months), slowly but surely, intentional, goal-directed behavior emerges. Instead of simply prolonging interesting events, babies intentionally use their schemes to reach a goal. They have become active problem solvers who use objects as tools, circumvent barriers, remove obstacles, and are undeterred by detours. Piaget (1952) describes Laurent's determined efforts toward a goal:

> I present a box of matches above my hand, but behind it, so that he cannot reach it without setting the obstacle aside. But Laurent, after trying to take no notice of it, suddenly tries to hit my hand as though to remove or lower it; I let him do it to me and he grasps the box. — I recommence to bar his passage, but using as a screen a sufficiently supple cushion to keep the impress of the child's gestures. Laurent tries to reach the box, and, bothered by the obstacle, he at once strikes it, definitely lowering it until the way is clear. (P. 217)

On this occasion, Laurent combined two schemes, grasping (which he temporarily set aside) and striking, to reach the coveted matchbox.

Babies' capabilities are expanding rapidly during this period, because for the first time they can imitate behavior they have never performed. As noted earlier, this advance means that observational learning is possible. Games like peekaboo take on new excitement, because the baby now can be an active participant instead of a fascinated ob-

In the latter part of their first year, babies are active learners and imitators who delight in such games as "Where's your nose?" *(Elizabeth Crews)*

server. Babies are ready to play "Where's your nose?" or "Where's your belly button?" because now they can connect a series of sounds with the response they have seen their parents make — pointing to the appropriate part of their bodies.

Substage 5 — Tertiary Circular Reactions

Babies in this stage of sensorimotor thought (twelve to eighteen months) often behave like little scientists. Faced with a problem, they now set about solving it through the process of trial and error. They cannot predict the results of a new action, but must first try it out. They often become so caught up in their experimentation that they may vary their schemes simply to see what will happen, as if they are working away at understanding the world. Piaget (1952) described Laurent's experiments with gravity:

Laurent is lying on his back. . . . He grasps in succes-

sion a celluloid swan, a box, etc., stretches out his arms, and lets them fall. He distinctly varies the position of the fall. Sometimes he stretches out his arm vertically, sometimes he holds it obliquely, in front of or behind his eyes, etc. When the object falls in a new position (for example on his pillow), he lets it fall two or three times more on the same place, as though to study the spatial relation; then he modifies the situation. (Pp. 268–269)

With this advance, the infant's schemes become **tertiary circular reactions.** They differ from secondary circular reactions in that they are intentional adaptations to specific situations. The baby who once explored objects by taking them apart now tries to put them back together, stacking blocks or nesting cups. When a toy is out of reach, the baby will pull on the tablecloth beneath it — a procedure that brings the toy within grasp. Piaget (1968) now describes the infant's behavior as "intelligent"; but it is an action-oriented intelligence, one based on perceptions and movements rather than on words and concepts.

Substage 6 — Beginning of Symbolic Thought

The final stage of sensorimotor thought (eighteen to twenty-four months) is really a transitional period between the sensorimotor and preoperational stages. Babies now can represent objects by means of symbols, an advance that allows them to think about their own actions and events involving others. In the baby's daily life, two important changes show up. First, because babies can visualize their own actions, they can solve problems in their heads, working out a solution with mental combinations and then applying it. They no longer must go through a lengthy trial-and-error test. Piaget (1952) describes Jacqueline's mental solution of a problem:

Jacqueline . . . arrives at a closed door — with a blade of grass in each hand. She stretches out her right hand toward the knob but sees that she cannot turn it without letting go of the grass. She puts the grass on the floor, opens the door, picks up the grass again and enters. But when she wants to leave the room things become complicated. She puts the grass on the floor and grasps the doorknob. But then she perceives that in pulling the door toward her she will simultaneously chase away the grass which she placed between the door and the threshold. She therefore picks it up in order to put it outside the door's zone of movement. (P. 339)

The second change is babies' ability to defer their imitations. No longer must their imitations of mommy or daddy immediately follow the parent's actions. These imitations are not always conducive to family harmony. At sixteen months, for example, Jacqueline watched with amazement as another toddler threw a horrendous temper tantrum, screaming, stamping his feet, and trying to push his way out of his playpen. Placed in her own playpen the next day, Jacqueline screamed and shoved and stamped her foot lightly several times in succession (Piaget, 1951). Clearly, the little girl had stored some mental representation of the little boy's actions.

Along with the ability to form mental images comes the capacity for pretend play. Because toddlers can mentally represent objects, they can pretend that a box is a cup or that a cup is a hairbrush. This ability is a striking advance over play during the fifth substage, when youngsters might pretend to drink tea from a cup that they could see and hold. Within another year, they will be engrossed in full-blown dramatic play.

MENTAL REPRESENTATION BY INFANTS AND TODDLERS

As toddlers move out of the sensorimotor period, their skill at representing information symbolically grows by leaps and bounds. Compared with younger toddlers, two- and three-year-olds have an amazing grasp of symbols, as our exploration of language acquisition in Chapter 7 will demonstrate. As their symbolic skills grow, they easily represent their experiences in thought. Then, on later occasions, they can draw on this experience to understand others, to solve problems, and to enrich their play.

The Object Concept

Two-year-olds believe that a hairbrush remains the same, even though it may appear on the bathroom shelf on one day and on the bedroom dresser the next. They also believe that the hairbrush continues to exist, even though it is tucked away in a drawer or closed up in a cupboard. These ideas about the identity and permanence of objects make up the **object concept**. The object concept is not present at birth but is slowly built up as a result of the infant's sensory, perceptual, and motor interactions with the environment. Piaget (1952, 1954), who studied the object concept by hiding objects and observing his children's reactions to their sudden disappearance, maintained that the construction is not complete until toward the end of the second year. By this time, youngsters have reached the last substage of the sensorimotor period.

Out of Sight, Out of Existence During the first few months, babies react to the disappearance of objects in a peculiar manner. When an object being watched by a baby of less than four months disappears from sight, the baby either keeps gazing at the spot where it was last visible or acts as if the object had never been in view. The baby in Substages 1 and 2 does not search for the object but behaves as though it no longer existed. Indeed, Piaget concluded that this is exactly the baby's attitude: when a toy vanishes, it has ceased to exist; when the toy reappears, it has been recreated.

During the next four months or so, the baby in Substage 3 often searches for an object that disappears from view. If a cup falls from the highchair tray, the six-month-old may lean toward the floor to see where it went. But this visual search occurs only when the baby sees the object starting to move away. At this point in the development of the object concept, an object seems to exist for babies only as long as they can continue looking at it. If you suddenly drop a napkin over an object that is in the baby's grasp, the baby either simply withdraws the hand or keeps holding the object but behaves as if unaware that it is still in his or her grasp.

The Beginnings of Object Permanence In observations of his own children, Piaget (1952, 1954) found that during the last four months of their first year, they searched for objects that they saw him place behind a screen. Yet their search was strictly limited. For instance, Piaget moved a toy behind a screen while one of his children was

(top) This infant of about six months has not yet developed a concept of object permanence. She looks intently at a toy elephant that is in front of her *(left),* but when the toy is blocked from view *(right),* she seems to have forgotten its existence. *(George Zimbel/Monkmeyer)*

(bottom) This older infant knows that objects that disappear continue to exist. When the object this baby sees *(left)* is shielded from view by a towel *(middle),* the baby searches for it and crawls under the towel to find the object *(right). (George Zimbel/Monkmeyer)*

watching. The child retrieved it. Piaget hid the toy again, and the child again recovered the toy. Then the game changed. With his child watching, Piaget hid the toy behind a screen located in a different place. Surprising as it may seem, the child insisted on searching for the toy in the original location. Psychologists call this the $A\overline{B}$ error, and Piaget concluded that it demonstrated the failure to dissociate the objects of the world from the infant's own actions on them. In repeating their earlier successful movement, babies were trying to reinstate a pleasant sensorimotor experience — play with the toy (Flavell, 1985).

Babies in Substage 5 are not deceived when a toy is hidden in a new place. Even if the toy is moved several times, they immediately search at the final location. But they are fooled when the toy is moved and they do not see the researcher moving it. When the object concept is fully developed, as it is during Substage 6, toddlers search for a toy in all possible places. According to Paul Harris (1983), this thoroughness indicates two advances in mental representation. The youngsters have developed, first, the ability to represent the toy despite its invisibility and, second, the ability to represent where the toy might be. Other researchers (Bertenthal and Fischer, 1983) have suggested that the complete search indicates a cognitive advance

that is also a social advance: youngsters now understand that a person can surreptitiously move an object from one place to another.

Egocentrism

If Piaget is correct about the $A\overline{B}$ error, its source is the Substage 4 baby's **egocentrism,** or inability to differentiate the self from the world. The infant's frame of reference for spatial relations is himself or herself. Babies reach toward the same spot because that is where they have seen the toy in relation to their bodies. In laboratory studies, nine-month-old babies do seem to locate objects in reference to themselves (Acredolo and Evans, 1980). However, if given some striking marker — such as blinking lights and garish stripes — they will switch from an egocentric viewpoint to using the landmark. Tested at home, babies show less evidence of egocentrism. A crawling nine-month-old appears to use familiar surroundings as landmarks, doing as well on tests as sixteen-month-olds do in the laboratory (Acredolo, 1979).

After reviewing the research, Paul Harris (1983) concluded that the $A\overline{B}$ error is not the result of egocentrism. He believes that as babies begin to rely on landmarks, they use the landmarks even after a toy has been moved to another hiding place. They have linked the toy with the first hiding place, and so they search for it there. Others have found that when babies are allowed to search immediately (within a second) after the toy is hidden in a second place, the AB error disappears. As babies get older, the permissible delay between hiding the toy at place B and the baby's successful search lengthens — from one second at seven months to as much as ten seconds among twelve-month-olds (Diamond, 1985). Adele Diamond (1985) believes that such results indicate that the baby is struggling with two factors: the fragile memory of the toy's new hiding place and the response that originally brought him or her the toy. The tendency to repeat the old, successful response may be so strong that at times the baby searches the old hiding place even when he or she accurately recalls the toy's new position.

Even after toddlers grasp the object concept, said Piaget, they are still egocentric in other ways. They appear to think that another person sees things the way they see them and experiences the same behavior and the same thoughts and feelings about things as themselves. Yet research indicates that two-year-olds are not so egocentric as Piaget believed. When toddlers are asked to show a picture to another person, eighteen-month-olds hold it flat — to share the picture with the other person. Twenty-four-month-olds turn the picture around so that its back is to them. What is more, if the other person covers his or her eyes with a hand, some eighteen-month-olds and all twenty-four-month-olds will uncover the person's eyes before they show the picture (Flavell, 1985).

In another study (Flavell, Shipstead, and Croft, 1978), two-and-one-half-year-olds could hide a Snoopy doll behind a tabletop screen so that the experimenter could not see Snoopy from where she sat (see Figure 6.6). The youngsters apparently could distinguish what they saw from what another person might see, could think about what the other person saw, and could both produce and recognize some physical situations in which another person could not see some object that they could see.

From such studies, John Flavell (1985) has concluded that toddlers' and young children's understanding of other people's perceptions goes through two stages. At Level 1, children recognize

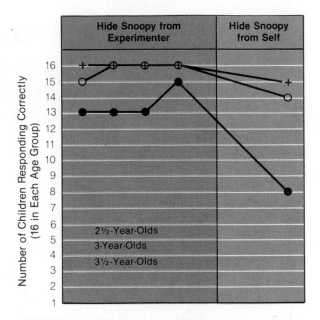

FIGURE 6.6 When young children were asked on four occasions to hide a Snoopy doll so the experimenter could not see it, even two-and-a-half-year-olds did well; but when asked to hide Snoopy from themselves, the youngest children's performance dropped sharply. *(Adapted from Flavell, Shipstead, and Croft, 1978)*

that another person may not always see the same object that they see. Children know *whether* another person does or does not see the object. At Level 2, children understand that even though they and another person see the same object, the two may have different perceptions if they view it from different places. Children are beginning to understand *how* another person perceives an object. Apparently, the object concept continues to develop after children leave infancy behind them.

Search Strategies

When infants search for a hidden toy, they engage in an extremely important task. Finding objects that are out of sight, whether car keys, tax returns, or other people, will be an essential skill throughout life. By tracing the development of search strategies, we can follow the growth of essential problem-solving skills (Wellman and Somerville, 1982).

During the first year, babies recognize the need

IS THIS ROCK REAL?
CONFUSING APPEARANCE
AND REALITY

Suppose that you show a three-year-old a gray sponge that looks exactly like a hunk of granite. You let the three-year-old handle the sponge, heft it, and squeeze it. Its light, squishy character betrays its identity. Then you hold up the sponge and ask the child two questions: "When you look at this with your eyes right now, does it look like a rock, or does it look like a sponge?" and "Is this really and truly a rock, or is it really and truly a sponge?"

You may be surprised to find that the three-year-old will give you the same answer to both questions. Although the object would fool a stone mason who had not touched it, the youngster will say that it not only *is* a sponge, but that it also *looks like* a sponge.

Undeterred, you now show the three-year-old a glass of milk that is surrounded by a green filter. The filter makes the milk look green. You remove the glass from behind the filter and hand it to the youngster, who inspects it. Clearly, it is a glass of white milk. You put it back and ask: "What color is the milk? Is it green or is it white?" The three-year-old will say that it not only looks green but that it actually *is* green.

John Flavell (1986), who has carried out a series of such experiments, has found that three-year-olds find it difficult to distinguish between appearance and reality. Yet their errors tend to be consistent. If you ask them about an object's size (say you put a small white stone beneath a strong magnifying glass) or its color, they seem fooled by appearance. Most say that the object *is* the way it looks: big in the case of the magnified stone; green in the case of the milk. They seem fooled by appearances. However, when you ask about an object's identity, they give "reality" answers, insisting that an object *looks like* what it actually is.

Flavell has not been able to figure out why reality is more important to youngsters in the one instance (the sponge) and appearance in the other (the milk). But he has discovered that the appearance-reality distinction is not an American problem. When he and his associates tried similar experiments with Chinese children of the same age in Beijing, they found the same pattern of errors. And when Flavell's group trained a group of 16 three-year-olds in the difference between "real" and "looks like," they continued to make the same errors in both kinds of situation.

By the time children are five years old, they answer such questions correctly. Is part of the problem language? Children have heard their parents say such things as "It looks like we're going to be late" when they mean "I think we're going to be late." This is a common second meaning of the term. However, Flavell (Pillow and Flavell, 1985) believes that confusion over language does not completely explain the three-year-olds' curious pattern of errors. Perhaps, says Flavell (1985), children simply are trying very hard to show that they aren't being fooled by the sponge boulder. Or perhaps three-year-olds find it nearly impossible to sort out information from different channels. They "know" that the object is a sponge; but their eyes tell them that it is a rock. Developmentalists are trying to discover the reasons for the young child's confusion — and how he or she comes to understand the difference between appearance and reality. The solution to this mystery might throw light on how the child gradually comes to a more important understanding: that a person can have more than one mental representation of the same object or event and that two people can represent the same object or event differently (Flavell, 1986).

to search only if they watch as an object is hidden. They are aware that there is something to search for, but their strategies seem inconsistent, and they are easily distracted. As we have seen, when babies are in their own homes, they locate objects by using landmarks much earlier than they do in the psychology lab.

Toddlers search when they see an object hidden; and when tested in their homes, eighteen-month-olds prove to be skilled searchers. In one study (DeLoache, 1980), mothers hid a stuffed Big Bird toy while the toddlers watched, then set a kitchen timer, telling the youngsters that they could go find the toy when the bell rang. In nearly 70 percent of the cases, the toddlers jumped up and got the coveted toy as soon as the bell sounded. Children this age also can use distinctive cues. For example, eighteen-month-olds find it easier to remember which box holds a small toy when the correct box differs radically in size or color from the other boxes (Daehler and Greco, 1985).

While waiting to search for a toy they have seen hidden, young toddlers (eighteen to twenty-four months old) use rudimentary memory strategies to remember a hiding place (DeLoache, Cassidy, and Brown, 1985). Although they have attractive toys to play with while they wait, the youngsters talk about the toy or its hiding place, look toward the hiding place, point at it, or move toward it. They are more likely to use these early strategies in the laboratory than at home, yet their searches at home are just as successful. The strange surroundings of the lab seem to make them less secure generally or less confident about their ability to find the toy. This uncertainty apparently leads them to keep monitoring the situation.

When a researcher surreptitiously changes a toy's hiding place, older toddlers (twenty-five to thirty months) seem to use their general knowledge to figure out where the toy might be (De-Loache and Brown, 1984). When Big Bird was spirited away from beneath a couch cushion, one thirty-month-old searched under the couch and beside it for the toy. And when another toddler discovered that a toy was missing from a desk drawer, he said, "Did Mickey Mouse fall out?" and then searched behind the desk. Youngsters this age quickly catch on to the experimenter's role, an ability that testifies to their representational capacity. When one twenty-nine-month-old girl found that a toy was missing, she ran to the experimenter's bag, yelling, "In your bag!" Then said, "Jackie, *you* took him." The girl had combined her memory of the experimenter's earlier moving of the toy with an inference about a probable new hiding place.

Young toddlers do not have to see an object hidden. They will search for a misplaced toy, and although they sometimes search persistently, they do not search comprehensively. When there are three possible locations for the toy, for example,

sixteen-month-olds make an exhaustive search about 75 percent of the time. Two-year-olds look in all possible places on every trial (Sophian and Wellman, in press). Within a few months, the sixteen-month-olds will be looking for objects if another person makes a verbal suggestion ("Where is your teddy bear?"), and they will search in a suggested location ("It's under your crib.") (Wellman and Somerville, 1982).

When there are many possible locations for an item, three-year-olds are much more efficient searchers than two-years-olds. In one study, youngsters looked through eight trash cans to find Oscar the Grouch (Wellman, Somerville, Revelle, Hauke, and Sophian, 1984). When the lids on the cans remained open (providing a cue that the can had been searched), two-year-olds looked in every can on most of the trials. But when the lids closed automatically, their performance deteriorated badly. In contrast, three- and four-year-olds were fairly proficient searchers whether the lids remained open or closed. Two-year-olds were also more likely than three- and four-year-olds to look in the same can more than once. They may be thorough but not very efficient searchers. Both tendencies suggest that two-year-olds look in likely places as they catch sight of them, whereas older youngsters plan their simple search sequences in advance.

Pretend Play

Play begins in sheer sensorimotor activity and evolves into symbolic social action. In the process, it incorporates the child's increasing ability to symbolize and imagine. Children everywhere engage in pretend play. The impetus for its development seems to come from within the child, leading Flavell (1985) to suggest that it is an evolved activity. Before children are a year old, pretend play is not possible. When babies less than a year old are given a toy metal tea set to play with, they will mouth, chew, or bang the various pieces. But infants who have passed their first birthday begin to show symbolic activity: they may try to drink, pour, or stir a cup of tea (Fenson, Kagan, Kearsley, and Zelazo, 1976). In this early pretend play, children carry out familiar activities away from their customary settings, but the play is not social. They

At first, toddlers need props that resemble real objects for their symbolic play. But these preschoolers could still "give the baby a bath" if they had a block of wood or a clothespin to bathe instead of a doll. *(Michael Weisbrot & Family)*

pretend to feed themselves or "wash" their own face with a dry cloth (Rubin, Fein, and Vandenberg, 1983).

According to Lev Vygotsky (1978), pretend play helps children free themselves from situational constraints and allows them to separate meaning from action. For example, when a little girl stamps the ground and pretends that she is riding a horse, she has detached the meaning of her action from a real action (an actual horseback ride). Vygotsky contended that in their symbolic play, toddlers must use props that resemble real objects. They are caught by the physical properties of the objects. They can pretend that a stick is a horse, but they cannot imagine a postcard as one.

Youngsters seem to go through a stage when their props must be realistic, but most emerge from it earlier than Vygotsky anticipated. When they are about eighteen months old, children begin to use substitute objects for realistic ones in their play. In one study (Jackowitz and Watson, 1980), 46 percent of the sixteen-month-olds and 62 percent of the twenty-three-month-olds could pretend that a toy car was a telephone or a cup of tea. However, all of the younger children and 62 percent of the older children needed some sort of

prop to carry out their pretense. When a little boy was left without a prop and asked to imitate a researcher who drank tea from a cup, the child searched the carpet until he found a piece of lint, then pretended to drink from it.

At first, children can substitute only one object in a pretend play sequence. When Greta Fein (1975) studied a group of twenty-four-month-olds, she found that nearly all of them could feed a toy horse invisible milk from a toy cup. When given a substitute (such as a wooden block) for either the horse or the cup, 70 percent still could pretend to feed the horse. But when the toddlers had to use substitutes for both horse and cup, only 33 percent could manage the pretense.

Among three-year-olds, solitary pretend play blossoms into dramatic play with other children. At first youngsters take familiar roles, acting out sequences that follow their expectations. If their play partner violates their expectations, they rearrange roles ("I'm not the baby anymore. I'm the daddy.") (Matthews, 1977). All the young players understand the nature of the fantasy game: a Playdough hamburger is never eaten, and the child who plays "Daddy" is aware of his own identity and may step out of the role to give directions ("Now you say that I'm supposed to go to work."). This ability indicates a giant step in cognitive development; youngsters realize that they can play a role and be themselves at the same time. They also realize that they can switch back and forth from self to role. This ability has led some researchers to suggest that pretend play may lay the groundwork for further cognitive advances (Rubin, Fein, and Vandenberg, 1983).

In this chapter, we have watched the action-oriented infant slowly become the symbol-using child who can recall the past, who may stop to think before acting, and whose flexible mind can switch from being a three-year-old to playing "mommy." Babies accomplish this feat by becoming active explorers. As tireless investigators of their surroundings, they use old responses on new objects and then modify these responses, assimilating and accommodating their skills as they learn to adapt to a widening world. In the next chapter, we will see how the same process turns them into competent communicators who can express their ideas, needs, and demands in words.

LEARNING TO SOLVE PROBLEMS

Many toys present toddlers with problems to be solved. They put puzzles together, build towers out of blocks, drop colored wooden shapes into matching holes in a small mailbox, and so on. When they first play with one of these toys, youngsters must figure out how the toy works. As they get older, their strategies for solving these problems become increasingly flexible and sophisticated.

The way children react to their wrong moves in such play reveals a good deal about their problem-solving strategies, as Judy DeLoache, Susan Sugarman, and Ann Brown (1985) discovered when they watched youngsters between the ages of eighteen and forty-one months explore a set of nesting cups. Nesting cups come in graduated sizes, and the child's aim is to nest the cups within one another so that the entire set fits within the largest cup. As soon as they were given the set of five cups, the children started nesting them. Most youngsters made many errors in the process.

The youngest children often tried to correct their mistakes by brute force. They twisted, banged, or pressed hard to force a large cup inside a small one. One eighteen-month-old who had successfully nested all but the largest cup placed it on the top of the stack. When it didn't fit, the youngster took it off, put it on again, pressed hard, took it off, and gave up.

Another simple strategy that appeared most often among the younger children was to discard one of the cups and try another. Finally, they often used a costly strategy of tearing up their stack and starting all over—even if they had nested four cups successfully.

As children got older, their strategies became more sophisticated. They reordered the stack in some way. Sometimes they rearranged it, taking some of the cups apart and putting them back in a different order. Latest to develop were two especially effective strategies. In one, children reversed the relationship between two cups. If one cup was too large to fit inside another, they placed the bottom cup on the top. Children who used this strategy seemed aware that two cups could be related in more than one way. In the other strategy, they took apart the stack at one place and simply inserted another cup. Children who used this strategy were simultaneously considering the relationship of the inserted cup to the next larger and the next smaller cup.

All the children knew when they had made a mistake. When one cup would not fit inside another, the youngsters got immediate feedback on their errors. In fact, there was no age difference in the likelihood that a child would try to correct a mistake. All age differences were in the methods used to correct errors. No eighteen-month-old, for example, ever reversed the relationship between two cups. And the older the child, the more likely he or she was to restructure the stack extensively. This gradual development of strategies reflects children's growing ability to regulate their cognitive processes. It also indicates an increasing flexibility in their thought and actions.

SUMMARY

1. The study of cognitive development has switched its focus from changes in observable behavior to discovering what happens within the child between the stimulus and the response. Today, **learning** is defined as the process of acquiring new information, and re-

searchers study **cognition,** which includes all the processes of representing information and using it.

2. As babies grow older, the qualities of a stimulus that *attract* their attention do not change, but the qualities that *hold* it do. They prefer increasingly complex sights and watch objects as long as they can gain information from them. Attention becomes increasingly selective; toddlers are best at remembering interesting information.

3. As they get older, babies habituate more quickly, and there are wide individual differences in the speed and efficiency of habituation. Young babies who habituate quickly and rapidly and who show immediate, renewed interest in novel stimuli tend to have higher than average scores on cognitive tests as six-year-olds. Much of babies' learning is the result of conditioning, as babies come to associate an action with its consequences. Yet when young children are rewarded for some activity they normally enjoy, they become less likely to engage in that activity. Apparently, such rewards undermine intrinsic motivation by making children feel that they are being controlled. The responsiveness of the environment and the joy of solving a problem appear to spur learning in babies. When babies or toddlers find that they are powerless to control the environment, they may develop **learned helplessness,** in which they become apathetic and make no effort to solve problems or initiate social interaction.

4. In some studies, newborns have imitated the facial expressions of adults. Because young babies are supposedly unable to form the representations required for such imitations, it has been suggested either that the researchers inadvertently influenced their results or that the babies' expressions are automatic responses to a releasing mechanism, perhaps set off by the moving features of the adult face. Toward the end of the first year, researchers agree, babies can imitate novel behavior; this advance makes observational learning possible. During the second year, deferred imitation appears, so that imitation no longer must come immediately after the youngster observes the novel behavior.

5. Babies begin forgetting almost immediately, through a selective, gradual process. Memory improves with age, and the improvement seems primarily based on quicker registration of stimuli in memory. When infants are allowed to look at an object until it bores them, age differences in memory disappear. Infants of any age seem most likely to remember those responses that have had an effect on their world. Instances of **recall** begin appearing at about seven months, and parental assistance plays an important part in helping babies to remember. Intentional memory improves steadily among toddlers, but they do poorly on formal tests of memory. Most toddlers are unaware of strategies that will help them register information in memory, but widespread experience with television and nursery school may be changing this situation.

6. The **sensorimotor stage,** Piaget's first period of cognitive development, is divided into six substages, each representing an advance in cognitive development. The first substage covers the neonatal period, when babies' responses are primarily reflexive. During Substage 2, babies produce **primary circular reactions,** in which they repeat unlearned actions because of the pleasurable stimulation that accompanies them. Babies in Substage 3 produce **secondary circular reactions,** in which they repeat learned responses. During Substage 4, babies can perform intentional acts to reach some goal. Substage 5 brings out **tertiary circular reactions,** which are intentional adaptations to specific situations and which the baby uses to solve problems through trial and error. Finally, in Substage 6, babies can represent objects by means of symbols and can defer their imitations. Now they can solve problems mentally and begin to use language.

7. The **object concept** develops slowly and usually is not complete until the second half of the second year. It begins to form during Substage 3, when babies search for objects that they see disappearing, but not until Substage 6 do babies search in all possible places for a vanished toy. Now they can represent the invisible toy as well as the place where it might be hidden; they can also understand that someone might move an object when they are not watching. Piaget be-

lieved that babies and young children are characterized by **egocentrism.** Babies, he said, cannot distinguish between self and the world; toddlers believe that another person sees things exactly as they see them and experiences the same thoughts and feelings as themselves. Research indicates that babies are less egocentric at home than in the lab and that toddlers emerge from egocentrism earlier than Piaget believed.

8. Toddlers develop increasingly effective search strategies; by the time they are three years old, they are efficient searchers. They use cues, simple memory strategies, their store of general knowledge, and plan their search sequences in advance. Pretend play develops during the second year, when toddlers can represent objects symbolically. At first toddlers must use props, and their ability to substitute items in a play sequence is limited. Three-year-olds move from solitary pretend play into dramatic play with other children. This ability to assume roles and to switch back and forth from self to role represents a major cognitive advance.

KEY TERMS

cognition
egocentrism
learned helplessness
learning

object concept
primary circular reaction
recall

secondary circular reaction
sensorimotor stage
tertiary circular reaction

STUDY TERMS

egocentrism Among babies, the inability to distinguish between the self and the external world; among young children, the belief that everyone sees the world and responds to it exactly as the child does.

learned helplessness A condition in which repeated failure in situations over which a person has no control leads to apathy and a refusal to try.

object concept The understanding that objects remain the same although they may move from place to place (*object identity*) and that they continue to exist when out of sight (*object permanence*).

recall The ability to remember information in the absence of the object or information to be remembered.

sensorimotor stage The first stage in Piaget's theory of cognitive development; it lasts through most of the first two years of life. During this stage, knowledge develops from the infant's sensations and physical actions.

CHAPTER 7

Cognition: The Emergence of Language

Two-and-a-half-year-old Scott watched with fascination as his grandfather chopped at a small log with a hatchet. Each time the sharp blade bit into the wood, chips flew through the air. Finally, the toddler could restrain himself no longer. When his grandfather paused between strokes, the child's words came tumbling out: "I want to hatch wood." Clearly, Scott did not expect to sit on the log like a mother hen until it gave birth to twigs. Instead he coined a word to extend his vocabulary so that he could talk about something important to him—a chance to wield the hatchet. Scott is on his way to being a skilled communicator. He understands the meaning of words and the way they are put together to convey ideas. His conversion of a noun *(hatchet)* into a verb *(hatch)* shows that he even grasps one of the processes used in English to form new words.

Scott still has a long way to go. When his grandfather refused to hand over the hatchet, saying, "Sorry, Scotty. Not this time," the little boy asked plaintively, "Why I can't have it?" He does not understand the rule for "wh-" questions; he did not place the auxilliary verb *(can't)* in front of the subject *(I)*. Yet in only a couple of years, Scott has accomplished an amazing feat. Then he could not say a word; today he knows hundreds of words and

159

uses them to get things done in the world. How did he master this complicated system of symbols? What did he have to do? What did he have to know?

Before children go off to kindergarten, they have mastered their native language. They can turn their thoughts and intentions into patterns of sounds that others can understand, and they can decipher the sound patterns produced by others. To reach this level of skill, children must understand the sounds, meaning, and structure of their native tongue. And if their mastery is to be of much value to them, they also must become skilled at using it to reach their goals.

In this chapter, we discuss the way children master their native language. Before we trace the child's journey, we consider what capabilities children must develop before language acquisition becomes possible. We take up the first attempts at speech, looking at what children say with their first words and what they mean. Next we follow children's grasp of syntax, tracing the gradual growth of their sentences in length and complexity. Finally, we investigate the various theories that attempt to explain how children acquire language.

GETTING READY TO TALK

Long before they say their first words, babies are deep into the task of acquiring language. Before a baby can say "Dada," substantial progress occurs in four areas of development. Physical maturation is important; language acquisition appears to be impossible until a child reaches a certain age. Perceiving and producing the sounds of speech are essential; unless babies can separate speech from the other noises in the world, language acquisition could not occur. Social interaction plays a vital role; without the society of other human beings, a child will not learn to speak. Cognitive advances obviously are essential; until babies have developed a certain understanding of the world, they cannot talk.

Maturational Readiness

Why does it take so long for most infants to talk? Why do most youngsters say their first words near

their first birthdays? Whether they live in a mansion or a tent, on a farm in Kansas, the streets of Calcutta, the steppes of Russia, or a Pacific atoll, children begin to talk at about the same age. In fact, it is almost impossible to keep them from talking. Normal children who have regular contact with older speakers invariably learn to talk. If experience has such a small effect, then we might suspect that speech is in our genes and that physiological maturation plays an important part in the emergence of language.

Young babies cannot speak even if they know what they want to say. Speech occurs when air from the lungs passes over the vibrating vocal cords in the larynx. The position of the tongue, teeth, and lips determines the shape of the vocal cavity and, therefore, the sounds that escape the lips. At birth, the baby has little control over the flow of air through the larynx, the tongue fills the toothless mouth, and the vocal cords are positioned so high that only minute changes in the shape of the vocal tract are possible (Sachs, 1985). This arrangement means that the young baby cannot produce the sounds of speech. In fact, the baby's vocal tract is shaped more like that of an adult chimpanzee than an adult human (Stark, 1986).

As the baby's head and neck grow and the cheeks lose fat, the oral cavity becomes larger. The tongue no longer takes up the available mouth space, and the vocal cords have a wider range of possible positions. At about six months, teeth begin to erupt. While the mouth and throat are growing, the baby is also gaining command over the body. Soon he or she will be able to control the muscles of the lips and tongue, the flow of air through the larynx, and the position of the vocal cords. These changes make it possible for the older baby to produce the wide range of sounds necessary for speech.

The control of speech sounds is not simply the result of increases in the baby's size and strength. As we saw in Chapter 5, maturation of the cortex is closely linked with control over various parts of the body. In the sensorimotor cortex, where an extremely large area is devoted to control of the lips, tongue, and jaw, connections among neurons are multiplying and becoming stronger. Similar events are taking place in specialized areas of the brain's left hemisphere, where the production and reception of language sounds are processed.

Although this baby cannot understand any words, she detects her father's mood by the stress and intonation of his voice. *(George Malave/Stock, Boston)*

This growth of connections goes on throughout the first two years (Goldman-Rakic, Isseroff, Schwartz, and Bugbee, 1983), which is precisely the period when the foundations of language are developing.

Speech Perception and Production

Before they can acquire language, babies must separate speech from the other noise in the environment. Indeed, they seem born prepared to do just that, and their perception of speech sounds races far ahead of their ability to produce them.

Perceiving Speech   Newborns not only distinguish between human and nonhuman sounds, they apparently recognize voices that are important to them. As we saw in Chapter 4, newborns will alter their sucking pattern in order to hear their own mother's voice (DeCasper and Fifer, 1980). Very soon, differences in adult stress and intonation can affect a baby's emotional state and behavior. Long

before babies understand the words they hear, they respond to cues in the rate, volume, and melody of adult speech. From these cues, babies sense when an adult is playful or angry, whether the adult is attempting to initiate or end the interaction, and so on.

Just as significant for language development as the response to intonation is evidence that a tiny baby can make fine distinctions between speech sounds. By the time babies are a month old, they can tell the difference between most language sounds (Aslin, Pisoni, and Jusczyk, 1983). Using similar habituation techniques, other researchers have found that six-week-old infants (the youngest age tested) distinguish between "bad" and "bag," a situation in which only the final sound differs (Jusczyk, 1977). Infants younger than one month have not been tested in this manner, so babies may come into the world ready to make precisely those perceptual discriminations that are necessary if they are to acquire human language.

If the language spoken around a baby does not discriminate between two sounds, the baby even-

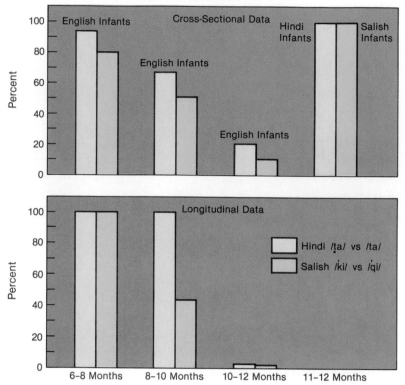

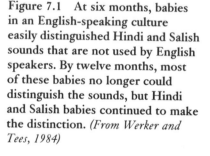

Figure 7.1 At six months, babies in an English-speaking culture easily distinguished Hindi and Salish sounds that are not used by English speakers. By twelve months, most of these babies no longer could distinguish the sounds, but Hindi and Salish babies continued to make the distinction. *(From Werker and Tees, 1984)*

tually will be unable to detect the difference between them. In a longitudinal study, Janet Werker and Richard Tees (1984) traced the gradual loss of this ability. When they were six to eight months old, infants from an English-speaking culture easily distinguished between the contrasting "t's" ("tar"/"star") that change the meaning of words in Hindi but not in English. But by the time the babies were ten to twelve months old, they could no longer tell the difference between the sounds. Over the same period, these babies also lost the ability to distinguish between two sounds that change the meaning of words in Salish (a northwestern Native American language) but not in English (see Figure 7.1). Heredity had prepared the babies to distinguish these sounds, but experience had closed the door to their use. Apparently, experience and the heredity of the species both play a role in the decoding of speech sounds.

From Crying to Babbling   Although babies can discriminate early among the sounds they hear,

most are at least a year old before they can produce sounds that can be identified as words. It is much easier to perceive differences between sounds than to acquire motor control over the various muscles and organs involved in producing speech. Babies go through five overlapping stages in their production of prelinguistic sounds, with some progressing through these stages more rapidly or more slowly than the average baby (Sachs, 1985; Stark, 1986).

Stage I: Reflexive Crying and Vegetative Sounds (0 to 8 weeks). A baby's first sounds are cries. After about three weeks, his or her vocalizations gradually increase in frequency and variety. Some sounds are only vegetative noises—burps, coughs, and sneezes that help keep the airway open. During this stage, the baby's physical immaturity sharply restricts the variety of possible sounds.

Stage II: Cooing and Laughter (8 to 20 weeks). Sounds of joy, called **cooing**, now appear, usually during social interaction: while babies watch a parent's smiling face or listen to singing or talking. These pleasurable sounds, which also are heard after babies eat and while they look at or handle objects, are made in the back of the mouth. Babies cry less now, perhaps because they have additional ways of expressing themselves. They also burst into peals of sustained laughter when something delights them.

Stage III: Vocal Play (16 to 30 weeks). This is a transitional stage between cooing and true babbling. As the size and shape of the oral cavity change and maturation progresses in the brain, the baby's noises change from a gurgling "coo" or "goo" to single, distinctive syllables, such as "da" or "ba." The baby produces these sounds, which are secondary circular reactions, while exploring and mapping the possibilities of the vocal tract.

Stage IV: Reduplicated Babbling (25 to 50 weeks). Babies now begin to babble, producing strings of alternating vowels and consonants, such as "bababababa." These sound sequences give the impression that the baby is uttering a string of syllables. Such repetitions indicate a greatly improved control over the muscles that govern speech. This control, together with babies' coordination of their speech with the perception of sound, is probably the primary function of babbling.

Stage V: Nonreduplicated Babbling and Expressive Jargon (9 to 18 months). As babies near the end of the first year, babbling changes again. The string of syllables may alternate consonants and take on a variety of stress and intonational patterns. The rising and falling pitch of this **expressive jargon** begins to sound like adult speech. Infants often produce long, complex sequences of meaningless sounds with the pitch contour of adult sentences. These sequences often appear in situations where language is appropriate, as when a child "talks" on a toy phone or "reads" a picture book. This period of expressive jargon often overlaps with the production of the child's first real words.

Social Precursors to Language

If children are to be competent speakers, they must be able to get things done with words. In fact, we can consider words as a form of "meaningful social behavior" (Bruner, 1976). Studying language as a

Long before babies can say "bow-wow" or "doggie," they use touching, pointing, and gazing to influence others in social situations. *(Suzanne Szasz)*

social act, in which the speaker is trying to accomplish something, is known as **pragmatics**. This approach leads researchers to look at the context in which language is used. They find that language seems to emerge from social interactions between baby and caregiver. Because they acquire language in social situations, children seem to grasp its pragmatic aspects early. In fact, before babies can talk, they influence others by touching, pointing, and gazing. These acts can be considered prelinguistic **speech acts** in which the communication is intended to help the baby achieve some goal (Bruner, 1983).

The Caregiver's Role From a baby's first days, parents speak to their child in special ways, a form of speech researchers call "baby talk" or **motherese**. As we saw in Chapter 4, the intonation, tempo, and rhythm of parental speech changes. The pitch of parents' voices becomes higher; the rise and fall of intonation is exaggerated; parents say only a few words at a time, pausing between utterances; and they often repeat words and phrases (Fernald and Simon, 1984). This speech directed toward young babies seems to have little formal structure, for it consists largely of interjections, naming, and playful sounds that are often imitations of the baby's own gurglings and coos. Parents also draw out their syllables, giving moth-

The playful sounds of early motherese provides the face-to-face interaction that helps lay the foundation for language acquisition. *(Suzanne Szasz)*

erese the characteristics of a pleasant melody (Papoušek, Papoušek, and Bornstein, 1985). The adult seems to be both conveying affection and capturing the child's attention for the task at hand. Motherese appears in societies around the world; its presence has been documented in at least fifteen cultures, and it is used by parents, childless adults, and older children alike (Ferguson, 1977; Jacobson, Boersma, Fields, and Olson, 1983). For this reason, some researchers have begun to call it simply "child-directed speech" (Snow, 1986).

Toward the end of the first year, motherese changes in quality. It moves closer to adult speech, but parents continue to speak more slowly, using simple sentences and inserting pauses into their words. They use very short sentences, replace difficult consonants with easy ones, substitute nouns for pronouns, and repeat phrases or whole sentences. Parents increase their emphasis on meaning and seem to be making the infant aware of the verbal world that surrounds them.

Adults also talk to children primarily about the here and now. They comment on what they are doing, or what the infant is doing or is about to do. They limit their vocabularies, and they select words that are most useful for the infant, words that relate to what babies are interested in. The adult is not trying to teach the child language; instead, the adult is trying to maintain interaction with the child (Shatz, 1984).

The result of baby talk is anything but babyish. The content and the intonation of the communication are childish, but the dialogue pattern is strictly adult (Bruner, 1981). How important is motherese? Researchers are uncertain whether this special speech is necessary to ensure normal language development. Heavy doses of motherese early in life seem to speed the acquisition of a baby's first few words. In a longitudinal study, Marc Bornstein and Margaret Ruddy (1984) found that mothers who encouraged their four-month-old babies to pay attention to objects and events around them (by using motherese and gestures) fostered the babies' early language acquisition. At twelve months, these babies had larger vocabularies than babies whose mothers gave them little encouragement. Among another group of youngsters, those who were especially responsive to motherese at three months tended to perform especially well on tests of linguistic functioning at twelve years (Roe, McClure, and Roe, 1982). Although some researchers believe that motherese is unlikely to help a child learn language rules and structure (Gleitman and Wanner, 1982), others have found that the structure of mothers' speech to their twenty-six-month-olds predicted aspects of their children's later language growth (Hoff-Ginsberg, 1986). In fact, a number of developmentalists believe that without some minimal exposure to motherese, infants might never become competent speakers.

Turn-Taking   Other aspects of child-caretaker interaction seem to be as important as motherese in stimulating linguistic development. Almost from the beginning, parents encourage babies to "take their turn" in conversation. At first the caregiver supplies both sides of the conversation. During these dialogues, even though young babies may not be trying to communicate, they are learning about the nature of human conversation.

When babies begin to play peekaboo, they are learning an essential conversational skill — how to take turns. *(Alice Kandell/Photo Researchers)*

In the course of these interactions, parents pay close attention to the baby's reactions, and as the infant's competence increases, the conversations change. At first, parents simply call the infant's attention to some object or event, perhaps saying, "Look!" Gradually, they demand more and more participation from the baby — first in the form of a gesture or a smile, then a vocalization that somewhat resembles a label, then a label that the parent can recognize. At this point, the parent may repeat a question ("What's that?") until the infant supplies an answer (Bruner, 1981).

Carrying on a conversation requires infants to master a number of language conventions: they must learn to take turns, speaking at the proper time and not interrupting their partners; they must learn to make eye contact and to indicate that they are paying attention. Turn-taking and other nonverbal conversational skills grow out of early games, such as peekaboo, in which baby and adult share experiences and exchange roles in ritualized ways.

Cognitive Precursors to Language

The basis for the child's ability to understand and speak a language is an understanding of the world. Until a number of cognitive advances occur, a child cannot use words meaningfully.

Object Permanence Before children can talk, they must have some notion that there is an enduring world of objects and people. A child who cannot remember the existence of vanished objects cannot attach labels to objects with any consistency and so cannot speak about them. As children develop the notion of object permanence, the nature of their early vocabulary shows a characteristic change. Most children begin to communicate with words at about the time they enter Substage 5 of the sensorimotor period (Harding and Golinkoff, 1979) (see Chapter 6). At this time, they understand that an object can be moved from one hiding place to another but are fooled if the experimenter secretly changes the object's location; in Substage 6, they are not tricked by such surreptitious moves. When researchers followed a group of twelve-month-olds for a year, they found that most youngsters in Substage 5 were using words that indicated *visible* movements of objects, such as "hi," "bye," "move," "stuck," "uh-oh," and "thank you" (Tomasello and Farrar, 1984). Not until they reached Substage 6 did words that indicate *invisible* movements (involving the disappearance or reappearance of objects) enter their vocabulary. Now they were saying "allgone," "more," "find," and "another."

Development of Concepts Concepts give us

ways of organizing the world, so that we have to store less information in order to think about it. Each concept consists of a set of features that are associated with one another so that they form a unit in memory (Clark, 1983). Concepts can refer to individuals (Miss Piggy) or to groups that share certain properties—either objects (Muppet, bird), situations (walking), or states (asleep, alive). When talking about the group described by a concept, we generally call it a *category*.

When children learn a word, they actually are learning to which concept or category the word refers. In most cases, children first learn the concept, then figure out what word refers to it (Macnamara, 1972). In fact, babies begin sorting the world into concepts before they know any words. Research indicates that most babies are forming concepts by the time they are ten months old. In one study (Younger and Cohen, 1983), four- to ten-month-old babies looked at projected drawings of imaginary animals. Each drawing mixed five features taken from schematic drawings, such as a feathered, fluffy, or horselike tail; a cowlike, elephantlike, or giraffelike body. Each baby looked at four different animals from the same category (having at least three correlated features) until he or she habituated. Then the baby saw a new animal: either another animal with familiar but uncorrelated features or an animal with all new features. All babies found the animal with new features fascinating, but only ten-month-olds were similarly fascinated by the animal with familiar but uncorrelated features. Apparently, the older babies had formed a category—they had extracted the correlation among the features and generalized it to a new situation. To these older babies, the uncorrelated features seemed as peculiar as wings on a giraffe would seem to you.

Imitation   When babies form concepts, they are representing objects or events mentally. Once babies begin to imitate events after they have occurred, they clearly are storing internal images of sights and sounds. As we saw in Chapter 6, deferred imitation first appears in Substage 6 of the sensorimotor period. Children who imitate the way Mommy stirs with a wooden spoon or the way an older sibling rocks a doll show that they have developed the memory abilities required for the acquisition of language. Before they can speak, children also must be able to imitate the sound patterns of language that they hear about them.

Symbolic Play   An infant's first words also emerge at about the same time as the infant begins to use symbolic gestures and to engage in pretend play. A baby girl who pushes a building block along the floor, pretending that it is a car, or runs her fingers through her hair, pretending that she is combing it, has demonstrated symbolic play. Children engaged in symbolic play are translating their experience into symbols, then combining them according to specific rules (playing house, driving a car, combing hair, and so on). This is exactly what children must do in order to use language, an indication that the same rules underlie the development of play and the development of language (Ungerer and Sigman, 1984). Indeed, such play is closely related to both the child's use of words and his or her comprehension of others' speech. At the same time that children begin connecting two or more symbolic gestures in play (pouring pretend tea, drinking it, then wiping their mouths), they are beginning to combine two or more words in a single utterance (Bates, Bretherton, Beeghly-Smith, and McNew, 1982).

Intention   Until babies are about nine months old, none of their signals indicates true intent; instead, they seem to be built-in reactions to a particular internal state (Bates, 1979). About the age of nine or ten months, babies undergo a great change in their behavior. Now if they want a toy that is out of reach, they look at a nearby adult, then at the toy, then back at the adult. If there is no response, they may fuss loudly to attract attention. Quickly, the grasp toward the elusive toy becomes an intentional signal, perhaps a repetitive opening and shutting of the hand, and the fussing sound becomes short, regular noises, such as "uh, uh" or "eeeee." These first signals change in volume and insistence, depending on whether the adult responds. This is a great moment, says Elizabeth Bates (1979), in the dawn of language. It shows the child's intent to communicate as well as the realization that there are mutually agreed upon signals, such as pointing, that can be used for mutually agreed upon purposes. Earlier, the infant may have wanted to communicate but lacked any shared notion of conventional ways to express intention.

Symbolic play is so closely connected to the development of language that an observer can predict whether a child has reached the two-word stage by watching the youngster at silent play. *(Linda Ferrer/Woodfin Camp & Associates)*

The way is now open for the baby's first words. This next advance, which comes at about twelve months, will require another realization — that an arbitrary symbol (a word) can refer to a particular object. This understanding indicates that the baby has grasped another aspect of language: **semantics**, which refers to the arbitrary meaning conveyed by language forms.

Once children have developed intent, their early communications arc far more successful than we would expect from their tentative grasp of symbols. These communications succeed because adults are good at guessing children's intentions. Youngsters give clues to their intentions in intonation and gesture. In addition, because children's communicative needs are always embedded in an ongoing context of activity, it is generally possible to figure out what they are trying to say.

The process works both ways. Children assess a communication in terms of its context, often figuring out what a parent wants even if they don't understand all the words they hear. When the context is ambiguous, they assume that language demands action, and so they do whatever seems appropriate (Shatz, 1983). Because toddlers' action often matches whatever the parent had requested or ordered, parents often overestimate their child's linguistic knowledge.

EARLY WORDS AND SENTENCES

When an infant shifts from babbling to words, something very important has happened. Instead of simply playing with sound, the baby is planning and controlling speech (de Villiers and de Villiers, 1979). As a result, the infant's utterances shrink in length. One word has to do the work of many, because babies' limited cognitive processing ability does not permit them to plan and produce a longer utterance before they run out of working memory.

First Words

First words tend to be either a single syllable ("ma") or a duplicated syllable ("mama"), consisting of a consonant followed by a vowel. The sounds are those that are easy for the baby to say, so no matter what a child's native language, the first words generally contain consonants that are produced at the front of the mouth, such as "b," "p," "d," or "m." The first syllable may occur when infants release their lips while vocalizing, producing such sounds as "ma" or "ba." The very first words may not be recognizable as such; babies

Table 7.1
The First Seven "Words" in One Child's Linguistic Development

Utterance	Age in Months	Meanings
uh?	8	An interjection. Also demonstrative, "addressed" to persons, distant objects, and "escaped toys."
dididi	9	Disapproval (loud). Comfort (soft).
mama	10	Refers vaguely to food. Also means "tastes good" and "hungry."
nenene	10	Scolding.
tt!	10	Used to call squirrels.
piti	10	Always used with a gesture and always whispered. Seems to mean "interest(-ed), (-ing)."
deh	10	An interjection. Also demonstrative. Used with the same gesture as above.

Source: Adapted from David McNeill, *The Acquisition of Language: The Study of Developmental Psycholinguistics* (New York: Harper & Row, 1970), p. 22; based on material from Werner F. Leopold, *Grammar and General Problems in the First Two Years*, Speech Development of a Bilingual Child: A Linguist's Record, Vol. 3 (Evanston, Ill.: Northwestern University Press, 1949), p. 6.

often copy animal sounds, pick up some sound from the environment, or invent words, applying one of their own sounds (such as "uh" or "deh") in a consistent manner (de Villiers and de Villiers, 1978). For example, two weeks before she produced her first conventional word, eleven-month-old Sarah began to say "di" to mean "Look at that" (Stoel-Gammon and Cooper, 1984). Sarah produced only this one invented word, but some babies use many of them, and they cover a variety of situations. A few seem to indicate emotion, as did "dididi," which one little girl spoke loudly to indicate disapproval and softly to indicate satisfaction (see Table 7.1).

Many of the first conventional words accompany actions or changes or some kind. They are likely to refer to the appearance or disappearance of some person ("Daddy!"), animal ("doggy"), or thing ("ball"); or else to a change in condition ("all gone") or situation ("up"). Words come quickly; in a study of three children's early linguistic development (Stoel-Gammon and Cooper, 1984), Daniel (whose first words were "light," "uh-oh," and

"what's that") had a fifty-word vocabulary within four months. Sarah (who first produced "baby," "mommy," and "doggie") took five and one-half months to reach that point, and Will (who began with "uh-oh," "all done," and "light") required six and one-half months.

Children simplify these early words. They may drop an initial consonant ("addy," for "daddy," "poon" for "spoon") or a final consonant ("du" for "duck," "ba" for "ball"). If an adult word has two syllables, children often make the second syllable a duplicate of the first ("baba" for "button"). Or they may use duplication to stretch out a one-syllable word ("coat-coat," "go-go"). Individual vocabularies vary widely, both in the consonants used and the form of words. Apparently, each child uses words whose sounds or syllable types they can produce easily, while avoiding words with sounds or syllable types they cannot articulate (Stoel-Gammon and Cooper, 1984).

From the content of their early vocabulary, we can tell quite a bit about the way in which infants and toddlers perceive and arrange their worlds. They talk about familiar objects as well as such important events as comings ("hi"), goings ("bye-bye"), and games ("peekaboo"). One of their first few words is likely to be "baby," which they generally use to refer to themselves. Very early, toddlers also talk about situations, usually referring to the outcomes of actions ("up," "broken," "stuck," "off"), and transient states of objects ("dirty," "wet"). Most children are about two years old before they talk about the permanent state of objects ("red" or "little") (Clark, 1983).

What Do First Words Mean?

During the one-word stage, which generally lasts until toddlers are about eighteen months old, their one-word utterances have to do the work of an entire sentence. Because youngsters mean more than they can say with a single word, their one-word sentences are called **holophrases**. The child may have an entire proposition in mind but can convey only one part of it at a time.

Most simple utterances can be understood only in context, as we saw in the discussion of intent. When a parent sees the toy on the floor or the empty cup of milk, the meaning of the child's "gone" is clear. The context of a situation goes far beyond the arrangement of objects and people in

As this youngster "reads" to the stuffed bear, most of her words are the names of familiar objects. *(Emily Siroka/Woodfin Camp & Assoc.)*

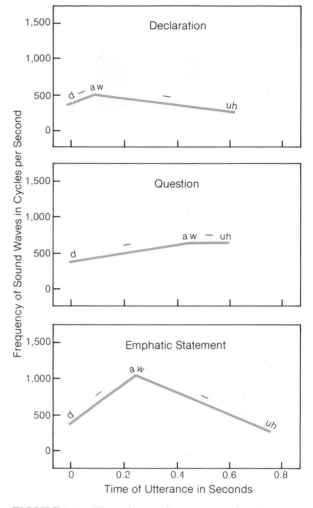

FIGURE 7.2   Three intonation patterns for the word *door* spoken by an infant at the one-word stage. *(After Menyuk, 1971)*

the environment. It includes beliefs, assumptions, actions, prior remarks, knowledge, and intentions (Ochs, 1979). When it is mealtime, whether a small boy says "up" or "chair," the mother knows that the toddler wants the tray removed so that he can climb into the highchair. Children's gestures —pointing, waving, stamping their feet, jerking or nodding their heads—often provide clues to meaning.

Intonation is an especially strong clue to a child's intent. Its ability to clarify meaning was evident in a study using tapes of a toddler saying "door" in several situations (Menyuk and Bernholtz, 1969). When the researchers played the tapes for listeners, there was general agreement about whether the child's use of "door" was a declaration, a question, or an emphatic statement (see Figure 7.2). When the word was spoken with a falling pitch (frequency contour), listeners judged the utterance as referring to a door ("That's a door"). When the same word was uttered with a rising intonation, listeners interpreted it as a question ("Is that a door?" or "Are you going to open the door?"). When the intonation rose sharply and then fell, it was heard as an emphatic assertion or demand ("Open the door!" "Close the door!"). Thus a single word can convey a number of meanings, depending on how a child says it.

Overextending Words

After children have learned a word, they may ex-

tend its meaning to cover other objects or actions that resemble it in some way; this process is called **overextension.** When an infant extends a word, usually it is possible to find some perceived similarity of form or function among the objects and events it includes. Most overextensions are based on appearance, with up to 90 percent of such overextensions based on shape (Clark, 1983). For example, one child extended "baw" from its original meaning, "ball," to refer to apples, grapes, eggs, squash, the clapper of a bell, and anything round. Some overextensions are based on movement, size, taste, texture, or sound.

Do children's overextensions signify a confusion in the meaning of words? Sometimes they

A toddler who says the single word "door" can be understood only in context. The word might mean "Open the door," "Close the door," or any of several other statements. *(Sybil Shelton/Monkmeyer)*

may. As noted earlier, in most cases children have concepts before they have words for them, but the child's concept may be very different from that of the adult. If the child's concept of "bow-wow" is a four-legged animal, then the child's overextension is just what it seems to be. Yet children often know that their overextensions are "wrong." Many youngsters who refer to all animals as "bow-wow," when asked to point to the "bow-wow," always pick a dog from a group of animals. They never point to a cat or a sheep (Gruendel, 1977). In such cases, the child knows that a cat is not a "bow-wow" but has no special word for "cat."

Sometimes children's extensions may reveal greater sensitivity than we give them credit for. The child may be trying to draw attention to a perceived similarity, as when a youngster calls a grapefruit a moon (roundness). If the child's grasp

of language were firmer, she or he might say "It's like a moon" or "It's round." In various studies (for example, Hudson and Nelson, 1984), children as young as twenty months have deliberately used language metaphorically. For example, one toddler (who knew the correct name for puppets and for paper bags) put a bag over his hand and said "puppet."

Learning New Words

Children pick up words in the context of some specific situation, and a word's initial meaning depends on the way the child represents the linguistic context (the structure of the utterance) and the nonlinguistic context (the physical situation) (Carey, 1982). For example, a toddler who has an older brother may at first believe that the meanings of "boy" and "brother" are identical.

In proposing how children acquire words, Clark (1983) has suggested that as youngsters become aware of a gap in their vocabulary, they search for the conventional word used in their language community to fill it. When they hear a new word, they assume that the word's meaning contrasts with the words already in their vocabulary, and they try to fit this new word to a concept for which they have no label. Until they find a word that will fill the gap, they rely on three devices as "place-holders." First, they temporarily overextend many words. Second, they rely on general-purpose words. When they need a noun, they use "that" or "thing"; when they need a verb, they resort to "do," "make," or "go." Finally, children coin new words — for objects, situations, or events. These new words are different from the invented quasi-words that children used as twelve-month-olds. Now their new words follow the word-formation patterns of English. They add suffixes; one five-year-old came up with "hateable" to describe the food in a hospital. They convert nouns to verbs; a toddler who hits an object with a stick may say "I sticked it." And they create compound words. One youngster called a psychologist who worked with rats a "ratman" and another called someone who smiled a lot a "smileperson." By the time children are coining words in this way, they have traveled a long way on the road of language acquisition. Figure 7.3, which charts the highlights of language development in the first two years, shows just how far they have come.

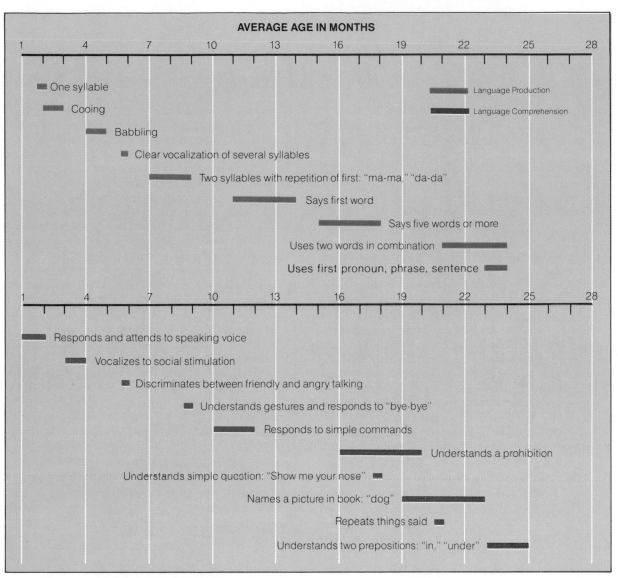

FIGURE 7.3 Highlights of language development during the first two years of life. The ages shown are approximate, and the length of the bars reflects the age range that researchers have reported for the appearance of a particular linguistic advance. *(Adapted from Lenneberg, 1967; McCarthy, 1954; Bayley, 1969)*

PUTTING WORDS TOGETHER

Toward the end of the one-word period, toddlers make sequences of separate one-word utterances that seem to relate to a larger meaning. Yet they speak each word separately, with its own falling intonation. For example, one eighteen-month-old girl looked at researcher Ronald Scollan (1979), held her foot threateningly above his tape recorder and said, "Tape. Step." Within two months, she was combining two words in a smooth utterance, saying such things as "Wash clothes" with no pause between the words.

The two-word stage is significant because it marks a striking advance in children's ability to code their understanding in linguistic terms and to project their ideas into the world of human interaction. It begins when children can process two words at a time without running out of space in working memory.

SUBDIVIDING THE WORLD

When two-year-olds coin such words as "feather-hat" or "lionbook" to fill gaps in their vocabulary, exactly what are they doing? They may be saying that there is a feather on the hat and a lion in the book. But they may be creating subcategories—dividing their world into even smaller conceptual chunks. In that case, their compound words would function as do adult subcategories; for example, *spaniel, collie,* and *poodle* are subcategories of *dog.*

At Stanford University, Eve Clark, Susan Gelman, and Nancy Lane (1985) tested young children to see how they interpreted the compound words they heard. By the time children were three years old, most interpreted such compounds appropriately. They knew which was the main word and which the modifier. When shown four pictures (a hat; a mouse; a hat on a mouse; and a hat on a fish), they point to the hat on the mouse if asked "Show me the mousehat." Most two-year-olds had not grasped the idea, and four-year-olds made almost perfect scores. But the children had not yet demonstrated that they interpreted compound words as denoting subcategories. In a further study, Clark and her colleagues placed children in situations that encouraged them to form compound words. Although two-year-olds formed some compounds, they were more likely to use simple nouns to describe the pictured objects. Three- and four-year-olds coined com-pound words that subcategorized the objects almost as often as adults did. When the children formed compounds, they prefaced them with articles ("a," "the")—a further indication that they realized that they were labeling categories and not attaching proper names. Like adults, the children were more likely to coin compound words when they were describing inherent categories ("pumpkinhouse" for a house made out of a pumpkin) than when they were describing accidental juxtapositions ("spiderchair" for a chair with spiders on it).

Children apparently interpret compound words much as adults do, as picking out a contrast within a single category. Four-year-olds are alert to grammatical clues that tell them to look for such contrasts. In another study (Gelman and Markman, 1985), four-year-olds showed that they understood the use of adjectives to pick out contrasts. When faced with four pictures (two identical caps, a spotted cap, and a geometric figure), they chose the figure if asked to point to "the fep." But if they were asked to point to "the fep one," they chose the spotted cap. Apparently, four-year-olds have worked out the conceptual relationship between nouns and adjectives. When they hear an adjective—even if they do not know its meaning—they focus on the category and look for contrasts within it.

Semantic Relations in Two-Word Sentences

Despite this limit on the length of their sentences, children are able to express a wide variety of ideas. They do this by combining their two words in a series of patterns that are based on semantic relations. From the study of Adam, Eve, and Sarah, Roger Brown (1970) discovered that all the children's two-word statements could be described by four patterns in which the youngsters referred to some object or event and seven patterns that depended on the relation between the two words in the utterance (see Table 7.2). These relations, such as actor, possessor, and location, reflect the situational meaning of words. Formal categories, such as nouns and verbs, subjects and objects, are absent from children's speech at this early age. Because they rely on semantic relations in forming their speech patterns, children often treat words from the same adult category (verbs such as *want* and *tickle*) differently. As Michael Maratsos (1983) has concluded, the structure of children's two-word utterances does not seem to follow general rules of English **syntax,** or the structural principles for forming sentences.

In fact, trying to analyze two-word utterances by formal grammatical rules that govern the distribution of word classes like nouns and verbs is futile. Such an analysis would treat the sentence

Table 7.2
Meanings in Two-Word Utterances

Reference		Relations	
Identification (demonstrative + object)	That (or it or there) + cat	Attributive (attribute + object)	Big + train, red + book
Notice (greeting + name)	Hi + mommy	Possessive (possessor + object)	Adam + checker
Recurrence	More (or 'nother) + milk	Locative 1 (object + location)	Sweater + chair
Nonexistence	Allgone (or no more) + rattle	Locative 2 (action + location or goal)	Go + store
		Agent + action	Adam + put
		Agent + patient (recipient of action)	Mommy + sock
		Action + patient	Put + book

Note: These eleven patterns show the range of meanings expressed in two-word utterances.

Source: Adapted from Brown, 1970; Maratsos, 1983.

"Baby chair" as the same, no matter how it was used (Bloom, 1970). But an eighteen-month-old boy may say "Baby chair" and mean "Baby is sitting in her highchair," or he may say "Baby chair" and mean "That is baby's highchair." In both cases, he is using only nouns, yet in the first he is indicating the baby's location and in the second, her possession of the chair.

Telegraphic Speech

The utterances of children who run around saying "Baby chair" and "Daddy shoe" resemble the statements of a telegram, stripped to their barest essentials. So it is not surprising that psychologists call two-word utterances **telegraphic speech**. At this stage, the words children choose are content words, full of information. All the little "functional" words (articles, prepositions, conjunctions) that would enable listeners to distinguish between the two uses of "Baby chair" are absent. How, then, do children make their meaning clear?

They rely on two grammatical devices that are basic tools of human language: intonation and word order. As they did in the two-word stage, they use intonation to distinguish a statement from a question. Now they also use another intonational device, *stress.* This vocal emphasis easily distin-

guishes the two possible meanings of "Baby chair." If the little boy wanted to indicate possession, he would emphasize the first word, saying "*baby* chair" ("That is baby's chair"). By emphasizing the second word, saying "Baby *chair,*" he could convey location ("Baby is in the chair") or destination ("Put baby in the chair"). The context of the utterance would indicate which he meant.

Instead of using the two-word limit in any order to produce a random collection of words, children combine their words in patterns that generally fit comfortably into the word order of English sentences (Brown, 1973). The typical English sentence follows a subject-verb-object word order, and many of children's early sequences conform to this order, which listeners find easy to follow. Such sequences include agent + action, agent + patient (recipient of the action), and action + patient. Toddlers produce such sentences as "Daddy throw," "Daddy ball," and "Throw ball," and they do not say "Throw Daddy" or "Ball throw." Yet children in this stage have not developed a general concept of word order, and each of their patterns follows its own separate rule. Once youngsters leave the two-word stage, the patterns come together and children grasp the general rules governing word order (Maratsos, 1983).

Although toddlers may not use a general rule in

producing sentences, they seem to use it in interpreting the speech of others. When asked to act out simple sentences (such as "The cat kissed the dog"), in which word order is the only cue to meaning, children in the two-word stage correctly portray the sentence, making the cat—not the dog—the one who does the kissing (de Villiers and de Villiers, 1978).

The Tendency to Overregularize

Once children have figured out a rule, they go through a period when a major strategy seems to be "Avoid exceptions" (Slobin, 1973). When they apply this strategy across the board, as they often do, they attempt to make the language more systematic than it actually is. Errors caused by this strategy disclose their control of a language rule. In English **overregularization** shows clearly when children use the past tense of verbs. The regular way to form the past tense for English verbs is to add *-ed: walk, walked.* Yet many common verbs form their past tenses in an irregular manner: *go, went; break, broke.* Children often learn a number of the irregular past forms as separate words and produce correct sentences: "It broke"; "Daddy went out"; "I fell." After using these correct past tense forms for many months, they discover the rule for forming regular past tenses. The irregular forms now may disappear from their speech, to be replaced by overregularized forms. The child of three or four may say, "It breaked"; "Daddy goed out"; "I falled."

As children get older, a curious pattern of redundant usage develops. Five- and six-year-olds begin to drop forms like "eated," "goed," and "maked," and in their place may use a doubled past form, like "ated," "wented," and "maded" (Kuczaj, 1978). By the time children are seven, they will have nothing to do with the redundant form; most have ceased to overregularize the verb in any way.

What looks like regression in the younger children is actually a sign of progress in their analysis of language. Clearly, children have not heard the overregularized forms from their parents; instead, they construct the forms to conform with the regularities they have noticed in the speech of others. And so a change from "went" to "goed" indicates that children have, on their own, discovered a reg-

ular pattern in English. In order to *avoid exceptions,* they are indicating the idea of the past in a regular way in their speech.

When children overregularize their speech, it often seems impervious to gentle efforts at correction, as the following conversation reported by Jean Berko Gleason (1967) shows:

CHILD: My teacher holded the baby rabbits and we patted them.
MOTHER: Did you say your teacher held the baby rabbits?
CHILD: Yes.
MOTHER: What did you say she did?
CHILD: She holded the baby rabbits and we patted them.
MOTHER: Did you say she held them tightly?
CHILD: No, she holded them loosely.

Although his mother substituted the correct form of the verb twice in this short dialogue, the little boy persisted in repeating "held" as "holded," tenaciously clinging to his own linguistic structure. Apparently, regularity is more powerful in its influence on children than is previous practice, reinforcement, or immediate imitation of adult forms. The child at this level of development seeks regularity and is deaf to exceptions (Bellugi, 1970).

As children gradually become aware of their overregularization, the correct forms seem to filter in and out of consciousness. Dan Slobin (1978) reports a conversation with his young daughter, who was in a transitional phase. Slobin asked her if the babysitter had read a book the previous night, and Heida replied, first using the correct past tense "read," then switching to "readed." During the exchange, Slobin said, "That's the book she readed, huh?" His own overregularization alerted Heida to the correct form and she replied in an annoyed tone, "Yeah. . . . read!" and followed up with the comment, "Dumdum!" Although Heida was shifting back to "read," she may still have been saying "goed" or "maked," because children eliminate their overregularization errors slowly. They must learn, one by one, that only a single past tense form exists for each irregular verb (Kuczaj, 1978).

Children also overregularize when forming plurals. English has some irregular plural forms, many of them common words: *feet, mice, men, children.* These irregular forms, like irregular verb past-tense forms, must be learned as separate vocabulary items. Researchers have found that the child who has been correctly using irregular plural forms (*feet, men, mice*) may, for a time, overgeneralize the newly discovered rules of formation and say "foots," "mans," "mouses"—another example of the kind of regularization that appears in the child's use of verbs. A child may even learn the irregular form but apply the plural rule anyway, saying the redundant "feets," "mens," "mices."

Understanding Complex Constructions

Children's ability to understand and produce complex sentences develops slowly. At first they are unable to handle several language rules at once. As they acquire new constructions, they rely on their knowledge of the world and the immediate context to help them in the task. The gestures and actions of others often serve as clues to the meaning of their words. And because others generally talk about the immediate situation, children tend to apply whatever they have heard to some nearby object or event. This practice sometimes betrays them. For example, children assume that people talk about things in the order that they occur. So when a parent says, "Eat your pie after you eat your broccoli," children are likely to believe that they have been told to eat their dessert first. We can see children's gradual grasp of various constructions by looking at their acquisition of questions.

Children discover a great deal by asking questions that begin with *who, what, where, where, why, how,* and *how come*. Questions are more difficult than statements because the child must use two rules in order to produce the correct form. They not only must begin with the question word, but in all but one of these forms, they also must place the auxiliary verb immediately after their *wh-* word. (The exception is *how come*, in which the child simply attaches the question words to the beginning of the statement: "How come Lauren is laughing?"). If children are to use the *wh-* rules correctly, they must say, "Why is David crying?" or "When will Santa Claus come?" In most cases, this rule requires them to separate the auxiliary and the verb by placing the noun between them—a violation of standard English word order.

Stanley Kuczaj and Nancy Brannick (1979)

Because children begin asking about the world before they know the general rules for forming questions, they are likely to produce such queries as "Why Cathy is crying?" at the sight of a friend in distress. *(Rohn Engh/The Image Works)*

have traced the child's gradual grasp of these rules. In learning to ask these questions, children begin by placing the *wh-* tag at the beginning of the sentence. Using this single rule produces correct *how come* questions, but fails with the others. Children say such things as "What he can ride in?" or "Who the girl will kiss?" This kind of construction is not surprising, because youngsters hear it in their parents' speech—embedded in other sentences. For example, adults say "Have you found out where you can catch the bus?" and "Did I tell you what he was singing?"

After using the incorrect form for a time, children realize that some adjustment is necessary, and they correctly place the auxiliary after the *wh-* tag —but only with *what* and *where*. Their *who, when, why,* and *how* questions are still incorrect. Apparently, children do not learn a second general rule, but begin by learning some of its specific applications (Kuczaj and Brannick, 1979). Once they understand the rule, however, they generalize it to all *wh-* questions, so that their formerly correct *how come* questions now are wrong. They produce such overregularizations as "How come can the dog sleep on the couch?" Just as with the acquisition of past tenses and plurals, children's language goes through a stage when it gets worse before it gets better.

TALKING ABOUT THINKING

When children begin to contemplate their own knowledge and beliefs, they have taken a giant step in cognitive development. When they understand that others also carry out such contemplation, they have made another advance. Yet researchers have found it difficult to assess this aspect of the young child's development (Miscione, Marvin, O'Brien, and Greenberg, 1978). A team of researchers at the University of Michigan decided that by carefully monitoring young children's speech, they might be able to find out. Starting at about two and one-half years, children begin using mental verbs, such as *think, know,* and *remember,* but these words often are conventional ways of holding the floor while a person decides what to say next ("you know") or softening the edge of a request ("I think I'd like a cookie").

Marilyn Shatz, Henry Wellman, and Sharon Silber (1983) carried out two studies in which they monitored young children's speech and noted the context whenever a child used a verb that referred to mental processes. In the first study, they collected samples of a little boy's speech, taping Abe's conversation twice a week from the time he was twenty-eight months old until he was four years old. In the second study, they regularly taped the conversation of thirty two-year-olds over a six-month period.

The analysis showed that early in the third year of life, children begin using mental verbs, but that at first the words do not refer to mental states or to mental processing. Until children are at least thirty months old, they use the terms to aid social interaction, as when they preface a remark with "Know what?" or tag a remark with "you know." Or else they say "I don't know," which the researchers regarded as often used to indicate a negative attitude.

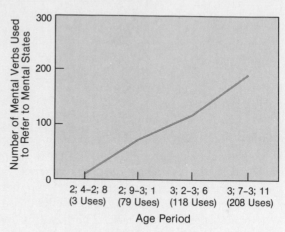

One child's use of mental verbs. (Information from Shatz, Wellman, and Silber, 1983)

Children probably pick up these expressions long before they understand their derivation.

Once children begin referring to mental states, the verbs proliferate in their conversation (see graph, "One Child's Use of Mental Verbs"). Three-year-olds say such things as "I was teasing you; I was *pretending* 'cept you didn't *know* that"; "The people *thought* Dracula was mean, but he was nice"; and "I *thought* there wasn't any socks, but when I looked I saw them." Shortly after children use words to refer to their own minds, children also use them to refer to the thoughts of others. Some researchers (for example, Shatz, 1983) contend that children cannot take part in a mature conversation until they understand that others also have beliefs, thoughts, and goals. Shatz and her colleagues seem to have located that important date near the child's third birthday.

Children do not proceed directly toward adult grammar. Instead, they construct and discard a variety of provisional grammars as they go along. As a result of these changing strategies, sentences that are correctly interpreted at one age may be misinterpreted later. The rapidity with which children acquire language, developing and discarding rules as they go, indicates that human beings are born prepared to learn language but that extensive experience is needed for its acquisition. Exactly how children acquire a command of their native language is still a matter of debate.

EXPLANATIONS OF LANGUAGE ACQUISITION

From thousands of studies, we can piece together a convincing description of the child's dawning grasp of language. We know *what* happens, but no one has yet been able to provide a satisfactory explanation of *how* children acquire language. Part of the problem undoubtedly arises because investigators split up the process of language acquisition into tiny parcels, such as the acquisition of negatives, or the grasp of a verb's meaning, or how children master the art of dialogue. An explanation that seems to handle the way a child gains mastery of some aspect of syntax is unlikely to tell us much about the acquisition of phonology, semantics, or pragmatics — and vice versa. An adequate explanation must take into account the maturational, cognitive, and social precursors of language; it must explain the diversity of children's first words, how they figure out the rules of syntax, and how early acquisition leads into the adult's mature command of language. For years, developmentalists veered between two explanations of language: the behavioristic and the biological. The first, said psychologist George Miller, was impossible; the second was miraculous (see Bruner, 1983). A third explanation, which stresses social and cognitive interaction, has tried to fill the gap between the impossible and the miraculous, but success remains elusive.

Biological Theories

In biological approaches, language development is primarily a matter of maturation because, according to linguist Noam Chomsky (1975; 1979), the structure of language is laid down in our genes. He called this innate capacity a **language acquisition device,** or **LAD,** and believed that it allows children to speak just as wings allow birds to fly. All human languages, despite their surface differences, share an underlying deep structure, which he calls a *universal grammar.* This grammar consists of principles, conditions, and rules for producing sound, meaning, and structure. The grammatical categories of subject, predicate, object, and verb are part of this universal grammar.

Because biological constraints characterize the grammar children will construct, they take the bits and pieces of language they hear, analyze them, and fit them to the universal grammar. Only in this way, says Chomsky, can we explain how children in a given community — each hearing entirely different and mostly fragmentary language — come up with the same rich, complex language system. In this view, language is partly predetermined, in the same way that genes determine the pattern of sexual maturation, and — given experience — children inevitably acquire language.

Biological theories assume that brain maturation is deeply involved in language acquisition. According to Eric Lenneberg (1967), language can be acquired only during a sensitive period in human development. The period begins when children are about two years old and lasts until they reach sexual maturity. At that time, the ability to learn a language declines, and by the late teens it is difficult — or even impossible — to acquire a first language. The end of the sensitive period, said Lenneberg (1973), coincides with the maturation of the brain; the mature brain has lost its plasticity and can no longer make the adjustments that the acquisition of language requires.

Some researchers believe that the case of Genie, a California girl who grew up in almost total isolation, indicates that a weakened version of Lenneberg's claim may be true (Curtiss, 1977). Genie was discovered when she was nearly fourteen, and her social experiences had been limited to spoon feeding by her almost blind mother. No one spoke to her, and whenever she made a noise, her father beat her. When Genie was found, she was severely disturbed and had no language. Although she slowly learned to understand the language of others, the syntax of her own language is impaired. Genie lacks many basic linguistic structures, such as passive sentences and *wh-* questions. Yet some aspects of Genie's development fail to support biological theories. Her speech is rule-governed and productive, and she can speak of people and objects that are not present. In addition Genie's sharply restricted childhood affected her cognitive development. Her store of concepts and world knowledge on which children build their language was so limited that this restriction, together with her emotional disturbance, may explain her problems with language.

According to biological theories of language acquisition, the existence of a sensitive period for language acquisition helps explain why youngsters who grow up in bilingual households speak both languages with ease. *(David S. Strickler/The Picture Cube)*

Behavioristic Theories

Given the problems with the "miraculous" theory of language acquisition, what about the "impossible" theory? Behaviorists, among them B. F. Skinner (1957) and Sidney Bijou and Donald Baer (1965), see language as simply vocal behavior that is reinforced by the action of another person. Because mothers generally talk to babies while they care for them, using words to express affection, a mother's speech becomes reinforcing. Babies also can reinforce themselves by listening to their own vocalizations. As they mature and gain control over their speech apparatus, babies begin to direct the sounds they produce, and the more closely their babbling resembles their mothers' speech, the more reinforcing their vocalizations become. When babies babble, their mothers often reward them with attention, thereby providing additional reinforcement.

When babies begin to label the objects in their world, their parents reinforce them with attention or approval. The reinforcement is for the sound itself, but the child soon responds to the sight of the object (ball, sock, doll) with the label. Other words are learned because the child receives tangi-ble rewards for producing them, as when the words "cookie" or "bottle" are followed by the objects they represent.

How do children acquire rules for combining words? They learn patterns of words (such as "the boy's X," "on the X," or "hit the X") into which they can insert new items. These patterns, called *grammatical frames*, function in sentences just as sounds function in words. Children build sentences out of grammatical frames, a process that allows them to produce sentences that are different from the sentences they hear. Gradually, children accumulate a patchwork of thousands of separately acquired frames, patterns, responses, and rules. On this base, they develop language by making small generalizations, inferences, and analogies (Whitehurst, 1982).

Social-learning theorists would add that imitation plays a major role in the acquisition of speech and that both comprehension and speech are based on observational learning (Bandura, 1977). Parents (and others) serve as models for their children, who imitate the speech they hear. They imitate grammatical frames as well as vocabulary, substituting their own words in frames they have heard others use. As noted in Chapter 2, imitation does not have to be immediate. A child can learn by observing and imitating the forms of adult speech when a later occasion warrants it. When a small girl says "I seed two mouses," says Albert Bandura, she is modeling structures she has heard in the speech of others—but modeling them "too well." Indeed, some social-learning theorists have summed up children's acquisition of language as "delayed selective imitation" (Whitehurst and Vasta, 1975).

Social-Cognitive Interaction Theories

The interaction approach to language acquisition agrees with the biological contention that maturation is vital and that until children reach a certain cognitive level, they cannot acquire language. It also agrees with the behaviorist contention that social interaction is the place to look for the emergence of language. But interaction theorists maintain that innate mechanisms cannot, by themselves, explain the child's grasp of language. The basis for linguistic competence also goes beyond conditioning and observational learning to include nonlinguistic aspects of human interaction: turn-taking, mutual gazing, joint attention, context, assumptions, and cultural conventions. The forms of language are acquired so children can carry out communicative functions (Bates, 1979).

Investigators with these interactionist views see general cognitive development and pragmatics as the keys to language development in a child. They point out that until children reach a certain stage of cognitive development, language is impossible and maintain that the nonlinguistic aspects of babies' social interactions build the pre-speech bases of language (Bruner, 1983). Instead of the unfolding of preprogrammed behavior, language is the product of the child's active interaction with an environment provided by other human beings. As Jean Berko Gleason and Sandra Weintraub (1978) point out, cognitive development can result from interaction with the physical world, but children cannot acquire language merely through simple exposure to it as passive listeners.

Will we ever have a satisfactory explanation of language development? Michael Maratsos (1983)

According to behaviorists, youngsters learn words rapidly because parents reinforce a child's early attempts to label objects. *(Charles Harbutt/Archive)*

believes that our knowledge of language acquisition is in a transitional state. He suggests that some of our most important findings either do not fit any of the current theories or else do not seem relevant to them. His advice seems to be to check back again in a few years. In the meantime, some variety of the interactionist approach may be most promising (Bohannon and Warren-Leubecker, 1985). Because interactionist theories borrow freely from the other major approaches, they give us the broadest available view of language acquisition.

SUMMARY

1. During the first year, the baby's vocal tract changes in shape and structure, and areas of the cortex involved with language mature. From birth, babies can detect slight distinctions between sounds that are critical to the perception of speech, and within a few months they respond to changes in intonation and stress. Babies go through five overlapping stages in their production of prelinguistic sounds. **Cooing,** or sounds of joy, first appear at about eight weeks. Around nine months, when babies enter the fifth stage, they use **expressive jargon,** babbling with the intonation and pitch of adult speech. Very early, babies grasp the **pragmatic** aspect of language: its social function. During interactions with their parents, babies learn many conventions of language use, including turn-taking. Without some exposure to the simplified speech known as **motherese,** infants might never become competent speakers. Among the cognitive precursors to language are object permanence, the development of concepts, the ability to imitate others, symbolic play, and the development of intent. The cognitive precursors culminate in the baby's awareness of **semantics.**

2. At first, infants speak in one-word sentences known as **holophrases,** and these simple utterances can be understood only in context. **Overextension,** in which a word's meaning is extended to cover other objects or actions, is fairly common among young children. When children discover a gap in their vocabulary, they either overextend another word to cover it, fall back on general purpose words, or coin a new word.

3. Two-word utterances are called **telegraphic speech.** Children in the two-word stage combine their two words in patterns that are based on semantic relations; these utterances do not follow the general rules of English **syntax.** Children in this stage have begun to use stress (vocal emphasis) to express meaning.

4. As children begin to acquire language rules, their language is marked by **overregularization,** in which they apply rules without exception. Asking questions follows a gradual course. First, children simply place the *wh-* tag at the beginning of a sentence. Then they begin using the auxiliary verb after the tag but learn it through specific instances. Once they understand the rule, they overregularize it.

5. Biological theories of language acquisition, such as that proposed by Noam Chomsky, assert that language development is largely a matter of brain maturation and that biological constraints characterize the universal grammar that underlies all languages. Chomsky called the innate language capacity a **language acquisition device (LAD).** Behavioristic theories assert that language is simply vocal behavior reinforced by the action of others; rules are acquired as children learn word patterns, known as grammatical frames. Social-learning theorists add observational learning and imitation to the behavioristic account. Social-cognitive interaction theorists agree that maturation is important but assert that nonlinguistic aspects of human interaction are equally important and that language is acquired for its pragmatic function. None of these theories yet provides a satisfactory explanation of language development, but some sort of interaction theory gives the broadest available view.

KEY TERMS

cooing

expressive jargon

holophrases

language acquisition device (LAD)

motherese

overextension

overregularization

pragmatics

semantics

speech act

syntax

telegraphic speech

STUDY TERMS

overextension A generalization in the child's meaning of a word so that it includes a number of dissimilar objects or events.

overregularization A temporary error in language acquisition in which the child applies a rule rigidly, making the language more regular than it actually is.

pragmatics The study of language's social purposes, in which each utterance used for communication is intended to help the speaker achieve some goal.

semantics The study of the arbitrary meanings conveyed by language forms, which provide the basis for an essential property of language: its ability to transmit meaning.

syntax The structural principles that determine the form of sentences.

CHAPTER 8

Personality: Becoming a Person

THE DEVELOPMENT OF ATTACHMENT
The Stages of Attachment / Separation Distress / Wariness of Strangers

VARIATIONS IN ATTACHMENT
Mothers / Fathers / Infant Responsiveness / Maternal Deprivation

THE EFFECTS OF CLASS AND CULTURE
Socioeconomic Differences / Cultural Differences / Multiple Caregiving

THE DEVELOPMENT OF SOCIABILITY
Attachment and Sociability / Self-concept / Competence and Autonomy / Boy or Girl / Peers and Siblings

Thirteen-month-old Christine Nowicki and her three-year-old sister Kate wake up each morning at six and eat breakfast with their orthodontist father in the kitchen. Later their mother comes, picks up Christine, and holds her while she talks with Kate about the coming day. When the housekeeper arrives, mother leaves for her own dental practice. In the Nowicki family, father takes care of morning child-care duties, and mother takes over in the evening (Shreve, 1984).

As little as ten years ago, the Nowicki family would have been considered an oddity. Even then, however, nearly one-third of all mothers of young children who lived with their husbands worked. Today, these employed mothers are in the majority (U.S. Department of Labor, 1986). Among divorced mothers of small children, a majority have been employed outside the home since 1970—when the first tabulations were made. Today, the unusual mother is not the one who goes out to work but the one who stays home with her children (L. Hoffman, 1984a). The American family has moved so far from its traditional image that our old views of infancy and early childhood may need radical change.

Today's baby is likely to spend a good part of the day separated from his or her mother. This separation does not seem to harm mother-child interaction, although it may change its nature. As we shall see, changes in the mother's interaction with her baby may be accompanied by changes in the way the father relates to the infant. Another consequence of the new family is the acceleration of the baby's social development. Today's infants may become social at a much earlier age. Whether babies go into conventional day care or into the home of a sitter who cares for other children, they come into sustained contact with unfamiliar peers and adults at a much earlier age than previous generations of American children did. In many other cultures, early peer contact traditionally has been the norm.

This chapter traces the beginnings of that social development in infants and toddlers. We start by tracing the development of the baby's first social bond with primary caregivers and discover that this attachment can take different forms. After a look at the effects of maternal deprivation, we examine class and cultural differences in child care and the question of substitute care. We find that attachment plays an important role in the baby's developing trust in the world and in the growing sense of self. Our exploration of the relationship between social bonds and the development of autonomy leads us to consider the way that early social interactions encourage independence in boys and encourage dependence in girls. Finally, we watch the baby become a social toddler and note the influence of peers and siblings on this development. By the end of the chapter, we will have examined a number of ways in which the important lessons of the child's first few years lay the groundwork for later development.

THE DEVELOPMENT OF ATTACHMENT

Human babies are born prepared by millions of years of primate evolution to respond to the sights and sounds of people and to behave in ways that elicit responses from them. Developmentalists who take an ethological view, among them John Bowlby (1969) and Mary Ainsworth (Ainsworth, Blehar, Waters, and Wall, 1978), have argued that the baby's inborn tendencies, such as crying or fussing when distressed, keep adults nearby and so help the baby to survive. Adults, in turn, have been prepared by evolution to respond to the baby's signals, providing care and giving the infant opportunities for social interaction.

These tendencies are considered the foundation of complex systems of social behavior that begin in the family. In most cultures, mothers and infants are involved for a time in a close symbiotic relationship in which the child is almost an extension of the mother's being. For this reason, many investigators have concentrated on the development of **attachment,** the special bond between infant and caregiver.

Our understanding of the development and consequences of attachment is heavily indebted to research with animals, and such research has dispelled some early assumptions about the nature of the bond. For many years, psychoanalysts and learning theorists assumed that babies develop close bonds with their caregivers because the caregiver satisfies the baby's physical needs. J. P. Scott (1962) has noted that this assumption leads to an unromantic conclusion: Infants love us only because we feed them. Research with monkeys has demonstrated, however, that there is more to attachment than being fed. In one series of studies by Harry F. Harlow and Margaret Harlow (1966; 1969), infant monkeys were raised in cages with two surrogate mothers. One mother substitute was covered with soft terrycloth; the other, equipped with a feeding mechanism, was made of hard wire mesh. If feeding were the major factor in attachment, the infant monkeys would have become attached to the wire mother, which fed them. But the monkeys spent much more time clinging to the cloth mother, which gave them no nourishment at all.

The monkeys seemed genuinely attached to the cloth mother. Given a choice of things to observe in a machine that allowed them to see various objects, they looked at the cloth mother much more often than at the wire mother. When monkeys raised with these artificial mothers were put in a strange place or when frightening objects were placed near them, they ran to the security of the cloth, but not the wire, mother. At first, the baby

monkeys seemed terrified, but when allowed to cling to their cloth mother, they soon calmed down. Eventually, the monkeys used the cloth mother as a base for exploring the world, leaving to manipulate strange objects but often returning to cling to their soft, snuggly mother, as monkeys raised with real mothers do. The wire mothers were never used in this way.

Baby monkeys may have become attached to the terrycloth mother because contact is important to the formation of attachment in monkeys. At birth, young monkeys cling to their mothers; it seems to be as natural to them as scanning and vocalizing are to human babies. A soft terrycloth mother encourages clinging, but a cold, hard mesh mother does not; and the difference leads to lasting effects. After a year's separation, a monkey will run to embrace its soft terrycloth mother, holding on passionately to its soft form. But after a similar separation from wire mothers, monkeys show no affection at all when they are reunited.

The Stages of Attachment

Attachment in people and in monkeys follows a similar pattern (see Table 8.1), but the response of the human baby to his or her mother develops more slowly than the monkey's attachment to its mother. In human beings, the bond takes many months to appear, involves a complex intermeshing of behavior between infant and caregiver, and assumes widely different forms.

Attachment in human babies refers to the early love relationship between the baby and the caregiver (usually one or both parents). Babies show this bond by reacting in characteristic ways. They smile and greet the caregiver joyously; when the caregiver leaves, they usually cry. A crucial aspect of behavior that signifies attachment is that it is directed toward some people and not toward others.

A baby's earliest responses to people are indiscriminate and do not reflect attachment. This ini-

When frightened by a toy bear *(top)*, monkey babies in the Harlow experiments ran to the cloth-covered mother for comfort *(middle)* and rejected the wire mother that fed them *(bottom)*. *(Harry F. Harlow, University of Wisconsin Primate Laboratory)*

Table 8.1
Stages of Attachment

Stage	Description	Age
I.	Indiscriminate social responsiveness (accepts comfort from anyone)	Birth to 2 months
II.	Discriminate social responsiveness (prefers familiar figures but does not protest when parents leave)	2 to 7 months
III.	Specific attachment (separation from caregiver leads to clear distress)	7 to 30 months
IV.	Goal-directed partnership (no longer distressed at caregiver's deparature; can work toward shared goals)	From 30 months

tial, indiscriminate stage of responsiveness lasts for about the first two months of life. During this time, the baby's cries bring milk, dry diapers, an end to physical discomfort; they also bring the pleasures of close human contact. But the baby will accept such aid and comfort from anyone. Toward the end of this period, the baby becomes a social being, cooing and smiling. Because these coos and social smiles are directed toward anyone, it appears that their onset is primarily controlled by maturation.

During the next stage of attachment, which lasts from two months until about seven months, babies begin to discriminate among the people around them (see Figure 8.1). At five months, they may smile at familiar faces as often as or even more often than they did before, but the smiling at strangers that was so prevalent at about two or three months drops off and even disappears. Gradually, the baby comes to recognize those people who consistently relieve his or her distress. At the sight of their faces, the baby feels an upsurge of positive emotion and responds socially with bright-eyed smiles, coos, and arm-waving. Although at this stage, babies may respond in special ways to specific people, they are unlikely to have developed a true attachment to a caregiver. For example, if a parent leaves a five-month-old baby with a sitter, the baby is unlikely to protest.

By the time they are eight months old, most babies have developed the intense bond that signifies true attachment. This third stage generally begins at about seven months and lasts until the infant is two or two and one-half years old. Before true attachment can emerge, the baby must realize not only that the same people react to his or her needs in the same predictable ways, but also that people continue to exist after they disappear from view. Most babies studied by Silvia Bell (1970) were aware of their mothers as objects who continued to exist when out of sight slightly before the babies showed a similar awareness of the continued existence of physical objects. Although person permanence may not always appear before object permanence (Levitt, Antonucci, and Clark, 1984), it seems likely that the comings and goings of the human caregiver may induce the baby to pay attention to the location of this very important "object." After all, the caregiver's activities are closely associated with the satisfaction of the baby's needs.

Some time after their second birthday, toddlers stop showing such visible distress each time their mothers leave. They have entered the fourth and final stage of attachment, which begins around two or two and one-half years and lasts throughout life. In this mature attachment, the original relationship becomes a partnership as the child comes to understand the caregiver's feelings and motives. The emotional bond remains strong, and the child still wants to be near the parent, but give and take has entered the relationship. The child now can use words and hugs and other devices in an attempt to influence the parent's plans — what child wants to be left at home when parents go to a party or away for the weekend? But when parents do leave,

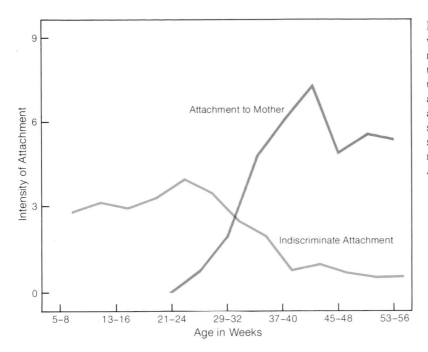

FIGURE 8.1   During the early weeks of life, most infants prefer not to be separated from the person they are with regardless of who that person is. Such "indiscriminate attachments" begin to decline at about the same time that the infant starts to show preferences for specific persons, such as the mother. *(Adapted from Schaffer and Emerson, 1964)*

the child continues to feel secure, as long as he or she knows where the parents have gone and when they are likely to return.

In their studies of attachment, researchers have focused on the third stage, when infants are distressed at a caregiver's absence. Their unhappiness generally shows itself in separation distress and stranger wariness.

Separation Distress

When a mother leaves her ten-month-old baby in an unfamiliar place, the baby is likely to cry and stop playing. When the mother leaves, the baby may reach for her and, if able, may crawl in pursuit of her. Such a reaction to an attachment figure is called **separation distress.** Although the adaptive function of attachment is to keep the infant alive, the bond also provides the baby with emotional security. Because an attachment figure acts as a secure base for the baby, the figure's presence prevents or reduces any fear the baby may experience when confronted with an unusual situation.

Separation distress appears to be a universal phenomenon, although it may emerge at slightly different ages in various cultures. For example, Ugandan babies begin to protest as early as six months when separated from their mothers (Ainsworth, 1967), but most Guatemalan babies do not object until they are nine months old (Lester, Kotelchuck, Spelke, Sellers, and Klein, 1974). In all cultures that have been studied, separation distress is apparent by eight or nine months and remains high until about eighteen months, when it begins to decline (Kagan, 1984).

When they find themselves in a strange situation, most nine- to twelve-month-old babies become concerned if their primary caregivers are not nearby. For example, Mary Ainsworth and Barbara Wittig (1969) found that when in a strange place, a baby's first action is to establish contact with his or her caregiver. After a time, the baby ventures out on short forays to explore the strange environment but always returns to the caregiver between expeditions. Most of us are familiar with this concern on the part of older infants and toddlers. For example, when a mother brings her toddler on a first visit to a friend's home, the young child may cling to (indeed, hide behind) the parent. Only after the child becomes accustomed to the new setting is she or he likely to let go of mother's leg. Young monkeys behave similarly, whether reared normally or with a cloth, surrogate mother; both venture forth only gradually from the physical security of their mothers.

When this baby's primary caregiver left her in a strange place, she was overcome by fear and began to cry, a response known as separation distress. *(Cour. by Laszlo Hege)*

Yet an attachment figure does more than act as a secure haven. The presence of the attachment figure allows babies to maintain their emotional bonds, learn about the world by observing their caregiver's actions, and exchange information they discover on their expeditions (Hay, 1980). For example, Harriet Rheingold and Carol Eckerman (1970) saw no distress among infants placed in a novel situation who followed the separation-and-return pattern. The infants they studied seemed to share their joy and excitement with attachment figures. Babies apparently use attachment figures both to reduce their fear and to share in the pleasure of life, and the same general pattern of behavior seems to serve both purposes.

Wariness of Strangers

The baby's wariness of strangers usually develops a month or two after specific attachments emerge. **Wariness of strangers** appears to be a natural reaction that complements attachment and helps the baby to avoid situations, people, or objects that might endanger life. Babies' reactions to strangers appear to pass through four phases. At first, there seems to be no difference in babies' emotional response to strangers and familiar persons. Later,

babies respond postively to strangers, although not as positively as they do to people they know. Then they go through a period of reacting uneasily to strangers; if an attachment figure is present, they look back and forth between the stranger and the caregiver as though trying to decide how the caregiver is reacting to the stranger. At this time, babies merely become sober and stare at the stranger. It is not until they are around eight months old that some babies respond to strangers with fear and withdrawal, looking away, frowning, whimpering, or even crying. This reaction is particularly intense when the baby's attachment figure is absent (Sroufe, Waters, and Matas, 1974).

When a stranger approaches, the caregiver's reaction (expression, tone of voice, and gestures) may either reassure the baby or increase his or her wariness. For example, when mothers of nine-month-old infants frowned at an approaching stranger and said hello in an abrupt and unfriendly tone, the babies reacted warily. Their hearts speeded up, their smiles disappeared, and some of them were visibly distressed. But when the mother smiled at both baby and stranger and said hello in a cheerful, friendly tone, the babies relaxed. Their hearts slowed, many of them smiled, and fewer showed any sign of distress (Boccia and Campos, 1983).

The way a stranger approaches also influences babies' reactions. Most babies become fearful if a stranger arrives and immediately reaches for them, touches them, or picks them up (Sroufe, 1977). When babies are given time to evaluate the stranger, however, many show little distress. As Mary Anne Trause (1977) found, if a stranger pauses before walking up to a year-old baby, the baby may smile, but if the stranger walks over rapidly, the infant probably will frown, turn away, or even burst into tears. The slower approach seems to give the baby time to decide whether the stranger may be dangerous.

An encounter with a stranger is a social situation, one in which the stranger's sex, appearance, and manner also affect the baby's reaction (Clarke-Stewart, 1978). In lab experiments, where strangers act out a rigid script, babies show more wariness or fear than they do when the stranger is allowed to interact naturally with them. Babies are much less likely to show wariness in

Many factors affect a toddler's response to a stranger: the sex, appearance, and manner of the stranger; the reaction of the toddler's caregiver; and whether the encounter takes place in a familiar setting. *(Elizabeth Crews)*

their own homes. In a longitudinal study, Russel Tracy, Michael Lamb, and Mary Ainsworth (1976) studied babies in their own homes from the time they were three weeks old until they were more than a year old. Every three weeks the investigators observed the babies for four hours. Once the babies began to crawl, they tended to follow their mother from place to place and to play comfortably in the presence of strangers. Although no baby at any age ever followed a stranger, few cried or showed other distress at a stranger's approach. The psychologist's laboratory may be a strange and perhaps frightening place to a baby. Babies respond to its strangeness by exploring and vocalizing less than they do at home.

VARIATIONS IN ATTACHMENT

Babies become attached to their mothers, their fathers, their siblings, and their substitute caregivers, but the nature of the bond is not always the same. A baby's temperament certainly affects the way parents respond to their child, so the quality of the attachment bond may depend as much on the baby's style as on that of the parents. Yet most research has explored parents' styles and practices.

For at least twenty-five years, researchers have been studying characteristics of caregiver and culture that might affect the way attachment develops.

Mothers

Some mothers often play with their babies, others usually restrict game time to the periods when they take care of the baby's needs. Some pick up the baby at the first hint of distress; others let the infant "cry it out." Researchers have discovered that the way a mother interacts with her child may affect just how secure the baby actually feels in various situations.

After studying mothers and their babies in a strange situation, Mary Ainsworth and her colleagues (1978) discerned three major kinds of attachment: secure, avoidant, and ambivalent. Infants with a **secure attachment** seem comfortable in a strange place as long as their mother is nearby. At first they react pleasantly to a stranger's approach but are clearly distressed when their mothers leave. When their mothers return, these babies actively seek them out, and the contact quickly ends their distress. About two-thirds of babies react in this way. The rest, who are less securely attached, fall into two roughly equal groups. The first group, who have an **avoidant attachment,** seem almost oblivious to their mothers' presence. They explore without checking back; they show no distress when their mothers leave; and when their mothers return, the babies do not seek contact with them. They seem almost too independent. The second group, who have an **ambivalent attachment,** seem the least secure. Although their mothers are present, the strange room and the stranger both distress them, and they stay close to their mothers' side. They are extremely upset when their mothers leave, but when their mothers return they alternate between seeking contact (perhaps holding out their arms to their mother) and angrily squirming to get away when picked up.

What is it about a mother's style of interaction that affects the quality of her baby's attachment? Ainsworth believed that a mother's sensitivity to her infant's needs was vital to the development of a secure attachment, and most research has supported this finding. Among babies of poor, unmarried mothers, those who developed secure attachments tended to have mothers who were cooperative with them and sensitive to their needs (Egeland and Farber, 1984). After reviewing a number of longitudinal studies, Michael Lamb and his colleagues concluded that securely attached babies generally had mothers who were warm, responsive, not intrusive, and not abusive (Lamb, Thompson, Gardner, and Charnov, 1985). Insecurely attached babies generally had mothers who lacked some or all of these qualities.

In trying to link these maternal qualities with the attachment bond, we might note that warm mothers show affection freely, often touch their infants tenderly, smile a good deal, and talk to them. Responsive mothers are dependable about answering their babies' cries of distress and pleas for attention — and they are quick to do so. Sensitive mothers are accurate at reading their babies' signals, whether they are calls for assistance or signs of fatigue, fear, or a desire to play. Unintrusive mothers are likely to cooperate with their babies' efforts to accomplish a new goal — even when the goal of a one-year-old is to spoon in the oatmeal all by himself or herself. And of course, nonabusive mothers do not abuse their infants — either physically or psychologically. Among a group of infants who had been abused or ne-

glected, only 29 percent of the twelve-month-olds and 23 percent of the eighteen-month-olds were securely attached to their mothers (Schneider-Rosen, Braunwald, Carlson, and Cicchetti, 1985). All of the maternal qualities that are linked with secure attachment are likely to make a baby feel less fearful and more secure.

If secure attachment to a mother has important effects on a baby's social development, we might expect to find its effects persisting past infancy. Some investigators have found such a connection and believe that babies with secure attachments are likely to become competent, independent toddlers. For example, Leah Matas, Richard Arend, and Alan Sroufe (1978) gave two-year-olds a series of increasingly difficult problems. Toddlers who had been rated as securely attached at both twelve and eighteen months attacked the problems with an enthusiasm rarely shown by toddlers who earlier had been rated as having ambivalent or avoidant attachments. When they reached the final problem, which was too difficult for them to solve, securely attached toddlers were less likely to throw tantrums and more likely to accept help from their mothers than were toddlers with insecure attachments. Similar results appeared among a group of three-year-olds who played a game in their homes with a stranger (Lütkenhaus, Grossmann, and Grossmann, 1985). The game was a race to build a tower by stacking wooden rings on a peg. Securely attached youngsters (as rated at twelve months) began the game without hesitation and increased their effort when they fell behind. Insecurely attached youngsters were hesitant to start and tended to slow down or give up when they fell behind.

The links between secure attachment and later competence have been traced even further. Among a group of four-year-olds, those with secure attachments during infancy showed less emotional dependence on their nursery-school teachers (Sroufe, Fox, and Pancake, 1983). They were competent, confident, and sought their teachers' assistance only when a task was clearly beyond their capabilities. Four-year-olds whose attachment during infancy had been rated as insecure behaved quite differently. They seemed to need frequent contact, approval, and attention from their nursery-school teachers and clung to them so closely that the relationship interfered with their play with other children. For example, when the children were in a group with the teacher, the insecurely attached youngsters either sat next to the teacher or climbed on her lap.

Such behavior is not necessarily *caused* by insecure early attachments, but it is predicted by them (Sroufe, Fox, and Pancake, 1983). It reflects the nature of the child's continuing relationship with primary caregivers. Unless the nature of the relationship changes, it continues to affect the child's development through the daily behavior of the mother and the child's interactions with her. For example, among the two-year-olds who worked a series of problems, mothers of securely attached infants offered hints when their child reached the difficult problem (Matas, Arend, and Sroufe, 1978). Their hints were subtle enough to allow the children to feel that they had solved the problem themselves. In contrast, most mothers of insecurely attached children allowed their children to become frustrated before they offered help, and then the mothers often solved the problem themselves.

Fathers

In traditional two-parent families, most fathers spent little time with their young babies. So for a long while, fathers were regarded as relatively unimportant in their children's early development. As fewer families meet the definition of the traditional family, in which the father is the sole wage earner and the mother stays in the home, more fathers are taking part in child care. When researchers began to look at fathers and babies, they found that infants become attached to both parents at about the same time, although the nature of the attachment may be somewhat different (Parke, 1981).

The quality of the baby's attachment to his or her father may vary, just as it does with mothers. Some infants are securely attached to one parent and insecurely attached to the other, and the secure attachment is as likely to be with the father as with the mother (Main and Weston, 1981). Among a group of twenty-month-olds, most of those who were securely attached to their fathers had fathers who were sensitive to their toddler's needs, were not aggravated by the child, and were unruffled by their lack of knowledge about child rearing (Easterbrooks and Goldberg, 1984).

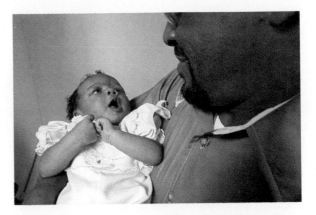

Fathers can be competent, nurturant caregivers who play boisterous, rough-and-tumble games with their babies. *(William Hubbell/Woodfin Camp & Associates)*

A father's attachment to his baby can be just as deep as that of a mother. Fathers make nurturant, competent caregivers, and they can become intensely involved with their babies. When Ross Parke and Douglas Sawin (1976) observed parents in the hospital with their newborn infants, they found that middle-class fathers and mothers spent an equal amount of time with their babies. Both parents looked and smiled at their babies, talked to and kissed them, explored their bodies, and gave them their bottles. Given the opportunity, lower-class fathers also were nurturant and competent with their newborn babies. When, for example, their baby became distressed during a feeding, both father and mother showed their sensitivity in the same way; they stopped the feeding, looked at the baby, and patted the infant solicitously.

Mothers and fathers may behave similarly in the hospital, but considerable research indicates that once they are home, their daily interactions with their babies are sharply different (Lamb, 1981). Perhaps because mothers are generally responsible for most child care, mothers generally pick up their babies to care for them. When fathers pick them up, it is usually to play. Mothers play traditional games like peekaboo and pat-a-cake; fathers engage in rough-and-tumble play, regardless of the infant's sex. Yet fathers do distinguish between sons and daughters: they tumble boys more than girls, laugh more with them, and are more likely to feed and diaper a son than a daughter. Once babies have reached their first birthdays, fathers spend more time with sons.

Increasing numbers of fathers have assumed the responsibility of infant care. This shift in society has led researchers to wonder whether fathers who play the traditional maternal role behave differently from other fathers. When Tiffany Field (1978) compared primary caregiving fathers with fathers who served as traditional secondary caregivers and traditional mothers, she found that all groups attended to the babies' basic needs. But being a primary caregiver did affect a father's actions. Like traditional mothers, they laughed less and smiled more than traditional fathers. They also imitated their babies' facial expressions and vocalizations more often. This change in the nontraditional fathers' behavior may be the result of more experience with the baby. Like traditional mothers, they have discovered that babies enjoy being imitated. But despite their new experience, the nontraditional fathers resembled traditional fathers in other ways. They played more games and poked at their babies more than mothers did. And they were less likely than mothers to hold the babies' arms and legs.

As babies pass their first birthday, they begin to respond differently to fathers and mothers. This change is probably a response to differences in the way fathers and mothers behave with them. When observed in their homes, girls may prefer either parent, and boys generally prefer their fathers. (Being tossed in the air is more fun than having your nose wiped.) But when the infants are with both parents in a stressful situation, a preference for the primary caregiver appears — as attachment theory would predict. Both boys and girls go to their mothers for security and comfort (Lamb, 1981).

Infant Responsiveness

For a long time, the effect of an infant's characteristics on a caregiver were overlooked (Bell and Harper, 1977). But a baby's reactions — or lack of them — clearly influence the tone of the parent-infant relationship. Sometimes the baby's characteristics may affect the quality of attachment. In one longitudinal study (Egeland and Farber, 1984), babies who later developed ambivalent attachments were less alert and active as newborns and seemed to develop more slowly, both physi-

cally and mentally, than other babies. They were less sociable than other babies and may have been more difficult to care for.

Some infant characteristics seem to affect the timing of the bond. Babies who actively resist cuddling tend to develop attachments later than cuddlers. Noncuddlers seem to derive little comfort from being snuggled, and their attachment during the first year is less intense than that of cuddlers. As infant and mother adapt to each other's styles, however, the difference between cuddlers and noncuddlers seems to disappear. Among one group of babies, those who actively resisted contact did not necessarily prevent social interaction with their parents. Instead, each baby and the parents gradually evolved a system of interaction that did not depend on physical contact (Schaffer and Emerson, 1964b).

Fussiness may be another infant characteristic that impedes the development of secure attachment. In another longitudinal study (Belsky, Rovine, and Taylor, 1984), babies who were especially fussy at three and nine months tended to have either avoidant or ambivalent attachments at one year. Do fussy babies take longer to develop attachment, or does their fussiness affect the way their parents care for them? Certainly, it is difficult to be the parent of a fussy infant; as we saw in Chapter 4, mothers and fathers respond to a baby's cry with annoyance, irritation, and distress. Despite the unpleasantness of the cries, parents of babies who fuss often tend to wait longer before picking up their child than do parents of babies who rarely fuss (Dunn, 1977). This tendency may have its explanation in the tale of the boy who cried wolf; parents of fussy babies may interpret their signals of distress as being simply bids for attention. Or if the baby does not quiet easily, the parents may decide that because responding has little effect, they might as well ignore the cries until they become intolerable.

Babies who quiet easily have happier effects on their parents. Because they soothe immediately, their response tends to reinforce their parents' attention and makes the parents feel more secure as caregivers. Because parents need to feel that they can respond to their baby's signals and satisfy his or her needs, the baby whose signs are easy to read enhances the parents' feeling of competence (Goldberg, 1977). The baby whose signals say clearly, "I'm hungry," "I'm bored," or "I'm wet,"

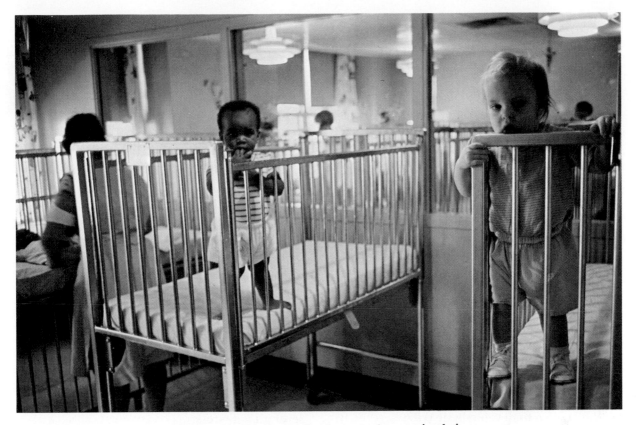

If children reared in institutions are to develop normally, they must have a stimulating environment and a stable relationship with a caregiver or an older child. *(Elliot Erwitt/ Magnum)*

who sucks vigorously and smiles freely is also the one who is most likely to make parents feel successful and competent.

Later, the baby's relative speed of development may affect relationships with parents. The baby who walks early, say at nine or ten months, but does not learn to respond to commands until fourteen or fifteen months, is likely to require more parental patience, provoke more irritation, need more physical restraint, and generally get into more trouble than the child who walks later. The baby who walks late, however, may provoke parental anxiety and concern in other ways. Alarmed at their child's slowness, parents may frequently pull the baby upright or even drag him or her along in attempts to speed development. The parents may even view the baby's relative slowness as a reflection of their own failure and begin to ignore the infant.

Maternal Deprivation

The emotional bond between baby and parent has dominated our story of infant and toddler development. As we have seen, the individualized care of a parent for a child seems to encourage healthy emotional and cognitive development. Basic to this relationship are reciprocal interaction (the baby does something, the caregiver responds, the baby responds in turn), warmth and affection, and the caregiver's responsiveness to the baby's signals.

Babies in Institutions What happens if a baby has no mother at all? Is development severely affected? Early studies of children reared in institutions revealed devastating effects on their social and intellectual development. As toddlers, such children often could not speak, walk, or even feed themselves (Spitz, 1949). It is now clear that the environment of the institution was responsible for some of these harmful effects.

A general lack of environmental stimulation radically slowed the children's cognitive development. Babies spent the day in cribs, without being turned over or picked up. Their world was limited to what they could see from their cribs. They had no rattles, no stuffed animals, no mobiles; they simply stared at bare walls. The babies in Lebanese institutions, who were described in Chapter 5, made rapid gains in both cognitive and physical development when introduced to interesting objects for only a few minutes each day.

The babies' social deficits came from a lack of mothering, not from the lack of a mother. Because the institutions had too few attendants, the emphasis was on running the institution. Babies were fed, bathed, and changed on schedule. Instead of being held at mealtime, they ate from a bottle propped on a pillow. No one played with them. Their desires were ignored, and their cries were unanswered. This experience gave them a feeling of ineffectiveness, and their response was to give up and fall silent. Unable to depend on anyone, they probably failed to develop basic trust.

The severe effects found in these youngsters do not appear when institutions have a stimulating environment (which encourages cognitive development) and a staff large enough so that a child has one or more warm, responsive relationships (which encourage social development). In one Greek institution—the Mitera Babies Center in Athens—babies get consistent mothering by a limited number of caregivers. In most cases, one nurse takes responsibility for primary care. Infants in this orphanage become attached to their primary caregiver at about the same time as other infants develop attachments to their parents (Dontas, Maratos, Fafoutis, and Karangelis, 1985).

Can development proceed in a relatively normal manner when youngsters do not become attached to an adult caregiver? Research with monkeys suggests that a peer relationship can provide some of the security a child gets from the caregiver. Monkeys raised without mothers or mother surrogates but with other baby monkeys for company are more normal in their adult social and sexual behavior than are monkeys raised with a surrogate mother but without peer contact (Suomi and Har-

low, 1975). Similarly, a young institutionalized child has a better chance to develop normally if she or he forms a warm relationship with another child. But when children in institutions do not become attached to a caregiver or an older child within the institution during their first two years, their social development suffers. As eight-year-olds, they tend to cling to caregivers, to demand attention, and to show shallow, indiscriminate friendliness (MacDonald, 1985). They are often restless, disobedient, and unpopular with other children.

Separation   Sometimes babies or toddlers are separated from their parents, usually because of long or repeated hospitalizations, or they are permanently separated from their first caregivers, as when a youngster is adopted from a foster home. What effect does this have on social development? Separation before children are six months old seems to have little effect, but once the attachment relationship begins to form, some children become distressed. They seem especially vulnerable from about six months until they are about two years old—the period when infants are susceptible to separation distress.

This vulnerability may have led to the apparent depression John Bowlby (1973; 1980) observed in older infants and toddlers who had been temporarily separated from their parents and placed in hospitals or other institutions. They became withdrawn, inactive, made no demands on the environment, cried intermittently, and seemed to feel increasing hopelessness and sadness. Later, they began to interact in a pleasant but shallow manner with institutional caregivers. When their parents visited, they responded in an aloof and detached way.

Such separations do not always have a permanent effect on children. Brief separations, such as hospital stays of a week or less, seem to have no lasting effect (Rutter, 1979). Lengthier separations sometimes leave their mark. Among children between the ages of six months and three years who were hospitalized for lengthy, recurrent periods, the effects were still apparent in adolescence (MacDonald, 1985). Yet Bowlby (1973) and his associates found no obvious signs of impaired relationships with parents among older boys and girls who had been hospitalized for long periods during the first two years.

Babies who are adopted from the Mitera Babies' Center (described earlier) face the same adjustment as babies adopted from foster homes. But the institution provides a two-week transition period when the adoptive parents spend their days with the baby in the institutional setting, giving the baby a chance to adapt to new caregivers. By the end of the period, most babies have already begun to transfer their primary attachments (Dontas et al., 1985). In another study, researchers could find no difference in attachment between adopted eighteen-month-olds and infants the same age who lived with their biological parents (Singer, Brodzinsky, Ramsay, Stein, and Waters, 1985). All these youngsters had been adopted by the time they were ten months old. Neither of these groups has been followed into later childhood in order to rule out the possibility of some sleeper effect (see Chapter 3).

Reversing the Effects   Good environments often can make up for early deprivation. As we saw in

Chapter 4, most SGA infants overcome their early handicaps if they go home to an advantaged environment. Can a good environment make up for the lack of a warm, responsive relationship during infancy? There is no simple answer. A child who is placed in a good environment at age three has three years of deprivation to overcome; but a child who is placed in a good environment at age ten must overcome ten years of deprivation. So the earlier the change is made, the better the changes of reversing the effects.

Children *can* develop attachments after the early sensitive period, but whether they can overcome all the effects of early deprivation is uncertain. Among a group of eight-year-olds who had been adopted between the ages of four and six, most had formed warm relationships with adoptive parents, but they still showed the indiscriminate affection, the restlessness, and the unpopularity with their peers typical of eight-year-olds who remained in institutions (Tizard and Hodges, 1978).

Yet some children seem to surmount devastat-

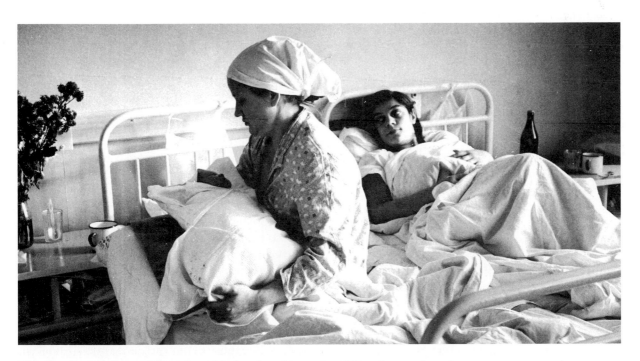

This Russian newborn will get more kissing, hugging, and cuddling than an American baby but also will be held more tightly and have less freedom of movement. (*Martine Franck/VIVA/Woodfin Camp & Associates*)

ing early experiences. When a group of refugee children were brought to the United States and placed in adoptive homes, most seemed to overcome the ill effects of their early deprivation. At the time they came to this country, these thirty-eight youngsters (most of whom were Korean or Greek) ranged in age from five months to ten years. Six years later, when these children were between the ages of six and sixteen, a team of researchers studied them. On the average, these children (who had had to learn a new language and adapt to a new culture) were socially competent, physically healthy, and had above average IQs. Only two were rated by psychologists as clinically disturbed and in need of professional help (Clarke and Clarke, 1977).

Just how completely the effects of early deprivation can be reversed depends in good part on the age of the child, the child's temperament and genetic susceptibility to adverse environmental influence, the severity of the early deprivation, and the quality of the new environment — both materially and emotionally (MacDonald, 1985; Rutter, 1979). Improvements are likely to occur in most cases, but complete reversal is less likely. Even among children who make impressive improvements, subtle effects may still be apparent.

THE EFFECTS OF CLASS AND CULTURE

No matter where they live, young children become attached to their caregivers, but the nature of that relationship varies widely across classes and cultures. Differences in the basic parent-infant relationship may leave different marks on the growing child.

Socioeconomic Differences

Social class has a powerful influence on a child's development, because it affects values, lifestyle, child-rearing practices, and even parents' views of their children's competence. Lower-class parents spend less time in child care than middle-class parents do, and they have more children to care for (Hoffmann, 1984a). When Jerome Kagan and Steven Tulkin (1971) studied ten-month-old middle-

and lower-class babies, they found that social class affected the mothers' attitudes toward their babies and the way they interacted with them. Mothers in both classes held, tickled, kissed, and bounced their babies, but other maternal behavior often differed. A middle-class mother was more likely than a lower-class mother to vocalize within two feet of her baby, to imitate the baby's sounds, to engage in long bouts of social interaction, to reward her baby with words, and to encourage her baby to walk. About two-thirds of the lower-class mothers used food to soothe their babies, but less than one-third of the middle-class mothers solved problems with food.

When Kagan and Tulkin tested these babies in the laboratory, they found no class differences in the levels of the babies' reactions to speech, whether they heard words or nonsense syllables. But middle-class babies quieted more dramatically to highly inflected, highly meaningful speech than to other verbal stimuli. They were also more likely than lower-class babies to look at a stranger after they heard such speech. In addition, middle-class infants quieted more to their mothers' voices than to strangers' voices, and they vocalized more than lower-class infants did after listening to recordings of their mothers' voices.

Cultural Differences

The nature of the relationship between parent and child tends to differ from one culture to the next, often in ways that reflect the culture's values. These differences affect development in various ways. Research with Ugandan infants, whose mothers generally interact more extensively with them than Western mothers do, supports the notion that experiences with the caregiver speed the development of attachment (Ainsworth, 1967). These babies formed specific attachments somewhat earlier than did a group of babies in Scotland (Schaffer and Emerson, 1964a).

Close human contact is also a prominent feature of early life among the !Kung San, a much-studied band of hunter-gatherers who live a nomadic life in Africa's Kalahari Desert under conditions that may be like those of our early ancestors. !Kung San babies spend most of their first year or so either on their mothers' laps or carried in a sling on their mothers' hips. The babies have continual access to the breast and nurse frequently. When they cry, their mothers respond immediately, and the babies' whims are gratified. Yet when these "indulged" babies are two to five years old, they do not hang onto their mothers, as casual observers from our own society might expect. Far from being spoiled or dependent, they show considerable independence, interacting less with their mothers and more with other children than English children of the same age (Konner, 1977). The course of infancy among the !Kung San suggests that in an environment like the one in which humanity may have evolved, a sensitive, immediately responsive caregiver is part of child rearing. And as we have seen, this is just the sort of caregiver that seems to have a securely attached child.

Wide variations exist in the child-rearing practices of Western industrialized societies. Urie Bronfenbrenner (1970) has described some of the differences he observed between the Soviet Union and the United States. Russian babies were held most of the time, even when they were not being fed. Russian babies seemed to get much more hugging, kissing, and cuddling than American babies did, but they were also held more tightly and allowed little freedom of movement. Russian mothers seemed so solicitous and protective that they curtailed the babies' mobility and initiative.

A very different maternal style prevails in Germany. Researchers have found that German mothers seem interested in promoting independence in their babies (Grossmann, Grossmann, Spangler, Suess, and Unzner, 1985). As soon as babies can crawl, German mothers discourage their infants from staying near them. When the babies are unhappy, German mothers are more likely to stop their tears with toys, words, or food than by picking them up. German babies are much more likely than American babies to develop avoidant attachments. In fact, German mothers regard as spoiled babies who become highly distressed when their mothers leave them in an unfamiliar place.

Multiple Caregiving

In today's world, multiple caregiving is a frequent form of infant care, even among babies who are not in institutions. In such surroundings, the lack of a central caregiver seems to produce no ill effects on children. After reviewing the research, Alison Clarke-Stewart and Greta Fein (1983) concluded

Children who grow up on a kibbutz develop normally; they become attached to their *metapelet* as well as to their mother and father. *(Louis Goldman/Rapho Photo Researchers)*

that when the main attachment figure shares caregiving with other people, as when mothers work or when the baby is part of an extended family, children thrive as long as other caregivers provide stable relationships.

Children reared in Israeli kibbutzim show normal social and emotional development. In the early kibbutzim, infants were reared communally in residential nurseries and saw their parents for only a few hours each day or on weekends. In most kibbutzim today, babies join their families at four o'clock each afternoon and stay until the next morning. In all kibbutzim, the caregiver, or *metapelet*, takes care of the infant's daily needs and training; the parents primarily provide emotional gratification. Babies become attached to their mothers, their fathers, and to the metapelet, although they develop somewhat different relationships with each one (Sagi et al., 1985). Such studies suggest that parents may be absent for significant

Table 8.2
The Changing American Family

| | Intact Families | | | | Mother-Headed | |
	1970 (%)	1975 (%)	1980 (%)	1985 (%)	1975 (%)	1985 (%)
0 to 1 year	24.0	30.8	39.0	49.4	38.5	38.0
2 years	30.5	37.1	48.1	54.0	49.1	55.7
3 years	34.5	41.2	51.5	55.1	53.5	54.8

Note: The proportion of mothers with young children who work outside the home continues to climb in intact families. In families maintained by women, where no father is present, there has been a slight decline over the past decade in the proportion of mothers of infants who work outside the home. This slight decline may reflect increased government assistance or a decline in unskilled jobs.

Source: U.S. Department of Labor, Bureau of Labor Statistics, *Monthly Labor Review,* February, 1986.

amounts of time without radically influencing attachment patterns, as long as someone who cares is present.

With the enormous rise in employment among mothers of young children, multiple caregiving is fast becoming typical of American families (see Table 8.2). In intact families, 50.7 percent of the mothers with children younger than three years old are employed outside the home; in single-parent families headed by widowed, separated, or divorced mothers, 44.5 percent are employed outside the home (U.S. Department of Labor, 1986). A considerable proportion of infants and toddlers are in substitute care. Sometimes parents share child care by working different shifts. Sometimes a grandparent or other relative comes into the home, or the child is taken to a day-care home. And sometimes a child is placed in day care. Infants are less likely to be placed in day care than in one of the other arrangements: in a recent study of employed mothers, only 5.2 percent of those with infants younger than one year old placed them in day care (Klein, 1985). Among toddlers and preschoolers, 18.8 percent of youngsters whose mothers work part time and 29.8 percent of youngsters whose mothers work full time are in day care (L. Hoffman, 1984b).

When parents work split shifts, or when fathers take over primary child care or share it, the influence of the father may increase. Instead of being simply a playmate, fathers also are seen as comforting caregivers. But when mothers take over

the traditional after-work playtime and fathers do not compensate with playful interactions on weekends and in the morning, the influence of the father may decrease (L. Hoffman, 1984a).

With half of all babies' mothers in the labor force, the attachment bond between babies and their employed mothers has become the focus of research. Most studies show no rise in the proportion of insecure attachments among the babies of working mothers (Barglow, Vaughan, and Molitor, 1987; Gottfried and Gottfried, in press), but none of these studies may provide an accurate measure of the baby's emotional bond. Because the security of the attachment relationship is assessed by placing the child in a strange situation, some researchers have questioned the validity of such measures when applied to the children of employed mothers or youngsters with considerable exposure to care outside the home (Weinraub, Jaeger, and L. Hoffman, in press). For such infants, the experimental setting does not seem truly "strange," and it may not evoke typical attachment behavior. Even with the typical study, a return to work before the baby is three months old does not seem to affect the security of attachment to the mother any more than does a return later in the first year (L. Hoffman, 1984b). With older infants and toddlers, the transition to day care may seem bumpy at first. Separation anxiety is apparent, and the youngsters are clearly distressed when their mothers leave—just as they are when parents go out and leave them with a sitter in the evenings.

Like mission specialist Anna Fischer, the first mother to make a space flight, mothers who work outside the home make up for their absence with direct, intensive interaction at other times. *(AP/Wide World Photos)*

But they adjust quickly, and before long they have no objection to being dropped off at the center. Indeed, some are eager to get to their favorite activities (Ragozin, 1980).

Mothers who are absent from their young children during working hours seem to make up for it after work and on weekends (Easterbrooks and Goldberg, 1985). Employed mothers do spend less time on child care but devote just as much time to direct, intensive interaction with their children as do homebound mothers (L. Hoffman, 1984b). However, the nature of their interaction may change. Employed mothers seem to engage in more social and verbal play with their babies and to handle them more vigorously than homebound mothers do. Some researchers have suggested that the traditional differences in fathers' and mothers' play with their infants may disappear (Pederson, Cain, Zaslow, and Anderson, 1981). The robust, rough-and-tumble play typical of father and infant may be the way in which any parent reestablishes contact after a separation.

Researchers have been investigating the effects of substitute care on infants' social and cognitive development (see box). However, exactly what effect the daily separation will have on a particular child is impossible to predict. Among the factors that interact with the mothers' daily absence are the sex of the child (girls seem to do better than boys), the age of the child when substitute care begins, the family's socioeconomic level, the mother's educational level, the presence of additional stress in the home (separation, divorce, a jobless or ill father), the mother's feelings about her work, and the quality of the substitute care (L. Hoffman, 1984).

THE DEVELOPMENT OF SOCIABILITY

As infants grow, their significant relationships broaden beyond the important attachment to parents. A little girl finds that she must contend with her older brother as a potential threat or boon to her well-being, just as she will have to contend with his friends, her own toddler playmates, and perhaps a younger sibling. Within the first two years of life, the rudimentary development of personality that we call *sociability* first appears. But all infants and toddlers are not equally sociable; they regard other people with varying degrees of positive expectations, warmth, and trust. Although their temperament has some effect on youngsters' sociability, their early experiences play an extremely important role in the way they approach others.

DAY CARE AND THE VERY YOUNG

Politicians and preachers often fret about the separation of employed mothers from their infants and toddlers. Their worries seem to be based primarily on their preconceptions, because most studies have failed to find any adverse effects (Hoffman, 1984b). Yet some developmentalists have wondered whether day care is the appropriate place for infants and have suggested that either having a sitter come into the home or taking the baby to the home of the sitter (an arrangement called *family day care*) might be more appropriate for the very young (Scarr, 1984).

Which is better for infants—day care or some other form of substitute care? One of the few studies to compare various forms of substitute care was carried out in Bermuda, where the government asked a team of psychologists to undertake a longitudinal study of day care. On this island, 64 percent of the babies are in substitute care during their first year, and 84 percent are in such care before they are two (McCartney, Scarr, Phillips, and Grajek, 1985; Scarr, 1983; Schwartz et al., 1981).

Among Bermudan children, those who had spent their first two years at home with mother, with a relative or sitter who came into the home, or in family day care did equally well. There was no difference among them in social or cognitive development. But children who had been placed in day-care centers before their second birthday seemed to be less competent in communicating with others, less attentive, less socially responsive, more apathetic, and to have more behavior problems.

After analyzing all aspects of the caregiving situations, the researchers concluded that day care's negative effects on infants were probably related to a lack of attention from a caring adult. In the day-care centers, each adult took care of about eight babies—a ratio that is considered far too high by most developmental psychologists. When a person must care for eight babies, there is little time to do more than feed and change them. The Bermudan infants got little playtime with a caregiver and did not have enough toys in front of them to hold their interest.

This conclusion was supported by a study of American toddlers in various day-care situations. When day-care workers had fewer toddlers to care for, they played and talked more with the young-

Toddlers and preschoolers in day care are more advanced socially, intellectually, and emotionally than youngsters who stay at home with their parents. (Charles Gupton/Stock, Boston)

sters, were more responsive to their social overtures, expressed more affection toward them, restricted their activities less, and were less likely to respond negatively to the youngsters' distress (Howes, 1983).

Older toddlers do well in groups. In fact, among Bermudan children, those who move from home or other substitute care into day care after their second birthday do best of all. Their cognitive and social development is more advanced than that of children who stay home with their mothers during the preschool years or those who remain in family day care.

In an American study, a team headed by Alison Clarke-Stewart (1984) followed the development of toddlers and preschoolers in various forms of substitute care. They studied middle-class youngsters between the ages of twenty-two and forty-two months who had started day care anywhere from three to six months earlier. Among these children, those in substitute care were more competent and mature on every count than children who stayed home with their mothers, and children who were in day-care centers instead of with sitters or in day-care homes were the most advanced of all. Youngsters in day-care centers reached various developmental milestones in social competence, intellectual knowledge, and emotional maturity about nine months earlier than children who stayed at home. Psychologists generally agree that cognitively oriented day-care programs improve intellectual functioning among disadvantaged youngsters. In this study, day care of any kind boosted intellectual functioning among middle-class youngsters as well. Clarke-Stewart believes that day care probably speeds development rather than sending it in a new direction. She notes that among the oldest children, who were five years old at the time the study ended, the gap between home-reared and center-reared children was beginning to close.

These American children were close in age to the Bermudan children who responded favorably to day care. Yet in the Bermuda study, eight-year-old children who were started in day-care centers before they were two years old still lagged behind youngsters who had spent the first two years at home or in family day care; the difference was apparent in both social and cognitive development. The lesson from these studies seems to be that the *quality* of the day-care environment is an important factor. Among Bermudan children, disadvantaged three-year-olds who attended a high-quality government day-care center designed to enrich development had better language skills, were more considerate, and more sociable than children who attended any of the other centers.

Clearly, parents who place children in day care should visit the centers before they enroll their children, looking not only at the space and equipment provided but also at the ratio of adults to children and the interaction between staff and children. Such inspections are easier if parents obtain one of the rating guides written for their use by developmental psychologists (Clarke-Stewart, 1982; Scarr, 1984).

Attachment and Sociability

The results of studies showing the importance of the emotional bond between infants and their caregivers are in harmony with Erik Erikson's (1963) theory of personality development. The child's first task is to resolve the conflict between trust and mistrust in situations involving others. Babies who have developed secure attachments show evidence of basic trust, which reflects the history of their interactions with the social world. Their experiences with their parents have led them to expect that parents can be counted on. As they generalize these expectations to other people, their basic trust colors their future social interactions. Gradually, a rudimentary sense of personal identity emerges. Infants realize that their memories, images, and anticipated sensations are firmly linked with familiar and predictable things and people. This comfortable certainty about the world and their place in it allows babies to venture into new realms of experience.

Once their initial wariness of strange situations and people is overcome, infants display a natural disposition toward affiliative and exploratory behavior. These early interactions promote their social development — a necessity in a social species like ours. Babies' inclination to explore encourages them to find out about the world and promotes their sense of competence. Just as the presence of an attachment figure may reduce wariness in infants, so may it enhance affiliation and exploration. If the attachment figure is missing or unreliable, infants are likely to become wary and refuse to investigate new situations. Such youngsters find it difficult to develop competence, autonomy, or sociability.

Self-concept

As babies begin to distinguish themselves from the world, they develop a sense of the self as an active, independent agent who can cause his or her own movements in space. This realization, which depends on cognitive development, seems to emerge at about the time a baby is twelve to fifteen months old. Once the concept of self as agent has developed, the baby can develop a sense of self as an object — a "thing" that has unique features and can be recognized (Harter, 1983). This blossoming self-awareness in turn influences the baby's interest in others and how he or she relates to them.

The Emergence of Self-concept In most babies, the concept of self as object gradually develops toward the end of the second year. The emergence

A self-concept develops slowly. By the time they are eighteen months old, most youngsters can recognize themselves in a mirror. *(George Zimbel/Monkmeyer)*

of this self-concept has been explored in a series of studies by Michael Lewis and Jeanne Brooks-Gunn (1979). These researchers decided that self-concept had been demonstrated when a baby clearly recognized herself or himself in a mirror. Babies without a self-concept treat the reflection as another baby. So Lewis and Brooks-Gunn placed babies before a mirror after first surreptitiously dabbing rouge on their noses. No babies under a year seemed to recognize that the smudged nose in the mirror belonged to them, but among babies from fifteen to eighteen months old, 25 percent immediately touched their noses, and by twenty-four months, 75 percent grabbed for their noses as soon as they looked in the mirror.

This gradual development in babies' ability to recognize themselves appears to be related to their level of cognitive development. As we saw in Chapter 7, babies develop the object concept slowly, in a process that extends well into the second year. Most babies do not understand that the nose in the mirror is their own until they also understand that objects continue to exist when out of sight (Bertenthal and Fischer, 1978). Apparently, the concept of object permanence is basic to babies' sense of their own continuing identities.

Yet cognitive development is not the only influence on the development of self-recognition; social experience also seems to be involved. In another study (Lewis, Brooks-Gunn, and Jaskir, 1985), insecurely attached infants recognized themselves in the mirror some months before securely attached infants did so. At sixteen months, for example, 12.5 percent of the securely attached and 40 percent of the insecurely attached infants recognized themselves, and at twenty months, 26.4 percent of the securely attached and 75 percent of the insecurely attached infants grabbed for their noses. Most of the insecurely attached babies had developed avoidant attachments and showed heightened attention to the environment. The researchers speculate that because these babies rely less on their mothers for security and more on themselves than securely attached infants do, they develop self-concepts earlier.

Self-concept and Empathy   Infants' increasing sense of self may play an essential role in the development of empathy. Until they conceive of themselves as a separate self, they are unlikely to be able to put themselves in another's place. Martin Hoffman (1984), who believes that younger infants show the basis for empathy, has traced its emergence in children. During the first year, babies cannot distinguish between themselves and another person in distress. He describes an eleven-month-old girl who saw another child fall and begin to cry. The baby girl, looking as if she were about to cry herself, put her thumb in her mouth and buried her face in her mother's lap — her customary reaction to her own distress or injury. As the concept of person permanence develops, infants begin to understand that the distress they observe is not their own and that the other person needs comfort. But at first, they go through a period when they try to comfort themselves as well as the person in distress.

Throughout the second year, youngsters assume that the distressed person feels exactly as they do and will respond to the same sort of comfort. For example, if a toddler's friend becomes distressed, the youngster will come to the friend's aid by fetching his or her own mother — even though the distressed toddler's mother is also present. Finally, some time after their second birthday, toddlers begin to understand that other people may respond differently to a distressing situation. At last, they have a rudimentary ability to put themselves in the other person's place.

Competence and Autonomy

Once infants can sit up, the world changes. Their hands are freed for exploration, and they can both experience the world tactually and reach out to initiate physical contact. Crawling and walking give them further opportunities to satisfy their curiosity and to initiate and sustain social interactions. Each time children's physical abilities increase and their perceptual world widens, the potential for learning more about the social world expands. They learn what people do, how they react, and what they do and do not like. They learn that touching brings a smile, tugging gets attention, and hitting brings a reprimand. They learn whom to seek out and whom to avoid.

As their competence increases, babies find increasing satisfaction in exploring the social world. Although they show distress at being left by their parents, they show no distress when they decide to move away from their attachment figures to explore their surroundings. Toddlers become adventuresome in their explorations, and girls are as brave as boys in their forays from mother. The age-related nature of exploration became apparent when Harriet Rheingold and Carol Eckerman (1970) placed forty-eight children between one and five years old in an L-shaped yard, arranged so that a child could wander out of his or her mother's sight. In most cases, the researchers could predict how far a child would travel from mother simply by knowing the age of the child; sex was not a factor.

The nature of infant explorations indicate that during the second year of life, a youngster's need for physical contact declines. The decline apparently is spurred by the child's desire to be competent, to find out about the world of people and objects, and to bask in the attention and smiles of new people. Novelty, complexity, and change draw infants away from the comfortable familiarity of attachment figures.

The child's new independence does not signal the end of attachment. The desire to be close to familiar and loved people and the desire to try out new experiences and expand competence appear to coexist throughout an individual's life. Youngsters with secure attachments feel safe to explore and to develop a sense of the self as an independent agent. From their explorations, they bring back new knowledge and abilities that they may incorporate into increasingly complex, interesting interactions with the people they love.

Toward the end of the second year, children make their first concentrated push toward **autonomy,** which is the feeling of self-control and self-determination. Parents suddenly realize that their sunny, independent toddler has become stubborn and disagreeable. The child has entered the period of social development sometimes called "the terrible twos," and family life often seems difficult. No matter what parents suggest, no matter what they ask, the toddler's consistent response is "no!"

This "negativistic crisis" develops as a child becomes aware of the distinction between self and others and between the child's own will and the will of others. Until now, youngsters have depended on caregivers for the satisfaction of their needs. As toddlers become more aware of their competence and their effects on the world, they strive for autonomy. They want to do things for themselves. The toddler who invariably says "no" is trying to discover the limits of his or her capability and initiative: the self. Parents frequently note that the clash of wills seems to have no practical point; the child is concerned not with an issue but with a principle. What often looks like deliberate defiance is a test of social relationships and responses as a youngster tries to discover what effect she or he can have on others. As we trace the course of development, it will become clear that this developing sense of competence and autonomy will be important throughout life.

Boy or Girl

Before infants learn whether they are girls or boys, they must discover what a girl or boy is. The voyage to this discovery begins before they are aware they have embarked on it, for girls and boys are treated differently right from the start. Babies are wrapped in pink or blue blankets in the hospital nursery and surrounded with sex-typed clothes

WHEN MOMMY AND DADDY FIGHT

A mother who was recovering from flu was overwhelmed by her messy, dirty house. The children's toys covered the floor, dirty dishes littered the kitchen, and food had been left out of the refrigerator to spoil. Enraged at the shambles and at her husband, she yelled, "I don't care if this house stays messed up forever. I am not picking up another damn thing." Through her anger, she heard the squeaky voice of her twenty-month-old daughter say, again and again, "Mommy, shut up. Mommy, shut up. Mommy, shut up" (Cummings, Zahn-Waxler, and Radke-Yarrow, 1981, p. 1276).

This incident was reported by a mother who took part in a study of infants' reactions to other people's emotional displays. By the time babies in this study were a year old, they became extremely upset by angry exchanges between their parents. Infants between twelve and twenty months showed their agitation in several ways. Some showed anger themselves, hitting or pushing one or both parents. Some became distressed, crying, looking concerned, or hiding their head under a blanket to shut out the sounds. Some ignored the event, staring ahead without expression. And some hugged and kissed their parents, in an attempt to distract or reconcile them — this response was most frequent in families where the parents quarreled frequently. According to the mothers' reports, the more often the parents fought, the more distressed the children were over each incident.

Wondering if youngsters' social and emotional functioning was altered by exposure to such quarrels, Mark Cummings, Ronald Iannotti, and Caroline Zahn-Waxler (1985) set out to study the effect of adult conflict on two-year-olds. Because family quarrels are not accessible to researchers, they staged quarrels between adults. After serving juice to the toddlers and coffee to the mothers, these adults switched from friendly interaction to a bitter quarrel over washing dishes while the toddlers played in the same room.

When the adults began to argue, 42.5 percent of the toddlers showed distress. They either froze in place, tried to shut out the quarrel by covering their faces or ears, ran to their mothers for comfort, looked anxious, cried, asked to leave ("Go home now"), scolded the quarrelers ("Bad ladies"), or tried to end the quarrel ("Stop!"). A month later, the same youngsters came back to the laboratory, and another quarrel erupted in front of them. This time, 63.8 percent of the youngsters showed distress.

Among toddlers who witnessed two quarrels, the background anger spilled over into their play. After the fight had subsided on their second visit, the incidence of aggressive acts among the watching youngsters increased sharply. This reaction was especially noticeable among boys and among toddlers of either sex who previously had been rated as aggressive. Girls tended to become distressed, anxious, or withdrawn.

Small children clearly are affected by the quarrels of others, and it would seem that the effect is magnified among youngsters who live in families where parents fight frequently. The researchers note that public concern over the influence of televised aggression overlooks an influence that may be even more powerful — and one that cannot be turned off.

and toys at home. Their gender may even affect the way they are fed, for one study showed that middle-class mothers were more likely to breast-feed a daughter than a son (Lewis, 1971).

If parents treat their own infants as they do the young infants of other people, gender affects interactions with their babies in subtle ways. In one study, Caroline Smith and Barbara Lloyd (1978) found that switching the label on a six-month-old baby changed the ways that mothers of first-born babies interacted with the infant. Told that the baby was a boy, mothers encouraged "him" to crawl, walk, and behave vigorously. Told that the baby was a girl, they never encouraged motor activity and never offered "her" a hammer as a plaything. Similar differences appeared when Hannah Frisch (1977) changed gender labels on a fourteen-month-old baby. Even a commitment to feminism did not wipe out the differences. Adults who were sympathetic to feminism often urged a "girl" to ride a tricycle but never encouraged "boys" to play with a baby doll.

These adults were playing with an unfamiliar baby. Perhaps they were simply acting on the only available information: the baby's age and gender. How do they regard their own infants? From the first, parents perceive gender differences in their newborns. Although girl babies are hardier than boys, as we saw in Chapter 3, parents see their newborn daughters as softer, more vulnerable, and less alert than their newborn sons, and fathers see their sons as stronger and hardier than their daughters (Huston, 1983). When parents see baby girls as soft, dainty, and fragile, they are likely to treat them gently; when they see baby boys as strong and tough, they are likely to treat them more roughly. Fathers seem to be especially conscious of gender differences. As noted earlier, they tumble their sons about more, play more roughly with them, and use toys less than they do with their daughters.

Clear differences in parental behavior turned up in a study by Beverly Fagot (1978), who observed families with an only child who was just under two years old. She discovered that parents often responded differently to the same activity, depending on their child's gender. Girls were never encouraged when they played with blocks, and only girls tended to be discouraged when they manipulated objects. As a result, boys explored the physical world freely, but girls were often criticized for it. Girls also were encouraged to be helpers and to ask for assistance when they tried to do things. The parents were unaware that they were training their daughters to be dependent and their sons to be independent.

When their children are about three years old, parents make this message even stronger. If asked to work on some task with their child, parents communicate higher expectations to their sons and demand more independent action from them. With daughters, they are quick to offer help and are more interested in the interpersonal aspects of the situation (Huston, 1983). As Lois Hoffman (1977) has pointed out, it is not so much that daughters are trained in dependency as that they are deprived of the training in independence that boys get practically from birth.

When infants go off to day care, teachers do their part in deepening these differences. In a lon-

Parents train daughters in dependency by setting lower expectations for daughters than for sons and by stepping in sooner with help. *(Ray Ellis/Photo Researchers)*

gitudinal study, Fagot and her associates videotaped infants in play groups (Fagot, Hagan, Leinbach, and Kronsberg, 1985). When teachers interacted with thirteen-month-olds, they responded with attention to boys who cried, whined, screamed, or grabbed at them but tended to ignore girls who acted this way. Teachers paid attention to girls when they tried to communicate, whether they babbled, spoke a recognizable word, or gestured. Yet there was no difference in the overall behavior of the boys and girls — merely a selectivity of the teachers' responses. The researchers believe that teachers' expectations about boys and girls (that boys will be assertive and aggressive and that girls will be verbal) shaped their interpretations of ambiguous behavior by infants who were just learning to interact with peers and adults outside the family. Within a year, these same youngsters had learned to act as their teachers expected them to. At twenty-four months, the boys were more assertive and grabbed for objects more often than girls; girls talked more and screamed, whined, and cried for attention less often than boys.

Infants learn about sex differences in other ways, too. At about eighteen months, they begin to learn gender labels and to apply them to others, generally relying on hair and clothes as cues. By the time they are two, most can identify females in pictures as "girl" or "mommy," even when the pictured models have short hair or wear long pants. But most two-year-olds are not sure of their own sex. They cannot always sort their own pictures by gender, nor do they always answer correctly when asked, "Are you a girl?" or "Are you a boy?" By the time they are three, that question gives them no problem (Thompson, 1975).

Peers and Siblings

The influence of parents and teachers can be strengthened or moderated by the influence of other children. Peers and siblings have somewhat different roles, because peers are at approximately the same stage of development as the child whereas siblings are either older or younger. When playing with peers, children are interacting with equals, an experience youngsters can get from no one else.

Peers In the past, investigators simply did not look for social interaction among infants, perhaps because of the general belief that young babies are too egocentric for such sociability. Yet babies are clearly interested in one another, even if they lack the social skills that make sustained interaction possible (Hartup, 1983). For example, when six-month-old babies meet for the first time, each tugs at the other's hair, pokes at eyes, and handles the other's toys. Yet the interaction goes smoothly, for neither baby frowns, fusses, resists, or withdraws from the situation (Hay, Nash, and Pedersen, 1983).

Babies are more sociable at home than in the strange surroundings of the psychological laboratory, and they are also more sociable with acquaintances than with young strangers. When Jacqueline Becker (1977) observed pairs of nine-month-olds playing together at home for ten sessions, she found that the infants were more interested in each other than in toys or their mothers. The more times the babies were together, the more attention they paid to each other, and the more complex their play became. Their increased social competence transferred to other situations. When these babies were given a chance to play with an unfamiliar peer, they interacted more with the new baby than did infants who had less experience playing with peers.

One of the reasons social interaction was discounted by earlier researchers may have been

Before they are two years old, children begin to develop cooperative, satisfying, and enjoyable patterns of social play. *(William MacDonald)*

babies' inexperience with peers. Not many years ago, infants had little experience outside the home, but the dramatic increase in employment among mothers of young children has led to interaction with peers at a much earlier age. For example, fourteen-month-olds with extensive nursery-school experience watched other babies more, smiled and vocalized at them more, and made more physical contact with them than did twenty-four-month olds in other studies (Field and Roopnarine, 1982).

During the last half of the second year, toddlers are playing games with one another, modifying their behavior to their playmates' activity. They invite one another to join in a game, imitate one another's actions, and by eighteen months, some are playing reciprocal games that involve turns—such as throwing a ball back and forth (Ross, 1982). Friction is frequent between toddlers, although the amount seems to vary widely. When Dale Hay and Hildy Ross (1982) observed twenty-one-month-olds playing in pairs, they recorded 2.3 squabbles in each fifteen-minute play period. Yet some toddlers never disagreed, and others fought almost once each minute.

As toddlers reach their second birthday, many are beginning to cooperate in pretend play. Previous research had indicated that youngsters did not begin cooperative pretend play until they were well past their second birthdays (Rubin, Fein, and Vanderberg, 1983), but the ability seems to emerge earlier when children have more experience with their peers. For example, among a group of toddlers in community day-care centers, half of the youngsters between the ages of twenty-one and twenty-three months were playing games that required them to take pretend roles: mother and baby, sister and brother, mommy and daddy (Howes, 1985). As in earlier research, all of the older toddlers (thirty-two and thirty-three months) played these games.

Siblings　Siblings play an important role in one another's lives. Whether children have older or younger siblings, many siblings — or none at all — influences personality development. From interactions with their siblings, children develop expectations about the way other people will behave.

When a first-born toddler acquires a baby brother or sister, the world suddenly changes. The toddler is no longer the center of the universe and has to stand by as parental attention and concern is focused on the new baby. Unlike the other people in the toddler's world, the baby is not at all concerned with the toddler's needs. In a study of English toddlers, nearly every child was disturbed and unhappy at the birth of a baby brother or sister (Dunn, 1983; Dunn and Kendrick, 1982). Most misbehaved, demanded attention, and were jealous when their father played with the baby. Yet these toddlers were also interested in the new baby and showed affection. Many tried to entertain the baby, were concerned when the infant cried, and tried to help out with infant care. One mother described her toddler son's concern for his baby sister:

> He hates anything to happen to her . . . hates to hear her cry. He moves small toys in case she puts them in her mouth and covers stickle bricks [prickly toy bricks that interlock] with a cloth. (Dunn and Kendrick, 1982, p. 97)

In this study, the toddlers' new status also made many of them more independent; they began dressing themselves, feeding themselves, going to the toilet alone, and playing more by themselves.

Others, however, temporarily regressed; they insisted that their mothers dress them, take them to the toilet, or feed them. When this sort of behavior appeared, it usually lingered throughout the first year after the baby's birth.

Older brothers and sisters often act as models and teachers with the baby. Studies have shown that twelve- and eighteen-month-old infants carefully watch their older brothers or sisters, often taking over their abandoned toys and imitating their actions. Their preschool siblings in turn talk to their baby brothers and sisters and offer them toys (Lamb, 1978). In fact, young siblings often have close interests, enjoy the same things, and seem to understand one another.

Familiarity gives siblings ample opportunity to annoy each other. At first, most of the hostility comes from the older child, who may grab toys from an infant sibling, teasing, threatening, kicking, hitting, biting, or pinching the younger child (Abramovitch, Corter, and Lando, 1979). By the time the second-born child is eighteen months old, he or she is able to retaliate. In one study, all younger siblings were physically aggressive, and all knew exactly how to tease or annoy an older brother or sister (Dunn and Munn, 1985). They destroyed the older child's possessions, took away favorite toys, or deliberately provoked them. For example, the mother of one pair told the researcher that the older child was afraid of spiders and hated a particular toy spider. Immediately, the toddler dashed to the next room, rummaged through the toy box, and returned with the toy spider. The toddler then shoved the spider at the older sibling, who burst into tears.

The relationship between young siblings seems to be highly ambivalent. Conflict between siblings appears in every study, but so does affection. A mother described her eight-month-old daughter's reactions to her toddler brother:

> She thinks he's marvelous. Hero-worships him. If he plays with her foot, she kills herself laughing. She doesn't cry till he goes out of the room. (Dunn and Kendrick, 1982, p. 93).

In many families, the infant sibling becomes attached to the older brother and sister and often goes to him or her for comfort.

Generalizing about the effects of young siblings on one another is difficult. Siblings can be comforters, teachers, devious manipulative bullies, or sensitive companions (Dunn, 1983). One pair of young siblings might have a parent-child relationship; another pair, a peer relationship. We can assume that these relationships have an influence on infants and toddlers, even though we cannot specify those effects.

SUMMARY

1. Studies of monkeys and human infants have shown the complex nature of **attachment.** In human babies, the relationship takes months to develop; it goes through four stages: indiscriminate social responsiveness (birth to two months); discriminate social responsiveness (two to seven months); specific attachment (seven to thirty months); and goal-directed partnership (from thirty months). Once infants develop a specific attachment, they are likely to show **separation distress** when the caregiver leaves and **wariness of strangers.**

2. The quality of the attachment bond may vary. About two-thirds of babies develop a **secure attachment;** the rest develop insecure bonds — either **avoidant attachment** or **ambivalent attachment** (the least secure). Babies with secure attachments generally have warm, responsive mothers who are neither intrusive nor abusive. Babies with secure attachments tend to become competent, independent toddlers. Babies also become attached to their fathers, whose interactions are generally more boisterous and playful than those of the baby's mother. A baby's characteristics influence the parent-infant relationship, perhaps affecting the quality or the timing of the attachment bond.

3. Babies can be reared successfully in institutions — as long as they develop one or more warm, responsive relationships with caregivers. The failure to develop such a relationship may permanently impair social development. Although children can develop attachments after the sensitive period, they may not be able to overcome all the effects of early deprivation.

4. Lower-class parents spend less time in child-care than middle-class parents do. Lower-class parents also interact differently with their babies, which may account for the middle-class baby's attentiveness to language. Cultural differences may also affect the nature of the parent-child relationship. When caregiving is shared, babies thrive as long as they develop stable relationships with the additional caregivers. Most research indicates that attachments among babies of working mothers are just as secure as among babies whose mothers stay home.

5. Babies with secure attachments show evidence of basic trust. Early personality and sociability are largely a product of interaction with parents. At about fifteen months, babies develop a sense of themselves as active, independent agents who can cause their own movements in space. Afterward, they develop a sense of themselves as an object with unique features. This aspect of self-concept, which depends on the development of object permanence, emerges gradually toward the end of the second year; it is demonstrated by the baby's recognition of himself or herself in a mirror. As the toddler's need for physical contact declines, he or she begins to develop **autonomy.**

6. Parents treat boys and girls different from birth, and these differences in treatment encourage independence in boys and dependence in girls. Because day-care workers expect boys to be aggressive and assertive and girls to be verbal, they respond to the infants' ambiguous behavior in a way that encourages the kind of development they expect. Babies engage in social interaction with their peers toward the end of the first year, and early experience with peers seems to speed the development of sociability. Siblings influence one another's social development, and most relationships are ambivalent. The quality of the sibling bond varies dramatically from one family to the next.

KEY TERMS

ambivalent attachment
attachment
autonomy

avoidant attachment
secure attachment

separation distress
wariness of strangers

STUDY TERMS

attachment   The primary social bond that develops between infant and parent or caregiver and that provides the baby with emotional security; attachment is demonstrated by the child's tendency to seek out the caregiver for comfort when distressed and for play when happy.

autonomy   A feeling of self-control and self-determination.

separation distress   A baby's distress at being parted from an attachment figure; the reaction appears by eight or nine months and begins to decline when the child is about a year and one-half old.

wariness of strangers   A natural reaction of babies to strangers that helps infants avoid potentially dangerous situations; it appears at about eight months and is heightened when the baby's attachment figure is absent.

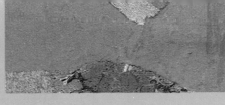

PART IV

The
Industrious Child

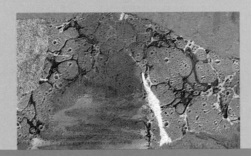

Between the ages of four and eleven, children undergo profound changes in every aspect of development. At four, they are still in what Erikson called the "play age," when they are full of surplus energy and take intense enjoyment in the exercise of mind and muscle. Their growing bodies, widening experiences, and rapidly developing understanding soon propel them from the narrow world of the nursery into the wider world of the schoolchild. Now children turn from initiative to industry, as their growing independence from the family opens them to new influences from peers, school, and community. Through this maze of influence, children move, selecting here, rejecting there, but always acting on the environment and influencing others as much as others influence them. During the school years, children seem eager and ready to learn various cultural skills. A tremendous surge in cognitive capabilities allows them to develop new and more realistic ways of understanding the world, operating in it competently, and perceiving the logical and causal relationships within it. All these developmental changes grow out of the continuous interaction of child and society.

CHAPTER 9

Personality: Growing Up in the Family

Nine-year-old Samantha Drake gets up every morning at 6:30 and goes into her mother's room. For half an hour, she lies in her mother's bed and watches her mother get ready to go to her job as a senior data analyst. Samantha's parents were divorced several years ago, and her mother has custody of her. Her father has remarried; every other weekend Samantha visits him and her stepmother. At first the divorce was difficult for Samantha; she blamed herself for her parents' broken marriage. She cried every night. For a long time, Samantha thought her parents would get back together, but eventually she realized that they never would. She says she's happy now, living with her mother, her dog, her cat, and her hamsters in a suburb of Houston, Texas. She makes straight A's at school, and her open, friendly manner indicates that she has indeed come to terms with her parents' divorce. Time, the school counselor, and a therapist she saw for a while after her father remarried have helped her adjust. Samantha's position is not unusual; many of her friends have stepparents, and parents of two other friends are getting divorces (Gelman, 1985).

How does the experience of living in a one-parent family affect the way that Samantha—and other children like her—master the developmental tasks of childhood? With one out of four American families headed by a single parent, this is an important question, and many psychologists are trying to answer it. Their findings will help us understand how the socialization process contributes to the development of personality. **Socialization** is the process of absorbing the attitudes, values, and customs of a society. It describes the ways in which pressures from parents, peers, teachers, other adults, and the media encourage acceptable behavior in children and discourage undesirable behavior. As a result of these pressures, children learn to behave in culturally approved ways, paying at least lip service to the dominant values, ideals, and motivations of the groups that include them.

The family is perhaps the major influence in the socialization process. By the time children are four years old, they are moving into a wider world of peers, school, and community. Yet the family is still the most powerful force in the child's development—and will remain so throughout middle childhood. In this chapter, we focus first on parents as agents of socialization, looking closely at different styles of discipline and their possible effects on the development of personality, morality, and sex roles. Then we examine siblings' roles in the socialization process. Once more we pick up the issue of maternal employment—this time concentrating on the school-aged child. Next we consider the effects on children of divorce and of growing up in a one- or two-parent family. This topic leads us to explore the special aspects of living with stepparents. Finally, we discuss how considering the family as a system of interacting relationships helps us understand the dynamics of family life.

PARENTS AS SOCIALIZERS

Parents contribute to the socialization process in at least five ways: by assuming the role of love providers and caregivers; by serving as identification figures; by acting as active, often deliberate, socialization agents; by providing the bulk of the child's experiences; and by participating in the development of the child's self-concept. Various theorists have stressed different aspects of the parents' roles, but each aspect probably plays some part in the child's acceptance of cultural attitudes and values. Yet children are not passive blobs of clay, to be molded by the strong fingers of parental instruction and example. In every instance, the process is interactive, with the child's temperament and capabilities influencing the methods used by parents and their effectiveness. Instead of considering parents as doing things *to* their children or *for* their children, we might look at each aspect of parental socialization as being something that parents do *with* their children (Maccoby and Martin, 1983).

Parents as Loving Caregivers

During the child's first year, the parents' primary responsibilities are to meet their baby's needs and to provide him or her with love. This role of caregiver and love provider continues throughout childhood, but its dominance of the relationship fades as other functions become more powerful. This aspect of the parent-child relationship has three important influences on the child. First, as we saw in Chapter 8, the dependability of a loving caregiver helps the baby meet the major developmental task of infancy—developing basic trust (Erikson, 1963). Second, this loving relationship may provide the toddler with the capacity to form emotional relationships (Bowlby, 1951). Finally, in carrying out the role of loving caregiver, parents prime the child for future socialization. Children are readily influenced by someone they love who also loves them—especially if they must depend on that person for the satisfaction of their needs. So the relationship enhances the parents' effectiveness as agents of socialization.

Parents as Identification Figures

The notion of parents as identification figures comes from the psychoanalytic view of development. During the process of **identification**, children internalize their parents' values and standards. This process occurs during the phallic period, when youngsters try so hard to become like the same-sexed parent that they take the parent's beliefs as their own. Learning theorists (Bandura and Walters, 1963) contend that it is simpler to regard the parent as a model, whom the child copies, than as an identification figure in the Freudian sense. In this view, children imitate models who are warm, powerful, and competent — as most parents seem to their children. Instead of seeing themselves as similar to the parent and trying to react as they think the parent would, they simply imitate the parent's actions and statements. Whether children identify with parents or simply imitate them, the process occurs without the parents' awareness or intention.

Parents as Active Socialization Agents

Sometimes parents intend their actions to have a socializing effect — as when they discipline or instruct a youngster in the right and wrong ways of doing things. At other times, parents' actions are socializing the child, but the parents seem oblivious to the effects of their actions.

Dispensers of Rewards and Punishments
When parents reward or punish a child, they are applying a powerful socialization technique. In the view of social-learning theorists, children do not blindly repeat rewarded behavior or automatically avoid behavior that is punished. Instead, they use reward and punishment as information when organizing and planning their actions. Rewards and punishments come continually, not just when the parent is disciplining the child. A five-year-old carries his plate into the kitchen after dinner, and his mother smiles and pats him on the arm. Another five-year-old reaches for a piece of bread and spills her glass of milk; her mother frowns and says, "Not again!" As we saw in Chapter 2, subtle approval reinforces a child's action, but a frown or the withdrawal of attention punishes it.

Teachers of Values
Parents often pass along explicit instructions that they hope will come to guide the child's future conduct. These instructions may take the form of specific skills (throwing a baseball, making cookies, weeding the garden), or they may be moral guidelines, which parents either believe in themselves or want their children to believe. These instructions generally are issued in the context of some activity. A child who comes

Parents can be powerful models; children not only dress up in their parents' clothes but also imitate their parents' walks, gestures, actions, and values. *(Burk Uzzle/Magnum)*

home crying after a fight with a peer may be told, "If he hits you, hit him back." A child who catches a small fish may be told, "Throw the fish back now so it will live." In such situations, children also learn about courtesy ("Tell the lady, 'Thank you'"), sex roles ("Dolls are for girls"), prejudice ("She's not the kind of person you should play with — she lives in the projects"), politics ("The Republicans are just out to help the rich get richer"), property ("That doesn't belong to you; give it back to Jimmy"), and other aspects of getting along with other people. Children tend to accept these rules, and unless subsequent experiences convince them otherwise, continue to regard them as truth. Many such guidelines are never challenged and remain part of a person's basic beliefs throughout life.

Disciplinarians   Parents become disciplinarians when children break some rule or do something their parents disapprove of. The effect of this discipline or socialization rests on the act itself (which misdemeanor is punished) and the form that the discipline takes. Parents simply may assert their superior power—by yelling, shouting, threatening, or hitting the child. They may withdraw their love for a time. Or they may give the child some reason for behaving acceptably. Parents often use some combination of these forms, and the effect of any discipline depends on which form dominates the balance (M. Hoffman, 1984). As we shall see in the discussion of discipline, parents' actions and the context in which they occur frequently have unanticipated results.

Parents as Providers of Experience

Parents control so much of the child's world that they determine the sort of experiences their child will have. This aspect of parental socialization actually sets the ground rules for the child's self-socialization, because from what children see and experience, they draw conclusions about the nature of the world and the people in it. These conclusions form the basis of **social cognition,** the term for children's understanding of themselves, other people, and society.

At home, children learn what men and women are like. From the behavior of their parents, they learn whether one sex is more capable than the other, has a larger say in the running of the household, or is more affectionate. Parents teach children how to approach other people and what to expect from them, as well as what aspects of the world children should fear.

Children learn about the nature of the world by watching their parents interact with their siblings. Sometimes observational learning inscribes a deeper lesson in children than they would derive from suffering the consequences themselves: seeing a sibling spanked may lead the child to exaggerate the pain of a spanking.

Finally, children learn about the nature of the world from the environment provided by parents. The environment provides certain experiences and withholds others. Parents may take their children to museums or ballgames, or always leave them at home. They may encourage children to play on their own outdoors, with freedom to experiment and investigate, or insist that children stay inside unless a supervising adult is present.

Parents as Builders of Self-concept

Parents help socialize a child by affecting the development of self-concept. The way they treat the child and the way they perceive that child contribute to the way the child thinks about herself or himself. If parents overprotect a child, for example, the child often may feel in need of protection although he or she actually needs no outside assistance. For example, an overprotected child may be unprepared to negotiate difficulties with peers or to take responsibility for his or her own academic performance. Similarly, a little girl who is treated as if she were fragile, cute, and incompetent may come to see herself in those terms.

Parents attribute qualities to their children and treat them as though they possessed those qualities. Sometimes they even label the child ("You're stupid"; "You're daring"; "You're a clown"). The children accept those labels and build them into their self-concept. Then they behave as if the parents' attributions were correct. For example, the tallest boy in a short family may be treated as "the tall one" and carry himself as though he were tall. If he is actually short for his age, his peers eventually may correct his misconception, but for a time he may reap the benefits of being tall by acting tall.

DISCIPLINE

Before children can crawl or walk, parents have little reason to discipline them. Once children can move around by themselves, however, parents must step in to preserve the child's safety and their own sanity. During the preschool years, the majority of mother-child interaction is devoted to discipline. Mothers of four-year-olds spend about 60 percent of their interaction time trying to interfere with their child's activities (M. Hoffman, 1983).

If the parents' efforts are successful, their children develop **self-regulation,** the ability to control their own behavior so that it is appropriate to the prevailing situation (Maccoby and Martin, 1983). Self-regulation encompasses more than refraining from some forbidden act or postponing some pleasure; it also enables children to achieve various aims and goals they have chosen. Because parental discipline may affect the development of children's morality, cognition, and personality, researchers have devoted a good deal of attention to it.

Disciplinary Styles

When a creeping baby reaches out and begins to jerk on a lamp cord, a parent's aim is to get the infant to stop what he or she is doing. So the parent uses the only disciplinary style that is effective with infants: power assertion. In **power-assertive discipline,** the force of the discipline resides in the parent's overwhelming power. The parent may pick up the baby and remove him or her bodily from the source of temptation. The parent may shout "No!" and pull the baby's hand away or even slap the baby's hand. With older children who are developing the capacity to regulate their own behavior, parents may use other power-assertive techniques, such as threats, commands, spankings, and the withdrawal of privileges. But whatever the specific action, power-assertive techniques are based primarily on the child's fear of punishment (M. Hoffman, 1984).

The second disciplinary style relies on the withdrawal of love. In **love-withdrawal,** the power of the discipline lies in the child's fear that he or she will lose the emotional support, affection, and approval of the parent. This technique involves nonphysical expressions of the parent's anger of disapproval (M. Hoffman, 1984). When using this style of discipline, parents may withdraw physically (turning their back on the child), refuse to speak or listen to the child, tell the child that they dislike him or her, or threaten to leave the child.

In the third style, **inductive discipline,** the power of the discipline lies in appeals to the child's reason, pride, or desire to be grown up and to the child's concern for others. Parents use reason and explanations to make the child realize the harmful consequences of the forbidden action—either to the child or to other people. These explanations often encourage youngsters to take the role of another.

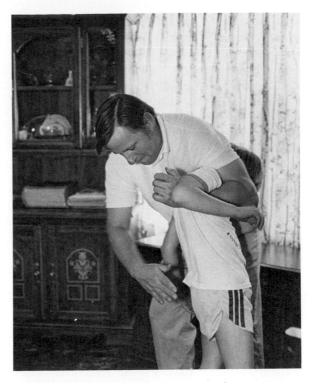

The assertion of physical power secures immediate compliance, but parents who rely primarily on power-assertive discipline may find that their children grow into self-centered individuals who learn to behave so that they do not get caught. *(Tom Ballard/ E.K.M.-Nepenthe)*

Love-withdrawal and power-assertion are both effective in the immediate situation. They get children to stop whatever they are doing and pay attention. However, when used heavily, they may be counterproductive. The prospect of abandonment or of losing a parent's love may be so frightening that the reason for the parent's withdrawal becomes lost on the child. Children whose parents depend on love-withdrawal may learn to repress all their emotions (M. Hoffman and Saltzstein, 1967). They may show little aggression or overt anger, but they also may show little excitement or joy in happy situations.

Any form of power assertion stops a child's activity, but the consistent use of physical punishment seems least effective in the long run (Perry and Bussey, 1984). Frequent physical punishment is likely to lead a child to associate fear and anger with the parents or the home situation. The child then avoids the parents and picks up his or her values elsewhere. In addition, the parent who hits a child is modeling physical aggression. The parent demonstrates that when you disapprove of someone's behavior, it is okay to hit that person (Walters and Grusec, 1977). If the child identifies with the parent, the lesson is especially effective. Intense punishment may also cause such a strong emotional reaction that the child fails to connect his or her misbehavior with the consequences. If the child forgets why he or she was punished, a spanking becomes an exercise in futility.

After reviewing the research, Gene Brody and David Shaffer (1982) concluded that parents who rely primarily on power assertion of any sort tend to have self-centered children whose aim in resolving moral problems is avoiding punishment. They may have learned to behave so that they will not get caught.

Induction appears to be the most effective disciplinary technique in establishing self-regulation. Children whose parents regularly use this technique are most likely to internalize their parents' standards and to abide by the rules even when parents or other adults are not around. They are also more likely to feel empathy with others and guilty when they act in a way that harms others or when they break a rule. In short, they develop a conscience.

Why does induction seem to be more successful for developing internalized moral standards? Martin Hoffman (1984) suggests that induction:

1. Helps the child to understand that he or she has caused another's distress
2. Provides a gradually increasing store of emotionally linked information about consequences and moral values, which helps the child identify situations in which some particular action is appropriate
3. Creates the perception that moral standards and guilt feelings come from within the child, instead of being imposed from without.

Inductive discipline seems related to the development of **prosocial behavior,** which describes any action that promotes or benefits another person. It includes generosity, coming to the aid of another person, and cooperation. For example, researchers have found that children who were rated by their peers as generous and helpful had parents who consistently pointed out the consequences of the children's actions on other people (Brody and Shaffer, 1982). Similarly, nine- and ten-year-olds who were told that stopping an unsupervised task in order to play would put an extra load of work on another person worked longer and harder than other children — whether the others were simply prohibited from playing or told that stopping work would increase their own labors (Kuczynski, 1983).

In a study of older elementary school children, researchers found that children whose parents used inductive discipline were more likely than other children to accept the responsibility for their transgressions, to be regarded by their classmates as considerate of other children, to judge an act as being right or wrong independent of rewards or punishment, and to connect transgressions with guilt (Hoffman and Saltzstein, 1967).

Nearly as important as the parent's style of discipline is its consistency. When parents ignore a child's misbehavior one week and the next week punish the same act, the child becomes confused. Patterns of parenting may interact with inconsistent discipline to produce highly aggressive children. An aggressive child often comes from a home with undemanding, unresponsive parents who use power assertion but apply it inconsistently (Becker, 1964). Yet even parents who customarily use inductive discipline may begin with love-withdrawal or power assertion (M. Hoffman, 1984). Once they have halted the child's misbehavior, they proceed to explain why the child's behavior is harmful or inappropriate.

The Context of Discipline

The way a parent disciplines a child depends on the sort of relationship that has been established between them. That relationship is influenced by many factors, including the child's temperament and the parent's perception of the child (see Chapter 4). What parents believe about acceptable behavior in children, about the capabilities of children, and about the responsibilities of a parent affects their child-rearing practices. No two sets of parents approach the responsibility of child rearing in exactly the same way, and no two chil-

Table 9.1
Patterns of Parenting

	Responsive	*Unresponsive*
Demanding, controlling	Authoritative parents Disciplinary style: primarily inductive; some power assertion	Authoritarian parents Disciplinary style: primarily power assertion
Undemanding, low in control	Permissive parents Disciplinary style: inductive	Rejecting-neglecting parents Disciplinary style: sporadic power assertion

Source: Adapted from Maccoby and Martin, 1983.

dren in a family establish exactly the same relationship with their parents. Because a child's development is affected by so many different factors, it is impossible to single out precisely the parental practices that lead to competent children and then to prescribe them — like daily doses of vitamins.

Yet certain parental characteristics tend to be associated with certain qualities in children — although just how strongly the child's own personality affects these parental characteristics is uncertain. The connection between parents' styles and children's personalities appeared in a longitudinal study by Diana Baumrind (1967; 1986). Baumrind views the parent-child relationship in terms of how much parents demand of a child (including how heavily they exercise their control), and how responsive they are to the child's interests and needs (see Table 9.1). Demanding parents exert firm control over their children; undemanding parents tend to let the children do as they please. Responsive parents tend to be accepting and place their children's needs first; unresponsive parents tend to reject their children and see their own needs as primary (Maccoby and Martin, 1983).

In the course of her study, Baumrind gathered information on parents from interviews, standardized tests, and observations in the home. She watched the children in nursery school and talked to teachers and parents. When the children were eight or nine years old, she studied them again to see whether the characteristics she had found in nursery school endured. Baumrind found four major patterns of parenting: authoritarian, permissive, authoritative, and rejecting-neglecting.

Authoritarian parents are unresponsive and demanding; they see obedience as a virtue. When the

child's actions or beliefs conflict with the parents' view of proper conduct, the child is punished with forceful power assertion. Respect for authority, work, and the preservation of order are important. Parents expect the child to accept without question their word on matters of right and wrong.

Permissive parents are responsive and undemanding. They avoid outright physical control, rely on reason alone, and consult with the child about matters of policy. Permissive parents are nonpunitive, accepting, and affirmative; they demand little from their children in the way of household responsibilities or orderly behavior. The children regulate their own activities and are not pushed to obey standards set up by others.

Authoritative parents are responsive and demanding. They believe that control is necessary, but they use reason as well as power assertion to achieve it. When directing their children's activities, authoritative parents use a rational, issue-oriented method and encourage a verbal give and take that the authoritarian parent does not tolerate. The aim is the child's responsible conformity to group standards without the loss of his or her independence.

Rejecting-neglecting parents are unresponsive and undemanding. Such parents seem indifferent to their children; their aim seems to be to spend as little time with their children and to exert as little effort as possible. Rejecting-neglecting parents pay little attention to any aspect of the parental role that inconveniences them, and so their children do not have to meet standards concerning aggression or homework (Maccoby and Martin, 1983).

Daughters and sons fare differently under these regimes. As four-year-olds, children of both per-

Authoritative parents, who are warm and encourage their children's individuality but exert firm control buttressed by reason, seem to produce the most competent children. *(Dennis MacDonald)*

missive and authoritarian parents turn out similarly. Girls tend to set low goals for themselves and to withdraw in the face of frustration. Boys tend to be hostile. Baumrind speculates that the preschool children of permissive and authoritarian parents are so much alike because both kinds of parents tend to shield their children from stress, inhibiting the development of assertiveness and the ability to tolerate frustration. As she sees it, both passive permissiveness and overprotection produce dependent children. Other studies indicate that four-year-olds whose parents are rejecting-neglecting tend to be demanding youngsters, who are less compliant and more aggressive than the offspring of parents who are involved with their children (Maccoby and Martin, 1983).

By the time these children are about nine years old, the picture changes somewhat (Baumrind, 1986) (see Table 9.2). Daughters of authoritarian parents seem to be high in social assertiveness (they participate comfortably in social interaction, sometimes taking the lead in group activities) but only average in social responsibility (they are about as generous and helpful, friendly and cooperative as their peers). They tend to be high in cognitive competence (they enjoy intellectual challenge and show originality in thought). Boys

of authoritarian parents do not differ from other boys in social assertiveness or social responsibility, but they tend to be low in cognitive competence. At the age of nine, daughters of permissive parents tend to be high on social responsibility but low on social assertiveness. Sons do not differ from other boys. Both girls and boys tend to be low in cognitive competence. Compared with other youngsters, children of rejecting-neglecting parents tend to be low in all areas of development: social responsibility, social assertiveness, and cognitive competence.

As preschoolers, daughters of authoritative parents tend to be independent and socially responsible. Sons are are also socially responsible but no more independent than average. According to Baumrind, these youngsters develop social responsibilities because their parents impose clearly communicated, realistic demands on them. At the age of nine, sons and daughters of authoritative parents both do well. They tend to show high social assertiveness, social responsibility, and cognitive competence. Firm but reasonable parental control, combined with some degree of choice by the children, also appears to encourage self-confidence and high self-esteen (Maccoby and Martin, 1983).

Table 9.2
Outcome of Parental Styles*

	High	*Low*
Social responsibility	Authoritative boys	Rejecting-neglecting girls
	Authoritative girls	Rejecting-neglecting boys
	Permissive girls	
Social assertiveness	Authoritative boys	Rejecting-neglecting boys
	Authoritative girls	Rejecting-neglecting girls
	Authoritarian girls	Permissive girls
Cognitive competence	Authoritative boys	Authoritarian boys
	Authoritative girls	Permissive boys
	Authoritarian girls	Permissive girls
		Rejecting-neglecting girls
		Rejecting-neglecting boys

* Parental styles seem consistently related to social and cognitive outcomes in older children. When a parental style does not appear in the table, the children tend to be average on that dimension.

Source: Information from Baumrind, 1986.

SEX ROLES

All the factors that encourage sex-typed behavior in infants and toddlers continue to push girls and boys into separate roles. Gradually, through the socialization process that begins in the family and is perpetuated by peers, school, and the mass media, children acquire the behavior and qualities that we think of as typically masculine or feminine. These outer manifestations of gender, known as **sex roles,** encompass behavior that society considers appropriate and desirable for each gender. These prescribed sex roles become magnified and transformed into **sex-role stereotypes**— simplified, fixed conceptions about the behavior and traits typical — or even possible — in each sex. Such exaggerated stereotypes probably make the acquisition of sex roles easier for children. In order to understand sex roles and their stereotypes, we first need to examine the emergence of another aspect of psychological sexuality--gender identity (see Table 9.3).

Gender Identity

Besides learning an appropriate sex role, children must develop the sense that they themselves are either male or female (Money and Ehrhardt, 1972). This invisible inner role, known as **gender identity,** develops by the time they are three years old. Most three-year-olds, says Sandra Bem (1983), not only know whether they are boys or girls but are also beginning to categorize the world by gender. They know whether toys, clothing, tools, games, and occupations are suitable for girls or boys, and they select and interpret new information through the filter of their naive theories about gender. This filter may lead them to ignore

Table 9.3
Aspects of Being Male or Female

Sex role	Outward behavior considered appropriate or desirable for males or females
Sex-role stereotype	Simplified, exaggerated conceptions of sex roles and characteristics of males and females
Gender identity	Private sense of being male or female
Gender constancy	The understanding that gender is permanent and that the child's own gender will never change
Gender schema	Informal theories about maleness and femaleness that children apply to all information that comes their way

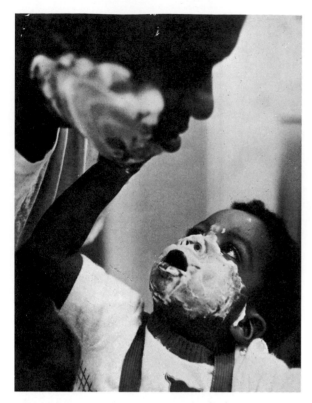

This little boy is developing his own notions of what it is to be male; imitating his father's actions contributes to the process. *(Burk Uzzle/Magnum Photos)*

information that doesn't fit their theories (mother replacing a worn out electrical switch) or distort their perceptions to fit the theories (recalling a male nurse from a television show as female) (Huston, 1985). Once children apply these theories, which Bem calls **gender schemas,** to themselves, they begin forming feminine or masculine self-concepts.

The process is gradual, and the preschoolers' elementary knowledge of their own gender is only the first step. Lawrence Kohlberg (1966) believed that children's understanding of gender is not complete until they acquire **gender constancy.** With the acquisition of that concept, the child understands that boys always become men and girls always become women and that maleness and femaleness cannot be changed. More important, the child realizes that no one can wave a magic wand and change his or her own gender. Kohlberg argued that until children are about six or seven years old, they do not understand this eternal

aspect of gender — even if they can describe exactly how to tell naked boys from girls. Until then, most children believe that a change of hair styles and clothing will transform a boy into a girl and vice versa.

Children may be most rigid about filtering the world through the lens of their gender schema while they are still learning about the permanence of their gender (Ruble, 1984). Older children, who have learned that adhering to sex-typed activities is not essential to being male or female, often seem to relax their vigil. Although their knowledge of sex-typing is more extensive than the six-year-old's, they believe that it is all right for males and females to engage in activities typed for the other sex. In fact, they tend to say that most behavior is equally appropriate for either sex and are becoming aware that most aspects of sex roles are culture-bound (Carter and Patterson, 1982). Yet among boys, this new-found tolerance applies primarily to other people. Boys' preferences, behavior, and attitudes tend to become increasingly masculine throughout childhood. Girls act on their new beliefs; many even begin to prefer masculine activities and interests (Huston, 1985).

Cultural Values and Social Change

Socialization operates to prepare children for the adult roles they will occupy. Much of the difference in the way parents and other social agents treat children reflects differing expectations about boys' and girls' adult roles (L. Hoffman, 1977). When the baby-boom generation was being born, girls were expected to spend most of their adult life as mothers, and boys were expected to be the sole breadwinners for their future families. In 1947, less than 30 percent of the female population was in the labor force — and nearly nine out of ten employed women were either single, widowed, or divorced. Only 20 percent of the married men had economic assistance from working wives (U.S. Bureau of the Census, 1982).

As in other societies around the world, children's toys allowed children to play at adult social roles without any of the physical, emotional, or economic consequences that accompany mistakes made when engaging in the real thing (Bruner, 1972). Dishes, dolls, brooms, and toy sewing machines let little girls practice the skills of child care, cooking, and homemaking — the roles their mothers filled. Trucks, tools, building equipment, and doctor kits let little boys practice the skills of driving, construction, and doctoring—the roles their fathers filled. (Little girls got *nurses'* kits.) When girls grow up to occupy a nurturant role, socialization patterns encourage them to become empathic and attuned to the emotions of others. When boys grow up to run social institutions and fend for the family, socialization patterns encourage them to become independent achievers and may even discourage the development of empathy.

In the 1980s, homemaking is not a full-time job, and motherhood occupies a much smaller proportion of a woman's life than it did forty years ago. Because women live longer today and have fewer children, they spend more years involved in occupational pursuits than in mothering. As we saw in Chapter 8, employment outside the home is the norm for today's woman. Women's move into the marketplace has been accompanied by men's increased participation in child care and household tasks. As Lois Hoffman (1977; Eccles and Hoffman, 1984) has pointed out, traditional sex-role training no longer prepares girls to fit their new adult roles—or boys to be nurturant caregivers. Even so, a girl still learns that society has defined her role as spouse and parent as primary and her vocational role as secondary; the reverse is true for boys. There is a lag between social changes in adult sex roles and society's perception of appropriate sex-role socialization.

Yet the convergence of adult roles may be followed by changes in the socialization of children (Hoffman, 1977). Some parents are making conscious efforts to produce independent daughters with broad vocational interests and nurturant, empathic sons, but they have not entirely shaken off the socialization styles of their own parents. Traditional sex differences still appear in their children (Huston, 1983). Slowly, but eventually, the way parents treat their sons and daughters may become more similar. If so, sex-role differences may diminish in future generations.

Parental Socialization

The differences in the way parents treat their infant and toddler sons and daughters continue in the ways they socialize older children. Often, parents teach expected sex roles directly. They may tell

Every culture establishes its own standards of behavior for each gender; in the culture of these children a boy can care for a younger sibling and still feel masculine. (© *Leonard Speier, 1980*)

their sons that "boys don't cry" or their daughters that "girls don't get in fist fights." They also are likely to teach skills in a gender-specific manner. Girls may learn to vacuum the house, do the laundry, or fix a meal when mother is late at the office. Boys are more likely to learn how to repair a broken stair, fix a bicycle tire, or mow the lawn. (The *boy's* mother will bring home a pizza for dinner.)

Indirectly, parents encourage the adoption of sex roles by the experiences they provide the child. Parents choose many of their children's toys, and girls' toys tend to encourage compliance but boys' toys encourage independence and originality. Sex-typed toys have other influences on children. Play with blocks, building materials, tools, and model kits encourages manipulation, develops skills connected with mathematics and spatial relationships, and provides boys with information

Children's toys tend to reinforce traditional sex roles. Like other boys' toys, model kits encourage manipulation, develop skills connected with math and spatial relations, and provide boys with information about the physical world. *(Liane Enkelis/Stock, Boston)*

about the physical world. Playing house or with Barbie dolls encourages girls to develop verbal skills (Eccles and Hoffman, 1984).

Parents' perceptions of their children lead them to expect more competence and independence from boys than from girls. When youngsters have a task to complete, parents are more likely to let a son figure out his own mistakes but step in to help a daughter as soon as she gets in trouble (Huston, 1983). Parents also give boys more freedom. They are allowed to investigate wider areas of the community without asking their parents' permission and run errands at an earlier age (Saegart and Hart, 1976). Such differences in socialization may affect personality and self-concept along gender-related lines. Boys tend to check with their mothers less often and to become more independent, exploratory, and assertive. Girls tend to continue checking frequently with their mothers, to be less assertive and more dependent, to miss many chances to develop a sense of competence, and may pick up their parents' fears about moving around freely in the world (Huston, 1983).

Parental patterns of reward and punishment also influence children's adoption of sex roles. Boys are more likely to be punished for violating sex roles, a practice that may make them more responsive than girls to sex-typed labels. It's okay to be a tomboy, but sissies are frowned on. Parents do not seem to mind if their daughter climbs trees,

rejects ribbons and skirts, and becomes a rabid fan of the Denver Broncos, but they are uneasy when their son shows an interest in dolls, asks to take ballet lessons, and says that professional football is brutal. Fathers show much more concern than mothers about appropriate sex-role behavior, perhaps because they hold more traditional views of sex roles than mothers do (L. Hoffman and Nye, 1974). When Judith Langlois and Chris Downs (1980) observed parents interacting with their three- to five-year-old children, the difference in mothers' and fathers' behavior became clear. Mothers showed no inclination to push their children into traditional sex roles, but fathers interfered actively to stop inappropriate play. If a son played with housekeeping toys or a daughter played with an army set, fathers talked negatively, ridiculed the play, or suggested that the child play with another toy. They balanced this punishment with rewards for playing with sex-appropriate toys.

Parents' attitudes toward sex roles and their own behavior may have the strongest effect on older children. At first, whether parents are liberated or traditional, youngsters display stereotypical attitudes and behavior. Then, with gender constancy firmly developed, children gradually become able to distinguish between cultural stereotypes and their parents' specific beliefs and attitudes about sex roles (Fagot, 1982). For example,

THE EYE OF THE BEHOLDER

Our perception of others' behavior often depends on the label we attach to that person. Do labels also affect our views of sex differences in behavior? When adults watch a crying baby, they assume that they are hearing cries of anger when told the baby is a boy and cries of fear when told the baby is a girl (Condry and Condry, 1976). John Condry and David Ross (1985) wondered if the same effect was responsible for the belief that boys are more aggressive than girls. In other words, they suspected that people would be more likely to perceive aggression among boisterous boys than among sweet girls who were playing just as roughly. So they videotaped a pair of preschoolers playing together in the snow. The play was ambiguous, but it could be interpreted as an attack by one child on the other. Because the youngsters were dressed in snowsuits, viewers could not detect their sex.

The researchers played the tape for men and women enrolled in a child development class, then asked them to rate the children's behavior. The results disproved the researchers' hypothesis. When viewers believed that both children were boys, they thought the play was least aggressive and most affectionate, and they evaluated the fighting children most favorably. In all the rest of the conditions (fighting girls, a boy attacking a girl, or a girl attacking a boy), viewers said that the play was highly aggressive. The sex of the observer made no difference: women were as likely as men to attribute the most aggression to the girls. When Condry and Ross analyzed their data more carefully, they discovered that observers who had no experience with children tended to see no difference in aggression, whether they thought they were watching girls or boys. But observers who had experience with children consistently saw the boys as less aggressive.

How can we explain these results? Condry and Ross concluded that experience with young children destroys the belief that kids are all alike. Such experience convinces young adults that boys are more aggressive than girls, and so they *discount* what they see. When two boys are wrestling in the snow, experienced observers say, "Boys will be boys." Expecting boys to fight, they judge the activity in terms of their gender schema for boys. Or perhaps they interpret the ambiguous scuffle as a bout of rough-and-tumble play, which is not hostile but affectionate. When they see two girls fighting, the activity so violates their expectations that they overestimate the level of aggression. The results of their experiment have led Condry and Ross to wonder if most observational research (because it is conducted by experienced viewers) *underestimates* sex differences in children's aggression.

---

there is no relationship between the sex role attitudes and future role aspirations of six- to eight-year-old girls and their mothers. But the attitudes and aspirations of ten- to twelve-year-old girls tend to correspond with those of their mothers (Meyer, 1980).

Sex roles probably are strengthened when children identify with the parent of the same sex and model their behavior on that parent's example (Eccles and Hoffman, 1984). In most families, mothers' education and occupations fall below those of fathers. Unless daughters get extra encouragement, they are unlikely to aim as high as their brothers or look for a job that falls outside the typical woman's sphere of work (teaching, nursing, librarianship, clerical jobs). Even in homes where parents' education and occupation are roughly equal, the major responsibility for household tasks and child care is likely to fall to the mother, while the father usually takes charge of the yard and keeps the family automobiles running. Thus, identification may strongly affect children's expectations and limit daughters' aspirations.

Sex Differences

With boys and girls getting such different treatment from parents, it comes as no surprise to find that girls and boys differ in interests and behavior.

Some researchers also have found differences in personality and cognitive capabilities. Boys tend to be more aggressive, more physically active, and more competitive than girls. They also seem to have superior visual-spatial ability and mathematical skills (but not arithmetic skills). Girls seem to have superior verbal skills as well as a greater need for emotional connections with other people. They are more empathic and nurturant than boys, less confident about their abilities, more likely to seek help and reassurance from others, and tend to avoid risks. When they fail, they are quicker than boys to take responsibility for their shortcomings (L. Hoffman, 1977; Huston, 1983).

In all these areas, the abilities and behavior of boys and girls overlap. The findings describe only the average behavior of a group. Some girls are more aggressive than the average boy, some boys more empathic than the average girl. In most cases, the average differences, although statistically significant, are not very large.

Yet there are problems with studies in nearly every one of these areas. Many experiments designed to test sex differences center on situations that are likely to produce stereotypical responses (Ruble, 1984). For example, ten-year-old girls may be assertive when playing a game with other girls but hesitant about asserting themselves in a situation that includes boys. Other factors that can evoke different responses from boys and girls are the sex of the experimenter, the children's familiarity with the situation, and their interest in the topic of the experiment. In the accompanying box, "The Eye of the Beholder," we can see that the experimenter's familiarity with children also may affect his or her perceptions.

Some researchers believe that a few sex differences have a biological basis. Before birth, hormones affect brain development and determine whether the mature individual will produce hormones continually (as males do) or on a cyclical basis (as females do). They also may lead to sex differences in brain organization. As a result, boys and girls may differ in perceptual and cognitive skills. For example, after reviewing the research, Diane McGuinness (1985) concluded that girls' superior performance in reading rests on sharper hearing (they find it easier to distinguish the sounds of language) and faster integration of verbal and visual stimuli. Boys, she says, do better in mathematics because of their superior spatial ability. Other researchers are convinced that sex differences are the result of socialization. After a similar review of research, Anne Fausto-Sterling (1985) concluded that none of the studies has successfully demonstrated a biological basis for sex differences in cognition. For example, there are no sex differences in spatial ability among Eskimos, who live in a large, almost featureless, snowclad environment, where the ability to detect minute detail is linked to survival.

The other sex difference usually traced to a biological base is aggression. Researchers have suggested that prenatal sex hormones predispose boys toward aggression. In a study of children whose mothers had taken male hormones during pregnancy (Reinisch, 1981), the boys had a much stronger tendency to be physically aggressive than their brothers who had not been exposed to the additional prenatal hormones (see Figure 9.1). The girls were also more aggressive than their unexposed sisters. (In this study, children told researchers how they would react in situations that involved conflict with other youngsters, but no one actually observed the children in conflict.)

The great overlap between the behavior of boys and girls indicates that any biological push toward different skills or traits must be small. Because behavior can only be expressed within an environment, the cultural influence is also important. Socialization can heighten sex differences or diminish them, depending on whether a culture considers a particular ability or behavior as an asset.

SIBLINGS

During childhood and adolescence, siblings are "always there." This enforced proximity makes the sibling relationship a source of companionship and conflict. Its ambivalent nature may provide children with unique learning experiences (Furman and Buhrmester, 1985). The quality of those experiences depends on a host of factors: the child's position in the family birth order, the spacing between the siblings, the sex of the sibling, and the number of children in the family. In Chapter 8, we saw how the birth of a sibling radically changes a first-born toddler's life, destroying the toddler's position as center of the universe but allowing the youngster to dominate the baby brother or sister.

Among sibling pairs in a longitudinal study, the older child's domination of the sibling relationship continued after both children started school (Abramovitch, Corter, Pepler, and Stanhope, 1986). As time passed, sibling pairs of the same sex tended to become more harmonious, but mixed-sex pairs teased, threatened, and competed more. Yet the thread of hostility that ran through these relationships was not major; most of the time, siblings played together and provided each other with affection, praise, approval, and comfort. Other studies have shown that ill will develops among siblings primarily when children perceive that parents are meeting the needs of one child and not the other (Bryant, 1982). In such cases, each child harbors hostility toward the other.

When it comes to outright aggression — kicking, hitting, biting, hair pulling, and throwing things — the boys are far ahead of the girls. Among four-year-olds, sex differences in family fighting are small, but once the youngest child is at least ten years old, the rate of physical aggression in all-boy families is more than twice the rate in all-girl families (Straus, Gelles, and Steinmetz, 1980). Even so, all physically aggressive acts decline with age; preschoolers battle much more often than older siblings.

Most studies of sibling interaction have focused on infants and preschoolers. With older children and adults, researchers have simply considered such factors as birth order, spacing, and family size, looking for correlations between these variables and personality traits or cognitive abilities. Although we lack a clear understanding of the process within the family that leads to various effects, it appears that the number of siblings in a family affects each child's intellectual development in a systematic way. According to **confluence theory,** which was developed by Robert Zajonc and Gregory Markus (1975; Zajonc, 1983), the intellectual development of a family is like a river, with input from each family member flowing into it. This river determines the intellectual level of the family; the younger the child, the less the child contributes. As families get larger, children's intellectual development suffers, because the level of the

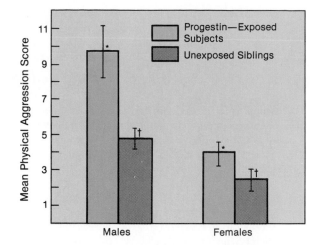

FIGURE 9.1   When asked how they would solve disputes with other youngsters, those who had been exposed to prenatal male hormones had a stronger tendency to choose physical aggression than their siblings of the same sex. Asterisk (*) indicates significant difference between progestin-exposed and unexposed subjects ($p < .01$); dagger (†) indicates significant difference between unexposed males and unexposed females ($p < .02$). *(From Reinisch, 1981)*

surrounding intellectual environment drops. As Zajonc (Zajonc and Hall, 1987) puts it, "Any adult you can add to the family — grandparent, uncle, aunt — and any infant you can subtract raises the intellectual quality of the environment."

A child's place in the family birth order, known as **ordinal position,** accentuates the effect: the more older siblings a child has, the lower his or her intellectual level. Instead of interacting primarily with adults, as a first-born child does, the fourth- or fifth-born interacts mostly with other children. The more closely children are born together, the more detrimental the effects become. The last-born child carries an extra burden because he or she never gets a chance to play teacher to a younger sibling, an experience that stimulates intellectual development. (According to Zajonc, because they also are deprived of the teaching function, only children do not do as well as first-born children in small families.)

Studies in Western Europe, North America, India, Nigeria, and Israel generally have confirmed the existence of the pattern (Zajonc, 1983). Yet confluence theory has not been universally accepted. Some developmentalists agree that family

COUNTRY IN A QUANDARY: THE ONLY CHILD IN CHINA

Alarmed by population growth that threatened its social and economic development plans, the government of China put its weight behind family planning. Official government policy now limits families to a single child. The effects of the policy are beginning to appear; in the cities of Beijing, Shanghai, and Tianjin and in several provinces, more than 70 percent of couples have only one child.

Cooperation is essential to the success of a socialist society; the individual who acts primarily in his or her own self-interest is unlikely to adapt comfortably to modern Chinese life. Should the Chinese government begin to worry about the possible effects of its family-planning program? Some child specialists in China have become concerned about the issue and are investigating the effects of growing up in a one-child Chinese family. Shulan Jiao, Guiping Ji, and Qicheng Jing (1986) compared only children in the Beijing area with children who had siblings. The children were matched pairs of kindergartners (four to six years old) or primary school students (nine to ten years old). Researchers had the children's classmates rate the children by answering questions about the youngsters in each group (for example, "When you play a game, who is the one who usually is the leader and offers new ideas?").

In their classmates' judgment, only children were significantly more likely than children with siblings to act according to their own interest and to refuse to share things with their peers. Only children also were less persistent at tasks, were less cooperative, and were held in lower regard by their peers. Of the fifteen children who were rated as most cooperative by their classmates, one was an only child. Of the fifteen children who were rated as best liked, a leader, and the child you would ask for advice and help, two were only children. Of the fifteen children

Chinese parents are under continual pressure to adhere to the government's "one-child" family policy; researchers wonder how the policy's success will affect future generations of Chinese. *(Owen Franken/Stock, Boston)*

who were rated as not sharing with other children and acting according to their own interest, eleven were only children.

When researchers looked at family backgrounds, they found that neither parents' occupations nor family structure affected the results. They now plan to examine socialization practices in the family to see if they can discover why growing up single seems to lead to "undesirable" personality traits. If the differences that appeared in the ten-year-old Chinese children persist to adulthood, what will happen to Chinese society? Are the strength of these results due to some aspect of Chinese culture, or if the United States moves toward the one-child family, will its citizens become less cooperative and more self-interested? No one yet knows the answers to these questions.

size, ordinal position, and spacing affect intellectual development but maintain that confluence theory's predictions are right for the wrong reason (L. Hoffman, 1983). Instead of pointing to a di-

minished intellectual environment in large families, they suggest that we look at other aspects of socialization. Perhaps a lack of parental attention is responsible. Parents have only so much attention to spread among their offspring, and each subsequent child receives less attention. As for the last-born's burden, it may not be related to the lack of opportunity to play teacher. Instead, the last-born might feel less competent and less efficient than his or her older siblings. This feeling of incompetence could lead to lowered self-efficacy and slowed intellectual development.

MATERNAL EMPLOYMENT

Among school-aged children, it is the child of the mother who is *not* employed who lives in an "abnormal" family (see Table 9.4). Among intact families, 68.1 percent of mothers are employed outside the home; among families headed by mothers, 75.7 percent are employed (U.S. Bureau of Labor Statistics, 1986). In most cases, having an employed mother seems to benefit the school-age child. Compared with children whose mothers are at home, the children of employed mothers probably see more of their fathers. The fathers are less likely to have a second job, and so they have more time for the family. The fathers also help out more at home, and so the children see a male in a nontraditional role. Children of employed mothers also have to help out at home; they are more likely to have household responsibilities than children of homebound mothers. Such responsibilities, when they are not unreasonable, often contribute to a child's sense of self-esteem (L. Hoffman, 1984a; Medrich, Roizen, and Rubin, 1982). Discipline in lower-income homes is more consistent when the mother is employed. In these families and in one-parent families, employed mothers tend to have structured rules for their children and to enforce the rules consistently (L. Hoffman, 1979; 1984a).

Daughters seem to reap special benefits from having a mother in the work force. They tend to be independent, high achievers with high self-esteem. Why should maternal employment have this effect? Mothers serve as role models, preparing their daughters for the sort of roles they will occupy as adults. Daughters admire their working mothers more than do daughters of homebound mothers. Accompanying this admiration is higher esteem for the female role and a stronger belief in

Table 9.4
Employed Mothers

Children	Intact Families (%)	Mother Headed (%)
3 to 5 years	58.6	61.2
6 to 13 years	68.1	75.7
14 to 17 years	67.0	78.5

Note: In 1985, more mothers were employed outside the home than were at home with their children.

Source: Data from U.S. Bureau of Labor Statistics, *Monthly Labor Review,* February 1986.

women's competence (Baruch, 1972; Vogel, Broverman, Broverman, Clarksun, and Rosenkrantz, 1970). Their fathers are also more likely to approve of competence in women and to encourage it. High-achieving women often have had a close relationship with their own warm and encouraging father, and the father's approval and participation in child care probably provided this sort of support (L. Hoffman, 1980).

Sons derive some benefit from having employed mothers. They seem better adjusted and hold less traditional views of both sexes; they see women as more competent and men as warmer than do sons of homebound mothers (Vogel et al., 1970). However, the blurring of traditional sex roles is not as pronounced among sons of blue-collar fathers, who sometimes admire their fathers less than do sons of homebound mothers. Because many wives of blue-collar men enter the work force primarily because of pinched finances, this view may reflect a perception of both father and son that the father has failed in his job of family provider. Blue-collar sons, as well as daughters, do better in school when their mothers are employed. This higher academic achievement also characterizes sons and daughters of employed mothers in poor families — including black families (L. Hoffman, 1980).

In the middle class, sons may not fare so well academically. Sons of employed mothers tend to make lower scores on achievement tests in mathematics and language than sons of homebound mothers (Gold and Andres, 1978). Researchers have tried to understand this effect, and some have suggested that it might be the result of heavy so-

Most children whose mothers work outside the home are expected to help with household chores, a responsibility that tends to increase a child's self-esteem. *(Michael Heron/Woodfin Camp & Associates)*

cialization by today's full-time homemaker. Close, extended contact with the full-time, middle-class mother may induce boys to conform to adult standards — and thus to perform well in school. This notion is supported by a study that looked at the effect of full-time mothering during the pre-school years of school-aged children (Moore, 1975). Sons who had experienced full-time mothering tended to be inhibited and conforming, but at school they outperformed sons whose mothers had been employed. Perhaps these boys are responding somewhat as girls do to heavily traditional sex-role socialization: with low levels of independence and good grades.

DIVORCE

One night after dinner, Jeanne and Bill Buff sat down in the living room with Andy, their seven-year-old son. "Do you know how Mommy and Daddy don't hug and kiss anymore and fight a lot?" Jeanne asked him. "Well," she added, "sometimes parents stop loving each other. . . . Daddy's not going to live with us anymore" (Gelman, 1985). Nearly half of the children born in the 1980s will go through a similar experience, their lives disrupted by their parents' divorce or separation (Hetherington and Camara, 1984). A child's immediate reaction to the painful announcement is likely to be some mixture of anger, fear, depression, and guilt (Hetherington, 1979).

Once the rupture takes place (usually, the father moves out of the house), child and parents enter a difficult period. Life changes in unpleasant, unsettling ways. There is a loss of routine; regular events, such as meals and bedtimes, no longer arrive on schedule. The division of labor within the home changes. The family and the house seem disorganized (Hetherington, Cox, and Cox, 1982). There are specific losses; planned activities and family vacations are canceled. Money may become scarce. The family may have to move (often to a poorer neighborhood), losing friends, neighbors, and perhaps a familiar school in the process (Hetherington, 1979).

There is a loss of emotional security; youngsters often watch in bewilderment as the secure nest they had taken for granted is shaken. Most of us assume that children are aware of parental discord, but research suggests that the divorce is often a shock to the child (Wallerstein and Kelly, 1979). Parents often conceal their difficulties from children; in families where parents argue, children tend to accept the arguments as part of family life. The parents' emotional distress after the break so changes their behavior that children

SURVIVAL SKILLS FOR THE LATCHKEY CHILD

School-aged children of employed mothers are too old for regular day-care facilities; many go to a neighbor's house after school or come home to father, a grandparent, or an aunt. But millions of them are **latchkey children**; they come home to an empty house and take the responsibility for their own care after school. No one knows just how many latchkey children there are; estimates run from more than 2 million to as many as 10 million. Most writers and researchers have expressed concern about the welfare of latchkey children, but little research has been done to ascertain whether self-care at an early age has any ill effects on a child's development.

In the few studies that have been carried out, differences sometimes appear between latchkey children and those who are under the care of an adult. Among black fifth-graders in Philadelphia, unsupervised girls were more likely to have school problems and to be low achievers than supervised girls (Woods, 1972). Among a group of city children, unsupervised youngsters seemed fearful (Long and Long, 1982). Some children said that they turned up the volume on the television so that they wouldn't hear scary noises. But fifth- and seventh-grade latchkey children who lived in the country were not afraid, and there were no differences between them and supervised children on any measures (Galambos and Garbarino, 1983).

Among fourth and seventh graders in North Carolina, researchers also drew a blank (Rodman, Pratto, and Nelson, 1985). They could find no differences between supervised and unsupervised children in self-esteem, feelings of competence and control, social adjustment, or interpersonal rela-

tions. Whether the children were boys or girls, black or white, fourth or seventh graders, middle or lower class, or lived in intact or single-parent families, they made similar scores on rating scales and were rated similarly by their teachers.

Yet parents whose children are on their own after school often are uneasy about the youngsters' safety. In Connecticut, Parents Anonymous, a private, nonprofit organization that sponsors public education about child abuse and neglect, has prepared a five-week course to help latchkey children and their parents contend with the problems of self-care. The course also makes them aware of the opportunities for growth that can accompany the children's taking of responsibility (Collins, 1984). Parents learn about their children's possible fears and the feeling of many latchkey children that they are prisoners in their homes each afternoon — not allowed to answer the phone, go to the door, or have friends over. Children talk about the rules their parents have established and, in role-playing sessions, learn how to communicate their feelings to their parents.

In ways that do not make the children excessively fearful, instructors teach the children how to be safe at home and how to avoid being sexually assaulted. They learn how to answer the door ("Look out the window and see who it is; never let a stranger in") and how to answer the telephone ("Never say that you're home alone"). The course tries to make children feel more responsible at home and to develop their general sense of responsibility. It also tries to give parents confidence in their children's ability to care for themselves.

---

may feel as if they are living with strangers (Hetherington and Camara, 1984). Their parents' moods may swing unpredictably from euphoria to depression, and the custodial parent, usually the mother, may be depressed, angry, impatient, and erratic in dispensing discipline for most of the first year.

The child's response to these disruptions depends on many things, including temperament and past experience, but the effect of the child's age and sex seem particularly important. The loss of routines is most disturbing for young children. Familiar, predictable routines give children a sense of security; such minor changes as the time and nature of meals can upset young children. Young children find their new situation difficult to understand. Often they think that the divorce is their fault—that something they did drove their parents apart—and they feel guilty. (Even older children may feel this way.) Young children also misinterpret the parent's moods and frequently feel that the parent's anger or sadness is their own fault. These feelings are understandable, because their egocentrism leads them to interpret the event from their own point of view. They may even fear that their own relationship to the parent could dissolve, just as the marriage did. ("If Mommy doesn't love Daddy anymore, maybe someday she won't love me either.")

At all ages, children are angry at one or both of the parents. They also tend to focus on their own losses, and their resentment may be expressed in aggressiveness, a refusal to comply with the parent's wishes, whining, nagging, dependence, and withdrawal of affection (Hetherington and Camara, 1984). Older children also may be embarrassed about the divorce. The embarrassment becomes acute if one of the parents has a new sexual partner or begins dating. Preadolescent children and adolescents, who are struggling with their own budding sexuality, find it especially difficult to deal with their parents as sexual beings. Yet these older children understand the situation better than young children do. They tend to distort it less and have more resources outside the family to help them handle this difficult transition period (Kelly and Wallerstein, 1975).

One of the most carefully documented difficulties of the first year after the divorce is the conflict that may develop between the custodial mother and her young son. In a longitudinal study of divorced families with four-year-olds, Mavis Hetherington, Martha Cox, and Roger Cox (1982) found an unpleasant cycle of interaction between mothers and their sons. The mothers, feeling depressed, anxious, and incompetent, would make ineffective and inconsistent attempts to exert discipline; the boys would respond with increased aggressiveness and noncompliance; the mothers would feel increased anxiety and incompetence and step up their power-assertive disciplinary attempts; the boys would become even more aggressive and noncompliant. This pattern of escalating power-assertion, on the one hand, and aggression

and noncompliance, on the other, affected the boys' behavior at school, where they became increasingly aggressive throughout the first year after the divorce. Although their aggression then began to wane, six years after the divorce these boys were still perceived as more aggressive than their peers.

Eventually, children come to terms with their new situation. Within two years after the divorce, most children have fewer problems than those who live in a home filled with marital discord. Girls seem to handle the adjustment better than boys; they are doing as well at the two-year mark as girls in intact families where there is little conflict (Hetherington and Camara, 1984). Why do boys seem more vulnerable than girls to the stress that accompanies divorce? Boys seem more vulnerable to any kind of family stress, including marital discord and unemployment. In fact, the detrimental effect of divorce on boys may be as much the stress of discord *before* the breakup as the stress of adjusting to a broken family. The personality of children who took part in a longitudinal study was assessed when they were three, four, and seven years old (Block, Block, and Gjerde, 1986). Some of the families later divorced. When researchers looked at their data, they found that boys in these families had shown the aggression and lack of impulse control connected with divorce as early as eleven years before their parents separated.

Other observations provide additional clues to boys' greater vulnerability, (L. Hoffman, 1986). First, when parents are under stress, their interactions with their sons suffer greater disruption than their interactions with their daughters (Elder, 1984; Hinde, 1985). Second, parents see boys as sturdier and less vulnerable than girls. This perception may lead parents to use boys instead of girls as targets of their frustrations. And it may account for the fact that boys are more exposed to parental discord than girls. Parents are more likely to quarrel in front of their sons (Hetherington, Cox, and Cox, 1982). Finally, peers and teachers view boys more negatively and give them less support during stressful periods than they give girls (Hetherington and Camara, 1984). Taken together, these factors suggest that boys are exposed to more stress than girls. As we shall see in the next section, how well a boy does after divorce also may depend on which parent he lives with.

An increasing number of fathers are heading single-parent homes, learning to juggle both parental roles—as single mothers always have done. *(Mark Antman/The Image Works)*

THE SINGLE PARENT

Because few couples today stay together "for the sake of the children," up to half of all youngsters will spend at least part of their childhood in a single-parent home; in nearly 90 percent of the cases, the custodial parent is the mother. The growing number of unwed mothers has further swelled the number of children in single-parent homes; by 1984, more than a quarter of all American families were headed by only one parent (Gelman, 1985). When researchers study single-parent families, they generally look for problems, and so their search may miss possible benefits. After an interview study with children and parents, Robert Weiss (1979) concluded that life with a single parent also has its positive aspects. He discovered that in families with school-age and adolescent children, the experience can lead to greater responsibility, self-sufficiency, and maturity. In these families, each child is expected to do his or her share to keep the household running—and most do. These children have more power than children in an intact family, and most develop a peer-like relationship with the custodial parent. As a seventeen-year-old who had lived in a one-parent family for six years told him:

In the long run—I feel sort of like I shouldn't say it—but a lot of kids are better off if their parents do get divorced, because you grow up a lot quicker. (Weiss, 1979, p. 111)

Many children find more problems than growth in the single-parent family. Whether the family is headed by mother or father, youngsters miss the chance to see successful interaction between men and women (Lamb and Bronson, 1980). Other effects depend on the child's sex and the sex of the parent. Boys are more likely to have problems when mothers are the custodial parent, girls when fathers have custody. These findings have led some developmentalists to suggest that boys may do better when living with their fathers, girls with their mothers (Santrock, Warshak, and Elliot, 1982). They stress that children who grow up with only one parent escape much of the influence of the missing parent's gender, so that they lack a role model as well as a person whose childhood experiences equip them to deal with the specific problems related to growing up male or female. However, other factors may also be involved.

Life Without Father

Consistent differences appear between groups of children who have fathers and those who do not, but factors other than the absence of the male parent may be responsible. Economics is surely important. Nearly half of all families headed by women fall beneath the poverty line, a fact of life in the 1980s that has led economists to talk about the "feminization" of poverty (Seaberry, 1985). As the relative number of female-headed families has increased, their economic position has decreased. The situation of minority families headed by women is especially grim: 86 percent of such black families are below the poverty line (Hill, 1983).

Emotional stress is another factor; many single mothers are under acute stress, and it affects their behavior with their children. Some of the stress is financial. Most single mothers have to struggle to provide their children with the necessities. Counselors who work with children of single parents speak of nine- and ten-year-olds who worry about the light bill or the rent (Gelman, 1985). Some of the stress is role overload. The single mother has to deal with all the tasks, responsibilities, and demands that would ordinarily be shared by two (Weiss, 1979). Some of the stress may come from social isolation. The single mother may be so hemmed in by responsibilities and poverty that she becomes a lonely captive in a child-centered world.

These factors probably interact with the absence of the male parent to produce the effects on children's development that researchers consistently find. The absence of the father may be felt as the lack of masculine influence. For optimum development, a child may need the presence of a male role model. Or the father's absence may be felt as the absence of another adult who would have enriched the child's environment. Confluence theory predicts that the subtraction of one adult from the family will depress a child's cognitive development (Zajonc and Hall, 1987), and researchers have found that the level of cognitive and social stimulation in single-parent homes is lower than when both parents are present (MacKinnon, Brody, and Stoneman, 1982). Children in single-parent homes also get less adult attention (Medrich, Roizen, and Rubin, 1982).

For whatever reason, neither boys nor girls in mother-headed households do as well in school as children from intact families (Hetherington, Camara, and Featherman, 1983). Their scores on achievement and IQ tests are lower, their grades are lower, they are more likely to repeat a grade, and they tend to leave school earlier. The effect is especially marked on mathematical skills (Shinn, 1978). Boys' intellectual development and academic performance suffer much more than that of girls, and the deepest effects appear if the boys are younger than five at the time the father leaves (Radin, 1981). The absence of a father seems most harmful among children in working-class families and among very bright children in lower-class families.

Some studies also find that boys without fathers have trouble developing self-control. They tend to be more aggressive and may run the risk of becoming juvenile delinquents (Guidubaldi, Perry, and Cleminshaw, 1983). Earlier we saw the escalating cycle of aggressiveness that custodial mothers and sons often fall into. Some researchers believe that the climate and tone of the home and the kind of supervision the boy receives are greater factors in the development of delinquency than the absence of the father (Herzog and Sudia, 1973).

Sex-role development has received most attention in studies of single-parent families. In the section on sex roles, we saw that fathers seem to be a dominant influence on the acquisition of sex roles. What happens when the father is missing? In the case of boys, his early loss appears to weaken or slow the acquisition of a male sex role — but does not prevent it (Biller, 1981). Boys tend to prefer feminine activities and shun activities involving competition and physical contact; they make less masculine scores on sex-role tests (Huston, 1983). Sometimes, however, they may show an exaggerated masculinity, as if to compensate for the absence of their father. When the father leaves after the boy starts school, the effects are much less pronounced.

The mother's behavior may be as important in this trend as the father's absence. Mothers in single-parent families sometimes overprotect their sons and discourage their independence (Lynn and Sawrey, 1959; Stolz et al., 1954). In longitudinal studies, boys developed stronger masculine attributes when their mothers reinforced them for sex-typed behavior, encouraged their independence, and had positive attitudes toward the missing father (Huston, 1983).

Evidence that the father's absence affects a girl's sex-role development is scant. Most studies indicate that girls are less affected than boys, al-

Some researchers believe that girls fare best when the custodial parent is the mother but boys do best when the father has custody. *(Lenore Weber, Taurus)*

though some studies find that girls from mother-headed homes tend to reject the role of wife and mother or have difficulties in achieving satisfactory sexual relationships (Biller, 1981). Perhaps the father's early departure affects girls as it does boys, but the influence does not show until girls reach adolescence. In a study of working-class girls, Hetherington (1972) found that high-school girls who had lost their fathers before they were five years old seemed uncertain about their actions around men. When taking part in an interview, they were either painfully shy (if their fathers had died) or excessively seductive (if their parents had divorced). But college women who had lost their fathers before they were five did not show the same inappropriate responses to men (Hainline and Feig, 1978). Either middle-class girls have wider opportunities than working-class girls to learn how to behave with the other sex, or else practice in socialization during high school helps most girls overcome the problem.

Life Without Mother

Between 1970 and 1982, the number of single-father families more than doubled (Collins, 1983). With families headed by single fathers reaching the 600,000 mark, researchers have begun to look at the effects of life without mother. In a group of single-father families, boys were more mature and sociable than boys who lived in single-mother families (Santrock, Warshak, and Elliott, 1982). Among these same families, girls' social development was slow; the girls were less sociable, less independent, and more demanding than girls in single-mother families.

In father-headed families, it is the girl who lacks a role model. Whether a girl adopts a strong female sex role may depend on the father's parenting style. In the same study of father-headed families, when fathers were attentive to their daughters, the girls tended to behave in masculine ways. But when fathers were authoritarian, their daughters tended to behave in a highly feminine manner. (As we saw earlier, when mothers are authoritarian, their sons tend to be extremely aggressive.) Because girls in father-headed families often are expected to assume some of the maternal responsibilities (household duties and care of younger siblings), they have an opportunity to learn the feminine role (Lamb and Bronson, 1980).

Puberty may be an especially difficult time in father-headed families. Fathers expect their wives to discuss menstruation and sexual matters with daughters, and the responsibility makes them uncomfortable. This may leave girls without any individual adult counsel and guidance in the area of sexuality. Some evidence indicates that girls from father-headed families are more likely than other girls to have an illegitimate pregnancy (Fox, 1978).

Today's single fathers are an unusual group, because their assumption of child-rearing responsibilities requires them to reject traditional sex roles. This high involvement with their children, in which they perform the duties that traditionally fall to the mother, may lead their sons and daughters to develop more flexible views of masculinity (Lamb, Pleck, and Levine, in press).

THE RECONSTITUTED FAMILY

Most children spend only a few years in a single-parent family. Within five years, up to 75 percent of divorced people have remarried; researchers estimate that about 35 percent of today's children will spend part of their lives in a stepfamily (Glick, 1984). The reconstituted family may solve some problems for children, but it also puts them under additional stress. Many children dream about reuniting their parents, and the new marriage abruptly ends those fantasies. Accepting the stepparent may even make the child feel disloyal to the noncustodial parent. Adjustment to the reconstituted family is most difficult for children between the ages of nine and fifteen. The new parent has entered a working system, and the entry of this new parental figure dethrones the child from the peer-like relationship he or she has developed with the custodial parent. It comes as no surprise, then, to find that older children tend to reject a stepparent, no matter how loving and attentive he or she is (Hetherington, Cox, and Cox, 1982).

In nine out of ten reconstituted families, the new parent is a stepfather. His success in assuming the parental role and how well the family functions depend in good part on the way in which he handles discipline. He is unlikely to be successful if he either abdicates authority, giving the mother little support in child rearing, or becomes extremely involved, restrictive, and authoritarian. Both those patterns were found to be prevalent in a study by Hetherington and her colleagues (Hetherington, Cox, and Cox, 1982). But when the stepfather was authoritative and warm and when his involvement was welcomed by the mother, children did better

than those in divorced, single-parent families or in intact families filled with marital discord. In families with authoritative stepfathers, relationships also improved between the biological mother and her children. The presence of a stepfather seemed to be good for young boys, who often developed warm attachments to their new father and found a role model in him. Daughters seemed to have more difficulty than boys in establishing a warm relationship with a stepfather (Clingempeel, Brand, and Ievoli, 1984).

When the new parent is a stepmother, boys have more problems than girls. They are less socially competent than boys in single-father families or girls who live in families with stepmothers (Santrock, Warshak, and Elliot, 1982). In a study of stepmother families with nine- to twelve-year-old children, Glenn Clingempeel and Sion Segal (1986) found that when children develop a warm relationship with the stepmother, the adjustment of both boys and girls improves, but the difference is striking for girls. Stepdaughters who felt that their stepmothers loved them had higher self-concepts, were less withdrawn and fearful, less aggressive, and more socially competent. Girls developed better relationships with their stepmothers if the biological mother did not visit frequently, probably because her visits increased conflicts within the daughter over whether her liking for her stepmother made her disloyal to her biological mother.

Time helps smooth family friction. It seems to take stepfathers about two years to develop warm relationships with their stepchildren and to establish themselves in a disciplinary role (P. Stern, 1978). In Clingempeel and Segal's study, the longer the stepmother and the biological father had lived together (both before and after marriage), the warmer the relationship between the children and their stepmother, and the better adjusted the children were.

Relationships in reconstituted families often are complicated by children from each parent's former marriage. In such cases, families with stepfathers are not as happy as other reconstituted families, even if the stepfather does not have custody of his own children (Clingempeel, 1981). When the stepfather brings his own children into the new family, family functioning suffers. Marital conflict often develops. Parents tend to disagree

Life with a stepparent at first may be bumpy; it takes about two years for stepfathers to establish themselves in the parental role and to develop warm relationships with their new children. *(Donald Dietz/Stock, Boston)*

about child-rearing practices. Each parent becomes dissatisfied with the way the other parent handles his or her responsibilities. And all family members believe that each parent gives preferential treatment to his or her own children (Hetherington and Camara, 1984).

PHYSICAL CHILD ABUSE

> He'd come to the table like any typical kid, and he'd spill his milk. Well, I'd take him and hit him about ten or fifteen times, but I wouldn't remember if I'd hit him ten times or five times except, you know, he'd have great big welts on him. . . . I have hit him hard enough to break my hand. (O'Brien, Schneider, and Traviesas, 1980, pp. 234-235)

These words were spoken on the television program *60 Minutes* by a woman who had repeatedly beaten her school-age son. Although few parents batter their children, the incidence of child abuse seems alarmingly high: during 1981, there were 850,000 reported cases of child abuse or neglect in the United States (American Humane Association, 1983).

Physical child abuse is the physical injury of a child because of intentional acts or failures to act on the part of his or her caregiver; the acts or omissions must violate the community's standards concerning the treatment of children (Parke and Collmer, 1975). Why do parents abuse their children? Researchers have no simple answer. The beating of a child seems to be the result of many interacting factors: characteristics of the parent, characteristics of the child, patterns of family interaction, socioeconomic stress, family isolation, and cultural acceptance of violence (Starr, 1979). All these factors correlate with child abuse, but no single factor—or combination of factors—clearly distinguishes the abusing from the nonabusing family (Gelles and Cornell, 1985).

The Abusing Parent

After more than two decades of investigation, researchers cannot predict which parents will abuse their child. Comparisons of child abusers and nonabusers have turned up few personality differences between the parent who scolds the milk-spilling child and the one who hits — and keeps on hitting. Seymour Feshbach (1980) believes that differences in attitudes and values are more important than personality differences in contributing to child abuse. He points out that most abusing parents have unrealistic expectations of children; they tend to believe that their children are capable of adultlike behavior and see any misdeeds as intentional defiance. They may label the child as incorrigible, "crazy," or "dumb." When such parents also suffer from low self-esteem, the probability of abuse increases. Low self-esteem leads a parent to react to the "deliberate" misbehavior of a child with anger; anger increases the likelihood that the parent will strike out at the child; remorse and guilt after the incident further lower the parent's self-esteem, and the parent becomes even more vulnerable to the angry response.

The notion of a generational cycle of abuse also has been popular. In this view, child abusers are likely to have had a childhood marked by physical or emotional abuse or neglect. As children, they learned from their own parents to be aggressive. They also learned that parents criticize and disregard their young children while making demands on them (Parke and Collmer, 1975). Being abused in childhood does make a person more likely to abuse his or her own children, but the connection is not nearly as strong as researchers once supposed (Gelles and Cornell, 1985). The majority of child abusers were not abused as children. Like low self-esteem, a history of child abuse is just one more strand in the tangled web that leads to child abuse.

The Abused Child

The characteristics of the child also seem to contribute to the likelihood of abuse. Something about the child's appearance or temperament may somehow distance the parent from the child and increase the chances that the parent will be abusive. Just being male puts a child at greater risk of being seriously injured (Straus, Gelles, and Steinmetz, 1980). Earlier, we saw that boys may become targets for their parents' frustrations, either because they are perceived as especially sturdy, because the culture permits more violence in connection with males, or because boys are more demanding and difficult to care for than girls. The same problem exists among monkeys, except there the trend is much stronger; researchers have found that abused monkey babies are four times more likely to be males (Suomi and Ripp, 1983).

Any characteristic that makes a youngster different from other children (such as prematurity or a physical or mental handicap) places him or her at increased risk throughout childhood. For example, 10 percent of babies have low birth weights, but 40 percent of battered children had low weights at birth (Bell and Harper, 1977). Yet most "different" children are *not* abused and not all abused children are "different." Finally, during family interactions, a child may learn to behave in ways that evoke abuse from parents. In fact, the experience of being battered may change the child's behavior in ways that make future abuse more likely.

Researchers have found that, early in life, abused children differ from children who have never been abused. The emotional reactions of abused infants are depressed, as if they had learned that being too happy, interested, sad, or afraid was risky (Gaensbauer, 1982). In observational studies, abused toddlers are more aggressive than other children (George and Main, 1979). At day-care centers, they may assault, threaten, or harass the caregiver. They also avoid the friendly advances of children and adults, a reaction that might help to maintain abuse at home. As we saw in Chapter 1, abused toddlers seem to lack empathy (Main and George, 1985). Instead of responding sympathetically to the distress of other children, they become fearful or angry and may even attack a crying child.

Older abused children often seem excessively compliant, passive, and obedient. They seem stoical and accept whatever happens. Yet some abused children are more like the toddlers — they are negative and aggressive. A very small group is sweet and compliant one minute and impulsive and disruptive the next. After studying abused children, Ruth and Henry Kempe (1978) concluded that these children never developed the basic sense of trust that is the major developmental task of infancy. They find it hard to trust adults, make only superficial friendships, and discard new friends at the slightest hint of rejection. In school, most are underachievers, lonely, and friendless.

The Context of Abuse

Although child abuse is found in every socioeconomic class, in every ethnic group, in the country and the suburbs as well as in the city, it is more likely to occur when parents have few social supports. When incomes and educational levels are low, when the neighborhood is unstable, when the mother is the sole parent, and when day care is not available, the incidence of child abuse increases (Garbarino and Crouter, 1978). Apparently, the combination of economic stress, the constant burden of child care, lack of support from friends, and ignorance of where help might be obtained can set up a situation in which a child's crying, whining, or aggressiveness can provoke vicious, even deadly, blows from an overwhelmed parent.

Within the abusing family, interaction proceeds differently from the way it does in other families. The difference was apparent when researchers observed families as they built with Tinker Toys, tossed bean bags, or discussed how they would spend lottery winnings (Burgess and Conger, 1978). Abused children and children who had not been abused behaved in a similar fashion, but the parents reacted differently. Mothers of abused children spoke less often to their children than other mothers, and they had less positive contact with them. They also carried out 77 percent more negative acts. Fathers of abused children were much less likely to comply with requests than other fathers, whether the requests came from the mother or the children.

Researchers (Gil, 1970) have found that 63 percent of abusive incidents develop out of some disciplinary action taken by the parents. As we might expect, abusive and nonabusive parents handle discipline differently. In a study of lower-middle and working-class children between four and eleven years old, abusive and nonabusive parents both used some physical punishment, but abusive parents applied it more frequently and used harsher methods (Trickett and Kuczynski, 1986). Two major differences appeared in the behavior of abusive parents. First, they used punishment indiscriminately, no matter what the transgression. Nonabusive parents tailored their methods to the offense. Sometimes they merely told the child to stop whatever he or she was doing. Nonabusive parents also used reasoning along with punishment when a child was aggressive, destructive, or dishonest. They relied on reason alone when the child violated some family rule (coming home late, leaving clothes on the floor, going somewhere without permission). Second, abusive parents

Each child is a contributing member of the family system, and every interaction between any two family members is affected by other relationships within the family. *(Greg Brull/West Stock)*

tended to become angry when their children were dishonest, aggressive, destructive, or broke family rules; nonabusive parents became depressed, anxious, or doubtful. Nonabusive parents were more successful in their disciplinary actions; their children were less likely to defy them or to become angry when their parents intervened than abused children were. Interaction between abusive parents and their children seemed in many ways like the coercive cycle that often develops between divorced mothers and their sons. In abusive families, such cycles apparently escalate to the point of violence. The failure of abusive parents to use reasoning may help explain why abused children were less compliant and more aggressive; as we saw earlier, reasoning helps a child internalize rules and regulations.

THE FAMILY AS A SYSTEM

By looking separately at various aspects of the child's socialization, we may get an oversimplified view of social development. Influence within the family does not run in one direction; while children are being socialized by others, they are also active socializing agents (Bell and Harper, 1977). The child influences the parents, younger and older siblings, grandparents, and other relatives.

The child also may act in ways that affect the family structure and important family events. When we explore the effects of a specific relationship, it is easy to forget that every relationship occurs within a context of interacting influences.

The family is a social system with interrelated parts, a system that is established with the parents' marriage. Over the years, the system's structure changes as new members are added, reach new developmental stages, or depart (Hill and Mattessich, 1979). Each member of the family system has a changing series of roles, depending on that person's age, gender, and relationship to other family members. For example, a baby boy fills the roles of infant, son to his mother, and son to his father. When the boy is three years old and a baby sister joins the family, his roles as son remain, but he now assumes the roles of preschooler and older sibling. The relationships between him and his parents (and thus the way they respond to — and affect — one another) will change as a result of the new family structure.

In this view, the child is an interdependent, contributing member of the family system, part of the process that controls his or her behavior (Minuchin, 1985). The child's own characteristics contribute to this process. Earlier, we saw an example of the child's contribution in the coercive cycle between divorced mother and agressive son. The cycle of power assertion by the mother, aggression and noncompliance by the son, increased power assertion by the mother, increased aggression by the son, and so on, formed a looping spiral, so that it was impossible to blame either party for the son's aggressiveness. Similarly, it is too simple to say that an overprotective mother creates a fearful and anxious child (Minuchin, 1985). Instead, the mother and child are caught up in a pattern, in which the mother responds to the child's fears with concerned behavior, which may make the child more fearful, which makes the mother more concerned, and so on.

Mother and child interact within the larger family system. Their interaction is also affected by the relationship of child to father, the relationship between the parents, the mother's relationship with other children in the family, and the child's relationship with other siblings. The marital relationship is especially important. With small infants, even the mother's competence at feeding her baby is affected by her husband. When the husband esteems her maternal role, she is more competent at the task than when there is marital tension and conflict (Pederson, 1975). A little later, the influence of the marital relationship appears when researchers rate a baby's attachment. Parents of securely attached babies tend to be highly satisfied with their marriages, but parents of insecurely attached babies tend to have unhappy marriages (Goldberg and Easterbrooks, 1984). Among a group of parents with small children, those who had a good marriage were more confident about being parents and had fewer problems controlling their children's behavior (Frank, Hole, Jacobson, Justkowski, and Huyck, 1986).

The family system exists in a larger social system, which influences the child, the other family members, and the family itself. For example, the demands of the culture (such as compulsory schooling, college, job transfers, retirement) affect the family structure (Hill and Mattessich, 1979). Other influences on the child, on other family members, and on the family system include the social milieu within which the family operates, the schools, the child's peer group, and television. In the next chapter, we explore these influences.

SUMMARY

1. Personality grows out of the process of **socialization,** in which the child absorbs the attitudes, values, and customs of society. The process is interactive, with children's characteristics affecting the way parents respond to them and with children playing an active role in their own socialization. Parents contribute to the socialization process through their roles as love provider and caregiver, identification figure, and active socialization agent. They also pro-

vide the bulk of the child's experiences and influence the child's developing self-concept. In the Freudian view, children internalize their parents' values and standards through the process of **identification.** In the learning view, children imitate their parents because their mothers and fathers are warm, powerful, and competent models. By controlling most of children's experiences, parents contribute to the development of their children's **social cognition,** which refers to a child's understanding of self, others, and society.

2. If parents' disciplinary efforts are successful, children develop **self-regulation,** the ability to control their behavior so that it is appropriate to the situation. Discipline may be **power-assertive** (which relies on the parents' superior force); it may take the form of **love-withdrawal** (which relies on the child's fear of losing the parent's affection and approval); or it may be **inductive** (which relies on appeals to the child's pride or reason). Although both power assertion and love-withdrawal are effective in the immediate situation, inductive discipline appears to be the most successful in developing self-regulation. Children whose parents use inductive discipline also seem most likely to show **prosocial behavior,** which includes generosity, cooperation, and helping others. Major parental styles are **authoritarian** (demanding and unresponsive parents), **permissive** (undemanding but responsive parents), **authoritative** (demanding but responsive parents), and **rejecting-neglecting** (undemanding and unresponsive parents). Children seem to fare best when their parents are authoritative.

3. Children learn to act as boys or girls through a lengthy process that has five aspects: **sex roles** (outwardly masculine or feminine behavior); **sex-role stereotypes** (simplified, exaggerated versions of sex roles); **gender identity** (the inner knowledge that one is male or female); **gender constancy** (the understanding that one's sex will never change); and **gender schemas** (naive theories about gender that one uses to filter new information). Recent social changes in adult sex roles have not yet been incorporated in the socialization of children. Parents influence their children's adoption of sex roles, using all the techniques they employ in other forms of socialization, but fathers seem to be most concerned with this aspect of child-rearing. Boys and girls differ in personality: boys are more aggressive, more active, and more competitive; girls are more empathic, more nurturant, more likely to seek assistance and avoid risks, and seem less confident. They differ in cognitive capability; boys excel in visual-spatial ability and mathematics; girls excel in verbal skills. Some researchers believe that these differences have a biological basis, but all agree that they are heavily influenced by socialization practices.

4. Siblings tend to get along more harmoniously when they are the same sex, but boys tend to be more physically aggressive than girls at all ages. According to **confluence theory,** family size and spacing influence cognitive development. The child's **ordinal position** (position in the family birth order) accentuates these effects; the more older brothers and sisters a child has, and the more closely the siblings are spaced, the lower the child's intellectual environment.

5. Most children's mothers are employed outside the home, and most children seem to profit from this arrangement. Daughters of employed mothers tend to be independent high achievers with high self-esteem. Sons tend to be better adjusted than boys whose mothers are not employed outside the home. Among working-class boys, maternal employment seems to improve academic performance but may diminish the father in the boys' eyes. Among middle-class boys, maternal employment may lower academic performance.

6. When parents divorce, children's routines are upset, their emotional security suffers, and they become angry at one or both parents. Girls generally adjust better than boys; within two years girls are doing as well—both emotionally and academically—as children in intact families. Boys seem to be more vulnerable to the stress that accompanies divorce.

7. When children live with only one parent, they tend to get less social and cognitive stimulation and less adult attention than children in intact homes. The absence of a father seems to be felt most by boys: their school performance suffers and they take longer to acquire the male sex role

than boys in intact families. The absence of a mother has a deeper effect on girls, who tend to be less sociable, less independent, and more demanding than girls in intact families. When the family is reconstituted by the addition of a stepparent, some of these problems are lessened, but others may arise. Stepparents usually find the situation easier when, first, they have no children of their own and, second, they and the stepchild are the same sex: boys are more likely to accept a stepfather, girls to accept a stepmother.

8. Child abuse has no single cause; it seems to result from the interaction of the parent's characteristics, the child's characteristics, family interaction patterns, socioeconomic stress, family isolation, and the cultural acceptance of violence. Although being abused in childhood makes a person more likely to abuse his or her own children, the connection is not as strong as once was believed. Being abused affects the way a child interacts with other children and adults and may lead the child to behave in ways that encourage further abuse.

9. The family is a changing social system with interrelated parts. The child is a contributing member of the system who fills a series of roles that change as the child develops. While the child is being socialized by parents and siblings, the child in turn is socializing them, and each family interaction takes place within a context of interacting influences.

KEY TERMS

authoritarian parents	inductive discipline	rejecting-neglecting parents
authoritative parents	latchkey children	self-regulation
confluence theory	love-withdrawal	sex role
gender constancy	ordinal position	sex-role stereotype
gender identity	permissive parents	social cognition
gender schema	power-assertive discipline	socialization
identification	prosocial behavior	

STUDY TERMS

authoritarian parents   Parents who demand that the child meet high standards but are relatively cold and unresponsive to the child.

authoritative parents   Parents who demand that the child meet high standards but are warm and responsive to the child.

confluence theory   The theory that the size of the family and the spacing of the children affects the cognitive development of each child; the larger the family and the closer the spacing, the lower the child's IQ.

gender schema   Self-constructed theory made up of sex-related associations for each gender, which organizes a person's perceptions of the world and determines the way new information will be organized.

identification   The internalization of another person's values and standards in an attempt to become like that person.

inductive discipline   A disciplinary technique whose power lies in appeals to pride or concern for others. It relies heavily on reason and explanations, and it attempts to induce empathy or role-taking.

love-withdrawal   A disciplinary technique whose power lies in instilling fear of losing emotional support, affection, or approval. It includes withdrawing physically, refusing to speak or listen to a person, telling the person that one dislikes him or her, or threatening to leave the person.

permissive parents   Parents who place few demands on the child but are warm and responsive to the child.

power-assertive discipline   A disciplinary technique whose force resides in power; when used with children, it includes blows, threats, commands, removing the child bodily, and the withdrawal of privilege.

rejecting-neglecting parents   Parents who place few demands on the child and are relatively cold and unresponsive to the child.

socialization   The process by which an individual acquires the behavior, attitudes, values, and roles expected from its members by a society.

Personality: Expanding Social Interaction

Eleven-year-old Matt watched the other boys run to the edge of the pier and jump into the swirling water below. One by one, they bobbed to the top and swam away. He took a hesitant step forward, then stopped and stared. His friends began calling to him: "Come on!" "Jump!" Matt could only dog paddle; the ten feet between him and the water seemed like a hundred. "What's the matter, sissie," yelled another boy, "are you scared?" The demands of his friends were stronger than his fear. Matt shut his eyes and jumped into the deep water.

The influence of children's peer groups can be extremely important in shaping their development. Within the peer group, children may find emotional security; norms for their behavior; instruction in cognitive, motor, and social skills; and stimulating company. In learning to get along with peers, children also learn to adjust to life (Asher, 1978). At the same time, children are learning what the adult society expects. Some of this instruction comes from television—an influence that begins socializing children into the wider world as soon as they can follow the flickering pictures on the screen. Other instruction comes in the classroom—from books and films, and from teachers who tell them what is good and bad, what they can do, must do, and dare not do. But much of what a child learns at school takes place on the playground. Matt may learn from playing basketball with his peers that cheating is not tolerated, or he may learn from playground intrigues that a person should stand up for his close friends.

In this chapter, we turn from the influence of the family to influences of the wider world. We begin by considering specific ways in which peers exert their influence. After exploring the connection between social skills and popularity, we take up the structure of the peer group and the ways in which peer pressure can alter children's behavior. Peers are friends as well as socializers, and we trace the course of friendship and the qualities children look for in their friends. After we examine the ways in which play socializes a child, we explore an agency that is designed to serve a socializing function: the school. There, we find, socialization may proceed in an unintended as well as a deliberate fashion. From among the other socializing influences in the child's world, we have chosen to examine television, because it occupies the largest portion of the child's waking hours. Accidents of birth help determine how children experience socializing influences, and so we close by considering the effects of social class, ethnic group, and cultural influence.

When children play with their peers, they have their first opportunity to relate to their equals. Competition is not hidden, and each child gets a chance to make the group's rules. *(Alan Carey/The Image Works)*

PEERS AS SOCIALIZERS

The influence of peers on the socialization process begins earlier today than it did a generation ago, when few mothers of infants and small children worked outside the home. At any age, peer influence is different from family influence in several respects. First, children must earn their membership in the peer group. At home, family membership is their birthright. No matter how gross their misbehavior, they cannot lose their relationships with parents and siblings. Even if their parents are abusive, the relationship is not severed. When children enter the peer group, however, they run the risk of rejection. No one has to accept them.

Second, the peer group gives children (unless they are twins) their first chance at interaction with equals. Within the family, each member has

different responsibilities and different powers. Older family members (whether siblings or parents) dominate younger members, but they also restrain their powers in some way. For example, when parents play a game with a child, they generally hold back, either allowing the child to win or making sure that the child's loss is not humiliating. Similarly, in arguments they do not insult the child; when punishing the child, they restrain the force of their spanks or slaps. In other ways, however, parents exert their power: they make the family's rules and enforce the discipline. When the child enters the peer group, he or she finds both open competition and a chance to help make social rules.

Finally, the peer group also gives children their first opportunity to compare themselves with others their own age. In **social comparison,** children can assess how well their own performance compares with that of other children. When their performance exceeds that of peers, they are likely to feel pride and enhanced self-esteem. When their performance does not measure up, they are likely to become dejected, and their self-esteem may suffer. Through social comparison, children also can readjust any clearly erroneous self-concepts that developed within the family. The short boy who was treated as "the tall one" in a short family soon may discover that he is not tall.

How Peers Socialize Children

By interacting with peers, children learn many essential social skills. They learn how to dominate or to protect someone, how to assume responsibility, how to reciprocate favors, how to appreciate another's viewpoint, and how to assess their physical, social, and intellectual skills realistically (Perry and Bussey, 1984). These lessons are learned by such processes as reinforcement, modeling, and social comparison.

Peer Reinforcement When peers show that they approve of a child's actions, the child becomes more likely to act that way again in the future. Reinforcement can take the form of praise, joining in the activity, imitating the child's actions, showing concern for the child, or simply watching the child attentively. Popular children tend to dispense praise and approval generously. In addition to providing such direct reinforcement, they are lavish with indirect reinforcement (attention and conversation) and approach other youngsters in a friendly manner. As a result, they receive a good deal of reinforcement in return (Masters and Furman, 1981).

Reinforcement works somewhat differently in encouraging aggression. When attacked children become passive, cry, or assume a defensive posture, they reinforce the young attacker, who often mounts another foray against the same victim. But when an attacked child fights back, the punishment changes the offender's behavior. The attacker usually finds a new victim or behaves differently toward the former victim, or both. Victims who launch successful counterattacks

Peers use reinforcement and punishment to enforce appropriate behavior; among these girls a good kicker will be praised. *(Ann Chwatsky)*

sometimes become aggressive themselves. Apparently, the success of their own aggression is reinforcing; it teaches former victims that aggression can be useful (Hartup, 1983).

Peers use punishment to pressure children into sex roles. In observational studies, five-year-olds often make direct attempts to change the behavior of a boy who begins playing with a doll or a girl who begins hammering (Lamb, Easterbrooks, and Holden, 1980). They criticize the activity, ask the youngster to stop playing with the toy, complain loudly, or physically intervene to stop the play. Regardless of the kind of punishment they receive, children usually stop cross-gender play at once.

Peer Modeling When some action is modeled by peers, the effect on the watching child's behavior is often as powerful as that of reinforcement or punishment. By observing another child, children may learn how to do something they either could not do (such as working a computer) or would not have thought of (such as walking a fence rail). They may learn what happens when one acts in a certain way (destroying property can get children into trouble), or how to behave in a strange situation (attending the first meeting of a scout troop).

Immediate imitation of a peer model declines sharply as children reach school years, and is rare among nine- to eleven-year-olds. In a study by Rona Abramovitch and Joan Grusec (1978), children who were leaders were imitated most by

Children act as models for one another, and when a popular child devises a new way to play "Space Invaders," his friends are likely to adopt his variation on the game. *(Paul Fusco/Magnum)*

other children, but these leaders also imitated others. Immediate imitation, say the investigators, may help establish and maintain a child's social influence. The decline in immediate imitation among older children does not indicate that the practice is waning. Older children may tend to save their imitations for a later occasion and so avoid being called a "copycat."

Modeling by peers influences all sorts of behavior. In various studies, it has increased or decreased generosity and aggression, led children to wait longer for rewards, helped them overcome their fear of dogs, increased sociability, and made them bold enough to break out of sex-role stereotypes (Hartup, 1983). In Chapter 9, we saw that boys' behavior is more strongly sex-typed than girls'. It is not surprising, then, that girls are more likely than boys to follow the lead of a model who carries out some activity that is clearly associated with the other gender.

Because adults and peers both can serve as models, we might wonder which model a child is likely to follow when the examples conflict. The answer seems to depend on the situation and the sort of behavior that is modeled. For example, when it comes to learning new ways to express aggression, children are more likely to imitate other children than adults (Hicks, 1965).

Social Comparison Although children compare themselves to others at an early age, most children do not begin to judge their skill or achievements by comparing their own behavior to that of others until they are at least seven years old (Harter, 1983). This lag may be due to the fact that young children are aware of their limited abilities. In many instances, they do not expect to do well and so are not especially interested in evaluating their skills. For example, after children carried out a task, Diane Ruble and her associates (Ruble, Boggiano, Feldman, and Loebl, 1980; Ruble, Parsons, and Ross, 1976) told the youngsters how well their peers had done on the same task. Six-year-olds were not bothered when they failed and paid little attention to information about others' performance when judging their own relative success. But eight-year-olds were distressed at failure and paid close attention to information about the way they measured up to their peers. When children first begin comparing their own performance to that of others, it is likely to be in situations in which they are allowed to reward themselves on the basis of their performance. Under such conditions, even six-year-olds may use social comparisons in deciding how well they have done (France-Kaatrude and Smith, 1985).

The interest that developmentalists have begun to take in social-comparison derives from its possible influence on self-efficacy. If children decide that they cannot run well, throw a ball accurately, make friends, or do arithmetic problems, their ability at any of these skills is likely to suffer.

Social Skills and Popularity

Children must earn their place in the peer group, and their social skills play a major role in determining their acceptance or rejection by others. Socially competent children, who are welcomed into the group, are skilled at initiating new relationships and maintaining old ones and at resolving conflicts (Hartup, 1983). Yet popularity is not solely a matter of social competence. Children's expectations, their behavior, and the responses of others form an interlacing web, so that it is difficult to say which comes first. In addition, factors outside a child's control may affect the responses of others. Research has shown, for example, that physical attractiveness affects a child's popularity. Black, Anglo, and Hispanic children believe that

From the time that children are about eight years old, they begin comparing their own performance with that of their peers. How well they feel they measure up may affect their feelings of competence. *(Lawrence Frank)*

attractive peers are smarter, friendlier, more likeable, and more likeable, and more willing to share than unattractive peers (Langlois and Stephan, 1977).

Once a child has earned popularity or been denied it, peers interpret the child's behavior in line with that reputation. Among a group of second and fifth graders, popular children were given the benefit of the doubt (Hymel, 1986). When they did something unpleasant, the other children attributed their behavior to some situational factor ("He didn't do it to be mean; it was just a joke"). If an unpopular child committed a similar act, the other children tended to hold the child accountable and to blame the youngster's disposition or hostile intent ("That's the kind of person she is"). This pattern of interpretation makes life easier for popular children and more difficult for the unpopular.

Initiating and Maintaining Relationships
When socially competent children try to enter a group of playing children, they are alert to any social cue (such as facial expressions) and respond in a pleasant and agreeable manner (Dodge, Pettit, McClaskey, and Brown, 1986). They comply with the playing children's wishes, provide requested information, and match their nonverbal behavior to that of the playing children. They avoid disrupting the play that is in progress and are usually welcomed into the group. Because peers judge children by their behavior as they first attempt to join in play, most socially competent children are popular playmates.

When unpopular children try to enter a group, they use techniques that seem to doom them to failure. Instead of playing quietly alongside the other children and gradually slipping into the group, they call attention to themselves. They ask irrelevant questions, talk about themselves, disagree with the other children, and present their opinions and feelings in a way that disrupts the flow of group play (Putallaz, 1983). It is no wonder that the group generally gives them the cold shoulder.

Children who get along well with their peers are friendly and generous with approval, as we have seen. They are rarely aggressive and are usually the children who remind others of the rules and establish group norms (Coie and Kupersmidt, 1983). In one study of nine- to eleven-year-olds (Nakamura and Finck, 1980), socially competent children were better than unpopular children at understanding the feelings and motives of other children and at anticipating problems and figuring out solutions.

Managing Aggression and Resolving Conflicts

Among monkeys, aggression is incorporated into social play. Within the peer group, young monkeys learn how to keep their boisterous scuffles playful; they threaten one another, wrestle, and bite without causing actual harm to their opponent (Perry and Bussey, 1984). As we saw in Chapter 5, human children use rough-and-tumble play in much the same way. Rough-and-tumble play among eight- and nine-year-olds is not serious, and usually no one gets angry (see the box "Does Rough-and-Tumble Play Turn Mean?" on page 258).

Through interaction with their peers, children learn how to express aggression appropriately and how to control it. It takes a long time to reach this point. Preschoolers quarrel frequently, usually over toys. Among six- to eight-year-olds, the number of squabbles declines, but the fighting may turn hostile (Hartup, 1974). At about this time, children also begin to give up blows in favor of words, and verbal aggression (threats, taunts, and insults) becomes prevalent.

Gradually, through the socialization processes described earlier, children learn when aggression is acceptable and when it is not. They also learn other methods of resolving their conflicts. Through a series of studies with preschoolers, kindergartners, and first graders, Kenneth Rubin

and Linda Krasnor (1986) discovered that socially competent children have the most strategies for solving problems and are able to adapt them in order to achieve their goal. Children who cannot get along with their peers tend to have trouble thinking about the problem; they seem to try out the first response that comes to mind — usually an assertive or aggressive strategy. If their attempt fails, instead of trying a different approach, they persist with the original strategy.

When social conflicts end in aggression, it usually means that one child has interpreted another child's intentions as hostile. An important difference between aggressive and nonaggressive children may be the way in which they interpret the intentions of others. In a study, Kenneth Dodge and Daniel Somberg (1987) discovered that in some situations, aggressive and nonaggressive boys interpret the actions of others similarly: when they are relaxed and when the boys' intentions are clear. In such situations, most boys respond benignly to clearly accidental damage and aggressively to damage that is clearly intentional. But when another boy's behavior is ambiguous, aggressive boys are more likely to interpret the damage as intentional, but nonaggressive boys tend to give the other child the benefit of the doubt. If they feel threatened, however, aggressive boys' abilities to interpret another child's intentions deteriorate, and their tendency to interpret ambiguous damage as intentional climbs sharply (see Figure 10.1). An aggressive boy who feels threatened even may have trouble interpreting accidental damage accurately. This tendency to assume the worst may help explain why highly aggressive children often are rejected by their peers and become social isolates.

The Isolated Child

When children are asked to name their friends, about 10 percent of the members in any group are not named at all (Asher and Renshaw, 1981). Some of these children are labeled "least liked" by the others; they have been *rejected* by their peers. The rest simply are not mentioned; they are *neglected* by their peers. Rejected and neglected children are both social isolates, but the neglected child may later be accepted — or even become popular (Asher, Hymel, and Renshaw, 1984). In a study of children moving from elementary to middle school, 80 percent of

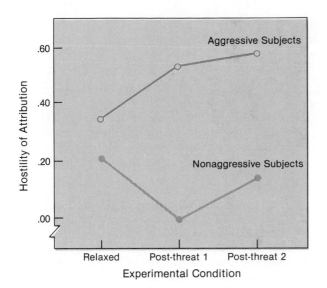

FIGURE 10.1 When boys are in a relaxed situation, aggressive boys may be somewhat more likely to attribute hostile intentions to the ambiguous acts of others than nonaggressive boys are, although the difference is not significant. But when the boys are threatened, the aggressive boys' tendency to assume the worst of others is heightened. *(From Dodge and Somberg, 1987)*

the neglected children were accepted by their peers at the new school (Newcomb and Bukowski, 1984).

By observing children during their first encounter in a new group, researchers can trace the development of a child's social status. Kenneth Dodge (1983) observed second-grade boys who were brought together each day in summer play groups and found that children who became social isolates tried to enter new groups as often as other children did. But because they lacked social skills, their encounters tended to be short and unproductive, and they roamed through the group, trying first one child then another. Eventually they quit striving for acceptance and began playing alone. Aggressive and antisocial boys were rejected by the group. They insulted, threatened, and hit the others and disrupted the other boys' games. Boys who were neglected by the group tended to be shy and less attractive than other boys.

Although neglected children are no more likely than the average child to have social or emotional problems, rejection can have serious conse-

quences for children. Youngsters who are rejected by their peers have problems at home and in the classroom as well as on the playground (French and Waas, 1985). They are more likely than other children to drop out of school, to develop emotional problems, and to become juvenile delinquents (Hartup, 1983). They usually are unhappy, lonely children. Realizing that many rejected children lack the social skills that would gain them acceptance, researchers have developed various programs to teach these skills. In some cases, the results of the programs seem lasting.

Structure of the Peer Group

The peer group seems to be an inevitable part of socialization. When children interact regularly, sooner or later they develop a structured group with its own standards and code of conduct. Young children are group members without knowing it. According to Willard Hartup (1983), preschoolers and kindergartners have little sense of belonging to a group. Even seven- and eight-year-olds see the group as a series of unilateral relations. Older children discern a little more cohesion; nine- to twelve-year-olds view the group as made up of interlocking pairs. Not until adolescence do children see the peer group as a community of like-minded people.

Their lack of group awareness does not prevent preschoolers from developing **dominance hierarchies**, rankings that reflect the relative social power of group members. These hierarchies are so similar to those found among macaques and chimpanzees that some developmentalists believe that the rankings evolved among our early ancestors — and in a similar manner (Rajecki and Flanery, 1981). Children climb the dominance ladder by means of physical attack, threats, or struggles over objects. Even in preschool play groups, children show by their actions that they know who wields power in the group; the roles of leaders and followers are solidly established. Yet if asked who is the "toughest" or "strongest," preschoolers often claim the title for themselves (Strayer, Chapeski, and Strayer, 1978). Gradually, children become aware of the rankings. By kindergarten, 62 percent agree on dominance ratings, and by second grade, 72 percent are in accord (Edelman and Omark,

CAN WE SPOT FUTURE DELINQUENTS?

From the very beginning, some youngsters have trouble getting along with their peers and teachers. Developmentalists have wondered whether aggression and antisocial behavior among young children warn of future trouble with society or whether these children are simply slower than others in learning self-control. In Philadelphia, George Spivack, Janet Marcus, and Marshall Swift (1986) studied about 500 inner-city youngsters who were enrolled in kindergarten. Periodically over the next fifteen years, they checked back on them, hoping to discover whether later delinquency was foreshadowed by specific early-warning signals in the early school years. By the close of the study, 37 percent of the boys and 15 percent of the girls had had at least one brush with the police.

What sort of behavior in primary school was associated with later delinquency? Among both boys and girls, future delinquents tended to tease and torment their classmates, interfering with their work. They often had to be reprimanded by teachers for making noise and disturbing other children. They were impatient and impulsive youngsters who started work too quickly and worked sloppily and fast. They were unwilling to go back over what they had done. They were defiant in the classroom, disrespectful to teachers, resisted instructions, and broke classroom rules. Somewhat less important was their tendency to interrupt the class with irrelevant comments and blurt their thoughts without thinking.

Children who show these signs are likely to have problems with adults and may be rejected by their peers. Although these youngsters may enter school without hostile intent, their behavior seems designed to provoke their teachers into anger and their peers into annoyance, if not rejection. As angry interchanges and rebuffs snowball, suggest the researchers, the disruptive behavior is intensified. By adolescence, the youngster has acquired an antisocial label and is treated as such.

Although these early signs of difficulty were consistently associated with trouble in high school and difficulty with the police, not all young children who behaved in this disruptive manner later got into trouble. Other factors, such as absences, grades, and the responses of peers, teachers, and family to the child undoubtedly played a part in determining which children would be involved in serious misconduct. In fact, the path toward such behavior may begin at home. Spivack and his associates speculate that their research may even have picked up children who started out as "difficult" infants (see Chapter 4). Such children, unless they have unusually firm, patient, consistent, and tolerant parents, may come into school showing this high-risk pattern of behavior. As we saw in Chapter 4, it may be the mismatch of child's and parent's temperaments that predicts later psychological problems.

The behavior signs that turned up in this study cannot tell us which children *will* get into trouble; many children with the high-risk profile did *not* have later trouble with the law. The signs tell us which children may need some sort of preventive intervention to forestall later difficulties. Other research with similar children has had promising results (Spivack and Shure, 1982). When such youngsters were taught to slow down and think before they acted and to develop an awareness of other's needs, beliefs, and attitudes, they became less disruptive and impulsive.

1973). The most aggressive child is not always the most dominant. In play groups, the most belligerently aggressive child may always withdraw or submit in favor of another child who—although less aggressive—is on the top rung of the group's dominance ladder (Strayer, 1984). By enabling children to anticipate and avoid aggressive encounters, the dominance hierarchy helps keep the group functioning smoothly.

As children get older, brute force becomes less important, and social power goes to the competent—those who can help the group reach its goals. In early childhood, power depends on keeping possessions and knowing how to use them. In middle childhood, it depends on being good at games and knowing how to organize them. As children enter adolescence, the early maturers take over—but only those who also possess athletic or social skills (Hartup, 1983).

Power is not the only force that keeps the group functioning. Friendships, coalitions, and subgroups are just as important as dominance—in monkey troops as well as among children (Hinde, 1983). These interactions, which include children's prosocial behavior, take place outside the dominance hierarchy. Children's sharing and assistance to one another make up a network of reciprocity that reflects bonds of friendship within the group (Strayer, 1984).

Conformity

No matter what status children hold in a group, its norms exert a great deal of influence on their behavior. Some of these norms reflect the standards of the larger culture, and some are restricted to the group. A norm generated by the group can be as trivial as leaving the laces on your sneakers untied or wearing a single earring.

Conformity to peer pressure goes beyond adhering to the group code. It refers to changing your perceptions or attitudes if they conflict with those of your peers. This sort of conformity seems to depend on the child's understanding of social rules, his or her motives, and the nature of the peer group (Hartup, 1983). For example, a child with low self-esteem who feels the need for the group's approval is more likely to conform in a dubious situation than a child whose self-esteem is high (Aboud, 1981).

Conformity emerges when children are about five years old. Before that time, they are apparently too egocentric to be concerned about peer approval or pressure. When the group's judgment is clearly erroneous, conformity is highest among five-year-olds and declines steadily with age. Many five-year-olds can look at two checkers spread out on a table and seem convinced that there are three if several peers unanimously agree that they see three. When the difference between the

The child who is considered a leader by peers is generally popular, good at games, and knows how to organize the group's activities. *(Jane Brown)*

child's judgment and that of the group is slight, however, children's conformity steadily increases until they are about eleven years old and then declines throughout adolescence (Allen and Newtson, 1972).

The solidarity of the group increases its power over the individual members. In studies designed to explore the influence of group membership, Muzafer and Carolyn Sherif and their associates (1953; Sherif, Harvey, White, Hood, and Sherif, 1961) discovered that competition between groups increased the cohesiveness of each group and produced considerable friction between the groups. The boys in these groups were attending a summer camp, where they played, hiked, swam, and shared cabins only with members of their own group. Competition in tugs of war, baseball, and football turned the groups against each other. The boys in one group looked down on members of the other group, and the situation eventually exploded into open warfare. The hostility further solidified each group and increased its influence over the behavior of its members. Boys who were not hostile participated in intensely aggressive acts for the

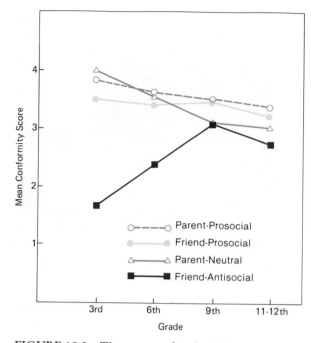

FIGURE 10.2   The course of antisocial peer pressure on children follows a characteristic course, rising sharply from third to sixth grade, then declining during the high-school years as adolescents begin to accept conventional standards. *(From Berndt, 1979)*

sake of the group. In this instance, the structured group overpowered the children's internalized standards and led them to engage in behavior that they would normally avoid.

This sort of influence is what parents have in mind when they worry about the influence of the peer group on their child. Will their ten-year-old who refuses to tie his shoelaces because of group norms also vandalize a schoolroom or try drugs because "all the kids do it"? Thomas Berndt (1979) decided to ask children about situations in which peer pressure and parental standards conflict. He discovered that antisocial conformity increased sharply from the third to the ninth grade. The older the schoolchild, the more likely she or he was to cheat, steal, soap windows on Halloween, trespass, or destroy property at the urging of peers. During high school, conformity to antisocial peer pressure declined. At no time was peer pressure ever *stronger* than parental influence, although among ninth graders both were equally strong (see Figure 10.2).

PEERS AS FRIENDS

All of us know what a friend is, but the meaning of friendship changes over childhood. To a preschooler, a friend is somebody you play with, and affection has little to do with the relationship (Selman, 1981). As children grow older, doing things together continues to be extremely important, but affection and support soon enter the relationship. When asked, "How do you know that someone is your best friend?" a fourth grader replied:

> I sleep over at his house sometimes. When he's playing ball with his friends he'll let me play. When I slept over, he let me get in front of him in 4-squares [a playground game]. He likes me.

Asked the same question, a sixth grader said:

> If you can tell each other things that you don't like about each other. If you get in a fight with someone else, they'd stick up for you. If you can tell them your phone number and they don't give you crank calls. If they don't act mean to you when other kids are around. (Berndt, 1986)

After reviewing the research, Carolyn Shantz (1983) summed up such changes by concluding that friendships slowly change over childhood in three major ways.

1. Friendships change from a purely behavioral relationship to an emotional relationship. Young children play together and give each other things; adolescents care for each other, share their thoughts and feelings, and comfort each other.

2. Friendships change from a self-centered relationship to a mutual relationship. Friends satisfy the young child's needs and wants; adolescent friends satisfy each other's needs and wants.

3. Friendships change from a smooth, brief relationship to a sometimes bumpy, enduring relationship. Young children's friendships rupture at the first disagreement; adolescents' friendships persist through stormy quarrels.

The Quality of Friendship

How do children choose their friends? Most are drawn to youngsters who resemble them in some way. Friends are usually the same age, the same gender, and the same ethnic background. They often have similar attitudes, interests, and personality characteristics. For example, if one friend is shy, the other is likely to be shy as well (Hartup, 1983). The older the friends, the more closely their attitudes and personalities mesh.

When compared with friendless children, youngsters with friends usually are more generous and helpful and have higher moral standards (McGuire and Weisz, 1982). Janice Nelson and Frances Aboud (1985) suggest that friendship may contribute to prosocial behavior and morality. In a study with third- and fourth-grade children, these researchers found that when children settled conflicts with friends, they did it in a manner that might promote more mature judgment. With friends, children explained their position more fully and criticized their friends' position more than they did with acquaintances. Apparently, friends feel secure enough with one another to risk retaliation or hurt feelings that may accompany criticism. Children are also more likely to shift their own position after a disagreement with a friend than with an acquaintance, an indication that they consider the friend's arguments more carefully.

How Friendships End

Children's friendships frequently break up. When Thomas Berndt and Sally Hoyle (1985) interviewed children about their friends in the fall and again in the spring, they discovered that the stability of friendships showed a marked increase between the first and fourth grades. First-grade boys kept many of the kindergarten friends who were in other first-grade classrooms, but during the year, first-grade girls tended to end friendships with old friends who were not in their classroom. The researchers speculate that because boys tend to play in large groups and girls tend to interact in pairs or small groups, it was easier for the boys to maintain their friendships with friends in other classrooms. Perhaps for the same reason, girls in both grades tended to limit the size of their friendship group, making fewer new friends during the year than boys did.

What leads children to rupture a friendship? In a study of kindergartners, third graders, and sixth graders, aggressiveness was a common cause for ending a friendship (Berndt, 1986). The notions that friends should be loyal, intimate, and trustworthy first emerged among the third graders, but only a few of them felt that way. The rest agreed with the kindergartners, who saw no reason to break off a friendship simply because a friend was disloyal or gossiped about personal information the child had disclosed. Sixth graders tended to break off friendships when the friend spread rumors about them or failed to support them against other people. Among these older children, faithfulness was most important to girls: about half the girls and a fifth of the boys had broken off a friendship when the friend was unfaithful (perhaps failing to invite them to a party or ignoring them in favor of other people). Studies consistently show that girls' friendships are more intimate and more exclusive than those of boys; apparently this exclusivity leads girls to worry more about being rejected by a friend.

PLAY AS SOCIALIZATION

Before we can see how play influences children's development, we have to decide what it is. Members of a professional football team are not playing when they go out on the gridiron, but ten-year-olds engrossed in a game of touch football are. Skipping a stone across the water is play; throwing the same stone with intent to harm is not. Catherine Garvey (1977) has proposed that an activity is not playful unless it meets four conditions:

1. It must be pleasurable
2. It must be an end in itself, not a means to some goal
3. It must be spontaneous and freely chosen by the player
4. It must involve some active engagement on the part of the player.

This definition encompasses the circular reactions of babies, the toddler riding a tricycle, the preschooler pretending to be Superman, and the child (or adult) collecting stamps, painting a picture, playing baseball, caught up in a video game, or matching wits across a chessboard.

Forms of Play

Children's cognitive level and social experience largely determine the nature of their play. Each of the four major types of play is most prevalent at a different age, and each demands a different sort of cognitive activity (Smilansky, 1968). The simplest, least mature form of play is functional. The child engaged in **functional play** makes simple, repetitive movements, with or without an object. It appears early in the circular reactions of infancy: babies bang the side of the crib or shake a rattle, purely for the pleasure that they derive from the motion (see Chapter 6). Although functional play declines sharply with age, it probably never disappears. We can see it in the four-year-old who runs around the room to no apparent purpose or the adolescent who drums rhythmically on the table. Studies have traced its decline from 53 percent of the two-year-old's activity to 14 percent among six- and seven-year-olds (Rubin, Fein, and Vandenberg, 1983). Too much functional play is a signal of trouble. Preschoolers who spend much of their playtime simply repeating some physical movement usually lack social competence and are rejected by their peers (Rubin and Maioni, 1975).

Children engrossed in **constructive play** are manipulating objects to construct or create something. They may be stacking blocks into a tower, drawing a horse, putting together a jigsaw puzzle, modeling a clay figure, or building a model rocket. This sort of play accounts for up to half of the activity among four- to six-year-olds in school settings (Rubin, Fein, and Vandenberg, 1983). It probably occupies less of children's free time, and there are wide individual differences in the amount of constructive play.

Because constructive play requires children to manipulate objects, to fit them together, or to solve some sort of problem, it helps children learn *how* to solve problems. In one study (Cheyne and Rubin, 1983), the more figures children had constructed using Tinker Toy-type materials (wooden dowels and connecting cubes), the faster they were able to solve a construction problem that required them to join sticks in order to get a marble out of a transparent box, and the fewer hints they needed.

Pretend play, whose emergence we explored in Chapter 6, incorporates the child's increasing ability to symbolize and imagine. Most children are deep into "let's pretend" by the time they are three or so. Using their increasing role-taking ability, they engage in a great deal of fantasy play. It mingles elements from the roles they see enacted around them ("I'm Daddy getting the baby dressed for bed"), from television ("We're on a ship, and there are sharks around us"), and from seemingly pure fantasy ("This is the time I learned how to fly"). Any available prop seems to generate a string of associations, which children weave into play that is sometimes infinitely flexible ("We can all walk on water") and sometimes extremely rigid ("You can't be a fireman because you don't have a hat on"). By the time they are five years old, children may react with fear to a playmate who has been assigned a terrifying role. Their delighted shrieks at the approach of a lumbering playmate who is pretending to be a Frankenstein monster may be tinged with a touch of real fear.

Pretend play seems to enhance social and cognitive skills. Highly imaginative youngsters tend to score higher on various cognitive tests; they are also more cooperative, friendlier, less aggressive, more independent, and more empathic than children who rarely pretend (Rubin, Fein, and Vandenberg, 1983). They are also likely to be happy children—if smiles, laughter, and similar indications of mood are used as a measure of happiness (Singer and Singer, 1979). In a study of preschoolers (Connolly and Doyle, 1984), youngsters who spent a good deal of their time in pretend play with their peers were more popular and had a better command of social skills than other children. Peers happily joined them in their bouts of pretend play, which were lengthy and characterized by lots of talking. Some researchers have proposed that pretend play that requires children to assume fantastic roles (Star Wars, jungle explorers) benefits children more than pretend play in which they assume familiar roles (mommy, daddy, baby, teacher, doctor) (Saltz and Brodie, 1982). Pretending to be a fantastic character places greater cognitive demands on the child and requires—if not develops—more sophisticated imagery and symbolic representations.

If imaginative play is to flourish and expand after a child is about five years old, it seems to require social nurturance. According to Jerome and Dorothy Singer (1981), unless parents are tolerant of fantasy, imagine along with their children, or provide them with specific opportunities for make-believe, the amount of fantasy play is likely to decline — or even disappear. Children between the ages of nine and thirteen still enjoy make-believe activities and fantasy games, but their interest may be suppressed if parents and teachers discourage such "nonsense."

The final form of play is **games with rules:** formal, rule-governed, competitive games. Such games begin to appear among older preschoolers, and their frequency increases during early elementary school, apparently peaking at about the fifth grade (Eifermann, 1971). At the same time, pretend play begins to wane. Competitive games, such as checkers, marbles, card games, or board games, require children to consider the other person's intentions and skill. For this reason, games are believed to decrease egocentrism and develop children's ability to deal with the demands of the social world (Rubin, Fein, and Vandenberg, 1983).

Children's games are centered on shared rules. Although a leader may break a rule, children with low group status usually find themselves under tremendous pressure to conform. This slavish attention to detail probably serves children in several ways. They learn that social commerce must be regulated if interaction is to be sustained. (At a younger age, if they do not like the rules, they merely drift away from their peers.) They learn that once a formal structure has been set up, they can relax, enjoying themselves within its confines without worrying about being rejected. And rules provide a means by which new arrivals may rapidly find a place in the group.

Play as Social Involvement

Games are a form of play with high social involvement. But children's play is not all social. Play can be solitary; a youngster plays alone or watches other children play without attempting to join. Social activity begins with parallel play, in which two children play side by side, each intent on his or her own toy and each perhaps keeping up a running monologue that amounts to thinking out loud. True social involvement appears in group play, when at least two children are playing together. When this sequence of development was first

Pretend play gives children a chance to practice adult roles and enhances social and cognitive skills, but unless parents encourage such fantasy, it declines at about the time children start school. *(Leonard Speier)*

proposed, investigators supposed that children went through the forms of play in order, with solitary play being the least mature and group play the most advanced (Parten, 1932). Once a child was firmly into group play, earlier forms supposedly disappeared or declined to almost nothing. Today, however, researchers stress that all early varieties of play persist into elementary school and that each has a purpose.

Solitary play can take any of the forms of play. Children who engage in solitary constructive play tend to be socially competent youngsters who are busy at some goal-directed activity. They may be involved in a building project with Legos or Tinker Toys, working at some craft, practicing basketball throws, or solving puzzles. But as we might expect, lengthy stretches of solitary functional play among four- and five-year-olds are associated with a lack of social competence. So is solitary pretend play after a child is about four years old. When other children are available, solitary pretend play is associated with social rejection, poor role-taking ability, and difficulty in figuring out solutions to interpersonal problems (Rubin, 1982).

Parallel play also appears in other forms of play. Sometimes it appears to be a social strategy. Socially competent children use parallel play to work themselves into play with the group (Bakeman and Brownlee, 1980). Parallel constructive play is also common and healthy, as when two children sit side by side drawing, working in clay, or making sepa-

DOES ROUGH-AND-TUMBLE PLAY TURN MEAN?

Rough-and-tumble play does not disappear when children grow out of the nursery. On any playground, older boys can be seen scuffling and tumbling about, while girls tend to engage in a milder variety of chase and flee, in which there is little physical contact. Some researchers have suggested that as boys near puberty, their rough-and-tumble games often become hostile encounters (Neill, 1976). Instead of fun and games, they turn into serious struggles for dominance.

In an attempt to trace the evolution of rough-and-tumble play, Anne Humphreys and Peter Smith (1987) combined naturalistic observation with a study in which children rated their classmates on liking (like/in-between/don't like) and strength (strong/in-between/weak). Six weeks of observation indicated that the incidence of rough-and-tumble play remained steady across childhood; whether children were seven or eleven years old, 10 percent of their playground time was spent in some form of rough-and-tumble play.

During the next twelve weeks, Humphreys and Smith concentrated on ten children in each class who spent the most time in rough-and-tumble play. No evidence of hostility appeared. It became apparent that, at all ages, acceptance of an invitation to rough-and-tumble play was optional. Only about a third of attempts to start an interchange were accepted by the other child. In the rest of the cases, the partner either responded with some other social interaction or else broke off contact. Less than 4 percent of the rough-and-tumble bouts led to injury, and in most cases the injured child was comforted by the play partner. After a bout of rough and tumble ended, the partners usually stayed together. This friendliness was supported by the ratings children made of their classmates. At every age, rough-and-tumble play occurred between children who liked one another.

Among seven- and nine-year-olds, there was no indication of a struggle for dominance. Class ratings indicated that strength played no part in a child's choice of a partner for rough and tumble. The chosen partner might be stronger, weaker, or equal in strength to the initiator. At these ages, rough-and-tumble play seemed purely social. Among eleven-year-olds, however, children consistently chose rough-and-tumble partners who were slightly weaker than themselves. By now the friendly nature of rough and tumble had become tinged with either the quest for dominance or a desire to practice fighting skills. Despite this change, Humphreys and Smith saw no indication of hostility or a serious dominance struggle. They suggest that the aggressiveness reported by other researchers may simply reflect the increased roughness that eleven-year-olds put into their games.

---

rate models (Rubin, 1982). However, when children spend lengthy periods in other kinds of parallel play—especially functional play—they are usually socially immature or in some sort of emotional distress. For example, during the first two years following their parents' divorce, boys show higher levels of solitary and parallel functional play than do boys in intact homes (Hetherington, Cox, and Cox, 1979).

SCHOOLS AND SOCIALIZATION

Children spend a major part of childhood in the society of the school, and the school socializes them in many of the same ways that families and peer groups do. As members of that small society, they are supposed to acquire basic academic skills, but the school's influence extends far beyond the curriculum. During their six hours of daily schooling (five days a week, nine months a year), children are carrying out tasks, relating to other people, and living within the confines of rules that differ in many ways from those of the family system. At school, the rules are impersonal; the relationships between the child and other people are relatively brief; the adults who run the society hold different—if not conflicting—views; and the child's performance is periodically and publicly compared with that of others (Hess and Holloway, 1984). These experiences interact with the influence of family, peers, religion, and media to affect children's feelings of competence and the way they regard themselves and others.

Teachers as Socializers

In passing along the content of the academic curriculum, teachers instruct, try to motivate, and evaluate the children in their classroom. In turn, the children are supposed to adopt the role of receptive learners who are task-oriented, responsible, and maintain an acceptable level of academic achievement. Teachers also pass along a "hidden curriculum" that stems from the need to manage children so that the classroom remains orderly and under control. When teachers are successful, their students take the role of pupil. Pupils are obedient, respect authority, cheerfully share materials and the teacher's time, and control their impulses and wishes for immediate gratification. How quickly they learn these roles has a profound effect on children's school experience (Hess and Holloway, 1984; Kedar-Voivodas, 1983).

Teachers find it easy to teach students who fit either the receptive learner or the pupil role. When student teachers rated children, they preferred such children and expected those who adopted the role of receptive learner to get the highest grades (Feshbach, 1969). When asked about children who have an independent and exploring attitude, are willing to challenge authority, and insist on explanations, the teachers' replies suggested that youngsters who adopt this role of active learner may find that their quest for knowledge is complicated by antagonism. Teachers said that they wouldn't like to have such children in

When teachers perceive a child as a high achiever, they inadvertently treat the youngster in ways that contribute to his or her school success. *(Elizabeth Crews)*

their class and expected that they would get poor grades.

We might dismiss this study on the grounds that student teachers are unsure of themselves and threatened by bright children who are not satisfied with pat answers. Yet research consistently shows that experienced teachers also respond in predictable ways to children's characteristics (Minuchin and Shapiro, 1983). They like children who conform to school routine, are high achievers, and who make few demands. Their ideal students are apparently high-achieving "pupils." Teachers seem indifferent to children who are silent or withdrawn, and they rarely talk to such youngsters. They actively reject children who continually demand inappropriate attention and consider them behavior problems.

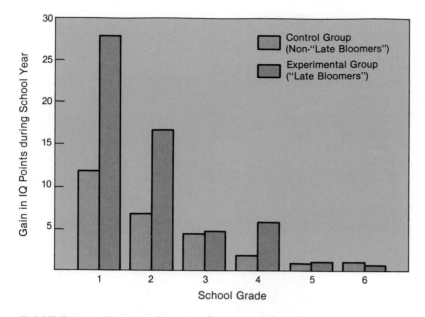

FIGURE 10.3   Teachers in each of the six grades of an elementary school were led to believe that certain of their pupils had been discovered to be "late bloomers" on the basis of a special test and would show great academic gains during the year. In fact, the pupils were selected at random. Intelligence tests were given both at the beginning and at the end of the school year. This figure shows the relative IQ gains during the year of the control group (pupils not expected to be "late bloomers" by their teachers) and the experimental group (pupils who were expected to be "late bloomers"). Both groups gained in the lower grades, but the experimental group gained more. However, in the upper grades there was little effect, perhaps because the teachers already had strong expectations about the pupils based on their performances in earlier grades. *(After Rosenthal, 1966)*

Children's success in school seems to be affected by teachers' perceptions of their ability. Whether a child does well in school may depend in part on whether the teacher expects the youngster to succeed. Twenty years ago, Robert Rosenthal and Lenore Jacobson (1968) demonstrated the effect of teachers' expectations on children's school performance. They picked elementary-school students at random and told their teachers that these students would make great cognitive strides during the school year. (To back up their claims, the researchers said that the children had made unusually high scores on special tests.) Later in the year, the teachers rated these students as more interested in school, more curious, and happier than other students. Among younger students, the prediction came true — the intellectual

"bloomers" in the first grade gained an average of 15 IQ points more than other children. Among fifth and sixth graders, the prediction had little effect, perhaps because the school records of these students contradicted the predictions (see Figure 10.3).

Why should teachers' expectations have such an effect on young children's school performance? Probably because the teachers' expectations led them to treat the intellectual bloomers in ways that made them likely to bloom (Brophy, 1983; Cooper, 1979). When teachers perceive students as high achievers, the teachers give them more opportunities to participate in class and more time to respond. If the children come up with the right answers, they get more praise than low achievers; if they are wrong, they are criticized for not trying.

The teacher assumes that low achievers probably do not know the answer and so calls on them less. They are criticized, not for lack of effort, but for messy papers or some other extraneous flaw.

Individual characteristics of teachers also can influence children's attitudes toward learning and their sense of autonomy. The effect may become established during the first few weeks of the school year. In a study of fourth- to sixth-grade classrooms (Deci, Neziek, and Sheinman, 1981), teachers who ran their classes with strict control tended to have students who were extrinsically motivated. They worked primarily for grades, showed little curiosity, and disliked challenges. The children also had little confidence in their ability. When teachers encouraged children to take part of the responsibility for their work and to consider all aspects of a situation, students tended to be intrinsically motivated. They worked primarily in order to master a skill or concept, showed curiosity, and preferred challenges. These children also had confidence in their ability. A series of teachers with similar attitudes could have a lasting effect on a child's sense of autonomy and self-worth.

Can Teachers Instill Learned Helplessness?

Some children have learned to approach academic tasks with little expectation of success; their main goal is to avoid the teacher's negative appraisal of their work. Carole Dweck and Elaine Elliot (1983) have found that these children fall into two groups. Most of those in the first group are accustomed to poor grades, and they approach tests or other achievement situations in a state of high anxiety. Unable to devise strategies for solving problems, they try to figure out the teacher, and look for clues in his or her behavior. The performance of highly anxious children degenerates rapidly when they are placed under time pressure. In one study of fifth and sixth graders (Hill and Eaton, 1977), anxious children's performance crumbled when there was not enough time to complete an arithmetic test. Compared with children who felt little anxiety, they took twice as long to work each problem, made three times as many mistakes, and cheated twice as often. When they had all the time

they needed, they performed as well as the other children.

A second group of children with low expectations of success have average or better IQs and often have a history of good test scores in various school subjects. These children are the victims of learned helplessness, which we explored in Chapter 6. Because they believe that they cannot succeed, they do not try very hard. They may refuse to try even when they could easily succeed. As we saw in Chapter 6, learned helplessness seems to develop when individuals are consistently placed in situations where their efforts have no effect.

Their pessimistic view of their own ability may lead "helpless" children to give up on difficult material. By altering the introductory sections in a simple booklet on psychology, Barbara Licht and Dweck (1984) caused the performance of helpless children to plunge. When the beginning sections were written in a confusing style, "helpless" children did poorly on the entire booklet, even on material that was written clearly. Yet children who had confidence in their own ability apparently saw their initial difficulty as due to lack of effort and responded by trying harder (see Table 10.1). These mastery-oriented children learned and understood the material. The difference in performance was not due to the helpless children's lack of ability, because when all the material was clearly written, helpless children did as well as mastery-oriented children. When their first encounter proved difficult, children who had learned to be helpless quit trying, and their scores on a review booklet showed little improvement.

Dweck and her colleagues (Dweck, Davidson, Nelson, and Enna, 1978) believe that the teacher's responses to children's academic failures are likely to promote learned helplessness in girls but not in boys. While observing in classrooms, Dweck noted that when boys failed at a task, teachers generally attributed the failure to lack of effort, to not following instructions, or to the messiness of the work. Because none of these criticisms has anything to do with ability, boys might believe that they have failed because they haven't worked hard enough. When girls failed, teachers almost always ascribed their failure to errors in the work itself; sometimes they even accompanied their criticism with praise for the girl's effort. Such criticism,

Table 10.1
Children's Attributions and Mastery of New Material

	Learning Condition	
Attributional Style	No Confusion (%)	Confusion (%)
Material mastered on first attempt		
Helpless	29.51	5.04
Mastery-oriented	34.16	24.43
Material mastered on final attempt		
Helpless	76.57	34.65
Mastery-oriented	68.36	71.88

Note: When introductory material was confusing, children who had developed learned helplessness learned much less than mastery-oriented children. Yet when all the material was clear, helpless and mastery-oriented children learned approximately the same amount.

Source: Licht and Dweck, 1984.

Dweck concluded, might lead girls to decide that they were incapable of academic success.

Teachers, Schools, and Sex Roles

Teachers' treatment of boys and girls differs in more than just separate styles of criticism. Some of these differences may be as important as criticism in explaining why, after years of outscoring boys on math tests, girls begin to fall behind when they reach the seventh grade. After reviewing the research, Jacquelynne Eccles and Lois Hoffman (1984) concluded that boys and girls have different experiences in the classroom. Teachers interact more with boys than with girls in math and science classes, and they expect boys to do better than girls. These differences are most extreme among bright students. When a boy and a girl both show superior math ability, teachers praise the boy more than they praise the girl. In addition, girls with superior math ability often escape the teacher's notice, but boys with similar ability are identified. As a result, few girls are encouraged to consider math, science, or other nontraditional majors in college.

When Eccles (1985) asked nearly 700 fifth- to twelfth-grade children about their attitudes toward mathematics, she found strong acceptance of the notion that math is for boys. Girls and boys agreed that math is more useful for boys than for girls. Boys liked math better than girls did, thought they were better at it, said that they didn't have to work as hard at it, and expected to get better grades in future math courses. As girls got older, they liked math even less and were more likely to take the minimum number of high school courses in it. Yet girls and boys performed equally well in their math courses.

School also pushes children into other aspects of traditional sex roles. Classroom tasks are doled out according to stereotype: girls are class secretaries, and boys are team captains; boys help girls with math assignments, girls help boys with English assignments. Children line up by sex to go to the cafeteria, the library, or the playground. In order to motivate and control the boys, teachers often pit one sex against the other in academic competition (Delamont, 1980).

Until recently, girls had few opportunities to participate in organized sports. As a result, they missed the lessons in social skills that athletic participation can provide (Eccles and Hoffman, 1984). For years, only boys got these lessons in competitiveness, confidence, teamwork, persistence in the face of difficult odds, and leadership. Athletic competition teaches children how to lose. Girls are still less likely to go out for sports than boys. So academically talented girls may go through elementary and high schools without ever

Although boys and girls tend to perform equally well in their math courses, both sexes see the subject as more useful for boys—who generally like math better than girls do. *(Elizabeth Crews)*

experiencing failure. As a result, they may never develop strategies for dealing with such disasters.

Even the structure of the school may mold students' expectations along the lines of traditional sex roles (Minuchin and Shapiro, 1983). Women teachers are clustered in the early grades, and male teachers in high school. In junior and senior high school, men teach math, science, and shop. Women teach languages and literature. At all educational levels, men hold most of the administrative positions, and women hold most of the clerical positions. In the typical primary school, a group of women teachers and clerks is bossed by a male principal. This lesson about the gender-related distribution of power in the adult world around them is not lost on children.

SOCIALIZATION BY TELEVISION

Children watch television for entertainment and sometimes for instruction, but what they get from the "tube" is continual socialization into the attitudes, values, and behavior they see before them. Only 2 percent of American families do not own a television set, and most children spend more than three hours each day watching. By the time they are sixteen years old, they have spent more time watching television than attending school, interacting with family members, or playing with other children (Nielsen Television Index, 1982). Thirty-five years ago, the child growing up in Moccasin, Montana, was limited in her knowledge of the world by geography and personal experience. That sort of geographic and cultural isolation has ended. Today youngsters in remote villages watch people in every corner of the globe. Before their eyes passes a parade of war, murder, mayhem, divorce, adultery, birth, death, poverty, and riches. Educational opportunities also present themselves: the underwater explorations of Jacques Cousteau, "Sesame Street," science specials, symphony orchestras, operas live from the Met. Television must affect every aspect of a child's socialization. Reflecting the concerns of parents, educators, and developmentalists, most research into television's effects has focused on aggression, although some investigators have looked at prosocial behavior and sex-role stereotyping.

Aggression

The average adolescent has seen more than 18,000 murders on television. The situation may be worsening. Although the level of televised violence has remained fairly steady over the last twenty years, its quality has changed. According to Sally Smith (1985), today's TV violence is more intense and realistic; violent acts often are connected with humor, the line between heroes and villains is becoming blurred, and more violent acts are committed by people with psychological problems. Further concern has been aroused by the widespread broadcasting of rock videos, which are often filled with images of menace and cruelty. In these videos, violence against people and property is ripped out of any justifying context — and it has no consequences. How does this stepped-up, decontextualized violence affect children? Does it teach them new forms of violence? Does it reduce their inhibitions against antisocial behavior?

Two government commissions have analyzed hundreds of studies exploring the effects of TV violence on children, but researchers still argue over the effects of watching violent programs (Freedman, 1984). Without any doubt, a correlation exists between aggressive behavior and the habitual viewing of violent programs, but this link does not tell us that watching the programs causes aggression. It is just as probable that aggressive children are drawn to violent television programs. When researchers try to tease out the connection, their results may be affected by uncontrolled variables. For example, unless they are studying children in a boarding school, researchers have no way of controlling the home television diet of their subjects.

Controlled experiments have shown conclusively that watching violent programs increases later aggression in the laboratory (Freedman, 1984). Clearly, television violence has some impact on its viewers. Yet several problems with these experiments keep us from applying them with confidence to everyday situations. First, in the lab, children respond with fake aggression. Hitting a plastic Bobo doll is not the same as hitting a person. Second, in these experiments, children have the tacit approval of the adult experimenter. If an adult indicates that it's okay to hit something, the child has no reason to inhibit aggression and can freely join in the "fun." Third, the effects of a single exposure to aggressive stimuli cannot tell us much about the effects of the continual bombardment of violence offered by television. Daily exposure to such fare may produce more profound changes in a child's behavior. Finally, experiments detect only the immediate effects of violent television. They tell us only what the child will do in the first twenty minutes or so after he or she sees the program. We cannot rule out the possibility that the effects disappear within an hour or so.

Even so, the results of research on TV violence are disquieting. A continual bombardment of TV violence seems to dull children to its horrors; when they see a violent act, they tend to react with indifference. Third graders who watched a violent detective program and then were asked to supervise younger children were significantly slower to intervene or to call for adult assistance when a fight broke out than other child supervisors who had watched a baseball game (Drabman and Thomas, 1976). There is reason to believe that this slowness to respond is linked to a diminished emotional response by the children. When children watch violence, they sweat slightly, and skin resistance to electrical conduction decreases. But witnessing televised violence appears to take the edge off this reaction. Compared with children who had just watched a volleyball game, children who had just finished watching a violent police drama reacted less to an ostensibly real fight on a TV monitor (Thomas, Horton, Lippincott, and Drabman, 1977).

At first, children cannot distinguish between fantasy and reality. Four-year-olds respond to violent cartoons as aggressively (hitting, punching, and kicking a Bobo doll) as they do to films of human violence (Bandura, Ross, and Ross, 1966). Once they can make the distinction between fantasy and reality, they are more likely to be influenced by realistic violence. Seymour Feshbach (1972) showed children a film that included scenes of a violent riot. When the watching children believed that the riot was part of a newsreel, they showed much more subsequent aggression than children who believed that the riot had been staged for a motion picture. Other researchers have found that the younger the child, the more likely he or she is to respond to a televised violent event as if it had no motivation and no consequences (Parke and Slaby, 1983). In one study, kindergartners and second graders tended to forget the reason for a violent act and its consequences when commercials separated the consequences from the act (Collins, Berndt, and Hess, 1974). But they had no trouble remembering the violence. The insertion of commercials did not disrupt the memory of fifth graders. They recalled motivation and consequences and used them in judging the act.

Although correlational studies cannot establish whether televised aggression causes children to behave aggressively, longitudinal studies indicate that heavy TV viewing probably has some influence on later aggression. In one study the amount of television violence that boys watched in the third grade was correlated with their aggression at age nineteen (Eron, Huesmann, Lefkowitz, and Walder, 1972; see Figure 10.4). This relationship was stronger than the link between their preference for violent television at both ages or the link between their third-grade aggressiveness and their preference for violent TV at that time.

Similar trends appeared in a later cross-cultural study. The same investigators followed three waves of American and Finnish first and third graders over a three-year period (Huesmann, Lagerspetz, and Eron, 1984). In both countries, heavy watchers of TV violence at the beginning of the study were likely to be highly aggressive children at the study's close. In the original study, the connection appeared only among boys (Eron et al., 1972). This time, American girls' viewing of TV violence also was linked with future aggression, a finding that led the investigators to suggest that recent changes in the socialization of American girls (new emphasis on assertiveness and physical activity) were responsible. No relationship was found among Finnish girls. Yet television violence alone did not make these children aggressive. The researchers discovered that besides absorbing heavy doses of television violence, the most aggressive children in their study believed that the shows accurately portrayed life, identified strongly with the aggressive characters they watched, performed poorly in school, were unpopular with peers, often fantasized about aggression, and came from low-status homes, where the parents had little education and the mother was aggressive.

Many developmentalists are convinced that heavy doses of violent television have a negative effect on children, yet they admit that research establishing the effects is not conclusive. They

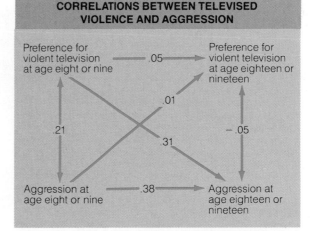

FIGURE 10.4   When 211 boys who were studied as eight- and nine-year-olds were restudied after a lapse of ten years, their preference for violent television programs as youngsters correlated positively with the amount of aggression they displayed as eighteen- or nineteen-year-olds. Although correlation does not indicate causation, the relative strength of this correlation is impressive. *(Adapted from Eron, Huesmann, Lefkowitz, and Walder, 1972)*

believe that violent TV probably does increase aggressiveness, desensitize children to the horrors of violence, and persuade them that a Rambo-like use of aggression is an acceptable way to solve human problems. Yet our chances of finding a definitive answer to the question are slim because so many interacting variables are involved in the development of aggression.

Prosocial Behavior

If links exist between television and children's aggressiveness, it stands to reason that similar links should appear between television and prosocial behavior. Yet in one study, Aimee Dorr (1979) found that kindergarten children often forgot the prosocial themes and behavior in the programs they watched; violent scenes and striking characters were more likely to stick in their memory. With increasing age, children remembered more prosocial aspects of the programs, perhaps because of their increased social understanding.

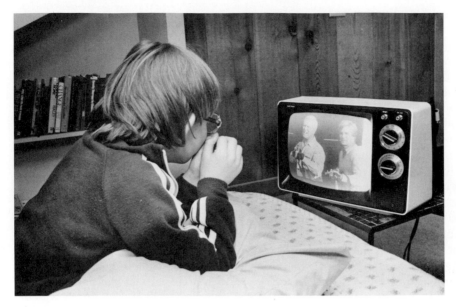

Heavy viewing of television violence probably desensitizes children and increases violence, but so many factors are involved that researchers have found it difficult to establish television's long-term effects. *(Mark Antman/ The Image Works)*

There seems little doubt that children can learn helpful, generous behavior from television, but it is more difficult to show that they act on this knowledge. Aletha Stein and Lynette Friedrich (1975) showed four episodes of "Mr. Roger's Neighborhood" to kindergarten children. These programs focused on (1) understanding others' feelings of jealousy, fear, and anger and on (2) such prosocial actions as expressing sympathy, helping, and sharing. Children who watched the programs learned their prosocial messages. They knew more about each of the themes than did a group of children who watched neutral films. But when placed with a child who needed assistance, most of the Mr. Rogers viewers were no more helpful than those who watched the neutral films. Yet there was some good news in the study. If watching prosocial films was combined with an opportunity to role play the parts with hand puppets, children did provide more assistance. The role-playing experience apparently made it easier for children to understand the feelings and needs of people in distress.

Since this research was completed, similar studies have demonstrated the same sort of effects, although none of the increases in prosocial behavior has been dramatic. Marian Radke-Yarrow and her associates (1983) believe that the weak effect of prosocial television may be due to the nature of the medium. These researchers point out that children continually see people in danger or need on the nightly news. They observe people and organizations responding to that distress, but these incidents are islands surrounded by commercials and by programs that evoke emotions that are incompatible with concern for others. Such regular experience may desensitize children to human needs and stifle their impulses to give assistance.

Television and Sex Roles

Most television shows purvey stereotypical views of male and female roles and personality. Children accept what they see. They say that they get their information about possible occupations from television and that they believe the information is accurate (Greenberg, 1982). Yet no matter what the program, men and women generally are portrayed in stereotypical occupations. Most television heroines unmask villains by luck or accident. In children's programs, men are aggressive, constructive, and helpful; their activities bring them tangible rewards. But women tend to be deferential, passive, and ignored; if they are too active, they are punished (Sternglanz and Serbin, 1974). Over the past several years, competent, assertive leading roles have been developed for women, but the old

PEERS AND TV COMMERCIALS — INTERACTING SOURCES OF INFLUENCE

Saturday morning TV fare sometimes seems more commercial than entertainment, full of pitches for sugared cereals, snacks, soft drinks, clothes, and toys directed at children. Over the course of a year, the average child watches 20,000 television commercials (Federal Trade Commission, 1978). Do children dutifully ask for the brands they see advertised, or do other factors temper their demands? Researchers at the University of Georgia decided to find out whether peers influenced children's reactions to the persuasive messages they see on the tube. Zolinda Stoneman and Gene Brody (1981) showed television commercials for various salty snacks to fourth-grade black and white children, then asked them to choose their favorite foods. As manufacturers would hope, television was powerful: children who had seen the commercials were much more likely to choose salty snacks than children who had watched an ad-free educational program.

When peers were involved, the situation changed. After some of the children watched the commercials, a peer (who had been coached) came into the room and chose his or her favorite snacks before the children made their selection. Sometimes the peer chose the salty snacks, and sometimes the peer avoided them. When the peer chose the kind of snacks that had been promoted in the commercials,

the power of the commercial was enhanced. The number of children who also chose salty snacks rose significantly. But when the peer avoided the salty snacks, TV's power declined sharply. Children became more likely to select other kinds of food as their favorites.

Black children's choices followed this pattern only when the peer model was also black. They followed the black peer's choice closely; if the peer refused the salty snacks, his or her disdain convinced black children that the advertised chips or pretzels were simply no good. When a white peer chose the salty snacks, the endorsement boomeranged; fewer black children selected them than did black children who saw no commercials at all. Apparently, the context in which children see a commercial is as important as its message.

Parents and educators may be relieved to discover that children are not simply passive consumers of TV messages. The children remembered what they had seen advertised (90 percent to 100 percent correctly). Getting the TV message does not guarantee that a child will act on it. As the researchers pointed out, television is part of a vast interactive system of influences. Family members, admired adults, and children's own experiences can exert conflicting or reinforcing pressures on the media message.

programs never die, they simply move into reruns. This practice may bear on findings that prime-time viewing has no relation to children's stereotypical views of sex roles, but heavy TV viewing after school and on Saturday morning does show such correlations (Greer, 1980).

Few commercials shatter sex-role stereotypes. After analyzing 300 commercials, researchers reported that the difference between female and male sex roles in these commercials was far greater than it is in society (Mamay and Simpson, 1981). Some ads now feature female bank managers or

traveling sales representatives, but the women in most ads are mothers, housewives, or sex objects who defer to men's needs, wishes, and preferences. It is the authoritative male who confronts women shoppers with twelve-hour cold caplets, corrects their choice of detergent, convinces them that their husbands prefer stuffing to potatoes, and delivers the smooth, authoritative, voice-over commentary in most commercials.

The average child watches more than 20,000 television commercials each year. So we should not be surprised to find that heavy television viewers (children who watch more than twenty-five hours each week) have significantly more stereotypical notions about sex roles than children who watch ten hours or fewer each week (Frueh and McGhee, 1975). And the older the child, the more ingrained the stereotype.

THE EFFECT OF SOCIAL CLASS

Whether a child's father drives a delivery truck or delivers babies affects many aspects of development. Social class, which is traditionally determined by the father's occupation, has a pervasive influence. It helps to determine children's physical environment, the neighborhood they live in, their playmates, their access to health care, the composition of their diet, their parents' child-rearing practices, the authority structure of their family, its stability, the number of brothers and sisters they have, and the sort of education they get. It is no wonder that researchers automatically control for its influence when they study various other factors that affect development (L. Hoffman, 1984a). Earlier we touched on the interaction of social class and maternal employment. Here we single out two additional aspects of social-class influence: child-rearing practices and the relationship between school and family.

Parents in different classes treat their children differently. Working-class parents tend to rely on power-assertive discipline, whereas middle-class parents are more likely to use inductive discipline (Hess, Shipman, Brophy, and Baer, 1968). As we saw in Chapter 9, heavy doses of power-assertive discipline are associated with children's low self-esteem, aggressiveness, slowed cognitive development, and behaving morally simply to avoid punishment. The pressure of the parents' absolute power may erode the child's sense of self-efficacy. She or he also misses out on the verbal enrichment that accompanies inductive discipline and promotes verbal fluency. Inductive discipline also rewards the middle-class child for skillful reasoning (because explaining your intentions can ward off punishment) and teaches him or her that the world is largely orderly and rational. Perhaps these differences reflect in part the work experiences of

adults in each class. Working-class parents are themselves more likely to be given orders by their bosses, but middle-class parents are more likely to be given explanations (L. Hoffman, 1984a). In addition, Melvin Kohn (1979) has noted that working-class parents tend to base their punishments on the consequences of their child's behavior, but middle-class parents more heavily weigh the child's intent.

These differences may also reflect class differences in home conditions. Working-class life often involves more stress than life in the middle-class, and a parent under stress may find it difficult to give reasons and weigh intent. It is also easier to forgive a child's unintentional destruction of an expensive vase when there is plenty of money to buy a new one. Such class differences in child-rearing techniques may have significance for children's development: the working-class child may be encouraged to conform and the middle-class child encouraged to be autonomous.

Social class partly determines the quality of a child's experience in school. Because schools are based on middle-class values, the middle-class child usually makes a smooth transition to the classroom. His or her speech, manners, and dress conform to the teacher's expectations. Because middle-class parents generally work at occupations that require extended schooling, the middle-class child is likely to find the school setting meaningful (L. Hoffman, 1984a). In contrast, the child from a low-income family may feel like a stranger in a strange land, primed for hostility by the maternal admonishment, "Keep out of trouble" (Hess and Shipman, 1968). He or she may have to learn new ways of behaving and new speech conventions. The school's goals may seem alien and its curriculum irrelevant. The middle-class child's way is also smoothed by the ease with which his or her parents move in the school setting. Middle-class parents usually attend parent conferences, Parent-Teacher Organization meetings, and school functions. Parents from low-income families may avoid contact with the school (L. Hoffman, 1984a).

Parents' expectations have been associated with children's achievement in school, and there are consistent class differences in how well parents expect their children to do, both in the classroom and in problem-solving situations (Seginer, 1983). Asked to predict their four-year-olds' performance on several tasks, for example, middle-class parents consistently expected their children would do at least as well as the average child, but working-class parents expected their children would do less well than average (Marcus and Corsini, 1978). When children attempted the tasks, both groups of children made similar scores. Low expectations by parents may lead not only to poor school performance but to lowered self-efficacy as well.

The mismatch between the schools and children from low-income families has led to concerted attempts to involve parents from these families in the schools. After reviewing a number of such programs, Robert Hess and Susan Holloway (1984) found that when the school can involve low-income parents, their children's school attendance increases, they are less disruptive in class and less aggressive on the playground, their classroom work improves, and they are more likely to complete their homework.

ETHNIC INFLUENCES ON SOCIALIZATION

A child's membership in an ethnic group has specific effects on development, but pinning them down is a difficult task. In the United States, ethnic minorities tend to be concentrated among low-income families, so that what at first appears to be an ethnic influence often turns out to be a socioeconomic effect (Zill, 1985). Developmentalists now understand that most studies of ethnic differences in development have compared development of low-income black children with middle-class whites. Such designs confuse class differences with racial differences. Further complicating the picture is the existence of subcultural differences within each ethnic group, due either to different cultural heritages or to socioeconomic differences within the ethnic group.

The traditional black American family has been partially shaped by African traditions (Sudarkasa, 1981). Instead of being based on the marital relationship, the African family was an extended fam-

Middle-class children have a head start in the middle-class world of school, and their advantage is increased by their parents' expectations. *(Leonard Speier)*

ily organized around adult siblings of the same sex, along with their spouses, children, and, perhaps, divorced siblings of the other sex. Despite changes during their experience in the United States, blood relationships remained central in black American families, and children were socialized to think in terms of their responsibilities to parents, siblings, and other close relatives. Although many middle- and upper-class black families seem to have adopted the marriage-centered family, the extended family still provides a source of emotional and material support, especially for families headed by a single parent. Members of the extended family are available and may even live under the same roof. They provide friendship and social interaction and can be a vital source of advice, financial support, and child care—sometimes informally adopting children of relatives (Wilson, 1986).

In addition to their strong reliance on the family, black families at all socioeconomic levels tend to have a strong sense of religiosity, an active involvement by both parents in child rearing and decision making, and a continual need to defend themselves against discrimination (H. McAdoo, 1982). Most black parents say that race has affected the way they bring up their children. Aware of the racism that their children will encounter, mothers feel that it is crucial to develop self-esteem and self-confidence in their sons and daughters (Peters, 1981). Boys may have a special need for self-esteem, because many researchers see them as especially vulnerable to racism. When black parents teach their children about race, girls generally are instructed in a more egalitarian manner than boys, who hear about racial manners in a problack, antiwhite context (Branch and Newcombe, 1986). But all black children are socialized to live in two worlds—in the world of the black community, where they must be accepted if they are to have friends, and the world of the white community, where they must be accepted if they are to survive.

CULTURAL INFLUENCES ON SOCIALIZATION

Our focus thus far has been on the way children develop in the United States. How typical of the world's children is the pattern of socialization we have described? Child-rearing patterns in any society reflect the values that are needed for an adult to function successfully. In a hunting society, for example, parents—and other adults—encourage their sons to show courage, strength, dexterity, and timing. These are the qualities that make an effective hunter; they are vital both to successful life as a man and to the survival of the society. When parents encourage these traits in their young sons, they are not deliberately trying to produce good hunters. Instead, they are encouraging qualities they believe are intrinsically desirable—good for all men in any society. This conviction comes from living in a society in which the most successful men are invariably brave, strong, dextrous, and have swift reaction times (L. Hoffman, 1984a).

Most parents in our society are not especially concerned if their sons' reaction time is somewhat slow, but they try to make certain that their children are independent, skillful in social interactions, competitive, and have a strong sense of self-efficacy. They also insist that they get as much schooling as possible. Parents see these qualities as intrinsically desirable; actually, they are simply qualities that lead to success in American society. If these same parents lived in a herding society, however, they would do everything they could to stamp out independence in their children, for they would regard it as a negative trait. Unfortunate innovations in herding techniques can threaten a family's food supply for many months.

Some child-rearing practices are based on cultural beliefs about the nature of children or the nature of the world. Among the Kwoma of New Guinea and the Zinacantecans of Mexico, for example, the belief that children are in danger from supernatural forces leads them to keep their babies close by, calm, and quiet—lest they call attention to themselves (Super and Harkness, 1982). This cultural stifling of emotional expression stands in sharp contast to American practice, in which parents encourage emotional expression in the belief that inhibited emotions can cause lasting psychological harm.

Even disciplinary techniques vary from one country to the next. Although Japan and the United States are both complex industrial societies that place a premium on educational achievement, they discipline their preschoolers differently. In one study (Conroy, Hess, Azuma, and Kashiwagi, 1980), Japanese mothers, who believe that preschoolers should be indulged but receptive to the suggestions of adults, relied on appeals to feelings and consequences when faced with an unruly child. They reminded the child how misbehavior makes the mother feel or how the child would feel if someone treated him or her that way, and they pointed out the consequences of the behavior to the child or others. American mothers were more likely to use power assertion or to remind the child of the rules governing the situation ("The puzzle belongs to Chris"). Because American mothers rely more heavily on power assertion and Japanese mothers on induction, Japanese youngsters probably internalize moral standards at an earlier age. When American mothers of preschoolers are compared with German mothers, however, it is the German mothers who are more likely to use power assertion as a disciplinary strategy (Parke, Grossmann, and Tinsley, 1981).

Cultural differences also exist in the influence and function of the peer group. Only in industrialized societies are infants, toddlers, and preschoolers brought together with children of their own age. In most societies, a baby graduates from maternal care into a group composed of children of all ages. Older children look after younger ones, and the child is absorbed into the group. Some researchers believe that parallel play is probably unknown in preindustrial societies and developed in societies that segregate children by age (Konner, 1975).

The peer group can be a force for stabilization or for social change. In Israel, where self-confidence, independence, and new ways of doing things are important, children are expected to be adventurous and full of mischief. There the peer group has more influence than parents, and Israeli children proudly say that they will break adult rules at the suggestion of the peer group (Shouval, Kav Venaki, Bronfenbrenner, Devereux, and Kiely, 1975).

In the Soviet Union, instead of being a force for youthful ideas, the peer group transmits the government's social values to children. The Soviet government has deliberately used the peer group in this way, in order to bring adult values into harmony with the needs of the system. The interests of the social group are considered more important than the interests of the individual, and children soon learn to subordinate themselves to the group. This is accomplished by keeping Soviet children in a series of "nested social units" that carry the responsibility for the child's behavior. These units include the row of double-seated desks in the classroom, the classroom itself, the entire school, and the various youth organizations to which children belong (Bronfenbrenner, 1973). Rewards or punishment are administered to the entire group, so that one child's misbehavior puts his or her social unit in jeopardy.

Research from other cultures reminds us that most studies of development reported in this book reflect Western conceptions of the individual. Western emphasis on competition, school achievement, and autonomy determines the research questions we ask as well as the way we interpret the results.

SUMMARY

1. Peer influence differs from family influence because children must earn a place in the peer group, because in the group they interact with equals, and because the group gives them an opportunity for **social comparison,** in which they can assess their own performance against that of other children. Peers socialize one another through reinforcement, modeling, and social comparison.

2. Many factors determine a child's acceptance by the peer group, including some, such as physical attractiveness, that are outside the child's control. Popular children tend to be friendly, socially competent, and good at understanding others and at solving problems. As children reach school age, they quarrel less often, but their arguments are more often hostile than were their preschool squabbles over toys. Unlike other children, aggressive youngsters tend to interpret ambiguous ac-

tions as intentionally hostile, especially when they feel threatened. Some children are neglected by their peers, others actively rejected. Neglected children are unlikely to have social or emotional problems, but rejected children often develop such problems and may drop out of school or become juvenile delinquents.

3. The peer group has structure, standards, and a code of conduct. Peer groups develop **dominance hierarchies,** rankings that reflect the relative social power of group members. Friendships, coalitions, and subgroups are outside the dominance hierarchy but are just as important to the group's functioning. Conformity to group norms emerges when children are about five years old, increases throughout childhood, and then begins to decline in adolescence. Antisocial conformity is sharpest in early adolescence, when conflict between parents' and peers' standards is sharpest.

4. Over childhood, friendships change from purely behavioral, self-centered, smooth but brief relationships to emotional, mutual, bumpy but enduring relationships. Children usually choose friends who resemble them in some way, and the process of friendship may contribute to prosocial behavior and the development of morality. At any age, aggressiveness will end a friendship; only among older children do friendships break up because of disloyalty.

5. Play is pleasurable; it is an end in itself; it is spontaneous; and it involves active engagement. **Functional play,** which consists of simple, repetitive movements, is most prevalent in infants and young children and rapidly declines with age. **Pretend play,** which incorporates elements of imagination or fantasy, is prevalent among preschoolers but declines in school-age children unless it is encouraged. **Constructive play,** which consists of constructing or creating something, and **games with rules** are first seen among preschoolers; both are prevalent throughout childhood. Play also varies in its social involvement; it can be solitary play, parallel play (in which children play side by side but separately), or group play.

6. Teachers respond in predictable ways to children. They prefer conforming high achievers who make few demands. Whether a teacher expects children to do well or not affects the way a teacher treats a child — and may affect the child's performance. Some children with little expectation of success in school are highly anxious; others suffer from learned helplessness, which may be promoted by the way teachers respond to students' failures. The school experience also enforces traditional sex roles and stereotypical views of boys' and girls' capabilities.

7. Watching violent TV programs increases the likelihood of immediate violence in controlled experiments, but such studies cannot be applied to daily life because, first, aggression in the lab is fake; second, the adult experimenter gives the children tacit approval to be aggressive; and, third, the effects of a single exposure say nothing about the effects of habitual viewing. The habitual viewing of violent TV programs is associated with aggressive behavior, but there is no simple cause and effect relationship. Many other aspects of socialization interact in the development of aggression. Children can learn prosocial behavior from television, but influences on their behavior seem weak. Television, especially commercials, strengthens stereotypical views of sex roles.

8. Social class affects child rearing. Working-class parents tend to use power-assertive discipline and encourage conformity in their children, whereas middle-class parents tend to use inductive discipline and encourage autonomy. Low-income children are at a disadvantage in school, which is based on middle-class values.

9. Some apparently ethnic influences on socialization are actually socioeconomic effects. However, black children are socialized to function in two worlds: the white and the black. The prevalence of racism leads black parents to make an extra effort to develop their children's self-esteem and self-confidence.

10. A society's child-rearing patterns encourage the values that are required for successful

functioning in that society. Some child-rearing patterns are based on cultural beliefs about the nature of the child or the nature of the world. Cultures also vary in the role they allot to the peer group, which may act as a force for stabilization or a force for social change.

KEY TERMS

constructive play
dominance hierarchy

functional play
games with rules

pretend play
social comparison

STUDY TERMS

dominance hierarchy   Ranking that reflects the relative social power of group members.

functional play   Play that consists of simple, repetitive movements; it is the simplest, least mature form of play.

social comparison   Process by which a person assesses his or her own performance or ability by comparing it with that of other people in a reference group.

CHAPTER 11

Cognition: Thinking and Reasoning

AN INTELLECTUAL REVOLUTION
Appearances Become Less Powerful / Attention Becomes Decentered / Thinking Becomes Reversible / Learning Becomes Self-regulated and Strategic / Language Becomes Instrumental for Thinking

CONCRETE-OPERATIONAL THOUGHT
Conservation / Causal Reasoning / Number Knowledge and Number Skills

ADVANCES IN INFORMATION PROCESSING
Attention / Memory / Problem Solving / Metacognition

SOCIAL COGNITION
Understanding What Others Know / Role-Taking / Morality

More and more children are on speaking terms with computers. Six-year-old Alex, who often plays tic-tac-toe with friends, is frustrated when he plays with Merlin, because the toy never makes mistakes (as his friends do) and never eases up to let him win (as most adults do). After losing steadily to Merlin, Alex bursts out, "He cheats. It's not fair." Children's notions about the capacity of computers to cheat undergoes a progression that parallels their cognitive development. Five- and six-year-olds believe that cheating requires some kind of physical action. This belief convinces many that computers can't cheat because they don't have hands or eyes. Others are not so sure; they suggest that the computer does have eyes. "Tiny eyes. You just can't see them." Eight-year-olds believe that cheating requires neither human anatomy nor any visible action. And some are convinced that computers cheat — "from the inside." Others say that a computer can't cheat because "it can't press by itself." For them, computers clearly lack autonomy. Older children are convinced that computers cannot cheat, because they regard cheating as the result of deliberate intent. But some contend that you can program a computer to cheat, perhaps by writing the program so that it moves twice in a row. Sherry Turkle

(1984) collected these increasingly sophisticated views in the course of a clinical study with nearly 100 children between the ages of four and fourteen.

In this chapter, we trace similar changes in all aspects of children's thinking. We pick up children while they are still "childish." They have not yet undergone the great intellectual revolution of childhood that turns youngsters into flexible, capable thinkers. After exploring the major themes of that revolution, we look at its consequences and examine the new conceptual knowledge and logical thought of the concrete-operational child. Then we turn to the advances in information-processing skills that make logical thought possible: changes in attention, memory, problem solving, and children's increasing knowledge about thought itself. Finally, we trace the development of social cognition. We watch as children gradually come to understand what others know, think, and intend, and we explore the development of their reasoning about moral issues.

AN INTELLECTUAL REVOLUTION

Young children's words and actions often are amusing, and fond parents frequently relate charming stories about the exploits of their preschool children. These tales reflect the thought of preschoolers, which Piaget found so different from the thought of the schoolchild that he placed it in a separate stage, which he called **preoperational thought.** He described this thought as intuitive, inflexible, contradictory, and focused on individual events. The preschool child, he maintained, is not capable of the flexible, rigorous, and logical thought that characterizes mental **operations.**

Our view of young children's thought was radically changed by Piaget's research. His recognition that children do not see the world as adults do led to new ways of looking at cognitive development. Although preschool children probably are more capable thinkers than Piaget believed, he asked the right questions about their thought, and his view of the way the child's mind gradually

develops has been extremely useful.

As Piaget proposed, the thought of preschool children differs from the more systematic thought of the schoolchild in major ways. The changes in children's thinking between the ages of four and ten are so great that they seem to reflect an intellectual revolution. Although we cannot point to a specific day or week — or even year — when this intellectual revolution occurs, we can describe the changes that distinguish the thinking of four-year-olds from that of ten-year-olds.

Appearances Become Less Powerful

Appearances seem to overwhelm preschoolers. We have already encountered the preschooler's nagging worry that gender is not necessarily permanent. As we saw in Chapter 9, young boys (or girls) believe that playing with girls' (or boys') toys might transform then into girls (or boys). Preschoolers also seem to believe that irrelevant changes in the appearance of objects or people change their identity (Flavell, Green, and Flavell, 1986). Nearly twenty years ago, Rheta DeVries (1969) convincingly demonstrated the way that appearance overpowers the young child's understanding of reality. She introduced children to Maynard, a black cat. Even the youngest, who were only three years old, agreed that Maynard was a cat. DeVries told each child in turn to keep watching the cat. She screened the cat's head from sight and placed on it a realistic mask resembling a fierce dog. Then she turned the cat around and asked the children once more to identify the animal. Three-year-olds were sure that it had become a dog. They said that the animal with the dog's head had a dog's bones and a dog's stomach under its skin. Most four-year-olds said that they would not be fooled: the cat would remain a cat even if DeVries put a dog's mask over its head. Yet once the transformation was completed, they changed their minds. The sight of the dog's head on a cat's body (even though the animal never left their field of vision) overwhelmed their earlier assertion that its species would remain unchanged. But five- and six-year-olds were not influenced by the mask. They had developed the concept of **identity,** which is the understanding that objects and people remain the same even if irrelevant properties are changed. These children maintained that a cat was a cat, no matter how it looked.

Irrelevant changes in objects also fool young children. If you show a ball of clay, then smash it into a flat pancake, the four-year-old will be convinced that there is less clay in the pancake than there was in the ball. Most four-year-olds are ready to accept things as they seem to be. They judge reality on the basis of what is before their eyes, even if they watch the transformation and see that you have not taken away any clay (Flavell, 1985).

The power of appearance wanes during the early school years. Older children are not easily fooled. They can infer reality even when objects or events are distorted, hidden, or camouflaged.

Attention Becomes Decentered

When observing a scene or solving a problem, young children usually concentrate on a single prominent feature of the stimulus. This captive attention, called **centration,** excludes all other aspects of the stimulus. When youngsters are asked to judge which glass holds the most cola, for example, they center on the height of the liquid in the glass and pay no attention to its width. To a four-year-old, a tall, narrow glass always holds more cola than a short, squat glass. The dominant aspect of a stimulus probably captures the young child's attention so effectively because she or he **encodes,** or registers, only that aspect of the stimulus in memory. This rudimentary encoding limits the ways in which a child can think about an object or a situation. As children get older, their attention becomes decentered. They can pay attention to more than one aspect of a stimulus or problem. They can think about it more comprehensively, considering the width as well as the height of a glass before judging how much cola it contains.

Thinking Becomes Reversible

Young children's thinking generally is confined to the immediate state of an object or situation. They seem unable to consider its previous or future states, and they do not seem to think about the sort of action that might transform an object from one state into another. When a four-year-old watches

This seven-year old is in the middle of an intellectual revolution; she is on the brink of discovering that an action, such as pouring milk from one-size container to another, can be mentally reversible. *(Richard Hutchings/Photo Researchers)*

cola poured from a squat glass into a tall, narrow glass, for example, he or she does not seem to realize that pouring the cola back into the squat glass would restore the level of liquid to its original level. Piaget said that the young child's thinking lacked **reversibility,** which is the understanding that irrelevant changes in appearance can be reversed and that such changes tend to compensate for one another. (As the cola level rises in the tall glass, its quantity is also restricted by the narrow sides.) Similarly, although most preschoolers can solve very simple problems in addition or subtraction, their understanding that subtraction reverses the effect of addition is still implicit and they can apply it only with very small numbers $(4 + 2 - 2)$ and only when there are no conflicting visual cues (Gelman and Baillargeon, 1983).

Ten-year-olds understand that pouring cola back into a squat glass restores the original situation. They can also apply this operation of reversibility to new situations. When a fifth-grade class visited a large airport, they discovered that if they walked backwards at just the right speed on the moving sidewalk, they stayed in the same place. They learned that compensation between actions can exactly cancel each other and so preserve an invariant relationship. The laughing ten-year-olds who blocked the sidewalk in the terminal could figure out how to compensate for the walkway's movement because their thought was reversible.

Learning Becomes Self-regulated and Strategic

Ask a four-year-old to carry out some simple task, such as setting the table, and chances are that the job will not be completed. The forks and spoons may be in place, but unless an adult monitors the project, reminding the youngster of each step, the task is likely to be abandoned or major items omitted. Most young children seem to be creatures of impulse. They find it difficult to develop a plan (first put a knife, fork, and spoon at each place; next get the napkins, and so on), initiate it, and then carry it out.

This inability to plan and regulate their own behavior interferes with young children's ability to learn, to solve problems, and to communicate effectively. In most instances, their difficulty is not caused by a lack of necessary mental equipment but by a failure to grasp the need to plan a course of action and to understand the strategies that make learning or problem-solving easier. Even when they develop a helpful strategy, they confine it to isolated situations and do not apply it in other places where it would be appropriate (Brown, Bransford, Ferrara, and Campione, 1983). When children are acquiring various strategies, most seem to go through a stage described as a **production deficiency,** when they are capable of executing the strategy but do not use it spontaneously (Flavell, 1985). As children get older, their use of these strategies becomes automatic.

Language Becomes Instrumental for Thinking

Language plays a critical role in the intellectual revolution of childhood. Increasingly, language helps guide thinking. Infants and toddlers can form simple concepts without language (see Chapter 6), but unless they are able to assign names to concepts, children may find it impossible to combine these elementary concepts into complex conceptual structures. Language not only speeds the acquisition of new concepts, but allows children to reason more rapidly and effectively as well.

Language and Memory Language facilitates memory. Children's dawning awareness of this

fact is responsible for part of the improvement that appears in memory during childhood. In a classic study, John Flavell, David Beach, and Jack Chinsky (1966) demonstrated how the spontaneous use of language helps children solve simple memory problems. The researchers showed children pictures of familiar objects, pointing to some they wished the children to remember. Fifteen seconds later, they asked the children to point to the same pictures in the same order. Five-year-olds remembered fewer pictures than eight-year-olds, apparently because most eight-year-olds repeated the names of the pictures they had to remember. Almost none of the five-year-olds did this, an indication that children do not automatically use their command of language when it would be helpful. The failure to rehearse the names verbally provides an example of a production deficiency. When researchers instructed other nonrehearsers to whisper the names of objects they were to remember, they recalled as many objects as children who spontaneously repeated the names to themselves (Keeney, Cannizzo, and Flavell, 1967). Yet when allowed to memorize items in any way they liked, most of the young children whose recall had improved so strikingly when they rehearsed stopped using the strategy.

Language and Self-control Language also seems vital to the development of self-control, an advance that is basic to children's socialization (see Chapter 9). Harriet and Walter Mischel (1983) used simple treats to discover how children learned to control themselves when sorely tempted. If youngsters are told that they can have one marshmallow immediately or two marshmallows if they are willing to wait, most say that they will wait. But four-year-olds usually overestimate their self-control. They want to look at the marshmallows while they wait. Because the four-year-old's attention is centered, this strategy makes the reward so tempting that after a few minutes, most give up and take the single marshmallow. Six-year-olds know that covering the rewards makes waiting bearable. They also have discovered how to use language to control their behavior. They sing or keep telling themselves, "If you wait, you get two marshmallows; if you don't, you get only one." Eight-year-olds can control themselves even when the marshmallows are not covered. Their

In this conservation experiment, a child looks at two rows of seven evenly spaced checkers. After she agrees that both rows have the same number, the researcher bunches together the checkers in one row. At this point, children who do not understand conservation say that the undisturbed row contains more checkers. *(William MacDonald)*

attention is decentered, and they have learned to use language to turn their thoughts away from the delicious sweet taste of the rewards. They tell themselves to think about the marshmallows' abstract qualities (cottony or cloudlike), a strategy that makes waiting easier. Again, researchers have found a production deficiency: preschoolers who are instructed to think about the marshmallows as clouds or cotton balls can delay their gratification for nearly fifteen minutes. But without instructions, they are likely to think about the chewy, sweet, soft taste and wait no longer than five minutes.

CONCRETE-OPERATIONAL THOUGHT

As the profound intellectual revolution of childhood is completed, the charming but illogical thought of the preoperational child gives way to the **concrete-operational thought** of the schoolchild. This change, said Piaget (Piaget and Inhelder, 1969), is a decisive turning point, because children now are capable of logical thought. Although they can apply logic only to concrete objects, their thought has become flexible. This flexibility allows them to manipulate their mental representations as easily as they manipulate physical objects (Siegler, 1986). The logical thought of the school years does not suddenly spring out of nowhere. It is based on concepts that developed during earlier years. As infants, children learned that objects continue to exist when out of sight. As preschoolers, they learned that people and animals and objects can change their appearance without losing their identity. Without these basic concepts of object permanence and identity, children could not grasp such principles as conservation.

Conservation

Children who understand **conservation** know that irrelevant changes in the external appearance of an object have no effect on the object's quantity — its weight, length, mass, or volume. In the best known test of conservation, children watch an experimenter fill two glasses of the same size and shape to an equal level with colored water. The children are asked whether the two glasses contain the same amount of water. When the children assert that the amounts are the same, the researcher pours the water from one of the glasses into a tall, narrow glass, so that the levels of colored water in the two glasses differ. A nonconserver, when asked whether each glass now contains the same amount of water, will say, "No! This one has more water in it because it is higher." Nonconservers have not completed the intellectual revolution. Unable to reverse the action mentally, they focus on the present state of the liquid. Their attention centers on the dominant dimension (the liquid's height), and they mistake appearance for reality (Flavell, 1985).

When seven-year-old Larry watches the transformation, he is not fooled. He points out that although the tall glass is higher, it is also narrower. His thought is reversible, and he can prove to himself that the amount of water has remained the same by imagining the liquid in its previous state. Larry clearly understands the conservation of quantity. Because Larry understands the conservation of liquid quantities, he also understands the conservation of number. If you place two rows of checkers in front of him, then spread out one row

so that it appears longer than the other, he will tell you that the rows are still equal. Larry is as convinced of this fact as he is of his knowledge that $2 + 2 = 4$. Once children grasp the conservation of number or liquids, they adamantly insist that nothing the researcher can do will convince them that they are wrong (Miller, 1986).

Children understand the conservation of number before they understand the conservation of liquid or solid quantity (such as balls of clay). Why is the conservation of number so much easier for children to grasp? Probably, says Robert Siegler (1981), because children have more cues to guide them when judging discrete quantities (like checkers) than when judging continuous quantities (like water). Faced with two rows of coins, a child can count them, line up the rows in one-to-one correspondence, or notice what the researcher does to transform one row. When children have to judge glasses of water or balls of clay, their only cue is the manipulations of the experimenter.

As Piaget discovered (Piaget and Inhelder, 1969), children's understanding of this concrete operation is not complete once they understand the conservation of quantity. The various aspects of conservation emerge slowly, and it is several years before children understand it completely. First, children understand the conservation of quantity (with number leading the way) and the conservation of continuous length (see Figure 11.1). Then, at about the age of nine or ten, they grasp the notion that weight is also conserved. Finally, at about ten or eleven, they understand the conservation of volume; they discover that the amount of water displaced by an object is not affected if its shape is changed (Piaget and Inhelder, 1941). Other researchers have confirmed Piaget's basic findings about the sequence of these acquisitions (Tomlinson-Keasy, Eisert, Kahlel, Hardy-Brown, and Keasey, 1979; Uzgiris, 1964).

Developmental psychologists still do not understand exactly how children acquire conservation concepts or why they seem to acquire them in a particular order. Conservation is an extremely complex cognitive skill, which reflects the development of specific cognitive processes and the child's growing store of experiences. As John Flavell (1985) has pointed out, decentration, more exhaustive encoding, reversibility, and the development of cognitive strategies are essential to the child's ability to think about quantity, length, weight, and volume. An increase in **cognitive capacity,** or the amount of information that children can keep in mind at one time, is also critical. When young children try to solve problems, most of the space they have for processing information is used up by such basic tasks as encoding or retrieving information (Case, Kurland, and Goldberg, 1982). As they get older, they process information rapidly and often automatically. When less space is needed for basic processes, more is available to hold and manipulate information. This increase enables children to consider more than one dimension or think about the transformations involved.

Many of Piaget's experiments have been replicated by other developmental psychologists, and their results support many of his findings. An increasing number of researchers, however, have found that young children seem to understand more about some aspects of conservation than the experiments reveal (Siegler, 1986). When the context of the experiment is changed, so that the children pour the water themselves, more of them solve the problem correctly. As Margaret Donaldson (1979) has pointed out, the conditions of the experiment push children toward the wrong answer. When the experimenter pours the water, he or she generally says, "Now watch what I do." This indicates to the child that the action is important and will affect whatever follows. The influence of the experimenter's words became apparent when Susan Rose and Marion Blank (1974) did not ask children about the quantity of the two items before manipulating their appearance. Six-year-olds who were tested with only the final question made fewer errors on the task at hand and

FIGURE 11.1   In each of these problems, the researcher calls attention to the original situation and asks the child whether the two displays are equal. Then, with the child watching, the researcher transforms the items as shown in the second picture of each pair and once more asks if the displays are equal. If the child says that they are the same (either because the researcher's manipulations did not affect the display or because the transformation can be reversed), the child has demonstrated a grasp of conservation.

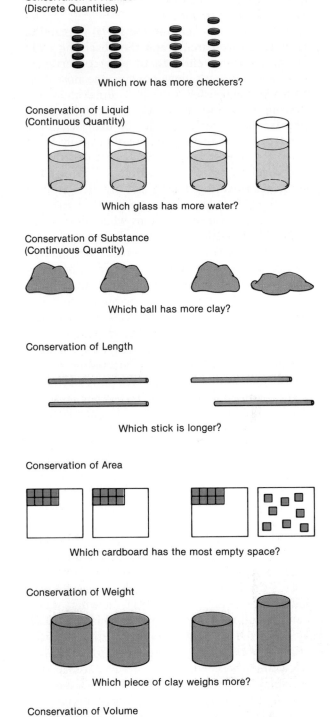

Conservation of Number
(Discrete Quantities)

Which row has more checkers?

Conservation of Liquid
(Continuous Quantity)

Which glass has more water?

Conservation of Substance
(Continuous Quantity)

Which ball has more clay?

Conservation of Length

Which stick is longer?

Conservation of Area

Which cardboard has the most empty space?

Conservation of Weight

Which piece of clay weighs more?

Conservation of Volume

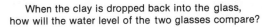

When the clay is dropped back into the glass,
how will the water level of the two glasses compare?

scored much higher a week later when tested in the manner devised by Piaget.

It appears that changing the social interaction between the researcher and the observing child allows additional children to pass conservation tests. But in Piaget's view, not even the most skillful teacher can teach a preoperational child that pouring water into a tall, narrow glass does not increase the water's quantity or that twisting a necklace into a curve does not shorten it. Yet a number of investigators have been able to teach three- and four-year-old children to pass conservation tests. With training and practice, Rochel Gelman (1982a) has taught preschoolers to solve number conservation problems when there are as many as ten checkers in a row. In her study, the children learned to ignore perceptual cues and rely instead on one-to-one correspondence, by mentally lining up the rows of checkers. In Piaget's view, these children may be passing the test, but they are not displaying conservation. He would say that recounting the checkers or using one-to-one correspondence neither requires concrete operations nor reflects an understanding of the transformation that has occurred.

Do young children actually know more about conservation than Piaget's tests indicate? Perhaps young children who pass conservation tests are simply maintaining their belief in the objects' identity says Kurt Acredolo (1982). Their thought is not reversible, and they do not understand that the change in the less dominant dimension can compensate for change in the dominant dimension. Acredolo believes that children probably recognize the identity rule (saying, "You just spread the checkers") before they understand compensation.

This explanation squares with the results of a study by Dorothy Field (1981), in which most four-year-olds who learned to recognize the identity of altered substances could still solve conservation problems five months after the training ended, but those who learned reversibility and compensation explanations could not. Further support comes from a study by Gilbert Botvin and Frank Murray (1975), in which nonconservers learned the concept from other children. Botvin and Murray put first graders in groups of five, each group made up of three nonconservers and two conservers. After a researcher asked each child to answer questions about weight and mass conservation, the group talked about conservation problems until they could agree on an answer. After they had reached an agreement, the researcher questioned each child.

Most of the nonconservers learned to conserve mass, weight, and number. During earlier group discussions, original conservers tended to explain the transformation by talking about the reversibility of the change. But new conservers tended to give "identity" explanations. They noted that nothing had been added to or subtracted from the original amount or that the change had been irrelevant. Their grasp of conservation seemed to rely on an understanding of identity, not on reversibility, which may be the way most children develop their comprehension.

Causal Reasoning

One day when Piaget and his daughter were out walking, four-year-old Lucienne looked up at the sun and said, "Oh, it's walking like us. Yes, it has little paws and we can't see them." Asked where it was walking, she replied, "Why, on the sky. The sky's hard. It's made of clouds." Then she discovered the sun was following them. "It's doing that for fun, to play a joke on us. . . ." Asked whether the sun knew that Piaget and Lucienne were there, she said, "Of course it does; it can see us!" (Piaget, 1951, p.252).

Piaget studied preschoolers' thoughts about the causes, purposes, and activities of such things as dreams; night and day; the sun, moon, and clouds; and mountains and rivers. He asked them why boats float and how steam engines operate. From their replies to his questions, he concluded that young children sought single, final, humanlike causes for things that are difficult to explain. This search seemed driven by three concepts: finalism, artificialism, and animism. **Finalism** refers to the belief that nothing happens by accident. Even the most trivial occurrence has a simple and direct cause. Four-year-olds say that a river flows because "it wants to" and that clouds move "in order to hide the sun." **Artificialism** refers to the child's inability to separate physical causes from nonphysical causes. They believe that either God or people have built everything in the world. The child's God bears little resemblance to the adult's concept of a cre-

THE DIFFERENCE BETWEEN CLASSES AND COLLECTIONS

When four-year-olds are asked to sort objects, they have little trouble putting all the toy cars in one pile and all the dolls in another. At this level, known as **basic categories,** the members are most like one another and most different from members of other categories. But few four-year-olds can sort all the vehicles (car, plane, truck) into one pile and all the toy furniture (bed, chair, table) into another. Such **superordinate categories** are highly generalized and usually based on function. The members look least like one another.

Do youngsters fail at this task because the items look so different? Or are they simply too inexperienced to have learned the features that determine class membership? Piaget contended that the problem was the result of the young child's mental organization. Until children were seven or eight years old, he said, they could not think about objects as simultaneously belonging to two different classes: an object could not be both a carrot *and* a vegetable or a truck *and* a vehicle. He demonstrated this contention by testing their ability to understand **class inclusion,** a concrete operation based on the knowledge that a superordinate class (vegetables) is always larger than any of its basic classes (carrots, peas). Piaget showed children twenty wooden beads (three white and seventeen brown) (Piaget, 1932/1965). Then he asked them whether there were more wooden beads or more brown beads in the box. Young children invariably said, "More brown beads." Piaget explained this by saying that the youngsters could not think of an entire class and its subclass at the same time, so they could not compare them. Instead they compared the two subclasses, correctly reporting that there are more brown beads (than white beads).

Some developmentalists have pointed out that Piaget phrased the question in a tricky way that might lead young children to misinterpret it (Daehler and Bukatko, 1985). Most comparisons they hear refer to mutually exclusive relations: "Are there more nickels or dimes on the table?" No one —except a developmental psychologist—ever asks them if there are more nickels or more coins.

How researchers refer to the superordinate class is important. Ellen Markman (1981) has found that using collective nouns instead of class nouns enables young children to compare class with subclass. When she asked, "Who would have a bigger party, someone who invited the boys or someone who invited the children?" most kindergartners incorrectly said "boys." But when she asked, "Who would have a bigger party, someone who invited the boys or someone who invited the class?" the kindergartners correctly said "class." Why should changing a single word turn an insoluble problem into an easy one? Markman points out that members of a collection are related in some way; members of classes are not. A boy is a child, but he is *part of* a class. This part-whole relationship, which is missing from categories, gives collections an internal structure and a psychological integrity. That makes the class-inclusion problem much easier to think about. Even young children can keep the whole collection in mind while thinking about its subparts.

But class-inclusion may be even more difficult that Piaget believed. Markman's (1981) further studies indicate that children do not understand the logical basis of the class-inclusion question until they are ten or eleven years old. Younger children still do not realize that, no matter how many objects are involved, the superordinate class always is larger.

ator; instead, children see God as a giant or magician who builds things in the way that people do. At various times, Piaget's children told him that lakes were filled by watering cans; that the sky was cut out and painted; and that a house on a riverbank was built before the river "because it's much harder to make streams and rivers and the lake" (Piaget, 1951, p. 249).

These pictures from *How the Mouse Was Hit on the Head by a Stone and So Discovered the World* show the world through the eyes of five- and six-year-old children. In the book by Etienne Delessert, which was produced with the assistance of Piaget, a mouse who never before had left his underground home one day discovers the world while digging a tunnel. *(top)* The mouse discovers the sky and clouds. *(bottom)* He talks to the moon.

Table 11.1
Children's Correct Judgments about the Animacy of Objects

	Object			
Age	Block (%)	Toy Worm (%)	Person (%)	Rabbit (%)
3-year-olds	69.2	53.8	84.6*	69.2
4-year-olds	93.3	86.6	93.3	100
5-year-olds	93.7	100	100	100

* Underlined proportions are significantly greater than chance (less than one chance in one thousand).

Source: M. Bullock, "Animism in Childhood Thinking: A New Look at an Old Question," *Developmental Psychology,* 21 (1985), 222, Table 3.

Animism refers to the child's tendency to ascribe thoughts, feelings, and life itself to inanimate objects. Three-year-olds may believe that any object that can affect people in any way is alive. The sun is alive—but only when it is shining; a gun is alive because it shoots. Soon children limit life to things that normally move, even though others may move them. The sun is still alive, and so is a bicycle, but a gun is not. About the time children start school, they limit life to things that move by themselves. A bicycle is no longer alive, but a battery-powered robot is. Finally, children limit life to plants and animals.

When Piaget (1929) asked children about the world, he often asked them about things they may never have thought about. He pointed out that their answers did not reflect a coherent belief system and that any child may move back and forth from one notion of animism to another, depending on the situation. There is some indication that young children's thought is not as animistic as Piaget assumed. Researchers found that three-year-olds may attribute life to inanimate objects—but only when they lack the knowledge they need for an informed decision (Bullock, 1985). Five-year-olds are almost as accurate as adults in judging the animacy of objects (see Table 11.1).

Piaget (1930) believed that children's interactions with machines contribute heavily to their gradual grasp of naturalistic explanations. As they try to make their toys function, produce physical effects, or overcome physical resistance in objects,

they begin to learn about the nature of physical causality. Yet his questions probed areas of nature in which children had little experience. Asking preschoolers what causes the wind to blow and the rain to fall may be as futile as asking a literary critic to explain subatomic physics. When children lack necessary knowledge, they make up animistic but plausible answers.

If preschoolers are asked about the causes of simple actions, they demonstrate a much better grasp of causality than the children Piaget questioned. One aspect of causality is that causes always precede effects. Three-to five-year-olds watched a ball roll down a runway; a few seconds later a jumping jack popped up from a hole in the box; then another ball rolled down the runway (Bullock and Gelman, 1979). When asked which ball made the jack jump, the children chose the first ball. Even when the first ball rolled down a runway that was physically separated from the box and the second ball ran down the connected runway, the children chose the ball that preceded the jack's jump.

Striking as these results are, they do not indicate that young children completely understand causality. They know that the cause must occur just before the event, but they do not seem to understand that it must always do so. As Piaget (1930) would have expected, when one event sometimes (but not always) follows another, five-year-olds are easily confused; they say that the first event causes the second. Eight-year-olds do not make this mistake (Siegler, 1986). It takes many years before children develop a complete understanding of causality; in fact, many adults do not understand some of the basic physical principles involved.

Number Knowledge and Number Skills

Children's knowledge of number builds on the baby's ability to recognize the difference between small numbers of objects. As we saw in Chapter 6, young babies seem to know the difference between two objects and three objects (Antell and Keating, 1983). No one suggests that young babies count the number of objects in a display; instead they **subitize**, a perceptual process that allows them to detect differences in patterns. Adults seem to use the same process when dealing with groups of five or less, and five-year-olds apparently use it with groups no larger than three (Chi and Klahr, 1975).

When young children passed simple tests in the conservation of numbers, some of them may have been subitizing. Rochel Gelman (1972) showed children two plates, one containing two green toy mice and the other containing three. Then she trained them to choose the "winner." Counting was never mentioned by the experimenter, but the winner was always the plate with more mice. After the children learned that the three-mouse plate always won, Gelman covered the plates and worked unseen "magic" on the winner plate. Sometimes she substituted a red mouse for a green one; sometimes she bunched up the row of mice so that it matched the loser plate; sometimes she removed one of the mice. No matter how Gelman changed the array on the winner plate, the three-year-olds chose it as winner whenever it had three mice (no matter what their color or spacing) but showed surprise when a mouse was missing and usually rejected the plate. Given that the children were not reversing a transformation, perhaps they were subitizing.

Gelman believes that they simply counted the mice. In fact, most of the children did just that, although the experimenter never suggested that the child might choose the winner that way. For example, a two-and-a-half-year-old was shown the plates after the three mice on the winner plate had been bunched together. Once the child had "conserved," the experimenter pointed to the two-mouse plate and asked the youngster about its quantity:

EXPERIMENTER:	How many on this [the two-item] plate?
CHILD:	Um-m, one, two.
EXPERIMENTER:	How many on this [the three-item] plate?
CHILD:	One, two, six!
EXPERIMENTER:	You want to do that again?
CHILD:	Ya, one, two, six!
EXPERIMENTER:	Oh! Is that how many there were at the beginning of the game?
CHILD:	Ya. (Gelman and Gallistel, 1978, p. 91)

Gelman and Randy Gallistel (1978) have found that most two-year-olds have begun to count—even though many of them can count only as far as two. They count, even if they do not know their language's words for number. They may use letters to count or they may invent their own words. They may borrow number words but invent their own sequence, as did the youngster in the example, who counted "one, two, six." These youngsters use their number words consistently. In this instance, "six" always stands for three. Before they are three, children point at objects they are counting or touch them, saying their number words aloud. When they are a little older, they will count to themselves, and announce only the total. But if a five-year-old is asked to count a good many objects, he or she will count them aloud.

Young children seem to be compulsive counters. They count toys, cracks in the sidewalk, raisins in their cereal bowl, flies on the windowsill, chocolate chips in their cookies, how many times they can bounce a ball, and the number of gifts grandparents bring to a sibling. Because children's own counting words do not go far, they must eventually learn the number system. Youngsters learn the first twenty number words by rote. Until they do so, Robert Siegler and Mitchell Robinson (1982) discovered, children stop counting before they reach twenty. These children, most of them three-year-olds, have not yet discovered the structure of the number system. When they figure out the counting rule for combining digits with decades, they can go as far as ninety-nine (see Figure 11.2). Most four-year-olds have grasped

FIGURE 11.2 Basic counting rules. By the time children can count much past twenty, they have mastered the rule that allows them to combine decades with digits. If they keep following the process shown here, they can count as far as ninety-nine before the rule fails them. In this model, the digit list (1 through 9) indicates the order in which numbers are connected with decade names. The rule applicability list indicates the places (e.g., 20, 30) where the rule that combines decades with digits is applied. *(From Siegler and Robinson, 1982)*

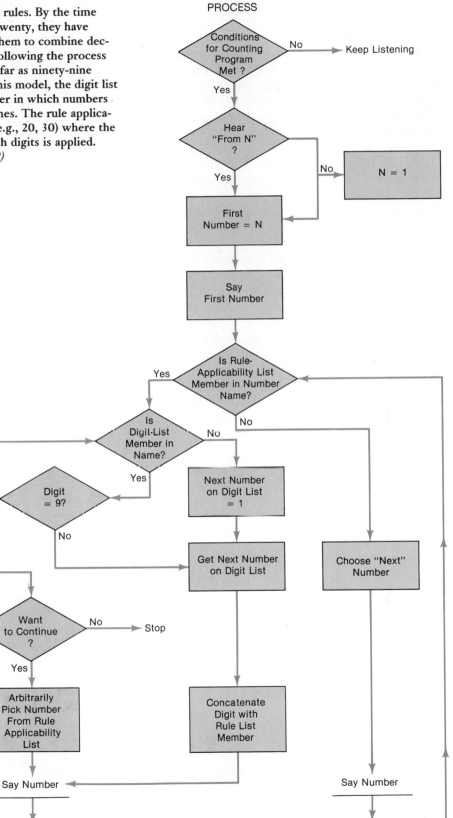

this rule, although they may not count as far as ninety-nine on request. When they stop, it is almost always on a number that ends in nine (such as thirty-nine). If the experimenter helps them out with the next decade (forty, forty-one), they pick up the count and continue to the end of the decade (forty-nine). Some four-year-olds and many five-year-olds have discovered a second counting rule and can combine hundreds. These children count until they get tired or bored. They usually choose a number that ends in nine or zero for a stopping place, because that seems to complete the task neatly.

Counting and reasoning about numbers are separate understandings, but counting provides the basis for mathematical reasoning by giving a child a way to represent number (Gelman and Gallistel, 1978). Studies indicate that preschoolers know more about mathematical reasoning than developmentalists once assumed (Gelman and Baillargeon, 1983; Siegler, 1986). As we saw in the section on conservation, young children can solve simple conservation problems by using one-to-one correspondence. They also understand mathematical magnitude: when comparing numbers, they know that greater numbers indicate "more" (six is bigger than three). They understand simple addition and subtraction and have an implicit understanding that one process reverses the other. (In Chapter 12, we will trace their understanding of these mathematical skills.) But they can apply these skills only to very small numbers of objects. They also may fail to apply knowledge they have demonstrated in one area (mathematical magnitude) to problems in another (addition). Children seem to discover the connection between various skills only after they use them enough to become proficient (Siegler and Robinson, 1982).

ADVANCES IN INFORMATION PROCESSING

As children grow, their thought appears to change in both quality and quantity; their store of information increases, and their understanding of it deepens. Their processing skills function with increasing speed and efficiency, allowing them to handle complex information that would only have confused them in earlier years.

Attention

Children's concepts of the world depend on which of its aspects get their attention. As their thought processes become increasingly sophisticated, they look at objects more systematically and attend to their most important aspects. Once they enter school, where they learn to read and to think about events and problems that are removed from daily life, they must use these skills in a different way. For example, when children learn to read, they must discriminate among letter forms, pay close attention to the shapes of letters and to their sequence, but ignore the shading of the print and the size of the letters. Once the letters have been discriminated, children must use them in combination to gain immediate access to meaning — as immediately as the sight of a medium-sized, four-footed animal with a wagging tail calls forth the concept *dog* (Gibson, 1974).

Scanning   The way that children look at things and the things they notice reflect their interests, their expectations about the world, and their strategies for acquiring information (Day, 1975). When preschoolers look at a picture, for example, their attention first is caught by the center of interest, and they scan downward from that point. They glance randomly from point to point in a display, and they tend to stop scanning before they have all the information they need. In one study, children looked at simple drawings of houses and tried to decide whether the houses were the same or different (Vurpillot and Ball, 1979). When they differed, the changes always appeared in one of the windows, where curtains, blinds, a birdcage, or a window box might have been added. Five-year-olds scanned unsystematically, and they failed to inspect every window. Nine-year-olds, who had learned what aspects of the environment it pays to notice, compared each pair of windows in turn and examined every window in the drawing.

Like these nine-year-olds, older children tend to scan exhaustively and systematically, beginning from the top of a picture, page, or pattern. Most

CULTURAL SUPPORT FOR COGNITIVE SKILLS

When you have to balance your checkbook, you probably whip out your hand-held calculator and punch in the numbers. But no matter how much you use the handy gadget, it will not improve your ability to do mental arithmetic. In many Asian classrooms, children learn to use an abacus, a form of calculator that has been used for thousands of years. The abacus is so popular that children take lessons after school to improve their skill, and nationwide abacus contests bring fame to the most proficient (Stigler, 1984). Instead of acting as a crutch, however, the abacus improves the arithmetic skills of its users.

This became apparent when James Stigler (1984) tested eleven-year-old Taiwanese experts with a series of addition problems. As he had expected, the youngsters were fast and accurate with their mechanical calculators. Their fingers flew over the abacus, clicking the beads up and down. What he had not expected was to find that they were just as accurate and even faster when they solved the problems in their heads. Some of the problems were extremely difficult to solve without pencil and paper $(23,987 + 47,310 + 98,216 + 52,148 + 11,635)$, yet they presented little problem for the children.

Why should concentrated use of an abacus improve a child's arithmetic skills? Consider the way you calculate on one of these machines. Each column in the accompanying diagram of the abacus represents a column in arithmetic notation: the first column on the end is the ones column, the next column inward is the tens column, the next is the hundreds, and so on. The single bead above the divider in each column stands for five, and each of the beads below stands for one. When the beads in a column are moved away from the center divider, the value of the column is zero. To represent one, you move a lower

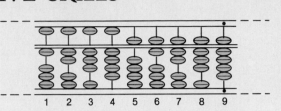

This abacus shows the number 123,456,789. The number reads from left to right, with the counter above the bar standing for 5 in each column. (From Stigler, 1984)

bead in the ones column against the divider; to represent five, you move the upper bead against the divider. Thus to represent 652, you would move the upper bead and the first lower bead in the hundreds column against the divider, as well as the upper bead in the tens column, and the first two lower beads in the ones column.

All the numbers are represented in a physical form before your eyes. Stigler believes that the Taiwanese children form a mental image of the abacus and, when adding in their heads, imagine that they are carrying out the same motions they would use when solving the problem on an actual abacus. He supports this hypothesis by noting that the children's mental mistakes—although infrequent—almost always consisted on an error of five or the omission of an entire column. Other researchers have found that abacus experts have no problem recalling a list of numbers while trying to follow spoken words, but their memory for numbers drops sharply when they try to carry out a simultaneous task involving visual imagery (Hatano and Osawa, 1983).

also have learned to scan without being distracted by irrelevant information, as younger children are. Older children's scanning techniques are also efficient; once they have the information they need

for a task, they stop scanning. As children grow older, they also scan more rapidly. Their speed increases because they are processing visual information more rapidly, because they are integrating

Once children enter school, they find they must deploy their attention in new ways, such as discriminating one letter from another. *(Elizabeth Crews/Stock, Boston)*

information across glances, or because each fixation of their eyes picks up information from a wider field (Day, 1975).

Selective Attention Young children may be inefficient scanners because they lack conscious control over their attention. When they begin a task, their attention is easily captured by the prominence of some stimulus. The result is a playful, rapid, and impulsive response to aspects of the world around them. As children get older, their attention becomes systematic and goal-oriented, with the relevance and informativeness of stimuli becoming increasingly important (Wright and Vliestra, 1975). They gain increasing control over their attention and become able to direct it toward information they need and to ignore information that is irrelevant to the task (Flavell, 1985).

As children gain control over their attention, they find it easier to adapt it to the requirements of specific situations (Flavell, 1985). Developmental changes in adaptability appeared when researchers switched instructions on a task (Hale, Taweel, Green, and Flaugher, 1978). Sometimes they told children to remember the shape of objects; at other times, they told the children to remember both shape and color. Shape was the most striking dimension of the stimulus and the one most likely to capture a young child's attention. When told to remember color as well as shape, five-year-olds'

memory for shape did not change, but their memory for color improved sharply. The instructions had different effects on nine-year-olds. Their attention to shape declined as their attention to color increased. Although five-year-olds were able to adapt their attention somewhat, they were not able to withdraw any of their attention from the dominant dimension. Older children were able to transfer their attention when the situation demanded it.

Children's increasing ability to adapt their attention to the demands of a situation reflects their growing ability to plan ahead. They prepare themselves to gather particular kinds of information, so that when the task begins they are using appropriate strategies. In one study, researchers sometimes asked children to match animal pictures by size, sometimes by color, and sometimes by shape (Pick and Frankel, 1973). It made no difference whether second graders knew ahead of time which matching standard would be used. Their performance was no faster or more accurate when they had advance knowledge. But sixth graders matched faster and more accurately when told beforehand than when they received the information after the matching had begun. This growing ability to use appropriate strategies was reflected earlier in the discussion of scanning. Flavell (1985) likens the person with planned, adaptive control of attention to the orchestra conductor who calls forth first one instrument, then another, then a combination, depending on the the effect demanded by the score.

Memory

Memory improves throughout childhood. In Chapter 6, we met the infant who recognized a mobile and remembered how to control it and the toddler who could remind a parent of a promised treat. In this chapter, we follow children as they become skillful rememberers. What *is* memory, anyway? And why do children get better at it as they grow older? Memory is not a single process, a passive storehouse of our experiences, or an isolated intellectual skill. When we speak of **memory**, we are talking about a collection of cognitive processes — the same processes involved in perceiving, thinking, and learning (Kail, 1984; Paris and Lindauer, 1977). When these processes are applied to the storage and retrieval of information, we find it convenient to refer to them as *memory.* Three major factors are responsible for the dramatic improvement in children's memory as they get older. First, they become skilled at integrating new information with what they already know about the world. Second, they acquire and use increasingly efficient methods of storing and retrieving information. Finally, they develop an awareness of the factors that influence their ability to remember.

The Role of Knowledge If you listened to a lecture about new ways of programming a computer, you might be baffled by the specialized terminology and unable to remember much of what you heard. But a computer programmer who heard the same lecture would find it interesting, be able to talk about the ideas presented, and apply them to her work the next day. You were unable to comprehend and retain the material because you lack the rich network of computer-related concepts that the programmer drew on with ease as she listened to the lecture, integrating what she heard with her knowledge about programming.

When you sat down to hear the lecture, you placed yourself in a position much like that of four- or five-year-olds as they go about their daily business. A good deal of what they encounter bears little or no relation to their relatively small store of knowledge about the world. When they come upon new information, they may not have any related concepts to connect it with in memory, so that the material is difficult to store and or retrieve (Flavell, 1985). Whether they are trying to learn new facts, new techniques, or new ideas, young children remember best information that they can associate with things they already know about or can do.

Their limited store of knowledge becomes a hindrance even on simple tasks like learning word lists. When youngsters are asked to memorize lists of words, they get progressively better with age. Yet when the lists are varied so that each age group gets a list of words that are meaningful to them, younger children recall as many words as older children do (Richman, Nida, and Pittman, 1976). In Chapter 1, we met the four-year-old with the enormous store of dinosaur knowledge (Chi and Koeske, 1983). He knew much more than the

Reading music is a skill that requires attention and the application of memory strategies; when the child begins to play a carefully rehearsed piece, the notes on the sheet music act as external retrieval cues. *(Leonard Speier)*

average adult about the habits of the stegosaurus and the triceratops. In fact, when adults are uninformed about a topic, knowledgeable children can best them in learning new, related material. In one study, Michelene Chi (1978) pitted children who were expert chess players against graduate students and research assistants who were indifferent players. Chi arranged chess pieces on boards as if a game were in progress, removed them, then asked each subject to replace the pieces. The children's memories were far superior to the adults' for the chess positions. Yet when Chi tested both groups by asking them to remember a list of ten numbers, the adults did much better than the children.

Background knowledge helps us to remember because of the constructive nature of memory. Instead of storing isolated items and retrieving exact copies of what we have stored, we interpret the information we encounter, make inferences about it, and construct a representation of what we have seen or heard. When we remember something, we reconstruct our memory, produce a logical interpretation of the original information, and perhaps flesh it out with guesses and pertinent knowledge we have picked up since we stored the representation (Flavell, 1985; Paris and Lindauer, 1977).

As children's understanding develops, their memories sometimes may seem to improve with the passage of time. Such an interaction of stored information and new understanding appeared when Jean Piaget and Bärbel Inhelder (1973) showed children a group of ten sticks (arranged from tallest to shortest) and asked them to draw the arrangement from memory. Only the six- and seven-year-olds produced an array that matched the graduated model they had seen. After six months, the same children were asked to redraw the sticks. This time many of the younger children produced copies that were closer to the original than were their first drawings. As the children's comprehension developed, they understood that objects can be arranged by size (a concept known as *seriation*) and recalled the display in a way that reflected their new understanding. Piaget and Inhelder found it difficult to separate memory from thought, because children seemed to structure stored information to conform with their cognitive schemes.

The Role of Strategies   **Strategies** are voluntary, conscious techniques that we use in order to remember specific information. Strategies can be obvious: a child may drape her scarf and mittens on the doorknob in the evening so that she won't forget to take them the next day or write a note ("mittens!") and stick it under a magnet on the refrigerator door — just as her parents do. Even kindergartners are aware of such external strategies, although they may forget to use them. Children begin to use strategies as they come to understand that unless they take some deliberate action, they will be unable to recall important information when they need it. As we have seen, youngsters are able to use strategies long before they adopt them on their own. Their first use of strategies may occur in situations that encourage their use or under conditions that give children more time to study the material (Flavell, 1985). Much of the improvement in memory that appears during childhood is the result of children's increased use of strategies. However, on memory tasks that do not require the use of strategies for efficient performance, preschoolers do almost as well as adults (Brown, Bransford, Ferrara, and Campione, 1983).

Encoding Strategies   One of the earliest internal strategies discovered by children is **rehearsal**, which involves repeating material that is to be remembered. A child may rehearse silently or aloud. As we saw earlier, children who repeated the names of pictures they were required to remember did a better job of recalling them than children who did not. Until recently, developmentalists believed that preschoolers do not use rehearsal as a memory aid, but many of today's preschoolers have begun to use the technique — at least in some situations (Weissberg and Paris, 1986). Perhaps watching programs like "Sesame Street" teaches young children that the strategy is helpful. When children first begin rehearsing, they use the technique inefficiently, and their improvement on memory tasks is slight. But as they become more skilled, the content of their rehearsal changes (Ornstein and Naus, 1978). Instead of repeating a single word, or perhaps two, over and over, they begin repeating a series of words, varying them with each repetition. This technique, which makes memory more efficient, is found only among older children. It indicates some sort of plan for the task and helps a child organize recall.

Clustering, or grouping items to be remembered around some common element, is one of the most effective aids to memory. Children who use such **organization** (for example, grouping all the animals, all the toys, and all the furniture to be recalled in a word list) remember many more words than children who do not. Five-year-olds do not deliberately use this strategy. Yet when asked to recall material by category, they remember items they did not recall spontaneously. Many eight-year-olds who do not sort items by category before learning them are aware that such organization makes recall easier (Corsale and Ornstein, 1980). Most children are nine or ten years old before they consistently reorganize material that they are trying to learn (Paris and Lindauer, 1982).

Retrieval Strategies   Rehearsal and organization are encoding strategies; children use them at the time they learn material in order to help them recall later. Other strategies are retrieval strategies, which are used at the time children try to remember. External cues are one kind of retrieval strategy—the strategically placed mittens, notes, shopping lists, or landmarks. Simple retrieval cues can sharply increase the efficiency of children's memory. When researchers cue children by giving them associated names as cues, the children remember many additional words from a memorized list. In one study (Hall, Murphy, Humphreys, and Wilson, 1979), an investigator said "thirsty" to cue recall of the word "water." Such cues were more helpful to fifth graders than to second graders. The older children recalled 52 percent of the words, as compared with the younger children's recall of 33 percent. However, the second graders apparently were not using the cues in the conscious, systematic manner employed by fifth graders (Kail, 1984). The younger children seemed to be responding with common word associations (you say "sit" and about a third of second graders say "down"). When simply responding to word associations in this way, second graders still produced 30 percent of the words and fifth graders' production dropped to 31 percent. Other studies have shown that when six- and seven-year-olds are given a picture that serves as a category label, they recall only one word and then move on to another category (Kobasigawa, 1977). Eleven-year-olds try to remember as many words from each category as they can before moving on.

Internal cues, which are generated by the person trying to remember the information, also can be helpful aids to memory. The simplest internal strategy is to keep trying to remember. This is an early strategy and one that people use all their lives. Organized search, such as going through the alphabet when trying to remember someone's name, develops much later, although—once again—six- and seven-year-olds can use it if told to do so (Flavell, 1985).

Strategies for Recalling Complex Material
Most studies of memory strategies focus on the recall of simple material: word lists, pairs of pictures, and the like. But such rote memory accounts for only a small proportion of the demands life

Plays and pageants at Sunday school and kindergarten give youngsters a chance to show off their ability to recall information they have memorized. *(Michael Weisbrot & Family)*

places on children. Enjoying and following a movie require a child to recognize the characters, infer the plot and motivation, and integrate what they see on the screen with knowledge about the world they already possess. When studying history, the goal is not to recall the text sentence by sentence, but to remember what happened, the factors that probably affected the event being studied, and its consequences.

There are many effective strategies for learning and remembering complex material. They include scanning a text before reading it, in an attempt to get some idea of its content and organization; underlining; taking notes; deliberately searching for main ideas or themes; asking yourself questions to see if you understand what you have read; summarizing what you have read; and reviewing (Paris and Oka, 1986). These strategies develop later than the strategies used in rote recall; in most studies, they begin appearing spontaneously at about the sixth grade (Flavell, 1985). When older children and adolescents were asked to learn a passage of about 400 words, only 6 percent of the fifth graders took notes, compared with 21 percent of the seventh and eighth graders, and 50 percent of the high-school students. When these students were given extra study time, all but the fifth graders remembered more information from the passage (Brown and Smiley, 1978). Good readers acquire the strategies before poor readers—who may never discover them without assistance.

The Role of Metamemory   Whether children deliberately use memory strategies may depend on how well they understand the way memory works. This understanding, known as **metamemory,** includes an awareness that situations call for remembering, a knowledge of factors that make memory tasks easier or more difficult, and an understanding of the usefulness of various memory skills. Between the ages of five and twelve, children make giant strides in their awareness of the demands of memory, their acquisition of strategies, and their spontaneous use of them (Paris and Lindauer, 1982). The first glimmer of metamemory appears in toddlers—although their knowledge is probably not conscious. As we saw in Chapter 6, toddlers look toward a toy's hiding place, point at it, or distinguish it in some way in order to keep from forgetting where the toy is hidden (De Loache, Cassidy, and Brown, 1985).

Although many four-year-olds know that noise makes it hard to remember and that it is easier to remember a few items than to remember a lot of them, most do not seem to realize what remembering actually entails. In one study, four-year-olds said that a boy who found his coat hanging in a closet had "remembered" where it was—whether or not the boy had seen the coat placed there (Wellman and Johnson, 1979). Until children are about nine years old, most of them do not understand that remembering is a form of knowing that is based on past experiences (Kail, 1984).

Kindergartners and first graders know that events that happened a long time ago are hard to recall, that telephone numbers are quickly forgotten, and that once something is learned, it is easier to relearn the same material than to learn something new (Kreutzer, Leonard, and Flavell, 1975). When asked how to remember something, these children usually suggest external memory aids, such as asking other people, tape recordings, written notes, or a string on a finger. However, most of them do not seem to understand how external aids work. In one study, first graders said that a cue was effective no matter where it was placed or when it was seen (Fabricius and Wellman, 1983). They also thought that putting a note inside their desk at school could remind them to stop by a friend's house on the way *to* school. Long before children begin using internal memory strategies, they are able to use them when told to do so. Yet, as we saw earlier, they then discard the strategies and go back to their old methods.

Why the delay in adopting memory strategies? Perhaps younger children do not believe that they need do anything special to remember. Kindergartners wildly overestimate their ability to remember objects (Yussen and Levy, 1975). They also seem unaware that some memory tasks are more difficult than others. About half of them believe that recall is no more difficult than recognition and that recalling something verbatim is as easy as paraphrasing it (Kail, 1984). In contrast, third and fifth graders understand that remembering related items is easier than remembering things that are completely dissimilar and that telling a story in your own words is easier than repeating the story verbatim (Flavell, 1985; Myers and Paris, 1978). Another reason for children's failure to adopt strategies may be that they do not understand their value. Even when children use a strategy like rehearsal or organization at a researcher's request, the children may not realize that their improved performance is the result of the method taught them by the researchers (Paris, 1978).

Researchers have assumed that as children begin to understand the way memory operates, they begin acquiring the strategies that make it more efficient. Using a group of first and second graders, Scott Paris, Richard Newman, and Kelly McVey (1982) tested that assumption. They divided the children into two groups and had them try to remember twenty-four common objects from pictures pasted on index cards. Both groups were shown how to use various memory strategies, but only the experimental group heard the researchers explain why each strategy would help them to remember the pictures. Several days later children who had been told about the usefulness of memory strategies learned and recalled more pictures than children who had only been told how to use the strategies (see Figure 11.3). When children understand the value of strategies, they seem ready to adopt them, an indication that the simultaneous advance in metamemory and the use of memory skills is no coincidence.

Problem Solving

The toddler who solves the problem of reaching the cookie jar by pushing a chair over to the kitchen counter becomes the preschooler who applies strategies and mental rules. As children's

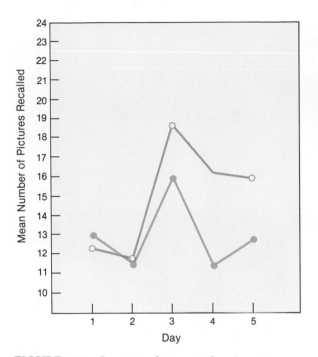

FIGURE 11.3   In a test of memory for pictures, children were shown on the third day how to use organization to enhance recall. Children in Group ○ were told *why* the strategy would help them remember; children in Group ● got no explanation. *(From Paris, Newman, and McVey, 1982)*

knowledge accumulates and their memories improve, they can tackle more difficult problems with success. Each time they encounter a new problem, they relate new information with old information and apply it to the task at hand.

Robert Siegler (1978; 1986) believes that children solve problems by applying mental rules. When they tackle an unfamiliar problem, they rely on some standard rule that has served them successfully in the past. Because children apply the same rules consistently to a variety of problems, their thinking is similar in many situations. As children grow older, they develop increasingly sophisticated rules that allow them to solve a wider range of problems.

Although studies generally show a progression in problem solving with age, getting older is not the only important influence on problem solving. The context of a problem also determines whether children can solve it. If the context in which a problem is presented changes, children may apply different aspects of their knowledge to it. When researchers asked Brazilian street children to solve arithmetic problems, they found that problems the children solved easily in one context baffled them in another (Carraher, Carraher, and Schliemann, 1983). These nine- to fifteen-year-olds had had little formal schooling, but they worked as street vendors in the city, selling popcorn, coconuts, corn on the cob, and the like. If a problem was set in the context of their street transactions ("How much do a coconut and a corn on the cob cost?"), the children solved it 98 percent of the time. If it was a similar transaction but did not involve the goods sold by the children ("A banana costs 85 cruzeiros, and a lemon costs 63 cruzieros. How much do the two cost together?"), the children solved it 74 percent of the time. But if the same problem was presented out of a natural context ("How much is 85 and 63?"), they solved it only 37 percent of the time.

Children's cognitive development takes place in a series of social contexts provided by the culture in which they live. These contexts either arrange for the child to have certain problem-solving experiences or withhold them (Laboratory of Comparative Human Cognition, 1983). A child whose major experience with addition takes place in a classroom, where out-of-context problems are worked at a desk, would probably find it difficult to handle the transactions the Brazilian children managed with ease.

Metacognition

A seven-year-old busy at homework complains bitterly to a parent because the sound of the television newscast makes it difficult for him to keep his attention focused on the task. A nine-year-old refuses to play a game of Chutes and Ladders because "it's a boring baby game." A twelve-year-old decides to reread a paragraph in a textbook because she realizes that she has missed the author's point. All these children are demonstrating **metacognition,** or knowledge about cognition and the ways in which people control cognitive activity. It includes an understanding of the way personal abilities, cognitive strategies, and the difficulty of a task affect performance (Paris and Cross, 1983). Metamemory is one aspect of metacognition, and we could also talk about meta-attention, metareasoning, metaproblem solving, metalanguage, metacommunication, and metacreativity—although people rarely do.

When watching a child draw a crude human figure, it is easy to forget that all children's drawings are aspects of problem solving. *(Jeffrey Foxx/Woodfin Camp & Associates)*

Metacognitive knowledge includes everything children know and believe about the human mind and its activity (Flavell, 1985). This knowledge is generally stable; once children acquire the knowledge that noise makes it hard to concentrate, for example, they do not lose it. Much of it can be stated; a child can say that sometimes her father doesn't understand her explanations. Some of it is wrong; a child may believe that it is just as easy to remember a list of unrelated words as a list of familiar animals. Most of it takes a long time to develop; children's knowledge about cognition keeps developing into late adolescence and even into adulthood (Brown et al., 1983). This progression became apparent when researchers questioned a group of schoolchildren about attention (Miller and Bigi, 1979). First graders believed that noise level was the primary factor that affected the deployment of attention, but fifth graders knew that motivation, mental effort, and resistance to temptation were also important.

Executive Management of Thinking Children's control over their learning, thinking, and problem solving is referred to as the *executive management* of thinking. Executive management encompasses the evaluation, planning, and regulation of thinking skills. Children's increasing proficiency as thinkers, problem solvers, rememberers, and readers reflects changes in these three areas (Paris and Lindauer, 1982).

The first aspect of executive management is to evaluate current knowledge and performance. Children often fail to take their own "mental temperature." And so they do not realize when they do not understand. When beginning to prepare for a spelling test, for example, seven-year-olds often are unaware of whether they already know their spelling words or whether they need to study them (Flavell, Friedrichs, and Hoyt, 1970). Young children frequently have inflated notions about their own cognitive skills. As we saw earlier, they overestimate their ability to remember. Nor do they know why some of their attempts at intellectual tasks succeed and why others fail (Paris and Lindauer, 1982). By the time they are ten or twelve years old, they will have some idea about whether they failed because they lacked the ability, lacked the appropriate information, or just didn't try hard enough.

The second aspect of executive management is planning the actions that will allow the child to reach specific goals. Preschoolers sometimes show evidence of metacognitive planning, but most children do not regularly plan their thinking until they are eight or nine years old. When taking a second memory test on a list of words, first graders often chose to study the words they had recalled correctly on the first test, but third graders tended to study words they had missed (Masur, McIntyre, and Flavell, 1973). Some primary-school children do not plan because they are unaware of the strategies they can use to improve their performance or lack the knowledge to apply them properly.

The final aspect of executive management is self-regulation of performance; children learn to check and adjust their cognitive activity. First and second graders tend to apply rules blindly. When learning to read, they do not check their understanding of what they have read; when doing arithmetic problems, they do not check their answers against their knowledge (Paris and Lindauer, 1982). They may defend incorrect answers in the face of clearly contradictory evidence.

As children grow older, they know more about cognition, and they become more expert at managing their cognitive processes. This progress is not simply the result of age, but of experience, expertise, and social contexts that make discovery of these skills probable (Brown, 1980).

SOCIAL COGNITION

The cognitive advances that we have traced through childhood are not limited to understanding the physical world and carrying out the kinds of tasks children encounter at school. They also influence social cognition, which refers to the way children reason about themselves and others in social situations. Some time ago, Piaget (1932/

1965) spent hours watching children play marbles and found that as the youngsters developed, their understanding of the rules changed. Children between the ages of six and ten regarded the rules for marbles as imposed from the outside by authorities. No one could change them, and even to think about it was naughty. Among twelve-year-olds, the understanding of the rules changed. Although they still respected the rules, they were ready to change them if everyone agreed. The development of flexible and realistic rules among older children may have been affected by the cooperative nature of their interactions with peers as well as by their improved reasoning skills.

As children's thinking develops, their notions of what other people see, feel, like, and understand changes. Social cognition encompasses more than children's understanding of their interactions with others. It includes the way they think about right and wrong, good and evil, politics and society. In this section, we examine children's deepening understanding of what others know, what others are like, and how to make moral judgments.

Understanding What Others Know

Children gradually come to understand what another person sees. As noted in Chapter 6, two- and three-year olds' knowledge of other people's visual perceptions is still at Level 1. These youngsters are not totally egocentric. They recognize that another person does not always see the same objects they see, but all they understand is whether or not the object is visible to the other person (Flavell, 1985). Four- and five-year-olds are beginning to understand that even though the other person can see objects in the child's field of vision, they may appear differently to him or her. They have entered Level 2 but have a long way to go before they understand exactly *how* visual perspectives differ.

Of all social-cognitive tasks, understanding another person's visual experience is the most cognitive and the least social (Shantz, 1983). It depends more on the development of the child's spatial representations than on the child's understanding of others. In most tests of this skill, children look at a group of photographs and chose the one that shows how the three-dimensional scene in front of them would appear to a person viewing it from

STAY OUT OF THE TURTLE ROOM
—HOW GOALS INFLUENCE
PROBLEM-SOLVING

Most of us have had the experience of being driven to a new restaurant and then discovering that we cannot find it again on our own. On the first trip, we were without a goal, and so we paid no attention to turns, distances, or landmarks. Something similar happens when children explore an area. What they remember depends on the purpose with which they conducted their exploration.

In a recent study, Mary Gauvain and Barbara Rogoff (1986) had schoolchildren explore a 12-foot square funhouse that had been constructed by dividing the space into rooms with blankets, sheets, wooden screens, and blinds (see diagram). Each room was decorated to match its name on the map and, like all funhouses, it contained dead-end rooms. Before the children explored the structure, they were given a goal by the researchers. Half the children were supposed to learn the general layout of the funhouse; they were told to "pay special attention to where all the rooms and hallways are." The rest of the children were supposed to learn the most direct route through the funhouse; they were told to "pay special attention to the best path for getting through the funhouse without getting stuck."

The funhouse walls were five feet high, and the researchers placed mirrors above them so that they could watch the way the children explored the rooms. Afterward, each child described the funhouse and drew a rough map of it. They also told the researchers the quickest way to get through it (forwards and backwards), answered specific questions about the layout ("Which room would you be in if you walked through the wall with Bert and Ernie on it?"), and then filled in an outline map, labeling each room and indicating the location of all doorways.

Age had no effect on the children's performance: younger children (six- and seven-year-olds) and older children (eight- and nine-year-olds) remembered about the same amount of information. But a child's goal had a significant effect on what she or he remembered. Children in both the layout group and the route group remembered equally well how to get through the funhouse. When it came to recalling the general plan, however, children in the layout group remembered much more information. The chil-

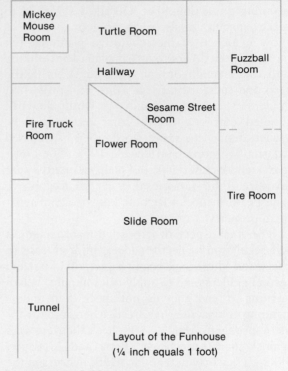

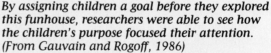

Layout of the Funhouse
(¼ inch equals 1 foot)

By assigning children a goal before they explored this funhouse, researchers were able to see how the children's purpose focused their attention. (From Gauvain and Rogoff, 1986)

dren's purpose had affected the way they explored the funhouse. Those whose problem was to learn the layout tended to spend more time in the funhouse; but even when the amount of time was equal, those whose problem was to learn the layout had a better memory for the relation between the rooms. Children learning the route apparently focused their attention on those aspects of the funhouse and paid no attention to information that they did not expect to need. They learned the landmarks (go past the Sesame Street room; turn left at the turtle room) and strung them together in a route but did not integrate the route into any sort of mental map. Once again, children demonstrated that knowledge is influenced by the purposes of the knower.

another angle. This technique may underestimate the skill of preschoolers, because some of them have trouble matching what they see to a photograph. They often choose a photograph that shows items hidden from their own view but that they know are included in the display (Liben and Belknap, 1981). When they are allowed to rotate the display to produce the other person's view instead of selecting a picture, most three-year-olds can solve the problem (Borke, 1975).

Once they had mastered the picture-matching skill, 60 percent of the preschoolers in one study correctly chose the picture that showed what a person viewing the display from another position would see (Gzesh and Surber, 1985). A sizable minority (27 percent) did make egocentric errors, choosing the picture that matched their own view. The proportion of children who chose the correct picture rose from 76 percent of first graders to 90 percent of fifth graders, but few of their errors were egocentric. Most of the children's difficulty came from their inability to make inferences based on spatial concepts. Children (and adults) did better on simple displays than on complicated ones and better when the other person was viewing the display from across the table than from the side or one of the corners.

Children's progress in understanding what others know is reflected in the way they communicate. If children are egocentric, they assume that the listener knows everything about the situation that they do. But if they adapt their speech to the needs of their listener, they show some awareness of those needs. Does a child's speech change when the listener cannot see? In one study, preschoolers played a simple game, in which they had to specify which of two toy passengers got to ride down a small hill (Maratsos, 1973). At every age, the children adapted their messages in some way to the speaker's inability to see. Three-year-olds did not give any more verbal information, but they did not point, as they did when playing the game with a sighted person. Four- and five-year-olds gave additional information. When the situation is complicated, the objects that must be described have many attributes, and the child has to figure out the rules, even eight-year-olds have trouble adapting their messages for a blindfolded player (Flavell, Botkin, Fry, Wright, and Jarvis, 1968).

Does a child's speech change when talking to younger, less competent speakers? Four-year-olds

Even young children adapt their speech when talking to babies and toddlers. They use shorter sentences and talk about fewer things. *(Michael Weisbrot & Family/Stock, Boston)*

adapt their speech when talking to two-year-olds. They use shorter sentences and talk about fewer things. Children's roles and their goals also affect the way in which they adjust their speech. They talk differently to two-year-olds when playing informally than when showing them how to work a new toy (Shatz and Gelman, 1977).

Although preschoolers make an effort to adapt their speech to others' needs, their understanding of those needs may be rudimentary. When Ralph Roberts and Charlotte Patterson (1983) studied children's attempts to communicate with others, they discovered that most four- and five-year-olds seemed to know when they had necessary information that their listener lacked. But few of them understood exactly what information was necessary for the other person to identify an object the child was describing. The majority of six-year-olds did understand which information was critical. All the children who passed a test of visual perspective gave the needed information to the other person, an indication that understanding what others know progresses through the same levels as understanding what others see.

As they become more experienced and skillful in understanding others, the way children judge the adequacy of communication changes. When others are talking to them, five- and six-year-olds rarely complain or ask for clarification when they are given misleading messages. Do they know when a message is ambiguous, incomplete, or contradictory? Usually they blame themselves for any misunderstanding; they may say that they are unsure about how to interpret the message but judge that it was adequate (Robinson and Robinson, 1983). Placed in the same situation, a nine-year-old will ask for more information.

Although they realize that they do not understand, young children often fail to signal their misunderstanding. Preschoolers apparently lack the planning and monitoring ability to handle such a task. Even when they have been told what to do (ask questions) and when to do it (when unsure of the speaker's message), they find it difficult to carry out the plan. Among kindergartners, failure to ask for clarification may be another example of production deficiency, because they can follow a plan provided by someone else. Fourth graders speak up whether or not a plan has been provided.

Role-Taking

Without the ability to take another's role, children would find it difficult to understand what others were like. Earlier we explored the emotional basis of role-taking — the development of empathy (see Chapters 8 and 9). There we saw that the rudimentary understanding that others may *feel* different in a distressing situation emerges at some time during the third year (M. Hoffman, 1984). But gradually children become aware that other people do more than perceive and feel. They develop a cognitive component to role-taking: the understanding that others' thoughts, motives, or intentions may differ from their own.

Until children reach this level of understanding, they see others as distinguished primarily by their external appearance and activities. Until they are about eight years old, children tend to describe other people in such terms; they seem to believe that a person *is* what she or he owns, where she or he lives, and how she or he looks (Shantz, 1983). Older children, who realize that these outward qualities are superficial, describe other people in terms of traits, abilities, and regularities in their behavior. In fact, children do not seem to expect regularities in behavior until they are about nine or ten years old. When researchers asked children to predict a youngster's behavior in one situation (giving up playtime to help another child rake leaves) from his or her behavior in another situation (sharing lunch with a hungry child), five- and six-year-olds expected none — unless the situation was identical (Rholes and Ruble, 1984). Nine-

and ten-year-olds expected a child to be consistently generous.

Children begin to understand intention before they are aware of any consistency in people's inner qualities. As we saw in the discussion of causal reasoning, preschoolers seem to assume that all acts are intentional; there are no accidents in their world. Yet there is some glimmer of the difference between intent and mistakes. When researchers studied children's judgment of simple actions, even three-year-olds knew that neither they nor other people meant to commit slips of the tongue in tongue-twisters ("She sells seashells by the sea shore") or make mistakes when trying to rub their stomachs and tap their heads at the same time (Shultz, 1980). Yet when asked to judge a series of actions in stories or films, four-year-olds say that the character intended even accidental events (knocking a box of cookies into the garbage can) to happen (Smith, 1978). Five-year-olds have made great strides. In this same study, they not only distinguished between voluntary (walking across a room) and involuntary (sneezing) actions but also between intentional and unintentional consequences of voluntary acts (knocking over a cereal box when you are trying to pick it up). Their distinctions were the same as those adults would make.

Children can infer people's intentions long before they can infer their thoughts. About the same time that they are distinguishing people on the basis of their inner qualities, children begin to understand the recursive nature of thought. They discover that they (and others) can think about thinking — and even think about thinking about thinking. Few seven-year-olds (only about 20 percent) can understand what are called "one-loop recursions" ("The boy is thinking that the girl is thinking of him") (Miller, Kessel, and Flavell, 1970). Understanding increases with age, from 40 percent of eight-year-olds to 50 percent of twelve-year-olds. Some twelve-year-olds can even handle "two-loop recursions" ("The boy is thinking that the girl is thinking of him thinking of her"). Understanding the recursive nature of thought is important, says Flavell (1985), because communication between adolescents and adults often presupposes this sort of knowledge ("I thought you already knew I'd sold my car").

This progression in the ability to infer another's thoughts and intentions is reflected in chil-

Table 11.2
Stage of Social Role-Taking

Stage 0	
Egocentric viewpoint (about 3 to 6 years)	Children cannot distinguish between their own thoughts and feelings and those of another. Children do not realize that other people's thoughts, feelings, intentions, and motivation may differ from their own.
Stage 1	
Social-informational role-taking (about 6 to 8 years)	Children know that others have their own views but believe that those views differ from theirs because they are based on different information. Children cannot judge their own actions from another's viewpoint.
Stage 2	
Self-reflective role-taking (about 8 to 10 years)	Children know that others' views are based on their own purposes or set of values. They can anticipate another person's judgment of their own actions. Yet they still cannot consider their own view and that of another at the same time.
Stage 3	
Mutual role-taking (about 10 to 12 years)	Children know that both they and another person can simultaneously consider their own view and that of the other. They can step outside an interaction with another person and see how a third party would interpret it.
Stage 4	
Social and conventional system role-taking (about 12 to 15 years and older)	Children are aware of the shared point of view of the social system (social conventions). Children realize that mutual awareness of views does not always lead to complete understanding.

Source: Adapted from Selman, 1976.

dren's increasing ability to take the role of another. By asking children about the feelings, thoughts, and intentions of characters in a series of stories, Robert Selman (1976; 1980) charted the development of role-taking ability. The stories revolved around dilemmas of childhood, as when a little girl who had been forbidden to climb trees discovers that she can rescue a friend's cat from a tree only by climbing after it. Selman believes that children move through five stages of role-taking, which are described in Table 11.2. These stages are related to children's ability to understand other differences between their own perspective (such as visual experience) and that of another. In Selman's view, children first understand the recursive nature of thought when they are about ten years old and have entered the stage of mutual role-taking.

Morality

When Piaget (1932/1965) questioned Swiss children about the rules that governed their marble games, he was studying their moral judgment. He believed that the rule system of children's games embodied their understanding of right and wrong. Earlier we saw how the socialization process contributes to the development of internalized moral standards (see Chapter 9). Now we follow Piaget's lead and explore the development of children's ability to reason about moral issues and how they justify their moral judgments.

Piaget's Theory   Piaget believed that young children's view of morality was limited by egocentrism and their deep respect for adults. Their loss of egocentrism and their experiences with their peers led not only to a realization that rules could be changed but also to a move from one stage of morality to another.

Young children were governed by the **morality of constraint,** in which virtuous conduct is based on obedience to authority. Transgressions are inevitably punished, perhaps by accidents or some other misfortune—a concept known as **immanent** justice. In one of his studies, Piaget (1932/1965) told children about a boy who stole some apples and then fell through a rotten bridge into the river. The younger children (86 percent of the six-year-olds and 73 percent of the seven- and eight-year-olds) felt that the boy had been justly punished. Asked if the boy would have fallen into the water if he had not stolen, a seven-year-old gave a typical answer: "No . . . Because he would not have done wrong" (Piaget, 1932/1965, p. 254). In the second stage, known as the **morality of cooperation,** morality is based on what is expected, fair, or just. Transgressions are not always punished, but a fair punishment should not be arbitrary. The culprit should receive a similar injury (one blow for each blow struck) or should make some kind of restitution.

Piaget realized that both of these moralities could exist side by side, that a child might apply the morality of constraint to one action and the morality of cooperation to another. As children grew older, they increasingly judged moral situations in terms of the morality of cooperation.

Kohlberg's View of Moral Reasoning   Building on Piaget's analysis of moral development, Lawrence Kohlberg (1969; Colby, Kohlberg, Gibbs, and Lieberman, 1983) proposed that moral reasoning passes through a series of six stages. Each succeeding stage builds on the preceding stage, reorganizing that understanding into a more complex and balanced view of morality. These stages were based on the replies to a series of moral dilemmas by fifty-eight boys between the ages of ten and sixteen. The boys responded to nine dilemmas, in which human needs or welfare conflicted with the commands of authority or obedience to the law. For example, the boys had to decide whether a physician should supply a dying, pain-ridden cancer patient with a large dose of pain killer that would surely kill her.

None of the decisions reached by the boys affected the way Kohlberg designed the stages; he was interested in the moral reasoning that justified the decisions. A person at any stage may decide either way in a given situation. What distinguishes the stages is the type of concerns that are indicated for self, authority, and society.

Children advance through the stages in an unvarying progression. They must understand the reasoning typical of one stage before they can begin to understand the greater complexities of the next. Each move to a new stage of understanding follows a cognitive conflict that arises when children encounter levels of moral reasoning that are somewhat more advanced than their own. The conflict leads to a reorganization of thought. Kohlberg's first four stages parallel Stages 1 to 4 in Selman's theory of social role-taking, and each stage indicates increased skill in taking another's roles. In each of Kohlberg's stages, children look at moral issues in a new and different way, although they continue to understand the reasoning of previous stages.

The proposed six stages form three basic developmental levels of moral reasoning, distinguished by what defines right or moral action. The first two stages form what is called the **premoral level,** because values simply reflect external pressure, and the dominant motives are to avoid punishment (Stage 1) and to serve your own needs and interests (Stage 2). The next two stages form the **conventional level,** with value placed in maintaining the conventional social order and the expectations of others. The dominant motives are to be a good person in your own (and other's) eyes (Stage 3) and to avoid breakdowns in the social system (Stage 4). The final two stages form the **principled level;** at this level, value resides in principles and standards that can be shared. The dominant motives are a sense of obligation to the social contract (Stage 5) and the belief in the validity of universal moral principles (Stage 6). Because it is often difficult to distinguish between stages at any level (Kurtines and Greif, 1974), our discussion focuses on the levels of moral reasoning.

Several factors affect the speed with which children (and adults) move through the various levels. After following the boys in the original study for twenty years, Kohlberg and his associates (Colby et al., 1983) concluded that the levels were related to age (see Figure 11.4). Most of the individuals in this study continued to rely on conventional reasoning, but the proportion of premoral reasoning declined steadily after the age of ten, and the use of Stage 3 reasoning began declining in adolescence. Principled reasoning did not appear until the boys reached young adulthood—and it developed in only 10 percent of them. Socioeconomic level also was related to progression through the stages, an indication that the type of experience the boys encountered affected their

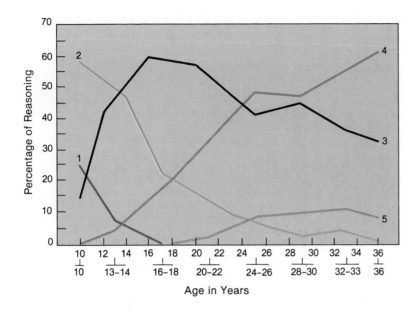

FIGURE 11.4   This figure shows the mean proportion of reasoning at each of Kohlberg's stages for each age group. As the boys matured, premoral reasoning (Stages 1 and 2) gradually disappeared, and advanced conventional reasoning (Stage 4) became more prevalent than early conventional reasoning (Stage 3). Postconventional reasoning (Stage 5) first appeared toward the end of adolescence but never accounted for more than 10 percent of moral thought. *(From Colby, Kohlberg, Gibbs, and Lieberman, 1983)*

moral reasoning. Each stage appeared earlier among the middle class, with only one working-class man ever reaching the principled level. Formal education was a third important factor. In the final analysis, every man who reasoned on the principled level had completed college.

In its final form, Kohlberg's model of moral development represents a response to criticism of the original version. He revised the scoring system to reflect the structural moral features of people's reasoning instead of its content. He eliminated Stage 6, which was difficult to distinguish from Stage 5 — and which none of the original subjects reached under the revised scoring system. In fact, the new scoring system drops the proportion of principled reasoners from 40 percent to 10 percent.

What were the major criticisms of Kohlberg's original system? Research had indicated that there was little uniformity in people's moral reasoning (M. Hoffman, 1984). A person who justified a decision by principled reasoning in one situation might fall back on conventional reasoning in another. It seemed that reasoning about right and wrong depended more on context and on personal needs than Kohlberg's principled stages suggested (Saltzstein, 1983). Individuals did not always progress forward through the stages, and one out of fourteen actually slipped backward (Rest, 1983). Elizabeth Simpson (1974) concluded that the theory is culturally biased and not universal,

because it is based on a social organization and values that fit only Western culture. Kohlberg's focus on issues of equality, rights, and justice reflects the values of a constitutional democracy. The formal abstract thinking that characterizes principled reasoning seems to require a level of education that puts it beyond most of the people in the world.

Because no females were included in Kohlberg's research, argues Carol Gilligan (1982), the system contains a built-in masculine bias. Women are socialized to equate goodness with helping others and tend to see moral problems as the result of conflicting responsibilities. Kohlberg's theory equates moral development with the acceptance of justice, so that moral problems arise from competing rights. Because women base their reasoning on the values of compassion, responsibility and obligation, they automatically are placed at a lower stage of moral development than men. To most women, Kohlberg's morality of rights and noninterference seems to justify indifference and lack of concern. Gilligan believes that a theory of moral development that applies to both sexes must incorporate an ethic of care as well as an ethic of justice.

Martin Hoffman (1984) carries these criticisms further, contending that the theory's most fundamental problem is still Kohlberg's basic assumption that a universal principle of justice or fairness exists. If the premise is not accepted, there are no grounds for assuming that moving toward a morality based on justice indicates an advance in moral reasoning.

Is there any relation between people's level of reasoning on Kohlberg's scale and their moral behavior? There does appear to be some connection between the two, but the connection is not impressive. In an analysis of seventy-five studies, Augusto Blasi (1980) found that moral judgment and behavior were significantly related in 76 percent of the studies but that the connection was not strong. Moral judgment is only one player in a large cast, suggests James Rest (1983). People differ in the way they apply their thinking to a particular situation, in the degree to which religious or ideological doctrines influence their sense of fairness, in the way they interpret possible courses of action, in the way they integrate the various considerations that affect a situation, in the course of action they select, and in the way they execute their decision.

A somewhat different approach to moral reasoning has been put forward by William Damon (1977), who separates the domain into four areas: (1) friendship, (2) justice and fairness, (3) obedience and authority, and (4) social rules and conventions. He argues that children develop separate moral concepts in each area, so that their judgments would not be consistent in all situations. Preschoolers think that it is naughtier to violate a moral code (stealing cookies) than to violate a social convention (talking during naptime) (Smetana, 1985).

In a study that explored the domain of justice and fairness, children as young as five were able to separate accidental damage not only from intentional damage, but also from damage due to negligence (Shultz, Wright, and Schleifer, 1986). They assigned the most responsibility when damage (a smashed model airplane, a lost balloon, a ripped poster, a wrecked kite, a torn beach ball) was intentional, least when it was accidental. Although five-year-olds assigned more blame for accidental damage than older children did (see Figure 11.5), they considered negligence in assigning blame and

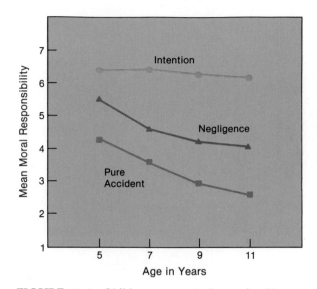

FIGURE 11.5   Children were asked to assign blame for similar types of damage, depending on whether the damage was caused by intent, negligence, or accident. Even five-year-olds were able to make the distinction. *(From Shultz, Wright, and Schliefer, 1986)*

weighed whether the culprit had made restitution when recommending punishment. The researchers contend that although these children cannot justify their moral judgments in terms that would place them very high on Kohlberg's scale, they use the same ideas as their elders do. But they are unable to reveal their understanding in the context of a typical moral reasoning experiment.

Children's understanding of others and of their moral responsibilities develops slowly, hand in hand with their ability to apply their growing cognitive skills to the physical world. Although young children are more capable than researchers once believed, their lack of experience and their inability to handle much information at one time makes it difficult for them to show their abilities in most situations. In the next chapter, we watch children applying their developing ability to learn and reason in the context of the classroom.

SUMMARY

1. According to Piaget, the **preoperational thought** of the preschool child is intuitive, inflexible, contradictory, and focused on individual events. Preschoolers are incapable of mental **operations** (flexible, rigorous, and logical thought). Preschoolers are probably more capable than Piaget believed, but an intellectual revolution does occur sometime between the ages of four and ten. As a result of this revolution, children's thought changes in five ways. (1) They acquire the concept of **identity** and understand that objects and people remain the same even if irrelevant properties are changed. (2) **Centration,** in which children's attention is so captured by a prominent feature of the stimulus that they **encode** only that aspect, gives way to decentered attention. (3) Thinking gains **reversibility,** so that children can mentally reverse processes or changes in appearance. (4) Learning becomes self-regulated and strategic. (5) Language becomes instrumental for thinking. As children acquire various strategies, they show **production deficiencies,** in which they are capable of executing a strategy but do not use it spontaneously.

2. The schoolchild is capable of **concrete operational thought,** in which he or she can think flexibly and apply logic to concrete objects. A typical concrete operation is **conservation,** in which children understand that irrelevant changes in an object's external appearance do not affect its quantity. After the conservation of liquid and solid quantity is established, other aspects of conservation emerge more slowly. Children's ability to conserve depends on the changes of the intellectual revolution, as well as on increased **cognitive capacity.** Before children grasp the essential reversible aspects of conservation, they conserve by applying the concept of identity.

3. According to Piaget, young children's understanding of causality is guided by three concepts: **finalism** (believing nothing happens by accident), **artificialism** (inability to separate physical from nonphysical causes), and **animism** (the tendency to believe that objects are alive). Preschool children are less animistic than Piaget believed, and they seem to ascribe thoughts, feelings, or life to inanimate objects primarily when they lack the knowledge required to make a correct judgment. They also understand that causes precede effects, but their grasp of causality is incomplete.

4. When shown up to three objects, children often **subitize,** and detect the difference between arrays without counting. However, even two-year-olds count, although many can count only as far as two. By the time they start kindergarten, most children understand the structure of the number system and have grasped some rudiments of mathematical reasoning.

5. When preschoolers scan, their attention is caught by the center of interest, and they scan from that point, they glance randomly, and tend to stop scanning before they have the needed information. Older children scan exhaustively and systematically, without being distracted by irrelevant information. Part of this difference may be due to the young child's lack of conscious control over his or her attention.

6. **Memory** is the application of cognitive processes to the storage and retrieval of information. Children's memory improves with age because of their increased knowledge store, their grasp of **strategies** (voluntary, conscious techniques that aid memory), and their understanding of how memory works **(metamemory).** Storage strategies include **rehearsal** (repeating material that is to be remembered) and **organization** (grouping items around some common element), and children show production deficiences in the development of each one. As metamemory develops and children understand the value of strategies, they begin developing and using them. Children apparently solve problems by applying mental rules, which become more sophisticated with age. The context of a problem often determines whether a child will be able to solve it.

7. **Metacognition** refers to our knowledge about

cognition and the ways in which cognitive activity is controlled. Children's control over their learning, thinking, and problem solving is referred to as the *executive management* of thinking. When applying executive management, children evaluate their current knowledge and performance, plan actions that will allow them to reach their goal, and show self-regulation (checking their progress and adjusting their cognitive activity).

8. Understanding what another person can see is the least social and most cognitive aspect of social cognition. Preschoolers attempt to adapt their speech to the needs of others, but their understanding of those needs seems to parallel their grasp of the other person's visual perspective. Five- and six-year-olds' inability to plan and monitor their thinking seems connected with their difficulty in judging the adequacy of others' communications.

9. Until children understand that others may have different thoughts, motives, or intentions, they see others primarily in terms of their external appearances and activities. Children find it easier to infer intentions than to infer thoughts and do not understand the recursive nature of thought until they are about eight years old. At this time, children begin to see others in terms of traits and abilities. As children are able to infer thoughts and intentions, they become increasingly skilled at role-taking.

10. According to Piaget, most young children are governed by the **morality of constraint.** They stress obedience to authority and believe in **immanent justice** (the inevitable punishment of transgressions). Older children are more likely to follow the **morality of cooperation.** They stress fairness and justice and know that transgressions are not always punished. After assessing boys' reactions to posed moral dilemmas, Lawrence Kohlberg proposed that moral reasoning goes through six stages, in a progressive series of developmental levels: the **premoral level,** the **conventional level,** and the **principled level.** The levels seem related to age and formal education and may describe the development of moral judgment only among men in constitutional democracies. The connection between moral reasoning and behavior is positive, although not strong. William Damon contends that moral judgment varies because children develop separate moral concepts in the realms of friendship, justice and fairness, obedience and authority, and social rules and conventions.

KEY TERMS

animism	finalism	premoral level
artificialism	identity	preoperational thought
basic categories	immanent justice	principled level
centration	memory	production deficiency
class inclusion	metacognition	rehearsal
cognitive capacity	metamemory	reversibility
concrete-operational thought	morality of constraint	strategy
conservation	morality of cooperation	subitize
conventional level	operations	superordinate category
encode	organization	

STUDY TERMS

centration   The concentration of attention on a prominent feature of a stimulus, to the exclusion of all other aspects of the situation.

concrete-operational thought   Thought during the third stage of Piaget's theory, which begins when children are about seven and lasts until about age eleven. Thought is flexible and logical but only in regard to concrete objects and situations.

conservation   The understanding that irrelevant changes in the physical appearance of objects do not affect their quantity, mass, weight, or volume; conservation is one of Piaget's concrete operations.

identity   In Piaget's theory, the understanding that objects and people remain the same even if irrelevant properties are changed.

metacognition   Knowledge about cognition and an understanding of the ways in which a person can control his or her own cognitive activity.

metamemory   An understanding of the workings of memory; one aspect of metacognition.

operations   Flexible and rigorous cognitive processes that first appear during the concrete-operational stage.

preoperational thought   Thought during the second stage in Piaget's theory, which begins at about two years and lasts until about seven years. Children record their experiences symbolically, but their thought is intuitive, inflexible, contradictory, and focuses on individual events.

production deficiency   The failure to use a skill or capacity that a person possesses.

reversibility   The understanding that irrelevant changes in appearance can be reversed and that such changes tend to compensate one another; reversibility is one of Piaget's concrete operations.

CHAPTER 12

Cognition: Intelligence and Schooling

Ronald was a quiet fourth grader who rarely spoke up in class. He never caused trouble, and his teacher usually let him work alone at his desk. But Ronald gradually fell further behind in his work. Concerned, the teacher began to watch him more closely. She discovered that Ronald spent his seatwork time drawing pictures and watching the other students. Then he tried to copy someone else's work. By the middle of the year, Ronald had slipped to nearly the bottom of the class in reading and math. His teacher recommended him for psychoeducational testing. The school psychologist administered several tests, including a standard intelligence test, and over several months talked regularly with Ronald. From the report prepared by the psychologist, the teacher learned that Ronald's IQ score was above average; he should have been performing much better in the classroom. Ronald's problem seemed one of attitudes and expectations, not ability. Ronald's father did not live at home, and his mother had the entire responsibility for the care of Ronald, his two brothers, and his sister. She had warned Ronald not to cause trouble at school, because she was too busy to come in and straighten things out with the teacher. She paid little attention to her children's school progress, and Ronald had adopted her low expectations

309

for his academic success. He spent more time avoiding the teacher than trying to learn. His low motivation and his pessimistic view of his own abilities kept Ronald from succeeding at tasks he was clearly capable of handling.

Without the testing program, Ronald probably would have been labeled as "mentally slow" and consigned to school failure. Yet in recent years, IQ tests have come under vigorous attack. In some places, the tests have been misused. They have been used to excuse bad education for minority groups. They have pinned the lethal label "retarded" on children whose major problem was lack of exposure to the dominant culture, and they have set up self-fulfilling prophecies by persuading teachers that certain children could not succeed. But IQ tests also have rescued other children, by revealing that their school failure was not due to cognitive problems. They have identified gifted children whose talents had gone unnoticed by their teachers. And they have provided children in disadvantaged homes a way to move out of poverty (Tyler, 1976).

In this chapter, we investigate the nature of intelligence and its connection with school. In an attempt to decide just what intelligence is, we look at various theories of intelligence and their implications for schooling. Then we examine the tests themselves, discover how they are constructed and scored, and explore alternative ways to measure cognitive skills. Considering what influences IQ scores gives us an opportunity to examine the controversy over race and IQ. Next we take up the question of exceptional intellectual development in both gifted and retarded children. With this background, we turn to schooling. We look at the development of skill in reading, writing, and arithmetic, and we note the connection between metacognitive skills and success in all academic areas. The chapter closes with a consideration of motivation and the role it plays in successful learning.

WHAT IS INTELLIGENCE?

When we say that someone is intelligent, what do we mean? If we looked at intelligence from an evolutionary standpoint, we would say that it reflected our ability to adapt to the demands of the environment. Without it, our species could not have survived long enough to leave any descendants. This description, although accurate, is not especially helpful when we try to analyze the concept of intelligence. Researchers have been trying to come up with a satisfactory definition for decades but have not been able to reach any agreement. Deciding just what characterizes intelligence is important because our definition of intelligence affects the way we try to assess it and how we train intellectual skills — or whether we even attempt to train them.

Information-Processing Views

Researchers who take an information-processing view believe that intelligence derives from the processes used to represent and manipulate information. Differences in intelligence develop because people vary in the efficiency and speed with which they carry out these basic processes.

When analyzing the primary abilities that determine intelligence, Raymond Cattell (1971) and John Horn (1968) found that they could group most of them into two categories: fluid and crystallized intelligence. **Fluid intelligence** is based on the ability to perceive, encode, and reason about information. It includes abstract, nonverbal reasoning, and problem-solving skills, and it reflects the ability to deal with novel information and novel situations. Fluid intelligence is developed through casual learning; its skills are neither taught in school nor pushed by the culture (Horn, 1984). **Crystallized intelligence** is based on the ability to understand relationships, make judgments, and solve problems that depend on schooling or cultural experience. It includes verbal skills and mechanical knowledge, and it reflects the ability to handle well-learned information in familiar situations. Crystallized intelligence is developed as a person learns facts and absorbs information that is emphasized by the culture.

An information-processing view put forth by Joseph Campione and Ann Brown (1979) uses a different two-part system of intelligence. The first part, called the **architectural system,** is biologically based and consists of basic cognitive processes. It includes memory capacity, the rate at which information is lost, and the speed with which the individual encodes, manipulates, and

Older children equate intelligence with a vast store of information. To them, the most intelligent child is the one who always wins at Trivial Pursuit. *(Miro Vintoniv/The Picture Cube)*

retrieves information. The second part, called the **executive system,** is heavily dependent on training and experience and consists of higher-order processes. It includes all organized knowledge, learning strategies, and metacognitive skills.

The **triarchic theory,** proposed by Robert Sternberg (1985), is a broad view of intelligence that includes social, educational, and situational factors that affect the development and exercise of intelligence. As its name implies, the triarchic theory encompasses three subtheories: the componential, the contextual, and the experiential. The *componential subtheory* breaks down the structures and mechanisms of intelligence into three types of components, each with its own function. Metacomponents are higher-order processes that correspond to executive control (see Chapter 11). They plan, monitor, regulate, and evaluate performance on any task. *Performance components* are lower-order processes that execute the plans and decisions of the metacomponents. *Knowledge-acquisition* components are lower-order processes involved in learning new information.

The other two subtheories are concerned with how the components of intelligence are used to deal with the world. The *experiential subtheory* refers to the attributes of tasks or situations that measure intelligence. It focuses on the individual's ability to deal with tasks and situations that are outside normal experience and to process infor-

mation automatically when carrying out complex tasks. The *contextual subtheory* places intelligence in a sociocultural setting that draws on the practical and social aspects of intelligence. It focuses on the mental activity involved in adapting to the environment, selecting a new environment, or shaping the present environment to match a person's needs. Sternberg's theory integrates the individual's inner world (components), experience, and the external world. It leads researchers to consider how people use their mental abilities to solve relevant problems in a variety of settings.

Factor Theories

A second group of theories is based on the attempt to understand intelligence in terms of abilities instead of processes. The task that faces adherents to **factor theories** is determining just what those abilities are and how many of them are involved. In their search for these abilities, most researchers use a technique called **factor analysis.** In factor analysis, the scores on a set of tests are correlated. Clusters of highly correlated scores indicate a factor that seems to underlie the differences among scores. This factor presumably reflects a common mental ability.

The first factor theory was put forth by Charles Spearman (1927), who proposed that intelligence was dominated by a single major factor, called *g* (general mental ability). Although other specific (*s*) factors existed, each of them was confined to a single ability. All intellectual activities relied on *g*, which involved seeing and manipulating the relations among bits of information.

Other theorists contended that intelligence was not as unified as Spearman had believed. Their research pointed to many more factors, although they could not agree on whether there were as few as seven or as many as 150. Louis Thurstone (1947) identified seven primary intellectual abilities: verbal comprehension, word fluency, number, space, memory, perceptual speed, and reasoning. Yet after Thurstone had identified these factors and devised tests for each of them, he discovered that people's scores on the various tests were correlated. A person who made high scores on a vocabulary test (which measured verbal comprehension) also tended to make high scores on arithmetic tests (number) or when recalling lists of unrelated words (memory). It appeared that some general mental ability might affect performance on many tasks.

Intelligence became much more complicated in J. P. Guilford's (1982) theory. Guilford first proposed a complex set of 120 interconnecting factors, although later analysis pushed the total to 150. He arranged these factors according to whether they involved what the person was thinking about (contents of thought), the mental processes used to think about them (operations), or the results of thinking (products). Each factor resulted from the interaction of one type of content (a list of words) with one of the operations (memory) and one kind of product (units). In this case, the activity would result in remembering a list of words.

Researchers still cannot agree on the number of factors that are involved in intelligence. Because they begin their search for factors by using different tests, each of which presents a different range of problems and demands different kinds of answers, disagreement over the type and number of factors is almost guaranteed. One factor is probably too few to describe intelligence adequately, but when the number of factors passes 100, it is impossible to chart the interrelation of the factors and distill the essential elements of intelligence. The question remains open.

Piaget's Cognitive Structures

In Piaget's (1976) theory, intelligence is demonstrated by the way people adapt to the environment. Underlying intelligence are the cognitive structures of thought, which differ sharply at different ages, and which he described in his stages of cognitive development. Babies develop intelligence by interacting with the environment. This interaction involves maturation, experience with the physical environment, the influence of the social environment, and the child's own self-regulatory processes, which keep trying to reestablish an equilibrium. The first signs of intelligence appear during the sensorimotor period, when the baby repeats actions in order to make interesting sights last (Substage 3). This intelligence, said Piaget, is controlled by things in the environment. Systematic intelligence does not appear until babies become conscious of the relation between their actions and the behavior of objects (Substage 5). This consciousness allows them to adapt their actions to specific situations and to solve problems through trial and error.

Because Piaget was primarily interested in the nature of the structures underlying children's thought (for example, reversibility, seriation), he paid little attention to the thought processes involved or how the components of a child's performance changed with age (Sternberg and Powell, 1983). Instead of analyzing individual differences among children in various situations (performance), he tried to discover what most children knew at successive points of development (competence).

HOW DO WE MEASURE INTELLIGENCE?

Their inability to agree on a single definition of intelligence has not stopped psychologists from trying to measure it. Early researchers tried to rate intelligence on the basis of sensitivity to physical stimuli and reaction times, but these nineteenth-century attempts almost convinced psychologists that the task was hopeless (Sternberg and Powell,

This child is working at items from the performance scale of the Stanford-Binet test. Such items as duplicating a block design depend less on cultural experience than do items on the verbal scale. *(Photos by John Oldenkamp with permission of the Houghton Mifflin Company from Terman and Merrill Stanford-Binet Intelligence Scale)*

1983). Then, in 1904, the French Ministry of Education hired psychologists Alfred Binet and Théophile Simon to construct a test that would identify children who were failing in school but who might be able to learn in special classes. They devised a set of problems that emphasized judgment, comprehension, and reasoning — the qualities that the two psychologists considered the core of intelligence (Binet and Simon, 1916).

The problems were grouped by age level; for example, all tests passed by 90 percent of normal five-year-olds were put at the five-year-level. Children's performance was rated in the same way. A seven-year-old who answered questions the way most nine-year-olds did was assigned a **mental age** of nine, as was a twelve-year-old who answered the questions similarly. Binet and Simon were so successful that psychologists around the world began translating the test into their own languages and using it to identify schoolchildren with learning problems as well as those who were doing exceptionally well. The **psychometric,** or mental-testing, approach was under way.

Modern Intelligence Tests

The Binet-Simon test would not have been adopted so rapidly unless psychologists and educa-

tors had needed some way to assess children's cognitive skills. If they could determine the basis of a child's difficulty in school, they reasoned, perhaps they could select a program that would give the youngster a better chance of succeeding at academic tasks. In 1916, Lewis Terman and his associates at Stanford University adapted the Binet-Simon test for American children. Over the years, the test, now known as the Stanford-Binet test, has been revised several times in order to reflect changes in the culture and the educational system. The current version, which was revised in 1972, can be given to individuals of any age, from two years to adulthood. *Individuals* is the key word, because the Stanford-Binet is an individual intelligence test administered to one child by a highly trained examiner.

The Stanford-Binet is made up of various subtests, grouped by age. Some of the tests assess verbal ability. For example, a child may be asked to tell what the pair of words *apple* and *peach* have in common or to answer questions about common activities. Other tests, known as *performance* tests, are nonverbal. They require the child to string beads, build blocks, match pictures, or to add features to an incomplete drawing. The examiner begins by asking the child questions from a level for a slightly younger person, then gradually moves up the scale, asking more difficult questions, until the child can answer none of them. Should the child have difficulty with the first questions, the examiner drops back to items for a younger child. From the pattern of answers, the examiner computes the child's score.

Another set of popular tests was constructed by psychologist David Wechsler, who needed a test to use with adult patients at Bellevue Hospital in New York City. After devising the Wechsler Adult Intelligence Scale (WAIS), he added the Wechsler Intelligence Scale for Children (WISC) and the Wechsler Preschool and Primary Scale of Intelligence (WPPSI) for children from four to six and one-half years old. Like the Stanford-Binet, the Wechsler tests are designed to be given individually. Unlike the Stanford-Binet, Wechsler's tests have separate verbal and performance scales, each with its own score. Tests on the verbal scale include general information questions ("How many nickels make a dime?"), general comprehension questions ("Why should people not waste fuel?"), arithmetic questions, similarities ("In what way are a shoe and slipper alike?"), vocabulary items, and tests of digit span (repeating a series of numbers). Tests on the performance scale require children to complete pictures (a rabbit with a missing ear), to arrange pictures in chronological order, to reproduce block designs, to assemble small objects, to match symbols with numbers on the basis of an arbitrary code, and to trace routes through mazes.

As the variety of subtests indicate, test makers assume that different tasks measure different aspects of intelligence. Some of the items in the tests depend on the child's experience. This is especially true of items on the verbal scale, except, perhaps, digit span. In Cattell and Horn's terms, these items test crystallized intelligence. Many of the items on the performance scale depend less on school experience; they may be tapping fluid intelligence. For example, a child should be able to assemble blocks in a design without having gone to school.

Scoring Intelligence Tests

Binet and Simon used a child's mental age as the score on their original tests. But unless educators knew the relation between a child's mental and chronological age, they had no way of assessing how retarded or advanced that child was compared with other youngsters of the same age. A child with a mental age of ten may be brilliant (if the chronological age is seven), a little slow (if the chronological age is eleven), or mildly retarded (if the chronological age is thirteen). To solve the problem, German psychologist William Stern (1914) suggested using the ratio between the child's mental and chronological ages to represent the child's level of intelligence. He called this ratio the child's *intelligence quotient*, or *IQ score*, which he produced by dividing the mental age by the chronological age and multiplying the result by 100 (to get rid of the decimals).

Although the tests are still called IQ tests, modern IQs no longer represent the ratio between a child's mental and chronological ages. Instead, the IQ is actually a "deviation IQ." Test makers construct the tests so that a child whose score is the same as the average score of all children of that age who take the test will make the standard score of 100. Today's scores show how far a child's IQ deviates from the average score of his or her own age group. About 68 percent of people fall within one standard deviation, or 15 points, of the average score of 100, and 95 percent fall within two standard deviations, or 30 points, of the average. This means that an IQ score is not an absolute measure of mental capacity. It is simply a descriptive statistic relating a child's present performance to that of other children of the same chronological age.

An Alternative Measure of Intelligence

IQ tests measure what a child knows at the moment he or she sits down to take the test. Some psychologists believe that this static assessment does not always reveal what the child might be able to learn. Recently, some psychologists have begun developing **dynamic assessment** tests, which evaluate what the child is prepared to learn, given a little assistance. Instead of measuring the child's current developmental level, these tests explore the child's zone of proximal development (see Chapter 2).

The need for such a test became clear to Reuven

FIGURE 12.1   In Exercise 1, the student is to trace broken lines so that some of the squares appear to be on top of others. This exercise helps students learn to control impulsiveness because darkening lines without thinking carefully leads to mistakes. In Exercise 2, the student who explains how the water disappeared from the pot is learning to see objects and events in relation to one another. *(From Feuerstein, Rand, Hoffman, and Miller, 1980)*

Feuerstein when he began working in Israel with displaced Jewish children who had survived the Holocaust (Chance, 1981). These children had spent most of their lives sleeping in doorways and struggling to survive life in concentration camps. Their IQ scores indicated that they were retarded, yet few had had any opportunity to learn. Feuerstein and his associates developed the Learning Potential Assessment Device, a performance scale that does not draw on knowledge of reading or arithmetic or the child's store of general knowledge. The testing session is actually a tutorial, in which the examiner's goal is to find out what the child *can* learn. And so the examiner intervenes continually, asking for explanations and giving them, asking for repetitions, summing up the test experiences, warning the child about possible difficulties, and attempting to prod the child into reflective, insightful thinking.

When the children were tested in this way, it became apparent that many "mentally retarded" children could become competent thinkers. Feuerstein discovered that most children who did poorly on IQ tests shared several tendencies. They were impulsive; they failed to recognize the discrepancies that were the key to thought problems; they viewed events and objects in isolation instead of in context; they routinely failed to make comparisons; and they had poor spatial orientation.

From his work with Israeli children, Feuerstein and his associates (Feuerstein, Rand, Hoffman, and Miller, 1980) developed a program known as FIE (Feuerstein's Instrumental Enrichment). The program, made up of more than 500 pages of increasingly complex pencil-and-paper exercises, teaches thinking skills (see Figure 12.1). It requires hour-long sessions with a teacher three times each week over a two- or three-year period. During the course of the program, children learn to identify basic principles of thinking and practice monitoring their use of these principles. The teacher continually bridges back and forth between the principles and their application to various aspects of life.

In the United States, Joseph Campione and his associates (Campione, Brown, Ferrara, and Bryant, 1984; Ferrara, Brown, and Campione, 1986) also have used dynamic assessment techniques to evaluate children's ability to grasp the principles of inductive reasoning. In initial sessions, children learn to work series-completion problems and progressive matrices. When a child is unable to solve a problem, he or she is given a series of hints (as many as but no more than necessary). Before the session ends, the child learns the rules that govern the problem's solution. In later sessions, the child gets similar problems as well as problems that require him or her to combine old rules or figure out slightly different rules. The ease with which children can do this indicates their ability to transfer their learning to new situations.

Such tests give educators a way to measure the

width of the child's zone of proximal development: they show just how much instruction a child requires in order to learn. One advantage of such tests is that they can uncover hidden potential—children who are ready to move ahead but who would be denied the opportunity on the basis of traditional tests. They also can pinpoint a child's strengths and weaknesses. Some of the children in these studies learned quickly but had trouble transferring that learning to a new situation; others learned slowly but transferred the learning swiftly.

INFLUENCES ON IQ SCORES

Since IQ tests were first developed to assess children with learning problems, they have been used widely in American schools. Although Stanford-Binet and Wechsler tests are used with only a few children, most youngsters periodically take some sort of group test that assesses IQ. As we have seen, the scores of most children fall between 85 and 115, and all but a handful score between 70 and 130. What influences determine whether a child scores near the bottom of that range or near the top? In searching for the determinants of IQ, researchers try to explain the **variance** in IQ scores, which means they try to account for the difference between the child's IQ and the average IQ of 100.

Heredity clearly has some effect on a child's score. As with other aspects of development, genes and environment interact to determine development. In Chapter 3, we saw that each person's genetic make-up results in an individual reaction range of possible responses to environmental situations. Each person's reaction range for the skills tapped by IQ tests is fairly wide (25 points), and aspects of the child's environment determine just where along that range IQ will develop.

Family Characteristics and IQ Scores

The home environment is one important influence on cognitive development. As we saw in Chapter 3, the home does not escape genetic influence, because the parents' genes (which the child shares) affect the parents' selection of experiences that are available to the growing child (Scarr and McCartney, 1983). Some family influences are general and experienced by all children in the family. These general influences, called "between-family influences," include whether the parents encourage achievement, how responsive they are to the child's questions and interests, the presence of stimulating toys and books in the home, educational opportunities provided by the parents, parents' teaching styles, whether they value intellectual achievement, and whether they provide models of such achievement. Behavioral geneticists who study adopted children conclude that these between-family differences explain only a small part of the variance in IQ scores (Plomin, DeFries, and McClearn, 1980).

Yet Lois Hoffman (1985) believes that adoption studies underestimate the home's general influence. They do not actually examine the quality of the environment. Hoffman questions whether the parents' IQ is an adequate measure of the home environment, particularly within the narrow range of IQ scores that adoptive parents represent.

One of the important between-family influences is the number of children in the home. As we saw in Chapter 10, children from large families tend to have lower IQ scores than children from small families. This relationship appears to have been consistent for at least the past century. Although IQ records were not available, researchers obtained scores from a vocabulary test (which correlates highly with WAIS scores) for more than 12,000 people born between 1894 and 1964. When they examined the test scores, the researchers discovered that no matter which birth year they examined, the more brothers and sisters a person had, the lower his or her score (Van Court and Bean, 1985).

Other family influences are not shared by all the children in the home. These influences, called "within-family influences," include interactions between siblings, different parental treatment received by different children, cohort differences, illness, separation, birth order, and spacing of children. They also include such individual factors as prenatal exposure to teratogens, premature birth, and malnutrition. Twin studies suggest that these factors account for as much of the variance in IQ scores as do between-family influences (Rowe and Plomin, 1981).

In Chapter 10, we discussed the effects of birth

The physical and psychological environment of the home can encourage cognitive development — or discourage it. (*Junebug Clark/Photo Researchers*)

order and spacing on intelligence. According to confluence theory, the birth of the second child is usually followed by a temporary drop in the IQ of the first-born child. This pattern appeared in the development of children who took part in a longitudinal study in which their IQs were tested every year. When Robert McCall (1984) examined these records, he discovered that within the first two years after the birth of the second child, the first-born's IQ dropped 10 points, compared with the IQ of only children. By the time the children were seventeen years old, the differences were no longer significant. Confluence theory explains this drop by pointing to the family intellectual atmosphere (Zajonc and Hall, 1987). When the new baby arrives, the older child no longer associates primarily with adults, and the levels of conversation and other activities decline. As the older child gets an opportunity to play teacher, his or her IQ score begins to rise again. However, McCall speculates that the decline may develop because the parents become preoccupied with infant care. This strains their relations with the older child and causes them to give the child less attention.

Racial Differences in IQ

By the time a child starts school, the average IQ score of black children is about 15 points below that of white children (Kennedy, 1969). Some psychologists believe that this difference can be traced to primarily environmental influences (Kamin, 1974). Black mothers are less likely to have prenatal care, more likely to have premature births, and less likely to have continuing medical care for their children than white mothers. Most of the between-family influences on IQ favor whites over blacks. Wide differences exist in the social, economic, cultural, motivational, nutritional, and medical situations of blacks and white. Finally, the tests require black youngsters to provide information that they have not encountered in their daily lives. Somehow, all these environmental influences interact to weaken the performance of black children on IQ tests.

A number of studies have indicated that conditions of life in the lower social class operate to depress IQ scores among whites as well as blacks (Hess, 1970; L. Hoffman, 1984a). Because of the history of discrimination in the United States, however, blacks are disproportionately represented in the lower class, so that what appear as racial differences in IQ are in large part social class differences. Yet even controlling for social class does not adequately handle the problem, because blacks are often clustered in the most impoverished part of the lower class.

A few psychologists believe that the differences are genetic. Perhaps the best-known proponent of

Cultural attitudes toward schooling and the belief that effort, not ability, is the secret of academic success may be responsible for the fact that on IQ tests, the average Japanese child scores 11 points higher than the average American child. *(Harriet Gans/The Image Works)*

this view is Arthur Jensen (1980), who contends that heredity accounts for between 50 and 75 percent of the variance between black and white IQ scores.

Jensen's conclusions have been highly controversial. As behavioral geneticists have pointed out (Scarr, 1981), Jensen makes the mistake of assuming that heritability is the same in blacks and whites. Actually, **heritability** is simply an estimate of the genetic contribution to a single trait *within* a given group. It says nothing about any genetic basis for differences in that trait *between* groups. The heritability of intelligence (or any other trait) can change from one year to the next, depending on the nature of the sample used to calculate it. If the group's environment changes radically, so does the heritability of the affected trait. A restricted environment depresses the genes' effects and decreases a trait's heritability; while a highly favorable environment allows the genes full expression and increases heritability. For that reason, says Sandra Scarr (1981), the traits measured by IQ have low heritability among blacks and much higher heritability among whites. In fact, Scarr (Scarr and Kidd, 1983) has suggested that the concept of heritability has so many limitations that it is difficult to apply in any meaningful way.

Racial differences in IQ almost as large as those

between black and white American children appear when test scores of white American children are compared with those of Japanese youngsters (Lynn, 1982). The average score of Japanese children is eleven points higher than the average score of American children. Today, Japanese children's IQs average between 108 and 115—the highest national average IQ in the world. Do these results indicate that Japanese are genetically superior in intelligence? If we relied on Jensen's arguments, we would have to say that they are. The high scores are apparent in children as young as six or seven years old.

The explanation is at least partly environmental. In recent decades, Japanese IQs have risen between 6 and 10 points, and the increase began with children born after World War II. The nutrition, prenatal care, and other factors that led to a postwar increase in birth weights, longevity, and adult height during the same period undoubtedly have had some effect on cognitive development. In addition, Japanese society puts a premium on intellectual skills that it expresses in educational attitudes and practices. Primary education in Japan is different from the education of American children in almost every aspect, as the accompanying box "Cultural Beliefs and School Achievement" indicates.

EXCEPTIONAL INTELLECTUAL DEVELOPMENT

The intelligence of most children and adults falls within a relatively narrow range. As we have seen, 95 percent of people have IQs between 70 and 130. Although differences in that span have important implications in the classroom, they usually go undetected at a picnic, a party, a dance, or a ballgame. Explaining the intellectual development of exceptional individuals—those whose intelligence falls on either side of that 60-point spread—has presented a challenge for psychologists.

Creativity and Talent

How do we explain the flowering of creative genius? Were the cognitive processes of Einstein, Darwin, Freud, Mozart, and Renoir different from those of a banker, a pediatrician, a firefighter, or an elementary school principal? Their creativity—and that of less gifted artists, writers, musicians, and scientists—apparently was not the result of exceptionally high IQs. There seems to be no correlation between IQ and creativity—although creative people generally have IQs at the higher end of the normal range (Wallach, 1985).

For years, psychologists searched for a cognitive skill that was responsible for creativity. This trait would not be tapped by IQ tests, and it would apply to all fields, much as Spearman's *g* applied to all intellectual endeavors. For a time, researchers supposed that creativity was the result of the ability to come up with many unusual ideas or associations, a skill they called **divergent thinking**. So they asked thousands of schoolchildren, musicians, artists, writers, and scientists to think of as many uses as possible for a brick, or everything they could think of that was white and edible, or all the possible occupations in which it would be appropriate to wear a bell on your clothes. Many of these tests turned out to correlate with IQ scores, and the few that did not could not account for creativity (Wallach, 1985). Some people who were good at divergent thinking were not at all creative.

Left without a general cognitive skill to explain creativity, researchers turned to personality. They found that most creative people shared a number of personality characteristics that were not related to IQ scores. Creative individuals showed independent judgment, intuition, flexibility, tolerance for ambiguity (they had no trouble with conflicting interpretations or outcomes), little concern for social norms, and a firm sense of themselves as creative (Janos and Robinson, 1985). This finding indicated that patterns of motivation and life styles might be more important in the encouragement of creativity than cognitive skills (Gallagher and Courtright, 1986).

Other psychologists decided that the notion of intelligence itself might be the problem. If we thought of intelligence as a unified characteristic, we were certain to have trouble with creativity, which just did not fit that construct. Instead, suggested Howard Gardner (1983), we should think of human beings as having "multiple intelligences." Gardner proposed the existence of seven different kinds of intelligence: linguistic, musical, logical-mathematical, spatial, bodily-kinesthetic, and two forms of personal intelligence (access to your own feelings and the ability to notice and make distinctions among other people). Traditional IQ tests measure some (but not all) aspects of linguistic, logical-mathematical, and spatial skills but make no attempt to measure any of the other intelligences. Each of these seven potentials has its own core components, which interact and build upon one another. For example, musical intelligence is based on the processing of tones and rhythms. Heredity, experience, and the interaction of the two determine the profile of each person's intellectual capacities. In this view, creativity is domain-specific. A person who is a creative musician is unlikely to be a creative politician (personal intelligence) or novelist (linguistic intelligence), although each of those intelligences draws on some aspects of the other domains.

How does a Mozart differ from the composer whose musical intelligence is high but who makes only modest strides in music? No matter how large the potential, musical intelligence by itself cannot produce a Mozart. If a person is to make significant creative contributions, other forces are equally important (Feldman, 1986). Mozart was born into a musical family that provided suitable models; he had a supportive environment; he devoted intensive effort to mastering music; and he lived in a society that nurtured and appreciated music. Individuals who make significant creative strides consistently have a background of nurtur-

CULTURAL BELIEFS AND SCHOOL ACHIEVEMENT

Most American parents seem satisfied with the education that their children are getting in elementary schools. Nearly 60 percent of the mothers of American fifth graders reported being "very satisfied" with their children's academic performance, compared with fewer than 10 percent of Taiwanese and Japanese mothers. But American children's knowledge of arithmetic falls far behind that of their Asian counterparts (Stevenson, Lee, and Stigler, 1986). Are Taiwanese and Japanese children brighter than American youngsters? Not at all. When Harold Stevenson and his colleagues (Stevenson et al., 1985) analyzed the cognitive skills of all three groups, they could find no major difference in the level, variability, and structure of these skills.

Yet differences in math achievement among the three countries are striking and the trend disquieting. Small or nonexistent differences among kindergartners become wide gaps among fifth graders, so much so that the average American youngster would be a candidate for remedial help in a Japanese or Taiwanese school (see graph). By fifth grade, the average math score in the *best* American class is about the same as the *worst* Taiwanese class and below the score of the *worst* Japanese class. Although American children read better than Japanese children at all levels tested (kindergarten, first grade, and fifth grade), they do not read as well as Taiwanese at any age, and Japanese fifth graders are beginning to close the gap.

Why should American youngsters know so much less about math than their Asian counterparts? Several factors appear to contribute to the developmental lag. American schoolchildren spend less time in academic activities, do less homework, and get less encouragement at home. American youngsters spend less than half as much class time on academic work (19.6 hours per week) as Chinese children (40.4 hours per week) and just over half as much time as Japanese children (32.6 hours per week). American youngsters are more likely to be out of the classroom during the school day. They spend 18.4 percent of their school time in the office, running errands for the teacher, or in the library, compared with less than 0.2 percent in Taiwan and Japan.

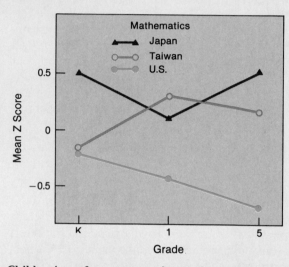

Children's performance on the mathematics test. When scores were averaged by class, the highest-scoring American class ranked below the lowest-scoring Japanese class and just above the lowest-scoring Chinese class. (From Stevenson, Lee, and Stigler, 1986)

American teachers spend a smaller proportion of their time imparting information than teachers in Taiwan and Japan, but they spend a lot more time giving directions.

The homework gap is impressive. According to their mothers, American first graders spend about 14 minutes each weekday on homework and fifth graders spend about 46 minutes. Chinese first graders spend 77 minutes each day, and fifth graders spend 114 minutes each day. Japanese first graders spend 37 minutes and fifth graders 57 minutes. The gap widens to enormous proportions on weekends, when American children do little or no homework and Asian children do almost as much as on weekdays—besides going to school half a day on Saturday.

At this point, the American observer begins to feel sorry for the Asian children slaving away at their desks. But more than 60 percent of Chinese children say that they *enjoy* homework; more than 60 percent of the Japanese children either enjoy it or feel neutral about it. On this side of the Pacific, 60 percent of American children don't like homework at all. How do parents feel about the situation? Parents in all countries thought that their children spent about the right amount of time, although Asian parents were much more likely than American parents to buy math and science workbooks to supplement their children's school assignments. And Asian parents spend significantly more time helping their children with their homework.

The heart of the matter is probably the difference in cultural beliefs about the essential ingredients of success and the value of academic achievement. Both Asian countries prize education, which may help to account for Chinese and Japanese youngsters' feelings about homework. When asked what it takes to succeed in school, American parents said that ability was as important as effort, but Japanese and Taiwanese parents stressed effort. Because American parents place less importance on diligent study, they are comfortable with current school practices—and their children fall farther behind each year. The Second International Mathematics Study compared the mathematics achievement of eighth graders in twenty countries (University of Illinois, 1984). Japanese children were best in the world at arithmetic, algebra, geometry, statistics, and measurement. American children ranked from eighth to eighteenth, depending on the area of math measured.

ance by others, training, and practice. They seem caught up by a powerful desire to become absorbed in their chosen field, and they apply themselves in a way that builds a rapid, extensive knowledge base. Finally, historical and cultural forces must mesh with the person's talent. In the nineteenth-century, scientists with little mathematical ability could make creative advances in their chosen field; today their work would be blocked by their low mathematical intelligence (Siegler and Kotovsky, 1986). Similarly, had Einstein been born in Thailand and raised as a Buddhist, he probably never would have changed Western physics (Feldman, 1986).

What Happens to Intellectually Gifted Children?

It took an extensive longitudinal study to convince the public that children with exceptionally high IQs were not eccentric, maladjusted creatures who became unhappy, friendless adults. In the 1920s, Lewis Terman (1959) collected more than 1,500 California schoolchildren with IQs of at least 135 (their average IQ was 150). He followed these children through their school days and into adult life, interviewing and testing them at regular intervals. The youngsters, who were affectionately known as "Termites," stayed two to four grades ahead of their same-aged schoolmates. Most of them became happy, successful adults. Their average income was four times the national average; their rates of mental illness and suicide were lower than in the general population. Many became national figures in their chosen professions, but none was a creative genius. In fact, as a whole, the group is low on artistic creation (Goleman, 1980).

During the 1960s, researchers looked at the 100 most successful and the 100 least successful men in the group, using professional prestige and income as yardsticks. The major difference between the groups lay in the areas of personality and motivation. Those in the top group had higher levels of aspiration, more drive, and were more persistent than those in the low group. These differences translated into larger incomes, more stable home lives (they were more likely to be married and less likely to be divorced), greater participation in physical sports and recreation, fewer problems with alcohol, and lower death rates.

When the Termites reached their sixties, investigators asked them what had given them most satisfaction in their lives (Goleman, 1980). Men and women agreed that they derived the most satisfaction from their families. Gifted men found that their occupations provided most satisfaction outside the family, but women got more satisfac-

Musical intelligence may be based on the way a child processes tones and rhythms, but if this ability is to flourish into creative genius, family encouragement and modeling are probably essential. *(Michal Heron/Woodfin Camp & Associates)*

tion out of friends, their overall pleasure in life, and cultural events. Yet researchers found the highest satisfaction with their occupation among single employed women and the lowest satisfaction among homemakers who had never had children.

Because less than half of the women in the Terman study were employed full-time in 1960, no analysis of the most and least successful was made. Those who were employed were concentrated in education and high-level clerical and accounting jobs. Although 10 percent of the men were lawyers or judges and 15 percent were scientists, engineers, or architects, less than 2 percent of the women had entered those five professions. The majority of these gifted women devoted their time and energy to their families, and those who did not earned considerably less than their male counterparts.

Most of the Termites were born about 1910, and so their choice of family over career undoubtedly was influenced by gender-role socialization. But what about today's gifted youth? As sex roles are broadening and more women are pursuing careers, are intellectually gifted girls entering traditionally masculine professions in great numbers? Probably not. As Jacquelynne Eccles (1985b) discovered, gifted girls are less likely than gifted boys

to enroll in accelerated programs, to join gifted programs when invited, to remain in the accelerated math track after summer enrichment programs, or to say that they would like to major in math or science. Eccles believes that gender-role socialization affects gifted girls today in about the same way as it affected the girls in Terman's study. The girls' interests and values lead them away from studying math and science. When they do show such interest, parents, educators, and peers tend to discourage it. Gifted girls are less likely than boys to consider such careers, are less likely to perceive themselves as succeeding in them, and regard the cost of engaging in them as too high (giving up more attractive options, going against their gender schema, etc.).

Despite gifted girls' reluctance to enter accelerated programs, some psychologists and educators have concluded that radical acceleration might be the best way of meeting the gifted child's needs. Academically gifted children often become bored or frustrated in school, because they already have mastered most of the curriculum. Some schools try to combat this with an "enriched curriculum," but often the enrichment turns out to be simply more of the same work the other students are doing. (Instead of solving fifteen algebra problems each evening, the gifted child solves thirty.) According to Halbert Robinson (1983), most gifted children expend so little effort in elementary and high school that many never develop good study habits or learn to persevere in the face of difficulty. The demands of higher education may discourage them or even lead them to drop out of college or graduate school. In the program developed by Robinson at the University of Washington, academically precocious five-year-olds are enrolled in a program that allows them to enter college at the age of fourteen.

Some educators have been reluctant to place children in college at such a young age on the grounds that they will be socially isolated and emotionally maladjusted. But most gifted children seem to take such advancement in stride. More than 200 studies have searched for any negative effects from educational acceleration, and not a single one has found any sign of severe or permanent social or emotional harm (Daurio, 1979; Keating, 1979; Robinson, 1983). In one five-year study that matched accelerated adolescents with gifted adolescents who were not accelerated (Pollins, 1983), both groups were well adjusted, socially mature, and effective in interpersonal relations. The accelerated students felt that their fast movement through school had affected their social and emotional development positively, and their educational aspirations were higher than those of the nonaccelerated group.

Mental Retardation

Low scores on an IQ test are not enough to classify children (or adults) as **mentally retarded;** the youngsters also must show impairment in their ability to adapt their behavior to the demands of the environment (American Association on Mental Deficiency, 1977). A child whose scores were more than two standard deviations below normal, but who was able to dress herself, make friends, and meet the other demands of daily life would not be considered mentally retarded. More than 90 percent of mentally retarded people can lead productive lives and require little assistance from others. They can hold jobs, marry, and become successful parents. Their development is primarily characterized by slowness. Out on the playground, they often are indistinguishable from other youngsters.

Stephen Baccus, at age twelve, is typical of academically precocious children who enter college before other children have finished elementary school. Such acceleration seems to have no ill effects and may raise the youngsters' educational aspirations. *(Diego Goldberg/Sygma)*

Genes, biology, and environment are all implicated in mental retardation. About 20 percent of retardation is the result of genetic and biological factors (Robinson and Robinson, 1976). Down's syndrome, Klinefelter's syndrome, and PKU (which we explored in Chapter 3) are among the genetic disorders that lead to mental retardation. Biological causes of retardation include many of the teratogens discussed in Chapter 3, such as lead, alcohol, cocaine, and some prescription drugs. Severe anoxia during the birth process sometimes is followed by retardation, as is birth before a fetus is thirty-three weeks old.

Like most mentally retarded individuals, this adolescent can look forward to a productive, self-sufficient life. *(Elizabeth Crews)*

Even biologically caused retardation is affected by environment. As we saw in Chapter 3, babies with these conditions who grow up in disadvantaged homes are most likely to be retarded. Children with Down's syndrome who grow up at home generally have IQs that are substantially higher than those of Down's children who grow up in institutions (Edgerton, 1979). The power of the environment in the development of retardation becomes especially clear when we recall the institutionalized toddlers in Chapter 8 who could not walk, talk, or feed themselves. Such extreme deprivation is rare, although cases do turn up from time to time.

The mildly retarded child's classroom problems are the result of specialized deficits in cognitive processes. Mentally retarded children have a smaller store of knowledge than normal children,

and their metacognitive knowledge is generally meager. When given memory tasks, they fail to use strategies to help them master the material. Dynamic assessment tests have shown that mentally retarded children have trouble transferring knowledge to new situations (Campione, Brown, Ferrara, Jones, and Steinberg, 1985). When mentally retarded children with a mental age of ten years were matched with normal ten-year-olds, there was no difference between the groups during the learning period. But at the second session, differences appeared. The mentally retarded children required hints to solve the same kind of problems they had earlier solved with few errors. When the children had to transfer their learning to new kinds of problems, the differences widened sharply. Although they had learned to solve the original problems as well as the normal children, the mentally retarded children were unable to use their knowledge flexibly.

SCHOOLING

The cognitive skills that are measured by IQ tests are applied most consistently in the classroom. Reading, writing, and arithmetic draw heavily on these skills, which is the reason that IQ scores are such good predictors of academic performance. Yet there is more to school success than academic cognition. Children's motivation and beliefs may have a powerful effect on their ability to learn.

Academic Cognition

Academic cognition differs from the cognition that children use in everyday life in three ways (Brown, Bransford, Ferrara, and Campione, 1983). Academic cognition is *effortful*. Instead of the relatively effortless, undemanding thought that children bring to most daily activities, in their schoolwork they must make deliberate, often painful, attempts to learn. Academic cognition is *individual*. Instead of being measured by their success in getting things done with others, progress through school is measured in terms of independent competence. Finally, academic cognition is *decontextualized knowledge*. When students learn

Experience in day-care centers and nursery schools teaches preschoolers the group routines that used to be acquired in kindergarten. *(Elizabeth Hamlin/Stock, Boston)*

facts stripped from their context, motivation and any practical use of information are neglected.

Reading In today's schools, many kindergartners are learning to read. A generation ago, formal reading instruction was invariably postponed until first grade, but most American five-year-olds have already been socialized to school — the traditional task of kindergarten (Anderson, Hiebert, Scott, and Wilkinson, 1985). At nursery school or day-care centers, they learn to adapt to the group routines required to make classroom instruction possible. They learn to sit quietly and listen to instructions; they listen to stories, perhaps take field trips to the post office and the fire station, and learn to participate in group activities.

Although the average child entering kindergarten today knows more about reading than children did a few decades ago, many have not yet discovered what this mysterious business of reading is all about. Like the five-year-old who memorized the story, closed his eyes, recited it, and proudly proclaimed, "Look, I can read with my eyes shut!" they may not realize that effort or skill is required. Some still do not know that you read a page from left to right and a book from front to back or even that printed words can be turned into speech. They may believe that a story's meaning comes

from the pictures (Paris, Lipson, and Wixson, 1983). Unsurprisingly, children who come into kindergarten with a store of knowledge about reading and writing progress much more rapidly than children who have had little exposure to books.

In the primary grades, children work at phonological decoding and identifying words. They learn to discriminate speech sounds, so that when the teacher asks them the first sound of the word *cup*, they can separate it from the rest of the syllable. This may be more difficult than you might think. Although they had been talking and understanding others' speech for several years, few five-year-olds were able to tap a desk twice when they heard the word "it" and three times when they heard "hit" (Liberman, Shankweiler, Fischer, and Carter, 1974). Unless they can divide a word into its sounds, children will have trouble reversing the process, blending sounds into words when they try to read. Most children know about fourteen letters when they enter kindergarten, but they must learn the rest of the letter names and then connect each of the letters with specific sounds (Anderson et al., 1985).

Associating combinations of letters with meaning draws on children's phonological knowledge and their visual recognition of individual words.

The first task that faces the beginning reader is to learn the letter names and to connect each letter with specific sounds. *(Elizabeth Crews)*

Both approaches require the children to search their memories for the correct word, but each approach requires a slightly different manner. In the *phonics* approach, children translate the visual pattern on the page into its sound, using the sound as a cue. In the *visual* approach—often called *look-and-say*—children use images of printed words to develop a vocabulary of words that they recognize automatically. Children who have not developed phonological decoding and automatic word recognition by the time they are eight or nine years old often have trouble learning to read fluently. Most reading programs teach children to use both approaches.

During early instruction, children may not read for pleasure or to acquire new information (Chall, 1979). The task of identifying words occupies such a large share of their processing resources that there is little left over for other tasks. Gradually, children become able to read quickly and make few errors. Word identification becomes virtually automatic, so that children devote little of their processing space (in the form of attention and memory) to the task. The child who reads fluently identifies words as adults do, using information from individual letters, the word as a whole, and the surrounding context (McClelland and Rumelhart, 1981).

If the processes do not become automatic, the child develops major reading problems. When third graders were asked to read an unfamiliar story aloud, good readers moved along at about 100 words per minute. But poor readers, whose identification skills had not become automatic, could manage only about 50 to 70 words per minute—a rate so slow that they often forgot the words they had decoded before they could grasp their meaning (Lesgold, Resnick, and Hammond, 1985). Such poor readers often rely primarily on the context of the surrounding sentence, as beginning readers do. Their patterns of errors reveal this technique. During their early months in the first grade, most youngsters' reading errors consist of substituting another word that makes sense in the situation but may not resemble the correct word. By the end of the year, as they gain reading skill, their substitution errors also resemble the visual form of the word.

Reading comprehension depends in good part on children's metacognitive knowledge about reading. Good readers are those who are aware of the demands of various reading tasks and have figured out how to adapt their reading skills to the material at hand. They know that their goals are different when reading an adventure story and when reading their science textbook. They know when to skim, when to check back to see if they have understood the text, when to summarize, ask themselves questions about the material, take notes, or underline important ideas.

Poor readers lack this knowledge. When researchers asked second and sixth graders what they did when they ran across words that they didn't know in a story, the good readers said that they either asked someone else or looked up the word in a dictionary (Myers and Paris, 1978). Poor readers couldn't say what they would do.

Table 12.1
Percentage of Students at or above the Five Reading Proficiency Levels

Reading Skills and Strategies	Age	1971	1975	1980	1984
Rudimentary (150)	9	90.4*	93.3	94.4	93.9
	13	99.7†	99.6	99.8	99.8
	17	99.7	99.9	99.9	100.0
Basic (200)	9	58.3*	61.7	65.1	64.2
	13	92.3*	92.8*	94.3	94.5
	17	96.6	97.5	97.9	98.6
Intermediate (250)	9	15.6*	14.0*	17.0	18.1
	13	57.0	57.5	59.3	60.3
	17	80.0*	82.0	82.8	83.6
Adept (300)	9	1.1	.7	.8	1.0
	13	9.3*	9.7*	10.9	11.3
	17	37.2	36.1*	34.8*	39.2
Advanced (350)	9	0.0	0.0	0.0	0.0
	13	.2	.2	.3	.3
	17	4.9	3.5	3.1	4.9

* Statistically significant differences from 1984.
† No significance test is reported when the proportion of students is either >95.0 or <5.0.

Source: National Assessment of Educational Progress, 1985.

Poor readers may be as competent intellectually as good readers but have low comprehension because of their failure to set reading goals and apply strategies efficiently and flexibly to meet them. They are passive, not active readers, and their passivity may be due to problems with motivation and attitude (Johnston and Winograd, 1985). Such problems may be the result of experiences as preschoolers, later experiences at home and on the playground, or experiences within the classroom.

How well do American children learn to read? According to periodic national assessments, they do not read as well as we would hope, but they read better than they did fifteen years ago (National Assessment of Educational Progress, 1985). Virtually all children learn to read at a rudimentary level; almost all nine-year-olds can read well enough to follow simple directions or read a few simple sentences and answer factual questions (see Table 12.1). Most reach the basic reading level, which requires them to read and comprehend simple stories and expository passages. They can read signs, newspaper ads, TV listings, recipes, order blanks in catalogues, and simple articles in magazines and newspapers. Four out of five eventually reach an intermediate level of reading skills, at which they can comprehend relatively long stories and expository passages. To be successful at college or in business or government, children should reach at least the adept reading level, at which they can understand, summarize, and explain stories, poems, expository passages, graphs, and charts. Few nine-year-olds can be expected to read at this level, and only 1 percent do. The problem facing society is that fewer than 40 percent of seventeen-year-olds are adept readers, and fewer than 5 percent have the reading skills required for excellence. Only advanced readers, who can understand financial and technical documents and scientific reports, can hope to reach the top of various businesses and professions. Reading at this level requires students to understand sophisticated syntax and to restructure and synthesize ideas in material they have read.

Although writing draws on some of the same skills required for reading, writing seems to be more difficult for children to master. *(John Blaustein/Woodfin Camp & Associates)*

Writing Writing complements reading. Instead of grasping meaning from the printed page, the child attempts to transform meaning into written words. Writing ability is highly correlated with reading achievement and draws on some of the same skills (Loban, 1962), yet writing seems to give children more problems than understanding what they read. In 1984, only 38 percent of the seventeen-year-olds in a national survey could produce a detailed, well-organized description of an object, and only 20 percent could write an effective, persuasive letter (Applebee, Langer, and Mullis, 1986). This represents an improvement over the performance of seventeen-year-olds in 1979 but is simply a return to the writing levels of seventeen-year-olds in 1974.

Researchers have been analyzing the writing process in the hope of finding ways to improve the writing ability of American children. They have found that competent writing is not a straightforward process of planning, drafting, and revising, as most educators had assumed. Instead, writing is a recursive process, in which writers move back and forth among the various processes (Applebee, 1984). After some initial planning, expert writers revise as they write, alter their plans as they go along, and insert new material as they revise.

This is not the case with young children when they first begin to write. When asked to compose stories, descriptions, or essays, they usually have trouble thinking of something to say. Often they seem to run dry after producing a sentence or two. Part of the problem is their small store of knowledge; the more children know about a topic, the higher the quality of their essays (Langer, 1984). However, much of the problem seems to lie in the planning and monitoring processes, which draw on the same metacognitive skills as reading does. Youngsters seem unable to formulate their goals and then keep them in mind while they write.

These metacognitive problems lead children to adopt a strategy known as "knowledge telling," which produces a series of unconnected sentences about a topic (Scardamalia and Bereiter, 1984). Instead of planning the composition, they begin writing about one aspect of the topic — which leads them into a new composition. Asked to write about his visit to the museum, for example, a boy may decide to write first about the dinosaur exhibit. After writing, "We saw the bones of dinosaurs," he may continue for several sentences to put down everything he can think of about dinosaurs. Then he stops writing and hands in a composition on dinosaurs, having forgotten the original topic. When children use the knowledge-telling strategy, they engage in none of the recursive writing that moves back and forth among the processes, and whatever revising they do is limited to changing a single word here or there (Nold, 1980).

This approach to writing actually hinders the child's thinking about the topic. Yet professional writers report that they understand a topic better after writing about it. Asked about the writing process, British novelist E. M. Forster once said, "How can I know what I think until I see what I say?" When children write in a recursive fashion, writing can become learning for them, too (Applebee, 1984). Studies have shown that the more a child manipulates the information in the process of writing, the better he or she comes to understand that information. Researchers have found that when students take notes or simply respond to short-answer study questions, they learn far less about a subject than when they write essays that require them to reorganize the information and apply the concepts in a new context (Newell, 1984).

Mathematics Today's children enter school knowing more about mathematics than their parents did. Many preschoolers can already solve addition problems—as long as the sum is less than 10. Their parents were first graders before they were as knowledgeable (Siegler, 1986). When formal instruction in arithmetic begins, children soon discover that they must learn their "number facts." Generations of school children have learned number facts, rattling off "7" when the teacher flashes the card that says "3 + 4 = ?" and "3" when the card says "10 - 7 = ?" Generations of educators have assumed that children always memorize these facts by rote and associate the combinations without understanding them.

Researchers have come to the conclusion that the educators have been partly mistaken. According to Arthur Baroody (1985), children learn some facts by association, but they also rely on rules and strategies that they have worked out. For example, once they figure out that 0 stands for *nothing,* they begin applying an informal rule—"when nothing is added to a number, the number does not change." They figure out that when adding 1, the answer is always the next number in the counting sequence. When they are introduced to multiplication, they discover that simply adding a zero multiplies by 10 or that when multiplying by 5, the answer always ends in a 5 or a 0. Instead of storing some 400 basic combinations for addition, subtraction, multiplication, and division, children seem to develop internalized rules, procedures, and principles that interact with a network of specific number combinations. They memorize some number facts, use rules to generate others, and rely on counting to come up with others. If children were taught mathematical thinking strategies instead of having to come up with them on their own, they might begin to appreciate the regularities and relationships that are the essence of mathematics instead of regarding it as memorization and mechanical routines.

Teachers who are determined that children learn their number facts by rote often discourage youngsters from counting on their fingers to solve problems in addition or subtraction. However, this prohibition may slow their acquisition of number facts instead of speeding it up (Siegler, 1986). Each time children retrieve an answer from memory, that answer is more strongly associated with the combination—whether the answer is right or wrong. Each association formed by an incorrect answer interferes with children's attempts to learn the right answer. Older children and brighter children do not have to use their fingers because they have either learned the combinations or figured out a rule that allows them to reconstruct the answer.

Often a gap develops between children's understanding of mathematical principles and the number problems they work in the classroom. The gap is so wide among first graders that some believe that it is all right to come up with one answer on a number sentence (3 + 4 = 7) and a different answer on the same word problem ("Andrea had three crayons and her teacher gave her four more crayons"). It takes some time for children to learn that the symbols they manipulate mechanically on paper stand for something (+ means a joining together) or to connect Andrea's crayons with the formal symbolism of an arithmetic problem (Hiebert, 1984). Some never succeed. (For an analysis of children's difficulties with word problems, see the accompanying box.).

A separation between symbols and the mathematical principles they stand for is more prevalent than most educators think, suggests Lauren Resnick (in press). Most youngsters see mathematics as a puzzle-like system in which they apply arbi-

WHY ARE WORD PROBLEMS SO DIFFICULT?

Many children who solve numerical problems with some skill still have difficulty with word problems. At home they may know that because Mother is on a business trip, there will be only three plates on the dinner table instead of four. They know that if they have $6 and want to buy a videocassette that costs $13, they must save or borrow $7. But told that David gave six marbles to Jim and now has nine marbles, many children cannot figure out how many marbles David started with. When children were presented with the problem of David and his marbles, 51 percent of the third graders and 33 percent of the fifth and sixth graders came up with the wrong answer (Morales, Shute, and Pelegrino, 1985). In fact, some of the problems that the older children found especially easy (Nancy has six marbles. Eve has three marbles. How many marbles does Nancy need to give away to have as many as Eve?) were among the most difficult for the third graders.

Why did so many third graders find problems that required such simple computations $(6 + 9; 6 - 3)$ so difficult? The children's errors were rarely mistakes in addition or subtraction. Instead, they made conceptual errors; they selected the wrong procedure to use in solving the problem. Apparently, when children did not understand the problem, they relied on surface cues (such as the word "more" or "less") when deciding whether to add or subtract.

Problems with the same mathematical structure often have different conceptual structures. Look at the following problems:

1. Eddie and Roy have 11 marbles altogether.
   Eddie has 4 marbles.
   How many marbles does Roy have?
2. Jane has 12 marbles.
   Mary has 7 marbles.
   How many marbles does Jane have more than Mary?

Both problems are solved in an identical manner $(11 - 4; 12 - 7)$, but the first problem requires the child to join and separate sets (Eddie's and Roy's marbles), and the second problem requires them to compare two sets (Jane's and Mary's marbles). Studies suggest that unless children understand such concepts as one-to-one correspondence, class inclusion, and part-whole relationships, they cannot solve simple word problems (Carpenter and Moser, 1982). Before they can represent a problem correctly, they must be able to grasp its conceptual basis.

In order to explore the source of those youngsters' misunderstanding, Romelia Morales and her associates (1985) returned to the classrooms after a lapse of three months and asked the children to sort the word problems, which were typed on index cards. Before sorting the problems, the children read them out loud so that the researchers could be certain that no reading problems were involved. Afterward, the children explained their reasons for sorting the cards as they did. The older children not only categorized the problems by major type, but were also able to distinguish subcategories within each type. The younger children tended to sort by surface structure, relying on word cues. At any age, the ability to sort problems systematically by concept could have predicted a child's earlier success at solving the problems correctly. Apparently, when children recognize the mathematical concept that underlies a problem, they find it much easier to choose good solutions.

trary rules that they have learned. Those who learn the rules correctly (even though they do not understand the principles behind them) get along all right in class, but they are unlikely to care much about the subject. Some children forget steps in the routines they have learned—or else they never learn them. So they figure out a plausible routine and apply it. Researchers call these erroneous routines *bugs*. With one common bug, children treat each column in a subtraction problem as unrelated to the other columns and routinely subtract the smaller number from the larger in each column. They turn in papers with such solutions as:

A.　　342　　B.　　5090
　　　−281　　　　　− 452
　　　　141　　　　　5040

In problem A, the bug is "Always subtract the smaller number from the larger number," so the child subtracts 1 from 2 (correctly), but then subtracts 4 from 8 as he or she moves to the tens column. In problem B, the bug is "Whenever there is a 0 on top, 0 is written as the answer."

Such procedures violate basic mathematical principles. For example, the bug for problem A violates the principle that underlies subtraction: noncommutativity. In addition, which is commutative, it makes no difference in which direction a child proceeds. Children who develop such bugs are applying intelligent reasoning to the problem. Their solution is a failure because they have a confused understanding of basic math principles.

Academic Motivation

Asked what he said to himself when he knew how to do his schoolwork, one youngster in a primarily black, inner-city, middle school said, "I pat myself on the shoulder. Then I'll be very happy inside" (Rohrkemper and Bershon, 1984, p. 141). But another child in the same school had less pleasant experiences. When she didn't grasp a teacher's explanation she kept silent: "You're afraid of people that would say, 'You can't do this easy stuff; you're stupid.' And that hurts me to be called names. I can't take it too well." Other students responded to classroom difficulties by just "putting down anything" to get the task over or by castigating themselves ("I say, 'I'm so dumb'") (Rohrkemper and Bershon, 1984, p. 135). As these examples suggest, children's attitudes toward school, the way they feel about themselves, and their beliefs about their ability to master the curriculum influence their academic achievement. The influence is so heavy that increasing numbers of cognitive psychologists have begun to look at the effects of motivation on children's learning and thinking.

Attributions for Success or Failure　Kindergartners believe that effort and ability are the same: children who try hard are smarter than children who do not try. If you try harder, you will become smarter. They overestimate their own ability, but because they believe that with effort they can be smarter, these inflated estimates are not surprising (Harter, 1983). When they begin first grade, children expect to do well in school. Whether they are bright, average, or somewhat slow, most believe that they are near the top of the class. Yet when asked about their classmates, they can tell you who is struggling and who is doing well (Stipek, 1981). This discrepancy may arise in part because to children on the threshold of formal education, success means finishing a task. Any problems they have with early reading or numbers do not bother them.

This optimistic outlook soon begins to change. From about the age of seven, children start to see intellectual competence as a stable personal characteristic, and their estimates of their own ability begin to match their teacher's estimate (Dweck and Elliott, 1983). They become less confident of success and increasingly vulnerable to failure. And they have become aware of their class standing; they are starting to use social comparison in assessing their own performance.

Succeeding or failing at an academic task can have widely different effects on the way children approach their schoolwork, depending on the way they interpret the outcome (Weiner, 1974). Children may interpret their successes or failures as due to causes inside them (ability, effort, mood) or causes in the outside world (difficulty, luck, the teacher not liking them). Some causes are stable (ability); others are transient (mood). Some causes are under the child's control (effort); others are not (ability). There seems to be a general tendency for all of us to take credit for our successes and to blame our failures on some aspect of the situation. Yet a child's past academic experiences color his or her interpretation of these outcomes. Successful children and children who are struggling often interpret the same outcome in different ways. When researchers asked fifth graders about the causes of success or failure in situations involving math and reading, good students tended to attribute their successes to ability and effort and their failures to difficult assignments or luck (Marsh, 1986). Poor students were more likely than good students to attribute their failures to lack of effort or ability.

A child who attributes a failure to transient internal causes and says, "I didn't do it careful enough," may try harder on the next lesson, but a child who attributes it to stable, internal causes and says, "I'm just not very good at math," may put out just enough effort to get by—or even fail to finish the assignment. Researchers see the way children interpret their failures as intimately bound up with their perceptions of their personal worth (Covington, 1984). If they attribute their failures to lack of effort, they may feel guilty for not trying harder, but they escape the humiliation of feeling incompetent. Effort is within their control, and if they apply themselves, they may succeed next time.

If they attribute their failures to lack of ability, they convict themselves of incompetence, and their sense of self-worth is damaged. They are publicly humiliated, and their future is unpromising. Ability is beyond their control, and having failed today, they are likely to fail tomorrow and tomorrow and tomorrow. Some older children are so afraid to discover that they lack ability that they simply quit trying. If they never apply themselves, they can always say, "I should have tried harder." They will never have to face the possibility that they are incompetent. Other students give up because they have become convinced that they lack ability, and they are afraid to fail.

Beliefs and Self-perceptions   Children who have given up are regarded as passive academic failures. They have developed learned helplessness and no longer see their efforts as having any bearing on the outcome of their school endeavors. As we saw in Chapter 10, the reactions of the teacher to the student's classroom efforts may be one factor in the development of passive failure. Whether teachers believe children are not trying or lack ability to do the work also may be important. When teachers believe a child's academic problems are due to lack of effort, they become angry and tend to withhold any help. But when teachers believe that the child is incapable of doing the work, they pity the youngster. Pity leads them to provide extra help, praise the student excessively

for success at easy tasks, and to refrain from criticism. Studies suggest that even six-year-olds attribute a teacher's anger as a signal that they have not tried hard enough and pity as a signal that they are incompetent (Graham, 1984). The solicitous behavior of the teacher who feels sorry for the failing child may encourage passive failure. For example, a teacher who pities the child who is failing in beginning reading demands less and less work from the child. Whenever the child hesitates, the teacher swiftly supplies the troublesome word, ends the child's recitations quickly, and often interrupts the child (Johnston and Winograd, 1985). This takes further control away from the child and proves to the child that he or she is incompetent.

Working against learned helplessness is the teacher's praise. No matter what a child's level of ability, praise from the teacher for schoolwork (but not for good behavior) is related to the child's perception of his or her ability. Appropriate praise from the teacher for good behavior is related to the child's perception of his or her effort. In a study of 11 second- and sixth-grade Michigan classrooms, these influences were as strong among sixth graders as among second graders and among girls as among boys (Pintrich and Blumenfeld, 1985). Such effects indicate the importance of matching students' tasks to their abilities in order to provide more students with opportunities for teacher approval.

Boys are more likely than girls to believe that their grades depend on whether the teacher likes them. Girls tend to believe that success depends on their own efforts, but whether girls or boys, children who see themselves as responsible for their successes or failures do best in school. Although school achievement is clearly related to these beliefs, children's IQ scores are *not*. Apparently, unless children know the rules for achieving success and avoiding failure in the classroom, they are unlikely to become highly motivated, self-regulated learners (Connell, 1985; Dweck and Elliott, 1983).

Self-regulated Learning

When schooling succeeds, the classroom is characterized by **self-regulated learning,** in which children plan, evaluate, and regulate their own learn-

Praise from teachers for academic accomplishments strengthens youngsters' perceptions of their ability and effort. *(Elizabeth Crews)*

ing skills and develop a lasting interest in learning (Paris and Cross, 1983). They are motivated to learn, possess the skills that enable them to learn, and adapt those skills to the learning situation. Self-regulated learners combine skill with will. They expect to be successful in the future because they have been successful in the past.

Many good students become self-regulated learners more or less on their own. They learn to coordinate their knowledge, their learning strategies, and their motivation, and they feel competent in the classroom. At present, however, most students are not self-regulated learners, and many of those who are cannot put into words exactly what they do. The average student uses self-regulating processes inconsistently, and the poor student has little grasp of them (Corno and Rohrkemper, 1985). Telling a student who lacks strategies and is afraid of failing to try harder is unlikely to induce self-regulation. Instead, the youngster who tries but lacks strategic knowledge required for success is merely practicing failure and learning that he or she has no control over the outcome.

Some researchers have concluded that more children could become self-regulated learners if they were taught some of the skills that good students already possess and knew *why* those skills

lead to successful learning. In the hope of helping children become self-regulated readers, Scott Paris and his associates (Paris, Cross, and Lipson, 1984; Paris and Jacobs, 1984; Paris and Oka, 1986) developed the Informed Strategies for Learning (ISL) program. Third and fifth graders got direct knowledge about effective reading strategies (skimming, rereading, paraphrasing, making inferences, and checking) and opportunities to practice them. Teachers demonstrated the strategies in structured group discussions, then gradually required the students to generate the strategies on their own. The students learned how to use the strategies, when to use them, and why they were likely to be helpful. Students shared their experiences, talking about the benefits, ease, and difficulties connected with the use of each strategy. Compared with children in control groups, children at every reading level increased their comprehension and their metacognitive knowledge about reading. The children became more aware of the cognitive processes involved in reading, the strategies involved, and the factors that made the task easier or more difficult.

Will these children become self-regulated readers? No one expects a short program to end reading failure and keep children motivated. Yet those youngsters who were convinced that the strategies they learned were both useful and necessary might be on their way to that goal. They have been given the essential tools, but their self-con-

cepts, their achievement histories, and the way they evaluate their successes or failures will also determine the outcome.

SUMMARY

1. Theorists never have been able to agree on an explicit definition of intelligence. In information-processing views, intelligence depends on the efficiency and speed with which individuals carry out the basic processes used to represent and manipulate information. Intelligence seems to consist of **fluid intelligence,** which is based on the ability to perceive, encode, and reason about information and is neither taught in school nor pushed by the culture, and **crystallized intelligence,** which is based on the ability to understand relationships, make judgments, and solve problems that depend on schooling or cultural experience. In Brown and Campione's theory, intelligence consists of a biologically based **architectural system** and a training- and experience-based **executive system.** In Sternberg's **triarchic theory,** the development and use of intelligence depends on (1) the components of intelligence (metacomponents, performance components, and knowledge-acquisition components); (2) the attributes of tasks or situations that measure intelligence; and (3) the sociocultural setting in which intelligence is displayed. **Factor theories** examine intelligence in terms of abilities instead of processes, and researchers search for basic abilities using the technique of **factor analysis.** Piaget saw intelligence in terms of the cognitive structures that underlay intelligent action.

2. The **psychometric,** or mental-testing, approach to intelligence was developed by Binet and Simon, who devised standardized tests to assess a child's **mental age.** Modern tests, such as the Stanford-Binet or one of the Wechsler tests, assess intelligence in terms of deviation IQ, which relates performance in terms of its deviation from the standard score of 100. Some

researchers are developing **dynamic assessment** tests, which evaluate what a child is prepared to learn with assistance, instead of what the child already has learned.

3. Researchers still disagree about explanations for the **variance** in IQ scores, which refers to individual differences between measured IQ and the average IQ of 100. Heredity and environment interact to produce intelligence, with genes setting the possible reaction range. Among environmental influences in the family, those general influences that are experienced by all family members are known as "between-family influences"; those that are specific to a particular member are known as "within-family influences." Jensen's proposal that heredity accounts for the majority of variance between IQ scores of blacks and whites has been strongly criticized. Critics point out that **heritability** of intelligence accounts only for the genetic contribution within a particular group and cannot be generalized to explain group differences.

4. At one time, some psychologists assumed that creativity was the result of **divergent thinking,** or the ability to come up with unusual ideas or associations. Others have supposed that personality characteristics are crucial. Gardner suggests that regarding human beings as having seven "multiple intelligences" helps account for creativity. Although a minimum IQ may be necessary for creativity, great creative genius requires a delicate balance of environmental forces. Intellectually gifted children generally grow up to be successful, well-adjusted individuals, and it appears that they may do best in school if placed in an accelerated program. **Mentally retarded** children or adults have IQ

scores more than two standard deviations (30 points) below normal and show an impaired ability to adapt to the demands of the environment. Retardation can be caused by genes, biology, or environment, and retarded children have specialized deficits in cognitive processes.

5. When learning to read, children must learn to discriminate speech sounds and associate letter combinations with meaning. This latter task draws on the child's ability to decode visual patterns into sounds and to recognize words automatically. Children's reading comprehension depends on their metacognitive knowledge about reading. Writing gives children more problems than reading, in part because children's planning and monitoring processes are so poorly developed that they cannot formulate goals and keep them in mind while they write. In mastering arithmetic, children memorize some number facts, develop rules to generate others, and rely on counting for the rest. When mathematic symbols and the principles they stand for are separated, children see math as a system with arbitrary rules and often try to solve problems by using "bugs" that violate math principles.

6. The way children interpret their school successes and failures determines what sort of effect these will have on children's motivation and attitudes toward school. Children may assume that the causes are inside them or in the outside world, stable or transient, under their own control or outside it. Children who attribute their failures to lack of effort may try harder next time; those who attribute them to lack of ability often quit trying. Children who give up are passive academic failures, who suffer from learned helplessness. Children who are successful students engage in **self-regulated learning,** in which they plan, evaluate, and regulate their own learning skills. Such children are motivated to learn, skilled at learning, and expect to be successful.

KEY TERMS

architectural system
crystallized intelligence
divergent thinking
dynamic assessment
executive system

factor analysis
factor theories
fluid intelligence
heritability
mental age

mentally retarded
psychometrics
self-regulated learning
triarchic theory
variance

STUDY TERMS

architectural system   The biologically based part of intelligence, consisting of basic cognitive processes.

crystallized intelligence   Verbal skills, mechanical knowledge, and the ability to handle well-learned information in familiar situations; crystallized skills are taught in schools and emphasized by the culture.

dynamic assessment   Evaluating what a child is prepared to learn with assistance; a measure of the child's zone of proximal development.

executive system   The acquired part of intelligence, consisting of organized knowledge, learning strategies, and metacognitive skills.

fluid intelligence   Abstract, nonverbal reasoning and problem-solving skills, which are acquired without formal instruction.

heritability   An estimate of the genetic contribution to a single trait within a given group.

PART V

Adolescence: Building an Identity

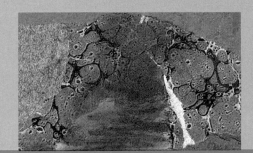

The physical changes of adolescence turn children into men and women. Sexual development obviously has wide psychological and social consequences, but the gradual transformation of dependent child into independent adult may be even more important. Moving out of the sheltered world of the child into the unprotected terrain of adulthood brings new risks and new opportunities. As the prospect of striking out on one's own becomes real, the personality that developed in late childhood faces an inevitable test. Life's joys as well as its pains arise from this confrontation between the needs of a developing personality and the demands of society. Out of the inevitable conflict emerges an identity that reflects the adolescent's sense of self. This unit shows how boys and girls react to the transformations of adolescence and how cultural changes affect the ranges of choices that society presents to them.

CHAPTER 13

The Changes of Adolescence

BIOLOGICAL CHANGES
Sexual Maturation in Girls / Sexual Maturation in Boys / Reactions to Physical Change

COGNITIVE CHANGES
Formal Operations / Understanding Social Institutions / Understanding People / Adolescent Egocentrism / Prevalence of Formal Thought

CHANGES IN THE SELF
Identity / Sexual Identity / Sex Roles and Intellectual Development

CHANGES IN FAMILY LIFE
Shifting Family Roles / Quest for Autonomy

CHANGES IN FRIENDSHIP AND SOCIAL LIFE
Friendships / The Peer Group / Relations with the Other Sex

CHANGES IN THE SCHOOL EXPERIENCE

What does it mean to become an adolescent? It means change in every aspect of a young person's life. Physically, cognitively, and socially, the nineteen-year-old is a different creature from the eleven-year-old. Some changes are apparent to all — the rapid growth, the deepening voice, the development of body hair, breasts, or penis. These changes are so predictable that when they are late or do not occur at all, both child and family are alarmed. Other changes are not nearly so obvious. Significant changes in the way adolescents think, although invisible, are at least as important as the signs of physical maturity. Their new capacity to think abstractly or to use and understand general concepts, such as the ideas of justice or liberty or community, allows adolescents to grasp and discuss moral and political questions. Yet changes in thinking are often so subtle and take place so gradually that they go unnoticed.

Many observers feel that the most important changes of adolescence are psychosocial: in relation to others, especially the family, the child moves from dependency to the beginnings of independence. The tempo of that movement and its conditions form a major theme of family life, with adolescent and parent preoccupied with what the adolescent can and cannot do, when he or she can do it, and how it will be done. Perhaps the most subtle change of all involves the adolescent's identity — the emerging sense of self that synthesizes so many elements of life. When these transitional years are complete, the girl or boy who embarked on adolescence as a child emerges as an adult.

As the material for this chapter was gathered, a largely unemphasized aspect of adolescent development became apparent. We know less than we think we do about this period. Much of the writing on adolescence has been based on armchair observation, extrapolations from anthropological fieldwork, and studies of emotionally disturbed young people (Adelson, 1985b). Only within the past four or five years have researchers begun to apply the same techniques to adolescents that have been so successful with younger children. For a long time, the psychology of adolescent development was the psychology of white, middle-class boys. In the past few years, researchers have begun to study adolescent girls, but most of the studies still focus on young people in the middle class. We still know little about the way that adolescence is experienced by other classes and ethnic groups.

In this chapter, we begin with the most obvious aspect of adolescence, the biological changes that usher in this stage of life. After surveying sexual maturation and youngsters' reactions to changes in their bodies, we consider the cognitive changes of adolescence. During the years from twelve to eighteen, differences develop in the way a youngster thinks about problems, institutions, and other people. Next we take up changes in self-concept and identity. All the changes we have considered to that point affect the way the family system operates, and so we explore how puberty alters relations between parents and child. Then we turn to changes in the adolescent's social life, which alters dramatically as friends and peers take on a new importance and the adolescent embarks on a sexual life. The chapter closes with a look at the adolescent in school.

BIOLOGICAL CHANGES

In the beginning, adolescence is a biological phenomenon. Early adolescence is characterized by **puberty,** the lengthy biological process that changes the immature child into a sexually mature person (Peterson, 1985). Since childhood, the endocrine system has been capable of initiating this change, but its functioning has been suppressed. Throughout childhood, both boys and girls produce low levels of **androgens** (male hormones) and **estrogens** (female hormones) in relatively equal amounts. Then, in response to some still unexplained biological signal, the hypothalamus tells the pituitary gland to begin the hormonal production found in adult men and women. The pituitary gland stimulates other endocrine glands, a surge in hormone production occurs, and the child enters puberty (see Figure 13.1). The reproductive glands — the **ovaries** in girls and the **testes** in boys — and the adrenal glands secrete hormones directly into the bloodstream; they create a balance that includes more androgens in boys and more estrogens in girls. These new hormonal levels lead directly to the dramatic physical changes of puberty, and within about four years, the child's body has been transformed into the body of an adult. Puberty is now complete, but hormone secretion continues to increase throughout adolescence and into young adulthood, peaking at about the age of twenty (Offer and Sabshin, 1984).

Although we talk about puberty as if it were a smooth, single process, it is actually a series of correlated events that reflect a group of interrelated processes (Brooks-Gunn and Warren, 1985). Youngsters progress through these events at different rates, with one girl reaching full breast development in two years, for example, while another takes five years to complete the same sequence of growth. Nor do all events follow the same timetable; breast development may be rapid in a girl whose pubic hair is developing more slowly than most girls'. This lack of harmony produces a growth trend known as **asynchrony.** Because puberty is characterized by uneven growth, at any given time during maturation, some body parts may be disproportionately large or small. Youngsters often complain that their hands and feet are too big. As growth progresses, body proportions usually become much more harmonious.

Because hormones are responsible for the physical changes of puberty, authorities once assumed that many of the behavioral changes of adolescence could be traced directly to hormonally caused increases in the sex drive. Yet no research has indicated that typical teenage behavior, such as interest

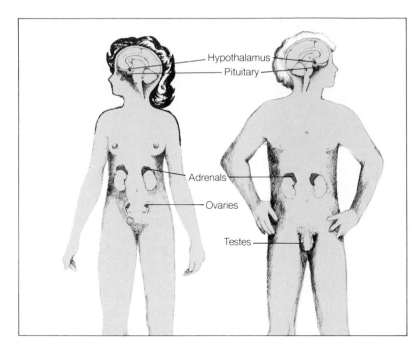

FIGURE 13.1   The endocrine system, showing only the major glands involved in pubertal changes. The hypothalamus (a part of the brain with neural and endocrine functions) signals the pituitary gland, which in turn stimulates hormonal secretions from other endocrine glands. This process produces many of the changes typifying adolescent physical and pubertal development.

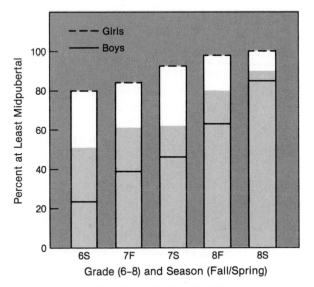

FIGURE 13.2   Until a majority of children in a classroom are clearly into adolescence ("midpubertal"), only those who have reached puberty begin acting in typical adolescent fashion. But once the 50 percent mark is passed—by spring of the sixth grade—the critical point is reached, and all the youngsters, whether or not they have entered puberty, become typical adolescents. *(From Petersen, 1985)*

in the opposite sex or increased conflict with parents, is directly related to hormone levels. Whatever contribution hormones make to adolescent behavior is heavily influenced by peer standards. For example, research indicates that a youngster's grade in school, not his or her pubertal status, is the best predictor of dating, preoccupation with the other sex, endless talking on the telephone, and wrangles with parents (Petersen, 1985). Although early-maturing youngsters are the first to behave in this way, once a majority of youngsters in a school grade are visibly pubertal, the entire class begins to act like "typical adolescents" (see Figure 13.2). When a class reaches "critical mass" (which occurred toward the end of the sixth grade in the Petersen study), many prepubertal youngsters begin dating—perhaps to keep from being dropped by their more sexually mature peer group.

Sexual Maturation in Girls

Although a girl's growth spurt can start at any time between the ages of seven and thirteen years, the typical girl begins to grow at around age ten (Faust, 1977). Her height increases rapidly, with growth

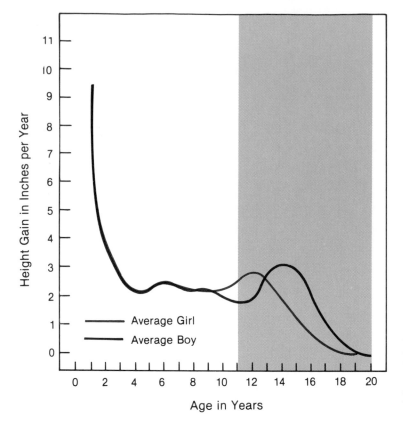

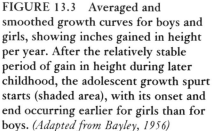

FIGURE 13.3   Averaged and smoothed growth curves for boys and girls, showing inches gained in height per year. After the relatively stable period of gain in height during later childhood, the adolescent growth spurt starts (shaded area), with its onset and end occurring earlier for girls than for boys. *(Adapted from Bayley, 1956)*

peaking at the age of twelve and continuing until she is about fifteen (see Figure 13.3). Her proportions change as her hips broaden more rapidly than her shoulders and she adds body fat. Her breasts begin to grow sometime during the middle of her tenth year and reach full size about three years later. As breasts enlarge, other changes occur. The areas around the nipples grow larger, more conical in form, and their color darkens. At the same time, a girl's vagina and uterus begin to mature, and her voice lowers. Pubic hair usually appears when a girl is about eleven, underarm hair about two years later.

Parents and adolescents often regard **menarche,** or the first incidence of menstruation, as the true indicator of puberty, but this event occurs relatively late in the pubertal sequence. Several years before a girl begins to menstruate, her estrogen production anticipates the cyclic rhythm of the menstrual cycle. Menarche may come as early as ten years or as late as seventeen. It is rare for a girl whose glands function normally to begin menstruating before she is nine or after she is eighteen.

For nearly a century, the average age of first menstruation has occurred earlier each decade. At the close of the nineteenth century, the average American girl began menstruating at age fourteen or fifteen; today she reaches menarche a few months after her twelfth birthday (Bullough, 1981). This trend toward the earlier onset of puberty, which probably was the result of better nutrition, less disease, and reduced social stress, now seems to have stopped (Malina, 1979).

We do not yet understand the relation of menstruation to fertility. The notion that menarche signals the attainment of full reproductive functioning is a misconception. Although some adolescent girls are soon able to conceive, about half of them remain infertile for a year or two after menarche (Offer and Sabshin, 1984). The older a girl when she begins to menstruate, the shorter this period of infertility.

Sexual Maturation in Boys

Boys generally begin their growth spurt about two years later than girls, and their growth peaks at the age of fourteen (see Figure 13.3). Although most reach their adult height by the age of sixteen, some do not even begin to grow rapidly until that age. Their pattern of growth is different from that of girls: boys' shoulders broaden more than their hips, and much of the increase in body size comes from muscle, not fat. The penis and scrotum usually begin their accelerated growth when a boy is around twelve and reach mature size within three to four years. Although the external genitalia of girls change little, in boys the changes in penis, testes, and scrotum are substantial. The shaft of the penis lengthens, and its head enlarges; the scrotum and testes grow larger and become pendulous. About a year and a half after his penis begins to grow, a boy is able to ejaculate semen (Tanner, 1978). By the time a boy is about fifteen, his semen contains mature sperm.

The growth of pubic hair accompanies the development of a boy's genitalia, with underarm and facial hair appearing about two years later. As the boy's larynx enlarges and his vocal cords lengthen, his voice deepens. Chest hair is the last male characteristic to appear, and it may not develop fully until well into young adulthood.

Reactions to Physical Change

Physical changes of the magnitude experienced by adolescents have a significant effect on how teenage boys and girls feel about themselves. Whether adolescents regard their adult bodies with pride, pleasure, embarrassment, or shame largely depends on the psychosocial context in which puberty occurs (Petersen, 1985). Reactions to puberty depend in good part on adolescents' childhood patterns of thoughts and feelings about sexuality, the reactions of the adolescents' parents and peers to their changed appearance, and the standards of the culture (both the local peer culture and the larger society).

Gender is another important influence on the youngster's reaction to physiological changes. The culture defines a particular body type as at-

Because today's adolescents are heavier, taller, and mature earlier than yesterday's adolescents, they often develop much higher levels of competence in athletic skills. *(Suzanne Szasz)*

tractive and sexually appropriate for each sex. Young people learn the characteristics of this mythical **body ideal** from peer and family expectations and from comparing their bodies to the images they see on television or in movies and magazines. The lesson is a harsh one for girls, due to the culture's stress on female beauty, and the requirement to attract a mate that is part of the traditionally feminine sex role. In a large survey of adolescents, most of the boys but just over half of the girls were proud of their bodies (Offer, Ostrov, and Howard, 1981). The rest said that they frequently felt ugly and unattractive. Adolescents who already feel unacceptable or who have low self-esteem may become anxious about their appearance, even though others find them as attractive as most of their peers (Petersen and Taylor, 1980). As we shall see in Chapter 14, the culture's unnaturally slim body ideal for girls is related to the development of eating disorders.

A girl's reaction to menstruation seems to depend in good part on how well she has been prepared for the event. Girls who know what to expect generally have fewer menstrual symptoms, including pain, and their symptoms are less severe than those of girls who reach menarche without preparation (Ruble and Brooks-Gunn, 1982). Another important influence on a girl's attitude toward menarche is its timing. Girls who begin to menstruate much earlier than their peers tend to

As their bodies change markedly, boys and girls compare themselves with the culture's body ideal and worry over how they appear to the other sex. *(Left, Richard Kalvar/Magnum; right, Abigail Heyman/Magnum)*

have more negative feelings about the process than those who reach menarche late or "on time." However, a girl's belief about the timing of menarche has more influence on her feelings about the event than its actual timing does. In one study, girls who were "on time" but who believed that they had reached menarche early tended to have the same negative feelings as girls who actually matured ahead of schedule (Rierdan and Koff, 1985).

The timing of puberty affects boys' and girls' feelings about their bodies—but in different ways. Boys who mature earlier than their peers tend to be most satisfied with their bodies, perhaps because they are taller and more muscular than other boys during early adolescence. Among girls in a longitudinal study, the cultural ideal of thinness again influenced the reaction to puberty (Blyth, Simmons, and Zakin, 1985). During early adolescence, girls who matured early generally felt worst about their weight, but as other girls ma-

tured, early maturers' feelings tended to fall into line. It was apparently the deposit of body fat and not the other visible aspects of puberty that bothered them. In general, maturational timing did not affect girls' self-esteem—except among girls who entered junior high school at about the time they reached menarche. When girls had to handle puberty and a new school at the same time, their self-esteem suffered.

What about the long-term effects of early maturity? Does it make a difference to a thirty-year-old whether puberty comes early or late? Early longitudinal studies indicate that, among boys, early maturers have an advantage that they retain throughout young adulthood (Jones, 1965). Early-maturing boys in these studies tended to be active in school activities. As adults, they tended to have higher occupational status, were more likely to work in supervisory or managerial positions, and to report more activity in clubs and organizations than late-maturing boys. Early maturers tended to be conventional, responsible, and socially poised. Late maturers had some positive characteristics; they appeared to be flexible and adaptive, and they were better able to tolerate ambiguity.

Most studies that have followed early- and late-maturing girls into adulthood have turned up few differences. The absence of any major effect is probably due to the traditional dependence of a woman's social life, status, and opportunities for achievement on her husband's status (Eichorn, 1963). However, recent studies that have followed Swedish girls into young adulthood indicate that early maturers are less likely than other girls to go on to college (Magnusson, Stattin, and Allen, 1985). Among these girls, the early maturers sought out older friends, had more contacts with boys, and saw themselves as more mature than other girls their age. Instead of setting their sights on careers, they were ready at an early age to marry and raise families.

COGNITIVE CHANGES

Adolescence ushers in a change in thinking that develops so unobtrusively that it may escape notice. This new way of thinking includes a number of separate skills that began to develop several years earlier but at first could be used only in isolation (Neimark, 1982). Not until adolescence do the skills become coordinated so that the child can apply them generally. When this happens, for the first time children are able to deal with the realm of the possible, the hypothetical, the future, the remote. They can even think about their own thoughts, as did the adolescent who remarked, "I found myself thinking about my future, and then I began to think about why I was thinking about my future." This new ability allows young people to see the world and the people in it, including themselves, in a different way. They speculate about what *might be* instead of accepting what *is*. Such changes affect their scientific reasoning, their understanding of principles, their grasp of society, and their understanding of other people.

Formal Operations

Piaget (1952) described the ability to deal with abstractions and logical possibilities as the stage of formal operations, and he regarded it as the culmination of cognitive development. Most of Piaget's explorations of **formal-operational thought** focused on scientific reasoning, in which children solved problems that required them to explain such concepts as force, inertia, and acceleration. When asked to account for some physical effect, a youngster who has acquired formal thought can isolate elements of the problem and systematically explore all possible solutions. By contrast, a concrete-operational child is likely to forget to test some solutions and to keep testing other solutions that have failed. The difference between these problem-solving approaches becomes clear when we look at the pendulum experiment, which was conducted by Bärbel Inhelder and Piaget (1958).

The two investigators gave youngsters strings of different lengths and objects of different weights, which a child could attach to a rod so that they swung like pendulums (see Figure 13.4). Each of the pendulums swung through its arc at a different speed. The child's task was to determine the factor or factors that accounted for the speed of the pendulum's swing. The four possible causes are (1) the weight of the object, (2) the length of the string, (3) the height from which the object is released, (4) the force of the initial push. Only the length of the string affects the speed of the pendulum. A child can discover this fact either by methodically trying all possible combinations of the four factors (varying a single factor on each trial) or by imagining trials of all possible combinations of factors. Either method, believed Piaget, required formal operations.

Among the children tested by Inhelder and Piaget, only fourteen- and fifteen-year-olds were able to solve the problem by themselves. The youngest children, who were apparently at the preoperational stage, went about the problem unsystematically. They could not vary the factors separately, and none of their trials could convince them that their own initial push was unrelated to the pendulum's speed. Eight- to thirteen-year-olds, who were apparently in the concrete-operational stage, varied some of the factors but found it difficult to

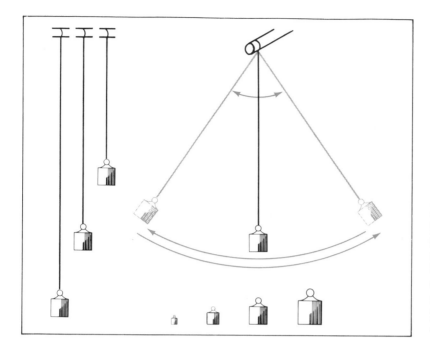

FIGURE 13.4   Illustration of a pendulum problem. The child is given a set of weights *(bottom)* and a string that can be shortened or lengthened *(left)*. The task is to determine which factor or factors account for the speed with which a pendulum traverses its arc. *(After Inhelder and Piaget, 1958)*

exclude any of them. They discovered that the length of the string had something to do with the solution but did not understand that it was the only factor involved. Fourteen- and fifteen-year-olds, who apparently were into the formal-operational stage, anticipated all possible combinations, tested them experimentally, and deduced both which factor affected the pendulum's speed and which factors were irrelevant.

Understanding Social Institutions

Most of what we know about the growth of thought in adolescence comes from studying the solution of problems in science, logic, and mathematics — problems that allow us to see how the child breaks down or combines the problem's elements. The trouble is that these tasks are narrow and unusual in daily life. Such tasks do not capture the common forms of adolescent thought. Another way to look at the movement of thought from the concrete to abstract is to ask children about the purpose of government and law.

When Joseph Adelson (1983; Adelson and Hall, 1987) and his colleagues interviewed more than 300 ten- to eighteen-year-olds in the United

States, England, and Germany, and another group of 450 American adolescents, they discovered a remarkable consistency in the development of children's thought. The preadolescent cannot answer coherently such questions as the purpose of government or law, cannot conceptualize "society" or "community," and can think of institutions only in personal terms. *Education* means *teacher*, *law* means *judge* or *police*. When asked, "What is the purpose of government?" a typical eleven-year-old said, "So everything won't go wrong in the country. They want to have a government because they respect him and they think he's a good man" (Adelson, 1983, p. 158). Like this youngster, preadolescents focus on the concrete; they speak of specific people, events, and objects. They cannot understand the relationship between the individual and the larger society. And so they evaluate all actions without respect for communal needs. As thought gradually becomes more abstract, adolescents begin to understand the invisible network of rules and obligations that bind citizens together. All eighteen-year-olds have some notion of the abstract, and nearly three-quarters are thinking at a high level of abstraction (see Table 13.1).

This dramatic shift in the way adolescents reorganize their perception of society also appears

Table 13.1
Levels of Abstraction in Adolescents' Concept of Government (Percent)

	Age			
	11	13	15	18
Concrete	57	25	07	00
Low-level abstraction	28	64	51	18
High-level abstraction	00	07	42	71
Don't know or not ascertained	15	05	00	13

Source: J. Adelson, "The Growth of Thought in Adolescence," *Educational Horizons* (Summer 1983), 158.

To young adolescents, who cannot handle abstractions, "law" means police, whose purpose is to suppress wayward behavior. *(Larry Mulvehill/Photo Researchers)*

in their thinking about law, politics, and principles. Until children are about fifteen years old, they see the law and other social institutions as primarily involved in suppressing wayward behavior. Children on the brink of adolescence tend to see government and law as purely restrictive. Asked how to teach lawbreakers not to commit additional crimes, they say, "Jail is usually the best thing, but there are others. . . . In the nineteenth century, they used to torture people for doing things. Now I think the best place to teach people is in solitary confinement" (Adelson, 1982, p. 9). Gradually, this authoritarian, punitive attitude gives way to the notion that the purpose of law and government is to protect and benefit the citizen. By the time they are eighteen, adolescents tend to see laws as benevolent ("to protect people and help them out") and as an aid to community ("so that the country will be a better place to live"). By this age, most see government as set up to benefit the average citizen (see Table 13.2).

The same shift from concrete to abstract thought allows adolescents to use moral and political principles in thinking about social issues. When asked to judge some social issue, eleven-year-olds may glibly fall back on some phrase, such as "freedom of religion" or "the majority rules," but probing reveals that they do not understand the principle. A twelve-year-old who champions "freedom of speech," for example, may urge the imprisonment of unpopular speakers, or one who says "the majority rules" may follow up with the comment that the smartest person ought to make all the decisions. Within three years, most of these

children will be able to grasp basic social principles and understand their application.

An understanding of such principles is, of course, necessary before an individual can begin to reason about moral issues at the principled level. Some evidence indicates that the failure to develop a high level of moral reasoning is in part the result of a failure to develop formal thought. In one study, a majority (60 percent) of people older than

Table 13.2
Adolescents' Opinions on the Purpose of Government (Percent)

	Age			
	11	13	15	18
Restriction	73	68	44	20
Restriction and benefit	12	18	33	38
Benefit	07	08	20	41
Other	08	05	03	01

Source: J. Adelson, "The Growth of Thought in Adolescence," *Educational Horizons* (Summer 1983), 159.

sixteen showed advanced formal thought, but only a small proportion (10 percent) also reasoned on a principled level (Kohlberg and Gilligan, 1971). In fact, few people reach this stage of moral development before young adulthood. In Chapter 11, we saw that premoral reasoning on Kohlberg's scale declines steadily after the age of ten and that adolescents tend to reason at the conventional level (Colby, Kohlberg, Gibbs, and Lieberman, 1983). Throughout adolescence, the boys in this original study increasingly tended to define moral actions in terms of avoiding breakdowns in the social system and became less likely to justify actions in terms of seeming to be good people in their own or others' eyes.

Understanding People

A similar progression occurs in adolescents' understanding of other people and their motivations. Until adolescence, children have only a limited understanding of human motivation. In their simple view of motives, they think in terms of getting mad, getting even, or teaching a lesson. The idea of gradations of motives and of variations in personality is beyond them. Similarly, they have only a limited time perspective. Their grasp on the effect of the past on the present — or of the present on the future — is feeble. Thus, they have almost no sense of others' inner conflicts, of the sources of conduct in personal history, or of the motives that would produce personal change. When Adelson (1982) asked eleven-year-olds why some people are law-abiding and others are not, their confused replies again showed a dependence on the concrete. As one child put it:

> Oh, well, someone — their mom and dad might separate or something and neither one wanted them or something like that, didn't like them very much and oh, if they happened to turn bad, I mean just, and they had trouble — pretty soon if they keep doing that and pretty bad conditions they'll probably get in a lot of trouble. (P. 12)

This child, who has a vague idea that rejection by parents and getting away with small infractions may be involved in later delinquency, does not generalize. Instead the youngster talks only about specific acts and specific feelings. By the age of

fifteen, this same child will be able to talk about problems in the abstract, saying that kids who come from broken families feel bad about themselves and become troublemakers.

As we saw in Chapter 11, children's ability to take another's role progresses hand in hand with cognitive development. Most young adolescents are in the stage of mutual role-taking. They know that both they and a friend can consider their own and each other's view at the same time. They also can understand how a third party might interpret their interaction with another person (Selman, 1980). The twelve-year-old in this stage can think about his or her friendships.

Not until they are about fifteen do children enter the final stage of role-taking, in which they can consider society's point of view as well. In one study, 14 percent of thirteen-year-olds and 57 percent of sixteen-year-olds had reached this stage (Byrne, 1973). These youngsters were beginning to grasp abstract principles and the concept of community. They were aware that people's thoughts and motivations can be influenced by factors that the person is not aware of. Children who have reached the final stage of role-taking also understand two-loop recursive thinking ("The boy is thinking that the girl is thinking of him thinking of her") (Flavell, 1985). Studies indicate that although only a handful of twelve-year-olds seem to use two-loop recursions, 65 percent of sixteen-year-olds use them spontaneously in conversation (Shantz, 1983).

Adolescent Egocentrism

The adolescent's new command of thought also may enmesh him or her in a different kind of egocentrism. According to David Elkind (1985), adolescents who can infer what other people are thinking tend to focus their inferences on what other people are thinking about the adolescent. This new egocentrism is a feature of early adolescence. By the time youngsters are fifteen or sixteen, it is already on the wane. While it lasts, adolescents tend to think in terms of what Elkind calls the "imaginary audience" and to believe in the "personal fable."

The **imaginary audience** refers to the adolescent's belief that other people share the adolescent's own preoccupation with himself or herself and hence are always noticing the young person's appearance, behavior, and actions. Continually on stage for the imaginary audience, the adolescent becomes highly self-conscious. The audience is one that the adolescent creates in his or her head — an accomplishment that is beyond the younger child. When combing his hair in front of a mirror, for example, the fourteen-year-old boy imagines how his peer group will admire his new haircut (Elkind, 1985).

When studying the adolescent's creation of the imaginary audience, researchers ask young people to imagine themselves in a number of revealing situations, such as discovering at school, just before you get up before the class to solve an algebra problem, that the side seam of your jeans is ripped (Elkind and Bowen, 1979). Then the youngsters tell how they would handle the situation. Those adolescents most in the thrall of the imaginary audience are likely to say that they would refuse to go to the chalkboard. Those who are less worried might say that they would hold a hand over the rip, and some say that they simply would ignore it.

The **personal fable** refers to the adolescent's feeling that he or she is personally unique and indestructible. The teenager's feeling of indestructibility is reflected in the complaint by the exasperated mother of a fifteen-year-old:

> As far as he is concerned, he can guzzle two six packs without getting drunk, he can drive a car without a lesson or a license, he can fly without wings. He probably feels that he could smoke, snort, sniff, inhale, swallow, or inject any substance at all without overdosing, becoming an addict, or losing his grip. . . . His response to everything is: "I know. *I know!*" (Karsh, 1987, p. 23)

The adolescent's uniqueness leads to the belief that his or her views and feelings are totally different from those of others. In fact, no one has ever experienced the world in the way that he or she is experiencing it (Harter, 1983). No one has ever loved as deeply, hurt as badly, or seen others' motivations with such clarity as the young adolescent.

Elkind believes that adolescent egocentrism is the result of the youngster's beginning grasp of formal operations, but other researchers have questioned this explanation. Their studies have

In later adolescence, thought is sufficiently abstract to let students build an understanding of the rules and obligations that bind citizens together, whether in student government or in the larger community. (*James L. Shaffer*)

found no consistent correlation between adolescent egocentrism and formal operations among sixth to twelfth graders (Lapsley, Milstead, Quintana, Flannery, and Buss, 1986). Because egocentrism seems to decline at about mid-adolescence, it may reflect the stage of mutual role-taking, which children enter before they have achieved formal operations (Lapsley and Murphy, 1985). In this view, as children pass into the final stage of role-taking, the imaginary audience loses its power, and the personal fable begins to crumble.

Prevalence of Formal Thought

The abstract, scientific thought that characterizes adolescence is not firmly established until children are at least fifteen years old (Inhelder and Piaget, 1958). Its development is not guaranteed. Most studies indicate that the emergence of formal operations depends on experience in formal education. For example, people who grow up in primitive villages seem unable to reason from hypotheses (If . . . then) (Kohlberg and Gilligan, 1971). Yet some people in societies without formal schooling develop abstract thought. Otherwise such structures as Stonehenge in England could not have been built (Neimark, 1982).

Nor is formal thought an all-or-nothing accomplishment. A person may achieve formal thought in one domain (such as history) and not another (such as physics). Finally, once attained, it can be lost—or at least discarded. The sort of logical reasoning we use in daily life rarely requires formal thought, and when daily life does not require formal thought, a person may cease to use it.

Yet adolescents retain most of their capacity for formal thought. If they did not, they could not function adequately. By the age of sixteen, almost all adolescents can think about abstractions and have developed a sense of community, some idea of rights, some ability to recognize future consequences, a grasp of inner motivation, a sense of the multiple determinants of action, and an understanding of political principles, their scope and limits. They may later lose such accomplishments, but only momentarily and usually in situations of psychological stress.

CHANGES IN THE SELF

During adolescence, youngsters face a variety of tasks whose outcome will affect the course of their future lives. Their emerging sexuality presents the possibility of intimacy with members of the other sex and the eventual formation of their own family. They can foresee the coming separation from their parents. They must make choices about schooling and vocations. They are striving for autonomy and dealing with issues of principles, politics, and religion. As they wrestle with these issues, they discover that their changed bodies evoke new expectations and behavior from friends, peers, and society.

With such change in every aspect of their lives, it is no wonder that adolescence is the time when boys and girls test their feelings about themselves, either consolidating their self-concepts or developing new ones. Most youngsters handle these issues of the self with little difficulty and successfully resolve the conflict between their own needs and social demands. But a few, who still have unresolved conflicts from earlier stages of development, reexperience these earlier conflicts and may return to earlier ways of resolving them. Whether the issue that flares up concerns matters of trust, autonomy, initiative, or industry depends on the adolescent's history, his or her individual strengths, and habitual ways of responding to stressful situations (Adelson and Doehrman, 1980). In the next chapter, we see how some adolescents respond to the revival of old conflicts and other intolerable stress—by becoming pregnant, addicted to drugs, or developing anorexia.

Yet only a minority of adolescents become young people in trouble. Most youngsters have coped with the developmental tasks of each stage, and their personalities remain relatively stable. As they encountered each developmental issue, they resolved it in an appropriate way. The vast majority of adolescents are happy, strong, and self-confident. They make friends easily, are not afraid of their sexuality, and see no major problems between themselves and their parents. They are hopeful about the future, look forward to adulthood, and believe that they can handle whatever challenges life has in store for them. This picture of the normal adolescent emerged from the replies of more than 20,000 teenagers who were studied by Daniel Offer and his colleagues (Offer and Sabshin, 1984). Because these young people ranged in age from thirteen to nineteen, some had not yet begun to work on the problem of identity; others had already achieved a sturdy sense of who they were and where they were going.

Identity

The achievement of identity is an essential task of adolescence. **Identity** is a coherent sense of individuality formed out of the adolescent's traits and circumstances. But such a definition barely begins to explain a complicated concept. According to Erik Erikson (1980), the adolescent's identity develops silently, over time, as many bits and pieces of the self come together in an organized way. These elements include inborn aspects of personality, such as temperament; developed aspects of personality, such as passivity, aggression, sensuality; talents and abilities; identification with models, whether parent, peer, or culture figure; ways of handling conflicts and regulating conduct; and the adoption of consistent social, vocational, and gender roles. Identity formation is a lifelong task that has its roots in early childhood, but it does not become central until adolescence. At that time, a youngster's physical development, cognitive

While various elements of identity are coming together, many adolescents go through a period of moratorium, when they postpone their commitment to an occupation, a religious faith, or a political conviction. *(Billy E. Barnes/Southern Light)*

skills, and social expectations mature enough to make the formation of a mature identity possible.

Erikson saw adolescence as a time of moratorium, a period when definitive choices are postponed while the various elements of identity are coming together. During that period, all the choices adolescents make (which courses to take in school, whether to go to college, whom to date, whether to take drugs, have sex, work after school, join a church, or work in a political campaign) contribute to the forging of identity. When the process does not go well, as when a variety of conflicts make the choices difficult — or even impossible — the result is a confused identity, in which the young person makes no commitments. Because Erikson's concept of identity is so complicated, assessing an adolescent's progress on this developmental task is extremely difficult.

Researchers found a way to get around the problem. They began classifying an adolescent's progress toward identity formation in terms of their status on the tasks of selecting an occupation and forging religious or political beliefs — clearly major components of identity. Building on Erikson's theory, James Marcia (1980) proposed that adolescent identity took one of four forms: foreclosure, moratorium, diffusion, or achievement.

In **foreclosure,** the adolescent is pursuing occupational and ideological goals, but the goals have been chosen by others — either parents or peers. (Ideological goals may be religious or political — or both.) Foreclosed adolescents have never experienced an "identity crisis," because they have uncritically accepted the values and expectations of others. In **moratorium,** the final choices have been put off. The adolescent is still struggling with occupational or ideological issues. He or she is in an identity crisis. In **identity achievement,** the adolescent has completed the struggle, made his or her own choices, and is pursuing occupational or ideological goals. Finally, in **identity diffusion,** the adolescent may have attempted to deal with these issues (or may have ignored them) but has made no choices and is not particularly concerned about making such commitments. Because such youngsters feel no pressure to choose, they are *not* in an identity crisis.

Adolescents whose identity moves from moratorium to identity achievement seem to have taken the preferred path — at least in contemporary cultures. Such young people are generally more independent, self-confident, flexible, and intellectually creative than other youngsters. Those whose identities are foreclosed tend to need the approval of others; they are conforming, respectful of authority, and they are more religious and behave in a more stereotypical fashion than other young people. In traditional societies, where young people automatically accept their parents' occupations and beliefs, most youngsters have foreclosed identities. Indeed, in such a society, an adolescent who made independent choices probably would be a misfit. Adolescents who have followed the identity diffusion pattern tend to be disturbed; they may lack a sense of direction, relate poorly to others, show a low level of moral reasoning, and may be heavy drug users. Yet they can seem charming and carefree.

Many youngsters enter young adulthood before they achieve their identity. Today, prolonged schooling probably keeps people in the moratorium status for a longer period than was once the case. Throughout adolescence, boys and girls can explore various fields, trying to find a match with their personal needs, interests, capacities, and values. But in early adolescence, most know little about the choices they soon must make, about the pathways that alternative choices may lead to, or about the irreversibility of some choices. For example, courses selected in high school often turn out to be irrevocable choices that determine whether a student's eventual occupation will be in the area of science or the humanities. Even so, as many as half of young people in college change their career goals before graduation.

Researchers have found that the process of identity formation may take somewhat different paths in boys and girls. When interviewed at the end of their junior or senior year in high school, boys who had achieved an occupational identity tended to be assertive, prefer difficult, challenging tasks, and to have little concern about others' opinions of them (Grotevant and Thorbecke, 1982). Girls who had achieved an occupational identity were quite different: they believed that hard work was important, but they avoided competition.

Perhaps this difference is due in good part to the context in which boys and girls form their identities. Boys are urged to make career decisions, a pressure that tends to push them toward a moratorium and later identity achievement. But even in a world of changing sex roles, girls tend to define their identities in terms of their relations with others. Instead of being concerned with autonomous thinking and carving out careers for themselves, they are primarily concerned with relationships and responsibilities (Gilligan, 1982).

Despite the fact that they are likely to spend most of their lives in the labor market, most girls feel little pressure to choose an occupation. During adolescence, they are likely to view employment as a temporary way station between high-school graduation and the birth of their first child. For them, marriage plays a dominant role in identity formation.

Yet some girls show a pattern of development in which achievement is as important as interpersonal success and traditionally feminine interests. This pattern was detected more than twenty years ago by Elizabeth Douvan and Joseph Adelson (1966), who found a group of girls with aspirations directed toward their own achievements rather than the status of their future husbands. These girls showed a greater interest in assuming adult roles and responsibilities than did traditionally feminine girls, and their perspective extended farther into the future. Girls in this group were feminine, but they dreamed of individual achievement. They tended to prefer risky jobs with opportunities for success over secure, less rewarding jobs.

Girls who followed this pattern tended to have parents who encouraged them to "stand on their own two feet." But more recent research has indicated that this pattern may be especially prevalent among girls who come from broken homes. Girls who grow up in stable homes are unlikely to achieve identity early. Among a group of girls in their last year of high school, those who had already achieved an identity tended to come from homes that had been broken by death or divorce (St. Clair and Day, 1979). Among the identity achievers, two-thirds came from broken homes, compared with only a fifth of the girls who showed other identity statuses. In Chapter 9, we saw that girls suffer less from divorce than boys. Home disruption may require earlier independence in girls, and perhaps lead them to the early realization that marriages are not always permanent and that they may have to think about occupational choices, much as boys do. Whatever the cause, girls in broken homes tend to make their own decisions about their future — and make them earlier than other girls.

Family conflict may affect boys differently. In one longitudinal study of boys, those from strife-ridden homes were more likely than other boys to have emotional conflicts (Offer and Offer, 1975).

The most stable transitions into adulthood appeared in boys who came from stable families and who accepted their parents' values and goals without question. These boys with foreclosed identities who seemed to grow up placidly, did well in school and had good relationships with others. Such boys generally accepted the role models they saw around them, and many went into the same occupations as their fathers. For example, the son of a tradesman, who has his own electrical or plumbing business or owns a small appliance store, begins learning the family business early in adolescence. For him, there is no identity crisis, because he never seriously considers any other occupation.

Sexual Identity

Sexual identity is an important aspect of the adolescent self. Adolescents' sexual identity has been developing since they realized, at about the age of three, that they were boys or girls and began learning the implications of that biological fact. How do the sexual impulses of puberty and a maturing body affect adolescents' perceptions of themselves as male or female? And what about the pressures from family and peers for sex-role conformity? Can they be resisted? And at what cost?

None of these questions can be answered satisfactorily, because there are no reliable data. But most observers believe that puberty brings with it an intensified feeling of gender. Boys begin to swagger and value muscles, and girls suddenly become super-feminine. These heightened sex-role displays probably are less the result of raging hormones than of social factors. First, youngsters whose bodies are blatantly announcing their sexual maturation to the world feel an inner uncertainty about their new situation. Adhering to a prescribed sex role is safer than experimenting with unconventional behavior. Second, the peer group demands conformity to sex roles, and straying too far outside the group's standards carries certain social costs.

Yet the pressure for adolescent sex-role conformity is not as restrictive as it might seem. Parents, peer groups, and society primarily tell youngsters what they must *not* do. Essentially, they prohibit a few extreme gender styles, such as that of the extremely effeminate boy. Because no

The demands of the peer group for conformity to sex roles contribute to a girl's tendency to become super-feminine during early adolescence. *(Leonard Speier)*

one tells youngsters what they *must* do, girls and boys have a wide variety of gender styles open to them.

Sex differences in adolescents' personal qualities show little change from childhood. Boys generally are more violent and more aggressive than girls. They also are more interested in mastery and less interested in interpersonal relationships. Girls are more at home with interpersonal relationships, and they are more caring and more concerned with the welfare of others. But even in areas where clear sex differences exist, the behavior, attitudes, and abilities of boys and girls largely overlap.

In large-scale studies of adolescents, boys and girls are more alike than different (Offer, Ostrov, and Howard, 1981; Ostrov and Sabshin, 1984). Yet there are some sharp differences. Girls, who tend to focus on interpersonal relationships, are more likely than boys to feel sad or lonely and to have their feelings hurt. Girls feel more strongly about social values (telling the truth, not hurting others) than boys do, and they are more likely to become upset if someone disapproves of them. Boys are more autonomous, worry less about the opinions of others, and are more likely to feel like leaders.

Sex Roles and Intellectual Development

When researchers try to untangle the relationship between gender and intellectual development, they find themselves caught in a complicated web. Some studies indicate a link between masculine personality qualities (aggression, dominance, competitiveness) and high scores in math and a similar connection between feminine personal qualities (compassion, understanding, gentleness) and high verbal scores (Huston, 1983). The relation seems to hold for both boys and girls, so that girls who see masculine qualities in themselves tend to do well in the supposedly masculine field of math, and boys who see feminine qualities in themselves tend to do well in the supposedly feminine verbal field.

The link between feminine qualities and verbal achievement seems plausible. Since early childhood, many youngsters have considered reading and writing as girls' activities. But why should the link between masculinity and math achievement be so prevalent? It all seems to depend on how we define masculinity and femininity. When researchers break down the concepts, both relationships are less straightforward. Among seventh and eighth graders who were tested by Carol Mills (1980), boys and girls with highly stereotyped interests and attitudes tended to do poorly in all academic fields. Stereotyped boys held macho values: they enjoyed fistfights, hunting, mechanics magazines, the military, and race-car driving. Stereotyped girls were "super feminine": they liked dress designing, nursing, and romantic stories.

Who tended to succeed in school? Girls and boys who saw themselves as mature (independent, self-sufficient, assertive) tended to do best in both academic fields. These qualities that predict

school success generally are associated with the masculine sex role, and the finding helps explain some of the association between masculinity and school achievement that often appears among college students. But the connection between sex roles and achievement is not complete. Boys who made high scores on math and verbal tests tended to be moody, unhappy, solemn and not cheerful. High-scoring girls tended to be the opposite. Mills sees this link between sex roles and achievement as an early adolescent stage. Among young adolescents, boys who do well in school are not considered "cool." Only in later adolescence do boys see academic achievement in positive terms. The sunny, high-achieving girls may also be an early-adolescent phenomenon. In later adolescence, they begin to see academic achievement as "not very feminine."

CHANGES IN FAMILY LIFE

When a child enters adolescence, the family system changes. The adolescent's new body, changing social relationships, and burgeoning mental powers affect the nature of family interactions. More or less compliant children, who saw their parents as wise and powerful dispensers of affection, discipline, and material goods, turn into "almost adults," who begin to assert their rights, question family rules, and see their parents as imperfect human beings. At the same time, they become less emotionally dependent on their parents. As adolescents move toward a more nearly peer-like relationship with their parents, some tension is inevitable. But generational warfare or continual turmoil is rare. In three out of four families, a child's transition into adolescence, with its accompanying changes in family roles, causes only minor and sporadic conflict (Hill, 1985). Whatever stress develops is handled effectively.

Perhaps one reason that family life remains relatively smooth is that most parents understand their teenage sons and daughters fairly well. In more than 100 normal families, researchers compared adolescents' image of themselves with their mothers' and fathers' perceptions of their child (Offer, Ostrov, and Howard, 1982). In most instances, parents and children agreed. For example,

GIRLS ON THE FOOTBALL TEAM

In October, 1985, a federal judge ruled that Jacqueline Lantz, a 4-foot 10-inch, 125 pound, sixteen-year-old, had the right to go out for football at a Yonkers high school. Within three weeks, the New York State Board of Regents rescinded regulations that prohibited girls from playing on teams with boys in contact sports (Maeroff, 1985). All teams in New York state high schools are open to girls, but they first must have their physical fitness evaluated by a special panel consisting of the school physician, a physical education teacher, and a physician chosen by the girls' parents.

The ruling did not lead to an immediate flood of female applicants. It came too late in the season for Lantz to get in much contact practice, and so she spent the remainder of the year on the bench. At a high school in upstate New York, another girl joined the junior-varsity squad but quit after three days. She decided that the risk of back injury was too great. In 1986, girls at two separate high schools signed up for football, and one played defensive back in the team's opening game. But Lantz passed up football in her senior year, choosing instead to go out for drama — an activity she planned to pursue in college (Hanley, 1986b).

Across the river in the state of New Jersey, girls have had a rough introduction to the sport. Elizabeth Balsley, a seventeen-year-old senior whose successful suit opened up New Jersey high-school football to girls, saw action in only one game her first season. When she joined the team the following year, some of her teammates objected. In an attempt to get her to quit the squad, three of them jumped her, knocking her to the ground, hitting her, and spitting on her. The school suspended the boys from class for several days and ordered them to sit out the team's next game (Hanley, 1986a). Things have gone better for fourteen-year-old Lina Garcia, who was a touch football star in junior high school. Garcia didn't have to petition to get on the team; she went out for freshman football at the coach's request. At 5 feet 3 inches and 120 pounds, she is about the same size as the boys on the team. She is enthusiastic and fast and has been accepted by her teammates, who helped her learn how to hit and how to take a hit. But she still has trouble catching passes (Hanley, 1986b).

Elizabeth Balsley was allowed to go out for football at her New Jersey high school only after she sued the school board. (Bettmann Newsphotos)

Some educators are reluctant to let girls play contact sports on the grounds that girls' body composition (more fat and less muscle mass per pound of body weight than boys) places them under additional risk of injury, but the courts have disagreed. Although the average girl is smaller, weaker, and slower than the average boy, the average girl does not go out for football and would not make the team if she did. The genetic gap in strength and muscular development between girls and boys probably has been accentuated by the sexes' different exercise patterns during childhood. If changes in sex roles lead to extensive participation in traditionally masculine sports during later childhood and early adolescence, the gap may narrow, producing a group of girls who will have little trouble making the varsity team.

Despite frequent disagreements between parents and their adolescent children, most adolescents believe that their parents are patient, supportive, and proud of their offspring. *(Thomas Hopker/Woodfin Camp & Associates)*

a boy's answer to a statement that explored how well he understood his parents was similar to the parents' estimate of how well the son thought he understood them. Where did the adolescent's self-image and his or her parents' perceptions part company? Primarily on sexual matters. Parents tended to underestimate the importance of having a boyfriend to their daughter or having a girlfriend to their son. They also underestimated their teenager's appreciation of dirty jokes. But they overestimated their child's attractiveness to the other sex — at least in their child's eyes.

The nature of family relations before puberty has a good deal to do with the way a child experiences adolescence. Communication between parent and child seems to be a key to a healthy adolescence. The better the communication between parent and child, the more positive an adolescent's self-image is likely to be (Offer, Ostrov, and Howard, 1982). Good communication seems to reflect a smoothly functioning family system, one in which parents are able to communicate their values, beliefs, and feelings to their children. Such families are likely to be loving and democratic, and

the parents are likely to set clear demands without being rigid. As Chapter 14 indicates, youngsters who grow up in families where parents are undemanding, rejecting, and unresponsive are at risk for a number of adolescent disorders. In such families, parents may fail to communicate their basic values.

Shifting Family Roles

No matter how loving and democratic the home, no matter how well parents understand their sons and daughters, as children enter adolescence, their interactions with parents change in subtle ways. The result is often a shift of power within the family. When Laurence Steinberg (1981) followed thirty-one intact, middle-class families in which the oldest child was a boy on the brink of puberty, he found that the boy's sexual maturation ushered in mother-son conflict. The pair began interrupting each other in family discussions, and the son became increasingly less deferential to his mother. Eventually, the mother backed off and began to defer to her son. The father retained his dominance over the boy — in fact, fathers' power seemed to increase.

Puberty also affects a girl's relationship with her parents, but the pattern of change is somewhat different. Menarche seems to usher in a period of temporary strain between mother and daughter. Among the seventh-grade girls in one study, those who recently had begun menstruating saw their mothers as less accepting and the family as being stricter and more controlling than did girls who had not yet reached menarche (Hill, Holmbeck, Marlow, Green, and Lynch, 1985). The girls also participated less in family activities, seemed less influenced by their families, and turned to them less often for guidance.

Minor parent-child conflict seems to peak in early adolescence, just before a youngster enters high school. Then disagreements wane, and relationships steadily become more harmonious. When researchers asked more than 300 seventh and eighth graders about family arguments, they reported that issues of school performance, household rules and chores, and adolescent privileges and freedoms dominated family disagreements (Richardson, Galambos, Schulenberg, and Petersen, 1985). Although one youngster out of ten complained about angry outbursts by their parents, most of these seventh and eighth graders said that their parents' disciplinary methods were fair.

Any family discord that accompanies the child's new status occurs within the context of general family harmony. These same seventh and eighth graders said that they were generally satisfied with family life and enjoyed sharing activities. Asked what they would change about their families, only 4 percent of the boys and 7 percent of the girls focused on their relationships with their parents. Most youngsters said that they went to their parents with their problems, and mothers were seen as a better source of comfort and understanding than fathers. More than two-thirds of these young adolescents felt comfortable discussing with their parents such issues as family relationships, their future goals and aspirations, and their relationships with same-sex peers. However, they drew the line at talking with parents about sexual issues or their relationships with adolescents of the other sex.

Quest for Autonomy

During adolescence, autonomy becomes an important issue for the first time since toddlerhood. According to Laurence Steinberg and Susan Silverberg (1986), youngsters are working on three major aspects of autonomy:

1. Emotional autonomy, in which they give up their childish dependence on parents and begin to perceive them as people
2. Resistance to peer pressure, in which they overcome a dependence on the peer group, its standards, and opinions
3. Self-reliance, in which they feel independent, assertive, and in control of their own lives.

After studying nearly 900 fifth to ninth graders, these researchers found that each aspect of autonomy has its own course of development (see Figure 13.5). These aspects of autonomy are related in a curious way. As emotional autonomy grows, resistance to peer pressure declines. Adolescents who are least dependent on their parents are most likely to succumb to peer pressure — whether the

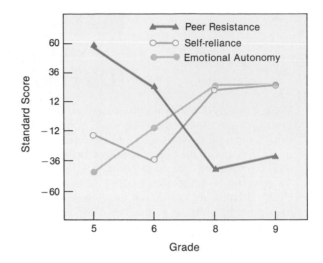

FIGURE 13.5   **The development of autonomy. During early adolescence, youngsters work at three aspects of autonomy: giving up their dependence on their parents (emotional autonomy); resisting peer pressure; and self-reliance. As self-reliance grows and dependence on parents wanes, young adolescents find it increasingly difficult to resist peer pressure.** *(From Steinberg and Silverberg, 1986)*

pressure is to leave shoelaces untied, drink Pepsi instead of Coke, smoke, or use drugs. This means that most children trade dependence on their parents for a period of dependence on their peers.

A similar shift in influence appeared among another group of more than 800 sixth and eighth graders (Krosnick and Judd, 1982). Whether sixth graders smoked cigarettes was influenced more by the parents' attitudes than by whether their peers smoked. Youngsters who said that their parents would be "really mad" if they smoked and who had been warned against smoking were less likely to use cigarettes than those whose parents would be "not mad at all" — even if their friends smoked. Among eighth graders, peer influence had become stronger and the effect of parental attitudes weaker, so that the example of peers was stronger than that of parents. As we saw in Chapter 10, other researchers have found that conformity to peers peaks in the ninth grade, just at the point where this study ends. In Thomas Berndt's (1979) research, conformity to antisocial peer pressure declined during the high school years. Sixteen- and seventeen-year-olds no longer felt so com-

SAME FAMILY, DIFFERENT WORLD

What happens in the family has important implications for every aspect of development. Most discussions of parental styles and sibling relationships imply that within the family, children share a common environment. But as we saw in Chapter 12, "within-family influences," those aspects of a child's life that are not shared by all children, may have powerful effects on the way that youngsters develop.

When Denise Daniels and her colleagues (Daniels, Dunn, Furstenberg, and Plomin, 1985) conducted separate interviews with pairs of adolescent siblings, they discovered that the adolescents had views of life within their families that differed substantially from their siblings'. Such differences in perception are not surprising. Twenty years ago, the Smothers Brothers became a popular comedy team by ending almost every sketch with the complaint, "Mom always loved you best!" In this case, there was some substance to the adolescents' perceptions. When researchers interviewed the mother of each pair, she confirmed the youngsters' reports—although the differences she saw were smaller than those perceived by the adolescents. These differences had little to do with an adolescent's age, gender, or birth order, which are often suggested as sources of within-family differences.

The traditional complaints by brothers and sisters, that parents lavish more time and affection on a sibling, expect a sibling to do fewer chores, or give a sibling more say in family decisions, turned out to be well-founded. Yet no one, parent or child, was asked to make comparisons between the sibling pairs. Instead, the youngsters reported how their parents treated them and how they got along with their sibling and other children. Mothers were asked about each child separately at different times in the course of a long interview.

Five aspects of the children's lives predicted which child in a pair would be rated as better adjusted. First, the closeness of the relationship between adolescent and mother was important. Better adjusted adolescents were more likely than their brother or sister to say that their mother spent enough time with them, gave them all the affection they wanted, and often did things together with them. Second was the friendliness of the sibling. Better adjusted adolescents reported fewer fights or disagreements in the sibling relationship than did their sister or brother. Third was the friendliness of peers. Better adjusted adolescents reported fewer fights or disagreements with other children. Fourth was the child's say in family decision making. Better adjusted adolescents believed that they had more say in making family rules, that parents talked over important decisions with them, and that they listened to the adolescent's side of any argument. Fifth was the child's home responsibilities. Better adjusted adolescents were expected to help more around the house, straightening up or cleaning, cooking and doing dishes.

Family interactions are always difficult to disentangle. Adolescents' and parents' perceptions of children's environments do not explain all the differences between siblings. Interpreting this study is not easy. It can give us no hint about which comes first, the differences in parental treatment or the adolescent's behavior. As the researchers point out, an adolescent who perceives that he or she is the best-loved child may develop strong self-esteem, but it is just as probable that a child with strong self-esteem gets more love from parents.

---

pelled to conform to their peers' wishes. They had begun to accept conventional adult standards for their behavior.

Autonomy may follow a different course of development in girls and boys. Steinberg and Silverberg (1986) found that, at any age, girls who felt self-reliant found it easiest to resist peer pressure. But among boys, there was no relation between self-reliance and resistance to peer pressure. A strongly self-reliant boy was as likely to succumb to peer pressure as a boy with little self-reliance. To the researchers' surprise, at every age girls

Adolescents spend the largest part of their waking hours in the company of their peers — a fact that helps explain the growth of peer influence in early adolescence. *(Leonard Speier)*

showed more autonomy than boys. They showed stronger emotional autonomy, were better at resisting peer pressure (whether it involved cheating on an exam or choosing where to spend the afternoon), and were more self-reliant. Twice as many ninth-grade girls as boys were high in both emotional autonomy and resistance to peer pressure.

CHANGES IN FRIENDSHIP AND SOCIAL LIFE

Throughout adolescence, friends and peers become increasingly important in a child's life. Their contribution to a youngster's social development may be especially important during early adolescence, when children are coming to terms with the physical and emotional changes in their lives (Crockett, Losoff, and Petersen, 1984). In most cases, this growing attachment to peers does not interfere with teenagers' relationship with their parents, but complements it.

When we consider how much time adolescents spend with their peers, the surprise is that peer influence is not more substantial than studies indicate. For the first time, we have a fairly accurate picture of the company teenagers keep. As part of the study reported in the box "What Teenagers Do All Day" (p.362), high-school students reported whom they were with each time their pager beeped (Csikszentmihalyi and Larson, 1984). When time with peers in the classroom (23 percent) and outside it (29 percent) was added together, it became apparent that the largest portion of most adolescents' waking hours is spent in the company of their contemporaries. Because teenagers are alone with parents for less than 5 percent of their time, with parents and siblings for about 8 percent, and with parents and friends together for another 2 percent, parents seem to have limited opportunities to influence their adolescent children. Some youngsters spend more time with peers than others. Among the high-school students in this study, too much time devoted to peers spelled trouble in other areas of the child's life. Teenagers who were with family more and peers less made better grades in school, were absent less often, and, according to their teachers, were "more intellectually involved" than other youngsters.

Friendships

Outgrowing the "fair-weather cooperation" that characterizes the child's friendships, the adolescent moves into an intimate relationship that is characterized by mutual sharing (Selman, 1981). Intimate friendships increase sharply between the ages of twelve and fourteen, perhaps because by then adolescents are equipped for this deepening relationship. Their new cognitive powers allow them to take the role of their friend, to see the friend's point of view, and to imagine how the friend understands them. As we saw earlier, adolescent egocentrism leads most adolescents to a preoccupation with how they impress other people (Elkind, 1985). As Carolyn Shantz (1983) describes the adolescent friendship, it is a mutual relationship, in which the friends care for each other, share their thoughts and feelings, and comfort each other. By now the bonds that link them are tough enough to endure some of the quarrels that rupture the friendships of nine- and ten-year-olds.

Most children get along well with their peers. Among one group of eighth graders, more than 80 percent said that they had a best friend, and the majority said that the friendship had lasted more than a year (Crockett, Losoff, and Petersen, 1984). Most children had one "best" friend and several "good" friends. They saw them every day at school, and about half visited each other's homes daily, with the rest exchanging visits at least weekly. Eighth graders lived up to the popular stereotype of the adolescent as a creature with a telephone grafted to one ear while a rock tape blasted in the background. Besides seeing their friends at school and at each other's homes, half the boys and four-fifths of the girls phoned their friends every day. The girls spent more than an hour each day on the phone; about a third talked for at least ninety minutes. Boys were less talkative; they averaged just over thirty minutes a day, with about one in ten spending an hour or more on the phone.

Girls' friendships progress from the activity-centered pairs of twelve-year-olds to the interdependent, emotional relationships of middle adolescence. The fourteen- to sixteen-year-old wants someone to confide in, someone who can offer emotional support and understanding. At this age, a friend must be loyal, trustworthy, and a reliable source of support in an emotional crisis (Douvan and Adelson, 1966). Many mid-adolescent boys' friendships tend to resemble those of the eleven- or twelve-year-old girl. The average boy is less concerned with closeness, mutual understanding, and emotional support, and more concerned with finding a congenial companion with whom to share activities. When fourteen-year-olds describe their friendships, the level of intimacy in girls' friendships is significantly higher than that of boys in every aspect of the relationship (Crockett, Losoff, and Petersen, 1984) (see Table 13.3). For example, 29 percent of the girls but only 8 percent of the eighth-grade boys said that they felt closest to a friend, and 64 percent of the girls but only 39 percent of the boys talked to friends about their problems. Despite this sex difference, many boys' friends are more than companions in fun. A mid-adolescent Wisconsin boy said:

> A best friend to me is someone you can have fun with and you can also be serious with about personal things, about girls, or what you're going to do with your life, or whatever. . . . A best friend is someone who's not going to make fun of you just because you do something stupid or put you down if you make a mistake. If you're afraid of something or someone, they'll give you confidence. (Bell, 1980, p. 62)

As girls move into later adolescence, the emotional intensity of their friendships subsides. The relationship is calmer; although the exchange of confidences remains important, older girls focus on sharing their personality, talents, and interests

Table 13.3
Average Intimacy Levels in Eighth-Grade Friendships (Percent)

	Boys	Girls	Significance (p-value)
Seeks friend for advice	2.60	3.80	.001
Wants to be like friend	2.48	3.10	.001
Feels accepted by friend	4.10	4.37	.025
Feels understood by friend	3.95	4.31	.022
Shares secrets/inner feelings with friend	3.29	4.07	.001
Friend seeks him or her for advice	3.00	3.93	.001
Importance of friend	4.29	4.68	.004
Satisfaction with relationship	4.48	4.54	NS

Note: Adolescents rated their friendships on a 5-point scale, in which 1 = "not at all"; 2 = "a little"; 3 = "some"; 4 = "mostly"; and 5 = "very much." Only in their satisfaction with the relationship was there no significant difference (NS) between girls and boys.

Source: Adapted from L. Crockett, M. Losoff, and A. C. Petersen, "Perceptions of the Peer Group and Friendship in Early Adolescence," *Journal of Early Adolescence,* 4 (1984), 173.

Girls are much more likely than boys to take their problems to a friend. *(Jim Whitmer)*

(Douvan and Adelson, 1966). At seventeen and eighteen, girls feel more secure in their own identity and no longer need to identify with an emotional clone. They worry less about loyalty, security, and trust, and many have turned to boys for intimacy. As for older boys, many spend their social lives in cliques and gangs instead of in pairs. This gender difference is part of the larger pattern of sex-role differences that make interpersonal relationships a major factor in the formation of identity among most girls.

The Peer Group

During early adolescence, the structure of the peer group changes. For the first time, youngsters see the group as a community of like-minded people (Hartup, 1983). Now cliques begin to form, with their special activities and the firm exclusion of outsiders. The clique's importance increases sharply during the junior high school years. In a study that followed more than 300 adolescents from the sixth to the eighth grade, boys and girls reported deeper involvement in cliques with each passing year (Crockett, Losoff, and Petersen,

1984). Cliques may be based on popularity, sports, activities, academics, or wealth, but the most prevalent standard for clique membership is popularity. Cliques may be made up of "average" or "unpopular" adolescents — who may resent the clique of popular youngsters. An eighth grader described such feelings in her Virginia school:

> Usually there's one group that's called the popular group, and everyone outside it is down on the people in that group. You know, they think those people are stuck up. Sometimes I think it's because everyone else is jealous of them. (Bell, 1980, p. 57)

What makes a young adolescent popular enough for the ruling clique? Athletic ability seems most important for boys, although by the eighth grade, appearance and personality have become nearly as important. For girls, appearance outweighs all other qualities by eighth grade, with personality running a poor second. Among young adolescents, academic achievement seems to play only a minor role in popularity, and boys see it as more important than girls do (see Figure 13.6).

Adolescents often deny that their group has a hierarchical formation, but as we saw in Chapter 10, such hierarchies are apparent even among nursery-school children. Sometimes the hierarchies are open, as they were among twelve- to fourteen-year-old boys at a summer camp who had no trouble telling a researcher which boys were leaders and which were followers (Savin-Williams, 1979). In half of the girls' cabins, however, the

WHAT TEENAGERS DO ALL DAY

The nature of the adults who emerge from adolescence is in good part shaped by what teenagers do and where they do it. But until recently, researchers have had only a vague notion of how adolescents spend their time. Then Mihaly Csikszentmihalyi and Reed Larson (1984) gave seventy-five boys and girls electronic pagers like those used by physicians. At random intervals between early morning and bedtime, the researchers beeped the youngsters. When signaled, the girls and boys filled out a questionnaire describing their activity at that moment and noting their mood, alertness, and concentration. The nearly 3,000 reports covered all aspects of the youngsters' lives — from eating breakfast or sitting in class to playing basketball or having sex.

The analysis of the teenagers' reports indicates that thirteen- to eighteen-year-olds spend 29 percent of their time productively (in class, studying, working at jobs), 31 percent maintaining themselves (eating, grooming, doing errands and chores, getting from one place to another), and 40 percent at leisure (talking, watching TV, in sports, games, and hobbies, reading, thinking, and listening exclusively to music). Of course, averaging all adolescents together can sometimes be misleading. The "average" adolescent spends 7.4 hours each week at a job, but when nonworking students are eliminated, average working time jumps to 18 hours per week for the 41 percent who are employed. Younger teenagers spend more time with their families than do older teenagers, who are away from home and socializing with friends about 10 hours longer each week. But in this study, it was the only difference in the way that young and old teens spend their time.

The single activity at which teenagers spend the most time is talking. They talk mostly with friends — spending three times as many hours each week in conversation with friends as parents and older adults combined. They talk a lot on the phone — 13 percent of their conversation takes this remote form. And they also talk while they are doing other things — studying, watching TV, eating. Their talk may be a form of recreation, but it is also a socializing activity, one in which youngsters exchange ideas and feelings and convey values and norms.

Schooling is another matter. While in class, American teenagers spend much less time than Japanese or Russian youngsters listening to the teacher

Solitude seems to be an essential part of life for American teenagers; they spend a quarter of their waking hours alone. (Elizabeth Crews/Stock, Boston)

— only about 4 hours each week. The rest of their time is spent listening to other students, in discussion groups, studying by themselves, or taking tests. Apparently, less direct socialization by adults goes on inside the American classroom. As we saw in Chapter 12, American children spend a good deal of their school time outside the classroom, and this continues to be true during the high school years. When class time and study time are added up, American adolescents get far less education than youngsters in other technologically advanced countries. They spend 38 hours each week either in class or studying. Russian teenagers spend 52 hours this way, Japanese adolescents spend 59 hours.

American youngsters use part of the time that other cultures devote to schooling at their jobs. But they also have considerably more leisure than adolescents in Japan, the Soviet Union, or West Germany — about 10 or 12 more hours each week. Besides talking, American teenagers watch TV intently for about an hour each day. For another 1.5 hours, the set is on, but most of their attention is on some other activity — talking, eating, and the like. Another 1.25 hours goes to some structured activity — playing basketball, drawing, making models, playing chess, dancing, playing the piano. Little time is spent on reading for pleasure — about half an hour each day. Although a few read books, most read the comics, Ann Landers, or news stories. Even less time is spent listening to music, although music is often a background for other activities.

By design or by chance, American adolescents spend 25.6 percent of their waking hours by themselves. Much of this solitary time passes in the privacy of their bedrooms — listening to music, studying, watching TV, doing chores, playing a guitar. Adolescents reported most of their low moods during these times. But few of their moods lasted longer than fifteen minutes or were extreme in either direction. Solitude seemed to be an essential part of their lives; it recharged them for another foray into the world. After being by themselves, they seemed to take extra enjoyment in their activities with friends and family.

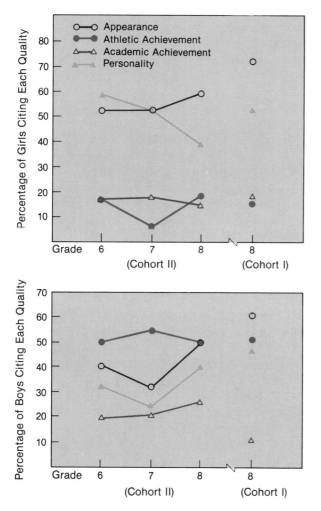

FIGURE 13.6 **What does it take to be popular? By eighth grade, appearance has become the major factor in popularity among girls. Although boys believe that appearance is important, they give equal weight to athletic achievement and rate academic achievement higher than girls do.** *(From Crockett, Losoff, and Petersen, 1984)*

girls professed not to know who was running things. Among both sexes, the leaders were self-confident, cool, mature, athletic, intelligent, and popular. Boy leaders asserted themselves physically, argued with others, and often threatened their cabinmates. Girls controlled by recognizing the status of their cabinmates, giving unsolicited advice to some, and shunning or ignoring others. Leaders took the biggest pieces of cake at dinner, the preferred seats at discussions, and the best sleeping sites near the campfire at cookouts. Leaders were useful to the group. The dominant girls, for example, often intervened in squabbles and patched interpersonal relationships. Among these young adolescents, social rankings not only made relationships within the group predictable but also reduced group friction and aggression.

During high school, teenagers become increasingly involved with peers as opposed to parents. With the gradual relaxation of parental rules, youngsters stay out later and have more of their meals away from home. Being a clique member may seem essential, as it did to a New York sixteen-year-old:

> Some people I know think it's cool to say that groups are the pits. They say they want to be an individual. But I mean, what fun is it to be an individual if you don't have a group of friends too? What are you going to do? Be an individual with yourself? Sit at home and say, "Oh, I'm an individual"? Sure. (Bell, 1980, p. 57)

By now, however, cliques are becoming less exclusive, and several of them may become linked together into a crowd. Older adolescents often move from one group to another, perhaps sticking with their clique for "good times," but seeking out a church group for serious conversation and sharing their personal feelings and problems with a friend or two (Csikszentmihalyi and Larson, 1984).

Young adolescents tend to belong to cliques whose members are of the same sex. At about midadolescence, when dating becomes important, the clique becomes heterosexual. Each member generally establishes a relationship with a member of the other sex, but the important structure is the group. This arrangement endures while the teenagers are learning the basic role characteristics that underlie heterosexual relationships; then the clique structure loosens (Dunphy, 1963). Its members become couples first and group members second.

Relations with the Other Sex

As they enter puberty, boys and girls already are interested in the other sex. When sixth graders were asked what they thought about most, about half of the boys said "girls," and somewhat more girls said "boys" (Crockett, Losoff, and Petersen, 1984). By eighth grade, 80 percent of the girls and about 65 percent of the boys were preoccupied with the other sex. Despite this sexual fascination, it is unclear just how much early boy-girl interaction is strictly sexual and how much is simply a variation of friendship.   .

Dating   The age at which formal dating begins varies from one school to another. At first, girls and boys may attend dances and parties in groups. The pairing off, even if prearranged, occurs at the event. This allows young teenagers to avoid the responsibility of dating arrangements and helps reduce their initial anxieties about heterosexual relations. It also spares boys the expense of picking up the tab for admission and spares the adolescents the pain of having parents chauffeur them on a date.

In the wake of the women's movement, not much of the traditional dating system has been washed away. Dating, also called "going out," still requires the boy to ask the girl, then pay for the movie or Big Macs. A sixteen-year-old suburban girl summed it up: "I could never, ever ask a guy out." And another explained that girls eased the expense of the date by eating before they left home

and then ordering the cheapest thing on the menu (Kolbert, 1986).

Long before they start dating, young adolescents believe that having a boyfriend or girlfriend is important. In a national sample, three-quarters said that having a boyfriend (or a girlfriend) was important to them (Offer, Ostrov, and Howard, 1981). Yet only about a quarter of the young adolescents in another study were dating by the end of the seventh grade, with the proportion climbing to about half within the next year (Crockett, Losoff, and Petersen, 1984). According to Sherman Feinstein and Marjorie Ardon (1973), boy-girl relationships pass through a series of four stages, with some youngsters moving along more rapidly than others. Most young adolescents are in the *stage of sexual awakening,* which is essentially a period of experimentation. They are not emotionally involved with their boyfriends or girlfriends, even though couples may pet on occasion. They are still anxious about the whole dating procedure and preoccupied with learning the ropes. This is especially true of boys, who may feel insecure, because they are behind the girls physiologically (and many are shorter than their dates). They know that the girls have opportunities to date older boys.

In the mid-adolescent *stage of practicing,* youngsters go through a rapid series of intense, short-term relationships. These pairings often feature the exchange of personal property — a boy may give a girl a football letter jacket or one of his earrings. Although youngsters see them as major commitments and take them seriously, they may be over in less than a week. Still unskilled at social relationships, youngsters may break off awkwardly. At the end of a seven-day relationship, one fifteen-year-old girl complained, "He didn't even tell me he broke up with me. He had his little sister do it" (Kolbert, 1986). During this stage, girls treat dating as a manipulative game, rather than a relationship based on mutuality and emotional interaction. What are the rules of the dating game? Steady dating is okay, but only if the boy and girl like each other a great deal or if they do not get too serious or sexually involved. Another fifteen-year-old girl who entered a steady relationship broke it off abruptly after a couple of weeks in response to sexual pressure, stating that she'd rather just be friends.

Typical of late adolescence is the *stage of accept-*

By the time they enter high school, half of American teenagers have begun the dating game. *(Glenn Cruickshank/West Stock)*

ance of the sexual role. Most youngsters are sixteen years old before they reach this level. At this stage, dating patterns are regular and stable, and anxiety no longer surrounds the dating process. Relationships last longer, and trustful love relationships begin to appear. Sexual experimentation is prevalent, and the incidence of sexual intercourse increases.

Both sexes enter the final stage, typified by the *development of a permanent love object,* when they have consolidated their identity and are ready to enter adulthood. Mature sexual relationships become possible, and the Eriksonian task of intimacy becomes prominent. Some young people move into this stage when they are about eighteen years old; others remain in the previous stage until they reach their mid-twenties.

Sexuality   Girls' childhood and early adolescent socialization generally makes them more competent than boys in interpersonal relationships. So

most girls incorporate sexual behavior into a social role and identity that already includes capacities for tenderness and sensitivity. Developmentalists generally assume that, because of their different socialization, boys are interested in sexuality first, and only later does the capacity for concerned, tender, and loving sexual relationships develop. Boys are certainly more interested than girls in the physical expression of sexuality. In a national sample, 86 percent of the thirteen- to fifteen-year-old boys and 87 percent of the sixteen- to eighteen-year-old boys agreed that "sexual experiences give me pleasure" (Offer, Ostrov, and Howard, 1981). When girls replied to the same statement, 60 percent of the younger girls and 76 percent of the older girls agreed. And although eight out of ten young adolescent boys "often think about sex," only five out of ten girls do.

According to the traditional view, sexuality is primarily "body-centered" for boys and "person-centered" for girls (Reiss, 1973). Researchers have assumed that the two approaches are on opposite ends of a single scale, so that youngsters who are high on one measure are necessarily low on the other. But studies with middle-class adolescents indicate that boys are as "person-centered" as girls when it comes to sexuality within a dating relationship (McCabe and Collins, 1979). Sixteen- and seventeen-year-old boys *are* more "body-centered" than girls of that age. They believe that sexual intimacies should progress much faster and farther than girls do (see Table 13.4). A heavy majority of boys but less than one in five girls believe that couples who go steady should be having sexual intercourse. Girls become more "body-centered" as they reach young adulthood: by the time they are nineteen, 58 percent believe that sexual intercourse is a desirable part of a steady relationship. And by the time they reach their mid-twenties, 90 percent of both sexes approve of sexual intercourse in such a context. Yet from the beginning, boys are just as insistent as girls that the relationship of dating couples be marked by sincerity, compatibility, understanding, affection, concern, tenderness, trust, security, mutual respect, and companionship. Agreement on these qualities ranged from 89 to 100 percent. Perhaps this agreement is the result of changes in society. Or perhaps the belief that a person could not be both body-centered *and* person-centered kept earlier researchers from asking adolescents how they felt.

Changing attitudes and expectations may have made some young people anxious and uncomfortable about sex. In the 1960s, only 7 percent of American teenagers thought that they were behind their peers in sexual experience. Ten years later, 21 percent felt that way (Offer, Ostrov, and Howard, 1981). But most adolescents feel that they are coping satisfactorily with sexual matters. Among young adolescents, 76 percent of the boys and 66 percent of the girls say that handling sex "in a right way" is not difficult. By late adolescence, 78 percent of the boys and 72 percent of the girls say that they have no trouble handling sex appropriately.

How do teenagers deal with sex? Despite their life in a sexually permissive society, boys' rate of sexual intercourse seems to have changed little since about 1950 (Miller and Simon, 1980). Boys may be having their first intercourse at a somewhat younger age, but the proportion of sexually experienced adolescents is about the same as it was when their fathers were teenagers. The change is among girls, whose rate of premarital intercourse is now about the same as that of boys. Our best information comes from national surveys of girls. As might be expected, between 1970 and 1979, the proportion of girls who had premarital intercourse increased steadily. Among adolescents between the ages of fifteen and nineteen, 49.8 percent of the unmarried girls had had intercourse in 1979 — up from 30.4 percent in 1971 (Zelnik and Kantner, 1980). But teenagers may be returning to a more conservative attitude toward sex. Fear of contracting AIDS, which seems to have affected sexual activity among all age groups, is likely to be a major force in this trend (Lyons, 1983).

Adolescents are not promiscuous. As we have seen, they strongly reject casual, indiscriminate sexual activity in favor of committed, caring relationships. In fact, most girls tend to restrict their sexual activity to partners whom they love and intend to marry (Zelnik, Kantner, and Ford, 1981). When looking at the number of teenagers who are having sexual intercourse, we tend to forget that half of older adolescents have never "gone all the way." Some are "technical virgins," who engage in extremely heavy petting and who have avoided only one sexual experience — vaginal intercourse. Many of these youngsters see intercourse as sacred and powerful — an experience that should be reserved for a deeply committed relationship. Others see premarital intercourse as ill-advised, stupid, or immoral (Rosen and Hall, 1984).

When adolescents make their sexual decisions, they are influenced by parents, peers, the media, their religious attitudes and beliefs, their own needs, and their own standards. Many get confusing signals from their parents, whose attitude seems to be, "Don't mess around, but if you do, be sure to be careful" (Furstenberg, 1980). Society has come to see some form of adolescent sexual experimentation as normal, and many parents and schools have swung from forbidding sexuality to preventing AIDS and teenage pregnancy. In a recent survey, 83 percent of Americans urged teaching twelve-year-olds about AIDS, and 84 percent said that school health clinics should make birth-control information available (*Time*, 1986). In Chapter 14, we examine the problem of teenage pregnancy.

Table 13.4
Desirable Sexual Activity in Dating Relationships (Percent)

	16–17-Year-Olds						19–20-Year-Olds					
	First Date		Several Dates		Going Steady		First Date		Several Dates		Going Steady	
	M	F	M	F	M	F	M	F	M	F	M	F
Hand holding	89	96	93	100	95	100	92	76	97	98	100	98
Light kissing	96	94	93	97	89	98	92	79	89	92	94	90
Necking	67	31	84	79	77	94	50	25	75	62	78	82
Deep kissing	60	31	89	79	97	90	58	25	83	73	97	98
Heavy breast petting	27	3	67	15	93	49	45	6	58	42	86	77
Nude embrace	9	6	40	9	70	31	45	4	53	19	78	71
Mutual masturbation	18	3	45	12	76	31	36	8	61	27	81	75
Intercourse	16	0	27	4	62	19	31	2	47	8	78	58

Source: Adapted from M. P. McCabe and J. K. Collins, "Sex Role and Dating Orientation," *Journal of Youth And Adolescence*, 8 (1979), 411.

CHANGES IN THE SCHOOL EXPERIENCE

The shift from elementary school to a middle or junior high school is a pivotal event of early adolescence. Accustomed to spending the day with a single teacher in a single classroom, youngsters suddenly find themselves moving from one classroom to another and encountering a different teacher for each subject. The veteran student, one of the senior citizens of the elementary school, becomes a rookie who is looked down upon by older students. Accompanying this disconcerting shift is the appearance of the competitive pressures of adolescence. Social popularity is now important. Organized athletics may be the key to successful school life — or at least to winning prestige among peers. Although rigid academic sifting may be postponed until high school, it appears for many in the junior high. Youngsters divide themselves (or are divided by the school) into collegebound and non-collegebound groups. With each passing year, students on these different academic tracks find themselves farther apart.

Some adolescents thrive in their new environment. They become stars in athletic or academic domains or else become immensely popular with their peers. Others may respond to these changes by withdrawing from competition. They find themselves unable to adapt to the changing requirements and the new academic demands. When they fail, they become discouraged, and their discouragement leads to further failure. Some who managed to get through elementary school without serious problems may develop learned helplessness.

The more changes a student encounters, the poorer he or she is likely to do in school. In a longitudinal study of sixth to eighth graders, grades tended to decline during junior high school for most students, perhaps because of the change in academic content or perhaps because grading became tougher (Schulenberg, Asp, and Petersen, 1984). But the decline was sharpest among those who transferred from the fifth grade to middle school and then switched again to a junior high school for seventh grade. The dual transition may have intensified the difficulty of their adjustment.

Researchers asked the junior high school students in this study whether they would rather be a star athlete, a straight A student, or the most popular student. More boys and girls chose straight A student than the other categories, although by eighth grade, girls were beginning to see popularity as more important than academic achievement. Nearly as many girls as boys said that they would like to be star athletes, but for both sexes the glamour of the athlete's life decreased between the sixth and eighth grades (see the box, "Girls on the Football Team," on page 355). However, for most students, athletics took precedence over music and student government as the preferred extracurricular activity.

In every culture, some adolescents are unable to cope with the enormous changes in their lives. In the next chapter, we explore the problems that arise when their resources are overwhelmed.

SUMMARY

1. **Puberty,** the lengthy biological process that changes an immature child into a sexually mature person, begins when the hypothalmus signals the pituitary gland to start producing adult levels of hormones. In response, girls' **ovaries** begin to secrete **estrogens** and boys' **testes** to secrete **androgens,** and the transformation begins. Puberty is characterized by a growth trend known as **asynchrony,** in which various processes of maturation proceed at different rates. **Menarche,** or the first incidence of menstruation, is usually taken as an indication of sexual maturity, but up to half of girls remain infertile for a year or two afterward. Boys begin to ejaculate semen at about thirteen or fourteen, and mature sperm appear at about fifteen. A youngster's reaction to puberty depends on his or her feelings about sexuality, reactions of others to his or her changed appearance, and cultural standards. Youngsters quickly learn the characteristics of the culture's **body ideal,** and deviations from this ideal influence an adolescent's self-concept and self-esteem. Boys who mature early seem to have a lasting advantage over their peers, but early maturity appears to reduce the likelihood that a girl will go on to college.

2. Most adolescents are capable of what Piaget called **formal-operational thought;** they can generate and test hypotheses, deal with logical possibilities, think about the future, and about thought itself. Some young people develop formal thought in one area and not another, and some — especially those who lack formal education — may not develop at all. In their understanding of government, law, politics, and principles, youngsters move from the concrete (teachers and police) to the abstract (education and law). Understanding abstract principles,

which requires formal thought, seems to be necessary if adolescents are to develop principled moral reasoning, as defined by Kohlberg. As adolescents develop an understanding of time and the effect of past events on the future, their understanding of others' motives deepens and their role-taking ability improves. In early adolescence, adolescent egocentrism develops. Young people think in terms of the **imaginary audience,** which is preoccupied with the adolescent's appearance and actions, and the **personal fable,** which is the adolescent's feeling that he or she is unique and indestructible.

3. Establishing an **identity,** an emerging sense of self that synthesizes roles and various aspects of personality, is a major developmental task of adolescence. A teenager's identity status may be one of **foreclosure,** in which occupational or ideological goals are chosen by parents; **moratorium,** in which the adolescent is struggling with occupational or ideological issues but the final choices have been postponed; **identity achievement,** in which the adolescent is pursuing self-chosen occupational or ideological goals; or **identity diffusion,** in which no choices have been made but the adolescent feels no pressure to make any. Young adolescents seem to have an intensified feeling of gender, in part because adhering to a sex role diminishes the uncertainty that they feel about their new position and in part because the peer group demands conformity to sex-role standards.

4. The nature of family life changes as adolescents move toward a more nearly peerlike relationship with their parents. Boys seem to take a more dominant role with their mothers but remain deferential to their fathers. Girls enter a period of strained relations with their mothers.

Young people establish three different aspects of autonomy: emotional autonomy, in which they lose their dependence on their parents; resistance to peer pressure; and self-reliance. At first, as emotional autonomy grows, young adolescents find it harder to resist peer pressure.

5. During adolescence, friendships tend to become intimate, mutual relationships, in which the friends care for each other, share their thoughts and feelings, and comfort one another. Girls' friendships tend to be more intimate than friendships between boys. Cliques become increasingly important during early adolescence, and clique members are of the same sex. In mid-adolescence, cliques become heterosexual, and in late adolescence they tend to become loose structures composed of couples.

6. Relationships with the other sex pass through four stages: (1) the stage of sexual awakening, when youngsters are experimenting with the routines of dating but are not emotionally involved; (2) the stage of practicing, which is characterized by a series of intense, short-term relationships; (3) the stage of acceptance of the sexual role, when dating patterns are stable and youngsters are no longer as anxious about dating; and (4) the development of a permanent love object, when adolescents are ready to develop the intimacy that characterizes adult sexual relationships. Although sexuality is considered "body-centered" for boys and "person-centered" for girls, the real difference between the sexes seems to be that "body-centered" aspects of sexuality are slow to develop in girls. These aspects of sexuality are not mutually exclusive, and — at least in the middle class — boys see sexuality within the dating relationship as both body-centered and person-centered.

7. At the same time as young people are encountering the competitive pressures of adolescence, they have to adjust to a new school system. Youngsters enter junior high valuing grades over popularity, but among girls, popularity soon becomes at least as important. As they progress through high school, a social separation appears between adolescents who are bound for college and those who are not.

KEY TERMS

androgens
asynchrony
body ideal
estrogen
foreclosure
formal-operational thought

identity
identity achievement
identity diffusion
imaginary audience
menarche

moratorium
ovaries
personal fable
puberty
testes

STUDY TERMS

foreclosure An identity status in which the adolescent is committed to an occupation or ideology that has been chosen by his or her parents or peers.

formal-operational thought Logical, abstract thought that can be applied to hypothetical situations; Piaget regarded it as the culmination of intellectual development.

identity A complex sense of self that develops during adolescence, when various life roles and aspects of the personality coalesce.

identity achievement An identity status in which the adolescent is committed to self-chosen occupational or ideological goals.

identity diffusion An identity status in which the adolescent has no occupational or ideological goal but is not particularly concerned about developing any.

moratorium An identity status in which the adolescent is struggling with occupational or ideological issues and may be in an identity crisis.

CHAPTER 14

The Stresses of Adolescence

CHANGE AND STRESS

NORMAL AND ABNORMAL ADOLESCENTS
The Myth of Adolescent Turmoil / The Myth of the Self-limiting Disturbance / The Myth of Conflict with Parents / The Myth of the Generation Gap

AREAS OF ADOLESCENT STRESS
Adolescent Drug Use / Adolescent Crime / Adolescent Suicide / Adolescent Pregnancy / Adolescent Eating Disorders

THE FUTURE OF ADOLESCENT STRESS AND DISTRESS

Steve Silverman, who is seventeen years old, has been in trouble since he was twelve. That was the year his beloved grandfather died and his father's back problems put him into the hospital. At about that time, Steve embarked on a series of destructive episodes. A psychologist decided that he had a learning disability, but neither remedial help at school nor a series of psychiatrists was much help. Steve began using cocaine. After an explosive, violent outburst in public, he was picked up by the police and placed in the psychiatric ward of a local hospital. His parents had him transferred to the adolescent unit of a private psychiatric hospital, one with educational facilities and a special drug-treatment program. Steve spent nine months there, and is now back home. He has a job at a meat-packing company and studies on the side for his high-school equivalency certificate. Every week he sees his psychiatrist. Steve is unenthusiastic about his job and finds reentering society a struggle, but his outbursts have stopped, and he is off drugs (Gelman, 1986).

Newspaper articles, weekly news-magazines, and local TV news seem to imply that Steve's situation is typical of many teenagers. Headlines that ask whether the psychiatric ward can fill in for the family are becoming increasingly common. Are teenagers in trouble? Is emotional upheaval a "normal" accompaniment of adolescence? The answer to both questions is a resounding no. As we will see in this chapter, adolescence may be accompanied by a variety of stresses, but the overwhelming majority of young people take these social pressures in stride. For most teenagers, adolescence is *not* the stormy struggle portrayed in print and videotape but a time of challenge and change.

In this chapter, after recalling the vast changes of adolescence, we explore the sort of stresses that may accompany them. Next we strip away the myths that have grown up about the perils of adolescence: the myth of adolescent turmoil, the myth of the self-limiting disorder, the myth of conflict with parents, and the myth of the generation gap. When stresses become too great, an adolescent's life may be disrupted in some characteristic manner. In turn, we take up five major ways in which adolescents express intolerable stress: substance abuse, crime, suicide, pregnancy, and eating disorders. In closing, we explore the reasons for past increases in adolescent disorders and look at a theory that predicts their decline.

CHANGE AND STRESS

Adolescence is almost by definition a period of transition, the bridge between late childhood and young adulthood. Its major characteristic is *change*, change in every area of the teenager's life, as we saw in Chapter 13. As puberty propels them into adolescence, young people find that they have crossed into a period in which others treat them differently. Now, instead of being seen against the background of their earlier childish abilities, they are seen against the background of the adults they will soon become. With their new time perspective, adolescents begin thinking about the adult years that stretch before them.

One way of looking at adolescence is to see it as a preparation for departure (Douvan and Adelson, 1966). During the teenage years, young people prepare to sever their attachment to parents and home and get ready to establish themselves as independent beings. The rate at which youngsters make these preparations varies widely. Some be-

come independent quickly, some slowly, some not at all. For the great majority, adolescence is the launching pad into self-sufficiency, a period when children learn and practice the academic, economic, and social skills that will turn them into well-functioning adults.

What does this extended preparation mean to young people? For one thing, their opportunities are wide and their horizons limited primarily by their imagination and capabilities. But the glittering promises require a series of choices. With wider possibilities, today's adolescents spend a good part of their lives confronting decisions that may be crucial to their future. First, they must decide which courses to take, then which colleges to apply for and which to accept, then which career to prepare for. At the same time, they are making other crucial decisions about dating, going steady, sexuality, and the like. In some societies, these choices are automatic, determined by the adolescent's status or background. A young person is expected or required to take up a particular profession or to marry a particular person — or at least a person from a specified group. Today's teenagers have freedom of choice in all these areas, but the freedoms come at some cost. They are accompanied by increased uncertainty and anxiety throughout the period of choosing.

All these elements — the lengthiness of adolescence, the myriad changes, the uncertainty about the future, the anxiety over choices — tend to make adolescence a stressful period. Every part of life is or seems to be shifting or unsettled. The adolescent's body and self as a whole are unstable. Hanging over everything else is an uncertainty about who or what the teenager will be. In this setting, the judgments made by others — other boys and girls, teachers, parents, even college entrance tests — seem to foreshadow the future. An adolescent who is shy and finds it difficult to make friends, one who does not seem to be sexually attractive to peers, or one who does poorly in school comes to believe that the present will continue into the future. Such an adolescent may decide that he or she is fated forever to remain unwanted, rejected, inadequate. Because they are seen as permanent, momentary disappointments and apprehensions are amplified.

Stresses also may develop within the family. There may be tension between teenager and parents over how much freedom he or she will be granted. Negotiations over rules and policies may lead the adolescent to test the limits of parental control. Such encounters have a great potential for generating conflict and bitterness on all sides. While struggling with these particularly adolescent issues, the young person is also encountering all the temptations and risks of adulthood — sex, drink, drugs. Choices that were once available primarily to individuals with more experience in living are suddenly there for the taking.

Beset with all these factors, the adolescent, already a creature of fluctuating moods, must live through nearly a decade of turbulence. People are so convinced of this that most see adolescence as a time of trouble, turmoil, and stress. This view of adolescence has led to four myths that pervade most private beliefs and popular accounts in the media.

Myth 1   Adolescence is a period marked by emotional disturbance, which is often severe. The disturbance develops when the adolescent is overwhelmed by the internal and external pressures just discussed.

Myth 2   Any disturbances that appear in adolescence are limited and do not continue into adult life. Most of the emotional storms that buffet adolescents subside as soon as youngsters reach adulthood.

Myth 3   The normal outcome of young people's need to separate from their parents is a period of intensified conflict and much open hostility.

Myth 4   There is invariably a generation gap between adolescents and their parents, which develops as adolescents challenge and then abandon the opinions and cherished values of their parents.

The problem with these myths is that they do not describe most adolescents.

NORMAL AND ABNORMAL ADOLESCENTS

It's not surprising that most people think of adolescence as a tempest-tossed period and of most adolescents as emotionally upset youngsters who

Adolescents tend to see the present situation as permanent. When an adolescent has trouble making friends, she may feel that she will remain friendless for the rest of her life. *(Elizabeth Crews)*

are camped on the far side of the generation gap. Most mental-health professionals have a similar view. A few years ago, Daniel Offer, Eric Ostrov, and Kenneth Howard (1981b) asked a group of psychiatrists, psychologists, and psychiatric social workers about the typical teenager. While pretending to be normal adolescents, the mental-health professionals filled out a personality test designed for adolescents. Then Offer and his colleagues compared the answers with those given by normal adolescents, juvenile delinquents, and seriously disturbed adolescents. In the eyes of these experts, the normal adolescent was worse off than actual delinquents or deeply disturbed youngsters in psychiatric hospitals. The professionals' "normal" answers portrayed mentally healthy adolescents as unhappy people with low self-esteem who found it difficult to deal with their moods, their families, and their friends, and who were confused

Boys with emotional problems are twice as likely as girls to see mental health professionals. *(Michael Weisbrot/Stock, Boston)*

about their educational and vocational goals. The normal adolescents simply did not feel this way about themselves at all.

When mental-health professionals subscribe to most of the adolescent myths, it is no wonder that the press and the public have adopted them. Yet none of the pictures of adolescents that have emerged from systematic research supports a single one of the myths.

The Myth of Adolescent Turmoil

The major myth of adolescence — that it is a period marked by heightened emotional disturbance — falls apart with even a cursory look at the evidence. On the whole, the degree of disturbance among adolescents is about the same as it is among adults. In both populations, about 20 percent report feelings of distress that seem troubling enough to require professional attention. Every systematic study that has been carried out confirms the view that eight out of ten adolescents are neither rebellious nor emotionally troubled.

The first national survey of adolescents, conducted by Elizabeth Douvan and Joseph Adelson

(1966), showed that most adolescents had a realistic view of themselves, had no major conflicts with their parents over discipline or values, and held conventional, realistic ambitions concerning their future vocational and family aims. Subsequent studies turned up similar results, with the proportion of troubled youngsters hovering around 20 percent in each one (Weiner, 1982). More recently, Offer, Ostrov, and Howard (1984) studied a randomly chosen group of Chicago high-school students, with similar results: 17 percent of the boys and 22 percent of the girls showed symptoms of emotional problems.

The Myth of the Self-limiting Disturbance

The second myth of adolescence — that adolescent disturbances fade away as adulthood arrives — is seriously misleading. Adolescents who are troubled are not likely to get better without some assistance. Longitudinal studies of adolescents in distress indicate that their problems do not diminish or disappear with the mere passage of time. The teenager with emotional problems usually becomes a distressed adult, and the more severe the symptoms, the more likely it is that the adult disorder will be serious or disabling (Adelson, 1985a).

Even worse, more than half of these troubled youngsters do not get the intervention that might help them overcome their problems. In the study of Chicago high-school students, more than half of the disturbed teenagers had received no professional help (Offer, Ostrov, and Howard, 1984). The school authorities were unaware of their serious problems. Yet these teenagers' views of themselves were very similar to that of youths who had been hospitalized for emotional disturbance. There are 18 million high-school students, and so there are probably 3.6 million (20 percent) troubled adolescents. If the Chicago students are typical, 1.8 million teenagers who need help are not getting it.

Boys were more likely than girls to have seen mental-health professionals. One-third of the disturbed boys but two-thirds of the disturbed girls had received no professional help. Why were boys more likely to get help than girls? Boys with emo-

Punk hairstyles are one of the issues over which parents and their adolescent children are most likely to clash. *(Ron Cooper/E.K.M.-Nepenthe)*

tional problems are more likely than girls to be engaged in obvious antisocial activity. About 65 percent of disturbed boys commit seriously delinquent acts or are picked up by the police, and so their problems are likely to come to the attention of authorities. But among girls, 62 percent suffer more or less in silence, never acting in a way that attracts any notice.

The Myth of Conflict with Parents

The third myth of adolescence — that hostility and conflict between parent and child are almost inevitable — also crumbles in the face of the evidence. Most teenagers say that they have good relationships with their parents. They look up to them and seek their advice on important matters. Whether researchers ask adolescents to respond to questionnaires or conduct probing clinical interviews, the results are similar. In the national Gallup Youth Survey, boys and girls between the ages of thirteen and eighteen told pollsters that they got along well with their parents (60 percent), that parental discipline was "about right" (82 percent), and that they would consult their parents instead of their friends if faced with a serious life decision (77 percent) (Adelson, 1985a).

The Myth of the Generation Gap

The final myth — that parents and adolescents differ sharply on values and important issues — also has little basis in fact. There are few signs of significant differences between the generations on important matters. This is true today, and it was also true during the 1960s, when the activism of a few students and the sensationalized counterculture that developed in the country's elite colleges and universities led to perceptions of an exaggerated gap between parent and child (Feather, 1980). Other exaggerations came from earlier studies of adolescents that translated the negative impact of peer standards on school achievement into the belief that adolescents' families progressively lost any ability to influence them.

Parental influence on adolescents remains stable and strong throughout the teenage years and into adulthood. Young people adhere to their parents' values in such matters as moral behavior, religion, achievement, academic performance, and job or career aspirations (Kandel and Lesser, 1972; Lerner and Knapp, 1975; Young and Ferguson, 1979). Studies of political attitudes also show close agreement between parent and child. When researchers compare the responses to political ques-

DOES WORKING INCREASE THE STRESSES OF ADOLESCENCE?

Working at a job is a normal part of growing up in the United States. By the time they graduate from high school, 80 percent of teenagers have had formal work experience (Steinberg, Greenberger, Garduque, Ruggiero, and Vaux, 1982). Most people believe that such employment prevents delinquency and gives adolescents a meaningful role in society (Carnegie Council on Policy Studies in Higher Education, 1980). Recent studies indicate that although paid employment during the high-school years has benefits, it is unlikely to be the cureall that many observers have suggested.

Among suburban teenagers in Orange County, California, working part-time had some positive effects. Among the tenth and eleventh graders studied by Laurence Steinberg and his colleagues (1982), working increased youngsters' responsibility on the job. Girls profited more than boys from this experience. Girls (but not boys) also became more self-reliant, more interested in jobs that allowed them to make decisions, and more likely to want additional education.

Some of the purported benefits of work did not appear. Working did not increase adolescents' tolerance or concern for other people. Although adolescents who worked did just as well in school as those who did not work, there were unexpected costs to employment. Teenagers who worked were less involved with school affairs. They felt more distant from their peers, although their jobs did not cut into the time they spent with other youngsters. Girls (but not boys) who worked more than twenty hours a week became more distant from family members. Work tended to develop cynical attitudes about its value among all adolescents except those from professional families. Those who worked tended to agree that "anyone who works harder than he or she has to is a little bit crazy." It also encouraged the acceptance of unethical behavior on the job by youngsters from white-collar families. Finally, working seemed to encourage some minor offenses: the more hours adolescents worked each week, the more likely they were to use marijuana. Although working did not affect alcohol use, it was associated with cigarette smoking among white- and blue-collar youngsters.

Most teenagers with steady employment are conspicuous consumers who are less involved in school affairs than other adolescents. *(Edward Lettau/Photo Researchers)*

Why should adolescents who work smoke more than other youngsters? Noting that marijuana use was best predicted by the time spent on the job, Steinberg and his colleagues suggest that job stress promotes the use of tobacco and marijuana. They speculate that teenagers who work more than twenty hours a week—as many of these youths did—may find that their health suffers and that they miss out on potentially important experiences with friends and family. Their long hours at work cause them to miss important experiences at school. They have no time to go out for sports, take part in the school play, join the staff of the school paper, or practice with the band.

These researchers would be less troubled if teenagers were socking their money away for college or contributing to their families. But most are not. Fewer than 20 percent are saving anything for life after high school (Greenberger and Steinberg, 1986). Employed teenagers generally are conspicuous consumers who spend their money on cars, gasoline, designer clothes, "boom boxes," and marijuana. In fact, working seems to increase materialism among boys and younger students. When youngsters work too long, too soon, work may not be the path to personal responsibility that most Americans expect it to be.

tions of adolescents, their parents, and their friends, it becomes clear that parents have a more powerful influence on their children's political beliefs than do peers (Jennings and Niemi, 1981).

Where do parents and their adolescent children part company? The major differences appear on relatively unimportant questions having to do with style, music, leisure pursuits, and the like. Parent and child are most likely to disagree over such issues as the earring in a boy's earlobe, a punk hairstyle, or the sounds of a heavy metal rock group. Disagreements also may arise over sex and drugs, but parents' and adolescents' values are rarely at opposite ends of the spectrum.

On every count, adolescence fails to live up to its press image. Yet not all the news is good. Today's adolescents are more troubled than teenagers of the 1950s. Over the past twenty-five years, there has been a clear and sometimes steep rise in some measures of adolescent disturbance.

AREAS OF ADOLESCENT STRESS

Newspaper headlines and newsweekly articles remind us that dealing with the tasks and stresses of adolescence is more than some young people can handle. Their inexperience may leave them unprepared to cope with the temptations and opportunities that come their way. When the stress becomes too great, teenagers may become involved in substance abuse or crime. Some develop eating disorders. Others may become pregnant, and a few, overwhelmed by the world's demands, commit suicide.

Adolescent Drug Use

Thirty years ago, the use of illegal drugs was rare among adolescents. Alcohol was a temptation, but few adolescents had an opportunity to try marijuana — or even knew anyone who had. Cocaine and other drugs were virtually unknown in most parts of the country. As illegal drugs became widely available, young people faced a new source of stress — pressure from peers to use these drugs. Over the past few decades, children have been introduced to drugs at increasingly younger ages, and many begin using them while still in elementary school.

Patterns of Use　　Alcohol is still the most popular drug: about half of junior high-school students and three-fourths of high-school students have tried it. More than 15 percent of thirteen-year-olds and 54 percent of high-school seniors have tried marijuana. Cocaine has been less popular; in 1985 it had been tried by 13 percent of high-school seniors (Kozel and Adams, 1986). With the wide availability of cheap freebased cocaine ("crack"), the incidence of cocaine use among young people may be increasing.

Alcohol is the "gateway" drug. Its use almost always precedes other drugs among adolescents. Students rarely use marijuana and other illegal drugs unless they also use alcohol. Among more than 27,000 young adolescents in New York State, most users progressed from alcohol to marijuana, then went on to pills and hard drugs (Welte and Barnes, 1985). The youngest junior high-school students, especially the girls, often began smoking cigarettes before they tried marijuana, but they, too, had used alcohol first.

Alcohol is the gateway drug; unless teenagers use alcohol, they generally do not use any other drug.
(*Joseph Szabo/Photo Researchers*)

When more teenagers use drugs than abstain, some kind of drug use becomes a "normal" aspect of adolescence. Among nearly 500 Philadelphia high-school students, the majority of users were not trying to escape reality, control their anger, or find a way to express their feelings, although about a third said that drugs made them feel "less tense or nervous" (Kovach and Glickman, 1986). Most said they used drugs "to get high," "to feel better," or "to get into music and other things." The peer group plays a strong role in drug use. About a third said that they used drugs because their friends used them. Alcohol and other drugs often serve a communal purpose. They strengthen social bonds, provide relaxation and ease, and initiate young people into the rituals of high school. At the same time, heavy use of alcohol or drugs is not a normal developmental phase. Heavy users are adolescents in trouble.

Excessive use of alcohol or drugs is associated with poor school performance, disrupted family life, and antisocial behavior. Among Philadelphia high-school students, those who used drugs at least weekly were more likely than nonusers to have repeated a grade, to have been suspended from school, and to have conflicts with their teachers (Kovach and Glickman, 1986). They had more crises in their families and conflicts with their parents. They rarely participated in family activities or helped out in emergencies. They were also more likely to have had trouble with the law. Heavy substance use is also a warning of future trouble, usually of an antisocial or self-destructive nature. In fact, most varieties of adult alcoholism have their roots in problem drinking during adolescence (Zucker, 1987).

The Background of Substance Abuse Drugs and alcohol are available to all adolescents, but some never use them, and others use them infrequently. Psychologists have looked for factors in the child and in the family that predict the abuse of drugs and alcohol. In a study that compared youngsters' personality during childhood with their use of drugs eight years later, Judith Brook and her colleagues (Brook, Whiteman, Gordon, and Cohen, 1986a) discovered that certain personality factors in childhood placed a child at risk for heavy drug use. Youngsters who were low achievers, tended to get angry and lose their temper, were often depressed, and had eating problems were most likely to abuse drugs as adolescents. But the progression was not inevitable. Youngsters at risk who learned to control their tempers, became high achievers, and developed high educational aspirations seemed to be protected against substance abuse.

Family factors also seem important. Adolescents who are problem drinkers generally have parents who give them little love or attention (Barnes, 1984) (see Table 14.1). They seem uninterested in their children and have little contact with them. These parents apparently have adopted the neglecting-rejecting parenting pattern, in which parents are undemanding, rejecting, and unresponsive (see Chapter 9). When the parents are also poor role models, perhaps being alcoholic or antisocial, cynical, and distrustful, their adolescents may progress from problem drinking to alcoholism (Zucker, 1987).

In another study, adolescents who had gone past marijuana and were using other illegal drugs tended to have mothers who were unconventional, impulsive, anxious, somewhat rebellious and psychologically unstable, and who found relations

Table 14.1
Parental Nurturance and Adolescent Problem Drinkers (Percent)

	Mother Nurturance		
	Low (N = 35)	Medium (N = 50)	High (N = 37)
Problem drinkers	26	24	8
Nonproblem drinkers and abstainers	74	76	92

	Father Nurturance		
	Low (N = 51)	Medium (N = 40)	High (N = 37)
Problem drinkers	26	18	5
Nonproblem drinkers and abstainers	74	83	95

Source: G. M. Barnes, "Adolescent Alcohol Abuse and Other Problem Behaviors: Their Relationships and Common Parental Influences," *Journal of Youth and Adolescence*, 13 (1984), 344.

with others difficult (Brooks, Whiteman, Gordon, and Cohen, 1986b). These mothers were dissatisfied with their children, spent little time with them, and exerted little control over their children's activities. They also made little objection to their children's use of tobacco or marijuana.

Peers play an important role in substance abuse, but the interaction is complicated and varies depending on the adolescent's age, gender, and social class. As we have seen, peer influence is strongest among younger adolescents. By the end of high school, adolescents are developing their own standards for substance use, standards that accommodate parental as well as peer guidelines (Pulkkinen, 1983).

National Trends in Drug Use   Over the long term, alcohol consumption has been declining in the United States. Americans drink less hard liquor and more wine and beer than they did only a few years ago. The quest for physical fitness has led many to switch to reduced-alcohol or nonalcoholic beer and wine or to wine coolers. Adolescent drinking trends generally follow those of the larger society. Smoking also has declined among the young; among high-school seniors, only 20

percent of the girls and 16 percent of the boys now use tobacco (*New York Times*, 1986b). Cigarette smoking is rapidly becoming class-linked; today most smokers are working class (Fuchs, 1983).

Marijuana use also has leveled off (see Table 14.2). After peaking in 1979, its use among high-school seniors declined and then leveled off. Daily marijuana use, which peaked in 1978 at 10.7 percent of high-school seniors, had dropped to 4.9 percent by 1985 (Kozel and Adams, 1986). Cocaine is the only drug to show an increase in recent years. Since 1975, the proportion of high-school seniors who have used cocaine has doubled.

Adolescent Crime

Crime and youth go hand in hand. No matter which society we look at or which era in history we choose, we find the crime rate peaking among young people. Why should adolescents commit more crimes than any other age group? No one is certain, but their susceptibility to crime may be related to the nature of adolescence — a period when parental control is loosened, but adult responsibilities have not yet begun to constrain behavior. This pattern is not new. In a classic study, Marvin Wolfgang (1973) followed nearly 1,000 boys in Philadelphia until they were twenty-six years old. Among these boys, born in 1945, 35 percent had been arrested by the time they were eighteen. These statistics are not unusual. In England, 20 percent of the boys in one major study were convicted of a serious offense by their seventeenth birthdays and 31 percent by their twenty-first birthdays (Farrington, 1979).

Age is the most important predictor of crime; both violent crimes and crimes against property peak between the ages of fifteen and eighteen and then decline (see Figure 14.1). Crime remains relatively high throughout the twenties, then declines sharply throughout the rest of adulthood. Crime is also overwhelmingly a masculine pursuit; at any age and in any country, males are more likely to become involved with the law than females. Among arrests for serious crimes in the United States, eight out of ten are among males (U.S. Bureau of Justice Statistics, 1983).

What Do Arrest Figures Mean?   Arrest figures are not reliable indicators of the actual level of

Table 14.2
Marijuana Use among High School Seniors (Percent)

	1975	1976	1977	1978	1979	1980	1981	1982	1983	1984	1985
Ever used	47.3	52.8	56.4	59.2	60.4	60.3	59.5	58.7	57.0	54.9	54.2
Used in past year	40.0	44.5	47.6	50.2	50.8	48.8	46.1	44.3	42.3	40.0	40.6
Used in past month	27.1	32.2	35.4	37.1	36.5	33.7	31.6	28.5	27.0	25.2	25.7
Used daily in past month	6.0	8.2	9.1	10.7	10.3	9.1	7.0	6.3	5.5	5.0	4.9

Source: N. J. Kozel and E. H. Adams, "Epidemiology of Drug Abuse: An Overview," *Science*, 234 (1986), 973.

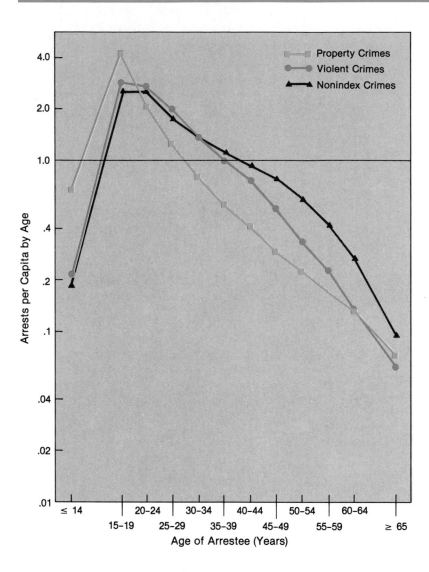

FIGURE 14.1   **Changes in crime rate with age. Proportion of arrests (in 1980) per proportion of the population at large in each age category for property and violent index crime and nonindex crime, plotted on a logarithmic axis. If arrests were equally spread over the life cycle, the curves would be horizontal at a value of 1.0. (Index crimes include larcency theft, burglary, aggravated assault, robbery, motor vehicle theft, forcible rape, murder, and arson. Nonindex crimes include status offenses and such crimes as embezzlement.)** *(From Wilson and Herrnstein, 1985)*

delinquency, because delinquent acts are both underreported and overreported. Many acts are never reported, the adolescents are not caught, or — if caught — are not arrested. Whether an arrest is made depends heavily on the arresting officer's discretion. Some authorities believe that delinquency is higher among middle-class adolescents than statistics indicate, because the middle-class youth is more likely to be let off with a warning in situations in which the lower-class youth is booked.

Overreporting occurs because many activities that can add a youngster to the delinquency records do not involve crimes against others. Acts in this category, called *status offenses,* include drinking, smoking marijuana, running away from home, cutting school, defying parental authority, and the like. As states have decriminalized many of these acts, an increasing number of youngsters who formerly would have gone to detention centers or reform schools are referred to some sort of therapy. In 1979, for example, 200,000 youths who had committed status offenses were held in juvenile justice facilities. By 1981, fewer than 23,000 status offenders were in such facilities (Gelman, 1986).

Many youths who commit status offenses never come into contact with the law. In fact, if all status offenders were charged, few adolescents would escape the label of delinquent. Some years ago, Martin Gold (1970) asked thirteen- to sixteen-year-old girls and boys to indicate (confidentially) which delinquent acts they had committed during the past year. Eighty-three percent admitted having broken some law, but most of the offenses involved such minor offenses as drinking alcoholic beverages or smoking marijuana.

Paths to Delinquency What sort of background characterizes the youth who commits a serious crime? Almost any negative factor you can think of is associated with delinquency, from poverty and broken homes to physical discipline and child abuse. Like other outcomes, criminality is the result of many interacting variables, some within the child, some within the family, and some in the larger society.

For the most part, delinquents tend to care little about others. Many have below average IQs, and they generally have problems at school. Lacking self-control, they are impulsive, highly aggressive, risk takers who seek excitement. Most abuse alcohol and other drugs. Many of these characteristics are linked with the quality of family life. Family life, of course, is affected by children as well as by parents. A child's temperament may help determine how he or she is treated by parents. Whatever genetic links exist, however, are trivial com-

Adolescent crime figures are often inflated by status offenses, such as smoking marijuana. *(Judy Herzl/The Picture Cube)*

pared with the influence of family and society.

Nearly forty years ago, Sheldon and Eleanor Glueck (1968) studied 500 delinquents and 500 youths who had no record of conviction. They concluded that delinquency was primarily determined by family factors: affection between the boy and each of his parents, the way the father disciplined the boy, the mother's supervision of the boy, and the cohesiveness of the family. Although they do not tell the entire story, these factors still play "a major part" in the development of delinquency. Other studies also have implicated disciplinary styles and emotional bonds between parent and child in the path to delinquency. For example, in a longitudinal study of Massachusetts boys, boys who became delinquents were more likely than other boys to have grown up in quarrelsome, chaotic homes where parents were cold and discipline was erratic or lax (McCord and McCord, 1959).

Children who grow up in such homes tend to develop weak emotional bonds with their parents. The final, lifelong stage of attachment (see Chapter 8) goes awry. These children have little wish to gain the approval of their parents and no certainty that their good behavior will earn them that ap-

When adolescent gangs set up the norm of delinquency, peer pressure can propel teenagers into trouble with the law. *(Edward Lettau/Photo Researchers)*

proval. When they fail to develop self-control or to internalize their parents' standards, they are at high risk for delinquency. As we saw in Chapter 9, erratic power-assertive discipline from cold parents also tends to produce highly aggressive youngsters, another characteristic of delinquents.

By adolescence, delinquents no longer share the family-related values that characterize most young people. When researchers had delinquent and nondelinquent boys fill out a self-image questionnaire, the lack of attachment that delinquents felt for their families distinguished the two groups (Ostrov, Offer, and Howard, 1982). Whether middle or working class, the nondelinquents had positive feelings about their families, but delinquents endorsed such statements as, "My parents are almost always on the side of someone else."

Social factors also are involved. Unemployment has no effect on the homicide rate, but it is linked with property crimes: robbery, burglary, and auto theft (Schapiro and Ahlburg, 1986). Low income also increases the likelihood of delinquency. Adolescents who grow up watching the luxury-filled world portrayed on television but have no way of obtaining these goods may simply take them. Peer pressure can be an important force, although it is not a case of "pure" adolescents succumbing to the persuasions of "evil" company. Instead, adolescent gangs may set up delinquency as the norm

for their members. Burglary, violence, and street-corner drug dealing are part of these youngsters' everyday world. In this context, the inability of the black, inner-city adolescent to find a job may make drug dealing or robbery seem like a sensible alternative.

Delinquency does not suddenly appear in adolescence. By the time a future delinquent is eight or nine years old, he or she has had trouble in school or has turned up at a child-guidance clinic. At this age, the trouble is not always antisocial in nature but encompasses a wide variety of aggressive and disruptive behavior. Longitudinal studies consistently show that such early misconduct is associated with later court convictions (Farrington, 1979). As we saw in Chapter 9, impatient, impulsive kindergartners who were defiant in the classroom, disrupted the class, and broke classroom rules ran a high risk of trouble with the law during adolescence (Spivack, Marcus, and Swift, 1986).

Adolescent Suicide

Suicide, once an uncommon cause of death among the young, is now the second leading cause of death among adolescents — exceeded only by accidents. What leads a youth to see life as so hope-

STOPPING THE CYCLE
OF JUVENILE CRIME

A large proportion of juvenile crime is the work of repeat offenders. So many factors are implicated in juvenile delinquency that, even when young offenders receive some kind of treatment, they frequently go on to criminal careers. A recent program, which takes an extremely broad approach to treatment of inner-city adolescents, shows signs of being more successful than most.

In Tennessee, Scott Henggeler and his colleagues (1986) have tested a program that uses a "multisystemic approach." This approach assumes that changing the interaction within and between the various settings in which a youngster lives is as important as changing the teenager's attitudes and feelings directly. Researchers worked with 57 delinquent adolescents individually, with the parents, and with the entire family. At the close of the four-year program, the youngsters in the treatment group had fewer behavior problems than a matched control group of offenders. And while family relations in the control group had deteriorated, relations within the treatment group had noticeably improved.

With the adolescent, the researchers worked on social skills. In many cases, a therapist developed a close relationship with the young offender. When a youngster already had a close relationship with a responsible adult, the therapist helped the adult change the child's pattern of social interactions. Within the peer group and school, the researchers encouraged the adolescent to become involved in group activities that would foster interpersonal skills. Within the families, the researchers encouraged authoritative parental styles (see Chapter 9), in which the parents set firm, consistent limits, but allowed the youngster to take responsibility and earn privileges. They worked on marital conflicts and tried to improve the relationship between the

youngster's parents. They showed families how to break the spiral of aggression, attack, and counterattack often found between aggressive boys and their parents (see Chapter 9).

Adolescents in the control group were assigned to existing programs. Many received individual counseling, family counseling was provided for some, and others were placed in alternative educational programs or vocational training.

By the close of the program, relations within the adolescents' families were warmer and more affectionate, whether the family was intact (38 percent) or was a mother-headed, single-parent family (62 percent). In intact families, the husband-wife relationship improved. In all the families, the relationship between the teenager and his or her parent (or parents) improved. Before entering the program, most of these adolescents either had been emotionally disengaged from their families or had lived in open parent-child conflict. Afterward, the adolescents talked more in family discussions, took more responsibility, began to contribute to family decisions, and took part in family social activities. Parents of these youngsters reported that they had fewer behavior problems to deal with, that their sons or daughters acted more maturely, and that they associated less with their delinquent peers.

Among families in the control group, relations between the mother and father had grown more distant and cold over the four-year period, as had relations between father and adolescent. There was no change in relations between mother and adolescent. The researchers suggest that the additional coldness in families already marked by disengagement and discord probably pushed the adolescent into closer association with delinquent peers — a factor that is a strong predictor of delinquent activities.

less that suicide is the solution? Is it a case of too many demands on today's youths? Unrealistic standards? As with other adolescent disorders, there is no simple answer to this troubling problem.

Race and gender heavily weight the chances that a young person will commit suicide. More whites kill themselves than blacks; more boys kill themselves than girls. Girls apparently make as many attempts at suicide, but they usually fail.

Boys and men generally are successful. What accounts for this difference? First, boys use more lethal means. The overwhelming majority shoot themselves; girls are most likely to use poison. Second, girls usually want to be rescued; their attempt is meant as a message. Boys (men, too) want to kill. They are trying to destroy someone else inside them, as well as themselves. Boys are unwilling to ask for help, even after they have made an unsuccessful attempt to kill themselves. Third, girls have better social support systems than boys. As we saw in Chapter 13, girls tend to have more intimate friendships and to exchange emotional confidences, but boys regard their friends as companions in fun. When adolescents talk about suicide, girls generally see it as a solution to emotional problems; boys, as a response to job problems (Simons and Murphy, 1985).

Adolescents who are likely to make a suicide attempt tend to have similar family backgrounds. Often they come from broken homes; when the home is intact, it is filled with strife, or else the youngster feels rejected by one or both parents. The loss of a father was related to future suicide in a long-term study of young men that began during their adolescence (Paffenbarger, King, and Wing, 1969). When those who later committed suicide were compared with controls, the future suicides were more likely to have lost a father, either by death or by divorce, before they were eighteen years old. Losing a mother had no effect on the suicide rate.

A family history of suicide is especially ominous. In one study, one-third of the adolescents who killed themselves had a relative who had either committed suicide or attempted it (Holden, 1986). A suicide attempt by a family member seems to make suicide a reasonable option. Why? The taboo against suicide is a powerful deterrent. When the family or the larger culture regards suicide as a horror, young people are unlikely to kill themselves. But a suicide attempt by a family member makes suicide an acceptable choice. This permission for suicide affects all age levels. Whenever a famous person commits suicide, the national suicide rate rises for the next few days.

Sometimes a wave of suicides seems to sweep through the young people in a community. In Omaha, Nebraska, three adolescents committed suicide within five days, and another four made unsuccessful attempts. The dead youths knew one another only casually. Sixteen-year-old Michele had troubles with her boyfriend and took an overdose of her mother's antidepressant medication. Fifteen-year-old Mark, a gregarious athlete, shot himself, as did eighteen-year-old Tom, a loner who was "disgusted with life" (Leo, 1986). Similarly, in Plano, a small Texas town north of Dallas, seven teenagers committed suicide within a year. In the sparsely populated countryside north of New York City, five boys killed themselves in one month. In such cases, the first suicide probably breaks the community taboo against such acts and makes it possible for other adolescents to consider suicide as a possible solution to their problems.

The adolescent who solves his or her problems with a gun, a rope, or an overdose of barbiturates is not a "normal" child who comes home one day and decides to commit suicide. After matching successful suicide victims to controls, psychiatrist Mohammad Shafii and his colleagues (1985) interviewed the adolescents' families, friends, and teachers. They found that most of the victims recently had undergone some sort of stress, tended to abuse alcohol or drugs (70 percent), had trouble with the law or had shown some other antisocial behavior (70 percent), were depressed (76 percent), and were rigid perfectionists who tended to isolate themselves from others (65 percent).

Many researchers have noted the link between depression and suicide. Both depressed adolescents and those who kill themselves are low in self-esteem, have failed to live up to their own impossibly high standards, have turned the anger they feel toward others against themselves, feel alone, helpless, and vulnerable, and are afraid of being alone and abandoned. The particular events that destroy self-esteem or signify failure vary from one youth to the next. Often the triggering incident is the breakup of a relationship. However, any experience that produces shame, guilt, and humiliation can precipitate a suicide attempt. Being arrested, beaten up, or raped often precedes suicide. The incident does not have to be violent. An adolescent boy may feel that life is not worth living when he is refused admittance to Harvard.

Psychiatrist Donald Cohen of Yale University has found that the characteristics of adolescents who kill themselves can be sorted into three basic patterns (see Holden, 1986). A majority, primarily

Youth Suicide: A Common Pattern

By JANE E. BRODY

The four suicides yesterday by teen-age friends in Bergenfield, N.J., are in one respect a rare phenomenon, but in others part of a pattern increasingly found in communities throughout the country.

According to Dr. David Shaffer, who has been conducting an in-depth study of 182 suicides among youths in the New York metropolitan area in the last two years, suicide pacts are extremely uncommon. However, in a high proportion of youth suicides, particularly among older teen-agers, drugs or alcohol are involved and school problems and antisocial behavior are commonplace.

Dr. Shaffer, a professor of child psychiatry at Columbia University, has also noted considerable "imitation" or "contagion" surrounding youth suicides.

Imitation Effect Feared

"The effect of highly publicized stories about teenage suicides is a significant increase in successful suicides and suicide attempts among young people," he said in an interview yesterday. "The current situation, I'm afraid, is ripe for imitation and will no doubt cause a great deal of anxiety about still more such deaths occurring."

Dr. Shaffer said he believed there were far more suicide clusters among youngsters than came to public attention. "A very high proportion of the suicide victims in our study knew others who had committed suicide or attempted it," he said.

In learning about the suicide of another child, children come to see suicide as an easy solution to their problems and a kind of "instant martyrdom," the psychiatrist added.

The "contagious" aspect of suicide is a well-known phenomenon and is said to account for the periodic clusters of suicides among young people in a single community. In recent years, for example, there were five suicides among youngsters in Westchester County and seven in the boom town of Plano, Tex.

Feelings of Guilt

In the current case, the picture is complicated by the fact that one victim, Thomas Rizzo, was with his best friend, Joe Major, last September when the latter fell or jumped to his death from a cliff of the Palisades.

Charlotte Ross, executive director of the Youth Suicide National Center, said that sometimes a friend knew of another's intention to kill himself and was racked with guilt for failing to thwart it.

"The one who remained silent feels totally responsible and may not be able to handle the guilt," she said, prompting him to opt for the same solution used by his friend.

Yesterday's deaths are among more than 5,000 known suicides that occur each year among Americans between the ages of 15 and 24, making suicide the second leading cause of death in this age group, after accidents.

The actual number of successful teen-age suicides is believed to be much greater, but many are recorded as accidents. Four other recent deaths among teenagers in Bergenfield, for example, were so recorded.

Certified deaths by suicide among teen-agers increased dramatically between 1960 and 1980, but the number has since begun to level off, possibly because of a decline in the use of mind-altering drugs and an increase in attention to children at risk of taking their own lives.

An estimated total of 400,000 teen-agers are said to attempt suicide each year, and most who succeed give one of more warnings of their suicidal intentions.

When a cluster of teen-age suicides appears, it is generally because an earlier suicide has broken the community taboo against self-destruction and made suicide a "thinkable" option. *(© 1987 by The New York Times Company. Reprinted by permission. 3/12/87)*

---

boys, have severe behavior problems: they may be delinquents; many are drug abusers. Another group, primarily girls, are depressed. And a third group, primarily boys, are uptight, ambitious perfectionists, who become extremely anxious when challenged socially or academically. Other researchers have noted that many boys who commit suicide have a history of depression, aggressive behavior, and impulsivity (Holden, 1986).

In a number of communities, alarmed parents, educators, and public officials have set up education programs to spread the word about the causes and effects of suicide to teenagers, their parents, educators, and the clergy. For example, three New Jersey pilot programs trained teachers and students to recognize youngsters who are potential suicides. However, psychiatrist David Shaffer of Columbia University believes that such programs are premature. He points out that no one knows whether they are effective, and he fears that the discussions involved may make suicide an option among some troubled youths (Williams, 1985). But researchers agree that teenagers who talk about suicide should be taken seriously. In one study of adolescent suicides, 85 percent of the youths had talked about their intent, and 40 percent had first made an unsuccessful try at killing themselves (Shafii et al., 1985).

Adolescent Pregnancy

Every year in this country, more than 500,000 babies are born to adolescent girls. Among whites, 23 percent of all first births are to teenagers; among blacks, the proportion is 45 percent. The majority of these babies are born to unmarried adolescents: 37 percent of the white babies and 87 percent of the black babies (Moore, 1985). The best estimate of scientists is that 35 percent of all adolescent girls who are sexually active become pregnant while they are teenagers (Zelnik, Kantner, and Ford, 1981). Pregnancy adds to the crucial decisions that already face teenagers, for the decisions made by pregnant adolescents change the course of their lives.

Hazards of Teenage Pregnancy The physical, economic, and social hazards that face young mothers and their babies have aroused the concern of many researchers. All sorts of complications increase sharply among adolescent mothers. When the mother is younger than sixteen, her risk of dying during pregnancy or childbirth is five times the national average (Bolton, 1980). Extremely young mothers face special risks because their pelvises are immature. The fetal head is often unable to pass safely through the immature pelvis, and so young teenagers are likely to have complicated deliveries and Caesarean sections (McCluskey, Killarney, and Papini, 1983).

No matter what the adolescent's age, her chances of developing complications are increased. Compared with other babies, more babies of adolescent mothers are born dead, and there are more cases of premature birth, low birth weight, respiratory distress syndrome, and neurological defects (Bolton, 1980). Most of the complications are unnecessary and not related to the mother's youth. They occur because many girls are reluctant to seek prenatal care and see a physician late in pregnancy — or not at all. Because most adolescents know little about nutrition or prenatal development, the girls may not eat properly, or they may expose the fetus to such hazards as alcohol, tobacco, or drugs. Older adolescents who have good prenatal care from early in the first trimester and who have proper nutrition and avoid cigarettes, drugs, and alcohol have babies as healthy as those of women in their twenties.

Adolescents face further hazards if they breast-feed their babies. Even though they take dietary supplements, they tend to lose large amounts of calcium and other minerals from their bones (Chan, Ronald, Slates, Hollis, and Thomas, 1982). Because their bones are still growing, it is difficult for adolescent girls to take in enough additional calcium and phosphorus to meet the simultaneous demands of milk production and new bone growth.

These physical hazards probably do not exceed the social and economic risks run by adolescent mothers. As the public has come to accept unmarried mothers, fewer teenagers have given their babies up for adoption. In some studies, as many as 95 percent have kept their babies (Group for the Advancement of Psychiatry, 1986). What happens to these young mothers? Their future seems to depend on the choices they make. Girls who stay at home with their parents and complete their education do best in the long run (Furstenberg, 1976). But most girls who keep their babies drop out of school, and few return. Nationwide surveys indicate that 80 percent of the adolescent mothers who become pregnant between the ages of fifteen and seventeen never complete high school (*New York Times*, 1985). These young women find themselves trapped in economic insecurity — without the skills that enable them to get a job and burdened with the emotional and economic responsibilities of caring for an infant. The care is usually more than they bargained for. The cuddly, sweet, smiling baby envisioned by pregnant girls turns into a colicky, wet crier, smelling of sour milk, who needs continual attention and keeps them awake at night. And within two years, 65 percent are pregnant again (Bolton, 1980).

Girls who "solve" their problem by getting married are not much better off. Although at first they are financially ahead of the unmarried girl, their advantage does not seem to be permanent. They usually drop out of school, and many find themselves divorced and without job skills (Moore, 1985). (As the box, "When Teenagers Become Mothers," indicates, the children of adolescent mothers also face serious problems.)

Why So Many Pregnancies? Although sexual activity has increased among adolescents, this increase does not account for the tide of teenage pregnancy. In Sweden, a society that is more sexually permissive than the United States, the rate of adolescent pregnancy is only about one-third that of American teenagers. American teenagers get pregnant at a rate that is two times higher than the rate in Canada, Great Britain, or France; seven times higher than in the Netherlands; and eighteen times higher than in Japan (Leavitt, 1986).

Most adolescents who become pregnant do not do so intentionally. Instead, they seem to have no motivation to avoid it (Moore, 1985). In fact, lack of motivation in general characterizes girls who become pregnant. They tend to have little interest in academic matters, and most are doing poorly in school and going nowhere (Furstenberg and Brooks-Gunn, in press).

Social trends play some part in teenage pregnancies and birth. As adolescent pregnancies have become more common and single-mother role models have appeared among celebrities and career women, the stigma that was once attached to out-of-wedlock pregnancies has nearly vanished. When Madonna's recording of *Papa Don't Preach* was released, officials of Planned Parenthood threw up their hands. "The message," said the executive director, "is that getting pregnant is cool and having the baby is the right thing and a good thing, and don't listen to your parents, the school, anybody who tells you otherwise" (Dullea, 1986). In his view, Madonna was offering teenagers a path to permanent poverty.

Changes in the black family also have affected the incidence of births to unmarried girls. Many black teenage mothers are the daughters of mothers who were teenage mothers. However, black women have become less likely to marry the father of their children, primarily because the job prospects for black men are dismal. By 1982, 56.7 percent of all black babies were born to unmarried mothers up from 37.6 percent in 1970 (U.S. Bureau of the Census, 1986).

The Case of Contraceptives   The immediate reason for adolescent pregnancy is the incorrect use of contraceptives, their sporadic use, or the failure to use them at all. Most sexually active teenagers know that contraceptives exist, but 27 percent never use them, and only 33 percent always use them (Hevesi, 1986). Why do so many adolescents play such a risky game? Most never seem to realize that pregnancy could happen to them. In one study of pregnant adolescents, no matter how much a girl knew about contraceptives and the risk of unprotected intercourse, she was surprised when she actually became pregnant (Smith, Nenney, Weinman, and Mumford, 1982). Another factor is feelings of guilt or ambivalence about sexual activity (Rosen and Hall, 1984). Girls who believe that premarital sex is improper tend to excuse their sexual activity if they are "swept away" by their emotions. Carrying contraceptives or taking birth-control pills indicates the intent to have sex and thus marks a girl as "bad" in her own eyes.

Some girls simply are misinformed. They believe that if they take one of their mother's birth-control pills before a date, they will be protected. Or they believe that intercourse in certain posi-

Most girls who get pregnant are doing poorly in school and lack the motivation to avoid pregnancy.
(Elinor S. Beckwith/Taurus)

tions is "safe." Six out of ten are not sure just when during a menstrual cycle they are most likely to conceive (Hevesi, 1986). Some have exaggerated fears of the side effects of contraceptives. And some are afraid that if they go to a clinic, their parents will learn that they are sexually active.

Adolescents who use contraceptives effectively tend to differ from sporadic or inefficient users in several ways. When Julie Spain (1980) interviewed fourteen- to eighteen-year-olds at a teen clinic, she found that girls who used contraceptives efficiently had thought about the future and realized that their present behavior had consequences for their future. Such girls tended to have their lives planned and could visualize their future career and family situations.

By contrast, girls who were sporadic users had trouble imagining themselves in the future. Either they had no goals, or else their goals were unrealis-

Although their provision of contraceptives has been controversial, many high schools that provide birth-control services have seen a drop in teenage pregnancies. *(Bernard Gotfryd/Woodfin Camp & Associates)*

tic and bore no relationship to their activities. Efficient contraceptive users also felt in control of their own lives; faced with a problem, they looked for a solution. Girls who were sporadic users saw their lives as controlled by external sources, did not look for alternatives, and rarely thought things through before acting.

Reducing Adolescent Pregnancies   The *number* of adolescent births is going down. In 1970, while the baby-boom generation swelled the adolescent section of the population, teenagers gave birth to 644,700 infants. By 1982, the number had dropped to 513,800. Among black teenagers, the birth *rate* had also dropped — from 97 births per 1,000 unmarried girls in 1970 to 87 births in 1982.

However, among white teenagers, the birth rate rose during that same period — from 11 per 1,000 in 1970 to 18 per 1,000 in 1982 (Moore, 1985).

Fears in some quarters that sex education courses increase sexual activity and pregnancy among adolescents seem groundless. Compared with adolescents who have not had sex education courses, adolescents who have completed courses show no additional sexual activity. These students also are less likely to have intercourse without contraceptives (Zelnik and Kim, 1982). But sex education by itself cannot solve the problem of teenage pregnancies.

In some places, high schools are providing contraceptives as part of their general health-care services. As a result, births among high-school girls in St. Paul, Minnesota, declined from 59 per 1,000 in 1977 to 37 per 1,000 in 1985 (Leavitt, 1986). When some high schools in Baltimore began providing birth-control services, the rate of pregnancies among students dropped 22.5 percent at a time when the pregnancy rate in other Baltimore high schools climbed 39.5 percent (Perlez, 1986). The presence of the clinics also seemed to slow the rate at which students became sexually active. After the clinics were installed, students in those high schools tended to postpone their first sexual activity by about six months. In most places, high-school clinics have been controversial. In fact, students themselves tend to say that they would prefer going off the school grounds to clinics — primarily because they fear that clinic personnel will notify school officials about their visits.

No program can eliminate adolescent pregnancies, but those that are most successful in reducing the rate provide adolescents with the motivation to avoid pregnancy.

Adolescent Eating Disorders

Eating disorders recently have emerged as a common adolescent problem. As recently as fifteen or twenty years ago, such terms as *anorexia* and *bulimia* were almost unknown except to clinical psychologists and psychiatrists. And most of them knew of these conditions only from descriptions in textbooks. Today, these disorders are so frequent that many colleges and universities offer counseling or therapy programs specifically designed for students who suffer from them. Eating disorders fall into three types: obesity, anorexia

WHEN TEENAGERS BECOME MOTHERS

Because bearing a child clearly constricts the adolescent girl's future, researchers have worried about the future of her child as well. Does her offspring show any ill effects for having so young a mother? In most cases, children born to adolescent mothers pay a penalty in both cognitive and social development. The problem has been to separate the children's socioeconomic handicaps from the handicap of having a mother who is little more than a child herself.

Children of adolescent mothers tend to score lower on school achievement tests and on IQ tests than children of older mothers. They are more likely to be retarded than children born to older mothers. Those who are not retarded have lowered educational aspirations. Among preschoolers, the cognitive differences are small, but they widen steadily as children go through school. By the time they are in high school, children of teenage mothers are much more likely than other youngsters to have repeated a grade. Among the children of black teenage mothers, 53 percent in one study had repeated a grade; in another study, 42 percent had repeated. Among children of older black mothers, 19 percent repeated a grade (Furstenberg and Brooks-Gunn, in press).

Socioeconomic factors account for most of this difference: Adolescent mothers generally are poor, unmarried, and have not completed high school. The majority grow up in a single-parent household. After allowing for all these socioeconomic factors, researchers found that having an adolescent mother added to the problem, but that the effect was small (Brooks-Gunn and Furstenberg, 1986).

Socially, teenagers' children are also at a disadvantage. In elementary school, they tend to be more active, impulsive, easily frustrated, and hyperactive than children of older mothers. Boys seem especially affected; they tend to be more aggressive and willful than other boys. When they reach high school, children of adolescent mothers have trouble at school; often they are suspended, expelled, or subjected to other disciplinary action (Brooks-Gunn and Furstenberg, 1986). Again, socioeconomic factors have some effect, but differences remain after researchers correct for them. For example, in one study, half of the fifteen- and sixteen-year-old children of teenage black mothers had been expelled or suspended from school in the past five years compared to only a quarter of the children of older black mothers (Furstenberg and Brooks-Gunn, in press). Finally, the daughters of teenage mothers are likely to become pregnant themselves, keeping the adolescent childbearing cycle going.

Some of the differences that appear in these children may be in part the result of the mother's immaturity and inexperience when her child is small. Although adolescent mothers are just as warm as other mothers, they are less responsive to their infants, talk less to them, are less sensitive to their needs, and tend to punish them more than older mothers do (Elster, McAnarney, and Lamb, 1983). In some studies, teenage mothers have been responsive but provided their babies with few opportunities for cognitive and emotional stimulation (Darabi, Graham, Namerow, Philliber, and Varga, 1984). Most adolescent mothers know little about child development and have unrealistic expectations of their children. As Jeanne Brooks-Gunn and Frank Furstenberg (1986) put it, they expect "too little, too late" from their children in cognition and language but may expect too much, especially in physical development, from preterm babies. Such differences may explain the high level of insecure attachments found among babies of adolescent mothers (Lamb, Hopps, and Elster, 1987).

When teenage mothers have adequate social support, their children's problems generally fade. Social support can alleviate stress, provide practical assistance, inform the mother about children's capabilities, and enhance the mother's self-esteem (Elster, McAnarney, and Lamb, 1983). Studies indicate that if there is another adult in the household, the youngsters' cognitive and social development is enhanced (Brooks-Gunn and Furstenberg, 1986). The additional adult may act as a buffer against negative events, provide social and emotional support for the mother, and provide direct support to the child. Teenagers can be good mothers, but socioeconomic stress and a lack of social support often prevent them from giving their babies a good start in life.

As Miss America and *Playboy* centerfold models became thinner, the pressure to diet intensified on teenage girls of normal weight. *(Bettmann Newsphotos)*

nervosa, and bulimia. Despite the distinctness of definition, they overlap somewhat in actuality, so that an adolescent with anorexia also may be bulimic, a once obese adolescent may become anorexic, and a youngster with bulimia also may be obese.

A common thread running through all the disorders is the culture's demand that women and adolescent girls be thin. The female body ideal is far thinner than the natural female figure, and that discrepancy has grown over the past few decades. Between 1959 and 1979, the weight and body size of the *Playboy* magazine centerfold model and the contestants in the Miss America contest decreased significantly, and since 1970, the contest winners have been thinner than the other contestants (Garner, Garfinkel, Schwartz, and Thompson,

1980). Because girls' self-concepts are strongly related to their attractiveness (Lerner, Orlos, and Knapp, 1976), these cultural changes have increased the pressure on girls to stay slim. As a result, most adolescent girls are dissatisfied with their weight and are preoccupied with efforts to reduce it. Such a situation sets up girls for eating disorders.

Obesity   About 15 percent of American adolescents are obese; their body weight exceeds the ideal weight for their height by at least 20 percent (Maloney and Klykylo, 1983). Because of social pressures, girls are much more disturbed about obesity than boys. Obese girls (and those who are not obese but believe that they weigh more than they should) generally are low in self-esteem, have a distorted image of their bodies (they see themselves as fatter than they actually are), and feel helpless and frustrated when their dieting is unsuccessful. They are ashamed about their weight, and the shame extends to their appetite for food. Some girls are so upset by their weight and so dissatisfied with their bodies that they become depressed (Rodin, Silberstein, and Striegel-Moore, 1985).

There is no single cause of obesity. As we saw in Chapter 5, genes, metabolism, eating habits, inactivity, and a heightened responsiveness to environmental cues are all implicated in its development. There are some indications that girls' attempts to lose weight can make staving off obesity even more difficult. At puberty, increased estrogen and progesterone levels promote the development of fat cells and the storage of body fat. These normal fat deposits send many girls onto rigid diets. But research suggests that dieting during this period, when hormonal production is being established, may disrupt the body's normal weight-regulation processes (Rodin, Silberstein, and Striegel-Moore, 1985).

Obesity has negative effects on a girl's future but is less threatening to a boy's. Fifty-two percent of nonobese girls but only 32 percent of the obese girls in high-school graduating classes went on to college. Among the boys, 53 percent of the nonobese and 50 percent of the obese boys entered college (Canning and Mayer, 1966). Because college education is an important determinant of socioeconomic level, such patterns could have a permanent effect and may help explain why obese women — but not obese men — tend to wind up at a lower socioeconomic status than their parents. At least part of this sex difference may be the result of discrimination by college admissions offices (Goldblatt, Moore, and Stunkard, 1965). In an increasing number of girls, the struggle against obesity leads to more serious eating disorders.

Anorexia Nervosa   **Anorexia nervosa** is a pattern of self-starvation brought about by fanatical dieting. To be diagnosed as anorectic, a girl must have lost more than 25 percent of her original body weight and have no known medical or psychiatric illness (Sorosky, 1986). Girls sometimes accelerate the weight loss by using laxatives, diuretics, and appetite suppressants. Their initial aim may be to achieve a "perfect" body by taking off a few pounds, but when they reach that goal, they select a new target of an even lower weight. The pattern continues, with the girl (up to 95 percent of anorectics are girls) becoming thinner and thinner. Eventually she resembles a skeleton: her ribs protrude, her face takes on a skull-like appearance, and her hands resemble claws. In most cases, she seems to enjoy the loss of each additional pound and denies that she is skinny. Yet she is often so malnourished that she must be hospitalized and forced to eat. Left untreated, anorexia nervosa is an extremely dangerous disorder. The victim may starve herself to death or die from the medical complications of malnutrition.

Anorexia develops out of a fear that the anorectic shares with most adolescent girls: the fear of becoming fat. When researchers compared anorectic girls with healthy girls, they found that both groups were "always on a diet," continually used will power to restrain their eating, and viewed their hunger as exaggerated and obscene (Thompson and Schwartz, 1982). Anorexia is most common among affluent, well-educated girls in developed countries, where the pressure to be slim and willowy is intense. Among young adults, it is likely to be found among those whose jobs demand rigid weight control: dancers, models, athletes (especially jockeys), and flight attendants (Sorosky, 1986).

Yet there seems to be something additional in the background of anorectic girls, or else most affluent teenagers would become anorectic. For one thing, most are high achievers. From her early years, the anorectic girl has driven to succeed, to be the straight A student, the "perfect child." One such young woman, while in college, took twenty units of course work each semester, held a full-time job, was captain of an athletic team, tutored disadvantaged children, and exercised strenuously for at least two hours a day.

Some clinicians believe that fear of sexuality is a major factor in anorexia (Maloney and Klykylo, 1983). The severe weight loss stops menstruation and shrinks the girl's breasts and hips until she no longer is recognized as female. Anorexia eliminates any possibility of pregnancy. In effect, it restores the girl to her prepubertal status, when she had no adult responsibilities.

Others believe that anorexia is the symptom of a deeply troubled, malfunctioning family, in which the girl's self-starvation maintains family stability. In this view, parents focus on protecting or blaming their child, a ploy that allows them to ignore their own conflicts and to see the girl as the primary family problem (Hsu, 1983). Still others believe that there is a genetic component to anorexia and that the girl's hypothalamus (which regulates eating) malfunctions.

Bulimia   The anorectic girl exerts rigid control over her eating, to the point of starvation. By contrast, in **bulimia,** sometimes called the "binge-purge syndrome," a girl goes through repeated episodes in which her eating is totally out of control. During her periodic food binges, she consumes large quantities of high-calorie foods — several pounds of chocolate bars perhaps or several large pizzas — in the course of an hour or two. In an attempt to manage her weight, the girl may induce vomiting after each binge or else train herself to throw up after each meal. Instead of vomiting, some bulimics use heavy doses of laxatives to control their weight. Others use diuretics or diet rigorously between binges. Those who purge themselves regularly run the risk of serious medical and dental problems.

Unlike anorectics, bulimics are aware that their binges are abnormal, are afraid that someday they will be unable to stop their eating, and feel ashamed and depressed after each episode. Although anorectics are by definition underweight,

After one of their periodic food binges, bulimics are ashamed and depressed. Most are aware that their eating patterns are abnormal. *(Susan Rosenberg/Photo Researchers)*

percent were vomiting at least once a month to control their weight.

Girls who become bulimic differ in several ways from the "normal" adolescent who is preoccupied with her weight. Genetic, family, and personality factors seem to interact in the production of bulimia (Johnson and Maddi, 1986). Not only do a large number of bulimics have symptoms of depression, but many of their close relatives (53 percent in one study) have major affective disorders (such as depression) as well (Hudson, Pope, Jonas, and Urgelun-Todd, 1983). This biological vulnerability may lead to bulimia when a girl with low self-esteem, who has trouble regulating her own behavior, grows up in a disorganized family that is filled with strife and conflict.

Once her weight drops below a certain point, the anorectic's disorder cannot be hidden. But bulimics can binge or binge and purge secretly for years without being discovered. Treatment for anorexia nervosa and bulimia depends on the therapist. Both disorders have been treated by psychoanalysis, family therapy, behavior therapy, cognitive therapy, group therapy, and biochemical methods. Often a therapist combines two types of treatment, such as cognitive therapy and antidepressants. Each approach seems promising.

THE FUTURE OF ADOLESCENT STRESS AND DISTRESS

Is the picture of adolescent disorders set forth in this chapter an enduring portrait of adolescence or simply a snapshot of the troubles that have beset adolescents over the last two decades? During the past few years, a major change has taken place in the way developmentalists view the adolescent experience. Not so long ago, our knowledge of adolescents came from studies (primarily of boys) that made no attempt to fit the findings into a historical perspective (Elder, 1980). Today, researchers generally try to consider how social and historical influences affect the way that young people mature.

After nearly twenty years of a steady rise in adolescent disorders, the numbers have turned around, and in many cases they have begun to de-

many bulimics are of average or above average weight. Like anorectics, bulimics are well-educated, affluent girls who are terrified of becoming fat. Bulimia is much more prevalent than anorexia and is especially common among college women. Among women under the age of 30, only one or two out of 100 are affected (Pyle and Mitchell, 1986), but in special groups, such as women students at private colleges, the rate may rise as high as 10 or even 25 percent. When researchers studied more than 1,000 high-school girls, they discovered that 4.9 percent were clearly bulimic (Johnson, Lewis, Love, Lewis, and Stuckey, 1984). But binge eating was not limited to the bulimic group. Nearly 17 percent of the "normal" group went on food binges at least weekly, and 9

According to the birth-cohort theory, competition among members of the crowded baby-boom generation was responsible for many of the increases in adolescent crime and suicide. *(Jacques Chenet/ Woodfin Camp & Associates)*

cline. Drug use peaked in 1979. Youthful crime (including adults up to the age of twenty-five) peaked in 1980. Suicide peaked in 1980. Out-of-wedlock births peaked in 1980.

How can we account for such startling changes? One intriguing theory explains the rise and subsequent fall as primarily an effect of the baby boom that produced a record crop of children between 1946 and 1964 (Easterlin, 1980; Fuchs, 1983). This **birth-cohort theory** holds that there is a strong relation between the "crowdedness" of a generation and the amount of disturbance felt by its members. Those born during a baby boom are

more likely to develop emotional problems than those born during a "baby bust," when there are few youngsters relative to the total population.

Children of a crowded generation find themselves competing with one another for limited resources. In each of life's races — for grades, admission to the best colleges, jobs, promotions, even for dates and mates — there are more runners to be edged out. Those who sense themselves falling behind or likely to fail tend to react with rage and resentment or with feelings of worthlessness and self-blame. Individuals who react with resentment tend to commit delinquent acts; those who react with feelings of worthlessness tend to become depressed or even commit suicide. As destructive or self-destructive acts accumulate, there is a sharp rise, not only in the number of such acts but also in the rate. The practical effects can be dramatic. If the number of youngsters born in a given year doubles, and if the rate of a particular act triples, there is a 600 percent increase. This is exactly what happened in the case of suicide by young white males.

The birth-cohort theory seems too simple to be true, but statistics seem to support it. When cohorts from 1933 to 1976 are compared, suicide correlates +.46 with the size of the cohort (Offer and Holinger, 1983). The recent cohort squeeze placed more youths in situations in which they tried and failed. Some felt crowded out and responded to the stress by killing themselves. In the 1980s, as the baby boomers moved out of adolescence and very young adulthood, the suicide rate among the young began to decline.

We can trace a similar pattern in the case of crime. During the past few years, the crime rate in the United States has been declining. Burglary, auto theft, robbery, and homicide are all down. A majority of crimes are committed by young men between the ages of fifteen and twenty-nine, and so the more young men in the population, the worse the crime statistics. Homicide, for example, correlates +.52 with cohort size (Offer and Holinger, 1983). Crime began to rise when the first wave of baby boomers hit adolescence, and it continued rising until this cohort moved into their thirties. The number of crimes rose because there was a larger share of people who were likely to commit crimes. But the per capita crime rate also rose: each 1,000 young men committed more crimes than did 1,000 young men in the 1960s.

Morton Schapiro and Dennis Ahlburg (1986) explain this rise in the crime rate in terms of birth-cohort theory. As job opportunities and income shrank for baby boomers, they found it increasingly difficult to equal their parents' economic position. Many could get only low-paying jobs or found no job at all. Psychological stress increased, and so did antisocial behavior. Young people who were at risk for delinquency (because of their family background and temperament) became more likely to turn to criminal acts.

The economists and demographers who discovered the correlation between cohort size and adolescent disorder tend to favor economic explanations of these trends. They stress competition among peers and the consequent crowding out of the less attractive, less able, or less fortunate. But there is another way to explain the trends. It may be a result of family size itself. As we saw in Chapter 12, confluence theory holds that family size explains the sharp decline — and subsequent rise — in SAT scores during this same period (Zajonc and Hall, 1987). Similar processes may be at work in the rise and fall of adolescent disorders. Children from larger families get less attention from their parents. As a result, they may identify less with their parents, get less moral instruction from them, or feel less loved. Over the years of growing up, any of these deficits could translate into higher levels of emotional disturbance.

If some version of the birth-cohort theory is correct, we might expect youthful disorders to continue their decline, at least until the end of the century. Yet many factors contribute to the degree of stress on adolescents, as we have seen in this chapter. Few social patterns have a single cause. The future of adolescent stress and distress is still uncertain.

SUMMARY

1. The adolescent years are spent in preparation for departure from the family. The lengthened period of adolescence in contemporary societies, together with young people's uncertainty about their future, and their anxiety over their choices can create stress.

2. Four myths have grown up about adolescence, but none has been supported by research. Ado-

lescence is *not* a period of unusual emotional turmoil; the rate of disturbance among adolescents is the same as among adults. When emotional disturbances do arise during adolescence, they do *not* fade away as the young person enters adulthood; teenagers with emotional problems become adults with emotional problems. Hostility and conflict between adolescent and parents are *not* inevitable; most teenagers get along well with their parents. A generation gap does *not* separate teenager and parents; most young people and their parents agree on basic values.

3. A majority of adolescents use some drugs at some time, but those who use drugs heavily are troubled youngsters. Excessive use of drugs or alcohol is associated with poor school performance, disrupted family life, and antisocial behavior. Alcohol is the gateway drug; teenagers almost always use it before progressing to other drugs.

4. In all societies, the crime rate is highest among the young and the male; in the United States, rates for violent crimes and crimes against property peak during adolescence. Delinquency is produced by interacting factors—some within the child, some within the family, and others within the larger society. Future delinquents generally are in trouble at school or have had severe enough home trouble to be taken to a child-guidance clinic by the time they are eight or nine years old.

5. Suicide, which is the second leading cause of death among adolescents, is concentrated among white males. Girls attempt suicide as often as boys, but boys use more lethal means, intend to kill instead of signal for help, and have poorer social-support systems than girls. Youngsters who commit suicide either have severe behavior problems, are depressed, or are uptight, ambitious perfectionists who become extremely anxious when challenged.

6. Adolescents who become pregnant run greatly increased risks of complication and death—both for themselves and their infants. Most of the risk is due to lack of prenatal care, but girls in early adolescence face additional risks because of their immature pelvises. Girls who keep their babies also face social and economic problems; they are burdened with responsibility for a baby but lack job skills. The high rate of adolescent pregnancy seems due to a lack of motivation to avoid pregnancy and social acceptance of out-of-wedlock births. Adolescents who do not use contraceptives generally believe that they will never become pregnant; feel guilty or ambivalent about premarital sex; are misinformed about the mechanics of conception; are afraid of contraceptives' side effects; or fear that their parents will discover their sexual activity.

7. Most adolescents with eating disorders are girls, and the disorders develop in good part because of the culture's unnaturally thin female body ideal. Obese teenagers tend to have low self-esteem, believe that they are much heavier than they actually are, and feel frustrated and helpless over their failures to lose weight. **Anorexia nervosa,** a pattern of self-starvation brought on by fanatical dieting, is found among high achievers. Other factors that may be involved include a fear of sexuality, a malfunctioning family that uses the daughter's disorder to remain stable, and a genetically based malfunction of the hypothalamus. **Bulimia,** which is characterized by periodic food binges often followed by purging, seems to result from the interaction of genetic, family, and personality factors.

8. Stress-related disorders among adolescents have risen over the past twenty years, but many of the disorders seem to have peaked, and some are declining. According to the **birth-cohort theory,** this pattern is the result of the baby boom, which led to increased stress on members of crowded cohorts as they competed for the culture's limited resources. Some suggest that the diluted parental attention received by children in large families may be as important as economic stress in explaining the pattern.

KEY TERMS

anorexia nervosa   birth-cohort theory   bulimia

STUDY TERMS

anorexia nervosa   An eating disorder characterized by self-starvation brought about by fanatical dieting; it is found primarily among affluent, well-educated girls in developed countries.

birth-cohort theory   The theory that the twenty-year rise, peak, and subsequent decline of stress-related dis-orders among adolescents is due to increased economic and social stress on members of crowded birth cohorts.

bulimia   An eating disorder characterized by periodic eating binges, often followed by purging; it is found primarily among affluent, well-educated girls in developed countries.

PART VI

Early and Middle Adulthood

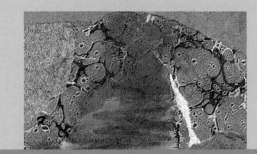

Our society has no rite or social ceremony to mark the passage from adolescence to adulthood. There is no single age at which a person becomes mature. So we will arbitrarily define early adulthood as the years from eighteen until forty, using the end of high school as a convenient marker for entry into adulthood. A familiar saying has it that "life begins at forty," and that is where we begin middle adulthood. One popular marker for the close of middle adulthood is eligibility for full Social Security benefits. We accept that date, because people in their early sixties now have more in common with adults in their fifties than with their elders. These chapters tell the story of young people struggling to establish intimacy and carving out occupational niches. They continue with the story of the "command generation" — middle-aged adults whose broadened responsibilities place them in charge of society.

CHAPTER 15

Young Adulthood: Selecting the Options

Susan, Scott, Donna, and David are all eighteen, and high school is behind them. They are on the brink of adulthood, with many common experiences ahead of them. But much of their experience as adults will be sharply different because of two major factors: gender and education.

Susan is college bound. She thinks that she will major in journalism or communications and hopes to become a writer for television or, perhaps, a newscaster. At eighteen, the notion of being an anchorwoman on the evening news appeals to her. Scott will also go to college. Scott is even less certain about his future than Susan. He thinks that he will major in psychology, but his ultimate goal is vague. At eighteen, he is wavering between law and business. Donna has no plans for college. While in high school, she majored in business and now hopes to get a job as a secretary. She is engaged to her high-school sweetheart and plans to marry within a year. Until then, she will live at home. David left high school before he graduated. A friend helped him get a job at the local automobile assembly plant, but David lost his job when the plant cut back on production. He now is working in a local lumberyard and still lives at home. David hopes to get his own apartment soon.

For Susan and Scott, decisions concerning careers and marriage still lie ahead. College is a half-way point in the progress toward true adulthood, a period that allows them to postpone their decisions concerning careers and marriage. For a time, they are free from adult responsibilities. Most college students still depend on their families for at least part of their financial support. Yet they are likely to be living away from home, where they no longer come under direct parental supervision. Donna and David will miss out on the pause enjoyed by the college-bound. For them, the decade of the twenties will not be a time of exploration, as it is for Susan and Scott, but a time when issues are settled and it is time to get down to the business of living — of job, marriage, children, and responsibility.

In this chapter, we see how changes in society have altered young adulthood since the parents of Susan, Scott, Donna, and David were eighteen years old. The situations they will face, the choices they must make as they live through the years from eighteen to thirty-nine will become clear as we trace the course of development in young adults. After looking at recent social changes, we briefly consider physical development during the young adult years. Next we examine various explanations of the changes that occur during the years between eighteen and forty. With that background, we are ready to take up major aspects of the young adult's life, beginning with the way maturity and gender affect self-concept and self-esteem. Next we investigate work, a part of our lives that is so important that most of us would work even if we did not have to support ourselves. After considering the institution of marriage and its alternatives, we look at parenthood and its effects on us as couples and individuals, and the twentieth-century addition to the cycle of many families — divorce and remarriage.

SOCIAL CHANGE

Changes in society affect the attitudes and behavior of all its members. Men and women have "social clocks" in their heads to help them judge their own and other people's behavior as being early, late, or on time (Hagestad and Neugarten, 1985).

The appropriate time for a particular developmental event may change from one generation to the next. In 1960, for example, nearly 90 percent of Chicago adults agreed that women should marry between the ages of nineteen and twenty-four; in 1980, only 40 percent believed that women should marry that early (Hagestad and Neugarten, 1985). Over the past two decades, the strength of social clocks has weakened. Traditional norms and expectations have changed, and the appropriate times for such events as marriage, careers, and parenthood are becoming tied less closely to chronological age. It sometimes seems as if we are witnessing the development of what Bernice Neugarten (1979) has called an **age-irrelevant society**, in which there is no single appropriate age at which to take on the role of parent, student, worker, grandparent, and so forth. Today there is little surprise at the twenty-eight-year-old mayor, the fifty-year-old retiree, the sixty-five-year-old father of a preschooler, or the seventy-year-old student. In an age-irrelevant society, developmental tasks remain the same, but adults do not feel that their social clocks are particularly early or late if they postpone or accelerate the social roles of adulthood.

An increasing number of young adults are postponing marriage. In 1956, the average woman married at twenty; by 1980, the average age was twenty-two, and by 1986, it had climbed to twenty-four (Salholz et al., 1986). The postponement is greatest among middle-class women, primarily because an increasing proportion are completing college, going on to graduate and professional schools, and then entering the professions. Families are changing as well. Women are waiting longer to start their families after they are married. The majority are using some form of birth control, with the pill the most popular method among all women who are postponing pregnancy (U.S. Bureau of the Census, 1986).

Hand in hand with planned parenthood go smaller families. The majority of couples either have or want two children, and the proportion of women who say that they expect to have only one child has risen during the past decade. It is higher among women who have graduated from high school than among women with a college education, among women in their early thirties than women in their twenties (U.S. Bureau of the Census, 1986).

Yet marriage is less popular than it has been for some years. Perhaps because more people are living together without marrying, the marriage rate has been declining, with the rate among eligible young women the lowest since this marker was established in 1940 (*New York Times,* 1986a). At the same time, the divorce rate has been rising. But in 1985, Americans still married twice as often as they divorced, with more than four out of ten marriages involving people who had been married before.

Another social change has taken place in physical appearance. Good nutrition, sanitation, and preventive medicine have combined to make women and men in the later portions of young adulthood look younger and more attractive than their parents and grandparents were at that age. The thirty-five-year-old of the 1930s or 1940s seemed visibly older than the thirty-five-year-old of the 1980s.

PHYSICAL CHARACTERISTICS

During young adulthood, most people are at the peak of their physical agility, speed, and strength. These are the years when our bodies, inside and out, are at their best. Men tend to be proud of their bodies, women not. When 300 college-age men and women were asked to rate their own bodies, women (no matter how slim) saw themselves as somewhat heavier than the male ideal and much heavier than their own ideal for the female body (Fallon and Rozin, 1985). Men (even those who were heavy) saw themselves as matching both the female and their own ideal body weights. Neither sex was on target in their notion of the other sex's standard for attractiveness. Men's ideal woman was heavier than women believed, and women's ideal man was lighter than men believed.

Despite the attractiveness of youth, many of the physical hallmarks of aging begin, almost imperceptibly, in young adulthood. Around the age of twenty, slow, continuing changes affect the workings of the human body (Weg, 1983). Muscle tone and strength, which generally peak between the ages of twenty and thirty, decline after that. Visual acuity and hearing begin to decline in the twenties. The first tiny wrinkles begin to appear beside the

Young adults are adept at sports that require speed and strength, but as they move into their thirties, they find that their reaction time begins to slow. *(C. Petit-J. M. Loubat/Agence Vandystadt/Photo Researchers)*

eyes, and the skin is aging—especially among those who cultivate a suntan. The ultraviolet rays of the sun interfere with the production of DNA and protein synthesis in the skin. In response, skin cells regenerate more slowly, and the skin thins and becomes wrinkled (Wantz and Gay, 1981).

Changes also occur deep inside the body. Even if weight remains constant, the proportion of fatty tissue to muscle begins to increase. In addition, the volume of blood pumped by the heart and the amount of air that can be drawn into the lungs in a single breath begin to decline in the twenties—decreasing about 1 percent per year (Perlmutter and Hall, 1985). Changes in the arteries are also occurring, with hard, yellow, fatty plaques appearing on the arterial wall of individuals who are susceptible to atherosclerosis. Poor diet and lack of exercise have begun to contribute to the development of chronic diseases that will not become apparent until middle or late adulthood.

Few young adults are concerned over these changes, although the thirty-year-old may be carefully plucking out an occasional gray hair. Perhaps our lack of concern comes from the sense of peak physical fitness and performance. Reaction times generally are at their peak until about the age of twenty-six. In any competitive situation or in any situation that demands rapid response, young adults usually come out ahead. The young excel in sports that demand strength and speed, such as basketball, boxing, tennis, skiing, and baseball. The slowing of their reaction time is one reason that most professional athletes begin to "feel their age" when they enter their thirties.

THEORIES AND ISSUES OF YOUNG ADULTHOOD

As people move through adulthood, they focus their energies and motivations on different developmental tasks. Among the major tasks faced by young adults are completing their education, entering the work force, marrying, and becoming parents. Everyone faces these tasks, for even the decision *not* to marry or have children is a way of handling this aspect of development. The various theories of adult development seek to explain these patterns of growth and change and to identify dominant themes that characterize adult lives. Some theorists believe that the course of development they have charted applies to people in any society; others are more cautious and regard their theories as applying primarily to adults in a Western technological society. When theories clash, the disagreements point up important issues in adult development that have not been resolved by research.

Erikson's Psychosocial Theory

Erik Erikson's (1982) view of adult development derives from his eight-stage theory of the life cycle. As we saw in Chapter 2, Erikson proposed that development consists of the progressive resolution of inevitable conflicts between needs and social demands. At each of the eight stages, a person must at least partially resolve the major developmental conflict of that stage before he or she can move on to the problems of the next.

The major task facing young adults is the development of intimacy, an advance that presupposes the earlier development of identity during adolescence (see Chapter 13). The alternative to intimacy is isolation. When adults resolve the conflict successfully, they are able to commit themselves to a relationship that demands sacrifice and compromise. They are able to love another person more or less unselfishly. If isolation dominates intimacy, their emotional relationships are cold and unspontaneous, and there is no real emotional exchange. A person may establish sexual relationships without developing intimacy, especially if he or she fears the emotional fusion involved in a committed relationship. When this pattern of noncaring sexual relationships characterizes a person's life, he or she may feel extremely isolated (Erikson and Hall, 1987). Erikson's psychosocial theory is meant to be a universal theory, applying to both genders and all societies. He points out that cultural differences change the way the developmental tasks of each stage are met.

Carol Gilligan (1982) believes that the developmental tasks are also very different for men and women because of differing socialization practices. Throughout childhood, women meet developmental tasks (autonomy, industry, identity) within a context of relationships, so that achieving intimacy does not present a great departure from their earlier development. Many women are working on identity and intimacy simultaneously. This is not true for men, Gilligan maintains, because during their earlier development relationships were not stressed. Intimacy requires men to change their adolescent identity.

Levinson's Seasons

Another stage theory of adult development has been formulated by Daniel Levinson (Levinson, Darrow, Klein, Levinson, and McKee, 1978), who has said that it portrays "the seasons of a man's life." He regards his theory as building on Erikson's psychosocial theory but with a shift of emphasis. Erikson concentrates on development within the individual; Levinson looks at the individual's relation to society. Levinson picks up men at about the age of seventeen and takes them through an orderly sequence that alternates between stable and transitional phases. During the stable phases, men pursue their goals more or less tranquilly, because the pertinent developmental tasks have been solved. The transitional phases can lead to major changes in a man's life structure, because at these times men are questioning the pattern of their lives and exploring new possibilities. Levinson based his theory on a series of indepth interviews with forty men (black as well as white; working class as well as middle class) and has made no attempt to apply it to women. In fact, he says that his theory may apply only to American men in the last part of the twentieth century.

Levinson sees the years from seventeen to twenty-two as a time of transition to early adulthood. In a development similar to Erikson's identity achievement, men work at becoming psychologically independent from their parents. By the age of twenty-two, they have become autonomous and move into a stable phase during which they are trying to establish themselves in the adult world. At the same time, they are learning to relate to women and establishing a home and family—developing intimacy, in Erikson's terms. Within six years, when they are about twenty-eight, they go into another transitional phase. This time they see flaws in the pattern of their lives and make new choices. Then, at about thirty-three, they are ready to settle down. Career consolidation becomes a major goal, and men concentrate on developing their skills and deepening the bases of experience. They also work at reaching the major goals that they have set for themselves, whether that entails becoming a corporate executive or owning their own truck. But along with this urge to get their lives in order and to achieve their goals comes an urge to be free and unattached. Men in their thirties want to be, as Levinson puts it, "open to new possibilities, ready to soar, wander, quest in all directions as the spirit moves one."

Gould's Transformations

Roger Gould's (1975; 1978) theory of adult development applies to both sexes, but all 524 men and women whose experiences form the basis of his theory were middle-class whites. From their re-

College students can prolong the decisions that launch them into true adulthood, but young adults in the working class take up adult responsibilities early. *(Frank Siteman/Taurus Photos)*

sponses to an exhaustive questionnaire, Gould concluded that adult development progresses through a series of transformations. In each transformation, a person reformulates his or her self-concept, faces childish illusions, and resolves conflicts.

In Gould's theory, young adults move through four phases. In the first phase, which begins in late adolescence and lasts until the age of twenty-two, people are forging an identity and moving away from their parents' world. With autonomy established, they move into the second phase, where they apply themselves to attaining their goals. Between the ages of twenty-eight and thirty-four, they pass through a transitional stage, in which they question some of their early goals and reevaluate their marriages. Many are pinched economically. At about the age of thirty-five, their discontent deepens, and the awareness of approaching middle age becomes acute. Life may seem painful, difficult, and uncertain. During this unstable period, which lasts until they are about forty-three, some may tear apart the fabric of their lives and put it together in a new way. A long-time bachelor may marry, a person who married early may get a divorce; a homebound mother may decide to go back to school or get a job; a childless couple may decide to start a family. Gould's theory parallels Levinson's life seasons but provides information about women as well as men. Both theories were developed about the same time — in the 1970s — with Levinson studying men in the northeastern United States and Gould studying men and women in California.

Gutmann's Parental Imperative

In the theory developed by David Gutmann (1975), personality development in men and women revolves around the **parental imperative.** He believes that the species has evolved to produce men and women with characteristics that ensure the emotional and physical safety of infants and children. In early human societies, a father's aggression, autonomy, competence, and control protected his child from predators and sent the father out to hunt for large game. Nurturance, sympathy, gentleness, and understanding kept the mother near her child and provided emotional security.

According to Gutmann, women and men are born with the potential for these sex roles. Through years of socialization, they become comfortable with the prescribed traits and enjoy exercising them. When they become parents, fathers become more traditionally masculine: their concern is the security (physical and economical) of their family. Because being a passive, dependent, sympathetic father might interfere with the ability to bring home the necessary resources or to defend his child, men suppress any urges to be dependent or sympathetic. New mothers become more traditionally feminine: their concern is for the care and nurturance of the child. Because an aggressive, insensitive mother might harm her baby or drive off her mate, women suppress any urges to be assertive, masterful, or aggressive. Not until the

last child leaves home is each sex free to express those aspects of the self that have been muffled by parental responsibilities.

Although Gutmann's theory is meant to apply to all societies in all historical periods, sharply restricted parental roles may not be so important in a modern technological society. When mothers and fathers share in providing their children's material support, care, and emotional security, parenthood may demand less intense changes in role and personality than Gutmann's theory suggests.

Issues in the Young Adult Years

Some theories of adult development place great importance on transitions in the life cycle. *Transitions* refer to the way we restructure our lives or reorder our goals in response to our changing experiences. Getting married, taking a new job, having children, being fired, buying a home, moving to another city are the sort of events that lead to such transitions.

The Nature of Transitions   How stressful are these changes? Researchers disagree about whether life transitions are times of physical and psychological distress. Levinson (Levinson et al., 1978) maintains that transitions are highly stressful. Among his forty men, twenty-five (62 percent) went through either a moderate or a severe crisis during the "Age Thirty Transition," which begins at about the age of twenty-eight. Only seven men (18 percent) said that those years were unruffled by psychological stress. Neugarten (1979) disagrees; she has found that transitions are stressful only when unexpected. When an event is anticipated and seen as part of the normal course of life, it causes little stress. But when the event is not part of the normal life course, or if it conflicts with a person's social clock, coming too early or too late, it can cause great stress and precipitate an emotional crisis. A three-year study of American women supported Neugarten's view (Baruch, Barnett, and Rivers, 1983). When asked about crises in their lives, these women rarely mentioned anticipated developmental events (such as marriage or childbirth). Instead, they reported events that upset the course of their lives (divorce, an automobile accident, a job transfer) or events that

Life's transitions are more likely to be stressful when they are unexpected; transitions that are expected or "on-time" cause little upheaval. *(John Lei/Stock, Boston)*

conflicted with their social clocks (the early death of a parent).

The major conflict between Levinson and Neugarten may arise from differing views of a transition's source. Neugarten sees the social or physical event as the cause of the transition. Levinson would agree that the event (such as a divorce) may trigger a transition, but he would argue that the process had been building within the person as old developmental tasks lost their relevance and new tasks appeared. In his view, the divorce is the result of the inner process and not its cause. The debate continues, and in Chapter 17 we shall meet it again when considering the transitions of middle adulthood.

The Timing of Adulthood   Another issue that has no simple resolution is the timing of adulthood. When does a person become mature? Chronological age is not much help here, because one person seems mature at twenty and another still seems hopelessly immature at forty. Some elements of maturity are common to all theories of adult development. All theorists regard the ability to be intimate, to give and accept love, and to be affectionate and sexually responsive as necessary to the attainment of maturity. All stress the ability to be sociable, to have friends, to be devoted to others, and to nurture them. All agree that mature individuals have a sense of their abilities and goals,

an interest in productive work, and the ability to do it.

One way to look at maturity is to think of it in terms of an ability to cope successfully with events and decisions that most people face at characteristic times in their lives. In terms of Erikson's theory, maturity in early adulthood would include:

1. A successful resolution of the developmental tasks of childhood and adolescence
2. The ability to commit the self to a close relationship with another (intimacy) and some concern with guiding the next generation and with productive work (generativity) (Whitbourne and Waterman, 1979).

Another way to look at maturity is in terms of people's perceptions. What makes a person feel grown up? Researchers asked more than 2,000 married men and women which event in their lives was most important in making them feel that they were really an adult (Hoffman and Manis, 1979). Becoming a parent and supporting oneself were the most consistent markers of maturity, but as Table 15.1 indicates, sex and ethnic group figured into people's perceptions.

No matter how we define adulthood, it is cumulative and changing. Maturity involves a continual adjustment to constantly changing expectations and responsibilities. Although people can be

Table 15.1
What Made You Feel Like an Adult?

| | Women | | | | | Men | | |
| | Parents | | | Nonparents | | Parents | | Non-parents |
Life Event	White	Black	Hispanic	White	Black	White	Black	White
Becoming a parent	40.2	34.8	33.3	11.1	14.3	31.6	11.5	5.3
Getting married	19.8	21.7	21.2	19.9	35.7	15.0	3.8	13.7
Supporting yourself	13.9	14.1	15.2	34.8	21.4	24.7	46.2	47.4
Getting a job	8.1	3.3	6.1	9.1	14.3	9.1	7.7	6.3
Finishing school	5.8	8.7	18.2	7.3	0.0	5.6	3.8	5.3
Moving out of parental home	5.1	10.9	3.0	9.8	7.1	7.8	23.1	7.4
Other	7.1	6.5	3.0	8.0	7.1	6.2	3.8	14.8
N	1,113	92	33	287	14	320	26	95

Note: When asked which event was (or might be) most important in making them feel like an adult, mothers and white fathers chose parenthood. For nonparents, "supporting yourself" was the most common reply by whites; blacks regarded marriage as the crucial event.

Source: L. W. Hoffman and J. D. Manis, "The Value of Children in the United States: A New Approach to the Study of Fertility," *Journal of Marriage and the Family*, 41 (1979), 589.

mature without marrying, having children, or working hard at a career, mature adults are aware of who they are and where they want to go, and they work toward those goals. The phrase "getting it all together" accurately sums up the young adult's struggle toward maturity.

SELF-CONCEPT AND SELF-ESTEEM

As people move from adolescence to young adulthood, they rarely experience a sharp discontinuity between their adolescent and adult selves. Yet we would expect some sort of change in **self-concept,** which is the organized, coherent, and integrated pattern of our perceptions about ourselves (Thomae, 1980). Physical appearance, social roles, and abilities are closely related to self-concept, and all of them change during young adulthood. When Jack Block (1971) looked at changes in personality over this period, he found both continuity and change in women and men. As they moved into adulthood, both sexes showed less self-centered impulsiveness and an increased ability to cope with problems. Other studies indicate that during young adulthood, men and women have similar levels of self-esteem, and both sexes value themselves more highly than they did as adolescents (Frieze, Parsons, Johnson, Ruble, and Zellman, 1978).

Any examination of self-concept that does not look at men and women separately, however, may be misleading. Men and women measure their lives against such radically different standards that different factors probably influence their self-concepts (Hagestad and Neugarten, 1985). The concepts men and women have about themselves reflect the impact of sex-role stereotypes and their own gender schema. As we have seen, girls are traditionally socialized to be dependent, passive, emotionally expressive, and warm, whereas boys learn to be assertive, independent, and to think rationally. Brought up in this way, young women are less likely than men to have a sense of control over their lives, successes, and failures. Young men believe in their power to control their fates, but women are more likely to believe that outside powers are in control.

Men and Self-esteem

Self-esteem in young men rises steadily after they leave high school, but there is no sharp shift as they move from high school to college or the world of work. Among 1,600 young men who were followed for five years after high school, the gradual rise seemed to reflect the increase in status, opportunities, and privileges that comes with increasing maturity (Bachman, O'Malley, and Johnston, 1978). As adolescents, the men's family background, their own intellectual ability, and their academic achievement had contributed heavily to their self-esteem. When the men became engaged in their careers, these factors faded in importance, and job status became more important. Higher-status jobs led to higher self-esteem. Men who were unemployed five years after high school showed declines in self-esteem, and the self-esteem of unemployed high-school dropouts declined the most.

Among a group of men who attended college, overall self-concept remained stable, but elements of their self-perceptions showed some change (Mortimer, Finch, and Kumka, 1982). Their feelings of competence declined during college, only to rebound on graduation. And with graduation, they began seeing themselves as less impulsive, less conventional, and less as dreamers. Once again, self-esteem suffered during periods of unemployment or among men forced to take jobs beneath their abilities and skills.

Women and Self-esteem

Men generally express their needs for self-control and mastery in their jobs, but women with a high need of achievement may not always express that need directly. Some do, pursuing a career or becoming involved in politics or community work. Others meet their need for achievement indirectly and derive satisfaction from the successes of their husbands and children.

Toward the close of young adulthood, self-esteem sometimes slips in high-achieving women who devote themselves to their families. Judith Birnbaum (1975) compared highly intelligent full-time homemakers (all were honor graduates from college) with married professional women (all

Among men, increased self-esteem is often connected with a high-status job. (*Joseph Schuyler/Stock, Boston*)

were mothers) and single professional women. She found that homemakers had the lowest self-esteem and the lowest sense of personal competence — even in the areas of social skills and child care. They tended to feel lonely and missed a sense of challenge and creative involvement. Apparently, as their children started school and no longer required extensive care, these women found the role of wife and mother inadequate for expressing their need to achieve.

Sex Roles and Self-esteem

Perhaps as a result of the women's movement in this country, young men's and women's concepts of masculinity and femininity are changing. Among many young adults, sex-role stereotypes are breaking down, and those whose personalities do not fit traditional stereotypes for either gender show the highest self-esteem (Spence, 1979). These women and men are **androgynous;** they are high both in personality traits considered masculine (they are self-reliant, independent, and assertive) and in traits considered feminine (they are affectionate, sympathetic, and understanding).

Among the college students studied by Janet Spence (1979), 32 percent of the men and 27 percent of the women fit in this description. A considerable number of these students (25 percent of the men and 28 percent of the women) were low in both masculine and feminine traits; their self-esteem was also low. Only one in three students fit the traditional sex-role stereotype (high in their own gender's traits and low in traits ascribed to the other gender). Among this group of traditional students, the men's self-esteem was generally higher. It seems that women who are not independent, self-reliant, and assertive have lower self-esteem than men. This aspect of the traditional sex role may explain why many women see themselves as less competent than men.

Most young women and men seem comfortable with androgyny. Among one group of young adults, men felt easy about expressing their "feminine" qualities, as women did about expressing their "masculine" side (Reedy, 1977). Both sexes wanted to see themselves as self-confident, intelligent, independent, loving, and understanding. This new way of thinking about masculinity and femininity has widened the possibilities for both sexes.

Many young adults have shifted their attitudes about what it means to be male or female, and an increasing number feel comfortable with androgyny. *(Michael Weisbrot & Family)*

WORK

Work occupies a considerable portion of the adult lifespan, and its influence touches almost every part of our lives. It defines our position in society, and, if we are fortunate, it gives meaning to our lives, provides satisfying activity, an outlet for creativity, and a source of social stimulation (Perlmutter and Hall, 1985). Our self-concept is so bound up with our work that most of us define ourselves in terms of what we do. "I'm with IBM," we say, or "I'm a teacher," or "I'm just a housewife" — a self-disparaging response that has become common now that the majority of women are in the labor force. When we are about to introduce a friend to a new person, the usual bit of information we pass along is the person's occupation: "I want you to meet Jerry. He runs that shoestore on Chestnut Drive." At some level, we apparently realize the importance of work, as

Freud did when he summed up the requirements for a healthy life as *lieben und arbeiten* (to love and work). Social class and gender have far-reaching effects on this vital part of our existence; they influence the kind of work we do, where, and when we do it. They even influence the course of our careers.

Importance of Work

The work we do affects personality, family life, social relations, and attitudes. To say that work affects personality may sound odd, but when we consider that the work environment is a stimulus that is present over a long period of time, we can see that prolonged exposure could have a cumulative effect on personality (Garfinkel, 1982). When workers were followed for ten years, the major influence seemed to come from the complexity of the work. According to Melvin Kohn (1980), the degree to which a person's job requires thought and independence affects many aspects of personality. Job complexity seems to lead to increased intellectual flexibility, which in turn affects a person's values, self-concept, and attitudes toward society. In another study, workers in a manufacturing plant who participated in solving problems and making work-related decisions showed an increase in interpersonal skills, communication skills, and the ability to listen to others (Crouter, 1984).

The emotional tone of the work situation also carries over into a worker's daily life. Research indicates that employees' social relations in the workplace set a prevailing mood that affects psychological well-being (Repetti, 1985). The quality of an employee's social relations (as rated by coworkers and by himself or herself) are related to self-esteem, levels of anxiety, and tendencies toward depression.

Work can be a source of stress, especially when a person becomes overinvolved in a job and devotes long hours to it (L. Hoffman, 1986). Many aspects of work can produce stress: unemployment, too little money, low status, unpleasant job-related tasks, a conflict between job values and personal values, a lack of control and autonomy, frustration or low morale, physical danger, and the job's intrusion into other areas of a person's life. Overinvolvement can lead to intolerable stress, even when a worker is highly successful.

When work-related stress leads to depression, it tends to be most disturbing in those who have few social roles. Rena Repetti and Faye Crosby (1984) studied more than 400 women and men whose jobs ranged from waitress and truck driver to physician and lawyer. They discovered that single people (whose major social role is worker) were most likely to be depressed, and parents (whose major social roles include worker, spouse, and parent) were least likely to be depressed. Within each group, those in low-prestige occupations showed more depression than those in high-prestige occupations.

Work can be a source of enormous satisfaction, especially when it gives the worker a sense of creating, producing, or achieving something (Garfinkel, 1982). Workers at all levels find employment highly satisfying when their jobs are challenging, financially rewarding, give them whatever resources they need to do the job well, and when their working conditions are comfortable (Seashore and Barnowe, 1972). Jobs that give people no chance to be creative or to learn new things, no freedom to decide how the job should be done, and do not allow them to use their skills are alienating.

Work-related stress is most likely to lead to depression in single people who have few social roles.
(Michael Phillip Manheim/Southern Light)

Choosing an Occupation

Many people wander into their occupations by accident. Such apparently irrelevant factors as decisions in some other area of life, the location of their homes, luck, and gender may determine which career or job awaits them.

Some of the decisions that determine which ticket a person draws in the great occupational lottery are made in high school, as we saw in Chapters 13 and 14. Among other important influences is where a young person lives. Residence helps decide occupational choice in two ways. First, the nature of local industries determines what sort of job is available. This factor is especially important in occupational decisions of working-class adults. If they live in Silicon Valley, they get a job assembling computers; if they live in Idaho, they get a job in the lumber industry; if they live in Texas, they work in the oilfields. Second, people can only work in occupations that they know about. Adults in the community provide the role models that turn a child's thoughts to various jobs and careers. A young woman who grows up in Iowa may think of becoming a plant geneticist who breeds new varieties of corn, but she is less likely to consider becoming a translator at the United Nations.

Most jobs and many careers depend on luck — the luck of knowing someone who is already working in an organization. Such informal con-

People enter occupations that they know about; most of those who work on commercial fishing boats have grown up near the sea. *(Therese Frare/The Picture Cube)*

tacts seem more important than classified ads or employment agencies, for they fill between 50 and 90 percent of all blue-collar jobs (Reid, 1972). The proportion may be similar for some white-collar careers, where the easiest way for a new worker to break in is through contacts within the "old-boy" network. This informal collection of friends, acquaintances, and former coworkers of both sexes becomes increasingly important as a person climbs the career ladder.

Sex Differences in the Work Force

Gender is an accident of birth that has far-reaching effects on the availability of jobs and careers, on individual work patterns, and on the way occupational choices are made. When children are involved, a mother's employment may affect both partners and their marital relationship.

Sex Differences in Work Patterns   The early working years are fairly similar for men and women, but at about the time the young working man makes his shift from casual to committed work and the young middle-class man's career is beginning to stabilize, the paths of men and most women separate. Most men and those women who remain single tend to have orderly occupational lives. When they leave college, they take entry-level positions. After some shifting in a search for

the right position, one that allows them to advance, they settle down in their chosen field. During the years from their mid-twenties to their mid-thirties, they are becoming established in their field. At about the age of thirty-five, when they have become experienced and knowledgeable, they devote themselves to consolidating their careers (Super, 1957).

Some women follow a different path. They leave the labor market at just the time when men and single women are establishing themselves. Whether they go back to work when their last child is three, six, or eighteen years old, the interruption nearly always proves detrimental to their careers (Hoffman and Nye, 1974). In recent years, an increasing number of women have either eliminated or shortened this break in their work pattern. Either they go back to work immediately, or else they return as soon as their infant becomes a toddler. Interruptions in employment take women off their occupational track and are partly responsible for the fact that women who work full time earn only $637 for every $1,000 earned by men (U.S. Bureau of the Census, 1984). Another factor that contributes to the income gap is married women's willingness to accept low-paying jobs that mesh comfortably with other aspects of their lives.

Maternal Employment and Morale   Mothers who are employed outside the home usually bear the major responsibility for housework and child care. Does this double load of work produce so much stress that it damages a mother's morale? Usually not; instead, most employed mothers have relatively high morale. They show less depression, fewer psychosomatic symptoms, and fewer signs of stress than mothers who stay at home (L. Hoffman, 1986; Kessler and MacRae, 1982). Employment builds the working-class mother's self-esteem by giving her a sense of achievement, challenge, stimulation, and a chance for adult companionship (L. Hoffman, 1984a). Among middle-class women in one study, mothers with professional careers had high self-esteem, rarely felt lonely, and saw themselves as personally competent and worthwhile (Birnbaum, 1975). They complained about having too little time, but they seemed under no excessive strain. Yet role overload can lead to excessive stress. Low morale is most likely to develop when the mother has several preschool children, has a handicapped child, cannot find adequate child care, has no adult support, or if either spouse is chronically ill. In some cases, the overload can be reduced by switching to part-time employment, a solution that reduces much of the stress (L. Hoffman, 1984b).

How does a woman's employment affect the quality of her marriage? Researchers have found no clear effect of maternal employment on the marital relationship (L. Hoffman, 1986). Some marriages seem to improve, especially in cases where the mother wants to work, the father does not oppose her employment, or where the couple is middle class. Some marriages deteriorate, especially in cases where the woman would rather be at home, her husband opposes her employment, or where the couple is working class. Although the divorce rate is higher among families with employed mothers, most researchers feel that a mother's employment does not lead to divorce. Instead, by making it possible to fund a divorce, employment provides an escape hatch from a failed marriage.

MARRIAGE

Most of us marry at least once in our lives, although we tend to be older, if not wiser, when we make such a legal commitment than we were twenty years ago. More than nine out of ten Americans eventually marry, and 96 percent of us say that the married state is the ideal form of life (Yankelovich, 1981). We've believed this for a long time: in 1984, less than 6 percent of adults past the age of sixty-five had always been single (U.S. Bu-

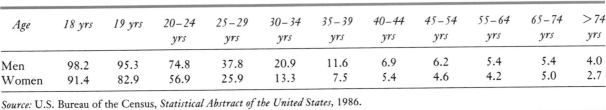

When women drop out of the labor force after childbirth, they generally find the interruption is detrimental to their later careers. *(Teri Leigh Stratford/ Photo Researchers)*

reau of the Census, 1986) (see Table 15.2). Yet we're not as eager to enter marriage as we were in 1960, when about 72 percent of women and 47 percent of men between the ages of twenty and twenty-four were married. Today, only 43.1 percent of women and 25.2 percent of men are married at that age (U.S. Bureau of the Census, 1986). These figures indicate that we are returning to the marriage patterns of the last century, when women married at the same age as they now do (U.S. Bureau of the Census, 1983). In every era, women marry younger than men, primarily because they tend to marry men who are several years older than they are.

The recent trend toward delayed marriage is in part a reflection of increased college enrollment. People who go to college often postpone marriage

Table 15.2
Americans Who Have Never Married (Percent)

Age	18 yrs	19 yrs	20–24 yrs	25–29 yrs	30–34 yrs	35–39 yrs	40–44 yrs	45–54 yrs	55–64 yrs	65–74 yrs	>74 yrs
Men	98.2	95.3	74.8	37.8	20.9	11.6	6.9	6.2	5.4	5.4	4.0
Women	91.4	82.9	56.9	25.9	13.3	7.5	5.4	4.6	4.2	5.0	2.7

Source: U.S. Bureau of the Census, *Statistical Abstract of the United States,* 1986.

Couples are waiting longer to marry than they did only a few years ago; increased college enrollment and women's tendency to delay marriage until they have established themselves in a career have contributed to the trend. *(Suzanne Szasz)*

until they have finished their education, and young women who are establishing careers postpone marriage longer than any other group. The delay is heightened by other changes in society: a widening acceptance of couples who live together without marriage, a new acceptance of the single stage as an appropriate way of life, and perhaps a hesitation to marry fostered by high divorce rates. In line with their earlier assumption of other adult responsibilities, working-class couples are more likely than middle-class couples to follow the early marriage pattern of the 1960s. One reason that working-class couples seem reluctant to delay marriage is its role in making them independent. Middle-class adults usually leave home to go to college; working-class adults usually leave home to marry.

Choosing a Mate

Selecting a mate is not simply a matter of the heart. Some of the same social factors that determine friendship also influence our choice of a spouse. Before a couple can marry, they must meet, and so where a person lives and where he or she goes to school limit the pool of possible mates. People who live in the same area and have the same educational experiences tend to be of similar religion, race, ethnic background, and socioeconomic

status, and so do married couples. Even couples who tumble head over heels at their first meeting are unlikely to develop a lasting, intimate relationship unless they also have common interests, backgrounds, and goals (Wong, 1981).

Except for star-crossed lovers like Romeo and Juliet, a first meeting rarely leads to the immediate conviction that the pairing will be permanent. Instead, there is a series of meetings — either dates or informal contacts that result from common friends, common classes in school, or common interests. These meetings are probably more relaxed among college students, among whom neither is particularly interested in a permanent relationship, than among working-class adults, who are more likely to be ready to consider marriage. External influences often affect our readiness to marry. Sometimes a working-class adult may be more interested in getting away from a conflict-ridden home than in building a life with a marital partner. Class or ethnic standards concerning the "right" age for marriage, income, job security, and the person's own inclinations toward the married state may combine either to keep a person from thinking about marriage or lead the person to perceive most members of the other sex as possible marital partners (Ankarloo, 1978). When a person is in the latter state, the choice of a mate is probably close at hand, and relationships may be initiated in a more deliberate and less playful fashion.

Once partners develop a committed relationship, sexual intimacy often follows. Among unmarried nineteen-year-old women, about 66 percent have had sexual intercourse (U.S. Bureau of the Census, 1986). Because working-class adults are less likely to use contraceptives than those in the middle class, many marry sooner than they had planned because the woman becomes pregnant (Chilman, 1983). Casual sexual relationships seem to be on the decline in this country, although they certainly have not disappeared. Fear of AIDS, a usually fatal disease transmitted by contaminated blood or semen, is changing the way people view casual sex. Originally concentrated among gay men (75 percent of the cases) or transmitted during transfusions or drug injections by contaminated blood or needles, recently AIDS has been moving into the heterosexual population through sexual intercourse. Suddenly, singles bars have become less popular, and many women have become wary about sexual relationships outside a committed relationship. As one woman put it, "It may not be the person you know. It may be the person that person knows" (Clark, Gosnell, and Hager, 1986). Some gynecologists report that a number of their single patients have discarded their birth-control pills and temporarily have given up sex.

Once couples reach the stage of commitment, their friends and families begin to see them as a unit. One is never invited to a party without the other. Gradually, the two begin to think of themselves as "us" and become aware that they depend on each other. If they have openly declared their intention to marry, one—or both—may go through a period of anxiety, wondering if he or she has made the right decision.

Making Marriage Work

Marriage establishes the family as a social system, and each partner has to adjust to the social roles connected with the institution of marriage. Before the first year of marriage is over, couples develop a way of handling the division of power. This division is central to the establishment of marital roles. In traditional marriages, the man dominates the relationship. He has the final say, and the woman either accepts his decisions or attempts to exert her influence in subtle, less direct ways (Falbo and Peplau, 1980) (see Table 15.3). Some marriages never have fit the traditional mold, but the majority still follow this pattern.

So how do most couples adjust? Women generally report making more concessions to keep the marriage running than men do, in good part because the traditional woman follows the basic rule, "If the family does well, I do well." According to John Scanzoni and Greer Fox (1980), this assumption leads a woman to submerge her own interests with the interests of her husband and children. By contrast, the man's basic assumption is, "If I do well, the family does well." In following this rule, he puts his individual interests first, "for the sake of the group." Changing sex roles and the increasing tendency of women to view their own employment as important and satisfying eventually may lead to a readjustment of the power balance. When women begin to assume that attaining

Table 15.3
Stereotypical Perceptions of Power Use*

Type of Power	More Associated With
Helplessness	Female
Nagging	Female
Sexuality	Female
False information	Female
Indirect information (presented unobtrusively)	Female
Appeal to a common identity ("because we are friends")	Female
Expert	Male
Direct information	Male
Legitimate (inherent in sex role)	Male
Coercion	Male
Reward	Male

* Sex-role stereotypes have produced our expectations concerning the appropriate uses of power by women and men. As a result, when one gender uses methods perceived as being the province of the other, people who hold stereotypical notions of power use often react in a negative manner.

Source: Frieze, Parsons, Johnson, Ruble, and Zellman, 1978, p. 317; based on P. Johnson, 1976.

their own interests also helps the family and men accept the notion that both partners operate on these assumptions, more marriages will be egalitarian partnerships in which decisions are made jointly. Yet among 300 couples studied in Seattle, San Francisco, and New York, men were reluctant to give up the traditional marriage (Blumstein and Schwartz, 1983). Among these middle-class, well-educated couples, most women wanted equal partnerships, but most men wanted to preserve their dominance.

Young couples vary widely in the satisfaction that they derive from their marriage, and some of the differences can be traced to personality characteristics. Emotional maturity, the ability to express emotions, consideration for others, self-esteem, and adaptability all have been linked with happy marriages. Emotionally immature adults seem unprepared to face the normal crises of family life (Cole, Cole, and Dean, 1980). Immaturity also may be associated with unrealistic views of marriage. When people begin a marriage with unrealistically high expectations, the reality of married life becomes dissatisfying by comparison (Spanier and Lewis, 1980).

THE EARLY STAGES
OF MARRIAGE

Most couples marry in a romantic haze, with little thought for the way that they will solve the problems of living together. As they build their marriage and deal with issues of power, authority, and control, most couples pass through three predictable phases, according to Lawrence Kurdek and Patrick Schmitt (1986), who studied a group of childless couples.

During the first year, called the *blending phase*, couples merge their lives. This is a time of learning to live together. Dirty dishes have to be washed, bathrooms scrubbed, and individual habits adjusted. Both may be accustomed to reading the first section of the morning paper with their coffee. One may leave the toothpaste uncapped and undergarments on the bedroom floor; the other may be a stickler for neatness. Personality characteristics that were unnoticed or soft-pedaled before marriage may emerge sharply. In adjusting to their new situation, the couple's task is to start thinking of themselves as part of an interdependent pair, in which the actions of one have consequences for the other (Golan, 1981). Despite these early problems, the quality of the relationship tends to be good. Passionate love is usually intense, and levels of sexual activity are high.

The second and third years of marriage are devoted to *nesting*. The couple makes a home together and explores their compatibility — or lack of it. Passionate love is on the wane, and it becomes clear that the ideal of sexual perfection is not being met. This trend is heightened among women or men who think that they are being taken advantage of by their partners. Compared with couples who feel that their marriage gives them a fair deal, such couples tend to be dissatisfied with their sexual relationship and to feel less loving or close after sex (Hatfield, Greenberger, Traupmann, and Lambert, 1982). During this marital phase, both partners may feel simultaneously attracted by the marriage and repelled by it. This is often a time of stress, disillusionment, and conflict over the amount of time that should be devoted to shared activities. Many marriages break apart during this period.

If couples make it through the third year, they enter the *maintaining phase*. By this time, sexual intercourse is less frequent. During the maintaining phase, family traditions are established, and each partner's individuality reappears. Couples who stay together until they reach this phase of marriage find that marital stress declines, many of the conflicts of the nesting period are resolved, and the quality of the relationship improves.

Cohabitation

Nearly four times as many unmarried men and women live together today as did in 1970; the number of unmarried couples of all ages has increased from 523 million to 1,988 million (U.S. Bureau of the Census, 1986). Of these couples, 47 percent of the adults involved previously had been married to someone else; the rest had never been married. Living together, or **cohabitation,** became popular on college campuses toward the close of the 1960s. By 1978, at least a quarter of college students were sharing quarters with a member of the other sex. As "Three's Company" reminded us, cohabitating does not necessarily involve sex (or even friendship), but it often does.

The commitment to the relationship ranges from slight (in which the partners see the arrangement as a temporary convenience and feel free to have intimate relationships with other people) to intense (in which the partners regard it as either a way station to marriage or a permanent substitute for it) (Macklin, 1980). For most college-age cohabitors, however, the arrangement seems to be a new step in the courtship process. It functions in the same way as going steady or testing the waters to see if the relationship might be strong enough for marriage.

Cohabitation is especially popular on college campuses, where about a quarter of the students share living quarters with a member of the other sex. (*Joel Gordon*)

Married and cohabiting couples of the same age appear to derive about the same amount of satisfaction from their relationships, and among young adults, both kinds of couples are similar in many ways (Macklin, 1978). When cohabitating couples marry, they do not differ from couples who had never cohabitated. They are just as satisfied with their marriages, are as emotionally close, have the same amount of conflict, and have the same degree of egalitarianism as the more traditional couples. Although young adults who have cohabitated say that it promotes their personal growth (Chilman, 1983), it does not seem to have any effect on their marriages.

The official definition of cohabitation limits it to male-female couples, but many homosexuals live together in a similar fashion. In fact, both cohabiting and homosexual couples (whether gay men or lesbians) pass through the same blending, nesting, and maintaining phases in their relationship as married couples do (Kurdek and Schmitt, 1986).

Most studies of male homosexuals have been rendered outdated by recent medical events. The most comprehensive study, now more than ten years old, showed that only 10 percent of gay men lived in close-coupled relationships that resembled traditional marriages, in which each partner promised to be faithful to the other (Bell and Weinberg, 1978). Another 18 percent lived in a stable sexual relationship but also engaged in sexual relationships with others. Fifteen percent resembled the swinging singles of the heterosexual world; the rest either had no partners or could not be classified. When AIDS began to sweep through the gay community in the early 1980s, it became apparent that the more sexual partners gay men had, the greater their risk for AIDS (Levine, 1982). In response to this threat, most gay men reevaluated their sexual practices. Many began confining their sexual partners to members of a small group or entered a close-coupled relationship. Although fear of AIDS has accelerated the prevalence of committed relationships among gay men, there already had been some indication that marriagelike relationships were on the rise (Macklin, 1980).

Lesbians seem more likely than gay men to live in stable, committed relationships. In the same study that showed only 10 percent of gay men in close-coupled relationships, 28 percent of lesbians were close-coupled, and another 17 percent lived in committed relationships but were free to have sexual relationships with others (Bell and Weinberg, 1978). The difference between lesbian and gay relationships has been attributed to different patterns of childhood socialization. In a gay masculine relationship, both partners have been socialized to be independent; in a lesbian relationship, both partners have been socialized to be nurturant and to have a strong interest in love and affection. Some researchers believe that this socialization pattern leads to warm, caring, and tender relationships that may suffer from emotional overinvolvement by both partners (Nichols and Lieblum, 1983).

Staying Single

Singlehood is on the rise in the United States, in part because so many adults are postponing marriage. Some will never marry. Researchers expect that the proportions of Americans who spend their lives in singlehood will rise from its present 5 or 6 percent to about 8 or 9 percent when adults now in their twenties reach old age (Glick, 1979). Not all single adults live by themselves; some cohabit, others move in with a friend or relative. Others never leave home.

At one time, people who stayed single faced public disapproval. In 1957, 80 percent of Americans believed that women who chose to remain unmarried must be "sick," "neurotic," or "immoral" (Yankelovich, 1981). The same charge was not made about single men although the early colonists looked on single men with disfavor. In an attempt to steer them into marriage, the various colonial governments taxed bachelors and collected the money every week (Scanzoni and Scanzoni, 1981). Times have changed. Today, 75 percent of Americans see single women as healthy people who have decided to follow a different way of life (Yankelovich, 1981).

It's easier to be single today than it was twenty-five years ago. Microwaves, frozen foods, clothes that do not need ironing, and improved transportation all make the details of living easier. Television makes the single life less lonely. At one time, women married for security. Today many are financially independent; they can marry for companionship. Economic freedom has made them more selective in their search for a mate.

People who prefer the single life say that it has many advantages: personal freedom, career opportunities, sexual availability and diversity, and a chance for self-improvement (Stein, 1975). In one study, single individuals were as physically and emotionally healthy as those who married (Rubinstein, Shaver, and Peplau, 1979). In some ways, single women are better off than single men. Women who have never married have more education, higher incomes, and better mental health than single men (Macklin, 1980).

HAVING CHILDREN

Americans are having fewer children and having them later in life, but most eventually become parents. Much about parenthood remains the same today as it always has, but changes in society alter the experience in ways that have radical effects on parents' lives. Cheap, effective contraceptives have wrought some of the changes. They have led to a decline in family size, which means that men and women spend fewer years actively engaged in child rearing. In our great-grandparents' day, it was not uncommon for a woman to give birth again at about the same time as her eldest daughter became a mother. Contraceptives also have made it easy to postpone the first birth and allow women to establish careers and couples to establish some financial security before they embark on parenthood. This control over the timing of parenthood makes children more welcome.

Because of technological changes, parenthood is less onerous today. All the innovations that make single life easier, along with such devices as disposable diapers, ease the drudgery of parenthood. They make it possible for mothers to enter (or stay in) the labor market. But high divorce rates and increases in the number of unwed mothers mean that more adults experience at least part of their parenthood without the support of a marital partner.

Pregnancy

Parenthood actually begins with pregnancy. As soon as parents are aware that they are to have a child, their relationship begins to change. For some couples, pregnancy is a highly stressful time;

for others, it is a time of personal growth. The emotional course of the pregnancy may stabilize the marriage or disrupt it (Osofsky and Osofsky, 1984). Some of a woman's feelings about her pregnancy are positive: she may feel special, fertile, and womanly, excited and impatient. Other feelings are negative: she may be fearful, exhausted, worried about her unborn child, and concerned about her ability to cope with motherhood (Grossman, Eichler, and Winickoff, 1980). Because she feels vulnerable, the reactions of her partner have an important influence on the way she feels about her pregnancy. As one pregnant woman wrote, "I am not now the self-sufficient woman he knows and loves. After work I need somebody to mother me" (Kates, 1986). How do most men respond? They generally feel excited and proud, but negative feelings also are common. A man may worry about how the baby's birth will change the marital relationship, be envious of his wife's ability to carry a child, jealous of the coming baby, feel an overwhelming sense of responsibility, or feel like a bystander—shut out from the mystery and intimacy of the childbearing process (Osofsky and Osofsky, 1984).

In a study of 100 middle-class couples who were expecting their first or second child, the quality of the marital relationship affected the course of the pregnancy (Grossman, Eichler, and Winickoff, 1980). When marital satisfaction was high and when couples shared in decision making, physical and emotional problems were few. And when the baby had been wanted at the time of conception, complications during pregnancy decreased.

Most couples embark on their first pregnancy with little idea of what becoming a parent entails (Alpert and Richardson, 1980). Women often become so preoccupied with the physical aspects of pregnancy that they do not think about how the baby will change family life and social roles until after the baby is born. The more that expectant parents know, the better they seem to adjust to their changed lives. In a longitudinal study of young couples expecting their first child, couples who knew what to expect during pregnancy, childbirth, and their child's first year coped better with all aspects of the process (Entwisle and Doering, 1981). Support from families and friends also made the experience easier to handle.

Couples are generally excited and proud as the birth of their first child approaches, but some negative feelings are not unusual. *(Joel Gordon)*

Adjusting to Parenthood

The birth of the first child causes a major upheaval in a couple's life. It changes a person's social roles, friendship patterns, family relationships, personality, values, and community involvements. Many women claim that the greatest change in their lives came about not as a result of their marriage but with the birth of their first child. Earlier, we saw that people view becoming a parent as a major mark of adulthood. It introduces a new form of responsibility for both parents. Now they must protect and nurture another life, a being who comes into the world virtually helpless.

Is parenthood a rewarding, exciting experience? Or is it an unpleasant, harrowing time? It

Table 15.4
How Have Children Changed Your Life?* (Percent)

	Women		Men	
	< 13 yrs education	> 13 yrs education	< 13 yrs education	> 13 yrs education
All change positive	47.2	35.5	40.0	36.0
More positive than negative	10.8	13.5	14.5	28.0
Balance of positive and negative	8.9	8.5	1.8	6.0
Neutral	17.8	22.0	29.1	12.0
More negative than positive	8.2	13.6	10.9	14.0
All change negative	7.1	14.2	3.6	4.0

* Most parents of preschoolers in a national sample derived more pleasure than pain from their children. All parents were younger than forty, and no single-parent families were included in the sample.

Source: Hoffman and Manis, 1978.

seems to be both. Among parents of preschoolers in a large national sample, from 95 percent to 98 percent of mothers and fathers — no matter what their level of education — said that they derived a great deal of satisfaction from being parents (Hoffman and Manis, 1978). When asked to list the joys of parenthood, they placed their emotional ties to their children at the top of the list. But "fun" ran a close second. Parents enjoyed watching their children's activities and playing with them. Self-fulfillment and a new sense of maturity also were important satisfactions. Many parents had only good things to say about the experience (see Table 15.4). The disadvantages of having children, said these parents, were that children tied you down and were expensive.

The demands and responsibilities of parenthood alter the marriage relationship. As couples make the transition, those whose marriages are based on romance are likely to find the experience much more stressful than those whose marriages are based on the idea of partnership (Belsky, 1981). Marital satisfaction may decrease. Couples communicate less; they find the spontaneity that characterized their social and sexual lives greatly reduced. They report more tensions and anxieties, more disagreements over money, and less mutual understanding during the early years of parent-

hood than at any other time. All of this stress may not be due to parenthood; childless couples show similar stress and conflict during the second and third years of their marriage — about the time that most couples have their first child (Kurdek and Schmitt, 1986).

Yet most couples feel that their children bring them closer together (Hoffman and Manis, 1978). Their new closeness seems to be in good part the result of the shared task of child rearing, which gives them a common goal. Other factors that unite the couple are the shared joys of children and the sense that children are "part of us." When couples feel pushed apart by children, the estrangement seems to grow out of the diminished time they have together, disagreements over child-rearing, or the husband's feeling that the wife is so absorbed in the children that she forgets him. It seems that parenthood intensifies pleasures and dissatisfactions, and the situation of the particular marriage determines which way the scales are tipped.

Parenthood changes other aspects of family life. It changes people's values and attitudes so that they are more oriented toward the interests of the family than the interests of society (Michaels, Hoffman, and Goldberg, 1982). Yet it also changes their community involvement. They become more likely to vote (Adelson and Hall, 1987), and as their children grow they begin to become more involved with school, church, and other community activities. The couple's social life shifts noticeably (L. Hoffman, 1978). They see less of friends who are childless and develop new friendships with parents of their children's friends. More of the couple's social life is spent with their parents, because the presence of grandchildren strengthens the bonds between generations.

Timing of Parenthood

The latest baby boom has been concentrated among women in their thirties. Between 1980 and 1983, the birth rate among women between thirty and thirty-five rose 15 percent (*New York Times,* 1984b). Is the experience of parenthood affected by the age of the parents? Researchers are finding both material and psychological factors at work.

When members of a couple are in their early twenties, just out of school, the birth of a child may be especially stressful. Neither is established in an occupation. Few couples at this age own a home, and most are paying for furniture and cars. In most cases, they have no savings and are stretching to make two salaries cover all expenses. Such young couples still are getting used to the idea of marriage.

Often both parents still have a lot of growing up to do. Among the couples in a study that examined the timing of parenthood, women who gave birth in their late teens or early twenties found themselves having to mother both their baby and their husband (Daniels and Weingarten, 1982). Yet there are advantages to becoming a parent while still so young. Young parents have enough energy to keep up with their children's seemingly incessant activities. And twenty or twenty-five years later, when the children strike out on their own, the parents are still relatively young. Their free time comes during middle age, when parents who waited to start their families are still struggling with adolescent children.

When couples postpone childbearing for several years, they have had an opportunity to work through the initial adjustment to marriage. Couples who wait until they are in their thirties to start

Couples who wait until they are past thirty to start their families often find the experience less stressful—both financially and psychologically—than couples who have children in their early twenties. (*Frank Siteman/E.K.M.-Nepenthe*)

a family encounter less pressure, and the marital relationship undergoes less strain. By this time, they generally have assets and may even own their own home. With one or both established in an occupation, their income is higher, and they can afford some of the luxuries that make life easier. Both are also likely to be more mature. In the study of parenthood timing, fathers in such families tended to be nurturant and aware of the mothers' emotional needs (Daniels and Weingarten, 1982). Unlike most younger fathers, they tended to assume part of the household duties and to become involved in child care. When mothers of first babies are observed in the laboratory, older mothers seem more sensitive to their babies' needs than younger mothers, and the emotional tone of the mother-infant relationship is generally more positive (Ragozin, Basham, Crnic, Greenberg, and Robinson, 1982). In addition, the older the mother at the time that her first baby is born, the more pleasure she reports from interacting with her infant.

DOES PARENTHOOD INTENSIFY SEX ROLES?

According to research and theory, sex roles become more pronounced when people become parents. In a typical study, young fathers rated themselves as more masculine and young mothers rated themselves as more feminine than did other men and women of their age (Abrahams, Feldman, and Nash, 1978). This was true whether the parents were compared with cohabiting couples, childless married couples, or married couples expecting their first child. But such studies are cross-sectional, and they do not show us whether the experience of parenthood actually intensified sex roles.

Only a longitudinal study can reveal the changes as they occur. When Shirley Feldman and Barbara Aschenbrenner (1983) followed a group of well-educated middle-class couples who were expecting their first child, they discovered that parenthood had some surprising effects. During the last trimester of pregnancy and again when their baby was seven or eight months old, each couple's masculinity and femininity were rated. As expected, the women felt more feminine after their babies were born. They showed an increase in nurturance, warmth, sensitivity, responsiveness to babies, and tolerance for others' shortcomings. But so did their husbands. On each of these aspects of femininity, men's scores increased. Yet the fathers' increased femininity did not lower their masculine ratings. They were just as independent, decisive, and self-reliant as they had been before their babies were born.

Although both partners changed similarly, the results were different. Women saw a greater difference between masculine and feminine roles than they had while they were pregnant, but men saw the difference diminishing. How can we explain these changes? Feldman and Aschenbrenner believe that fatherhood has a much stronger impact on men's sex typing than psychologists had suspected. Even though parenthood may increase the divergence in sex roles, as the women noted, the men may respond to the new nurturant qualities they observe in themselves. The researchers also point out that the couples in their study may not have been typical. They were middle-class, well-educated couples, and about a third of the women had returned to work by the time of the second testing. All of the men helped with household tasks to some extent, and 36 percent shared equally in such responsibilities. Finally, the men were deeply involved with their babies. They helped with child care. Most had coached their wives during childbirth and had been present in the delivery room at their baby's birth. Perhaps recent changes in sex roles, which are concentrated in the middle class, are leading to changes in the way that men experience fatherhood.

Childless or Child-Free?

Compared with the rate in the 1960s, the rate of childless couples today is high. Yet we cannot say that voluntary childlessness is becoming a social trend (L. Hoffman, 1982). Because birth rates are climbing among women in their thirties, what seems to be an increase in childlessness is primarily a postponement of births.

Although many people pity couples who are childless by choice, the decision not to have children does not destine a couple to unhappiness, misery, and loneliness. Couples without children appear to be no different from couples with children in their self-esteem, life satisfaction, or maturity (Silka and Kiesler, 1977). Many young childless couples, especially husbands, report greater satisfaction with their lives than do couples with young children. Without the responsibility of children, couples are not tied down, they have more time for each other, and they have money for luxury items and time-saving devices.

Will people who have decided to remain child-free one day regret their decision? In Erikson's theory of adult development, human beings have a need for generativity (Erikson and Hall, 1987), and Gutmann's (1975) parental imperative centers around the protection and nurturance of children. But in Gutmann's theory, the imperative does not begin to operate until it is triggered by the birth of a child. And Erikson points out that what he calls "the procreative urge" can be effectively expressed through creativity and productivity, as well as by caring for the children of others—whether as teachers, medical personnel, day-care workers, or adoptive parents.

Single Mothers

A thirty-three-year-old, unmarried junior high school teacher is artificially inseminated and gives birth to a daughter. A thirty-eight-year-old unmarried computer executive adopts a baby from Mexico. A thirty-five-year-old unmarried school psychologist asks a friend from college to father her child (Kantrowitz, Michael, Rotenberg, Williams, and Greenberg, 1985). Across the country, an increasing number of children are being born to single women in their twenties and thirties who have good jobs and financially secure futures. Either they have postponed marriage and feel that biology will not allow them to wait any longer, or else they are women who know that they want children but are not certain that they want husbands. These highly publicized cases obscure the situation of most unmarried women who are having children. The vast majority do not have the financial prospects of the "new single mother." These women have less education, have fewer financial resources, get less prenatal care, and are more likely to bear a low-birth-weight baby than their married counterparts (Ventura, 1985) (see Figure 15.1).

Many lone parents did not start out that way but have acquired the position as the consequence of divorce or death. Nineteen percent of American households consist of mothers and their children; less than 3 percent consist of fathers and their children (U.S. Bureau of the Census, 1986). Many of these single-parent families contain more than one child. Most of the information we have about single-parent families comes from studies of mother-headed households, but the information available on father-headed households indicates that many of the problems are similar, no matter which sex is in charge.

The major problem, as we saw in Chapter 9, is that one person is saddled with the responsibilities carried by two people in intact families. Most single mothers or fathers say that this role overload, in which they must see that meals are prepared, house and clothes are clean, financial affairs are in order, property (house, yard, and car) is maintained, and children reared, is the most stressful aspect of their situation. Despite this strain, most single parents feel proud and happy about their accomplishments. They find themselves developing new aspects of their personalities. Women, cast on their own, become more self-reliant; men, forced to assume a maternal role, become more nurturant (Weiss, 1979).

The role of single parent also affects the way a man or woman performs on the job. Fathers say that child care limits their job mobility, cuts into their working hours and earnings, changes their work priorities, and hampers job transfers (Keshet and Rosenthal, 1978). It also limits their behavior on the job and restricts the kind of work they do, their promotions, and their relations with co-workers and supervisors. Employed mothers (and more than 75 percent are employed) face similar restrictions.

DIVORCE

Married couples have become increasingly less likely to persist in a dismal relationship. In the United States, about one out of three first marriages ends in divorce (Jacobson, 1983). Social changes may have made a rising divorce rate inevitable. The same developments that have led to a rise in singlehood have made people less likely to cling to an unsatisfactory marriage. Women no longer must rely on men for economic security. Technological changes have made the one-adult (or one-adult plus children) household manageable. Society has removed the social stigma that once accompanied the divorced state.

Along with the removal of these barriers to divorce came the demand that marriage reach a level of happiness that it had never been expected to provide, creating a burden perhaps too heavy for the institution to bear. At one time, our definition of a happy marriage was one in which people drifted along comfortably from day to day, feeling that things were "okay." Only a highly unpleasant situation drove them to sever the marital bond. Today we expect marriage to provide romantic

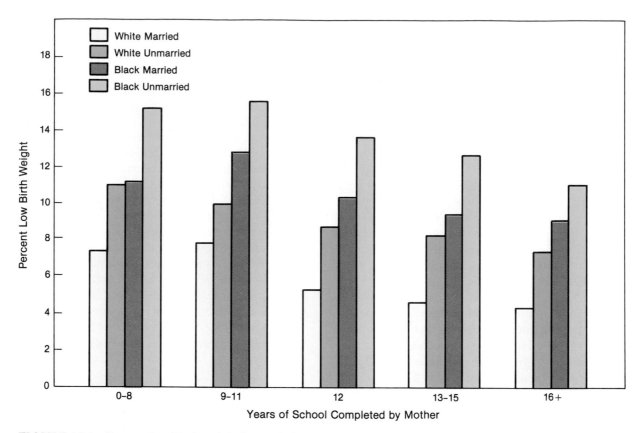

FIGURE 15.1   Percent low birth weight by marital status and educational attainment of mother, 1982. *(From Ventura, 1985; information from NCHS, Division of Vital Statistics)*

love, personal growth, and self-fulfillment for both partners. If it does not, we may be quick to end it.

Some relationships seem to last in spite of it all; others quickly break apart. Most divorces among young adults take place within the first four years of marriage (Glick, 1980). What places a marriage at high risk? Marrying when the first child has already been conceived. Being younger than nineteen when you marry, if you're a woman, or twenty-one, if you're a man. Being older than thirty when you marry. Being black. (Being Hispanic reduces your chances of divorce.) Low income and low education increase the likelihood of divorce, although a wife's advanced education and career placement (which make her less dependent on the marriage) also seem to increase divorce.

In attempting to explain why some seemingly satisfactory marriages break up, Graham Spanier and Robert Lewis (1980) suggest that outside forces often may play an important role. They see

marital stability as determined by the balance of costs and rewards perceived by each partner. Satisfaction with a lifestyle, the rewards of interacting with the spouse, and the social and personal resources of the marriage may equal the dissatisfactions that are present. But should some alternative attraction, such as another possible mate or a crucial career decision, upset the balance, the marriage may founder.

Once the process of divorce begins, it takes a long time to complete. Divorces appear to pass through three phases (Golan, 1981). The first phase begins when people realize that a basic conflict threatens the marital relationship. Their inability to resolve it starts the dissolution of their emotional bond. Unpleasant feelings—anger, guilt, bitterness, inadequacy, loneliness—accompany their interactions. They may begin merely enduring each other's company or even avoid it. Finally, they separate. But long after they have ceased to love each other, their attachment endures. Away from the partner, each suffers an emotional distress much like the separation anxiety that develops in infants and toddlers (see Chapter 8). They are still angry at the former partner and distrustful, but they are also preoccupied by him or her and often jealous (Hetherington and Camara, 1984). They are always eager for news of the absent partner. Is she seeing someone else? Did he go to the Johnson's party? Not all divorcing people go through this anxiety; but even those who have asked for the divorce in order to marry someone else often go through periods of deep pain. Once it becomes clear that reconciliation is out of the question and divorce proceedings are underway, each partner may be pervaded with loneliness.

Once the divorce has been granted, people move into the second phase, in which they adjust to the reality of the divorce. It is generally an unhappy period. They may relish their new freedom, but some soon find that their expectations about life after divorce were unrealistic. They may feel cast adrift, rootless, and anxious. They have lost a primary social role (wife, husband) and have assumed a new role (divorced adult) for which society has developed no standards and few expectations. Most find themselves shut out of their former social activities, which were centered around married couples. Many, especially women, find themselves in serious financial straits. Some become depressed.

Yet some people come through a divorce with a heightened feeling of well-being and show evidence of personal growth. In a study of working-class women who were in the process of getting a divorce, Prudence Brown (1976) found that less traditional sex-role attitudes were associated with psychological well-being. Other characteristics that predicted personal growth from the experience included having an active social life, making new friends, having little social contact with the former husband, reaching a separation status consistent with their goals, having a high income, not having been divorced before, and having a religious affiliation.

Toward the end of the second year, most divorced adults have begun to move into the third phase, in which they reconstruct their lives. Their financial situation has improved, their new households are established, their new social lives are underway. Those who were unduly attached to their former spouse may have broken those bonds by means of a new intimate relationship (Hetherington and Carrara, 1984). With their rebuilding underway, many are ready to remarry, and hope for success on their next try.

REMARRIAGE

About 40 percent of all marriages involve people who have been married before (Glick, 1980). Most remarriages take place about three years after the divorce, and young adults are the most likely to remarry. Second marriages appear to be less stable than first marriages. Some researchers have suggested that this greater readiness to divorce may not be due to the fact that remarriages are necessarily unsatisfactory. Remarried individuals have already proved willing to end a difficult marital relationship, and their earlier experience has provided them with knowledge about how to do it (Glick, 1980).

Remarriages differ in several ways from first marriages, according to Frank Furstenberg (1982). People approach a second marriage with expectations and habits formed during their first marriages. They judge the new marriage against the first. They also recall what went wrong the first time around and may consciously develop a new style of interaction. Second, contact with the previous spouse often affects the marriage, especially if the first marriage produced children. Relationships become complicated, and financial ties from the first marriage (support payments, property, insurance policies, wills) may affect the economic situation of the new marriage. As we saw in Chapter 9, playing stepparent often is a difficult task.

Third, people who remarry are older, more experienced, and perhaps have moved up in social status since they entered their first marital relationship. A thirty-two-year-old who is established in an occupation does not approach marriage in the same way as a twenty-three-year-old, perhaps just out of school. The age spread between the partners is also greater in second marriages. In remarriages, the man is usually six years older than the woman; in first marriages, the age gap is only two or three years. A divorced man generally marries someone younger than his first wife, and a divorced woman generally marries someone older than her first husband (Glick, 1980). Finally, the social background may have changed. Shifts in cultural standards can alter expectations and responsibilities in such areas as contraceptive use, sex roles, economic expectations, women's employment, and child care.

Second marriages usually are not as romantic as first marriages, but the level of marital satisfaction, happiness, and worry seems to be about the same as in the average first marriage. People in a second marriage have less trouble communicating with their partner, they find their new partner more tolerant than the old one, and they believe that the new marriage is more of a partnership than the old one was. The less romantic aura of the second marriage may help explain why remarried people say that their marital problems have changed. Instead of worrying about their spouses' immaturity, sexual problems, and their own unreadiness for marriage, remarried people worry about children and money (Messenger, 1976).

SUMMARY

1. The appropriate times for such events as marriage, careers, and parenthood are becoming less tied to age, especially in the middle class, making this an **age-irrelevant society.** Young adults are marrying later, postponing the births of their children, and having smaller families.

2. During young adulthood, men and women are at the peak of physical agility, strength, and speed. However, within the body, organs are aging; by the thirties, reflexes have slowed.

3. In Erikson's psychosocial stage theory, young adults face the task of developing intimacy. However, this universal task is different for women and men because of their earlier socialization. In Levinson's stage theory, men go through an orderly sequence that alternates between tranquil, stable phases and transitional phases during which men question the pattern of their lives and explore new possibilities. During young adulthood, they develop autonomy and intimacy and consolidate their careers. In Gould's theory, young adults go through four phases; during each phase they reformulate their self-concepts, face illusions, and resolve conflicts. In Gutmann's theory, personality development is heavily influenced by the **parental imperative,** in which the requirements of parenthood intensify traditional sex roles. One issue concerning adult development is the nature of transitions. Some maintain that the various transitions (such as marriage, parenthood, entering the job market) are highly stressful; others believe that they create stress only when they are unexpected and not considered part of the normal life course. A second issue is the timing of adulthood: when does a person become mature?

4. **Self-concept,** the organized, coherent, and integrated pattern of self-perceptions, shows both continuity and change during young adulthood. Self-esteem seems to rise in men throughout young adulthood, although it generally declines among the unemployed. Although women tend to feel less control over their lives than men do, their self-esteem generally is high. When high-achieving women become full-time homemakers, they may develop low self-esteem. An increasing number of young adults are **androgynous,** that is, high in personality traits attributed to both sexes.

5. Work affects personality, family life, social relations, attitudes, and values. Job complexity appears to be a major influence on personality. Work can be a source of stress, especially among those with few social roles. When work is challenging and rewarding, it also can be a source of satisfaction. Men and single women generally have orderly occupational histories, but other women may move in and out of the labor market. Employed mothers seem to have higher morale and show fewer symptoms of stress than mothers who stay at home.

6. Adults are marrying later in life than they did a few decades ago. Couples are likely to be similar in religion, race, ethnic background, and socioeconomic status. Marriage establishes the family as a social system, with marital roles affected by the way power is divided. In the majority of marriages, the man is dominant; only a small minority of marriages are egalitarian. Happy marriages are characterized by emotional maturity, the free expression of emotions, consideration for others, high self-esteem, and adaptability.

7. **Cohabitation,** in which unmarried couples live together, varies in commitment from slight to intense. For college couples, cohabitation seems to be a new step in the courtship process. Cohabiting couples and married couples seem to be much alike and derive the same satisfaction from their relationship. Cohabiting gay and lesbian couples are very similar to cohabiting or married heterosexual couples and go through the same processes in establishing their relationship. An increasing number of men and women are remaining single, in part because the single life is easier than it once was and in part because women no longer are economically dependent on men.

8. Parenthood begins with pregnancy, and the quality of the marital relationship affects the course of the pregnancy. When a person becomes a parent, social roles, friendship patterns, family relationships, personality, values, and community involvements all change. Parenthood seems to intensify both the pleasures and dissatisfactions of life, and children either can draw a couple together or push them apart. Couples who decide not to have children are similar to couples with children in self-esteem, maturity, and satisfaction with life. Single parents find role overload stressful.

9. The divorce rate has been rising, in part because couples break up unless their relationship provides romantic love, personal growth, and self-fulfillment. Most divorces take place within the first four years of marriage, when partners perceive more costs than rewards in the relationship. There are three phases to divorce: 1. the realization that the relationship is threatened by some basic conflict and the initial separation; 2. the divorce and adjustment to its reality; 3. the reconstruction of life as a single person and perhaps the preparation to remarry. Remarriages are different from first marriages because the remarried partner comes with expectations and habits formed during the first marriage; the marriage may be complicated by contact with the former spouse; the partner is now older, more experienced, and has a higher social status; and social expectations and responsibilities in areas that affect marriage may have changed.

KEY TERMS

age-irrelevant society
androgyny

cohabitation
parental imperative

self-concept

STUDY TERMS

age-irrelevant society A society in which major life events, such as marriage, schooling, and retirement, are not closely tied to chronological age.

androgynous A person whose self-concept incorporates both masculine and feminine characteristics.

parental imperative The notion that parenthood exerts a controlling influence over adult personality, based on the proposal that basic personality differences between the sexes have evolved in order to protect and nurture children.

self-concept The organized and integrated pattern of perceptions related to the self, including self-esteem and self-image.

CHAPTER 16

Intellectual
Development in Early
and Middle Adulthood

Whether adults are lawyers or homemakers, lab technicians or truck-drivers, they use a wide variety of problem-solving procedures in daily life. Donna, who is both businesswoman and mother, draws on her intelligence as heavily when managing her family as she does when managing her employer's office. When one of her children seems out of sorts, she checks for symptoms of illness and decides whether to keep the youngster home from school, what sort of medication to use, and whether to call the family physician. If she decides on home medication, she draws on her knowledge that her youngest child needs a smaller dose than the older children do. She plans menus ahead, marketing once a week to get the necessary ingredients, and doubles the quantities in most recipes in order to feed her family. She writes a letter to the editor of the local paper, protesting the schoolboard's recent cut in field trips. She pays the monthly bills, balances her bank account, and estimates how much she and her husband must save each month for the family vacation next summer. When her youngest child has trouble with her homework, Donna interrupts the novel she is reading to go over the assignment and make certain that her daughter understands it.

427

As they handle daily tasks, adults use a variety of problem-solving procedures. The thought involved in the successful solution of life's practical problems depends on a store of general knowledge and accumulated facts. It also requires the possession of such basic skills as reading, calculating, and writing. Finally, problem solving requires adults to use such metacognitive techniques as planning; generating hypotheses, then applying them; checking progress toward a solution; and revising the hypotheses as needed. In short, daily thinking in adult life requires sophisticated intelligence.

In this chapter, we begin by examining the major approaches toward the study of intelligence in adults. After exploring the psychometric and practical views of intelligence, we consider the possibility that the Piagetian theory of intelligence might require an additional stage to accommodate adult thought. Then we look at a view of adult cognitive development that is based on the life tasks customarily encountered in the various stages of adulthood. We take up the matter of intellectual change and evaluate possible declines and the ways in which adults can compensate for them. Next we consider a factor that is often omitted in discussions of cognition: the effects of personality, lifestyle, and health on intelligence. The chapter closes with an overview of adult education and an analysis of the adult student's major objectives.

INTELLIGENCE

The problem of defining intelligence does not disappear when psychologists try to trace intellectual development in adults. If anything, it becomes more complicated. Because most adults are no longer engaged in formal education, there is no basic pool of information that all are trying to master at the same time. Each person, depending on his or her occupation and interests, is mastering an increasingly specialized body of knowledge — whether it is how to keep an automobile engine running or how to manage a successful corporation. Although a person's knowledge base — the store of accumulated facts and knowledge — is

certainly one aspect of intelligence, it is an inadequate yardstick for assessing thought in a specialized world.

Researchers have considered alternative ways of looking at intelligence in adults. Some have suggested that the ability to make plans and choices and to correct them as necessary is a good measure of intelligence. Some have pointed to quick-wittedness — the rapidity with which a person responds to a problem or situation. Some have relied on academic skills and educational achievements. Some have used test scores. And others believe that the ability to reason in practical, everyday situations is the hallmark of intelligence. None of these alternatives is entirely satisfactory, for each view captures a different aspect of intelligence. When studying the development of intelligence across the life span, most researchers tend to use either a psychometric or a practical approach.

Psychometric Intelligence

Because no special theory underlies the psychometric approach, researchers make few assumptions about the nature of thought or its development (Perlmutter, in press). Instead, they trace changes in intelligence across the life span by measuring adults' performance on standardized tests. In Chapter 12, we saw how such tests, based on factor theories of intelligence, were devised to assess children's ability to succeed in school. By testing large groups of adults of various ages, researchers hope to show age-related changes in various aspects of intelligence.

Not all researchers are comfortable with the psychometric approach to adult intelligence. They believe that several factors make IQ tests poor measures of adult intelligence. Most of the tests have been standardized on young adults and may not be relevant to the functioning of intelligence in middle-aged and older individuals. Items on mental tests require the sort of reasoning that is valued in the classroom. Each task is clearly defined, includes all the information needed for its solution, has only one correct answer, and usually there is only one method of reaching that answer (Wagner and Sternberg, 1986). To produce such items, test makers must abstract the tasks from life. To solve

Although IQ tests are useful tools in predicting competence for some entry-level positions, they tap only a portion of the intellectual skills needed for success in the adult world. *(Ken Robert Buck/ The Picture Cube)*

them, a person must ignore influences that the test maker has eliminated, even though they would affect the problem if encountered in reality. This demand may seem unsatisfactory to adults who are no longer in school. They often find the premises of such stripped problems oversimplified. Presented with such a problem, a fifty five or sixty year-old may rebel against having to "stick to the facts," because his or her experience indicates that the solution called for is impractical (Labouvie-Vief, 1985).

The results of IQ tests are strongly related to success in school and are good predictors of competence in entry-level positions for such professions as engineering, piloting, and computer programming (Willis and Schaie, 1986). This relation makes them a useful tool with some young adults. But test results are only modestly related to success on most jobs, with a correlation of about +.20 (Wagner and Sternberg, 1986). Apparently, IQ tests tap only a portion of the intellectual competencies that are important in the adult world—a finding that is not surprising, given our discussion of intelligence in Chapter 12. Dissatisfied with an approach that limits intelligence to academic skills, an increasing number of developmentalists have focused on practical applications of intelligence.

Practical Intelligence

Underlying practical approaches to intelligence is the view that development is an active, lifelong process of adaptation to the environment (Dixon and Baltes, 1986). Because human development takes place in a social context, intelligence is best studied within the context in which it is used. Thus the appropriate measure of adults' intelligence is their ability to solve the demanding tasks they encounter in their daily lives. In this contextual view of intelligence, researchers assume that accumulated general knowledge, experience, and individual expertise in various domains affect the way that people think about and meet these tasks. Adults should do well on tasks that draw on skills they use frequently in their occupational or daily lives and do less well on tasks that draw on skills they rarely use—or have not used since they left school. Given the great diversity of adult experience and expertise, similar differences appear among individuals in the nature of their thought and the developmental pattern of cognitive skills.

The closeness of practical intelligence to everyday functioning makes it a more valuable way of looking at intelligence with each decade that passes in an adult's life. When we assess middle-aged and older adults solely in terms of psychomet-

Comparing the size and cost of articles in the supermarket requires people to relate their knowledge, expertise, and basic cognitive skills to a practical problem. *(Charles Gupton/Stock, Boston)*

a comparative measure of performance on basic intellectual skills when taken out of context. Yet practical intelligence may be more important in successful living. For example, researchers have discovered that there is no relation between a person's ability to make intelligent choices (comparing size and cost of similar items in the supermarket) and his or her score on formal tests of the arithmetic operations involved (Scribner, 1986). The key may be to look at intelligence as made up of two general processes, as Paul Baltes and his associates have suggested (Baltes, Dittmann-Kohli, and Dixon, 1984).

In this **dual-process model,** intellectual functioning consists of mechanics and pragmatics. The **mechanics of intelligence** include the basic operations of thought used in processing information and solving problems. These functions and abilities probably reach full development by the end of adolescence, and they are measured by performance scales on IQ tests or other tests of fluid intelligence. The **pragmatics of intelligence** include all the procedures that relate stored knowledge, expertise, and the basic cognitive skills (mechanics) to daily life. These functions and abilities continue to develop during adulthood, as knowledge is elaborated, maintained, and transformed. Verbal scales on IQ tests or tests of crystallized intelligence measure some aspects of these pragmatics but not all. The pragmatics of intelligence also encompasses methods of maintaining professional knowledge and productivity and the sort of interpretive knowledge we call *wisdom.*

When developmentalists were primarily interested in the early part of the life span, wisdom was rarely, if ever, mentioned in discussions of intelligence. Wisdom grows out of experience, and so no matter how highly educated adolescents or young adults become, they are unlikely to be wise. Wisdom is different from knowledge, because it requires more than the possession of facts. Wise people understand the significance of what they know, and they show their wisdom in sound judgment concerning the conduct of life, the factors that influence life, and the developmental tasks that they face (Dixon and Baltes, 1986). Wisdom is an aspect of intelligence that is likely to increase across adulthood, because its development is fostered by wide experience.

ric intelligence, we are likely to underestimate their intellectual readiness to take on various tasks, their ability to adapt to various situations, and their handling of situations in daily life (Dixon and Baltes, 1986).

The Dual-Process Model of Intelligence

Even if psychometric tests are not the best measure of intelligence across adulthood, they give us

WHEN PICKING THE PONIES, DON'T RELY ON IQ

Handicapping horses involves assigning the odds for or against a horse's chance of winning a particular race. An expert handicapper takes into account seven aspects of the horse's record: best lifetime speed, the speed at its last race, the horse's past speed during the first and last quarter miles, the horse's maneuvers during a race, the quality of the horses it has run against in the past, the jockey, and the track conditions. Considering the way these variables interact and deciding a horse's chances of winning is a complex cognitive task. If psychometric tests measure a person's general intelligence, then expert handicappers must have high IQs. But if there is no relation between such expertise and IQ, then some important aspects of intelligence are not being measured by IQ tests.

Determined to find out, Stephen Ceci and Jeffrey Liker (1986) spent three years studying middle-aged and older men who attended harness races almost every day during the racing season. All the men in their study had an extensive factual knowledge of harness racing. All bought and read the "early form," a racing form published the day before the race that gave full statistics on the horses but no odds. The men were separated into "expert handicappers" and "nonexperts" on the basis of their ability to handicap ten regular races. (When their picks were compared with the post-time odds of the paid track handicappers, the experts did as well as the professionals.) Each man also took a standard IQ test.

There was no relation between IQ and track expertise. One expert, a construction worker with an IQ of 85, picked the top horse in all ten races and picked the top three horses in the correct order in five of the races. He had been coming to the track for sixteen years. One nonexpert, a lawyer with an IQ of 118, picked the top horse in only three races and the top three horses only once. He had been coming to the track for fifteen years. Overall, the experts' IQs ranged from 81 to 128; nonexperts' from 83 to 130. Experience clearly was important, but it was not the sole factor in the development of handicapping expertise. The "nonexperts" had from seven to twenty-three years' experience in following the races.

Ceci and Liker asked each man to handicap fifty pairs of unnamed horses, based on the statistics given them by the experimenters. In response to questions, they explained their reasoning in assessing the odds. Computer analysis showed that the experts consistently used a complex interaction of the seven variables to handicap the horses. The nonexperts used this complex form of reasoning only occasionally. When experts and nonexperts were matched on experience and factual knowledge about racing, the expert with an IQ of 81 reasoned in a more complex manner than the nonexpert with an IQ of 130. Ceci and Liker (1987) concluded that the challenges we meet in daily life, such as handicapping horses, force us to develop practical intelligence — specific styles and modes of thought that are unrelated to successful performance on academic tasks.

STAGES OF INTELLECTUAL DEVELOPMENT

During childhood, intelligence changes rapidly. As children acquire experiences, facts, and thinking skills, their understanding of the world and its ways widens and becomes more sophisticated. The changes are so predictable and so characteristic that it tells us a lot about a ten-year-old if we know that she thinks like most eight-year-olds or like most twelve-year-olds. This developmental pace makes cognitive development in children relatively easy to study. Cognitive changes in adults

Older adults may make better jurors than young adults do, because experience makes people better at coordinating conflicting information and drawing on several sources for a conclusion. *(Southern Light)*

develop slowly and are less predictable than in children. We have not learned much about the intelligence of a forty-year-old man if we are told that he thinks like most thirty-five-year-olds. This different pace has made it difficult for researchers to study adults' intellectual development.

Extending Piagetian Theory

For decades, there was almost no research into cognitive development during adulthood. Most theorists focused on childhood and had little to say about intellectual changes after adolescence. As we saw in Chapter 13, Piaget regarded the formal operations of adolescence as the culmination of cognitive development. Because many adolescents were slow to develop formal operations (at least the sort of deductive reasoning from hypotheses that Piaget studied), there seemed little reason to look for further advances in the way adults thought.

With the emergence of interest in development across the life span, the situation changed. Once psychologists discovered that life was not simply a downhill course after adolescence, they began to look for signs of cognitive development among adults. Klaus Riegel (1975) proposed that we add a fifth and final stage to Piaget's theory — the stage of **dialectical operations**, also called *postformal*

thought. As we saw in Chapter 2, dialectical theorists propose that people reach new levels of functioning through their interactions with society. Experiences during adulthood lead to questions, doubts, and contradictions that may produce a further reorganization of thought.

How do the cognitive operations of dialectical thought differ from formal operations? In the formal-operational stage, thought and actions were supposed to be consistent with adult logic. By resolving the contradictory conceptions that developed toward the close of childhood, the adolescent had attained a state of equilibrium. Riegel suggests that adults in the dialectical stage no longer require a state of equilibrium. Cognitive imbalance does not bother them. They understand, for example, that people (and objects) often have contradictory features. A person can be loving and cold, generous and greedy, strong and weak at the same time. Realizing the impossibility of discovering absolute truth, they understand that their own assumptions and ways of thinking influence the knowledge that they glean from the world. This realization enables them to accept contradiction as the basis of all thought and development. We might say that their thought involves a continuing dialectic. Faced with conflicting viewpoints, they no longer have to discard one or the other but can integrate them into a larger framework (Kramer, 1983).

Some research indicates that middle-aged adults

REASONING ABOUT SOCIAL DILEMMAS

How important is formal-operational thought when we face the messy dilemmas of life? Such problems require us to apply intellectual skills to highly emotional issues. If adults develop postformal thought, then we would expect middle-aged men and women to show more advanced reasoning on social dilemmas than adolescents or young adults.

Psychologist Fredda Blanchard-Fields (1986) gave three dilemmas to a group of 20 adolescents (fourteen- to sixteen-year-olds taking college-track courses), 20 young adults (college students in their twenties), and 20 mature adults (thirty-five- to forty-six-year-olds). Each person read the dilemmas, described the conflict involved, judged the issue, and explained his or her stand. The first dilemma, which was not emotional, asked them to resolve conflicting accounts of a fictional war by participants of the opposing sides. The second dilemma consisted of a conflict between an adolescent boy and his parents over a visit to the grandparents. The third was a conflict of views between a man and woman over whether to abort an unplanned pregnancy. Each person also took a test of formal reasoning, the vocabulary subscale of an IQ test, and a test of emotional maturity.

Nearly all the subjects showed some grasp of formal operations, but such understanding bore no relation to the level of reasoning shown on the dilemmas. In all three dilemmas, most adults in their thirties and forties tried to reconcile the differences in both accounts. They tried to focus on the facts, separating them from the interpretations of the people involved. In the grandparent story, for example, some weighed the adolescent's need for peer approval against the family needs of his parents. Many saw each perspective as a valid, unique, and irreconcilable frame of reference. They apparently had reached the stage of dialectical operations. Few young adults were able to do this. They were aware that discrepancies between individuals' accounts of an event are to be expected, yet they were likely to say that the truth could be reached if a neutral party were present. On the nonemotional task, the adolescents reasoned in a similar manner, but in the emotional dilemmas, most of them took one side or the other. Although they indicated awareness of the opposing view, they were much less likely than either of the adult groups to try to deal with it.

A few adolescents and a larger group of young adults reasoned as efficiently as the oldest group. They saw each perspective as unique and valid. What tended to predict "postformal" reasoning in younger people? Educational level made no difference in performance, but IQ scores and the test of emotional maturity did. Younger adults who scored high on these measures were less likely to see the world in black and white and more likely to try to reconcile opposing viewpoints. When older adults scored low on these measures, they tended to reason like adolescents.

Maturity apparently enables adults to separate a person's account of an event from the event itself. It also leads to a more accurate reporting of conflicting positions and a respect for them. Such an advance is consistent with several views of cognitive development. It could reflect postformal (or dialectical) reasoning, the application of pragmatic intelligence, or the attainment of the responsible stage of thought.

are more adept than younger people at integrating conflicting information (Labouvie-Vief, 1985). When they encounter a person whose words contradict his or her facial expressions or gestures, middle-aged adults tend to take both sources of information into account. In the same situation, young adults tend to accept the words and ignore the other evidence. And in situations such as jury duty, when conclusions must be made on the basis of varied — and often conflicting — information, older adults seem to be more likely than young adults to coordinate the sources and thus less likely to base their conclusions on isolated information. (The accompanying box, "Reasoning about Social Dilemmas," describes a recent study exploring such differences.)

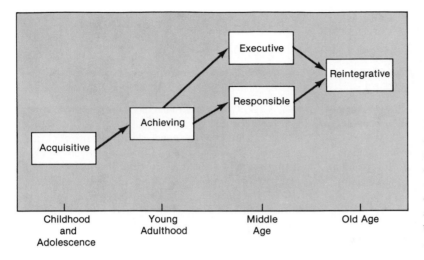

FIGURE 16.1 **Stages of adult cognitive development. Warner Schaie's theory relates cognition to developmental tasks. The first stage (childhood and adolescence) is devoted to acquiring knowledge; adult stages reflect different ways of using knowledge.** *(From Schaie, 1977/78)*

Stages of Adult Cognition

Riegel built his view of cognitive development on Piaget's system. Warner Schaie (1977/78) has developed a stage approach to adult intelligence that relates cognition to developmental tasks. His view of intelligence across adulthood is compatible with Erikson's system (see Chapters 15 and 17). In Schaie's theory (see Figure 16.1), cognitive changes *before* adulthood reflect increasingly efficient ways of acquiring new information; changes *during* adulthood reflect different ways of using information. For that reason, he places childhood and adolescence together in a single stage: the **acquisitive stage.** Throughout this period, young people are engaged in learning new skills and in amassing a store of knowledge, but the knowledge is primarily acquired for future use. It is a time of learning for learning's sake, of acquiring knowledge without knowing whether it ever will be useful. The motivating question is, "What should I know?" Indeed, by demanding that young people spend most of their day in school, society insists that they devote themselves to the acquisition of knowledge.

During the three stages Schaie proposed for young and middle adulthood, the question is, "How should I use what I know?" Young adulthood is the time of Schaie's second stage, the **achieving stage.** The time has arrived to apply the knowledge that has been accumulating for years. Young adults already on the job immediately begin applying their knowledge toward their occupa-

tional goals. Those in college continue to acquire knowledge, but this time the acquisition has immediate application to vocational interests. During the achieving stage, young people also apply their knowledge in their personal lives, as many marry and begin families. They also may apply their knowledge in the pursuit of their hobbies, whether they hang glide, ski, paint, or restore classic cars. During this stage, the consequences of problem solving may be enormous, especially when the problem involves such decisions as whether (or whom) to marry, whether (or when) to have children, which occupation to enter.

The achieving stage prepares young adults for the cognitive stages of middle adulthood: the **responsible stage** and the **executive stage.** These stages require them to apply their intelligence in a socially responsible manner. The responsible stage begins first. During this stage, people apply themselves to practical problems of living and to their obligations to family members and fellow employees. Many people go on to the executive stage, in which the responsibility moves from a person's immediate family and coworkers to society. Now adults are concerned with managing organizations—a department at work, a factory team, a service club. Their interest also turns to complex community or national issues—town zoning, school boards, taxes, or foreign policy.

Schaie sees late adulthood as spent in the **reintegrative stage.** It is a time when the demand to acquire knowledge has slackened and the consequences of decisions are limited. The motivating question becomes, "Why should I know?" Instead of stretching themselves over occupation, family matters, and community or national issues, older adults may focus on a single area. Perhaps retirement leaves them free to become active in politics, church affairs, or community betterment. Perhaps they devote their skills to their relations with their spouse and grandchildren. Some may continue to follow a profession but cut back on their involvement in other areas of life.

Passage from one of these stages to another is determined not by age but by developmental tasks. During the acquisitive stage, people must remain flexible. They do not know what the shape of their lives will be or in what sort of context they will exercise their skills. They excel at the sort of context-free thought demanded by schools. As they move into adulthood, they begin making commitments — to occupations, to a spouse, to child rearing. Situations arise and are resolved within the context of home or work. Problems no longer are sharply defined, and answers are no longer clear. Instead of being concerned with "the facts" and the "correct" solution, adults are involved with handling ambiguous situations and understanding the implications for themselves and others (Labouvie-Vief, 1985). As developmental tasks change during adulthood, the nature of thinking and intelligence appear to change as well.

During the responsible stage of middle adulthood, people apply their intelligence to practical problems involving their fellow employees. *(Charles Harbutt/Archive)*

DOES INTELLIGENCE CHANGE WITH AGE?

A central issue in the study of adult intelligence is whether the cognitive skills measured by IQ tests change as people age. The body is physically programmed to age, so it seems only natural to assume that cognitive functions decline in the same inevitable way. About thirty years ago, most psychologists assumed that the course of cognitive development paralleled physical maturation and decline. Intellectual ability improved throughout the first two decades of life, then remained level for a number of years, only to begin a steady, inevitable decline (Labouvie-Vief, 1985).

But there were problems with this picture of

intellectual skills. First, the date of decline kept getting pushed later and later into adulthood (Schaie, 1983a). In 1916, scores indicated that IQ peaked at age sixteen; people in their late twenties had already begun to think less efficiently. In 1939, IQ seemed to peak in the late twenties; by the 1950s, IQ was rising until the early thirties. People seemed to be sharp as ever until they were about forty. Second, there was a pool of old people who continued to function at a high level long after their mental processes should have slowed if the predictions were accurate. Supreme Court justices, public officials, writers, painters, sculptors, musicians, philosophers, psychologists, architects, and actors in their seventies, eighties, and even in their nineties made important contributions to society. The quantity of their productive activity tended to decline during these later decades, but its quality seemed to remain stable (Perlmutter, in press).

Analyzing the Decline

Yet scores on psychometric measures continued to decline with age. Why were declines in test scores so consistent while the performance of many adults remained high? After reviewing the evidence, psychologists Roger Dixon and Paul Baltes (1986) concluded that intellectual development in adulthood follows three principles:

- Mechanics of mental functioning (the basic operations used to process information) decline with age, but well-practiced functions and skills stabilize or even improve.

- Older adults often fail to apply their full mental capacity, which means that they have a reserve capacity that may be drawn upon in certain situations. When they are interested, try hard, practice, or are highly motivated, their intellectual performance improves.

- When some aspects of mental functioning decline, other aspects compensate, so that drops in performance tend to be localized and much smaller than test measures would lead us to expect.

Put succinctly, intellectual functioning in middle and late adulthood depends on practice, motivation, and expertise.

This more complex picture of development means that a single IQ score is probably not a useful measure of adult intelligence. A global measure of IQ tells us very little about changes in the way people think. If various aspects of intelligence change in different ways, the same IQ score may mean different things at different ages. By looking more closely at test performance, we may get a clearer picture of what sort of decline is inevitable and why it is less debilitating than scores would indicate.

Cross-Sectional Studies In cross-sectional studies, adults' IQ scores begin a gradual drop between the age of about forty and seventy. After that time,

it becomes sharper, but not precipitous. When we look at scores more closely, it becomes apparent that not all aspects of intelligence age in the same way. Scores on the verbal scale show little decline, and some subscores remain steady or even increase. The decline seems to be concentrated in the performance, or nonverbal scale, where some subscores begin to decline early in middle age and then continue to drop across the rest of the life span. This pattern, known as the **classic aging pattern,** seems universal. It is found in men and women, in whites and blacks, in middle-class and working-class individuals (Botwinick, 1977).

Studies of fluid and crystallized intelligence also show how various components of thought follow different patterns across adulthood. Fluid intelligence scores, which reflect the mechanics of mental functioning, begin to drop early in the thirties and continue dropping across the remaining years. With each passing decade, adults do worse on abstract, nonverbal reasoning and problem solving and on tasks that require them to deal with novel information. What accounts for this decline? According to John Horn (1982), with each passing decade adults find it more difficult to organize information when they first encounter a problem. They find it more difficult to keep their attention focused on the matter at hand, and they find it more difficult to form expectations about a task.

This decline in fluid intelligence is unlikely to trouble middle-aged adults, because its loss is matched by a rise in crystallized intelligence (see Figure 16.2). Until they are about sixty-five years old, adults keep getting better at solving problems that depend on manipulating well-learned information in familiar situations. As for specific skills, adults in their early sixties do better than those in their twenties, thirties, or forties on vocabulary tests, tests that require them to understand analogies, and tests of divergent thinking. As we saw in Chapter 12, tests of divergent thinking assess original thought. Horn (1982) believes that crystallized intelligence improves in part because more information accumulates with each passing decade. Older adults have more information to draw on and seem to have organized it in a more efficient and flexible manner.

Some developmentalists still believed that cross-sectional studies were not providing an ac-

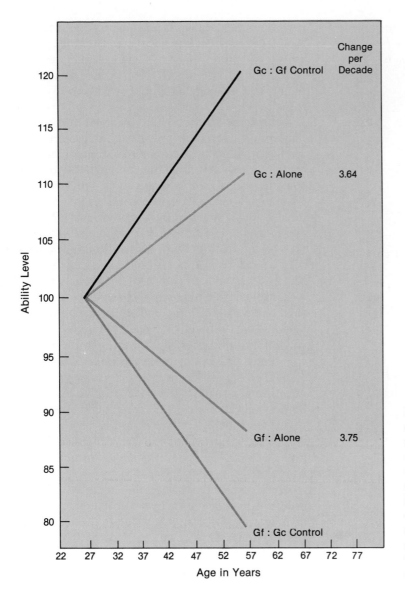

FIGURE 16.2   Aging of fluid and crystallized intelligence. Throughout middle adulthood, crystallized intelligence (Gc) rises with age, but fluid intelligence (Gf) declines. When fluid intelligence is controlled, the rise in crystallized intelligence becomes sharper; when crystallized intelligence is controlled, the drop in fluid intelligence becomes sharper. The figures to the right indicate the rise or fall in IQ points per decade. *(From Horn, 1982)*

curate picture of adult intelligence. When researchers took another look at their tests, they realized that several factors were contributing to the drops in IQ scores that appeared in virtually every study. First, each time IQ tests were restandardized, older adults had to achieve higher scores to maintain their IQs at their previous levels. Advances in education and living standards and the influence of radio, films, and television have led to more difficult IQ tests. On today's tests, a score of 114 is substantially equivalent to a score of 100 in 1937 (Flynn, 1984). Second, most IQ tests are timed, with speed affecting scores on many subtests (Willis, 1985). When ratings of intelligence rest on the speed with which answers are supplied, a slowing of perceptual speed or a tendency to deliberate over answers will lead to a drop in scores. Third, tests are standardized on groups of young adults, most of whom are either in school or fresh from their academic careers. They are accustomed to taking tests and reasoning on tasks that have been taken out of context. Adults who have not been in school for thirty or more years are unaccustomed to formal testing situations and may find it difficult to stay within the premises of the tasks.

Throughout middle adulthood, people get better at manipulating well-learned information in familiar situations; this woman is probably much better at solving crossword puzzles than she was at twenty-five. *(Michael Weisbrot & Family)*

Fourth, health, cognitive experiences, and lifestyle affect our store of information and the way we process it. Groups of middle-aged and older adults may include individuals with chronic diseases (which become more prevalent with each passing decade). Their average educational level also is probably lower than that of younger adults. More than 85 percent of today's young adults have graduated from high school; about 55 percent of adults who are fifty-five or older have completed high school (U.S. Bureau of the Census, 1986). When researchers compared groups of adults whose educational level was the same, they found almost no IQ decline until the age of sixty-five (Botwinick, 1977). Other sorts of cohort effects are also important. The world has become increas-ingly complex, and this complexity has affected the nature of education, jobs, and daily life. As we saw in Chapter 1, historical change, such as continual exposure to TV from birth, also may affect people's knowledge and thought patterns.

Longitudinal Studies These cohort differences led some researchers to wonder if longitudinal studies might not give us a more optimistic view of intelligence. They could help untangle any distortion due to cohort effects and could show changes within individuals. The most important longitudinal study, conducted by Warner Schaie (Schaie and Hertzog, 1983), was also sequential in design (see Chapter 1). It followed two groups of adults over a fourteen-year period and compared their IQ scores with those of four cross-sectional groups. Ages ranged from twenty-two to sixty-seven at the time of the first testing, and so the data cover all periods of adulthood.

Cohort differences affected scores on several of the subtests. Growing up in a younger cohort led to higher scores on tests of reasoning, verbal meaning, and space. Space and inductive reasoning both are measures of fluid intelligence, whereas verbal meaning (recognition vocabulary) is a crystallized skill. Growing up in an older cohort led to higher scores on word fluency (vocabulary retrieval).

Over a fourteen-year period, adults' IQ scores did show declines in various components, but the drop was smaller than that found in the cross-sectional groups. Cohort effects apparently magnify such declines. The longitudinal groups showed greater rises in scores during young adulthood and less decline during middle age (see Figure. 16.3). Statistically reliable declines appeared during the fifties in all cohorts, but the declines were too small to affect intellectual performance in a noticeable manner. Between the ages of forty-six and sixty, the decline amounted to only 3 IQ points. Older adults in the longitudinal study showed some decline in all subtests. Pointing out that the test used was highly speeded, Schaie speculates that much of this decline is due to a slowing in adults' ability to carry out most intellectual processes.

An important advantage of longitudinal studies is their ability to discern changes within individuals. They remind us that even if the average IQ

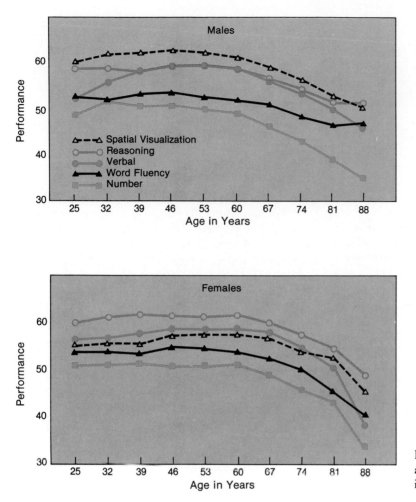

FIGURE 16.3   In longitudinal studies, aging affects different mental abilities in different ways. *(From Schaie, 1983b)*

declines during later life, many people show no drop in IQ until they are well into their seventies, and a few are in their early eighties before the first measurable decline appears (Schaie, 1984). Some of the factors that lead to IQ change during middle adulthood became clear in the California Generational Studies (Eichorn, Hunt, and Honzik, 1981). As a group, the adults in these studies showed a small increase in IQ between the age of eighteen and midlife (when they were between thirty-six and forty-eight years old). Yet some individuals showed large gains or drops in IQ. Most women and men whose IQs rose sharply during the period had either traveled extensively outside the United States, married a spouse whose IQ was at least 10 points higher than their own adolescent IQ, or both. Most men and women whose IQs declined sharply drank heavily and had serious health problems.

Terminal Drop   Some researchers have suggested that the connection between health and IQ is reflected in **terminal drop,** a critical decline in IQ scores that appears shortly before death. The drop is not related to age (time since birth); instead it is related to mortality (distance from death). It is apparently the result of physical deterioration or damage. In a longitudinal study of German men and women, the link appeared strongest among those who died before the age of sixty-five (Riegel and Riegel, 1972). In some longitudinal studies, these sharp declines appear as long as five years before death; in others, the declines are limited to the last ten months of life. Just how the declines

Their accumulated knowledge, practice in job-related skills, and deeper commitment to their work explain why professionals in their fifties and early sixties are generally more efficient than their younger co-workers. *(Robert Houser/Photo Researchers)*

affect various aspects of intelligence has not been settled. Some researchers have found the clearest drop in verbal information skills; some have found it in performance skills; others have found it in both (Botwinick, 1977). Because of these conflicting results, the concept of terminal drop remains controversial.

Compensating for IQ Declines

Do the changes that appear in the scores of most middle-aged and older adults have a significant effect on their lives? Unless an individual has some debilitating disease, declines in the mechanics of intelligence are small. Until late in life, they have little perceptible effect on people's ability to solve most of the problems that they encounter. After reviewing more than a dozen studies, researchers concluded that most workers, especially those in the professions, tend to become more efficient on the job as they age (Waldman and Avolio, 1983). They are as accurate as younger adults and tend to work more steadily. They have fewer accidents and are absent less often (Stagner, 1985). In one study of the printing industry, efficiency and accuracy peaked among workers in their fifties, then declined slightly among workers past the age of sixty — except for one group (Clay, 1956). Proofreaders in their sixties were still more accurate and productive than workers in their twenties and thirties.

This productive performance on the job relies on the qualities already mentioned: practice, motivation, and expertise. Older employees are more involved in their work and more committed to their organization than younger employees. In addition, skills related to an activity that has been thoroughly mastered, whether related to occupation or hobbies, often continue to improve (Perlmutter, in press). Such improvement may be related to an efficiently organized knowledge base and the earlier development of strategic, job-related skills.

Finally, adults may acquire new, compensating skills that prevent deterioration in performance after the mechanics of thinking have slowed. For example, reaction time is a component of typing skill. When their reaction time is tested, older typists are slower than younger typists. Yet they type just as fast as the young. Studies have shown that older typists compensate for their slowed reactions by looking farther ahead in the material they are copying than younger typists do (Salthouse, 1984). When researchers arrange the material so that typists cannot see ahead, the speed of older typists drops, but the younger typists are as fast as ever. Performance in decision making also shows no decline. Older bridge players may take longer to bid a hand, and older chess players may deliberate longer before moving a piece on the board, but both play as well as younger adults do (Charness, 1985).

Aspects of Intellectual Change

Our picture of intelligence across adulthood is not a simple one. Three views of adult intelligence have been common among developmentalists. Some have proposed that intelligence becomes more highly developed in adults; some have proposed that it tends to remain stable throughout life; and some have proposed that it declines. Each view is too simple. A more accurate picture would be to say that all three notions accurately describe the process, with the combination varying from one person to another. The pattern of intellectual change seems almost as complex as thinking processes themselves.

A helpful way to look at adult intelligence is in terms of four conceptions suggested by Roger Dixon and Paul Baltes (1986). They propose that the development of intelligence in adulthood is (1) multidimensional, (2) multidirectional, and characterized by (3) interindividual variability and (4) intraindividual plasticity. Adult intelligence is multidimensional because it is composed of many separate mental abilities. Each of these abilities may have its own distinct structure, function, and possibility for change. Adult intelligence is multidirectional because each of these abilities may follow its own pattern of progress, stability, or decline. Adult intelligence is characterized by interindividual variability, because the pattern of developmental process differs from one individual to the next. Finally, adult intelligence shows intraindividual plasticity, because throughout life people are adaptable. They can change their way of approaching and solving problems. They can acquire new information, develop new strategies, and perfect old ones.

HOW HEALTH AND LIFE STYLE AFFECT COGNITION

When well into this eighties, British philosopher Bertrand Russell had a long discussion of technical mathematics with three mathematicians. Afterward, one of them said, "It was not merely that his brain was beautifully clear for somebody of eighty-seven; it was beautifully clear for anybody at any age" (Clark, 1975, p. 549). The example of exceptional older people has led some developmentalists to conclude that cognitive decline is not an inevitable accompaniment of age. In Schaie's (1984) longitudinal study, nearly half the subjects showed no decline of any kind over a fourteen-year period that took many of them into their seventies. Because of such findings, researchers have looked for the factors that affect cognition during adulthood. Earlier we noted that education seems to be one such factor. Personality, lifestyle, and chronic disease appear to be other important factors.

How does personality affect the way we think? Research indicates that personality patterns may affect cognitive functioning in highly stressful situations. Some people are highly competitive, hostile when thwarted, and behave as if they were always racing the clock. Others are relaxed and give no indication that they feel the pressure of time. In most situations, the clock racers (known as *Type A's*) are highly productive and frequently outperform the relaxed *Type B's*. But in highly stressful situations, Type A people seem to have a strong need to maintain control, and this can get them into trouble (Glass, 1977). In one study, Type A's and Type B's solved a group of problems, thinking out loud as they worked at the solutions (Brunson and Matthews, 1981). After they had completed the problems, they began work on a second set. But this time the problems were unsolvable. As they struggled with one unsolvable problem after another, Type A's became increasingly frustrated and annoyed. They said that the test was too hard and that they lacked the ability to handle it. Instead of trying new attacks, they gave up and kept producing the same incorrect answer even though the researchers had said that it was wrong. Type B's responded in a completely different manner. They seemed unhappy and bored, but they were not angry. Instead, they kept trying to find a solution and seemed to think that they would eventually succeed.

Lifestyles also have an important influence on adult cognition. They can predict the course of IQ in later adulthood. Schaie (1984) has found that middle-aged people whose lives are high in environmental stimulation, especially those who continue to pursue educational interests, generally retain their intellectual abilities during later adulthood. Apparently, the complexity of a person's environment is related to the absence of cognitive decline. Those who are engaged in intellectually stimulating work, for example, continue to develop their mental abilities. Those who assume management positions during young adulthood continue to show increases in IQ throughout middle adulthood (Willis, 1985).

Some researchers have suggested that intelligence may begin to decline when adults retire and withdraw from full participation in the economic and social life of the society (Labouvie-Vief, 1985). In Schaie's study, large declines in IQ were associated with being poor, socially isolated, widowed or divorced, and having stopped working (Gribbin, Schaie, and Parham, 1980). The sharpest drops were among women living in relatively inaccessible environments who withdrew from social activities after being widowed. Adults who retained a highly active lifestyle, full of social and

Adults who embark on a regular exercise program generally find that it improves their reaction time, attention span, and memory. *(Herve Donnezan/Rapho/ Photo Researchers)*

intellectual activity, performed best on IQ tests.

Exercise also seems to foster mental fitness. The reaction time of young adults who are out of shape resembles that of older adults. Yet when these unfit adults embark on a vigorous exercise program, their reaction times improve considerably (Tweit, Gollnick, and Hearn, 1963). Other studies have shown a similar connection between exercise and cognition in older adults (Wiswell, 1980). Those who are in poor condition have slower reaction times, more trouble paying attention, and poorer memories than older adults who have kept in shape.

Why should exercise have any effect on cognition? Exercise seems to relieve anxiety and reduce tension. In one study, walking for fifteen minutes

gave more effective relief to highly anxious men than a dose of tranquilizers (deVries and Adams, 1972). Regular exercise also reduces blood pressure and improves the condition of the circulatory system. It reduces cholesterol levels, causes an increase in the number of red blood cells, and improves the condition of blood vessels around the heart.

The effect of exercise on blood pressure and the circulatory system is especially important, because some researchers have found a connection between these factors and IQ declines. In one study, young adults with high blood pressure had lower IQ scores than either young or middle-aged adults with normal blood pressure (Schultz, Elias, Robbins, Streeten, and Blakeman, 1986). When the middle-aged adults were retested after a lapse of six years, those with normal blood pressure showed an increase on the verbal scale and stable scores on the performance scale. The hypertensive adults had stable scores on both scales. Although these adults had high blood pressure, they had no other physical ailments.

Other studies have connected cardiovascular disease with declines in the ability to solve problems that require formal-operational reasoning (La Rue and Jarvik, 1982). Middle-aged and older adults tried to solve the pendulum problem (see Chapter 13) and two other Piagetian tests of formal reasoning as well as analogous practical tasks. Age had no effect on scores, but health did. Researchers also have found an association between cognition and kidney function (Osberg, Mears, McKee, and Burnett, 1982). Kidney disease, kidney failure, and the need for dialysis were associated with intellectual decline.

The close relation between health and intellectual functioning was apparent among adults who took part in a twenty-one-year longitudinal study of aging at Duke University (Manton, Siegler, and Woodbury, 1986). Long after the close of the study, when most of the participants had died, researchers divided them into five groups on the basis of their past scores on IQ subtests and other cognitive variables, including memory and reaction time. Those whose scores were lowest tended to have high blood pressure and to be in the poorest health. Those whose scores were highest tended to have the best physical and mental health. Other factors that affected cognitive functioning

Women and men of all ages enroll in adult education courses, and most of these returning students have above-average incomes and education. *(Will McIntyre/ Photo Researchers)*

were race, education, and socioeconomic status. Age itself was not important.

Among healthy adults, education and a highly active life style appear to be the best defense against declining intelligence in middle and late adulthood. Perhaps the current popularity of physical fitness programs and increased enrollments in adult education will increase the proportion of older adults whose IQs remain stable.

ADULT EDUCATION

Anyone who doubts the popularity of adult education need only drop by a community college or public high school on a weekday evening. Courses are offered in everything from gourmet cooking, yoga, and obedience training for dogs to psychology, computer science, and economics. As a society, the United States seems to have switched from viewing education as a vaccine (a large dose during childhood and adolescence provides immunity against the need for further learning) to viewing education as a lifelong learning process (Birren and Woodruff, 1973). Participation in formal adult education classes provides a potent stimulus for intraindividual changes in intelligence.

The return to school should not be surprising, because more than a decade ago, people in their early thirties told researchers about their dissatisfaction with the state of their knowledge (Flanagan and Russ-Eft, 1976). Only 54 percent of these adults were satisfied with the development of their minds and the knowledge they had accumulated through formal schooling and experience. In every other area of their lives, their satisfaction was much higher.

Who enrolls in adult education? Women and men of every age can be found in these classes, but the majority are young and middle-aged adults with higher than average income and education. At least 12 percent of adults take part in such courses; participation drops sharply after the age of fifty-five. Only 4.5 percent of adults in late middle age and older groups are enrolled (Willis, 1985). Because completion of high school seems to be the marker of further interest in education, experts are predicting that enrollments will increase in the over-fifty-five group as soon as more highly educated cohorts reach late middle age (Birren and Woodruff, 1973).

The Adult Student's Objectives

Adults have many reasons for returning to school, and their goals shift slightly with age. In a study of community college students, younger adults emphasized their desire to get a job, a general education, and more money (Daniel, Templin, and Shearon, 1977). Older adults who were enrolled in courses for credit saw contributing to society as their primary goal, followed closely by becoming a more cultured person and earning more money. Older adults in noncredit courses were intent on learning interesting things, meeting interesting people, and contributing to society. In most cases, students had more than one reason for coming back to school.

Few studies of the middle-aged adult's educational goals exist, but Sherry Willis (1985) has suggested four broad objectives that are related to occupational and personal development. Many adults are preparing themselves for second careers. Some are individuals who have worked in occupations that provide early retirement: armed forces personnel, police officers, firefighters, or airline pilots. They are in their forties or fifties and are not ready to withdraw from the world of work. Some are victims of "burnout." They have lost all interest in their present occupation, often because it requires an intense emotional involvement or the daily grappling with overwhelming problems. Burnout is fairly common among nurses and mental health counselors (Stagner, 1985). Some are women who are entering the labor market after spending fifteen or twenty years rearing children. These women often enroll in regular college classes to begin or complete an interrupted education. Finally, some are workers displaced by basic changes in the American economy. Former steelworkers, oilfield employees, farmers, and middle managers enroll in courses that train them for new jobs.

A second educational objective is combating technological or sociocultural obsolescence. This goal may be occupational. Physicians or other professionals return to school in order to keep abreast of changes that affect their work. For others, the training may be provided or subsidized by their employers. Business and industry provide education for more adults than colleges and universities. Workers whose factories have been automated are retrained to handle robot-dominated assembly lines. Office workers who have been using automatic typewriters and calculators learn to operate information-processing equipment. Some corporations subsidize university classes. For example,

Harvard, Stanford, and MIT each provide a three-month course in advanced management for bankers and other mid-level executives in their forties. The course, which is paid for by employers, prepares these men and women to climb the corporate ladder. In 1986, seventy-three universities provided some sort of management education for executives, and about 15,000 middle-aged American executives were enrolled in the courses (Wayne, 1986).

Sometimes the struggle against obsolescence is motivated by the need to survive. Rapidly changing technology can create knowledge gaps that are wide enough to make daily life difficult. When every corner of existence has been invaded by the computer chip, and stories on the evening news routinely refer to missile "throw-weights," genetic codes, and the workings of the immune system, adults may find that yesterday's educational level no longer equips them to handle the practical problems of life.

A third educational objective is the generation of satisfactory retirement roles. In this instance, the goal is personal satisfaction instead of economic gain. Adults enroll in courses that help them to develop leisure pursuits after retirement. Some are acquiring skills and information that help them to serve as semiprofessional volunteers in the human services. Others are developing hobbies and other leisure interests.

Finally, understanding the biological and psychological changes of adulthood may become an important objective of many older adults. Through human history, adults have taken the aging process for granted, accepting the physical and cognitive changes that they assumed were inevitable. As we shall see in Chapter 18, researchers have developed ways of teaching cognitive strategies that may stave off or reverse declines in learning, memory tasks, or problem solving.

The Problem of Adult Illiteracy

Not everything in the field of adult education is coming up roses. In recent years, concern has mounted about the rate of adult illiteracy in the United States. Among 158 countries that belong to the United Nations, the United States ranks forty-ninth in the literacy rate. That figure is likely to get

LEARNING THE ELDERHOSTEL WAY

Sometimes adults in their early sixties wish to return to school but are not interested in preparing for a second career or pursuing a degree. For them, colleges and universities across the country have developed a series of inexpensive, short-term courses meant to challenge the older adult and expose him or her to new ideas. The concept is called *Elderhostel,* because it is a combination of adult education and hosteling. Students live in campus dorms and eat in college dining halls. Regular faculty members teach the courses, which run from one to three weeks. The first Elderhostel program was offered by five New Hampshire colleges in 1975; 220 adults enrolled. By 1982, the program had expanded to all fifty states, and enrollment had reached 55,000.

Elderhostel programs have been popular because they offer adults change, a chance to travel, and the opportunity to develop new interests and catch up on old ones. Who enrolls in these courses? Most students have been to college: in one survey only 10 percent had never attended college, and the majority had a graduate degree or a professional background (*AARP News Bulletin,* 1983). The majority are in their late sixties and have an income that is above the average for retired individuals. About two-thirds are

women. People who attend seem to enjoy the experience; nearly 60 percent in one study had attended at least one previous Elderhostel session (Romaniuk and Romaniuk, 1982).

The motivation of first-timers and experienced Elderhostelers is somewhat different. First-timers are attracted by the experience of living on campus, getting to know new people, and the chance of a change in daily routines. For experienced Elderhostelers, the major motives are traveling to new places and learning something new (Romaniuk and Romaniuk, 1982).

Who profits most from the Elderhostel experience? In a study of 900 Elderhostelers, Michael Brady (*AARP News Bulletin,* 1983) found that the least typical students seemed to get the most out of the courses. Those with less education and lower incomes were extremely enthusiastic, as were older students. Those in their seventies and eighties appreciated the courses more than students in their sixties.

No matter what the Elderhosteler's background or motives, attendance is likely to foster mental fitness and reduce the chances of intellectual decline.

larger, because the high-school dropout rate is increasing.

How bad is the situation? Estimates vary. The U.S. Census Bureau (1986) reports that between 17 million and 21 million adults, or approximately 13 percent of the population, are illiterate. Jonathan Kozol (1985) claims that the correct figure is 60 million adults, or approximately one-third of the population. No one is certain just how many illiterate adults actually live in the United States, and the guesses depend on whether we look at completely illiterate people, who cannot read or write at all, or at **functional illiterates,** people who lack the basic reading and writing skills required for productive performance in American society.

Functional illiteracy has had almost as many

definitions as people who have written about the topic. Because there is little agreement about the minimum skill required for literacy, national assessments of reading ability have deemphasized literacy and begun to describe levels of literacy. Virtually all individuals who stay in school until they are thirteen years old have a rudimentary literacy and can read well enough to follow simple directions, as we saw in Chapter 12. If functional literacy is limited to reading simple newspaper articles, signs, newspaper ads, TV listings, recipes, and catalogue order blanks, 94.5 percent meet the test. But if we require people to read and understand long stories or articles, only 83.6 percent of those who are still in school at the age of seventeen are functionally literate (National Assessment of Educational Progress, 1985). Unless they can read at this level, they cannot profit from vocational education.

One major problem is that not everyone stays in high school until the age of seventeen. Those who drop out are often those who cannot read at all or, at best, can manage to puzzle out the program listings in *TV Guide*. At least a third of the illiterate are more than sixty years old and may have grown up in states that had no compulsory education laws (Deigh, 1986). Many of the rest come from poverty areas, such as the inner cities or Appalachia. But some are working-class adults who struggled for a while and then dropped out. There is Hal, a Yonkers plumber with three children, who refused to go into a store unless a family member accompanied him. He couldn't read the labels on merchandise, couldn't write a check, couldn't even draw money out of his bank account. Hal quit

school at the end of junior high school because the other youngsters teased him for his inability to read. He hid his illiteracy on the job by asking other people to read the blueprints with him. He refused to answer a telephone at work because he might have to write down a message. Hal entered an adult literacy program for adults with normal IQs and is learning to read (Spear, 1985).

After surveying the research on intelligence in adulthood, what can we expect of our cognitive powers as we move through middle age and approach later adulthood? What seems clear is that we have some control over what happens to us. If we can stay healthy, keep active, and continue to use our minds, we are unlikely to experience major cognitive declines. Werner Schaie and Sherry Willis (1986) summed up the typical pattern of cognition across adulthood by saying, "Those who live by their wits die with their wits."

SUMMARY

1. Most research on adult intellectual development explores either psychometric intelligence or pragmatic intelligence. Psychometric studies trace intelligence across adulthood through performance on IQ tests and rest on few assumptions about the nature of thought or its development. Pragmatic studies grow out of the view that the process of adapting to the environment is an active, lifelong process. They take a contextual view of intelligence, in which intelligence is demonstrated by the application of knowledge, expertise, and experience to problems of daily life. The **dual-process model** of intelligence draws on both these traditions. In this model, the **mechanics of intelligence,** which are basic information-processing operations, can be measured through psychometric tests of fluid abilities, but only some aspects of the **pragmatics of intelligence** can be measured through psychometric tests of crystallized abilities.

2. Some researchers have proposed that adult cognitive development may include a stage that goes beyond formal operations: the stage of

dialectical operations. Adults who reach this stage are able to accept contradictions and integrate conflicting viewpoints. In another view of adult cognition, development through adolescence consists of stages that reflect increasingly efficient ways of acquiring new information; they can be encompassed in a single **acquisitive stage.** Adult cognition consists of stages that reflect different ways of using information. In the **achieving stage** of young adulthood, knowledge is applied toward starting families and reaching occupational goals. In the **responsible stage** of middle adulthood, knowledge is used to fulfill family and occupational obligations. In the **executive stage** of middle adulthood (which not all attain), knowledge is used to manage organizations. In the **reintegrative stage** of late adulthood, knowledge is used to fulfill personal interests. Passage from one stage to another is determined by developmental tasks, not by age.

3. Adult intellectual development appears to follow three principles: (1) a decline in the speed and efficiency of the mechanics of mental func-

tioning, which can be partly offset by practice; (2) a failure to apply full mental capacity, which can be partly offset by motivation; (3) a further compensation for declining functions by the development of expertise. Cross-sectional studies reflect the **classic aging pattern** of development: scores on fluid abilities (mechanics) begin to decline in middle adulthood, but scores on crystallized abilities (knowledge) continue to rise until later adulthood. Some of the decline in test scores may be due to the requirements of the test, cohort differences, or health problems. Longitudinal studies show greater increases in young adulthood and smaller declines in middle adulthood. Test scores of older adults may be affected by **terminal drop,** a decline in IQ scores that in some studies appears shortly before death.

4. Personality may affect intellectual functioning in stressful situations, with highly competitive, clock-racing individuals becoming so frustrated and annoyed that they quit trying. Lifestyle affects intellectual functioning; adults who live in a stimulating environment and pursue educational interests tend to retain a high level of functioning, whereas those who withdraw from life tend to show declines. Exercise affects intellectual functioning, and those in poor condition show slowed reaction times, attention problems, and poor memories. Cardiovascular and kidney disease are connected with intellectual decline.

5. The majority of those enrolled in adult education classes are young and middle-aged adults with above average incomes and education. The adult who returns to school is usually working toward at least one of four goals: (1) preparing for a second career; (2) combating technological or socio-cultural obsolescence; (3) establishing satisfactory retirement roles; (4) understanding the biological and psychological changes of adulthood. Approximately 13 percent of the population may be illiterate, but up to one-third may be **functional illiterates,** who lack the reading and writing skills necessary for productive performance.

KEY TERMS

achieving stage
acquisitive stage
classic aging pattern
dialectical operations

dual-process model
executive stage
functional illiterate
mechanics of intelligence

pragmatics of intelligence
reintegrative stage
responsible stage
terminal drop

STUDY TERMS

classic aging pattern   A typical pattern of changes in IQ scores with age, in which scores on verbal (or crystallized) abilities either remain steady or increase, while scores on performance (or fluid) abilities begin to decline in early middle-age.

dialectical operations   A fifth stage of adult cognitive development that goes beyond Piaget's stage of formal operations; an individual in this stage no longer seeks mental equilibrium but accepts contradiction as the basis of thought and development.

dual-process model   A view of cognition, in which intellectual functioning consists of the basic cognitive skills **(mechanics of intelligence)** and the procedures that relate these skills, stored knowledge, and expertise to daily life **(pragmatics of intelligence).**

terminal drop   A noticeable drop in IQ scores that appears shortly before death and is apparently the result of physical deterioration or damage.

CHAPTER 17

Middle Adulthood: Making the Most of It

448

As Susan reaches age forty, she is engrossed in her work and her horizons are continuing to expand. She feels good about herself and thinks that she is more attractive than she used to be. Her undergraduate switch from journalism to psychology steered her into social work, and she finds it absorbing. She has a master's degree, which she financed by working for a year after graduation. After several love affairs and a live-in relationship with a young lawyer, which broke up when their goals and values clashed, Susan married a thirty-two-year-old engineer who works for a small corporation. When her first baby was born, Susan — then thirty-three — stayed at home for a year before going back to work part time. Five years ago, when her second baby was born, she stopped working for six months. Now that her younger child is in kindergarten, she has a new sense of freedom and is thinking of further training so that she can become a family therapist.

On the edge of middle age, forty-year-old Scott is a lawyer with a small private firm. After several unhappy years of high-pressure work with a big law firm in the city, he became a partner in a small, suburban firm near his home. The switch has made him a more relaxed, happier man. Scott is married to Samantha, another lawyer, who is three years younger than he. They lived together for two years before they were married. The decision to formalize their relationship came four years ago, when they decided to have a child. Although they are both absorbed in their careers, they get great satisfaction from their family life and have decided to have another baby.

At forty, Donna has been working full time for twelve years and runs the office of a local insurance agent. She is still married to Pete, her high-school sweetheart, and this year they are celebrating their twentieth wedding anniversary. On high-school graduation, Donna got a job in the office of a department store. When the first of her three children was born, she quit her job, but within a year she was doing part-time office work. Although Pete is a construction worker and makes good money when he works, he is often laid off. In order to make the mortgage payments, Donna kept working part time, taking only a few weeks off at the birth of her last two children. As soon as her third child was a year old, she started working full time. Donna hopes to send her daughter to the local college when she graduates from high school next year. She is satisfied with her marriage but, as with most of her friends, her social life centers around family gatherings and her women friends.

David, now forty, has been working steadily for the state department of transportation for the past ten years. His life has settled into a pattern. When he was twenty, his girlfriend became pregnant, and they married. But the marriage didn't last; in two years, they divorced. David still sees his son and contributes money each month to his support. At twenty-seven, David remarried, and his attitude toward work changed. He began looking for a solid job with benefits and retirement; he has worked his way up to foreman of a state road district. He has begun to put on weight, but it doesn't seem to bother him. David and his second wife, who is now thirty-three, have two children. Denise works as a receptionist in the office of a pediatrician, and they have saved enough money to think of buying a house.

In this chapter, we examine the developmental tasks that Susan, Scott, Donna, and David will encounter during the years that stretch before them. In many ways, the midlife years, from forty to sixty-five, are the most satisfying part of the life span. In today's affluent society, the majority of middle-aged adults are healthy and financially secure. Living through their period of maximum productivity and maximum rewards, they are part of "the command generation," the group that controls American society. We begin with recent social changes that have affected the experience of middle age in American society, then examine the changes in appearance, body function, and sexuality that accompany middle adulthood. Returning to the theories we discussed in Chapter 15, we see what sort of picture they paint of middle age. After exploring self-concept and self-esteem in midlife, we discover how men's and women's occupational lives differ at this period. The rest of the chapter is devoted to the family. In the section on marriage, we focus on changes in marital satisfaction and the sexual relationship, then examine midlife trends in divorce and remarriage. Parenthood at midlife, we find, can take three different paths: the birth of the first baby, the nurturance of adolescents, and the adjustment to the empty nest. Next we look at the middle-aged adult's relationship with his or her own parents and close with an exploration of what it means to become a grandparent.

SOCIAL CHANGE

As we near the close of the twentieth century, the nature of middle age is changing in this country. Fifty years ago, people in their forties and fifties looked "middle aged." Gray hair, a "middle-aged spread," a sedate lifestyle, and "mature" clothes set most of them apart from younger adults. Today, many still seem young. They are healthier, more physically active, and more attractive than their parents and grandparents were at the same age. When journalist Gloria Steinem reached fifty, an interviewer said that she didn't "look fifty." Steinem, who was born in 1934, replied, "This is what fifty looks like."

At midlife, most of today's couples are at an earlier stage of family development than their parents and grandparents were. Delayed marriage and childbearing postpone the time when children leave home, especially among the middle class. Parents tend to be older when their first-born leaves the nest, yet younger when the last-born departs. Because couples are having fewer children, the period of life devoted to childrearing has been curtailed for today's adults. When the nest begins to empty, it does so rapidly, perhaps in the space of two or three years, and parents get less time to adjust to the change. Working-class couples who have limited the size of their families but have not postponed parenthood may be in their mid-forties when their last child departs, a time when their grandparents and great-grandparents might have been anticipating the birth of their last child. Because we spend a greater proportion of the life span as a couple, the marital relationship takes on new importance and is subject to new stresses. In fact, Erik Erikson (Erikson and Hall, 1987) has suggested that the prospect of sixty years of married life may have played an important role in the growing tendency to divorce and remarry.

Fewer people die in middle adulthood, and the consequent rise in the proportion of older Americans means that today's middle-aged parents are likely to have living parents themselves and perhaps even grandparents. Unlike their mothers, few women today are widowed during middle age, although they are more likely than their mothers to be single, divorced, divorcing, or cohabiting. The rate of remarriage among middle-aged women has dropped since their mothers' day. At that time, the marriage rate among middle-aged widows was 16.5 per thousand, and among divorced women, it was 45.8 per thousand (U.S. Bureau of the Census, 1986). Today, middle-aged widows are marrying at the rate of 12 per thousand and middle-aged divorced women at the rate of 31.3 per thousand. The divorced or widowed male is more likely than his female counterpart to remarry during middle age—and to marry a younger woman. Some men are starting new families at a time when the nest is emptying for most men and women.

The world outside the home also has changed for people in middle adulthood. They are better educated. In 1970, just over half of adults older than twenty-five had completed high school. By 1984, three-quarters of those in middle adulthood had completed high school, and an increasing proportion of them had been to college (U.S. Bureau of the Census, 1986). As we saw in Chapter 16, many middle-aged adults are going back to school,

Men who are divorced or widowed during middle age are more likely than their female counterparts to remarry. *(Charles Feil/Stock, Boston)*

to prepare themselves either for occupational changes, or in the case of many women, for entry into the labor market. More middle-aged women are employed, either because they have always worked or because they are returning to the labor market as their children reach school age. Many farmers, factory workers, and miners whose occupations are evaporating have enrolled in vocational courses geared to high-technology jobs.

With the first wave of the post-World War II baby boom entering middle adulthood, differences can be seen between those who have entered their fifties and those who have just left young adulthood. Men and women in their fifties tend to be doing well, but many of those in their early forties are discovering that they will not live better than their parents and may not do nearly so well. Their parents and grandparents saw their real income increase sharply after the age of thirty, and they spent only about $15 on mortgage payments out of every $100 they earned. In contrast, the average man in his early forties has seen no increase in real income since he turned thirty, and he spends about $44 out of every $100 earned on mortgage payments (Thomas, 1986). Yet men and women in their early forties feel that they have freedom to do what they wish with their lives.

PHYSICAL CHANGES

During midlife, people begin to notice obvious changes in the way their bodies look and work. All the little changes that began in early adulthood progress steadily, and they force adults to realize that they are no longer young. The realization is unsettling, and it leads most to look backward, wishing that they could recapture their youthful appearance and vigor. The face that looks back at them from the mirror clearly has a few wrinkles, the skin no longer stretches so tightly over the body, the hair may thin and begin to gray.

In a culture that emphasizes youth, we might expect middle-aged women and men to be less happy about themselves and their physical appearance than younger adults are. Yet body image appears to be stable. People older than forty-five report just as much overall satisfaction with their bodies as do people younger than forty-five (Berscheid, Walster, and Bohrnstedt, 1973). Women do become concerned with their faces. Concern about facial attractiveness peaks in middle age. Women regard facial traces of aging as affecting their general attractiveness. Men are less concerned about their general attractiveness, and with good reason: both women and men say that age enhances a man's attractiveness (Nowak, 1977).

Functional Changes

Even if middle-aged adults can deny the visible traces of age, they cannot escape other signs. Their muscles do not work as strongly, as quickly, or as long as they used to, in part because muscle mass begins to shrink after people reach the age of forty. At least part of this shrinkage is the result of a less

active life; regular exercise in midlife can increase lean body mass (Buskirk, 1985). Muscle shrinkage is accompanied by that increase in fat known as "middle-aged spread."

Yet these early declines in muscle strength and speed of reaction have only marginal significance for most people's everyday life. They are not likely to be bothered much by these losses, because they have learned to compensate for them (Belbin, 1967). Daily life is not affected, because by paying attention to the features of various tasks, people discover how they can maintain or even improve their performance in the face of changing physical abilities. They may begin to carry only two bags of groceries at a time instead of four. At work, they may avoid jobs that depend on speed and instead look for jobs in which they can work at their own pace.

During middle age, many people, especially men, become concerned about their health. This worry has some basis, because the incidence of chronic and life-threatening illness rises during the middle years. The most common major disorders in otherwise healthy, middle-aged Americans are overweight, hypertension, and arthritis (Weg, 1983). The incidence of hypertension increases markedly in the mid-forties; about 15 percent of women and 21 percent of men between the ages of forty-five and fifty-four are hypertensive (U.S. Bureau of the Census, 1982). Midlife also marks the appearance of "maturity-onset diabetes," a form of diabetes in which the body produces normal levels of insulin, but the individual's tissues have become insensitive to it. During middle adulthood, the death rate begins to increase, and it accelerates as people approach the age of sixty. The most common cause of death in these years is heart disease, followed by cancer and stroke.

Yet more than three-quarters of middle-aged Americans have no chronic health problems and no limitations on their daily activities (U.S. Bureau of the Census, 1982). Despite their weakened immune systems, people between the ages of forty-five and sixty-four retain their resistance to diseases that they already have encountered. This, together with changes in lifestyle, means that middle-aged adults have fewer bouts of acute illness (infections, respiratory and digestive disease) than young adults.

Sexuality is still an important part of marriage for the majority of middle-aged couples. *(Chuck Fishman/Woodfin Camp & Associates)*

Not all the physical changes that we connect with middle age are necessary or due to the normal processes of aging. Some are due to disease. Some are due to abuse: smoking, alcohol, drugs, poor nutrition, and stress cause bodily deterioration. Some are due to disuse: regular exercise can maintain muscular strength and endurance, increase joint mobility, retard changes in the cardiovascular and respiratory systems, reduce obesity, and slow or prevent the bone loss of osteoporosis (deVries, 1983). By establishing good health habits, people can decrease their susceptibility to the physical changes of midlife. Good nutrition, exercise, a decrease in alcohol consumption, the elimination of cigarettes, and the avoidance of direct sunlight can retard many of the expected changes in health and appearance.

Sex and Sexuality in the Middle Years

Changes in the reproductive system provide women with the medical marker of middle age: **menopause,** or the cessation of menstruation. Before the menstrual cycle ceases, periods may become shorter, irregular, and farther apart. When women are about fifty, menstruation stops altogether. Ovulation and reproductive capacity have ended. Because menopause signals the end of reproductive capacity and youth, popular wisdom

says that menopause must be a psychological crisis. A menopausal woman, in the popular mind, is irritable, nervous, and depressed. She has headaches or backaches and is always tired. Psychology and physiology are so intertwined that women who believe the myths about menopause may have a difficult time. Yet the notion that menopause is a developmental crisis is clearly wrong. From a developmental standpoint, menopause no longer signifies a "change of life." At fifty, women view their childbearing years as far behind them, and so there is no major discontinuity in their lives.

Some women dread menopause, but once they enter it, most discover that the discomfort is minor. The only symptoms of menopause that are consistently reported by women are hot flashes and sweating; these seem to affect from 75 to 85 percent of women (Harman and Talbert, 1985; Notman, 1980). Many of the symptoms popularly associated with menopause (nervousness, irritability, headaches, depression) are not found among all women or all societies. In addition, a woman may attribute almost any midlife physiological disturbance to menopause, whether there is any real connection or not. Things quickly improve, even for those who find the phase uncomfortable. Studies indicate that postmenopausal women typically feel better, more confident, and freer than before they entered menopause (Neugarten, Wood, Kraines, and Loomis, 1963).

At menopause, the body's production of female sex hormones (estrogen and progesterone) drops off to a negligible level. Afterward, a woman's risk of heart disease increases, and her bones may lose calcium, leading to osteoporosis. Estrogen replacement therapy prevents bone loss, reduces the risk of heart disease by 60 percent, and eliminates hot flashes in most women. For a time, physicians were reluctant to prescribe estrogen therapy, in the belief that it increased the likelihood of uterine cancer. It now seems that low doses of estrogen, given on a cyclic basis, and supplemented with progestin do not increase the risk (Harman and Talbert, 1985).

Unlike women, men at midlife do not lose their reproductive ability. During the forties, sperm production declines in some men, but recent research indicates no change in sperm count among healthy men of proven fertility (Nieschlag, Lammers, Freischem, and Wicklings, 1982).

How do these physiological changes affect sexual response? Many women find that vaginal lubrication tends to be slower and less intense and that the vagina is less elastic, leading to discomfort during intercourse. Estrogen therapy may alleviate this condition, as does an artificial lubricant. Regular sexual activity also seems to slow vaginal atrophy, perhaps because it is associated with higher estrogen levels in postmenopausal women (Leiblum, Bachmann, Kemmann, Colburn, and Swartzman, 1983). Although the intensity and duration of women's sexual response is reduced by age, the hormonal decreases of menopause generally cause only slight inconvenience.

The major change in a man's sexual response is in its speed. Men are slower to be aroused, slower to climax, and do not necessarily feel the urge to climax at every sexual encounter. Slowed physical arousal characterized the middle-aged men in one study, in which their penile responsiveness was measured while they watched erotic movies (Solnick and Birren, 1977). Among fifty-year-olds, penile diameter increased about six times more slowly than among men in their twenties. However, an older man can retain an erection for much longer than a younger man, primarily because it takes him longer to climax. Middle-aged men find that they need more direct stimulation to become aroused and that, after a climax, they require more time before they can be aroused again. These changes in sexual response affect the nature of the sexual experience but do not decrease its pleasure.

In the absence of major health problems (such as diabetes), loss of sexual responsiveness is likely to be due to psychological factors, not physiological ones. Men are more susceptible than women to such losses, and their incidence of sexual inadequacy rises sharply after the age of fifty. An important factor in reduced sexual responsiveness among middle-aged men appears to be the monotony of a repetitious sexual relationship (Masters and Johnson, 1974). Other factors may reduce a man's sexual interest or responsiveness. He may be so preoccupied with work that he has no physical or mental energy for sex. Overindulgence in food or alcohol can also leave him "too tired" for sex. Finally, a man may avoid sex because he fears impotence. If he finds himself unable to respond on one occasion because of fatigue and alcohol, he may start avoiding sex because he is afraid of another failure.

The majority of middle-aged men and women continue to be both interested in sex and sexually active. Among adults between the ages of forty-six and fifty, 90 percent of the men and 70 percent of the women expressed moderate to strong sexual interest (Pfeiffer and Davis, 1972). In general, the richer and more regular an individual's sex life has been, the more likely it is that his or her sexual interest and activity will be maintained throughout the middle years.

THEORIES AND ISSUES OF MIDDLE ADULTHOOD

Being middle-aged means being part of the age group that runs society and therefore means being in power, in command, and responsible. The middle years are characterized by a concern with expanding and asserting our adulthood and sometimes with developing a new way of life. As people enter middle adulthood, most find their energies focused on different issues. Yet some changes are related more closely to life circumstances than to chronological age, and so many middle-aged adults, such as those with young children, still are absorbed with some tasks of early adulthood. Other issues of middle adulthood, such as the acceptance of physical limitations and the prospect of mortality, are common to all adults. As they deal with the realization that life will end, individuals develop an increasing sense of not having enough time to do most of the things that they want to do.

There is often personal turmoil in the middle years. Yet when life changes are expected and occur on time, these years are fairly stable in terms of an individual's identity, coping capacities, influence, and productivity. Once people resolve their uncertainties about their past and future, life tends to become mellow. By returning to the theories we explored in Chapter 15, we can trace the way motivations tend to change as adults deal with their new developmental tasks.

Erikson's Psychosocial Theory

When people move into middle adulthood, said Erikson (1982), they face a struggle between generativity and the forces of self-absorption and stagnation. As we saw in Chapter 2, **generativity** involves a concern for future generations. Many people express this concern directly, by nurturing their own children and guiding them into adulthood. Some express it by working with other people's children, as teachers, physicians, or nurses, or by serving as mentors to younger workers in their profession. But Erikson saw generativity as being much wider than direct involvement with the young. He proposed that it can be expressed through creativity or productivity as well. The writer, the artist, and the musician satisfy the need for generativity through their creative output, but the carpenter can express it by building houses for future generations. Any of us can express it by helping to maintain or improve society (Erikson and Hall, 1987). According to Erikson, generativity is the driving power in human organizations. Women and men who express generativity in any of these ways develop *care,* the strength of middle adulthood, which includes the capacity for empathy as well as the willingness to accept responsibility for others.

The person who shows no concern for future generations or for society may find his or her life stagnating. Such people become preoccupied with themselves. They may become bored, find their lives frustrating, and feel a vague sense of loss,

Although life crises seem no more common at midlife than at any other time, some individuals do make radical breaks. Paul Gaugin greeted middle age by leaving his wife, five children, and his stockbroker's job in France and fleeing for Tahiti, where he spent the rest of his life painting. *(New York Public Library)*

even though they do not understand its source.

Little research has been done on later stages of Erikson's theory, but some longitudinal studies have supported its broad outlines. Among men who were followed into middle adulthood, only those who developed generativity seemed mature and skilled at coping with the world (Vaillant and Milofsky, 1980). Whether Harvard graduates or men from the inner city, generative men also had mastered the developmental tasks of earlier stages. They had successful marriages and stable occupations, and they enjoyed their children. Regardless of income, they were altruistic and active in some kind of public service. Men who had not developed generativity tended to have insecure identities and had trouble developing intimate relationships.

Levinson's Seasons

Among the men studied by Daniel Levinson and his associates (Levinson, Damon, Klein, Levinson, and McKee, 1978), the years between forty and forty-five served as a transition to middle adulthood. Men tended to reevaluate their lives at this time and to conclude that their youthful dreams for the future were out of reach. Levinson saw this period as a time of turmoil, when men whose illusions were gone reassessed their goals and tried to restructure their lives. A central issue at this time was discovering "what I really want." Some men in his study went so far as to change occupations, divorce their wives, or move to distant cities. As wrinkles, gray hairs, and minor declines in strength forced them to come to terms with their mortality, many began to act as mentors to younger adults.

Once through the transition period, men began building their lives on the basis of these new choices. Those who were successful found life productive and more satisfying than it had ever been. Those who had not been able to solve the tasks of the midlife transition spent the rest of their forties in a period of stagnation and decline. When they began the transition into their fifties, men who had escaped major changes during the midlife transition often found that turmoil had caught up with them. It was their turn to struggle with the mismatch between their goals and the paths their lives were taking. By the mid-fifties, men were in the period Levinson calls the culmination of middle adulthood. They settled into their lives, and many found the rest of the decade a time of great fulfillment. At sixty, the transition into late adulthood began, another five-year period of reappraisal, when men's choices would define the shape of their remaining years.

Gould's Transformations

The transformations of middle adulthood described by Roger Gould (1975; 1978) are similar to the seasons of Levinson's men. But Gould found the midlife transition beginning earlier, at about the age of thirty-five, and lasting until women and men were about forty-three years old. Gould also found turmoil, questioning, and radical life changes during this period. After weathering the storms of this transformation, women and men found the rest of their forties a time of stability and satisfaction. Many became more realistic about their goals and tended increasingly to agree that "I try to be satisfied with what I have and not to think so much about the things I probably won't be able to get." Friends, family, and marriage became their central concerns, and money seemed less important.

As they entered their fifties, women and men became increasingly aware of their mortality and sensed the running out of time. The personal relationships that were of concern in the forties took on increased importance. Marriage became more satisfying, children became a potential source of warmth and satisfaction, and parents were no longer seen as the cause of personal problems. People showed increased self-acceptance, and many expressed their generativity by becoming actively involved in their communities.

Jung's Concept of Middle Adulthood

Like Erikson, Carl Jung (1969) based his theory of adulthood on a psychoanalytic view of human development. Jung saw adult development as a process characterized by growth and change, in which we are guided by our aims for the future as well as our past experiences. He believed that healthy development involves striving to realize our full potential. Such self-actualization requires us to develop all parts of our personality, then unite them into a balanced, integrated self.

As we approach middle adulthood, said Jung, we may feel that we have our lives all worked out, from the course of our careers and family to our ideals and the principles that guide our behavior. But soon aspects of our personality that have been lying "in the lumber room among dusty memories" begin to assert themselves. In some people, there are gradual changes in personality; in others, new inclinations and interests develop. Not every-

At midlife, many adults become mentors; they take a personal interest in a younger employee, guiding the novice and smoothing his or her promotion and advancement. *(Ulrike Welsch)*

one changes in this way; some seem to feel threatened by impending change and respond by becoming rigid and intolerant. According to Jung, each of us has both masculine and feminine aspects, and among the unexpressed sides of personality that become apparent at midlife are men's femininity and women's masculinity. Once women's years of active mothering are finished and men no longer are absorbed in "making it," the other side of gender becomes apparent. Women become tough-minded and may go into business or develop an interest in broader social concerns; men become tender-hearted and less assertive. Those who stifle such inclinations may find themselves in emotional trouble, because the suppressed masculinity or femininity is likely to assert itself in some indirect, irrational way.

Jung saw midlife changes in personality, goals, and interests as natural. "We cannot live the afternoon according to the programme of life's morning," he wrote, "for what was great in the morning will be little in the evening, and what in the morning was true will at evening have become a lie" (1969, p. 399). As people pass through middle adulthood, they must set new goals instead of living with diminished forms of old ones. A great ballerina should not keep performing as her preci-

sion and grace decline; instead, she should become an equally great choreographer or teacher of ballet.

Gutmann's Parental Imperative

David Gutmann's (1980) parental imperative picks up Jung's idea of unexpressed gender potentials that reassert themselves in middle adulthood. In his view, once the "chronic emergency" of active parenting has passed, women become more aggressive, less affiliative, and more managerial or political. Men become less interested in their occupations and more interested in companionship and sensual enjoyments — good food, pleasant sights and sounds. Men become more dependent on their wives, but women become less dependent on their husbands. Gutmann sees this change as developmental, predictable, and a positive sign of growth.

Gutmann and Jung both see adults becoming more androgynous as they enter the second half of life. Research has supported some aspects of this claim. Gutmann's (1975) own research in the United States, Central America, and the Middle East has shown this progression in each society he has studied. Other researchers have found some-

Jung saw the midlife woman's emergence as a tough-minded business executive as the flowering of the masculine aspect of her personality. *(Ellis Herwig/ The Picture Cube)*

what similar trends. Among blue-collar workers in the United States, middle-aged women became more self-assertive, autonomous, and competent, while the same qualities decreased among men (Fiske, 1980). In one study, it was not freedom from the parental imperative but the arrival of grandchildren that was associated with increased androgyny (Feldman, Biringen, and Nash, 1981). Middle-aged parents whose children had left home showed traditional sex differences; only those who also had become grandparents showed androgynous tendencies. Compared with other middle-aged women and men, grandmothers were more autonomous, and grandfathers were more tender and compassionate. No one can be certain whether this tendency will appear in middle-aged

Americans of the twenty-first century. If today's young adults are free to express both sides of their gender potential, the tendency toward a reversal of sex roles in middle adulthood may diminish.

Issues in Theories of Middle Adulthood

Two controversies dominate discussions of personality in middle adulthood. Researchers cannot agree on whether personality remains stable over adulthood, and they cannot decide whether the "midlife crisis" is an inevitable part of human development.

Continuity vs. Change   When we reach middle adulthood, most of us seem to think our personality has changed a good deal since adolescence — and mostly for the better. A group of forty-five-year-old women and men who had taken a personality test at the age of twenty retook the same test. Then they took the test yet again, this time answering as they believed they had answered in their youth. Most indicated that they had been much less competent and less well adjusted as twenty-years-olds than they were in midlife. But when Diane Woodruff and James Birren (1972) compared the results, they discovered that the adults had filled out the tests similarly at twenty and at forty-five. The discrepancy was in their midlife view of their youthful selves. Although their personalities had remained relatively stable for twenty-five years, the adults perceived themselves as having changed.

What actually happens as we live through adulthood? Do we change, or does personality remain relatively stable? The question is not whether change is possible; researchers agree that it is. The controversy centers around how much change is probable and whether predictable developmental experiences change people in predictable ways. As we have seen, some theorists of adult development propose regular, age-related changes in personality, such as an increase in assertiveness among midlife women, that appear when people encounter various developmental tasks.

Yet in longitudinal studies, major dimensions of personality generally remain stable across adulthood (McCrae and Costa, 1984). Impulsive teenagers become impulsive adults, assertive teenagers still are assertive in old age, and shy teenagers still are shy even after they retire. Because longitudinal studies allow investigators to separate generational differences from maturational changes, their results may tell us more about personality development than do cross-sectional studies.

In another longitudinal study of Californians, researchers found an orderly progression in the development of many aspects of personality (Haan, Millsap, and Hartka, 1986). From adolescence to their mid-fifties, cheerful, confident people tended to become more cheerful and confident, fearful people became more fearful and distrusting, and so on. Personality seemed least stable during the transition into young adulthood, when people were taking on occupational roles and getting married. Once that transition was complete, personality tended to regain its consistency. Some people did show personality changes, but these shifts generally were associated with some unusual, unexpected experience (the early death of a spouse, an unexpected inheritance).

It seems that personality remains relatively stable as long as a person's life situation does not change in some radical fashion (Bengston, Reedy, and Gordon, 1985). Personality develops as a person, with all of his or her predispositions, interacts with environmental events. These events may be either common tasks (achieving economic independence) or individual events (an automobile accident). The relative stability of a person's personality may primarily reflect that person's psychosocial situation rather than the inevitable course of development.

The Midlife Crisis   Closely related to the question of stability in personality is the issue of the midlife crisis. According to Levinson (Levinson et al., 1978) and Gould (1978), the transition into middle age is almost invariably accompanied by a **midlife crisis** — a state of physical and psychological distress when developmental tasks threaten to overwhelm a person's internal resources and system of social support (Cytrynbaum et al., 1980). Among Levinson's men, for example, 80 percent went through such an upheaval in their early forties. The notion of midlife crisis has grabbed our

imagination, perhaps because of its popularization by journalist Gail Sheehy (1976), whose book about changes in the lives of midlife men and women became a national best seller. The idea so permeated popular writing on middle age that most people probably accept such a crisis as an inevitable part of life.

Yet most longitudinal studies have not uncovered a general crisis in midlife. Whether researchers looked at male Harvard graduates (Vaillant, 1977), middle-aged women (Baruch, Barnett, and Rivers, 1983), Californians of both sexes (Clausen, 1981), or at a national sample of more than 10,000 Americans (Costa et al., 1986), they were unable to find a predictable emotional upheaval in early midlife — or at any other age period they examined (see Figure 17.1). Certainly, some people have life crises during their forties, but at no greater rate than people in their twenties, thirties, fifties, or sixties. One researcher points out that divorce, job disenchantment, and depression occur at about the same frequency across the life span (Vaillant, 1977), and others note that midlife often is the most satisfying and rewarding period of life (Clausen, 1981).

Developmental events such as marriage, childbirth, job promotion, menopause, or retirement may be followed by changes in self-concept and identity. But when such events are "on time," arriving at whatever point in life our social clock has led us to expect them, most of us cope without caving in (Hagestad and Neugarten, 1985). The serenity of our lives may be ruffled, but no crisis develops. Two factors seem responsible for our ability to handle expected events. First, because we anticipate them, we work through them ahead of time, rehearsing them mentally until their actual occurrence poses no huge problem. Second, because most of our peers are going through similar transitions, we get social support from them and a sense that we are all "in the same boat." It is the unexpected event (the divorce, the automobile accident) or the expected event that arrives at the wrong time (the early death of a parent or spouse) that is likely to precipitate a crisis. Unexpected change in midlife is not always bad; it may even lead to positive growth. A young widow whose roles suddenly shift may discover dormant talents and abilities and find herself expressing new aspects of her personality.

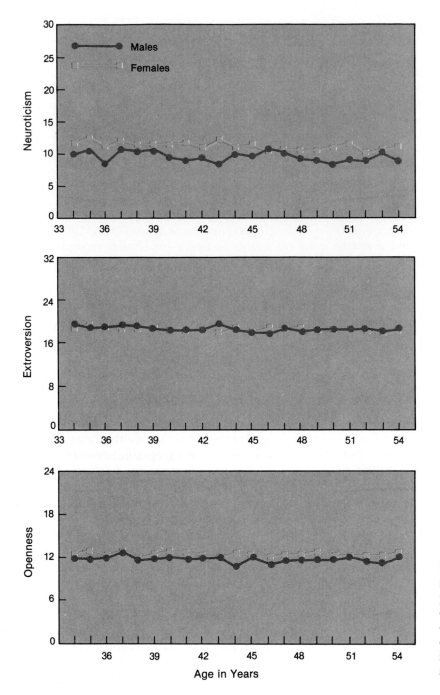

FIGURE 17.1   Personality ratings from a large national sample provide no evidence of a midlife crisis. Mean levels of neuroticism, extroversion, and openness to experience show remarkable stability between the ages of thirty-three and fifty-four. *(From Costa et al., 1986)*

SELF-CONCEPT AND SELF-ESTEEM

The way we respond to life's challenges and changes affects the way we feel about ourselves. Stress may be an inevitable part of changes in mid-dle adulthood, but as Richard Lazarus (1985) argues, the stress itself does not lower our self-esteem, erode our self-concept, or destroy our sense of self-efficacy. Our sense of self remains firm when we meet stress in certain ways:

1. When we can either tolerate or alleviate the distress

2. When we can maintain a sense of personal worth in the face of defeat

3. When we can maintain good relationships with friends and family members throughout the trial

4. When we can meet whatever challenge is connected with the stress.

People who expect to be defeated, who believe that success or failure depends on luck or fate, not only suffer diminished self-esteem but may also develop learned helplessness (Seligman, 1975).

Most adults feel better about themselves in midlife than they did during early adulthood. The sense of self-control and confidence that grows in the twenties and thirties continues to increase during the forties. Men in their forties tend to use more mature strategies in coping with personal problems and to assume greater responsibility for them than they did as adolescents and young adults (Vaillant, 1977). They also show a more realistic sense of their strengths and weaknesses. Instead of assuming the young adult's attitude of "I can handle anything" or "I want to do it all myself," middle-aged adults have a growing awareness that other people can be relied on for advice and help. Despite this new awareness, the sense of self-esteem tends to increase during middle adulthood.

To some extent, mental health at midlife depends on the match between what a person has and what he or she expects. In one study, unmarried women felt good about themselves because life had turned out much better than they had expected (Birnbaum, 1975). They discovered that satisfaction did not depend on being married and having children. People who had extremely high expectations of success, joy, or passion or who had been convinced that their children would be perfect may become depressed after they take stock at midlife.

WORK

When Studs Terkel (1974) interviewed Larry Ross, the middle-aged ex-president of a conglomerate, Ross told him why he was now a management consultant instead of a corporation executive:

I've always wanted to be a teacher. I wanted to give back the knowledge I gained in corporate life. . . . In every sales group, you always have two or three young men with stars in their eyes. They always sat at the edge of the chair. I knew they were comers. I always felt I could take 'em, develop 'em, and build 'em. . . . I'd like to get involved with the young people and give my knowledge to them before it's buried with me. (P. 540)

The place of work in a person's life undergoes a decided shift during middle adulthood. Occupation continues to be important, but attitudes toward work are likely to change, sometimes drastically.

Men's Work

For most men, work is no longer the all-absorbing interest it was during their thirties. Work is still vitally important, but men have climbed about as far as they had expected to go. At least for those who have reached their goals, the drive to get ahead subsides, and work seems more satisfying (Bray and Howard, 1983; Clausen, 1981). Many become mentors to younger workers; they provide their juniors with guidance and smooth their way to advancement.

The change becomes apparent at around the age of forty-five, when most men tend to cut back on their working time. Among men in a longitudinal study of Californians, this curtailment appeared in both working- and middle-class men, except for top executives and professionals (Clausen, 1981). These highly successful men increased the time they devoted to their occupation, adding about three hours each week to their work schedule. When such a pattern develops, men may devote so much time and energy to their careers that the quality of family life is diminished, the marital relationship erodes, and relationships with their children suffer (L. Hoffman, 1986).

By the time men enter their fifties, a relation between socioeconomic level and personality appears. Among these same Californians, several personality attributes could be ranked by occupational level. Men who had made it to the top scored lowest in anxiety, fearfulness, and punitiveness (Clausen, 1981). These men were also less likely to withdraw when frustrated or to feel victimized by life. Middle-class men who had managed to move up from the working class tended to be

Women who first enter the labor market at midlife often have a special enthusiasm for their work and derive great satisfaction from the social aspects of the job. *(Laimute E. Druskis/Taurus)*

warmer and more sympathetic than other men, to have developed intellectual skills and interests, and to hold conventional views.

Women's Work

The majority of single women follow an occupational path similar to that of men (Keating and Jeffrey, 1983). But married women, especially those with children, relate very differently to work at midlife. At a time when men are becoming less involved with their occupation, women are either becoming more involved or else making their first foray into the world of work. The freshness of their involvement may explain why many midlife women seem more excited about their work than men or single women who have been working continuously. Coming from the relative isolation of the homemaker's world, these new workers may find satisfaction primarily in the social aspects of the job. Most men and single women place more importance on work's financial rewards or its challenging aspects (Kessler and McRae, 1981).

When asked about the satisfactions that they derive from employment, women speak about the chance to work on their own, a sense of competence and accomplishment, and the joy of having a job that fits their interests and skills (Baruch and Barnett, 1986). These satisfactions far outweigh any distresses they encounter, and their major complaints center around overload: having too much to do and having to juggle conflicting tasks.

Women who have been holding back on their commitment to their occupation and those who have just joined the labor force may benefit especially from employment during the time when children leave the nest. The new commitment fills a gap left by the departing children and adds zest to their lives. Women who have been committed to a career throughout the child-rearing period miss out on this source of exhilaration. Consequently, they may either feel the loss of their children keenly or simply welcome the removal of a source of restraint in their lives.

MARRIAGE AT MIDLIFE

Delays in marriage and parenthood may be changing the experience of the marriage relationship at midlife. Earlier research on midlife marriage focused on how the marital partners related to adolescent children and how they adjusted to an empty nest after the children left home. As the family life

MIXING MARRIAGE AND A SECOND CAREER

Most of us follow the same general occupation throughout our working lives, but during midlife some people strike out in an entirely new direction. Either they become dissatisfied with their earlier line of work, or else they retire early. Some occupations (the military, law enforcement) provide for early retirement; sometimes a person can no longer meet the physical requirements of the job; sometimes he or she has accumulated enough assets to retire but takes up a new career to keep busy.

Curious about the way second careers are incorporated into the marital relationship, Leslie and Leonard Lieberman (1986) studied a group of men and women who had begun new careers in the field of art. Some of the men had been professionals; others had had business or blue-collar jobs. Some of the women had never been employed outside the home; others had held white-collar or professional jobs. Their new careers combined art and travel: after creating their work, they traveled to art and craft fairs across the United States, where they showed and sold their handiwork.

Among the sixty-eight artists interviewed by the Liebermans, several patterns appeared. Some wives and husbands had separate artistic careers; some worked jointly in the same medium; sometimes only one partner was an artist, but the other assisted in either producing the work (stretching canvas, framing), setting up the display, or handling sales. A few of the artists (six men, three women) received no support from their spouses. This pattern usually appeared when the spouse was still busy with her or his primary career.

How did the second career affect the marriages? One couple who worked as a team to create dried flower arrangements found their marriage more satisfying. According to the wife, "We have a lot of fun at this; he does some of the things that I do just because he likes being with me." The husband was even more enthusiastic, saying "Oh, my God— never in our entire life have we had a better time" (Lieberman and Lieberman, 1986, p. 222). A painter reported that helping with her second career had changed her husband; he no longer felt that sex roles should follow traditional standards.

In fact, for many of these couples, the income from their new career was secondary to other benefits. Starting a new—and often radically different —career provided them with challenging opportunities. But it was the context of the career that was especially satisfying. It allowed the couple to work together in ways that increased communication between them, enhanced their respect for one another, and provided companionship. As one man said

We will work until 1 A.M.; neither wants to quit. In general my wife and I are able to enjoy our total life together. After the sales are done we talk for two or three hours—in the past we never had that. (Lieberman and Lieberman, 1986, p. 223)

cycle entered a new phase, both partners had to adjust to new roles and develop new ways of seeing themselves in the context of changing relationships. Today's middle-aged couple may have infants or young children at home, so that in many ways their marriage may resemble the marriage of early adulthood. Most couples, of course, especially those in the working class, continue to encounter the traditional marital adjustments of midlife.

Marital Satisfaction

Cross-sectional studies generally show marital satisfaction starting to decline as soon as children are born and dropping to its lowest point when they reach adolescence. As soon as the nest is emptied, satisfaction rises and remains high throughout middle adulthood. It is reasonable to assume that once the strains of active parenting are passed and demands on income are reduced, couples enter

Once their active parenting duties are behind them, midlife couples often find a new freedom in their marriages. *(Eric Kroll/Taurus)*

a new era of freedom: freedom from financial responsibilities, freedom to be mobile, freedom from household responsibilities and chores connected with children, and freedom to be the people they want to be.

Some couples do feel this way. They report that after the children have left, they laugh more together, have more discussions, and work together more often on projects. Women especially are likely to feel more satisfied with their marriages once the children have left home, primarily because the possibilities of companionship increase. Wife and husband again can enjoy one another's company.

The problem with this portrait is that cross-sectional studies are not following the developmental course of marriages but giving us simulta-neous snapshots of marriages in different cohorts. Margaret Huyck (1982) suggests that marital statistics may show high satisfaction in the last part of middle adulthood because most unhappy couples have divorced by then. Hints that this may be true appear in national surveys. Between 1957 and 1976, the level of marital satisfaction rose substantially in this country and paralleled the rise in the divorce rate (Veroff, Douvan, and Kulka, 1981).

In one longitudinal study, neither the length of the marriage nor the stage of the family cycle had any effect on marital satisfaction (Skolnick, 1981). Couples were just as satisfied with adolescent children at home as they had been sixteen to eighteen years earlier, when they had had no parenting problems to contend with. Happily married couples in this study said that their marriages had improved with time and that they liked, admired, and respected each other. Such marriages, known as *companionate marriages,* are not typical. Researchers estimate that only about 20 percent of American marriages center around the close personal relationships that characterized these marriages.

Most American marriages tend to be *institutional marriages,* in which couples have established a utilitarian living arrangement that both partners find satisfactory. In these marriages, there are no emotional bonds between the partners. Instead, satisfaction comes from material possessions and from the children. Researchers have found three types of institutional marriages (Cuber and Harroff, 1965). In the first type, couples argue a lot but find fighting acceptable. In the second type, couples are distant and find their marriages boring. In the third type, couples live in dull, predictable, but comfortable contentment. These couples may indeed find marriage more satisfying after the children leave. Their satisfaction increases, not because they can do what they like, but because they have less to argue about and fewer demands on their time (Swenson, Eskew, and Kohlhepp, 1981). Each is free to follow his or her own interests.

The Sexual Relationship

For some couples, marital sex improves in midlife. The male requires longer to climax, which increases pleasure for both partners, and women no longer fear pregnancy. Yet many couples report sexual problems at midlife, ranging from impotence, to lack of interest, to extramarital affairs.

Sometimes middle-aged couples, who have watched the culture's rules for sexuality change since they reached young adulthood, feel that they have missed out on some of life's excitement. If either decides that he or she has been cheated, the disgruntled partner may grasp what seems a last chance for adventure and embark on an extramarital relationship. Successful middle-class men often find that they are more attractive to women than they were in their youth. The teenage boy with acne is now a corporate executive who looks much better relative to his age group than he did thirty-five years ago. Women executives in midlife may also find themselves more attractive to men as they begin to move in the corridors of power. Among midlife couples in the 1980s, men are more likely than women to have an affair, with more than half of men but only about a quarter of women reporting at least one extramarital relationship during middle age (Gould, 1980). This disparity may disappear when today's young adults enter middle age. The first extramarital relationship now comes earlier in the marriage, and middle-class, educated women in their twenties or thirties are about as likely to have an affair as their husbands are (Macklin, 1980).

A last grab at youth is not the only reason for an extramarital relationship. Some people become involved in an affair because they are dissatisfied with their marriages, because they are under pressure at home, seeking status, asserting their independence, or trying to punish a spouse. Men who find themselves impotent at home may try to reaffirm their waning sexual powers by seeking out a younger woman (Gould, 1980). Some men and women even find the guilt that frequently accompanies an extramarital relationship pleasurable and exciting. Men often remain detached from the relationship, separating "love" and "sex," as many did during adolescence. But women are more likely to become involved, as their attempt to confirm a romantic self-image turns into a full-blown love affair (Blumstein and Schwartz, 1983; Gould, 1980).

If the transgression is discovered, no matter what the reason for the affair, marital trust and intimacy often are destroyed. Participants may overendow these relationships with emotion and see the affair as "true love" or live under a heavy burden of guilt, while their spouses frequently are filled with hurt and anger. Affairs threaten American marriages, because they conflict with the socialization experience of the culture. In fact, when people are asked why they are *not* having an affair, they usually talk about the consequences to their marriage instead of referring to their love for their spouse or the fact that such a relationship would violate ethical or religious precepts (Hunt, 1974).

DIVORCE AND REMARRIAGE

When couples realize that their children soon will be leaving, their marriages may come under increased strain. As wife and husband begin thinking about life after children, they may size each other up and wonder how they will get along without the buffer of the children between them. Either or both may have changed so much over the past twenty years or so that the prospect of undiluted companionship seems unattractive. Like many other middle-aged couples, they may decide to get a divorce.

Although midlife marriages are less likely to end in divorce than marriages of young adults, the divorce rate is still considerable, especially during the years just after the children have left home. The divorce rate for people past forty-five has doubled since 1960 (Diegmueller, 1986). Some marriages that end at this time have been held together "for the sake of the children." Others end when some other major life event disrupts a marital relationship that had been satisfactory to both partners (Turner, 1980). One partner may develop a life-threatening illness or an emotional disorder. One of them may undergo a religious conversion or some other sharp shift in values. One of them may decide to make a radical career change. They may have a deeply disappointing experience with a child, perhaps the discovery of an involvement with drugs or the declaration of homosexuality. The husband may lose his job, and the wife may take on the breadwinner's responsibilities. As the couple adjusts to such an event, their unspoken agreements about the balance of power, their re-

When her first baby is delayed until midlife, a woman tends to enjoy her infant and find great satisfaction in motherhood. *(Eastcott/Momatiuk/The Image Works)*

spective duties, or other aspects of the marriage may be broken. The changes in marital roles may not be acceptable to one of the partners.

Yet some couples remain deeply dissatisfied with their marriages for years before they decide to divorce. In one study of California divorces, 36 percent of the men and 42 percent of the women said that their marriages had been conflict-ridden from the beginning, and 15 percent were unhappy for at least twelve years before deciding to divorce (Kelly, 1982). Among most middle-aged couples, the woman is the first to realize that the marriage is heading for disaster (Hagestad and Smyer, 1983). The signs may become apparent to her more than ten years before the decision to divorce is made. Middle-aged men are less aware of the depth of their marital troubles and may drift along complacently for another seven or eight years before realizing that the marriage is on shaky ground.

No matter which partner first realizes the seriousness of the problems, in the majority of cases, it is the woman who decides to seek a divorce (Kelly, 1982). (The woman almost always files suit for divorce, whether she or the man has decided to break up the marriage.) The decision usually is precipitated by some single event: infidelity, some critical outside event that throws the relationship into a new focus (moving, a new job), or some sort of "last straw" (a second suicide attempt, an alcoholic binge). The partner who makes the decision may feel guilty, sad, or apprehensive, but he or she escapes the feelings of humiliation or rejection felt by the other partner. By having gone through the grieving process earlier, the partner who seeks the divorce also may recover his or her self-esteem earlier and start to put a life back together sooner.

In some ways, divorce is more difficult for people in midlife than it is for young adults. Neither party may have had recent practice in developing new intimate relationships with the other sex, and the process is likely to take longer and be more stressful than it is for younger people. A middle-aged woman in a traditional marriage who has depended on her husband's position for her own identity and for her financial security may find divorce particularly distressing. Cathy Knapp of Houston, divorced at forty-one, said, "When I walked out of that courtroom, my feelings were, 'How am I going to survive?' I only had a high school education; I had not worked in years" (Diegmueller, 1986, p. 10). Knapp found a job and went back to college to work toward a paralegal degree as the first step in her occupational training. As more and more young women build occupations for themselves in young adulthood, the divorced woman who loses both identity and income will become increasingly rare.

Many people who divorce in midlife find new mates. The rate of marriage is higher for divorced men and women than for single people at any age. The major change in the middle years is that marriage rates for women drop below those for men. Several factors contribute to this situation. First, death rates increase for men in midlife, and the pool of possible mates for women is reduced. Second, as noted in Chapter 15, women tend to marry older men, and men marry younger women. This further reduces the pool of possible mates. Third, men are willing to marry someone with less education than they have, but women usually want a mate with similar educational background. This requirement again reduces their possibilities. In 1970, for example, among divorced women in their early forties, over 70 percent of those with some high school but less than 50 percent of those who had been to graduate school ever remarried (U.S. Bureau of the Census, 1971). The remarriage rate among men in their early forties remained above 70 percent no matter what their level of education.

PARENTHOOD AT MIDLIFE

Until recently, midlife parents were thought of as parenting adolescents and young adults. Today middle-aged couples have children of all ages. Some mothers with new babies are in their forties; in other cases, the new mother is in her twenties or thirties, but the new father is in his forties, his fifties, or even his sixties. These latter situations usually come in second marriages, and the father often has adolescent children by a former marriage. Other couples who have postponed parenthood or whose children have left the nest decide to adopt children.

Delayed Parenthood

Women who delay childbearing until their forties may find it difficult to conceive. Fertility declines only slightly until the age of thirty-five but drops sharply after that time (Menken, Trussell, and Larsen, 1986). Among women in their early forties, six out of ten may be sterile. Even those who are still fertile may take more than a year to conceive, a nerve-wracking delay when the biological clock is ticking away. Most men in midlife can father children; among men in their early fifties, the fertility rate is about 73 percent of what it was during their early twenties.

Once a couple conceives, concern does not end. The likelihood of certain birth disorders, such as Down's syndrome or spinal cord defects, rises with age. The forty-year-old mother has 1 chance in 100 of producing a child with Down's syndrome, but the chances rise to 1 in 45 among forty-five-year-old mothers (Omenn, 1983). When the woman does conceive, many middle-aged couples have amniocentesis to make certain that the fetus is normal (see Chapter 3). Historically, older women have had more miscarriages, more complications during pregnancy, more difficult deliveries, and have run a greater risk of dying in childbirth than women in their twenties (Vider, 1986). But advances in obstetrical techniques have greatly reduced these hazards, so that most healthy older mothers have normal pregnancies and healthy babies.

Middle-class couples who have midlife babies seem to become "professional parents," centering their lives around their young child. They are knowledgeable about all aspects of pregnancy and childcare. Many study prenatal development and child psychology as if they were cramming for an examination. Once the baby arrives, most seem absorbed by their infant and find parenthood enormously rewarding. They seem settled, relaxed, and calmer than younger parents do. The high levels of satisfaction among midlife parents seem in good part due to their lack of economic worries. Fifty-six-year-old Dick Lord, the president of a Manhattan advertising agency and the father of a toddler, summed it up,

> It all boils down to the economic thing. When the first kids were little, I was always scrambling. I couldn't turn off my work life, even on weekends. Now I feel secure. And I can have fun with the kids. (Wolfe, 1982, p. 30)

Among these affluent, middle-class families, fathers tend to be absorbed with their children and emotionally available to both children and wife. When children arrive during young adulthood, fathers are absorbed in their careers and so seem much less committed to child rearing and family life. No one knows how this difference in a youngster's early life will affect the socialization process.

Parenting Teenagers

Some family conflict is inevitable when children reach adolescence, because each generation is at a different point in its developmental agenda and faces different developmental tasks. Middle-aged parents and their almost grown children often argue over their changing roles, their various responsibilities, the children's strivings for autonomy, and what the parents may see as the disintegration of family ties. Yet as we saw in Chapter 14, in the majority of families, conflict is sporadic and mostly about minor matters.

Limit testing is part of the adolescent's search for identity and independence. It is a developmental issue not only for the teenager but for his or her middle-aged parents as well. Besides clashing over the setting of limits, parents and their adolescent children may have conflicts over sexuality, achievement, values, and breakdowns in communication (Rapoport, Rapoport, and Strelitz, 1977). Parents may have to pull back at exactly the moment when they want to hang on or even increase controls (L. Hoffman, 1985b). As the child copes with identity, autonomy, and sexuality, parents worry about all the disasters they read about in the paper or see on the evening newscast. Will their child get involved with drugs? With alcohol? Each report of an automobile accident, a teenage pregnancy, or a teenage suicide stirs new apprehension. The stakes and the dangers seem much greater than they were in the preteen years, but the opportunities for surveillance have shrunk.

The age at which a child enters adolescence and whether the child is a boy or girl appear to affect the way parents approach these issues. When daughters mature early, parents are most likely to report high levels of conflict and concern over their daughters' behavior (Savin-Williams and Small, 1986). Parents may feel that their daughter's early sexual maturation places her in situations that she is not equipped to handle.

No matter when boys mature, their arrival at puberty shifts the family balance of power. As we saw in Chapter 13, after a period of increased conflict between mothers and their adolescent sons, the mothers seem to back off and become deferential (Steinberg, 1981). The son apparently takes over the authority that was once the mother's and strips her of much of her power over family decisions.

This power shift puts the mother at a disadvantage when she tries to exert control over her son. In one study, mothers and their adolescent sons got along much better when the father was also present (Gjerde, 1986). Mothers became more secure, more affectionate, more consistent, and found it easier to keep control of the situation. In contrast, fathers got along better with their sons when the mother was not around. When the mother was gone, fathers were more involved with their sons, more responsive, and tended to treat them in an egalitarian manner. But when the mother was present, fathers tended to become critical and antagonistic toward their sons. The fathers' switch from easy interaction to an assumption of control may have relieved some of the stress on the mother and allowed her to relate more

positively to her son. These tensions may be eased for the employed mother, who is likely to encourage independence in her adolescent offspring (L. Hoffman, 1985).

The Empty Nest

Whether parenting adolescent children has been a joy or a trial, eventually the children leave home. Usually, the parents are in their mid-fifties before the last child departs. At one time, psychiatrists and psychologists assumed that this period was extremely difficult for parents and especially for women. Faced with the loss of their children, the loss of their youth, and the ordeal of menopause, women were supposed to be prone to a special kind of depression, called *involutional melancholia*. But when researchers began to separate theory from fact, the picture became quite different. The rate of depression among women turned out to be about the same whether women were younger than forty-five, between forty-five and fifty-five, or older than fifty-five (Weissman, 1979). That did not rule out the possibility of the **empty nest syndrome,** an emotional crisis that threatened a woman's defenses even if it did not plunge her into a depression.

Other researchers looked directly at the empty nest phenomenon. Bernice Neugarten (1970) and her associates compared midlife women whose children were all at home with those who had launched some of their offspring and with those whose nests were empty. The women whose children were gone were happier and more satisfied than either of the other groups. Other studies have confirmed Neugarten's results (Glenn, 1975; Lowenthal and Chiriboga, 1972). When Lillian Rubin (1975) interviewed midlife women, most women said that they were relieved when their last child left home. A typical response came from a fifty-year-old, middle-class homemaker:

> When the youngest one was ready to move out of the house, I was right there helping him pack. We love having the children live in the area, and we love seeing them and the grandchildren, but I don't need for any of them to live in this house ever again. I've had as much as I ever need or want of being tied down with children. (Rubin, 1979, p. 16)

Parents who prepare in advance for the time when their grown children leave find the transition to the empty nest is eased. *(Ken Heyman)*

When children leave the nest "on time," parents have prepared for the event. But the empty nest may well foster an emotional crisis when the child leaves home too early, as when a fifteen-year-old runs away. The nest that doesn't empty on time may also be a source of serious discomfort. Parents live under continual strain and have a sense of personal failure. One midlife father interviewed by psychologist Gunhild Hagestad (1984) exploded in angry bewilderment:

> Last night we had a confrontation. . . . A disgust on my part for a twenty-year-old not in school, not working, not putting anything into the house. . . . It's all taking. . . . food, car, clothing. (P. 151)

When children leave the nest on time, several factors affect their parents' reactions to the departure. If there is only one child or two children,

closely spaced, the nest empties rapidly. Parents may feel the pangs more sharply when children leave suddenly than when they have children leaving over a period of five to ten years. But no matter what the size and spacing of the family, the relationship between husband and wife also affects parental reactions. If the couple care deeply for each other, their response may be one of relief and delight. They have time for each other, can travel when they like, can return to the spontaneous intimacy and sexuality of the period before their first child was born. If the couple have a satisfactory institutional marriage, the response may still be positive, for each can pursue his or her own interests while living comfortably together—albeit without much affection. If the couple have a conflict-ridden, unhappy marriage, they may divorce.

Another factor that may affect reactions to the empty nest is the woman's relationship to her chil-

Middle-aged children provide frequent services and gifts for their older parents, and most parents reciprocate. *(Rae Russel)*

dren (Baruch, Barnett, and Rivers, 1983). Women who are *autonomous mothers* see their children as individuals. They enjoy doing things with their children, encourage their strivings for maturity, and like the kind of people they have become. These women are usually high in self-esteem and feel in control of their lives. They are likely to find the empty nest a pleasant place. Other women are *coupled mothers* who see their children as extensions of themselves. Children give meaning to the lives of coupled mothers; they make the women feel needed. Compared with autonomous mothers, coupled mothers are low in self-esteem and feel less in control of their lives. They are more likely to complain of anxiety or depression. Such mothers may find the empty nest a bleak and desolate place.

RELATING TO AGING PARENTS

Most middle-aged adults have living parents, and an increasing number can expect their parents to be alive when the adults themselves reach old age. Researchers estimate that more than a fourth of the women born in 1930 will have a mother living in 1990 (Winsborough, 1980). The nature of the parent-child bond changes as people age, but it generally remains firm over their half century or more of shared time. Some researchers believe that relationships between adult children and their parents are warmer and closer today than they have ever been. According to Andrew Cherlin (1983), such relationships were cold and distant in colonial America, apparently because the older father retained control of the land and ruled the family in an authoritarian manner. Cherlin proposes that adult children and their parents are likely to be closest and most affectionate when neither generation has to depend on the economic support of the other. Research supports this notion. In one study, relations between middle-aged adults and their parents were warmest when the aging parents were in good health and financially independent (Johnson and Bursk, 1977). The parents' attitudes toward their children also affect the relationship. When aging mothers approve of their daughters, are interested in them, and refrain from criticizing them, their midlife daughters respond with warmth and affection (Weishaus, 1979).

Although most adult children and parents are not dependent on one another, gifts and services

Table 17.1
Financial Aid between the Generations (Percent)

Older Adults	All Older Adults	Sex		Race		Age	
		Women	*Men*	*Black*	*White*	*<75*	*>75*
Percent who receive aid from children	11.3	11.9	10.2	18.2	8.6	8.9	14.3
Percent who need aid from children	18.6	22.1	13.0	42.1	9.8	21.3	15.0
Percent of those needing help who are getting it	34.6	31.6	42.9	37.5	30.0	29.4	44.4
Percent who give aid to children	47.2	42.6	53.3	52.8	44.3	54.8	36.4

Note: Among 160 older adults, more were providing financial assistance to their children than were getting it, and many of those who needed help were not getting it.

Source: L. W. Hoffman, K. A. McManus, and Y. Brackbill, "The Value of Children to Young and Elderly Parents," *International Journal of Aging and Human Development* (in press).

flow up and down the generational tree (Bengston, Cutler, Mangen, and Marshall, 1985). Middle-aged adult children assist their parents in a number of ways. They may provide economic support, personal care, help with transportation, share outings and holidays, prepare food, or help with home chores. Aging parents are appreciative, but they value their children's affection and respect more than they prize material assistance (Treas, 1983). In fact, as long as parents remain healthy and independent, they return similar gifts and services to their grown children (see Table 17.1).

Sometimes midlife adults must assume most of the responsibility for an aging parent. Although they still have adolescent children at home or are supporting young adults through college, they are faced with the burden of providing for their own parents. This simultaneous push from an older and a younger generation is known as a **life-cycle squeeze.** It is especially stressful when the parents have adult children whose own development is off-time (Hagestad, 1984). One midlife woman who complained of role overload had a jobless son in his late twenties; another had a daughter who had left her husband and moved back home. Women feel the squeeze more strongly than men, even when the two are providing the same level of care. Researchers believe that this increased stress may have two sources: the intimate relationship between mothers and daughters (Robinson and Thurnher, 1979) and the responsibilities (household management, child rearing, emotional support) that most women assume, even when they are employed outside the home (Brody, 1981).

In the future, midlife adults may face serious problems when an aging parent needs this sort of care. When today's youngsters are middle-aged, most will have only a single sibling with whom to share parental care. Only children will have to assume the entire burden themselves. Fewer daughters will be able to provide the sort of care that traditionally has been expected from daughters. The majority of middle-aged women are now in the labor force, and the trend toward women's commitment to an occupation is likely to increase. When a parent requires care, the daughter will have three options: she can quit her job, she can hire someone else to care for her parent, or she can place the parent in a nursing home. No matter which course she chooses, she is likely to feel guilty or resentful. Some researchers have looked into the future and have seen a family network that is overburdened by cross-generational demands (Bengston and Treas, 1980).

BECOMING GRANDPARENTS

As life expectancy has increased, the number of multigenerational families has risen rapidly. Many middle-aged adults become grandparents while their own parents are living. At least four out of ten older Americans are great-grandparents (Troll, Miller, and Atchley, 1979). In such four- (and even five!) generation families, the middle-aged grandparents are not the family elders, but an intermediate generation. Each parent-child linkage in that family is part of a chain, in which each person

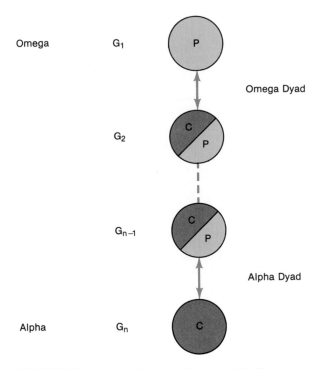

Omega G_1

Omega Dyad

G_2

G_{n-1}

Alpha Dyad

Alpha G_n

**FIGURE 17.2   A multigenerational model of
parent-child relations.** This four-generation model of
family relations shows the way each parent-child
linkage is part of a vertical chain, beginning with the
Omega generation (G_1), who have only a parental
role because their own parents all are dead, and
ending with the Alpha generation (G_n), who are still
immature and have only a child's role. Each circle is a
"generational station," which describes that generation in terms of its parental *(P)* or child *(C)* status.
(From Hagestad, 1984)

until she is thirty-five, he will be nearly ninety
when his grandchild is born. In one recent study,
grandparents' ages ranged from forty-five to
ninety (Thomas, 1986).

Such a span guarantees that no "typical" grandparent exists, because the wide range in ages means
a similar range of cohorts (who grew up under
widely different influences) and of life tasks that
are being dealt with. Yet in the popular mind, the
stereotypical grandfather is an elderly, white-
haired gentleman who whittles willow whistles
for his grandson, and when someone says "grandmother," most people think of a plump, white-
haired, cheerful old lady who cures scraped knees
with a kiss and always has a full cookie jar. Our
stereotypical grandparents actually resemble
great-grandparents. In our society, the average
woman becomes a grandparent when she is between forty-nine and fifty-one years old, the average man when he is between fifty-one and fifty-
three (Tinsley and Parke, 1984). When the first
grandchild is born, most grandparents are im-
mersed in their careers. Grandmother is too busy
to babysit, because she goes to the office each
day—or to the movie set. We often forget that
both Paul Newman and Elizabeth Taylor have
been grandparents for some time.

Most grandparents enjoy the experience. They
derive comfort, satisfaction, and pleasure from relating to the child of their child. Yet not all grandparents find the experience a delight. Adults who
are most likely to be ill at ease in the role tend to fall
at the extremes of the age span (Troll, 1980).
Those who are younger than fifty tend to make
uncomfortable grandparents, perhaps because
they see themselves as too young to be cast in a role
that carries a stereotype of agedness. Those who
are eighty or older may not enjoy the experience
because they have neither the energy nor the patience to deal with boisterous children. Other
studies indicate that grandmothers enjoy the role
somewhat more than grandfathers do and that satisfaction increases when grandparents feel some
responsibility for helping their grandchildren and
caring for them (Thomas, 1986).

Grandchildren seem to enjoy their grandparents as much as grandparents enjoy them. The
relationship has little of the tension that often
exists between parent and child. Because grandparents are not responsible for rearing the child,

except the oldest and the youngest simultaneously
occupies the roles of parent and child (Hagestad,
1984) (see Figure 17.2). Exactly how the particular link a person occupies affects the experience of
being a grandparent is uncertain, but it probably
changes the relationship in some way.

New grandparents come in a wide variety of
ages, from the grandmother in her late thirties
whose adolescent daughter has just given birth, to
the grandmother in her late sixties whose career-
committed daughter has had her long-postponed
baby. New grandfathers may be even older; consider the fifty-six-year-old father of a toddler
whom we met in the section on delayed parenthood. If this man's daughter postpones her family

WHAT DOES IT MEAN TO BE A GRANDPARENT?

Being a grandparent may mean day-to-day delight and an enriched life or disappointment and bitterness, depending on the expectations of the grandparents and the quality of the relationships with their grandchildren. When Helen Kivnick (1982) decided to find out just what it meant to most grandparents, she interviewed nearly 300 men and women about the experience.

The grandparents' replies clustered around five major dimensions. All grandparents experienced all the dimensions, but their emphasis varied — from grandparent to grandparent, from one grandchild to another, and from time to time with the same grandchild. Being a grandparent, they said, gave meaning to life. When this dimension was emphasized, activities with the grandchildren became important (to both child and grandparent), and grandparents incorporated the role into their identity. Another dimension focused around their role as a valued older adviser and resource person. When this dimension was emphasized, grandparents were concerned about the ways in which their grandchildren would remember them. A third dimension focused on the grandparent's sense of personal immortality through his or her descendants. A fourth dimension centered on the grandparents' reinvolvement with their past. When this dimension was emphasized, grandparents referred to the stories they told their grandchildren about the grandparents' own grandparents and to the way they relived experiences from their early life with their grandchildren. Finally, grandparents emphasized the classic grandparental role, in which they spoiled their grandchildren by indulging them and refusing to hold them to strict rules.

Grandparents did not mention other aspects of the grandparental role directly, but Hagestad (1981) believes that the chance to cuddle and hug a young grandchild is an important benefit in a culture that allows few expressions of intimacy. She also stresses the opportunity for grandparents to break the norms of middle-aged adult behavior by playing children's

Midlife grandparents often say that the relationship with their grandchild gives meaning to their lives. (Joseph Veroff)

games and acting in a carefree manner. For the staid, respectable adult, playing grandparent provides a holiday from propriety.

For these grandparents, their own experience as a grandchild affected the way they saw their relationship with their grandchildren. Grandmothers who had positive memories of being a grandchild and who had had a favorite grandparent were most likely to relive their own past in the relationship, to see their role as grandparent as central to their identity, and to see themselves as a valued elder. Grandfathers who had positive memories of their own grandparents were most likely to emphasize the joys of spoiling and indulging a grandchild.

From the interviews, Kivnick concluded that the experiences that go along with being grandparent and grandchild help individuals resolve the psychosocial conflicts connected with stages of the life cycle and can enhance psychological well-being.

they can enjoy the youngster without worrying about the consequences. The bond between grandparent and child seems to be closest while the child is young. As youngsters approach puberty

Four-generational families have become common, which means that many of today's grandparents are no longer the family elders. *(Paul Conklin)*

and feel too old for the stories and games they have shared with their grandparents, the relationship becomes more distant, but the affection remains.

Grandparents influence their grandchildren in many ways. Their direct influence as caregivers and playmates is fairly obvious. When 300 children were interviewed, they confirmed those roles and added others (Kornhaber and Woodward, 1981). The children saw their grandparents as historians who told them about their ethnic heritage and family history and traditions. They saw grandparents as mentors who guided and advised them. In this role, grandparents also served as

models who demonstrated the grandparent role and provided role models for aging as well as models of possible occupations. Finally, children saw their grandparents as buffers between themselves and their parents, comforters who often stepped in to smooth waters and reduce tensions. Other researchers note that grandparents also influence their grandchildren indirectly, by way of the children's parents (Tinsley and Parke, 1984). Grandparents model child-rearing skills, and they provide emotional and financial support, advice, and information.

SUMMARY

1. The nature of middle age is changing. Today's adults between the ages of forty and sixty-five look and feel younger and healthier than their parents and grandparents did. Many are at an earlier stage of family development and are more likely to have living parents, and fewer women are widowed. Today's midlife adults also are better educated, and the women are more likely to be employed.

2. Muscle strength and reaction time decline in

midlife and chronic disorders (especially obesity, hypertension, arthritis, and diabetes) begin to appear. Many of the physical changes associated with aging are not necessary; they develop when bodies are abused, contract some chronic disease, or are simply not used. **Menopause,** or the cessation of menstruation, which ends reproductive capacity in women, creates only minor discomfort for most women. Midlife men do not lose their reproductive capacity, although their sexual response is slowed. In healthy midlife adults, the loss of sexual responsiveness is probably the result of psychological factors.

3. According to Erikson, midlife brings on a struggle between generativity and stagnation. **Generativity** may be expressed through creativity and productivity as well as by having children or caring for them. Jung saw midlife personality changes as unexpressed aspects of the self emerge. Both Jung and Gutmann see unexpressed gender potentials reasserting themselves at midlife. In Levinson's and Gould's theories, most men and women face a **midlife crisis,** in which developmental tasks can cause physical and psychological distress. Most longitudinal studies have not supported this conjecture. Personality seems fairly stable across midlife, although personality may change when people encounter unexpected events that lead to radical change in their lives.

4. The stresses of midlife are unlikely to affect the sense of self unless a person expects defeat and believes that luck or fate determines success. Self-control and self-confidence generally increase across middle adulthood.

5. Work becomes less absorbing to men, and many cut back on their working time. Many midlife women become more absorbed in work, especially those who have just entered the job market or those whose children have just left home.

6. Although cross-sectional studies show a decline in marital satisfaction that lasts until children leave the nest, longitudinal studies show no changes in satisfaction related to age of children or length of marriage. Most marriages are institutional marriages: the couple has a satisfactory but not a happy or loving relationship. Extramarital affairs are relatively common during midlife; they may develop when one of the partners makes a last try at youth, becomes dissatisfied at home, feels pressure at home, seeks status, asserts his or her independence, or tries to punish a spouse.

7. Divorce rates have been climbing among midlife adults. Some divorces are due to changes in marital roles that one partner considers unacceptable; others develop when some event leads an already dissatisfied partner to end the marriage. Midlife women are less likely to remarry than men, because men's higher death rates, the tendency for women to marry men older than themselves, and women's insistence that their mates have an educational background similar to their own combine to produce a smaller pool of potential mates.

8. Parenthood in midlife depends on the couple's stage in the family cycle. Some have new infants or small children, some have adolescent youngsters, and others have — or soon will have — an empty nest. The older parents of young children are likely to be middle class and absorbed in the child. Parents of adolescents generally face sporadic family conflict as their children test limits, with the age and gender of the adolescent affecting the nature of the parents' reaction. The **empty-nest syndrome,** an emotional crisis that follows the departure of the last child, seems confined to mothers whose children leave home extremely early or who are overinvolved in their children and see them as extensions of themselves. Most women welcome the empty nest, which often ushers in a period of freedom and fosters a new intimacy in their marriage.

9. Gifts and services flow both ways between generations, with each generation providing whatever assistance it can to the other. When midlife adults must provide for their own parents at the same time as they are providing for their children, the adults may be caught in a **life-cycle squeeze.** Now that most midlife women are in the labor force, the needs of an aging parent may create extreme pressure — a pressure that is likely to increase as smaller families produce future generations in which the burden must be shouldered by fewer siblings.

10. There is no typical grandparent, because the wide range in age means a similar range of cohorts and current developmental tasks. Most grandparents enjoy their grandchildren, and those who do not tend to be younger than fifty or older than eighty. Grandparents influence their grandchildren in many ways: as caregivers, playmates, historians, mentors and role models, and as buffers between the grandchildren and their parents.

KEY TERMS

empty-nest syndrome
generativity

life-cycle squeeze
menopause

midlife crisis

STUDY TERMS

empty-nest syndrome   An emotional crisis produced by the departure of children from the home; occurs primarily when the children leave at an extremely young age or when the mother sees her children primarily as an extension of herself.

generativity   Ego strength of middle age in Erikson's theory; consists of procreativity, productivity, and creativity.

life-cycle squeeze   Stress, either emotional or economic, caused when the care of an aging parent and the responsibility for children overlap; it is aggravated when both husband and wife are employed and unavailable to provide care for the aging parent.

midlife crisis   A state of physical and psychological distress that arises when the developmental tasks of midlife threaten to overwhelm a person's internal resources and social supports.

PART VII

Later Adulthood

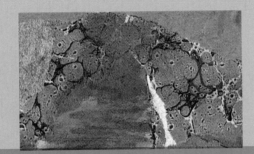

The years after age sixty-five place their own unique demands on the individual to grow, develop, and change. Equipped with more memories and a longer history, older individuals retain the human capacity and desire to control the environment and the human need to love and be loved. How they meet the developmental tasks of old age depends in good part on how they have met the tasks of previous life stages. Although most older adults are ready to relinquish their responsibility for society, many remain active and involved with younger generations. In fact, the growing pool of "young-old" adults, who are healthy and vigorous, is extending the phase of generativity far into old age. This means that for many people, life's final task — coping with death — comes later in the life span than it did for their parents and grandparents.

CHAPTER 18

Thought and Function in Later Adulthood

"When I have time—and I mean something on the order of half an hour—I can almost always recall a name if I have already recalled the occasion for using it," said B. F. Skinner (1983) at the age of seventy-nine.

"It's embarrassing when you have trouble finding the word you want, particularly when you are lecturing to an undergraduate class and must ask them to tell you the word you can't remember," said neuropsychologist Donald Hebb (1978) at the age of seventy-four.

These eminent psychologists agreed that faulty recall was one of the problems of growing old. Both had figured out ways to keep a sluggish memory from interfering with their professional work. Hebb, who kept a card in his wallet listing terms he had trouble remembering, began writing out his lectures instead of speaking from notes. Discussing his professional writing, Skinner said that his problem was not how to have ideas, but how to have them when he could use them. He found that a pocket notebook, a pad and pencil on his bedside table, and a tape recorder made his ideas accessible when he needed them. To remember names, he used such techniques as going through the alphabet, testing for the name's initial letter.

479

When words or names begin to elude them, many older women and men become anxious about their perceived cognitive loss. But forgotten words are not gone, just temporarily inaccessible during tension. Hebb noted that despite his forgetfulness during a lecture, he could still work the difficult crossword puzzles in the *London Observer*. Many older individuals become so afraid that they will forget that their very fear makes a memory lapse inevitable. Skinner's solution is to reduce the unpleasant consequences of a memory failure, thereby reducing anxiety and increasing the chances that the names will be recalled. Explain your failure gracefully, he says:

> Appeal to your age. Flatter your listener by saying that you have noticed that the more important the person, the easier it is to forget the name. Recall the amusing story about forgetting your own name when you were asked for it by a clerk. If you are skillful at that sort of thing, forgetting may even be a pleasure. (Skinner, 1983, p. 240)

Although names may be temporarily forgotten and objects misplaced, most older adults are unlikely to have serious memory problems. As our investigation of cognition will show, cognitive losses among healthy adults are not nearly so large as people believe. After discussing myths and misconceptions about mental decline, we look at the biological changes of later adulthood and their implications for cognitive functioning. Next we investigate learning and problem solving in later life. We then return to the topic of memory, and discover why recall sometimes becomes a problem. After looking at changes in encoding, storage, and retrieval, we close the chapter by exploring strategies that reduce memory failure.

MYTHS ABOUT AGING

What do you think it is like to grow old? Myths and misperceptions about aging are even more widespread than myths about adolescence. The chances are that your expectations are nothing like the experience of most women and men in this society. To find out, take the following abbreviated quiz, which taps knowledge about aging. It was devised by medical sociologist Erdman Palmore (1977; 1980), who coordinated the longitudinal studies of aging at Duke University that have helped explode myths about growing old. Decide whether each of the following statements is true or false; then check your score to see how many misconceptions you need to shed.

1. The majority of old people are senile.
2. All five senses tend to decline in old age.
3. Most old people have no interest in, or capacity for, sexual relations.
4. Lung vital capacity tends to decline in old age.
5. The majority of old people feel miserable most of the time.
6. Physical strength tends to decline in old age.
7. At least one-tenth of the aged are living in long-stay institutions, such as nursing homes, mental hospitals, or homes for the aged.
8. Aged drivers have fewer accidents per driver than drivers under age sixty-five.
9. Most older workers cannot work as effectively as younger workers.
10. About 80 percent of the aged are healthy enough to carry out their normal activities.
11. Most old people are set in their ways and are unable to change.
12. Old people usually take longer to learn something new.
13. It is almost impossible for most old people to learn something new.
14. The reaction time of most old people tends to be slower than the reaction time of younger persons.
15. In general, most old people are pretty much alike.
16. The majority of old people report that they are seldom bored.
17. The majority of old people are socially isolated and lonely.

All odd-numbered statements in this quiz are false; all even-numbered statements are true. Few people answer all items correctly; even college professors tend to miss about three. No matter what their age, sex, or race, most college students miss about six, and high-school graduates do no better than chance—they miss about nine (Palmore, 1980).

Slowed information processing may delay older adults' mastery of their home computer, but most eventually become proficient operators. *(Grapes/Michaud/Photo Researchers)*

Palmore's quiz addresses only a few of the misconceptions about cognition among the elderly. Most people believe that older men and women, even if they are not senile, have lost the capacity to change and grow. According to stereotypes, older adults forget where they had lunch yesterday but remember the distant past with clarity. They have trouble learning, but even if they could learn quickly, they would not want to (Butler, 1975). Such erroneous beliefs have led to **ageism,** which is prejudice against old people. The view that old people are incompetent at best and perhaps even senile is partly responsible for society's tendency to discriminate against them, ignore them, or fail to take them seriously. Yet most old people are capable of handling the tasks of daily life, and some are among the most capable and intelligent members of society. Perhaps a look at the biological changes of old age that relate to cognition will give us an accurate picture of thought processes after the age of sixty-five.

BIOLOGICAL CHANGES

People who answer true to the first statement in Palmore's quiz are probably afraid to grow old. Yet the assumption that old age means confused thought, disorientation, and the inability to handle the problems of living is wrong. When the condition commonly called *senility* develops, it is never the result of aging itself. Aging is associated with changes in the brain and nervous system, but in healthy individuals the practical consequences are relatively minor.

Sensory Capacities and Processing Speed

Stimulation from the environment reaches the brain through the sensory systems. As people age, all five senses become less acute, which makes access to knowledge about the world more difficult to obtain. Most people also take longer to process information. It takes them longer than it once would have to figure out how to operate a microwave oven or to record a TV program on their VCR.

What is the practical effect of less acute sensory systems? Suppose that you smeared Vaseline over the lenses of your glasses and put cotton plugs in your ears, then pulled on a pair of rubber gloves. With much of your sensory information cut off, your movements would probably slow, and you would become extremely cautious. This situation may resemble the world of many older individuals, leading psychologist Diane Woodruff (1983) to

Age-related changes in vision can make night driving especially difficult for older adults. *(Frank Siteman/The Picture Cube)*

suggest that older men and women are in a state of sensory deprivation. Yet there are ways to compensate for some — but not all — of these sensory losses. Such losses are not uniform, and many older individuals are not so isolated from the world around them. As with aging in other bodily systems, wide interindividual differences appear in the degree of sensory deterioration that develops. Some eighty-year-olds can read small print without glasses, hear as well as some twenty-five-year-olds, play the piano with skill, or detect subtle changes in a cook's use of spices.

Vision   Most older people have no severe visual impairment, but few see as well as they did in their thirties. Changes in vision occur slowly. Many of them begin while people are in their forties. By the time they reach later adulthood, people are more bothered by glare, see less well in the dark, require more light to see clearly, and have more trouble seeing objects well than they once did (Kline and Schieber, 1985). Their eyes also adjust more slowly to sudden changes in illumination, so that it takes them longer to regain their vision when moving from light to dark or back again. The visual field constricts, so that some peripheral vision is lost. Glasses and appropriately placed lights can solve many of the visual problems of aging.

The effect of visual changes on many older in-

dividuals may be most noticeable when they try to drive at night. They have trouble reading highway signs under night-driving conditions (which gives them less time than younger drivers to react). They also take longer to recover from the glare of oncoming headlights or changes in illumination as they pass from lighted intersections to darkened stretches of road than they did when they were younger. It is not surprising that many older drivers will not get behind the wheel after dark. Some older individuals, however, are no more sensitive to glare or shifts of illumination than the average younger driver (Sterns, Barrett, and Alexander, 1985).

Hearing   The ability to hear high frequency tones begins to decline after the age of forty-five and becomes marked among people in their late seventies. By this time, about 75 percent have noticeable hearing problems, with hearing loss generally more severe among men than among women (Olsho, Harkins, and Lenhardt, 1985). Older adults have the most difficulty when straining to follow a conversation against background noise or when words overlap or are interrupted. When hearing loss is great, they may miss so many of the words that they either guess at the course of the conversation (which often leads to embarrassment when the guess is wrong) or else withdraw and stop listening. The difficulty can be partially overcome when other people lower their voices, speak slowly and distinctly, and look directly at the older person's face, providing visual cues.

For some older people, the deterioration of hearing may become so pronounced that normal conversations seem like clandestine whispers. In fact, older people with paranoid disorders (who believe that others are persecuting them) often have a history of extreme hearing loss (Post, 1980). The connection led Philip Zimbardo and his colleagues (Zimbardo, Andersen, and Kabat, 1981) to use hypnosis to induce temporary deafness in college students in order to see if the experience made them suspicious. Students who did not know why they had suddenly lost their hearing began to think, feel, and act differently. They became irritable, hostile, tense, and unfriendly. Although they said that they were not suspicious, their scores on tests of paranoia climbed. Other students, who had been made temporarily deaf but who knew that the condition was hypnotically induced, showed no such changes. Perhaps some older people's hearing loss develops so slowly that they do not realize that they are becoming deaf. Their attempt to explain their loss of hearing in some logical manner may be responsible for psychological reactions similar to those of college students who could not explain their deafness.

Processing Speed　As people age, it takes them longer to dial a telephone, zip up a jacket, unwrap a stick of gum, decide whether the trouble with a defective lamp is in the switch or the plug, and balance their checkbooks. This slowness seems to affect every kind of behavior. What causes the slowdown? Psychologists have not been able to determine exactly what sort of biological change is responsible for slowed execution of actions. Some have suggested that aging in the body's **peripheral nervous system** is responsible. This network of nerves and sensory receptors transmits sensations from the outside world to the central nervous system and motor commands to muscles. Pointing to the sensory changes that accompany aging, researchers have proposed that as people age, the quality of this transmission declines. It takes longer for stimulation from the environment to reach the brain and for commands from the brain to reach and activate the muscles involved.

Sensory slowing may contribute to slowed behavior, but Timothy Salthouse (1985) believes that it can account for only a small portion of the slowdown. If sensory slowing were the answer, the differences in speed between younger and older adults would remain the same on simple and complex tasks. On both tasks, transmitting sensory information and motor commands would take the same amount of time; the complexity occurs in the processing of information after it is received. But age does not affect behavior in this way; as tasks become more complex, age differences increase. Salthouse maintains that activity in the entire central nervous system (brain and spinal cord) slows with age, so that all aspects of information processing take longer. The only activities that escape this general slowdown are those that have become automatic, such as the highly practiced skill of the typist.

Brain and Nervous System

If behavioral slowing is due to slowed activity in the central nervous system, perhaps biological changes in the brain are responsible. Yet researchers have been unable to determine the effects of normal aging on the brain and spinal cord. Most of the information that we have about biological changes comes from the examination of brain tissue after death. At that time, it is difficult to separate the effects of normal aging from the effects of cardiovascular disease, respiratory function, brain disease, damage from drugs and alcohol, and other destructive forces (Bondareff, 1985).

The brain apparently shrinks with age. As tissue shrinks, the spaces deep within the brain (called *ventricles*) expand. By the age of seventy, the average person has lost 5 percent of brain mass; by the age of ninety, the loss approaches 20 percent. Yet the studies on which these estimates are based include people with varying degrees of disease. When researchers look only at brains of people whose cognitive functions were normal, they find considerably less shrinkage (Adams, 1980). A technique known as the **computerized axial tomography (CAT) scan** enables researchers to reconstruct cross sections of the living brain at any depth or at any angle. In a study using this technique, researchers studied the brains of adults and discovered that the brain begins to shrink slightly when people are in their thirties (Takeda and Matsuzawa, 1985). The shrinkage, which increases each decade thereafter, appears to be part of the normal course of aging, because only healthy adults took part in this study.

A factor that probably contributes to cognitive decline is a reduced concentration of certain chemicals that transmit signals in the brain. Neurons may stop manufacturing one of the essential transmitters. Without the transmitter,connections between neurons are lost, and neuronal circuits are disrupted. After enough circuits are destroyed, functions fail. This process eventually leads to the destruction of neurons themselves, but long before the neurons actually die, the damage is done (Bondareff, 1985). Many individuals show little or no effect from such neuronal loss, perhaps because as connections between some neurons are disrupted, new connections develop among other cells. Although brain cells cannot replace themselves, the new growth seems to compensate for part of the loss. These new fibers are more common in the brains of people in their late seventies and eighties than in the brains of fifty-year-olds, and William Bondareff (1985) believes that they may prevent a progressive decline in functioning during late old age.

In some older individuals, so many connections are disrupted that cognitive functioning is impaired. The nature of the impairment depends on the pattern of neuronal loss. Marcel Kinsbourne (1980) suggests that if the loss is spread diffusely across wide areas of the brain, all functions remain intact but processing is slowed. The person finds it difficult to cope with changing situations, responds sluggishly, and lacks mental alertness. Attention is impaired, so that when trying to carry out simultaneous tasks (driving a car and talking), one task interferes with the other. If the loss is concentrated in particular areas of the brain, the range of responses constricts. The person loses some normal behavioral options and relies heavily on others. Depending on the site of damage, a person might become impulsive or hesitant, continually find his or her attention caught by some detail, or able only to take a wide-ranging, superficial view.

Recordings of brain waves provide another measure of central nervous system activity. Until people are about eighty years old, the very fast brain waves that accompany concentration and thought are as prevalent as ever. However, as healthy people reach their late seventies, the proportion of very slow brain waves increases. If these slow waves spread across the brain, IQ scores decline (Marsh and Thompson, 1977). Researchers believe that increased slow-wave activity indicates a reduced flow of blood through brain tissue and a slowed metabolism within the brain. As metabolism slows, neurotransmitter production declines, and the disruptive chain of events described earlier begins (Bondareff, 1985).

Many developmentalists believe that cognitive declines traceable to the disruption of neuronal circuits or the loss of neurons primarily affect older adults who are in poor health. Until recently, most studies of cognitive changes in older adults were conducted in nursing homes, where few of the residents are in good health.

Disease

Most declines in cognitive functioning are more closely related to health than to age (Siegler and Costa, 1985). As we saw in Chapter 16, hypertension and cardiovascular disease are associated with IQ test declines during middle age. Older adults show the same connection; those with cardiovascular problems do worse on memory tasks than those who are healthy, and researchers speculate that much of the age-related decline that appears in experimental studies is caused by undiagnosed cardiovascular disease (Barrett and Watkins, 1986).

A small group of older adults show various forms of serious mental deterioration, known as *organic brain disorders*. Researchers estimate that about 5 percent of the elderly have moderate to severe organic brain disorders, and another 10 percent have mild disorders (La Rue, Dessonville, and Jarvik, 1985). These disorders have different causes but produce similar changes in cognitive processes and behavior. The signs of organic brain disorders include (1) a severe loss of intellectual ability that interferes with social or occupational functioning; (2) impaired memory; (3) impaired judgment or impaired thought processes (American Psychiatric Association, 1980). Organic brain disorders produce the deterioration of thought and personality commonly called "senility."

Multiinfarct Dementia Up to 20 percent of adults with organic brain disorders have **multiinfarct dementia,** a condition caused by vascular disease. It develops when blockage in small arteries repeatedly cuts off the blood supply to various parts of the brain. The blockages, which are actually a series of tiny "strokes," may go unnoticed; the first symptoms may be headaches or dizziness. Sometimes, however, spotty memory loss or an attack of confusion are the first signs of trouble (Butler and Lewis, 1982). A major difference between multiinfarct dementia and other organic brain disorders is the existence of periods when the person seems lucid and memories return (Sloane, 1980). Diagnosis is important, because medical treatment of hypertension and the underlying vascular disease can markedly slow the course of this disorder.

Alzheimer's Disease The commonest form of dementia is **Alzheimer's disease,** which affects about half of the adults with organic brain disorders. Another 12 percent have both Alzheimer's disease *and* multiinfarct dementia (Butler and Lewis, 1982). A certain diagnosis of Alzheimer's disease is possible only after death. The brains of Alzheimer's victims show four characteristic changes. First, they are infested with twisted clumps of nerve fibers, called *neurofibrillary tangles*. A few of these tangles appear in most aging brains, but only in Alzheimer's victims do they spread throughout the cortex and the hippocampus. Second, similar concentrations of *plaques,* which are patches of debris from dead neurons wrapped around a special protein, are found outside the nerve cells. Third, the fibers that bring impulses into nerve cells have atrophied. Fourth, the brain has shrunk markedly (see Figure 18.1). Physicians usually diagnose the disease by eliminating other possible causes.

What causes Alzheimer's disease? Researchers have discovered that a defective gene on chromosome 21 (the same chromosome involved in Down's syndrome) is responsible for at least 10 percent of the cases (St. George-Hyslop et al., 1987). Another gene located nearby on the same chromosome is responsible for the production of

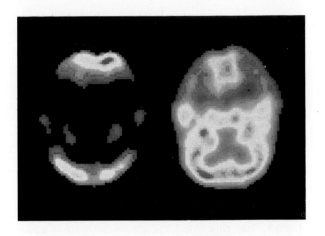

FIGURE 18.1   The difference between the normal brain of a seventy-two-year-old adult *(right)* and the brain of a seventy-three-year-old with Alzheimer's disease *(left)* shows clearly in this PET scan. PET scans are made by injecting radioactive glucose into the body and tracing the brain's uptake of the substance. More active brain sites take up more glucose, and the presence of the decaying radioactive ions shows brain function. *(NIH/Science Source-Photo Researchers)*

the special protein that is at the core of plaques and neurofibrillary tangles (Goldgaber, Lerman, McBride, Saffiotti, and Gajdusek, 1987). Other cases of Alzheimer's disease may be caused by a combination of genetic and special environmental conditions. Researchers still are not certain what conditions initiate the disease or why no genetic involvement can be found in many cases.

When Alzheimer's disease develops, its progression is always the same (Coyle, Price, and De-Long, 1983). The brain's supply of the transmitter acetylcholine is drastically reduced, primarily because the supply of enzyme that synthesizes this transmitter is depleted. Neurons deep within the brain, in an area where acetylcholine is produced, die. Their dying fibers, which stretch to other parts of the brain, form plaques. Starved of essential acetylcholine, neurons in other areas of the brain die, especially those in the hippocampus, a brain structure that is involved in the formation of memories (Hyman, Van Hoesen, Domasio, and Barnes, 1984), and in areas adjacent to it, blocking nerve impulses from entering or leaving this important structure (Clark, 1984).

Alzheimer's disease develops very slowly, and memory loss frequently is the first sign. The loss becomes severe and soon bears little relation to the memory lapses of normal aging. A person who is aging normally misplaces the car keys; a person with Alzheimer's disease forgets that he or she ever owned a car. The ability to write checks or to make change disappears. The same book can be read over and over, because the person cannot remember having read it. The ability to read remains for some time, long after the ability to understand what the person has read departs. A son handed his mother a greeting card from an old friend. The mother, a victim of Alzheimer's disease, read the card aloud from beginning to end in a monotone, then read "A Hallmark Card," and the price code across the bottom (Leroux, 1981). None of the words had any meaning for her.

Researchers have discovered that recall is the first cognitive process to decline (Vitaliano, Russo, Bren, Vitiello, and Prinz, 1986). When patients with mild Alzheimer's disease were compared with normal individuals, scores on recall tests distinguished between the groups, but scores on tests of attention and recognition memory were similar in both groups. As the disease progresses, attention and recognition memory begin to fail. Patients with mild and moderate Alzheimer's disease made equally poor scores on recall tests, but only among those with moderate cases had attention and recognition deteriorated. Two years later, the disease had progressed among patients with formerly mild cases; they also had developed problems with attention and recognition memory.

As the disease develops, people may dress for a snowstorm in midsummer, forget the names of their children, fail to recognize a spouse, or, while sitting in their living room, ask when they will be going home. They cannot feed or dress themselves. In the disease's final stages, people cannot speak or walk. Eventually, they die, often from pneumonia, urinary tract infections, or other complications that develop in bedridden patients.

There is no cure for Alzheimer's disease, although researchers have been experimenting with various drugs that increase the supply of acetylcholine (Clark, 1984). The progression of the disease cannot be halted, but simple aids, such as notes around the house ("Your lunch is in the refrigerator" on the refrigerator door; "Turn off the burner" above the stove; "Write down the name and number" beside the telephone; "Don't go out; I will be home at 3:30" on the front door) increase the period during which people with Alzheimer's disease can function independently.

Delirium As many as 20 percent of people with organic brain disorders have a reversible condition that responds to treatment. This acute disorder, known as **delirium**, is the result of disturbed metabolism throughout the brain. Patients with delirium show the symptoms of organic brain disorder but also may hallucinate, show paranoia, and display such physiological symptoms as fever, muscular tremors, rapid heartbeat, sweating, dilated pupils, and elevated blood pressure.

Delirium has many causes: acute alcohol intoxication, brain tumors, liver disease, cardiovascular disease, strokes, fever, emphysema, malnutrition, or any drug that affects the central nervous system. Often more than one of these factors is involved (Sloane, 1980). When the underlying cause or causes are treated, the delirium passes and the patient regains his or her mental faculties. Frequently, delirium develops in older people with cardiovascular disease who mistakenly take multiple doses of some prescribed medication.

LEARNING AND THINKING

In 1983, Frederick F. Bloch received his Ph.D. in history at New York University (*New York Times*, 1983). The topic of his dissertation was the common soldier in the Victorian British Army. This news would be unremarkable except for Bloch's age. He was eighty-one years old. It took him fifteen years to earn his doctorate, a program he embarked on after he sold his paper-export business and retired. Bloch's plans included a little teaching at NYU and writing a book on minorities in nineteenth-century Britain. The example of people like Bloch demonstrates convincingly that older adults can learn and that their thought processes need not deteriorate.

Few older adults engage in enterprises that produce such tangible evidence of their successful learning. Because we cannot see learning, but can

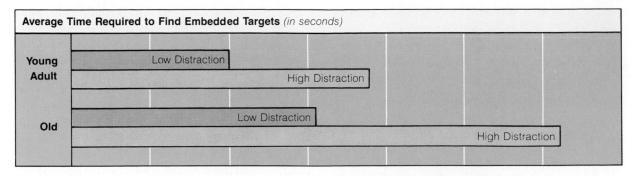

FIGURE 18.2   The performance of older adults may suffer when incidental information distracts their attention from the task at hand. In this study, adults tried to detect visual symbols embedded among other symbols. As the distraction of the background increased, the superiority of the young adults' performance over that of older adults climbed sharply. *(From Cerella, Poon, and Williams, 1974; based on data collected by Arnold and Farkas)*

only infer it from people's behavior, the process is difficult to study in older people. They may learn many things but have no occasion to use the knowledge they have acquired. Suppose that older adults are placed in a situation that calls for such knowledge but fail to use it. Did they fail to learn? There is no way to be certain. Perhaps they are simply too tired to use the knowledge or lack the motivation or opportunity to use it.

Older adults probably cannot learn as swiftly or as competently as they once did. Studies consistently show that younger adults outperform them on most aspects of learning. Yet because studies of learning are nearly always cross-sectional, it has been impossible to say exactly when an individual's learning skills begin to decline or how rapid the decline is likely to be. Researchers find it difficult to eliminate cohort effects or the effects of poor health, such as silent cardiovascular disease or early, undiagnosed Alzheimer's disease. Perhaps by looking at age-associated declines in concentration, reaction time, and learning speed, we can sort out the research findings.

Attention

Aging in the central nervous system makes it difficult for older adults to concentrate their attention on a task, according to some researchers. They have failed, however, to agree on just how atten-

tion is affected. Some suggest that older adults find it difficult to focus their attention because they are distracted by information that has nothing to do with the learning task (see Figure 18.2). Yet in some situations, older adults may be no more distractible than younger adults are. When researchers tested the ability of men and women to find particular letters in a visual display, college students' performance suffered as much from the presence of irrelevant information as that of older adults (Madden, 1983). This study seemed to indicate that older adults' problem was in concentrating their attention on relevant information, whether or not distractors were present.

What about those common situations of daily life in which few of us pay close attention to our activities? On the way to the airport, we try to remember whether we have done all the necessary chores. Did we lock the front door? Did we turn down the thermostat? Did we water the plants? Studies indicate that older adults store such information as younger people do; they know whether they had planned such activities and can usually say whether they carried them out (Kausler, Lichty, and Freund, 1985). Although there is some decline in older adults' accuracy at identifying which tasks they actually have completed, they are just as efficient as young adults at knowing which tasks they had planned to do.

Some researchers suggest that older adults' attention is not defective but simply inefficient

When they have an incentive and are given plenty of time, older people are efficient learners. This woman, who was never taught to read or write, is now on the road to literacy. *(Mark Mittelman)*

(Craik and Byrd, 1982). Although they still have the ability to learn, they either fail to attend to all aspects of a task, or else they simply do not make the effort required. In this view, older adults have a limited supply of mental energy. Because learning requires a deliberate application of attention that drains mental energy, older adults are unlikely to make a conscious effort to learn.

When people apply their attention to a learning task, they process the information at hand more deeply than when they have no interest in learning. They reorganize the information, elaborate it, make inferences about it, and relate it to other knowledge. Left to their own devices, older adults supposedly do not carry out this deep processing, but when the situation makes such processing easy

or accessible, they do so (Craik and Byrd, 1982).

In a study that required adults to respond to target letters by pressing a corresponding key for each letter, older adults seemed to have little trouble focusing their attention (Madden, 1985). Healthy, well-educated older adults benefited from cues that preceded the letter's appearance on the monitor just as college students did, and when the lapse between the cue and the target letter was very brief (200 milliseconds), they were more accurate than the younger adults. The results of this study fail to support the notion that older adults lack the mental energy for deliberate concentration. In every situation, however, older adults took much longer to press a key, an indication that their reaction time had slowed noticeably.

Reaction Time and Response Speed

Earlier we saw that older adults are slower at carrying out simple actions, such as zipping a jacket, than young or middle-aged adults are. They also learn new tasks more slowly in the laboratory and tend to make more errors after they learn them. In a typical test of motor-skill learning, the task was to keep a stylus on a penny-sized silver target as it moved in a clockwise direction (Wright and Payne, 1985). At the beginning of the task, seventy-year-olds were less efficient than nineteen-year-olds, and the difference widened with practice. Both groups improved over thirty trials, but younger adults improved much more rapidly than their elders. However, laboratory experiments (which generally give only a few minutes or hours of practice) are not able to mimic the sort of improvement with practice that goes on in daily life, where practice includes many thousands of "trials" (Salthouse, 1985).

Tasks such as following the target or key pressing would seem to depend heavily on reaction time. In key-pressing studies, adults often must learn to choose between two responses: press the key under your right index finger if the red light goes on; press the key under your left index finger if the green light goes on. Older adults have no trouble learning these responses, but their reaction time is slow; it takes them a fraction of a second longer to press the key after the light begins to glow than it does younger people. This difference is statistically significant in the psychology laboratory, but it is so small as to be meaningless in most daily tasks. As we might expect, there are wide individual differences in processing speed; in every study, some older adults react more quickly than the average young person. Yet most older adults may not respond as rapidly as they can. In one study, older men were reinforced for their correct responses (Baron and Menich, 1985). A message on the computer screen announced: "Right. You have earned one credit." After receiving such feedback, they began answering more quickly. However, reinforcement did not wipe out the difference between the speed of younger and older men; it merely reduced it.

The slowdown is much less noticeable among healthy older adults, who generally react about as fast as younger people who are out of condition (Salthouse, 1985). Most researchers accept some slowing in reaction time as an inevitable accompaniment of aging. But perhaps they are wrong. When Roberta Rikli and Sharman Busch (1986) tested a group of highly active women in their late sixties against a group of highly active college students, there were no significant age differences in reaction time. The older women had been following a program of vigorous activity (a minimum of 30 minutes of vigorous activity at least three times a week) for ten years or more. Physical activity had little effect on reaction time among the young; inactive college students reacted as swiftly as active college students did. The results indicate that a highly active life style may prevent the sort of cognitive slowing with age that researchers believe is responsible for most of the observed decline in reaction time.

Older adults clearly take longer to learn than do the young. Yet the differences are small in practical terms, and older adults' slowness does not interfere with most learning. Some of this slowness in learning may be due to the speed with which researchers require them to learn (Arenberg and Robertson-Tchabo, 1977). Perhaps when older adults have more time to respond, they can compensate for their slowness by some other means.

Pace of Learning

Some researchers have suggested that when older adults are allowed to learn at their own pace, they learn as much as younger learners. When required

to learn a list of words, for example, older adults may need fifteen trials to learn a list mastered by young adults in six trials (Kausler, 1982). Several factors may affect the speed at which older adults learn. First, older adults are often *cautious*. Instead of responding quickly on tests, they deliberate before responding. If they are not certain about the answer, they often do not respond at all. In many tests, the older learner's mistakes are errors of omission, but the younger learner's mistakes are wrong answers (Arenberg and Robertson-Tchabo, 1977).

Second, older adults may become *anxious*. When placed in an experimental situation, older adults may become so apprehensive that they do poorly. Nearly twenty years ago, researchers tested this notion by giving half of the adults in their study an injection that reduced their level of arousal (Eisdorfer, Nowlin, and Wilkie, 1970). Older adults who had received the calming drug made better scores on the learning task than those who had received an injection of sterile water.

Finally, information from other situations may *interfere* with the learning task. When older adults begin a learning task, previously established habits may affect their general approach to the experimental situation (Arenberg and Robertson-Tchabo, 1977). If the initial instructions are complicated, older adults may develop misconceptions about the task that the experimenter cannot correct. Or they may fail to use the strategies that the experimenter has asked them to employ, and revert instead to their own customary, but inappropriate, strategies.

Problem Solving

Older adults' lives are filled with problems of all shapes and sizes. Some are as trivial as opening a "child-proof" medicine bottle or deciding which brand and size of supermarket products to buy. Some are worrisome but can usually be solved: what to do when the refrigerator stops making ice or how to get into a locked apartment when the key has been left inside. The solutions to others can have serious consequences. Is the protection of Medicare sufficient, or is a supplementary Medigap policy a wise idea? If so, which kind? Is it best to sell a Nebraska home and move to the sunny Southwest, buy a condominium in the town where a child lives, or simply stay put?

Older adults solve the daily problems they encounter, although most are neither as fast nor efficient as they once were. *(Chuck Beckley/Southern Light)*

Faced with a problem, an adult may use any of a variety of strategies to solve it. The aggravation of the child-proof cap may be solved by carefully following the instructions on the cap, by destroying the plastic bottle and placing the tablets in another container, or by asking the pharmacist to use a different kind of cap. Adults may meet problems by applying old strategies rigidly, by adjusting their strategies to meet the new situation, by devising new strategies, by ignoring the problem, or by manipulating the environment so that the problem changes (as when older adults refuse to buy medication in child-proof containers) (Reese and Rodeheaver, 1985).

There are no studies to show how older adults actually go about solving such everyday problems, but on laboratory tasks they generally do worse than young adults. Some laboratory tasks require deductive reasoning. In a typical study, adults read the description of three-course meals, with four alternatives for each course (Hartley, 1981). Two of the twelve dishes had been poisoned, so that eating either of them was fatal. (Safe meals contained neither of the poisoned foods.) To discover which foods were tainted, a person made up a three-course meal, and the experimenter said whether the person who ate it would live or die. Solving the problem required thinking in terms of "*either* oysters *or* pie or *both*." Older adults were much less likely to solve the problem than either young or middle-aged adults were, and those who were successful required more tries to figure out the answer. Older adults seemed to have trouble understanding that discovering that one food might be poisoned did not eliminate the possibility that another food at the meal was also poisoned. They also persisted with inefficient strategies, often stuck with their hunches, and failed to test all possibilities.

Whether older adults also are less competent at solving practical problems is uncertain. Nancy Denney and A. M. Palmer (1981) tried to simulate practical problems in the laboratory. They asked adults how they would handle such situations as a refrigerator that was warm inside, a flooded basement, being stranded on a highway in a blizzard, witnessing a mugging, and receiving a threatening telephone call. Middle-aged adults provided the most competent solutions, with both young adults and older adults apparently less able to handle the problems by themselves and more likely to depend on others. However, it is risky to generalize from such findings. The best solution for such situations would differ from person to person, depending on their experience in related situations and their physical condition.

Some older adults solve abstract problems as well as younger men and women. They play cognitive games efficiently, apply deductive logic, organize elements of the problem, and devise (and follow) systematic strategies. In the poisoned-food game, older adults who do well tend to be well educated and to have high fluid-intelligence scores (Reese and Rodeheaver, 1985). In fact, when older and younger adults are matched on tests of nonverbal intelligence, there is no age-related decline in problem solving (Denney, 1982). Cohort influence may play a role here, with the generally lower educational levels of today's older adults handicapping their performance on the sort of task that may come easily to those with extensive education.

Can Learning and Thinking of Older Adults Be Modified?

Perhaps older adults fail to use effective strategies when learning or solving problems because they have had no occasion to use such strategies in many years. Such a "disuse" effect is familiar among younger people. When English-speaking adults who have learned French do not use the language for years, they believe that they have forgotten how to speak it. But should they spend a month or two in France, their command of the language returns and they speak it as well as they ever did. The same sort of process affects some psychomotor skills. Donald Kausler (1982) reports the experience of an eighty-year-old man who had not typed for decades. When he sat down at the typewriter, he was no faster than he had been after his first week of introductory typing years before, but after a month of daily practice, he regained his skill. If disuse is a major factor in older adults' failure to use effective strategies, then direct training might improve their learning and problem-solving skills.

Acting on this assumption, researchers have used various techniques to encourage the adoption of effective strategies among older adults (Denney, 1982). No matter what technique is used, the training is usually effective. Presented with the same sort of problem they solved during training, older adults tend to use the new strategies. The question is whether adults who use them effectively on specific problems will transfer the strategies to problems that are not obviously similar. As a general rule, transfer tends to be limited to similar situations.

In an intervention program that used video-games to speed information processing in older adults, transfer was apparent (Clark, Lanphear, and Riddick, 1987). Videogames demand controlled attention. Players must notice similarities and differences quickly, focus their attention selectively, and concentrate on the task in a sustained way. The games provide immediate feedback; there is no doubt about the correctness or incorrectness of the player's responses. Seven weeks of daily play at Pac Man and Donkey Kong resulted in an enormous increase in older adults' scores on the games, as we might expect. What the researchers wanted to know was whether experience at Pac Man translated into more efficient responses in other situations. Older adults' skill did transfer; they became faster and more accurate in a key-pressing task of reaction time after making choices. The researchers believe that playing the game affected the older adults' information-processing strategies, and encouraged them to adopt a strategy that reduced the time required to select a response. For example, some may have begun keeping critical stimulus-response pairs (Pac Man "ghost"/Reverse direction) in their working memory.

Researchers have wondered why older adults seem to use efficient strategies only after some sort of intervention program. Perhaps they begin work on a problem without even considering which strategies they might use. Perhaps they consider the strategies but do not understand their value, or they feel that the strategies are too difficult to use. Alan Hartley and Joan Anderson (1986) tried to discover which explanation was correct. One group of adults was pushed to generate strategies. They were asked to describe all the strategies they could think of that might be helpful in solving the problem. A second group of adults read written descriptions of possible strategies and judged how good each strategy would be in solving the problem. Older adults generated just as many strategies as young adults did, but their strategies were less efficient than those proposed by young adults. Older adults were also less accurate than the young at judging relative effectiveness of strategies. Apparently, the age difference in problem solving is primarily a production deficiency. Older adults use inefficient strategies, but when convinced of a strategy's value, they adopt it.

MEMORY IN LATER LIFE

Because problem solving and learning both depend on the ability to acquire, retain, and recall information, memory declines may be responsible for much of whatever cognitive decline appears in later adulthood. At the beginning of the chapter, we met two eminent psychologists in their seventies who complained about memory lapses. Skinner (1983) recommended memory cues as an aid to

CAN INTERVENTION STUDIES REVERSE COGNITIVE DECLINE?

When cognition follows the classic aging pattern, declines are concentrated in intellectual skills tapped by nonverbal measures. Once such a decline occurs, is it permanent? Or can the sort of training that has been successful with problem-solving strategies reverse the apparent deterioration? Working with members of a longitudinal study of IQ, Warner Schaie and Sherry Willis (1986) have shown that long term declines can be reversed.

Adults in this group, whose ages ranged from sixty-four to ninety-five, had taken IQ tests in 1970, 1977, and 1984. Over the fourteen-year period, nearly half had shown no cognitive decline in inductive reasoning or spatial orientation, the two skills selected for intervention. Some had declined in one skill, but not the other (nearly one-third); and some had declined in both skills (nearly one-fourth). The reasoning test requires a person to figure out the rule governing a series of letter or numbers. During the training program, adults learned four major rules that govern such series as well as three strategies that helped them identify the pattern (scanning the series, saying the series aloud in order to hear the pattern, and underlining repeated letters in the series). They then applied their new knowledge not only to problems using letters, but also to patterns of musical notes and travel schedules. The training program in spatial orientation relied primarily on instruction and practice in cognitive strategies that enable people to rotate objects mentally. The strategies included learning terms for various angles, practice in manually rotating three-dimensional forms, practice in mentally rotating drawings of familiar objects, and learning to focus on one or two features of the abstract figure when mentally rotating it. Each adult entered one of the training programs, which consisted of five one-hour sessions.

After the completion of the program, each person was retested. Among adults whose scores had declined, four out of ten completely reversed the drop; their scores were as high as they had been fourteen years earlier (see graph). Another two out of ten showed improvement, although their scores had not returned all the way to the 1970 level. Among adults whose scores had been stable for fourteen years,

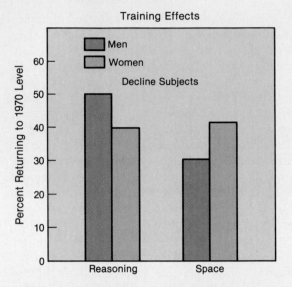

A five-hour training course was sufficient to return many older adults' scores on IQ subtests to their previous levels. (From Schaie and Willis, 1986)

more than half showed significant gains in reasoning and four out of ten showed significant gains in spatial orientation. Neither age nor education nor income level affected this pattern.

The training effects were ability-specific. That is, significant score increases appeared only in the cognitive skill covered by the intervention program. People's scores on other IQ subtests showed no change. Such a result indicates that the improvements in spatial orientation or inductive reasoning were real improvements and not simply signs of test sophistication or improved response speed resulting from practice. None of the training was identical to the content of the IQ test; instead it focused on strategies. Older adults' application of these strategies to new content areas indicated that the training transferred.

The good news from this study is that relatively healthy older adults have flexible minds. Cognitive decline that appears in most IQ tests may be the result of disuse — not the sign of mental deterioration.

daily activities. He found that he could remember to take an umbrella on a day that threatened rain by hanging the umbrella over the doorknob as soon as the thought crossed his mind. Hebb (1978) was not quite as optimistic, saying that such a strategy worked best for him when the object was big enough to trip him as he went out the door.

Memory research rarely focuses on such everyday tasks as remembering to carry an umbrella or take prescribed medication. Instead, most studies try to determine how aging affects various aspects of the information-processing system that are involved in the storage and retrieval of information (see Figure 2.1 on p. 42). As we saw in Chapter 2, information from the environment enters the sensory register as a fleeting sense impression, where it is stored briefly — for less than a second. If the information catches our attention, it moves into the phase of short-term memory, which is a temporary holding and organizing system. In short-term memory, information is encoded, and we are conscious of its presence. As information fades out of consciousness, it is either lost or stored in long-term memory. When we need information, it is retrieved from long-term memory, activated, and returned to short-term memory, where we are aware of it. Problems with memory may arise during any of these processes.

Older adults consistently do worse than young or middle-aged adults on various memory tasks, but just which aspect of the memory system may be responsible for these age differences is not clear (Howe and Hunter, 1986). Older people take longer to memorize a list of words and make more mistakes when recalling them, whether the list consists of unrelated items, items that can be grouped by category, or pairs of previously unassociated words (river/stone). However, when they are asked to memorize and recall previously related word pairs (ham/eggs; dream/sleep), older adults generally do as well as younger people (Gillund and Perlmutter, in press).

Encoding

Before information can be encoded, it must be present in the sensory register. Its presence there prolongs the period when it is available for identi-fication and selection for encoding, a step that permanently records the information. Sensory memory, either for sights or for sounds, appears to be relatively unaffected by aging (Kausler, 1982; Poon, 1985). The capacity of short-term memory seems similarly unaffected by aging. There are few age differences in digit or word span tests, in which people repeat a string of digits or words that they have just heard. Older adults also show the same *recency effect* as younger adults; if researchers read aloud a list of words that exceeds the capacity of short-term memory, older adults remember the last few words (which are still in short-term memory) as well as younger adults do (Craik and Rabinowitz, 1984). In practical terms, this means that after looking up a phone number, for example, older adults are generally as good as younger people at remembering the number long enough to dial it.

Yet when older people must manipulate or reorganize information in some way, as when they must repeat a phone number in reverse order, age differences in short-term memory become apparent (Erber, 1982). Reorganization is an important aid when information is to be encoded for permanent storage; it is one sort of encoding strategy. When encoding material, older adults may not be using such strategies. Some researchers believe that the failure to use efficient encoding strategies indicates that older adults' processing abilities have deteriorated: they can no longer use strategies that they once employed. Other researchers are convinced that the problem is not a processing deficiency, but a production deficiency. That is, older adults are capable of encoding information efficiently, but they do not make spontaneous use of helpful memory strategies. This view was supported by a study in which older adults had to organize a word list by category, a procedure that forced them to think about the meaning of each word (Mitchell and Perlmutter, 1986). On an unexpected test of recall, the age difference disappeared. Older adults recalled about as many words as young adults did.

Storage

How efficient is the older adult's retention of material? That probably depends more on the thor-

IT WAS SIXTY YEARS AGO, BUT IT SEEMS JUST LIKE YESTERDAY

Most of us believe that older people forget what happened last week or last month but can remember events from their childhood and youth with clarity. This view of memory in old age may be another of our many myths about aging. Certainly, many old people can give elaborate accounts of youthful incidents, but according to Timothy Salthouse (1982), four problems keep us from accepting those reminiscences as evidence for a clear memory of early days. First, the information in the stories may be as much fiction as fact. Second, the stories may primarily describe incidents that were highly important or memorable for one reason or another ("what I was doing when I heard about Pearl Harbor"; "the first time I saw your grandmother"; "the time I finally got the best of the neighborhood bully"). Memories of less important incidents may have faded. Third, much of the material may be inference, not memory. Describing her sixth birthday, your great-grandmother may supply details that were probably accurate (six candles on the cake) or common to most birthdays. Fourth, the incident may not be remembered from long ago but from the time it was last told. Each time we recall an incident, we rehearse it and elaborate on it. Instead of being a sixty-year-old memory, the story actually may be a memory that is no more than six months—or six weeks—old.

Because of these problems, establishing the quality of remote memories has eluded laboratory researchers. Some have asked adults of varying ages about newsworthy events that happened in the past. These studies have produced conflicting results, with some showing the memories of older people superior (Perlmutter, 1978), some showing no difference (Botwinick and Storandt, 1974), and some

showing superior memory in the young (Squire, 1974). Yet there is no way to make certain whether people are remembering from personal experience or from reading historical accounts. Moreover, some people do not recall past events because they paid little attention to them at the time. A person who has no interest in baseball is unlikely to recall who won the World Series thirty years ago—or even last year.

Another method used to tap remote memories is to give adults single-word cues (garden, Christmas, school) and ask them to respond with "the first life event that occurs to you." When Dennis Holding and his associates used this method, the responses failed to support the notion that older adults remember their early experiences best (Holding, Noonan, Pfau, and Holding, 1986). The recollections of adults in their seventies followed the same pattern found in college students: more than two-thirds of their memories came from the recent past —the quarter of their lives immediately preceding the test. Both young and old found recent memories the easiest to retrieve and easiest to date after they had been recalled. The major age difference in the study was the speed with which memories were retrieved and dated. Older adults took about twice as long as the young to come up with appropriate memories.

Although establishing the accuracy of anyone's memory for remote events has been difficult, many researchers have concluded that older adults recall incidents from their distant past with considerable accuracy but that they are just as good at remembering things that happened recently (Erber, 1981).

oughness with which he or she processes it than on age. Information that is reorganized, elaborated, or related to other knowledge enters long-term memory, which provides a relatively permanent record. This deep processing interprets the information and integrates it with information that a

person already possesses. Such information is unlikely to be lost, although it may become momentarily unavailable.

Early studies indicated substantial age differences in the "loss" of recently learned material from storage. When asked to recall material that they had learned the previous week, younger adults remembered far more than older adults. Researchers suggested that older adults had trouble remembering because they were highly susceptible to interference from other stored information. Later studies showed that it was not interference but inefficient learning that was responsible for most age differences. When researchers arranged memory tasks so that older adults learned the material as thoroughly as younger adults, age differences virtually disappeared (Kausler, 1982). Interference can cause forgetting, but the young are just as susceptible to it as the old.

Retrieval

Although encoding problems apparently are responsible for a major part of the age difference on memory tasks, the retrieval process may add to the problem. Sometimes the material may be stored but elude the older person's search. This conjecture is supported by older adults' ability to recognize material that they have previously encountered. When adults recognize a word list that they have not been able to recall, for example, the deficiency is in the search process. Seeing the original list seems to act as a cue, which makes it easier for them to retrieve the information (Perlmutter, 1979). When adults can neither recall nor recognize the information, they have failed to encode it efficiently.

Age differences appear in both recognition and recall memory, but experiments indicate a much smaller decline in recognition. In some conditions, older adults' recognition memory is as good as that of younger adults. When shown a series of photographs and line drawings, for example, adults in their late sixties later recognized the pictures as accurately as college students did (Park, Puglisi, and Smith, 1986). Both young and old found it easier to recognize photographs or drawings that were highly detailed, an indication that both had processed the details. Yet four weeks later, when they returned to the lab, age differences appeared. College students' recognition was more accurate, and older adults turned in many more "false alarms" (claiming to recognize pictures that were not part of the original set).

In some situations, the characteristics of the people studied determine whether age differences appear on tests of recognition. When testing adults on their ability to recognize words, researchers found that those in their seventies with high verbal IQs recognized words as efficiently as did college students with similar IQs (Bowles and Poon, 1982). But among adults with low verbal IQs, those in their seventies did much worse than young adults with similar IQs. Apparently, a large store of knowledge can compensate for processing declines related to recognition.

Age differences in recall are generally larger when people expect to be tested. In such tests, people memorize a word list, then try to repeat the words spontaneously (a procedure known as *free recall*). Age differences in free recall first appear when people reach their thirties, and the gap between twenty-year-olds and their elders gets wider with each passing decade. However, when a retrieval cue (such as the name of a category) is presented at the time of testing, age differences shrink (Craik, 1977). Because stored information is organized by meaning, the category name activates related concepts. This narrows the search task; it requires less processing. Younger adults profit less from the retrieval cue, perhaps because they supply their own retrieval cue during free recall.

Memory for Prose

Most assessments of memory depend on adults' ability to recall isolated words. Except for shopping lists, such tasks are rarely encountered in daily life. More important is the ability to read and recall meaningful information. In such cases, the goal is to recall the gist of the text, not its literal wording. Does the older adult's ability to recall what he or she has read in newspapers, magazines, and books show a decline with age?

Whether age differences disappear in the comprehension of articles depends on several factors (Dixon, Hultsch, Simon, and Von Eye, 1984). One important factor is whether the article is well organized, so that its main points are not buried somewhere in the middle of the text. Another important factor is verbal ability. Among adults who make high scores on vocabulary tests, there are no age differences in the ability to extract the most

Older adults of high verbal ability can recall the gist of a newspaper article they have just read as well as a younger person. *(Barbara Rios/Photo Researchers)*

important ideas from a prose passage. Whether adults are in their twenties, their forties, or their eighties, their scores are almost identical. Among adults who make low scores on vocabulary tests, there are consistent age differences in the ability to extract the most important ideas, with young adults doing the best and older adults doing the worst. In general, it seems that age differences in text recall are minimal or even nonexistent when the original text is well-organized, when both old and young are familiar with the topic, and when they have above average verbal ability (Hultsch and Dixon, 1984).

Metamemory

Is older adults' failure to use strategies on memory tasks related to declines in their knowledge about the memory system? If the relation between production deficiencies and metamemory is the same

for children and adults, this could account for the failure. As we saw in Chapter 11, once children's understanding of the memory system deepens and they become convinced of the value of memory strategies, they adopt them. Until that time, they do not use strategies spontaneously even if they know how to use them.

When researchers investigated this possibility, they discovered that knowledge about the effectiveness of strategies is only one aspect of metamemory. It also includes knowledge of basic memory processes (for example, knowing that it is easier to remember interesting facts than facts that are dull), knowledge of our own mental capacity (for example, knowing whether we are good at remembering names), awareness of any changes in the ability to remember, knowing that emotional states affect the ability to remember (for example, it is harder to remember when upset), motivation (the belief that having a good memory and performing well on memory tasks is important), and the perception of some control over the ability to remember. After analyzing metamemory in this way, Roger Dixon and David Hultsch (1983) compared adults' knowledge of metamemory's various aspects with their ability to recall the gist of prose passages that they had read. The aspects of metamemory that were associated with the ability to recall text changed with age. Younger adults' performance depended on their knowledge of strategies, the general workings of the memory system, and their own capacity to remember. Although understanding the memory system was also important for older adults, their motivation and the belief that they had some control over their memories were equally important. With age, attitudes apparently come to have an increasingly powerful effect on the ability to remember.

When the situation concerns meaningful information, older adults have little trouble predicting what they know. Using questions about movies, sports, and current events that had been failed in a recall test (for example, "What was the former name of Muhammad Ali?"), researchers presented the questions in a multiple-choice form (Lachman and Lachman, 1980). As adults answered, they indicated how certain they were that their answers were correct. All age groups were able to answer additional questions, but older adults (average age sixty-eight) answered more of them than younger adults did. The researchers attributed this difference to older adults' cautiousness; on the recall test, the old were less likely to guess when uncertain of the answer. What about the "feeling of knowing"? It was the same in all age groups. No age differences appeared in either the efficiency of retrieving additional knowledge or the relation between accuracy and adults' confidence in their answers (see Figure 18.3). Older adults apparently can monitor the accessibility of their stored knowledge as efficiently as younger adults.

Training Programs

Although older adults' memory performance is marked by production deficiencies, they already are using some memory strategies. They make lists, put objects in prominent positions, take notes at meetings, carry an appointment book, keep a "birthday book," and provide themselves with other simple retrieval cues. Their environment provides other external cues, just as it does for the young. Catalogues in the mailbox, ads in the media, the change of seasons, the migration of birds, all remind them when to prepare for spring gardening, for holidays, and the like. In fact, when retrieval difficulties appear, the lack of appropriate external cues may be responsible. Irene Hulicka (1982), who was given a series of youthful letters between an eighty-year-old man and his seventy-five-year-old sister, prepared twenty questions about trips, friends, celebrations, and family problems that were detailed in the letters. The eighty-year-old could answer only four of the questions, his sister only three. Later the pair, who had been separated for several years, met in Hulicka's presence. She again asked them the twenty questions, as well as ten new ones. By providing each other with retrieval cues, they were able to answer nine of the new questions and all but one of the old ones.

The abundance of external retrieval cues (seasonal catalogs from suppliers, calendars, and the like) enables older people to keep running their businesses efficiently whether or not they have begun to experience minor memory problems. *(James Knowles/ Stock, Boston)*

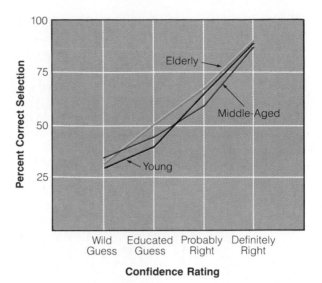

FIGURE 18.3 When asked about meaningful material, older adults' "feeling of knowing" was as accurate as that of young and middle-aged adults. Older adults' percentage of correct answers in relation to confidence in their choices was just as high as younger people's. *(From Lachman and Lachman, 1980)*

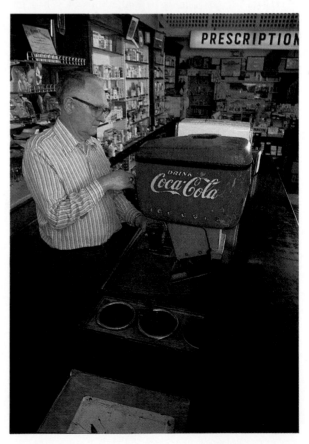

HOW OLDER ADULTS
ASSESS MEMORY DECLINES

Seemingly healthy older adults frequently complain about memory failures. Younger adults also forget things, but their memory lapses seem less frequent, and they rarely are upset by forgetfulness (Cavanaugh, Grady, and Perlmutter, 1983). Many older adults are upset by their memory failures, perhaps because they have accepted the myth that a deteriorating memory is an inevitable part of old age.

The most frequent memory lapse among older men and women in Cambridge, England, was finding that they could not recall a word that was "on the tip of their tongue" (Sunderland, Watts, Baddeley, and Harris, 1986). Other major complaints were forgetting where they had put an object; having to go back and check to see if they had done a task; forgetting something they had been told the previous day; forgetting to take an object with them; during a conversation, forgetting what they had just said; and confusing the details of something they had just heard.

Despite such common complaints, research indicates that older adults may exaggerate the degree of their mental lapses. When researchers ask about memory problems, they often find that older adults' complaints of forgetfulness are not related to their scores on objective tests of memory. Instead, the complaints are strongly related to measures of depression (O'Hara, Hinrichs, Kohout, Wallace, and Lemke, 1986). Compared with older adults who are not depressed, depressed adults complain more about forgetting names, faces, words, phone numbers, and where they put things. They rate their memory as poorer than that of most other adults of their own age, and they are more likely to say that their memory is not nearly as good as it was in young adulthood. But when given a free-recall test, they remember as many words as nondepressed adults do. In other words, the older adult who complains most bitterly about memory lapses tends to perform just as well on tests of memory as the adult who has no particular complaint.

Why should depressed adults believe that their memory is so poor? Perhaps their depression leads them to focus on the unpleasant aspects of their lives. They complain about their appetite, their loss of interest in activities, their fatigue, their inability to make decisions—and their memory lapses. Aware of the myths about aging, they may be especially sensitive to each sign of a failing memory and exaggerate its importance (Zarit, 1980).

Older adults who believe such myths may become so worried about the consequences of a deteriorating memory that their general efficiency and psychological well-being suffer (Hulicka, 1982). Yet the slight memory impairment that accompanies aging does not interfere with daily life among adults who are free from organic brain disorders. Although most older people are convinced that their memory has declined since their youth, few regard such memory failures as much of a handicap (Sunderland et al., 1986).

Problems with names, faces, words, telephone numbers, and where they put things still bother many older adults. Memory-training programs can minimize such problems. Programs in which adults learn new encoding strategies have been successful in improving memory skills, even among adults with mild brain disorders (Poon, 1985). Most of these programs rely on imagery, a memory strategy that is extremely effective but one that is less common than rehearsal or organization.

Imagery can be especially effective in helping people connect names with faces. In one training program, researchers taught a group of retired middle managers how to connect a prominent facial feature with a person's name (Yesavage, Rose, and Bower, 1983). After selecting the facial feature (large mouth), these older adults learned to create an image from a person's name ("Whalen" becomes a whale), then to visualize that image in connection with the prominent feature (a whale stuck in a person's mouth). Finally, they were to

Older people take longer to complete minor tasks primarily because the rate at which they process information has slowed. *(Rohn Engh/The Image Works)*

decide whether the created image was pleasant or unpleasant. This final step required them to think about the image, so that they processed it more thoroughly during encoding. After brief training, older adults' recall of names doubled. Such programs are even more effective when they are preceded by a pretraining program that reduces older adults' anxiety about their memory problems (Yesavage and Jacob, 1984).

In a self-teaching program, older adults who had complained of memory lapses learned a variety of memory techniques (Scogin, Storandt, and Lott, 1985). Each adult who enrolled received a ninety-two-page manual that contained a guided course of 16 one-hour study periods. They learned to create interacting images, to chunk large amounts of material into compact form (remembering "110011001100" as "three 1100s"), to organize material by category, and to use the method of loci. This last technique involves visualizing a familiar location, such as a person's home, then placing each item to be remembered at a different location (a loaf of bread on the sofa, a bottle of milk on the coffee table, a pound of hamburger by the front door, and so on). To recall the items, you take a mental walk through the house and call off each item as you pass it. The self-training significantly improved their scores on free recall of word lists and on recalling names and faces. Although their memory performance had improved, these adults continued to complain about their failing memories. As the accompanying box, "How Older Adults Assess Memory Declines," indicates, memory complaints of older adults are not related to their memory proficiency.

The self-training study indicates that older adults can improve their memory without elaborate or expensive training programs. Yet not everyone profits from such programs, and no single method works for all adults or in all situations

(Poon, 1985). Will older adults continue to use these memory techniques in their daily lives? No one is certain. The use of imagery requires time at encoding; after taking the self-training program, older adults' study time on memory tasks increased significantly. As we have seen, older people seem to have diminished mental energy. If they find these techniques to be too much trouble, they are likely to discard them. The key to continued use is probably motivation. When older adults have some goal that the techniques would help them reach and are convinced of the techniques' usefulness, they are likely to continue using them.

SUMMARY

1. Most people have many misconceptions about growing old. These misconceptions are partly responsible for the development of **ageism,** which is prejudice against old people.

2. Some sensory loss occurs with age, but the losses are not uniform and vary greatly from one person to the next. Motor actions, decisions, and problem solving take longer than they once did. Some believe that slowed transmission in the **peripheral nervous system** is responsible, but others believe that activity throughout the central nervous system slows.

3. By using **computerized axial tomography (CAT) scans,** researchers have established that the brain shrinks with age, beginning when people are in their thirties. Reduced production of neurotransmitters, which can lead to neural death, may be implicated in cognitive slowing, although new connections between neurons make up for much of the loss. Health, not age, is the primary predictor of cognitive decline. Severe loss of intellectual ability, serious memory impairment, and impaired thought processes are caused by organic brain disorders. Irreversible disorders include **multiinfarct dementia** (caused by cardiovascular disease) and **Alzheimer's disease** (apparently caused by defective genes or a combination of genetic and environmental circumstances). **Delirium,** which reflects disturbed metabolism throughout the brain, has many causes and can be reversed.

4. Older adults seem to have more trouble than young adults in learning new material, perhaps because their limited supply of mental energy makes them reluctant to concentrate on the task at hand. Slowed reaction time may also be a problem, although health seems to play a larger role than age in the slowing of reaction time. Factors that may slow older adults' learning include caution, anxiety, and interference by old habits. On laboratory tasks, older adults are worse than young adults at problem solving, in part because they tend to use inefficient strategies. The problem seems to be a production deficiency, because older adults can use efficient strategies when asked to do so.

5. Neither the sensory register nor the capacity of short-term memory appears to decline with age, although when older adults must manipulate material in short-term memory, they do not perform as well as younger people. Older adults' failure to use efficient encoding strategies seems to be primarily a production deficiency. When they process the material thoroughly, older adults seem to store it as well as the young do.

6. Age differences are greater in recall than in recognition, but recall differences shrink when retrieval cues are available. Age differences in recalling well-organized text disappear among adults of high verbal ability who are familiar with the topic. With age, motivation and a belief in the ability to control memory become as important in recall as an understanding of the memory system. Memory-training programs can minimize some of the problems that older adults have with names, faces, phone numbers, and the like.

KEY TERMS

ageism

Alzheimer's disease

computerized axial tomography
(CAT) scan

delirium

multiinfarct dementia

peripheral nervous system

STUDY TERMS

Alzheimer's disease   The most prevalent organic brain disorder; this debilitating, irreversible brain disorder is characterized by increasingly serious memory loss and deterioration of attention, judgment, and personality.

delirium   A reversible organic brain disorder that reflects disturbed metabolism throughout the brain.

multiinfarct dementia   An irreversible organic brain disorder that is the result of cardiovascular disease and that develops when blood supply to the brain is interrupted repeatedly.

CHAPTER 19

Self and Society:
Living Successfully

The past twenty-five years have treated our quartet of adults relatively well. None has major health problems, and only one has economic worries. As they have aged, each has traveled down a different path, meeting the developmental demands, first of early adulthood, then of middle-age. At sixty-five, Susan has a successful career as a family therapist. She plans to continue working for several years but has decided to cut back on her practice. Her husband retired two years ago but on occasion consults for his old firm. Their economic situation is solid, and both are in good health. Susan gave up smoking ten years ago and is heavier than she used to be, but she swims regularly. Her husband still jogs three times a week. They have talked about moving to a retirement community in Arizona but have decided to wait. Their older child presented them with a grandson last year, and they want to stay nearby through his preschool years.

Scott is now the head of his law firm and the wealthiest of the four. He has no intention of retiring and expects to be involved with the firm in some way as long as he is healthy. He dreads retirement because it symbolizes old age to him. Five years ago he had a heart attack, but by watching his diet and exercising, he has kept in good shape. During midlife, Scott and Samantha drifted apart. Ten years ago, there was an amicable divorce and Scott remarried. His second wife, Sally, is ten years younger than he and is a partner in a local real estate firm. Scott and Sally play golf regularly, go to Europe in the spring, and go to a condominium on Antigua in the winter.

Donna will retire this year, although she has mixed feelings about the prospect. She looks forward to gardening but is not eager to spend all her time at home with her husband. They are not close, and their relationship is strained. Pete has a bad back and took early retirement, and so his Social Security is smaller than they had expected. When Donna retires, she will have Social Security, supplemented by a small pension from the insurance agency. Although their house is paid for, money will be tight. Donna's eldest daughter did go to college, where she majored in business, a move that placed her in the middle class. She is divorced and lives nearby with her two adolescent children. The other two children are also married and have children. Donna's life revolves around her children and grandchildren.

David is ready to retire from the state department of transportation. He has high blood pressure but manages to control it with medication. Together with Social Security, his pension will be adequate, once the mortgage is paid off. Denise plans to work for another seven years, until she is sixty-five. Then they may sell their house and buy a trailer. Their marriage is good, and they enjoy each other's company. Their largest problem is trying to decide whether to travel for a few years or to settle in a Florida trailer development.

What can our four adults expect in old age? In this chapter, we find that the last stage of life is fulfilling for some and disappointing for others. Once more we begin with a look at the influences of social change on development. After considering the physical changes that typify the last decades of life, we return to theories discussed earlier and see how they apply to late adulthood. In tracing the final development of self-concept, we also take up the stresses of old age and the importance of social support. Because few older adults work past the age of sixty-five, our exploration of the occupational sphere of life focuses primarily on retirement. Our examination of family life explores the effects of retirement on the marital relationship, divorce and remarriage, children, and grandchildren. Next we look at the living arrangements of

older adults and find that they generally are determined by whether one is young-old or old-old.

SOCIAL CHANGE

Today's older Americans are different from the generations that will follow them. Their outlook and previous experiences are much more traditional. Few of today's sixty-five- and seventy-year-olds cohabited before marriage, although a considerable number of them have picked up the notion from their grandchildren. Faced with a reduction in Social Security benefits or their widow's pension if they remarried, many older women simply moved in with a male companion and lover. Changes in pension laws have reversed this trend, which peaked in 1970, when 34 percent of cohabiting couples were at least sixty-five years old. Today, when the number of cohabiting couples in the United States has quadrupled, the number of older couples has dropped by 35 percent (U.S. Bureau of the Census, 1986).

Different cohorts age in different ways, and changes in life patterns are the result of historical events during the cohort's lifetime (Hagestad and Neugarten, 1985). Today's older adults are finding that old age has changed dramatically since their grandparents reached the age of sixty-five. In 1900, about 4 percent of the population (3 million people) had reached their sixty-fifth birthdays, and about 40 percent of the babies born that year would live to celebrate their sixty-fifth birthdays in 1965. In 1984, 11.5 percent of the population (26 million people) were at least sixty-five years old, and about 80 percent of the babies born that year probably will live to celebrate their sixty-fifth birthdays in 2049. The rise in the proportion of the over sixty-five crowd obscures the even more dramatic rise in the oldest group of all—Americans past the age of eighty-five.

What is the quality of these extra years of life? Much better for some, and worse for others. Older Americans who do not develop a debilitating disease are healthier and more vigorous than their counterparts of several generations ago. They look, feel, and act younger than their parents and grandparents did at the same age. These young-old (and many have passed their eightieth birthdays)

Table 19.1
Relative Health of Older Adults

Health Indicators	Years				
	1961–1965	*1966–1970*	*1971–1975*	*1976–1981*	*% Change 1961–1981*
Days of restricted activity	2.33	2.23	2.15	2.11	−10
Days of bed disability	2.34	2.18	2.09	2.05	−12
Injuries per 100 persons	0.69	0.63	0.62	0.60	−13
Acute conditions per 100 persons	0.59	0.53	0.48	0.50	−15
Visual impairments (percent)	4.93	NA*	4.32	4.09	−17
Severe visual impairments (percent)	7.45	NA	7.23	6.74	−10
Hearing impairments (percent)	4.70	NA	5.54	3.84	−18

Note: Information from the National Center for Health Statistics' surveys of 120,000 people over the past twenty years indicates that relative to that of the rest of the population, the health of adults older than sixty-five has improved substantially. The figures in the table are ratios. For example, in 1961, older adults spent 2.34 days in bed from illness or injury for every day spent in bed by people younger than sixty-five. By 1981, that figure had dropped to 2.05 days in bed.

* NA = Data not available.

Source: Palmore, 1986.

consistently tell researchers, "I am much younger than my mother — or my father — was at my age" (Neugarten and Hall, 1987). Between 1961 and 1981, for example, older people's health improved substantially compared with the health of the rest of the population (Palmore, 1986) (see Table 19.1). For most people, significant health-related problems do not arise until at least the age of seventy-five.

Since 1900, the living arrangements of older adults have changed past all recognition. When the twentieth century began, few older adults had their own households. Whether it was a house, an apartment, or a room in a boarding house, only 29 percent of married older adults and 11 percent of single older adults had independent living arrangements. By 1975, 84 percent of married adults and 67 percent of unmarried adults had their own households. Two factors have fostered this trend. One is affluence. The typical older adult has more assets than he or she did at the turn of the century. Fewer older adults are forced by circumstance to live with a child or other kin (usually a sibling). The second factor is the low birth rate during the Great Depression. By 1975, older Americans had fewer living children than their parents and grandparents had when they entered old age. In fact, 20 percent had no living children at all (Thornton and

Freedman, 1983). As the parents of the baby-boom generation retire (and the first wave are just beginning to do so), they will have more living children to depend on. But as long as their health and finances permit, most will choose to live independently. When today's young adults retire, the situation of the 1970s will return. The increase in single adults and the decrease in family size will lead to a generation of older Americans with few living children.

An increasing number of couples will enter older adulthood at discrepant stages of the life span. As an ever larger proportion of middle-aged women are employed outside the home, more men are going to find that, although they are ready to retire, their wives are still deeply absorbed with their occupations. Because most women are younger than their husbands, this trend will be magnified — and the greater the age discrepancy, the more acute the problem will become. Another enormous social change has fostered this problem. In 1870, there were no problems with retirement. Most men died at the age of sixty-one, still hard at work, and those who were still alive could not retire because there were no pensions and no Social Security (Miernyk, 1975). Today's older Americans have years of leisure that were unknown to previous generations.

The exterior signs of aging—white hair, sagging skin, and wrinkles—are less important than invisible changes in the ability to adapt to stress. *(Abigail Heyman/Magnum)*

PHYSICAL CHANGES

To most people, getting older means the continued loss of beauty, strength, and vigor. Although physical changes occur during all phases of adulthood, they have little effect on daily life until people are well into later adulthood. Not until the late seventies or eighties do the cumulative changes of aging begin to interfere with people's effectiveness and daily habits (Weg, 1983a).

Typical Signs of Aging

There are wide individual differences in the rate of aging, but eventually the typical changes catch up with us. The hair turns white and becomes sparse. The skin loses its natural moisture and elasticity, and wrinkles trace their patterns on the face. As the skeletal structure changes, people tend to get

shorter, but the shrinkage in height is not so great as earlier cross-sectional studies had indicated (Rossman, 1977). Lack of exercise may accelerate muscle shrinkage, and joints may stiffen, impairing strength and movement. As calcium is lost, bones become spongy and fragile, so that they break more easily. Fractures still knit, but it takes much longer for bones to repair themselves than it once did (Tonna, 1977).

Within the older adult's body, other changes take place. These invisible changes have a profound effect on a person's ability to adapt to stress and change. In healthy, active subjects, the heart works as well as it ever did when people are resting. But when they are exposed to the stress of exercise or emotional upset, their hearts do not react as fast or as well as they once did (Lakatta, 1985). Afterward, the older heart takes longer to return to its normal level of beating and pumping. Even during mild exertion, the circulatory system no longer carries blood as well as it once did. As arterial walls stiffen and become less elastic, circulation slows and blood pressure may rise. Less air can be drawn into the lungs with each breath, a condition that leads to shortness of breath and discomfort after exertion.

About a third of older people complain that they sleep badly, but most spend seven to eight hours out of every twenty-four in sleep, just as younger adults do. The perception of poor sleep may arise because of changed sleep patterns and changes in the quality of sleep. Older adults tend to wake during the night and make up for the disturbance by napping during the day. In one recent study of middle-class adults between the ages of sixty-five and ninety-five, the average adult slept eight hours and eighteen minutes when sleep was recorded in the home (Ancoli-Israel, Kripke, Mason, and Kaplan, 1985).

Insomnia is not a normal accompaniment of aging, but it may be caused by depression, too much caffeine or alcohol, or the use of sleeping pills. The pills interfere with sleep because a person builds up a tolerance for the drug, and it seems to increase the incidence of apnea (when breathing stops for at least ten seconds) and irregular heartbeat. Older adults who have trouble sleeping may find that they sleep more deeply and wake less frequently if they spend less time in bed, avoid daytime naps, and stop using sleeping pills (Woodruff, 1985).

Sexuality in the Later Years

Changes in sexual response that were apparent during middle age continue in the later years of life. Among men, erection takes even longer than it did in midlife. Orgasmic contractions are fewer but just as pleasurable, and seminal fluid is expelled with much less force. Semen may still contain sperm; in studies, the proportion of semen samples containing living sperm drops from 68.5 percent among sixty-year-olds to 48 percent among eighty-year-olds (Harman and Talbert, 1985). Among women, orgasms are shorter and less intense, but sexual response is unimpaired (Weg, 1983b).

Despite the promise of continued pleasure, sexual activity declines during later adulthood, and a majority of men report impotence by the age of seventy-five (Harman and Talbert, 1985). Much of the impotence reported before the age of eighty or ninety is psychological, but an increasing proportion is physiological. Any disease or disorder that affects the male hormone balance, nerve pathways, or blood supply to the penis can lead to impotence. A disorder like emphysema may not directly cause impotence, but the body may respond to the medical threat by sacrificing sexual function in order to support systems that are vital to health (Schumacher and Lloyd, 1981). Among the major factors associated with impotence are chronic disease (anemia, diabetes), drugs (alcohol, marijuana, tranquilizers, hypertensive medication), malnutrition, and fatigue (Weg, 1983b). These same factors also can reduce sexual responsiveness and interest among women.

Because society does not see older people as sexy, interested in sex, or sexually active, some healthy adults give up sexual activity during their later years. For these people, the sexless older years are the result of a self-fulfilling prophecy; they lose their desire for sex because they are "supposed to." In some cases, adults who have thought of sex as a duty, or as unpleasant, use their age as an acceptable excuse for ending sexual relations.

How Much Physical Decline Is Inevitable?

When researchers report that older adults tend to have fragile bones, or high blood pressure, or little

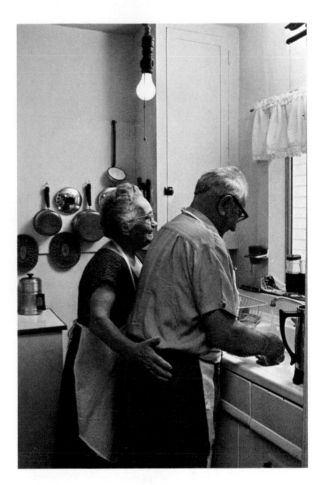

Contrary to popular belief, sexual interest and activity can continue as long as life itself; all that's required is an interested — and interesting — partner. *(Wayne Miller/Magnum)*

stamina, we generally assume that these results are the inevitable accompaniments of age. Yet most of these studies include many adults who suffer from some degenerative disease. In fact, some of the early studies that cast such a pall over the prospect of aging were done in institutions, where nearly *all* the subjects were frail or ill. The fate of these old-old seventy- and eighty-year-olds is not necessarily the fate of future generations of older Americans.

As we saw in Chapter 17, hidden disease, disuse, and abuse probably are responsible for a majority of the changes that we assume are a natural part of aging. The aged, weathered, wrinkled skin that we take for granted is primarily the result of

Older adults tend to think they should take it easy, but those who continue to exercise are likely to have a healthier — and longer — old age. *(Ulrike Welsch/Photo Researchers)*

exposure to sun and wind. Osteoporosis was once believed to be inevitable, especially among post-menopausal women. But a diet deficient in calcium and a lack of exercise may be critical to its development. Women between the ages of sixty-nine and ninety-five who participated in regular exercise sessions over a three-year-period had a 4.2 percent *increase* of bone density; women who did not exercise lost 2.5 percent of their bone density in the same period (Buskirk, 1985). Emphysema was once thought to be a part of normal aging. Today researchers know that, like lung cancer, it is caused by smoking and other types of environmental damage.

Regular exercise may prevent many of the common effects of aging. It prevents the characteristic shrinkage of muscle tissue, improves joint mobility, increases respiratory endurance, improves circulation, and reduces the risk of heart disease by about 50 percent (U.S. Public Health Service, 1979). Although older adults who run regularly would never win a 100-yard dash, their endurance remains high.

If Americans exercised throughout their lives, never smoked, never abused alcohol or other drugs, and watched their diet, most would remain young-old long after they entered old age. Instead of being hampered by some degenerative disease,

they might remain vigorous and active until shortly before their death. Perhaps they would simply "wear out." In one longitudinal study of older adults, those who had the least illness and lived the longest tended to be those who exercised heavily (Palmore, 1974). Those who died prematurely tended to be smokers; those who were frequently ill tended to be either obese or thin.

Many of today's older adults do not understand the value of exercise and believe that it is dangerous for the old to be active. Actually, "take it easy" probably is the worst advice an old person can get.

THEORIES AND ISSUES OF LATER ADULTHOOD

The early portion of life is spent gathering experience and increasing strength. During middle adulthood, this experience and strength are put to productive social use. The developmental tasks of the later years are personal. Older people's major task is to understand and accept their life and to use their long experience to deal with personal changes or loss (Fiske, 1980). During later adulthood, people face three separate issues. They must adjust to decreasing physical strength and health. Some become preoccupied with their physical condition and focus on every ache and pain. Others seem to accept what cannot be changed and find enjoyment in their relationships with other people and in activities that do not require strength or stamina.

Adjusting to retirement is another issue of later adulthood. People whose identity is based on their occupation face the problem of redefining themselves once they retire. Some may become demoralized. Some cultivate their other roles—spouse, grandparent—or find new ones. At eighty-six, Bill Cota says you have to "keep moving." Cota is a combination Mr. Fixit and village elder in his Iowa village. He fixes leaky faucets, mends children's bikes, and passes the collection plate at church. Cota shakes his head when he talks about a retired neighbor who doesn't keep moving: "All he does is count his losses . . . Now that's no good" (Donosky, 1982, p. 58).

The third major issue confronted by older adults is coming to terms with their own mortality. Some face death with fear, some with anger and resentment, some with resignation. Others use the confrontation to find meaning in their lives, either from the way their influence will live on through their children or their contributions to society, from their part in a meaningful biological cycle, or from their religious convictions. When contemplating death, Florida Scott-Maxwell (1979), then in her eighties, wrote:

> I feel the solemnity of death, and the possibility of some form of continuity. Death feels a friend because it will release us from the deterioration of which we cannot see the end. (P. 138)

As people deal with these issues, their motivations may change in characteristic ways. Various aspects of the process have drawn the attention of theorists.

Erikson's Psychosocial Stages

When adults enter the final stage of life, said Erikson (1982), their task is to see their lives as whole and coherent. They need to accept their own life as they lived it, see meaning in it, and believe that they did the best they could have done under the circumstances. If they succeed at this task, they will have developed **ego integrity**. Ego integrity can be gained only after a struggle with despair. When despair dominates, the person fears death, and although he or she may express disdain for life, continues to yearn for a chance to live it over again. When integrity dominates, the person possesses the strength of old age, which is wisdom. With wisdom, the adult is able to accept limitations. The wise adult knows when to accept change and when to oppose it, when to sit quietly, and when to fight.

The passage into later adulthood does not end a person's generativity. As the ranks of older adults grow larger, Erikson predicts that older people will remain involved in matters of the world much longer (Erikson and Hall, 1987). He sees later adulthood as a more productive and creative period than it has been in the past—one in which the eighty-year-old artist, writer, or musician will no longer seem exceptional.

Levinson's Seasons

Levinson's (Levinson, Darrow, Klein, Levinson, and McKee, 1978) chart of adult male development stops at the age of sixty-five, after the transition to old age. Despair is often part of that transition, because men generally feel that the youth within them is dying. Their contribution to society nearly complete, men enter the struggle between integrity and despair described by Erikson. The arrival of later adulthood generally is accompanied by a disruption of identity as men retire and lose most of their power and authority. A major problem is to find a new balance of involvement between self and society—both in the world and in the family. Ideally, work and play blend. Free from financial pressure and the world's pressures, a man can apply his creative energies to whatever engages his deepest interests.

In Levinson's view, late adulthood covers the years from sixty-five to eighty. He realized that the group of adults older than eighty was growing rapidly, and so he proposed a new, final stage, called *late-late adulthood*. During this period, a man comes to terms with dying—a process that Erikson saw as beginning during late adulthood. Development consists of finding new meaning in life and death, both generally and in personal terms.

Jung's Concept of Later Adulthood

Jung saw older adults as still striving to develop the self, for he believed that the search for an integrated personality rarely was completed. Within each person, he saw conflicting forces and tendencies that needed to be recognized and reconciled. Part of this recognition is reflected in the tendency for each sex to express traits usually associated with the other. As we saw in Chapter 17, Jung proposed that this tendency first appeared in midlife. Both Jung and Gutmann (1980) see the expression of hidden gender potential as increasing during late adulthood.

During later adulthood, men's expression of femininity and women's expression of masculinity are accompanied by another attempt to reconcile conflicting tendencies. Jung proposed that within each person was an orientation toward the external world, which he called **extraversion,** and an orientation toward the inner, subjective world, which he called **introversion.** During young adulthood and most of middle adulthood, people express their extraversion. Once the family is grown and the career is over, women and men are free to cultivate their own concerns, reflect on their values, and explore their inner world. "For a young person," wrote Jung (1969), "it is almost a sin, or at least a danger, to be too preoccupied with himself; but for the aging person it is a duty and a necessity to devote serious attention to himself" (p. 399). This change of orientation leads to a steadily developing trend toward introversion among older adults.

Disengagement Theory

Nearly forty years ago, researchers from the University of Chicago began studying people between the ages of forty and ninety who lived in the Kansas City area. By following these adults over the years, the researchers hoped to trace the course of personality, attitudes, and values as people aged and to discover typical adaptational patterns. From these studies came conflicting theories of personality and motivation in later adulthood.

After studying older adults in Kansas City for five years, Elaine Cumming and William Henry (1961) proposed that the typical pattern of adjustment to old age could best be described as disengagement. As people aged, said Cumming and Henry, their capacities changed and so did their preferences. By choice, they gradually withdrew from social roles and decreased their involvement with others. As Jung had proposed, they became highly introverted, not in order to reconcile the conflicting aspects of personality, but in preparation for incapacity and death. At the same time, society gradually withdrew from the old and handed over to the young the roles and responsibilities once held by the old. Disengagement supposedly was a universal, biologically based process, welcomed by the old and highly satisfactory to both older adults and society. Cumming and Henry believed that it represented the best way for adults to adapt to later adulthood and that those who disengaged would be more satisfied with life than those who remained active and engaged.

As a general picture of personality in later adulthood, **disengagement theory** has been rejected by most researchers. Although adults do lose some social roles as they age, most do not become disengaged. Anthropological research showed that in some cultures, older adults remained highly involved with both society and other people (Featherman, 1981). Several longitudinal studies showed no evidence of general disengagement and no sign that disengagement made later life more satisfying. In a study at Duke University, it was the highly active adults, not the disengaged, who were most satisfied with life (Palmore, 1970).

Yet this counterview also oversimplifies the issue. During the 1960s, researchers pitted disengagement theory against **activity theory.** The disengagement theorists said that life satisfaction among older adults hinged on withdrawing emotionally and physically from roles and activities. The activity theorists claimed that life satisfaction hinged on social integration and high involvement. Today's view is that each is right — for some people (Maddox and Campbell, 1985). Although socially involved older adults are more likely than others to say that they are satisfied, some disengaged adults are just as content. It seems that there are many ways to adapt to aging and that each is a continuation of a person's way of adapting in young and middle adulthood. Disengaged older adults were disengaged midlife adults and disengaged young adults.

GETTING OLDER OR GETTING BETTER?

Alberta Hunter (AP/Wide World Photos)

Georgia O'Keeffe (Dennis Brack/Black Star)

Among the oldest Americans, those past the age of eighty, is a group who seem twenty to thirty years younger than their age—at least as far as their productivity is concerned. A look at their achievements provides ample proof that disengagement does not characterize all old people. It also assures us that life can be exciting, productive, creative, and full of meaning until the very end.

George Abbot At ninety-two, this playwright-director wrote a book (*Try-Out*); at one hundred, he directed a revival of a Broadway musical and completed writing a new play.

George Burns At eighty, he won the Academy Award for best supporting actor for the film *Oh, God*. At eighty-eight, he starred in the film *Oh God! You Devil*.

Erik Erikson At eighty, this psychoanalyst and influential theorist published a book that summed up his thought concerning development and proposed changes in Freud's psychosexual theory. At eighty-four, he collaborated with his wife and a psychologist on a study of old age.

Ruth Gordon At eighty-three, she won an Emmy award for her appearance in an episode of "Taxi." At eighty-four, she appeared in the movie *Any Which Way You Can*. When she was eighty-five, her book, *Shady Lady,* was published.

Alberta Hunter While in her eighties, this talented jazz singer was not only giving occasional concerts but also drawing capacity crowds to her regular weekend performances at a Manhattan jazz club.

Harry Lieberman   At eighty, he began painting and kept it up until he died in 1983, at the age of 106. His watercolors and oil paintings, done in two-dimensional primitive style, have been exhibited in museums and galleries across the country.

Odilon Long   At eighty-one, this former telephone company employee was the oldest Peace Corps volunteer in service. He taught vocational skills, such as welding and carpentry, in a remote area of southwest Haiti that had neither plumbing nor electricity.

Scott O'Dell   At the age of eighty-eight, he finished the manuscript of his twenty-fourth book for children and the next day began work on his twenty-

fifth. Although he did not begin writing for children until he was more than sixty, he has won national and international literary awards for his work.

Georgia O'Keeffe   At the age of ninety, this artist was still busy with her painting and sculpture. In the same year, she received the Presidential Medal of Honor. When she was eighty-nine, she produced a book (*Georgia O'Keeffe*) and at ninety-five had a solo exhibition of her work.

Pablo Picasso   At ninety-one, this painter was still at work, concentrating on drawings and prints. He continued to work in oils until he was ninety. At the age of seventy-nine, he married for the last time.

Issues in Later Adulthood

When a thirty-five-year-old man cannot remember where he left his glasses, we assume that he misplaced them. When a seventy-year-old man cannot remember where he left his glasses, we assume that his memory is failing. It is easy to fall back on aging as the explanation for any aspect of behavior that seems prevalent among older adults. For a long time, physicians, psychologists, and sociologists held similar assumptions, as the discussion of depression in the box on "Is Aging a Depressing Experience?" indicates. But as we saw in Chapter 18, until recently, both cohort effects and the ravages of degenerative disease were confused with the effects of normal aging on cognitive processes. Similar confusion exists in the areas of personality and social relations.

The circumstances in which we grow up powerfully affect attitudes. Events that affect the whole society (depression, war, assassinations, prosperity), politics, and technological advances influence the way we feel about many issues. Because an entire cohort feels the impact of general circumstances at the same point in development, this shared experience and perspective tend to affect their attitudes similarly.

Cohort effects on attitudes are especially plain in the area of politics. People are supposed to start out liberal, even radical, and to become more con-

servative with age. Political polls support this notion. Older adults are more likely than younger people to oppose school busing, legalization of marijuana, women's rights, homosexuals' rights, pornography, abortion, and protest politics; to oppose federal aid to education or federal activity in civil rights; to be hawks in matters of foreign policy; and to be members of the Republican party (Cutler, 1983).

What happens to this age difference when we look at cohort effects? There is a great gap between the educational level of young and old cohorts. Over the past century, the average level of schooling has risen for each succeeding cohort. Increased education accounts for some — but not all — of age differences in opinion. For example, in 1972, 18 percent of adults younger than thirty but 52 percent of those older than fifty said that premarital intercourse was always wrong. After correcting for education, 20 percent of the young adults and 47 percent of the older adults opposed premarital intercourse. The generation gap shrinks from 34 to 27 points (Glenn, 1980).

When we first look at results from Gallup polls, it appears that with age, people gravitate to the Republican party (see Table 19.2). In each national poll between 1946 and 1958, the proportion of Republicans steadily increases as we move down the column from the twenty-one-year-olds to the sixty-five-year-olds. But when we follow each co-

Table 19.2
Age and Identification with Republican Party (Percent)

Age Intervals	Cohort Labels	1946	1950	1954	1958
	A				
	B				
21–24		46	41	42	43
	C				
25–28		54	43	45	51
	D				
29–32		51	44	39	49
	E				
33–36		59	50	47	49
	F				
37–40		59	53	51	42
	G				
41–44		70	58	56	44
	H				
45–48		58	58	52	34
	I				
49–52		58	50	89	62
53–56		60	60	66	47
57–60		65	75	58	63
61–64		58	86	75	55
65–68		70	60	90	66
Total		57	51	50	48

Note: Results from successive Gallup polls seem to indicate that as adults age, they tend to become Republicans. But when we follow each cohort's political identification, it becomes clear that age does not a Republican make.

Source: Cutler, 1983.

Although some older people slow down, others remain deeply engaged in society — like this woman who is active in the foster grandparents' program.
(Timothy Eagan/Woodfin Camp & Associates)

hort by moving diagonally across the chart, we find that there is no drift toward the Republican party with age. The changes that we see reflect changes in the general political environment (Cutler, 1983).

If there is no drift toward the Republican party with age, why do older adults tend to be Republicans? People in later adulthood today were socialized before the Great Depression of the 1930s, when the Republican party dominated the political process. They cast their first vote before the country swung behind the liberalism of the Roosevelt era. As a result of their shared experience, older adults see conservatism in political terms: a sound fiscal policy, limited spending, and a balanced budget. To them, liberalism means big government and socialism. The majority see themselves as conservative and identify with the Republican party. By contrast, midlife adults, who were socialized during the Great Depression and World War II, cast their first votes while the country was generally liberal. They see conservatism in social as well as political terms: free enterprise, limited government, and a resistance to change and new ideas. To them, liberalism means an acceptance of

Even in conservative times, older adults are likely to show less conservative shifts than younger people on issues like Social Security or Medicare because both affect their self-interest. *(Michael D. Sullivan/Texastock)*

change, new ideas, and progressive policy (Hudson and Strate, 1985). In the year 2000, common wisdom might say that people get more liberal as they get older and that they tend to become Democrats. The trend toward conservatism that has been apparent in all aspects of society during recent years could make this prediction come true.

Yet this general conservatism is likely to cause some shift in the political orientation of all cohorts — even those socialized in a climate of liberalism. Each cohort responds to general trends in society. When society moves in a liberal direction, each cohort becomes more liberal; when it moves in a conservative direction, each cohort becomes more conservative. Age affects the trend in two ways:

1. When the issue does not affect the cohort's self-interest, the older the cohort, the smaller the change in attitude
2. When the issue affects the cohort's self-interest, cohort members are likely to change more or less than average, depending on the way the issue affects them.

We can see this effect in older adults' strong support for Social Security and young adults' support for day care.

SELF-CONCEPT AND SELF-ESTEEM

What happens to self-concept and self-esteem as a person ages? Can they withstand the fading of strength and youthful beauty and the withdrawal of the productive work role? It appears that they can. Self-esteem remains as high in old age as it ever was. Cross-sectional studies consistently show that the self-esteem of older adults is at least as high as the self-esteem of younger people (Bengston, Reedy, and Gordon, 1985). Some studies indicate no difference with age; others show that older people have higher self-esteem than either young or midlife adults. Self-concept also tends to remain positive in old age, despite the loss of some social roles (Thomae, 1980).

Perhaps self-esteem and self-concept remain high because many older adults do not see themselves as old. Many adults in their mid-seventies — and even older — continue to think of themselves as middle-aged. Said an eighty-four-year-old retired schoolmaster, "I tend to look upon other old men as *old men* — and not include myself. It is not vanity; it is just that it is still natural for me to be young in some respects" (Blythe, 1979, p. 185). As long as older adults refuse to see them-

IS AGING A DEPRESSING EXPERIENCE?

Depression is one of the most common psychiatric disorders that afflicts older adults, even though it is not a normal aspect of aging. Major depression is probably present in no more than 2 to 6 percent of older Americans, but 10 to 15 percent of them are depressed enough to need some sort of therapeutic intervention (La Rue, Dessonville, and Jarvik, 1985). The issue surrounding depression among old people is its cause. Does depression develop in response to the social losses and physical declines of old age, or does it have some physiological cause — or causes?

When psychologists refer to depression, they are not talking about sadness of a lonely person on a rainy afternoon or grief over the loss of a loved one. As a psychiatric disorder, depression includes emotional and physical symptoms. The depressed person feels hopeless, worthless, and worn out. He or she loses all interest in most activities and pastimes and finds it impossible to concentrate or make decisions. Appetite and sleep patterns shift sharply — the person may lose or gain weight, have insomnia, or sleep all day. Some consider suicide (Klerman, 1983).

Researchers have not been able to isolate "the" cause of depression, but physiological and social factors have been implicated. Aging often is accompanied by losses — the loss of occupation, the loss of a spouse, the loss of financial security, the loss of prestige and status, the loss of friends or relatives. Sometimes a major loss in one of these areas precedes the depression. But age alone, when controlled for social class, is not associated with depression. In one longitudinal study, people between the ages of sixty and eighty showed a decrease in depression over a five-year-period (Lieberman, 1983). When major losses were followed by depression, they usually had changed the circumstances of a person's life in some way. Social isolation was not strongly associated with major depression. Yet suddenly being separated from people who are important parts of their lives may contribute to mild depression in some older adults.

Most older people seem to handle the loss of work, status, prestige, spouse, child, or friend — unless several of these losses occur at the same time. But when they become physically disabled, they sometimes become depressed (Jarvik, 1983). Another factor that fosters depression may be illness. Depressive symptoms often accompany heart disease, cancer, infectious diseases (such as tuberculosis or hepatitis), metabolic disorders, Parkinson's disease, and other conditions. Particularly ripe for depression are older men with several chronic illnesses who have recently had surgery (La Rue, Dessonville, and Jarvik, 1985).

Sometimes depression is a side effect of various medications given for illness. Drugs can cause true depression, aggravate a mild depression, or produce symptoms that resemble depression (Klerman, 1983). The list of drugs involved encompasses most of those given older adults for such conditions as hypertension, Parkinson's disease, tuberculosis, cancer, heart conditions, and estrogens given for the prevention of osteoporosis. Many older adults take several different drugs (prescribed and over the counter), and the drugs' interaction also can induce depression. Physicians often find it difficult to recognize drug-induced depression because it may not arise for as long as fourteen months after the patient begins taking a drug.

Illness does not always accompany depression. Among depressed patients, about 29 percent of older men and 35 percent of older women show no evidence of medical illness or sensory impairment (La Rue, Dessonville, and Jarvik, 1985). There is not always an obvious change in a person's life that precedes the depression. What about these cases? Chemicals that transmit signals in the brain are involved in major depression. Several different brain chemicals have been implicated, and researchers believe that the balance of these transmitters in the brain may be the key to some depression (Davis, Segal, and Spring, 1983). Often depression lifts when patients are given drugs that block certain transmitters, prevent their destruction, or increase their production.

Does the stress of life events upset brain chemistry? Does an imbalance in brain chemistry alter reactions to life events? Disentangling the many interacting causes of depression is difficult, but it appears that depression develops when life situations interact with personality and brain chemistry.

selves as old, they do not have to accept the negative status that is often associated with age.

Those who retain their middle-aged self-concepts tend to be better adjusted and have higher morale than those who see themselves as old (Turner, 1979). Because older adults do not *feel* old, such self-deception makes it possible for them to sense a continuity with the rest of life that is not supported by either the reality of the body or the views of others.

Older adults seem to keep their middle-aged self-concepts by erecting barriers against events that might lead to a loss of self-esteem or self-concept. These barriers are constructed of two factors: their own judgment and their persistence in thinking in terms of old roles (Atchley, 1980). Older people tend to depend less on feedback from others and more on their own judgment in daily life. Often they simply pay no attention to cues from other people that signal their age or dependence. In addition, despite the changes in their social roles, they generally continue to think of themselves in terms of their former roles. A widow may think of herself as Mrs. Chapman, and a retired man (or woman) may think of himself (herself) as a carpenter or a lawyer. Just as retired military officers, judges, physicians, and elected officials take their titles with them when they vacate their posts, many older adults retain their status while giving up their roles (Streib, 1985).

But what if circumstances make it impossible to hang onto earlier status? Self-concept among older adults depends in good part on the comparison between the person's current status and his or her earlier situation. The self-concept of a healthy retired physician who has a sizeable portfolio of investments and is still addressed respectfully as "Doctor" is probably as high as it was in midlife, but the self-concept of a retired factory worker who suffers from emphysema, lives on Social Security, and gets neither attention nor respect is likely to have shrunk.

Sex Differences in Aging

Traditional sex differences in self-concept narrow as people move into later adulthood. As predicted by Jung and Gutmann, the androgynous trend that began with the arrival of the first grandchild continues. Regardless of social class, many older men see themselves as fairly cooperative and nurturant and as less dominant than they once did. Many older women see themselves as more assertive, less dependent, more capable of solving problems, and as exerting more authority at home than when they were younger (Bengston, Reedy, and Gordon, 1985; Chiriboga and Thurnher, 1976). As we saw in Chapter 17, Gutmann attributes this shift to the ending of the parental imperative. Another factor may be involved. As men retire, they abruptly lose power and influence in the public sphere. They may indeed feel less dominant. Older women, whose lives traditionally have been spent cultivating family relationships, are freed from the restrictions of child care but retain their emotional power over their grown children (Fry, 1985).

When self-concept and self-esteem suffer, older women and men tend to respond in different ways. Women are more likely than men to develop an exaggerated fear of disease, called **hypochondriasis**. People with hypochondriasis have symptoms of physical illness without any apparent organic cause. Most are disengaged from society and absorbed in themselves (Verwoerdt, 1981). Many are healthy but believe themselves to be suffering from a multitude of disorders. Some researchers believe that hypochondriasis is a response to accumulated stress, perhaps the result of prolonged criticism, isolation, or a decline in marital satisfaction following a spouse's disability (Busse, 1976).

Until the last years of life, women are also more likely than men to become depressed. Between the ages of sixty-five and eighty, women are twice as likely to become depressed as men (Greenblatt and Chien, 1983). But among adults over eighty, both mild and severe depression are more common among men (Gurland, Dean, Cross, and Golden, 1980). Depressed people sometimes commit suicide, and this shift may help explain why suicide rates are highest among white men between the ages of eighty and eighty-four. Men in this group kill themselves at the rate of 51.4 per 100,000 (Zarit, 1980). Among the very oldest adults, those past eighty-five, twelve times as many men as women commit suicide (Levy, Derogatis, Gallagher, and Gats, 1980). In addition to being depressed, most men who have suicidal thoughts are unmarried, have few friends, and do not believe in an afterlife (Kastenbaum, 1985).

The emotional support, aid, and services provided by families can reduce the effects of stress on older adults. *(Erika Stone/Photo Researchers)*

Coping with Stress

Unrelieved stress or stress that is beyond an adult's coping ability can erode self-esteem. It also can be responsible for the deterioration of physical and mental health. Some stresses are specific and major: the death of a spouse, major surgery. Others are chronic: an unhappy marriage, estrangement from a grown child. Some are small, continual events: running out of money before the Social Security check arrives; the fear of being mugged on a trip to the grocery; misplacing the only pair of reading glasses; or struggling with a defective can opener. As we saw in Chapter 17, it is the way a person responds to stress and not the stress itself that affects body, self-concept, and self-esteem.

Older adults actually encounter fewer stressful events than the young. But many of the stresses of younger adults' lives have pleasant aspects. Leaving home, getting married, having a baby, buying a house, getting a promotion are all stressful, but they also bring challenge and reward. Many of the stresses of later adulthood are primarily negative: poor health, reduced income, death of a spouse (Chiriboga and Cutler, 1980). In addition, the older adults' aging body magnifies the destructiveness of each stress, even though he or she may not perceive the event as especially stressful. An aging immune system makes adults more vulnerable to the physical effects of stress (House and Robbins, 1983). The strain is magnified if they already suffer from some degenerative disease, such as heart trouble or diabetes.

Many factors can modify the destructiveness of stress on older adults. Experience with stress in earlier stages of life seems to prepare a person for the losses and stresses of age. Older people whose early lives have been smooth and stress-free often seem unable to cope with stress (Fiske, 1980). Being able to anticipate a stressful event seems to make it less destructive. If a stress is anticipated, older adults often can work it through ahead of time. Then when the event arrives, whether it is major surgery or retirement, they may be able to cope effectively.

Social support is another factor that helps to reduce stress. Networks of family, friends, and acquaintances provide social support, which helps older adults maintain their social identity; and networks provide emotional support, material aid, information, and services (Antonucci, 1985). When researchers followed the older residents of New York City's single-room occupancy hotels over a three-year period, they found that social support helped hotel residents to cope with the stresses of deteriorating neighborhoods, family illness, muggings, personal injury due to crime, and financial problems (Cohen, Teresi, and Holmes, 1985). The support both cushioned the impact of stressful events on the older adults and had a direct effect on their health.

In another study, Neal Krause (1986a) traced the way in which specific kinds of social support eased specific stresses among older adults in the Galveston, Texas, area. Emotional support (a personal relationship that was caring, loving, trusting, and empathic), tangible help (someone who provided material aid or services), and informational support (provision of information that helped resolve the stress) enabled bereaved adults to avoid depression. Only emotional support reduced depression among adults who had been mugged, robbed, involved in automobile accidents, or enmeshed in lawsuits. But no sort of social support reduced the stressful effects of financial problems. Older adults who were having trouble paying their bills or who had suffered major financial losses were similarly depressed, whether or not they had strong social support.

When older adults are moved from one nursing home to another, they often go into a decline or die. In an attempt to discover what predicted successful adaptation to the stressful move, Morton Lieberman and Sheldon Tobin (1983) studied older men and women who were about to be moved from one institution to another. Personality played a role in these adults' abilities to cope with major stress. Passive adults, who either withdrew or cooperated nicely with the staff, tended to deteriorate after the move. But aggressive adults, who were rebellious and nonconforming, quarrelsome and even hostile, tended to weather the move unimpaired. Some even improved in functioning. Another factor that enabled these adults to adapt to the move was their view that they had mastery and control over their lives. As we shall see in Chapter 20, a sense of control over the environment helps people to cope with stress that might otherwise become destructive.

WORK AND RETIREMENT

Work is an important part of life. It provides a sense of competence, an identity, a way of organizing life and its routines, social stimulation, friendships, a chance to get out of the house, and much of life's satisfaction. The transition from work to retirement is a major change — and one that is difficult to anticipate. Yet most people seem eager to retire. The proportion of older Americans in the work force has been dropping steadily ever since Social Security and private pensions were established. In 1900, about 68 percent of men older than sixty-five and 9 percent of older women were still employed. By midcentury, when Social Security covered a large part of the labor force, about 50 percent of the men and 10 percent of the women were still working after sixty-five. Today's older workers have virtually abandoned the labor market: only about 15 percent of the men and less than 8 percent of the women are still working (Greenhouse, 1986).

A large proportion of today's retired men and women left the labor force before they were sixty-five. Among men, early retirement has been on the increase. At a time when more women between the ages of fifty-five and sixty-four are in the labor force than ever before, the proportion of male workers has declined rapidly: from nearly 85 percent in 1965 to just over 67 percent — a drop of more than 20 percent over two decades (Greenhouse, 1986). In the same period, women's employment rose slightly: from 41 percent to a little more than 42 percent.

The Decision to Retire

Why do some people retire early, others retire on time, and a small group keep working as long as they are physically able? Many factors go into the decision to retire, and not all are within the worker's control.

Early Retirement A major factor in the surge toward early retirement is the availability of Social Security payments at the age of sixty-two and even earlier payments from private pension funds. In

Most people enjoy their retirement and find life as satisfying as those who are still working. *(Peter Menzel/ Stock, Boston)*

1978, 68 percent of all eligible older workers retired early (Ward, 1984), even though they knew that their Social Security payments would be substantially reduced. When workers choose to retire before the age of sixty-five, their health, money, and the availability of employment are major factors in the decision. The largest group of early retirees are in poor health. Work has become so burdensome that they are willing to accept reduced, often inadequate, Social Security or pension benefits. Another group of early retirees enjoys good health, has no financial worries, and has positive attitudes toward retirement (Robinson, Coberly, and Paul, 1985). Pat Christy, a New York State junior high school teacher who retired at the age of fifty-six, is a member of this group. After three years, she is still enthusiastic about her decision, has started a union chapter of retired teachers, and has become the first woman commodore of her sailing club, the Narrasketuck Yacht Club. Christy thinks that she was "born to retire" (Collins, 1986b).

On-Time Retirement Although health heavily influences the decision to retire early, it does not seem to play a major role in the retirement plans of people who work until they are sixty-five. The lack of connection between health and later retirement decisions is particularly clear in *longitudinal* research (Palmore, George, and Fillenbaum, 1982). Although retired workers queried in *cross-sectional* studies often report that their health was a major factor in their decision to retire on time, Erdman Palmore and his colleagues suggest that retired workers exaggerate the influence of their health when recalling their decision. Poor health is a socially acceptable reason for retiring, and it denies the notion that a worker has been rejected by his or her employer.

Late Retirement Workers who stay on the job after the age of sixty-five are likely to be middle-class professionals or people who own small businesses. People with high levels of education and high status jobs have more opportunities to work and more incentives to work longer (Palmore, George, and Fillenbaum, 1982). A positive attitude toward work helps keep workers in the labor force. Those who say that they prefer work to leisure or that they would work even if they had plenty of money frequently work past retirement age—or else retire and go to work part time for another company.

Some older people keep working because they cannot afford to retire. In one survey of people past sixty-five who still were employed, 46 percent of the women and 39 percent of the men said that the need for money kept them on the job (Collins, 1986a). If working time were flexible, the proportion of older workers might increase. Up to one-half of workers surveyed in two large companies said that they would not retire if they could work part time and still get a portion of their pension benefits (Robinson, Coberly, and Paul, 1985).

The Nature of Retirement

Once they have retired, people may find that retirement has many aspects that they did not anticipate. Most people look forward to shutting off the alarm clock and living a leisurely life that is one long vacation. But gardening every day is much less fun than gardening on weekends, just as spending the entire day with a spouse may be less gratifying than a relationship confined to evenings and weekends. Some retired workers may find that they miss their work routines and contact with colleagues. After studying retired workers, researchers have concluded that retirement is not an event, but a process that progresses through the phases described in the accompanying box, "Phases of Retirement."

Most people enjoy their retirement. In a longitudinal study of 5,000 men, 80 percent of retirees said that retirement fulfilled or exceeded their expectations, and 75 percent said that, given it all to do over again, they would retire at the same age — or perhaps even earlier (Parnes, 1981). Only about 13 percent of whites and 17 percent of blacks said that they had retired too soon.

People who are healthy and have enough money to meet their needs find retirement the most satisfying. In fact, when individuals who retired because of poor health are eliminated from the comparison, retired adults are just as satisfied with life as those who are still working (see Table 19.3). Despite the common belief that health deteriorates after retirement, studies show no support for the idea (Robinson, Coberly, and Paul, 1985). Many retired workers say that their health actually has improved since they left their jobs, but it seems that the change is primarily in their perceptions. When researchers compared claims of improved health with men's health records at the time of

Table 19.3
Satisfaction among Adults (Percent)

"Very Happy" With	Nonretired (N = 503)	All Retired (N = 299)	Healthy Retired (N = 185)
Housing	70	67	72
Local area	68	64	66
Health condition	59	47	62
Standard of living	62	54	59
Leisure activities	54	57	65
Things overall	59	51	60

Note: When adults with twelve years of education were compared, there was no difference between healthy retired people (all except those who retired for health reasons) and workers in their satisfaction with most areas of life, except that retired adults were happier with their leisure activities.

Source: Parnes, 1981, p. 188.

retirement, they could find no change in health (Ekerdt, Bosse, and LoCastro, 1983).

No matter how much people dislike their jobs, when they retire they lose something — if only a means of keeping busy. Asked what they missed most about their jobs, retirees in a national survey said that money was the biggest loss; the loss of contact with people at work ran a close second (Harris, 1981). Less important but frequently mentioned factors included: the work itself, the feeling of being useful, things happening around them, the respect of others, and having a fixed schedule every day. If retirement is only a loss, men and women are unlikely to find it gratifying. A key to the effects of retirement on life satisfaction is whether the experience adds some new element to life. Those who retire *to* a new life are likely to find retirement more satisfying than those who retire *from* a job.

MARRIAGE IN LATER ADULTHOOD

Most older men are married, but the majority of older women are not. Because of men's shorter lifespan and greater age, the ranks of husbands are rapidly depleted; by the age of seventy-five, only a minority of women are still married. Less than a quarter still have living husbands.

PHASES OF RETIREMENT

Retirement is a major role transition, and most adults tend to work through it in fairly similar ways. Robert Atchley (1976) has detected six phases in the process, although he notes that some people skip some phases or repeat others. Before retirement, workers go through the *preretirement phase*. At first, workers see retirement as a vaguely positive thing that will happen someday, much as an adolescent sees his or her future career. Once the retirement date is set, workers begin to separate themselves emotionally from their jobs. They become "short-timers," and their commitment to the company may weaken as they visualize it functioning without them. Many fantasize about retired life. When the fantasies are fairly accurate, they may ease the transition to retirement. But when fantasies are unrealistic, they may create expectations that lead to disappointment.

After the retirement luncheon, the cake, and the gold watch, workers are physically separated from the job and the *honeymoon phase* begins. Workers try to live out their preretirement fantasies: golf, tennis, cards, travel, gardening, fishing, self-improvement, playing grandparent. The worker, says Atchley, is like a child in a room full of toys, darting from one to another in a state of bliss, limited only by available funds. Although for some the honeymoon lasts for years, among 2,000 men in a longitudinal study it seemed sweetest during the first six months (Ekerdt, Bosse, and Levkoff, 1985).

Eventually, the honeymoon is over. Some workers, especially those whose fantasies were unrealistic, move into the *disenchantment phase*. They feel empty, let down, and may even become depressed. The beautiful castle they built in the air has tumbled down, and they must rebuild their retirement structure. Among retirees in the longitudinal study, life satisfaction and levels of physical activity were lowest at the end of the first year (Ekerdt, Bosse, and Levkoff, 1985).

As disenchanted retirees explore new ways of structuring their time and new avenues of involvement, they enter a *reorientation phase*. They may turn to family and friends or be drawn into senior center activities. They search for realistic choices that will offer moderate levels of satisfaction. Toward the end of the second retirement year, men in the longitudinal study had not regained their initial optimism, but their levels of physical activity and life satisfaction had begun to rise (Ekerdt, Bosse, and Levkoff, 1985).

When individuals find a predictable, satisfying life style, they have entered the *stability phase*. They know what others expect of them and understand their own capabilities and limitations. They are self-sufficient adults who have mastered the retirement role. Some are busy, some are not, but they have adapted to retirement in a way that suits them. People who retire with realistic expectations of retirement may move directly into this phase from the honeymoon period, bypassing entirely the phases of disenchantment and reorientation.

Finally, people may move out of the retirement role altogether. The *termination phase* develops when the stable life structure no longer is relevant. For some, this comes when they decide to go back to work. For most, it comes when they find it impossible to handle household chores and care for themselves. Giving up their independence and able-bodied status, they move into the sick and disabled role.

Being married is a demanding state at any age, and the later years are no exception. For many couples, the most significant transition is the husband's retirement. A man suddenly finds himself without his occupation and shorn of his daily contacts with fellow workers. Yet most husbands look forward to retirement more than their wives do. Women who do not work outside the home must adjust to having their husbands home all day. Norah Keating and Priscilla Cole (1980) studied the impact of a husband's retirement on the relationships of 400 retired male teachers and their wives. They found that 42 percent of the men discovered that their retirement had created problems in their marriage. Wives took a dimmer view; 78 percent of the women reported marital problems, which included decreased personal freedom, too much togetherness, and too many demands on their time.

A wife's reaction depends on her view of the marriage. Those who look on "home maintenance" as their primary marital responsibility seem to have a more difficult time adjusting to their husbands' retirement than do women who regard "affection and caring" as their primary responsibilities (Kerckhoff, 1966). Women who are home maintainers find it disconcerting to have their husbands around the house all day. Such feelings were voiced by former First Lady Betty Ford, who said, "I'm glad we will have more time to spend together, dear. But don't come home to lunch."

Most studies of retirement have looked at couples in which the wife has not worked steadily. When working wives retire, they face the same loss of income and social contacts as husbands do, but they lose independence as well. The thought of losing that independence may make them more reluctant to give up an occupation, especially if they began their careers in midlife and are still absorbed in their work. As occupationally absorbed wives indicate their reluctance to tie their retirement to their husband's age, male retirement may involve additional stress for many couples. Some older couples may adjust to the changes in marital roles. When fifty-eight-year-old Peggy Zeitler's husband retired, she kept working as a secretary at a Long Island community college. This led to a role reversal in the Zeitler family, which the Zeitlers settled amicably. Her husband, a former bank vice-president, says, "My wife is very direct about it. She's just not ready to retire. But it works out well for both of us. It's the first time in 40 years that I can stay in bed and wave goodbye to my wife" (Collins, 1986a, C1).

Regardless of whether one or both spouses have occupations, retirement brings new demands: worries over money, disagreements about moving into a smaller house or apartment, or health problems (Stinnett, Carter, and Montgomery, 1972). Yet most married couples who reach later adulthood together probably have lived through enough stress to weather this period. Their major conflicts—over divisions of responsibility and power, sex, money, children, and in-laws—have been settled. Most couples who were unable to work out solutions to such problems divorced earlier.

Couples who continue sexual activity in later adulthood are likely to be those for whom sexual activity has always been frequent and the husband is highly interested in sex and enjoys it. Among couples in the Duke Longitudinal Study, the husband's declining health and lack of interest were the primary reasons couples gave for reducing or stopping sexual activity (Pfeiffer, Verwoerdt, and Davis, 1972). In only a quarter of the cases did the wife's lack of interest play a major part in the decision.

Many couples continue to enjoy sexual activity well into their later years. After reviewing the research, Alex Comfort (1980) reported that in one study, 25 percent of adults between the ages of seventy-five and ninety were still sexually active. Older people often tend to find gentler, caring lovemaking more important than a focus on orgasm. Sexual activity becomes less a matter of compelling passion and more an expression of person-oriented intimacy (Weg, 1983b). Erik Erikson describes it as a "generalized sexuality, which has something to do with play and the importance of the moment" (Erikson and Hall, 1987, p. 132).

Whether or not they continue regular sexual activity, most older couples describe their marriage as "happy" or "very happy." Only newlyweds find their marriages as satisfying as older adults do. The upswing in satisfaction that begins after children leave home continues into the later years, so that 90 percent of the couples in one study said that their marriage was harmonious most of the time (Rollins and Feldman, 1970). One reason marriage seems so satisfying may be its comparison with the alternatives. When older adults look around at their peers who are single, divorced, or widowed, they may decide that in old age the solitary life leaves much to be desired.

DIVORCE AND REMARRIAGE

When a couple who have been married for forty years divorce, they are likely to show much more psychological stress than younger people in their

In later life, marriage may be better than ever. For the first time, a couple can enjoy each other's companionship at their own pace. *(Guy Gillette/Photo Researchers)*

situation. Over the years, they have become firmly entrenched in the established social order as a married couple (Burrus-Bammel and Bammel, 1985). The loss of marital roles as well as occupational roles can disrupt their sense of identity.

The number of older adults who divorce is rising. The government keeps no statistics on "over-sixty-five" divorces, but about 100,000 Americans older than fifty-five are divorced each year (Cain, 1982). Why should an older couple sever deep-seated bonds after forty years of marriage? Among a group of older divorcees in Michigan, women who initiated the divorce said that their husbands were either chronic alcoholics who refused to get help, tyrants, or womanizers. But in most cases, husbands had initiated the divorce in order to marry another woman. These husbands had been deeply involved in the aggressive pursuit of their careers, and their decision to leave the marriage usually coincided with their retirement.

These women, socialized to see marriage as their life's occupation, had based their primary identity on their marital role. When their marriages failed, some felt that their entire lives were failures. After reacting with shock, dismay, and denial, most set about to build a new life structure. But as one sixty-five-year-old woman said, "Divorce after sixty is a double whammy. You're too old to start all over, and you're too young to toss it all in" (Cain, 1982, p. 90). Women who had adapted best generally had a confidante with whom they could share their problems and fears. When married children lived nearby, the reminder of their maternal and grandmaternal roles also helped.

Unless divorced men and women remarry, their prospects for satisfactory lives diminish, and their levels of psychological stress rise (Burrus-Bammel and Bammel, 1985). Divorced older men generally stay single for only a short time. As we have seen, the intention to take a new partner is the deciding factor in many late adult divorces. But divorced older women rarely reenter the ranks of the married. Only 11.5 percent of divorcees older than fifty remarry, and so the proportion of women past sixty-five who find new husbands must be extremely small. Because there are four women for every man in this age group, there simply are not enough men to go around.

WIDOWHOOD

The loss of a husband or wife is a source of intense emotional stress. The surviving spouse goes through a lengthy period of bereavement, which we explore in Chapter 20. It may be years before widows or widowers completely adjust to their new status. Yet widowhood seems to be the "normal" situation of older women. There are nearly 8 million older widows in this country, but only 1.5 million older widowers (U.S. Bureau of the Census, 1986). Most widowers remarry, but nearly all older widows spend the rest of their days without a partner.

Women seem to adapt to the solitary life of a widow much better than men adjust to life as a widower. Either is more likely to die than a married person, but the death rate among widowers skyrockets. They are seven times more likely to die than married men. This extremely high death rate probably develops for several reasons:

1. Widowers with good health and financial resources generally remarry and leave the pool of widowers dominated by men with poor health and little money
2. The new tasks that a widower must assume (cooking and other domestic chores) are more closely related to survival than the tasks assumed by a widow (yard work, home repair)
3. Wives usually maintain a couple's social ties with relatives and friends, so that the widower often finds himself socially isolated and lonely.

Nearly eight out of ten widows live by themselves. Most are reluctant to move in with their children, and only those who are very poor or frail live with some relative. Few express any interest in remarrying, so the lack of potential marriage partners may not distress them. Among the widows studied by Helena Lopata (1973), more than 75 percent said that they would not consider remarriage. They gave several reasons. Most either wanted to be independent or said that they were tired of playing the subordinate role of wife. Some said that they did not want to go through the burden of caring for another invalid. Finally, some said that marriage was simply out of the question, perhaps because they had so idealized their late husbands that no other man could meet their standards.

Much of what we know about today's elderly widows may not apply to most midlife women when they are widowed, as most will be. Because they will have more personal resources, their adjustment may be very different. More than half of the women who entered late adulthood toward the close of the 1970s were immigrants to the United States. Only about half had graduated from high school, fewer than one in ten had a college degree, and fewer than one in eight had a professional or technical background (Neugarten and Brown-Rezanka, 1978). Most of tomorrow's older widows will have relatively high levels of education as well as an occupation and see themselves as workers as well as wives and mothers. They will be used to handling money and getting things done by themselves. If, as some researchers believe, many of the negative consequences associated with widowhood are actually the result of the widow's low socioeconomic level (Balkwell, 1981), the widow of the twenty-first century may find adjustment much easier.

FAMILY RELATIONS IN LATER ADULTHOOD

The household unit established by marriage generally shrinks to husband and wife in later adulthood and finally ends when one partner dies. But the larger family goes on, and the connections between older parents and the family systems initiated by their children and their children's children remain firm, relatively close, and usually frequent. When distance makes face-to-face visits impossible, telephone calls and letters act as substitutes. Older parents and their children prefer the freedom and independence of their own households, but the bonds between them are so strong that researchers refer to Americans as living in **modified extended families,** a term describing generations that live in separate dwellings but are linked by mutual aid and affection (Litwack, 1960).

Children

Gifts, services, influence, and affection travel up and down the generational tree, as we saw in Chapter 17. Both sides generally see their relations as close, but older adults may perceive the relationship as being closer than their children do. The tendency for older parents to see deeper trust, respect, understanding and affection may reflect each party's **generational stake** in the relationship (Bengston and Cutler, 1976). Aging parents have a stake in a close relationship; it indicates that their children are perpetuating the parents' ideals. But children have a stake in a more distant relationship; it indicates their own autonomy and distinctness from their parents. These stakes lead old adults to deny differences between the generations and their children to magnify them.

The strength of the bond between aging parents and their children shows in the frequency of their contacts. Daughters visit or call their parents more often than sons do, and they tend to contact mothers somewhat oftener than fathers (Hoffman, McManus, and Brackbill, in press). Three out of four older parents live within half an hour's drive of at least one child and see that child often. In a national sample of nearly 4,000 older adults, distance determined contact (Moss, Moss, and Moles, 1985). More than half of those who lived in the same neighborhood saw their child daily; the rest saw them several times each week. Those who lived between two and ten miles from their children generally saw them at least once a week and contacted them by phone about twice a week. As families scattered across the country, contact diminished. Older adults who lived more than 500 miles from their children saw them at least once a year, about half had a monthly letter, and about a third had a monthly phone call.

A close, warm relationship with grown children tends to be a strong predictor of older parents' view of their own health and their life satisfaction (Snow and Crapo, 1982). If the connection is so strong, what happens to childless adults? Are they

Recreation centers and organized activities, such as this bridge group, make it easy for older people who move into retirement communities to find new friends. *(L. L. T. Rhodes/Taurus)*

frail and disgruntled? Results from one national study seemed to indicate that childless adults were just as happy as adults with grown children (Glenn and McLanahan, 1981). This study included adults as young as fifty in the sample. When researchers studied an older sample (average age seventy-two) of Canadians, they found that childless adults were wealthier, healthier, and more satisfied with their health than older parents (Rempel, 1985). But they were also more likely to be lonely. Those with children tended to have more friends, were better integrated into the community, and were more satisfied with life than the childless.

At the close of life, loneliness and social isolation may await many childless old people. Among Americans past the age of sixty-five, the childless were more likely to be socially isolated than those with children (Bachrach, 1980). Childless adults were more likely to live alone, and most did not make up for lack of contact with children by cultivating other people. Among the middle class, however, childless adults in good health who had many nonfamily roles (volunteer work, church activities, clubs, community organizations, paid employment) were not isolated. But even for this group, as health declined and roles dwindled, iso-

Table 19.4
Young Adults and Their Grandmothers

	Grandchild's Relation to Grandmother					
Perceived Attachment of Parents	Maternal Grandmother			Paternal Grandmother		
	Close	Not Close			Close	Not Close
Only mother close	20*	8	Only father close		4	22
Both parents close	20	8			17	9
Mother not close	3	12	Father not close		1	22

Note: Close bonds are present between young adults and their grandmothers when the young adult perceives the grandparent-parent relationship as close and when the young adult had access to the grandmother during childhood.

* Numbers are frequencies.

Source: Adapted from Matthews and Sprey, 1985.

lation tended to increase. The isolating effects of childlessness are likely to be felt most keenly among the old-old who are ill and frail.

Grandchildren

Older grandparents are less likely than the middle-aged to be their grandchildren's playmates. When Jeanne Thomas (1986b) compared grandparents ranging in age from forty-five to ninety, she found that once they were into their seventies, grandparents also felt less responsibility for their grandchildren's care and discipline and were hesitant to step forward with child-rearing advice. Similar feelings were voiced in a study of great-grandmothers (Wentowski, 1985). These women were not as involved with their great-grandchildren as they had been with their grandchildren, in part because they had less strength than they had had when their grandchildren were born. They had passed most grandparental responsibilities on to their own children. As one great-grandmother said:

> When you're a grandparent, you love 'em, you're glad to have them come, you fix 'em food, do things for 'em, because they're precious to you. When you're a great-grandparent, you're older and you can't do as much. It's different. (Wentowski, 1985, p. 594)

Several factors affect the strength of the bond between grandparents and their grandchildren.

When Sarah Matthews and Jetse Sprey (1985) investigated the bond between college students and their grandparents, it became clear that the gender of the grandparent, the gender of the intervening child (the midlife parent), and the nature of the relationship between that child and the grandparent were all crucial. If young adults perceived their parents' relationships with a grandparent as close, the young adult grandchildren were likely to develop a close relationship with the grandparent themselves, and vice versa. In no case did grandchildren have a close relationship with a grandmother, for example, if neither parent was close to her (see Table 19.4). Most young adults felt closer to both maternal grandparents than to either paternal grandparent and closest of all to their maternal grandmother. Having access to the grandparent during childhood also increased the sense of closeness. Whether grandchildren's relationship was close or distant, however, had no effect on grandchildren's belief that they were obliged to help their grandparents whenever help was needed.

LIVING ARRANGEMENTS OF OLDER ADULTS

When someone mentions the living arrangements of older adults, retirement communities and nursing homes spring to mind. Actually, these two situations are home to only a small minority of adults past the age of sixty-five. About 5 percent live in some kind of institution, and another 8 percent live in some kind of age-segregated housing — which includes government housing projects as well as middle-class retirement communities. A much larger 18 percent live with an adult child (Gelman, 1985b). The rest (69 percent) live in houses, condominiums, apartments, or hotels in cities, towns, and rural communities. Thus, more than seven out of ten adults over the age of sixty-five live independently.

How the Young-Old Live

The young-old are nearly always independent. Only 1.4 percent of adults younger than seventy-five live in nursing homes. Most live alone or with a spouse. The tendency is to "age in place," to stay in the house where they reared their children and which many own (70 percent). This arrangement has much in favor of it. The house is full of memories, its familiarity gives the older person a feeling of competence, and home ownership conveys status to the older person (Lawton, 1985). Because most have paid off their mortgages, housing costs (taxes, insurance, and maintenance) often are less than the cost of renting an apartment. Only when costs outweigh comforts (as when taxes rise sharply or utility bills from heating and cooling a large house mount) do many older people consider selling their home and moving into smaller quarters.

As health declines and old-old age approaches, some sort of adjustment often must be made. Sometimes an unmarried child comes back home to live with a widowed parent — usually a mother. Sometimes simple alterations, such as grab bars in the bathroom, higher toilet seats, handrails, remote controls for appliances, phone amplifiers, nightlights, and knob turners for arthritic fingers can prolong an older person's independence for several years.

The young-old adults who move into retirement communities generally are healthy and relatively affluent. Older adults find life in these communities extremely satisfying, and most live highly active lives (Lawton, 1985). Morale is high among residents, fear of crime is low, and residents are spared the annoyance of noisy children. No youthful neighbors serve as continual reminders that one is aging. The presence of peers with common problems encourages friendships, the development of support networks, and social activities. Yet retirement communities deprive residents of the social and intellectual stimulation that comes from mingling with other age groups. And by removing the healthy young-old from the community, they rob children of interaction with older people that might destroy the stereotypes of aging. The same benefits and drawbacks are present in other forms of age-segregated housing, whether we look at public housing, mobile parks, or some form of community that provides special care, such as common dining halls.

How the Old-Old Live

As life expectancy increases, the group of Americans who are older than eighty-five is expanding rapidly. Today, there are 2.2 million Americans who have passed their eighty-fifth birthdays, up from half a million in 1960. Eventually, many will be unable to lead independent lives. There may be an accident — a fall that leaves them with a broken hip. Arthritis may progress to the point where they are no longer mobile. Early Alzheimer's disease may affect memory so that they no longer can function without assistance. Finally, they may have to move in with children or enter a nursing home or other care facility.

Most older adults who live with their children are either past eighty-five or the victims of some chronic degenerative disease. Earlier (see Chapter 17) we considered the stress that such situations place on the caregiving child. Being dependent on a child, which reverses the original parent-child relationship, also may place older adults under considerable stress. In a study of ninety older adults who were receiving care from family members, many reported that the prospect of continued dependence loomed so large in their minds that they found it difficult to think of anything else (Rakowski and Clark, 1985). The situation was especially stressful for those without religious faith.

Sometimes home care — whether by family or

Many nursing homes are attempting to provide a stimulating environment and to give their patients the feeling of control over their environment. *(Alan Carey/The Image Works)*

friends—is impossible. Today, 23 percent of adults older than eighty-five live in nursing homes (Gelman, 1985). The majority are women. Most are either single or widowed and are either childless or have only one living child. They generally need assistance to carry out such daily activities as bathing, dressing, using the toilet, and eating.

Some older adults get along better than others in nursing homes. As we saw earlier, assertive, aggressive people tend to adapt but passive people tend to decline. Some older people find increased satisfaction in life after moving into a nursing home. Individuals who improve tend to be from lower socioeconomic groups; need help in such basic activities as dressing, bathing, or eating; have a number of friends; belong to several social groups; and generally have been living with someone besides a spouse and sharing a bath with nonfamily members (Moos and Lemke, 1985).

The quality of the nursing home also plays a role in the outcome. Many nursing homes provide unstimulating environments and do little more than warehouse their charges. Adults in these homes may decline or die after admission. Yet in other nursing homes, patients improve. Researchers have compared various nursing-home environments in an attempt to discover what qualities of the institution provide positive support (Moos and Lemke, 1985). The quality of the staff is one factor: patients improve in nursing homes with relatively high professional staff-to-patient ratios,

more registered nurse hours per patient, and better medical records. Food arrangements are another: better meal services led to improved patients, perhaps because when nursing homes emphasized food services there was more communication and social interaction. A third factor is control: nursing homes that emphasized autonomy and personal control tended to have patients who improved.

Conditions in nursing homes often encourage dependency. Studies by Margaret Baltes and her associates indicated that when residents indicated the desire to dress or feed themselves and handle other aspects of self-care, they got no encouragement from the staff or other residents (Baltes, Honn, Barton, Orzech, and Lago, 1983). Their attempts at independence were simply ignored, but any indication that they would like assistance brought prompt help in a manner that probably encouraged dependency.

No single solution meets the needs of all older people. The individual's health and personal characteristics, family situations, and the quality and structure of the nursing home interact to determine whether an older adult would be more satisfied living independently, with children, or in a nursing home. From a social standpoint, the more alternatives that are available, the more likely it is that individual needs will be met.

Our picture of the last stage of life is not yet complete. In the next chapter, we examine life's final task—coming to terms with death.

SUMMARY

1. Americans are living longer, with nearly 12 percent of the population over sixty-five years old, and the quality of later adulthood has changed. Most are healthier and more vigorous than old people were at the beginning of the century, and they are more likely to have their own households, to live above the poverty line, and to have few adult children.

2. Changes in the circulatory and respiratory systems reduce the ability of the aging adult to adapt to stress and change. Sexual response is slower, but sexual pleasure is undiminished. Although many older adults lose interest in sex, sexual activity can continue indefinitely among those who remain healthy. Most of the physical changes that we associate with old age are not inevitable but are caused by such factors as too much sun, lack of exercise, poor nutrition, and smoking.

3. The major developmental tasks of later adulthood are adjusting to decreasing physical strength and health, adjusting to retirement, and coming to terms with death. Erikson's theory focuses on coming to terms with mortality, and those adults who find meaning in their lives develop **ego integrity.** Levinson sees the adjustment to retirement as the first major task of later adulthood. Jung proposed that later adulthood was characterized by a change in orientation, as people shifted from **extraversion** to **introversion.** This view was echoed in **disengagement theory,** in which withdrawal from the world was seen as the most satisfactory adjustment to old age. Yet according to **activity theory,** adults who remain involved in society find the most satisfaction in old age. Either course may lead to a satisfactory old age, depending on the person's adaptation during earlier adulthood.

4. Self-esteem remains high in later adulthood, with adults who retain their middle-aged self-concepts tending to have high self-esteem. When self-concept is damaged, the sexes may react differently. **Hypochondriasis** (an exaggerated fear of disease) is more common in women, whereas suicide is more common among men. The stresses of later adulthood (poor health, reduced income, death of a spouse) may be modified by earlier experiences with stress, the anticipation of the event, social support, or the sense of control.

5. Although poor health is a major factor in the decision to take early retirement, it is not connected with retirement decisions among people who work until they are sixty-five years old. Most people enjoy retirement, and there is no support for the notion that health deteriorates after people retire.

6. Retirement may create marital problems, especially among wives who regard home maintenance as their primary marital responsibility. With an increasing proportion of women in the labor market, male retirement could be an additional source of marital stress when men retire before their wives are ready to stop working. Yet most older couples report satisfying marriages.

7. Divorce in later adulthood may be highly stressful and disrupt the divorcing adult's sense of identity. After a divorce those who fail to remarry tend to remain under stress and to find diminished satisfaction in life. Men generally remarry, but women do not, primarily because of a scarcity of partners.

8. Women adapt to widowhood better than men adapt to life as widowers. Men tend to remarry quickly, and among those who do not, the death rate rises sharply. Most widows live by themselves and few wish to remarry.

9. The American family is a **modified extended family,** in which generations who live apart are linked by aid and affection. Parents and their adult children each have a **generational stake** in their relationship, with parents wanting a close relationship and children wanting a more distant relationship. Contacts between older adults and their grown children are frequent, limited primarily by distance. Childless older adults seem as satisfied as those with children, but adults without children run the risk of social isolation. Older grandparents tend to feel less responsibility for their grandchildren and are more hesitant to give advice than are middle-aged grandparents.

10. Young-old adults tend to live independent lives, but many adults past eighty-five live with their children, and about a quarter live in some care facility. The most successful nursing homes have a high professional staff-to-resident ratio, good meal service, and emphasize autonomy and personal control. Residents who feel that they have some control over their environment tend to be happier, healthier, more alert, and more active than residents who feel that they have little control.

KEY TERMS

activity theory
disengagement theory
ego integrity

extraversion
generational stake
hypochondriasis

introversion
modified extended family

STUDY TERMS

activity theory   The theory that life satisfaction in old age depends on being highly involved with others and integrated in society.

disengagement theory   The theory that life satisfaction in old age depends on a gradual withdrawal from society and a decreasing involvement with other people; the process is regarded as a mutual one, with society gradually withdrawing from the old.

ego integrity   In Erikson's theory, the older adult's acceptance of his or her own life as meaningful and coherent, with the accompanying belief that the adult handled life tasks in the best possible way under the given circumstances.

modified extended family   A family structure in which each unit has its own separate dwelling, but family members are held together by bonds of aid and affection; typical of the contemporary American family.

CHAPTER 20

The End of Life

DEATH AS A DEVELOPMENTAL TASK

THE LENGTH OF LIFE
Life Expectancy / Disease, Age, and Stress / Longevity

DEVELOPMENTAL CHANGES IN ATTITUDES TOWARD DEATH

THE PROCESS OF DYING
Preparing for Death / The Dying Trajectory / How and Where We Die

CONCEPTS OF DEATH
Medical Concepts of Death / Historical Concepts of Death

GRIEVING

BURIAL CUSTOMS

CONCEPTS OF IMMORTALITY

One of the things that gives life its urgency and meaning is the fact that it ends. For some, death comes too soon and interrupts a busy life, filled with plans and projects. For others, death comes too late or too slowly, making a dignified and appropriate end impossible. But no matter when the end comes, dealing with our own death is life's last developmental task. Most of us postpone the confrontation as long as possible. Our culture encourages us to avoid thinking about the end. People "pass on," "pass away," or "depart" — but they seldom die. As our reluctance to put death into words indicates, the fear and denial of death are common human experiences.

When death touches us closely, we feel many different emotions — fear, anger, sadness, loneliness, helplessness, resentment, inevitability, finality. In this chapter, we begin our exploration of death by looking at the factors that contribute to longevity. Then we look at the human fear of extinction and the way that anxieties about death change across adulthood. We consider the ways in which older people prepare for death, then evaluate the psychological changes that take place when people realize that death is close. Next we turn to concepts of death and examine various medical definitions of death, and changes in death's meaning for people in Western societies. At every death, there are survivors. We see how people face the death of their loved ones and examine the role of mourning in coping with the inevitable grief. We close with a consideration of the human desire for immortality.

DEATH AS A DEVELOPMENTAL TASK

For most of life, we strive to keep death at a distance. Crossing the border into old-old age brings decline, the loss of capacities, and death into focus. The struggle between despair and integrity is forced on us. Erikson (1978) saw the person facing death as struggling against the dread of ultimate non-being and disgust over human failings and pretenses. The task is to find meaning in life, either through the cycles of generation or through the belief systems provided by the culture. Some people embark on this search for meaning by reviewing their lives, by examining their past in the light of their approaching death. When the person is successful, death loses its sting.

According to anthropologist Ernest Becker (1973), the fear of death haunts humanity and is a major force behind most human activity. When Becker himself faced death from cancer, he found meaning through his belief in God, although he emphasized that he did not feel any more religious because he was dying. In an interview taped in the hospital less than three months before he died, Becker said:

> What makes dying easier is to be able to transcend the world into some kind of religious dimension. I would say that the most important thing is to know that beyond the absurdity of one's life, beyond the human viewpoint, beyond what is happening to us, there is the fact of the tremendous creative energies of the cosmos that are using us for some purposes we don't know. To be used for divine purposes, however we may be misused, this is the thing that consoles. I think of Calvin when he said, "Lord, Thou bruises me, but since it is You, it is all right." I think one does, or should try to, just hand over one's life, the meaning of it, the value of it, the end of it. This has been the most important to me. I think it is very hard for secular men to die. (Keen, 1974, pp. 191–192)

Some people respond to the closeness of death with a process of self-reflection that changes their relationship to mortality. They may disengage and withdraw from life's daily activities. Others show little trace of their awareness of death's approach. They stay busy, take one day at a time as they always have, make no concession to the end that they know is near (Kastenbaum, 1985).

Whether people die at home or in a hospital, they must adjust to the patient role. For some, there is the need to control pain. For all, there is the need to retain dignity and self-concept. How they handle these final tasks depends on the situation in which they die and the amount of control that they have over the circumstances.

THE LENGTH OF LIFE

Only in recent times has death been associated primarily with advanced age. In earlier times, youth afforded little protection from death. Parents expected that some of their young children would die. The prospect was so certain that before the marriage ceremony, young Swedish couples used to walk to the local graveyard and select burial sites for some of their future children (Kastenbaum, 1985). Sanitation, improved nutrition, and medical advances have sharply reduced the death rate among the young, so that today the best predictor of approaching death is advanced age.

Life Expectancy

Life expectancy, or the number of years the average person can expect to live, has increased considerably over the centuries. In ancient Greece, life expectancy was about twenty years; by the Middle Ages, it had climbed to about thirty-three years. The big leap in life expectancy in the United States occurred during this century. In 1900, life expectancy was only forty-seven years, but babies born today can expect to live until they are nearly seventy-five years old (U.S. Bureau of the Census, 1986).

This dramatic increase in life expectancy does not mean that the human life span has lengthened, but that more people are reaching old age. Life expectancy is only an average. When it is calculated, all deaths of infants (who lived for less than a year), as well as other untimely deaths, drag down the final figure. In the eighteenth century, only three out of every ten people lived past the age of twenty-five. As late as 1900, one out of every six newborns died before their first birthday (Yin and Shine, 1985). Today, at least nineteen out of every twenty live to become adults. Improved nutrition and sanitation have been responsible for the major decreases in infant and early childhood mortality (McKeown, 1978). The pasteurization of milk probably saved more babies than any other single advance. Medical science played little part in lengthening life expectancy until the twentieth century, when immunization, antibiotics, and surgery began to save lives.

The near elimination of some major causes of death has changed the way we die. Degenerative diseases such as heart disease, cancer, and stroke have replaced infectious diseases such as pneumonia, tuberculosis, and intestinal disorders as the leading causes of death. Heart disease ranked fourth as the cause of death in 1900; today it is the most common cause of death. Two out of three deaths among people past the age of sixty-five are caused by cardiovascular disease (heart attack, stroke, atherosclerosis) (Brody and Brock, 1985). Even this disease is beginning to loosen its fatal grip. The death rate from cardiovascular disease has declined by more than 30 percent since 1950. No single factor seems responsible for this astonishing drop, but researchers conjecture that a number of factors, including improved medical services, advances in the treatment of heart disease, improved control of high blood pressure, decreased smoking, increased leisure activities, changed eating habits, and modified life styles, have combined to produce the drop (Levy and Moskowitz, 1982). Cancer, which ranked eighth in 1900, is the second most common cause of death in the United States. And strokes, which ranked fifth in 1900, are now the third most common cause of death (U.S. Bureau of the Census, 1986).

Disease, Age, and Stress

Age tends to make older people more susceptible to disease, and disease tends to make people age faster. The circle is a vicious one: the processes work together and result in the loss of health and,

A century ago, when the typical cause of death was infectious disease, this woman would have run a high risk of dying young. Today, most people live until old age, when they die of cardiovascular disease or cancer. *(Michael Weisbrot & Family)*

finally, in death. The saying, "Nobody ever dies of old age," has more than a glimmer of truth in it. Autopsies indicate that 26 percent of individuals past the age of eighty-five die from "natural causes" (Kohn, 1982). In these "natural" deaths, degenerative disease is present, but its ravages are not severe enough to have caused death in a stronger, more vital person. With age, the body's ability to withstand any given insult (flu, anesthesia, side effects of medication, broken hip) deteriorates until even a small stress leads to death (Fries, 1984).

Older people are especially affected by the close relationship between stress and disease. Life changes create stress, which involves physiological and psychological responses to environmental demands or threats. Some of the most stressful life changes are characteristic of later life: death of a spouse, death of a close family member, personal illness, retirement, change in the health of a family member, and sexual difficulties (Holmes and Rahe, 1967). If events mount and if older adults' sense of control has been seriously eroded, stress can become destructive. As we saw in Chapter 19, adults who believed that they could control what

PERSONALITY, STRESS, AND DISEASE

Heart disease, which shows up with increasing frequency during middle adulthood, has been linked to a pattern of behavior known as *Type A,* which appears at least to double a person's chances of developing heart disease. Type A behavior is competitive, forceful, speeded-up, and sometimes hostile. The Type-A person is "aggressively involved in a chronic, incessant struggle to achieve more and more in less and less time, and if required to do so, against the opposing efforts of other things or persons" (Friedman and Rosenman, 1974). No matter how well these clock-racers do, they tend to have a nagging feeling that they could achieve more, if only they tried a little harder. When things go wrong, Type A's tend to blame themselves, even when they clearly had no control over the outcome (Brunson and Matthews, 1981).

How can personality translate into heart disease? Researchers hold differing views; some say that Type A's overrespond to stress (Glass, 1977). Placed in a stressful situation, their physiological reactions are intense and place a good deal of wear and tear on their hearts. As we saw in Chapter 16, Type A's have a strong need to maintain control in a stressful situation and become highly frustrated and annoyed when they fail (Brunson and Matthews, 1981). Other researchers believe that Type A's underreact (Carver, DeGregorio, and Gillis, 1981). When working, they do not feel the symptoms of fatigue or stress that warn other people to slow down.

Whatever the explanation, the reaction is not good for their health. What happens to Type A's who survive until retirement? Because their impatient, competitive behavior seems to show itself most clearly at work, perhaps it subsides when they no longer are part of the labor force. In a longitudinal study of retired men, researchers found such a reaction (Howard, Rechnitzer, Cunningham, and Donner, 1986). The men first were evaluated three months before they retired, then again a year later. In the meantime, some of the men took part in an exercise program that consisted of exercises, followed by jogging or walking. At the final evaluation, there was little change in the relaxed Type B's, but the extreme Type A's (10 percent of the group) were less hostile, less depressed, and less anxious than they had been at the first testing. Those in the exercise program whose cardiovascular fitness improved the most also showed the greatest reduction in anger, hostility, and aggressiveness. They became more like Type B's. It appears that Type A's tendency toward hostility and aggressive competition flourishes when they are placed in an environment that encourages such behavior. With decreased work demands and more free time, their aggressive, competitive behavior subsides.

---

happened to them fared best when transferred from one institution to another. In another study, the health of older people who were forced to relocate from a decaying neighborhood to a housing project suffered compared with the health of older adults in a control group (Kasl, Ostfeld, Brody, Snell, and Price, 1980).

According to Judith Rodin (1986), as people age, the relation between a sense of control and the quality of their health increases. How can a sense of control reduce the destructive effects of stress? Rodin lists several ways. First, when people believe that they can prevent, end, or lessen the severity of some stress, its power to bother them is diminished. Second, a sense of control over unpleasant events decreases the physiological responses to stress, lowers blood pressure and heart rate, reduces gastric ulceration, and lowers the level of factors in the blood that promote the formation of plaques in the arteries. Animal studies indicate that uncontrollable stress reduces the immune system's ability to fight cancer (Laudenslager, Ryan, Drugan, Hudson, and Maier, 1983). Finally, people who feel some control over their environments are more likely to take actions that improve or maintain their health. They are more likely to seek health-related information, care for themselves, adhere to medical routines, and inter-act actively with health-care providers.

Although the sense of control is extremely valu-able, there are situations in which it can be detri-mental. Rodin (1986) points out that people vary in the amount of control that they can cope with. Some older people become anxiety-ridden when given responsibility for themselves and their health. When people are given control but lack sufficient information to handle a situation, the sense of control can itself cause stress.

Longevity

Some people appear to sail through their later years active, vigorous, and the picture of robust health. Others seem to spend those years in physi-cians' offices and in hospitals. To judge by the healthy, old age is merely a different period of life; to judge by the ill, it is a dismal period. Researchers interested in developmental change over the life span have advanced several different ideas about why some people seem to age faster and die sooner than others.

Theories of Aging   Aging refers to the increasing inability of a person's body to maintain itself and to perform its operations as it once did. The result is that with the passing of time, the probability of dying by natural causes increases. Although this definition describes the biological process, it does not explain why people age.

A number of theories have attempted to explain why aging occurs, but none has yet been accepted as the primary cause of aging by scientists who study these processes (Rockstein and Sussman, 1979). Researchers still are considering nine major theories. The first six theories focus on ac-cumulated damage to the human body, especially individual cells.

- The *wear-and-tear theory* maintains that the human body simply wears out with constant use, as a complex machine would.
- The *waste-product theory* proposes that damag-ing substances build up within the cells and in-terfere with their function.
- The *error theory* is based on the fact that during a

person's life span, most cells in the body repro-duce themselves again and again. According to this theory, errors build up during the repeated copying of the cells' genetic message. Eventu-ally, the messages that control the orderly be-havior of the cells become so full of errors that the cells no longer function normally.

- The *cross-linkage theory* is based on the fact that molecules within the tissues of our bones and bodies and the DNA of our cells become linked so solidly together that they are immobilized and cannot function properly. The process is like that used to tan leather, in which the cross-linkage of molecules turns hides into leather.
- The *free-radical theory* is based on the fact that normal cell processes produce unstable mole-cules whose free electrons latch onto other mol-ecules. This latching initiates the aging process, causing cross-linkage and even damaging the normal genetic machinery.
- The *autoimmune theory* proposes that, as an in-dividual ages, the body's immune system begins to attack normal body cells. The body ages be-cause it can no longer distinguish between its own cells and germs, viruses, or cancer cells (Walford, 1983).

Other theories of aging propose some kind of genetic control of the aging process.

- The *genetic program theory* says that regulatory genes turn on and off during development. Just as some genes program puberty, others program aging.
- The *pacemaker theory* proposes that aging is controlled by specific pacemakers in the body, probably located in the brain. When the timer sends out its signal, the body's hormone balance is upset and aging begins.
- The *running-out-of-program theory* supposes that the genetic program spelled out at concep-tion eventually runs out. As DNA is used up, cell function ends.

Each of these theories assumes that human beings have a natural life span, that is, a maximum number of years that a person can expect to live under the best of conditions. Most researchers have set the human life span at about 100 years

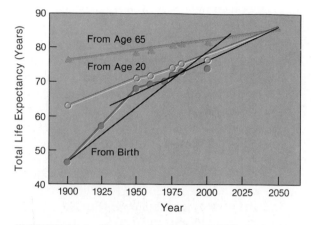

FIGURE 20.1 **Projected estimates of life expectancy in the United States.** The lines representing improvement in life expectancy at different ages can be extrapolated into the future to give a maximum estimate for the natural life span in the absence of premature death. Here projections from birth *(solid circles)* are made for the past eighty years and for the most recent decade to indicate the similarity of the estimated life span with different assumptions. The life span is approximated by the points of intersections with projections from age sixty-five *(solid triangles)* or age twenty *(open circles)*. Estimates from the Office of the Actuary for the year 2000 suggest a projection slightly less than age eighty-five. *(From Fries and Crapo, 1981. National Center for Health Statistics, 1977. Figures for the year 2000 are estimates from the Office of the Actuary.)*

(Fries and Crapo, 1981). If our natural life span is 100, we still have a long way to go before the average citizen can expect to live that long (see Figure 20.1).

Factors in Longevity Although we have no consensus on a theory of aging, we can agree on factors that influence life expectancy. What affects our chances of living a long life? Our genes, our gender, our race, the environment, the food we eat, how active we are, the stability of our social roles, our marital status, our attitude toward aging, and how long we expect to live.

Heredity is an important factor in determining how long an individual lives. One of the best predictors of longevity is having four grandparents who lived long and healthy lives. People with such a heritage live longer because tendencies toward

heart disease, hypertension, and some kinds of cancer appear to run in families. Placed in the environmental conditions that encourage one of these diseases, a person who has inherited a tendency to develop the ailment is likely to do so.

Gender is also important. Women generally outlive men in societies where women no longer perform hard physical labor and where their chances of dying in childbirth are small. Since 1950, the gap between male and female longevity has been increasing in most countries, including Japan, which has the highest male life expectancy in the world (Myers and Manton, 1984). In our society, although more boy babies are born than girl babies, girls begin to outnumber boys by the close of adolescence. By later adulthood, there are 135 women for every 100 men. Although increased smoking among women may narrow the gap between male and female longevity, it is unlikely to close it. Today, the life expectancy of a white American baby boy is 71.5 years, and for a white baby girl it is 78.8 years (U.S. Bureau of the Census, 1986).

In this country, a person's ethnic background also affects the length of time that he or she can expect to live. The life expectancy of a black baby boy is 64.9 years, and for a black baby girl it is 73.5 years (U.S. Bureau of the Census, 1986). But, during late adulthood, a shift in racial differences occurs. As black women and men reach the age of sixty-five, the difference almost disappears, and among those in their mid-eighties, the black survival rate surpasses that of whites (see Table 20.1). Studies indicate that the cross-over takes place at the age of seventy-three for men and at eighty-five for women (Wing, Manton, Stallard, Hames, and Tryoler, 1985).

How do researchers explain this reversal? Most believe that socioeconomic factors play some part in the cross-over. Earlier we saw that nutrition, sanitation, and medical care are responsible for general increases in life expectancy. Because black socioeconomic levels are generally lower in comparison with whites, blacks are more likely than whites to die young. Those who survive into old age are likely to be robust, hardy individuals. Different blood pressure patterns in the two races may also play a role. Blacks are more likely than whites to die from high blood pressure through midlife, while whites are more likely to die from a different form of high blood pressure in old age

Many factors affect longevity; in this society, a white woman whose grandparents all lived to a healthy old age is likely to outlive other people. *(Burk Uzzle/Magnum)*

Table 20.1
Life Expectancy in Old Age (In Years)

Age	White Men	White Women	Black Men	Black Women
Birth	71.5	78.8	64.9	73.5
Age 65	14.5	18.9	13.3	17.2
Age 85	5.5	7.0	6.8	9.2

Source: U.S. Bureau of the Census, 1982; 1986.

(Wing, Manton, Stallard, Hames, and Tryoler, 1985).

Increasing Longevity Heredity, gender, and ethnic background are beyond our control, but many environmental factors that affect longevity are not. In the hope of discovering those factors, researchers have studied groups of long-lived people.

From time to time, stories appear about communities where most people live past 100 and a few live decades beyond that age. In every instance, careful studies have exploded the reports (Mazess and Forman, 1979; Medvedev, 1974). In some places, a number of baptismal records carried the same names, so that birth dates were confused. In others, in order to escape military service, young men took the names of older brothers who

People in Soviet Georgia remain healthy and active throughout life. Their diets are high in fiber and low in saturated fats, and they retain their social roles and responsibilities. *(Eve Arnold/Magnum)*

had died. In still others, the age distribution as reported to investigators was skewed, so that many people claimed to be 100 or 110, but almost no one said she or he was seventy or eighty. This abnormal age distribution aroused suspicions, and when researchers returned to these communities after a lapse of several years, they found people who were claiming to be ten years older than they had been four years previously. In a study of Vilcabamba, an Ecuadorean community noted for longevity, a systematic exaggeration of age was found in people who were more than seventy years old (Mazess and Forman, 1979). Not one of the community's reputed centenarians had actually reached the age of 100. Many exaggerated their ages by more than twenty years.

Older people in these societies, although they may not be past 100, do seem vigorous and remain active throughout life. In Vilcabamba, the average "100-year-old" was actually about eighty-four, and the average "130-year-old" was about ninety-five. Perhaps these old people retain their vigor in part because retirement does not exist in their agrarian communities, and so they can keep their social roles and responsibilities far into old age.

In our own country, people who live long and well have a number of common characteristics (Woodruff, 1977). Findings from interviews with people between the ages of eighty-seven and 103 indicate that most of these individuals have parents who lived a long time, that they are happily married, and that they are sexually active. In fact, a good marriage appears to add five years to life.

Another characteristic of long-lived Americans is their retention of physical and intellectual abilities. Their reaction times also tend to be faster than those of the average old person. They are physically and socially active, and few give in to social or physical change. If they are widowed, most remarry; they develop hobbies, and they take long walks and get plenty of exercise (Palmore and Jeffers, 1971). Long-lived Americans are rarely anxious, most have always been independent, and they enjoy living. Most are religious, but few are extremely orthodox. They tend to be moderate eaters, of normal weight, and they never have slept

In all parts of the world, long-lived people tend to be married. It appears that a happy marriage may add five years to the life span. *(Betsy Cole/Stock, Boston)*

long hours. Some drink, and some never have. Some smoke occasionally (Rose and Bell, 1971). By necessity, they tend to be highly adaptable. They prefer to live in the present, with all its problems, rather than in the past (Jewett, 1973). How long people live, however, may be less important than the quality of their lives. Perhaps a more reasonable goal than avoiding aging is stretching out the productive middle years of life into later adulthood.

DEVELOPMENTAL CHANGES IN ATTITUDES TOWARD DEATH

"Men fear death as children fear to go in the dark," wrote Sir Francis Bacon more than 350 years ago. Many writers and researchers have assumed that every human being fears death. Earlier we saw that Ernest Becker (1973) believed that the fear of death was present in everyone, although it might be so disguised that we could not recognize it.

So certain are many researchers that we all harbor a deep-seated fear of death that they build the fear of death into studies meant to investigate its existence (Marshall, 1980). When questionnaires

provide a place for people to say that they are *not* afraid to die, the answer is often interpreted as a "denial" of death fears. In a study that attempted to discover which aspects of death terrify people, one research team designed a questionnaire that lacked any way for respondents to say that they felt no fear (Diggory and Rothman, 1961). What do we fear about death? The end of all experience seems the worst aspect of death for most people, although the pain of dying, the prospect of an unknown future, the end to their personal plans, and the grief of friends and family are also important (Shneidman, 1971).

At every age, some people are highly anxious about the possibility of death, and others show little or no concern. Yet the fear of death shows characteristic trends across the life span. Most young people find it difficult to think of death in personal terms. As life expectancy has increased and death has been pushed into extreme old age, young adults' lives are rarely touched by it. Their first personal experience with death is likely to be with the death of a grandparent—and as more grandparents live to become great-grandparents, even that encounter is occurring at an older age. So it is not surprising that most researchers find the fear of death to be low throughout young adulthood, although not all studies agree (Kalish and Reynolds, 1976).

Midlife adults are likely to view their own deaths with more concern. The middle-aged person has experienced death at first hand—grandparents and parents may have died. Even more sobering, a close friend may have died suddenly of a heart attack or cancer. When those close to them begin to die with their goals and projects unfinished, men and women tend to become apprehensive about death arriving when they are least ready for it. Perhaps because of this initial confrontation with death, the fear of death tends to peak during middle age. Among 1,500 adults in a national sample, the middle-aged were most fearful of death and more likely than the young or old to believe that "death always comes too soon" (Riley, 1970).

Once people move into old age, the fear of death seems to decline. In fact, some studies have found less fear among the old than among any other group (Kalish and Reynolds, 1976). Why is death generally less frightening to older people? According to Richard Kalish (1976), three factors may contribute to the diminished fear of death among the old. First, older people may place less value on their lives than the young. They have finished many of their life projects, they may be in poor health, or they may have financial problems. Second, they may no longer feel that death is unfair. Once they reach the end of their alloted life span, they may feel that they have had all the years they deserve. Finally, older people may have become used to the idea of their own deaths. Each time they deal with the deaths of others, they may rehearse their own death. By the time their own death draws near, they have been socialized to accept it.

As people decide that their own end is drawing near, they prepare themselves for death. The preparation often begins several years before a person actually dies.

THE PROCESS OF DYING

As losses mount and the body's frailty becomes obvious, the old-old begin their psychological preparation for death. This period is determined not by chronological age, but by a person's social, physical, and mental situation (Marshall, 1980). An eighty-five-year-old, married and in good health, who has friends and an interest in the world may not yet have begun his or her preparation. Yet a sixty-five-year-old, widowed and in frail health, who is friendless and has lost interest in others, may have completed it.

Preparing for Death

The major developmental task connected with the end of life is, as we saw, a basic reassessment of life (Erikson, 1978). Somehow the aging person must find a solution to the inevitable decline and loss that signal the approach of death. When energy wanes and climbing out of the bathtub requires planning, physical declines cannot be denied. Even when memory remains sharp, an old-old individual becomes confused when trying to manipulate complicated ideas. Social losses accelerate: spouse, kin, and friends die. One by one, familiar celebrities die, and the aged appearance of those who are still seen on television provides sharp reminders of the inexorable passage of time.

Time becomes scarce. It no longer stretches endlessly ahead, but dwindles down to a few precious years—or less. Such awareness may lead people to rearrange their lives and to make choices. Possessions that once seemed dear may seem ephemeral. Instead of adding to a record collection or personal library, for example, a person may turn to thoughts of whether it should be sold after his or her death or given now to a new, appreciative owner. Many have already arranged their lives to their own satisfaction. When older adults were asked what they would do if they discovered that they would die within six months, about a third said that they would make no changes at all, and somewhat more said that they would read, contemplate, or pray (Kalish and Reynolds, 1976). Few older adults said that they would make drastic changes in their lives (such as traveling or seeking new experiences), try to tie up loose ends, or focus on their concern for others.

Yet many older married people are more concerned about their spouse's life expectancy than their own. Those who have accepted their impending death often hope that it will be postponed until after the spouse dies. When Victor Marshall

One way that people prepare for death is by reviewing their past; this often takes the form of storytelling, which helps them weave the past into a meaningful perspective. *(Cornell Capa/Magnum)*

(1980) asked an eighty-seven-year-old man how long he hoped to live, the man replied:

> As long as my wife does—longer, 'cause I want to look after her. Outside of that, I think I'm old enough. I mean you lose your outlook on life to some extent, realize your time is limited. (P. 131)

As part of their preparation for death, many old people turn inward. They withdraw from activities and may try to make sense of their lives by a process known as **life review**. According to Robert Butler (1975), the awareness of death leads people to reflect on their past, to look back over the events of their lives in an attempt to adjust to their eventual deaths. They take up old conflicts, review old relationships, and try to come to terms with their past actions in light of their present situation. As older adults probe past conflicts, they may feel anxiety, guilt, depression, or despair. But when the conflicts can be resolved, they may overcome de-

spair and emerge with integrity, having discovered meaning in their lives.

Butler saw life review as a universal developmental process that was a part of Erikson's struggle between integrity and despair. He believed that the task involved problem solving and was a sign of maturity. When successful, it led to serenity; when unsuccessful, the person was left in turmoil. Yet studies indicate that not all older people review their past lives (Kastenbaum, 1985) and that those who do are not always restructuring the past in a way that promotes integrity. Morton Lieberman and Sheldon Tobin (1983) believe that when life review occurs, its purpose may not be to resolve past conflicts or to accept one's present life as inevitable, but to rework that life and create a personal myth. Instead of promoting integrity, such a review allows the person to reaffirm his or her current self-concept.

Life review may be a developmental task that is limited to societies in which people expect to live into old age. When death is common, unpredictable, and uncontrollable—as likely to come at the age of fifteen or twenty-five as at seventy-five or eighty—people may not fear it (Ariès, 1981). In such societies, there may be no reason to reflect on past conflicts and come to terms with death. Victor Marshall (1980) proposes that instead of regarding life review as a universal process, we consider it a twentieth-century response to predictable death in old age.

The Dying Trajectory

Unless death comes suddenly, perhaps from accident or a massive heart attack, people go through a **dying trajectory,** which refers to the interval between the time a person realizes that death is imminent and death itself (Glaser and Strauss, 1968). This trajectory may last for weeks or months, or it may be over in a few days. For some, it takes the shape of a slow, downhill process, as when death comes from emphysema. For others, it may be a kind of staircase, as when periods of remission occur during the course of cancer.

When death comes slowly, as it does with most older people, the dying trajectory is leisurely and less intense. The life review has been completed months or years before, and the recognition of death is followed by days, weeks, or months of time for people to adapt to the idea of death. Mansell Pattison (1977) describes three somewhat different phases of the dying trajectory: acute, chronic, and terminal. The acute phase begins when people learn that they are going to die very soon. Most people react with anxiety and try to cope with their fears by using a variety of psychological defense mechanisms. Denial is one common response. The patient either denies the diagnosis ("The lab mixed up my tests with someone else's"; "it's a benign tumor") or denies its implication ("I can lick it"). Denial is not necessarily bad or immature. It can be a healthy way of confronting the initial news that one is going to die. The denial acts as a buffer, protecting the patient from shock and postponing the necessity of dealing with imminent death. After all, diagnoses sometimes *are* wrong; people sometimes recover after their physician has decided that their condition is terminal. Denial and other typical reactions,

such as rage and aggression, probably are more common in young, midlife, or young-old people. The very old, who often have completed their preparation for death, may sublimate their anxiety, react with humor, or even look forward to the end.

During the chronic phase, people realize that they are gravely ill and threatened by death but continue to hope that they will get better. As they come to terms with death, their anxiety gradually declines. However, they may have other emotions to work through: loneliness, fear of suffering, and fear of the unknown. Finally, people enter the terminal phase, in which they have given up all hope of recovery. Anxiety slowly fades away, and they accept the certainty and immediacy of death.

After working with more than 200 dying persons, Elisabeth Kübler-Ross (1969) proposed that individuals approaching death pass through five separate stages. At first the dying person denies the possibility of his or her death, saying "No, not me" and refusing to believe that the diagnosis is true. In the second stage, the person becomes filled with rage. The dominant reaction changes to "Why me?" and the dying person is filled with anger because his or her life is being cut short and with envy at the good fortune of healthy people. In the third stage, the dying person attempts to bargain for life, trying to buy time from God, the physician or nurse, or loved ones. The person believes that if he or she only does the right thing (devotes years of service to the church, promises to donate his or her body to science), death can be postponed. The fourth stage is one of depression. The patient is not depressed over the loss of health or job, but over the prospect of losing everything—family, friends, home, possessions. The final stage is acceptance. Depression and anger depart. The patient quietly expects death but feels peace instead of anxiety. He or she feels distant from the world. Even patients in this final stage cling to a tiny glimmer of hope. Perhaps a new, experimental drug will bring a cure. Perhaps a remission of the cancer will bring more "good" time. When this last glow of hope dies, says Kübler-Ross, so does the patient.

Although Kübler-Ross's stages of death sound plausible, they apparently do not reflect the experience of most dying people (Kastenbaum, 1985; Schneidman, 1980a). The stages she has proposed come not from statistical data compiled by trained observers, but from her own intuitive conclusions, drawn from her close interactions with dying people. Researchers have found that dying people may experience only some of the stages described by Kübler-Ross. Or they may experience them in a different order. Or they may move back and forth among the stages in a period of hours, or even minutes. In the course of a conversation, for example, a dying man may talk to a friend with complete honesty about his approaching death, then surprise the friend with the declaration that he will leave the hospital the following week and must think about finding a new job. Another problem with these stages is their failure to allow for individual differences, both in the kind of death that a person faces and the way that he or she meets it. A patient's gender, cultural background, personality, developmental level, and surroundings (whether at home, in an intensive-care unit, or a nursing home) interact with the nature of the terminal illness so as to make each death different. Patients dying from congestive heart failure, a brain tumor, or emphysema have different problems and perhaps different reactions to their fates.

How and Where We Die

Most people want to die at home. Over the past few decades, however, fewer people have been dying there. Most of us die in hospitals or nursing homes (Kastenbaum, 1980). The picture drawn in so many Victorian novels of the family gathering around the bedside of the dying older person to bid farewell and receive a blessing has been nearly obliterated by life-extending technology. Instead, most people die in a strange environment, isolated, cared for by strangers, and subjected to bureaucratic routines. Often they are connected to respirators, intravenous feeding tubes, and monitoring equipment that may prolong life in the form of a comatose existence.

An Appropriate Death   When people die in this manner, they have lost all control over the circumstances of their death. Such a death deprives a person of dignity, especially when medical personnel keep trying to "heal" a person who is far along in the dying trajectory. Because hospitals are devoted to healing, the staff tends to see a dying

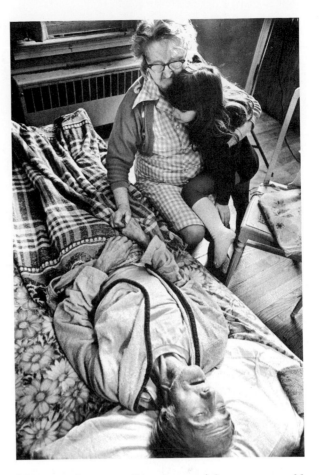

Many people want to die at home; eighty-one-year-old Frank Tugend, who died at home after a three-year battle with organic brain disease, had the comfort of family life around him until the very end. *(Mark and Dan Jury)*

patient as a failure. When a patient dies, staff members may feel guilty and wonder if some additional treatment might have changed the dying process into healing (Perlmutter and Hall, 1984).

Many researchers who work with dying patients have urged a change in hospital procedures. Avery Weisman (1972) believes that people should be allowed to die an **appropriate death,** protected from demeaning medical procedures but free from pain and allowed to participate in medical decisions. An appropriate death is possible only when patients are kept informed, and many physicians find it difficult to tell patients that they are dying. Families often collaborate in this pretense.

Why do physicians and family so often withhold such news? Many physicians believe that hearing the truth about their condition would confuse patients, cause them mental anguish, and destroy their hopes. Besides, say many physicians, people don't really want to know that they are dying. Sissela Bok (1978) points out that deceiving patients deprives them of the opportunity to make important decisions about the nature of their dying and the way that they will spend their last days. It not only deprives them of a dignified and appropriate death, but also may stand in the way of deepening relationships with loved ones that might take place if the person were aware of death's imminence.

Many people prefer to know the truth. In a study of cancer patients, 80 percent said that they wanted to be told if their illness was fatal (Gilbertsen and Wangensteen, 1961). These patients felt that knowledge of impending death helped them understand their illness and gave them peace of mind. It also permitted them to get their affairs in order.

Even when the truth is withheld, the dying often discover their condition. When patient, physician, hospital staff, and family all know that death is near but are unwilling to discuss it, a problem exists. Barney Glaser and Anselm Strauss (1965) have called this situation "the ritual drama of mutual pretense." Although the pretense may offer dignity and privacy to the dying, it also deprives them of emotional support from their family and prevents them from dealing openly with their concerns about death. The pretense that the patient will recover generally breaks down. But by that time, he or she may be so sedated and so close to death that all intimate communication and any chance for the patient to control the nature of final treatment may be impossible.

Over the past two decades, people have begun to emphasize their need to have some control over the time and place of their deaths. One response to this demand has been the establishment of **hospices,** where people can die gracefully. In hospices, no extraordinary measures are used to prolong life. There are no blood transfusions, intravenous feedings, or respirators. The aim of the hospice is to provide a humane, dignified environment for the dying. St. Christopher's, the first hospice, was established thirty years ago in England by Dame Cicely Saunders. Home and hospice care are coordinated, with hospice personnel supervising home care as long as it is feasible. Patients who go to a hospice generally stay at home at least two weeks longer than patients who are transferred to a regular hospital, and some never have to transfer to the hospice at all (Schulz, 1978). Whether at home or in the hospice, the dying patient gets medication that relieves pain but leaves him or her alert. Friends and family may visit at any hour. Hospices offer dying people a warm, homelike atmosphere in which they can face death without placing the burden of care on their families.

Many patients who have accepted the idea of dying still fear a lingering and painful death. Yet the majority of terminally ill patients die without pain, and death seems to come more easily to old people than to the young. As the moment of death finally approaches, most people feel increasingly drowsy and are unaware of what is going on around them. Drugs, the disease, and the psychological distancing of the dying patient from the world as death approaches all tend to contribute to this drowsiness. Some researchers believe that as death approaches, the brain releases a chemical that makes the moment of death pleasant instead of painful (Thomas, 1976). For most, then, death comes painlessly and peacefully.

Choosing to Die   Many dying people believe that they should have the right to chose death when the circumstances of their lives are no longer acceptable. They believe that death is better than a life filled with pain or considerable physical or mental incapacity. Because the granting of this right can entail suicide or murder, patients who wish to die or those who help them frequently run into conflict with the law.

The practice of **euthanasia,** or encouraging a "good" or "easy" death, takes two forms: passive and active (Morison, 1971). In passive euthanasia, medical personnel do everything possible to ease pain and discomfort but take no extraordinary life-prolonging measures. Life is not extended by machines, drugs, transfusions, or intravenous feedings. When administered by hospices, this passive approach has aroused little controversy. But it is often difficult to carry out in regular hospitals, especially if physicians already have begun to use extraordinary measures to extend life.

In a hospice, terminally ill patients can die in a supportive, homelike atmosphere, confident that their existence will not be prolonged by technology. *(John Moss/Photo Researchers)*

Whether the patient is conscious or comatose, the question of "pulling the plug" may arise, and a court battle may follow.

In active euthanasia, death is hastened by the use of drugs or some other simple procedure. A growing number of people have begun to favor active euthanasia. From time to time, researchers ask Americans, "When a person has a disease that cannot be cured, do you think doctors should be allowed by law to end the patient's life by some painless means if the patient and his or her family request it?" The proportion who agree to this proposal rose from 36 percent in 1950 to 53 percent in 1973 and 63 percent in 1977 (Ward, 1980).

In the Netherlands, active, voluntary euthanasia has become accepted, although it is against Dutch law (Clines, 1986). Physicians administer a combination of barbiturates and curare when there is no hope of recovery from an illness and when the pain is so great that drugs cannot control it. People who seek (and receive) euthanasia in the Netherlands must be fully conscious. Physicians consult family members at each step in the decision-making procedure, but the patient remains in control and must sign the authorization. Families are not permitted to request it on behalf of someone who is unable to make his or her own decision.

Because many people would like to have some control over the manner of their deaths, an increasing number have begun to write **living wills.** These documents give patients an opportunity to decide how they will die by setting forth the circumstances at the time when the patients can make reasonable decisions. The standard living will specifies that when recovery from extreme physical or mental disability is impossible, physicians are not to use medication, artificial means, or "heroic measures" to keep the person alive. It often requests pain-killing medication, even when it is likely to hasten the person's death. Although the will is not legally binding, it gives physicians and families some guidance at the time when their decisions can affect the quality of a loved one's death.

CONCEPTS OF DEATH

What is death? When does it occur? What does it mean to be dead? Each culture's belief system provides its members with some strategy for handling the idea of death (Shneidman, 1980a). Death is the great human mystery, and historically, it has been related to religion and explained in a religious context. But medical advances have so complicated the definition of death that clergy and court find themselves increasingly involved in medical decisions concerning life and death.

Medical Concepts of Death

Recognizing death used to be easy. A person was dead when the heart stopped beating and the lungs no longer drew in and expelled air. This straightforward answer loses a good deal of its value when physicians can revive a person whose heart has stopped, restore life to a person who has drowned in freezing water, or keep a body breathing and its heart beating long after the brain has ceased to function. The question of organ transplants has further complicated the situation. When can physicians legally and ethically remove a heart from a "dead" body?

These problems have led to three different definitions of death: clinical death, cerebral death, and brain death. In **clinical death,** the heart stops and the person no longer breathes. This is the familiar definition of death, and one that works in societies without advanced medical technology. Today many people who would otherwise be clinically dead are kept alive for months or even years, as machines breathe for them, keep their hearts pumping, and drip nourishment into their veins. Yet even when heart and lungs fail, a person is not yet dead. He or she is only "about to die." Death comes when the stoppage of circulation persists long enough for the brain to die.

These technological advances have led an increasing proportion of medical personnel and the courts to rely on the vitality of the brain as an indicator of life. The switch has led to two definitions of death: cerebral death and brain death. The difference between them (and between them and clinical death) becomes clear when we look at the case of Karen Ann Quinlan, the young woman whose drug-induced coma led to a court decision with an unexpected outcome. For a year after she lapsed into a deep coma, Karen breathed through a respirator. Then the Superior Court ruled that the machine could be turned off, if physicians agreed that there was no reasonable possibility that she would return to a "cognitive, sapient state" (Schulz, 1978). The respirator was shut off, but Karen Ann Quinlan continued to breathe on her own. In a deep coma, kept alive by intravenous feeding, she lived on for more than ten years.

By the standards of clinical death, Karen Ann Quinlan was indeed alive during her coma. She was breathing on her own, her heart was beating, and blood flowed to all her tissues. Yet the withdrawal of her feeding tube would soon lead to her death. Judged by the measure of **cerebral death,** Karen Ann Quinlan already had been dead for more than ten years, and the feeding tube could be withdrawn. Cerebral death refers to the death of the cortex, the part of the brain that controls voluntary action, thought, and memory. When it ceases to function, EEG tracings show a straight line, and the cortex is dead. The person can no longer move, think, see, hear, or remember. But was Karen Ann Quinlan actually dead? Judged by the concept of **brain death,** she was still alive. In brain death, *all* parts of the brain have ceased to function. Even though her cortex and midbrain (which controls reflexes) were both dead, her brainstem (which controls body functions) was still working. As long as any part of the brain lives, a person cannot be declared brain dead.

At least eighteen states accept brain death as the definition of death. In all of them, brainstem function is enough to prevent a diagnosis of death. The stringent standard of brain death proposed by the Ad Hoc Committee of the Harvard Medical School (Beecher, Adams, and Barger, 1968) has been adopted in many places. Under this standard, the absence of EEG tracings (cerebral death) is only one of four criteria used to establish brain death. The other three are: a total lack of response to any stimulus, even when it causes intense pain; no movement for one hour and, when a person is taken off the respirator, no breathing for three minutes and no reflexes (flat, dilated pupils) and no brain stem activity. These four tests are repeated twice at an interval of twenty-four hours. Before the tests are used, physicians must be certain that the coma is not the result of drugs or of hypothermia, in which a body temperature lower than 90 degrees Fahrenheit depresses brain activity. Whether brain death or cerebral death is used, today's dominant medical standard allows physicians to withdraw from a respirator any person whose entire brain has stopped functioning.

Historical Concepts of Death

Today we tend to believe that all human beings have always felt about death as we do, whether they lived in Topeka or Tahiti, in ancient Rome or contemporary Los Angeles. But a look at the record shows that attitudes toward death change from time to time even in the same society.

According to historian Philippe Ariès (1981), the meaning of death in predominantly Christian societies has gone through several major transformations since the Middle Ages. Cultural attitudes toward death, he says, reflect prevailing concepts of self-awareness and individuality. Changes in our notions of the self are followed by changes in our feelings about death. Consequently, many contemporary ideas about death were actually invented during the past century or two.

Until about A.D. 1200, death was both expected and accepted. Only sudden death was truly fearful, and people calmly contemplated their own deaths. Death was tame. It did not extinguish the individual's existence but marked the loss of a community member. The dead merely slept until the Second Coming of Christ, when all would be redeemed. In the late Middle Ages, as growing awareness of the self developed, death was no longer accepted so calmly. It was seen as personal extinction, the death of the self. All feared the moment of death, because at that instant the soul was judged and passed immediately to its punishment or reward. No longer did it slumber peacefully until the moment of universal redemption.

During the seventeenth and eighteenth centuries, death and life became intertwined. People thought about death a great deal and tried to prepare for it throughout life. This made death remote but also imminent. The concept of mortality was accepted, but the thought of personal death filled people with anxiety. At the beginning of the nineteenth century, the focus shifted from the self to the family. Personal death was no longer the concern; instead people worried about the death of others—family and friends. Being separated by death was a major emotional crisis. By then the belief in hell had waned, and the rewards of heaven got little attention. Instead, people concentrated on a happy reunion with loved ones after death.

Toward the end of the nineteenth century, as death began to be pushed toward a later part of the life span, people began to deny its existence. The concept and the spectacle of death were hidden, and death became invisible. Terminally ill people were encouraged to believe that they could recover. The dying were sent to the hospital so that

Grieving is a normal way of adjusting to the death of a loved one, but it may be a year or two before the survivors begin to reorganize their lives. *(top, Leonard Speier; bottom, Costa Manos/Magnum)*

they would not die at home. Death became as taboo as sex had been during the Victorian era. The management of grief was handed over to the undertaker, who removed it from daily life and concentrated it at the funeral. Death was no longer a natural event, but a failure of medicine or a terrible accident.

In the past two decades, there has been a revolt against the invisible death. Appalled by the undignified death of the isolated patient whose life has been artificially extended, people are trying to restore the possibility of the appropriate, dignified death. As we have seen, this has led to the establishment of hospices and the invention of the living will.

GRIEVING

Death introduces a highly emotional, stress-laden period for the survivors. It severs an emotional bond and ushers in a painful reaction we call *grief*. Researchers who have studied the reaction of grief-stricken survivors call it the "most severe psychological trauma most people will encounter in the course of their lives" (Parkes and Weiss, 1983). The trauma is most acute when the death is untimely. As we have seen, losses are more disruptive when they are "off time" and violate our expectations. We expect death to come in old age, when the person has completed a long, full life. So grief at the death of old people is usually less intense than when a child or young adult dies. Mourning for a young person, especially when the death is accidental, may be prolonged.

When a loved one dies, our reactions may resemble a physical illness. Our limbs feel heavy, we sigh, our throat gets tight, our breath is short, we have a sort of restless apathy, an empty feeling in the pit of the stomach. We lose our appetite, have trouble sleeping, and suffer pangs of acute distress (Parkes and Weiss, 1983). Because these reactions are "normal," there must be a reason for them. The outward behavior of grief-stricken adults resembles that of young children who have been separated from their caregiver as well as the behavior of nonhuman social animals who have been separated from mother or mate. They may cry out, search restlessly for the missing person, and attack whatever or whoever tries to stop their search. Because of this similarity, John Bowlby and Murray Parkes (1970) see grief as a sort of separation anxiety (see Chapter 8). In temporary separations, its major purpose is to reunite the pair, and it is generally effective. In such cases, grief is adaptive. When grief is a response to death, it may serve a different purpose. As a signal of distress, it tells other people that the person is in need of assistance and protection. In response, people treat the bereaved person as if he or she were sick or wounded and, for a time, do not hold them to the rules of normal social behavior. Even outbursts of anger are tolerated. Grief for a loved one often goes on for several years. If mourning is prolonged beyond that time, as described in the accompanying box, "When the Grieving Doesn't Stop," the prospect of recovery may be dim.

When death is not sudden, the survivors have a chance to prepare for their coming ordeal. Some researchers believe that foreknowledge allows a person to go through a period of anticipatory grief, so that they get an earlier start on their bereavement (Kübler-Ross, 1969). However, Murray and Parkes and Robert Weiss (1983), who have studied grief in widows and widowers, believe that grieving does not actually begin until the death, despite the warning. None of the survivors they studied had entered into the stages of grief early. Although foreknowledge did not seem to reduce later grief, it did seem to make recovery easier.

One reason seemed to be that the survivors may have felt less guilt. The knowledge that a spouse was about to die intensified the bond between the pair and brought them closer together. They were able to resolve quarrels, say their goodbyes, and know that they had been available to the spouse during his or her last weeks or months. This rounding-off of their relationships enabled them to enter mourning without some of the recriminations and regrets that survivors of sudden deaths felt. Foreknowledge also may lessen grief by allowing the survivors to prepare for their future while living with the prospect of loss. They do this not by grieving, but by making practical plans. By rehearsing the death, they can anticipate what adjustments they will have to make in their lives after the loved one dies. Finally, it helps the survivors make sense of their lives. When at last the death comes, it is part of a process that they understand, no matter how much they hate it.

BURIAL CUSTOMS

When a person dies, relationships are disrupted, and a family must be reorganized. One way of getting life back on track is through some sort of ritual for disposal of the dead. Every society has rules for these rites, and anthropologists have

WHEN THE GRIEVING DOESN'T STOP

Most women and men eventually adapt to the loss of a spouse, but some still grieve deeply years after the event. Younger adults, for whom the death of a husband or wife is "off-time," appear to be more distressed than older adults, and their grief seems to be deeper (Breckenridge et al., 1986). When studying younger widows and widowers, Murray Parkes and Robert Weiss (1983) found that prolonged, insurmountable grief could be associated with the circumstances of the death, the character of the marriage, or the personality of the surviving spouse.

Unanticipated grief is associated with the circumstances of the death. It develops when the surviving spouse has less than three days' warning that death is imminent or less than two weeks' notice that an illness will be fatal. Stripped of the forewarning that allows people to prepare for bereavement, widows and widowers have trouble accepting the reality of their loss. Four years later they still may be socially withdrawn, anxious, lonely, and depressed. One widower in his forties, whose wife died in childbirth, began drinking and withdrew from family and work responsibilities. When reinterviewed three years after his wife's death, he said: "I'll tell you the honest truth. I've let things go that I know I can do. I've let things go. I haven't got the—what would you call it?—the push? Well, I haven't got the push to do it" (Parkes and Weiss, 1983, p. 198).

When the marriage has been unhappy and filled with conflict, **conflicted grief** may develop. We might expect a person freed from an unhappy marriage to grieve less, not more, than other people. But this seems to be the case only during the first six months or so. By the first anniversary of the spouse's death, when most widows and widowers show signs of coming to terms with their loss, those with conflicted grief are in deep mourning. Some are still guilty, angry, anxiety-ridden, and depressed three years later. The odd pattern may develop because these survivors feel guilt for early wishes that their partner would die and grief for the good marriage they never had—and now would never know. Three years after her husband's death, a widow in her thirties who had earlier described her marriage as unhappy and empty was depressed. "Halfway down I feel like I wouldn't care if I died tomorrow," she said. "And then, deeper down, I feel like I do care. I can't explain it. Like sometimes I try to make the kids be enough for me, and sometimes I feel they're not" (Parkes and Weiss, 1983, p. 116).

Prolonged grief associated with personality tends to appear in individuals who were highly dependent on their spouse. They develop **chronic grief.** Without the emotional support and presence of their partner, they are unable to carry out the routine responsibilities connected with their social roles. Deeply insecure, they seem unable to fashion a new life for themselves. Four years after his wife's death, a widower in his thirties was still sad and grief-stricken; he felt unable to care for his young son, who lived with the wife's parents. "I'm not really able to do anything," he said. "I'm very restless. In the evening I try to be with company. That's the way in which I try to hide my loneliness" (Parkes and Weiss, 1983, p. 214).

Not all surviving spouses who had lacked forewarning, had unhappy marriages, or who had been highly dependent on the dead spouse develop prolonged grief. Its development depends in part on the specific characteristics of the individual (self-esteem, resilience, capacity for optimism) and in part on the absence of others who hold the bereaved person in high esteem and can provide needed protection and support.

found that they serve both social and personal needs (Bowlby, 1980). First, the funeral helps the survivors. It emphasizes the fact of death and gives them a way to express their grief in public. Second, the funeral helps maintain the society. It provides a way to note the loss and an acceptable channel for people's fear and anger. Social continuity is assured. Third, it strengthens social cohesiveness. The scattered family gathers to provide support for its bereaved members. Friends and acquaintances draw near. This support demonstrates to all that they can expect the same sort of aid when

Burial customs give survivors a way to express their grief publicly, and mourning customs (such as dark clothes and mourning periods) help them to resolve that grief. *(Dan Chidester/The Image Works)*

death strikes their small family circle. Fourth, it gives the living an opportunity to express their gratitude to the deceased. Finally, the funeral also provides a way of helping the dead, by carrying out last wishes and praying for his or her future welfare. In some societies, the rites make the dead person's rebirth a certainty.

No matter which society we look at, burial customs proceed under the assumption that the bereaved person is shocked and socially disoriented. In most societies, there is also a general belief that although the body has died, relationships between the deceased and the living continue for a time. When the relationships are seen as harmful, the rituals protect the living. Among the Swazi in Africa, for example, the rites safeguard the living from attacks by inhabitants of the spirit world. The Washo Indians of California burned the dead person's home to make certain that he or she would not return to harm the living (Leming and Dickinson, 1985). When relationships are seen as beneficial, the rituals preserve the bonds. The Japanese custom of building an altar within the home, where the dead person's photograph and ashes are placed, is meant to maintain the relationship. In many cultures, the survivors are expected to be angry with whomever they blame for the death. This is especially true in societies where death frequently strikes the young. When anger is ex-

pected, the ceremonies provide a way to direct or express it. Finally, most ceremonies define the mourning period, so that the survivors know when they are to take up their usual social roles again (Bowlby, 1980).

As mourning customs have faded from Western societies, some researchers have become concerned about the ability of survivors to resolve their grief (Parkes, 1972). Without social expectations and markers (dark clothes, armbands, specified periods of mourning, and the like), the bereaved often are insecure and confused. The funeral serves an important function by forcing on the survivors the realization that their loved one is dead. As long as people avoid confronting this finality, they find it difficult, if not impossible, to resolve their grief. For this reason, some authorities believe that the survivors should view the body whenever possible (Lindemann, 1944; Pine, 1975). The sight of the body removes all possibility of denying the death.

Among the widows in one study, some refused to believe that their husband actually had died until they saw his lifeless body (Parkes, 1972). Viewing the body is especially important in the death of a child, believes Elisabeth Kübler-Ross (Kübler-Ross and Goleman, 1976). In her work with bereaved parents, she has found that when parents are prevented from seeing their child's body, their grief may never be resolved. She tells of one mother who, five years after her daughter's death, still turned down her bed every night.

Yet some relatives find the sight of the body extremely unpleasant. In one study, half of the widows and a quarter of the widowers were upset by viewing the body; in another group, some were haunted by what they regarded as a horrifying sight, and others found the memory pleasant (Parkes, 1972). When the husband had suffered, the sight seemed to convince widows that he finally was at rest. Said one widow, "I like to think of him like that. He was smiling and looked peaceful. You could see he was all right" (Parkes, 1972, pp. 156–157). Funerals and mourning rites also help the survivors by placing the death within a meaningful context. For religious individuals, the concept of an afterlife may make the resolution of grief easier.

CONCEPTS OF IMMORTALITY

We simply cannot imagine our own death, said Sigmund Freud (1915/1957). Whenever we attempt it, we find ourselves surviving as spectators, looking on at the world without us. This convinced Freud that, deep in our hearts, each of us is convinced that he or she is immortal. Robert Lifton (1971) believes that our conviction of immortality is not as unshakable as Freud proposed. Instead, says Lifton, we have a need to maintain a *sense* of immortality in the face of inevitable biological death. This need is not simply a denial of death, but an urge to hold onto a continuous symbolic relationship to life.

Lifton proposed that human beings seek immortality in four different ways. Most societies provide their members with some form of immortality, and in most cultures it takes the form of an afterlife. This sort of immortality is theological. Religious faith assures our immortality by providing us with an afterlife. Some people seek immortality in other ways—although a person is not restricted to a belief in a single form of immortality. In biological immortality, we see ourselves as living on through our descendants or through future generations of our own society. In influential

immortality, we see ourselves living on through our creative works (literature, paintings, music, buildings, institutions) or through our human influences (the lives we touch that go on to touch other lives). People often say that a person lives as long as someone remembers him or her. In natural immortality, we see ourselves as surviving through nature itself. Our bodies decay, become part of the earth, and survive through the natural cycle of life.

In Western society, those who reject theological immortality see death as the end of existence. In their view, the death of the physical body ends life, awareness, consciousness. They seek immortality through biological, influential, or natural forms. Individuals who take this scientific perspective are outnumbered by those who take a religious perspective and believe that the soul continues to exist after the death of the body (Siegel, 1980). Among the people in one survey, well over half believed that they would live on in some form after their deaths (Kalish and Reynolds, 1976). The belief in an existence after death was held most widely among the elderly. Most of those who believed in an afterlife expected to find some kind of paradise.

The religious promise of immortality can help us to make sense out of the cycle of life and death. According to Robert Kastenbaum (1985), the concept of everlasting life compensates us for the additional time we have lost on earth. If eternity waits in the wings, we can endure the suffering of terminal illness. Yet few terminally ill people seem to rely on the promise of eternal life. In a national sample of nearly 400 older adults with terminal illness, just over 3 percent said that the thought of surviving after death was their major support (Kastenbaum, Kastenbaum, and Morris, in prep.). Although almost 50 percent said that they were deeply religious, only three women and ten men mentioned eternal life. Biological immortality did not comfort them either. Just over 2 percent said that living on through their descendants was a great comfort to them. Not some form of immortality, but love from their family and friends was the greatest comfort to these dying adults. Other studies have produced somewhat similar results. In another sample, 40 percent of older adults said that memories of a full life were their greatest comfort as they faced death, and 25 percent said that they were sustained by love from family and friends (Peterson, 1980). Among these adults, 35

The relationships of young and old, present and past, symbolize the continuity of human development. *(Elliott Erwitt/Magnum)*

to make sense out of life (Marshall, 1980). Belief in an afterlife does not always allay the fear of death. In some studies, the people most afraid of death were those who believed in hell but were not sure of their own salvation (Nelson and Nelson, 1975). In other studies, older people who had deep religious feelings or who were highly active in religious activities had thought more about their own deaths and were better able to deal with the prospect of dying (Chiriboga and Gigy, 1975).

Religious faith often helps survivors. Among a group of younger widows, those who were devout said that their religious beliefs had been a major source of comfort (Glick, Weiss, and Parkes, 1974). Although ideas of an afterlife did not seem to lessen the intensity of early grief, as the widows' sorrow began to subside, the notion of immortality bolstered their morale. Only 6 percent of these widows believed that death was the end of existence, although 34 percent were not certain that there was an afterlife. Twenty-two percent were deeply convinced that they would be reunited with their husbands in an afterlife, and 34 percent hoped for an afterlife but were not sure that there would be a reunion. One widow said: "My religion helped me an awful lot. It's really helped me overcome grief to know — well, in our religion, life is eternal — to know that Dave is going on" (Parkes and Weiss, 1983, p. 119).

All of us are survivors, but all survivors eventually die. By objective standards, people have successfully prepared themselves for a developmental task if they handle it well. The problem with death is that it is impossible to determine whether anyone has dealt with it successfully. Dying is a personal and unique experience, and everyone must experience it alone. Perhaps the most sensible preparation for the end of life, then, is a life well lived from the beginning.

percent found the greatest comfort in religion.

Researchers have found that whether religious feelings help people to accept death depends on the context of the religious beliefs, their strength, and the person's ability to use religious meanings

SUMMARY

1. In Erikson's theory, the last developmental task is coming to terms with death by finding meaning in life. People respond to death's approach in various ways: with self-reflection, disengagement, or the continuation of daily activities.

2. **Life expectancy** (the average number of years that a person lives) has increased dramatically, but most of the increase has come about because premature deaths have been sharply reduced. Older people are more susceptible to disease, in part because their immune systems

are less efficient and in part because of a diminished sense of control. The latter is closely related to the quality of health. In some situations, however, a sense of control may be detrimental. Some theories of aging focus on accumulated damage to the body, especially in individual cells, whereas others focus on genetic control of the aging process. Longevity involves both genetic and environmental factors. Long-lived people have common characteristics, including sexual, physical, and social activity, moderate habits, independence, adaptability, and a tendency to live in the present rather than the past.

3. The fear of death seems to be low among young adults, probably because they find it difficult to think of death in personal terms. Fear of death tends to peak in middle adulthood, then declines among older adults. Older adults may place less value on their lives than the young, may no longer feel that death is unfair, and may have been socialized to accept their own death.

4. In preparing for death, many older adults go through the process of **life review,** in which they reflect on their past and try to resolve old conflicts. Unless their death is sudden, people go through a **dying trajectory,** the interval between their realization that they are dying and their actual death. The dying trajectory may be acute, chronic, or terminal. Kübler-Ross has proposed that dying people go through five stages (denial, rage, bargaining for life, depression, and acceptance), but the stages are intuitive and not supported by research.

5. Most people die in an institution, where it may be difficult for them to have an **appropriate death.** In such a death, people retain some control over the way in which they die. The establishment of **hospices** has made a dignified, appropriate death possible for more people. **Euthanasia** can be passive — no extraordinary life-prolonging methods are used — or active — death is hastened by drugs. **Living wills** allow people to retain control over the manner of their deaths.

6. There are three medical concepts of death: **clinical death** arrives when the heart stops beating and the lungs stop working; **cerebral death** arrives when the cortex ceases to function; and **brain death** arrives when all parts of the brain cease functioning. In Western societies, the acceptance of death changed over the centuries to a denial of death, an attitude that recently has been questioned.

7. Grieving is a normal way of coping with the death of a loved one. Prolonged grief may take the form of **unanticipated grief** (when death comes without warning), **conflicted grief** (when the surviving spouse has had an unhappy, conflict-ridden marriage), or **chronic grief** (when the surviving partner was extremely dependent on the dead spouse).

8. Burial customs serve both social and personal needs. Funerals help the survivors accept the fact of death and give them a way to express public grief; maintain society by providing a channel for fear and anger; and strengthen social cohesiveness. As mourning customs have begun to disappear in Western societies, survivors may lose ways to resolve their grief.

9. Human beings seek immortality through belief in an afterlife (theological immortality), through descendants or future generations of the society (biological immortality), through creative works (influential immortality), or through becoming part of the natural cycle (natural immortality). The religious promise of immortality helps many people to make sense out of the cycle of life and death, although it does not allay the fear of death unless a person is sure of salvation. The idea of immortality also helps survivors by reassuring them of the continued existence of their loved one.

KEY TERMS

appropriate death
brain death
cerebral death
chronic grief
clinical death

conflicted grief
dying trajectory
euthanasia
hospice

life expectancy
life review
living will
unanticipated grief

STUDY TERMS

brain death   The cessation of function by all parts of the brain, including the cortex (which controls voluntary action, thought, and memory) and the brainstem (which controls body functions).

cerebral death   The cessation of function by the cortex (which controls voluntary action, thought, and memory).

clinical death   The cessation of body function (heart and lungs).

life expectancy   The average number of years that members of a particular group can expect to live.

life review   The process of reflecting on the past in an attempt to resolve old conflicts and come to terms with death; whether it is a universal developmental process, a developmental task limited to societies with long life expectancies, or simply a way that some people use to adjust to their own deaths has not been established.

Glossary

accommodation   Piaget's term for the modification of schemes to incorporate new knowledge that does not fit them.

achieving stage   In Warner Schaie's theory of adult cognition, the stage during young adulthood when knowledge is applied toward vocational and family goals.

acquired immune deficiency syndrome (AIDS)   A disease that attacks the immune system, so the individual has no protection against infection. It can be passed through the placenta from mother to unborn child.

acquisitive stage   In Warner Schaie's theory of adult cognition, the period of childhood and adolescence when knowledge is acquired in increasingly efficient ways.

active sleep   See **REM sleep.**

activity theory   The theory that life satisfaction in old age depends on being highly involved with others and integrated into society.

acuity   The ability to see objects clearly and to resolve detail.

adolescence   The period from puberty until the assumption of adult economic and social roles.

adulthood   The period from the assumption of adult economic and social roles until death.

afterbirth   The placenta, its membranes, and the remainder of the umbilical cord, all expelled during the final stage of labor.

age-irrelevant society   A society in which major life events, such as marriage, schooling, retirement, are not closely tied to chronological age.

ageism   Prejudice against old people, in which they are seen as incompetent; it leads to discrimination against older adults.

allele   The alternative form of a gene found at a given site on a chromosome.

Alzheimer's disease   The most prevalent organic brain disorder; this debilitating, irreversible brain disorder is characterized by increasingly serious memory loss and deterioration of attention, judgment, and personality.

ambivalent attachment   The least secure form of the attachment bond, in which the infant becomes extremely upset when the caregiver leaves but, on reunion, alternates between seeking contact and angrily squirming to get away.

amniocentesis   A procedure used to detect fetal abnormalities in which a sample of amniotic fluid is taken and chromosomal analyses performed on fetal cells within it.

amnion   The inner membrane of the sac that surrounds and protects the developing zygote.

androgens   Male hormones.

androgynous   A person whose self-concept incorporates both masculine and feminine characteristics.

animism   The belief that inanimate objects have thoughts, feelings, and life.

anorexia nervosa   An eating disorder characterized by self-starvation brought about by fanatical dieting; found primarily among affluent, well-educated girls in developed countries.

anoxia   The absence of oxygen; a birth complication that may occur in a breech or transverse delivery.

Apgar score   A common scoring system, developed in 1962 by Virginia Apgar, by which the newborn's color, heart rate, reflex irritability, muscle tone, and respiratory effort are assessed.

appropriate death   A dignified death, in which the dying person is protected from demeaning medical procedures, kept as free from pain as possible, and allowed to participate in medical decisions.

architectural system   The biologically based part of intelligence, consisting of basic cognitive processes.

artificialism   The belief, caused by the inability to separate physical from psychological causes, that either God or humans have built or made everything in the world.

assimilation   Piaget's term for the incorporation of new knowledge into existing schemes.

asynchrony   A growth trend typical of adolescence, in which different body parts mature at different rates.

attachment   The primary social bond that develops between infant and parent or caregiver and that provides the baby with emotional security; attachment is demonstrated by the child's tendency to seek the caregiver for comfort when distressed and for play when happy.

authoritarian parenting   A parental style in which parents demand that the child meet high standards but are relatively cold and unresponsive to the youngster.

authoritative parenting   A parental style in which parents demand that the child meet high standards but are warm and responsive to the youngster.

autonomy   A feeling of self-control and self-determination.

avoidant attachment   An insecure form of the attachment bond, in which the infant pays little attention to the caregiver and seems almost too independent.

basic category   Category formed at the level at which members

557

are most like one another and most different from members of other categories (for example, flower, bird, bed, doll).

birth-cohort theory   The theory that the twenty-year rise, peak, and subsequent decline of stress-related disorders among adolescents is due to increased economic and social stress on members of crowded birth groups.

body ideal   The body type defined by the culture as ideally attractive and sex-appropriate.

bonding   The process through which parents form an emotional attachment to their baby.

brain death   Death defined as the cessation of function by all parts of the brain, including the cortex (which controls voluntary action, thought, and memory) and the brainstem (which controls body functions).

bulimia   An eating disorder characterized by periodic eating binges, often followed by purging, found primarily among affluent, well-educated girls in developed countries.

canalization   Genetic programming that is extremely difficult to deflect from its course and that is self-stabilizing when temporarily deflected.

case study   A study in which researchers follow individuals over months or years and use in-depth interviews and observation.

catch-up growth   A period of rapid growth that returns a child to his or her normal growth curve after a condition that has been retarding growth is eliminated.

centration   The concentration of attention on a prominent feature of a stimulus, to the exclusion of all other aspects of the situation.

cephalocaudal development   The progression of growth from head to foot; in which the head develops and grows before the torso, arms, and legs.

cerebral death   Death defined as the cessation of function by the cortex (which controls voluntary action, thought, and memory); the patient may still breathe, and his or her heart may still beat.

cervix   The pinhead-sized opening that separates the vagina from the uterus.

childhood   The period from age two until puberty.

chlamydia   A common bacterium that may inhabit the vagina and enter the baby during labor; it may cause eye infections or pneumonia.

chorion   The outer membrane of the sac that surrounds and protects the developing embryo.

chorionic villi sampling   A procedure used to detect fetal abnormalities; cells are removed from the fingerlike projections of the chorion and the chromosomes examined.

chromosomes   Beadlike strings of genes present in every cell of the body; except in the gametes, they occur in pairs.

chronic grief   A form of prolonged grief in which the surviving spouse has been completely dependent on the dead spouse, so that he or she is unable to carry out the routine responsibilities connected with social roles.

classic aging pattern   A typical pattern of changes in IQ scores with age; scores on verbal (or crystallized) abilities either remain steady or increase, whereas scores on performance (or fluid) abilities begin to decline in middle age.

classical conditioning   A simple form of learning, in which one stimulus is associated with another, so that the first evokes the response that normally follows the second stimulus. Also called *respondent conditioning.*

class inclusion   The knowledge that a basic class *(flower)* is always larger than any of its subordinate classes *(poppy).*

clinical death   Death defined as the cessation of body function; the heart has ceased to beat, the lungs no longer draw in and expel air.

clinical study   A study consisting of in-depth interviews, sometimes supplemented by questionnaires and tests.

codominant   Alleles for single-gene traits that are not determined by a simple dominant-recessive arrangement; the allele's expression depends on environmental conditions.

cognition   All intellectual processes, including perception, memory, the use of symbols, thought, and imagination.

cognitive capacity   The number of symbols that the mind can include at one time.

cohabitation   An arrangement in which unmarried couples live together.

cohort   The members of a particular age group; a group of people of the same age.

computerized axial tomography (CAT) scan   An X-ray technique that enables researchers to reconstruct cross-sections of the living brain at any depth or angle.

concrete-operational stage   Thought during the third stage in Piaget's theory; it begins when children are about six and lasts until around age eleven. Thought is flexible and logical but only in regard to concrete objects and situations.

conditioned reflex   An involuntary response that, through conditioning, follows a formerly neutral stimulus.

conditioning theory   Any behavior-learning theory that interprets developmental changes in terms of a person's learning to associate one event with another.

conflicted grief   A form of prolonged grief that sometimes develops in the surviving spouse when the marriage had been unhappy and full of conflict; it apparently develops because of guilt feelings.

confluence theory   The theory that the size of the family and the spacing of the children affect the cognitive development of each child; the larger the family and the closer the spacing, the smaller the child's IQ.

conservation   The understanding that irrelevant changes in the physical appearance of objects do not affect their quantity, mass, weight, or volume; one of Piaget's concrete operations.

constructive play   Play that consists of manipulating objects to construct or create something.

constructivist   Piaget's term for the child's understanding of reality. Knowledge comes from the child's actions on objects; from this knowledge, the child constructs an understanding of the world.

control group   A group with the same characteristics as the experimental group in a study but that does not undergo the experimental treatment.

conventional level   The middle level in Kohlberg's theory of moral reasoning; at which value is placed on maintaining the conventional social order and on the expectations of others.

convergence   The mechanism by which the slightly different images seen by each eye come together to form a single image.

cooing   The sounds of joy made by babies from about the third month of age.

correlation   A numerical expression of how closely two sets of measures correspond. Correlations range from $+1.00$ (perfect positive correlation) to -1.00 (perfect negative correlation).

cortex   The mantle of neural cells that covers the two cerebral hemispheres; it is heavily involved in sensation, speech, learning, memory, and voluntary movements.

co-twin control   A method of study in which one of a pair of twins undergoes some experience that is withheld or delayed in the other twin.

cross-sectional design   An experimental design that compares the performance of different age groups on a single occasion.

crystallized intelligence   Verbal skills, mechanical knowledge, and the ability to handle well-learned information in familiar situations; crystallized skills are taught in schools and emphasized by the culture.

delirium   A reversible organic brain disorder that reflects disturbed metabolism throughout the brain.

deoxyribonucleic acid (DNA) The complex chemical containing the genetic code that guides development.

dependent variable A factor in a study that changes as the result of the introduction of an independent variable.

development Any age-related change in body or behavior from conception to death.

dialectical operations A fifth stage of cognitive development that goes beyond Piaget's stage of formal operations; an individual in this stage no longer seeks mental equilibrium but accepts contradiction as the basis of thought and development.

dialectical theory Developmental theory that sees development as proceeding in a dialectic between the individual and society, with each interaction leading to a higher level of functioning.

disengagement theory The theory that life satisfaction in old age depends on a gradual withdrawal from society and a decreasing involvement with other people; the process is regarded as a mutual one, with society gradually withdrawing from the old.

divergent thinking The ability to come up with many unusual ideas or associations.

dominance hierarchy Ranking that reflects the relative social power of group members.

dominant gene The allele whose corresponding trait appears in an individual when the allele is paired with a different allele for the same trait.

Down's syndrome A condition that results when an extra chromosome 21 is present in the zygote or when extra material from chromosome 21 becomes attached to another chromosome. It produces various physical abnormalities and mental retardation in the afflicted child.

dual-process model A view of cognition, in which intellectual functioning consists of basic cognitive skills (mechanics of intelligence) and the procedures that relate these skills, stored knowledge, and expertise to daily life (pragmatics of intelligence).

dying trajectory The interval between the time a person realizes that death is imminent and the moment of death; the character of the trajectory varies, depending on the cause of death.

dynamic assessment Evaluation of what a child is prepared to learn with assistance; a measure of the child's zone of proximal development.

ego The conscious self, which in Freudian theory guides behavior and mediates the perpetual conflict between id and superego.

egocentrism Among babies, the inability to distinguish between the self and the external world; among young children, the belief that everyone sees the world and responds to it as the child does.

ego integrity In Erikson's theory, the older adult's acceptance of his or her own life as meaningful and coherent, with the accompanying belief that the adult has handled life tasks in the best possible way under the circumstances.

embryo The developing organism from the second to the eighth week of development within the uterus.

embryonic period The second to sixth week of prenatal development; during this period, the organism begins to take shape and organ systems form.

empty-nest syndrome An emotional crisis produced by the departure of children from the home; occurs primarily when the children leave at an extremely young age or when the mother sees her children primarily as an extension of herself.

encode To register information in memory.

equilibration Piaget's developmental principle, which states that the organism always tends toward biological and psychological balance.

estrogens Female hormones.

ethologist Scientist who studies human or animal behavior in evolutionary terms.

euthanasia Any method of hastening death with the intention of making the dying process easy; euthanasia may be passive (when life-prolonging measures are withheld) or active (when drugs or some other process is used to speed death).

evoked potential A characteristic electrical response in the brain that is evoked by a new stimulus, such as a sight or a sound.

executive stage In Warner Schaie's theory of adult cognition, the period in middle adulthood when knowledge is applied to managing organizations.

executive system The acquired part of intelligence, consisting of organized knowledge, learning strategies, and metacognitive skills.

experiment A study in which researchers can control the arrangement and manipulation of conditions, in order to systematically observe particular phenomena.

experimental group Group of research subjects that undergoes the experimental treatment.

expressive jargon Babbling that has the intonation and pitch of speech; it occurs in infants toward the end of the first year.

extinguish To eliminate a response that is not reinforced.

extraversion In Jung's theory, a major personality orientation, in which a person is primarily interested in the external world.

factor analysis A technique in which scores on a series of tests are correlated in the hope of finding clusters of highly correlated scores that reflect a common ability.

factor theories Theories of intelligence based on abilities uncovered through factor analysis.

Fallopian tube The passage leading from either ovary to the uterus.

fetal alcohol syndrome A condition that afflicts many babies born to alcoholic mothers; the infants may be small for gestational age, have abnormal head and facial features, and be mentally retarded.

fetus The developing organism from eight weeks after conception until birth.

field study A study in which the investigator introduces some factor into the natural situation that changes it.

finalism The belief that nothing happens by accident.

fixated In Freudian theory, to become stalled emotionally at an immature level of personality development, where behavior is dominated by the traits characteristic of that level.

fluid intelligence Abstract, nonverbal reasoning and problem-solving skills, which are neither taught in school nor emphasized by the culture.

fontanel The soft area at the crown of a newborn's head that is unprotected by cartilage.

foreclosure An identity status in which the adolescent is committed to an occupation or ideology that has been chosen by his or her parents.

formal operational thought Logical, abstract thought that can be applied to hypothetical situations; it develops during the final stage in Piaget's theory, which roughly corresponds to adolescence. Piaget regarded formal-operational thought as the culmination of cognitive development.

functional illiterate A person who can read and write at a rudimentary level but lacks the basic reading and writing skills required for productive performance in American society.

functional play Play that consists of simple, repetitive movements; the simplest, least mature form of play.

games with rules Formal, rule-governed, competitive games; the last form of play to develop.

gametes Mature reproductive cells; spermatozoa and ova.

gender constancy The understanding that gender will never change, that boys always become men and girls always become women.

gender identity The inner experience of gender; the unchanging sense of self as male or female.

gender schema Self-constructed theory made up of sex-related associations for each gender, which organize a person's perceptions of the world and determine the way that new information is organized.

generational stake An individual's personal interest in the relationship between generations, which affects his or her perception of that relationship.

generativity Ego strength of middle age in Erikson's theory; made up of procreativity, productivity, and creativity.

genes Microscopic particles of DNA that contain instructions for the development of physical traits and behavioral dispositions; located at specific sites on chromosomes.

genetic epistemology Piaget's basic approach to development, focusing on the development of intelligence.

genital herpes An acute viral infection of the genital tract, usually transmitted through sexual contact.

genotype The specific combination of alleles that makes up each individual's genetic inheritance.

germinal period The first two weeks after conception, when the zygote is primarily engaged in cell division.

gestational age The age of the fetus as calculated from the date of conception.

gestation period The period of prenatal development, calculated from fertilization (thirty-eight weeks) or from the date of the last menstruation (forty weeks).

gonorrhea A sexually transmitted bacterial disease that can infect a newborn during birth.

grasping reflex The newborn's unlearned tendency to clutch any small object placed in the hand; it is strongest in the first month of life and disappears at about three or four months.

habituation Reduced response to a stimulus after repeated or continuous encounters with it; a primitive kind of learning analogous to becoming bored with the stimulus.

heritability An estimate of the genetic contribution to a single trait within a given group.

heterozygous The condition in which the alleles at a given chromosome site are different; in such cases, the dominant gene generally determines the appearance of the affected trait.

holophrases One-word sentences of the toddler that depend on context to communicate meaning.

homozygous The condition in which the alleles at a given chromosome site are identical.

hospice An institution where people can die with dignity; patients are kept pain free, and no life-prolonging measures are used.

hydrocephaly A condition in which fluid accumulates within the skull and presses on the brain; often appears in individuals with spina bifida.

hypochondriasis An exaggerated fear of disease, generally characterized by physical symptoms that have no organic basis.

hypothesis A prediction based on theory, which can be tested by the gathering of appropriate information.

id The aspect of the personality that, in Freudian terms, contains the unconscious impulses or drives.

identification The internalization of another person's values and standards in an attempt to become like that person.

identity In Piaget's theory, the understanding that objects and people remain the same even if irrelevant properties are changed. In Erikson's theory, a complex sense of self that develops during adolescence, when various life roles and aspects of the personality coalesce.

identity achievement An identity status in which the adolescent is committed to self-chosen occupational or ideological goals.

identity diffusion An identity status in which the adolescent has no occupational or ideological goals but is not particularly concerned about the situation.

imaginary audience An aspect of adolescent egocentrism in which the adolescent acts with the assumption that others share the adolescent's own concern with himself or herself and thus are close observers of the adolescent's appearance and actions.

imitation Copying or reproducing observed behavior.

immanent justice Punishment perceived as an inevitable consequence of breaking rules; characteristic of Piaget's morality of constraint.

independent variable The factor in a study that is selected or changed in some way by the investigator.

inductive discipline A disciplinary technique whose power lies in appeals to pride or concern for others, relies heavily on reason and explanations, and attempts to induce empathy or role-taking.

infancy The period in development from birth to a child's second birthday.

information-processing theory A theory of cognition that sees individuals as processing information much as a computer does; thought and behavior are believed to be built on a small set of primitive processes.

interaction A spiraling developmental process in which hereditary characteristics influence the environment, which in turn affects further development, and vice versa.

introversion In Jung's theory, a basic personality orientation in which the person withdraws interest from the external world and is primarily oriented toward the self.

Klinefelter's syndrome A condition resulting from the presence in boys of an extra female sex chromosome (XXY); the boys are sterile, have rounded bodies, and may be somewhat retarded.

kwashiorkor A serious, often fatal, disease that develops in children who may get enough calories but whose diets are severely deficient in protein.

language acquisition device (LAD) According to Noam Chomsky, the innate human language capacity that ensures the acquisition of language by any child who is exposed to spoken language.

latchkey children Youngsters who come home from school to an empty house and take responsibility for their own care, so called for the house key that the child must carry.

learned helplessness A condition in which repeated failure in situations over which a person has no control leads to apathy and refusal to try.

learning The process of acquiring new information.

libido Freud's term for the life instinct, the "psychic energy" that fuels all human motivation; these energies and desires come from the id.

life-cycle squeeze Stress, either emotional or economic, caused when the care of an aging parent and the responsibility for children overlap; it is aggravated when both husband and wife are employed and unavailable to provide care for the aging parent.

life expectancy The average number of years that members of a particular group can expect to live.

life review The process of reflecting on the past in an attempt to resolve old conflicts and come to terms with death; whether it is a universal developmental process, a developmental task limited to societies with long life expectancies, or simply a way that some people use to adjust to their own deaths has not been established.

living will A document that asks physicians not to use life-prolonging measures when recovery from extreme physical or mental disability is impossible.

longitudinal design An experimental design that follows the same subjects over time and compares their behavior at different ages.

love-withdrawal A disciplinary technique whose power lies in the fear of losing emotional support, affection, or approval. It includes withdrawing physically, refusing to speak or listen to a person, telling the person that one dislikes him or her, or threatening to leave the person.

maturational theory Theory of development that sees development as self-regulating and unfolding according to a maturational timetable.

mechanics of intelligence The basic cognitive skills used to process information and solve problems; skills similar to abilities of fluid intelligence. See **dual-process model**

meiosis The form of cell division followed in gametes; produces four cells, each containing twenty-three single chromosomes.

memory The application to information storage and retrieval of cognitive processes involved in perceiving, thinking, and learning.

menarche The first incidence of menstruation.

menopause The cessation of menstruation; the medical marker of middle age in women, which usually occurs at about the age of fifty.

menstrual age The age of the fetus as calculated from the beginning of the mother's last menstrual period.

menstrual cycle The hormonal cycle characterized by the periodic discharge of blood and tissue from the uterus; each cycle occurs monthly from puberty to menopause, except during pregnancy and lactation.

mental age Level of intelligence determined by comparing one child's ability with the age at which an average child makes a given score; based on the concept that intellectual abilities increase with age.

mentally retarded Scoring at least two standard deviations (thirty points) below normal on IQ tests and also showing an impaired ability to adapt to the demands of the environment.

metacognition Knowledge about cognition and an understanding of the ways in which a person can control his or her own cognitive activity.

metamemory An understanding of the workings of memory; one aspect of metacognition.

midlife crisis A state of physical and psychological distress that arises when the developmental tasks of midlife threaten to overwhelm a person's internal resources and social supports.

modified extended family A family structure in which each unit has its own separate dwelling but family members are held together by bonds of aid and affection; typical of the contemporary American family.

morality of constraint According to Piaget, the first stage of morality, in which virtuous conduct is based on obedience to authority. Sometimes called *objective morality*.

morality of cooperation According to Piaget, the second stage of morality, in which virtuous conduct is based on what is expected, fair, or just. Sometimes called *subjective morality*.

moratorium An identity status in which the adolescent is struggling with occupational or ideological issues and may be in an identity crisis.

Moro reflex A newborn's unlearned response, in which the neonate thrusts out the arms and curls the hands when support for the neck and head is removed; disappears by five or six months of age.

motherese The altered, simplified speech used by parents with infants; also called *baby talk* or *child-directed speech*.

multiinfarct dementia An irreversible, organic brain disorder that results from cardiovascular disease and develops when blood supply to the brain is repeatedly interrupted.

mutation A change in the chemical structure of a single gene, which produces a new allele that carries new genetic information.

naturalistic study A study in which researchers observe and record behavior without interfering with it in any way.

neonate The technical term for an infant during the first month of independent life.

neuron A neural cell in the central nervous system.

norms Typical patterns of growth or performance; they describe the approximate ages at which important attributes and skills appear.

obesity Extreme overweight, a condition in which there is an excessive proportion of fat to muscle; genes and environment are usually involved in its development.

object concept The understanding that objects remain the same although they may move from place to place (object identity) and that they continue to exist when out of sight (object permanence).

object identity see **object concept**

object permanence see **object concept**

observational study Any study in which a researcher observes people as they go about daily activities and carefully records their behavior. See **naturalistic study** and **field study.**

operant conditioning A form of learning in which a response is strengthened or changed as a result of reinforcement. Sometimes called *instrumental conditioning.*

operations Flexible and rigorous cognitive processes that first appear during the concrete-operational stage.

ordinal position The child's position in the family birth order.

organization The grouping of items that are to be remembered around some common element (for example, all the animals, all the flowers).

ovaries The female reproductive glands, which mature and release ova.

overextension A generalization in a child's use of a word so that its meaning includes dissimilar objects or events.

overregularization A temporary error in language acquisition in which the child applies a rule rigidly and makes the language more regular than it actually is.

ovum The female reproductive cell; the largest cell in the human body.

parental imperative The notion that parenthood exerts a controlling influence over adult personality, based on the proposal that basic personality differences between the sexes have evolved in order to protect and nurture children.

peripheral nervous system That part of the nervous system that connects the central nervous system (brain and spinal cord) with all parts of the body, sending sensory information to the brain and transmitting commands to the various muscles and organs.

permissive parenting A parental style in which the parents place few demands on the child but are warm and responsive to the child.

personal fable An aspect of adolescent egocentrism in which the adolescent believes that he or she is unique and indestructible.

phenotype Physical or behavioral traits as they appear in the individual, reflecting the influence of genetic and environmental influences.

phenylketonuria (PKU) An inherited inability to metabolize phenylalanine, a component of milk and other foods.

placenta A pliable structure of tissue and blood vessels that transmits nourishment and wastes between mother and fetus.

placing reflex The newborn's unlearned tendency to lift up a foot and place it on top of a surface; generally disappears between the third and fourth months after birth.

polygenic   The capacity for several genes to have an equal and cumulative effect in producing a trait.

positron emission tomography (PET)   A method of studying brain function in which injections of radioactive glucose produce maps of brain activity.

postpartum depression   Emotional letdown that often follows the birth of a child; frequently called *baby blues*.

power-assertive discipline   A disciplinary technique whose force resides in power; it includes blows, threats, commands, removing the offending person bodily, and withdrawing privileges.

pragmatics   The study of language's social purposes.

pragmatics of intelligence   The procedures that relate stored knowledge, expertise, and basic cognitive skills to daily life; see **dual-process model.**

premoral level   The most primitive level in Kohlberg's theory of moral reasoning; value is placed on physical acts and needs, not on people or social standards.

prenatal period   The first stage of development; the period from conception to birth.

preoperational thought   Thought during the second stage in Piaget's theory, which begins at about eighteen months or two years and lasts until about seven years; during this stage children record their experiences symbolically and use language, but their thought is intuitive, inflexible, contradictory, and focused on individual events.

pretend play   Play that involves fantasy or role-taking.

primary circular reaction   The repetition of unlearned behavior (such as sucking or kicking) for the stimulation it provides; characteristic of Substage 2 of Piaget's sensorimotor period.

principled level   The third, and highest, level in Kohlberg's theory of moral reasoning; value is placed in self-chosen principles and standards that have a universal logical validity and therefore can be shared.

production deficiency   The failure to use a skill or capability that a person possesses.

prosocial behavior   All actions that promote or benefit another person.

proximodistal development   The progression of physical and motor growth from the center of the body to the periphery, which first appears during the embryonic period; for example, a baby learns to control shoulder movements before arm or finger movements.

psychometrics   Mental testing; the branch of psychology that has developed intelligence tests.

psychosexual theory   Freud's psychodynamic theory of personality development, which focuses on the changing seat of sensual pleasures in the individual.

psychosocial theory   Erikson's psychodynamic theory of personality development, which focuses on the individual's interactions with society.

puberty   The biological process that turns a child into a sexually mature individual.

punishment   Any unpleasant outcome of an action that makes it less likely that the action will be repeated.

quiet sleep   Sleep in which there is no movement of the eyes, respiration is slowed, and brain waves show an uneven pattern; also called *non-REM sleep.*

reaction range   The range of possible responses within which a genetic trait can express itself.

recall   The ability to remember information in the absence of the object or information to be remembered.

recessive gene   The allele whose corresponding trait fails to appear in an individual who carries it; the subordinate member of a pair of alleles.

reflex   An unlearned response to a specific stimulus that is not affected by motivation and that is common to all members of the species.

rehearsal   An encoding strategy in which a person repeats information that is to be remembered.

reinforcement   Any consequence following an action (response) that makes it likely that a person will repeat the action (response).

reintegrative stage   In Warner Schaie's theory of adult cognition, the period of later adulthood when knowledge is applied to personal interests.

rejecting-neglecting parenting   A parental style in which the parents place few demands on the child and are relatively cold and unresponsive to the youngster.

REM sleep   Sleep that is characterized by rapid eye movements (REM), rapid respiration, and a relatively even pattern of brain waves; also called *active sleep.*

respiratory distress syndrome   A lung condition (formerly called *hyaline membrane disease*) in which the preterm infant cannot maintain necessary surfactin levels.

responsible stage   In Warner Schaie's theory of adult cognition, the period during middle adulthood when knowledge is used to fulfill family and vocational obligations.

reversibility   The understanding that irrelevant changes in appearance can be reversed and that such changes tend to compensate one another; one of Piaget's concrete operations.

rooting reflex   The newborn's unlearned tendency to turn the head and mouth in the direction of any object that gently stimulates the mouth area; disappears by three or four months of age.

rubella   Commonly called *German measles,* this disease can cause abnormalities in the developing fetus if contracted by the mother during the first trimester of pregnancy.

scheme   Piaget's term for patterns of action (banging, sucking) or mental structures (classification of objects) that are involved in the acquiring and structuring of knowledge.

secondary circular reaction   The repetition of learned behavior (such as shaking a rattle) because the event interests the baby. These reactions characterize Substage 3 of Piaget's sensorimotor period.

secure attachment   A form of the attachment bond in which infants are comfortable in a strange place as long as their caregiver is present; when separated from the caregiver, the infant actively seeks the caregiver and is comforted by contact with him or her.

self-concept   The organized and integrated pattern of perceptions related to the self, including self-esteem and self-image.

self-efficacy   An individual's judgment of his or her competence in a particular situation, which influences whether the individual takes part in some activity, how hard he or she works at it, and how long the individual perseveres in the face of obstacles.

self-regulated learning   Learning in which children are motivated to learn, possess the skills that enable them to learn, plan and regulate those skills, and adapt them to the learning situation.

self-regulation   The ability to control one's behavior so as to fulfill an intention.

semantics   The study of the arbitrary meanings conveyed by language forms.

sensorimotor stage   The first stage in Piaget's theory, which lasts through most of the first two years of life, when knowledge develops from the infant's sensations and physical actions.

separation distress   A baby's distress at being parted from an attachment figure; the reaction appears by eight or nine months of age and begins to decline when the baby is about one and one-half years old.

sequential design   A design that combines elements from cross-sectional and longitudinal designs in a single study.

sex role   Socially prescribed pattern of behavior and attitudes considered characteristic of either gender.

sex-role stereotype   Simplified, exaggerated concept concerning the behavior and traits typical of either gender.

sleep apnea   A temporary halt to breathing during sleep.

small for gestational age (SGA)   The condition in which a baby is underweight for his or her gestational age.

social cognition   The way that people reason about themselves and others in social situations.

social comparison   Process by which an individual assesses his or her own performance or ability by comparing it with that of other people in a reference group.

socialization   The process by which an individual acquires the behavior, attitudes, values, and roles expected from its members by society.

social-learning theory   A behavior-learning theory that sees development as the result of conditioning, observation, and imitation and regards stimuli as information.

sonogram   A picture produced by bouncing sound waves off an object, used to guide tests for birth defects and to detect the presence of twins and other visible complications of pregnancy.

speech act   An utterance used for communication and intended to help the speaker achieve some goal.

spermatozoon   The male reproductive cell — a sperm.

spina bifida   A protrusion of spinal cord nerves through an opening in the back, caused by the failure of the neural tube to close during prenatal development.

stage   A particular pattern of abilities, motives, or behavior that is predicted by a specific theory of development.

stepping reflex   The newborn's unlearned tendency to straighten out the legs at the hip and knee as if to stand, when held with feet touching a surface; usually disappears by three or four months of age.

strategy   A technique used to encode or retrieve information, such as scanning, rehearsal, or organization.

subitize   To detect numerical differences in patterns by an almost automatic perceptual process, without any counting.

successive approximation   A technique used by behaviorists to shape new behavior; after rewarding behavior that only vaguely resembles the desired action, the teacher demands that, for each subsequent reward, the behavior more closely approaches the desired response.

sudden infant death syndrome (SIDS)   The unexpected death, during sleep, of an apparently healthy infant; also called *crib death*.

superego   Freud's term for the conscience, which he saw as developing in early childhood when a child internalizes parental values and standards.

superordinate category   A category determined primarily by function (for example, vehicle, furniture, toy); the most abstract level of categorization.

surfactin   A liquid that coats the air sacs of the lungs and enables infants to transmit oxygen from the air to the blood.

syntax   The structural principles that determine the form of sentences.

syphilis   A sexually transmitted disease that can affect almost any organ or tissue in the body; the spirochete that causes it can pass across the placental barrier during pregnancy and infect the fetus.

telegraphic speech   Utterances of children in the two-word stage; utterances stripped to the basic content words.

temperament   Early, observable differences in babies' emotional responses, motor actions, and attention.

teratogen   Any influence that can disrupt fetal growth or cause malformation in the developing organism.

term   The gestational age of 266 days from conception.

terminal drop   A noticeable drop in IQ scores that appears shortly before death and apparently is the result of physical deterioration or damage.

tertiary circular reaction   An intelligent, systematic adaptation to a specific situation, characteristic of Substage 5 of Piaget's sensorimotor period.

testes   The male reproductive glands, which manufacture and release sperm.

theory   A set of logically related statements that generates testable hypotheses and explains some aspect of experience.

triarchic theory   Sternberg's three-part theory of intelligence that includes social, educational, and situational factors in addition to cognitive components of the information-processing system.

Turner's syndrome   A condition resulting from the absence in girls of one female sex chromosome (X0); the girls generally are short and lack secondary sex characteristics; have retarded spatial skills but normal verbal skills.

ultrasound   The technique that produces sonograms.

umbilical cord   The flexible cord, containing two arteries and one vein, that connects the developing organism to the placenta.

unanticipated grief   A form of prolonged grief that sometimes develops when death comes without warning and survivors have had no time to prepare for it.

unconditioned reflex   A response to a stimulus that occurs naturally and without any learning.

unconscious   In Freud's theory, the part of the mind that contains forgotten or repressed memories and impulses.

variable   A factor that can vary in size or strength and that may affect the results of a study.

variance   A statistic that describes the distribution of individual scores.

vernix   The white, greasy substance that lubricates the fetus for passage through the birth canal.

visual accommodation   The ability to alternate focus in order to see objects at different distances clearly.

wariness of strangers   A natural reaction of babies to strangers that helps infants avoid potentially dangerous situations; it appears at about eight months of age and is heightened when the baby's attachment figure is absent.

zone of proximal development   Vygotsky's term for the area in which children, with the help of adults or more capable peers, can solve problems they are unable to solve by themselves.

zygote   Fertilized ovum, formed by the union of spermatozoon and ovum; refers to the developing organism during the first two weeks of development.

Bibliography

AARP News Bulletin. 1983. "Study Concludes Less Educated Get More from College Classes." *24,* Jul.–Aug., 3. (Ch. 16)

Aboud, F. E. 1981. "Egocentrism, Conformity, and Agreeing to Disagree." *Developmental Psychology,* 17, 791–799. (Ch. 10)

Abrahams, B., S. S. Feldman, and S. C. Nash. 1978. "Sex Role Self-Concept and Sex Role Attitudes." *Developmental Psychology,* 14, 393–400. (Ch. 15)

Abramovitch, R., C. Corter, and B. Lando. 1979. "Sibling Interaction in the Home." *Child Development,* 50, 997–1003. (Ch. 8)

——, ——, D. J. Pepler, and L. Stanhope. 1986. "Sibling and Peer Interaction." *Child Development,* 57, 217–229. (Ch. 9)

——, and J. E. Grusec. 1978. "Peer Imitation in a Neutral Setting." *Child Development,* 49, 60–65. (Ch. 10)

Abramson, P. 1985. "Genentech's Drug Problem." *Newsweek,* Nov. 25, 70. (Ch. 5)

Abravanel, E., and H. Gingold. 1985. "Learning via Observation during the Second Year of Life." *Developmental Psychology,* 21, 614–623. (Ch. 6)

——, and A. D. Sigafoos. 1984. "Exploring the Presence of Imitation during Early Infancy." *Child Development,* 55, 381–392. (Ch. 6)

Acheson, R. M. 1960. "Effects of Nutrition and Disease on Human Growth." In *Human Growth,* ed. J. M. Tanner, 73–92. NY: Pergamon Pr. (Ch. 5)

Acredolo, K. 1982. "Conservation-Nonconservation." In *Children's Logical and Mathematical Cognition,* ed. C. J. Brainerd, 1–31. NY: Springer-Verlag. (Ch. 11)

Acredolo, L. P. 1979. "Laboratory vs. Home." *Developmental Psychology,* 15, 666–667. (Ch. 6)

——, and D. Evans. 1980. "Developmental Changes in the Effects of Landmarks on Infant Spatial Behavior." *Developmental Psychology,* 16, 312–318. (Ch. 6)

Adams, R. D. 1980. "Morphological Aspects of Aging in the Human Nervous System." In *Handbook of Mental Health and Aging,* ed. J. E. Birren and R. B. Sloane, 149–160. Englewood Cliffs, NJ: Prentice-Hall. (Ch. 18)

Adamson, L. B., and R. Bakeman. 1985. "Affect and Attention." *Child Development,* 56, 582–593. (Ch. 1)

Adelson J. 1982. "Rites of Passage." *American Educator,* Summer, 6–33ff. (Ch. 13)

——. 1983. "The Growth of Thought in Adolescence." *Educational Horizons,* Summer, 156–162. (Ch. 13)

——. 1985a. "Adolescence for Clinicians." In *From Research to Clinical Practice,* ed. G. Stricker and R. Keisner, 313–326. NY: Plenum. (Ch. 14)

——. 1985b. "Observations on Research in Adolescence." *Genetic, Social, and General Psychology Monographs,* 111, 249–254. (Ch. 13)

——, and M. J. Doehrman. 1980. "The Psychodynamic Approach to Adolescence." In *Handbook of Adolescent Psychology,* ed. J. Adelson, 99–116. NY: Wiley-Interscience. (Ch. 13)

——. Interview by E. Hall. 1987. "Children and Other Political Naïfs." In E. Hall, *Growing and Changing,* 88–102. NY: Random House. (Chs. 13, 15)

Ainsworth, M. D. S. 1967. *Infancy in Uganda.* Baltimore: Johns Hopkins Univ. Pr. (Ch. 8)

——, M. C. Blehar, E. Waters, and S. Wall. 1978. *Patterns of Attachment.* Hillsdale, NJ: Lawrence Erlbaum Assoc. (Ch. 8)

——, and B. A. Wittig. 1969. "Attachment and Exploratory Behavior of 1-Year-Olds in a Strange Situation." In *Determinants of Infant Behavior,* ed. B. M. Foss, vol. 4, 111–136. London: Methuen. (Ch. 8)

Aldous, J., E. Klaus, and D. W. Klein. 1985. "The Understanding Heart." *Child Development,* 56, 303–316. (Ch. 1)

Allen, V. L., and D. Newtson. 1972. "Development of Conformity and Independence." *Journal of Personality and Social Psychology,* 22, 18–30. (Ch. 10)

Alpert, J. L., and M. S. Richardson. 1980. "Parenting." In *Aging in the 1980s,* ed. L. W. Poon, 441–454. Washington, DC: Amer. Psychological Assn. (Ch. 15)

American Association on Mental Deficiency. 1977. *Manual on Terminology and Classification of Mental Retardation.* Rev. ed. Washington, DC: Amer. Assn. on Mental Deficiency. (Ch. 12)

American Humane Association. 1983. *Annual Report, 1981.* Denver: Amer. Humane Assn. (Ch. 9)

American Psychiatric Association. 1980. *Diagnostic and Statistical Manual of Mental Disorders.* 3rd ed. Washington, DC: Amer. Psychiatric Assn. (Ch. 18)

Ancoli-Israel, S., D. F. Kripke, W. Mason, and O. J. Kaplan. 1985. "Sleep Apnea and Period Movements in an Aging Sample." *Journal of Gerontology,* 40, 419–425. (Ch. 19)

Anderson, G. C., A. K. Burroughs, and C. P. Measel. 1983. "Nonnutritive Sucking Opportunities." In *Infants Born at Risk,* ed. T. Field and A. Sostek, 129–146. NY: Grune & Stratton. (Ch. 4)

Anderson, R. C., E. H. Hiebert, J. A. Scott, and I. A. G. Wilkinson. 1985. *Becoming a Nation of Readers.* Washington, DC: Nat. Inst. of Education. (Ch. 12)

Ankarloo, B. 1978. "Marriage and Family Formation." In *Transitions,* ed. T. K. Hareven, 113–134. NY: Academic Pr. (Ch. 15)

Antell, S. E., and D. P. Keating. 1983. "Perception of Numerical Invariance in Neonates." *Child Development,* 54, 695–701. (Chs. 6, 11)

Antonucci, T. C. 1985. "Personal Characteristics, Social Supports, and Social Behavior." In *Handbook of Aging and the Social Sciences,* 2nd ed., ed. R. H. Binstock and E. Shanas, 94–128. NY: Van Nostrand Reinhold. (Ch. 19)

Apgar, V., and L. S. James. 1962. "Further Observations on the Newborn Scoring System." *American Journal of the Diseases of Children, 104,* 419–428. (Ch. 3)

Appelbaum, M. I., and R. B. McCall. "Design and Analysis in Developmental Psychology." 1983. In *Handbook of Child Psychology,* 4th ed. ed. P. H. Mussen, vol. 1, 415–476. NY: Wiley. (Ch. 1)

Applebee, A. N. 1984. "Writing and Reasoning." *Review of Educational Research, 54,* 577–596. Princeton, NJ: Educ. Testing Service. (Ch. 12)

———, J. A. Langer, and I. V. S. Mullis. 1986. *Writing Trends across the Decade, 1974–1984.* National Assessment of Educational Progress. (Ch. 12)

Arenberg, D., and E. A. Robertson-Tchabo. 1977. "Learning and Aging." In *Handbook of the Psychology of Aging,* ed. J. E. Birren and K. W. Schaie, 421–449. NY: Van Nostrand Reinhold. (Ch. 18)

Ariès, P. 1962. *Centuries of Childhood.* NY: Vintage. (Ch. 1)

———. 1981. *The Hour of Our Death.* NY: Knopf. (Ch. 20)

Asher, S. R. 1978. "Children's Peer Relations." In *Social and Personality Development,* ed. M. E. Lamb, 273–296. NY: Holt, Rinehart and Winston. (Ch. 10)

———, S. Hymel, and P. D. Renshaw. 1984. "Loneliness in Children." *Child Development, 55,* 1456–1464. (Ch. 10)

———, and P. D. Renshaw. 1981. "Children without Friends." In *The Development of Children's Friendships,* ed. S. R. Asher and J. M. Gottman, 273–296. NY: Cambridge Univ. Pr. (Ch. 10)

Ashmead, D. H., and M. Perlmutter. 1980. "Infant Memory in Everyday Life." In *New Directions in Child Development,* ed. M. Perlmutter, no. 10, 1–16. San Francisco: Jossey-Bass. (Ch. 6)

Aslin, R. N. 1977. "Development of Binocular Fixation in Human Infants." *Journal of Experimental Child Psychology, 23,* 133–150. (Ch. 4)

———, D. B. Pisoni, and P. W. Jusczyk. 1983. "Auditory Development and Speech Perception in Infancy." In *Handbook of Child Psychology,* 4th ed., ed. P. H. Mussen, vol. 2, 573–687. NY: Wiley. (Chs. 4, 7)

Atchley, R. C. 1976. *The Sociology of Retirement.* NY: Halstead Pr. (Ch. 19)

———. 1980. *The Social Forces in Later Life.* 3rd ed. Belmont, CA: Wadsworth. (Ch. 19)

Babson, S. G., M. L. Pernoll, G. I. Benda, and K. Simpson. 1980. *Diagnosis and Management of the Fetus and Neonate at Risk.* 4th ed. St. Louis: Mosby. (Chs. 3, 4)

Bachman, J. G., P. M. O'Malley, and J. Johnston. 1978. *Youth in Transition,* vol. 6. Ann Arbor: Inst. for Social Research. (Ch. 15)

Bachrach, C. A. 1980. "Childlessness and Social Isolation among the Elderly." *Journal of Marriage and the Family, 42,* 627–637. (Ch. 19)

Bakeman, R., and J. R. Brownlee. 1980. "The Strategic Use of Parallel Play." *Child Development, 51,* 873–878. (Ch. 10)

Balkwell, C. 1981. "Transition to Widowhood." *Family Relations, 30,* 117–127. (Ch. 19)

Baltes, M. M., S. Honn, E. M. Barton, M. J. Orzech, and D. Lago. 1983. "On the Social Ecology of Dependence and Independence in Elderly Nursing Home Residents." *Journal of Gerontology, 38,* 556–564. (Ch. 19)

Baltes, P. B., F. Dittmann-Kohli, and R. A. Dixon. 1984. "New Perspectives on the Development of Intelligence during Adulthood." In *Life-Span Development and Behavior,* ed. P. B. Baltes and O. G. Brim, Jr., vol. 6, 33–76. NY: Academic Pr. (Ch. 16)

———, H. W. Reese, and J. R. Nesselroade. 1977. *Life-Span Developmental Psychology.* Monterey, CA: Brooks/Cole. (Ch. 1)

Bandura, A. 1969. "Social-Learning Theory of Identificatory Processes." In *Handbook of Socialization Theory and Research,* ed. D. A. Goslin, 213–262. Chicago: Rand McNally. (Ch. 2)

———. 1977. *Social Learning Theory.* Englewood Cliffs, NJ: Prentice-Hall. (Chs. 2, 7)

———. 1982. "Self-Efficacy Mechanism in Human Agency," *American Psychologist, 37,* 122–147. (Ch. 2)

———, D. Ross, and S. A. Ross. 1963. "Imitation of Film-Mediated Aggressive Models." *Journal of Abnormal and Social Psychology, 66,* 3–11. (Ch. 10)

———, and D. H. Schunk. 1981. "Cultivating Competence, Self-Efficacy, and Intrinsic Interest through Proximal Self-Motivation." *Journal of Personality and Social Psychology, 41,* 586–598. (Ch. 2)

———, and R. H. Walters. 1963. *Social Learning and Personality Development.* NY: Holt, Rinehart and Winston. (Chs. 2, 9)

Banks, M. S., and P. Salapatek. 1983. "Infant Visual Perception." *Handbook of Child Psychology,* 4th ed., ed. P. H. Mussen, vol. 2, 435–571. NY: Wiley. (Chs. 4, 5)

Barglow, P., B. E. Vaughn, and N. Molitor. 1987. "Effects of Maternal Absence Due to Employment on the Quality of Infant-Mother Attachment in a Low Risk Sample." *Child Development 58,* 945–954. (Ch. 8)

Barnes, G. M. 1984. "Adolescent Alcohol Abuse and Other Problem Behaviors." *Journal of Youth and Adolescence, 13,* 329–348. (Ch. 14)

Barol, B. 1986. "Cocaine Babies." *Newsweek, 108,* Jul. 28, 56–57. (Ch. 3)

Baron, A., and S. R. Menich. 1985. "Age-Related Effects of Temporal Contingencies on Response Speed and Memory." *Journal of Gerontology, 40,* 60–70. (Ch. 18)

Baroody, A. J. 1985. "Mastery of Basic Number Combinations." *Journal for Research in Mathematics Education, 16,* 83–98. (Ch. 12)

Barrett, T. R., and S. K. Watkins. 1986. "Word Familiarity and Cardiovascular Health as Determinants of Age-Related Recall Differences." *Journal of Gerontology, 41,* 222–224. (Ch. 18)

Baruch, G. K. 1972. "Maternal Influences upon College Women's Attitudes toward Women and Work." *Developmental Psychology, 6,* 32–37. (Ch. 9)

———, and R. C. Barnett. 1986. "Role Quality in Multiple Role Involvement and Psychological Well-Being in Midlife Women." Working Paper no. 149. Center for Research on Women. Wellesley, MA: Wellesley Coll. (Ch. 17)

———, ———, and C. Rivers. 1983. *Life Prints.* NY: McGraw-Hill. (Chs. 15, 17)

Bates, E. 1979. *The Emergence of Symbols.* NY: Academic Pr. (Ch. 7)

———, I. Bretherton, M. Beeghly-Smith, and S. McNew. 1982. "Social Bases of Language Development." In *Advances in Child Development and Behavior,* ed. H. W. Reese and L. P. Lipsitt, vol. 16, 7–75. NY: Academic Pr. (Ch. 7)

Baumrind, D. 1967. "Childcare Practices Anteceding 3 Patterns of Preschool Behavior." *Genetic Psychology Monograph, 4,* 1, pt. 2. (Ch. 9)

———. 1986. *Familial Antecedents of Social Competence in Middle Childhood.* Unpublished monograph. Institute of Human Development, University of California, Berkeley. (Ch. 9)

Bayley, N. 1956. "Individual Patterns of Development." *Child Development, 27,* 45–74. (Ch. 5)

———. 1969. *Manual for the Bayley Scales of Infant Development.* NY: Psychological Corp. (Chs. 5, 7).

Becker, E. 1973. *The Denial of Death.* NY: Free Pr. (Ch. 20)

Becker, J. M. 1977. "A Learning Analysis of the Development of Peer-Oriented Behavior in 9-Month-Old Infants." *Developmental Psychology, 13,* 481–491. (Ch. 8)

Becker, W. C. 1964. "Consequences of Different Kinds of Parental Discipline." In *Review of Child Development Research,* ed. M. L. Hoffman and L. W. Hoffman. vol. 1. NY: Russell Sage Found. (Ch. 9)

Beecher, H. W., R. D. Adams, and A. C. Barger. 1968. "A Definition of Irreversible Coma." *Journal of the American Medical Association, 205,* 337–340. (Ch. 20)

Belbin, R. M. 1967. "Middle-Age." In *Middle Age,* ed. R. Owen, 98–106. London: Cox and Wyman. (Ch. 17)

Bell, A. P., and M. S. Weinberg. 1978. *Homosexualities.* NY: Simon & Schuster. (Ch. 15)

Bell, R. 1980. *Changing Bodies, Changing Lives.* NY: Random House. (Ch. 13)

Bell, R. Q., and L. V. Harper. 1977. *Child Effects on Adults.* Hillsdale, NJ: Lawrence Erlbaum Assoc. (Chs. 8, 9)

Bell, S. M. 1970. "The Development of the Concept of Object as Related to Infant-Mother Attachment." *Child Development, 41,* 291–311. (Ch. 8)

Bellugi, U. 1970. "Learning the Language." *Psychology Today, 4,* December, 32–35ff. (Ch. 7)

Belsky, J. 1981. "Early Human Experience." *Developmental Psychology, 17,* 3–23. (Ch. 15)

———, M. Rovine, and D. G. Taylor. 1984. "The Pennsylvania Infant and Family Project." *Child Development, 55,* 718–728. (Ch. 8)

Bem, S. L. 1983. "Gender Schema Theory and Its Implications for Child Development." *Signs, 8,* 598–616. (Ch. 9)

Bengston, V. L., and N. E. Cutler. 1976. "Generations and Intergenerational Relations." In *Handbook of Aging and the Social Sciences,* ed. R. H. Binstock and E. Shanas, 130–159. NY: Van Nostrand Reinhold. (Ch. 19)

——, ——, D. J. Mangen, and V. W. Marshall. 1985. "Generations, Cohorts, and Relations between Age Groups." In *Handbook of Aging and the Social Sciences*, 2nd ed., ed. R. H. Binstock and E. Shanas, 304–338. NY: Van Nostrand Reinhold. (Ch. 17)

——, M. N. Reedy, and C. Gordon. 1985. "Aging and Self-Conceptions." In *Handbook of the Psychology of Aging*, 2nd ed., ed. J. E. Birren and K. W. Schaie, 544–593. NY: Van Nostrand Reinhold. (Chs. 17, 19)

——, and J. Treas. 1980. "The Changing Family Context of Mental Health and Aging." In *Handbook of Mental Health and Aging*, ed. J. E. Birren and R. B. Sloane, 440–428. Englewood Cliffs, NJ: Prentice-Hall. (Ch. 17)

Berg, W. K., and K. M. Berg. 1979. "Psychophysiological Development in Infancy." In *Handbook of Infant Development*, ed. J. D. Osofsky, 283–343. NY: Wiley-Interscience. (Ch. 4)

Berndt, T. J. 1979. "Developmental Changes in Conformity of Peers and Parents." *Developmental Psychology*, 15, 608–616. (Chs. 10, 13)

——. 1986. "Children's Comments about Their Friends." In *Minnesota Symposia on Child Psychology*, ed. M. Perlmutter. vol. 18. Hillsdale, NJ: Lawrence Erlbaum Assoc. (Ch. 10)

——, and S. G. Hoyle. 1985. "Stability and Change in Childhood and Adolescent Friendships." *Developmental Psychology*, 21, 1007–1015. (Ch. 10)

Berscheid, E., E. Walster, and G. Bohrnstedt. 1973. "Body Image." *Psychology Today*, 7, Nov., 119–131. (Ch. 17)

Bertenthal, B. I., and K. W. Fischer. 1978. "Development of Self-Recognition in Infants." *Developmental Psychology*, 14, 44–50. (Ch. 8)

——, and ——. 1983. "The Development of Representation in Search." *Child Development*, 54, 846–857. (Ch. 6)

Bijou, S. W. 1976. *Child Development*. Englewood Cliffs, NJ: Prentice-Hall. (Ch. 2)

——, and D. M. Baer. 1965. *Child Development*. Vol. 2. NY: Appleton-Century-Crofts. (Ch. 7)

Biller, H. D. 1981. "Father Absence, Divorce, and Personality Development." In *The Role of the Father in Child Development*, 2nd ed., ed. M. E. Lamb, 489–552. NY: Wiley-Interscience. (Ch. 9)

Binet, A., and T. Simon. 1916. *The Development of Intelligence in Children*. Baltimore: Williams & Wilkins. (Ch. 12)

Birnbaum, J. A. 1975. "Life Patterns and Self-Esteem in Gifted Family-Oriented and Career-Committed Women." In *Women and Achievement*, ed. M. T. S. Mednick, S. S. Tangi, and L. W. Hoffman, 396–419. NY: Halstead Pr. (Chs. 15, 17)

Birnholz, J. C., and B. R. Benacerraf. 1983. "The Development of Human Fetal Hearing," *Science*, 222, 516–518. (Ch. 3)

Biron, O., J.-G. Mongeau, and D. Bertrand. 1977. "Familial Resemblance of Bodyweight and Weight/Height in 374 Homes with Adopted Children." *Journal of Pediatrics*, 91, 555–558. (Ch. 5)

Birren, J. E., and D. S. Woodruff. 1973. "Human Development over the Life Span through Education." In *Life-Span Developmental Psychology*, ed. P. B. Baltes and K. W. Schaie, 305–337. NY: Academic Pr. (Ch. 15)

Blanchard-Fields, F. 1986. "Reasoning on Social Dilemmas Varying in Emotional Saliency." *Psychology and Aging*, 1, 325–333. (Ch. 16)

Blasi, A. 1980. "Bridging Moral Cognition and Moral Action." *Psychological Bulletin*, 88, 593–637. (Ch. 11)

Blass, E. M., J. R. Ganchrow, and J. E. Steiner. 1984. "Classical Conditioning in Newborn Humans 2–48 Hours of Age." *Infant Behavior and Development*, 7, 223–236. (Chs. 4, 6)

Block, J. 1971. *Lives through Time*. Berkeley, CA: Bancroft Books. (Ch. 15)

Block, J. H., J. Block, and P. F. Gjerde. 1986. "The Personality of Children prior to Divorce." *Child Development*, 57, 827–840. (Ch. 9)

Blomberg, S. 1980. "Influence of Maternal Distress during Pregnancy on Postnatal Development." *Acta Psychiatrica Scandinavica*, 62, 405–417. (Ch. 3)

Bloom, L. M. 1970. *Language Development*. Cambridge: MIT Pr. (Ch. 7)

Blumstein, P., and P. Schwartz. 1983. *American Couples*. NY: William Morrow. (Ch. 15, 17)

Blurton-Jones, N. 1976. "Rough-and-Tumble Play among Nursery School Children." In *Play*, ed. J. Bruner, A. Jolly, and K. Sylva, 352–363. NY: Basic Books. (Ch. 5)

Blyth, D. A., R. G. Simmons, and D. F. Zakin. 1985. "Satisfaction with Body Image for Early Adolescent Females." *Journal of Youth and Adolescence*, 14, 207–226. (Ch. 13)

Blythe, R. 1979. *The View in Winter*. NY: Harcourt Brace Jovanovich. (Ch. 19)

Boccia, M., and J. Campos. 1983. "Maternal Emotional Signaling." Paper presented at the meeting of the Society for Research in Child Devt. Detroit. (Ch. 8)

Bohannon, J. H. III, and A. Warren-Leubecker. 1985. "Theoretical Approaches to Language Acquisition." In *The Development of Language*, ed. J. B. Gleason, 173–226. Columbus, OH: Charles E. Merrill. (Ch. 7)

Bok, S. 1978. *Lying*. NY: Pantheon. (Ch. 20)

Bolton, F. G., Jr. 1980. *The Pregnant Adolescent*. Beverly Hills, CA: Sage. (Ch. 14)

Bondareff, W. 1985. "The Neural Basis of Aging." In *Handbook of the Psychology of Aging*, 2nd ed., ed. J. E. Birren and K. W. Schaie, 95–112. NY: Van Nostrand Reinhold. (Ch. 18)

Borke, H. 1975. "Piaget's Mountains Revisited." *Developmental Psychology*, 14, 240–243. (Ch. 11)

Bornstein, M. H. 1984. "Perceptual Development." In *Developmental Psychology*, ed. M. H. Bornstein and M. E. Lamb, 81–131. Hillsdale, NJ: Lawrence Erlbaum Assoc. (Ch. 4)

——. 1985. "Habituation of Attention as a Measure of Visual Information Processing in Human Infants." In *Development of Audition and Vision during the First Year of Postnatal Life*, ed. G. Gottlieb and N. A. Krasnegor, 253–300. Norwood, NJ: Ablex. (Chs. 4, 6)

——, and A. A. Benasich. 1986. "Infant Habituation." *Child Development*, 57, 87–99, (Ch. 6)

——, J. Gaughran, and P. Homel. 1986, in press. "Temperament." In *Measurement of Emotions in Infants and Children*, vol. 2. ed. C. E. Izard and P. B. Read. NY: Cambridge Univ. Pr. (Chs. 4, 8)

——, and M. G. Ruddy. 1984. "Infant At-

tention and Maternal Stimulation." In *Attention and Performance*, ed. H. Bouma and D. G. Bouwhuis, vol. 10, 433–445. London: Lawrence Erlbaum Assoc. (Ch. 7)

——, M. D. Sigman. 1986. "Continuity in Mental Development from Infancy." *Child Development*, 57, 251–274. (Chs. 6, 12)

Botvin, G. J., and F. B. Murray. 1975. "The Efficacy of Peer Modeling and Social Conflict in the Acquisition of Conservation." *Child Development*, 46, 796–799. (Ch. 11)

Botwinick, J. 1977. "Intellectual Abilities." In *Handbook of the Psychology of Aging*, ed. J. E. Birren and K. W. Schaie, 580–605. NY: Van Nostrand Reinhold. (Ch. 15)

——, and M. Storandt. 1974. *Memory, Related Functions and Age*. Springfield, IL: Charles C. Thomas. (Ch. 18)

Bowlby, J. 1951. *Maternal Care and Mental Health*. Geneva: World Health Org. (Ch. 9)

——. 1969. *Attachment and Loss*. Vol. 1., *Attachment*. NY: Basic Books. (Chs. 2, 8)

——. 1973. *Attachment and Loss*. Vol. 2., *Separation*. NY: Basic Books. (Ch. 8)

——. 1980. Attachment and Loss. Vol. 3, *Loss*. NY: Basic Books. (Chs. 8, 20)

——, and C. M. Parkes. 1970. "Separation and Loss." In *The Child in His Family*, ed. E. J. Anthony and C. Koupernik, vol. 1. NY: Wiley. (Ch. 20)

Bowles, N. L., and L. W. Poon. 1982. "An Analysis of the Effect of Aging on Recognition Memory." *Journal of Gerontology*, 37, 212–219. (Ch. 18)

Branch, C. W., and N. Newcombe. 1986. "Racial Attitude Development among Young Black Children as a Function of Parental Attitude." *Child Development*, 57, 712–721. (Ch. 10)

Bray, D. W., and A. Howard. 1983. "The AT&T Longitudinal Studies of Managers." In *Longitudinal Studies of Adult Psychological Development*, ed. K. W. Schaie. NY: Guilford Pr. (Ch. 17)

Breckenridge, J. N., D. Gallagher, L. W. Thompson, and J. Peterson. 1986. "Characteristic Depressive Symptoms of Bereaved Elders." *Journal of Gerontology*, 41, 163–168. (Ch. 20)

Broadbent, D. E. 1954. "The Role of Auditory Localization in Attention and Memory Span." *Journal of Experimental Psychology*, 47, 191–196. (Ch. 2)

Brody, E. M. 1981. "Women in the Middle and Family Help to Older People." *Gerontologist*, 21, 471–480. (Ch. 17)

Brody, G. H., and D. R. Shaffer. 1982. "Contributions of Parents and Peers to Children's Moral Socialization." *Developmental Review*, 2, 31–75. (Ch. 9)

Brody, J. A., and D. B. Brock. 1985. "Epidemiologic and Statistical Characteristics of the US Elderly Population." In *Handbook of the Biology of Aging*, 2nd ed., ed. C. E. Finch and E. L. Schneider, 3–26. NY: Van Nostrand Reinhold. (Ch. 20)

Brody, J. E. 1984. "Infection Linked to Sex Surpasses Gonorrhea." *New York Times*, Jun. 5, C1ff. (Ch. 3)

Brody, L. R., P. R. Zelazo, and H. Chaika. 1984. "Habituation-Dishabituation to Speech in the Neonate." *Developmental Psychology*, 20, 114–119. (Ch. 4)

Bronfenbrenner, U. 1970. *Two Worlds of Childhood*. NY: Russell Sage Found. (Chs. 8, 10)

———, P. Moen, and J. Garbarino. 1984. "Child, Family, and Community." In *Review of Child Development Research*, ed. R. D. Parke, vol. 7, 283–328. Chicago: Univ. of Chicago Pr. (Ch. 5)

Brook, J. S., M. Whiteman, A. S. Gordon, and P. Cohen. 1986a. "Dynamics of Childhood and Adolescent Personality Traits and Adolescent Drug Use." *Developmental Psychology, 22*, 403–414. (Ch. 14)

———, ———, ———, and ———. 1986b. "Some Models and Mechanisms for Explaining the Impact of Maternal and Adolescent Characteristics on Adolescent Stage of Drug Use." *Developmental Psychology, 22*, 460–467. (Ch. 14)

Brooks-Gunn, J., and F. F. Furstenberg, Jr. 1986. "The Children of Adolescent Mothers." *Developmental Review, 6*, 224–251. (Ch. 14)

———, and M. P. Warren. 1985. "Measuring Physical Status and Timing in Early Adolescence." *Journal of Youth and Adolescence, 14*, 163–190. (Ch. 13)

Brophy, J. E. 1983. "Research on the Self-Fulfilling Prophecy and Teacher Expectations." *Journal of Educational Psychology, 75*, 631–661. (Ch. 10)

Brown, A. L. 1980. "Metacognitive Development and Reading." In *Theoretical Issues in Reading Comprehension*, ed. R. Spiro, B. Bruce, and W. Brewer. Hillsdale, NJ: Lawrence Erlbaum Assoc. (Ch. 11)

———, J. D. Bransford, R. A. Ferrara, and J. C. Campione. 1983. "Learning, Remembering, and Understanding." In *Handbook of Child Psychology*, 4th ed., ed. P. H. Mussen, vol. 3, 77–166. NY: Wiley. (Chs. 11, 12)

———, and S. S. Smilcy. 1978. "The Development of Strategies for Studying Texts." *Child Development, 49*, 1076–1088. (Ch. 11)

Brown, P. 1976. "Psychological Distress and Personal Growth among Women Coping with Marital Dissolution." Ph.D. diss. University of Michigan. (Ch. 15)

Brown, R. 1970. *Psycholinguistics*. NY: Free Pr. (Ch. 7)

———. 1973. *A First Language*. Cambridge: Harvard Univ. Pr. (Ch. 7)

Brozan, N. 1985. "Fetal Health." *New York Times*, Mar. 9, 15. (Ch. 3)

Bruner, J. S.. 1970. "The Growth and Structure of Skill." In *Motor Skills in Infancy,"* ed. K. J. Connelly. NY: Academic Pr. (Ch. 5)

———. 1972. "Nature and Uses of Immaturity." *American Psychologist, 27*, 687–708. (Ch. 9)

———. 1976. "From Communication to Language." *Cognition, 3*, 255–287. (Ch. 7)

———. 1981. "Intention in the Structure of Action and Interaction." In *Advances in Infancy*, ed. L. P. Lipsitt and C. K. Rovee-Collier, vol. 1, 41–56. Norwood, NJ: Ablex. (Ch. 7)

———. 1983. *Child's Talk*. NY: Norton. (Ch. 7)

Brunson, B. I., and K. A. Matthews. 1981. "The Type A Coronary-Prone Behavior Pattern and Reactions to Uncontrollable Stress." *Journal of Personality and Social Psychology, 40*, 906–918. (Chs. 16, 20)

Bryant, B. K. 1982. "Sibling Relations in Middle Childhood." In *Sibling Relationships*, ed. M. E. Lamb and B. Sutton-Smith, 87–122. Hillsdale, NJ: Lawrence Erlbaum Assoc. (Ch. 9)

Bullock, M. 1985. "Animism in Childhood Thinking." *Developmental Psychology, 21*, 217–225. (Ch. 11)

———, and R. Gelman. 1979. "Preschool Children's Assumptions about Cause and Effect." *Child Development, 50*, 89–96. (Ch. 11)

Bullough, V. L. 1981. "Age at Menarche." *Science, 213*, 365–366. (Ch. 13)

Burgess, R. L., and R. D. Conger. 1978. "Family Interaction in Abusive, Neglectful, and Normal Families." *Child Development, 49*, 1163–1173. (Ch. 9)

Burrus-Bammel, L. L., and G. Bammel. 1985. "Leisure and Recreation." In *Handbook of the Psychology of Aging*, 2nd ed., ed. J. E. Birren and K. W. Schaie, 848–863. NY: Van Nostrand Reinhold. (Ch. 19)

Bushnell, E. W. 1985. "The Decline of Visually Guided Reaching During Infancy." *Infant Behavior and Development, 8*, 139–156. (Ch. 5)

Buskirk, E. R. 1985. "Health Maintenance and Longevity." In *Handbook of the Biology of Aging*, 2nd ed., ed. C. E. Finch, and E. L. Schneider, 894–931. NY: Van Nostrand Reinhold. (Chs. 17, 19)

Buss, A. H., and R. Plomin. 1984. *Temperament*. Hillsdale, NJ: Lawrence Erlbaum Assoc. (Ch. 4)

Busse, E. W. 1976. "Hypochondriasis in the Elderly." *Journal of the American Geriatric Society, 24*, 145–149. (Ch. 19)

Butler, J. A., B. Starfield, and S. Stenmark. 1984. "Child Health Policy." In *Child Development Research and Social Policy*, ed. H. W. Stevenson and A. W. Siegel, vol. 1, 110–188. Chicago: Univ. of Chicago Pr. (Ch. 5)

Butler, R. N. 1975. *Why Survive?* NY: Harper & Row. (Chs. 18, 20)

———, and M. I. Lewis. 1982. *Aging and Mental Health*, 3rd ed. St. Louis: Mosby. (Ch. 18)

Byrne, D. 1973. "The Development of Role-Taking in Adolescence." Ph.D. diss. Harvard: Graduate School of Education. (Ch. 13)

Cain, B. S. 1982. "Plight of the Gray Divorcee." *New York Times Magazine*, Dec. 19, 89–93. (Ch. 19)

Campbell, W. J. 1982. "US Rebuffed, Infant Formula Code Adopted." *Boston Globe*, May 21, p. 3. (Ch. 5)

Campione, J. C., and A. L. Brown. 1979. "Toward a Theory of Intelligence." In *Human Intelligence*, ed. R. J. Sternberg and D. K. Detterman, Norwood, NJ: Ablex. (Ch. 12)

———, ———, and R. A. Ferrara. 1982. "Mental Retardation and Intelligence." In *Handbook of Human Intelligence*, ed. R. J. Sternberg. NY: Cambridge Univ. Pr. (Ch. 12)

———, ———, ———, and N. H. Bryant. 1984. "The Zone of Proximal Development." In *New Directions for Child Development*, ed. B. Rogoff and J. V. Wertsch, vol. 23, 77–92. San Francisco: Jossey-Bass. (Chs. 2, 12)

———, ———, R. S. Jones, and E. Steinberg. 1985. "Breakdowns in the Flexible Use of Information." *Intelligence, 9*, 297–315. (Ch. 12)

Campos, J. J. 1976. "Heart Rates." In *Developmental Psychobiology*, ed. L. P. Lipsitt. Hillsdale, NJ: Lawrence Erlbaum Assoc. (Ch. 5)

———, K. C. Barrett, M. E. Lamb, H. H.

cioemotional Development." In *Handbook of Child Psychology*, 4th ed., ed. P. H. Mussen, vol. 2, 783–915. NY: Wiley. (Ch. 4)

Canning, H., and J. Mayer. 1966. "Obesity—Its Possible Effect on College Acceptance." *New England Journal of Medicine, 275*, 1172–1174. (Ch. 14)

Carey, S. 1982. "Semantic Development." In *Language Acquisition*, ed. E. Wanner and L. R. Gleitman, 347–389. Cambridge: Cambridge Univ. Pr. (Ch. 7)

Carnegie Council on Policy Studies in Higher Education. 1980. *Giving Youth a Better Chance*. San Francisco: Jossey-Bass. (Ch. 14)

Carpenter, T. P., and J. M. Moser. 1982. "The Development of Addition and Subtraction Problem-Solving Skills." In *Addition and Subtraction*, ed. T. P. Carpenter, J. M. Moser, and T. Romberg, 9–24. Hillsdale, NJ: Lawrence Erlbaum Assoc. (Ch. 12)

Carraher, T. N., D. W. Carraher, and A. D. Schliemann. 1983. "Mathematics in the Streets and in Schools." Unpublished manuscript. (Cited in Siegler, 1986.) (Ch. 11)

Carter, D. B., and C. J. Patterson. 1982. "Sex Roles as Social Conventions." *Developmental Psychology, 18*, 812–824. (Ch. 9)

Carver, C. S., E. DeGregorio, and R. Gillis. 1981. "Challenge and Type A Behavior among Intercollegiate Football Players." *Journal of Sport Psychology, 3*, 140–148. (Ch. 20)

Case, R., D. M. Kurland, and J. Goldberg. 1982. "Operational Efficiency and the Growth of Short-Term Memory Span." *Journal of Experimental Child Psychology, 33*, 386–404. (Ch. 11)

Cattell, P. 1940. *The Measurements of Intelligence of Infants and Young Children*. NY: Psychological Corp. (Ch. 5)

Cattell, R. B. 1971. *Abilities*. Boston: Houghton Mifflin. (Chs. 12, 16)

Cavanaugh, J. C., J. G. Grady, and M. Perlmutter. 1983. "Forgetting and Use of Memory Aids in 20- and 70-Year-Olds' Everyday Life." *International Journal of Aging and Human Development, 17*, 113–122. (Ch. 18)

Ceci, S. J., and J. K. Liker. 1986. "A Day at the Races." *Journal of Experimental Psychology: General, 115*, 255–266. (Ch. 16)

———, and ———. 1987. "Academic and Nonacademic Intelligence." In *Practical Intelligence*, ed. R. J. Sternberg and R. K. Wagner, 119–142. NY: Cambridge Univ. Pr. (Ch. 16)

Cerella, J., L. W. Poon, and D. M. Williams. 1974. "Age and the Complexity Hypothesis." In *Aging in the 1980s*, ed L. W. Poon. Washington, DC: Amer. Psychological Assn. (Ch. 18)

Cernoch, J. M., and R. H. Porter. 1985. "Recognition of Maternal Axiliary Odors by Infants." *Child Development, 56*, 1593–1598. (Ch. 4)

Chabon I. 1966. *Awake and Aware*. NY: Delacorte Press. (Ch. 3)

Chall, J. S. 1979. "The Great Debate." In *Theory and Practice of Early Reading*, ed. L. B. Resnick and P. A. Weaver. Hillsdale, NJ: Lawrence Erlbaum Assoc. (Ch. 12)

Chan, G. M., N. Ronald, P. Slater, J. Hollis, and M. R. Thomas. 1982. "Decreased Bone Mineral Status in Lactating Adolescent Mothers." *Journal of Pediatrics, 101*, 767–770. (Ch. 14)

Chance, P. 1981. "The Remedial Thinker." *Psychology Today, 15,* Oct., 63–73. (Ch. 12)

Charness, R. 1985. "Aging and Problem-Solving Performance." In *Aging and Human Performance,* ed. N. Charness. NY: Wiley. (Ch. 16)

Cherlin, A. 1983. "A Sense of History." In *Aging in Society,* ed. M. W. Riley, B. B. Hess, and K. Bond, 5–24. Hillsdale, NJ: Lawrence Erlbaum Assoc. (Ch. 17)

Cheyne, J. A., and K. H. Rubin. 1983. "Playful Precursors of Problem Solving in Preschoolers." *Developmental Psychology, 19,* 577–584. (Ch. 10)

Chi, M. T. H. 1978. "Knowledge Structure and Memory Development." In *Children's Thinking,* ed. R. S. Siegler, 73–96. Hillsdale, NJ: Lawrence Erlbaum Assoc. (Ch. 11)

———, **and D. Klahr.** 1975. "Span and Rate of Apprehension in Children and Adults." *Journal of Experimental Child Psychology, 19,* 434–439. (Ch. 11)

———, **and D. R. Koeske.** 1983. "Network Representation of a Child's Dinosaur Knowledge." *Developmental Psychology, 19,* 29–39. (Chs. 2, 11)

Chilman, C. 1983. *Adolescent Sexuality in a Changing American Society.* 2nd ed. NY: Wiley. (Ch. 15)

Chiriboga, D., and L. Cutler. 1980. "Stress and Adaptation." In *Aging in the 1980s,* ed. L. W. Poon, 347–362. Washington, DC: Amer. Psychological Assn. (Ch. 19)

———, **and L. Gigy.** 1975. "Perspectives on Life Course," In *Four Stages of Life,* ed. M. F. Lowenthal, M. Thurnher, and D. Chiriboga, 62–83. San Francisco: Jossey-Bass. (Ch. 20)

———, **and M. Thurnher.** 1976. "Concept of Self." In *Four Stages of Life,* ed. M. Lowenthal, M. Thurnher, and D. Chiriboga. San Francisco: Jossey-Bass. (Ch. 19)

Chomsky, N. 1975. *Reflections on Language.* NY: Pantheon. (Ch. 7)

———. 1979. *Language and Responsibility.* NY: Pantheon. (Ch. 7)

Chugani, H. T., and M. E. Phelps. 1986. "Maturational Changes in Cerebral Function in Infants Determined by [18]FDG Positron Emission Tomography." *Science, 231,* 840–843. (Ch. 5)

Claridge, G., and G. Mangan. 1983. "Genetics of Human Nervous System Functioning." In *Behavior Genetics,* ed. J. L. Fuller and E. C. Simmel, 33–88. Hillsdale, NJ: Lawrence Erlbaum Assoc. (Ch. 3)

Clark, E. V. 1983. "Meanings and Concepts." In *Handbook on Child Psychology,* 4th ed., ed. P. H. Mussen, vol. 3, 787–840. NY: Wiley. (Ch. 7)

———, **S. A. Gelman, and N. M. Lane.** 1985. "Compound Nouns and Category Structure in Young Children." *Child Development, 56,* 84–94. (Ch. 7)

Clark, J. E., A. K. Lanphear, and C. C. Riddick. 1987. "The Effect of Videogame Playing on the Response Selection Processing of Elderly Adults." *Journal of Gerontology, 42,* 82–85. (Ch. 18)

Clark, M. 1984. "A Slow Death of the Mind." *Newsweek,* Dec. 3, 56–62. (Ch. 18)

———, **M. Gosnell, and M. Hager.** 1986. "Women and AIDS." *Newsweek,* July 14, 60–61. (Ch. 15)

Clark, R. W. 1975. *The Life of Bertrand Russell.* NY: Knopf. (Ch. 16)

Clarke, A. M., and A. D. B. Clarke. 1977. *Early Experience.* NY: Free Pr. (Ch. 8)

Clarke-Stewart, K. A. 1978. "Recasting the Lone Stranger." In *The Development of Social Understanding,* ed. J. Glick and K. A. Clarke-Stewart, 109–176. NY: Gardner Pr. (Ch. 8)

———. 1982. *Daycare.* Cambridge: Harvard Univ. Pr. (Ch. 8)

———. 1984. "Day Care." In *Minnesota Symposia on Child Psychology,* ed. M. Perlmutter, vol. 17, 61–100. Hillsdale, NJ: Lawrence Erlbaum Assoc. (Ch. 8)

———, **and G. G. Fein.** 1983. "Early Childhood Programs." In *Handbook of Child Psychology,* 4th ed. ed. P. H. Mussen, vol. 2, 917–1000. NY: Wiley. (Ch. 8)

Clausen, J. A. 1981. "Men's Occupational Careers in the Middle Years." In *Present and Past in Middle Life,* ed. D. H. Eichorn, J. A. Clausen, N. Haan, M. P. Honzik, and P. Mussen, 321–351. NY: Academic Pr. (Chs. 15, 17)

Clay, H. M. 1956. "A Study of Performance in Relation to Age at Two Printing Works." *Journal of Gerontology, 11,* 417–424. (Ch. 16)

Clement, J., L. J. Schweinhart, W. S. Barnett, A. S. Epstein, and D. P. Weikart. 1984. *Changed Lives.* Ypsilanti, MI: High/Scope Press. (Ch. 1)

Clines, F. X. 1986. "Dutch Are Quietly Taking the Lead in Euthanasia." *New York Times,* Oct. 31, A4. (Ch. 20)

Clingempeel, W. G. 1981. "Quasi-kin Relationships and Marital Quality in Stepfather Families." *Journal of Personality and Social Psychology, 41,* 890–901. (Ch. 9)

———, **E. Brand, and R. Ievoli.** 1984. "Stepparent-Stepchild Relationships in Stepmother and Stepfather Families." *Family Relations, 33,* 465–473. (Ch. 9)

———, **and S. Segal.** 1986. "Stepparent-Stepchild Relationships and the Psychological Adjustment of Children in Stepmother and Stepfather Families." *Child Development, 57,* 474–484. (Ch. 9)

Cohen, C., J. Teresi, and D. Holmes. 1985. "Social Networks, Stress, and Physical Health." *Journal of Gerontology, 40,* 478–486. (Ch. 19)

Coie, J. D., and J. B. Kupersmidt. 1983. "A Behavioral Analysis of Emerging Social Status in Boys' Groups." *Child Development, 54,* 1400–1416. (Ch. 10)

Colby, A., L. Kohlberg, J. Gibbs, and M. Lieberman. 1983. "A Longitudinal Study of Moral Judgment." *Monographs of the Society for Research in Child Development, 48,* no. 200. (Chs. 11, 13)

Cole, C. L., and A. L. Cole, and D. G. Dean. 1980. "Emotional Maturity and Marital Adjustment." *Journal of Marriage and the Family, 42,* 533–539. (Ch. 15)

Cole, M., and S. Scribner. 1978. "Introduction." In *Mind in Society,* ed. L. S. Vygotsky, 1–14. Cambridge: Harvard Univ. Pr. (Ch. 2)

Collins, G. 1983. "Single-Father Survey Finds Adjustment a Problem." *New York Times,* Nov. 21, B17. (Ch. 9)

———. 1984. "Course for 'Latchkey' Children and Parents." *New York Times,* Mar. 19, C10. (Ch. 9)

———. 1986a. "As More Men Retire Early, More Women Work Longer." *New York Times,* Apr. 3, C1ff. (Ch. 19)

———. 1986b. "Retirement Planners Focusing on Women." *New York Times,"* Apr. 14, C1ff. (Ch. 19)

Collins, W. A., T. J. Berndt, and V. I. Hess. 1974. "Observational Learning of Motives and Consequences for Television Aggression." *Child Development, 45,* 799–802. (Ch. 10)

Comfort, A. 1980. "Sexuality in Later Life." In *Handbook of Mental Health and Aging,* ed. J. E. Birren and R. B. Sloane, 885–892. Englewood Cliffs, NJ: Prentice-Hall. (Ch. 19)

Condry, J. C., and S. Condry. 1976. "Sex Differences." *Child Development, 47,* 812–819. (Ch. 9)

———, **and D. F. Ross.** 1985. "Sex and Aggression." *Child Development, 56,* 225–233. (Ch. 9)

Connell, J. P. 1985. "A New Multidimensional Measure of Children's Perception of Control." *Child Development, 56,* 1018–1041. (Ch. 12)

Connolly, J. A., and A.-B. Doyle. 1984. "Social Fantasy Play and Social Competence." *Developmental Psychology, 20,* 797–806. (Ch. 10)

Conroy, M., R. D. Hess, H. Azuma, and K. Kashiwagi. 1980. "Maternal Strategies for Regulating Children's Behavior." *Journal of Cross-Cultural Psychology, 11,* 153–172. (Ch. 10)

Cooper, H. M. 1979. "Pygmalion Grows Up." *Review of Educational Research, 49,* 389–410. (Ch. 10)

Corno, L., and M. M. Rohrkemper. 1985. "The Intrinsic Motivation to Learn in Classrooms." In *Research on Motivation and Education,* ed. C. Ames and R. Ames, vol. 2, 53–90. Orlando, FL: Academic Pr. (Ch. 12)

Corsale, K., and P. A. Ornstein. 1980. "Developmental Changes in Children's Use of Semantic Information in Recall." *Journal of Experimental Child Psychology, 30,* 231–245. (Ch. 11)

Costa, P. T., Jr., et al. 1986. "Cross-Sectional Studies of Personality in a National Sample." *Psychology and Aging, 1,* 144–149. (Ch. 17)

Covington, M. V. 1984. "The Self-Worth Theory of Achievement Motivation." *The Elementary School Journal, 85,* 5–20. (Ch. 12)

Coyle, J. T., D. L. Price, and M. R. DeLong. 1983. "Alzheimer's Disease." *Science, 219,* 1184–1190. (Ch. 18)

Craik, F. I. M. 1977. "Age Differences in Human Memory." In *Handbook of the Psychology of Aging,* ed. J. E. Birren and K. W. Schaie, 384–420. NY: Van Nostrand Reinhold. (Ch. 18)

———, **and M. Byrd.** 1982. "Aging and Cognitive Deficits." In *Aging and Cognitive Processes,* ed. F. I. M. Craik and S. Trehub, 191–211. NY: Plenum. (Ch. 18)

———, **and J. C. Rabinowitz.** 1984. "Age Differences in the Acquisition and Use of Verbal Information." In *Attention and Performance,* ed. L. Long and A. Baddeley, vol 10. Hillsdale, NJ: Lawrence Erlbaum Assoc. (Ch. 18)

Crain, W. C. 1985. *Theories of Development.* 2nd ed. Englewood Cliffs, NJ: Prentice-Hall. (Ch. 2)

Cravioto, J., and E. Delicardie. 1970. "Mental Performance in School Age Children." *American Journal of Diseases of Children, 120,* 404. (Ch. 5)

Crockett, L., M. Losoff, and A. C. Peter-sen. 1984. "Perceptions of the Peer Group and Friendship in Early Adolescence." *Journal of Early Adolescence, 4,* 155–181. (Ch. 13)

Crook, C. K. 1979. "The Organization and Control of Infant Sucking." In *Advances in Child Development and Behavior,* ed. H. W. Reese and L. P. Lipsitt, vol. 14, 209–253. NY: Academic Pr. (Ch. 4)

———, **and L. P. Lipsitt.** 1976. "Neonatal Nutritive Sucking." *Child Development, 47,* 518–522. (Ch. 4)

Crouter, A. C. 1984. "Participative Work as an Influence on Human Development." *Journal of Applied Developmental Psychology, 5,* 71–90. (Ch. 15)

Csikszentmihalyi, M., and R. Larson. 1984. *Being Adolescent.* NY: Basic. (Ch. 13)

Cuber, J. F., and P. B. Harroff. 1965. *Sex and the Significant Americans.* Baltimore: Penguin. (Ch. 17)

Cumming, E., and W. E. Henry. 1961. *Growing Old.* NY: Basic. (Ch. 19)

Cummings, E. M., R. J. Iannotti, and C. Zahn-Waxler. 1985. "Influence of Conflict between Adults on the Emotions and Aggression of Young Children." *Developmental Psychology, 21,* 495–507. (Ch. 8)

———, **C. Zahn-Waxler, and M. Radke-Yarrow.** 1981. "Young Children's Responses to Expressions of Anger and Affection by Others in the Family." *Child Development, 52,* 1274–1282. (Ch. 8)

Curtiss, S. R. 1977. *Genie.* NY: Academic Pr. (Ch. 7)

Cutler, N. E. 1983. "Age and Political Behavior." In *Aging,* 2nd ed., ed. D. S. Woodruff and J. E. Birren, 409–442. Monterey, CA: Brooks/Cole. (Ch. 19)

Cytrynbaum, S., et al. 1980. "Midlife Development." In *Aging in the 1980s,* ed. L. W. Poon, 463–474. Washington DC: Amer. Psychological Assn. (Ch. 17)

Daehler, M. W., and D. Bukatko. 1985. *Cognitive Development.* NY: Knopf. (Chs. 6, 11)

———, **and C. Greco.** 1985. "Memory in Very Young Children." In *Cognitive Learning and Memory in Children,* ed. M. Pressley and C. J. Brainerd. NY: Springer-Verlag. (Ch. 6)

Damon, W. 1977. *The Social World of the Child.* San Francisco: Jossey-Bass. (Ch. 11)

Daniel, D. E., R. G. Templin, and R. W. Shearon. 1977. "The Value Orientation of Older Adults toward Education." *Educational Gerontology, 2,* 33–42. (Ch. 16)

Daniels, D., J. Dunn, F. F. Furstenberg, Jr., and R. Plomin. 1985. "Environmental Differences within the Family and Adjustment Differences within Pairs of Adolescent Siblings." *Child Development, 56,* 764–774. (Ch. 13)

Daniels, P., and K. Weingarten. 1982. *Sooner or Later.* NY: Norton. (Ch. 15)

Darabi, K., E. Graham, P. Namerow, S. Philliber, and P. Varga. 1984. "The Effect of Maternal Age on the Well-Being of Children." *Journal of Marriage and the Family,* 933–936. (Ch. 14)

Darwin, C. [1872] 1955. *The Expression of the Emotions in Man and Animal.* NY: Philosophical Library. (Ch. 2)

Daurio, S. P. 1979. "Educational Enrichment vs. ⌀ œrf¿ Æ̆ Æ In *Educating the Gifted,* ed.

W. C. George, S. J. Cohn, and J. C. Stanley, 13–63. Baltimore: Johns Hopkins Univ. Pr. (Ch. 12)

Davis, J. M., and C. K. Rovee-Collier. 1983. "Alleviated Forgetting of a Learned Contingency in 8-Week-Old Infants." *Developmental Psychology, 19,* 353–365. (Ch. 6)

———, **N. L. Segal, and G. K. Spring.** 1983. "Biological and Genetic Aspects of Depression in the Elderly." In *Depression and Aging,* ed. L. R. Breslau and M. R. Haug, 94–113. NY: Springer. (Ch. 19)

Day, M. C. 1975. "Developmental Trends in Visual Scanning." In *Advances in Child Development and Behavior,* ed. H. W. Reese, vol. 10, 154–193. NY: Academic Pr. (Ch. 11)

DeCasper, A. J., and W. P. Fifer. 1980. "Of Human Bonding." *Science, 208,* 1174–1176. (Chs. 4, 7)

———, **and M. J. Spence.** 1986. "Prenatal Maternal Speech Influences Newborns' Perception of Speech Sounds." *Infant Behavior and Development, 9,* 133–150. (Chs. 3, 4)

Deci, E. L., J. Neziek, and L. Sheinman. 1981. "Characteristics of the Rewarder and Intrinsic Motivation of the Rewardee." *Journal of Personality and Social Psychology, 40,* 1–10. (Ch. 10)

Deigh, R. 1986. "Curse It, Count It, Cure It." *Insight,* Sept. 29, 10–14. (Ch. 16)

Delamont, S. 1980. *Sex Roles and the Schools.* London: Methuen. (Ch. 10)

DeLoache, J. S. 1980. "Naturalistic Studies of Memory for Object Location in Very Young Children." In *New Directions in Child Development,* ed. M. Perlmutter, no. 10, 17–32. San Francisco: Jossey-Bass. (Ch. 6)

———, **and A. L. Brown.** 1984. "Where Do I Go Next?" *Developmental Psychology, 20,* 37–44. (Ch. 6)

———, **D. J. Cassidy, and A. L. Brown.** 1985. "Precursors of Mnemonic Strategies in Very Young Children's Memory." *Child Development, 56,* 125–137. (Chs. 6, 11)

———, **S. Sugarman, and A. L. Brown.** 1985. "The Development of Error Correction Strategies in Young Children's Manipulative Play." *Child Development, 56,* 928–939. (Ch. 6)

Denney, N. W. 1982. "Aging and Cognitive Change." In *Handbook of Developmental Psychology,* ed. B. B. Wolman, 807–827. Englewood Cliffs, NJ: Prentice-Hall. (Ch. 18)

———, **and A. M. Palmer.** 1981. "Adult Age Differences on Traditional and Practical Problem-Solving Measures." *Journal of Gerontology, 36,* 323–328. (Ch. 18)

Dennis, W. 1960. "Causes of Retardation among Institutional Children." *Journal of Genetic Psychology, 96,* 47–59. (Ch. 5)

———, **and P. Najarian.** 1957. "Infant Development under Environmental Handicap." *Psychological Monographs, 71,* 436. (Ch. 5)

———, **and Y. Sayegh.** 1965. "The Effect of Supplementary Experiences upon the Behavioral Development of Infants in Institutions." *Child Development, 36,* 81–90. (Ch. 5)

de Villiers, J. G., and P. A. de Villiers. 1978. *Language Acquisition.* Cambridge: Harvard Univ. Pr. (Ch. 7)

———, **and** ———. 1979. *Early Language.* Cambridge: Harvard Univ. Pr. (Ch. 7)

deVries, H. A. 1983. "Physiology of Exercise and Aging." In *Aging,* 2nd ed., ed. D. S. Woo-

druff and J. E. Birren, 285–304. Monterey, CA: Brooks/Cole. (Chs. 17, 20)

———, **and G. M. Adams.** 1972. "Electromyographic Comparison of Single Doses of Exercise and Meprobamate as to Effects on Muscle Relaxation." *American Journal of Physical Medicine, 52,* 120–141. (Ch. 16)

deVries, M., and A. J. Sameroff. 1984. "Culture and Temperament." *American Journal of Orthopsychiatry, 54,* 83–96. (Ch. 4)

DeVries, R. 1969. "Constancy of Generic Identity in the Years 3 to 6." *Monographs of the Society for Research in Child Development, 34,* no. 127. (Ch. 11)

Diamond, A. 1985. "Development of the Ability to Use Recall to Guide Action, as Indicated by Infants' Performance on AB̄." *Child Development, 56,* 868–883. (Ch. 6)

Dick-Read, G. 1944. *Childbirth without Fear.* NY: Harper & Bros. (Ch. 3)

Diederen, I. 1983. "Genetics of Schizophrenia." In *Behavior Genetics,* ed. J. L. Fuller and E. C. Simmel, 189–216. Hillsdale, NJ: Lawrence Erlbaum Assoc. (Ch. 3)

Diegmueller, K. 1986. "Divorce." *Insight, 2,* Oct. 13, 8–13. (Ch. 17)

Diggory, J. and D. Rothman. 1961. "Values Destroyed by Death." *Journal of Abnormal and Social Psychology, 63,* 205–210. (Ch. 20)

DiPietro, J. A. 1981. "Rough and Tumble Play." *Developmental Psychology, 17,* 50–58. (Ch. 5)

Dixon, R. A., and P. B. Baltes. 1986. "Toward Life-Span Research on the Functions of Pragmatics of Intelligence." In *Practical Intelligence,* ed. R. J. Sternberg and R. K. Wagner, 203–235. NY: Cambridge Univ. Pr. (Ch. 16)

———, **and D. F. Hultsch.** 1983. "Metamemory and Memory for Text Relationships in Adulthood." *Journal of Gerontology, 38,* 689–694. (Ch. 18)

———, ———, **E. W. Simon, and A. von Eye.** 1984. "Verbal Ability and Text Structure Effects on Adult Age Differences in Text Recall." *Journal of Verbal Learning and Verbal Behavior, 23,* 569–578. (Ch. 18)

Dodge, K. A. 1983. "Behavioral Antecedents of Peer Social Status." *Child Development, 54,* 1386–1399. (Ch. 10)

———, **G. S. Pettit, C. L. McClasky, and M. M. Brown.** 1986. "Social Competence in Children." *Monographs of the Society for Research in Child Development, 51,* no. 213. (Ch. 10)

———, **and D. R. Somberg.** 1987. "Hostile Attributional Biases among Aggressive Boys Are Exacerbated under Conditions of Threat to the Self." *Child Development, 58,* 213–224. (Ch. 10)

Donaldson, M. 1979. *Children's Minds.* NY: Norton. (Ch. 11)

Donosky, L. 1982. "Keeping Your Work Clothes on." *Newsweek,* Nov. 1, 58. (Ch. 19)

Dontas, C., O. Maratos, M. Fafoutis, and A. Karangelis. 1985. "Early Social Development in Institutionally Reared Greek Infants." *Monographs of the Society for Child Development, 50,* no. 209, 136–146. (Ch. 8)

Dorr, A. 1979. "Children's Reports of What They Learn from Daily Viewing." Paper presented at the biennial meeting of the Society for Research in Child Devt. San Francisco, Mar. (Ch. 10)

Douvan, E., and J. Adelson. 1966. *The Adolescent Experience.* NY: Wiley. (Chs. 13, 14)

Drabman, R. S., C. D. Cordua, D. Hammer, G. J. Jarvie, and W. Horton. 1979. "Developmental Trends in Eating Rates of Normal and Overweight Children." *Child Development, 50,* 211–216. (Ch. 5)

———, and **M. H. Thomas.** 1976. "Does Watching Violence on Television Cause Apathy?" *Pediatrics, 57,* 329–331. (Ch. 10)

Dubowitz, L. M. S., V. Dubowitz, and C. Goldberg. 1970. "Clinical Assessment of Gestational Age in the Newborn Infant." *Journal of Pediatrics, 77,* 1. (Ch. 3)

Dullea, G. 1986. "Madonna's New Beat Is a Hit, But Song's Message Rankles." *New York Times,* Sept. 18, B1ff. (Ch. 14)

Dunn, J. 1977. *Distress and Comfort.* Cambridge: Harvard Univ. Pr. (Ch. 8)

———. 1983. "Sibling Relationships in Early Childhood." *Child Development, 54,* 787–811. (Ch. 8)

———, and **C. Kendrick.** 1982a. *Siblings.* Cambridge: Harvard Univ. Pr. (Ch. 8)

———, and ———. 1982b. "The Speech of 2- and 3-Year-Olds to Infant Siblings." *Journal of Child Language, 9,* 579–595. (Ch. 8)

———, and **P. Munn.** 1985. "Becoming a Family Member." *Child Development, 56,* 480–492. (Ch. 8)

Dunphy, D. C. 1963. "The Social Structure of the Urban Adolescent Peer Group." *Sociometry, 26,* 230–246. (Ch. 13)

Dunst, C. J., and B. Lingerfelt. 1985. "Maternal Ratings of Temperament and Operant Learning in 2- to 3-Month-Old Infants." *Child Development, 56,* 555–563. (Ch. 6)

Durant, W., and A. Durant. 1963. *The Story of Civilization.* vol. 8, NY: Simon & Schuster. (Ch. 3)

Dweck, C. S., W. Davidson, S. Nelson, and B. Enna. 1978. "Sex Differences in Learned Helplessness." *Developmental Psychology, 14,* 268–276. (Ch. 10)

———, and **E. S. Elliott.** 1983. "Achievement Motivation." In *Handbook of Child Psychology,* 4th ed., ed. P. H. Mussen, vol. 4, 643–691. NY: Wiley. (Chs. 6, 10, 12)

Easterbrooks, M. A., and W. A. Goldberg. 1984. "Toddler Development in the Family. *Child Development, 55,* 740–752. (Ch. 8)

———, and ———. 1985. "Effects of Early Maternal Employment on Mothers, Toddlers, and Fathers." *Developmental Psychology, 21,* 774–783. (Ch. 8)

Easterlin, R. 1980. *Birth and Fortune.* NY: Basic. (Ch. 14)

Eccles, J. S. 1985a. "Sex Differences in Achievement Patterns." In *Nebraska Symposium on Motivation,* ed. T. Sonderegger. Lincoln: Univ. of NE Pr. (Ch. 10)

———. 1985b. "Why Doesn't Jane Run?" In *The Gifted and the Talented,* ed. F. D. Horowitz and M. O'Brien, 251–295. Washington, DC: Amer. Psychological Assn. (Ch. 12)

———, and **L. W. Hoffman.** 1984. "Sex Roles, Socialization, and Occupational Behavior." In *Child Development Research and Social Policy,* ed. H. W. Stevenson and A. E. Siegel, 367–420. Chicago: Univ. of Chicago Pr. (Chs. 9, 10)

Edelman, M. S., and D. R. Omark. 1973.

"Dominance Hierarchies in Young Children." *Social Science Information, 12,* 103–110. (Ch. 10)

Edgerton, R. B. 1979. *Mental Retardation.* Cambridge: Harvard Univ. Pr. (Ch. 12)

Egeland, B., and E. A. Farber. 1984. "Infant-Mother Attachment." *Child Development, 55,* 753–771. (Ch. 8)

Ehrman, L., and J. Probber. 1983. "Fundamentals of Genetics and Evolutionary Theories." In *Behavior Genetics,* ed. J. L. Fuller and E. C. Simmel, 1–32. Hillsdale, NJ: Lawrence Erlbaum Assoc. (Ch. 3)

Eibl-Eibesfeldt, I. 1970. *Ethology.* NY: Holt, Rinehart and Winston. (Ch. 2)

Eichorn, D. H. 1963. *Biological Correlates of Behavior.* Chicago: Nat'l. Soc. for the Study of Education. (Ch. 13)

———. 1979. "Physical Development." In *Handbook of Infant Development,* ed. J. D. Osofsky, 253–282. NY: Wiley-Interscience. (Ch. 5)

———, **J. A. Clausen, N. Haan, M. P. Honzik, and P. H. Mussen, eds.** 1981. *Present and Past in Middle Life.* NY: Academic Pr. (Ch. 1)

———, **J. V. Hunt, and M. P. Honzik.** 1981. "Experience, Personality, and IQ." In *Present and Past in Middle Life,* ed. D. H. Eichorn, J. A. Clausen, N. Haan, M. P. Honzik, and P. H. Mussen, 89–116. NY: Academic Pr. (Ch. 16)

Eifermann, R.R. 1971. "Social Play in Childhood." In *Child's Play,* ed. R. E. Herron and B. Sutton-Smith. NY: Wiley. (Ch. 10)

Eisdorfer, C., J. Nowlin, and F. Wilkie. 1970. "Improvement of Learning in the Aged by Modification of the Central Nervous System." *Science, 170,* 1327–1329. (Ch. 18)

Ekerdt, D. J., R. Bosse, and S. Levkoff. 1985. "An Empirical Test for Phases of Retirement." *Journal of Gerontology, 40,* 95–101. (Ch. 19)

———, ———, and **J. S. LoCastro.** 1983. "Claims that Retirement Improves Health." *Journal of Gerontology, 38,* 231–236. (Ch. 19)

Elder, G. H., Jr. 1974. *Children of the Great Depression.* Chicago: Univ. of Chicago Pr. (Chs. 1, 9)

———. 1980. "Adolescence in Historical Perspective." *Handbook of Adolescent Psychology,* ed. J. Adelson, 3–46. NY: Wiley-Interscience. (Ch. 14)

———. 1984. "Families, Kin, and the Life Course." In *Review of Child Development Research,* ed. R. D. Parke, vol. 7, 80–136. Chicago: Univ. of Chicago Pr. (Ch. 9)

Elkind, D. 1985. "Egocentrism Redux." *Developmental Review, 5,* 218–216. (Ch. 13)

———, and **R. Bowen.** 1979. "Imaginary Audience Behavior in Children and Adolescents." *Developmental Psychology, 15,* 38–44. (Ch. 13)

Elster, A. B., E. R. McAnarney, and M. E. Lamb. 1983. "Parental Behavior of Adolescent Mothers." *Pediatrics, 71,* 494–503. (Ch. 14)

Emde, R. N., J. Swedberg, and B. Suzuki. 1975. "Human Wakefulness and Biological Rhythms after Birth." *Archives of General Psychiatry, 32,* 780–783. (Ch. 4)

Entwisle, D. R., and S. G. Doering. 1981. *The First Birth.* Baltimore: Johns Hopkins Univ. Pr. (Ch. 15)

Erber, J. T. 1981. "Remote Memory and Age." *Experimental Aging Research, 1,* 189–199. (Ch. 18)

———. 1982. "Memory and Age." In *Review of Human Development,* ed. T. M. Field, A. Huston, H. C. Quay, L. Troll, and G. E. Finley, 569–585. NY: Wiley. (Ch. 18)

Erikson, E. H. 1963. *Childhood and Society.* 2nd ed. NY: Norton. (Chs. 5, 8, 9)

———. 1978. "Reflections on Dr. Borg's Life Cycle." In *Adulthood,* ed. E. H. Erikson, 1–32. NY: Norton. (Ch. 20)

———. 1980. *Identity and the Life Cycle.* NY: Norton. (Ch. 13)

———. 1982. *The Life Cycle Completed.* NY: Norton. (Chs. 2, 15, 17, 19)

———. **Interview by E. Hall.** 1987. "The Father of the Identity Crisis." In *Growing and Changing,* E. Hall, 128–140. NY: Random House. (Chs. 2, 15, 17, 19)

Eron, L. D., L. R. Huesmann, M. M. Lefkowitz, and L. O. Walder. 1972. "Does Television Cause Aggression?" *American Psychologist, 27,* 253–263. (Ch. 10)

Fabricius, W. V., and H. M. Wellman. 1983. "Children's Understanding of Retrieval Cue Utilization." *Developmental Psychology, 19,* 14–21. (Ch. 11)

Fagan, J. F., III. 1979. "The Origins of Face Perception." In *Psychological Development from Infancy,* ed. M. H. Bornstein and W. Kessen, 83–113. Hillsdale, NJ: Lawrence Erlbaum Assoc. (Ch. 6)

Fagot, B. I. 1978. "The Influence of Sex of Child on Parental Reactions to Toddler Children." *Child Development, 49,* 459–465. (Ch. 8)

———. 1982. "Adults as Socializing Agents." In *Review of Human Development,* ed. T. M. Field, A. Huston, H. C. Quay, L. Troll, and G. E. Finley, 304–315. NY: Wiley-Interscience. (Ch. 9)

———. 1985. "Beyond the Reinforcement Principle." *Developmental Psychology, 21,* 1097–1104. (Ch. 1)

———, **R. Hagan, M. D. Leinbach, and S. Kronsberg.** 1985. "Differential Reactions to Assertive and Communicative Acts of Toddler Boys and Girls." *Child Development, 56,* 1499–1505. (Ch. 8)

Falbo, T. and L. A. Peplau. 1980. "Power Strategies in Intimate Relationships." *Journal of Personality and Social Psychology, 38,* 618–628. (Ch. 15)

Fallon, A., and P. Rozin. 1985. "Sex Differences and Perception of Desirable Body Shapes." *Journal of Abnormal Psychology, 94,* 102–105. (Ch. 15)

Fantz, R. L. 1961. "The Origin of Form Perception." *Scientific American, 204,* May, 66–72. (Ch. 6)

———, **J. F. Fagan, III, and S. B. Miranda.** 1975. "Early Visual Selectivity." In *Infant Perception,* ed. L. B. Cohen and P. Salapatek, vol. 1, 249–345. NY: Academic Pr. (Ch. 6)

Farnham-Diggory, S. 1978. *Learning Disabilities.* Cambridge: Harvard Univ. Pr. (Ch. 3)

Farrington, D. P. 1979. "Longitudinal Research on Crime and Deliquency." In *Crime and Justice,* ed. N. Morris and M. Tonry, vol. 1, 289–348. Chicago: Univ. of Chicago Pr. (Ch. 14)

Faust, M. S.   1977. "Somatic Development of Adolescent Girls." *Monographs of the Society for Research in Child Development, 42,* no. 169. (Ch. 13)

Fausto-Sterling, A.   1985. *Myths of Gender.* NY: Basic Books. (Ch. 9)

Feather, N. T.   1980. "Values in Adolescence." In *Handbook of Adolescent Psychology,* ed. J. Adelson, 247–294. NY: Wiley-Interscience. (Ch. 14)

Featherman, D. L.   1981. "The Life-Span Perspective in Social Science Research." Unpublished paper, prepared for the Social Science Research Council. University of Wisconsin. (Ch. 19)

Federal Trade Commission.   1978. *FTC Staff Report on Television Advertising to Children.* Washington, DC: US Gov't. Printing Office. (Ch. 10)

Fein, G. G.   1975. "A Transformational Analysis of Pretending." *Developmental Psychology, 11,* 291–296. (Ch. 6)

Feinstein, S., and M. Ardon.   1973. "Trends in Dating Patterns and Adolescent Development." *Journal of Youth and Adolescence, 2,* 157–166. (Ch. 13)

Feldman, D. H.   1986. *Nature's Gambit.* NY: Basic Books. (Ch. 12)

Feldman, S. S., and B. Aschenbrenner.   1983. "Impact of Parenthood on Various Aspects of Masculinity and Femininity." *Developmental Psychology, 19,* 278–289. (Ch. 15)

——, Z. D. Biringen, and S. C. Nash.   1981. "Fluctuations of Sex-Related Self-Attributions as a Function of Stage and of Family Life Cycle." *Developmental Psychology, 17,* 24–35. (Chs. 15, 17)

Fenson, L., J. Kagan, R. B. Kearsley, and P. R. Zelazo.   1976. "The Developmental Progression of Manipulative Play in the First 2 Years." *Child Development, 47,* 232–236. (Ch. 6)

Ferguson, C. A.   1977. "Baby Talk as a Simplified Register." In *Talking to Children,* ed. C. E. Snow and C. A. Ferguson, 219–236. NY: Cambridge Univ. Pr. (Ch. 7)

Fernald, A., and T. Simon.   1984. "Expanded Intonational Contours in Mothers' Speech to Newborns." *Developmental Psychology, 20,* 104–113. (Chs. 4, 7)

Ferrara, R. A., A. L. Brown, and J. C. Campione.   1986. "Children's Learning and Transfer of Inductive Reasoning Rules." *Child Development, 57,* 1087–1099. (Ch. 12)

Feshbach, N. D.   1969. "Student Teacher Preferences for Elementary School Pupils Varying in Personality Characteristics." *Journal of Educational Psychology, 60,* 126–132. (Ch. 10)

Feshbach, S.   1972. "Reality and Fantasy in Filmed Violence." In *Television and Social Behavior,* ed. J. P. Murray, E. A. Rubenstein, and G. A. Comstock, vol. 2, 318–345. Washington, DC: US Gov't. Printing Office. (Ch. 10)

——.   1980. "Child Abuse and the Dynamics of Human Aggression." In *Child Abuse,* ed. G. Gerbner, C. J. Ross, and E. Zigler, 48–60. NY: Guilford Pr. (Ch. 9)

Feuerstein, R., Y. Rand, M. B. Hoffman, and R. Miller.   1980. *Instrumental Enrichment.* Baltimore: Univ. Park Pr. (Ch. 12)

Field, D.   1981. "Can Preschool Children Really Learn to Conserve?" *Child Development, 48,* 326–334. (Ch. 11).

Field, T. M.   1978. "Interaction Behaviors of Primary versus Secondary Caretaker Fathers." *Developmental Psychology, 14,* 183–184. (Ch. 8)

——.   1981. "Infant Arousal, Attention, and Affect during Early Interaction." In *Advances in Infancy,* ed. L. P. Lipsitt, vol. 1, 57–100. Norwood, NJ: Ablex. (Ch. 4)

——.   1983. "Early Interactions and Interaction Coaching of High-Risk Infants and Parents." In *Minnesota Symposia on Child Psychology,* ed. M. Perlmutter, vol. 16, 1–33. Hillsdale, NJ: Lawrence Erlbaum Assoc. (Chs. 1, 4)

——, and J. L. Roopnarine.   1982. "Infant-Peer Interactions." In *Review of Human Development,* ed. T. M. Field, A. Huston, H. C. Quay, L. Troll, and G. E. Finley, 164–179. NY: Wiley-Interscience. (Ch. 8)

——, et al.   1985. "Pregnancy Problems, Postpartum Depression, and Early Mother-Infant Interaction." *Developmental Psychology, 21,* 1152–1156. (Ch. 4)

Fischer, K. W., and M. W. Watson.   1981. "Explaining the Oedipus Conflict." In *New Directions for Child Development,* ed. K. W. Fischer, no. 12, 79–92. San Francisco: Jossey-Bass. (Ch. 2)

Fiske, M.   1980. "Tasks and Crises of the Second Half of Life." In *Handbook of Mental Health and Aging,* ed. J. E. Birren and R. B. Sloane, 337–373. Englewood Cliffs, NJ: Prentice-Hall. (Chs. 17, 19)

Flanagan, J. C., and D. Russ-Eft.   1976. *An Empirical Study Aid in Formulating Educational Goals.* Palo Alto: American Inst. for Research. (Ch. 16)

Flavell, J. H.   1982. "Structures, Stages, and Sequences in Cognitive Development." In *Minnesota Symposia on Child Psychology,* ed. W. A. Collins, vol. 15, 1–28. Hillsdale, NJ: Lawrence Erlbaum Assoc. (Ch. 2)

——.   1985. *Cognitive Development.* 2nd ed. Englewood Cliffs, NJ: Prentice-Hall. (Chs. 1, 2, 6, 11, 13)

——.   1986. "Development of Children's Knowledge about the Appearance-Reality Distinction." *American Psychologist, 41,* 418–425. (Ch. 6)

——, D. R. Beach, and J. M. Chinsky.   1966. "Spontaneous Verbal Rehearsal on a Memory Task as a Function of Age." *Child Development, 37,* 283–299. (Ch. 11)

——, P. T. Botkin, C. L. Fry, Jr., J. W. Wright, and P. E. Jarvis.   [1968] 1975. *The Development of Role-Taking and Communication Skills in Children.* Huntington, NY: Robert Krieger. (Ch. 11)

——, A. G. Friedrichs, and J. D. Hoyt.   1970. "Developmental Changes in Memorization Processes." *Cognitive Psychology, 1,* 324–340. (Ch. 11)

——, F. L. Green, and E. R. Flavell.   1986. "Development of Knowledge about the Appearance-Reality Distinction." *Monographs of the Society for Research in Child Development, 51,* no. 212. (Ch. 11)

——, S. G. Shipstead, and K. Croft.   1978. "Young Children's Knowledge about Visual Perception." *Child Development, 49,* 1208–1211. (Ch. 6)

Flynn, J. R.   1984. "The Mean IQ of Americans." *Psychological Bulletin, 95,* 29–51. (Chs. 1, 16)

Forssberg, H.   1985. "Ontogeny of Human Locomotor Control." *Experimental Brain Research, 57,* 480–493. (Ch. 5)

Fox, G. L.   1978. "The Family's Role in Adolescent Sexual Behavior." Paper presented to the Family Impact Seminar. Washington, DC, Oct. (Ch. 9)

France-Kaatrude, A.-C., and W. P. Smith.   1985. "Social Comparison, Task Motivation, and the Development of Self-Evaluation Standards in Children." *Developmental Psychology, 21,* 1080–1089. (Ch. 10)

Frank, S., C. B. Hole, S. Jacobson, R. Justkowski, and M. Huyck.   1986. "Psychological Predictors of Parents' Sense of Confidence and Control and Self-Versus Child-Focused Gratifications." *Developmental Psychology, 22,* 348–355. (Ch. 9)

Freedman, D. G.   1979. "Ethnic Differences in Babies," *Human Nature, 2,* Jan. 36–43. (Ch. 1)

Freedman, J. L.   1984. "Effect of Television Violence on Aggressiveness." *Psychological Bulletin, 96,* 227–246. (Ch. 10)

French, D. C., and G. A. Waas.   1985. "Behavior Problems of Peer-Neglected and Peer-Rejected Elementary-Age Children." *Child Development, 56,* 246–252. (Ch. 10)

Freud, S.   [1905] 1955. "Three Essays on the Theory of Sexuality." In *The Standard Edition of the Complete Psychological Works of Sigmund Freud,* vol. 7, 125–145. London: Hogarth (Ch. 2)

——.   [1915] 1957. "Thoughts for the Times on War and Death." In *The Standard Edition of the Complete Psychological Works of Sigmund Freud,* vol. 14, 275–300. London: Hogarth. (Ch. 20)

Friedman, M., and R. H. Rosenman.   1974. *Type A Behavior and Your Heart.* NY: Knopf. (Ch. 20)

Fries, J. F.   1984. "The Compression of Morbidity." *Gerontologist, 24,* 354–359. (Ch. 20)

——, and L. M. Crapo.   1981. *Vitality and Aging.* San Francisco: Freeman. (Ch. 20)

Frieze, I. H., J. E. Parsons, P. B. Johnson, D. N. Ruble, and G. I. Zellman.   1978. *Women and Sex Roles.* NY: Norton. (Ch. 15)

Frisch, H. L.   1977. "Sex Stereotypes in Adult-Infant Play." *Child Development, 48,* 1671–1675. (Ch. 8)

Frodi, A. M., M. E. Lamb, L. A. Leavitt, and W. L. Donovan.   1978. "Fathers' and Mothers' Responses to Infant Smiles and Cries." *Infant Behavior and Development, 1,* 187–198. (Ch. 4)

Frueh, T., and P. E. McGhee.   1975. "Traditional Sex Role Development and Amount of Time Spent Watching Television." *Developmental Psychology, 11,* 109. (Ch. 10)

Fry, C. L.   1985. "Culture, Behavior, and Aging in the Comparative Perspective." In *Handbook of the Psychology of Aging,* 2nd ed., ed. J. E. Birren and K. W. Schaie, 216–244. NY: Van Nostrand Reinhold. (Ch. 19)

Fuchs, V. R.   1983. *How We Live.* Cambridge: Harvard Univ. Pr. (Ch. 14)

Furman, W., and D. Buhrmester.   1985. "Children's Perceptions of the Qualities of Sibling Relationships." *Child Development, 56,* 448–461. (Chs. 1, 9)

Furstenberg, F. F., Jr.   1976. *Unplanned Parenthood.* NY: Free Pr. (Ch. 14)

————. 1980. "Burdens and Benefits." *Journal of Social Issues, 36*, 64–87. (Ch. 13)

————. 1982. "Conjugal Succession." In *Life-Span Development and Behavior*, ed. P. B. Baltes and O. G. Brim, Jr., vol. 4, 107–146. NY: Academic Pr. (Ch. 15)

————, and J. Brooks-Gunn. In press. *Adolescent Mothers in Later Life*. NY: Cambridge Univ. Pr. (Ch. 14)

Gaensbauer, T. J. 1982. "Regulation of Emotional Expression in Infants from 2 Contrasting Caretaker Environments." *Journal of the American Academy of Child Psychiatry, 21*. (Ch. 9)

Galambos, N. L., and J. Garbarino. 1983. "Identifying the Missing Links in the Study of Latchkey Children." *Children Today*, Jul.–Aug., 2–4ff. (Ch. 9)

Gallagher, J. J., and R. D. Courtright. 1986. "The Educational Definition of Giftedness and Its Policy Implications." In *Conceptions of Giftedness*, ed. R. J. Sternberg and J. E. Davidson, 112–127. NY: Cambridge Univ. Pr. (Ch. 12)

Ganchrow, J. R., J. E. Steiner, and M. Daher. 1983. "Neonatal Facial Expressions in Response to Different Qualities and Intensities of Gustatory Stimuli." *Infant Behavior and Development, 6*, 473–484. (Ch. 4)

Garbarino, J., and A. Crouter. 1978. "Defining the Community Context for Parent-Child Relations." *Child Development, 49*, 606–616. (Ch. 9)

Gardner, H. 1983. *Frames of Mind*. NY: Basic. (Ch. 12)

Garfinkel, R. 1982. "By the Sweat of Your Brow." In *Review of Human Development*, ed. T. M. Field, A. Huston, H. C. Quay, L. Troll, and G. E. Finley, 500–507. NY: Wiley-Interscience. (Ch. 15)

Garner, D. M., P. E. Garfinkel, D. Schwartz, and M. Thompson. 1980. "Cultural Expectations of Thinness in Women." *Psychological Reports, 47*, 483–491. (Ch. 14)

Garvey, C. 1977. *Play*. Cambridge, MA: Harvard Univ. Pr. (Ch. 10)

Gauvain, M., and B. Rogoff. 1986. "Influence of the Goal on Children's Exploration and Memory of Large-Scale Space." *Developmental Psychology, 22*, 72–76. (Ch. 11)

Gelles, R. J., and C. P. Cornell. 1985. *Intimate Violence in Families*. Beverly Hills, CA: Sage. (Ch. 9)

Gelman, D. 1985a. "Playing Both Mother and Father." *Newsweek, 106*, Jul. 15, 42–50. (Chs. 9, 14)

————. 1985b. "Who's Taking Care of Our Parents?" *Newsweek, 106*, May 6, 61–68. (Ch. 19)

————. 1986. "Treating Teens in Trouble." *Newsweek*, Jan. 20, 52–54. (Ch. 14)

Gelman, R. 1972. "Logical Capacity of Very Young Children." *Child Development, 43*, 75–90. (Ch. 11)

————. 1982a. "Accessing One-to-One Correspondence." *British Journal of Psychology, 73*, 209–220. (Ch. 11)

————. 1982b. "Basic Numerical Abilities." In *Advances in the Psychology of Human Intelligence*, ed. R. J. Sternberg, vol. 1. Hillsdale, NJ: Lawrence Erlbaum Assoc. (Ch. 6)

————, and R. Baillargeon. 1983. "A Review of Some Piagetian Concepts." In *Handbook of Child Psychology*, 4th ed., ed. P. H.

Mussen, vol. 3, 167–230. NY: Wiley. (Chs. 2, 11)

————, and C. R. Gallistel. 1978. *The Child's Understanding of Number*. Cambridge, MA: Harvard Univ. Pr. (Ch. 11)

Gelman, S. A., and E. M. Markman. 1985. "Implicit Contrast in Adjectives vs. Nouns." *Journal of Child Language, 12*, 125–143. (Ch. 7)

Gentile, A. M., et al. 1975. "The Structure of Motor Tasks." *Mouvement, 7*, 11–28. (Ch. 5)

George, C., and M. Main. 1979. "Social Interactions of Young Abused Children." *Child Development, 50*, 306–318. (Ch. 9)

Gesell, A. L. 1925. *The Mental Growth of the Preschool Child*. NY: Macmillan. (Ch. 5)

————. 1956. *Youth*. NY: Harper & Row. (Ch. 2)

————, and F. L. Ilg. 1946. *The Child from Five to Ten*. NY: Harper & Row. (Ch. 2)

————, ————, and L. B. Ames. 1940. *First Five Years of Life*. NY: Harper. (Ch. 2)

Gibson, E. J. 1969. *Principles of Perceptual Learning and Development*. NY: Appleton-Century-Crofts. (Ch. 6)

————. 1974. "Trends in Perceptual Development." In *Minnesota Symposia on Child Psychology*, ed. A. D. Pick, vol. 8, 24–54. Minneapolis: Univ. of MN Pr. (Ch. 11)

————, and E. S. Spelke. 1983. "The Development of Perception." In *Handbook of Child Psychology*, 4th ed., ed. P. H. Mussen, vol. 3, 1–76. NY: Wiley, 1983. (Ch. 1)

————, and R. D. Walk. 1960. "The Visual Cliff." *Scientific American, 202*, April, 67–71. (Ch. 5)

Gil, D. G. 1970. *Violence Against Children*. Cambridge: Harvard Univ. Pr. (Ch. 9)

Gilbertsen, V. A., and O. H. Wangensteen. 1961. "Should the Doctor Tell the Patient that the Disease Is Cancer?" In *The Physician and the Total Care of the Cancer Patient*. NY: American Cancer Society. (Ch. 20)

Gilligan, C. 1982. *In a Different Voice*. Cambridge: Harvard Univ. Pr. (Chs. 11, 13, 15)

Gillund, G., and M. Perlmutter. In press. "The Relation between Semantic and Episodic Memory across Adulthood." In *Language, Comprehension, Memory, and Aging*, ed. L. L. Light and D. M. Burke. NY: Springer. (Ch. 18)

Gjerde, P. F. 1986. "The Interpersonal Structure of Family Interaction Settings." *Developmental Psychology, 22*, 297–304. (Ch. 17)

Glaser, B. G., and A. L. Strauss. 1965. *Awareness of Dying*. Chicago: Aldine. (Ch. 20)

————, and ————. 1968. *Time for Dying*. Chicago: Aldine. (Ch. 20)

Glass, D. C. 1977. *Behavior Patterns, Stress, and Coronary Disease*. Hillsdale, NJ: Lawrence Erlbaum Assoc. (Ch. 16, 20)

Gleason, J. B. 1967. "Do Children Imitate?" *Proceedings of the International Conference on Oral Education of the Deaf, 2*, 1441–1448. (Ch. 7)

————, and S. Weintraub. 1978. "Input Language and the Acquisition of Communicative Competence." In *Children's Language*, ed. K. Nelson, vol. 1, 171–222. NY: Gardner Pr. (Ch. 7)

Gleitman, L. R., and E. Wanner. 1982. "Language Acquisition." In *Language Acquisition*, ed. E. Wanner and L. R. Gleitman, 3–48. Cambridge: Cambridge Univ. Pr. (Ch. 7)

Glenn, N. D. 1975. "Psychological Well-

Being in the Postparental Stage." *Journal of Marriage and the Family, 37*, 105–110. (Ch. 17)

————. 1980. "Values, Attitudes, and Beliefs." In *Constancy and Change in Human Development*, ed. O. G. Brim, Jr., and J. Kagan, 594–640. Cambridge: Harvard Univ. Pr. (Ch. 19)

————, and S. McLanahan. 1981. "The Effects of Offspring on the Psychological Well-Being of Older Adults." *Journal of Marriage and the Family, 43*, 409–421. (Ch. 19)

Glick, I. O., R. S. Weiss, and C. M. Parkes. 1974. *The First Year of Bereavement*. NY: Wiley-Interscience. (Ch. 20)

Glick, P. C. 1979. "Future American Families." *The Washington COFO MEMO, 2*, Summer/Fall, 2–5. (Ch. 15)

————. 1980. "Remarriage." *Journal of Family Issues, 1*, 455–478. (Ch. 15)

————. 1984. "Marriage, Divorce, and Living Arrangements." *Journal of Family Issues, 5*, 7–26. (Ch. 9)

Glueck, S., and E. Glueck. 1968. *Delinquents and Nondelinquents in Perspective*. Cambridge: Harvard Univ. Pr. (Ch. 14)

Golan, N. 1981. *Passing through Transitions*. NY: Free Press. (Ch. 15)

Gold, D., and D. Andres. 1978. "Developmental Comparisons between 10-year-old Children with Employed and Nonemployed Mothers." *Child Development, 49*, 74–84. (Ch. 9)

Gold, M. 1970. *Delinquent Behavior in an American City*. Belmont, CA: Brooks/Cole. (Ch. 14)

————. 1981. "Pregnant Pauses." *Science 81, 3*, January/February, 34–39. (Ch. 3)

Goldberg, S. 1977. "Social Competence in Infancy." *Merrill-Palmer Quarterly, 23*, 163–177. (Ch. 8)

Goldberg, W. A., and M. A. Easterbrooks. 1984. "Role of Marital Quality in Toddler Development." *Developmental Psychology, 20*, 504–514. (Ch. 9)

Goldblatt, P. B., M. E. Moore, and A. D. Stunkard. 1965. "Social Factors in Obesity." *Journal of the American Medical Association, 192*, 1039–1044. (Ch. 14)

Goldfield, E. C., and G. F. Michel. 1986. "The Ontogeny of Infant Bimanual Reaching during the First Year." *Infant Behavior and Development, 9*, 81–90. (Ch. 5)

Goldgaber, D., M. I. Lerman, O. W. McBride, U. Saffiotti, and D. C. Gajdusek. 1987. "Characterization and Chromosomal Localization of a cDNA Encoding Brain Amyloid of Alzheimer's Disease." *Science, 235*, 877–880. (Ch. 18)

Goldman-Rakic, P. S., A. Isseroff, M. L. Schwartz, and N. M. Bugbee. 1983. "The Neurobiology of Cognitive Development." In *Handbook of Child Psychology*, ed. P. M. Mussen, 4th ed. vol. 2, 281–344. NY: Wiley. (Chs. 5, 7)

Goleman, D. 1980. "1,528 Little Geniuses and How They Grew." *Psychology Today, 13*, Feb., 28–53. (Ch. 12)

Goodall, M. M. 1980. "Left-Handedness as an Educational Handicap." In *Problems of Handicap*, ed. R. S. Laura, 55–66. Melbourne: Macmillan. (Ch. 5)

Gottesman, I. I. 1974. "Developmental Genetics and Ontogenetic Psychology." In *Minnesota Symposia on Child Psychology*, ed. A. D.

Pick, vol. 8, 55–80. MN: Univ. of Minnesota Pr. (Ch. 3)

Gottfried, A. E., and A. W. Gottfried, eds. In press. *Maternal Employment and Children's Development.* NY: Plenum Press. (Ch. 8)

Gottfried, A. W., and K. Bathurst. 1983. "Hand Preference across Time Is Related to Intelligence in Young Girls, Not Boys." *Science,* 221, 1074–1076. (Ch. 5)

Gottlieb, G. 1983. "The Psychobiological Approach to Developmental Issues." In *Handbook of Child Psychology,* 4th ed., ed. P. H. Mussen, vol. 2, 1–26. NY: Wiley. (Ch. 4)

Gould, R. E. 1980. "Sexual Problems." In *Midlife,* ed. W. H. Norman and T. J. Scaramella, 110–127. NY: Brunner/Mazel. (Ch. 17)

Gould, R. L. 1975. "Adult Life Stages." *Psychology Today,* 8, Feb., 74–78. (Chs. 15, 17)

———. 1978. *Transformations.* NY: Simon & Schuster. (Chs. 15, 17)

Gould, S. J. 1977. *Ontology and Phylogeny.* Cambridge: Belknap Pr. of Harvard Univ. Pr. (Ch. 5)

Graham, S. 1984. "Teacher Feelings and Student Thoughts." *The Elementary School Journal,* 85, 91–104. (Ch. 12)

Greenberg, B. S. 1982. "Television and Role Socialization." In *Television and Behavior,* ed. D. Pearl, L. Bouthilet, and J. Lazer. Washington, DC: Nat'l. Inst. of Mental Health. (Ch. 10)

Greenberger, E., and L. D. Steinberg. 1986. *When Teenagers Work.* NY: Basic. (Ch. 14)

Greenblatt, M., and C. Chien. 1983. "Depression in the Elderly." In *Depression and Aging,* ed. L. D. Breslau and M. R. Haug, 193–207. NY: Springer. (Ch. 19)

Greenhouse, S. 1986. "Surge in Prematurely Jobless." *New York Times,* Oct. 13, D1ff. (Chs. 2, 19)

Greer, L. D. 1980. "Children's Comprehension of Formal Features with Masculine and Feminine Connotations." Master's thesis. University of Kansas. (Cited in Huston, 1983.) (Ch. 10)

Gribbin, K., K. W. Schaie, and I. A. Parham. 1980. "Complexity of Lifestyle and Maintenance of Intellectual Abilities." *Journal of Social Issues,* 36, 47–61. (Ch. 16)

Griffiths, R. 1954. *The Abilities of Babies.* NY: McGraw-Hill. (Ch. 5)

Grossman, F. K., L. S. Eichler, and S. A. Winickoff. 1980. *Pregnancy, Birth, and Parenthood.* San Francisco: Jossey-Bass. (Chs. 3, 15)

Grossmann, K., K. E. Grossmann, G. Spangler, G. Suess, and L. Unzner. 1985. "Maternal Sensitivity and Newborns' Orientation Responses as Related to Quality of Attachment in Northern Germany." *Monographs of the Society for Research in Child Development,* 50, No. 209, 232–256. (Ch. 8)

Grotevant, H. D., and W. L. Thorbecke. 1982. "Sex Differences in Styles of Occupational Identity Formation in Late Adolescence." *Developmental Psychology,* 18, 396–405. (Ch. 13)

Group for the Advancement of Psychiatry. Committee on Adolescence. 1986. *Crises of Adolescence.* NY: Brunner/Mazel. (Ch. 14)

Gruendel, J. M. 1977. "Referential Overextension in Language Development." *Child Development,* 48, 1567–1576. (Ch. 7)

Guidubaldi, J., J. D. Perry, and H. K. Clemin-

shaw. 1983. "The Legacy of Parental Divorce." *School Psychology Review,* Summer. (Ch. 9)

Guilford, J. P. 1982. "Cognitive Psychology's Ambiguities." *Psychological Review,* 89, 48–59. (Ch. 12)

Gunderson, V., and G. P. Sackett. 1982. "Parental Effects on Reproductive Outcome and Developmental Risk." In *Advances in Developmental Psychology,* ed. M. E. Lamb and A. L. Brown, vol. 2, 85–124. Hillsdale, NJ: Lawrence Erlbaum Assoc. (Ch. 3)

Gurland, B. J., L. Dean, P. S. Cross, and R. Golden. 1980. "The Epidemiology of Depression and Dementia in the Elderly." In *Psychopathology in the Aged,* ed. J. O. Cole and J. E. Barrett, 37–62. NY: Raven Pr. (Ch. 19)

Gutmann, D. L. 1975. "Parenthood." In *Life-Span Developmental Psychology,* ed. N. Datan and L. H. Ginsberg, 167–184. NY: Academic Pr. (Ch. 15)

———. 1980. "The Post-Parental Years." In *Midlife,* ed. W. H. Norman and T. J. Scaramella, 38–52. NY: Brunner/Mazel. (Chs. 17, 19)

Gzesh, S. M., and C. F. Surber. 1985. "Visual Perspective-Taking Skills in Children." *Child Development,* 56, 1204–1213. (Ch. 11)

Haan, N., R. Millsap, and E. Hartka. 1986. "As Time Goes by." *Psychology and Aging,* 1, 220–232. (Ch. 17)

Hagestad, G. O. 1984. "The Continuous Bond." In *Minnesota Symposia on Child Psychology,* ed. M. Perlmutter, vol. 17, 129–158. Hillsdale, NJ: Lawrence Erlbaum Assoc. (Ch. 17)

———, and B. L. Neugarten. 1985. "Age and the Life Course." In *Handbook of Aging and the Social Sciences,* 2nd ed., ed. R. H. Binstock and E. Shanas, 35–61. NY: Van Nostrand Reinhold. (Chs. 15, 17, 19)

———, and M. Smyer. 1983. "Divorce at Middle-Age." In *Dissolving Personal Relationships,* ed. S. Weissman, R. Cohen, and B. Cohler. NY: Academic Pr. (Ch. 17)

Hahn, S. R., and K. E. Paige. 1980. "American Birth Practices." In *The Psychobiology of Sex Differences,* ed. J. E. Parsons, 145–175. NY: McGraw-Hill. (Ch. 3)

Hainline, L. 1978. "Developmental Changes in the Scanning of Faces and Nonface Patterns by Infants." *Journal of Experimental Psychology,* 25, 90–115. (Ch. 6)

———, and E. Feig. 1978. "The Correlates of Father Absence in College-Aged Women." *Child Development,* 49, 37–42. (Ch. 9)

Haith, M. M. 1980. *Rules that Babies Look by.* Hillsdale, NJ: Lawrence Erlbaum Assoc. (Ch. 4)

———, T. Bergman, and M. J. Moore. 1977. "Eye Contact and Face Scanning in Early Infancy." *Science,* 198, 853–855. (Chs. 4, 6)

Hale, G. A., S. S. Taweel, R. Z. Green, and J. Flaugher. 1978. "Effects of Instructions on Children's Attention to Stimulus Components." *Developmental Psychology,* 14, 499–506. (Ch. 11)

Hall, J. W., J. Murphy, M. S. Humphreys, and K. P. Wilson. 1979. "Children's Cued Recall." *Journal of Experimental Child Psychology,* 27, 501–511. (Ch. 11)

Hanley, R. 1986a. "Football Players Sus-

pended for Attacking Girl on Team." *New York Times,* Oct. 15, B2. (Ch. 13)

———. 1986b. "Girls Playing Football, but not Many." *New York Times,* Sept. 19, B2. (Ch. 13)

Harding, C., and R. Golinkoff. 1979. "The Origins of Intentional Vocalizations in Prelinguistic Infants." *Child Development,* 50, 33–40. (Ch. 7)

Harlow, H. F., and M. K. Harlow. 1966. "Learning to Love." *American Scientist,* 54, 244–272. (Ch. 8)

———, and ———. 1969. "Effects of Various Mother-Infant Relationships on Rhesus-Monkey Behaviors." In *Determinants of Infant Behavior,* ed. B. M. Foss, vol. 4, 15–36. London: Metheun. (Ch. 8)

Harman, S. M., and G. B. Talbert. 1985. "Reproductive Aging." In *Handbook of the Biology of Aging,* 2nd ed., ed. C. E. Finch and E. L. Schneider, 457–510. NY: Van Nostrand Reinhold. (Chs. 17, 19)

Harris, L., and Associates. 1981. *Aging in the Eighties.* Washington, DC: Nat'l. Council on Aging. (Ch. 19)

Harris, P. L. 1983. "Infant Cognition." In *Handbook of Child Psychology.* 4th ed., ed. P. H. Mussen, vol. 2, 689–782. NY: Wiley. (Chs. 2, 6)

Harter, S. 1983. "Developmental Perspectives on the Self-System." In *Handbook of Child Psychology,* 4th ed., ed. P. H. Mussen, vol. 4, 275–385. NY: Wiley. (Chs. 8, 10, 12, 13)

Hartley, A. A. 1981. "Adult Age Differences in Deductive Reasoning Processes." *Journal of Gerontology,* 36, 700–706. (Ch. 18)

———, and J. W. Anderson. 1986. "Instruction, Induction, Generation, and Evaluation of Strategies for Solving Search Problems." *Journal of Gerontology,* 41, 650–658. (Ch. 18)

Hartup, W. W. 1974. "Aggression in Childhood." *American Psychologist,* 29, 336–341. (Ch. 10)

———. 1983. "Peer Relations." In *Handbook of Child Psychology,* 4th ed., ed. P. H. Mussen, vol. 4, 102–196. NY: Wiley. (Chs. 8, 10, 13)

Hatano, G., and K. Osawa. 1983. "Digit Memory of Grand Experts in Abacus-Derived Mental Calculation." *Cognition,* 15, 95–110. (Ch. 11)

Hatfield, E., D. Greenberger, J. Traupmann, and P. Lambert. 1982. "Equity and Sexual Satisfaction in Recently Married Couples." *Journal of Sex Research,* 18, 18–32. (Ch. 15)

Hay, D. F. 1980. "Multiple Functions of Proximity Seeking in Infancy." *Child Development,* 51, 636–645. (Ch. 8)

———, A. Nash, and J. Pedersen. 1983. "Interaction between 6-Month-Old Peers." *Child Development,* 54, 557–562. (Ch. 8)

———, and H. S. Ross. 1982. "The Social Nature of Early Conflict." *Child Development,* 53, 105–113. (Ch. 8)

Hebb, D. O. 1978. "On Watching Myself Grow Old." *Psychology Today,* 12, Nov., 15–23. (Ch. 18)

Heller, D. 1985. "The Children's God," *Psychology Today,* 19, Dec., 22–27. (Ch. 1)

Henggeler, S. W., et al. 1986. "Multisystematic Treatment of Juvenile Offenders." *Developmental Psychology,* 22, 132–141. (Ch. 14)

Hertzog, C., K. W. Schaie, and K. Gribbin. 1978. "Cardiovascular Disease and

Changes in Intellectual Functioning from Middle to Old Age." *Journal of Gerontology*, *33*, 872–883. (Ch. 16)

Herzog, E., and C. F. Sudia. 1973. "Children in Fatherless Families." In *Review of Child Development Research*, ed. B. M. Caldwell and H. N. Ricciuti, vol. 3, 141–232. Chicago: Univ. of Chicago Pr. (Chs. 9, 10)

Hess, R. D. 1970. "Social Class and Ethnic Influences on Socialization." In *Carmichael's Manual of Child Psychology*, 3rd ed., ed. P. H. Mussen, vol. 2, 457–557. NY: Wiley. (Ch. 12)

———, and S. D. Holloway. 1984. "Family and School as Educational Institutions." In *Review of Child Development Research*, vol. 7, ed. R. D Parke, 197–222. Chicago: Univ. of Chicago Pr. (Ch. 10)

———, and V. C. Shipman. 1968. "Early Experience and the Socialization of Cognitive Modes in Children." *Child Development*, *34*, 869–886. (Ch. 10)

———, ———, J. Brophy, and D. M. Baer. 1968. *The Cognitive Environment of Urban Preschool Children*. Chicago: Univ. of Chicago Pr. (Ch. 10)

Hetherington, E. M. 1972. "Effects of Father Absence on Personality Development in Adolescent Daughters." *Developmental Psychology*, *7*, 313–326. (Ch. 9)

———. 1979. "Divorce." *American Psychologist*, *34*, 852–858. (Ch. 9)

———, and K. A. Camara. 1984. "Families in Transition." In *Review of Child Development Research*, ed. R. D. Parke, vol. 7, 398–439. Chicago: Univ. of Chicago Pr. (Chs. 9, 15)

———, ———, and D. L. Featherman. 1983. "Achievement and Intellectual Functioning of Children from One-Parent Households." In *Achievement and Achievement Motives*, ed. J. Spence. San Francisco: Freeman. (Ch. 9)

———, M. Cox, and R. Cox. 1979. "Play and Social Interaction in Children Following Divorce." *Journal of Social Issues*, *35*, 26–49. (Ch. 10)

———, ———, and ———. 1982. "Effects of Divorce on Parents and Children." In *Nontraditional Families*, ed. M. E. Lamb, 233–288. Hillsdale, NJ: Lawrence Erlbaum Associates. (Ch. 9)

Hevesi, D. 1986. "Harris Poll Reports Teenagers Favor Contraceptives at Clinics." *New York Times*, Dec. 17, B12. (Ch. 14)

Hicks, D. J. 1965. "Imitation and Retention of Film-Mediated Aggressive Peer and Adult Models." *Journal of Personality and Social Psychology*, *2*, 97–100. (Ch. 10)

Hiebert, J. 1984. "Children's Mathematics Learning." *Elementary School Journal*, *84*, 497–513. (Ch. 12)

Hill, J. P. 1985. "Family Relations in Adolescence." *Genetic, Social, and General Psychology Monographs*, *111*, 233–248. (Ch. 13)

———, G. N. Holmbeck, L. Marlow, T. M. Green, and M. E. Lynch. 1985. "Menarcheal Status and Parent-Child Relations in Families of 7th-Grade Girls." *Journal of Youth and Adolescence*, *14*, 301–316. (Ch. 13)

Hill, K. T., and W. O. Eaton. 1977. "The Interaction of Test Anxiety and Success-Failure Experiences in Determining Children's Arithmetic Performance." *Developmental Psychology*, *13*, 205–211. (Ch. 10)

Hill, M. S. 1983. "Trends in the Economic Situation of US Families and Children." In *American Families and the Economy*, ed. R. Nelson and F. Skidmore. Washington, DC: Nat'l. Academy Pr. (Ch. 9)

Hill, R., and P. Mattessich. 1979. "Family Development Theory and Life-Span Development." In *Life-Span Development and Behavior*, ed. P. B. Baltes and O. G. Brim, vol. 2, 161–204. NY: Academic Pr. (Ch. 9)

Hinde, R. A. 1983. "Ethology and Child Development." In *Handbook of Child Psychology*. 4th ed., ed. P. H. Mussen, vol. 2, 27–94. NY: Wiley. (Chs. 2, 10)

———. 1985. "Categorizing Individuals." Paper presented at the Biennial Meeting of the Society for Research in Child Development. Toronto, April. (Ch. 9)

Hoff-Ginsberg, E. 1986. "Function and Structure in Maternal Speech." *Child Development*, *22*, 155–163. (Ch. 7)

Hoffman, L. W. 1977. "Changes in Family Roles, Socialization, and Sex Differences." *American Psychologist*, *32*, 644–657. (Chs. 8, 9)

———. 1978. "Effects of the First Child on the Woman's Role." In *The First Child and Family Formation*, ed. W. Miller and L. Newman. Chapel Hill: Univ. of NC Pr. (Ch. 15)

———. 1979. "Maternal Employment." *American Psychologist*, *34*, 859–865. (Ch. 9)

———. 1980. "The Effects of Maternal Employment on the Academic Attitudes and Performance of School-Aged Children." *School Psychology Review*, *9*, 319–336. (Ch. 9)

———. 1983. "Population Psychology." Paper presented at Inter-Amer. Congress of Psychology. Quito, July. (Ch. 9)

———. 1984a. "Work, Family, and the Socialization of the Child." In *Review of Child Development Research*, ed. R. D. Parke, vol. 7, 223–282. Chicago: Univ. of Chicago Pr. (Chs. 8, 9, 10, 15)

———. 1984b. "Maternal Employment and the Young Child." In *Minnesota Symposia on Child Psychology*, ed. M. Perlmutter, vol. 17, 101–128. Hillsdale, NJ: Lawrence Erlbaum Assoc. (Chs. 8, 15)

———1985a. "The Changing Genetic/Socialization Balance." *Journal of Social Issues*, *41*, 127–148. (Chs. 3, 12)

———. 1985b. "Social Change and the Effects of Maternal Employment on the Child." Paper presented at the International Seminar on the Educational Role of the Family. Japan, Mar. (Ch. 17)

———. 1986. "Work, Family, and the Children." In *Psychology and Work*, ed. M. S. Pallak and R. O. Perloff, 169–220. Washington, DC: Amer. Psychological Assn. (Chs. 9, 15, 17)

———, and J. D. Manis. 1978. "Influences of Children on Marital Interaction and Parental Satisfactions and Dissatisfactions." In *Child Influences on Marital and Family Interaction*, ed. R. Lerner and G. Spanier, 165–213. NY: Academic Pr. (Ch. 15)

———, and ———. 1979. "The Value of Children in the United States." *Journal of Marriage and the Family*, *41*, 583–596. (Ch. 15)

———, K. A. McManus, and Y. Brackbill. In press. "The Value of Children to Young and Elderly Parents." *International Journal of Aging and Human Development*. (Ch. 19)

———, and F. I. Nye. 1974. *Working Mothers*. San Francisco: Jossey-Bass. (Chs. 9, 15)

Hoffman, M. L. 1983. "Affective and Cognitive Processes in Moral Internalization." In *Social Cognition and Social Development*, ed. E. T. Higgins, D. N. Ruble, and W. Hartup. NY: Cambridge Univ. Pr. (Ch. 9)

———. 1984. "Moral Development." In *Developmental Psychology*, ed. M. H. Bornstein and M. E. Lamb, 279–324. Hillsdale, NJ: Lawrence Erlbaum Assoc. (Chs. 8, 9, 11)

———, and H. D. Saltzstein. 1967. "Parent Discipline and the Child's Moral Development." *Journal of Personality and Social Psychology*, *5*, 45–57. (Ch. 9)

Hofsten, C. von. 1982. "Eye-Hand Coordination in the Newborn." *Developmental Psychology*, *18*, 450–461. (Ch. 5)

———. 1983. "Catching Skills in Infancy." *Journal of Experimental Psychology: Human Perception and Performance*, *9*, 75–85. (Ch. 5)

———. 1984. "Developmental Changes in the Organization of Prereaching Movements." *Developmental Psychology*, *20*, 378–388. (Ch. 5)

Holden, C. 1980. "Identical Twins Reared Apart." *Science*, *207*, 1323–1328. (Ch. 1)

———. 1986. "Youth Suicide." *Science*, *233*, 839–841. (Ch. 14)

Holding, D. H., T. K. Noonan, H. D. Pfau, and C. S. Holding. 1986. "Data Attribution, Age, and the Distribution of Lifetime Memories." *Journal of Gerontology*, *41*, 481–486. (Ch. 18)

Holmes, J. H., and R. H. Rahe. 1967. "The Social Readjustment Rating Scale." *Journal of Personality and Social Psychology*, *11*, 213–218. (Ch. 20)

Hooker, D. 1952. *The Prenatal Origin of Behavior*. Lawrence: Univ. of KN Pr. (Ch. 3)

Horn, J. L. 1968. "Organization of Abilities and the Development of Intelligence." *Psychological Review*, *75*, 242–259. (Chs. 12, 16)

———. 1982. "The Theory of Fluid and Crystallized Intelligence in Relation to Concepts of Cognitive Psychology and Aging in Adulthood." In *Aging and Cognitive Processes*, ed. F. I. M. Craik and S. Trehub, 237–278. NY: Plenum. (Chs. 12, 16)

———. 1984. "Remodeling Old Models of Intelligence." In *Handbook of Intelligence*, ed. B. B. Wolman. Englewood Cliffs, NJ: Prentice-Hall. (Chs. 12, 16)

House, J. S., and C. Robbins. 1983. "Age, Psychosocial Stress, and Health." In *Aging in Society*, ed. M. W. Riley, B. B. Hess, and K. Bond, 175–198. Hillsdale, NJ: Lawrence Erlbaum Assoc. (Ch. 19)

Howard, J. H., P. A. Rechnitzer, D. A. Cunningham, and A. P. Donner. 1986. "Change in Type A Behavior a Year after Retirement." *Gerontologist*, *26*, 643–649. (Ch. 20)

Howe, M. L., and M. A. Hunter. 1986. "Long-Term Memory in Adulthood." *Developmental Review*, *6*, 334–364. (Ch. 18)

Howes, C. 1983. "Caregiver Behavior in Center and Family Day Care." *Journal of Applied Developmental Psychology*, *4*, 99–107. (Ch. 8)

———. 1985. "Sharing Fantasy." *Child Development*, *56*, 1253–1258. (Ch. 8)

Hsu, L. K. G. 1983. "The Aetiology of Anorexia Nervosa." *Psychological Medicine*, *13*, 231–237. (Ch. 14)

Hubel, D. H., and T. N. Wiesel. 1963. "Receptive Fields of Cells in the Striate Cortex of Very Young, Visually Inexperienced Kittens." *Journal of Neurophysiology, 26,* 994–1002. (Ch. 5)

Hudson, J., and K. Nelson. 1984. "Play with Language." *Journal of Child Language, 11,* 337–346. (Ch. 7)

Hudson, J. I., H. G. Pope, Jr., J. M. Jonas, and D. Urgelun-Todd. 1983. "Family History Studies of Anorexia Nervosa and Bulimia." *British Journal of Psychiatry, 142,* 133–138. (Ch. 14)

Hudson, R. B., and J. Strate. 1985. "Aging and Political Systems." In *Handbook of Aging and the Social Sciences,* 2nd ed., ed. R. H. Binstock and E. Shanas, 554–585. NY: Van Nostrand Reinhold. (Ch. 19)

Huesmann, L. R., K. Lagerspetz, and L. D. Eron. 1984. "Intervening Variables in the TV Violence-Aggression Relation." *Developmental Psychology, 20,* 746–775. (Ch. 10)

Hulicka, I. M. 1982. "Memory Functioning in Late Adulthood." In *Aging and Cognitive Processes,* ed. F. I. M. Craik and S. Trehub, 331–351. NY: Plenum. (Ch. 18)

Hultsch, D. F., and R. A. Dixon. 1984. "Memory for Text Materials in Adulthood." In *Life-Span Development and Behavior,* ed. P. B. Baltes and O. G. Brim, Jr., vol. 6, NY: Academic Pr. (Ch. 18)

Humphreys, A. P., and P. K. Smith. 1987. "Rough and Tumble, Friendship, and Dominance in Schoolchildren." *Child Development, 58,* 201–212. (Ch. 10)

Hunt, M. 1974. *Sexual Behavior in the 1970s.* NY: Dell. (Ch. 17)

Hunter, M. A., E. W. Ames, and R. Koopman. 1983. "Effect of Stimulus Complexity and Familiarization Time on Infant Preferences for Novel and Familiar Stimuli." *Developmental Psychology, 19,* 338–352. (Ch. 6)

Huston, A. C. 1983. "Sex-Typing." In *Handbook of Child Psychology,* 4th ed., ed. P. H. Mussen, vol. 4, 387–467. NY: Wiley. (Chs. 1, 8, 9, 13)

————. 1985. "The Development of Sex-Typing." *Developmental Review, 5,* 1–17. (Ch. 9)

Huyck, M. H. 1982. "From Gregariousness to Intimacy." In *Review of Human Development,* ed. T. M. Field, A. Huston, H. C. Quay, L. Troll, and G. E. Finley, 471–484. NY: Wiley-Interscience. (Ch. 17)

Hyman, B. T., G. N. Van Hoesen, A. R. Damasio, and C. L. Barnes. 1984. "Alzheimer's Disease." *Science, 225,* 1168–1170. (Ch. 18)

Hymel, S. 1986. "Interpretations of Peer Behavior." *Child Development, 57,* 431–445. (Chs. 10, 13)

Inhelder, B., and J. Piaget. 1958. *The Growth of Logical Thinking from Childhood to Adolescence.* NY: Basic Books. (Ch. 13)

Interprofessional Task Force on Health Care of Women and Children. 1978. *The Development of Family-Centered Maternity/Newborn Care in Hospitals.* Chicago: Interprofessional Task Force. (Ch. 3)

Istomina, Z. M. 1975. "The Development of Voluntary Memory in Preschool-Age Children." *Soviet Psychology, 13,* 5–64. (Ch. 6)

Jackowitz, E. R., and M. W. Watson. 1980.

"Development of Object Transformation in Early Pretend Play." *Developmental Psychology, 16,* 543–549. (Ch. 6)

Jacobson, G. F. 1983. *The Multiple Crises in Marital Separation and Divorce.* NY: Grune & Stratton. (Ch. 15)

Jacobson, J. L., D. C. Boersma, R. B. Fields, and K. L. Olson. 1983. "Paralinguistic Features of Adult Speech to Infants and Small Children." *Child Development, 54,* 436–442. (Ch. 7)

Jacobson, S. W. 1979. "Matching Behavior in the Young Infant." *Child Development, 54,* 436–442. (Ch. 6)

————, G. G. Fein, J. L. Jacobson, P. M. Schwartz, and J. K. Dowler. 1984. "Neonatal Correlates of Prenatal Exposure to Smoking, Caffeine, and Alcohol." *Infant Behavior and Development, 7,* 253–265. (Ch. 3)

————, ————, ————, ————, and ————. 1985. "The Effect of Intrauterine PCB Exposure on Visual Recognition Memory." *Child Development, 56,* 853–860. (Ch. 3)

James, W. [1890] 1950. *The Principles of Psychology.* Vol. 1. NY: Dover. (Ch. 4)

Janos, P. M., and N. M. Robinson. 1985. "Psychosocial Development in Intellectually Gifted Children." In *The Gifted and Talented,* ed. F. D. Horowitz and M. O'Brien, 149–196. Washington, DC: Amer. Psychological Assn. (Ch. 12)

Jarvik, L. F. 1973. "Discussion." In *Intellectual Functioning in Adults,* ed. L. F. Jarvik, C. Eisdorfer, and J. E. Blum, 65–67. NY: Springer. (Ch. 1)

————. 1983. "The Impact of Immediate Life Situation on Depression." In *Depression and Aging,* ed. L. D. Breslau and M. R. Haug, 114–120. NY: Springer. (Ch. 19)

Jelliffe, D. B., and E. F. P. Jelliffe. 1979. *Human Milk in the Modern World.* NY: Oxford Univ. Pr. (Ch. 5)

Jennings, M., and R. G. Niemi. 1981. *Generations and Politics.* Princeton: Princeton Univ. Pr. (Ch. 14)

Jensen, A. R. 1980. *Bias in Mental Testing.* NY: Free Pr. (Ch. 12)

Jewett, S. 1973. "Longevity and the Longevity Syndrome." *Gerontologist, 13,* 91–99. (Ch. 20)

Jiao, S., Ji, G., and Jing, Q. (Ching, C. C.). 1986. "Comparative Study of Behavioral Qualities of Only Children and Sibling Children." *Child Development, 57,* 357–361. (Ch. 9)

Joffe, J. M. 1965. "Genotype and Prenatal and Premating Stress Interact to Affect Adult Behavior in Rats." *Science, 150,* 1844–1845. (Ch. 3)

Johnson, C., C. Lewis, S. Love, L. Lewis, and M. Stuckey. 1984. "Incidence and Correlates of Bulimic Behavior in a Female High School Population." *Journal of Youth and Adolescence, 13,* 15. (Ch. 14)

————, and K. L. Maddi. 1986. "The Etiology of Bulimia." *Adolescent Psychiatry,* vol. 13, 253–273. Chicago: Univ. of Chicago Pr. (Ch. 14)

Johnson, D. D. 1980. "Reunion of Identical Twins, Raised Apart, Reveals some Astonishing Similarities." *Smithsonian,* Oct. 48–56. (Ch. 1)

Johnson, E., and B. Bursk. 1977. "Relationships between the Elderly and Their Adult

Children." *Gerontologist, 27,* 90–96. (Ch. 17)

Johnson, E. M., and D. M. Kochlar (eds.). 1983. *Teratogenesis and Reproductive Toxicology.* NY: Springer. (Ch. 3)

Johnson, P. 1976. "Women and Power." *Journal of Social Issues, 32,* 99–110. (Ch. 15)

————, and D. W. Salisbury. 1975. "Breathing and Sucking during Feeding in the Newborn." In *Parent-Infant Interaction.* Amsterdam: CIBA Foundation Symposium 33, new series, ASP. (Ch. 4)

Johnston, P. H., and P. N. Winograd. 1985. "Passive Failure in Reading." *Journal of Reading Behavior, 17,* 279–301. (Ch. 12)

Jones, M. C. 1965. "Psychological Correlates of Somatic Development." *Child Development, 39,* 899–911. (Ch. 13)

Jung, C. G. 1969. *The Structure and Dynamics of the Psyche.* Princeton: Princeton Univ. Pr. (Chs. 17, 19)

Jusczyk, P. W. 1977. "Perception of Syllable-Final Stop Consonants by 2-Month-Old Infants." *Perception and Psychophysics, 21,* 450–454. (Ch. 7)

Kagan, J. 1958. "The Concept of Identification." *Psychological Review, 65,* 296–305. (Ch. 2)

————. 1984. *The Nature of the Child.* NY: Basic. (Ch. 8)

————, and R. E. Klein. 1973. "Cross-Cultural Perspectives on Early Development." *American Psychologist, 28,* 947–961. (Ch. 1)

————, and S. R. Tulkin. 1971. "Social Class Differences in Child Rearing during the First Year." In *The Origins of Human Social Relations,* ed. H. R. Schaffer, 165–186. NY: Academic Pr. (Ch. 8)

Kail, R. 1984. *The Development of Memory in Children.* 2nd ed. NY: W. H. Freeman. (Chs. 6, 11)

————, and J. W. Hagen. 1982. "Memory in Childhood." In *Handbook of Developmental Psychology,* ed. B. W. Wolman, 350–366. Englewood Cliffs, NJ: Prentice-Hall. (Ch. 2)

Kalish, R. A. 1976. "Death and Dying in a Social Context." In *Handbook of Aging and the Social Sciences,* ed. R. H. Binstock and E. Shanas, 483–507. NY: Van Nostrand Reinhold. (Ch. 20)

————, and D. K. Reynolds. [1976] 1981. *Death and Ethnicity.* Farmingdale, NY: Baywood Publishing. (Ch. 20)

Kalnins, I. V., and J. S. Bruner. 1973. "The Coordination of Visual Observation and Instrumental Behavior in Early Infancy." *Perception, 2,* 307–314. (Ch. 6)

Kamin, L. J. 1974. *The Science and Politics of IQ.* Potomac, MD: Lawrence Erlbaum Assoc. (Ch. 12)

Kandel, D. B., and G. S. Lesser. 1972. *Youth in Two Worlds.* San Francisco: Jossey-Bass. (Ch. 14)

Kantrowitz, B., and N. Joseph. 1986. "Building Baby Biceps." *Newsweek, 107,* May 26, 79. (Ch. 5)

————, R. Michael, L. Rotenberg, E. Williams, and N. F. Greenberg. 1985. "Mothers on Their Own." *Newsweek,* Dec. 23, 66–67. (Ch. 15)

Karsh, E. 1987. "A Teen-Ager Is a Ton of Worry." *New York Times,* Jan. 3, 23. (Ch. 13)

Kasl, S. V., A. M. Ostfeld, G. M. Brody, L. Snell, and C. A. Price. 1980. In *Second Conference on the Epidemiology of Aging,* ed. S. G.

Haynes and M. Feinleib, 211–236. Nat'l. Inst. of Health Pub. no. 80-969. Bethesda, MD: US Dept. of Health and Human Services. (Ch. 20)

Kastenbaum, R. 1980. "Death, Dying and Bereavement in Old Age." In *Aging*, 2nd ed., ed. H. Cox, 200–207. Guilford, CT: Dushkin. (Ch. 20)

———. 1985. "Dying and Death." In *Handbook of the Psychology of Aging*, 2nd ed., ed. J. E. Birren and K. W. Schaie, 619–643. NY: Van Nostrand Reinhold. (Chs. 19, 20)

———, B. K. Kastenbaum, and J. Morris. In preparation. "Strengths and Preferences of the Terminally Ill." (Cited in Kastenbaum, 1985.) (Ch. 20)

Kates, J. 1986. "Hers." *New York Times*, Sept. 18, C2. (Ch. 15)

Kausler, D. H. 1982. *Experimental Psychology and Human Aging*. NY: Wiley. (Ch. 18)

———, W. Lichty, and J. S. Freund. 1985. "Adult Age Differences in Recognition Memory and Frequency Judgments for Planned vs. Performed Activities." *Developmental Psychology*, 21, 647–65. (Ch. 18)

Kaye, K., and A. J. Wells. 1980. "Mothers' Jiggling and the Burst-Pause Pattern in Neonatal Feeding." *Infant Behavior and Development*, 3, 29–46. (Ch. 4)

Keating, D. P. 1979. "The Acceleration/Enrichment Debate." In *Educating the Gifted*, ed. W. C. George, S. J. Cohn, and J. C. Stanley, 217–220. Baltimore: Johns Hopkins Univ. Pr. (Ch. 12)

Keating, N. C., and P. Cole. 1980. "What Do I Do with Him 24 Hours a Day?" *Gerontologist*, 20, 84–89. (Ch. 19)

———, and B. Jeffrey. 1983. "Work Careers of Ever Married and Never Married Retired Women." *Gerontologist*, 23, 416–421. (Ch. 17)

Kedar-Voivodas, G. 1983. "The Impact of Elementary Children's Roles and Sex Roles on Teacher Attitudes." *Review of Educational Research*, 53, 414–437. (Ch. 10)

Keen, S. 1974. *Voices and Visions*. NY: Harper & Row. (Ch. 20)

Keeney, T. J., S. R. Cannizzo, and J. H. Flavell. 1967. "Spontaneous and Induced Verbal Rehearsal in a Recall Task." *Child Development*, 38, 953–966. (Ch. 11)

Keil, F. C. 1981. "Constraints on Knowledge and Cognitive Development." *Psychological Review*, 88, 197–227. (Ch. 6)

Kelly, J. B. 1982. "Divorce." In *Handbook of Developmental Psychology*, ed. B. B. Wolman, 734–750. Englewood Cliffs, NJ: Prentice-Hall. (Ch. 17)

———, and J. S. Wallerstein. 1975. "The Effects of Parental Divorce." *American Journal of Orthopsychiatry*, 45, 253–254. (Ch. 9)

Kempe, R. S., and H. C. Kempe. 1978. *Child Abuse*. Cambridge: Harvard Univ. Pr. (Ch. 9)

Kennedy, W. A. 1969. "A Follow-Up Normative Study of Negro Intelligence and Achievement." *Monographs of the Society for Research in Child Development*, 34, no. 126. (Ch. 12)

Kerckhoff, A. 1966. "Husband-Wife Expectations and Reactions to Retirement." In *Social Aspects of Aging*, ed. I. H. Simpson and J. C. McKinney, 160–172. Durham, NC: Duke Univ. Pr. (Ch. 19)

Keshet, H. F., and K. M. Rosenthal. 1978. "Fathering after Marital Separation." *Social Work*, 23, Jan., 11–18. (Ch. 15)

Kessler, R. C., and J. A. McRae, Jr. 1981. "Trends in the Relationship between Sex and Psychological Distress." *American Sociological Review*, 46, 443–453. (Ch. 17)

———, and ———. 1982. "The Effects of Wives' Employment on the Mental Health of Married Men and Women." *American Sociological Review*, 47, 216–227. (Ch. 15)

Kinsbourne, M. 1980. "Attentional Dysfunctions and the Elderly." In *New Directions in Memory and Aging*, ed. L. W. Poon, J. L. Fozard, L. S. Cermak, D. Arenberg, and L. W. Thompson, 113–130. Hillsdale, NJ: Lawrence Erlbaum Assoc. (Ch. 18)

Kivnick, H. Q. 1982. "Grandparenthood." *Gerontologist*, 22, 59–66. (Ch. 17)

Klaus, M. H., and J. H. Kennell. 1976. *Maternal-Infant Bonding*. St. Louis: Mosby. (Ch. 4)

Klein, R. P. 1985. "Caregiving Arrangements by Employed Women with Children under 1 Year of Age." *Developmental Psychology*, 21, 403–406. (Ch. 8)

Kleitman, N. 1963. *Sleep and Wakefulness*. Chicago: Univ. of Chicago Pr. (Ch. 4)

Klerman, G. L. 1983. "Problems in the Definition and Diagnosis of Depression in the Elderly." In *Depression and Aging*, ed. L. D. Breslau and M. R. Haug, 3–19. NY: Springer. (Ch. 19)

Kline, D. W., and F. Schieber. 1985. "Vision and Aging." In *Handbook of the Psychology of Aging*, 2nd ed., ed. J. E. Birren and K. W. Schaie, 296–331. NY: Van Nostrand Reinhold. (Ch. 18)

Kobasigawa, A. 1977. "Retrieval Strategies in the Development of Memory." In *Perspectives on the Development of Memory and Cognition*, ed. R. V. Kail, Jr., and J. W. Hagen, 177–201. Hillsdale, NJ: Lawrence Erlbaum Assoc. (Ch. 11)

Koepke, J. E., M. Hamm, M. Legerstee, and M. Russell. 1983. "Neonatal Imitation." *Infant Behavior and Development*, 6, 97–102. (Ch. 6)

Kohlberg, L. 1966. "A Cognitive-Developmental Analysis of Children's Sex-Role Concepts and Attitudes." In *The Development of Sex Differences*, ed. E. E. Maccoby, 82–173. Stanford: Stanford Univ. Pr. (Ch. 9)

———. 1969. "Stage and Sequence." In *Handbook of Socialization Theory and Research*, ed. D. A. Goslin, 347–480. Chicago: Rand-McNally. (Ch. 11)

———, and C. Gilligan. 1971. "The Adolescent as a Philosopher." *Daedalus*, 100, 1051–1086. (Ch. 13)

Kohn, M. 1979. "The Effects of Social Class on Parental Values and Practices." In *The American Family*, ed. D. Reiss and H. A. Hoffman, 45–68. NY: Plenum. (Ch. 10)

———. 1980. "Job Complexity and Adult Personality." In *Themes of Work and Love in Adulthood*, ed. N. J. Smelser and E. H. Erikson, 193–210. Cambridge: Harvard Univ. Pr. (Ch. 15)

Kohn, R. R. 1982. "Causes of Death in Very Old People." *Journal of the American Medical Association*, 247, 2793–2797. (Ch. 20)

Kolata, G. B. 1978. "Behavioral Teratology." *Science*, 202, 732–734. (Ch. 3)

———. 1979. "Developmental Biology." *Science*, 206, 315–316. (Ch. 3)

———. 1985. "Finding Biological Clocks in Fetuses." *Science*, 230, 929–930. (Ch. 4)

———. 1986. "Obese Children." *Science*, 232, 20–21. (Ch. 5)

Kolbert, E. 1986. " 'Going Out.' " *New York Times*, Dec. 13, 19ff. (Ch. 13)

Konner, M. 1975. "Relations among Infants and Juveniles in Comparative Perspective." In *Friendship and Peer Relations*, ed. M. Lewis and L. A. Rosenblum, 99–130. NY: Wiley. (Ch. 10)

———. 1977. "Infancy among the Kalahari San." In *Culture and Infancy*, ed. P. H. Leiderman, S. R. Tulkin, and A. Rosenfeld, 287–328. NY: Academic Pr. (Ch. 8)

Kopp, C. B. 1979. "Perspectives on Infant Motor System Development." In *Psychological Development from Infancy*, ed. M. H. Bornstein and W. Kessen, 9–36. Hillsdale, NJ: Lawrence Erlbaum Assoc. (Ch. 5)

———. 1983. "Risk Factors in Development." In *Handbook of Child Psychology*, 4th ed., ed. P. H. Mussen, vol. 2, 1081–1188. NY: Wiley. (Chs. 3, 5)

Korner, A. F., C. A. Hutchinson, J. A. Koperski, H. C. Kraemer, and P. A. Schneider. 1981. "Stability of Individual Differences of Neonatal Motor and Crying Patterns." *Child Development*, 52, 83–90. (Ch. 4)

Kornhaber, A., and K. L. Woodward. 1981. *Grandparents/Grandchild*. Garden City, NY: Anchor Pr. (Ch. 17)

Kovach, J. A., and N. W. Glickman. 1986. "Levels and Psychosocial Correlates of Adolescent Drug Use." *Journal of Youth and Adolescence*, 15, 61–78. (Ch. 14)

Kozel, N. J., and E. H. Adams. 1986. "Epidemiology of Drug Abuse." *Science*, 234, 970–974. (Ch. 14)

Kozol, J. 1985. *Illiterate America*. Garden City, NY: Anchor Pr. (Ch. 16)

Kramer, D. A. 1983. "Post-Formal Operations?" *Human Development*, 26, 91–105. (Ch. 16)

Krause, N. 1986. "Social Support, Stress, and Well-Being among Older Adults." *Journal of Gerontology*, 41, 512–519. (Ch. 19)

Kreutzer, M. A., C. Leonard, and J. H. Flavell. 1975. "An Interview Study of Children's Knowledge about Memory." *Monographs of the Society for Research in Child Development*, 40, no. 159. (Ch. 11)

Krosnick, J. A., and C. M. Judd. 1982. "Transition in Social Influence at Adolescence." *Developmental Psychology*, 18, 359–368. (Ch. 13)

Kübler-Ross, E. 1969. *On Death and Dying*. NY: Macmillan. (Ch. 20)

———. Interview by D. Goleman. 1976. "The Child Will Always Be There." *Psychology Today*, 10, Sept., 48–52. (Ch. 20)

Kuczaj, S. A., II. 1978. "Children's Judgments of Grammatical and Ungrammatical Irregular Past-Tense Verbs." *Child Development*, 49, 319–326. (Ch. 7)

———, and N. Brannick. 1979. "Children's Use of '*Wh*'- Question Modal Auxilliary Placement Rule." *Journal of Experimental Child Psychology*, 28, 43–67. (Ch. 7)

Kuczynski, L. 1983. "Reasoning, Prohibitions, and Motivations for Compliance." *Developmental Psychology*, 19, 126–134. (Ch. 9)

Kurdek, L. A., and J. P. Schmitt. 1986. "Early Development of Relationship Quality in Heterosexual Married, Heterosexual Cohabiting, Gay, and Lesbian Couples." *Developmental Psychology*, 22, 305–309. (Ch. 15)

Kurtines, W., and E. B. Greif. 1974. "The Development of Moral Thought." *Psychological Bulletin, 8*, 453–470. (Ch. 11)

Laboratory of Comparative Human Cognition. "Culture and Cognitive Development." In *Handbook of Child Psychology*, 4th ed., ed. P. H. Mussen, vol. 1, 295–356. NY: Wiley. (Ch. 11)

Labouvie-Vief, G. 1985. "Intelligence and Cognition." In *Handbook of the Psychology of Aging*, 2nd ed., ed. J. E. Birren and K. W. Schaie, 500–530. NY: Van Nostrand Reinhold. (Ch. 16)

Lachman, J. L., and R. Lachman. 1980. "Age and the Actualization of World Knowledge." In *New Directions in Memory and Aging*, ed. L. W. Poon, J. L. Fozard, L. S. Cermak, D. Arenberg, and L. W. Thompson, 285–311. Hillsdale, NJ: Lawrence Erlbaum Assoc. (Ch. 18)

Lakatta, E. G. 1985. "Heart and Circulation." In *Handbook of the Biology of Aging*, 2nd ed., ed. C. E. Finch and E. L. Schneider, 377–413. NY: Van Nostrand Reinhold. (Ch. 19)

Lamb, M. E. 1978. "Interactions Between 18-Month-Olds and Their Preschool-Aged Siblings." *Child Development, 49*, 51–59. (Ch. 8)

———. 1981. "The Development of Father-Infant Relationships." In *The Role of the Father in Child Development*, 2nd ed., ed. M. E. Lamb, 459–488. NY: Wiley-Interscience. (Ch. 8)

———, and M. H. Bornstein. 1986. *Development in Infancy*. 2nd ed. NY: Random House. (Ch. 4)

———, and S. K. Bronson. 1980. "Fathers in the Context of Family Influences." *School Psychology Review, 9*, 336–353. (Ch. 9)

———, M. A. Easterbrooks, and G. W. Holden. 1980. "Reinforcement and Punishment among Preschoolers." *Child Development, 51*, 1230–1236. (Ch. 10).

———, K. Hopps, and A. B. Elster. 1987. "Strange Situation Behavior of Infants with Adolescent Mothers." *Infant Behavior and Development, 10*, 39–48. (Ch. 14)

———, and C.-P. Hwang. 1982. "Maternal Attachment and Mother-Neonate Bonding." In *Advances in Developmental Psychology*, ed. M. E. Lamb and A. L. Brown, vol. 2, 1–40. Hillsdale, NJ: Lawrence Erlbaum Assoc. (Ch. 4)

———, J. H. Pleck, and J. Levine. In press. "The Role of the Father in Child Development." In *Advances in Clinical Child Psychology*, ed. A. Kazdin. vol. 8. NY: Plenum. (Ch. 9)

———, R. A. Thompson, W. P. Gardner, and E. L. Charnov. 1985. *Infant-Mother Attachment*. Hillsdale, NJ: Lawrence Erlbaum Assoc. (Ch. 8)

Lancioni, G. E. 1980. "Infant Operant Conditioning and Its Implications for Early Intervention." *Psychological Bulletin, 88*, 516–534. (Ch. 6)

Langer, J. A. 1984. "The Effects of Available Information on Responses to School Writing Tasks." *Research in the Teaching of English, 28*, 27–44. (Ch. 12)

Langlois, J. H., and A. C. Downs. 1980. "Mothers, Fathers, and Peers as Socialization Agents of Sex-Typed Play Behaviors in Young Children." *Child Development, 51*, 1237–1247. (Ch. 9)

———, and C. F. Stephan. 1977. "The Effects of Physical Attractiveness and Ethnicity on Children's Behavioral Attributions and Peer Preference." *Child Development, 48*, 1694–1698. (Ch. 10)

Lapsley, D. K., M. Milstead, S. M. Quintana, D. Flannery, and R. R. Buss. 1986. "Adolescent Egocentrism and Formal Operations." *Developmental Psychology, 22*, 800–807. (Ch. 13)

———, and M. N. Murphy. 1985. "Another Look at the Theoretical Assumptions of Adolescent Egocentrism." *Developmental Review, 5*, 201–217. (Ch. 13)

La Rue, A., C. Dessonville, and L. F. Jarvik. 1985. "Aging and Mental Disorders." In *Handbook of the Psychology of Aging*, 2nd ed., ed. J. E. Birren and K. W. Schaie, 664–702. NY: Van Nostrand Reinhold. (Chs. 18, 19)

———, and L. F. Jarvik. 1982. "Old Age and Biobehavioral Change." In *Handbook of Developmental Psychology*, ed. B. B. Wolman, 791–806. Englewood Cliffs, NJ: Prentice-Hall. (Ch. 16)

Lasky, R. E., et al. 1981. "The Relationsip between Physical Growth and Infant Behavioral Development in Rural Guatemala." *Child Development, 52*, 219–226. (Ch. 5)

Laudenslager, M. L., S. M. Ryan, R. C. Drugan, R. L. Hudson, and S. F. Maier. 1983. "Coping and Immunosuppression." *Science, 221*, 568–570. (Ch. 20)

Lawton, M. P. 1985. "Housing and Living Environments of Older People." In *Handbook of Aging and the Social Sciences*, 2nd ed., ed. R. H. Binstock and E. Shanas, 450–478. (Ch. 19)

Lazarus, R. 1985. "Stress and Adaptational Concerns." *American Psychologist, 40*, 770–780. (Ch. 17)

Leakey, R. E., and R. Lewin. 1977. *Origins*. NY: Dutton. (Ch. 5)

Leavitt, H. 1986. "School Clinics vs. Teen Pregnancies." *Insight*, Dec. 22, 26. (Ch. 14)

Lee, C. L., and J. E. Bates. 1985. "Mother-Child Interaction at Age 2 Years and Perceived Difficult Temperament." *Child Development, 56*, 1314–1325. (Ch. 4)

Leming, M. R., and G. E. Dickinson. 1985. *Understanding Dying, Death, and Bereavement*. NY: Holt, Rinehart and Winston. (Ch. 20)

Lenneberg, E. H. 1967. *Biological Foundations of Language*. NY: Wiley. (Ch. 7)

———. 1973. "Biological Aspects of Language." In *Communication, Language, and Meaning*, ed. G. A. Miller, 49–60. NY: Basic. (Ch. 7)

Leo, J. 1986. "Could Suicide Be Contagious?" *Time*, Feb. 24, 59. (Ch. 14)

Leonard, C. O. 1981. "Serum AFP Screening for Neural Tube Defects." *Clinical Obstetrics and Gynecology, 24*, 1121–1132. (Ch. 3)

Leopold, W. F. 1949. *Grammar and General Problems in the First Two Years*. Evanston, IL: Northwestern University Press.

Lepper, M. R. 1983. "Social Control Processes, Attributions of Motivation, and the Internalization of Social Values." In *Social Cognition and Social Behavior*, ed. E. T. Higgins, D. N. Ruble, and W. W. Hartup. NY: Cambridge Univ. Pr. (Chs. 6, 9)

———, D. Greene, and R. E. Nisbett. 1973. "Undermining Children's Intrinsic Interest with Extrinsic Rewards." *Journal of Personality and Social Psychology, 18*, 129–137. (Ch. 6)

Lerner, R. M., and J. R. Knapp. 1975. "Ac-

tual and Perceived Intrafamilial Attitudes of Late Adolescents and Parents." *Journal of Youth and Adolescence, 4*, 17–36. (Ch. 14)

———, J. B. Orlos, and J. R. Knapp. 1976. "Physical Attractiveness, Body Attitudes, and Self-Concept in Late Adolescence." *Adolescence, 11*, 313–326. (Ch. 14)

Leroux, C. 1981. *The Silent Epidemic*. Chicago: Alzheimer's Disease and Related Disorders Assn. (Ch. 18)

Lesgold, A., L. B. Resnick, and K. Hammond. 1985. "Learning to Read." In *Reading Research*, ed. T. G. Waller and G. E. MacKinnon, vol. 4, 107–138. NY: Academic Pr. (Ch. 12)

Lester, B. M., K. Kotelchuck, E. Spelke, M. J. Sellers, and R. E. Klein. 1974. "Separation Protest in Guatemalan Infants." *Developmental Psychology, 10*, 79–85. (Ch. 8)

Levine, A. S. 1982. "The Epidemic of Acquired Immune Dysfunction in Homosexual Men and Its Sequelae." *Cancer Treatment Reports, 66*, 1391–1395. (Ch. 15)

Levinson, D. J., C. N. Darrow, E. B. Klein, M. H. Levinson, and B. McKee. 1978. *The Seasons of a Man's Life*. NY: Knopf. (Chs. 1, 15, 17, 19)

Levitt, M. J., T. G. Antonucci, and M. C. Clark. 1984. "Object-Person Permanence and Attachment." *Merrill-Palmer Quarterly, 30*, 1–10. (Ch. 8)

Levy, R. I., and J. Moskowitz. 1982. "Cardiovascular Research." *Science, 217*, 121–129. (Ch. 20)

Levy, S. M., L. R. Derogatis, D. Gallagher, and M. Gatz. 1980. "Intervention with Older Adults and the Evaluation of Outcome." In *Aging in the 1980s*, ed. L. W. Poon, 41–61. Washington, DC: Amer. Psychological Assn. (Ch. 19)

Lewis, M. 1971. "Social Interaction in the First Days of Life." In *The Origins of Human Social Relations*, ed. H. R. Schaffer. NY: Academic Pr. (Ch. 8)

———, and J. Brooks-Gunn. 1979. *Social Cognition and the Acquisition of Self*. NY: Plenum Pr. (Ch. 8)

———, ———, and J. Jaskir. 1985. "Individual Differences in Self-Recognition as a Function of the Mother-Infant Attachment Relationship." *Developmental Psychology, 21*, 1181–1187. (Ch. 8)

Liben, L. S. and B. Belknap. 1981. "Intellectual Realism." *Child Development, 52*, 921–924. (Ch. 11)

Liberman, I. Y., D. Shankweiler, F. W. Fischer, and B. Carter. 1974. "Explicit Syllable and Phoneme Segmentation in the Young Child." *Journal of Experimental Child Psychology, 18*, 201–212. (Ch. 12)

Licht, B. G., and C. S. Dweck. 1984. "Determinants of Academic Achievement." *Developmental Psychology, 20*, 628–638. (Ch. 10)

Lieberman, L., and L. Lieberman. 1986. "Husband-Wife Interaction in Second Careers." *Journal of Family Issues, 7*, 215–229. (Ch. 17)

Lieberman, M. A. 1983. "Social Contexts of Depression." In *Depression and Aging*, ed. L. D. Breslau and M. R. Haug, 121–133. NY: Springer. (Ch. 19)

———, and S. Tobin. 1983. *The Experience of Old Age*. NY: Basic. (Chs. 19, 20)

Lieblum, S., G. Bachmann, E. Kemmann, D. Colburn, and L. Swartzman. 1983. "Vaginal Atrophy in the Postmenopausal Woman."

Journal of the American Medical Association, 249, 2195–2198. (Ch. 17)

Lifton, R. J. 1971. *History and Human Survival.* NY: Vintage. (Ch. 20)

Linde, E. V., B. A. Morrongiello, and C. K. Rovee-Collier. 1985. "Determinants of Retention in 8-Week-Old Infants." *Developmental Psychology,* 21, 602–613. (Ch. 6)

Lindemann, E. 1944. "Symptomatology and Management of Acute Grief." *Journal of Psychiatry,* 101, 141–148.

Lipsitt, L. P. 1979. "Critical Conditions in Infancy." *American Psychologist,* 34, 973–980. (Ch. 5)

———, W. Q. Sturner, and B. Burke. 1979. "Perinatal Indicators and Subsequent Crib Death." *Infant Behavior and Development,* 2, 325–328. (Ch. 5)

Litwak, E. 1960. "Reference Group Theory, Bureaucratic Career and Neighborhood Primary Group Cohesion." *Sociometry,* 23, 72–84. (Ch. 19)

Loban, W. 1962. "Language Development." Research Report No. 18. Urbana, IL: Nat'l. Council of Teachers of English. (Ch. 12)

Long, T. J., and L. Long. 1982. *Latchkey Children.* Washington, DC: Catholic Univ. of America. (ERIC Document Reproduction Service No. ED 211 229). (Ch. 9)

Lopata, H. Z. 1973. *Widowhood in an American City.* Cambridge: Schenkman. (Ch. 19)

Lorenz, K. 1942–1943. "Die Angeborenen former möglicher Ehfahrung." *Zeitschrift für Tierpsychologie,* 5, 239–409. (Ch. 2)

Lounsbury, M. L., and J. E. Bates. 1982. "The Cries of Infants of Differing Levels of Perceived Temperamental Qualities." *Child Development,* 53, 677–686. (Ch. 4)

Lovejoy, C. O. 1981. "The Origin of Man." *Science,* 211, 341–350. (Ch. 5)

Lowenthal, M. F., and D. Chiriboga. 1972. "Transition to the Empty Nest." *Archives of General Psychiatry,* 26, 8–14. (Ch. 17)

———, and C. Haven. 1968. "Interaction and Adaptation." *American Sociological Review,* 33, 20–31. (Ch. 19)

Lütkenhaus, P., K. E. Grossmann, and K. Grossmann. 1985. "Infant-Mother Attachment at 12 Months and Style of Interaction with a Stranger at the Age of 3 Years." *Child Development,* 56, 1538–1542. (Ch. 8)

Lynn, D. B., and W. L. Sawrey. 1959. "The Effects of Father Absence on Norwegian Boys and Girls." *Journal of Abnormal and Social Psychology,* 59, 258–262. (Ch. 9)

Lynn, R. 1982. "IQ in Japan and the United States Shows a Growing Disparity." *Nature,* 297, 222-223. (Ch. 12)

Lyons, R. D. 1983. "Sex in America." *New York Times,* Nov. 15, A1ff. (Ch. 13)

Maccoby, E. E., and J. A. Martin. 1983. "Socialization in the Context of the Family." In *Handbook of Child Psychology,* 4th ed., ed. P. H. Mussen, vol. 4, 1–101. NY: Wiley. (Ch. 9)

MacDonald, K. 1985. "Early Experience, Relative Plasticity, and Social Development." *Developmental Review,* 5, 99–121. (Ch. 8)

MacKinnon, C. E., G. H. Brody, and Z. Stoneman. 1982. "The Effects of Divorce and Maternal Employment on the Home Environment of Preschool Children." *Child Development,* 53, 1392–1399. (Ch. 9)

Macklin, E. D. 1978. "Review of Research on Nonmarital Cohabitation in the United States." In *Exploring Intimate Life Styles,* ed.

B. I. Murstein, 197–243. NY: Springer. (Ch. 15)

———. 1980. "Nontraditional Family Forms." *Journal of Marriage and the Family,* 42, 905–922. (Ch. 15, 17)

Macnamara, J. 1972. "Cognitive Basis of Language Learning in Infants." *Psychological Review,* 79, 1–13. (Ch. 7)

Madden, D. J. 1983. "Aging and Distraction by Highly Familiar Stimuli during Visual Search." *Developmental Psychology,* 19, 499–507. (Ch. 18)

———. 1985. "Adult Age Differences in Memory-Driven Selective Attention." *Developmental Psychology,* 21, 654–665. (Ch. 18)

Maddox, G. L., and R. T. Campbell. 1985. "Scope, Concepts, and Methods in the Study of Aging." In *Handbook of Aging and the Social Sciences,* 2nd ed., ed. R. H. Binstock and E. Shanas, 3–31. NY: Van Nostrand Reinhold. (Ch. 19)

Maeroff, G. I. 1985. "Regents to Let Girls Compete with Boys in the Contact Sports." *New York Times,* Nov. 15, A1ff. (Ch. 13)

Magnusson, D., H. Stattin, and V. L. Allen. 1985. "Biological Maturation and Social Development." *Journal of Youth and Adolescence,* 14, 267–284. (Ch. 13)

Main, M., and C. George. 1985. "Responses of Abused and Disadvantaged Toddlers to Distress in Agemates." *Developmental Psychology,* 21, 407–412. (Chs. 1, 9)

———, and D. R. Weston. 1981. "The Quality of the Toddler's Relationship to Mother and to Father." *Child Development,* 52, 932–940. (Ch. 8)

Malina, R. M. 1979. "Secular Changes in Size and Maturity." In *Monographs of the Society for Research in Child Development,* ed. A. F. Roche, no. 179, 59–102. (Ch. 13)

Maloney, M. J., and W. M. Klykylo. 1983. "An Overview of Anorexia Nervosa, Bulimia, and Obesity in Children and Adolescents." *Journal of the American Academy of Child Psychiatry,* 22, 99–197. (Ch. 14)

Mamay, P. D., and R. L. Simpson. 1981. "Three Female Roles in Commercials." *Sex Roles,* 7, 1223–1232. (Ch. 10)

Manton, K. G., I. C. Siegler, and M. A. Woodbury. 1986. "Patterns of Intellectual Development in Later Life." *Journal of Gerontology,* 41, 486–499. (Ch. 16)

Maratsos, M. P. 1973. "Nonegocentric Communication Abilities in Preschool Children." *Child Development,* 44, 697–700. (Ch. 11)

———. 1983. "Some Current Issues in the Study of the Acquisition of Grammar." In *Handbook of Child Psychology,* 4th ed., ed. P. H. Mussen, vol. 3, 705–786. NY: Wiley. (Ch. 7)

Marcia, J. E. 1980. "Identity in Adolescence." In *Handbook of Adolescent Psychology,* ed. J. Adelson, 159–187. NY: Wiley-Interscience. (Ch. 13)

Marcus, T. L., and D. A. Corsini. 1978. "Parental Expectations of Preschool Children as Related to Child Gender and Socioeconomic Status." *Child Development,* 49, 245–246. (Ch. 10)

Markman, E. M. 1981. "Two Different Principles of Conceptual Organization." In *Advances in Developmental Psychology,* ed. M. E. Lamb and A. L. Brown, vol. 1, 199–236. Hillsdale, NJ: Lawrence Erlbaum Assoc. (Ch. 11)

Marsh, G. R., and L. W. Thompson. 1977.

"Psychophysiology of Aging." In *Handbook of the Psychology of Aging,* ed. J. E. Birren and K. W. Schaie, 219–248. NY: Van Nostrand Reinhold. (Ch. 18)

Marsh, H. W. 1986. "Self-Serving Effect (Bias?) in Academic Attributions." *Journal of Educational Psychology,* 78, 190–200. (Ch. 12)

Marshall, V. W. 1980. *Last Chapters.* Monterey, CA: Brooks/Cole. (Ch. 20)

Masters, J. C., and W. Furman. 1981. "Popularity, Individual Friendship, and Specific Peer Interaction among Children." *Developmental Psychology,* 17, 344–350. (Ch. 10)

Masters, W. H., and V. E. Johnson. 1974. "Emotional Poverty." In American Medical Association, *The Quality of Life.* 101–108. Acton, MA: Publishing Sciences Group. (Ch. 17)

Masur, E. F., C. W. McIntyre, and J. H. Flavell. 1973. "Developmental Changes in Apportionment of Study Time among Items in a Multitrial Free Recall Task." *Journal of Experimental Child Psychology,* 15, 237–246. (Ch. 11)

Matas, L., R. Arend, and L. A. Sroufe. 1978. "Continuity of Adaptation in the Second Year." *Child Development,* 49, 547–556. (Ch. 8)

Matthews, S. H., and J. Sprey. 1985. "Adolescents' Relationships with Grandparents." *Journal of Gerontology,* 40, 621–626. (Ch. 19)

Matthews, W. S. 1977. "Sex Role Perception, Portrayal, and Preference in the Fantasy Play of Young Children." Paper presented at the biennial meeting of the Society for Research in Child Devt. New Orleans, Mar. (Ch. 6)

Maurer, D., and P. Salapatek. 1976. "Developmental Changes in the Scanning of Faces by Infants." *Child Development,* 47, 523–527. (Ch. 6)

Mazess, R. B., and S. H. Forman. 1979. "Longevity and Age Exaggeration in Vilcabamba, Ecuador." *Journal of Gerontology,* 34, 94–98. (Ch. 20)

McAdoo, H. P. 1982. "Stress Absorbing Systems in Black Families." *Family Relations,* 32, 479–488. (Ch. 10)

McCabe, M. P., and J. K. Collins. 1979. "Sex Roles and Dating Orientation." *Journal of Youth and Adolescence,* 8, 407–424. (Ch. 13)

McCall, R. B. 1979. *Infants.* Cambridge: Harvard Univ. Pr. (Ch. 4)

———. 1984. "Developmental Changes in Mental Performance." *Child Development,* 55, 1317–1321. (Ch. 12)

McCarthy, D. 1954. "Language Development in Children." In *Manual of Child Psychology,* 2nd ed., ed. L. Carmichael. NY: Wiley. (Ch. 7)

McCartney, K., S. Scarr, D. Phillips, and S. Grajek. 1985. "Day Care as Intervention." *Journal of Applied Developmental Psychology,* 6, 247–260. (Ch. 8)

McClelland, J. L., and R. E. Rumelhart. 1981. "An Interactive Model of the Effect of Context in Perception." *Psychological Review,* 88, 375–407. (Ch. 12)

McCluskey, K. A., J. Killarney, and D. R. Papini. 1983. "Adolescent Pregnancy and Parenthood." In *Life-Span Developmental Psychology: Nonnormative Events,* eds. E. J. Callahan and K. A. McCluskey, 69–113. NY: Academic Press. (Ch. 14)

McCord, W., and J. McCord. 1959. *Origins of Crime.* NY: Columbia Univ. Pr. (Ch. 14)

McCrae, R. R., and P. T. Costa, Jr. 1984. *Emerging Lives, Enduring Dispositions*. Boston: Little, Brown. (Ch. 17)

McGraw, M. B. 1935. *Growth*. NY: Appleton-Century-Crofts. (Ch. 5)

————. 1939. "Later Development of Children Specially Trained during Infancy." *Child Development, 10,* 1–19. (Ch. 5)

McGuinness, D. 1985. *When Children Don't Learn*. NY: Basic. (Ch. 9)

McGuire, K. D., and J. R. Weisz. 1982. "Social Cognition and Behavior Correlates of Preadolescent Chumship." *Child Development, 53,* 1478–1484. (Ch. 10)

McKenna, J. J. 1983. "Sudden Infant Death Syndrome in an Anthropological Context." Paper presented at the World Congress of Infant Psychiatry. Cannes, Apr. (Ch. 5)

McKeown, T. 1978. "Determinants of Health," *Human Nature, 1,* Apr. 60–67. (Ch. 20)

McNeill, D. 1970. *The Acquisition of Language*. NY: Harper & Row. (Ch. 7)

Mead, M. [1928] 1968. *Coming of Age in Samoa*. Reprint. NY: Dell. (Ch. 1)

————, and N. Newton. 1967. "Cultural Patterning of Perinatal Behavior." In *Childbearing*, ed. S. A. Richardson and A. F. Guttmacher. Baltimore: Williams & Wilkins. (Ch. 3)

Meadow, K. P. 1978. "The 'Natural History' of a Research Project as Illustration of Methodological Issues in Research with Deaf Children." In *Deaf Children*, ed. L. S. Liben, 21–40. NY: Academic Pr. (Ch. 4)

Medrich, E. A., J. Roizen, and V. Rubin. 1982. *The Serious Business of Growing Up*. Berkeley: Univ. of CA Pr. (Ch. 9)

Medvedev, Z. A. 1974. "Caucasus and Altay Longevity." *Gerontologist, 14,* 381–387. (Ch. 20)

Meltzoff, A. N. 1985. "Immediate and Deferred Imitation in 14- and 24-Month-Old Infants." *Child Development, 56,* 62–72. (Ch. 6)

————, and M. K. Moore. 1977. "Imitation of Facial and Manual Gestures by Human Neonates." *Science, 198,* 75–78. (Ch. 6)

————, and ————. 1983. "Newborn Infants Imitate Adult Facial Gestures." *Child Development, 54,* 702–709. (Ch. 6)

Menken, J., J. Trussell, and U. Larsen. 1986. "Age and Infertility." *Science, 233,* 1389–1394. (Ch. 17)

Menkes, J. H. 1980. *Textbook of Child Neurology*. Philadelphia: Lea & Febiger. (Ch. 4)

Menyuk, P. 1971. *The Acquisition and Development of Language*. Englewood Cliffs, NJ: Prentice-Hall. (Ch. 7)

————, and N. Bernholtz. 1969. "Prosodic Features and Children's Language Production." *MIT Research Laboratory of Electronics Quarterly Progress Reports, 93,* 216–219. (Ch. 7)

Meredith, H. V. 1963. "Change in the Stature and Body Weight of North American Boys during the Last 80 Years." In *Advances in Child Development and Behavior*, ed. L. P. Lipsitt and C. C. Spiker, vol. 1, 69–114. NY: Academic Pr. (Ch. 5)

————. 1984. "Body Size of Infants and Children around the World in Relation to Socioeconomic Status." In *Advances in Child Development and Behavior*. ed. H. W. Reese, vol. 18, 81–145. Orlando, FL: Academic Pr. (Ch. 5)

Messenger, L. 1976. "Remarriage between Divorced People with Children from Previous Marriages." *Journal of Marriage and Family Counseling, 2,* 193–200. (Ch. 15)

Meyer, B. 1980. "The Development of Girls' Sex-Role Attitudes." *Child Development, 52,* 508–514. (Ch. 9)

Michaels, G. Y., M. L. Hoffman, and W. Goldberg. 1982. Paper presented at the annual meeting of the Amer. Psychological Assn. Aug., Washington, DC. (Ch. 15)

Michaels, R. H., and G. W. Mellin. 1960. "Prospective Experience with Maternal Rubella and the Associated Congenital Malformations." *Pediatrics, 26,* 200–209. (Ch. 3)

Michel, G. F. 1981. "Right-Handedness." *Science, 212,* 685–687. (Ch. 5)

————, D. A. Harkins, and M. R. Ovrut. 1986. "Assessing Infant (6–13 Months Old) Handedness Status." Paper presented at 5th Internat'l. Conference on Infant Studies. Los Angeles, Apr. (Ch. 5)

Miernyk, W. H. 1975. "The Changing Life Cycle of Work." In *Life-Span Developmental Psychology*, ed. N. Datan and L. H. Ginsberg, 279–286. NY: Academic Pr. (Ch. 19)

Migdal, S., R. P. Abeles, and L. R. Sherrod. 1981. *An Inventory of Longitudinal Studies of Middle and Old Age*. NY: Social Science Research Council. (Ch. 1)

Miller, N. E., and J. Dollard. 1941. *Social Learning and Imitation*. New Haven, CT: Yale Univ. Pr. (Ch. 2)

Miller, P. H., and L. Bigi. 1979. "The Development of Children's Understanding of Attention." *Merrill-Palmer Quarterly, 2,* 235–250. (Ch. 11)

————, F. S. Kessel, and J. H. Flavell. 1970. "Thinking about People Thinking about People Thinking about . . ." *Child Development, 41,* 613–623. (Ch. 11)

Miller, P. Y., and W. E. Simon. 1980. "The Development of Sexuality in Adolescence." In *Handbook of Adolescent Psychology*, ed. J. Adelson, 383–407. NY: Wiley-Interscience. (Ch. 13)

Miller, S. A. 1986. "Certainty and Necessity in the Understanding of Piagetian Concepts." *Developmental Psychology, 22,* 3–18. (Ch. 11)

Mills, C. J. 1981. "Sex Roles, Personality, and Intellectual Abilities in Adolescents." *Journal of Youth and Adolescence, 10,* 85–112. (Ch. 13)

Minuchin, P. 1985. "Families and Individual Development." *Child Development, 56,* 289–302. (Ch. 9)

————, and E. K. Shapiro. 1983. "The School as a Context for Social Development." In *Handbook of Child Psychology*, 4th ed., ed. P. H. Mussen, vol. 4, 197–274. NY: Wiley. (Ch. 10)

Mischel, H. N., and W. Mischel. 1983. "The Development of Children's Knowledge of Self-Control Strategies." *Child Development, 54,* 603–619. (Ch. 11)

Miscione, J. L., R. S. Marvin, R. G. O'Brien, and M. T. Greenberg. 1978. "A Developmental Study of Preschool Children's Understanding of the Words 'Know' and 'Guess.'" *Child Development, 49,* 1107–1113. (Ch. 7)

Mitchell, D. B., and M. Perlmutter. 1986. "Semantic Activation and Episodic Memory." *Developmental Psychology, 22,* 86–94. (Ch. 18)

Mittenthal, S. 1984. "Amniocentesis." *New York Times*, Aug. 22, C1ff. (Ch. 3)

Money, J., and A. A. Ehrhardt. 1972. *Man & Woman; Boy & Girl*. Baltimore: Johns Hopkins Univ. Pr. (Ch. 9)

Moore, K. A. 1985. "Teenage Pregnancy." *New Perspectives*, Summer, 11–15. (Ch. 14)

Moore, T. W. 1975. "Exclusive Early Mothering and Its Alternatives." *Scandinavian Journal of Psychology, 16,* 256–272. (Ch. 9)

Moos, R. H., and S. Lemke. 1985. "Specialized Living Environments for Older People." In *Handbook of the Psychology of Aging*, 2nd ed., ed. J. E. Birren and K. W. Schaie, 864–889. NY: Van Nostrand Reinhold. (Ch. 19)

Morales, R. V., V. J. Shute, and J. W. Pellegrino. 1985. "Developmental Differences in Understanding and Solving Simple Word Problems." *Cognition and Instruction, 2,* 41–57. (Ch. 12)

Morison, R. S. 1971. "Death." *Science, 173,* 694–702. (Ch. 20)

Morsbach, G., and C. Bunting. 1979. "Maternal Recognition of Their Neonates' Cries." *Developmental Medicine and Child Neurology, 21,* 178–185. (Ch. 4)

Mortimer, J. T., M. D. Finch, and D. Kumka. 1982. "Persistence and Change in Development." In *Life-Span Development and Behavior*, ed. P. B. Baltes and O. G. Brim, Jr., vol. 4, 263–313. NY: Academic Pr. (Ch. 15)

Moss, M. S., S. Z. Moss, and E. L. Moles. 1985. "The Quality of Relationships between Elderly Parents and Their Out-of-Town Children." *Gerontologist, 25,* 134–140. (Ch. 19)

Muir, D., and J. Field. 1979. "Newborn Infants Orient to Sounds." *Child Development, 50,* 431–436. (Ch. 4)

Mukherjee, A. M., and G. D. Hodgen. 1982. "Maternal Ethanol Exposure Induces Transient Impairment of Umbilical Circulation and Fetal Hypoxia in Monkeys." *Science, 218,* 700–702. (Ch. 3)

Myers, G. C., and K. G. Manton. 1984. "Recent Changes in the US Age at Death Distribution." *Gerontologist, 24,* 572–575. (Ch. 20)

Myers, M., and S. G. Paris. 1978. "Children's Metacognitive Knowledge about Reading." *Journal of Educational Psychology, 70,* 680–690. (Chs. 11, 12)

Nakamura, C. Y., and D. N. Finck. 1980. "Relative Effectiveness of Socially Oriented and Task-Oriented Children and Predictability of Their Behaviors." *Monographs of the Society for Research in Child Development, 45,* no. 185. (Ch. 10)

National Assessment of Educational Progress. 1985. *The Reading Report Card*. ETS Report 15-R-01. Princeton, NJ: Educ. Testing Service. (Chs. 12, 16)

Navelet, Y., C. Payan, A. Guilhaume, and O. Benoit. 1984. "Nocturnal Sleep Organization in Infants 'At Risk' for Sudden Infant Death Syndrome." *Pediatric Research, 18,* 654–657. (Ch. 5)

Neill, S. R. St.-J. 1976. "Aggressive and Nonaggressive Fighting in 12- to 13-Year-old Preadolescent Boys." *Journal of Child Psychology and Psychiatry, 17,* 213–220. (Ch. 10)

Neimark, E. D. 1982. "Adolescent Thought." In *Handbook of Developmental Psychology*, ed. B. B. Wolman, pp. 486–502. Englewood Cliffs, NJ: Prentice-Hall. (Ch. 13)

Nelson, J., and F. E. Aboud. 1985. "The Resolution of Social Conflict between Friends." *Child Development, 56,* 1009–1017. (Ch. 10)

Nelson, L. D., and C. C. Nelson. 1975. "A Factor Analytic Inquiry into the Multidimensionality of Death Anxiety." *Omega, 6,* 171–178. (Ch. 20)

Nesselroade, J. R., K. W. Schaie, and P. B. Baltes. 1972. "Ontogenetic and Generational Components of Structural and Quantitative Change in Adult Behavior." *Journal of Gerontology, 27,* 222–228. (Ch. 1)

Neugarten, B. L. 1970. "Adaptation and the Life Cycle." *Journal of Geriatric Psychiatry, 4,* 71–87. (Ch. 17)

———. 1979. "Time, Age, and the Life Cycle." *American Journal of Psychiatry, 136,* 887–894. (Ch. 15)

———, and L. Brown-Rezanka. 1978. "A Midlife Woman in the 1980s." In US House of Representatives. Select Committee on Aging and Subcommittee on Retirement Income and Employment. *Women in Midlife,* part 1, 24–38. Washington, DC: US Gov't. Printing Office. (Ch. 19)

———. Interview by E. Hall. 1987. "Acting One's Age." In E. Hall, *Growing and Changing,* 113–127. NY: Random House. (Chs. 1, 19)

———, V. Wood, R. J. Kraines, and B. Loomis. 1963. "Women's Attitudes toward the Menopause." *Vita Humana, 6,* 140–151. (Ch. 17)

Newcomb, A. F., and W. M. Bukowski. 1984. "A Longitudinal Study of the Utility of Social Preference and Social Impact of Sociometric Classification Schemes." *Child Development, 55,* 1434–1447. (Ch. 10)

Newell, G. 1984. "Learning from Writing in Two Content Areas." *Research in the Teaching of English, 18,* 265–287. (Ch. 12)

New York Times. 1983. "A Sense of History." Jun. 9. (Ch. 18)

———. 1984. "Study Shows Births Up in Women in Their 30s." May 9, C8. (Ch. 15)

———. 1985a. "Infant Death Data Indicate High Risk Groups." Nov. 17, 21. (Ch. 5)

———. 1985b. "Young Unwed Mothers Learn a Trade." June 26, C1ff. (Ch. 14)

———. 1986a. "Marriage Rate Hits Low Mark." May 8, C11. (Ch. 15)

———. 1986b. "Report Asks States to Set Smoking Age at 18." Nov. 21, A18. (Ch. 13)

Nichols, M., and S. R. Lieblum. 1983. "Lesbianism as Personal Identity and Social Role." Unpublished manuscript. Rutgers University. (Ch. 15)

Nielsen Television Index. 1982. *National Audience Demographics Report.* Northbrook, IL: A. C. Nielsen. (Ch. 10)

Nieschlag, E., U. Lammers, C. W. Freischem, and E. J. Wicklings. 1982. "Reproductive Functions in Young Fathers and Grandfathers." *Journal of Clinical Endocrinological Metabolism, 55,* 676–681. (Ch. 17)

Ninio, A. 1983. "Joint Book Reading as a Multiple Vocabulary Acquisition Device." *Developmental Psychology, 19,* 445–451. (Ch. 6)

Nold, E. 1980. "Revising." In *Writing,* ed. C. Frederiksen, M. Whiteman, and J. Dominic. Hillsdale, NY: Lawrence Erlbaum Assoc. (Ch. 12)

Notman, M. 1980. "Adult Life Cycles." In *The Psychobiology of Sex Differences and Sex Roles,* ed. J. E. Parsons, 209–224. NY: McGraw-Hill. (Ch. 17)

Nowak, C. A. 1977. "Does Youthfulness Equal Attractiveness?" In *Looking Ahead,* ed.

L. E. Troll, J. Israel, and K. Israel, 59–64. Englewood Cliffs, NJ: Prentice-Hall. (Ch. 17)

O'Brien, D. H., A. R. Schneider, and H. Traviesas. 1980. "Portraying Abuse." In *Child Abuse,* ed. G. Gerbner, C. J. Ross, and E. Zigler, 231–238. NY: Oxford University Pr. (Ch. 9)

Ochs, E. 1979. "Introduction." In *Developmental Pragmatics,* ed. E. Ochs and B. B. Schieffelin, 1–17. NY: Academic Pr. (Ch. 7)

Offer, D., and P. C. Hollinger. 1983. "Toward the Prediction of Violent Deaths among the Young." Paper presented at the meeting of the Amer. Assn. for the Advancement of Science. Detroit, May. (Ch. 14)

———, and J. B. Offer. 1975. *From Teenage to Young Manhood.* NY: Basic. (Ch. 13)

———, E. Ostrov, and K. I. Howard. 1981a. *The Adolescent.* NY: Basic. (Chs. 13, 14)

———, ———, and ———. 1981b. "The Mental Health Professional's Concept of the Normal Adolescent." *Archives of General Psychiatry, 38,* 149. (Ch. 14)

———, ———, and ———. 1982. "Values and Self-Conceptions Held by Normal and Delinquent Males." *Journal of Psychiatric Treatment and Evaluation, 4,* 503–509. (Ch. 14)

———, ———, and ———. 1984. "Epidemiology of Mental Health and Mental Illness among Adolescents." In *Significant Advances in Child Psychiatry,* ed. J. Call. NY: Basic Books. (Ch. 14)

———, and M. Sabshin. 1984. *Normality and the Life Cycle.* NY: Basic. (Ch. 13)

O'Hara, M. W., J. V. Hinrichs, F. J. Kohout, R. B. Wallace, and J. H. Lemke. 1986. "Memory Complaint and Memory Performance in the Depressed Elderly." *Psychology and Aging, 1,* 208–214. (Ch. 18)

Olsho, L. W., S. W. Harkins, and M. L. Lenhardt. 1985. "Aging and the Auditory System." In *Handbook of the Psychology of Aging,* 2nd ed., ed. J. E. Birren and K. W. Schaie, 322–377. NY: Van Nostrand Reinhold. (Ch. 18)

Olson, G. M., and T. Sherman. 1983. "Attention, Learning, and Memory in Infants." In *Handbook of Child Psychology,* 4th ed., ed. P. H. Mussen, vol. 2, 1002–1080. NY: Wiley. (Chs. 4, 6)

Omenn, G. S. 1983. "Medical Genetics, Genetic Counseling, and Behavior Genetics." In *Behavior Genetics,* ed. J. L. Fuller and E. C. Simmel, 155–216. Hillsdale, NJ: Lawrence Erlbaum Assoc. (Chs. 3, 17)

Ornstein, P. A., R. G. Medina, B. P. Stone, and M. J. Naus. 1985. "Retrieving for Rehearsal." *Developmental Psychology, 21,* 633–641. (Ch. 1)

———, and M. J. Naus. 1978. "Rehearsal Processes in Children's Memory." In *Memory Development in Children,* ed. P. A. Ornstein, 69–100. Hillsdale, NJ: Lawrence Erlbaum Assoc. (Ch. 11)

Osberg, J. W., G. J. Mears, and D. McKee, and G. B. Burnett. 1982. "Intellectual Functioning in Renal Failure and Chronic Dialysis." *Journal of Chronic Disease, 35,* 445–457. (Ch. 16)

Oski, F. A., A. S. Honig, B. Helu, and P. Howanitz. 1983. "Effect of Iron Therapy on Behavior Performance in Nonanemic, Iron

Deficient Children." *Journal of Pediatrics, 71,* 877–880. (Ch. 5)

Osofsky, J. D., and K. Connors. 1979. "Mother-Infant Interaction." In *Handbook of Infant Development,* ed. J. D. Osofsky, 519–548. NY: Wiley-Interscience. (Ch. 4)

———, and H. J. Osofsky. 1984. "Psychological and Developmental Perspectives on Expectant and New Parenthood." In *Review of Child Development Research,* ed. R. D. Parke, vol. 7, 372–397. Chicago: Univ. of Chicago Pr. (Ch. 15)

Paffenbarger, R. S., Jr., S. H. King, and A. L. Wing. 1969. "Characteristics in Youth that Predispose to Suicide and Accidental Death in Later Life." *American Journal of Public Health, 59,* 900–908. (Ch. 14)

Palincsar, A. S., and A. L. Brown. 1984. "Reciprocal Teaching of Comprehension-Fostering and Comprehension-Monitoring Devices." *Cognition and Instruction, 1,* 117–175. (Ch. 2)

Palmore, E. B. 1970. "The Effects of Aging on Activity and Attitudes." In *Normal Aging,* ed. E. Palmore. Durham, NC: Duke Univ. Pr. (Ch. 19)

———. 1974. "Health Practices and Illnesses." In *Normal Aging II,* ed. E. Palmore, 49–55. Durham, NC: Duke Univ. Pr. (Ch. 19)

———. 1977. "Facts on Aging." *Gerontologist, 17,* 315–320. (Ch. 18)

———. 1980. "The Facts on Aging Quiz." *Gerontologist, 20,* 669–672. (Ch. 18)

———. 1986. "Trends in the Health of the Aged." *Gerontologist, 26,* 298–302. (Ch. 19)

———, L. K. George, and G. G. Fillenbaum. 1982. "Predictors of Retirement." *Journal of Gerontology, 37,* 733–742. (Ch. 19)

———, and F. C. Jeffers, eds. 1971. *Prediction of Life Span.* Lexington, MA: Heath. (Ch. 20)

Papoušek, H., and M. Papoušek. 1984. "Learning and Cognition in the Everyday Life of Human Infants." In *Advances in the Study of Behavior,* vol. 14, 127–163. NY: Academic Pr. (Ch. 4)

Papoušek, M., H. Papoušek, and M. H. Bornstein. 1985. "The Naturalistic Vocal Environment of Young Infants." In *Social Perception in Infants,* ed. T. M. Field and N. Fox, 269–297. Norwood, NJ: Ablex. (Ch. 4)

Paris, S. G. 1978. "Coordination of Means and Goals in the Development of Mnemonic Skills." In *Memory Development in Children,* ed. P. A. Ornstein, 126–146. Hillsdale, NJ: Lawrence Erlbaum Assoc. (Ch. 11)

———, and D. R. Cross. 1983. "Ordinary Learning." In *Learning in Children,* ed. J. Bisanz, G. Bisanz, and R. Kail, 137–169. NY: Springer-Verlag. (Chs. 11, 12)

———, ———, and M. Y. Lipson. 1984. "Informed Strategies for Learning." *Journal of Educational Psychology, 76,* 1239–1252. (Ch. 12)

———, and J. E. Jacobs. 1984. "The Benefits of Informed Instruction for Children's Reading Awareness and Comprehension Skills." *Child Development, 55,* 2083–2093. (Ch. 12)

———, and B. K. Lindauer. 1977. "Constructive Processes in Children's Comprehension and Memory." In *Perspectives on the Development of Memory and Cognition,* ed. R. V. Kail and J. W. Hagen, 35–60. Hillsdale,

NJ: Lawrence Erlbaum Assoc. (Ch. 11)
————, and ————. 1982. "The Development of Cognitive Skills during Childhood." In *Handbook of Developmental Psychology*, ed. B. W. Wolman, 333–349. Englewood Cliffs, NJ: Prentice-Hall. (Chs. 2, 11)

————, M. Y. Lipson, and K. K. Wixson. 1983. "Becoming a Strategic Reader." *Contemporary Educational Psychology, 8*, 293–316. (Ch. 12)

————, R. S. Newman, and J. E. Jacobs. 1985. "Social Contexts and Functions of Children's Remembering." In *Cognitive Learning and Memory in Children*, ed. M. Pressley and C. J. Brainerd, 81–115. NY: Springer-Verlag. (Ch. 6)

————, ————, and K. A. McVey. 1982. "Learning the Functional Significance of Mnemonic Actions." *Journal of Experimental Child Psychology, 34*, 490–509. (Ch. 11)

————, and E. R. Oka. 1986. "Children's Reading Strategies." *Developmental Review, 6*, 25–56. (Chs. 11, 12)

Park, D. C., J. T. Puglisi, and A. D. Smith. 1986. "Memory for Pictures." *Psychology and Aging, 1*, 11–17. (Ch. 18)

Parke, R. D. 1981. *Fathers*. Cambridge: Harvard Univ. Pr. (Ch. 8)

————, and C. W. Collmer. 1975. "Child Abuse." In *Review of Child Development Research*, E. M. Hetherington, vol. 5, 509–590. Chicago: Univ. of Chicago Pr. (Ch. 9)

————, K. Grossmann, and B. R. Tinsley. 1981. "Father-Mother-Infant Interaction in the Newborn Period." In *Culture and Early Interaction*, ed. T. H. Field, A. M. Sostor, P. Vietze, and P. H. Leiderman, 95–113. Hillsdale, NJ: Lawrence Erlbaum Assoc. (Ch. 10)

————, and D. B. Sawin. 1976. "The Father's Role in Infancy." *Family Coordinator, 25*, 365–371. (Ch. 8)

————, and R. G. Slaby. 1983. "The Development of Aggression." In *Handbook of Child Psychology*, 4th ed., ed. P. H. Mussen, 547–641. NY: Wiley. (Ch. 10)

Parkes, C. M. 1972. *Bereavement*. NY: Internat'l. Univ. Pr. (Ch. 20)

————, and R. S. Weiss. 1983. *Recovery from Bereavement*. NY: Basic. (Ch. 20)

Parmelee, A. H., Jr. and M. D. Sigman. 1983. "Perinatal Brain Development and Behavior." In *Handbook of Child Psychology*, ed. P. H. Mussen, vol. 2, 96–155. NY: Wiley. (Chs. 4, 5)

Parnes, H. 1981. *Work and Retirement*. Cambridge: MIT Press. (Ch. 19)

Parten, M. B. 1932. "Social Participation among Preschool Children." *Journal of Abnormal Psychology, 27*, 243–269. (Ch. 10)

Pattison, E. M. 1977. *The Experience of Dying*. Englewood Cliffs, NJ: Prentice-Hall. (Ch. 20)

Pavlov, I. P. 1927. *Conditioned Reflexes*. London: Oxford Univ. Pr. (Ch. 2)

Pederson, F. 1975. "Mother, Father, and Infant as Interactive System." Paper presented at the annual meeting of the Amer. Psychological Assn. Denver, Sept. (Ch. 9)

Pederson, F. A., R. Cain, M. Zaslow, and B. Anderson. 1981. "Variations in Infant Experience Associated with Alternative Family Role Organization." In *Families as Learning Environments for Children*. ed. L. Laesa and I. Sigel. NY: Plenum Pr. (Ch. 8)

Perlez, J. 1986. "Nine New York High Schools Dispense Contraceptives to Their Students." *New York Times*, Oct. 6, A1ff. (Ch. 14)

Perlmutter, M. 1978. "What Is Memory Aging the Aging Of?" *Developmental Psychology, 14*, 330–345. (Ch. 18)

————. 1979. "Age Differences in Adults' Free Recall, Cued Recall, and Recognition." *Journal of Gerontology, 34*, 533–539. (Ch. 18)

————. 1980. "Development of Memory in the Preschool Years." In *Childhood Development*, ed. R. Greene and T. D. Yawkey, 3–27. Westport, CT: Technemic. (Ch. 6)

————. In press. "Continued Cognitive Potential Throughout Life." In *Theories of Aging*, ed. J. E. Birren and V. L. Bengston. (Ch. 16)

————, and E. Hall. 1985. *Adult Development and Aging*. NY: Wiley. (Chs. 15, 20)

Perry, D. G., and K. Bussey. 1984. *Social Development*. Englewood Cliffs, NJ: Prentice-Hall. (Chs. 9, 10)

Peters, M. F. 1981. "Parenting in Black Families with Young Children." In *Black Families*, ed. H. P. McAdoo, 211–224. Beverly Hills, CA: Sage. (Ch. 10)

Petersen, A. C. 1985. "Pubertal Development as a Cause of Disturbance." *Genetic, Social, and General Psychology Monographs, 111*, 205–232. (Ch. 13)

————, and B. Taylor. 1980. "The Biological Approach to Adolescence." In *Handbook of Adolescent Psychology*, ed. J. Adelson, 117–155. NY: Wiley-Interscience. (Ch. 13)

Peterson, J. A. 1980. "Social-Psychological Aspects of Death and Dying and Mental Health." In *Handbook of Mental Health and Aging*, ed. J. E. Birren and R. B. Sloane, 922–942. Englewood Cliffs, NJ: Prentice-Hall. (Ch. 20)

Pfeiffer, E., and G. C. Davis. 1972. "Determinants of Sexual Behavior in Middle and Old Age." *Journal of the American Geriatrics Society, 20*, 151–158. (Ch. 17)

————, A. Verwoerdt, and G. C. Davis. 1972. "Sexual Behavior in Middle Life." *American Journal of Psychiatry, 128*, 1261–1267. (Ch. 19)

Piaget, J. 1929. *The Child's Conception of the World*. NY: Harcourt, Brace. (Ch. 11)

————. 1930. *The Child's Conception of Physical Causality*. London: Kegan, Paul. (Ch. 11)

————. [1932] 1965. *The Moral Judgment of the Child*. NY: Free Press. (Ch. 11)

————. 1951. *Play, Dreams and Imitation in Childhood*. NY: Norton. (Chs. 1, 6, 11)

————. 1952. *The Origins of Intelligence in Children*. NY: Internat'l. Univ. Pr. (Chs. 6, 13)

————. 1954. *The Construction of Reality in the Child*. NY: Basic. (Ch. 6)

————. 1965. *The Child's Conception of Number*. NY: Norton. (Ch. 11)

————. 1968. *On the Development of Memory and Identity*. Barre, MA: Clark Univ. Pr. (Ch. 6)

————. 1976. *The Psychology of Intelligence*. Totowa, NJ: Littlefield, Adams. (Ch. 12)

————, and B. Inhelder. 1941. *Le Developpement des Quantities Chez L'Enfant*. Neuchâtel: Delachaux et Niestle. (Ch. 11)

————, and ————. 1969. *The Psychology of the Child*. NY: Basic. (Ch. 11)

————, and ————. 1973. *Memory and Intelligence*. NY: Basic. (Ch. 11)

Pick, A. D, and G. W. Frankel. 1973. "A Study of Strategies of Visual Attention in Children." *Developmental Psychology, 4*, 348–357. (Ch. 11)

Pillow, B. H., and J. H. Flavell. 1985. "Intellectual Realism." *Child Development, 56*, 664–670. (Ch. 6)

Pine, V. R. 1975. *Caretaker of the Dead*. NY: Irvington. (Ch. 20)

Pintrich, P. R., and P. C. Blumenfeld. 1985. "Classroom Experience and Children's Self-Perceptions of Ability, Effort, and Conduct." *Journal of Educational Psychology, 77*, 646–657. (Ch. 12)

Plomin, R., J. C. DeFries, and G. E. McClearn. 1980. *Behavior Genetics*. San Francisco: Freeman. (Ch. 12)

Pollins, L. D. 1983. "The Effects of Acceleration on the Social and Emotional Development of Gifted Students." In *Academic Precocity*, ed. C. P. Benbow and J. C. Stanley, 139–159. Baltimore: Johns Hopkins Univ. Pr. (Ch. 12)

Pollitt, E., C. Garza, and R. L. Leibel. 1984. "Nutrition and Public Policy." In *Child Development Research and Social Policy*, ed. H. W. Stevenson and A. E. Siegel, vol. 1, 421–470. Chicago: Univ. of Chicago Pr. (Ch. 5)

Poon, L. W. 1985. "Differences in Human Memory with Aging." In *Handbook of the Psychology of Aging*, 2nd ed., ed. J. E. Birren and K. W. Schaie, 427–462. NY: Van Nostrand Reinhold. (Ch. 18)

Post, F. 1980. "Paranoid, Schizophrenia-like, and Schizophrenic States in the Aged." In *Handbook of Mental Health and Aging*, ed. J. E. Birren and R. B. Sloane, 591–615. Englewood Cliffs, NJ: Prentice-Hall. (Ch. 18)

Powell, G. F., J. A. Brasel, and R. M. Blizzard. 1967. "Emotional Deprivation and Growth Retardation Simulating Idiopathic Hypopituitarism." *New England Journal of Medicine, 276*, 1271–1278. (Ch. 5)

Prader, A., J. M. Tanner, and G. A. von Harnack. 1963. "Catch-up Growth Following Illness or Starvation." *Journal of Paediatrics, 62*, 646–659. (Ch. 5)

Prechtl, H. F. R. 1982. "Regressions and Transformations during Neurological Development." In *Regressions in Mental Development*, ed. T. G. Bever, 103–116. Hillsdale, NJ: Lawrence Erlbaum Assoc. (Ch. 4)

Price, G. G. 1984. "Mnemonic Support and Curriculum Selection in Teaching by Mothers." *Child Development, 55*, 659–668. (Ch. 6)

Pulkkinen, L. 1983. "Youthful Smoking and Drinking in a Longitudinal Perspective." *Journal of Youth and Adolescence, 12*, 253. (Ch. 14)

Putallaz, M. 1983. "Predicting Children's Socioeconomic Status from Their Behavior." *Child Development, 54*, 1417–1426. (Ch. 10)

Pyle, R. L., and J. E. Mitchell. 1986. "The Prevalence of Bulimia in Selected Samples." *Adolescent Psychiatry, 13*, 241–252. (Ch. 14)

Radin, N. 1981. "The Role of the Father in Cognitive, Academic, and Intellectual Development." In *The Role of the Father in Child Development*, 2nd ed., ed. M. Lamb, 379–428. NY: Wiley-Interscience. (Ch. 9)

Radke-Yarrow, M., C. Zahn-Waxler, and M. Chapman. 1983. "Children's Prosocial Dispositions and Behavior." In *Handbook of Child Psychology*, 4th ed., ed. P. H. Mussen, vol. 4, 469–546. NY: Wiley. (Ch. 10)

Ragozin, A. 1980. "Attachment Behavior of

Day-Care Children." *Child Development, 51,* 409–415. (Ch. 8)

———, R. B. Basham, K. A. Crnic, M. T. Greenberg, and N. M. Robinson. 1982. "Effects of Maternal Age on Parenting Role." *Developmental Psychology, 18,* 627–634. (Ch. 15)

Rajecki, D. W., and R. C. Flanery. 1981. "Social Conflict and Dominance in Children." In *Advances in Developmental Psychology,* ed. M. E. Lamb and A. L. Brown, vol. 1, 87–130. Hillsdale, NJ: Lawrence Erlbaum Assoc. (Chs. 2, 10)

Rakowski, W., and N. M. Clark. 1985. "Future Outlook, Caregiving, and Care Receiving in the Family Context." *Gerontologist, 25,* 618–623. (Ch. 19)

Ramsay, D. S. 1984. "Onset of Duplicated Syllable Babbling and Unimanual Handedness in Infancy." *Developmental Psychology, 20,* 64–71. (Ch. 5)

———. 1985. "Fluctuations in Unimanual Hand Preference in Infants Following the Onset of Duplicated Syllable Babbling." *Developmental Psychology 21,* 318–324. (Ch. 5)

———, and S. L. Weber. 1986. "Infants' Hand Preference in a Task Involving Complementary Roles for the Two Hands." *Child Development, 57,* 300–307. (Ch. 5)

Rapoport, R., R. Rapoport, and Z. Strelitz. 1977. *Fathers, Mothers, and Society.* NY: Basic. (Ch. 17)

Reedy, M. N. 1977. "Age and Sex Differences in Personal Needs and the Nature of Love." University of Southern California. (Ch. 15)

Reese, H. W., and D. Rodeheaver. 1985. "Problem Solving and Complex Decision Making." In *Handbook of the Psychology of Aging,* 2nd ed., ed. J. E. Birren and K. W. Schaie, 474–499. NY: Van Nostrand Reinhold. (Ch. 18)

Reid, G. 1972. "Job Search and Effectiveness of Job-Finding Measures." *Industrial and Labor Relations Review, 25,* 479–495. (Ch. 15)

Reinisch, J. M. 1981. "Prenatal Exposure to Synthetic Progestins Increases Potential for Aggression in Humans." *Science, 211,* 1171–1173. (Ch. 9)

Reiss, I. L. 1973. *Heterosexual Relationships inside and outside Marriage.* Morristown, NJ: Gen'l. Learning Pr. (Ch. 13)

Rempel, J. 1985. "Childless Elderly." *Journal of Marriage and the Family, 47,* 343–348. (Ch. 19)

Renninger, K. A., and R. H. Wozniak. 1985. "Effect of Interest on Attentional Shift, Recognition, and Recall in Young Children." *Developmental Psychology, 21,* 624–632. (Ch. 6)

Repetti, R. L. 1985. "The Social Environment at Work and Psychological Well-Being." Ph.D. diss. Yale University. (Ch. 15)

———, and F. Crosby. 1984. "Gender and Depression." *Journal of Social and Clinical Psychology, 2,* 57–70. (Ch. 15)

Resnick, L. B. In press. "Constructing Knowledge in School." In *Development and Learning,* ed. L. S. Liben and D. H. Feldman, Hillsdale, NJ: Lawrence Erlbaum Assoc. (Ch. 12)

Rest, J. R. 1983. "Morality." In *Handbook of Child Psychology,* 4th ed., ed. P. H. Mussen, vol. 3, 556–629. NY: Wiley. (Ch. 11)

Rheingold, H. L, and C. O. Eckerman. 1970. "The Infant Separates Himself from His Mother." *Science, 168,* 78–83. (Ch. 8)

Rholes, W. S., and D. N. Ruble. 1984. "Children's Understanding of the Dispositional Characteristics of Others." *Child Development, 55,* 550–560. (Ch. 11)

Richards, C. S., and L. J. Siegel. 1978. "Behavioral Treatment of Anxiety States and Avoidance Behaviors in Children." In *Child Behavior Therapy,* ed. D. Marholin II, 274–338. NY: Gardner Pr. (Ch. 2)

Richardson, R. A., N. L. Galambos, J. E. Schulenberg, and A. C. Petersen. 1984. "Young Adolescents' Perceptions of the Family Environment." *Journal of Early Adolescence, 4,* 131–154. (Ch. 13)

Richman, C. L., S. Nida, and L. Pittman. 1976. "Effects of Meaningfulness on Child Free-Recall Learning." *Developmental Psychology, 12,* 460–465. (Ch. 11)

Ridley, C. A., A. W. Avery, J. E. Harrell, L. A. Haynes-Clements, and N. McCunney. 1981. "Mutual Problem-Solving Skills Training for Premarital Couples." *Journal of Applied Developmental Psychology, 2,* 89–116. (Ch. 1)

Riegel, K. F. 1975. "Toward a Dialectical Theory of Development." *Human Development, 18,* 50–64. (Ch. 16)

———, and R. M. Riegel. 1972. "Development, Drop, and Death." *Developmental Psychology, 6,* 306–319. (Ch. 16)

Rierdan, J., and E. Koff. 1985. "Timing of Menarche and Initial Menstrual Experience." *Journal of Youth and Adolescence, 14,* 237–244. (Ch. 13)

Rikli, R., and S. Busch. 1986. "Motor Performance of Women as a Function of Age and Physical Activity Level." *Journal of Gerontology, 41,* 645–649. (Ch. 18)

Riley, J. W., Jr. 1970. "What People Think about Death." In *The Dying Patient,* ed. O. B. Brim, Jr., H. E. Freeman, S. Levine, and N. A. Scotch. NY: Russell Sage Found. (Ch. 20)

Roberts, R. J., Jr., and C. J. Patterson. 1983. "Perspective Taking and Referential Communication." *Child Development, 54,* 1005–1014. (Ch. 11)

Robertson, S. S. 1982. "Intrinsic Temporal Patterning in the Spontaneous Movement of Awake Neonates." *Child Development, 53,* 1016–1021. (Chs. 4, 5)

———, L. J. Dierker, Y. Sorokin, and M. G. Rosen. 1982. "Human Fetal Movement." *Science, 218,* 1327–1330. (Ch. 3)

Robinson, B., and M. Thurnher. 1979. "Taking Care of Parents." *Gerontologist, 19,* 586–593. (Ch. 17)

Robinson, E. J., and W. P. Robinson. 1983. "Children's Uncertainty about the Interpretation of Ambiguous Messages." *Journal of Experimental Child Psychology, 36,* 81–96. (Ch. 11)

Robinson, H. B. 1983. "A Case for Radical Acceleration." In *Academic Precocity,* ed. C. P. Benbow and J. C. Stanley, 139–159. Baltimore: Johns Hopkins Univ. Pr. (Ch. 12)

Robinson, P. K., S. Coberly, and C. E. Paul. 1985. "Work and Retirement." In *Handbook of Aging and the Social Sciences,* 2nd ed., ed. R. H. Binstock and E. Shanas, 503–527. NY: Van Nostrand Reinhold. (Ch. 19)

Roche, A. F. 1981. "The Adipocyte-Number Hypothesis." *Child Development, 52,* 31–43. (Ch. 5)

Rockstein, M., and M. Sussman. 1979. *Biology of Aging.* Belmont, CA: Wadsworth. (Ch. 20)

Rodin, J. 1983. "Insulin Levels, Hunger, and Food Intake." Based on Presidential Address, Div. 38, Amer. Psychological Assn. Anaheim, Aug. (Ch. 5)

———. 1986. "Aging and Health." *Science, 233,* 1271–1276. (Ch. 20)

———. Interview by E. Hall. 1987. "A Sense of Control." In E. Hall. *Growing and Changing,* 103–112. NY: Random House. (Chs. 1, 5)

———, L. Silberstein, and R. Striegel-Moore. 1985. "Women and Weight." In *Nebraska Symposium on Motivation,* ed. T. B. Sonderegger. Lincoln: Univ. of NE Pr. (Ch. 14)

Rodman, H., D. J. Pratto, and R. S. Nelson. 1985. "Child Care Arrangements and Children's Functioning." *Developmental Psychology, 21,* 413–418. (Ch. 9)

Roe, K. V., A. McClure, and A. Roe. 1982. "Vocal Interaction at 3 Months and Cognitive Skills at 12 Years." *Developmental Psychology, 18,* 15–16. (Ch. 7)

Roffwarg, H. P., W. C. Dement, and C. Fisher. 1964. "Preliminary Observations of the Sleep-Dream Pattern in Neonates, Infants, Children, and Adults." In *Monographs on Child Psychiatry,* ed. E. Harms, no. 2. NY: Pergamon Pr. (Ch. 4)

Rogoff, B. 1982. "Integrating Context and Cultural Development." In *Advances in Developmental Psychology,* ed. M. E. Lamb and A. L. Brown, vol. 2, 125–170. Hillsdale, NJ: Lawrence Erlbaum Assoc. (Ch. 2)

Rohrkemper, M. M., and B. L. Bershon. 1984. "Elementary School Students' Report of the Causes and Effects of Problem Difficulty in Mathematics." *The Elementary School Journal, 85,* 127–147. (Ch. 12)

Rollins, B. C., and H. Feldman. 1970. "Marital Satisfaction over the Life Cycle." *Journal of Marriage and the Family, 32,* 20–28. (Ch. 19)

Romaniuk, J. G., and M. Romaniuk. 1982. "Participation Motives of Older Adults in Higher Education." *Gerontologist, 22,* 364–368. (Ch. 16)

Rose, C. L., and B. Bell. 1971. *Predicting Longevity.* Lexington, MA: Heath. (Ch. 20)

Rose, S. 1973. *The Conscious Brain.* NY: Knopf. (Ch. 5)

Rose, S. A. 1983. "Behavioral and Psychophysiological Sequelae of Preterm Birth." In *Infants Born at Risk,* ed. T. Field and A. Sostek, 45–67. NY: Grune & Stratton. (Ch. 4)

———, and M. Blank. 1974. "The Potency of Context in Children's Cognition." *Child Development, 45,* 499–502. (Ch. 11)

———, and I. F. Wallace. 1985. "Visual Recognition Memory." *Child Development, 56,* 843–852. (Ch. 6)

Rosen, R., and E. Hall. 1984. *Sexuality.* NY: Random House. (Chs. 3, 13, 14)

Rosenthal, R. 1966. *Experimenter Effects in Behavioral Research.* Englewood Cliffs, NJ: Appleton-Century-Crofts. (Ch. 10)

———, and L. Jacobson. 1968. *Pygmalion in the Classroom.* NY: Holt, Rinehart and Winston. (Ch. 10)

Rosenzweig, M. R., E. L. Bennett, and M. C. Diamond. 1972. "Brain Changes in Response to Experience." *Scientific American, 226,* February, 22–29. (Ch. 5)

Ross, H. S. 1982. "Establishment of Social Games among Toddlers." *Developmental Psychology, 18,* 509–518. (Ch. 8)

Rossman, I. 1977. "Anatomic and Body Composition Changes with Aging." In *Handbook of the Biology of Aging*, ed. C. E. Finch and L. Hayflick, 189–221. NY: Van Nostrand Reinhold. (Ch. 19)

Rovee-Collier, C. K. 1984. "The Ontogeny of Learning and Memory in Human Infancy." In *Comparative Perspectives on the Development of Memory*, ed. R. Kail and N. E. Spear, 103–134. Hillsdale, NJ: Lawrence Erlbaum Assoc. (Ch. 6)

———, and M. J. Gekoski. 1979. "The Economics of Infancy." In *Advances in Child Development and Behavior*, ed. H. W. Reese and L. P. Lipsitt, vol. 13, 195–255. NY: Academic Pr. (Ch. 4)

Rovet, J., and C. Netley. 1982. "Processing Deficits in Turner's Syndrome." *Developmental Psychology*, 18, 77–94. (Ch. 3)

Rowe, D. C., and R. Plomin. 1978. "The Burt Controversy." *Behavior Genetics*, 8, 81–84. (Ch. 3)

———, and ———. 1981. "The Importance of Nonshared (E_1) Environmental Influences in Behavioral Development." *Developmental Psychology*, 17, 517–531. (Ch. 12)

Rubin, K. H. 1982. "Nonsocial Play in Preschoolers." *Child Development*, 53, 651–657. (Ch. 10)

———, G. Fein, and B. Vandenberg. 1983. "Play." In *Handbook of Child Psychology*, 4th ed., ed. P. H. Mussen, vol. 4, 693–774. NY: Wiley. (Chs. 6, 8, 10)

———, and L. R. Krasnor. 1986. "Social Cognitive and Social-Behavioral Perspectives on Problem Solving." In *Minnesota Symposia on Child Psychology*, ed. M. Perlmutter, vol. 18. Hillsdale, NJ: Lawrence Erlbaum Assoc. (Ch. 10)

———, and T. Maioni. 1975. "Play Preference and Its Relation to Egocentrism, Popularity, and Classification Skills in Preschoolers." *Merrill-Palmer Quarterly*, 21, 171–179. (Ch. 10)

Rubin, L. 1979. *Women of a Certain Age*. NY: Harper & Row. (Ch. 17)

Rubin, R. T., J. M. Reinisch, and R. F. Haskett. 1981. "Postnatal Gonadal Steroid Effects on Human Behavior." *Science*, 211, 1318–1324. (Ch. 3)

Rubinstein, C., P. Shaver, and L. A. Peplau. 1979. "Loneliness." *Human Nature*, 2, Feb. 58–65. (Ch. 15)

Ruble, D. N. 1984. "Sex-Role Development." In *Developmental Psychology*, ed. M. H. Bornstein and M. Lamb, 325–371. Hillsdale, NJ: Lawrence Erlbaum Assoc. (Ch. 9)

———, A. K. Boggiano, N. S. Feldman, and J. H. Loebl. 1980. "Developmental Analysis of the Role of Social Comparison in Self-Evaluation." *Developmental Psychology*, 16, 105–115. (Ch. 10)

———, and J. Brooks-Gunn. 1982. "The Experience of Menarche." *Child Development*, 53, 1557–1566. (Ch. 13)

———, J. E. Parsons, and J. Ross. 1976. "Self-Evaluative Responses of Children in an Achievement Setting." *Child Development*, 47, 999–997. (Ch. 10)

Ruff, H. A. 1984. "Infants' Manipulative Exploration of Objects." *Developmental Psychology*, 20, 9–20. (Ch. 6)

Rugh, R., and L. B. Shettles. 1971. *From Conception to Birth: The Drama of Life's Beginnings*. NY: Harper & Row. (Ch.3)

Rutter, M. 1979. "Maternal Deprivation, 1972–1978." *Child Development*, 50, 283–305. (Ch. 8)

Sachs, J. 1985. "Prelinguistic Development." In *The Development of Language*, ed. J. B. Gleason, 37–60. Columbus: Merrill. (Ch. 7)

Saegert, S., and R. Hart. 1976. "The Development of Sex Differences in the Environmental Competence of Children." In *Women in Society*, ed. P. Burnett. Chicago: Maaroufa Pr. (Ch. 9)

Sagi, A. 1981. "Mothers' and Non-Mothers' Identification of Infant Cries." *Infant Behavior and Development*, 4, 37–40. (Ch. 4)

———, et al. 1985. "Security of Infant-Mother, -Father, and -Metapelet Attachments among Kibbutz-Raised Israeli Children." *Monographs of the Society for Research in Child Development*, 50, no. 209, 257–275. (Ch. 8)

St. Clair, S., and H. D. Day. 1979. "Ego Identity Status and Values among High School Females." *Journal of Youth and Adolescence*, 8, 317–326. (Ch. 13)

St. George-Hyslop, P. H., et al. 1987. "The Genetic Defect Causing Familial Alzheimer's Disease Maps on Chromosome 21." *Science*, 235, 885–890. (Ch. 18)

Salholz, E., et al. 1986. "Too Late for Prince Charming?" *Newsweek*, 107, June 2, 54–61. (Ch.15)

Salkind, N. J. 1985. *Theories of Human Development*. 2nd ed. NY: Wiley. (Ch. 2)

Salthouse, T. A. 1982. *Adult Cognition*. NY: Springer-Verlag. (Chs. 1, 18)

———. 1984. "Effects of Age and Skill in Typing." *Journal of Experimental Psychology: General*, 113, 345–371. (Ch. 16)

———. 1985. "Speed of Behavior and Its Implications for Cognition." In *Handbook of the Psychology of Aging*, 2nd ed., ed. J. E. Birren and K. W. Schaie, 400–426. NY: Van Nostrand Reinhold. (Ch. 18)

Saltz, E., and J. Brodie. 1982. "Pretend-Play Training in Childhood." In *The Play of Children*, ed. D. J. Pepler and K. H. Rubin. Basel: Karger AG. (Ch. 10)

Saltzstein, H. D. 1983. "Critical Issues in Kohlberg's Theory of Moral Reasoning." *Monographs of the Society for Research in Child Development*, 48, 108–119. (Ch. 11)

Sameroff, A. J. 1968. "The Components of Sucking in the Human Newborn." *Journal of Experimental Child Psychology*, 6, 607–623. (Ch. 6)

———, and P. J. Cavanagh. 1979. "Learning in Infancy." In *Handbook of Infant Development*, ed. J. D. Osofsky, 344–392. NY: Wiley-Interscience. (Ch. 6)

Sandberg, E. C., N. L. Riffle, J. V. Higdon, and C. E. Getman. 1981. "Pregnancy Outcome in Women Exposed to Diethylstilbestrol in Utero." *American Journal of Obstetrics and Gynecology*, 140, 194–205. (Ch. 3)

Santrock, J. W., R. A. Warshak, and G. L. Elliott. 1982. "Social Development and Parent-Child Interaction in Father-Custody and Stepmother Families." In *Nontraditional Families*, ed. M. E. Lamb, 289–314. Hillsdale, NJ: Lawrence Erlbaum Assoc. (Ch. 9)

Savin-Williams, R. C. 1979. "Dominance Hierarchies in Groups of Early Adolescents." *Child Development*, 50, 923–935. (Ch. 13)

———, and S. A. Small. 1986. "The Timing of Puberty and Its Relationship to Adolescent and Parent Perceptions of Family Interactions." *Developmental Psychology*, 22, 342–347. (Ch. 17)

Scafidi, F. A., et al. 1986. "Effects of Tactile/Kinesthetic Stimulation on the Clinical Course of Sleep/Wake Behavior of Preterm Neonates." *Infant Behavior and Development*, 9, 91–106. (Ch. 4)

Scanzoni, J., and G. L. Fox. 1980. "Sex Roles, Family, and Society." *Journal of Marriage and the Family*, 42, 743–756. (Ch. 15)

Scanzoni, L., and J. Scanzoni. 1981. *Men, Women, and Change*. 2nd ed. NY: McGraw-Hill. (Ch. 15)

Scardamalia, M., and C. Bereiter. 1984. "Written Composition." In *Handbook of Research on Teaching*, 3rd ed., ed. M. Wittrock, 778–803. NY: Macmillan. (Ch. 12)

Scarr, S. 1981. *Race, Social Class, and Individual Differences in IQ*. Hillsdale, NJ: Lawrence Erlbaum Assoc. (Chs. 3, 12)

———. 1982. "On Quantifying the Intended Effects of Interventions." In *Facilitating Infancy and Early Childhood Development*, ed. L. A. Bond and J. M. Joffe, 466–484. Hanover, VT: Univ. Pr. of New England. (Ch. 3)

———. 1983a. "Child Care." Presented at Science and Public Policy Seminar, Fed. of Behavioral, Psychological, and Cognitive Sciences, Oct. 21. (Ch. 8)

———. 1983b. "An Evolutionary Perspective on Infant Intelligence." In *Origins of Intelligence*, 2nd ed., ed. M. Lewis, 191–223. NY: Plenum. (Chs. 1, 5, 6)

———. 1985. *Mother Care, Other Care*. NY: Basic. (Chs. 2, 8)

———, and K. E. Kidd. 1983. "Developmental Behavioral Genetics." In *Handbook of Child Psychology*. 4th ed., ed. P. E. Mussen, vol. 2, 345–433. NY: Wiley. (Chs. 3, 12)

———, and K. McCartney. 1983. "How People Make Their Own Environments." *Child Development*, 54, 425–435. (Chs. 3, 4, 12)

———, and P. Salapatek. 1970. "Patterns of Fear Development in Infancy." *Merrill-Palmer Quarterly*, 16, 53–90. (Ch. 5)

———, and R. A. Weinberg. 1983. "The Minnesota Adoption Studies." *Child Development*, 54, 260–267. (Ch. 3)

Schaffer, H. R. 1971. *The Growth of Sociability*. Baltimore: Penguin. (Ch. 4)

———. 1977. *Mothering*. Cambridge: Harvard Univ. Pr. (Ch. 4)

———, and P. E. Emerson. 1964a. "The Development of Social Attachments in Infancy." *Monographs of the Society for Research in Child Development*, 29, no. 94. (Ch. 8)

———, and ———. 1964b. "Patterns of Response to Physical Contact in Early Human Development," *Journal of Child Psychology and Psychiatry*, 5, 1–13. (Ch. 8)

Schaie, K. W. 1977. "Quasi-Experimental Research Designs in the Psychology of Aging." In *Handbook of the Psychology of Aging*, ed. J. E. Birren and K. W. Schaie, 39–58. NY: Van Nostrand Reinhold, 1977. (Ch. 1)

———. 1977/78. "Toward a Stage Theory of Adult Development." *International Journal of Aging and Human Development*, 8, 129–138. (Ch. 16)

———. 1983a. "Age Changes in Adult Intelligence." In *Aging*, 2nd ed., ed. D. S. Woodruff and J. E. Birren, 137–148. Monterey, CA: Brooks/Cole. (Ch. 16)

———. 1983b. "The Seattle Longitudinal Study." In *Longitudinal Studies of Adult Psy-*

chological Development, ed. K. W. Schaie. NY: Guilford Pr. (Ch. 16)

————. 1984. "Midlife Influences upon Intellectual Function in Old Age." *International Journal of Behavioral Development*, 7, 463–478. (Chs. 1, 16)

————, and C. Hertzog. 1983. "Fourteen-Year-Cohort-Sequential Analyses of Adult Intellectual Development." *Developmental Psychology*, 19, 531–543. (Ch. 16)

————, and S. L. Willis. 1986a. *Adult Development and Aging*. 2nd ed. Boston: Little, Brown. (Ch. 16)

————, and ————. 1986b. "Can Declines in Adult Intellectual Functioning Be Reversed?" *Developmental Psychology*, 22, 223–232. (Ch. 18)

Schapiro, M. G., and D. A. Ahlburg. 1986. "Why Crime Is Down." *American Demographics*. (Ch. 14)

Schmeck, H. M., Jr. 1985. "Study Finds High Risk from Acne Drug Early in Pregnancy." *New York Times*, Oct. 3, A20. (Ch. 3)

Schneider, B., S. E. Trehub, and D. Bull. 1980. "High-Frequency Sensitivity in Infants." *Science*, 207, 1003–1004. (Ch. 4)

Schneider-Rosen, K., K. G. Braunwald, V. Carlson, and D. Cicchetti. 1985. "Current Perspectives in Attachment Theory." *Monographs of the Society for Research in Child Development*, 50, no. 209, 194–210. (Ch. 8)

Scogin, F., M. Storandt, and L. Lott. 1985. "Memory-Skills Training, Memory Complaints, and Depression in Older Adults." *Journal of Gerontology*, 40, 562–568. (Ch. 18)

Schulenberg, J. E., C. E. Asp, and A. C. Petersen. 1984. "School from the Young Adolescent's Perspective." *Journal of Early Adolescence*, 4, 107–130. (Ch. 13)

Schultz, N. R., Jr., M. F. Elias, M. A. Robbins, D. H. P. Streeten, and N. Blakeman. 1986. "A Longitudinal Comparison of Hypertensives and Normotensives on the Wechsler Adult Intelligence Scale." *Journal of Gerontology*, 41, 169–175. (Ch. 16)

Schulz, R. 1978. *The Psychology of Death, Dying, and Bereavement*. Reading, MA: Addison-Wesley. (Ch. 20)

Schumacher, S., and C. W. Lloyd. 1981. "Physiological and Psychological Factors in Impotence." *Journal of Sex Research*, 17, 40–53. (Ch. 19)

Schwartz, G. M., C. E. Izard, and S. E. Ansul. 1985. "The 5-Month-Old's Ability to Discriminate Facial Expressions of Emotion." *Infant Behavior and Development*, 8, 65–77. (Ch. 6)

Schwartz, J. C., et al. 1981. "Center, Sitter, and Home Day Care before Age 2." Paper presented at the Amer. Psychological Assn. Meeting. Los Angeles, Apr. (Ch. 8)

Scollan, R. 1979. "A Real Early Stage." In *Developmental Pragmatics*, ed. E. Ochs and B. B. Schieffelin, 215–227. NY: Academic Pr. (Ch. 7)

Scott, J. P. 1962. "Genetics and the Development of Social Behavior in Mammals." *American Journal of Orthopsychiatry*, 32, 878–893. (Ch. 8)

Scott-Maxwell, F. 1979. *The Measure of My Days*. NY: Penguin. (Ch. 19)

Scribner, S. 1986. "Thinking in Action." In *Practical Intelligence*, ed. R. J. Sternberg and R. K. Wagner, 13–30. NY: Cambridge Univ. Pr. (Ch. 16)

Seaberry, J. 1985. "Poverty Rises in Families

with Children." *Washington Post*, Dec. 26, D1ff. (Ch. 9)

Seashore, S. E., and J. T. Barnowe. 1972. "Collar Color Doesn't Count." *Psychology Today*, 6, Aug., 119–128. (Ch. 15)

Seginer, R. 1983. "Parents' Educational Expectations and Children's Academic Achievement." *Merrill-Palmer Quarterly*, 29, 1–23. (Ch. 10)

Self, P. A., and F. D. Horowitz. 1979. "The Behavioral Assessment of the Neonate." In *Handbook of Infant Development*, ed. J. D. Osofsky, 126–164. NY: Wiley-Interscience. (Ch. 3)

Seligman, M. 1975. *Helplessness*. San Francisco: Freeman. (Ch. 17)

Seligmann, J. 1986. "Babies Born with AIDS." *Newsweek*, Sept. 22, 70–71. (Ch. 3)

Selman, R. L. 1976. "Social-Cognitive Understanding." In *Moral Development and Behavior*, ed. T. Lickona, 299–316. NY: Holt, Rinehart and Winston. (Ch. 11)

————. 1980. *The Growth of Interpersonal Understanding*. NY: Academic Pr. (Chs. 11, 13)

————. 1981. "The Child as a Friendship Philosopher." In *The Development of Friendships*, ed. S. R. Asher and J. M. Gottman. NY: Cambridge Univ. Pr. (Chs. 10, 13)

Semb, G, ed. 1972. *Behavior Analysis and Education*. Lawrence: Univ. of KN Pr. (Ch. 2)

Shafii, M., et al. 1985. "Psychological Autopsy of Completed Suicide in Children and Adolescents." *American Journal of Psychiatry*, 142, 1061. (Ch. 14)

Shantz, C. U. 1983. "Social Cognition." In *Handbook of Child Psychology*, 4th ed., ed. P. H. Mussen, vol. 3, 495–555. NY: Wiley. (Chs. 10, 11, 13)

Shatz, M. 1983. "Communication." In *Handbook of Child Psychology*, 4th ed., ed. P. H. Mussen, vol. 3, 841–889. NY: Wiley. (Ch. 7)

————. 1984. "Contributions of Mother and Mind to the Development of Communicative Competence." In *Minnesota Symposia on Child Psychology*, ed. M. Perlmutter, vol. 17, 33–60. Hillsdale, NJ: Lawrence Erlbaum Assoc. (Ch. 7)

————, and R. Gelman. 1977. "Beyond Syntax." In *Talking to Children*, ed. C. Snow and C. A. Ferguson, 189–198. NY: Cambridge Univ. Pr. (Ch. 11)

————, H. M. Wellman, and S. Silber. 1983. "The Acquisition of Mental Verbs." *Cognition*, 14, 301–321. (Ch. 7)

Sheehy, G. 1976. *Passages*. NY: Dutton. (Ch. 17)

Sherif, M., O. J. Harvey, B. J. White, W. R. Hood, and C. W. Sherif. 1961. *Intergroup Conflict and Cooperation*. Norman, OK: Inst. of Group Relations. (Ch. 10)

———— and C. W. Sherif. 1953. *Groups in Harmony and Tension*. NY: Harper & Row. (Ch. 10)

Shinn, M. 1978. "Father Absence and Children's Cognitive Development." *Psychological Bulletin*, 85, 295–324. (Ch. 9)

Shneidman, E. S. 1971. "You and Death." *Psychology Today*, 5, Jun. 43–45ff. (Ch. 20)

————. 1973. *Deaths of Man*. NY: Quadrangle. (Ch. 20)

————. 1980a. *Death*. 2nd ed. Palo Alto: Mayfield. (Ch. 20)

————. 1980b. *Voices of Death*. NY: Harper & Row. (Ch. 20)

Shouval, R. H., S. Kav Venaki, U. Bronfen-

brenner, E. Devereux, and E. Kiely. 1975. "Anomalous Reactions to Social Pressure of Israeli and Soviet Children Raised in Family vs. Collective Settings." *Journal of Personality and Social Psychology*, 32, 477–489. (Ch. 10)

Shreve, A. 1984. "The Working Mother as Role Model," *New York Times Magazine*, Sept. 9, pp. 39–43ff. (Ch. 8)

Shultz, T. R. 1980. "Development of the Concept of Intention." In *Minnesota Symposia on Child Psychology*, ed. W. A. Collins, vol. 13, 131–164. Hillsdale, NJ: Lawrence Erlbaum Assoc. (Ch. 11)

————, K. Wright, and M. Schleifer. 1986. "Assignment of Moral Responsibility and Punishment." *Child Development*, 57, 177–184. (Ch. 11)

Siegel, R. K. 1980. "The Psychology of Life after Death." *American Psychologist*, 35, 911–931. (Ch. 20)

Siegler, I. C., and P. T. Costa, Jr. 1985. "Health Behavior Relationships." In *Handbook of the Psychology of Aging*, 2nd ed., ed. J. E. Birren and K. W. Schaie, 144–166. NY: Van Nostrand Reinhold. (Ch. 18)

Siegler, R. S. 1978. "The Origins of Scientific Reasoning." In *Children's Thinking*, ed. R. S. Siegler, 109–149. Hillsdale, NJ: Lawrence Erlbaum Assoc. (Ch. 11)

————. 1981. "Developmental Sequences within and between Concepts." *Monographs of the Society for Research in Child Development*, 46, no. 189. (Ch. 11)

————. 1983. "Information Processing Approaches to Development." In *Handbook of Child Psychology*, 4th ed., ed. P. H. Mussen, vol. 1, 129–211. NY: Wiley. (Ch. 2)

————. 1986. *Children's Thinking*. Englewood Cliffs, NJ: Prentice-Hall. (Chs. 6, 11, 12)

————, and K. Kotovsky. 1986. "Two Levels of Giftedness." In *Conceptions of Giftedness*, ed. R. J. Sternberg and J. E. Davidson, 417–435. NY: Cambridge Univ. Pr. (Ch. 12)

————, and M. Robinson. 1982. "The Development of Numerical Understandings." In *Advances in Child Development and Behavior*, ed. H. W. Reese and L. P. Lipsitt, vol. 16, 241–312. NY: Academic Pr. (Ch. 11)

Silka, L., and S. Kiesler. 1977. "Couples Who Choose to Remain Childless." *Family Planning Perspectives*, 9, 16–35. (Ch. 15)

Simons, R. L., and P. I. Murphy. 1985. "Sex Differences in the Causes of Adolescent Suicide Ideation." *Journal of Youth and Adolescence*, 14, 423–434. (Ch. 14)

Simpson, E. L. 1974. "Moral Development Research." *Human Development*, 17, 81–106. (Ch. 11)

Singer, J. L., and D. G. Singer. 1979. "The Values of the Imagination." In *Play and Learning*, ed. B. Sutton-Smith, 195–218. NY: Gardner Pr. (Ch. 10)

————, and ————. 1981. *Television, Imagination, and Aggression*. Hillsdale, NJ: Lawrence Erlbaum Assoc. (Ch. 10)

Singer, L. M., D. M. Brodzinsky, D. Ramsay, M. Stein, and E. Waters. 1985. "Mother-Infant Attachment in Adoptive Families." *Child Development*, 56, 1543–1551. (Ch. 8)

Skinner, B. F. 1938. *The Behavior of Organisms*. NY: Appleton-Century-Crofts. (Ch.)

————. 1957. *Verbal Behavior*. NY: Appleton-Century-Crofts. (Ch. 7)

————. 1983. "Intellectual Self-Management in Old Age." *American Psychologist, 38,* 239–244. (Ch. 18)

Skolnick, A. 1981. "Married Lives." In *Present and Past in Middle Life,* ed. D. H. Eichorn, J. A. Clausen, N. Haan, M. P. Honzik, and P. H. Mussen, 269–298. NY: Academic Pr. (Ch. 17)

Slater, A., V. Morison, and D. Rose. 1984. "Habituation in the Newborn." *Infant Behavior and Development,* 7, 183–200. (Ch. 4)

Sloane, R. B. 1980. "Organic Brain Syndrome." In *Handbook of Mental Health and Aging,* ed. J. E. Birren and R. B. Sloane, 554–590. Englewood Cliffs, NJ: Prentice-Hall. (Ch. 18)

Slobin, D. I. 1973. "Cognitive Prerequisites for the Development of Grammar." In *Studies of Child Language Development,* ed. C. A. Ferguson and D. I. Slobin, 175–208. NY: Holt, Rinehart and Winston. (Ch. 7)

———. 1978. "A Case Study of Early Language Awareness." In *The Child's Conception of Language,* ed. A. Sinclair, R. J. Jarvella, and W. J. M. Levelt, 45–54. NY: Springer-Verlag. (Ch. 7)

Smetana, J. G. 1985. "Preschool Children's Conception of Transgressions." *Developmental Psychology,* 21, 18–29. (Ch. 11)

Smilansky, S. 1968. *The Effects of Sociodramatic Play on Disadvantaged Preschool Children.* NY: Wiley. (Ch. 10)

Smith, C., and B. Lloyd. 1978. "Maternal Behavior and Perceived Sex of Infant." *Child Development,* 49, 1263–1265. (Ch. 8)

Smith, M. C. 1978. "Cognizing the Behavior Stream." *Child Development,* 48, 736–743. (Ch. 11)

Smith, P. B., S. W. Nenney, M. L. Weinman, and D. M. Mumford. 1982. "Factors Affecting Perception of Pregnancy Risk in the Adolescent." *Journal of Youth and Adolescence,* 22, 207. (Ch. 14)

Smith, P. K. 1977. "Social and Fantasy Play in Young Children." In *Biology of Play,* ed. B. Tizard and D. Harvey, 123–145. Philadelphia: Lippincott. (Ch. 5)

Smith, S. B. 1985. "Why TV Won't Let Up on Violence." *New York Times,* Jan. 13, Section 2, 2ff. (Ch. 10)

Smith, S. D., W. J. Kimberling, B. F. Pennington, and H. A. Lubs. 1983. "Specific Reading Disability." *Science,* 219, 1345–1347. (Ch. 3)

Snow, C. E. 1986. "Conversations with Children." In *Language Acquisition,* 2nd ed., ed. P. Fletcher and M. Garman, 69–89. NY: Cambridge Univ. Pr. (Ch. 7)

Snow, R., and L. Crapo. 1982. "Emotional Bondedness, Subjective Well-Being, and Health in Elderly Medical Patients." *Journal of Gerontology,* 37, 609–615. (Ch. 19)

Solnick, R. L., and J. E. Birren. 1977. "Age and Male Erectile Responsiveness." *Archives of Sexual Behavior,* 6, 1–9. (Ch. 17)

Somerville, S. C., H. M. Wellman, and J. C. Cultice. 1983. "Young Children's Deliberate Reminding." *Journal of Genetic Psychology,* 143, 87–96. (Ch. 6)

Sontag, L. 1966. "Implications of Fetal Behavior and Environment for Adult Personalities." *Annals of the New York Academy of Science,* 134, 782. (Ch. 3)

Sophian, C., and H. M. Wellman. In press. "Selective Information Use and Perseveration in the Search Behavior of Infants and Young Children." *Journal of Experimental Child Psychology.* (Ch. 6)

Sorosky, A. D. 1986. "Introduction: An Overview of Eating Disorders." *Adolescent Psychiatry,* 13, 221–229. (Ch. 14)

Spain, J. 1980. "Psychological Aspects of Contraceptive Use in Teenage Girls." In *Psychological Aspects of Pregnancy, Birthing, and Bonding,* ed. B. L. Blum, 67–83. NY: Human Sciences Pr. (Ch. 14)

Spanier, G. B., and R. A. Lewis. 1980. "Marital Quality." *Journal of Marriage and the Family,* 42, 825–839. (Ch. 15)

Spear, L. 1985. "Literacy Program Focuses on Severely Disabled Adults." *New York Times,* Dec. 1, WC6–7. (Ch. 16)

Spearman, C. 1927. *The Abilities of Man.* NY: Macmillan. (Ch. 12)

Spence, J. T. 1979. "Traits, Roles, and the Concept of Androgyny." In *Psychology and Women in Transition,* ed. J. F. Gullahorn, 167–187. NY: Wiley. (Ch. 15)

Spitz, R. A. 1949. "The Role of Ecological Factors in Emotional Development." *Child Development,* 20, 145–155. (Ch. 8)

Spivack, G., J. Marcus, and M. Swift. 1986. "Early Classroom Behavior and Later Misconduct." *Developmental Psychology,* 22, 124–131. (Chs. 10, 14)

———, and M. B. Shure. 1982. "The Cognition of Social Adjustment." In *Advances in Child Psychology,* ed. B. B. Lahey and A. E. Kazdin, 323–372. NY: Plenum Pr. (Ch. 10)

Squire, L. R. 1974. "Remote Memory as Affected by Aging." *Neuropsychologia,* 12, 429–435. (Ch. 18)

Sroufe, L. A. 1977. "Wariness of Strangers and the Study of Infant Development." *Child Development,* 48, 731–746. (Ch. 8)

———, N. E. Fox, and V. R. Pancake. 1983. "Attachment and Dependency in Developmental Perspective." *Child Development,* 54, 1615–1627. (Ch. 8)

———, E. Waters, and L. Matas. 1974. "Contextual Determinants of Infant Affective Response." In *The Origins of Fear,* ed. M. Lewis and L. Rosenblum. NY: Wiley. (Ch. 8)

Stagner, R. 1985. "Aging in Industry." In *Handbook of the Psychology of Aging,* 2nd ed., ed. J. E. Birren and K. W. Schaie, 789–817. NY: Van Nostrand Reinhold. (Ch. 16)

Stark, R. E. 1986. "Prespeech Segmental Feature Development." In *Language Acquisition,* 2nd ed., ed. P. Fletcher and M. Garman, 149–173. NY: Cambridge Univ. Pr. (Ch. 7)

Starkey, P., and R. G. Cooper, Jr. 1980. "Perception of Numbers by Human Infants." *Science,* 210, 1033–1035. (Ch. 6)

———, E. Spelke, and R. Gelman. 1980. "Number Competence in Infants." Paper presented at the meeting of the Internat'l. Conference on Infant Studies. New Haven, CT: Apr. (Ch. 6)

Starr, R. H., Jr. 1979. "Child Abuse." *American Psychologist,* 34, 873–878. (Ch. 9)

Stechler, G., and A. Halton. 1982. "Prenatal Influences on Human Development." In *Handbook of Developmental Psychology,* ed. B. B. Wolman, 175–189. Englewood Cliffs, NJ: Prentice-Hall. (Ch. 3)

Stein, A. H., and L. K. Friedrich. 1975. "The Effects of Television Content on Young Children." In *Minnesota Symposia on Child Psychology,* ed. A. D. Pick, vol. 9, 78–105. Minneapolis: Univ. of MN Pr. (Ch. 10)

Stein, P. 1975. "Singlehood." *Family Coordinator,* 24, 489–505. (Ch. 15)

Steinberg, L. D. 1981. "Transformation in Family Relations at Puberty." *Developmental Psychology,* 17, 833–840. (Chs. 13, 17)

———, E. Greenberger, L. Garduque, M. Ruggiero, and A. Vaux. 1982. "Effects of Working on Adolescent Development." *Developmental Psychology,* 18, 385–395. (Ch. 14)

———, and S. B. Silverberg. 1986. "The Vicissitudes of Autonomy in Early Adolescence." *Child Development,* 57, 841–851. (Ch. 13)

Steiner, J. E. 1979. "Facial Expressions in Response to Taste and Smell Stimulation." In *Advances in Child Development and Behavior,* ed. H. W. Reese and L. P. Lipsitt, vol. 13, 257–296. NY: Academic Pr. (Ch. 4)

Steinschneider, A. 1975. "Implications of the Sudden Infant Death Syndrome for the Study of Sleep in Infancy." In *Minnesota Symposia on Child Psychology,* ed. A. D. Pick, vol. 9, 106–134. Minneapolis: Univ. of MN Pr. (Ch. 5)

Stephan, C. W., and J. H. Langlois. 1984. "Baby Beautiful." *Child Development,* 55, 576–585. (Ch. 4)

Stern, P. N. 1978. "Stepfather Families." *Issues in Mental Health Nursing,* 1, 50–56. (Ch. 9)

Stern, W. 1914. *The Psychological Methods of Testing Intelligence.* Baltimore: Warwick & York. (Ch. 12)

Sternberg, R. J. 1985. *Beyond IQ.* NY: Cambridge Univ. Pr. (Ch. 12, 16)

———, and J. S. Powell. 1983. "The Development of Intelligence." In *Handbook of Child Psychology,* 4th ed., ed. P. H. Mussen, vol. 3, 341–419. NY: Wiley. (Ch. 12)

Sterngianz, S. H., and L. A. Serbin. 1974. "Sex Role Stereotyping in Children's Television Programs." *Developmental Psychology,* 10, 710–715. (Ch. 10)

Sterns, H. L., G. V. Barrett, and R. A. Alexander. 1985. "Accidents and the Aging Individual." In *Handbook of the Psychology of Aging,* 2nd ed., ed. J. E. Birren and K. W. Schaie, 703–724. NY: Van Nostrand Reinhold. (Ch. 18)

Stevenson, H. W. 1983. "How Children Learn." In *Handbook of Child Psychology,* 4th ed., ed. P. H. Mussen, vol. 1, 213–236. NY: Wiley. (Chs. 2, 6)

———, S-Y. Lee, and J. W. Stigler. 1986. "Mathematics Achievement of Chinese, Japanese, and American Children." *Science,* 231, 693–699. (Ch. 12)

———, et al. 1985. "Cognitive Performance and Academic Achievement of Japanese, Chinese, and American Children." *Child Development,* 56, 718–734. (Ch. 12)

Stigler, J. W. 1984. "'Mental Abacus.'" *Cognitive Psychology,* 16, 145–176. (Ch. 11)

Stinnett, N., L. Carter, and J. Montgomery. 1972. "Older Persons' Perceptions of Their Marriages." *Journal of Marriage and the Family,* 34, 665–670. (Ch. 19)

Stipek, D. J. 1981. "Children's Use of Past Performance Information in Ability and Expectancy Judgments for Self and Other." Paper presented at the meeting of the Internat'l. Society for the Study of Behavioral Devt. Toronto, Aug. (Ch. 12)

Stoel-Gammon, C., and J. A. Cooper. 1984. "Patterns of Early Lexical and Phonological

Development." *Journal of Child Language, 11,* 247–271. (Ch. 7)

Stolz, L. M., et al.   1954. *Father Relations of War-Born Children.* Stanford: Stanford Univ. Pr. (Ch. 9)

Stoneman, Z., and G. H. Brody.   1981. "Peers as Mediators of Television Food Advertisements Aimed at Children." *Developmental Psychology, 17,* 853–858. (Ch. 10)

Straus, M. A., R. J. Gelles, and S. K. Steinmetz.   1980. *Behind Closed Doors.* Garden City, NY: Doubleday. (Ch. 9)

Strauss, M. S., and L. B. Cohen.   1980. "Infant Immediate and Delayed Memory for Perceptual Dimensions." Paper presented at the Internat'l. Conference on Infant Studies. New Haven, CT: Apr. (Ch. 6)

Strayer, F. F.   1984. "Biological Approaches to the Study of the Family." In *Review of Child Development Research,* ed. R. D. Parke, vol. 7, 1–19. Chicago: Univ. of Chicago Pr. (Ch. 10)

———, T. R. Chapeskie, and J. Strayer.   1978. "The Perception of Preschool Social Dominance." *Aggressive Behavior, 4,* 183–192. (Ch. 10)

Streib, G. F.   1985. "Social Stratification and Aging." In *Handbook of Aging and the Social Sciences,* 2nd ed., ed. R. H. Binstock and E. Shanas, 339–368. NY: Van Nostrand Reinhold. (Ch. 19)

Streissguth, A. P., H. M. Barr, and D. C. Martin.   1983. "Maternal Alcohol Use and Neonatal Habituation Assessed with the Brazelton Scale." *Child Development, 54,* 1109–1118. (Ch. 3)

———, et al.   1984. "Intrauterine Alcohol and Nicotine Exposure." *Developmental Psychology, 20,* 533–541. (Ch. 3)

Sudarkasa, N.   1981. "Interpreting the African Heritage in Afro-American Family Organization." In *Black Families,* ed. H. P. McAdoo, 37–53. Beverly Hills, CA: Sage. (Ch. 10)

Sulik, K. K., M. C. Johnston, and M. A. Webb.   1981. "Fetal Alcohol Syndrome." *Science, 214,* 936–938. (Ch. 3)

Sunderland, A., K. Watts, A. D. Baddeley, and J. E. Harris.   1986. "Subjective Memory Assessment and Test Performance in Elderly Adults." *Journal of Gerontology, 41,* 376–384. (Ch. 18)

Suomi, S. J.   1977. "Development of Attachment and Other Social Behaviors in Rhesus Monkeys." In *Attachment Behavior,* ed. T. Alloway, P. Pliner, and L. Kranes, vol. 3. NY: Plenum Pr. (Ch. 5)

———, and H. F. Harlow.   1975. "The Role and Reason of Peer Relationships in Rhesus Monkeys." In *Friendship and Peer Relations,* ed. M. Lewis and L. A. Rosenblum, 153–185. NY: Wiley. (Ch. 8)

———, and C. Ripp.   1983. "A History of Motherless Mother Monkey Mothering at the University of Wisconsin Primate Laboratory." In *Child Abuse,* 49–78. NY: Alan R. Liss. (Ch. 9)

Super, C. M.   1976. "Environmental Effects on Motor Development." *Developmental Medicine and Child Neurology, 18,* 561–567. (Ch. 5)

Super, C. M., and S. Harkness, eds.   1982. *New Directions for Child Development,* no. 8. San Francisco: Jossey-Bass. (Ch. 10)

Super, D. E.   1957. *The Psychology of Careers.* NY: Harper & Row. (Ch. 15)

Sutton-Smith, B.   1982. "Birth Order and Sibling Status Effects." In *Sibling Relationships,* ed. M. E. Lamb and B. Sutton-Smith, 153–166. Hillsdale, NJ: Lawrence Erlbaum Assoc. (Ch. 1)

Swenson, C. H., R. W. Eskew, and K. A. Kohlhepp.   1981. "Stages of Family Life Cycle, Ego Development and the Marriage Relationship." *Journal of Marriage and the Family, 43,* 841–853. (Ch. 17)

Takeda, S., and T. Matsuzawa.   1985. "Age-Related Brain Atrophy." *Journal of Gerontology, 40,* 159–163. (Ch. 18)

Takeuchi, T.   1972. "Biological Reactions and Pathological Changes in Human Beings and Animals Caused by Organic Mercury Contamination." In *Environmental Mercury Contamination,* ed. R. Hartung and B. D. Dinman. Ann Arbor: Ann Arbor Science. (Ch. 3)

Tan, L. E.   1985. "Laterality and Motor Skills in 4-Year-Olds." *Child Development, 56,* 119–124. (Ch. 5)

Tanner, J. M.   1978. *Fetus into Man.* Cambridge: Harvard Univ. Pr. (Chs. 5, 13)

Tauber, M. A.   1979. "Sex Differences in Parent-Child Interaction Styles during a Free-Play Session." *Child Development, 50,* 981–988. (Ch. 1)

Teitsch, K.   1985. "Medical Gains Seen in Care for Small Infants." *New York Times,* Nov. 10, 34. (Ch. 3)

Terkel, S.   1974. *Working.* NY: Pantheon. (Ch. 17)

Terman, L. M., ed.   1959. *Genetic Studies of Genius,* vol. 5. Stanford: Stanford Univ. Pr. (Ch. 12)

Thelen, E.   1979. "Rhythmical Stereotypies in Normal Human Infants." *Animal Behavior, 27,* 699–715. (Ch. 4)

———.   1981. "Rhythmical Behavior in Infancy." *Developmental Psychology, 17,* 237–257. (Ch. 6)

———.   1984. "Learning to Walk." In *Advances in Infancy Research,* ed. L. P. Lipsitt and C. Rovee-Collier, vol. 3, 213–250. Norwood, NJ: Ablex. (Ch. 5)

———.   1985. "Developmental Origins of Motor Coordination." *Developmental Psychobiology, 18,* 1–22. (Ch. 5)

———.   In press. "The Role of Motor Development in Developmental Psychology." In *Contemporary Topics in Developmental Psychology,* ed. N. Eisenberg. NY: Wiley. (Ch. 5)

———, D. M. Fisher, and R. Ridley-Johnson.   1984. "The Relationship between Physical Growth and a Newborn Reflex." *Infant Behavior and Development, 7,* 479–493. (Ch. 4, 5)

Thoenen, H., and D. Edgar.   1985. "Neurotrophic Factors," *Science, 229,* 238–242. (Ch. 3)

Thomae, H.   1980. "Personality and Adjustment in Aging." In *Handbook of Mental Health and Aging,* ed. J. E. Birren and R. B. Sloane, 285–309. Englewood Cliffs, NJ: Prentice-Hall. (Ch. 15, 19)

Thoman, E. B., A. F. Korner, and L. Beason-Williams.   1977. "Modification of Responsiveness to Maternal Vocalization in the Neonate." *Child Development, 48,* 563–569. (Chs. 4, 5)

Thomas, A., and S. Chess.   1977. *Temperament and Development.* NY: Brunner-Mazel. (Ch. 4)

Thomas, E.   1986. "Growing Pains at 40." *Time,* May 19, 22–41. (Ch. 17)

Thomas, J. L.   1986a. "Gender Differences in Satisfaction with Grandparenting." *Psychology and Aging, 1,* 215–219. (Ch. 17)

———.   1986b. "Age and Sex Differences in Perception of Grandparenting." *Journal of Gerontology, 41,* 427–423. (Ch. 19)

Thomas, L.   1976. "A Meliorist View of Disease and Dying." *Journal of Medicine and Philosophy, 2,* 212–221. (Ch. 20)

Thomas, M. H., R. W. Horton, E. C. Lippincott, and R. S. Drabman.   1977. "Desensitization to Portrayals of Real-Life Aggression as a Function of Exposure to Television Violence." *Journal of Personality and Social Psychology, 35,* 450–458. (Ch. 10)

Thomas, R. M.   1979. *Comparing Theories of Child Development.* Belmont, CA: Wadsworth. (Ch. 2)

Thompson, M. G., and M. Schwartz.   1982. "Life Adjustment of Women with Anorexia and Anorexic-Like Behavior." *International Journal of Eating Disorders, 1,* 47–60. (Ch. 14)

Thompson, S. K.   1975. "Gender Labels and Early Sex Role Development." *Child Development, 46,* 339–347. (Ch. 8)

Thompson, W. P.   1957. "Influence of Prenatal Maternal Anxiety on Emotionality in Young Rats." *Science, 125,* 698–699. (Ch. 3)

Thornton, A., and D. Freedman.   1983. "The Changing American Family." *Population Bulletin, 38,* no. 4, Oct. (Ch. 19)

Thurstone, L. L.   1947. *Multiple Factor Analysis.* Chicago: Univ. of Chicago Pr. (Chs. 12, 16)

Time.   1986. "How the Public Feels," Nov. 24, 58–59. (Ch. 13)

Tinsley, B. R., and R. D. Parke.   1984. "Grandparents as Support and Socialization Agents." In *Beyond the Dyad,* ed. M. Lewis. NY: Plenum Pr. (Ch. 17)

Tizard, B., and J. Hodges.   1978. "The Effect of Early Institutional Rearing in the Development of 8-Year-Old Children." *Journal of Child Psychology and Psychiatry, 19,* 99–118. (Ch. 8)

Tomasello, M., and M. J. Farrar.   1984. "Cognitive Bases of Lexical Development." *Journal of Child Language, 11,* 477–493. (Ch. 7)

Tomlinson-Keasey, C., D. C. Eisert, L. R. Kahlel, K. Hardy-Brown, and B. Keasey.   1979. "The Structure of Concrete-Operational Thought." *Child Development, 50,* 1153–1163. (Ch. 11)

Tonna, E. A.   1977. "Aging of Skeletal-Dental Systems and Supporting Tissue." In *Handbook of the Biology of Aging,* ed. C. E. Finch and L. Hayflick, 470–495. NY: Van Nostrand Reinhold. (Ch. 19)

Tracy, R. L., M. E. Lamb, and M. D. S. Ainsworth.   1976. "Infant Approach Behavior as Related to Attachment." *Child Development, 47,* 571–578. (Ch. 8)

Trause, M. A.   1977. "Stranger Responses." *Child Development, 48,* 1657–1661. (Ch. 8)

Treas, J.   1983. "Aging and the Family." In *Aging,* 2nd ed., ed. D. S. Woodruff and J. E. Birren, 94–109. Monterey, CA: Brooks/Cole. (Ch. 17)

Trevarthen, C.   1982. "Basic Patterns of Psychogenetic Change." In *Regressions in Mental Development,* ed. T. G. Bever, 7–46. Hillsdale, NJ: Lawrence Erlbaum Assoc. (Ch. 5)

Trickett, P. K., and L. Kuczynski. 1986. "Children's Misbehaviors and Parental Discipline Strategies in Abusive and Nonabusive Families." *Developmental Psychology, 22,* 113–123. (Ch. 9)

Troll, L. E. 1980. "Grandparenting." In *Aging in the 1980s,* ed. L. W. Poon, 475–481. Washington, DC: Amer. Psychological Assn. (Ch. 17)

———, **S. J. Miller, and R. C. Atchley.** 1979. *Families in Later Life.* Belmont, CA: Wadsworth. (Ch. 17)

Turkewitz, G., and P. A. Kenny. 1982. "Limitations on Input as a Basis for Neural Organization and Perceptual Development." *Developmental Psychobiology, 15,* 357–368. (Ch. 4)

Turkle, S. 1984. *The Second Self.* NY: Simon & Schuster. (Ch. 11)

Turner, B. 1979. "The Self-Concept of Older Women." *Research on Aging, 1,* 464–480. (Ch. 19)

Turner, N. W. 1980. "Divorce in Mid-life." In *Midlife,* ed. W. H. Norman and T. J. Scaramella, 149–177. NY: Brunner/Mazel. (Ch. 17)

Twain, M. [1876] 1936. *The Adventures of Tom Sawyer.* NY: Heritage Pr. (Ch. 6)

Tweit, A. H., P. D. Gollnick, and G. R. Hearn. 1963. "Effect of Training Program on Total Body Reaction Time of Individuals of Low Fitness." *Research Quarterly, 34,* 508–512. (Ch. 16)

Tyler, L. E. 1976. "The Intelligence We Test." In *The Nature of Intelligence,* ed. L. B. Resnick, 13–26. Hillsdale, NJ: Lawrence Erlbaum Assoc. (Ch. 12)

Ungerer, J. A, and M. Sigman. 1984. "The Relation of Play and Sensorimotor Behavior to Language in the 2nd Year." *Child Development, 55,* 1448–1455. (Ch. 7)

US Bureau of Justice Statistics. 1983. *Report to the Nation on Crime and Justice.* Washington, DC: US Govt. Printing Office. (Ch. 14)

US Bureau of Labor Statistics. 1986. "Rise in Mothers' Labor Force Activity Includes Those with Infants." *Monthly Labor Review, 109,* 43–45. (Chs. 8, 9)

US Bureau of the Census. 1971. *1970 Census of Population,* vol. 2, 4C. Washington, DC: US Govt. Printing Office. (Ch. 17)

———. 1982. *Statistical Abstract of the United States, 1982–1983.* Washington, DC: US Govt. Printing Office. (Chs. 9, 17)

———. 1983. *American Women.* Washington, DC: US Govt. Printing Office. (Ch. 15)

———. 1986. *Statistical Abstract of the United States.* Washington, DC: US Govt. Printing Office. (Chs. 13, 14, 15, 16, 17, 19, 20)

US Public Health Service. 1979. *Healthy People.* Dept. HEW Pub. No. 79-55071. Washington, DC: US Govt. Printing Office. (Ch. 19)

University of IL. 1984. "Preliminary Report." Urbana. (Ch. 12)

Uzgiris, I. C. 1964. "Situational Generality of Conservation." *Child Development, 35,* 831–841. (Ch. 11)

Valliant, G. E. 1977. *Adaptation to Life.* Boston: Little, Brown. (Chs. 2, 17)

———, **and E. Milofsky.** 1980. "Natural History of Male Psychological Health."

American Journal of Psychiatry, 137, 1348–1359. (Ch. 17)

Van Court, M., and F. D. Bean. 1985. "Intelligence and Fertility in the United States." *Intelligence, 9,* 23–32. (Ch. 12)

Ventura, S. J. 1985. "Recent Trends and Variations in Births to Unmarried Women." Paper presented at biennial meeting of the Society for Research in Child Devt. Toronto, Apr. (Ch. 15)

Veroff, J., E. Douvan, and R. Kulka. 1981. *The Inner American.* NY: Basic. (Ch. 17)

Verwoerdt, A. 1981. *Clinical Gerontology,* 2nd ed. Baltimore: Williams & Wilkins. (Ch. 19)

Vider, E. 1986. "Late Motherhood." In *Human Development 86/87,* ed. H. E. Fitzgerald and M. G. Walraven, 254–256. Guilford, CT: Dushkin. (Ch. 17)

Vintner, A. 1986. "The Role of Movement in Eliciting Early Imitations." *Child Development, 57,* 66–71. (Ch. 6)

Vitaliano, P. P., J. Russo, A. R. Bren, M. V. Vitiello, and P. N. Prinz. 1986. "Functional Decline in the Early Stages of Alzheimer's Disease." *Psychology and Aging, 1,* 41–46. (Ch. 18)

Vogel, S. R., I. K. Broverman, D. M. Broverman, F. Clarkson, and P. Rosenkrantz. 1970. "Maternal Employment and Perception of Sex Roles among College Students." *Developmental Psychology, 3,* 384–391. (Ch. 17)

Vurpillot, E., and W. A. Ball. 1979. "The Concept of Identity and Children's Selective Attention." In *Attention and Cognitive Development,* ed. G. A. Hale and M. Lewis, 23–42. NY: Plenum Pr. (Ch. 6)

Vygotsky, L. S. 1962. *Thought and Language.* Cambridge: MIT Press. (Ch. 2)

———. 1978. *Mind in Society.* Cambridge: Harvard Univ. Pr. (Chs. 2, 6)

Wagner, R. K., and R. J. Sternberg. 1986. "Tacit Knowledge and Intelligence in the Everyday World." In *Practical Intelligence,* ed. R. J. Sternberg and R. K. Wagner, 51–83. NY: Cambridge Univ. Pr. (Ch. 16)

Waldman, D. A., and B. S. Avolio. 1983. *Enjoy Old Age.* NY: Norton. (Ch. 16)

Walford, R. I. 1983. *Maximum Life Span.* NY: Norton. (Ch. 20)

Wallach, M. A. 1985. "Creativity Testing and Giftedness." In *The Gifted and the Talented,* ed. F. D. Horowitz and M. O'Brien, 99–124. Washington, DC: Amer. Psychological Assn. (Ch. 12)

Wallerstein, J. S., and J. B. Kelly. 1979. "Children and Divorce." *Social Work, 24,* 468–475. (Ch. 9)

Walters, G. C., and J. E. Grusec. 1977. *Punishment.* San Francisco: Freeman. (Ch. 9)

Wantz, M. S., and J. E. Gay. 1981. *The Aging Process.* Cambridge, MA: Winthrop. (Ch. 15)

Ward, R. A. 1980. "Age and Acceptance of Euthanasia." *Journal of Gerontology, 35,* 911–931. (Ch. 20)

———. 1984. *The Aging Experience.* NY: Harper & Row. (Ch. 19)

Waterlow, J. C. 1973. "Note on the Assessment and Classification of Protein-Energy Malnutrition in Children." *Lancet, 2,* 87–89. (Ch. 5)

———, **and P. R. Payne.** 1975. "The Protein Gap." *Nature, 258,* 113–117. (Ch. 5)

Watson, J. B. [1924] 1970. *Behaviorism.* NY: Norton. (Ch. 1)

———. 1928. *Psychological Care of Infant and Child.* NY: Norton. (Chs. 2, 8)

Watson, J. S., and C. T. Ramey. 1972. "Reactions to Response-Contingent Stimulation in Early Infancy." *Merrill-Palmer Quarterly, 18,* 219–228. (Ch. 6)

Wayne, L. 1986. "Attache-Case Education Is Enriching Everybody." *New York Times Education Life,* Jan. 4, Sec. 12, 72–76. (Ch. 16)

Weg, R. B. 1983a. "Changing Physiology of Aging." In *Aging,* 2nd ed., ed. D. S. Woodruff and J. E. Birren, 252–284. Monterey, CA: Brooks/Cole. (Chs. 15, 17, 19, 20)

———. 1983b. "The Physiological Perspective." In *Sexuality in the Later Years,* ed. R. B. Weg, 39–80. NY: Academic Pr. (Ch. 19)

Weinberg, R. S., D. Gould, and A. Jackson. 1979. "Expectations and Performance." *Journal of Sports Psychology, 1,* 320–332. (Ch. 2)

Weiner, B. 1974. *Achievement Motivation and Attribution Theory.* Morristown, NJ: Gen'l. Learning Pr. (Ch. 12)

Weiner, I. B. 1982. *Child and Adolescent Psychopathology.* NY: Wiley. (Ch. 14)

Weinraub, M., E. Jaeger, and L. W. Hoffman. In press. "Predicting Infant Outcome in Families of Employed and Non-Employed Mothers." *Early Childhood Research Quarterly.* (Ch. 8)

Weishaus, S. 1979. "Aging Is a Family Affair." In *Aging Parents,* ed. P. K. Ragan, 154–174. Los Angeles: Univ. of Sou. CA Pr. (Ch. 17)

Weisman, A. D. 1972. *On Dying and Denying.* NY: Behavioral Pub. (Ch. 20)

Weiss, R. S. 1979a. "Growing up a Little Faster." *Journal of Social Issues, 35,* 97–111. (Ch. 9)

———. 1979b. *Going It Alone.* NY: Basic. (Ch. 15)

Weissberg, J. A., and S. G. Paris. 1986. "Young Children's Remembering in Different Context." *Child Development, 57,* 1123–1129. (Chs. 6, 11)

Weissman, M. M. 1979. "The Myth of Involutional Melancholia." *Journal of the American Medical Association, 242,* 742–744. (Ch. 17)

Wellman, H. M., and C. N. Johnson. 1979. "Understanding of Mental Processes." *Child Development, 50,* 79–88. (Ch. 11)

———, **and S. C. Somerville.** 1980. "Quasi-Naturalistic Tasks in the Study of Cognition." In *New Directions for Child Development,* ed. M. Perlmutter, no. 10. San Francisco: Jossey-Bass. (Ch. 6)

———, **and** ———. 1982. "The Development of Human Search Ability." In *Advances in Developmental Psychology,* ed. M. E. Lamb and A. L. Brown, vol. 2, 41–84. Hillsdale, NJ: Lawrence Erlbaum Assoc. (Ch. 6)

———, **G. L. Revelle, R. J. Haake, and C. Sophian.** 1984. "The Development of Comprehensive Search Skills." *Child Development, 55,* 472–481. (Ch. 6)

Welte, J. W., and G. M. Barnes. 1985. "Alcohol." *Journal of Youth and Adolescence, 14,* 487. (Ch. 14)

Wentowski, G. J. 1985. "Older Women's Perceptions of Great-Grandmotherhood." *Gerontologist, 25,* 593–596. (Ch. 17)

Werker, J. F., and R. C. Tees. 1984. "Cross-Language Speech Perception." *Infant Behavior and Development, 7,* 49–63. (Ch. 7)

Werner, J. S., and M. Perlmutter. 1979. "Development of Visual Memory in Infants." In *Advances in Child Development and Behavior*, ed. H. W. Reese and L. P. Lipsitt, vol. 14, 2–56. NY: Academic Pr. (Ch. 6)

———, **and E. R. Siqueland.** 1978. "Visual Recognition Memory in the Preterm Infant." *Infant Behavior and Development, 1*, 79–94. (Ch. 4)

Whitbourne, S. K., and A. S. Waterman. 1979. "Psychosocial Development during the Adult Years." *Developmental Psychology, 15*, 373–378. (Ch. 15)

Whitehurst, G. J. 1982. "Language Development." In *Handbook of Developmental Psychology*, ed. B. B. Wolman, 367–386. Englewood Cliffs, NJ: Prentice-Hall. (Ch. 7)

———, **and R. Vasta.** 1975. "Is Language Acquired through Imitation?" *Journal of Psycholinguistic Research, 4*, 37–59. (Ch. 7)

Whiting, J. W. M. 1960. "Resource Mediation and Learning by Identification." In *Personality Development in Children*, ed. I. Iscoe and H. W. Stevenson, 112–126. Austin: Univ. of TX Pr. (Ch. 2)

Wiesenfeld, A. R., and C. Z. Malatesta. 1982. "Infant Distress." In *Parenting*, ed. L. W. Hoffman, R. J. Gandelman, and H. R. Schiffman, 123–139. Hillsdale, NJ: Lawrence Erlbaum Assoc. (Ch. 4)

Wilkinson, A. C. 1980. "Children's Understanding in Reading and Listening." *Journal of Educational Psychology, 72*, 562–574. (Ch. 2)

Willerman, L. 1979. "Effects of Families on Intellectual Development." *American Psychologist, 34*, 923–929. (Ch. 3)

Williams, L. 1985. "Out of Grief, A Drive to Cut Youth Suicide." *New York Times*, Nov. 11, A1ff. (Ch. 14)

Willis, S. L. 1985. "Educational Psychology of the Older Adult Learner." In *Handbook of the Psychology of Aging*, 2nd ed., ed. J. E. Birren and K. W. Schaie, 818–847. NY: Van Nostrand Reinhold. (Ch. 16)

Wilson, J. Q., and R. Herrnstein. 1985. *Crime and Human Nature.* NY: Simon & Schuster. (Ch. 14)

Wilson, M. N. 1986. "The Black Extended Family." *Developmental Psychology, 22*, 246–258. (Ch. 10)

Wing, S., K. G. Manton, E. Stallard, C. G. Hames, and H. A. Tryoler. 1985. "The Black/White Mortality Crossover." *Journal of Gerontology, 40*, 78–84. (Ch. 20)

Wingerson, L. 1979. "Evidence of Fetal Defense Mechanism." *New York Times*, Oct. 9, C1–2. (Ch. 3)

Winsborough, H. H. 1980. "A Demographic Approach to the Life Cycle." In *Life Course*, ed. K. W. Back. Boulder: Westview Pr. (Ch. 17)

Wiswell, R. A. 1980. "Relaxation, Exercise, and Aging." In *Handbook of Mental Health and Aging*, ed. J. E. Birren and R. B. Sloane, 943–958. Englewood Cliffs, NJ: Prentice-Hall. (Ch. 16)

Wohlwill, J. F. 1973. *The Study of Behavioral Development.* NY: Academic Pr. (Ch. 1)

Wolfe, L. 1982. "Mommy's 39, Daddy's 57 – and Baby Was Just Born." *New York*, Apr., 28–33. (Ch. 17)

Wolfenstein, M. 1955. "Fun Morality." In *Childhood in Contemporary Culture*, ed. M. Mead and M. Wolfenstein. Chicago: Univ. of Chicago Pr. (Ch. 2)

Wolff, G. 1935. "Increased Bodily Growth of School Children since the War." *Lancet, 228*, 1006–1011. (Ch. 5)

Wolfgang, M. 1973. "Crime in a Birth Cohort." *Proceedings of the American Philosophical Society, 117*, 404–411. (Ch. 14)

Wong, H. 1981. "Typologies of Intimacy." *Psychology of Women Quarterly, 5*, 435–443. (Ch. 15)

Woodruff, D. S. 1977. *Can You Live to Be 100?* NY: Chatham Sq. (Ch. 20)

———. 1983. "Physiology and Behavior Relationships in Aging." In *Aging*, 2nd ed., ed. D. S. Woodruff and J. E. Birren, 178–201. Monterey, CA: Brook/Cole. (Ch. 18)

———. 1985. "Arousal, Sleep, and Aging." In *Handbook of the Psychology of Aging*, 2nd ed., ed. J. E. Birren and K. W. Schaie, 261–295. NY: Van Nostrand Reinhold. (Ch. 18)

———, **and J. E. Birren.** 1972. "Age Changes and Cohort Differences in Personality." *Developmental Psychology, 6*, 252–259. (Ch. 17)

Woods, M. B. 1972. "The Unsupervised Child of the Working Mother." *Developmental Psychology, 6*, 14–25. (Ch. 9)

Woodson, R. H. 1983. "Newborn Behavior and the Transition to Extrauterine Life." *Infant Behavior and Development, 6*, 139–144. (Ch. 4)

World Health Organization. 1964. *Human Genetics and Public Health.* Geneva: World Health Org. (Ch. 3)

Wright, B. M., and R. B. Payne. 1985. "Effects of Aging on Sex Differences in Psychomotor Reminiscence and Tracking Proficiency." *Journal of Gerontology, 40*, 179–184. (Ch. 18)

Wright, J. C., and A. G. Vliestra. 1975. "The Development of Selective Attention." In *Advances in Child Development and Behavior*, ed. H. W. Reese, vol. 10, 195–239. NY: Academic Pr. (Ch. 11)

Yankelovich, D. 1981. *New Rules.* NY: Random House. (Ch. 15)

Yesavage, J. A., and R. Jacob. 1984. "Effects of Relaxation and Mnemonics on Memory, Attention, and Anxiety in the Elderly." *Experimental Aging Research, 10*, 211–214. (Ch. 18)

———, **T. L. Rose, and G. H. Bower.** 1983. "Interactive Imagery and Affective Judgments Improve Face-Name Learning in the Elderly." *Journal of Gerontology, 38*, 197–203. (Ch. 18)

Yin, P., and M. Shine. 1985. "Misinterpretations of Increases in Life Expectancy in Ger-ontology Textbooks." *Gerontologist, 25*, 78–82. (Ch. 20)

Young, J. W., and L. R. Ferguson. 1979. "Developmental Changes through Adolescence in the Spontaneous Nomination of Reference Groups as a Function of Decision Content." *Journal of Youth and Adolescence, 8*, 239–252. (Ch. 14)

Younger, B. A., and L. B. Cohen. 1983. "Infant Perception of Correlations among Attributes." *Child Development, 54*, 858–867. (Ch. 7)

Yussen, S. R. and V. M. Levy. 1975. "Developmental Changes in Predicting One's Own Span of Short-Term Memory." *Journal of Experimental Child Psychology, 19*, 502–508. (Ch. 11)

Zajonc, R. B. 1983. "Validating the Confluence Model." *Psychological Bulletin, 93*, 457–480. (Ch. 9)

———. Interview by E. Hall. 1987. "Mining New Gold from Old Research." In E. Hall, *Growing and Changing*, 79–87. NY: Random House. (Chs. 9, 12, 14)

———, **and G. B. Markus.** 1975. "Birth Order and Intellectual Development." *Psychological Review, 82*, 74–88. (Ch. 9)

Zarit, S. H. 1980. *Aging and Mental Disorders.* NY: Free Pr. (Chs. 18, 19)

Zelazo, P. R. 1983. "The Development of Walking." *Journal of Motor Behavior, 15*, 99–137. (Chs. 4, 5)

———. 1984. "'Learning to Walk.'" In *Advances in Infancy Research*, ed. L. P. Lipsitt and C. Rovee-Collier, vol. 3, 251–256. (Ch. 5)

Zelnick, M., and J. F. Kantner. 1980. "Sexual Activity, Contraceptive Use and Pregnancy among Metropolitan-Area Teenagers." *Family Planning Perspectives, 12*, 230–237. (Ch. 13)

———, ———, **and K. Ford.** 1981. *Sex and Pregnancy in Adolescence.* Beverly Hills, CA: Sage. (Chs. 13, 14)

———, **and J. Y. Kim.** 1982. "Sex Education and Its Association with Teenage Sexual Activity, Pregnancy, and Contraceptive Use." *Family Planning Perspectives, 14*, 117–126. (Ch. 14)

Zeskind, P. S., and C. T. Ramey. 1978. "Fetal Malnutrition." *Child Development, 49*, 1155–1162. (Ch. 1)

———, **and** ———. 1981. "Preventing Intellectual and Interactional Sequelae of Fetal Malnutrition." *Child Development, 52*, 213–218. (Chs. 1, 3)

Zill, N. 1985. *Happy, Healthy, and Insecure.* NY: Cambridge Univ. Pr. (Chs. 9, 10)

Zimbardo, P., S. M. Andersen, and L. G. Kabat. 1981. "Induced Hearing Deficit Generates Experimental Paranoia." *Science, 212*, 1529–1531. (Ch. 18)

Zucker, R. A. 1987. "The Four Alcoholisms." In *Nebraska Symposium on Motivation*, vol. 14. Lincoln: Univ. of NE Pr. (Ch. 14)

Acknowledgments and Copyrights

Chapter-Opening Photo Credits

Illustration and Table Credits

Cole Publishing Company, Pacific Grove, California 93940.

P. 520, Table 19.3 From H. Parnes, *Work and Retirement: A Longitudinal Study,* 1981, p. 188. Published by the MIT Press. © 1981 by the Massachusetts Institute of Technology.

P. 526, Table 19.4 Adapted from S. H. Matthews and J. Sprey, "Adolescents' Relationships with Grandparents: An Empirical Contribution to Conceptual Clarification," *Journal of Gerontology,* 40 (1985), pp. 621–626. Reprinted by permission of the *Journal of Gerontology.*

P. 538, Figure 20.1 From J. F. Fries and L. M. Crapo, *Vitality and Aging,* 1981, p. 75. Copyright © 1981 W. H. Freeman and Company.

Name Index

Subject Index

About the Authors

Lois Wladis Hoffman is Professor of Psychology at the University of Michigan where she serves as chair of the Developmental Psychology Department. She received her B.A. from SUNY-Buffalo, her M.S. from Purdue University, and her Ph.D. from the University of Michigan in 1958. Since 1967, she has taught the undergraduate course in Developmental Psychology, alternating terms since 1980 with Scott Paris. In 1981, she was given an award for outstanding teaching.

Professor Hoffman is perhaps best known for her work on the effects of maternal employment on the child. She coauthored two books on this topic with F. Ivan Nye, *The Employed Mother in America* (1963) and *The Working Mother* (1974); published many articles; and has given lectures in Europe, Asia, South America, and throughout the United States. She is also well known for her research on parent-child interaction and the child's social and personality development and on the value of children to parents.

Professor Hoffman's other books include the *Review of Child Development Research* (with M. L. Hoffman), *Women and Achievement* (with M. Mednick and S. Tangri), and *Parenting: Its Causes and Consequences* (with R. Gandelman and R. Shiffman).

She has served as President of Division 9 of the American Psychological Association. She has been on the editorial boards of *Developmental Psychology*, the *Journal of Applied Developmental Psychology*, *Women and Work*, the *Review of Child Development Research*, and other professional journals.

Scott G. Paris is Professor of Psychology and Education at the University of Michigan, where he serves as Director of the Center for Research on Learning and Schooling. Since receiving his B.A. from the University of Michigan in 1968 and his Ph.D. from Indiana University in 1972, Professor Paris has taught at Purdue

University (1973–1979) and Michigan. He has also been a visiting scholar at Stanford University, UCLA, the University of Auckland (New Zealand), and the Flinders University and the University of Newcastle (Australia). His research in developmental psychology has focused primarily on memory and problem-solving skills in children, while his research on education has investigated children's learning and reading. He has written more than 50 articles and book chapters; is a coauthor of *Psychology*, 2nd ed. (with H. Roediger et al.); and is a coeditor of *Learning and Motivation in the Classroom* (with G. Olson and H. Stevenson). He is a member of the editorial boards of *Child Development*, the *Journal of Educational Psychology, Developmental Review*, and *Reading Research Quarterly* and has created educational materials entitled "Reading and Thinking Strategies" for grades 3–6.

Elizabeth Hall is the coauthor of *Child Psychology Today* (2nd ed.), of *Sexuality* (both published by Random House), and of *Adult Development and Aging*. Before she turned to college textbooks, she was Editor-in-chief of *Human Nature*, a magazine about the human sciences. She was formerly Managing Editor of *Psychology Today*. Ms. Hall still interviews prominent psychologists for that magazine, and some of these conversations on developmental psychology have recently been published as *Growing and Changing: What the Experts Say* (Random House, 1987). She has also written a number of books for children; two of them, *Why We Do What We Do: A Look at Psychology* and *From Pigeons to People: A Look at Behavior Shaping*, received Honorable Mention in the American Psychological Foundation's National Media Awards.

Robert E. Schell is a lecturer in the psychology department at San Diego State University and a clinical and consulting psychologist in California. He received his Ph.D. from the University of Illinois and has held academic appointments at Michigan State University, Dartmouth College, and the Merrill-Palmer Institute. Professor Schell is the author of *Letters and Sounds* and has been a contributing author and consultant on several Random House texts. He has published articles in various journals, including *Child Development, Journal of Comparative and Physiological Psychology, Journal of Speech and Hearing Disorders*, and *Journal of Abnormal and Social Psychology*.